THE INTERACTIVE CASEBOOK SERIES^{SM}

CRIMINAL PROCEDURE

A Contemporary Approach

SECOND EDITION

Russell L. Weaver
PROFESSOR OF LAW & DISTINGUISHED UNIVERSITY SCHOLAR
UNIVERSITY OF LOUISVILLE, LOUIS D. BRANDEIS SCHOOL OF LAW

John M. Burkoff
PROFESSOR OF LAW EMERITUS
UNIVERSITY OF PITTSBURGH SCHOOL OF LAW

Catherine Hancock
GEOFFREY C. BIBLE & MURRAY H. BRING PROFESSOR OF CONSTITUTIONAL LAW
TULANE UNIVERSITY LAW SCHOOL

WEST
ACADEMIC
PUBLISHING

Interactive Casebook Series is a servicemark registered in the U.S. Patent and Trademark Office.

© 2015 LEG, Inc. d/b/a West Academic
© 2018 LEG, Inc. d/b/a West Academic
    444 Cedar Street, Suite 700
    St. Paul, MN 55101
    1-877-888-1330

West, West Academic Publishing, and West Academic are trademarks of West Publishing Corporation, used under license.

Printed in the United States of America

ISBN: 978-1-64020-087-6

Dedication

To Laurence, Ben and Kate, with love, RLW

Dedicated with love to Nancy, Amy & Sean,

David & Emmy, Emma, Molly,

Hannah, and Cyrus, JMB

For Elizabeth, Caitlin & Margaret, CH

Preface

This second edition of our interactive criminal procedure casebook continues the tradition of our prior criminal procedure casebook (which went through five editions), but continues to a second edition in the interactive format.

As with the prior books, our primary goal was to create a "teacher's book" – a book that contains thought provoking problems (referred to as "hypos" in the Interactive Casebook Series) designed to stimulate thought and produce interesting classroom discussion. The hypos are woven throughout the chapters and are designed to help students learn doctrine, illuminate trends in the law, and ultimately produce better learning. A secondary goal was to include a focus on teaching "skills." Many of the hypos place students in practical situations that they are likely to encounter in practice, and therefore encourage students to think about how they might handle those situations in real-life.

However, the interactive format allows us to offer a number of other features, including live hyperlinks and the ability to access the material interactively. Students will also find a variety of boxes in the text of the principal cases, Some of these boxes involve "food for thought" questions that will help them to understand how to address the more complex questions that arise in the "points for discussion" material and in the hypotheticals. The boxes also provide information about topics such as the attorneys' strategies in the cases and links to online sources that illustrate various facets of the litigation. There are also "FYI," and "Take Note" boxes. Also included are multiple choice questions that allow students to test their understanding and comprehension of the issues presented.

As with any book, tradeoffs are necessary. In order to prevent the book from being unduly voluminous and unwieldy, we have chosen not to include encyclopedic notes and references like those found in other books. The inclusion of too many notes impedes learning. Moreover, in the criminal procedure area, students have numerous high-quality secondary sources available to them, and students can consult those sources for expanded scholarly discussions of the law. By limiting the scope of notes, we were able to include more hypotheticals and to provide greater opportunity for critical thinking.

We welcome input from faculty and students who use this book. You can contact us at the following e-mail addresses: Professor Russell Weaver (russ. weaver@louisville.edu); Professor John Burkoff (burkoff@pitt.edu); and Professor Catherine Hancock (chancock@law.tulane.edu).

We give thanks to the many people who assisted us in the creation and revision of this book, including our research assistants and secretaries. We are particularly grateful to students who helped us find and correct errors.

Finally, we are thankful to our spouses, significant others, and children who supported us through the various stages of this project.

RLW, JMB, CH

Acknowledgments

Excerpts from the following articles have been reprinted by permission:

Monroe Freedman & Abbe Smith, "Misunderstanding Lawyer's Ethics (Book Review of Daniel Markovits, A Modern Legal Ethics: Adversary Ethics in a Democratic Age (2008))," 108 Mich. L. Rev. 925 (2010).

Bruce Green & Ellen Yaroshefsky, "Prosecutorial Accountability 2.0," 92 Notre Dame L. Rev. 51, 114–16 (2016).

W. William Hodes, "Seeking the Truth Versus Telling the Truth at the Boundaries of the Law: Misdirection, Lying, and 'Lying With an Explanation,' " 44 S. Tex. L. Rev. 53 (2002).

Richard Klein, "The Role of Defense Counsel in Ensuring a Fair Justice System," 36 The Champion 38 (June 2012).

David Luban, "The Conscience of a Prosecutor," 45 Val. U. L. Rev. 1 (2010).

Daniel Markovits, "Adversary Advocacy and the Authority of Adjudication," 75 Fordham L. Rev. 1367 (2006).

Robert P. Mosteller, "Why Defense Attorneys Cannot, But Do, Care About Innocence," 50 Santa Clara L. Rev. 1 (2010).

Deborah L. Rhode, "The Future of the Legal Profession: Institutionalizing Ethics," 44 Case W. Res. L. Rev. 665 (1994).

Daniel Richman, "Prosecutors and Their Agents, Agents and Their Prosecutors," 103 Colum. L. Rev. 749 (2003).

William H. Simon, "The Ethics of Criminal Defense," 91 Mich. L. Rev. 1703 (1993).

Abbe Smith, "Defending Those People," 10 Ohio St. J. Crim. L. 277 (2012).

Features of this Casebook

Throughout the book you will find various text boxes on either side of the page. These boxes provide information that will help you to understand a case or cause you to think more deeply about an issue.

 For More Information These boxes point you to resources to consult for more information on a subject.

 Food for Thought These boxes pose questions that prompt you to think about issues raised by the material.

 Take Note Here you will be prompted to take special notice of something that deserves further thought or attention.

 FYI A self-explanatory category that shares useful or simply interesting information relevant to material in the text.

 See It These boxes point you to visual information that is relevant to the material in the text.

 Go Online If there are relevant online resources that are worth consulting in relation to any matter being discussed, these boxes will direct you to them.

 Make the Connection When concepts or discussions that pertain to information covered in other law school courses appear in a case or elsewhere in this text, often you will find this text box to indicate the course in which you can study those topics. Here you may also be prompted to connect information in the current case to material that you have covered elsewhere in this course.

 It's Latin to Me The law is fond of Latin terms and phrases; when you encounter these for the first time, this box will explain their meaning.

 Practice Pointers Here you will find advice relevant to legal practice typically inspired by the actions (or inactions) of legal counsel in the cases or simply prompted by an important issue being discussed.

 What's That? These boxes explain the meaning of special legal terms that appear in the main text. *Black's Law Dictionary* definitions may be accessed by clicking on the hyperlinked term in the text.

Major Themes In the Executive Summaries at the end of each chapter, you will find here a discussion of some of the deeper themes and issues pertaining to the topic covered in that chapter.

 Ethical Issue These boxes point out potential ethics problems, and identify sources that can help address those issues.

 Global View These boxes offer comparative and international law perspectives.

 Hear It These boxes point you to audio information that is relevant to the material in the text, such as recordings of a case's oral argument at *oyez.org*.

 Who's That? Provides biographical information about a person mentioned in the text.

 Test Your Knowledge These boxes point you to multiple choice quizzes that provide immediate feedback to help gauge how well you're understanding the material.

Table of Contents

CHAPTER 19 *Freedom of the Press and Fair Trials*

Table of Cases

The principal cases are in **bold** type. Cases cited or discussed in the text are in roman type. References are to pages. Cases cited in principal cases and within other quoted materials are not included.

CRIMINAL PROCEDURE

A Contemporary Approach

SECOND EDITION

CHAPTER 1

Introduction to the Criminal Justice Process

Lawyers who work in the criminal justice system rely on many sources of law, including the constitutional case law of the United States Supreme Court. These important federal precedents are part of the bedrock knowledge of defense counsel and prosecutors who practice in municipal, state and federal courts, and roughly a dozen precedential criminal procedure decisions are handed down by the Court every year. This case law is the primary source material in most criminal procedure casebooks, but the significance of the Court's rulings can be difficult to understand in context because of the narrow doctrinal focus exhibited in any one individual decision. The Court's opinions rarely describe the procedures and lawyering activities that occurred *before* a case is briefed and argued in the rarified forum of the Court's chambers. Each opinion usually gives the reader only a tiny glimpse of the large backdrop of law, custom, and practice that surrounds each case. This Chapter provides a brief overview of that backdrop, which practicing lawyers take for granted as a frame of reference for understanding the Court's precedents.

Go Online

You can see just what cases are going to be or have been argued at the Supreme Court's website. *See* http://www.supremecourt.gov/.

A. Sources of Law That Create Legal Rights for Criminal Defendants and Regulate the Procedures of the Criminal Justice System

Certain federal constitutional rights are available to all defendants who are charged with crimes. These rights are established in particular provisions of the Bill of Rights, such as the Fourth, Fifth, Sixth, and Eighth Amendments, and by the Due Process and Equal Protection Clauses of the Fourteenth Amendment. A defendant in a federal prosecution is also entitled to rights that are provided by federal statutes, such as the federal Code of Criminal Procedure, 18 U.S.C. § 3001 *et seq.*

A defendant in a state prosecution is entitled to invoke not only federal constitutional rights, but also rights provided by state statutes, such as state codes of criminal procedure. More importantly, state defendants also have *state* constitutional rights that may provide greater protections than federal constitutional rights. Most state constitutions have provisions that are similar to the Bill of Rights, and each state supreme court is the final authority on the meaning of these provisions. From a state supreme court's point of view, federal Supreme Court interpretations of a particular right may provide a model for interpretation of the state constitutional version of that right. However, the federal model may be rejected by state courts whose state constitutions provide greater protections for state court defendants. While many rulings by the United States Supreme Court are "borrowed" by state supreme courts as interpretations of parallel state constitutional provisions, some rulings are rejected by state courts that interpret their state provisions as intended to take a different course.

In effect, the federal constitution creates a "floor" that establishes the minimum rights that must be recognized in *all* criminal prosecutions and criminal investigations, but the state courts are free to establish their own higher "floors" that establish higher entitlements to rights that will be enforced in state prosecutions. These higher levels of state constitutional rights may be found in state constitutional case law, in rulings based on interpretations of state statutes, or in

Make the Connection

This important point may be clearer to you when you read about and discuss the nature of particular federal constitutional rights later in this casebook. For example, in Chapter 4, you will discover that, under the Fourth Amendment, federal law enforcement officers need neither probable cause nor a warrant in order to use a canine sniff for drugs or explosives. However, some state supreme courts have interpreted their state constitutions as requiring either probable cause or reasonable suspicion before state law enforcement officers can use canines for this purpose.

rulings based on other legal sources. From a defense counsel's perspective, representation of a client in a particular state court requires a bedrock knowledge of that state's constitutional and statutory law, in order to raise all relevant state-law claims in tandem with arguments based on the federal constitution. State prosecutors also must possess the same bedrock knowledge in order to enable them to respond to all of these claims.

In addition to constitutional and statutory law, there are other sources of law that create rights for criminal defendants or regulate the criminal justice process in important ways. One case-law source is the body of judge-made rules that derive from a court's "supervisory" authority over the criminal court system and its evidentiary rules. One statutory source is the rules of court adopted by judges to govern procedure in particular courts. These sources exist in both federal and state jurisdictions. There are also "local" sources of law that create rights and regulate criminal procedure, such as city ordinances and municipal court rules.

Occasionally, it may be unclear whether a person is charged with a "crime," or only with a "civil" offense that does not entitle him or her to state and federal constitutional and statutory rights reserved for *criminal* defendants. When the Congress or a state legislature labels a sanction as criminal, courts recognize that this permits a defendant to invoke such rights. However, if the legislature labels a sanction as civil, this does not end the inquiry. The Supreme Court has ruled that it is theoretically possible for a defendant to persuade a court to treat a proceeding as criminal (sometimes "quasi-criminal") despite its legislative classification as civil. However, it is usually very difficult for defense counsel to win such an argument, without strong evidence that the statutory scheme is punitive in purpose or effect.

While the Supreme Court's federal constitutional precedents have been likened to a "code" of criminal procedure, they are neither as systematic nor as comprehensive as a legislative code. Instead, they reveal the Court's historical preoccupation with particular issues that raise fundamental questions about fairness in the treatment of people who are investigated for and charged with crime, and about the needs of law enforcement officers and officials to investigate and prosecute crimes effectively. For example, the Prohibition era provided the setting for the Court's early development of Fourth Amendment law defining police powers to perform searches and seizures, and the focus on the prosecution of drug crimes in recent decades has spurred the Court to establish many new Fourth Amendment precedents. Moreover, the Court's precedents are concentrated in particular fields of criminal procedure, so that some fields are heavily influenced by them and other fields are not. Even in fields where many precedents exist, the Court's decisions often provide sketchy guidance for lower courts that must attempt to interpret and enforce these holdings. Thus, in most areas of criminal procedure, the Court's decisions provide only a starting point for analyzing some issues.

When state legislatures and courts consider the need to define or interpret statutory codes governing criminal procedure, they are often influenced by the Federal Rules of Criminal Procedure and other federal statutes, and by the American Bar Association Standards for Criminal Justice. They may also be influenced by the American Law Institute's Model Code of Pre-Arraignment Procedure. However, there is no real pressure for the "nationalization" of criminal procedure doctrine and practice, in part because of the long history of state and local autonomy and diversity in this field. In fact, the politicization of "law and order" issues in recent decades has created the opposite kind of pressure for constant local experimentation with criminal procedure rules. Public criticism of the weaknesses of the criminal justice system is a permanent feature of the modern legal landscape, and political calls for reform of the system have affected many aspects of criminal procedure, ranging from the election of state supreme court justices based on their doctrinal views to legislative attempts to repeal or restrict various criminal procedure rules that benefit defendants, such as the writ of habeas corpus and exclusionary rules of evidence.

B. Prosecution Systems

1. Multiple Jurisdictions, Major and Minor Crimes

When a person commits a criminal act, he or she may violate simultaneously the criminal law of multiple jurisdictions, such as federal and state laws, or state laws and municipal ordinances. According to the Court's Double Jeopardy doctrine, multiple prosecutions for the same act by different "sovereign" governments are not prohibited by the Constitution. Therefore, if an act violates state and federal law, for example, it is up to the prosecutors in each jurisdiction to decide how to coordinate the two potential prosecutions. It is possible that a statute of limitations may bar prosecution in one jurisdiction, or that prosecution in one jurisdiction is particularly advantageous because of the penalty, the procedural rules, or for some other reason. Or, some prosecutors may lack resources that other prosecutors possess, and this difference may influence the timing and outcome of decisions to prosecute in only one or both jurisdictions.

In federal and state jurisdictions, most prosecutions are for minor crimes. While the definition of a "minor" crime is not uniform among the states, in most states a misdemeanor cannot be punished for more than one year in prison. Fewer than one tenth of state prosecutions are for felonies. By contrast, about one third of federal prosecutions are for felonies. Not surprisingly states have established different procedures

Go Online

You can view the most recent federal statistics on criminal victimization rates of U.S. residents at http://www.bjs.gov/index.cfm?ty=pbse&sid=6. In 2015, U.S. residents age 12 or older experienced an estimated 5.0 million violent victimizations (rape or sexual assault, robbery, aggravated assault, and simple assault). From 1993 to 2015, the rate of violent crime declined from 79.8 to 18.6 victimizations per 1,000 persons age 12 or older. In 2015, 0.98% of all persons age 12 or older (2.7 million persons) experienced at least one violent victimization, and 0.41% (1.1 million persons) experienced at least one serious violent victimization (rape or sexual assault, robbery, and aggravated assault). Among households in the United States, 7.60% (10.0 million) of all households experienced one or more property victimizations. https://www.bjs.gov/content/pub/pdf/cv15_sum.pdf

to deal with the millions of minor-crime prosecutions that occur every year. For example, a defendant who is charged with a misdemeanor may not be entitled to a preliminary hearing, grand jury review, pretrial discovery, or a jury trial. Also, prosecutions for minor crimes may be tried in municipal court before a magistrate who may not be a lawyer.

2. The Gap Between Law and Practice

When lawyers practice criminal law, they often find that the criminal procedure rules "on the books" may not be reflected in reality, and that a defendant's rights may be rarely invoked or enforced. This may be the result of defense counsel's advice to waive these rights, as when a defendant pleads guilty and thereby waives the right to trial by jury and the privilege against self-incrimination, among others. Or, it may be the case that defense counsel lacks the resources to pursue all potential legal arguments available to an indigent defendant, or that such counsel is incompetent under A.B.A. standards but probably not "ineffective" under federal constitutional standards. It may be that a defense counsel lacks evidence that will persuade a judge or prosecutor to accept a defendant's claim, as when a judge credits a police officer's testimony concerning an event and rejects the defendant's testimony. Even when a defendant has a good claim, he or she may nonetheless have no right to the assistance of appointed counsel to pursue such a claim. According to Supreme Court precedents, the Sixth Amendment guarantees trial counsel for indigent defendants only in those cases where he or she will receive a jail or prison sentence. For appeals, the Fourteenth Amendment guarantees indigent defendants a right to counsel only for the first appeal. Defendants who seek to pursue claims in other circumstances have no federal constitutional right to counsel, although they may have such rights based on state constitutional or statutory law.

The gap between law and practice also is created by the decentralized nature of prosecution systems. The federal system is the most centralized institution, because police and prosecutors generally answer to a single prosecutorial authority, the Department of Justice (DOJ) (although some federal agencies also have their own prosecution units). The DOJ attempts to create some uniformity among its agents through the promulgation of policy positions to be followed by all United States Attorneys' Offices and, for example, all Drug Enforcement Administration officers. By contrast, in state prosecution systems, police and prosecutors often work for different authorities, so that police actions may not be authorized by prosecutors, but only by the police department. Typically, state prosecutors have "territorial" jurisdiction over a particular county (which often overlaps with the jurisdiction of certain local prosecutors or city attorneys), and a variety of police departments also have overlapping jurisdictions within the same territory. This collection of autonomous groups in the prosecution system makes it difficult for uniform policies or practices to be implemented without the cooperation of all of the agents in the system.

Finally, both police and prosecutors are vested with considerable discretion, which further widens the gap between law and practice. For example, the police have substantial discretion to ignore criminal acts, or to arrest one person for a certain crime but not another person who has committed exactly the same crime. Prosecutors have discretion in their charging decisions, and in plea bargaining. Some of the Supreme Court's remedies for constitutional violations by police and prosecutors are assumed to be necessary in order to create incentives for these law enforcement agents and officials to adhere to constitutional obligations. Yet even the existence of incentives cannot always insure the proper recognition and enforcement of constitutional rights on the streets, or for that matter, in court.

C. The Roles of Prosecutors and Defense Counsel in Various Stages of a Criminal Prosecution

1. The Pre-Arrest Investigation Stage

One goal of most pre-arrest investigations, whether conducted by police or by prosecutors working together with police, is to obtain evidence that will satisfy the "probable cause" standard required both for arrest and for judicial validation of any decision to charge a person with a crime. This standard does not require as much evidence as the "preponderance" (more likely than not) standard for proving liability in a typical civil case. But the probable cause standard requires more proof than the lower "reasonable suspicion" standard that allows police to stop, question, frisk, and briefly detain people during pre-arrest investigations. A second goal of most pre-arrest investigations is to obtain sufficient evidence to satisfy the "beyond a reasonable doubt" standard required ultimately for conviction at trial. If this kind of evidence cannot be obtained before an arrest is made, then police and prosecutors will attempt to obtain it by using a variety of investigatory techniques after the arrest.

A prosecutor's first contact with a case usually occurs after police have engaged in some investigative procedures following the report of a crime, i.e. it is reactive not proactive, or after police have arrested a person following such a report and investigation. Police may not be able to make a

Food for Thought

Would our criminal justice system be fairer, do you think, if prosecutors were more involved in pre-arrest investigative activities?

crime-scene arrest, but they usually will interview the victim and any witnesses and collect evidence, in order to effectively preserve a record for later prosecution. Unlike the police activities portrayed in television dramas, investigations for most crimes do not go beyond these simple activities. When further investigation is called for, prosecutors sometimes may be asked to participate in police efforts to obtain a warrant for searches and seizures of a person's home, or in interviews of witnesses or interrogations of a person who is a possible suspect but not in custody. Occasionally, prosecutors may participate in investigations of unreported crimes. They may help to supervise "sting" operations, for example, or to advise the police concerning the use of undercover police agents or informants, or the use of police surveillance techniques such as electronic monitoring. Prosecutors may also investigate crimes through the use of grand jury proceedings, and rely on subpoenas to compel witnesses to testify and provide evidence to grand juries.

Defense counsel usually will not play a role in pre-arrest investigative activities by prosecutors and police, unless called upon to do so by a client. For example, a person with retained counsel may ask for advice concerning the advisability of agreeing to a police interview, and may decide to agree to the interview only in the presence of counsel. A witness who is required to appear before a grand jury may consult retained counsel during breaks in the course of the grand jury proceedings. A person who believes he or she may be the "target" of a grand jury investigation may also employ retained counsel to communicate with prosecutors concerning the case, in order to protect his or her interests, to gain immunity, or to attempt to influence the ultimate charging decision.

2. The Arrest Stage

There are two different kinds of arrests: the non-custodial "citation" arrest, and the "full-custody" arrest. Both require probable cause, but the citation arrest is used typically only for minor offenses such as traffic crimes. Many states and municipalities authorize police to issue an arrest citation for such crimes, in their discretion, and to release the arrested person after giving them the citation. The arrestee has the obligation to respond to the citation, either by pleading guilty and paying a fine, or by appearing in court to contest guilt. Even for minor offenses, however, police may retain the discretion to perform a full-custody arrest, and usually they will follow this practice when arresting a person for a serious crime. After forcibly detaining the arrestee, the police will take him or her to the police station for "booking," and then the arrestee will be jailed or possibly released to await the outcome of the prosecutor's review and decision to charge.

Most arrests are made without warrants, as authorized by the Supreme Court's precedents establishing a variety of exceptions to the Fourth Amendment's warrant requirement. Thus, police will seek an arrest warrant from a magistrate only when this is required by law, or when there is some practical reason to do so.

Prosecutors may work together with police in preparing the documents to present to a magistrate. The request for a warrant must be supported by sworn affidavits describing the investigation that led the police to believe there is probable cause that a crime has been committed by a particular person. The magistrate's hearing on the police request for an arrest warrant is *ex parte*, so that defense counsel usually have no role to play in this procedure.

It's Latin to Me

Ex parte. On or from one party only, usually without notice to or argument from the adverse party.

The power to make a full-custody arrest carries with it other powers. It entitles police to perform a full search of the arrestee's person at the scene of arrest, and to search the passenger compartment of a car when arresting a driver. Once a person is in custody, even more intrusive body searches may be allowed for arrestees who are going to be jailed. Even though these searches may be made without probable cause, a warrantless arrest must be based upon probable cause that will be reviewed by a magistrate at a hearing after the arrest. The Supreme Court's precedents establish 48 hours as the maximum deadline for such a hearing, but most states have a significantly shorter deadlines.

3. The Booking and Jailing Stage

People who have been subjected to a full-custody arrest will also undergo the booking process, which usually occurs at the police station or jail. The purpose of booking is to allow the police to keep a record of arrests, and to obtain photographs and fingerprints of arrestees. There is no connection between booking and the formal "charging" process, which occurs later. During booking, the arrestee is asked to supply biographical information, such as name and address, but should not be asked questions about the crime. After booking, police may allow people who are arrested for minor crimes to post "bail" immediately, and to be released on their own recognizance, pending the outcome of later decisions whether or not to file

FYI

"Between 1990 and 2004, 62% of felony defendants in State courts in the 75 largest counties were released prior to the disposition of their case. Beginning in 1998, financial pre-trial releases, requiring the posting of bail, were more prevalent than non-financial releases. This increase in the use of financial releases was mostly the result of a decrease in the use of release on recognizance, coupled with an increase in the use of commercial surety bonds." Thomas H. Cohen & Brian A. Reaves, U.S. Department of Justice, Office of Justice Programs, Bureau of Justice Statistics Special Report, "State Court Processing Statistics, 1990-2004: Pretrial Release of Felony Defendants in State Courts," (November 2007), http://www.bjs.gov/content/pub/pdf/prfdsc.pdf.

formal charges against them. However, people who lack the money to post bail will be jailed, as will people who are charged with serious crimes. Someone who is jailed may be subjected to a thorough search of his or her person, and a complete inventory of the new arrestee's possessions may be performed. State or local law, or police custom or practice may allow an arrestee to telephone a lawyer or a friend at this stage, but an arrested person who is indigent may not have contact with appointed defense counsel until the arraignment stage.

4. The Post-Arrest Investigation Stage

After an arrest, a prosecutor may participate in the same kinds of investigative activity that precedes an arrest, such as witness interviews or interrogations, and the procuring of search warrants. Additionally, a prosecutor may participate in activities that usually occur only after arrest, such as a "lineup,"where police require the arrestee to stand with a group of people who roughly resemble him or her, and ask a witness to attempt to identify the person who committed the crime. An indigent arrestee has no *per se* right to have appointed counsel present during a lineup. Not until the initiation of formal "adversarial judicial proceedings" does such a right to counsel exist. Nor does the arrestee have a right to have appointed counsel present at a photographic "showup," where police show a witness an "array" of photographs which includes a picture of the defendant, and ask the witness to attempt to identify the guilty party. A prosecutor also may participate in the interrogation of an arrested person, who is now entitled to *Miranda* warnings due to the existence of "custodial" interrogation. An arrestee may invoke the right to counsel by asking for a lawyer during an interrogation, thereby precluding further interrogation until counsel is present. *See* discussion in Chapter 6.

5. The Decision to Bring a Formal Charge by Filing a Complaint

When a person is arrested, the police have, in a sense, "charged" that person with committing a crime, but that is not a formal charge that will serve as the basis of a prosecution. The prosecution does not actually begin until a "complaint" is filed, either by the prosecutor or by the police. Many arrests do not result in the filing of complaint. In some cases, a supervising police officer will decide that no charge should be pursued. In many jurisdictions, a prosecutor will make this decision, although it is possible that the decision to drop a case may not be made until after the defendant's "first appearance," or even later, after the filing of an information or issuance of an indictment. When a prosecutor decides to drop a charge, it is often due to insufficient admissible evidence, or because of the unavailability of witnesses whose testimony is believed to be necessary for conviction. In making charging decisions, a prosecutor also may decide to change the original charge, or to add additional charges. It is common for a prosecutor to review all felony arrests before deciding which charges to pursue by filing a complaint, and to allow police to file a complaint for most misdemeanor charges without a prosecutor's review.

When a complaint is filed either by a prosecutor or by a police officer, the arrestee is now a "defendant." The complaint usually sets forth a description of the crime and a citation to the criminal code offense being charged. Either the police or the victim will sign the complaint, and swear to the truth of its allegations. The act of filing the complaint is not necessarily accompanied by other immediate formal judicial proceedings. However, this filing sets other procedures in motion under state or local law, such as the requirement that a defendant must make a "first appearance" in court within a certain time period. If the defendant is not in jail, there may be a time lapse

> **FYI**
>
> "Between 1990 and 2009, more than 3 in 5 felony defendants were charged with either a drug offense or property offense, and about 1 in 4 was charged with a violent offense. The percentage of defendants charged with a violent offense in 2009 (25%) approached that observed in 1990 (27%) after dropping to a low of 23% in 2004 and 2005. Drug defendants represented 33% of felony cases in both 1990 and 2009, but they accounted for 37% of cases between 1996 and 2006." Brian A. Reaves, "Felony Defendants in Large Urban Counties, 2009," (December 2013), https://www.bjs.gov/content/pub/pdf/fdluc09.pdf.

of several days before this hearing, but any defendant in jail must be brought "promptly" before a magistrate. Further, if a defendant was arrested without a warrant, the validity of probable cause for the arrest must also be determined promptly by a magistrate.

If the crime is a misdemeanor, the complaint will remain the "charging instrument" for the prosecutor, and the case usually will be tried in a lower-level court. However, if the crime is a felony, the complaint will be replaced with a different instrument after proceedings in the lower-level court are finished, and the case proceeds to the "court of original jurisdiction," where the trial will occur. In cases where the grand jury is involved, that charging document will be an "indictment," and in other cases, that document is called an "information." Defense counsel usually does not play a role at the charging stage, unless he or she has been retained by a client to communicate with the prosecutor and to attempt to negotiate the disposition of the charge.

6. The Defendant's First Appearance in Court

The defendant's first appearance in court occurs after the complaint is filed. This initial hearing—sometimes called the "presentment"—before the magistrate may occur as early as a few hours after arrest, or as late as several days after the arrest, depending on the defendant's custodial status and the nature of the arrest.

Usually, the hearing has three purposes. First, the magistrate informs the defendant of the charges set forth in the complaint, and typically describes the defendant's various rights, such as the right to remain silent and the right to counsel. Second, the magistrate must determine whether the defendant is indigent, and ask an indigent defendant whether he or she wishes to be represented by appointed counsel. Most defendants are indigent. Most often, these defendants will be represented by attorneys who are employed by a state or local public defender agency. However, some jurisdictions continue to use a system of appointing attorneys from the private Bar. A few jurisdictions allow a private law firm or other group to have a contract for representation of indigents.

The magistrate is supposed to take whatever steps are necessary to begin the process of having counsel appointed in a particular jurisdiction. Finally, the magistrate sets bail for the defendant at this hearing, assuming that this is necessary because the defendant is in custody. The magistrate may require the defendant to post cash or a bond that is secured from a professional bonding agency. In the alternative, the magistrate may decide to release a defendant, but impose conditions on that release. Some states allow the magistrate to perform a fourth function at this hearing, which is to review the grounds for probable cause for a warrantless arrest. For misdemeanor cases triable in the magistrate's court, a fifth function of the first appearance is to ask for the defendant's plea on the record. It is possible for a misdemeanor defendant to plead guilty, assuming that any right to counsel and other rights are properly waived. The magistrate's acceptance of a guilty plea is regulated by standards set forth in constitutional precedents as well as statutory law. In felony cases, the defendant's plea on the record will occur at the arraignment. While indigent defendants will not be represented by appointed counsel at the first appearance, retained defense counsel may participate in the hearing.

> "Indigent defense involves the use of publicly financed counsel to represent criminal defendants who are unable to afford private counsel. At the end of their case approximately 66% of felony Federal defendants and 82% of felony defendants in large State courts were represented by public defenders or assigned counsel." Caroline Wolf Harlow, U.S. Department of Justice, Office of Justice Programs, Bureau of Justice Statistics Special Report, "Defense Counsel in Criminal Cases," (November 2000), http://www.bjs.gov/content/pub/pdf/dccc.pdf.

7. The Preliminary Hearing or Grand Jury Stage

The preliminary hearing (sometimes called a preliminary examination) usually will usually be the first stage where an indigent defendant will be represented by appointed counsel, and thus for most defendants, it will be the first proceeding where the prosecutor and the defense counsel meet formally as adversaries. However, a preliminary hearing may not occur for a variety of reasons. A prosecutor may decide not to pursue the charge and file a *nolle prosequi* motion in order to have the complaint dismissed. Defense counsel may advise a client to plead guilty, and to waive the preliminary hearing in anticipation of the plea. Or, a prosecutor in some few jurisdictions may decide to avoid the disadvantages of a preliminary hearing by seeking an indictment from a grand jury.

It's Latin to Me

Nolle prosequi. A legal notice that a lawsuit or prosecution has been abandoned.

The primary disadvantage of a preliminary hearing, from a prosecutor's point of view, is that it provides advantages to defense counsel. Specifically, it allows defense counsel to cross-examine the "probable cause" witnesses who testify at the hearing, and thereby obtain a formal record that may be used for impeachment of these witnesses at trial. Defense counsel may also discover a prosecutor's evidence or strategy that would otherwise be difficult to learn about before trial. Typically, defense does not present evidence at a preliminary hearing, in order to avoid the very disadvantages that may provoke a prosecutor to avoid such a hearing. By taking the same witnesses to a secret grand jury proceeding where defense counsel is absent, the prosecutor, in jurisdictions permitting this avenue, may obtain a finding of probable cause while avoiding the need to have a magistrate to make this determination at a preliminary hearing.

See It

Do you want to view a preliminary hearing? Here's one you can watch involving a defendant accused of murdering his girlfriend and her unborn child. *See* https://www.youtube.com/watch?v=aJeomZoeSyE.

In any event, even if the prosecutor does decide to go forward with a preliminary hearing, and to minimize the exposure of witnesses by presenting a small amount of evidence, it is the rare case where a magistrate rejects a complaint for lack of probable cause. After all, another magistrate has previously concluded that probable cause existed for the arrest, and unless other evidence casts doubt upon that determination, the result of this second probable cause determination will be the same.

Once this decision is made, there are two possible routes that the prosecution will take, depending on the requirements of state law. In a majority of states, the defendant will then be "bound over" to the trial court, where the prosecutor will file an "information" which supplants the complaint.

In a few other states and in federal prosecutions, the defendant must be "bound over" to the grand jury, so that an indictment may issue from that body, and supplant the complaint. In states where a prosecutor has the option of using the grand jury or filing an information, the latter procedure is typically used. If the grand jury option must be used, this group is required to make an independent determination of probable cause, based on a prosecutor's presentation of evidence. Defense counsel do not have access to these secret proceedings. It is the rare case where a grand jury refuses to indict a defendant, whether or not the grand jury's proceeding was preceded by a preliminary hearing.

Once an indictment is issued or an information is filed, Supreme Court precedents create some limitations on a prosecutor's subsequent investigative activities. For example, if undercover police agents deliberately elicit incriminating statements from a defendant at this stage, such statements will not be admissible at trial on the charged offense. If a prosecutor wishes to conduct a lineup at this point, and does so in the absence of counsel, any identification obtained at the lineup will likewise be inadmissible.

8. The Arraignment Stage

The arraignment has two functions. It is a hearing in the trial court where the judge will inform the defendant of the felony charges in the indictment or information, and where the defendant will be asked to enter a plea to the charges on the record. Most defendants will enter a plea of not guilty, and the judge will then set the case for trial. An indigent defendant is entitled to representation by appointed counsel at arraignment. If counsel has not been appointed and a defendant asks for counsel, this will operate as a bar to further police interrogation about the charged crime until counsel is present, but will not necessarily cut off questioning about other crimes.

See It

Do you want to view an arraignment? Here's one you can watch involving a defendant charged with eight counts of attempted murder; five counts of terrorism, six counts of intimidation with a dangerous weapon; eight counts of assault on a peace officer with the intent to inflict serious injury; and eight counts of assault on a peace officer by use or display of a dangerous weapon. *See* https://www.youtube.com/watch?v=EKJLBNteq9U.

Once the arraignment occurs, plea negotiations may begin, although in some cases they may occur even earlier (or later). Defense counsel may advise a defendant to plead guilty because of the benefits offered by a prosecutor in exchange for a plea, whether in the form of an agreement to reduce charges or to recommend a lower sentence. However, a prosecutor may decline to offer such benefits, especially for serous charges. Most cases are nonetheless resolved by guilty pleas, but the rate of pleas varies among jurisdictions and as between crimes. If no guilty plea occurs, a prosecutor may either dismiss the charges or continue to investigate the case and prepare for trial. The prosecutor will seek discovery material from the defense as permitted by statutory law, such as a list of trial witnesses. In some jurisdictions, the defense must give the prosecution notice of the intent to raise certain defenses at trial, such as alibi or insanity. The prosecutor may also rely on expert witnesses to assist with forensic evidence, or with preparation for rebuttal of certain defenses.

Ideally, if defense counsel has the resources and time to investigate a case thoroughly, he or she may hire a private investigator to assist in interviewing witnesses and collecting evidence. Counsel will interview the defendant, examine the police report, and seek discovery of exculpatory material from the prosecutor, as well as other discovery material allowed by state or federal law, such as a list of trial witnesses. Counsel may seek to have an expert appointed for an indigent defendant to assist in trial preparation relating to crucial issues.

Defense counsel should attempt to follow the A.B.A. Criminal Justice Defense Function Standards concerning the proper representation of a criminal defendant. There are especially complex duties of preparation required by the A.B.A. Standards for capital cases. However, appointed defense counsel are sometimes burdened with large caseloads and have few or no resources for investigating a case thoroughly. In some jurisdictions, there are caps on the maximum fees that appointed counsel may receive, such as $1,000 for all the work involved in preparing and trying a capital case. In a few jurisdictions, these caps have been challenged on constitutional grounds, and legislative and judicial responses to these challenges have sometimes created resulted in increased resources available to defense counsel.

> **FYI**
>
> The 4th edition of the A.B.A. Criminal Justice Defense Function Standards, adopted in 2015, can be found at https://www.americanbar.org/groups/criminal_justice/standards/DefenseFunctionFourthEdition-TableofContents.html.

9. The Pre-Trial Motions Stage

As part of defense counsel's investigation of a case, certain pre-trial motions may be filed, such as a motion to compel disclosure of evidence, or for the appointment of expert witnesses to testify at trial concerning a mental-state defense like insanity. Other motions will be made in order to pursue a defendant's claims that the police or prosecutor violated the constitution or statutory law. These motions include a motion to exclude inadmissible evidence at trial, usually referred to as a "motion to suppress" evidence. Other standard motions include a motion to quash the indictment because of particular defects, a motion for reduction of bail, and a motion *in limine* to limit the prosecutor's examination of witnesses in some way.

Most motions to suppress are filed in order to exclude materials seized in unconstitutional searches, or incriminating statements by the defendants obtained in unconstitutional interrogations, or pre-trial identifications by witnesses obtained in an unconstitutional manner. In the small percentage of cases where a motion to suppress is granted, this ruling may result in a prosecutor's filing a *nolle prosequi* motion to dismiss, because the prosecutor now believes there is insufficient evidence of proof of guilt "beyond a reasonable doubt" to obtain a conviction at trial. However, the prosecutor may obtain additional evidence later and proceed with the same charge against the same defendant again, because the protection of the Double Jeopardy Clause does not attach until the jury is sworn at trial.

See It

Do you want to view a suppression hearing? Here's one you can watch involving a defendant charged with DUI (driving under the influence). *See* https://www.youtube.com/watch?v=NhmkC87Kzg4.

10. The Trial Stage

Defendants are guaranteed the right to a speedy trial, and some defendants will receive a trial within the time limits set by federal or state statutes, which often require that the trial occur within six months of the indictment. However, defense counsel may advise a defendant to waive the right to a speedy trial, e.g. in order to have more time for pretrial preparation, and even where the right is not waived, a statutory exception to the required deadline may apply.

Defense counsel and a prosecutor will conduct *voir dire* of the jury in most states, although in some state courts and the federal courts, the judge conducts voir dire. Based on the information obtained from juror questionnaires and the answers obtained from jurors during *voir dire* questioning, the prosecutor and defense counsel will

FYI

Of 100 defendants arraigned on serious felony charges in the 75 largest urban counties in the U.S., only 4 of them will actually go to trial. Sixty-five will plead guilty; 23 will have their cases dismissed; and 8 will be diverted or have some other outcome. Thomas H. Cohen and Tracey Kyckelhahn, U.S. Department of Justice, Office of Justice Programs, Bureau of Justice Statistics Bulletin, "Felony Defendants in Large Urban Counties, 2006," (May 2010), http://www.bjs.gov/content/pub/pdf/fdluc06.pdf.

challenge jurors "for cause" and with "peremptory challenges." This process is regulated by Supreme Court precedents governing jury selection, as well as by statutory laws that define the grounds for challenges and limit each side to a certain number of peremptory challenges.

Most cases are tried to a jury, although defense counsel may advise the defendant to waive the right to a jury trial in some cases. Only a small percentage of trials end in a mistrial because the jury cannot agree on a verdict. Supreme Court precedents limit the right to jury trial to cases where the maximum sentence is more than six months in prison, but some states provide for this right in other cases. Most states require that the jury verdict be unanimous, although Supreme Court precedents allow for non-unanimous, state court criminal verdicts. Most states also require a jury of twelve for serious felonies and capital cases, and some states use six-person juries for misdemeanors or less serious felonies. The Court's precedents hold that a unanimous jury of six is the smallest size that can be used for a criminal trial. Most trials end in conviction, and the conviction rates vary significantly for different crimes.

11. The Sentencing Stage

In most states, a convicted defendant in a non-capital case will be sentenced by the trial judge, but in a few states, the jury will sentence the defendant. In a capital case, the jury has the responsibility of choosing between life and death. Some states have adopted complex sentencing guidelines for non-capital cases, modeled on the federal sentencing guidelines. These guidelines, or the existence of statutory "mandatory minimum" sentences, may influence or limit the discretion of a sentencing judge.

Food for Thought

Would our system be fairer if the newly-convicted defendant was typically sentenced by the same jury of peers that just found him or her guilty, rather than by the trial judge?

An indigent defendant is entitled to representation by appointed counsel at the sentencing hearing, which is usually held some weeks after the trial so that the probation department may prepare a presentence report for the judge. This report will contain information about the defendant's history that the probation officer believes may be relevant to sentencing. At sentencing, defense counsel may try to challenge information in the report, and may produce new information for the judge's consideration. Usually, however, the role of a defense counsel and prosecutor is confined to argument concerning the appropriate exercise of judicial discretion, based on the facts in the presentence report. Defendants convicted of misdemeanors often receive a fine or community service, or both, instead of a jail sentence, but most defendants convicted of serious felonies receive a substantial prison sentence. Once a sentence is imposed, the state corrections system takes on the responsibility for administering it. The availability of parole and "good time" may mean that a defendant will not serve the same time as the sentence that is imposed by the judge.

12. The Appeal Stage

When a defendant appeals a conviction, Supreme Court precedents hold that this action does not implicate Double Jeopardy rights if the reversal is on a ground other than the sufficiency of the evidence. Accordingly, the defendant-appellant may usually be tried again if the conviction is reversed. The Court's precedents also hold that an indigent defendant is entitled to appointed counsel to pursue the first appeal "of right." While there is no federal constitutional right to such an appeal itself, all states have a long tradition of providing this right. For a state defendant, this appeal usually lies in the intermediate appellate court, or in the state supreme court of a state that has no such intermediate courts. For a federal defendant, the appeal lies in the federal Circuit Court of Appeals. In most states with intermediate appellate courts, once the defendant loses the first appeal of right, a further appeal to the state supreme court will be heard only if that court exercises its discretion and decides to hear the case. Supreme Court precedents do not establish a right to appointed counsel for indigent defendants for this second discretionary appeal, or for subsequent stages, such as the pursuit of a writ of certiorari from the Supreme Court. Only after the appeal process is exhausted will the conviction be termed "final." At that point, a convicted defendant may pursue the inaptly named "post-conviction remedies" that are available in state and federal court.

13. The "Post-Conviction" Remedies Stage

Once a conviction is final, see above, a state defendant usually must pursue his claims by filing a petition in the state trial court, seeking state "habeas" or "*coram nobis*" relief. A defendant may seek an evidentiary hearing on such claims, and some states provide that indigents have a right to appointed counsel at this stage. Even in states that do not provide counsel automatically at this stage, a trial court may decide to appoint counsel in a particular case in order to have the merits of the case briefed and argued, or in order to provide representation at the evidentiary hearing. Most requests for evidentiary hearings at this stage, however, are not granted. If a hearing is granted, it will be conducted as a civil proceeding. The losing party may appeal to the intermediate appellate court, and then to the state supreme court. At this point, a losing defendant usually will have "exhausted" his or her available post-conviction remedies in state court, and may file a petition for a writ of habeas corpus in federal district court, in order to pursue federal constitutional claims. A federal defendant begins the post-conviction process by filing that petition at the outset in federal district court. In non-capital cases, post-conviction relief is granted in a very small percentage of cases. In capital cases, however, there is a higher percentage of cases where relief is granted, especially in some federal circuits.

Executive Summary

Constitutional Criminal Procedure Rights. The Bill of Rights, especially the Fourth, Fifth, Sixth, and Eighth Amendments, through the Due Process and Equal Protection Clauses of the Fourteenth Amendment, is the source of most of the rights that individuals possess relating to law enforcement activity and in the criminal justice system.

State Constitutional Criminal Procedure Rights. State constitutions are often interpreted as providing greater individual rights in the criminal justice setting that Bill of Rights provisions as interpreted by the Supreme Court.

Dual Sovereignty. Multiple prosecutions for the same criminal act by the federal and state governments are not prohibited by the Constitution.

Prosecutors Are Generally Reactive Not Proactive. Most criminal activity comes to the attention of prosecutors after reports from law enforcement agents rather than resulting from a concerted investigative effort.

Major Themes

a. Law and Practice Often Different—The rights a particular Bill of Rights provides and the rights individuals actually receive may not be—and often are not—the same thing.

b. Discretion Pervasive—Law enforcement officers and prosecutors have wide discretion in who and how they investigate suspected criminal activity and in what and when criminal charges are filed.

c. Indigents Disadvantaged—Criminal defendants who have sufficient means to retain their own counsel, post bail, and hire experts and investigators, have an advantage in that regard over indigent defendants who have a limited entitlement to such things.

d. Plea Bargaining Is the Name of the Game—Most criminal defendants facing serious charges end up pleading guilty to lesser charges as a result of their acceptance of a plea bargain.

Charging Documents. An accused person may face charges filed in an "information" issued after a preliminary hearing or, in some states and in federal prosecutions, as a result of an "indictment" issued by a grand jury.

Discovery in Criminal Cases. The preliminary hearing is the principal means of discovery of the information possessed by the prosecution in criminal cases.

Most Defendants Do Not Actually Go To Trial. Most criminal defendants do not ultimately stand trial on the charges filed against them. Most defendants plead guilty instead, although many have the charges against them dismissed.

Finality of Convictions. A conviction is not "final" until the final appeal has concluded or opportunity to appeal has lapsed. Even then, a convicted defendant may seek to initiate post-conviction proceedings, such as seeking a writ of habeas corpus.

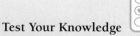

Test Your Knowledge

To assess your understanding of the material in this chapter, click here to take a quiz.

For More Information

• William J. Brennan, Jr., *The Bill of Rights and the States: The Revival of State Constitutions As Guardians of Individual Rights*, 61 N.Y.U. L. REV. 535 (1986)

• RUSSELL L. WEAVER, JOHN M. BURKOFF, CATHERINE HANCOCK & STEVEN I. FRIEDLAND, PRINCIPLES OF CRIMINAL PROCEDURE Ch. 1 (6th ed. 2018).

• Catherine M. Grosso & Barbara O'Brien, *Grounding Criminal Procedure*, 20 J. Gender Race & Just. 53 (2017).

• WAYNE LAFAVE, JEROLD ISRAEL, NANCY KING & ORIN KERR, CRIMINAL PROCEDURE 6th ed (West Academic Publishing 2016).

• Anna Lvovsky, *The Judicial Presumption of Police Expertise*, 130 Harv. L. Rev. 1995 (2017).

• Alexandra Natapoff, *Misdemeanors*, 85 S. CAL. L. REV. 1313 (2012).

• Robert E. Scott & William J. Stuntz, *Plea Bargaining As Contract*, 101 YALE L.J. 1909 (1992).

• William J. Stuntz, *The Pathological Politics of Criminal Law*, 100 MICH. L. REV. 505 (2001).

• William J. Stuntz, *The Uneasy Relationship Between Criminal Procedure and Criminal Justice*, 107 YALE L.J. 1 (1997).

Chapter 2

Fourteenth Amendment Due Process

A. Incorporation of the Bill of Rights

Federal criminal procedure, like other exercises in national governance, are subject to the United States Constitution. Notwithstanding the Bill of Rights' comprehensive and uncontroverted pertinence to federal investigative, prosecutorial and adjudicative processes, its applicability to the states is a more recent and debated phenomenon.[1]

Adoption of the Fourteenth Amendment represented a fundamental redistribution of power from the state to the national government. Although that Amendment heightened federal interest in and responsibility over civil rights, debate has persisted over whether the amendment enhanced the significance of the Bill of Rights and made it applicable to the states. United States Supreme Court opinions have advanced several analytical methods for applying the Bill of Rights to the states.

In the first half of the twentieth century, the leading method for determining how and whether the Bill of Rights was applicable to the states through the Fourteenth Amendment was the "fundamental rights" approach. The Bill of Rights is regarded as protecting rights that are fundamental, and provide a reference point for measuring which state practices are so shocking to the conscience that they are inconsistent with the concept of "ordered liberty." *Palko v. Connecticut*, 302 U.S. 319 (1937). The court evaluated each case under a totality of circumstances approach. For example, long before the Court held in *Gideon v. Wainwright* that the Sixth Amendment required appointment of counsel for state felony defendants, it had held that the Sixth Amendment right to counsel was not a "fundamental right" which the states had to follow. In other words, it did not "shock the conscience" for a state to refuse appointment of counsel for indigent defendant accused of felonies. *Betts v. Brady*, 316 U.S. 455 (1942). Decisions like *Betts* produced criticism that the rights of a state defendant were substantially limited in comparison with a federal defendant.

---

[1] U.S. Const., amend. XIX. The history of Reconstruction is discussed comprehensively in Charles Fairman, VII History of the Supreme Court of the United States, Reconstruction and Reunion (1987).

The second method used to evaluate the applicability of the Bill of Rights to the states through the Fourteenth Amendment was the "total incorporation" approach. All the protections of the Bill of Rights applied to the states. Critics of this approach relied on the lack of legislative history of the Bill of Rights to support any legislative intent that all the protections applied to the states. Although Justice Hugo Black was unable to convince a majority of his colleagues that the total incorporation approach was the proper course, his advocacy nevertheless influenced the "selective incorporation" approach used by the current Court.

In *Duncan v. Louisiana*, 391 U.S. 145 (1968), Justice White described the difference in the approaches.

> Selective incorporation represents a hybrid or compromise between the earlier analytical methods. Its advocates believe that Fourteenth Amendment Due Process includes rights which are essential to "ordered liberty," and that the protections in the Bill of Rights are the only fundamental protections. They also find that the fundamental rights approach is too subjective and unstructured.

In one sense recent cases applying provisions of the first eight Amendments to the States represent a new approach to the "incorporation" debate. Earlier the Court can be seen as having asked, when inquiring into whether some particular procedural safeguard was required of a State, if a civilized system could be imagined that would not accord the particular protection. For example, *Palko v. State of Connecticut* stated: "The right to trial by jury and the immunity from prosecution except as the result of an indictment may have value and importance. Even so, they are not of the very essence of a scheme of ordered liberty. Few would be so narrow or provincial as to maintain that a fair and enlightened system of justice would be impossible without them." The recent cases, on the other hand, have proceeded upon the valid assumption that state criminal processes are not imaginary and theoretical schemes but actual systems bearing virtually every characteristic of the common-law system that has been developing contemporaneously in England and in this country. The question thus is whether given this kind of system a particular procedure is fundamental—whether, that is, a procedure is necessary to an Anglo—American regime of ordered liberty. It is this sort of inquiry that can justify the conclusions that state courts must exclude evidence seized in violation of the Fourth Amendment, *Mapp v. State of Ohio;* and that state prosecutors may not comment on a defendant's failure to testify, *Griffin v. State of California.*

Of each of these determinations that a constitutional provision originally written to bind the Federal Government should bind the States as well it might be said that the limitation in question is not necessarily fundamental to fairness in every criminal system that might be imagined but is fundamental in the context of the criminal processes maintained by the American States. When the inquiry is approached in this way the question whether the States can impose criminal punishment without granting a jury trial appears quite different from the way it appeared in the older cases opining that States might abolish jury trial. A criminal process which was fair and equitable but used no juries is easy to imagine. It would make use of alternative guarantees and protections which would serve the purposes that the jury serves in the English and American systems. Yet no American State has undertaken to construct such a system. Instead, every American State, including Louisiana, uses the jury extensively, and imposes very serious punishments only after a trial at which the defendant has a right to a jury's verdict. In every State, including Louisiana, the structure and style of the criminal process—the supporting framework and the subsidiary procedures—are of the sort that naturally complement jury trial, and have developed in connection with and in reliance upon jury trial.

To determine whether a particular Bill of Rights protection applies to the states under the selective incorporation approach, it is necessary to look at 1) the entirety of the right, not just as it applies to a particular set of facts (as with the fundamental rights approach), and 2) whether the provision is fundamental to Anglo-American jurisprudence. In *Malloy v. Hogan*, 378 U.S. 1 (1964), Justice Brennan observed that if the right applies to the states, all aspects of the right will apply to every state case as it applies to every federal case.

We hold that the Fourteenth Amendment guaranteed the petitioner the protection of the Fifth Amendment's privilege against self-incrimination, and that under the applicable federal standard, the state court erred in holding that the privilege was not properly invoked. The state urges that the availability of the federal privilege to a witness in a state inquiry is to be determined according to a less stringent safeguard than is applicable in a federal proceeding. We disagree. We have held that the guarantees aspects of the Bill of Rights are all to be enforced against the States under the Fourteenth Amendment according to the same standards that protect those personal rights against federal encroachment. The Court thus has rejected the notion that the Fourteenth Amendment applies to the States only a "watered-down, subjective version of the individual guarantees of the Bill of Rights."

Despite criticism that the selective incorporation approach is arbitrary and prevents local experimentation, it was the basis for applying most of the Bill of Rights protections to the states in the second half of the twentieth century. Of the Bill of Rights provisions related to criminal procedure, the Court has refused to find that only two portions are expressly applicable to the states through the Fourteenth Amendment. The Eighth Amendment prohibition on excessive bail, although it may be regarded by the Court as fundamental, is not applicable to the states. As recently as the 1990's, the Court has noted that the Fifth Amendment requirement for a grand jury indictment in felony cases is inapplicable to the states. *Albright v. Oliver*, 510 U.S. 266 (1994).

McDonald v. City of Chicago, Illinois

561 U.S. 742 (2010).

JUSTICE ALITO announced the judgment of the Court.

Two years ago, in *District of Columbia v. Heller*, 554 U.S. 570 (2008), we held that the Second Amendment protects the right to keep and bear arms for the purpose of self-defense, and we struck down a District of Columbia law that banned the possession of handguns in the home. The city of Chicago and the village of Oak Park, a Chicago suburb, have laws that are similar to the District of Columbia's, but Chicago and Oak Park argue that their laws are constitutional because the Second Amendment has no application to the States. We have previously held that most of the provisions of the Bill of Rights apply with full force to both the Federal Government and the States. Applying the standard that is well established in our case law, we hold that the Second Amendment right is fully applicable to the States.

The Bill of Rights, including the Second Amendment, originally applied only to the Federal Government. In *Barron ex rel. Tiernan v. Mayor of Baltimore*, 7 Pet. 243, 8 L.Ed. 672 (1833), the Court, in an opinion by Chief Justice Marshall, explained that this question was "of great importance" but "not of much difficulty." In less than four pages, the Court firmly rejected the proposition that the first eight Amendments operate as limitations on the States, holding that they apply only to the Federal Government. The constitutional Amendments adopted in the aftermath of the Civil War fundamentally altered our country's federal system. The provision at issue in this case, § 1 of the Fourteenth Amendment, provides, among other things, that a State may not abridge "the privileges or immunities of citizens of the United States" or deprive "any person of life, liberty, or property, without due process of law."

The Court eventually initiated what has been called a process of "selective incorporation," i.e., the Court began to hold that the Due Process Clause fully incorporates particular rights contained in the first eight Amendments. The Court inquired whether a particular Bill of Rights guarantee is fundamental to our scheme of ordered liberty and system of justice.

The Court also shed any reluctance to hold that rights guaranteed by the Bill of Rights met the requirements for protection under the Due Process Clause. The

Court eventually incorporated almost all of the provisions of the Bill of Rights. Only a handful of the Bill of Rights protections remain unincorporated. Finally, the Court abandoned "the notion that the Fourteenth Amendment applies to the States only a watered-down, subjective version of the individual guarantees of the Bill of Rights," stating that it would be "incongruous" to apply different standards "depending on whether the claim was asserted in a state or federal court." Instead, the Court decisively held that incorporated Bill of Rights protections "are all to be enforced against the States under the Fourteenth Amendment according to the same standards that protect those personal rights against federal encroachment."

With this framework in mind, we now turn to whether the Second Amendment right to keep and bear arms is incorporated in the concept of due process. In answering that question, we must decide whether the right to keep and bear arms is fundamental to our scheme of ordered liberty, or whether this right is "deeply rooted in this Nation's history and tradition."

Our decision in *Heller* points unmistakably to the answer. In *Heller*, we held that the Second Amendment protects the right to possess a handgun in the home for the purpose of self-defense. Unless considerations of *stare decisis* counsel otherwise, a provision of the Bill of Rights that protects a right that is fundamental from an American perspective applies equally to the Federal Government and the States. We therefore hold that the Due Process Clause of the Fourteenth Amendment incorporates the Second Amendment right recognized in *Heller*.

Points for Discussion

a. Incorporated Rights

These decisions are cited by the *McDonald* Court as those in which the Court "eventually incorporated almost all of the provisions of the Bill of Rights":

> With respect to the First Amendment, see *Everson v. Board of Ed. of Ewing*, 330 U.S. 1 (1947) (Establishment Clause); *Cantwell v. Connecticut*, 310 U.S. 296 (1940) (Free Exercise Clause); *De Jonge v. Oregon*, 299 U.S. 353 (1937) (freedom of assembly); *Gitlow v. New York*, 268 U.S. 652 (1925) (free speech); *Near v. Minnesota ex rel. Olson*, 283 U.S. 697 (1931) (freedom of the press). With respect to the Fourth Amendment, see *Aguilar v. Texas*, 378 U.S. 108 (1964) (warrant requirement); *Mapp v. Ohio*, 367 U.S. 643 (1961) (exclusionary rule); *Wolf v. Colorado*, 338 U.S. 25 (1949) (freedom from unreasonable searches and seizures). With respect to the Fifth Amendment, see *Benton v. Maryland*, 395 U.S. 784 (1969) (Double Jeopardy Clause); *Malloy v. Hogan*, 378 U.S. 1 (1964) (privilege against self-incrimination); *Chicago, B. & Q.R. Co. v. Chicago*, 166 U.S. 226 (1897) (Just Compensation Clause). With respect to the Sixth Amendment, see *Duncan v. Louisiana*, 391 U.S. 145 (1968) (trial by jury

in criminal cases); *Washington v. Texas*, 388 U.S. 14 (1967) (compulsory process); *Klopfer v. North Carolina*, 386 U.S. 213 (1967) (speedy trial); *Pointer v. Texas*, 380 U.S. 400 (1965) (right to confront adverse witness); *Gideon v. Wainwright*, 372 U.S. 335 (1963) (assistance of counsel); *In re Oliver*, 333 U.S. 257 (1948) (right to a public trial). With respect to the Eighth Amendment, *see Robinson v. California*, 370 U.S. 660 (1962) (cruel and unusual punishment); *Schilb v. Kuebel*, 404 U.S. 357 (1971) (prohibition against excessive bail).

b. Rights Not Fully Incorporated

The *McDonald* Court cited these decisions to illustrate the "handful of the Bill of Rights protections that remain unincorporated":

> In addition to the right to keep and bear arms (and the Sixth Amendment right to a unanimous jury verdict), the only rights not fully incorporated are (1) the Third Amendment's protection against quartering of soldiers; (2) the Fifth Amendment's grand jury indictment requirement; (3) the Seventh Amendment right to a jury trial in civil cases; and (4) the Eighth Amendment's prohibition on excessive fines.

B. Retroactivity

Constitutional interpretation that generates a new rule of law presents an issue with respect to scope of application. Traditionally, the Court has allowed a prevailing litigant to be the beneficiary of a new rule. Initial determinations that illegally seized evidence must be excluded from trial, *Mapp v. Ohio*, 367 U.S. 643 (1961), or that persons in custodial interrogation must be informed of certain rights they possess, *Miranda v. Arizona*, 384 U.S. 436 (1966). thus redounded to the benefit of the individuals who first prevailed. Application at least to the prevailing litigant is justified for purposes of satisfying the case or controversy requirement and providing inducement for challenges that may improve the law.

Take Note

As the *McDonald* Court observed, the Court ultimately adopted the position that incorporated rights protections "are all to be enforced against the States under the Fourteenth Amendment according to 'the same standards that protect those rights from federal encroachment.'" However, the *McDonald* Court noted that "there is one exception to this general rule," and described that exception as follows:

> The Court has held that although the Sixth Amendment right to trial by jury requires a unanimous jury verdict in federal criminal trials, it does not require a unanimous jury verdict in state criminal trials. But that ruling was the result of an unusual division among the Justices, not an endorsement of the two-track approach to incorporation.

Beyond a party whose case engendered a constitutional rule change, the scope of a new principle's operation has been widely debated especially over the past few decades. During the 1960s, as federal case law became increasingly protective of defendant's rights, the Court asserted that the benefit of a new rule would not extend to persons whose convictions became final prior to its adoption. *Linkletter v. Walker*, 381 U.S. 618 (1965). In *Linkletter v. Walker*, 381 U.S. 618, 637–38 (1965), the Court thus applied the exclusionary rule in a forward-looking fashion except to the extent the litigant and persons who had not played out the full string of appeals. Reluctance to allow greater retroactivity reflected the sense that such a distribution of benefits would subvert the interest of finality, generate numerous retrials and undermine good-faith reliance by police and courts on the existing state of constitutional law.

Pursuant to the *Linkletter* doctrine, the benefits of a new rule did not extend to habeas corpus petitioners but could be claimed by persons whose cases still were on direct review. Further tightening of the retroactivity principles occurred thereafter.

FYI

In *Stovall v. Denno*, the Court determined that a newly imposed requirement of counsel at lineups[5] governed only police activity that post-dated the new rule.[6] Like claims would not be heard, therefore, even if asserted in cases for which a final judgment had not been rendered.

[5] *Gilbert v. California*, 388 U.S. 263 (1967); *United States v. Wade*, 388 U.S. 218 (1967).
[6] *Stovall v. Denno*, 388 U.S. 293, 299–301 (1967).

Non-retroactivity (except for the litigant) reflected the work of a Court that, in expanding the ambit of defendants' rights, locked onto prospectivity as a device for minimizing disruption of and costs to the criminal justice system. *See, e.g., Jenkins v. Delaware*, 395 U.S. 213, 219–22 (1969). Whatever virtues the Court attached to such a premise, however, were not consensually acknowledged. In *Desist v. United States*, Justice Harlan argued that prospectivity was a handmaiden of arbitrariness and judicial overreaching. Responding to a majority decision refusing to apply retroactively a rule requiring counsel at certain lineups, Harlan concluded that he could no longer "accept the rule first announced two years ago in *Stovall v. Denno*, and reaffirmed today, which permits this Court to apply a 'new' constitutional rule entirely prospectively, while making an exception only for the particular litigant whose case was chosen as the vehicle for establishing that rule. Indeed, I have concluded that *Linkletter* was right in insisting that all 'new' rules of constitutional law must, at a minimum, be applied to all those cases which are still subject to direct review by this Court at the time the 'new' decision is handed down. He went on to argue that:

Matters of basic principle are at stake. In the classical view of constitutional adjudication, criminal defendants cannot come before this Court simply to request largesse. This Court is entitled to decide constitutional issues only when the facts of a particular case require their resolution for a just adjudication on the merits. We do not release a criminal from jail because we like to do so, or because we think it wise to do so, but because the government has offended constitutional principle in the conduct of his case. When another similarly situated defendant comes before us, we must grant the same relief or give a principled reason for acting differently. We depart from this basic judicial tradition when we simply pick and choose from among similarly situated defendants those who alone will receive the benefit of a "new" rule of constitutional law.

The unsound character of the rule reaffirmed today is perhaps best exposed by considering the following hypothetical. Imagine that the Second Circuit in the present case had anticipated the line of reasoning this Court subsequently pursued in *Katz v. United States*, concluding—as this Court there did—that "the underpinnings of *Olmstead* and *Goldman* have been so eroded by our subsequent decisions that the 'trespass' doctrine there enunciated can no longer be regarded as controlling." Would we have reversed the case on the ground that the principles the Second Circuit had announced—though identical with those in *Katz*—should not control because *Katz* is not retroactive? To the contrary, I venture to say that we would have taken satisfaction that the lower court had reached the same conclusion we subsequently did in *Katz*. If a "new" constitutional doctrine is truly right, we should not reverse lower courts which have accepted it; nor should we affirm those which have rejected the very arguments we have embraced. Anything else would belie the truism that it is the task of this Court, like that of any other, to do justice to each litigant on the merits of his own case. It is only if our decisions can be justified in terms of this fundamental premise that they may properly be considered the legitimate products of a court of law, rather than the commands of a super-legislature.

Re-examination of prior developments in the field of retroactivity leads me irresistibly to the conclusion that the only solid disposition of this case lies in vacating the judgment of the Court of Appeals and in remanding this case to that court for further consideration in light of *Katz*. *Desist v. United States*, 394 U.S. 244, 258–59 (1969).

Harlan's reasoning had long-term significance. In *Griffith v. Kentucky*, the Court determined that a new rule should be applied to all cases pending on direct review. It observed that:

In Justice Harlan's view, and now in ours, failure to apply a newly declared constitutional rule to criminal cases pending on direct review violates basic norms of constitutional adjudication. First, it is a settled principle that this Court adjudicates only "cases" and "controversies." Unlike a legislature, we do not promulgate new rules of constitutional criminal procedure on a broad basis. Rather, the nature of judicial review requires that we adjudicate specific cases, and each case usually becomes the vehicle for announcement of a new rule. But after we have decided a new rule in the case selected, the integrity of judicial review requires that we apply that rule to all similar cases pending on direct review. Justice Harlan observed:

> "If we do not resolve all cases before us on direct review in light of our best understanding of governing constitutional principles, it is difficult to see why we should so adjudicate any case at all. In truth, the Court's assertion of power to disregard current law in adjudicating cases before us that have not already run the full course of appellate review, is quite simply an assertion that our constitutional function is not one of adjudication but in effect of legislation."

As a practical matter, we cannot hear each case pending on direct review and apply the new rule. But we fulfill our judicial responsibility by instructing the lower courts to apply the new rule retroactively to cases not yet final. Thus, it is the nature of judicial review that precludes us from "simply fishing one case from the stream of appellate review, using it as a vehicle for pronouncing new constitutional standards, and then permitting a stream of similar cases subsequently to flow by unaffected by that new rule."

Second, selective application of new rules violates the principle of treating similarly situated defendants the same. As we pointed out in *United States v. Johnson*, the problem with not applying new rules to cases pending on direct review is "the actual inequity that results when the Court chooses which of many similarly situated defendants should be the chance beneficiary" of a new rule. Although the Court had tolerated this inequity for a time by not applying new rules retroactively to cases on direct review, we noted: "The time for toleration has come to an end." *Griffith v. Kentucky*, 479 U.S. 314, 322–23 (1987).

Although arguing for retroactivity to cases in which convictions had not been finalized, Justice Harlan also distinguished collateral review from direct review. Given the unique purpose of the writ of habeas corpus, to ensure that states comply with federal principles at the time they were in force, he identified no logic for retroactivity in collateral proceedings except when punished conduct was beyond a state's law-making power or so fundamental as to be an implication of "ordered liberty." In *Teague v. Lane*, 489 U.S. 288 (1989), a plurality subscribed to Harlan's argument that retroactivity generally should not extend to habeas actions. This determination was notable not only for its investment in Harlan's thesis but for further narrowing the possibility of retroactivity in habeas proceedings.

The Court noted two limited exceptions suggested by Justice Harlan to the general prohibition on announcing or applying new rules in collateral proceedings. First, a new rule should be applied retroactively if it places "certain kinds of primary, private individual conduct beyond the power of the criminal law-making authority to proscribe." The second exception was that a new rule should be applied retroactively if it requires the observance of "watershed rules of criminal procedure." Although *Teague* did not generate a majority opinion, the reasoning of the O'Connor plurality was adopted soon thereafter in *Penry v. Lynaugh*, 492 U.S. 302, 314 (1989).

A critical determinant of retroactivity is whether a principle is driven by precedent or establishes a new rule. The *Linkletter* doctrine reflected Blackstonian theory that regarded new rulings as a discovery of the law as it actually existed. The *Teague* decision and its progeny rejected the notion that the law is decoded, and instead accepted the prior legal condition as a reality. In *Yates v. Aiken*, 484 U.S. 211, 216 (1988), the Court distinguished between a result generated by a rule that breaks new ground and an outcome that is dictated by precedent. It referenced Harlan's understanding "that most collateral attacks on final judgments should be resolved by reference to the state of the law at the time of the petitioner's conviction, and his sense that many 'new' holdings are merely applications of principles that were well settled at the time of conviction."

Justice Harlan in *Desist* had distinguished between rules that were genuinely new and holdings that applied established principles to different factual settings. In *Teague*, the plurality stressed that a new rule is announced "if the result was not *dictated* by precedent existing at the time the defendant's conviction became final." 489 U.S. at 301. Whatever room the *Teague* and *Penry* decisions left, for results ordained by existing precedent, was compressed further in *Butler v. McKellar*, 494 U.S. 407 (1990). The *McKellar* Court determined that a rule was new "if the outcome was susceptible to debate among reasonable minds." The depiction of a new rule elicited criticism by dissenting justices and commentators to the effect that the majority had gutted the writ of habeas corpus and thus "infringed upon legislative prerogatives." 494 U.S. at 432 (Brennan, J., dissenting). Supporting that perspective is the fact that the Court typically does not grant review unless reasonable minds differ over the applicability of existing law.

Butler v. McKellar

494 U.S. 407 (1990).

CHIEF JUSTICE REHNQUIST delivered the opinion of the Court.

Petitioner Horace Butler was convicted and sentenced to death for the murder of Pamela Lane. After his conviction became final on direct appeal, Butler collaterally attacked his conviction by way of a petition for federal habeas corpus. Butler relied on our decision in *Arizona v. Roberson,* decided after his conviction became final on direct appeal. We have held, however, that a new decision generally is not applicable in cases on collateral review unless the decision was dictated by precedent existing at the time the petitioner's conviction became final. *Penry v. Lynaugh*; *Teague v. Lane.* We hold that our ruling in *Roberson* was not so dictated and that Butler's claim is not within either of two narrow exceptions to the general rule.

Butler was indicted and convicted of murder, after the trial court denied his motion to suppress statements he had given to police. In a separate proceeding, the jury sentenced him to death. Butler lost his direct appeal and his petition for state collateral relief. His federal petition for habeas corpus relief was rejected by the trial court and Fourth Circuit. On the same day the Fourth Circuit denied his rehearing petitions, the Supreme Court issued its decision in *Roberson.*

We held in *Roberson* that the Fifth Amendment bars police-initiated interrogation following a suspect's request for counsel in the context of a separate investigation. On Butler's motion for reconsideration, the original Fourth Circuit panel considered Butler's new contention that *Roberson* requires suppression of his statements taken in the separate investigation of Lane's murder. Although the panel conceded that the substance of its prior conclusion "was cast into immediate and serious doubt" by our subsequent decision in *Roberson*, it nevertheless determined that Butler was not entitled to the retroactive benefit of *Roberson.* According to the panel, the *Edwards-Roberson* limitations on police interrogation are only tangentially related to the truth-finding function. They are viewed most accurately as part of the prophylactic protection of the Fifth Amendment right to counsel created to be "guidelines" for the law enforcement profession. The interrogation of Butler, while unquestionably contrary to present "guidelines," was conducted in strict accordance with established law at the time. The panel, therefore, denied Butler's petition for rehearing. A majority of the Circuit Judges denied, over a dissent, Butler's petition for a rehearing en banc. We granted certiorari, and now affirm.

The "new rule" principle validates reasonable, good-faith interpretations of existing precedents made by state courts even though they are shown to be contrary to later decisions.

Butler contends that *Roberson* did not establish a new rule and is, therefore, available to support his habeas petition. Butler argues that *Roberson* was merely an application of *Edwards* to a slightly different set of facts. In support of his position, Butler points out that the majority had said that *Roberson's* case was directly controlled by *Edwards.*

But the fact that a court says that its decision is within the "logical compass" of an earlier decision, or indeed that it is "controlled" by a prior decision, is not conclusive for purposes of deciding whether the current decision is a "new rule" under *Teague*. Courts frequently view their decisions as being "controlled" or "governed" by prior opinions even when aware of reasonable contrary conclusions reached by other courts. In *Roberson*, for instance, the Court found *Edwards* controlling but acknowledged a significant difference of opinion on the part of several lower courts that had considered the question previously. That the outcome in *Roberson* was susceptible to debate among reasonable minds is evidenced further by the differing positions taken by the judges of the Courts of Appeals for the Fourth and Seventh Circuits noted previously. It would not have been an illogical or even a grudging application of *Edwards* to decide that it did not extend to the facts of *Roberson*. We hold, therefore, that *Roberson* announced a "new rule."

The question remains whether the new rule in *Roberson* nevertheless comes within one of the two recognized exceptions under which a new rule is available on collateral review.

Under the first exception, "a new rule should be applied retroactively if it places 'certain kinds of primary, private individual conduct beyond the power of the criminal law-making authority to proscribe." This exception is clearly inapplicable. The proscribed conduct in the instant case is capital murder, the prosecution of which is, to put it mildly, not prohibited by the rule in *Roberson*. Nor did *Roberson* address any "categorical guarantees accorded by the Constitution" such as a prohibition on the imposition of a particular punishment on a certain class of offenders.

Under the second exception, a new rule may be applied on collateral review "if it requires the observance of 'those procedures that are "implicit in the concept of ordered liberty."'" *Teague*, however, discerned a latent danger in relying solely on this famous language from *Palko*: "Were we to employ the *Palko* test without more, we would be doing little more than importing into a very different context the terms of the debate over incorporation. Reviving the *Palko* test now, in this area of law, would be unnecessarily anachronistic." We believe that Justice Harlan's concerns about the difficulty in identifying both the existence and the value of accuracy-enhancing procedural rules can be addressed by limiting the scope of the second exception to those new procedures without which the likelihood of an accurate conviction is seriously diminished. "Because we operate from the premise that such procedures would be so central to an accurate determination of innocence or guilt, we believe it unlikely that many such components of basic due process have yet to emerge."

Because a violation of *Roberson's* added restrictions on police investigatory procedures would not seriously diminish the likelihood of obtaining an accurate determination—indeed, it may increase that likelihood—we conclude that *Roberson* did not establish any principle that would come within the second exception.

The judgment of the Court of Appeals is therefore *Affirmed.*

[JUSTICE BRENNAN dissented, joined by JUSTICES MARSHALL, BLACKMUN and STEVENS. He argued that the Court had narrowed the window for identifying a new rule in habeas proceedings. *Roberson* was not a "new rule,"was dictated by prior precedent, and therefore, should be retroactively applicable to cases on collateral review.]

Whorton v. Bockting

549 U.S. 406 (2007).

JUSTICE ALITO delivered the opinion of the Court.

This case presents the question whether, under the rules set out in *Teague v. Lane*, 489 U.S. 288 (1989), our decision in *Crawford v. Washington*, 541 U.S. 36 (2004), is retroactive to cases already final on direct review. We hold that it is not.

Respondent Marvin Bockting lived in Las Vegas, Nevada, with his wife, Laura Bockting, their 3-year-old daughter Honesty, and Laura's 6-year-old daughter from a previous relationship, Autumn. One night, while respondent was at work, Autumn awoke from a dream crying, but she refused to tell her mother what was wrong, explaining: "Daddy said you would make him leave and that he would beat my butt if I told you." After her mother reassured her, Autumn said that respondent had frequently forced her to engage in numerous and varied sexual acts with him.

The next day, Laura Bockting confronted respondent and asked him to leave the house. He did so but denied any wrongdoing. Two days later, Laura called a rape crisis hotline and brought Autumn to the hospital for an examination. At the hospital, Detective Charles Zinovitch from the Las Vegas Metropolitan Police Department Sexual Assault Unit attempted to interview Autumn but found her too distressed to discuss the assaults. Detective Zinovitch then ordered a rape examination, which revealed strong physical evidence of sexual assaults.

Two days later, Detective Zinovitch interviewed Autumn in the presence of her mother, and at that time, Autumn provided a detailed description of acts of sexual assault carried out by respondent; Autumn also demonstrated those acts using anatomically correct dolls. Respondent was then arrested, and a state grand jury indicted him on four counts of sexual assault on a minor under 14 years of age.

At respondent's preliminary hearing, Autumn testified that she understood the difference between a truth and a lie, but she became upset when asked about the assaults. Although she initially agreed that respondent had touched her in a way that "she didn't think he was supposed to touch her," she later stated that she could not remember how respondent had touched her or what she had told her mother or the detective. The trial court, found the testimony of Laura Bockting and Detective Zinovitch to be sufficient to hold respondent for trial.

At trial, the court held a hearing outside the presence of the jury to determine whether Autumn could testify. After it became apparent that Autumn was too distressed to be sworn in, the State moved under Nev.Rev.Stat. § 51.385 (2003) to allow Laura Bockting and Detective Zinovitch to recount Autumn's statements regarding the sexual assaults. Under the Nevada statute, out-of-court statements made by a child under 10 years of age describing acts of sexual assault or physical abuse of the child may be admitted if the court finds that the child is unavailable or unable to testify and that "the time, content and circumstances of the statement provide sufficient circumstantial guarantees of trustworthiness." Over defense counsel's objection that admission of this testimony would violate the Confrontation Clause, the trial court found sufficient evidence of reliability to satisfy § 51.385.

As a result of this ruling, Laura Bockting and Detective Zinovitch were permitted at trial to recount Autumn's out-of-court statements about the assaults. Laura Bockting also testified that respondent was the only male who had had the opportunity to assault Autumn. In addition, the prosecution introduced evidence regarding Autumn's medical exam. Respondent testified in his own defense and denied the assaults, and the defense brought out the fact that Autumn, unlike many children her age, had acquired some knowledge about sexual acts, since she had seen respondent and her mother engaging in sexual intercourse and had become familiar with sexual terms. The jury found respondent guilty of three counts of sexual assault on a minor under the age of 14, and the trial court imposed two consecutive life sentences and another concurrent life sentence.

Respondent took an appeal to the Nevada Supreme Court, which handed down its final decision more than a decade before *Crawford*. In analyzing respondent's contention that the admission of Autumn's out-of-court statements had violated his Confrontation Clause rights, the Nevada Supreme Court looked to *Ohio v. Roberts,* 448 U.S. 56 (1980), which was then the governing precedent of this Court. *Roberts* had held that the Confrontation Clause permitted the admission of a hearsay statement made by a declarant who was unavailable to testify if the statement bore sufficient indicia of reliability, either because the statement fell within a firmly rooted hearsay exception or because there were "particularized guarantees of trustworthiness" relating to the statement in question. Applying *Roberts,* the Nevada Supreme Court held that the admission of Autumn's statements was constitutional because the circumstances surrounding the making of the statements provided particularized guarantees of trustworthiness. The Court cited the "natural spontaneity" of Autumn's initial statements to her mother, her reiteration of the same account to Detective Zinovitch several days later, her use of anatomically correct dolls to demonstrate the assaults, and her detailed descriptions of sexual acts with which a 6-year-old would generally not be familiar.

Respondent then filed a petition for a writ of habeas corpus with the United States District Court for the District of Nevada. While this appeal was pending, we issued our opinion in *Crawford*, in which we overruled *Roberts* and held that "testimonial statements of witnesses absent from trial" are admissible "only where the declarant is unavailable, and only where the defendant has had a prior opportunity to cross-examine the witness." We noted that the outcome in *Roberts*-as well as the outcome in all similar cases decided by this Court-was consistent with the rule announced in *Crawford*, but we concluded that the interpretation of the Confrontation Clause set out in *Roberts* was unsound in several respects. First, we observed that *Roberts* potentially excluded too much testimony because it imposed Confrontation Clause restrictions on nontestimonial hearsay not governed by that Clause. At the same time, we noted, the *Roberts* test was too "malleable" in permitting the admission of *ex parte* testimonial statements.

On appeal from the denial of his petition for writ of habeas corpus, respondent contended that if the rule in *Crawford* had been applied to his case, Autumn's out-of-court statements could not have been admitted into evidence and the jury would not have convicted him. Respondent further argued that *Crawford* should have been applied to his case because the rule was either (1) an old rule in existence at the time of his conviction or (2) a "watershed" rule that implicated "the fundamental fairness and accuracy of the criminal proceeding." *Saffle v. Parks*, 494 U.S. 484, 495 (1990).

A divided panel of the Ninth Circuit reversed the District Court, holding that *Crawford* applies retroactively to cases on collateral review. The panel's decision conflicts with the decision of every other Court of Appeals and State Supreme Court that has addressed this issue. We granted certiorari to resolve this conflict.

In *Teague* and subsequent cases, we laid out the framework to be used in determining whether a rule announced in one of our opinions should be applied retroactively to judgments in criminal cases that are already final on direct review. Under the *Teague* framework, an old rule applies both on direct and collateral review, but a new rule is generally applicable only to cases that are still on direct review. A new rule applies retroactively in a collateral proceeding only if (1) the rule is substantive or (2) the rule is a " 'watershed rule of criminal procedure' implicating the fundamental fairness and accuracy of the criminal proceeding." *Saffle, supra,* at 495 (quoting *Teague, supra,* at 311 (plurality opinion)).

In this case, it is undisputed that respondent's conviction became final on direct appeal well before *Crawford* was decided. We therefore turn to the question whether *Crawford* applied an old rule or announced a new one. A new rule is defined as "a rule that was not '*dictated* by precedent existing at the time the defendant's conviction became final.'" *Saffle, supra,* at 488 (quoting *Teague, supra,* at 301 (plurality opinion)).

Applying this definition, it is clear that *Crawford* announced a new rule. The *Crawford* rule was not "dictated" by prior precedent. Quite the opposite is true: The *Crawford* rule is flatly inconsistent with the prior governing precedent, *Roberts,* which *Crawford* overruled. "The explicit overruling of an earlier holding no doubt creates a new rule." *Saffle, supra,* at 488. *Crawford* was quick to note that "the rationales" of our prior decisions had been inconsistent with the *Crawford* rule. "The 'new rule' principle validates reasonable, good-faith interpretations of existing precedents made by state courts even though they are shown to be contrary to later decisions." *Lockhart v. Fretwell,* 506 U.S. 364 (1993). Prior to *Crawford,* "reasonable jurists" could have reached the conclusion that the *Roberts* rule was the rule that governed the admission of hearsay statements made by an unavailable declarant.

Because the *Crawford* rule was not dictated by the governing precedent existing at the time when respondent's conviction became final, the *Crawford* rule is a new rule.

Because *Crawford* announced a "new rule" and because it is clear and undisputed that the rule is procedural and not substantive, that rule cannot be applied in this collateral attack on respondent's conviction unless it is a "'watershed rule of criminal procedure' implicating the fundamental fairness and accuracy of the criminal proceeding." *Saffle,* 494 U.S., at 495 (quoting *Teague,* 489 U.S., at 311 (plurality opinion)). This exception is "extremely narrow." We have observed that it is "unlikely" that any such rules "'have yet to emerge,'" *ibid.* In the years since *Teague,* we have rejected every claim that a new rule satisfied the requirements for watershed status. See, *e.g., Summerlin, supra* (rejecting retroactivity for *Ring v. Arizona,* 536 U.S. 584 (2002)); *Beard v. Banks,* 542 U.S. 406 (2004) (rejecting retroactivity for *Mills v. Maryland,* 486 U.S. 367 (1988)); *O'Dell, supra* (rejecting retroactivity for *Simmons v. South Carolina,* 512 U.S. 154 (1994)); *Gilmore v. Taylor,* 508 U.S. 333 (1993) (rejecting retroactivity for a new rule relating to jury instructions on homicide); *Sawyer v. Smith,* 497 U.S. 227 (1990) (rejecting retroactivity for *Caldwell v. Mississippi,* 472 U.S. 320 (1985)).

In order to qualify as watershed, a new rule must meet two requirements. First, the rule must be necessary to prevent "an impermissibly large risk" of an inaccurate conviction. *Summerlin, supra,* at 356. Second, the rule must "alter our understanding of the bedrock procedural elements essential to the fairness of a proceeding." *Ibid.* We consider each of these requirements in turn.

The *Crawford* rule does not satisfy the first requirement relating to an impermissibly large risk of an inaccurate conviction. To be sure, the *Crawford* rule reflects the Framers' preferred mechanism (cross-examination) for ensuring that inaccurate out-of-court testimonial statements are not used to convict an accused. But in order for a new rule to meet the accuracy requirement, "it is not enough to say that the rule is aimed at improving the accuracy of trial," *Sawyer,* 497 U.S., at 242 or that the rule "is directed toward the enhancement of reliability and accuracy in some sense." Instead, the question is whether the new rule remedied "an 'impermissibly large risk' " of an inaccurate conviction.

Guidance in answering this question is provided by *Gideon v. Wainwright,* 372 U.S. 335 (1963), to which we have repeatedly referred in discussing the meaning of the *Teague* exception. In *Gideon,* the only case that we have identified as qualifying under this exception, the Court held that counsel must be appointed for any indigent defendant charged with a felony. When a defendant who wishes to be represented by counsel is denied representation, *Gideon* held, the risk of an unreliable verdict is intolerably high. See *Mickens v. Taylor,* 535 U.S. 162 (2002). The new rule announced in *Gideon* eliminated this risk.

The *Crawford* rule is in no way comparable to the *Gideon* rule. The *Crawford* rule is much more limited in scope, and the relationship of that rule to the accuracy of the fact-finding process is far less direct and profound. *Crawford* overruled *Roberts* because *Roberts* was inconsistent with the original understanding of the meaning of the Confrontation Clause, not because the Court reached the conclusion that the overall effect of the *Crawford* rule would be to improve the accuracy of fact finding in criminal trials. Indeed, in *Crawford* we recognized that even under the *Roberts* rule, this Court had never specifically approved the introduction of testimonial hearsay statements. Accordingly, it is not surprising that the overall effect of *Crawford* with regard to the accuracy of fact-finding in criminal cases is not easy to assess.

With respect to *testimonial* out-of-court statements, *Crawford* is more restrictive than was *Roberts,* and this may improve the accuracy of fact-finding in some criminal cases. Specifically, under *Roberts,* there may have been cases in which courts erroneously determined that testimonial statements were reliable. But whatever improvement in reliability *Crawford* produced in this respect must be considered together with *Crawford's* elimination of Confrontation Clause protection against the admission of unreliable out-of-court non-testimonial statements. Under *Roberts,* an out-of-court non-testimonial statement not subject to prior cross-examination could not be admitted without a judicial determination regarding reliability. Under *Crawford,* on the other hand, the Confrontation Clause has no application to such statements and therefore permits their admission even if they lack indicia of reliability.

It is thus unclear whether *Crawford,* on the whole, decreased or increased the number of unreliable out-of-court statements that may be admitted in criminal trials. But the question is not whether *Crawford* resulted in some net improvement in the accuracy of fact-finding in criminal cases. Rather, "the question is whether testimony admissible under *Roberts* is so much more unreliable than that admissible under *Crawford* that the *Crawford* rule is one without which the likelihood of an accurate conviction is *seriously* diminished." *Crawford* did not effect a change of this magnitude.

The *Crawford* rule also did not "alter our understanding of the *bedrock procedural elements* essential to the fairness of a proceeding." This requirement cannot be met simply by showing that a new procedural rule is *based on* a "bedrock" right. We have frequently held that the *Teague* bar to retroactivity applies to new rules that are based on "bedrock" constitutional rights. Similarly, "that a new procedural rule is 'fundamental' in some abstract sense is not enough." *Summerlin,* 542 U.S., at 352.

Instead, in order to meet this requirement, a new rule must itself constitute a previously unrecognized bedrock procedural element that is essential to the fairness of a proceeding. In this case, it is apparent that the rule announced in *Crawford,* while certainly important, is not in the same category with *Gideon*. *Gideon* effected a profound and "sweeping" change. The *Crawford* rule simply lacks the "primacy" and "centrality" of the *Gideon* rule, and does not qualify as a rule that "altered our understanding of the bedrock procedural elements essential to the fairness of a proceeding," *Sawyer,* 497 U.S., at 242.

In sum, we hold that *Crawford* announced a "new rule" of criminal procedure and that this rule does not fall within the *Teague* exception for watershed rules. We therefore reverse the judgment of the Court of Appeals and remand the case for further proceedings consistent with this opinion.

It is so ordered.

Executive Summary

Application of the Bill of Rights to the States. Although the provisions of the Bill of rights were originally conceived as limitations on the power, many of these rights were held applicable against the states during the twentieth century.

Decisions Regarding Incorporation and Applicability. To determine whether a protection from the Bill of Rights applies to the states under the selective incorporation approach, it is necessary to look at 1) the entirety of the right, not just as it applies to a particular set of facts (as with the fundamental rights approach), and 2) whether the provision is fundamental to Anglo-American jurisprudence.

Incorporation of Criminal Rights. A number of criminal process provisions have been applied to the states, including the Fourth Amendment's prohibition against unreasonable searches and seizures, the Fifth Amendment's prohibitions against double jeopardy, compelled self-incrimination, and the Sixth Amendment's right to trial by jury, to compulsory process, to a speedy and public trial, the assistance of counsel, and to prohibitions against excessive bail and cruel and unusual punishment.

Retroactivity of New Constitutional Rules. When the courts announce a new constitutional rule, questions arise regarding whether the new rule should be retroactively applied. In general, the courts have been reluctant to extend the benefits of a new rule to someone whose conviction was final prior to announcement of the new rule. However, the benefits of a new rule were sometimes applied to those whose convictions were on direct review at the time the rule is announced.

Major Themes

a. Incorporation of Rights—Many provisions of the Bill of Rights have been incorporated into the Fourteenth Amendment, and are therefore applicable to the states.

b. Retroactivity—Whenever the courts announce a new constitutional rule, questions can arise regarding whether the rule should be applied retroactively to convictions that are already final. As a general rule, new rules are not applied retroactively except to cases that are still pending at the time that the new rule is announced.

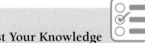

Test Your Knowledge

To assess your understanding of the material in this chapter, click here to take a quiz.

For More Information

• WAYNE R. LAFAVE, JEROLD H. ISRAEL, NANCY J. KING & ORIN S. KERR, CRIMINAL PROCEDURE (5th ed. 2009).

• RUSSELL L. WEAVER, JOHN M. BURKOFF, CATHERINE HANCOCK, JANET HOEFFEL, STEVE FRIEDLAND & STEPHEN SINGER, PRINCIPLES OF CRIMINAL PROCEDURE Ch. 2 (5th ed. 2015).

CHAPTER 3

The Right to Counsel

A. Generally

In 1938, the United States Supreme Court held that federal defendants who could not afford an attorney had a constitutional right to appointed counsel under the Sixth Amendment. *Johnson v. Zerbst*, 304 U.S. 458 (1938). Justice Black, writing for the majority, emphasized that "the Sixth Amendment stands as a constant admonition that if the constitutional safeguards it provides be lost, justice will not 'still be done.' It embodies a realistic recognition of the obvious truth that the average defendant does not have the professional legal skills to protect himself when brought before a tribunal with power to take his life or liberty, wherein the prosecution is presented by experienced and learned counsel. The Sixth Amendment withholds from federal courts, in all criminal proceedings, the power and authority to deprive an accused of his life or liberty unless he has or waives the assistance of counsel."

Betts v. Brady

316 U.S. 455 (1942).

MR. JUSTICE ROBERTS delivered the opinion of the Court.

Smith Betts was indicted for robbery in the Circuit Court of Carroll County, Maryland. Due to lack of funds he was unable to employ counsel, and so informed the judge at his arraignment. He requested that counsel be appointed for him. The judge advised him that this could not be done as it was not the practice in Carroll County to appoint counsel for indigent defendants save in prosecutions for murder and rape.

Without waiving his asserted right to counsel the petitioner pleaded not guilty and elected to be tried without a jury. At his request witnesses were summoned in his behalf. He cross-examined the State's witnesses and examined his own. The latter gave testimony tending to establish an alibi. Although afforded the opportunity, he did not take the witness stand. The judge found him guilty and imposed a sentence of eight years.

Was the petitioner's conviction and sentence a deprivation of his liberty without due process of law, in violation of the Fourteenth Amendment, because of the court's refusal to appoint counsel at his request?

The Sixth Amendment of the national Constitution applies only to trials in federal courts. The due process clause of the Fourteenth Amendment does not incorporate, as such, the specific guarantees found in the Sixth Amendment although a denial by a State of rights or privileges specifically embodied in that and others of the first eight amendments may, in certain circumstances, or in connection with other elements, operate, in a given case, to deprive a litigant of due process of law in violation of the Fourteenth. The phrase due process of law formulates a concept less rigid and more fluid than those envisaged in other specific and particular provisions of the Bill of Rights. Its application is less a matter of rule. Asserted denial is to be tested by an appraisal of the totality of facts in a given case. That which may, in one setting, constitute a denial of fundamental fairness, shocking to the universal sense of justice, may, in other circumstances, and in the light of other considerations, fall short of such denial. In the application of such a concept there is always the danger of falling into the habit of formulating the guarantee into a set of hard and fast rules the application of which in a given case may be to ignore the qualifying factors therein disclosed.

The question we are now to decide is whether due process of law demands that in every criminal case, whatever the circumstances, a State must furnish counsel to an indigent defendant. Is the furnishing of counsel in all cases whatever dictated by natural, inherent, and fundamental principles of fairness? The answer to the question may be found in the common understanding of those who have lived under the Anglo-American system of law. By the Sixth Amendment the people ordained that, in all criminal prosecutions, the accused should "enjoy the right to have the Assistance of Counsel for his defense." We have construed the provision to require appointment of counsel in all cases where a defendant is unable to procure the services of an attorney, and where the right has not been intentionally and competently waived. Though, as we have noted, the Amendment lays down no rule for the conduct of the States, the question recurs whether the constraint laid by the Amendment upon the national courts expresses a rule so fundamental and essential to a fair trial, and so, to due process of law, that it is made obligatory upon the states by the Fourteenth Amendment. Relevant data on the subject are afforded by constitutional and statutory provisions subsisting in the colonies and the states prior to the inclusion of the Bill of Rights in the national Constitution, and in the constitutional, legislative, and judicial history of the States to the present date.

The Constitutions of the thirteen original States, as they were at the time of federal union, exhibit great diversity in respect of the right to have counsel in criminal cases. It is evident that the constitutional provisions to the effect that a defendant should be "allowed" counsel or should have a right "to be heard by himself and his counsel," or that he might be heard by "either or both," at his election, were intended to do away with the rules which denied representation, in whole or in part, by counsel in criminal prosecutions, but were not aimed to compel the State to provide counsel for a defendant.

The constitutions of all the States, presently in force, save that of Virginia, contain provisions with respect to the assistance of counsel in criminal trials. Those of nine States may be said to embody a guarantee textually the same as that of the Sixth Amendment, or of like import. In the fundamental law of most States, however, the language used indicates only that a defendant is not to be denied the privilege of representation by counsel of his choice.

This demonstrates that, in the great majority of the States, it has been the considered judgment of the people, their representatives and their courts that appointment of counsel is not a fundamental right, essential to a fair trial.

On the contrary, the matter has generally been deemed one of legislative policy. In the light of this evidence, we are unable to say that the concept of due process incorporated in the Fourteenth Amendment obligates the States, whatever may be their own views, to furnish counsel in every such case. Every court has power, if it deems proper, to appoint counsel where that course seems to be required in the interest of fairness.

In this case there was no question of the commission of a robbery. The State's case consisted of evidence identifying the petitioner as the perpetrator. The defense was an alibi. Petitioner called and examined witnesses to prove that he was at another place at the time of the commission of the offense. The simple issue was the veracity of the testimony for the State and that for the defendant. As Judge Bond says, the accused was not helpless, but was a man forty-three years old, of ordinary intelligence, and ability to take care of his own interests on the trial of that narrow issue. He had once before been in a criminal court,

Make the Connection

Recall the discussion in Chapter 2(A) of the pre-incorporation "fundamental rights" approach to determining individual rights in the states. This is a perfect example. The Court here won't require states to respect Bill of Rights provisions unless they are "fundamental and necessary" to due process or "shocking to the universal sense of justice." What does this actually mean in this setting? What significance do you think we should give today to the fact that, when the Constitution was adopted, indigent defendants did not have the right to counsel?

pleaded guilty to larceny and served a sentence and was not wholly unfamiliar with criminal procedure.

Food for Thought

Is this accurate? Do you believe that a person who previously pleaded guilty in a criminal matter would now be somewhat familiar with criminal procedure? Really?

It is quite clear that in Maryland, if the situation had been otherwise and it had appeared that the petitioner was, for any reason, at a serious disadvantage by reason of the lack of counsel, a refusal to appoint would have resulted in the reversal of a judgment of conviction.

To deduce from the due process clause a rule binding upon the states in this matter would be to impose upon them a requirement without distinction between criminal charges of different magnitude or in respect of courts of varying jurisdiction. " 'Presumably it would be argued that trials in the Traffic Court would require it.'" And indeed it was said by petitioner's counsel both below and in this court, that as the Fourteenth Amendment extends the protection of due process to property as well as to life and liberty, if we hold with the petitioner, logic would require the furnishing of counsel in civil cases involving property.

As we have said, the Fourteenth Amendment prohibits the conviction and incarceration of one whose trial is offensive to the common and fundamental ideas of fairness and right, and while want of counsel in a particular case may result in a conviction lacking in such fundamental fairness, we cannot say that the Amendment embodies an inexorable command that no trial for any offense, or in any court, can be fairly conducted and justice accorded a defendant who is not represented by counsel.

The judgment is *Affirmed.*

MR. JUSTICE BLACK, dissenting, with whom MR. JUSTICE DOUGLAS and MR. JUSTICE MURPHY concur.

The petitioner, a farm hand, out of a job and on relief, was indicted in a Maryland state court on a charge of robbery. He was too poor to hire a lawyer. He so informed the court and requested that counsel be appointed to defend him. His request was denied. Put to trial without a lawyer, he conducted his own defense, was found guilty, and was sentenced to eight years' imprisonment. The court below found that the petitioner had "at least an ordinary amount of intelligence." It is clear from his examination of witnesses that he was a man of little education.

If this case had come to us from a federal court, it is clear we should have to reverse it, because the Sixth Amendment makes the right to counsel in criminal cases inviolable by the Federal Government. I believe that the Fourteenth Amendment made the Sixth applicable to the states. But this view, although often urged in dissents, has never been accepted by a majority of this Court and is not accepted today.

This Court has declared that due process of law is denied if a trial is conducted in such manner that it is "shocking to the universal sense of justice" or "offensive to the common and fundamental ideas of fairness and right." On another occasion, this Court has recognized that whatever is "implicit in the concept of ordered liberty" and "essential to the substance of a hearing" is within the procedural protection afforded by the constitutional guaranty of due process. The right to counsel in a criminal proceeding is "fundamental."

An historical evaluation of the right to a full hearing in criminal cases, and the dangers of denying it, were set out in the *Powell v. Alabama*, 287 U.S. 45 (1932), case, where this Court said: "What does a hearing include? Historically and in practice, in our own country at least, it has always included the right to the aid of counsel when desired and provided by the party asserting the right. Even the intelligent and educated layman lacks both the skill and knowledge adequately to prepare his defense, even though he have a perfect one. He requires the guiding hand of counsel in every step in the proceedings against him. Without it, though he be not guilty, he faces the danger of conviction because he does not know how to establish his innocence."

A practice cannot be reconciled with "common and fundamental ideas of fairness and right," which subjects innocent men to increased dangers of conviction merely because of their poverty. Whether a man is innocent cannot be determined from a trial in which, as here, denial of counsel has made it impossible to conclude, with any satisfactory degree of certainty, that the defendant's case was adequately presented.

Gideon v. Wainwright

372 U.S. 335 (1963).

MR. JUSTICE BLACK delivered the opinion of the Court.

Petitioner was charged in a Florida state court with having broken and entered a poolroom with intent to commit a misdemeanor. This offense is a felony under Florida law. Appearing in court without funds and without a lawyer, petitioner asked the court to appoint counsel for him, whereupon the following colloquy took place:

"The COURT: Mr. Gideon, I am sorry, but I cannot appoint Counsel to represent you in this case. Under the laws of the State of Florida, the only time the Court can appoint Counsel to represent a Defendant is when that person is charged with a capital offense. I am sorry, but I will have to deny your request to appoint Counsel to defend you in this case.

"The DEFENDANT: The United States Supreme Court says I am entitled to be represented by Counsel."

Put to trial before a jury, Gideon conducted his defense about as well as could be expected from a layman. He made an opening statement to the jury, cross-examined the State's witnesses, presented witnesses in his own defense, declined to testify himself, and made a short argument "emphasizing his innocence to the charge contained in the Information filed in this case." The jury returned a verdict of guilty, and petitioner was sentenced to serve five years in the state prison. Gideon subsequently filed a habeas corpus petition attacking his conviction on the ground that the trial court's refusal to appoint counsel for him was unconstitutional. The Florida Supreme Court denied him any relief without opinion. Since 1942, when *Betts v. Brady* was decided by a divided Court, the problem of a defendant's federal constitutional right to counsel in a state court has been a continuing source of controversy and litigation in both state and federal courts.

The Sixth Amendment provides: "In all criminal prosecutions, the accused shall enjoy the right to have the Assistance of Counsel for his defense." We have construed this to mean that in federal courts counsel must be provided for defendants unable to employ counsel unless the right is competently and intelligently waived. Betts argued that this right is extended to indigent defendants in state courts by the Fourteenth Amendment. In response the Court stated that, while the Sixth Amendment laid down "no rule for the conduct of the States, the question recurs whether the constraint laid by the Amendment upon the national courts expresses a rule so fundamental and essential to a fair trial, and so, to due process of law, that it is made obligatory upon the States by the Fourteenth Amendment." In order to decide whether the Sixth Amendment's guarantee of counsel is of this fundamental nature, the Court in *Betts* set out and considered "relevant data on the subject afforded by constitutional and statutory provisions subsisting in the colonies and the states prior to the inclusion of the Bill of Rights in the national Constitution, and in the constitutional, legislative, and judicial history of the States to the present date." On the basis of this historical data the

See It

You can watch the legendary actor, Henry Fonda, do a terrific job of playing the role of Clarence Gideon in the 1980 made-for-TV film, *Gideon's Trumpet*, based on the book by Anthony Lewis. *See* http://www.imdb.com/title/tt0080789/.

Court concluded that "appointment of counsel is not a fundamental right, essential to a fair trial." It was for this reason the *Betts* Court refused to accept the contention that the Sixth Amendment's guarantee of counsel for indigent federal defendants was extended to or, in the words of that Court, "made obligatory upon the states by the Fourteenth Amendment." Plainly, had the Court concluded that appointment of counsel for an indigent criminal defendant was "a fundamental right, essential to a fair trial," it would have held that the Fourteenth Amendment requires appointment of counsel in a state court, just as the Sixth Amendment requires in a federal court.

We accept *Betts v. Brady's* assumption, based as it was on our prior cases, that a provision of the Bill of Rights which is "fundamental and essential to a fair trial" is made obligatory upon the States by the Fourteenth Amendment. We think the Court in *Betts* was wrong, however, in concluding that the Sixth Amendment's guarantee of counsel is not one of these fundamental rights.

The fact is that in deciding as it did—that "appointment of counsel is not a fundamental right, essential to a fair trial"—the Court in *Betts v. Brady* made an abrupt break with its own well-considered precedents. In returning to these old precedents, sounder we believe than the new, we but restore constitutional principles established to achieve a fair system of justice. Not only these precedents but also reason and reflection require us to recognize that in our adversary system of criminal justice, any person haled into court, who is too poor to hire a lawyer, cannot be assured a fair trial unless counsel is provided for him. This seems to us to be an obvious truth. Governments, both state and federal, quite properly spend vast sums of money to establish machinery to try defendants accused of crime. Lawyers to prosecute are everywhere deemed essential to protect the public's interest in an orderly society. Similarly, there are few defendants charged with crime, few indeed, who fail to hire the best lawyers they can get to prepare and present their defenses. That government hires lawyers to prosecute and defendants who have the money hire lawyers to defend are the strongest indications of the widespread belief that lawyers in criminal courts are necessities, not luxuries. The right of one charged with crime to counsel may not be deemed fundamental and essential to fair trials in some countries, but it is in ours. From the very beginning, our state and national constitutions and laws have laid great emphasis on procedural and substantive safeguards designed to assure fair trials before impartial tribunals in which every defendant stands equal before the law. This noble ideal cannot be realized if the poor man charged with crime has to face his accusers without a lawyer to assist him. A defendant's need for a lawyer is nowhere better stated than in the moving words of Mr. Justice Sutherland in *Powell v. Alabama,* 287 U.S. 45 (1932):

> "The right to be heard would be, in many cases, of little avail if it did not comprehend the right to be heard by counsel. Even the intelligent

and educated layman has small and sometimes no skill in the science of law. If charged with crime, he is incapable, generally, of determining for himself whether the indictment is good or bad. He is unfamiliar with the rules of evidence. Left without the aid of counsel he may be put on trial without a proper charge, and convicted upon incompetent evidence, or evidence irrelevant to the issue or otherwise inadmissible. He lacks both the skill and knowledge adequately to prepare his defense, even though he have a perfect one. He requires the guiding hand of counsel at every step in the proceedings against him. Without it, though he be not guilty, he faces the danger of conviction because he does not know how to establish his innocence."

The Court in *Betts v. Brady* departed from the sound wisdom upon which the Court's holding in *Powell v. Alabama* rested. Florida, supported by two other States, has asked that *Betts v. Brady* be left intact. Twenty-two States, as friends of the Court, argue that *Betts* was "an anachronism when handed down" and that it should now be overruled.

We agree. *Reversed.*

MR. JUSTICE HARLAN, concurring.

When we hold a right or immunity to be "implicit in the concept of ordered liberty" and thus valid against the States, we do not automatically carry over an entire body of federal law and apply it in full sweep to the States. Any such concept would disregard the frequently wide disparity between the legitimate interests of the States and of the Federal Government, the divergent problems that they face, and the significantly different consequences of their actions.

> **Food for Thought**
>
> Why do you think that the Attorneys General from twenty-two states filed an *Amicus* Brief *in Gideon's behalf* rather than supporting the state of Florida? Do you think they were simply convinced at this point in time that *Betts* was wrongly decided? Or could they have had some tactical motivation for taking this position?

Points for Discussion

a. Providing Indigent Services

Representation for the literally millions of indigent criminal defendants charged in state and federal court each year is provided through a public-defender or contract-attorney system, or simply by an appropriate judge or judicial officer assigning the indigent's defense to a private attorney by order of appointment. In 2007, 964 public defender offices across the nation received nearly 6 million indigent defense cases. Misdemeanor cases accounted for about 40% of all cases received by state-based public defender offices and about 50% of the cases received by county-based offices. Donald J. Farole, Jr. & Lynn Langton, Public Defender Offices, 2007—Statistical Tables (Revised) (U.S. Dept. Of Justice, Bur. Of Justice Statistics, Nov. 2009), http://bjs.ojp.usdoj.gov/index.cfm?ty=pbdetail&iid=1758.

County-based public defender offices received more than 4 million cases in 2007. About three-quarters (73%) of county-based public defender offices exceeded the maximum recommended limit of cases received per attorney in 2007. County-based offices employed a median of 7 litigating public defenders. Donald J. Farole, Jr. & Lynn Langton, County-based and Local Public Defender Offices, 2007 (U.S. Dept. Of Justice, Bur. Of Justice Statistics, Sept. 2010), http://bjs.ojp.usdoj.gov/index.cfm?ty=pbdetail&iid=2211. State governments spent $2.3 billion on indigent defense in 2012. Erinn Herberman and Tracey Kyckelhahn, State Government Indigent Defense Expenditures, FY 2008-2012 – Updated (U.S. Dept. Of Justice, Bur. Of Justice Statistics, October 24, 2014), http://www.bjs.gov/content/pub/pdf/sgide0812.pdf.

"Of the 28 states and the District of Columbia that had state-administered indigent defense systems in 2013: Twenty-seven states and the District of Columbia had either governmental or nongovernmental public defenders providing representation for indigent clients; Eight states and the District of Columbia required indigent clients to pay both an application fee to receive representation and recoupment for legal services provided; In nine states the governor appointed the chief executives of the indigent defense delivery system; Six states reported fewer than 10 full-time equivalent investigators on staff for public defender offices. Between 2007 and 2013, 16 of the 22 states with state-administered public defender offices increased the number of full-time equivalent litigating attorneys. In 2013, state-administered systems closed an estimated 2,696,950 criminal, appellate, civil, and juvenile cases." Suzanne M. Strong, State-Administered Indigent Defense Systems, 2013 (U.S. Dept. of Justice, Bur. Of Justice Statistics (November 16, 2016), https://www.bjs.gov/index.cfm?ty=pbdetail&iid=5826.

Court-appointed counsel represented 66% of federal felony defendants in 1998. U.S. Dept. of Justice, Bur. of Justice Statistics, Defense Counsel in Criminal Cases (November 2000). However,

federal appellate and district judges express high regard for public defenders but low regard for court-appointed counsel and retained counsel. Retained counsel represent 25% and court-appointed counsel 33% of federal criminal defendants. If the quality of legal representation matters to criminal case outcomes, as recent studies suggest, a majority of indigent federal criminal defendants may be serving longer sentences by virtue of not having been represented by a federal public defender. The Constitution has been interpreted to place a floor under the quality of assistance of counsel tolerated in criminal cases, but one federal district judge described the work of defense attorneys other than public defenders as "exceedingly poor."

Richard A. Posner & Albert H. Yoon, What Judges Think of the Quality of Legal Representation, 63 Stanford Law Review 317, 341–42 (2011).

Unfortunately, skyrocketing caseloads and inadequate funding for such programs has led to what some commentators deem "a crisis of extraordinary proportions in many states throughout the country." Richard Klein & Robert Spangenberg, *The Indigent Defense Crisis* 25 (ABA Section of Criminal Justice 1993). See also *id.* ("Justice often does not reach impoverished urban centers or poor rural counties where limited funding for indigent defense cannot provide effective representation to those accused of crime."); Stephen B. Bright, *Turning Celebrated Principles Into Reality*, Champion 6 (January/February 2003):

> No constitutional right is celebrated so much in the abstract and observed so little in reality as the right to counsel. While leaders of the judiciary, legal profession and government give speeches every Law Day about the essential role of lawyers in protecting the individual rights of people accused of crimes, many states have yet to create and fund adequately independent programs for providing legal representation. As a result, some people—even people accused of felonies—enter guilty pleas and are sentenced to imprisonment without any representation. Others languish in jail for weeks or months—often for longer than any sentence they would receive—before being assigned a lawyer. Many receive only perfunctory representation—sometimes nothing more than hurried conversations with a court-appointed lawyer outside the courtroom or even in open court—before entering a guilty plea or going to trial. The poor person who is wrongfully convicted may face years in prison, or even execution, without any legal assistance to pursue avenues of post-conviction review.

Food for Thought

Do these comments and statistics make you wonder whether the *Gideon* decision has actually worked to accomplish what the Court thought or hoped that it would accomplish? Should more public monies be spent on indigent defense services? Is this realistic as a political matter?

See also Ethan Bronner, *Right to Lawyer Can Be Empty Promise for Poor*, New York Times p. A1 (March 16, 2013) ("The Legal Services Corporation says there are more than 60 million Americans—35 percent more than in 2005—who qualify for its services. But it calculates that 80 percent of the legal needs of the poor go unmet."); Attorney General Eric Holder, Jr., *Defendants' legal rights undermined by budget cuts*, Washington Post (August 22, 2013) ("Despite the promise of the court's ruling in *Gideon*, the U.S. indigent defense systems—which provide representation to those who cannot afford it—are in financial crisis, plagued by crushing caseloads and insufficient resources.").

See further Matt Apuzzo, *Holder Backs Suit in New York Faulting Legal Service for Poor*, New York Times p. A1 (Sept. 25, 2014):

Attorney General Eric H. Holder Jr., who last year declared a crisis in America's legal-defense system for the poor, is supporting a class-action lawsuit that accuses Gov. Andrew M. Cuomo and the State of New York of perpetuating a system that violates the rights of people who cannot afford to hire lawyers. The lawsuit claims that public defenders in New York are so overworked and overmatched that poor people essentially receive no legal defense at all. It describes a system in which indigent defendants navigate courts nearly alone, relying on spotty advice from lawyers who do not have the time or money to investigate their cases or advise them properly. Because of substandard legal aid, children are taken from their parents, defendants in minor cases are jailed for long periods and people are imprisoned for crimes for which they might have been acquitted, the civil rights lawyers who filed the suit said.

Although the United States is not a party to the case, Mr. Holder is using the same core legal arguments as the plaintiffs and the weight of the federal government to resolve what he sees as deep-seated unfairness in local criminal courts. His views will bring national attention to a case that has mainly been of interest in New York. After Mr. Holder weighed in last year in a similar case in Washington State, the judge strongly rebuked the public-defense systems in two cities there and ordered improvements.

If the New York lawsuit succeeds, the state could be forced to take over the public-defense system, which is now run by county governments. Such an outcome would also quite likely encourage similar lawsuits, and, in turn, additional intervention by the Justice Department.

Mr. Holder has made the right to legal representation part of a broad effort to address inequities in the criminal justice system. He has pushed to reduce harsh sentences that were adopted during the country's crack epidemic, for example, and to eliminate mandatory-minimum sentences for nonviolent drug crimes.

"To truly guarantee adequate representation for low-income defendants, we must ensure that public defenders' caseloads allow them to do an effective job," Mr. Holder said in a statement. "The Department of Justice is committed to addressing the inequalities that unfold every day in America's courtrooms."

And, finally, see Sara Mayeux, "Our Rickety Public Defense System Has Finally Collapsed. Here's How to Fix It," The Nation (May 9, 2016), http://

www.thenation.com/article/our-rickety-public-defense-system-has-finally-collapsed-heres-how-to-fix-it/:

> The persistence of crisis conditions in indigent defense suggests that the causes are deeply entrenched, and not a temporary reflection of shifting political views or economic vicissitudes. One long-term historical factor helping to explain America's weak commitment to indigent defense is the legal profession's own prestige hierarchy, which has long valorized advising corporations more than helping ordinary people. A second factor undermining indigent defense is simply the structure of American federalism. The New Orleans judge who recently ordered the release of defendants awaiting counsel wrote, by way of explanation, that "constitutional rights are not contingent on budget demands." But in practice, constitutional rights are often hamstrung by state-level budgets.

b. Excessive Caseloads & Appointments

In *State ex rel. Missouri Public Defender Com'n v. Waters*, 370 S.W.3d 592 (Mo. 2012), the Missouri Supreme Court ruled that a trial court exceeded its lawful authority by appointing the state public defender's office to represent a defendant in contravention of an administrative rule permitting a district defender office to decline additional appointments when it has been certified as being on limited availability after exceeding its caseload capacity for at least three consecutive calendar months. The court reasoned that overburdened defense counsel is ineffective counsel and

> simply put, a judge may not appoint counsel when the judge is aware that, for whatever reason, counsel is unable to provide effective representation to a defendant. Effective, not just pro forma, representation is required by the Missouri and federal constitutions.

Food for Thought

Can public defenders refuse to take additional cases until they are "caught up" with existing cases, and simply ask judges to appoint private attorneys at state expense? What else can they do? Should they (can they) sue the state (their employers) for relief? *See, e.g.,* Dave Collins, *Public defenders feel squeeze: Conn. cuts create caseload worries*, BOSTON GLOBE (July 21, 2011), ("The public defenders' office cut all 30 of its per diem independent contractor positions last week, including 16 lawyers, and laid off 12 temporary employees, including seven lawyers. All 42 of those workers helped keep caseload levels down, but needed to be cut regardless of any union savings deal. To meet the savings mandated by the Legislature, the public defenders' office is proposing laying off 24 full-time employees and eliminating another nine jobs through attrition or retirements. The agency has not decided yet how many of those positions will be lawyers or when the job cuts will be made."); Deborah Yetter, *State's Public Defender Can't Refuse Cases, Court Rules*, LOUISVILLE COURIER-JOURNAL, A–1, c. 1–6 (Sept. 20, 2008).

Does this make sense to you? Should (can?) courts force state or local governments to spend more on indigent defense, essentially making a "political" choice as between public spending priorities?

c. Who Is an "Indigent?"

The Supreme Court has never defined "indigency" for purposes of an indigent criminal defendant's right to the appointment of counsel. States use varying formulae and income levels to define indigency for these purposes. The American Bar Association, in ABA Standards for Criminal Justice, Providing Defense Services Standard 5–7.1 (3d ed. 1992), has recommended the following standard be applied: "Counsel should be provided to persons who are financially unable to obtain adequate representation without substantial hardship. Counsel should not be denied because of a person's ability to pay part of the cost of representation, because friends or relatives have resources to obtain counsel, or because bond has been or can be posted."

d. Making the Indigent's Family Pay

The Massachusetts Supreme Judicial Court has held that rules of court requiring the income of an otherwise indigent's defendant's girlfriend and mother to be attributed to him did not violate his right to counsel, and that it was not unconstitutional to place the burden of proving indigency on the defendant himself. *Com. v. Fico*, 462 Mass. 737, 971 N.E.2d 275 (2012). *See also Com. v. Porter*, 462 Mass. 724, 971 N.E.2d 291 (2012) (rule allowing defendant's spouse's income to be attributed to him for purposes of determining indigency held constitutional); *Com. v. Mortimer*, 462 Mass. 749, 971 N.E.2d 283 (2012) (rule allowing defendant's spouse's income to be attributed to him for purposes of determining indigency held constitutional). Is this fair? What do you think?

Argersinger v. Hamlin

407 U.S. 25 (1972).

MR. JUSTICE DOUGLAS delivered the opinion of the Court.

Petitioner, an indigent, was charged in Florida with carrying a concealed weapon, an offense punishable by imprisonment up to six months, a $1,000 fine, or both. The Florida Supreme Court followed the line we marked out in *Duncan v. Louisiana*, 391 U.S. 145, 159, as respects the right to trial by jury and held that the right to court-appointed counsel extends only to trials "for non-petty offenses punishable by more than six months imprisonment." We reverse.

The right to trial by jury, also guaranteed by the Sixth Amendment by reason of the Fourteenth, was limited by Duncan to trials where the potential punishment was imprisonment for six months or more. But the right to trial by jury has a different genealogy and is brigaded with a system of trial to a judge alone. While there is historical support for limiting the "deep commitment" to trial by jury to "serious criminal cases," there is no such support for a similar limitation on the right to assistance of counsel.

The Sixth Amendment extended the right to counsel beyond its common-law dimensions. But there is nothing in the language of the Amendment, its history, or in the decisions of this Court, to indicate that it was intended to embody a retraction of the right in petty offenses wherein the common law previously did require that counsel be provided.

The assistance of counsel is often a requisite to the very existence of a fair trial. The requirement of counsel may well be necessary for a fair trial even in a petty-offense prosecution. We are by no means convinced that legal and constitutional questions involved in a case that actually leads to imprisonment even for a brief period are any less complex than when a person can be sent off for six months or more.

Beyond the problem of trials and appeals is that of the guilty plea, a problem which looms large in misdemeanor as well as in felony cases. Counsel is needed so that the accused may know precisely what he is doing, so that he is fully aware of the prospect of going to jail or prison, and so that he is treated fairly by the prosecution.

In addition, the volume of misdemeanor cases, far greater in number than felony prosecutions, may create an obsession for speedy dispositions, regardless of the fairness of the result. We must conclude, therefore, that the problems associated with misdemeanor and petty offenses often require the presence of counsel to insure the accused a fair trial. Mr. Justice Powell suggests that these problems are raised even in situations where there is no prospect of imprisonment. We need not consider the requirements of the Sixth Amendment as regards the right to counsel where loss of liberty is not involved, however, for here petitioner was in fact sentenced to jail. And, as we said in *Baldwin*, "the prospect of imprisonment for however short a time will seldom be viewed by the accused as a trivial or 'petty' matter and may well result in quite serious repercussions affecting his career and his reputation."

We hold, therefore, that absent a knowing and intelligent waiver, no person may be imprisoned for any offense, whether classified as petty, misdemeanor, or felony, unless he was represented by counsel at his trial.

Food for Thought

Does this holding make sense? How can a judge sensibly and fairly make the decision whether or not he or she is going to sentence the defendant (if convicted) to at least a day in jail *in advance of hearing the facts*?

We do not sit as an ombudsman to direct state courts how to manage their affairs but only to make clear the federal constitutional requirement. How crimes should be classified is largely a state matter. The fact that traffic charges technically fall within the category of "criminal prosecutions" does not necessarily mean that many of them will be brought into the class where imprisonment actually occurs.

Under the rule we announce today, every judge will know when the trial of a misdemeanor starts that no imprisonment may be imposed, even though local law permits it, unless the accused is represented by counsel. He will have a measure of the seriousness and gravity of the offense and therefore know when to name a lawyer to represent the accused before the trial starts.

The run of misdemeanors will not be affected by today's ruling. But in those that end up in the actual deprivation of a person's liberty, the accused will receive the benefit of "the guiding hand of counsel" so necessary when one's liberty is in jeopardy.

Reversed.

MR. CHIEF JUSTICE BURGER, concurred in the result. MR. JUSTICE BRENNAN, with whom MR. JUSTICE DOUGLAS and MR. JUSTICE STEWART joined, concurred, adding:

Law students may provide an important source of legal representation for the indigent. More than 125 of the country's 147 accredited law schools have established clinical programs in which faculty supervised students aid clients in a variety of civil and criminal matters. These programs supplement practice rules enacted in 38 States authorizing students to practice law under prescribed conditions. Most of these regulations permit students to make supervised court appearances as defense counsel in criminal cases.

Given the huge increase in law school enrollments over the past few years, law students can be expected to make a significant contribution, quantitatively and qualitatively, to the representation of the poor in many areas.

MR. JUSTICE POWELL, with whom MR. JUSTICE REHNQUIST joins, concurring in the result.

Food for Thought

Is representation by a law student in criminal proceedings sufficient to meet the Sixth Amendment guarantee of the right to counsel? Would you want to have your spleen removed by a medical student? Is there a difference? What do you think? When he was alive, should we have arranged for a medical student to perform an endoscopy on Chief Justice Burger and *then* ask him if he thought this was adequate medical care? Too late now.

The flat six-month rule of the Florida court and the equally inflexible rule of the majority opinion apply to all cases within their defined areas regardless of circumstances. It is precisely because of this mechanistic application that I find these alternatives unsatisfactory. Due process embodies principles of fairness rather than immutable line drawing as to every aspect of a criminal trial.

While counsel is often essential to a fair trial, this is by no means a universal fact. Some petty offense cases are complex; others are exceedingly simple. Where the possibility of a jail sentence is remote and the probable fine seems small, or where the evidence of guilt is overwhelming, the costs of assistance of counsel may exceed the benefits. It is anomalous that the Court's opinion today will extend the right of appointed counsel to indigent defendants in cases where the right to counsel would rarely be exercised by nonindigent defendants. I would hold that the right to counsel in petty-offense cases is not absolute but is one to be determined by the trial courts exercising a judicial discretion on a case-by-case basis.

Food for Thought

Do you agree with Justice Powell? Was a "bright-line rule" really necessary here? Bright line rules are often appealing because they are seemingly easy to apply. However, sometimes these rules create anomalous results. It's hard to create a "one size fits all rule" and have it make sense in every situation. Case-by-case approaches, on the other hand, can produce unpredictable results and can be hard to apply. Which is better in this specific situation?

Points for Discussion

a. Right to Counsel For Fines?

In *Scott v. Illinois*, 440 U.S. 367 (1979), Scott was convicted of theft and fined $50 after a bench trial in which he was unrepresented. The Illinois statute set the maximum penalty for theft at a $500 fine and/or one year in jail. Scott challenged his conviction on the basis that *Argersinger* required the state to provide counsel whenever imprisonment was an *authorized* penalty. The Court rejected this challenge: "The central premise of *Argersinger*—that actual imprisonment is a penalty different in kind from fines or the mere threat of imprisonment—is eminently sound and warrants adoption of actual imprisonment as the line defining the constitutional right to appointment of counsel." Justice Brennan dissented: "The offense of 'theft' is certainly not a 'petty' one. It is punishable by a sentence of up to one year in jail. It carries the moral stigma associated with common-law crimes traditionally recognized as indicative of moral depravity. Scott's right to the assistance of appointed counsel is thus plainly mandated by the logic of the Court's prior cases, including *Argersinger* itself."

b. Suspended Sentences

In *Alabama v. Shelton*, 535 U.S. 654 (2002), the Supreme Court ruled 5-to-4 that the *Argersinger* and *Scott* day-in-jail rule applies to defendants who receive suspended sentences rather than actual incarceration. Shelton was convicted of assault and sentenced to 30 days in jail, but the trial court immediately suspended the sentence, placing him on probation for two years. The majority held that "the Sixth Amendment right to appointed counsel, as delineated in *Argersinger* and *Scott*, applies to a defendant in Shelton's situation. We hold that a suspended sentence that may 'end up in the actual deprivation of a person's liberty' may not be imposed unless the defendant was accorded 'the guiding hand of counsel' in the prosecution for the crime charged." The Court added that "a suspended sentence is a prison term imposed for the offense of conviction. Once the prison term is triggered, the defendant is incarcerated not for the probation violation, but for the underlying offense. The uncounseled conviction at that point 'results in imprisonment'; it 'ends up in the actual deprivation of a person's liberty.' This is precisely what the Sixth Amendment, as interpreted in *Argersinger* and *Scott*, does not allow."

c. Sentence Enhancement With Uncounseled Conviction

In *Baldasar v. Illinois*, 446 U.S. 222 (1980), the Supreme Court held that an uncounseled misdemeanor conviction, although lawful under *Scott*, could not be used to enhance a defendant's sentence for a subsequent misdemeanor conviction into a felony conviction under a sentencing enhancement statute. Subsequently, however, the Court reversed itself, overruling *Baldasar* and holding that "an uncounseled misdemeanor conviction, valid under *Scott* because no prison term was imposed, is also valid when used to enhance punishment at a subsequent conviction." *Nichols v. United States*, 511 U.S. 738, 749 (1994).

d. When Right to Counsel Attaches

Gideon and *Scott* focus upon the right to counsel at trial. The text of the Sixth Amendment embraces, however, "all criminal prosecutions," not just criminal trials. The Supreme Court has ruled, accordingly, that the right to counsel attaches prior to trial at any "critical stage of the criminal prosecution" after the "initiation of adversary judicial criminal proceedings—whether by way of formal charge, preliminary hearing, indictment, information, or arraignment." *Kirby v. Illinois*, 406 U.S. 682, 683, 689 (1972). A proceeding is a critical stage of the prosecution when "potential substantial prejudice to the defendant's rights inheres in the particular confrontation," and "the ability of counsel can help avoid that prejudice." *United States v. Wade*, 388 U.S. 218, 227 (1967). The right to counsel applies, for example, when a defendant appears at a sentencing proceeding, *Mempa v. Rhay*, 389 U.S. 128 (1967), when a defendant appears at a preliminary hearing, *Coleman v. Alabama*, 399 U.S. 1 (1970), and when a defendant first appears before a judge to be "told of the formal accusation against him and restrictions are imposed on his liberty," *Rothgery v. Gillespie County, Texas*, 554 U.S. 191, 194 (2008).

e. Choosing Retained Defense Counsel

A criminal defendant with adequate resources has the right to retain counsel of his or her choice. *United States v., Gonzalez-Lopez,* 548 U.S. 140 (2006); *Chandler v. Fretag,* 348 U.S. 3 (1954). However, such retained counsel must be admitted to practice in the jurisdiction in which the trial is being held, unless the trial court exercises its discretion to grant counsel special admission to the Bar for purposes of that trial only ("*pro hac vice* admission"). *Leis v. Flynt,* 439 U.S. 438 (1979).

> **It's Latin to Me**
>
> *Pro hac vice.* A lawyer who has not been admitted to practice in a particular jurisdiction but who is admitted there temporarily for the purpose of conducting a particular case.

f. Indigents Have No Right to Choose Counsel

Unlike criminal defendants who have adequate resources to employ their own counsel, indigent defendants do not have a right to "choose" their counsel. As the Court explained in *Wheat v. United States,* 486 U.S. 153, 159 (1988), "the essential aim of the Sixth Amendment is to guarantee an effective advocate for each criminal defendant rather than to insure that a defendant will inexorably be represented by the lawyer whom he prefers. A defendant may not insist on representation by an attorney he cannot afford or who for other reasons declines to represent the defendant." A judge may, however, as a discretionary matter, appoint an attorney that an indigent defendant desires, assuming that such attorney is available and agrees to accept the (typically minimal) compensation that is provided for such appointed services.

Moreover, 18 U.S.C. § 3599 entitles indigent federal criminal defendants to the appointment of counsel in capital cases, including habeas corpus proceedings. In *Christeson v. Roper,* 135 S.Ct. 891 (2015), a majority of the Supreme Court held that a federal district court abused its discretion in denying a habeas petitioner's request for substitution of his federally-appointed counsel due to counsel's conflict of interest. Such motions for appointment of new counsel should be evaluated in the "interests of justice," the majority ruled, and substitution of counsel was necessary under that standard in *Christeson* where appointed counsel labored under what the Court deemed an "obvious conflict of interest."

> ## Hypo 1: *License Revocation*
>
> Does a respondent in a driver's license revocation proceeding have a right to appointed counsel? Would your answer be any different if the judge made it clear in advance that no jail time would be imposed?

Hypo 2: *Post-Verdict Motions*

After the criminal trial has concluded and the defendant has been convicted, does the defendant have a continuing right to be represented by appointed counsel for purposes of filing post-trial motions, like a motion for new trial, for example? What if the defendant represented himself at trial, waiving his right to appointed trial counsel? In that case, should his waiver mean that he has also lost the right to have counsel appointed to make post-trial motions for him? *See State v. Pitts*, 131 Hawai'i 537, 319 P.3d 456 (2014).

Hypo 3: *Special Relationship with Counsel*

Defendants Emily and William Harris, members of the "Symbionese Liberation Army," were charged with kidnaping, robbery, assault with a deadly weapon and false imprisonment. Defendants asked the trial judge to appoint attorneys Susan Johnson and Leonard Weinberg to represent them. Both attorneys were willing to undertake the representation, had represented defendants in a prior related proceeding, and purported to have a special relationship with defendants. Many of the witnesses in the prior proceeding were likely to be witnesses in this proceeding. The defendants also asserted that these attorneys shared their political and social beliefs so that there was a sense of mutual trust and confidence between them. In their view, to appoint "strangers" in whom they had no such confidence and trust would be to deprive them of a true representation of their interests. Should the judge grant defendants' motion to appoint these attorneys? How would you argue this case for the State? How might defendants respond? How would you rule? Suppose that the judge felt that it would be better to appoint other attorneys based on their reputation among the local bench and bar, their experience in the trial of capital cases, and the fact that the other attorneys were certified as criminal law specialists by the State Bar? *See Harris v. Superior Court*, 19 Cal.3d 786, 140 Cal. Rptr. 318, 567 P.2d 750 (In Banc, 1977).

Hypo 4: *Physical Assault on Counsel*

When should a trial judge deny an indigent defendant the right to counsel and force him or her to proceed *pro se*? Suppose that a defendant told his appointed counsel "I know how to get rid of you," and later physically assaulted him. If you were the judge, how should you proceed? If counsel wants to withdraw, should you release him, and, if so, are you obligated to appoint alternate counsel for the defendant, or can you force him to proceed pro se? *See State v. Holmes*, 302 S.W.3d 831 (Tenn. 2010).

B. Waiver of the Right to Counsel

Faretta v. California

422 U.S. 806 (1975).

MR. JUSTICE STEWART delivered the opinion of the Court.

The Sixth and Fourteenth Amendments of our Constitution guarantee that a person brought to trial in any state or federal court must be afforded the right to the assistance of counsel before he can be validly convicted and punished by imprisonment. This clear constitutional rule has emerged from a series of cases decided here over the last 50 years. The question before us now is whether a defendant in a state criminal trial has a constitutional right to proceed *without* counsel when he voluntarily and intelligently elects to do so. Stated another way, the question is whether a State may constitutionally hale a person into its criminal courts and there force a lawyer upon him, even when he insists that he wants to conduct his own defense. It is not an easy question, but we have concluded that a State may not constitutionally do so.

Anthony Faretta was charged with grand theft in an information filed in the Superior Court of Los Angeles County, Cal. At the arraignment, the Superior Court Judge assigned to preside at the trial appointed the public defender to represent Faretta. Well before the date of trial, however, Faretta requested that he be permitted to represent himself. Questioning by the judge revealed that Faretta had once represented himself in a criminal prosecution, that he had a high school education, and that he did not want to be represented by the public defender because he believed that office was "very loaded down with a heavy case load." The judge responded that he believed Faretta was "making a mistake" and emphasized that in further proceedings Faretta would receive no special favors. Nevertheless, after establishing that Faretta wanted to represent himself and did not want a lawyer, the judge, in a "preliminary ruling," accepted Faretta's waiver of the assistance of counsel. The judge indicated, however, that he might reverse this ruling if it later appeared that Faretta was unable adequately to represent himself.

Several weeks thereafter, but still prior to trial, the judge *sua sponte* held a hearing to inquire into Faretta's ability to conduct his own defense, and questioned him specifically about both the hearsay rule and the state law governing the challenge of potential jurors. After consideration of Faretta's answers, and observation of his demeanor, the judge ruled that Faretta had not made an intelligent and knowing waiver of his right to the assistance

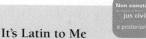

It's Latin to Me

Sua sponte. Without prompting or suggestion; on its own motion.

of counsel, and also ruled that Faretta had no constitutional right to conduct his own defense. The judge, accordingly, reversed his earlier ruling permitting self-representation and again appointed the public defender to represent Faretta. Faretta's subsequent request for leave to act as co-counsel was rejected, as were his efforts to make certain motions on his own behalf. Throughout the subsequent trial, the judge required that Faretta's defense be conducted only through the appointed lawyer from the public defender's office. At the conclusion of the trial, the jury found Faretta guilty as charged, and the judge sentenced him to prison. The California Court of Appeal affirmed the trial judge's ruling that Faretta had no federal or state constitutional right to represent himself.

In the federal courts, the right of self-representation has been protected by statute since the beginnings of our Nation. In *Adams v. U. S. ex rel. McCann*, 317 U.S. 269, 279 (1942), the Court recognized that the Sixth Amendment right to the assistance of counsel implicitly embodies a "correlative right to dispense with a lawyer's help." The defendant in that case, indicted for federal mail fraud violations, insisted on conducting his own defense without benefit of counsel. He also requested a bench trial and signed a waiver of his right to trial by jury. The prosecution consented to the waiver of a jury, and the waiver was accepted by the court. The defendant was convicted, but the Court of Appeals reversed the conviction on the ground that a person accused of a felony could not competently waive his right to trial by jury except upon the advice of a lawyer. This Court reversed and reinstated the conviction, holding that "an accused, in the exercise of a free and intelligent choice, and with the considered approval of the court, may waive trial by jury, and so likewise may he competently and intelligently waive his Constitutional right to assistance of counsel."

Food for Thought

Why would a defendant want to proceed *pro se*? How can such a decision make sense? After all, few defendants are well versed in the criminal law, the rules of evidence, or in criminal procedure. So, how can they effectively represent themselves (or think that they can)?

The *Adams* case does not, of course, necessarily resolve the issue before us. It held only that "the Constitution does not force a lawyer upon a defendant." Whether the Constitution forbids a State from forcing a lawyer upon a defendant is a different question. But the Court in *Adams* did recognize, albeit in dictum, an affirmative right of self-representation:

> "The right to assistance of counsel and the *correlative right to dispense with a lawyer's help* are not legal formalisms. They rest on considerations that go to the substance of an accused's position before the law.
>
> "What were contrived as protections for the accused should not be turned into fetters. To deny an accused a choice of procedure in circumstances in which he, though a layman, is as capable as any lawyer of making an intelligent choice, is to impair the worth of great Constitutional safeguards by treating them as empty verbalisms.
>
> "When the administration of the criminal law is hedged about as it is by the Constitutional safeguards for the protection of an accused, to deny him in the exercise of his free choice the right to dispense with some of these safeguards is to imprison a man in his privileges and call it the Constitution."

This Court's past recognition of the right of self-representation, the federal-court authority holding the right to be of constitutional dimension, and the state constitutions pointing to the right's fundamental nature form a consensus not easily ignored. We confront here a nearly universal conviction, on the part of our people as well as our courts, that forcing a lawyer upon an unwilling defendant is contrary to his basic right to defend himself if he truly wants to do so. This consensus is soundly premised. The right of self-representation finds support in the structure of the Sixth Amendment, as well as in the English and colonial jurisprudence from which the Amendment emerged. Because Sixth Amendment rights are basic to our adversary system of criminal justice, they are part of the "due process of law" that is guaranteed by the Fourteenth Amendment to defendants in the criminal courts of the States. The Sixth Amendment does not provide merely that a defense shall be made for the accused; it grants to the accused personally the right to make his defense. It is the accused, not counsel, who must be "informed of the nature and cause of the accusation," who must be "confronted with the witnesses against him," and who must be accorded "compulsory process for obtaining witnesses in his favor." Although not stated in the Amendment in so many words, the right to self-representation—to make one's own defense personally—is thus necessarily implied by the structure of the Amendment. The right to defend is given directly to the accused; for it is he who suffers the consequences if the defense fails.

The counsel provision supplements this design. It speaks of the "assistance" of counsel, and an assistant, however expert, is still an assistant. The language and spirit of the Sixth Amendment contemplate that counsel, like the other defense tools guaranteed by the Amendment, shall be an aid to a willing defendant—not an organ of the State interposed between an unwilling defendant and his right to defend himself personally. To thrust counsel upon the accused, against his considered wish, thus violates the logic of the Amendment. In such a case, counsel is not an assistant, but a master; and the right to make a defense is stripped of the personal character upon which the Amendment insists. It is true that when a defendant chooses to have a lawyer manage and present his case, law and tradition may allocate to the counsel the power to make binding decisions of trial strategy in many areas. This allocation can only be justified, however, by the defendant's consent, at the outset, to accept counsel as his representative. An unwanted counsel "represents" the defendant only through a tenuous and unacceptable legal fiction. Unless the accused has acquiesced in such representation, the defense presented is not the defense guaranteed him by the Constitution, for, in a very real sense, it is not *his* defense.

There can be no blinking the fact that the right of an accused to conduct his own defense seems to cut against the grain of this Court's decisions holding that the Constitution requires that no accused can be convicted and imprisoned unless he has been accorded the right to the assistance of counsel. For it is surely true that the basic thesis of those decisions is that the help of a lawyer is essential to assure the defendant a fair trial. And a strong argument can surely be made that the whole thrust of those decisions most inevitably lead to the conclusion that a State may constitutionally impose a lawyer upon even an unwilling defendant.

But it is one thing to hold that every defendant, rich or poor, has the right to the assistance of counsel, and quite another to say that a State may compel a defendant to accept a lawyer he does not want. The value of state-appointed counsel was not unappreciated by the Founders, yet the notion of compulsory counsel was utterly foreign to them. And whatever else may be said of those who wrote the Bill of Rights, surely there can be no doubt that they understood the inestimable worth of free choice.

It is undeniable that in most criminal prosecutions defendants could better defend with counsel's guidance than by their own unskilled efforts. But where the defendant will not voluntarily accept representation by counsel, the potential advantage of a lawyer's training and experience can be realized, if at all, only imperfectly. To force a lawyer on a defendant can only lead him to believe that the law contrives against him. Moreover, it is not inconceivable that in some rare instances, the defendant might in fact present his case more effectively by conducting his own defense. Personal liberties are not rooted in the law of averages. The right to defend is personal. The defendant, and not his lawyer or the State, will bear the personal consequences of a conviction. It is the defendant, therefore, who must be free personally to decide whether in his particular case counsel is to his advantage. And although he may conduct his own defense ultimately to his own detriment, his choice must be honored out of "that respect for the individual which is the lifeblood of the law."[46]

When an accused manages his own defense, he relinquishes, as a purely factual matter, many of the traditional benefits associated with the right to counsel. For this reason, in order to represent himself, the accused must "knowingly and intelligently" forgo those relinquished benefits. Although a defendant need not himself have the skill and experience of a lawyer in order competently and intelligently to choose self-representation, he should be made aware of the dangers and disadvantages of self-representation, so that the record will establish that "he knows what he is doing and his choice is made with eyes open."

Take Note

This is an important footnote. After the Court legitimized the concept of "standby counsel" here, the use of this technique became commonplace where defendants decided to "*go pro se*" in serious cases.

Here, weeks before trial, Faretta clearly and unequivocally declared to the trial judge that he wanted to represent himself and did not want counsel. The record affirmatively shows that Faretta was literate, competent, and understanding, and that he was voluntarily exercising his informed free will. The trial judge had warned Faretta that he thought it was a mistake not to accept the assistance of counsel, and that Faretta would be required to follow all the "ground rules" of trial procedure. We need make no assessment of how well or poorly Faretta had mastered the intricacies of the hearsay rule and the California code provisions that govern challenges of potential jurors on *voir dire*. For his technical legal knowledge, as such, was not relevant to an assessment of his knowing exercise of the right to defend himself.

In forcing Faretta, under these circumstances, to accept against his will a state-appointed public defender, the California courts deprived him of his constitutional right to conduct his own defense. Accordingly, the judgment before us is vacated.

---

[46] We are told that many criminal defendants representing themselves may use the courtroom for deliberate disruption of their trials. But the right of self-representation has been recognized from our beginnings by federal law and by most of the States, and no such result has thereby occurred. Moreover, the trial judge may terminate self-representation by a defendant who deliberately engages in serious and obstructionist misconduct. Of course, a State may—even over objection by the accused—appoint a "standby counsel" to aid the accused if and when the accused requests help, and to be available to represent the accused in the event that termination of the defendant's self-representation is necessary.

Whatever else may or may not be open to him on appeal, a defendant who elects to represent himself cannot thereafter complain that the quality of his own defense amounted to a denial of "effective assistance of counsel."

MR. CHIEF JUSTICE BURGER, with whom MR. JUSTICE BLACKMUN and MR. JUSTICE REHNQUIST join, dissenting.

This case is another example of the judicial tendency to constitutionalize what is thought "good." That effort fails on its own terms here, because there is nothing desirable or useful in permitting every accused person, even the most uneducated and inexperienced, to insist upon conducting his own defense to criminal charges. If we were to assume that there will be widespread exercise of the newly discovered constitutional right to self-representation, it would almost certainly follow that there will be added congestion in the courts and that the quality of justice will suffer.

MR. JUSTICE BLACKMUN, with whom THE CHIEF JUSTICE and MR. JUSTICE REHNQUIST join, dissenting.

I fear that the right to self-representation constitutionalized today frequently will cause procedural confusion without advancing any significant strategic interest of the defendant. I therefore dissent. Although the Court indicates that a *pro se* defendant necessarily waives any claim he might otherwise make of ineffective assistance of counsel, the opinion leaves open a host of other procedural questions. Must every defendant be advised of his right to proceed *pro se*? If so, when must that notice be given? If a defendant has elected to exercise his right to proceed *pro se*, does he still have a constitutional right to assistance of standby counsel? How soon must a defendant decide between proceeding by counsel or *pro se*? Must he be allowed to switch in midtrial? If there is any truth to the old proverb that "one who is his own lawyer has a fool for a client," the Court by its opinion today now bestows a *constitutional* right on one to make a fool of himself.

> **FYI**
>
> Is it *really* so foolish to want to represent oneself? *See, e.g.,* Erica J. Hashimoto, *Defending the Right to Self Representation: An Empirical Look at the Pro Se Felony Defendant*, 85 N.C. L. Rev. 423, 423-24 (2007):
>
> The data undermine both the assumption that most felony pro se defendants are ill-served by the decision to self-represent and the theory that most pro se defendants suffer from mental illness. Somewhat surprisingly, the data indicate that pro se felony defendants in state courts are convicted at rates equivalent to or lower than the conviction rates of represented felony defendants, and the vast majority of pro se felony defendants—nearly 80%—did not display outward signs of mental illness.
>
> The data also suggest an alternative explanation for the pro se phenomenon. The small, self-selected group of felony defendants who choose to represent themselves may make that choice because of legitimate concerns about court-appointed counsel. Without the right to represent themselves, those defendants would be in the untenable position of being represented by inadequate counsel with no alternative.

Point for Discussion

On Appeal

In *State v. Rafey*, 167 Wash.2d 644, 652, 222 P.3d 86, 89 (2009), the Washington Supreme Court recognized a convicted defendant's right to proceed *pro se* under the State of Washington's Constitution: "In both trial and appellate proceedings, courts must carefully balance the dissonant rights to counsel and to self-representation when a defendant seeks to proceed *pro se*." However, the court also warned that the right must be asserted in a timely manner. Are appellate proceedings so different from trial court proceedings that courts should *not* recognize a right to *pro se* representation in that setting? What do you think?

Hypo 1: *The Unabomber Case*

You are the federal judge assigned to hear the "Unabomber case." The defendant, Theodore Kaczynski, is the individual who was charged with having murdered a number of people with mail bombs. Defendant wants to conduct his own defense, but his own attorneys question his competency. The reality is that Kaczysnki is very bright, but his sanity is questionable (to put it mildly). How do you decide whether Kaczynski is competent to represent himself? How much weight should you give to the fact that Kaczynski may not be insane, but is, any event, clearly not in sound mental health?

See It

Here's how the FBI describes this case: "How do you catch a twisted genius who aspires to be the perfect, anonymous killer—who builds untraceable bombs and delivers them to random targets, who leaves false clues to throw off authorities, who lives like a recluse in the mountains of Montana and tells no one of his secret crimes? That was the challenge facing the FBI and its investigative partners, who spent nearly two decades hunting down this ultimate lone wolf bomber." *See* https://www.fbi.gov/history/famous-cases/unabomber.

Hypo 2: *Non-Investigating Great Advocate*

Defendant was represented at trial by a public defender. On several occasions during the trial, defendant expressed dissatisfaction with counsel's performance. Prior to jury selection, defendant filed a motion to dismiss his attorney. He claimed that his attorney was not investigating the case adequately. Defense counsel acknowledged the existence of some problems in investigating matters related to the case, but the judge nonetheless denied defendant's motion, noting that the defendant's attorney had been a "great advocate" for his client. Did the judge act properly? *State v. Flanagan*, 293 Conn. 406, 978 A.2d 64 (2009).

Iowa v. Tovar

541 U.S. 77 (2004).

Justice Ginsburg delivered the opinion of the Court.

The Sixth Amendment safeguards to an accused who faces incarceration the right to counsel at all critical stages of the criminal process. The entry of a guilty plea, whether to a misdemeanor or a felony charge, ranks as a "critical stage" at which the right to counsel adheres. Waiver of the right to counsel, as of constitutional rights in the criminal process generally, must be a "knowing, intelligent act done with sufficient awareness of the relevant circumstances." This case concerns the extent to which a trial judge, before accepting a guilty plea from an uncounseled defendant, must elaborate on the right to representation.

> **Hear It**
>
> You can hear the oral argument in *Tovar* at http://www.oyez.org/cases/2000-2009/2003/2003_02_1541.

Beyond affording the defendant the opportunity to consult with counsel prior to entry of a plea and to be assisted by counsel at the plea hearing, must the court, specifically: (1) advise the defendant that "waiving the assistance of counsel in deciding whether to plead guilty entails the risk that a viable defense will be overlooked"; and (2) "admonish" the defendant "that by waiving his right to an attorney he will lose the opportunity to obtain an independent opinion on whether, under the facts and applicable law, it is wise to plead guilty"? The Iowa Supreme Court held both warnings essential to the "knowing and intelligent" waiver of the Sixth Amendment right to the assistance of counsel.

We hold that neither warning is mandated by the Sixth Amendment. The constitutional requirement is satisfied when the trial court informs the accused of the nature of the charges against him, of his right to be counseled regarding his plea, and of the range of allowable punishments attendant upon the entry of a guilty plea.

On November 2, 1996, respondent Felipe Edgardo Tovar, then a 21-year-old college student, was arrested in Ames, Iowa, for operating a motor vehicle while under the influence of alcohol (OWI). At arraignment, the court's inquiries of Tovar began: "Mr. Tovar appears without counsel and I see, Mr. Tovar, that you waived application for a court appointed attorney. Did you want to represent yourself at today's hearing?" Tovar replied: "Yes, sir." The court soon after asked: "How did you wish to plead?" Tovar answered: "Guilty." Tovar affirmed that he had not been promised anything or threatened in any way to induce him to plead guilty.

Conducting the guilty plea colloquy required by the Iowa Rules of Criminal Procedure, the court explained that, if Tovar pleaded not guilty, he would be entitled to a speedy and public trial by jury, and would have the right to be represented at that trial by an attorney, who "could help Tovar select a jury, question and cross-examine the State's witnesses, present evidence, if any, in his behalf, and make arguments to the judge and jury on his behalf." By pleading guilty, the court cautioned, "not only would Tovar give up his right to a trial of any kind on the charge against him, he would give up his right to be represented by an attorney at that trial." The court further advised Tovar that, if he entered a guilty plea, he would relinquish the right to remain silent at trial, the right to the presumption of innocence, and the right to subpoena witnesses and compel their testimony.

Turning to the particular offense with which Tovar had been charged, the court informed him that an OWI conviction carried a maximum penalty of a year in jail and a $1,000 fine, and a minimum penalty of two days in jail and a $500 fine. Tovar affirmed that he understood his exposure to those penalties. The court next explained that, before accepting a guilty plea, the court had to assure itself that Tovar was in fact guilty of the charged offense. To that end, the court informed Tovar that the OWI charge had only two elements: first, on the date in question, Tovar was operating a motor vehicle in the State of Iowa; second, when he did so, he was intoxicated. Tovar confirmed that he had been driving on the night he was apprehended and that he did not dispute the results of the intoxilyzer test administered by the police that night, which showed that his blood alcohol level exceeded the legal limit nearly twice over.

After the plea colloquy, the court asked Tovar if he still wished to plead guilty, and Tovar affirmed that he did. The court then accepted Tovar's plea, observing that there was "a factual basis" for it, and that Tovar had made the plea "voluntarily, with a full understanding of his rights, and of the consequences of pleading guilty."

On December 30, 1996, Tovar appeared for sentencing on the OWI charge. Noting that Tovar was again in attendance without counsel, the court inquired: "Mr. Tovar, did you want to represent yourself at today's hearing or did you want to take some time to hire an attorney to represent you?" Tovar replied that he would represent himself. The court then engaged in essentially the same plea colloquy on the suspension charge as it had on the OWI charge the previous month. After accepting Tovar's guilty plea, the court imposed the minimum sentence of two days in jail and a $500 fine, plus a surcharge and costs.

On March 16, 1998, Tovar was convicted of OWI for a second time. He was represented by counsel in that proceeding, in which he pleaded guilty. On December 14, 2000, Tovar was again charged with OWI, this time as a third offense. Represented by an attorney, Tovar pleaded not guilty.

In March 2001, through counsel, Tovar filed a motion arguing that Tovar's first OWI conviction, in 1996, could not be used to enhance the December 2000 OWI charge from a second-offense aggravated misdemeanor to a third-offense felony. Tovar did not allege that he was unaware at the November 1996 arraignment of his right to counsel prior to pleading guilty and at the plea hearing. Instead, he maintained that his 1996 waiver of counsel was invalid—not "full knowing, intelligent, and voluntary"—because he "was never made aware by the court of the dangers and disadvantages of self-representation."

The court denied Tovar's motion. Tovar then waived his right to a jury trial and was found guilty. On the OWI third-offense charge, he received a 180-day jail term, with all but 30 days suspended, three years of probation, and a $2,500 fine plus surcharges and costs. The Iowa Court of Appeals affirmed, but the Supreme Court of Iowa reversed, holding that the colloquy preceding acceptance of Tovar's 1996 guilty plea had been constitutionally inadequate. We granted certiorari and we now reverse.

The Sixth Amendment secures to a defendant who faces incarceration the right to counsel at all "critical stages" of the criminal process. A plea hearing qualifies as a "critical stage."

Because Tovar received a two-day prison term for his 1996 OWI conviction, he had a right to counsel both at the plea stage and at trial had he elected to contest the charge.

Take Note

Note that, without much fanfare, the Court confirmed here that indigents have the right to counsel at guilty plea hearings.

A person accused of crime, however, may choose to forgo representation. While the Constitution "does not force a lawyer upon a defendant," it does require that any waiver of the right to counsel be knowing, voluntary, and intelligent. Tovar contends that his waiver of counsel at his first OWI plea hearing, was insufficiently informed, and therefore constitutionally invalid. In particular, he asserts that the trial judge did not elaborate on the value, at that stage of the case, of an attorney's advice and the dangers of self-representation in entering a plea.

We have described a waiver of counsel as intelligent when the defendant "knows what he is doing and his choice is made with eyes open." We have not, however, prescribed any formula or script to be read to a defendant who states that he elects to proceed without counsel. The information a defendant must possess in order to make an intelligent election will depend on a range of case-specific factors, including the defendant's education or sophistication, the complex or easily grasped nature of the charge, and the stage of the proceeding.

In Tovar's case, he first indicated that he waived counsel at his Initial Appearance, affirmed that he wanted to represent himself at the plea hearing, and declined the court's offer of "time to hire an attorney" at sentencing, when it was still open to him to request withdrawal of his plea. "Does the Sixth Amendment require a court to give a rigid and detailed admonishment to a *pro se* defendant pleading guilty of the usefulness of an attorney, that an attorney may provide an independent opinion whether it is wise to plead guilty and that without an attorney the defendant risks overlooking a defense?" This Court recently explained, in reversing a lower court determination that a guilty plea was not voluntary: "The law ordinarily considers a waiver knowing, intelligent, and sufficiently aware if the defendant fully understands the nature of the right and how it would likely apply in general in the circumstances—even though the defendant may not know the specific detailed consequences of invoking it." We have similarly observed: "If the defendant lacked a full and complete appreciation of all of the consequences flowing from his waiver, it does not defeat the State's showing that the information it provided to him satisfied the constitutional minimum."

In a collateral attack on an uncounseled conviction, it is the defendant's burden to prove that he did not competently and intelligently waive his right to the assistance of counsel. Tovar has never claimed that he did not fully understand the charge or the range of punishment for the crime prior to pleading guilty. Further, he has never "articulated with precision" the additional information counsel could have provided, given the simplicity of the charge. Nor does he assert that he was unaware of his right to be counseled prior to and at his arraignment. He suggests only that he "may have been under the mistaken belief that he had a right to counsel at trial, but not if he was merely going to plead guilty."

Food for Thought

As extensive as waiver-of-the-right-to-counsel colloquies may appear in theory, the reality is that many trial judges "fly through" them, and many other judges openly encourage such waivers. What effect to you think that the *Tovar* decision will have on that practical reality?

We note, finally, that States are free to adopt by statute, rule, or decision any guides to the acceptance of an uncounseled plea they deem useful. We hold only that the two admonitions the Iowa Supreme Court ordered are not required by the Federal Constitution.

For the reasons stated, the judgment of the Supreme Court of Iowa is reversed.

Indiana v. Edwards

554 U.S. 164 (2008).

JUSTICE BREYER delivered the opinion of the Court.

This case focuses upon a criminal defendant whom a state court found mentally competent to stand trial if represented by counsel but not mentally competent to conduct that trial

Hear It

You can hear the oral argument in *Edwards* at http://www.oyez.org/cases/2000-2009/2007/2007_07_208.

himself. We must decide whether in these circumstances the Constitution forbids a State from insisting that the defendant proceed to trial with counsel, the State thereby denying the defendant the right to represent himself. We conclude that the Constitution does not forbid a State so to insist.

In July 1999 Ahmad Edwards tried to steal a pair of shoes from an Indiana department store. After he was discovered, he drew a gun, fired at a store security officer, and wounded a bystander. He was caught and then charged with attempted murder, battery with a deadly weapon, criminal recklessness, and theft. His mental condition subsequently became the subject of three competency proceedings and two self-representation requests, mostly before the same trial judge:

1. First Competency Hearing: August 2000. Five months after Edwards' arrest, his court-appointed counsel asked for a psychiatric evaluation. After hearing psychiatrist and neuropsychologist witnesses (in February 2000 and again in August 2000), the court found Edwards incompetent to stand trial and committed him to Logansport State Hospital for evaluation and treatment.

2. Second Competency Hearing: March 2002. Seven months after his commitment, doctors found that Edwards' condition had improved to the point where he could stand trial. Several months later, however, but still before trial, Edwards' counsel asked for another psychiatric evaluation. In March 2002, the judge held a competency hearing, considered additional psychiatric evidence, and (in April) found that Edwards, while "suffering from mental illness," was "competent to assist his attorneys in his defense and stand trial for the charged crimes."

3. Third Competency Hearing: April 2003. Seven months later but still before trial, Edwards' counsel sought yet another psychiatric evaluation of his client. And, in April 2003, the court held yet another competency hearing. Edwards' counsel presented further psychiatric and neuropsychological evidence showing that Edwards was suffering from serious thinking difficulties and delusions. A testifying psychiatrist reported that Edwards could understand the charges against him, but he was "unable to cooperate with his attorney in his defense because of his schizophrenic illness"; "his delusions and his marked difficulties in thinking make it impossible for him to cooperate with his attorney." In November 2003, the court concluded that Edwards was not then competent to stand trial and ordered his recommitment to the state hospital.

4. First Self-Representation Request and First Trial: June 2005. About eight months after his commitment, the hospital reported that Edwards' condition had again improved to the point that he had again become competent to stand trial. And almost one year after that Edwards' trial began. Just before trial, Edwards asked to represent himself. He also asked for a continuance, which, he said, he needed in order to proceed *pro se*. The court refused the continuance. Edwards then proceeded to trial represented by counsel. The jury convicted him of criminal recklessness and theft but failed to reach a verdict on the charges of attempted murder and battery.

5. Second Self-Representation Request and Second Trial: December 2005. The State decided to retry Edwards on the attempted murder and battery charges. Just before the retrial, Edwards again asked the court to permit him to represent himself. Referring to the lengthy record of psychiatric reports, the trial court noted that Edwards still suffered from schizophrenia and concluded that "with these findings, he's competent to stand trial but I'm not going to find he's competent to defend himself." The court denied Edwards' self-representation request. Edwards was represented by appointed counsel at his retrial. The jury convicted Edwards on both of the remaining counts.

Subsequently, the Indiana Supreme Court concluded that this Court's precedents, namely, *Faretta,* and *Godinez v. Moran*, 509 U.S. 389 (1993), required the State to allow Edwards to represent himself. Our examination of this Court's precedents convinces us that those precedents frame the question presented, but they do not answer it. The two cases that set forth the Constitution's "mental competence" standard, *Dusky v. United States*, 362 U.S. 402 (1960), and *Drope v. Missouri*, 420 U.S. 162 (1975), specify that the Constitution does not permit trial of an individual who lacks "mental competency." *Dusky* defines the competency standard as including both (1) "whether" the defendant has "a rational as well as factual understanding of the proceedings against him" and (2) whether the defendant "has sufficient present ability to consult with his lawyer with a reasonable degree of rational understanding." *Drope* repeats that standard, stating that it "has long been accepted that a person whose mental condition is such that he lacks the capacity to understand the nature and object of the proceedings against him, to consult with counsel, and to assist in preparing his defense may not be subjected to a trial." Neither case considered the mental competency issue presented here, namely, the relation of the mental competence standard to the right of self-representation.

The Court's foundational "self-representation" case, *Faretta*, held that the Sixth and Fourteenth Amendments include a "constitutional right to proceed without counsel when" a criminal defendant "voluntarily and intelligently elects to do so." The sole case in which this Court considered mental competence and self-representation together is *Godinez*. That case focused upon a borderline-competent criminal defendant who had asked a state trial court to permit him to represent himself and to change his pleas from not guilty to guilty. The state trial court had found that the defendant met *Dusky's* mental competence standard, that he "knowingly and intelligently" waived his right to assistance of counsel, and that he "freely and voluntarily" chose to plead guilty. And the state trial court had consequently granted the defendant's self-representation and change-of-plea requests. This Court "rejected the notion that competence to plead guilty or to waive the right to counsel must be measured by a standard that is higher than (or even different from) the *Dusky* standard." The decision to plead guilty, we said, "is no more complicated than the sum total of decisions that a represented defendant may be called upon to make during the course of a trial." Hence "there is no reason to believe that the decision to waive counsel requires an appreciably higher level of mental functioning than the decision to waive other constitutional rights." And even assuming that self-representation might pose special trial-related difficulties, "the competence that is required of a defendant seeking to waive his right to counsel is the competence to waive the right, not the competence to represent himself."

Godinez does not answer the question before us now. In *Godinez*, the higher standard sought to measure the defendant's ability to proceed on his own to enter a guilty plea; here the higher standard seeks to measure the defendant's ability to conduct trial proceedings. To put the matter more specifically, the *Godinez* defendant sought only to change his pleas to guilty, he did not seek to conduct trial proceedings, and his ability to conduct a defense at trial was expressly not at issue.

We assume that a criminal defendant has sufficient mental competence to stand trial (i.e., the defendant meets *Dusky's* standard) and that the defendant insists on representing himself during that trial. We ask whether the Constitution permits a State to limit that defendant's self-representation right by insisting upon representation by counsel at trial on the ground that the defendant lacks the mental capacity to conduct his trial defense unless represented.

Several considerations taken together lead us to conclude that the answer to this question is yes. First, the Court's precedent points slightly in the direction of our affirmative answer. The Court's "mental competency" cases set forth a standard that focuses directly upon a defendant's "present ability to consult with his lawyer," a "capacity to consult with counsel," and an ability "to assist counsel in preparing his defense." These standards assume representation by counsel and emphasize the importance of counsel. They thus suggest (though do not hold) that an instance in which a defendant who would choose to forgo counsel at trial presents a very different set of circumstances, which in our view, calls for a different standard.

Second, the nature of the problem before us cautions against the use of a single mental competency standard for deciding both (1) whether a defendant who is represented by counsel can proceed to trial and (2) whether a defendant who goes to trial must be permitted to represent himself. Mental illness itself is not a unitary concept. It varies in degree. It can vary over time. It interferes with an individual's functioning at different times in different ways. The history of this case illustrates the complexity of the problem. In certain instances an individual may well be able to satisfy *Dusky's* mental competence standard, for he will be able to work with counsel at trial, yet at the same time he may be unable to carry out the basic tasks needed to present his own defense without the help of counsel.

Third, in our view, a right of self-representation at trial will not "affirm the dignity" of a defendant who lacks the mental capacity to conduct his defense without the assistance of counsel. To the contrary, given that defendant's uncertain mental state, the spectacle that could well result from his self-representation at trial is at least as likely to prove humiliating as ennobling. Moreover, insofar as a defendant's lack of capacity threatens an improper conviction or sentence, self-representation in that exceptional context undercuts the most basic of the Constitution's criminal law objectives, providing a fair trial.

Further, proceedings must not only be fair, they must "appear fair to all who observe them." An amicus brief reports one psychiatrist's reaction to having observed a patient (a patient who had satisfied *Dusky*) try to conduct his own defense: "How in the world can our legal system allow an insane man to defend himself?" The application of *Dusky's* basic mental competence standard can help in part to avoid this result. But given the different capacities needed to proceed to trial without counsel, there is little reason to believe that *Dusky* alone is sufficient. At the

> **FYI**
>
> Only a *minority* of states have followed Indiana's lead and determined that the competency standard to be met in order for a defendant to proceed *pro se* should be set higher than the competency standard to be met for merely standing trial represented by counsel.

same time, the trial judge, particularly one such as the trial judge in this case, who presided over one of Edwards' competency hearings and his two trials, will often prove best able to make more fine-tuned mental capacity decisions, tailored to the individualized circumstances of a particular defendant.

We consequently conclude that the Constitution permits judges to take realistic account of the particular defendant's mental capacities by asking whether a defendant who seeks to conduct his own defense at trial is mentally competent to do so. That is to say, the Constitution permits States to insist upon representation by counsel for those competent enough to stand trial under *Dusky* but who still suffer from severe mental illness to the point where they are not competent to conduct trial proceedings by themselves.

Indiana has also asked us to adopt, as a measure of a defendant's ability to conduct a trial, a more specific standard that would "deny a criminal defendant the right to represent himself at trial where the defendant cannot communicate coherently with the court or a jury." We are sufficiently uncertain, however, as to how that particular standard would work in practice to refrain from endorsing it as a federal constitutional standard here. We need not now, and we do not, adopt it.

Indiana has also asked us to overrule *Faretta*. We decline to do so. We recognize that judges have sometimes expressed concern that *Faretta*, contrary to its intent, has led to trials that are unfair. But recent empirical research suggests that such instances are not common. *See, e.g.,* Hashimoto, Defending the Right of Self-Representation: An Empirical Look at the *Pro Se* Felony Defendant, 85 N.C.L.Rev. 423, 427, 428 (2007) (noting that of the small number of defendants who chose to proceed pro se, roughly 0.3% to 0.5%" of the total, state felony defendants in particular "appear to have achieved higher felony acquittal rates than their represented counterparts in that they were less likely to have been convicted of felonies"). At the same time, instances in which the trial's fairness is in doubt may well be concentrated in the 20 percent or so of self-representation cases where the mental competence of the defendant is also at issue. If so, today's opinion, assuring trial judges the authority to deal appropriately with cases in the latter category, may well alleviate those fair trial concerns.

For these reasons, the judgment of the Supreme Court of Indiana is vacated, and the case is remanded for further proceedings not inconsistent with this opinion.

JUSTICE SCALIA, with whom JUSTICE THOMAS joins, dissenting.

The Constitution guarantees a defendant who knowingly and voluntarily waives the right to counsel the right to proceed *pro se* at his trial. A mentally ill defendant who knowingly and voluntarily elects to proceed *pro se* instead of through counsel receives a fair trial that comports with the Fourteenth Amendment. The Court today concludes that a State may nonetheless strip a mentally ill defendant of the right to represent himself when that would be fairer. In my view the Constitution does not permit a State to substitute its own perception of fairness for the defendant's right to make his own case before the jury—a specific right long understood as essential to a fair trial.

Food for Thought

Is it *fair* to convict a *pro se* defendant of a crime when any reasonable person could see that he or she did not have the slightest idea what he or she was doing? What do you think?

Because I think a defendant who is competent to stand trial, and who is capable of knowing and voluntary waiver of assistance of counsel, has a constitutional right to conduct his own defense, I respectfully dissent.

Points for Discussion

a. *Pro Se* Defendants, Mental Illness, and the Challenge for Trial Judges

Pro se defendants with mental problems are a real challenge for trial judges. Not only might such defendants do crazy and/or disruptive things in court, but the judge may have a reasonable fear that their lack of legal skills might lead to an unfair result. It is not surprising then to find trial judges, after *Edwards*, turning down an increasing number of putative *pro se* defendants' requests to represent themselves on competency grounds. Not only because it's "easier" on the judge, but also because of the judge's (perfectly legitimate) fears and doubts about the fairness of the proceedings. That said, as the *Edwards* Court made clear, *Faretta* is still good law. Criminal defendants do still have a constitutional right to represent themselves.

b. Waiver By Silence

What constitutes a good waiver? Suppose that the defendant fails to assert the right to counsel, and proceeds to represent himself or herself at trial. Has there been a waiver by virtue of the mere failure to make such an assertion? No. The Court has made it clear that such a waiver will not be presumed from mere silence. Trial judges, accordingly, need to take pains to make sure that waivers are clear on the record.

c. Good Waivers

The *Faretta* Court talked about a "knowing and intelligent" waiver of counsel and the *Tovar* Court similarly spoke of a waiver made by a defendant who "knows what he is doing." But *Tovar* and *Faretta* don't *really* require that a defendant make an "intelligent" choice in the dictionary meaning of that word. As Justice Blackmun pointed out in his dissent in *Faretta*, few decisions to waive counsel can be regarded as truly intelligent in that sense. In most instances, criminal defendants do not know the rules of evidence, and have studied neither criminal law nor criminal procedure. Under these circumstances, can even a fully competent defendant make a truly "knowing" and "intelligent" waiver of the right to counsel? In any event, the Supreme Court requires only that the defendant be competent to make the waiver, and that he or she has been given sufficient information on which to base the waiver decision.

Hypo 1: *Judge's Dilemma*

Assuming that defendants are entitled to make a less than (truly) intelligent choice, how should they do so? A robbery defendant has stated that he is aware of his right to counsel, but that he prefers to proceed *pro se*. In light of *Faretta's* requirement that a waiver be "knowing and intelligent," how should the trial judge proceed? Should the judge accept his request at face value? Should the judge interrogate him about his knowledge of the rules of evidence and the criminal law? Should it matter that the accused did not know, or was not able to recall, most (or any) of the exceptions to the hearsay rule? For that matter, can *you* recall them?

Hypo 2: *Judge's Dilemma #2*

If a *pro se* defendant has a valid objection to inadmissible evidence introduced by the prosecutor but fails to make the objection (because he or she doesn't know the applicable law), should the trial judge act *sua sponte* to keep the evidence out? Should the judge inform the *pro se* defendant of the law? Or should the judge say nothing and simply permit the prosecution to introduce otherwise inadmissible evidence?

Hypo 3: *Defendant Changes His Mind*

Where an indigent defendant has waived his right to counsel multiple times, but then changes his mind after trial, and decides that he does want counsel after all for purposes of filing a motion for new trial, should the trial judge have the discretion to deny that request? Or must the trial judge grant that request automatically? What do you think is the appropriate rule given the existing precedent? *See Marshall v. Rodgers*, 569 U.S. 58 (2013).

Exercise : *Pro Se Request*

You are the law clerk to a trial judge. Defendant Jane Jones has been charged with arson in your court and has demanded to proceed *pro se* at trial. She was examined by a clinical psychologist one year ago who found that Jones suffered from "an active psychotic disorder of a paranoid type" and has "auditory hallucinations, delusions of a bizarre and persecutory nature, and is intent on using the legal process as a vehicle for acting out many of her paranoid psychotic preoccupations." After interrogating Jones at length, your judge has told you that she believes that Jones understands the seriousness of the charge filed against her and comprehends the disadvantages of proceeding *pro se*, and that Jones told her that although she heard voices in the past, she no longer does. The file also discloses that Jones has extensive familiarity with the courts in that she has previously filed seventeen motions in state court, eleven in federal court, and has instituted two Court of Claims actions, one for damages for false arrest and the other for an assault allegedly committed on her at a state mental institution. Your judge has asked you to provide her with a bench memo (of no longer than 5 double-spaced pages) that summarizes the applicable federal law on this subject and recommends to her whether or not she should permit Jones to proceed *pro se*.

* * *

The *Faretta* Court indicated in a footnote that trial judges could appoint "standby counsel" to assist *pro se* defendants in presenting their cases, or simply to be available when and if the *pro se* defendant decides that he or she would rather be represented by counsel. As the following decision illustrates, however, standby counsel's appropriate role remains controversial.

McKaskle v. Wiggins

465 U.S. 168 (1984).

Hear It

You can hear the oral argument in *McKaskle* at http://www.oyez.org/cases/1980-1989/1983/1983_82_1135.

JUSTICE O'CONNOR delivered the opinion of the Court.

In *Faretta v. California*, this Court recognized a defendant's Sixth Amendment right to conduct his own defense. The Court also held that a trial court may appoint "standby counsel" to assist the *pro se* defendant in his defense. Today we must decide what role standby counsel who is present at trial over the defendant's objection may play consistent with the protection of the defendant's *Faretta* rights.

Carl Edwin Wiggins was convicted of robbery and sentenced to life imprisonment as a recidivist. In his petition for federal habeas corpus relief, Wiggins argued that standby counsel's conduct deprived him of his right to present his own defense, as guaranteed by *Faretta*. The Court of Appeals held that Wiggins' Sixth Amendment right of self-representation was violated by the unsolicited participation of overzealous standby counsel: "The rule that we establish today is that court-appointed standby counsel is 'to be seen, but not heard.' By this we mean that he is not to compete with the defendant or supersede his defense. Rather, his presence is there for advisory purposes only, to be used or not used as the defendant sees fit." We do not accept the Court of Appeals' rule, and reverse its judgment.

A defendant's right to self-representation plainly encompasses certain specific rights to have his voice heard. The *pro se* defendant must be allowed to control the organization and content of his own defense, to make motions, to argue points of law, to participate in *voir dire*, to question witnesses, and to address the court and the jury at appropriate points in the trial. The record reveals that Wiggins was in fact accorded all of these rights.

Before trial Wiggins moved the trial court to order preparation of a transcript of the first trial. He, not standby counsel, then waived receipt of the transcript and announced ready for trial. He filed and argued at least 12 *pro se* motions in pretrial proceedings. Wiggins alone conducted the defense's *voir dire* of prospective jurors and made the opening statement for the defense to the jury.

Wiggins filed numerous *pro se* motions in the course of the trial. He cross-examined the prosecution's witnesses freely, and registered his own objections. Throughout the trial Wiggins selected the witnesses for the defense, examined them, decided that certain questions would not be asked by the defense, and decided which witnesses would not be called. Against counsel's advice, Wiggins announced that the defense rested. Wiggins filed his own requested charges to the jury, and made his own objections to the court's suggested charge. He obtained the removal of one of the court's proposed charges over counsel's express objection, approved the verdict form supplied to the jury, and gave a closing argument to the and he argued his case to the jury at that stage as well.

Wiggins' complaint is directed not at limits placed on *his* participation in the trial, for there clearly were none. Wiggins contends that his right to present his defense *pro se* was impaired by the distracting, intrusive, and unsolicited participation of counsel throughout the trial.

Faretta's logic indicates that no absolute bar on standby counsel's unsolicited participation is appropriate or was intended. The right to appear *pro se* exists to affirm the dignity and autonomy of the accused and to allow the presentation of what may, at least occasionally, be the accused's best possible defense. Both of these objectives can be achieved without categorically silencing standby counsel.

In determining whether a defendant's *Faretta* rights have been respected, the primary focus must be on whether the defendant had a fair chance to present his case in his own way. *Faretta* itself dealt with the defendant's affirmative right to participate, not with the limits on standby counsel's additional involvement. The specific rights to make his voice heard that Wiggins was plainly accorded form the core of a defendant's right of self-representation.

We recognize, nonetheless, that the right to speak for oneself entails more than the opportunity to add one's voice to a cacophony of others. As Wiggins contends, the objectives underlying the right to proceed *pro se* may be undermined by unsolicited and excessively intrusive participation by standby counsel. In proceedings before a jury the defendant may legitimately be concerned that multiple voices "for the defense" will confuse the message the defendant wishes to convey, thus defeating *Faretta's* objectives. Accordingly, the *Faretta* right must impose some limits on the extent of standby counsel's unsolicited participation.

First, the *pro se* defendant is entitled to preserve actual control over the case he chooses to present to the jury. This is the core of the *Faretta* right. If standby counsel's participation over the defendant's objection effectively allows counsel to make or substantially interfere with any significant tactical decisions, or to control the questioning of witnesses, or to speak instead of the defendant on any matter of importance, the *Faretta* right is eroded.

Second, participation by standby counsel without the defendant's consent should not be allowed to destroy the jury's perception that the defendant is representing himself. The defendant's appearance in the status of one conducting his own defense is important in a criminal trial, since the right to appear *pro se* exists to affirm

Take Note

The ABA in its Criminal Justice Standards, The Defense Function, Standard 4-5.3(b) (4th ed. 2015), has recommended that "defense counsel whose duty is to assist a *pro se* accused only when the accused requests assistance may bring to the attention of the accused steps that could be potentially beneficial or dangerous to the accused, but should not actively participate in the conduct of the defense unless requested by the accused or as directed to do so by the court."

the accused's individual dignity and autonomy. In related contexts the courts have recognized that a defendant has a right to be present at all important stages of trial, that he may not normally be forced to appear in court in shackles or prison garb, and that he has a right to present testimony in his own behalf. Appearing before the jury in the status of one who is defending himself may be equally important to the *pro se* defendant. From the jury's perspective, the message conveyed by the defense may depend as much on the messenger as on the message itself. From the defendant's own point of view, the right to appear *pro se* can lose much of its importance if only the lawyers in the courtroom know that the right is being exercised.

Participation by standby counsel outside the presence of the jury engages only the first of these two limitations. A trial judge, who in any event receives a defendant's original *Faretta* request and supervises the protection of the right throughout the trial, must be considered capable of differentiating the claims presented by a *pro se* defendant from those presented by standby counsel. Accordingly, the appearance of a *pro se* defendant's self-representation will not be unacceptably undermined by counsel's participation outside the presence of the jury.

Thus, *Faretta* rights are adequately vindicated in proceedings outside the presence of the jury if the *pro se* defendant is allowed to address the court freely on his own behalf and if disagreements between counsel and the *pro se* defendant are resolved in the defendant's favor whenever the matter is one that would normally be left to the discretion of counsel.

Most of the incidents of which Wiggins complains occurred when the jury was not in the courtroom. In the jury's absence Wiggins' two standby counsel frequently explained to the trial judge their views and points of disagreement with Wiggins. Counsel made motions, dictated proposed strategies into the record, registered objections to the prosecution's testimony, urged the summoning of additional witnesses, and suggested questions that the defendant should have asked of witnesses. On several occasions Wiggins expressly adopted standby counsel's initiatives.

On several other occasions Wiggins strongly opposed the initiatives of counsel. He resisted counsel's suggestion that the trial be postponed so that the transcript of his prior trial could be prepared, and he waived counsel's right to a 10-day preparation period, which counsel wished to invoke. In the course of a pretrial discussion concerning a discovery request Wiggins indignantly demanded that counsel not participate further without invitation. Later, Wiggins successfully opposed the inclusion in the jury instructions of a charge that counsel felt should be included.

The most acrimonious exchange between standby counsel Graham and Wiggins occurred in the course of questioning a witness on *voir dire*. Wiggins suggests this exchange was typical of counsel's overbearing conduct, but he fails to place the incident in context. Wiggins had expressly agreed to have Graham conduct the *voir dire*, but Wiggins attempted to take over the questioning in midstream. Plainly exasperated, Graham used profanity and curtly directed Wiggins to "sit down."

Though several of these incidents are regrettable, we are satisfied that counsel's participation outside the presence of the jury fully satisfied the first standard we have outlined. Wiggins was given ample opportunity to present his own position to the court on every matter discussed. He was given time to think matters over, to explain his problems and concerns informally, and to speak to the judge off the record. Standby counsel participated actively, but for the most part in an orderly manner. Equally important, all conflicts between Wiggins and counsel were resolved in Wiggins' favor. The trial judge repeatedly explained to all concerned that Wiggins' strategic choices, not counsel's, would prevail. Not every motion made by Wiggins was granted, but in no instance was counsel's position adopted over Wiggins' on a matter that would normally be left to the defense's discretion.

Participation by standby counsel in the presence of the jury is more problematic. It is here that the defendant may legitimately claim that excessive involvement by counsel will destroy the appearance that the defendant is acting *pro se*. This, in turn, may erode the dignitary values that the right to self-representation is intended to promote and may undercut the defendant's presentation to the jury of his own most effective defense. Nonetheless, we believe that a categorical bar on participation by standby counsel in the presence of the jury is unnecessary.

In measuring standby counsel's involvement against the standards we have described, it is important not to lose sight of the defendant's own conduct. A defendant can waive his *Faretta* rights. Participation by counsel with a *pro se* defendant's express approval is, of course, constitutionally unobjectionable. A defendant's invitation to counsel to participate in the trial obliterates any claim that the participation in question deprived the defendant of control over his own defense. Such participation also diminishes any general claim that counsel unreasonably interfered with the defendant's right to appear in the status of one defending himself.

Although this is self-evident, it is also easily overlooked. A defendant like Wiggins, who vehemently objects at the beginning of trial to standby counsel's very presence in the courtroom, may express quite different views as the trial progresses. Even when he insists that he is not waiving his *Faretta* rights, a *pro se* defendant's solicitation of or acquiescence in certain types of participation by counsel substantially undermines later protestations that counsel interfered unacceptably.

The record in this case reveals that Wiggins' *pro se* efforts were undermined primarily by his own, frequent changes of mind regarding counsel's role. *Faretta* does not require a trial judge to permit "hybrid" representation of the type Wiggins was actually allowed. But if a defendant is given the opportunity and elects to have counsel appear before the court or jury, his complaints concerning counsel's subsequent unsolicited participation lose much of their force. A defendant does not have a constitutional right to choreograph special appearances by counsel. Once a *pro se* defendant invites or agrees to any substantial participation by counsel, subsequent appearances by counsel must be presumed to be with the defendant's acquiescence, at least until the defendant expressly and unambiguously renews his request that standby counsel be silenced.

Faretta rights are also not infringed when standby counsel assists the *pro se* defendant in overcoming routine procedural or evidentiary obstacles to the completion of some specific task, such as introducing evidence or objecting to testimony, that the defendant has clearly shown he wishes to complete. Nor are they infringed when counsel merely helps to ensure the defendant's compliance with basic rules of courtroom protocol and procedure. In neither case is there any significant interference with the defendant's actual control over the presentation of his defense. The likelihood that the defendant's appearance in the status of one defending himself will be eroded is also slight, and in any event it is tolerable. A defendant does not have a constitutional right to receive personal instruction from the trial judge on courtroom procedure. Nor does the Constitution require judges to take over chores for a *pro se* defendant that would normally be attended to by trained counsel as a matter of course.

Accordingly, we make explicit today what is already implicit in *Faretta*: A defendant's Sixth Amendment rights are not violated when a trial judge appoints standby counsel—even over the defendant's objection—to relieve the judge of the need to explain and enforce basic rules of courtroom protocol or to assist the defendant in overcoming routine obstacles that stand in the way of the defendant's achievement of his own clearly indicated goals. Participation by counsel to steer a defendant through the basic procedures of trial is permissible even in the unlikely event that it somewhat undermines the *pro se* defendant's appearance of control over his own defense.

At Wiggins' trial a significant part of standby counsel's participation both in and out of the jury's presence involved basic mechanics of the type we have described—informing the court of the whereabouts of witnesses, supplying

Wiggins with a form needed to elect to go to the jury at the punishment phase of trial, explaining to Wiggins that he should not argue his case while questioning a witness, and so on. When Wiggins attempted to introduce a document into evidence, but failed to mark it for identification or to lay a predicate for its introduction, counsel, at the trial court's suggestion, questioned the witness to lay an appropriate predicate, and Wiggins then resumed his examination. Similarly, the trial judge repeatedly instructed Wiggins to consult with counsel, not with the court, regarding the appropriate procedure for summoning witnesses.

Notwithstanding Wiggins' several general objections to the presence and participation of counsel, we find these aspects of counsel's involvement irreproachable. None interfered with Wiggins' actual control over his defense; none can reasonably be thought to have undermined Wiggins' appearance before the jury in the status of a *pro se* defendant.

Putting aside participation that was either approved by Wiggins or attendant to routine clerical or procedural matters, counsel's unsolicited comments in front of the jury were infrequent and for the most part innocuous. On two occasions Graham interrupted a witness' answer to a question put by Wiggins. The first interruption was trivial. When the second was made the jury was briefly excused and subsequently given a cautionary instruction as requested by Graham. Wiggins made no objection. Standby counsel also moved for a mistrial three times in the presence of the jury. Each motion was in response to allegedly prejudicial questions or comments by the prosecutor. Wiggins did not comment on the first motion, but he opposed the following two. All three motions were immediately denied by the trial court. Regrettably, counsel used profanity to express his exasperation on the second occasion. Finally, counsel played an active role at the punishment phase of the trial. The record supplies no explanation for the sudden change in this regard. Wiggins made no objection to counsel's participation in this phase of the trial. We can only surmise that by then Wiggins had concluded that appearing *pro se* was not in his best interests.

The statements made by counsel during the guilt phase of the trial, in the presence of the jury and without Wiggins' express consent, occupy only a small portion of the transcript. Most were of an unobjectionable, mechanical sort. While standby counsel's participation at Wiggins' trial should not serve as a model for future trials, we believe that counsel's involvement fell short of infringing on Wiggins' *Faretta* rights. Wiggins unquestionably maintained actual control over the presentation of his own defense at all times.

We are also persuaded that Wiggins was allowed to appear before the jury in the status of one defending himself. At the outset the trial judge carefully explained to the jury that Wiggins would be appearing *pro se*. Wiggins, not counsel, examined prospective jurors on *voir dire*, cross-examined the prosecution's witnesses, examined his own witnesses, and made an opening statement for the defense. Wiggins objected to the prosecutor's case at least as often as did counsel. If Wiggins' closing statement to the jury had to compete with one made by counsel, it was only because Wiggins agreed in advance to that arrangement.

By contrast, counsel's interruptions of Wiggins or witnesses being questioned by Wiggins in the presence of the jury were few and perfunctory. Most of counsel's uninvited comments were directed at the prosecutor. Such interruptions present little threat to a defendant's *Faretta* rights, at least when the defendant's view regarding those objections has not been clearly articulated. On the rare occasions that disagreements between counsel and Wiggins were aired in the presence of the jury the trial judge consistently ruled in Wiggins' favor. This was a pattern more likely to reinforce than to detract from the appearance that Wiggins was controlling his own defense. The intrusions by counsel at Wiggins' trial were simply not substantial or frequent enough to have seriously undermined Wiggins' appearance before the jury in the status of one representing himself.

Faretta affirmed the defendant's constitutional right to appear on stage at his trial. We recognize that a *pro se* defendant may wish to dance a solo, not a *pas de deux*. Standby counsel must generally respect that preference. But counsel need not be excluded altogether, especially when the participation is outside the presence of the jury or is with the defendant's express or tacit consent. The defendant in this case was allowed to make his own appearances as he saw fit. In our judgment counsel's unsolicited involvement was held within reasonable limits.

Food for Thought

The majority concludes that its new test for the limits on standby counsel's participation was not violated in this case. Do you think this conclusion was correct, i.e. even if the test is just fine, was it really satisfied on these facts?

The judgment of the Court of Appeals is therefore *Reversed.*

JUSTICE WHITE, with whom JUSTICE BRENNAN and JUSTICE MARSHALL join, dissenting.

The continuous and substantial intervention of standby counsel, despite Wiggins' repeated demands that he play a passive role, could not have had "anything but a negative impact on the jury. It also destroyed Wiggins' own perception that he was conducting *his* defense."

Under the Court's new test, it is necessary to determine whether the pro se defendant retained "actual control over the case he chose to present to the jury," and whether standby counsel's participation "destroyed the jury's perception that the defendant was representing himself." Although this test purports to protect all of the values underlying our holding in *Faretta*, it is unclear whether it can achieve this result.

As long as the *pro se* defendant is allowed his say, the first prong of the Court's test accords standby counsel at a bench trial or any proceeding outside the presence of a jury virtually untrammeled discretion to present any factual or legal argument to which the defendant does not object.

Although the Court is more solicitous of a *pro se* defendant's interests when standby counsel intervenes before a jury, the test's second prong suffers from similar shortcomings. To the extent that trial and appellate courts can discern the point at which counsel's unsolicited participation substantially undermines a *pro se* defendant's appearance before the jury, a matter about which I harbor substantial doubts, their decisions will, to a certain extent, "affirm the accused's individual dignity and autonomy." But they will do so incompletely, for in focusing on how the jury views the defendant, the majority opinion ignores *Faretta's* emphasis on the defendant's own perception of the criminal justice system, and implies that the Court actually adheres to the result-oriented harmless error standard it purports to reject.

As a guide for standby counsel and lower courts, moreover, the Court's two-part test is clearly deficient. Instead of encouraging counsel to accept a limited role, the Court plainly invites them to participate despite their clients' contrary instructions until the clients renew their objections and trial courts draw the line. Trial courts required to rule on *pro se* defendants' objections to counsel's intervention also are left at sea. They clearly must prevent standby counsel from overtly muzzling their *pro se* clients and resolve certain conflicts in defendants' favor. But the Court's opinion places few, if any, other clear limits on counsel's uninvited participation; instead it requires trial courts to make numerous subjective judgments concerning the effect of counsel's actions on defendants' *Faretta* rights.

In short, I believe that the Court's test is unworkable and insufficiently protective of the fundamental interests we recognized in *Faretta*.

Food for Thought

What more could the trial court have done in this case to protect Wiggin's *pro se* rights? One thing it could have done was to order standby counsel to remain silent, at least in front of the jury, unless spoken to or requested to speak by the defendant. Obviously, the majority was unwilling to impose that requirement. Would that have been a better result?

Hypo 1: *Meddling Law Professor*

Suppose that you graduated from law school, passed the bar (*congratulations!*), and were appointed to represent an indigent defendant in a criminal case. Your criminal procedure professor, interested to see how much you learned in law school, comes to observe. Unhappy with your performance, the professor offers interjections and suggestions while you are trying the case. Is a court likely to tolerate the professor's conduct? If not, should the court be any more willing to tolerate such conduct when a *pro se* defendant is involved as counsel? Is there a dispositive difference in these two situations?

Hypo 2: *Judicial Instructions*

Suppose that you are the judge in a criminal case involving a *pro se* defendant and standby counsel. Prior to trial, would you give standby counsel any special instructions regarding his or her role? What instructions? Suppose that counsel subsequently intrudes in the case inappropriately. How should you (still the trial judge) respond?

Hypo 3: *Standby Counsel's Role in Penalty Phase*

Defendant, who proceeded *pro se* at trial, was convicted of murder and faced the possibility of a death sentence. During the penalty phase of the proceeding, he elected not to present any evidence and instead relied in mitigation on the fact that he had confessed to some unsolved crimes and took responsibility for the murder for which he had been convicted. Standby counsel conducted his own mitigation investigation, and introduced mitigation evidence over defendant's objections, *inter alia*, establishing that defendant "was under the emotional or mental disturbance of cocaine dependency, and an antisocial personality disorder." Defendant was sentenced to death. Were the actions of standby counsel in presenting mitigation evidence over defendant's objections justified? Or did they unduly infringe upon defendant's Sixth Amendment right to proceed pro se? *Barnes v. State*, 29 So.3d 1010 (Fla. 2010).

> ## Hypo 4: *Pro Se Defendant at Sidebar?*
>
> Attorneys often "approach the Bench" and have conversations with the trial judge about various issues. This is called meeting "at sidebar." If a *pro se* defendant has standby counsel, should that *pro se* defendant have a right to participate in these sidebar conferences discussing legal issues instead of or in addition to standby counsel? Would it or should it make any difference if the defendant had previously been disruptive in court? *See Allen v. Com.*, 410 S.W.3d 125 (Ky. 2013).

C. Ineffective Assistance of Counsel

In *Powell v. Alabama*, 287 U.S. 45 (1932), the United States Supreme Court made it clear that a criminal defendant's constitutional right to counsel includes the right to the "effective" assistance of counsel.

However, the Court did not establish a test to determine when defense counsel violates the Sixth Amendment due to ineffective assistance of counsel until 1984.

Powell v. Alabama was the Supreme Court's decision in the widely-publicized "Scottsboro Boys" case, in which nine African-American teenagers were prosecuted for the rape of two white women. The trial court purported to appoint "all the members of the bar" to represent the defendants. But, despite the theoretical abundance of defense counsel, the reality was that no local lawyer would represent them. As a result, they were unrepresented at arraignment, and they were still unrepresented as late as the morning of trial. At that point, the judge hastily forced two lawyers to serve as counsel, but neither attorney was given time to prepare for trial, which began immediately. Unsurprisingly, the Scottsboro Boys were quickly convicted in a one-day trial and some were sentenced to death, and others received life sentences. But, in what can be seen as one of the earliest civil-rights decisions in this country, the Supreme Court reversed, holding that not only did the defendants have the right to counsel, but they were also entitled to the *effective* assistance of counsel, a right which they clearly had not received. (*Postscript*: Justice was only temporary. The defendants were re-convicted on remand, even though, in hindsight, the charges against them were clearly ludicrous and fabricated.)

See It

Watch and listen to Emory's Charles Howard Candler Professor and Chair of African American Studies, Carol Anderson, movingly discuss the extraordinary circumstances of this case. *See* https://www.youtube.com/watch?v=TmsYLmqx3wg.

Strickland v. Washington

466 U.S. 668 (1984).

Hear It

You can hear the oral argument in *Strickland* at http://www.oyez.org/cases/1980-1989/1983/1983_82_1554.

JUSTICE O'CONNOR delivered the opinion of the Court.

This case requires us to consider the proper standards for judging a criminal defendant's contention that the Constitution requires a conviction or death sentence to be set aside because counsel's assistance at the trial or sentencing was ineffective.

During a 10-day period in September 1976, respondent planned and committed three groups of crimes, which included three brutal stabbing murders, torture, kidnaping, severe assaults, attempted murders, attempted extortion, and theft. After his two accomplices were arrested, respondent surrendered to police and voluntarily gave a lengthy statement confessing to the third of the criminal episodes. The State of Florida indicted respondent for kidnaping and murder and appointed an experienced criminal lawyer to represent him.

Counsel actively pursued pretrial motions and discovery. He cut his efforts short, however, and he experienced a sense of hopelessness about the case, when he learned that, against his specific advice, respondent had also confessed to the first two murders. By the date set for trial, respondent was subject to indictment for three counts of first-degree murder and multiple counts of robbery, kidnaping for ransom, breaking and entering and assault, attempted murder, and conspiracy to commit robbery. Respondent waived his right to a jury trial, again acting against counsel's advice, and pleaded guilty to all charges, including the three capital murder charges.

In the plea colloquy, respondent told the trial judge that, although he had committed a string of burglaries, he had no significant prior criminal record and that at the time of his criminal spree he was under extreme stress caused by his inability to support his family. He also stated, however, that he accepted responsibility for the crimes. The trial judge told respondent that he had "a great deal of respect for people who are willing to step forward and admit their responsibility" but that he was making no statement at all about his likely sentencing decision.

Counsel advised respondent to invoke his right under Florida law to an advisory jury at his capital sentencing hearing. Respondent rejected the advice and waived the right. He chose instead to be sentenced by the trial judge without a jury recommendation.

In preparing for the sentencing hearing, counsel spoke with respondent about his background. He also spoke on the telephone with respondent's wife and mother, though he did not follow up on the one unsuccessful effort to meet with them. He did not otherwise seek out character witnesses for respondent. Nor did he request a psychiatric examination, since his conversations with his client gave no indication that respondent had psychological problems.

Counsel decided not to present and hence not to look further for evidence concerning respondent's character and emotional state. That decision reflected trial counsel's sense of hopelessness about overcoming the evidentiary effect of respondent's confessions to the gruesome crimes. It also reflected the judgment that it was advisable to rely on the plea colloquy for evidence about respondent's background and about his claim of emotional stress: the plea colloquy communicated sufficient information about these subjects, and by forgoing the opportunity to present new evidence on these subjects, counsel prevented the State from cross-examining respondent on his claim and from putting on psychiatric evidence of its own.

Counsel also excluded from the sentencing hearing other evidence he thought was potentially damaging. He successfully moved to exclude respondent's "rap sheet." Because he judged that a presentence report might prove more detrimental than helpful, as it would have included respondent's criminal history and thereby would have undermined the claim of no significant history of criminal activity, he did not request that one be prepared.

At the sentencing hearing, counsel's strategy was based primarily on the trial judge's remarks at the plea colloquy as well as on his reputation as a sentencing judge who thought it important for a convicted defendant to own up to his crime. Counsel argued that respondent's remorse and acceptance of responsibility justified sparing him from the death penalty. Counsel also argued that respondent had no history of criminal activity and that respondent committed the crimes under extreme mental or emotional disturbance, thus coming within the statutory list of mitigating circumstances. He further argued that respondent should be spared death because he had surrendered, confessed, and offered to testify against a codefendant and because respondent was fundamentally a good person who had briefly gone badly wrong in extremely stressful circumstances. The State put on evidence and witnesses largely for the purpose of describing the details of the crimes. Counsel did not cross-examine the medical experts who testified about the manner of death of respondent's victims.

The trial judge found several aggravating circumstances with respect to each of the three murders. He found that all three murders were especially heinous, atrocious, and cruel, all involving repeated stabbings. All three murders were committed in the course of at least one other dangerous and violent felony, and since all involved robbery, the murders were for pecuniary gain. All three murders were committed to avoid arrest for the accompanying crimes and to hinder law enforcement. In the course of one of the murders, respondent knowingly subjected numerous persons to a grave risk of death by deliberately stabbing and shooting the murder victim's sisters-in-law, who sustained severe—in one case, ultimately fatal—injuries.

With respect to mitigating circumstances, the trial judge made the same findings for all three capital murders. First, although there was no admitted evidence of prior convictions, respondent had stated that he had engaged in a course of stealing. In any case, even if respondent had no significant history of criminal activity, the aggravating circumstances "would still clearly far outweigh" that mitigating factor. Second, the judge found that, during all three crimes, respondent was not suffering from extreme mental or emotional disturbance and could appreciate the criminality of his acts. Third, none of the victims was a participant in, or consented to, respondent's conduct. Fourth, respondent's participation in the crimes was neither minor nor the result of duress or domination by an accomplice. Finally, respondent's age (26) could not be considered a factor in mitigation, especially when viewed in light of respondent's planning of the crimes and disposition of the proceeds of the various accompanying thefts.

In short, the trial judge found numerous aggravating circumstances and no (or a single comparatively insignificant) mitigating circumstance. He therefore sentenced respondent to death on each of the three counts of murder and to prison terms for the other crimes. The Florida Supreme Court upheld the convictions and sentences. In subsequent postconviction proceedings, a federal district court denied Strickland's petition for habeas corpus, but the court of appeals reversed.

In a long line of cases that includes *Powell v. Alabama*, 287 U.S. 45 (1932), *Johnson v. Zerbst*, 304 U.S. 458 (1938), and *Gideon v. Wainwright*, 372 U.S. 335 (1963), this Court has recognized that the Sixth Amendment right to counsel exists, and is needed, in order to protect the fundamental right to a fair trial. A fair trial is one in which evidence subject to adversarial testing is presented to an impartial tribunal for resolution of issues defined in advance of the proceeding. The right to counsel plays a crucial role in the adversarial system embodied in the Sixth Amendment, since access to counsel's skill and knowledge is necessary to accord defendants the "ample opportunity to meet the case of the prosecution" to which they are entitled.

The Court has recognized that "the right to counsel is the right to the effective assistance of counsel." Government violates the right to effective assistance when it interferes in certain ways with the ability of counsel to make independent decisions about how to conduct the defense. Counsel, however, can also deprive a defendant of the right to effective assistance, simply by failing to render "adequate legal assistance."

The Court has not elaborated on the meaning of the constitutional require-ment of effective assistance in cases presenting claims of "actual ineffectiveness." In giving meaning to the requirement, however, we must take its purpose—to ensure a fair trial—as the guide. The benchmark for judging any claim of ineffec-tiveness must be whether counsel's conduct so undermined the proper function-ing of the adversarial process that the trial cannot be relied on as having produced a just result.

The same principle applies to a capital sentencing proceeding such as that provided by Florida law. A capital sentencing proceeding like the one involved in this case is sufficiently like a trial in its adversarial format and in the existence of standards for decision, that counsel's role in the proceeding is comparable to counsel's role at trial—to ensure that the adversarial testing process works to produce a just result under the standards governing decision. For purposes of describing counsel's duties, therefore, Florida's capital sentencing proceeding need not be distinguished from an ordinary trial.

A convicted defendant's claim that counsel's assistance was so defective as to require reversal of a conviction or death sentence has two components. First, the defendant must show that counsel's performance was deficient. This requires showing that counsel made errors so serious that counsel was not functioning as the "counsel" guaran-teed the defendant by the Sixth Amendment. Second, the defendant must show that the deficient perfor-mance prejudiced the defense. This requires showing that counsel's errors were so serious as to deprive the

Food for Thought

Given the potential consequences of a capital sentencing hearing—*a sentence of death*—wouldn't it have been reasonable to have required defense counsel to do more than to provide merely *adequate* representation?

defendant of a fair trial, a trial whose result is reliable. Unless a defendant makes both showings, it cannot be said that the conviction or death sentence resulted from a breakdown in the adversary process that renders the result unreliable.

The proper standard for attorney performance is that of reasonably effective assistance. When a convicted defendant complains of the ineffectiveness of coun-sel's assistance, the defendant must show that counsel's representation fell below an objective standard of reasonableness. More specific guidelines are not appro-priate. The Sixth Amendment refers simply to "counsel," not specifying particular requirements of effective assistance. It relies instead on the legal profession's main-tenance of standards sufficient to justify the law's presumption that counsel will fulfill the role in the adversary process that the Amendment envisions. The proper measure of attorney performance remains simply reasonableness under prevailing professional norms.

Representation of a criminal defendant entails certain basic duties. Counsel's function is to assist the defendant, and hence counsel owes the client a duty of loyalty, a duty to avoid conflicts of interest. From counsel's function as assistant to the defendant derive the overarching duty to advocate the defendant's cause and the more particular duties to consult with the defendant on important decisions and to keep the defendant informed of important developments in the course of the prosecution. Counsel also has a duty to bring to bear such skill and knowledge as will render the trial a reliable adversarial testing process.

These basic duties neither exhaustively define the obligations of counsel nor form a checklist for judicial evaluation of attorney performance. In any case presenting an ineffectiveness claim, the performance inquiry must be whether counsel's assistance was reasonable considering all the circumstances. Prevailing norms of practice as reflected in American Bar Association standards and the like, *e.g.,* ABA Standards for Criminal Justice 4–1.1 to 4–8.6 (2d ed. 1980) ("The Defense Function"), are guides to determining what is reasonable, but they are only guides. No particular set of detailed rules for counsel's conduct can satisfactorily take account of the variety of circumstances faced by defense counsel or the range of legitimate decisions regarding how best to represent a criminal defendant. Moreover, the purpose of the effective assistance guarantee of the Sixth Amendment is not to improve the quality of legal representation, although that is a goal of considerable importance to the legal system. The purpose is simply to ensure that criminal defendants receive a fair trial.

Judicial scrutiny of counsel's performance must be highly deferential. It is all too tempting for a defendant to second-guess counsel's assistance after conviction or adverse sentence, and it is all too easy for a court, examining counsel's defense after it has proved unsuccessful, to conclude that a particular act or omission of counsel was unreasonable. A fair assessment of attorney performance requires that every effort be made to eliminate the distorting effects of hindsight, to reconstruct the circumstances of counsel's challenged conduct, and to evaluate the conduct from counsel's perspective at the time. Because of the difficulties inherent in making the evaluation, a court must indulge a strong presumption that counsel's conduct falls within the wide range of reasonable professional assistance; that is, the defendant must overcome the presumption that, under the circumstances, the challenged action "might be considered sound trial strategy." There are countless ways to provide effective assistance in any given case. Even the best criminal defense attorneys would not defend a particular client in the same way.

The availability of intrusive post-trial inquiry into attorney performance or of detailed guidelines for its evaluation would encourage the proliferation of ineffectiveness challenges. Criminal trials resolved unfavorably to the defendant would increasingly come to be followed by a second trial, this one of counsel's unsuccessful defense. Counsel's performance and even willingness to serve could be adversely affected. Intensive scrutiny of counsel and rigid requirements for acceptable assistance could dampen the ardor and impair the independence of defense counsel, discourage the acceptance of assigned cases, and undermine the trust between attorney and client.

Thus, a court deciding an actual ineffectiveness claim must judge the reasonableness of counsel's challenged conduct on the facts of the particular case, viewed as of the time of counsel's conduct. A convicted defendant making a claim of ineffective assistance must identify the acts or omissions of counsel that are alleged not to have been the result of reasonable professional judgment. The court must then determine whether, in light of all the circumstances, the identified acts or omissions were outside the wide range of professionally competent assistance. In making that determination, the court should keep in mind that counsel's function, as elaborated in prevailing professional norms, is to make the adversarial testing process work in the particular case. At the same time, the court should recognize that counsel is strongly presumed to have rendered adequate assistance and made all significant decisions in the exercise of reasonable professional judgment.

These standards require no special amplification in order to define counsel's duty to investigate, the duty at issue in this case. As the Court of Appeals concluded, strategic choices made after thorough investigation of law and facts relevant to plausible options are virtually unchallengeable; and strategic choices made after less than complete investigation are reasonable precisely to the extent that reasonable professional judgments support the limitations on investigation. In other words, counsel has a duty to make reasonable investigations or to make a reasonable decision that makes particular investigations unnecessary. In any ineffectiveness case, a particular decision not to investigate must be directly assessed for reasonableness in all the circumstances, applying a heavy measure of deference to counsel's judgments.

The reasonableness of counsel's actions may be determined or substantially influenced by the defendant's own statements or actions. Counsel's actions are usually based, quite properly, on informed strategic choices made by the defendant and on information supplied by the defendant. In particular, what investigation decisions are reasonable depends critically on such information. For example, when the facts that support a certain potential line of defense are generally known to counsel because of what the defendant has said, the need for further investigation may be considerably diminished or eliminated altogether. And when a defendant has given counsel reason to believe that pursuing certain investigations would be fruitless or even harmful, counsel's failure to pursue those investigations may not later be challenged as unreasonable. In short, inquiry into counsel's conversations with the defendant may be critical to a proper assessment of counsel's investigation decisions, just as it may be critical to a proper assessment of counsel's other litigation decisions.

An error by counsel, even if professionally unreasonable, does not warrant setting aside the judgment of a criminal proceeding if the error had no effect on the judgment. The purpose of the Sixth Amendment guarantee of counsel is to ensure that a defendant has the assistance necessary to justify reliance on the outcome of the proceeding. Accordingly, any deficiencies in counsel's performance must be prejudicial to the defense in order to constitute ineffective assistance under the Constitution.

Conflict of interest claims aside, actual ineffectiveness claims alleging a deficiency in attorney performance are subject to a general requirement that the defendant affirmatively prove prejudice. The government is not responsible for, and hence not able to prevent, attorney errors that will result in reversal of a conviction or sentence. Attorney errors come in an infinite variety and are as likely to be utterly harmless in a particular case as they are to be prejudicial. They cannot be classified according to likelihood of causing prejudice. Nor can they be defined with sufficient precision to inform defense attorneys correctly just what conduct to avoid. Representation is an art, and an act or omission that is unprofessional in one case may be sound or even brilliant in another. Even if a defendant shows that particular errors of counsel were unreasonable, therefore, the defendant must show that they actually had an adverse effect on the defense.

It is not enough for the defendant to show that the errors had some conceivable effect on the outcome of the proceeding. Virtually every act or omission of counsel would meet that test, and not every error that conceivably could have influenced the outcome undermines the reliability of the result of the proceeding.

The appropriate test for prejudice finds its roots in the test for materiality of exculpatory information not disclosed to the defense by the prosecution, and in the test for materiality of testimony made unavailable to the defense by Government deportation of a witness. The defendant must show that there is a reasonable probability that, but for counsel's unprofessional errors, the result of the proceeding would have been different. A reasonable probability is a probability sufficient to undermine confidence in the outcome.

In making the determination whether the specified errors resulted in the required prejudice, a court should presume, absent challenge to the judgment on grounds of evidentiary insufficiency, that the judge or jury acted according to law. An assessment of the likelihood of a result more favorable to the defendant must exclude the possibility of arbitrariness, whimsy, caprice, "nullification," and the like. A defendant has no entitlement to the luck of a lawless decisionmaker, even if a lawless decision cannot be reviewed. The assessment of prejudice should proceed on the assumption that the decisionmaker is reasonably, conscientiously, and impartially applying the standards that govern the decision. It should not depend on the idiosyncrasies of the particular decisionmaker, such as unusual propensities toward harshness or leniency. Although these factors may actually have entered into counsel's selection of strategies and, to that limited extent, may thus affect the performance inquiry, they are irrelevant to the prejudice inquiry. Thus, evidence about the actual process of decision, if not part of the record of the proceeding under review, and evidence about, for example, a particular judge's sentencing practices, should not be considered in the prejudice determination.

The governing legal standard plays a critical role in defining the question to be asked in assessing the prejudice from counsel's errors. When a defendant challenges a conviction, the question is whether there is a reasonable probability that, absent the errors, the fact-finder would have had a reasonable doubt respecting guilt. When a defendant challenges a death sentence such as the one at issue in this case, the question is whether there is a reasonable probability that, absent the errors, the sentencer—including an appellate court, to the extent it independently reweighs the evidence—would have concluded that the balance of aggravating and mitigating circumstances did not warrant death.

In making this determination, a court hearing an ineffectiveness claim must consider the totality of the evidence before the judge or jury. A verdict or conclusion only weakly supported by the record is more likely to have been affected by errors than one with overwhelming record support. Taking the unaffected findings as a given, and taking due account of the effect of the errors on the remaining findings, a court making the prejudice inquiry must ask if the defendant has met the burden of showing that the decision reached would reasonably likely have been different absent the errors.

A number of practical considerations are important for the application of the standards we have outlined. Most important, in adjudicating a claim of actual ineffectiveness of counsel, a court should keep in mind that the principles we have stated do not establish mechanical rules. Although those principles should guide the process of decision, the ultimate focus of inquiry must be on the fundamental fairness of the proceeding whose result is being challenged. In every case the court should be concerned with whether, despite the strong presumption of reliability, the result of the particular proceeding is unreliable because of a breakdown in the adversarial process that our system counts on to produce just results.

To the extent that this has already been the guiding inquiry in the lower courts, the standards articulated today do not require reconsideration of ineffectiveness claims rejected under different standards. With regard to the prejudice inquiry, only the strict outcome-determinative test, among the standards articulated in the lower courts, imposes a heavier burden on defendants than the tests laid down today. The difference, however, should alter the merit of an ineffectiveness claim only in the rarest case.

Although we have discussed the performance component of an ineffectiveness claim prior to the prejudice component, there is no reason for a court deciding an ineffective assistance claim to approach the inquiry in the same order or even to address both components of the inquiry if the defendant makes an insufficient showing on one. If it is easier to dispose of an ineffectiveness claim on the ground of lack of sufficient prejudice, which we expect will often be so, that course should be followed. Courts should strive to ensure that ineffectiveness claims not become so burdensome to defense counsel that the entire criminal justice system suffers as a result.

Take Note

Note that to defeat a claim of ineffectiveness, all the government must do is to establish that the defendant has failed to satisfy *either* one of these tests, not both.

Application of the governing principles is not difficult in this case. The facts as described above make clear that the conduct of respondent's counsel at and before respondent's sentencing proceeding cannot be found unreasonable. They also make clear that, even assuming the challenged conduct of counsel was unreasonable, respondent suffered insufficient prejudice to warrant setting aside his death sentence.

With respect to the performance component, the record shows that respondent's counsel made a strategic choice to argue for the extreme emotional distress mitigating circumstance and to rely as fully as possible on respondent's acceptance of responsibility for his crimes. Although counsel understandably felt hopeless about respondent's prospects, nothing in the record indicates that counsel's sense of hopelessness distorted his professional judgment. Counsel's strategy choice was well within the range of professionally reasonable judgments, and the decision not to seek more character or psychological evidence than was already in hand was likewise reasonable.

The trial judge's views on the importance of owning up to one's crimes were well known to counsel. The aggravating circumstances were utterly overwhelming. Trial counsel could reasonably surmise from his conversations with respondent that character and psychological evidence would be of little help. Respondent had already been able to mention at the plea colloquy the substance of what there was to know about his financial and emotional troubles. Restricting testimony on respondent's character to what had come in at the plea colloquy ensured that contrary character and psychological evidence and respondent's criminal history, which counsel had successfully moved to exclude, would not come in. On these facts, there can be little question, even without application of the presumption of adequate performance, that trial counsel's defense, though unsuccessful, was the result of reasonable professional judgment.

With respect to the prejudice component, the lack of merit of respondent's claim is even more stark. The evidence that respondent says his trial counsel should have offered at the sentencing hearing would barely have altered the sentencing profile presented to the sentencing judge. At most this evidence shows that numerous people who knew respondent thought he was generally a good person and that a psychiatrist and a psychologist believed he was under considerable emotional stress that did not rise to the level of extreme disturbance. Given the overwhelming aggravating factors, there is no reasonable probability that the omitted evidence would have changed the conclusion that the aggravating circumstances outweighed the mitigating circumstances and, hence, the sentence imposed. Indeed, admission of the evidence respondent now offers might even have been harmful to his case: his "rap sheet" would probably have been admitted into evidence, and the psychological reports would have directly contradicted respondent's claim that the mitigating circumstance of extreme emotional disturbance applied to his case.

Failure to make the required showing of either deficient performance or sufficient prejudice defeats the ineffectiveness claim. Here there is a double failure. More generally, respondent has made no showing that the justice of his sentence was rendered unreliable by a breakdown in the adversary process caused by deficiencies in counsel's assistance. Respondent's sentencing proceeding was not fundamentally unfair.

We conclude, therefore, that the District Court properly declined to issue a writ of habeas corpus. The judgment of the Court of Appeals is accordingly *Reversed.*

Justice Marshall, dissenting.

My objection to the performance standard adopted by the Court is that it is so malleable that, in practice, it will either have no grip at all or will yield excessive variation in the manner in which the Sixth Amendment is interpreted and applied by different courts.

I object to the prejudice standard adopted by the Court for two independent reasons. First, it is often very difficult to tell whether a defendant convicted after a trial in which he was ineffectively represented would have fared better if his lawyer had been competent. Seemingly impregnable cases can sometimes be dismantled by good defense counsel. On the basis of

Food for Thought

Is the *Strickland* ineffectiveness test a sensible and fair one? Is it unreasonably difficult for a defendant to satisfy? Does or should the Sixth Amendment right to counsel require *more* from a defense representative?

a cold record, it may be impossible for a reviewing court confidently to ascertain how the government's evidence and arguments would have stood up against rebuttal and cross-examination by a shrewd, well-prepared lawyer. The difficulties of estimating prejudice after the fact are exacerbated by the possibility that evidence of injury to the defendant may be missing from the record precisely because of the incompetence of defense counsel. In view of all these impediments to a fair evaluation of the probability that the outcome of a trial was affected by ineffectiveness of counsel, it seems to me senseless to impose on a defendant whose lawyer has been shown to have been incompetent the burden of demonstrating prejudice.

Second and more fundamentally, the assumption on which the Court's holding rests is that the only purpose of the constitutional guarantee of effective assistance of counsel is to reduce the chance that innocent persons will be convicted. In my view, the guarantee also functions to ensure that convictions are obtained only through fundamentally fair procedures. The majority contends that the Sixth Amendment is not violated when a manifestly guilty defendant is convicted after a trial in which he was represented by a manifestly ineffective attorney. I cannot agree. Every defendant is entitled to a trial in which his interests are vigorously and conscientiously advocated by an able lawyer.

Points for Discussion

a. Extrinsic Ineffectiveness

In a companion case to *Strickland*, *United States v. Cronic*, 466 U.S. 648 (1984), the Supreme Court rejected defendant's "extrinsic" claims of defense counsel's ineffectiveness in all but the rarest of cases. "Extrinsic" claims are those that focus upon alleged general problems with counsel or the case (e.g. counsel was too young and/or inexperienced, the case was too complex for this attorney and/or there was too little time to prepare) without accompanying claims of "actual" incidents of ineffectiveness. Cronic was indicted on mail fraud charges involving the transfer of over $9,400,000 in checks between banks in Florida and Oklahoma during a 4-month period. Shortly before the scheduled trial date, retained counsel withdrew. The court then appointed a young lawyer with a real estate practice to represent Cronic, but allowed counsel only 25 days for pretrial preparation even though it had taken the Government over four and one-half years to investigate the case and it had reviewed thousands of documents during that time. Cronic was subsequently convicted on 11 of the 13 counts in the indictment and received a 25-year sentence. The court of appeals overturned Cronic's conviction based on five extrinsic factors: " '(1) The time afforded for investigation and preparation; (2) the experience of counsel; (3) the gravity of the charge; (4) the complexity of possible defenses; and (5) the accessibility of witnesses to counsel.' " The Supreme Court reversed, however, holding that a criminal defendant can "make out a claim of ineffective assistance only by pointing to specific errors made by trial counsel."

b. Ineffectiveness Claims in Habeas Corpus Proceedings

In *Kimmelman v. Morrison*, 477 U.S. 365 (1986), the Court refused to extend *Stone v. Powell*, 428 U.S. 465 (1976) to Sixth Amendment claims of ineffectiveness. In *Stone*, the Court held that exclusionary rule arguments relating to Fourth Amendment violations could not be asserted on collateral review in federal habeas corpus proceedings if the defendant had a full and fair opportunity to raise the issues in state court. In *Kimmelman*, the Court held that this rule did not apply to claims of ineffective assistance where the principal allegation and manifestation of inadequate representation was counsel's failure to file a timely motion to suppress evidence allegedly obtained in violation of the Fourth Amendment.

c. Ethics & Ineffectiveness

In *Nix v. Whiteside*, 475 U.S. 157 (1986), Whiteside was convicted of second degree murder. At trial, Whiteside claimed self-defense and wanted to testify that he had seen something metallic (presumably a gun) in the victim's hand. However, Whiteside's attorney concluded that the testimony would be perjury and "advised him that if he did do that it would be my duty to advise the Court of what he was doing and that I felt he was committing perjury." Counsel also stated that he would attempt to withdraw from representing Whiteside if he insisted on committing perjury. Following his conviction, Whiteside sought a writ of habeas corpus, claiming that the attorney's conduct deprived him of effective assistance of counsel. The Court rejected this argument:

> An attorney's ethical duty to advance the interests of his client is limited by an equally solemn duty to comply with the law and standards of professional conduct; it specifically ensures that the client may not use false evidence. Whether counsel's conduct is seen as a successful attempt to dissuade his client from committing the crime of perjury, or whether seen as a 'threat' to withdraw from representation and disclose the illegal scheme, his representation of Whiteside falls well within accepted standards of professional conduct and the range of reasonable professional conduct acceptable under *Strickland*.

Hypo 1: *Cronic Problems*

Does the *Cronic* presumption of effective assistance in the absence of a showing of actual, prejudicial errors make sense? When defense counsel is inexperienced and is given insufficient time and resources to prepare his case, is it really fair to simply presume that counsel functioned effectively? Shouldn't ineffective assistance be presumed sometimes? What if defendant's counsel showed up for trial drunk and occasionally went to sleep during the trial. In such a situation, should defendant really have to show that counsel committed specific errors in order to gain reversal?

Hypo 2: Defense Counsel Ten Minutes Late

Defendant Donald was charged, *inter alia*, with felony murder. At trial, his defense counsel returned late from a break in the proceedings, totally missing ten minutes of the trial. Donald was convicted and subsequently sentenced to life imprisonment. Do you think that defense counsel's absence during ten minutes of the trial was (or should be deemed to be) ineffective assistance under *Cronic*, entitling Donald to a new trial? *See Woods v. Donald*, 135 S.Ct. 1372 (2015).

Hypo 3: *Missing Counsel*

Suppose that a defendant's attorney recommends that he talk to the police to explain his alibi to robbery/murder charges. However, counsel mistakenly believes that he cannot remain in the room during the questioning and therefore leaves. Notwithstanding counsel's absence, defendant explains his alibi and it leads the police to two witnesses who testify against him. Defendant is convicted. Should his conviction be reversed for ineffective assistance of counsel? *See People v. Frazier*, 2008 WL 782593 (Mich. Ct. App. 2008).

Hypo 4: *Failure to Object to Leg Restraints*

Was defense counsel ineffective under *Cronic* for failing to object to the fact that defendant was standing trial for first-degree murder while being forced by the sheriff to wear a leg restraint under his pants leg which prevented him from fully straightening his leg? Does it—should it—matter that the shackle was not visible to the jury? *See Zink v. State*, 278 S.W.3d 170 (Mo. 2009).

Missouri v. Frye

566 U.S. 133 (2012).

JUSTICE KENNEDY delivered the opinion of the Court.

The Sixth Amendment, applicable to the States by the terms of the Fourteenth Amendment, provides that the accused shall have the assistance of counsel in all criminal prosecutions.

Hear It

You can hear the oral argument in *Frye* at http://www.oyez.org/cases/2010-2019/2011/2011_10_444.

The right to counsel is the right to effective assistance of counsel. This case arises in the context of claimed ineffective assistance that led to the lapse of a prosecution offer of a plea bargain, a proposal that offered terms more lenient than the terms of the guilty plea entered later. The initial question is whether the constitutional right to counsel extends to the negotiation and consideration of plea offers that lapse or are rejected. If there is a right to effective assistance with respect to those offers, a further question is what a defendant must demonstrate in order to show that prejudice resulted from counsel's deficient performance.

In August 2007, respondent Galin Frye was charged with driving with a revoked license. Frye had been convicted for that offense on three other occasions, so the State of Missouri charged him with a class D felony, which carries a maximum term of imprisonment of four years. On November 15, the prosecutor sent a letter to Frye's counsel offering a choice of two plea bargains. The prosecutor first offered to recommend a 3-year sentence if there was a guilty plea to the felony charge, without a recommendation regarding probation but with a recommendation that Frye serve 10 days in jail as so-called "shock" time. The second offer was to reduce the charge to a misdemeanor and, if Frye pleaded guilty to it, to recommend a 90-day sentence. The misdemeanor charge of driving with a revoked license carries a maximum term of imprisonment of one year. The letter stated both offers would expire on December 28. Frye's attorney did not advise Frye that the offers had been made. The offers expired.

Frye's preliminary hearing was scheduled for January 4, 2008. On December 30, 2007, less than a week before the hearing, Frye was again arrested for driving with a revoked license. At the January 4 hearing, Frye waived his right to a preliminary hearing on the charge arising from the August 2007 arrest. He pleaded not guilty at a subsequent arraignment but then changed his plea to guilty. There was no underlying plea agreement. The state trial court accepted Frye's guilty plea. The prosecutor recommended a 3-year sentence, made no recommendation regarding probation, and requested 10 days shock time in jail. The trial judge sentenced Frye to three years in prison.

Frye filed for postconviction relief in state court. He alleged his counsel's failure to inform him of the prosecution's plea offer denied him the effective assistance of counsel. At an evidentiary hearing, Frye testified he would have entered a guilty plea to the misdemeanor had he known about the offer. A state court denied the postconviction motion, but the Missouri Court of Appeals reversed.

It is well settled that the right to the effective assistance of counsel applies to certain steps before trial. The "Sixth Amendment guarantees a defendant the right to have counsel present at all 'critical' stages of the criminal proceedings." Critical stages include arraignments, postindictment interrogations, postindictment lineups, and the entry of a guilty plea. With respect to the right to effective counsel in plea negotiations, a proper beginning point is to discuss two cases from this Court considering the role of counsel in advising a client about a plea offer and an ensuing guilty plea: *Hill v. Lockhart*, 474 U.S. 52 (1985); and *Padilla v. Kentucky*, 559 U.S. 356 (2010).

Hill established that claims of ineffective assistance of counsel in the plea bargain context are governed by the two-part test set forth in *Strickland*. In *Hill*, the decision turned on the second part of the *Strickland* test. There, a defendant who had entered a guilty plea claimed his counsel had misinformed him of the amount of time he would have to serve before he became eligible for parole. But the defendant had not alleged that, even if adequate advice and assistance had been given, he would have elected to plead not guilty and proceed to trial. Thus, the Court found that no prejudice from the inadequate advice had been shown or alleged.

In *Padilla*, the Court again discussed the duties of counsel in advising a client with respect to a plea offer that leads to a guilty plea. *Padilla* held that a guilty plea, based on a plea offer, should be set aside because counsel misinformed the defendant of the immigration consequences of the conviction. The Court made clear that "the negotiation of a plea bargain is a critical phase of litigation for purposes of the Sixth Amendment right to effective assistance of counsel." It also rejected the argument made by petitioner in this case that a knowing and voluntary plea supersedes errors by defense counsel.

When a plea offer has lapsed or been rejected, no formal court proceedings are involved. This underscores that the plea-bargaining process is often in flux, with no clear standards or time lines and with no judicial supervision of the discussions between prosecution and defense. Indeed, discussions between client and defense counsel are privileged. So the prosecution has little or no notice if something may be amiss and perhaps no capacity to intervene in any event. And, as noted, the State insists there is no right to receive a plea offer. For all these reasons, the State contends, it is unfair to subject it to the consequences of defense counsel's inadequacies, especially when the opportunities for a full and fair trial, or, as here, for a later guilty plea albeit on less favorable terms, are preserved.

The State's contentions are neither illogical nor without some persuasive force, yet they do not suffice to overcome a simple reality. Ninety-seven percent of federal convictions and ninety-four percent of state convictions are the result of guilty pleas. The reality is that plea bargains have become so central to the administration of the criminal justice system that defense counsel have responsibilities in the plea bargain process, responsibilities that must be met to render the adequate assistance of counsel that the Sixth Amendment requires in the criminal process at critical stages. Because ours "is for the most part a system of pleas, not a system of trials," it is insufficient simply to point to the guarantee of a fair trial as a backstop that inoculates any errors in the pretrial process. "To a large extent, horse trading between prosecutor and defense counsel determines who goes to jail and for how long. That is what plea bargaining is. It is not some adjunct to the criminal justice system; it is the criminal justice system." Scott & Stuntz, Plea Bargaining as Contract, 101 Yale L. J. 1909, 1912 (1992). In today's criminal justice system, therefore, the negotiation of a plea bargain, rather than the unfolding of a trial, is almost always the critical point for a defendant.

Take Note

Don't miss this important point. The five-justice majority in *Frye* recognized explicitly that plea bargaining—not an actual criminal trial—is "the name of the game" in U.S. criminal justice. That is how most criminal prosecutions are resolved, namely through pleas not in trials. Once the majority reached this conclusion, the holding that ineffective-assistance-of-counsel rules apply was ineluctable.

To note the prevalence of plea bargaining is not to criticize it. The potential to conserve valuable prosecutorial resources and for defendants to admit their crimes and receive more favorable terms at sentencing means that a plea agreement can benefit both parties. In order that these benefits can be realized, however, criminal defendants require effective counsel during plea negotiations. "Anything less might deny a defendant 'effective representation by counsel at the only stage when legal aid and advice would help him.' "

The inquiry then becomes how to define the duty and responsibilities of defense counsel in the plea bargain process. This is a difficult question. Bargaining is, by its nature, defined to a substantial degree by personal style. The alternative courses and tactics in negotiation are so individual that it may be neither prudent nor practicable to try to elaborate or define detailed standards for the proper discharge of defense counsel's participation in the process. This case presents neither the necessity nor the occasion to define the duties of defense counsel in those respects, however. Here the question is whether defense counsel has the duty to communicate the terms of a formal offer to accept a plea on terms and conditions that may result in a lesser sentence, a conviction on lesser charges, or both.

This Court now holds that, as a general rule, defense counsel has the duty to communicate formal offers from the prosecution to accept a plea on terms and conditions that may be favorable to the accused. Any exceptions to that rule need not be explored here, for the offer was a formal one with a fixed expiration date. When defense counsel allowed the offer to expire without advising the defendant or allowing him to consider it, defense counsel did not render the effective assistance the Constitution requires. Under *Strickland*, the question then becomes what, if any, prejudice resulted from the breach of duty.

To show prejudice from ineffective assistance of counsel where a plea offer has lapsed or been rejected because of counsel's deficient performance, defendants must demonstrate a reasonable probability they would have accepted the earlier plea offer had they been afforded effective assistance of counsel. Defendants must also demonstrate a reasonable probability the plea would have been entered without the prosecution canceling it or the trial court refusing to accept it, if they had the authority to exercise that discretion under state law. To establish prejudice in this instance, it is necessary to show a reasonable probability that the end result of the criminal process would have been more favorable by reason of a plea to a lesser charge or a sentence of less prison time. In a case, such as this, where a defendant pleads guilty to less favorable terms and claims that ineffective assistance of counsel caused him to miss out on a more favorable earlier plea offer, *Strickland's* inquiry into whether "the result of the proceeding would have been different," requires looking not at whether the defendant would have proceeded to trial absent ineffective assistance but whether he would have accepted the offer to plead pursuant to the terms earlier proposed.

In order to complete a showing of *Strickland* prejudice, defendants who have shown a reasonable probability they would have accepted the earlier plea offer must also show that, if the prosecution had the discretion to cancel it or if the trial court had the discretion to refuse to accept it, there is a reasonable probability neither the prosecution nor the trial court would have prevented the offer from being accepted or implemented. This further showing is of particular importance because a defendant has no right to be offered a plea, nor a federal right that the judge accept it. It can be assumed that in most jurisdictions prosecutors and judges are familiar with the boundaries of acceptable plea bargains and sentences. So in most instances it should not be difficult to make an objective assessment as to whether or not a particular fact or intervening circumstance would suffice, in the normal course, to cause prosecutorial withdrawal or judicial nonapproval of a plea bargain. The determination that there is or is not a reasonable probability that the outcome of the proceeding would have been different absent counsel's errors can be conducted within that framework.

These standards must be applied to the instant case. As regards the deficient performance prong of *Strickland*, the Court of Appeals found the "record is void of any evidence of any effort by trial counsel to communicate the formal Offer to Frye during the Offer window, let alone any evidence that Frye's conduct interfered with trial counsel's ability to do so." On this record, it is evident that Frye's attorney did not make a meaningful attempt to inform the defendant of a written plea offer before the offer expired. The Missouri Court of Appeals was correct that "counsel's representation fell below an objective standard of reasonableness." The Court of Appeals erred, however, in articulating the precise standard for prejudice in this context. As noted, a defendant in Frye's position must show not only a reasonable probability that he would have accepted the lapsed plea but also a reasonable probability that the prosecution would have adhered to the agreement and that it would have been accepted by the trial court. Frye can show he would have accepted the offer, but there is strong reason to doubt the prosecution and the trial court would have permitted the plea bargain to become final.

There appears to be a reasonable probability Frye would have accepted the prosecutor's original offer of a plea bargain if the offer had been communicated to him, because he pleaded guilty to a more serious charge, with no promise of a sentencing recommendation from the prosecutor.

The Court of Appeals failed, however, to require Frye to show that the first plea offer, if accepted by Frye, would have been adhered to by the prosecution and accepted by the trial court. Whether the prosecution and trial court are required to do so is a matter of state law, and it is not the place of this Court to settle those matters. The Court has established the minimum requirements of the Sixth

Food for Thought

How in the world can the defendant prove whether the prosecution would have honored its bargain? Or whether the Court would accept it? Are proofs like this too high a burden for a defendant who has not been advised of a favorable plea bargain to meet?

Amendment as interpreted in *Strickland*, and States have the discretion to add procedural protections under state law if they choose. A State may choose to preclude the prosecution from withdrawing a plea offer once it has been accepted or perhaps to preclude a trial court from rejecting a plea bargain. In Missouri, it appears "a plea offer once accepted by the defendant can be withdrawn without recourse" by the prosecution. The extent of the trial court's discretion in Missouri to reject a plea agreement appears to be in some doubt.

We remand for the Missouri Court of Appeals to consider these state-law questions, because they bear on the federal question of *Strickland* prejudice. If, as the Missouri court stated here, the prosecutor could have canceled the plea agreement, and if Frye fails to show a reasonable probability the prosecutor would have adhered to the agreement, there is no *Strickland* prejudice. Likewise, if the trial court could have refused to accept the plea agreement, and if Frye fails to show a reasonable probability the trial court would have accepted the plea, there is no *Strickland* prejudice. In this case, given Frye's new offense for driving without a license on December 30, 2007, there is reason to doubt that the prosecution would have adhered to the agreement or that the trial court would have accepted it at the January 4, 2008, hearing, unless they were required by state law to do so.

The judgment of the Missouri Court of Appeals is vacated, and the case is remanded for further proceedings not inconsistent with this opinion.

Justice Scalia, with whom The Chief Justice, Justice Thomas, and Justice Alito join, dissenting.

The Court acknowledges that Frye's conviction was untainted by attorney error. Given the "ultimate focus" of our ineffective-assistance cases on "the fundamental fairness of the proceeding whose result is being challenged," that should be the end of the matter.

The plea-bargaining process is a subject worthy of regulation, since it is the means by which most criminal convictions are obtained. It happens not to be, however, a subject covered by the Sixth Amendment, which is concerned not with the fairness of bargaining but with the fairness of conviction.

Food for Thought

Was Justice Scalia correct? Is "fairness" the "ultimate focus" of the Court's ineffective assistance cases?

"The Constitution is not an all-purpose tool for judicial construction of a perfect world; and when we ignore its text in order to make it that, we often find ourselves swinging a sledge where a tack hammer is needed." In this case, the Court's sledge may require the reversal of perfectly valid, eminently just, convictions. I respectfully dissent.

Point for Discussion

Poor Advice

In the companion case of *Lafler v. Cooper*, 566 U.S. 156 (2012), the same 5-to-4 majority of the Supreme Court, applied *Strickland* to a situation where a favorable plea offer was reported to the client (unlike Frye), but, on poor advice of counsel, was rejected. "In these circumstances," the majority ruled, "a defendant must show that but for the ineffective advice of counsel there is a reasonable probability that the plea offer would have been presented to the court (i.e., that the defendant would have accepted the plea and the prosecution would not have withdrawn it in light of intervening circumstances), that the court would have accepted its terms, and that the conviction or sentence, or both, under the offer's terms would have been less severe than under the judgment and sentence that in fact were imposed." Deficient performance was conceded, and the Court found prejudice because "respondent received a minimum sentence 31/2 times greater than he would have received under the plea." That said, the majority added:

> Even if a defendant shows ineffective assistance of counsel has caused the rejection of a plea leading to a trial and a more severe sentence, there is the question of what constitutes an appropriate remedy.

> The specific injury suffered by defendants who decline a plea offer as a result of ineffective assistance of counsel and then receive a greater sentence as a result of trial can come in at least one of two forms. In some cases, the sole advantage a defendant would have received under the plea is a lesser sentence. This is typically the case when the charges that would have been admitted as part of the plea bargain are the same as the charges the defendant was convicted of after trial. In this situation the court may conduct an evidentiary hearing to determine whether the defendant has shown a reasonable probability that but for counsel's errors he would have accepted the plea. If the showing is made, the court may exercise discretion in determining whether the defendant should receive the term of imprisonment the government offered in the plea, the sentence he received at trial, or something in between.

> In some situations it may be that resentencing alone will not be full redress for the constitutional injury. If, for example, an offer was for a guilty plea to a count or counts less serious than the ones for which a defendant was convicted after trial, or if a mandatory sentence confines a judge's sentencing discretion after trial, a resentencing based on the conviction at trial may not suffice. In these circumstances, the proper exercise of discretion to remedy the constitutional injury may be to require the prosecution to reoffer the plea proposal. Once this has occurred, the judge can then exercise discretion in deciding whether to vacate the conviction from trial and accept the plea or leave the conviction undisturbed.

* * *

Since the reasonableness of defense counsel's conduct is a very fact-specific inquiry under *Strickland*, sometimes it may be perfectly reasonable for counsel to engage in counter-intuitive conduct for good reasons, e.g. actually conceding the defendant's guilt or abandoning an insanity defense. Then again, defense counsel's strategic decisions are not entirely immune from second guessing. In this regard, consider the following Supreme Court decisions:

Florida v. Nixon

543 U.S. 175 (2004).

JUSTICE GINSBURG delivered the opinion of the Court.

This capital case concerns defense counsel's strategic decision to concede, at the guilt phase of the trial, the defendant's commission of murder, and to concentrate the defense on establishing, at the penalty phase, cause for sparing the defendant's life. Any concession of that order, the Florida Supreme Court held, made without the defendant's express consent—however gruesome the crime and despite the strength of the evidence of guilt—automatically ranks as prejudicial ineffective assistance of counsel necessitating a new trial. We reverse the Florida Supreme Court's judgment.

Defense counsel undoubtedly has a duty to discuss potential strategies with the defendant. *See Strickland v. Washington*, 466 U.S. 668 (1984). But when a defendant, informed by counsel, neither consents nor objects to the course counsel describes as the most promising means to avert a sentence of death, counsel is not automatically barred from pursuing that course. The reasonableness of counsel's performance, after consultation with the defendant yields no response, must be judged in accord with the inquiry generally applicable to ineffective-assistance-of-counsel claims: Did counsel's representation "fall below an objective standard of reasonableness"? The Florida Supreme Court erred in applying, instead, a presumption of deficient performance, as well as a presumption of prejudice; that latter presumption, we have instructed, is reserved for cases in which counsel fails meaningfully to oppose the prosecution's case. A presumption of prejudice is not in order based solely on a defendant's failure to provide express consent to a tenable strategy counsel has adequately disclosed to and discussed with the defendant.

On Monday, August 13, 1984, near a dirt road in the environs of Tallahassee, Florida, a passing motorist discovered Jeanne Bickner's charred body. Bickner had been tied to a tree and set on fire while still alive. Her left leg and arm, and most of her hair and skin, had been burned away. The next day, police found Bickner's car, abandoned on a Tallahassee street corner, on fire. Police arrested 23-year-old Joe Elton Nixon later that morning, after Nixon's brother informed the sheriff's office that Nixon had confessed to the murder.

Questioned by the police, Nixon described in graphic detail how he had kidnaped Bickner, then killed her. He recounted that he had approached Bickner, a stranger, in a mall, and asked her to help him jumpstart his car. Bickner offered Nixon a ride home in her 1973 MG sports car. Once on the road, Nixon directed Bickner to drive to a remote place; en route, he overpowered her and stopped the car. Nixon next put Bickner in the MG's trunk, drove into a wooded area, removed Bickner from the car, and tied her to a tree with jumper cables. Bickner pleaded with Nixon to release her, offering him money in exchange. Concerned that Bickner might identify him, Nixon decided to kill her. He set fire to Bickner's personal belongings and ignited her with burning objects. Nixon drove away in the MG, and later told his brother and girlfriend what he had done. He burned the MG on Tuesday, August 14, after reading in the newspaper that Bickner's body had been discovered.

Public Def. Investigation

The State gathered overwhelming evidence establishing that Nixon had committed the murder in the manner he described. In late August 1984, Nixon was indicted in Leon County, Florida, for first-degree murder, kidnaping, robbery, and arson. Assistant public defender Michael Corin, assigned to represent Nixon, filed a plea of not guilty and deposed all of the State's potential witnesses. Corin concluded, given the strength of the evidence, that Nixon's guilt was not "subject to any reasonable dispute." Corin thereupon commenced plea negotiations, hoping to persuade the prosecution to drop the death penalty in exchange for Nixon's guilty pleas to all charges. Negotiations broke down when the prosecutors indicated their unwillingness to recommend a sentence other than death.

Counsel's Strategy

Faced with the inevitability of going to trial on a capital charge, Corin turned his attention to the penalty phase, believing that the only way to save Nixon's life would be to present extensive mitigation evidence centering on Nixon's mental instability. Experienced in capital defense, Corin feared that denying Nixon's commission of the kidnaping and murder during the guilt phase would compromise Corin's ability to persuade the jury, during the penalty phase, that Nixon's conduct was the product of his mental illness. Corin concluded that the best strategy would be to concede guilt, thereby preserving his credibility in urging leniency during the penalty phase.

Corin attempted to explain this strategy to Nixon at least three times. Although Corin had represented Nixon previously on unrelated charges and the two had a good relationship in Corin's estimation, Nixon was generally unresponsive during their discussions. He never verbally approved or protested Corin's proposed strategy. Corin eventually exercised his professional judgment to pursue the concession strategy. As he explained: "There are many times lawyers make decisions because they have to make them because the client does nothing."

When Nixon's trial began on July 15, 1985, his unresponsiveness deepened into disruptive and violent behavior. On the second day of jury selection, Nixon pulled off his clothing, demanded a black judge and lawyer, refused to be escorted into the courtroom, and threatened to force the guards to shoot him. An extended on-the-record colloquy followed Nixon's bizarre behavior, during which Corin urged the trial judge to explain Nixon's rights to him and ascertain whether Nixon understood the significance of absenting himself from the trial. Corin also argued that restraining Nixon and compelling him to be present would prejudice him in the eyes of the jury. When the judge examined Nixon on the record in a holding cell, Nixon stated he had no interest in the trial and threatened to misbehave if forced to attend. The judge ruled that Nixon had intelligently and voluntarily waived his right to be present at trial.

The guilt phase of the trial thus began in Nixon's absence. In his opening statement, Corin acknowledged Nixon's guilt and urged the jury to focus on the penalty phase:

> "In this case, there won't be any question, none whatsoever, that my client, Joe Elton Nixon, caused Jeannie Bickner's death. That fact will be proved to your satisfaction beyond any doubt.

> "This case is about the death of Joe Elton Nixon and whether it should occur within the next few years by electrocution or maybe its natural expiration after a lifetime of confinement.

> "Now, in arriving at your verdict, in your penalty recommendation, for we will get that far, you are going to learn many facts about Joe Elton Nixon. Some of those facts are going to be good. That may not seem clear to you at this time. But, and sadly, most of the things you learn of Joe Elton Nixon are not going to be good. But, I'm suggesting to you that when you have seen all the testimony, heard all the testimony and the evidence that has been shown, there are going to be reasons why you should recommend that his life be spared."

During its case in chief, the State introduced the tape of Nixon's confession, expert testimony on the manner in which Bickner died, and witness testimony regarding Nixon's confessions to his relatives and his possession of Bickner's car and personal effects. Corin cross-examined these witnesses only when he felt their statements needed clarification and he did not present a defense case. Corin did object to the introduction of crime scene photographs as unduly prejudicial and actively contested several aspects of the jury instructions during the charge conference. In his closing argument, Corin again conceded Nixon's guilt and reminded the jury of the importance of the penalty phase: "I will hope to argue to you and give you reasons not that Mr. Nixon's life be spared one final and terminal confinement forever, but that he not be sentenced to die." The jury found Nixon guilty on all counts.

At the start of the penalty phase, Corin argued to the jury that "Joe Elton Nixon is not normal organically, intellectually, emotionally or educationally or in any other way." Corin presented the testimony of eight witnesses. Relatives and friends described Nixon's childhood emotional troubles and his erratic behavior in the days preceding the murder. A psychiatrist and a psychologist addressed Nixon's antisocial personality, his history of emotional instability and psychiatric care, his low IQ, and the possibility that at some point he suffered brain damage. The State presented little evidence during the penalty phase, simply incorporating its guilt-phase evidence by reference, and introducing testimony, over Corin's objection, that Nixon had removed Bickner's underwear in order to terrorize her.

In his closing argument, Corin emphasized Nixon's youth, the psychiatric evidence, and the jury's discretion to consider any mitigating circumstances; Corin urged that, if not sentenced to death, "Joe Elton Nixon would never be released from confinement." The death penalty, Corin maintained, was appropriate only for "intact human beings," and "Joe Elton Nixon is not one of those. He's never been one of those. He never will be one of those." Corin concluded: "You know, we're not around here all that long. And it's rare when we have the opportunity to give or take life. And you have that opportunity to give life. And I'm going to ask you to do that. Thank you." After deliberating for approximately three hours, the jury recommended that Nixon be sentenced to death.

In accord with the jury's recommendation, the trial court imposed the death penalty. Notably, at the close of the penalty phase, the court commended Corin's performance during the trial, stating that "the tactic employed by trial counsel was an excellent analysis of the reality of his case." The evidence of guilt "would have persuaded any jury beyond all doubt," and "for trial counsel to have inferred that Mr. Nixon was not guilty would have deprived counsel of any credibility during the penalty phase." The Florida Supreme Court subsequently reversed, finding ineffective assistance of counsel.

Issue + Holding

We granted certiorari to resolve an important question of constitutional law, i.e., whether counsel's failure to obtain the defendant's express consent to a strategy of conceding guilt in a capital trial automatically renders counsel's performance deficient, and whether counsel's effectiveness should be evaluated under *Cronic* or *Strickland*. We now reverse the judgment of the Florida Supreme Court.

An attorney undoubtedly has a duty to consult with the client regarding "important decisions," including questions of overarching defense strategy. That obligation, however, does not require counsel to obtain the defendant's consent to "every tactical decision." But certain decisions regarding the exercise or waiver of basic trial rights are of such moment that they cannot be made for the defendant by a surrogate. A defendant, this Court affirmed, has "the ultimate authority"

> **FYI**
>
> The Florida Supreme Court's decision in *Nixon* led to calls for the impeachment of three of the justices who decided that case. *See, e.g.,* http://www.tampabay.com/news/courts/florida-justices-under-attack-for-ruling-that-turned-on-defense-attorneys/1253953. Given the outcome of the Supreme Court's unanimous ruling in *Nixon*, reversing the Florida Supreme Court, do you think that those calls were justified?

to determine "whether to plead guilty, waive a jury, testify in his or her own behalf, or take an appeal." Concerning those decisions, an attorney must both consult with the defendant and obtain consent to the recommended course of action.

Corin was obliged to, and in fact several times did, explain his proposed trial strategy to Nixon. Given Nixon's constant resistance to answering inquiries put to him by counsel and court, Corin was not additionally required to gain express consent before conceding Nixon's guilt. The two evidentiary hearings conducted by the Florida trial court demonstrate beyond doubt that Corin fulfilled his duty of consultation by informing Nixon of counsel's proposed strategy and its potential benefits. Nixon's characteristic silence each time information was conveyed to him, in sum, did not suffice to render unreasonable Corin's decision to concede guilt and to home in, instead, on the life or death penalty issue.

Food for Thought

Suppose that, instead of remaining unresponsive, Nixon insisted that he was actually innocent (in the face of the same, overwhelming contrary evidence)? Would or should defense counsel in that instance have gone "all out" to try (futilely) to establish his innocence, thus creating a much higher risk of a death sentence?

Corin's concession of Nixon's guilt does not rank as a "failure to function in any meaningful sense as the Government's adversary." Although such a concession in a run-of-the-mine trial might present a closer question, the gravity of the potential sentence in a capital trial and the proceeding's two-phase structure vitally affect counsel's strategic calculus. Attorneys representing capital defendants face daunting challenges in developing trial strategies, not least because the defendant's guilt is often clear. Prosecutors are more likely to seek the death penalty, and to refuse to accept a plea to a life sentence, when the evidence is overwhelming and the crime heinous. In such cases, "avoiding execution may be the best and only realistic result possible."

Food for Thought

What if this had not been a capital case. Should the Court's ultimate holding have been the same? If Nixon had faced a potential sentence of 5 to 10 years in jail, for example, would defense counsel have been justified in sacrificing any chance at an acquittal, however remote, for a chance at arguing for a reduced sentence subsequently? What do you think?

Counsel therefore may reasonably decide to focus on the trial's penalty phase, at which time counsel's mission is to persuade the trier that his client's life should be spared. Unable to negotiate a guilty plea in exchange for a life sentence, defense counsel must strive at the guilt phase to avoid a counterproductive course. In this light, counsel cannot be deemed ineffective for attempting to impress the jury with his candor and his unwillingness to engage in "a useless charade."

To summarize, in a capital case, counsel must consider in conjunction both the guilt and penalty phases in determining how best to proceed. When counsel informs the defendant of the strategy counsel believes to be in the defendant's best interest and the defendant is unresponsive, counsel's strategic choice is not impeded by any blanket rule demanding the defendant's explicit consent. Instead, if counsel's strategy, given the evidence bearing on the defendant's guilt, satisfies the *Strickland* standard, that is the end of the matter; no tenable claim of ineffective assistance would remain.

Rule

Reversed.

Point for Discussion

Advice about Defense

In *Knowles v. Mirzayance*, 556 U.S. 111 (2009), the Supreme Court concluded that defense counsel's advice to his client that he withdraw his insanity defense because it was "doomed to fail"—advice that was accepted by his client—was also not ineffective assistance of counsel. As the Court made clear, "we are aware of no 'prevailing professional norms' that prevent counsel from recommending that a plea be withdrawn when it is almost certain to lose. The law does not require counsel to raise every available nonfrivolous defense. Counsel also is not required to have a tactical reason—above and beyond a reasonable appraisal of a claim's dismal prospects for success—for recommending that a weak claim be dropped altogether." What do you think? Was this really the *effective* assistance of counsel?

Rompilla v. Beard

545 U.S. 374 (2005).

JUSTICE SOUTER delivered the opinion of the Court.

This case calls for specific application of the standard of reasonable competence required on the part of defense counsel by the Sixth Amendment. We hold that even when a capital defendant's family members and the defendant himself have suggested that no mitigating evidence is available, his lawyer is bound to make reasonable efforts to obtain and review material that counsel knows the prosecution will probably rely on as evidence of aggravation at the sentencing phase of trial.

Rule

On the morning of January 14, 1988, James Scanlon was discovered dead in a bar he ran in Allentown, Pennsylvania, his body having been stabbed repeatedly and set on fire. Rompilla was indicted for the murder and related offenses, and the Commonwealth gave notice of intent to ask for the death penalty. Two public defenders were assigned to the case.

The jury at the guilt phase of trial found Rompilla guilty on all counts, and during the ensuing penalty phase, the prosecutor sought to prove three aggravating factors to justify a death sentence: *1* that the murder was committed in the course of another felony *2* that the murder was committed by torture; *3* and that Rompilla had a significant history of felony convictions indicating the use or threat of violence. The Commonwealth presented evidence on all three aggravators, and the jury found all proven. Rompilla's evidence in mitigation consisted of relatively brief testimony: five of his family members argued in effect for residual doubt, and beseeched the jury for mercy, saying that they believed Rompilla was innocent and a good man. Rompilla's 14-year-old son testified that he loved his father and would visit him in prison. The jury acknowledged this evidence to the point of finding, as two factors in mitigation, that Rompilla's son had testified on his behalf and that rehabilitation was possible. But the jurors assigned the greater weight to the aggravating factors, and sentenced Rompilla to death. The Supreme Court of Pennsylvania affirmed both conviction and sentence. Subsequently, a District Court granted Rompilla's habeas corpus petition on ineffectiveness grounds, and the Third Circuit Court of Appeals reversed. We granted certiorari, and now reverse.

Ineffective assistance under *Strickland* is deficient performance by counsel resulting in prejudice, with performance being measured against an "objective standard of reasonableness," "under prevailing professional norms." This case, like some others recently, looks to norms of adequate investigation in preparing for the sentencing phase of a capital trial, when defense counsel's job is to counter the State's evidence of aggravated culpability with evidence in mitigation. In judging the defense's investigation, as in applying *Strickland* generally, hindsight is discounted by pegging adequacy to "counsel's perspective at the time" investigative decisions are made, and by giving a "heavy measure of deference to counsel's judgments."

[handwritten margin note: Strickland standard]

A standard of reasonableness applied as if one stood in counsel's shoes spawns few hard-edged rules, and the merits of a number of counsel's choices in this case are subject to fair debate. This is not a case in which defense counsel simply ignored their obligation to find mitigating evidence, and their workload as busy public defenders did not keep them from making a number of efforts, including interviews with Rompilla and some members of his family, and examinations of reports by three mental health experts who gave opinions at the guilt phase. None of the sources proved particularly helpful.

Rompilla's own contributions to any mitigation case were minimal. Counsel found him uninterested in helping, as on their visit to his prison to go over a proposed mitigation strategy, when Rompilla told them he was "bored being here listening" and returned to his cell. To questions about childhood and schooling, his answers indicated they had been normal, save for quitting school in the ninth grade. There were times when Rompilla was even actively obstructive by sending counsel off on false leads.

The lawyers also spoke with five members of Rompilla's family (his former wife, two brothers, a sister-in-law, and his son), and counsel testified that they developed a good relationship with the family in the course of their representation. The third and final source tapped for mitigating material was the cadre of three mental health witnesses who were asked to look into Rompilla's mental state as of the time of the offense and his competency to stand trial, but their reports revealed "nothing useful" to Rompilla's case, and the lawyers consequently did not go to any other historical source that might have cast light on Rompilla's mental condition.

When new counsel entered the case to raise Rompilla's postconviction claims, however, they identified a number of likely avenues the trial lawyers could fruitfully have followed in building a mitigation case. School records are one example, which trial counsel never examined in spite of the professed unfamiliarity of the several family members with Rompilla's childhood, and despite counsel's knowledge that Rompilla left school after the ninth grade. Others examples are records of Rompilla's juvenile and adult incarcerations, which counsel did not consult, although they were aware of their client's criminal record. And while counsel knew from police reports provided in pretrial discovery that Rompilla had been drinking heavily at the time of his offense, and although one of the mental health experts reported that Rompilla's troubles with alcohol merited further investigation, counsel did not look for evidence of a history of dependence on alcohol that might have extenuating significance.

Before us, trial counsel and the Commonwealth respond to these unexplored possibilities by emphasizing this Court's recognition that the duty to investigate does not force defense lawyers to scour the globe on the off-chance something will turn up; reasonably diligent counsel may draw a line when they have good reason to think further investigation would be a waste. The Commonwealth argues that the information trial counsel gathered from Rompilla and the other sources gave them sound reason to think it would have been pointless to spend time and money on the additional investigation espoused by postconviction counsel, and we can say that there is room for debate about trial counsel's obligation to follow at least some of those potential lines of enquiry. There is no need to say more, however, for a further point is clear and dispositive: the lawyers were deficient in failing to examine the court file on Rompilla's prior conviction.

There is an obvious reason that the failure to examine Rompilla's prior conviction file fell below the level of reasonable performance. Counsel knew that the Commonwealth intended to seek the death penalty by proving Rompilla had a significant history of felony convictions indicating the use or threat of violence, an aggravator under state law. Counsel further knew that the Commonwealth would attempt to establish this history by proving Rompilla's prior conviction for rape and assault, and would emphasize his violent character by introducing a transcript of the rape victim's testimony given in that earlier trial. There is no question that defense counsel were on notice, since they acknowledge that a "plea letter," written by one of them four days prior to trial, mentioned the prosecutor's plans. It is also undisputed that the prior conviction file was a public document, readily available for the asking at the very courthouse where Rompilla was to be tried.

It is clear, however, that defense counsel did not look at any part of that file, including the transcript, until warned by the prosecution a second time. In a colloquy the day before the evidentiary sentencing phase began, the prosecutor again said he would present the transcript of the victim's testimony to establish the prior conviction.

With every effort to view the facts as a defense lawyer would have done at the time, it is difficult to see how counsel could have failed to realize that without examining the readily available file they were seriously compromising their opportunity to respond to a case for aggravation. The prosecution was going to use the dramatic facts of a similar prior offense, and Rompilla's counsel had a duty to make all reasonable efforts to learn what they could about the offense. Reasonable efforts certainly included obtaining the Commonwealth's own readily available file on the prior conviction to learn what the Commonwealth knew about the crime, to discover any mitigating evidence the Commonwealth would downplay and to anticipate the details of the aggravating evidence the Commonwealth would emphasize. Without making reasonable efforts to review the file, defense counsel could have had no hope of knowing whether the prosecution was quoting selectively from the transcript, or whether there were circumstances extenuating the behavior described by the victim. The obligation to get the file was particularly pressing here owing to the similarity of the violent prior offense to the crime charged and Rompilla's sentencing strategy stressing residual doubt. Without making efforts to learn the details and rebut the relevance of the earlier crime, a convincing argument for residual doubt was certainly beyond any hope.

At argument the most that Pennsylvania (and the United States as amicus) could say was that defense counsel's efforts to find mitigating evidence by other means excused them from looking at the prior conviction file. And that, of course, is the position taken by the state postconviction courts. Without specifically discussing the prior case file, they too found that defense counsel's efforts were enough to free them from any obligation to enquire further.

We think this conclusion of the state court fails to answer the considerations we have set out, to the point of being an objectively unreasonable conclusion. It flouts prudence to deny that a defense lawyer should try to look at a file he knows the prosecution will cull for aggravating evidence, let alone when the file is sitting in the trial courthouse, open for the asking. No reasonable lawyer would forgo examination of the file thinking he could do as well by asking the defendant or family relations whether they recalled anything helpful or damaging in the prior victim's testimony. Nor would a reasonable lawyer compare possible searches for school reports, juvenile records, and evidence of drinking habits to the opportunity to take a look at a file disclosing what the prosecutor knows and even plans to read from in his case. Questioning a few more family members and searching for old records can promise less than looking for a needle in a haystack, when a lawyer truly has reason to doubt there is any needle there. But looking at a file the prosecution says it will use is a sure bet: whatever may be in that file is going to tell defense counsel something about what the prosecution can produce.

The dissent thinks this analysis creates a "rigid, per se" rule that requires defense counsel to do a complete review of the file on any prior conviction introduced, but that is a mistake. Counsel fell short here because they failed to make reasonable efforts to review the prior conviction file, despite knowing that the prosecution intended to introduce Rompilla's prior conviction not merely by entering a notice of conviction into evidence but by quoting damaging testimony of the rape victim in that case. The unreasonableness of attempting no more than they did was heightened by the easy availability of the file at the trial courthouse, and the great risk that testimony about a similar violent crime would hamstring counsel's chosen defense of residual doubt.

Since counsel's failure to look at the file fell below the line of reasonable practice, there is a further question about prejudice, that is, whether "there is a reasonable probability that, but for counsel's unprofessional errors, the result of the proceeding would have been different." We think Rompilla has shown beyond any doubt that counsel's lapse was prejudicial; Pennsylvania, indeed, does not even contest the claim of prejudice.

If the defense lawyers had looked in the file on Rompilla's prior conviction, it is uncontested they would have found a range of mitigation leads that no other source had opened up. In the same file with the transcript of the prior trial were the records of Rompilla's imprisonment on the earlier conviction, which defense counsel testified she had never seen. The prison files pictured Rompilla's childhood and mental health very differently from anything defense counsel had seen or heard. An evaluation by a corrections counselor states that Rompilla was "reared in the slum environment of Allentown, Pa. vicinity. He early came to the attention of juvenile authorities, quit school at 16, and started a series of incarcerations in and out Penna. often of assaultive nature and commonly related to over-indulgence in alcoholic beverages." The same file discloses test results that the defense's mental health experts would have viewed as pointing to schizophrenia and other disorders, and test scores showing a third grade level of cognition after nine years of schooling.

The accumulated entries would have destroyed the benign conception of Rompilla's upbringing and mental capacity defense counsel had formed from talking with Rompilla himself and some of his family members, and from the reports of the mental health experts. With this information, counsel would have become skeptical of the impression given by the five family members and would unquestionably have gone further to build a mitigation case. Further effort would presumably have unearthed much of the material postconviction counsel found, including testimony from several members of Rompilla's family, whom trial counsel did not interview. Judge Sloviter dissenting in the Third Circuit, summarized this evidence:

> "Rompilla's parents were both severe alcoholics who drank constantly. His mother drank during her pregnancy with Rompilla, and he and his brothers eventually developed serious drinking problems. His father, who had a vicious temper, frequently beat Rompilla's mother, leaving her bruised and black-eyed, and bragged about his cheating on her. His parents fought violently, and on at least one occasion his mother stabbed his father. He was abused by his father who beat him when he was young with his hands, fists, leather straps, belts and sticks. All of the children lived in terror. There were no expressions of parental love, affection or approval. Instead, he was subjected to yelling and verbal abuse. His father locked Rompilla and his brother Richard in a small wire mesh dog pen that was filthy and excrement filled. He had an isolated background, and was not allowed to visit other children or to speak to anyone on the phone. They had no indoor plumbing in the house, he slept in the attic with no heat, and the children were not given clothes and attended school in rags."

The jury never heard any of this and neither did the mental health experts who examined Rompilla before trial. While they found "nothing helpful to Rompilla's case," their postconviction counterparts, alerted by information from school, medical, and prison records that trial counsel never saw, found plenty of " 'red flags' " pointing up a need to test further. When they tested, they found that Rompilla "suffers from organic brain damage, an extreme mental disturbance significantly impairing several of his cognitive functions." They also said that "Rompilla's problems relate back to his childhood, and were likely caused by fetal alcohol syndrome and that Rompilla's capacity to appreciate the criminality of his conduct or to conform his conduct to the law was substantially impaired at the time of the offense."

These findings in turn would probably have prompted a look at school and juvenile records, all of them easy to get, showing, for example, that when Rompilla was 16 his mother "was missing from home frequently for a period of one or several weeks at a time." The same report noted that his mother "has been reported ... frequently under the influence of alcoholic beverages, with the result that the children have always been poorly kept and on the filthy side which was also the condition of the home at all times." School records showed Rompilla's IQ was in the mentally retarded range.

Food for Thought

It may well be the case that the key fact to know in this case, like *Nixon*, is that this is a capital case. Is it possible that the Court is *sub silentio* requiring more of counsel in such cases than in non-capital cases given the gravity and finality of the potential penalty? If that is indeed the case, do you think that is an inappropriate approach? And if that is what a majority of the Court is really doing, should it just say so directly?

This evidence adds up to a mitigation case that bears no relation to the few naked pleas for mercy actually put before the jury, and although we suppose it is possible that a jury could have heard it all and still have decided on the death penalty, that is not the test. It goes without saying that the undiscovered "mitigating evidence, taken as a whole, 'might well have influenced the jury's appraisal' of Rompilla's culpability," and the likelihood of a different result if the evidence had gone in is "sufficient to undermine confidence in the outcome" actually reached at sentencing, *Strickland*.

The judgment of the Third Circuit is reversed, and Pennsylvania must either retry the case on penalty or stipulate to a life sentence.

JUSTICE O'CONNOR, concurring.

I write separately to put to rest one concern. The dissent worries that the Court's opinion "imposes on defense counsel a rigid requirement to review all documents in what it calls the 'case file' of any prior conviction that the prosecution might rely on at trial." But the Court's opinion imposes no such rule. Rather, today's decision simply applies our longstanding case-by-case approach to determining whether an attorney's performance was unconstitutionally deficient under *Strickland*. Trial counsel's performance in Rompilla's case falls short under that standard, because the attorneys' behavior was not "reasonable considering all the circumstances." In particular, there were three circumstances which made the attorneys' failure to examine Rompilla's prior conviction file unreasonable.

First, Rompilla's attorneys knew that their client's prior conviction would be at the very heart of the prosecution's case. The prior conviction went not to a collateral matter, but rather to one of the aggravating circumstances making Rompilla eligible for the death penalty. Second, the prosecutor's planned use of the prior conviction threatened to eviscerate one of the defense's primary mitigation arguments. Rompilla was convicted on the basis of strong circumstantial evidence. His lawyers structured the entire mitigation argument around the hope of convincing the jury that residual doubt about Rompilla's guilt made it inappropriate to impose the death penalty. In announcing an intention to introduce testimony about Rompilla's similar prior offense, the prosecutor put Rompilla's attorneys on notice that the prospective defense on mitigation likely would be ineffective and counterproductive. Third, the attorneys' decision not to obtain Rompilla's prior conviction file was not the result of an informed tactical decision about how the lawyers' time would best be spent. Their failure to obtain the crucial file "was the result of inattention, not reasoned strategic judgment." As a result, their conduct fell below constitutionally required standards.

JUSTICE KENNEDY, with whom THE CHIEF JUSTICE, JUSTICE SCALIA, and JUSTICE THOMAS join, dissenting.

Today the Court brands two committed criminal defense attorneys as ineffective—"outside the wide range of professionally competent counsel"—because they did not look in an old case file and stumble upon something they had not set out to find. To reach this result, the majority imposes on defense counsel a rigid requirement to review all documents in what it calls the "case file" of any prior conviction that the prosecution might rely on at trial.

The majority's analysis contains barely a mention of *Strickland* and makes little effort to square today's holding with our traditional reluctance to impose rigid requirements on defense counsel. While the Court disclaims any intention to create a bright-line rule, this affords little comfort. The Court's opinion makes clear it has imposed on counsel a broad obligation to review prior conviction case files where those priors are used in aggravation—and to review every document in those files if not every single page of every document, regardless of the prosecution's proposed use for the prior conviction.

One of the primary reasons this Court has rejected a checklist approach

> **Food for Thought**
>
> The dissenters say this case creates a "rigid requirement." The majority say it does not. Which side is correct? Isn't it true after decision in *Rompilla* that defense counsel in a capital case must always look at the file documents relating to a prior offense if the prosecution indicates that it intends to rely on that conviction for purposes of sentence enhancement? If it is true, is that an inappropriate result?

to effective assistance of counsel is that each new requirement risks distracting attorneys from the real objective of providing vigorous advocacy as dictated by the facts and circumstances in the particular case. The Court's rigid requirement that counsel always review the case files of convictions the prosecution seeks to use at trial will be just such a distraction.

Points for Discussion

a. AEDPA

A 5-to-4 majority of the Supreme Court ruled in *Williams v. Taylor*, 529 U.S. 362, 412 (2000), that the Antiterrorism & Effective Death Penalty Act of 1996 ("AEDPA"), 28 U.S.C. § 2254, "places a new constraint on the power of a federal habeas court to grant a state prisoner's application for a writ of habeas corpus with respect to claims adjudicated on the merits in state court." More particularly, the Court held, under this new provision,

> the writ may issue only if one of the following two conditions is satisfied—the state-court adjudication resulted in a decision that (1) "was contrary to clearly established Federal law, as determined by the Supreme Court of the United States," or (2) "involved an unreasonable application of clearly established Federal law, as determined by the Supreme Court of the United States." Under the "contrary to" clause, a federal habeas court may grant the writ if the state court arrives at a conclusion opposite to that reached by this Court on a question of law or if the state court decides a case differently than this Court has on a set of materially indistinguishable facts. Under the "unreasonable application" clause, a federal habeas court may grant the writ if the state court identifies the correct governing legal principle from this Court's decisions but unreasonably applies that principle to the facts of the prisoner's case.

More recently, the Supreme Court has added that "'clearly established Federal law' for purposes of the AEDPA includes only the holdings, as opposed to the *dicta*, of this Court's decisions." *See White v. Woodall*, 134 S.Ct. 1697, 1702 (2014). And the Supreme Court has also advised that the AEDPA also "prohibits the federal courts of appeals from relying on their own precedent to conclude that a particular constitutional principle is 'clearly established.'" *See Lopez v. Smith*, 135 S.Ct. 1, 2 (2014).

Most significantly, the fact that a state court may have made an *incorrect* constitutional ruling on an ineffectiveness inquiry no longer suffices—under this AEDPA provision—to entitle a defendant to habeas corpus relief. *See, e.g. Woodford v. Visciotti*, 537 U.S. 19 (2002) ("Under the 'unreasonable application' clause, a federal habeas court may not issue the writ simply because that court concludes in its independent judgment that the state-court decision applied *Strickland* incorrectly.

Rather, it is the habeas applicant's burden to show that the state court applied *Strickland* to the facts of his case in an objectively unreasonable manner.").

In *Rompilla*, the dissenters argued that "the Pennsylvania Supreme Court gave careful consideration to Rompilla's Sixth Amendment claim and concluded that 'counsel reasonably relied upon their discussions with Rompilla and upon their experts to determine the records needed to evaluate his mental health and other potential mitigating circumstances.' This decision was far from unreasonable under the AEDPA." The majority concluded, however, not only that defense counsel were ineffective, but that the state court decision finding them *not* to have been ineffective "was contrary to, or involved an unreasonable application of, clearly established Federal law, as determined by the Supreme Court of the United States," pursuant to the AEDPA. What do you think? Do you agree?

b. Decisional Consistency

Why was defense counsels' decision to focus on mitigation in the penalty phase of a capital case held in *Nixon* to be reasonable and the same decision held to be unreasonable in *Rompilla*? Does this difference in result make sense to you?

c. Limited Records For Review

In *Cullen v. Pinholster*, 563 U.S. 170 (2011), the Supreme Court ruled that an ineffectiveness inquiry in a federal habeas corpus proceeding under the AEDPA (*see* Point a, above) is limited to the record that was before the state court that adjudicated the claim on the merits; evidence that was presented only to the federal habeas court may not be considered. The *Cullen* majority conceded that "this test is 'difficult to meet,' and it is a 'highly deferential standard for evaluating state-court rulings, which demands that state-court decisions be given the benefit of the doubt.' "

The Supreme Court has also made clear that "whether a state court's decision resulted from an unreasonable legal or factual conclusion under the AEDPA does not require that there be an opinion from the state court explaining the state court's reasoning. Where a state court's decision is unaccompanied by an explanation, the habeas petitioner's burden still must be met by showing there was no reasonable basis for the state court to deny relief." *Harrington v. Richter*, 562 U.S. 86 (2011).

d. Mentally Ill Clients

In its 2007 decision in *Schriro v. Landrigan*, 550 U.S. 465 (2007), a 5–to–4 majority of the Court held that a federal district court did not abuse its discretion in declining to order a habeas corpus evidentiary hearing in a case where counsel failed to present significant mitigating evidence at a capital sentencing hearing where that failure was due to defendant's express request. As the majority pointed out, "it was not objectively unreasonable for the district court to conclude that a defendant who refused to allow the presentation of any mitigating evidence could not establish *Strickland* prejudice based on his counsel's failure to investigate further possible mitigating evidence." In dissent, Justice Stevens argued, however, that

> significant mitigating evidence-evidence that may well have explained respondent's criminal conduct and unruly behavior at his capital sentencing hearing-was unknown at the time of sentencing. Only years later did respondent learn that he suffers from a serious psychological condition that sheds important light on his earlier actions. The reason why this and other mitigating evidence was unavailable is that respondent's counsel failed to conduct a constitutionally adequate investigation.

What do you think? Should a mentally ill defendant's decisions against interest divest him of any opportunity to establish ineffective assistance after the fact?

e. Adequate Investigations

In *Bobby v. Van Hook*, 558 U.S. 4 (2009), the Supreme Court found that counsel was *not* ineffective for failing to adequately investigate and to present additional mitigating evidence at a capital sentencing hearing when defense counsel did present a great deal of evidence, but there could have been more:

> "Despite all the mitigating evidence the defense did present, Van Hook and the Court of Appeals fault his counsel for failing to find more. What his counsel did discover, the argument goes, gave them 'reason to suspect that much worse details existed,' and that suspicion should have prompted them to interview other family members-his stepsister, two uncles, and two aunts-as well as a psychiatrist who once treated his mother, all of whom 'could have helped his counsel narrate the true story of Van Hook's childhood experiences.' But there comes a point at which evidence from more distant relatives can reasonably be expected to be only cumulative, and the search for it distractive from more important duties. Given all the evidence they unearthed from those closest to Van Hook's upbringing and the experts who reviewed his history, it was not unreasonable for his counsel not to identify and interview every other living family member or every therapist who once treated his parents. This is not a case in which the defendant's attorneys failed to act while potentially powerful mitigating evidence stared them in the face or would have been apparent from documents any reasonable attorney would have obtained. It is instead a case, like *Strickland* itself, in which defense counsel's 'decision not to seek more' mitigating evidence from the defendant's background 'than was already in hand' fell 'well within the range of professionally reasonable judgments.' "

Is this decision consistent with the decision in *Rompilla*?

f. Advice on Deportation Risk

In *Padilla v. Kentucky*, 559 U.S. 356 (2010), the Supreme Court ruled that in order to satisfy the performance prong of *Strickland*, "counsel must inform her client whether his guilty plea carries a risk of deportation." Padilla claimed that his counsel not only failed to advise him about the deportation consequences of his guilty plea to charged marijuana offenses, but told him that he "did not have to worry about immigration status since he had been in the country so long." This advice was incorrect and, after his conviction, Padilla did indeed face deportation.

The Court held that "advice regarding deportation is not categorically removed from the ambit of the Sixth Amendment right to counsel. *Strickland* applies to Padilla's claim." That does not mean, the Court added, that criminal defense counsel must become experts on immigration law. Rather, "a criminal defense attorney need do no more than advise a noncitizen client that pending criminal charges may carry a risk of adverse immigration consequences."

The Supreme Court subsequently ruled that *Padilla* does not apply retroactively. *Chaidez v. United States*, 568 U.S. 342 (2013). Hence, a person whose conviction became final before *Padilla* was decided could not benefit from it.

g. Don't Skimp On Experts

In *Hinton v. Alabama*, 134 S.Ct. 1081 (2014), the Supreme Court unanimously found the conduct of defense counsel deficient where he failed to request additional funds to replace an inadequate "firearms and toolmark" expert. In *Hinton*, forensic comparisons of bullets recovered from the homicide defendant's revolver was critical evidence tying him to the crime scene. Operating under the mistaken belief that he could pay no more than $1,000, counsel went looking for a well-regarded expert, but found only one person who was willing to take the case for that amount of money. Counsel hired that expert even though he "did not have the expertise he thought he needed," concluding that—for that amount of money—he was "stuck" with him. As expected, the expert's testimony was weak and largely discredited, defendant was convicted, and subsequently sentenced to death.

The Court concluded that defense counsel "knew that he needed more funding to present an effective defense, yet he failed to make even the cursory investigation of the state statute providing for defense funding for indigent defendants that would have revealed to him that he could receive reimbursement not just for $1,000 but for 'any expenses reasonably incurred.' An attorney's ignorance of a point of law that is fundamental to his case combined with his failure to perform basic research on that point is a quintessential example of unreasonable performance under *Strickland*."

That finding of inadequate performance did not, in and of itself, establish ineffective assistance. The case was remanded for a determination whether this deficient performance actually prejudiced the defendant. What will the defendant have to prove on remand to show that this deficient performance prejudiced him?

* * *

What exactly constitutes "prejudice" under *Strickland*? Consider the following decisions:

Glover v. United States

531 U.S. 198 (2001).

JUSTICE KENNEDY delivered the opinion of the Court.

Petitioner, Paul Glover, contends that the trial court erred in a Sentencing Guidelines determination. The legal error, petitioner alleges, increased his prison sentence by at least 6 months and perhaps by 21 months. We must decide whether this would be "prejudice" under *Strickland v. Washington*, 466 U.S. 668 (1984). We reverse and remand for further proceedings.

Glover was the Vice President and General Counsel of the Chicago Truck Drivers, Helpers, and Warehouse Workers Union (Independent). Glover used his control over the union's investments to enrich himself and his co-conspirators through kickbacks. The presentence investigation report recommended that the convictions for labor racketeering, money laundering, and tax evasion be grouped together under United States Sentencing Commission, Guidelines Manual § 3D1.2 (Nov.1994), which allows the grouping of "counts involving substantially the same harm." The District Court ruled that the money laundering counts should not be grouped with Glover's other offenses. Glover's attorneys did not submit papers or offer extensive oral arguments contesting the no-grouping argument and, accordingly, Glover's offense level was increased by two levels, yielding a concomitant increase in the sentencing range. Glover was sentenced to 84 months in prison, which was in the middle of the Guidelines range of 78 to 97 months. On appeal, Glover's counsel (the same attorneys who represented him in District Court) did not raise the grouping issue. A short time after argument on Glover's appeal, a different panel of the Seventh Circuit held that, under some circumstances, grouping of money laundering offenses with other counts was proper under § 3D1.2. *United States v. Wilson*, 98 F.3d 281 (1996). A month later, the Seventh Circuit affirmed his conviction and sentence.

Glover filed a *pro se* motion to correct his sentence. The failure of his counsel to press the grouping issue, he argued, was ineffective assistance. The performance of counsel, he contended, fell below a reasonable standard both at sentencing, when his attorneys did not with any clarity or force contest the Government's argument, and on appeal, when they did not present the issue in their briefs or call the *Wilson* decision to the panel's attention following the oral argument. He further argued that absent the ineffective assistance, his offense level would have been two levels lower, yielding a Guidelines sentencing range of 63 to 78 months. Under this theory, the 84-month sentence he received was an unlawful increase of anywhere between 6 and 21 months.

[handwritten: Glover's Theory]

The District Court denied Glover's motion and the Court of Appeals affirmed. It appears the Seventh Circuit relied on *Lockhart v. Fretwell*, 506 U.S. 364 (1993). *Lockhart* holds that in some circumstances a mere difference in outcome will not suffice to establish prejudice. But this Court explained last Term that our holding in *Lockhart* does not supplant the *Strickland* analysis. Our jurisprudence suggests that any amount of actual jail time has Sixth Amendment significance. *Argersinger v. Hamlin*, 407 U.S. 25 (1972).

The Seventh Circuit's rule is not well considered in any event, because there is no obvious dividing line by which to measure how much longer a sentence must be for the increase to constitute substantial prejudice. Although the amount by which a defendant's sentence is increased by a particular decision may be a factor to consider in determining whether counsel's performance in failing to argue the point constitutes ineffective assistance, under a determinate system of constrained discretion such as the Sentencing Guidelines it cannot serve as a bar to a showing of prejudice. We hold that the Seventh Circuit erred in engrafting this additional requirement onto the prejudice branch of the *Strickland* test. This is not a case where trial strategies, in retrospect, might be criticized for leading to a harsher sentence. Here we consider the sentencing calculation itself, a calculation resulting from a ruling which, if it had been error, would have been correctable on appeal. We express no opinion on the ultimate merits of Glover's claim because the question of deficient performance is not before us, but it is clear that prejudice flowed from the asserted error in sentencing.

Take Note

As difficult as it may sometimes be to establish the prejudice prong of the *Strickland* test, it is not impossible as the decision in *Glover* illustrates.

The judgment of the Seventh Circuit is reversed.

Buck v. Davis

137 S.Ct. 759 (2017)

CHIEF JUSTICE ROBERTS delivered the opinion of the Court.

A Texas jury convicted petitioner Duane Buck of capital murder. Under state law, the jury could impose a death sentence only if it found that Buck was likely to commit acts of violence in the future. Buck's attorney called a psychologist to offer his opinion on that issue. The psychologist testified that Buck probably would not engage in violent conduct. But he also stated that one of the factors pertinent in assessing a person's propensity for violence was his race, and that Buck was statistically more likely to act violently because he is black. The jury sentenced Buck to death.

Buck contends that his attorney's introduction of this evidence violated his Sixth Amendment right to the effective assistance of counsel. The Sixth Amendment right to counsel "is the right to the effective assistance of counsel." A defendant who claims to have been denied effective assistance must show both that counsel performed deficiently and that counsel's deficient performance caused him prejudice.

Strickland's first prong sets a high bar. A defense lawyer navigating a criminal proceeding faces any number of choices about how best to make a client's case. The lawyer has discharged his constitutional responsibility so long as his decisions fall within the "wide range of professionally competent assistance." It is only when the lawyer's errors were "so serious that counsel was not functioning as the 'counsel' guaranteed by the Sixth Amendment" that *Strickland's* first prong is satisfied.

The District Court determined that, in this case, counsel's performance fell outside the bounds of competent representation. We agree. Counsel knew that Dr. Quijano's report reflected the view that Buck's race disproportionately predisposed him to violent conduct; he also knew that the principal point of dispute during the trial's penalty phase was whether Buck was likely to act violently in the future. Counsel nevertheless (1) called Dr. Quijano to the stand; (2) specifically elicited testimony about the connection between Buck's race and the likelihood of future violence; and (3) put into evidence Dr. Quijano's expert report that stated, in reference to factors bearing on future dangerousness, "Race. Black: Increased probability."

Given that the jury had to make a finding of future dangerousness before it could impose a death sentence, Dr. Quijano's report said, in effect, that the color of Buck's skin made him more deserving of execution. It would be patently unconstitutional for a state to argue that a defendant is liable to be a future danger because of his race. No competent defense attorney would introduce such evidence about his own client.

To satisfy *Strickland*, a litigant must also demonstrate prejudice—"a reasonable probability that, but for counsel's unprofessional errors, the result of the proceeding would have been different." Accordingly, the question before the District Court was whether Buck had demonstrated a reasonable probability that, without Dr. Quijano's testimony on race, at least one juror would have harbored a reasonable doubt about whether Buck was likely to be violent in the future. The District Court concluded that Buck had not made such a showing. We disagree.

In arguing that the jury would have imposed a death sentence even if Dr. Quijano had not offered race-based testimony, the State primarily emphasizes the brutality of Buck's crime and his lack of remorse. A jury may conclude that a crime's vicious nature calls for a sentence of death. In this case, however, several considerations convince us that it is reasonably probable—notwithstanding the nature of Buck's crime and his behavior in its aftermath—that the proceeding would have ended differently had counsel rendered competent representation.

Dr. Quijano testified on the key point at issue in Buck's sentencing. True, the jury was asked to decide two issues—whether Buck was likely to be a future danger, and, if so, whether mitigating circumstances nevertheless justified a sentence of life imprisonment. But the focus of the proceeding was on the first question. Much of the penalty phase testimony was directed to future dangerousness, as were the summations for both sides. The jury, consistent with the focus of the parties, asked during deliberations to see the expert reports on dangerousness.

Deciding the key issue of Buck's dangerousness involved an unusual inquiry. The jurors were not asked to determine a historical fact concerning Buck's conduct, but to render a predictive judgment inevitably entailing a degree of speculation. Buck, all agreed, had committed acts of terrible violence. Would he do so again?

Buck's prior violent acts had occurred outside of prison, and within the context of romantic relationships with women. If the jury did not impose a death sentence, Buck would be sentenced to life in prison, and no such romantic relationship would be likely to arise. A jury could conclude that those changes would minimize the prospect of future dangerousness.

But one thing would never change: the color of Buck's skin. Buck would always be black. And according to Dr. Quijano, that immutable characteristic carried with it an "increased probability" of future violence. Here was hard statistical evidence—from an expert—to guide an otherwise speculative inquiry.

And it was potent evidence. Dr. Quijano's testimony appealed to a powerful racial stereotype—that of black men as "violence prone." In combination with the substance of the jury's inquiry, this created something of a perfect storm. Dr. Quijano's opinion coincided precisely with a particularly noxious strain of racial prejudice, which itself coincided precisely with the central question at sentencing. The effect of this unusual confluence of factors was to provide support for making a decision on life or death on the basis of race.

This effect was heightened due to the source of the testimony. Dr. Quijano took the stand as a medical expert bearing the court's imprimatur. The jury learned at the outset of his testimony that he held a doctorate in clinical psychology, had conducted evaluations in some 70 capital murder cases, and had been appointed by the trial judge (at public expense) to evaluate Reasonable jurors might well have valued his opinion concerning the central question before them.

For these reasons, we cannot accept the District Court's conclusion that "the introduction of any mention of race" during the penalty phase was "de minimis." There were only "two references to race in Dr. Quijano's testimony"—one during direct examination, the other on cross. But when a jury hears expert testimony that expressly makes a defendant's race directly pertinent on the question of life or death, the impact of that evidence cannot be measured simply by how much air time it received at trial or how many pages it occupies in the record. Some toxins can be deadly in small doses.

The effect of Dr. Quijano's testimony on Buck's sentencing cannot be dismissed as "de minimis." Buck has demonstrated prejudice.

The judgment of the United States Court of Appeals for the Fifth Circuit is reversed, and the case is remanded for further proceedings consistent with this opinion.

Points for Discussion

a. Quick Plea Advice Not Ineffective

In *Premo v. Moore*, 562 U.S. 115 (2011), the Supreme Court concluded that a state postconviction court's conclusion that defense counsel did not perform deficiently in advising his client, Moore, to enter a quick no-contest plea to felony murder, without having brought a motion to suppress one of his confessions, was neither an unreasonable application of clearly established federal law, nor was the conclusion that he was not prejudiced unreasonable:

> The state court here reasonably could have determined that Moore would have accepted the plea agreement even if his confession had been ruled inadmissible. By the time the plea agreement cut short investigation of

Moore's crimes, the State's case was already formidable and included two witnesses to an admissible confession. Had the prosecution continued to investigate, its case might well have become stronger. At the same time, Moore faced grave punishments. His decision to plead no contest allowed him to avoid a possible sentence of life without parole or death. The bargain counsel struck was thus a favorable one—the statutory minimum for the charged offense—and the decision to forgo a challenge to the confession may have been essential to securing that agreement.

b. Insufficient Investigation Not Necessarily Prejudicial

In *Wong v. Belmontes,* 558 U.S. 15 (2009), the Court held that Belmontes was not prejudiced by the fact that defense counsel may have been ineffective for failing to investigate and present sufficient mitigating evidence during the penalty phase of his capital trial:

> It is hard to imagine expert testimony and additional facts about Belmontes' difficult childhood outweighing the facts of the victim's murder. It becomes even harder to envision such a result when the evidence that Belmontes had committed another murder—'the most powerful imaginable aggravating evidence,' is added to the mix. The notion that the result could have been different if only counsel had put on more than the nine witnesses he did, or called expert witnesses to bolster his case, is fanciful.

However, the Supreme Court subsequently emphasized that "we have never limited the prejudice inquiry under *Strickland* to penalty phase cases in which there was only 'little or no mitigation evidence' presented." *Sears v. Upton,* 561 U.S. 945 (2010). As the *Sears* Court explained:

> To assess the probability of a different outcome under *Strickland,* we consider the totality of the available mitigation evidence—both that adduced at trial, and the evidence adduced in the habeas proceeding—and reweigh it against the evidence in aggravation. That standard will necessarily require a court to "speculate" as to the effect of the new evidence—regardless of how much or how little mitigation evidence was presented during the initial penalty phase. This is the proper prejudice standard for evaluating a claim of ineffective representation in the context of a penalty phase mitigation investigation.

Why do you think that so many Supreme Court ineffective-assistance-of-counsel decisions arise out of capital sentencing hearings? Is it because counsel in that setting is often so bad or because judges are less concerned about achieving finality in those cases? Or is neither of those reasons persuasive?

c. Changing Technology and Ineffectiveness

In *Wright v. Van Patten,* 552 U.S. 120 (2008), the Supreme Court concluded that defense counsel's participation in a plea hearing (no contest) by speaker phone—rather than in person—was not presumptively prejudicial to his client: "Our precedents do not clearly hold that counsel's participation by speaker phone should be treated as a 'complete denial of counsel,' on par with total absence. Even if we agree with Van Patten that a lawyer physically present will tend to perform better than one on the phone, it does not necessarily follow that mere telephone contact amounted to total absence or 'prevented counsel from assisting the accused,' so as to entail application of *Cronic*. The question is not whether counsel in those circumstances will perform less well than he otherwise would, but whether the circumstances are likely to result in such poor performance that an inquiry into its effects would not be worth the time." Do you agree? Should the same result apply when defense counsel appears at trial by way of video conferencing? Or, sometime in the (distant?) future, defense counsel "appears" virtually, but not corporally?

d. Convicting the Innocent

A recent study estimates that if all death-sentenced defendants remained under sentence of death indefinitely, at least 4.1% of them would ultimately be exonerated. See Samuel R. Gross, Barbara O'Brien, Chen Huc, and Edward H. Kennedy, Proceedings of the National Academy of Science of the United States of America, *Rate of false conviction of criminal defendants who are sentenced to death*, http://www.pnas.org/content/111/20/7230.full (2014). *See also, e.g., Illinois abolishes death penalty; cites wrongful convictions*, The Washington Times (March 9, 2011) ("Illinois abolished the death penalty Wednesday, more than a decade after the state imposed a moratorium on executions out of concern that innocent people could be put to death by a justice system that had wrongly condemned 13 men."). Does this suggest that the Court's approach to ineffective assistance is too strict, too difficult to establish? But, on the other hand, aren't *some* erroneous convictions inevitable? Or not?

e. Structural Error and Ineffectiveness

Some trial errors are known as "structural errors," errors that cannot be deemed to be harmless. The purpose of the structural error doctrine is to ensure that certain basic, constitutional guarantees define the framework of any criminal trial. One such basic constitutional guarantee is the right to a public trial.

In *Weaver v. Massachusetts*, 137 S.Ct. 1899 (2017), the issue arose of the relationship between this kind of structural error and an ineffectiveness claim. During Weaver's trial on state criminal charges, the courtroom was completely occupied by potential jurors and closed to the public for two days of the jury selection process. Defense counsel neither objected to the closure at trial nor raised the issue on direct review. As a result, the Court was faced with "the question whether invalidation of the conviction is required, or if the prejudice inquiry is altered when the structural error is raised in the context of an ineffective-assistance-of-counsel claim."

The Court reasoned that

although the public-trial right is structural, it is subject to exceptions. Though these cases should be rare, a judge may deprive a defendant of his right to an open courtroom by making proper factual findings in support of the decision to do so. The fact that the public-trial right is subject to these exceptions suggests that not every public-trial violation results in fundamental unfairness. Thus, when a defendant raises a public-trial violation via an ineffective-assistance-of-counsel claim, *Strickland* prejudice is not shown automatically. Instead, the burden is on the defendant to show either a reasonable probability of a different outcome in his or her case or to show that the particular public-trial violation was so serious as to render his or her trial fundamentally unfair.

Hence, the Supreme Court ruled, "in the context of a public-trial violation during jury selection, where the error is neither preserved nor raised on direct review but is raised later via an ineffective-assistance-of-counsel claim, the defendant must demonstrate prejudice to secure a new trial." In *Weaver*, the Court held that Weaver failed to do this, i.e. he did not establish a reasonable probability that the jury would not have convicted him if his attorney had objected to the closure of the courtroom.

Do you think this is a sensible test? Why should a defendant whose trial was subject to a structural error, the failure to receive a basic constitutional guarantee, have to prove that he or she was prejudiced thereby? More importantly, just how would a defendant go about proving such prejudice? As Justice Breyer, joined by Justice Kagan, argued in dissent:

In my view, we should not require defendants to take on a task that is normally impossible to perform. Nor would I give lower courts the unenviably complex job of deciphering which structural errors really undermine fundamental fairness and which do not—that game is not worth the candle. I would simply say that just as structural errors are categorically insusceptible to harmless-error analysis on direct review, so too are they categorically insusceptible to actual-prejudice analysis in Strickland claims. A showing that an attorney's constitutionally deficient performance produced a structural error should consequently be enough to entitle a defendant to relief.

What do you think?

Hypo 1: *Failure to Challenge Government's Use of Flawed Scientific Evidence*

Defense counsel failed to challenge the government's use of Comparative Bullet Lead Analysis (CBLA) at defendant's first-degree murder trial in 1995. Although no longer generally accepted after 2003, CBLA evidence was commonly used at that time. Was defense counsel ineffective for failing to challenge the prosecution's use of that questionable evidence? Does it make sense to judge the reasonableness of defense counsel's conduct many years later, in hindsight? *See Maryland v. Kulbicki*, 136 S.Ct. 2 (2015).

Hypo 2: *Failure to Suppress*

Defendant is on trial for possession of narcotics. The prosecution has overwhelming evidence of guilt in the form of cocaine found in defendant's home. However, the evidence was obtained as a result of an illegal search. As in *Premo*, set out above, defense counsel fails to file a suppression motion and defendant is convicted. Was counsel ineffective under either *Strickland* or *Cronic*? *See, e.g., State v. Silvers*, 587 N.W.2d 325 (Neb. 1998).

Hypo 3: *Demeaning Client*

Should ineffectiveness be presumed where counsel referred to his client with a racist epithet and told him that he "hoped he gets life?" Counsel also stated that, if defendant "insists on going to trial," he would be "very ineffective." *See* Frazer v. United States, 18 F.3d 778 (9th Cir.1994).

Hypo 4: *Failure to Appear*

Do you think that criminal defense counsel should be deemed to be automatically ineffective when he failed to show up for most of the direct and cross-examination of an important prosecution witness—a victim—without any excuse for his absence? What if counsel failed to show up for any of the cross-examination? Would it make any difference in your analysis if counsel was prepared to finish the cross-examination, but asked for a recess to review what he had missed before proceeding? *See McKnight v. State*, 320 S.C. 356, 465 S.E.2d 352 (1995).

Hypo 5: *Prior Convictions*

Defendant is convicted of armed robbery. He had been convicted of this crime twice before. During *voir dire*, defense counsel asked the members of the venire whether they could judge defendant fairly and with an open mind if they learned he had been convicted of armed robbery twice previously. At no other point in the trial was the subject of defendant's prior convictions mentioned. Was counsel ineffective because he mentioned them during *voir dire*?

Hypo 6: *Failure to Advise*

Defense counsel failed to inform his client, who was considering pleading guilty to a drug offense, that the client's prior conviction for a narcotics paraphernalia offence would qualify as a sentencing enhancement mandating imprisonment for not less than five years. On advice of counsel, defendant pled guilty to manufacturing methamphetamine, second offense, and was sentenced to seven years' imprisonment. After Padilla, discussed above, was this ineffective assistance of counsel? *See Berry v. State*, 381 S.C. 630, 675 S.E.2d 425 (2009).

Hypo 7: *Failure to Call Eyewitness*

Do you think that trial counsel was ineffective where he failed to call an eyewitness to the shooting at issue even though he knew that her statements would contradict the eyewitness upon whom the prosecution's entire case relied, he knew that she had not identified the defendant on the night of the shooting, and he also knew that the witness had not identified the defendant later when she examined a photo array? Can you think of any tactical reason at all why counsel might have failed to put a witness like this on the stand? *See State v. Jenkins*, 355 Wis.2d 180, 848 N.W.2d 786 (2014).

Hypo 8: *You Get What You Pay For*

Massachusetts suffered from a shortage of lawyers willing to accept indigent appointments. The trial court concluded that the unavailability of lawyers was directly related to inadequate levels of compensation. Suppose that you are a trial court judge and you have a number of indigent defendants who are entitled to counsel but who remain unrepresented. What remedies are available to you? Should you: (1) order attorneys to accept indigent cases at prevailing compensation rates; (2) order the state to pay attorneys more for indigent representation; or (3) order that defendants be released and their cases be dismissed without prejudice? *See Lavallee v. Justices in the Hampden Superior Court*, 442 Mass. 228, 812 N.E.2d 895 (2004).

Hypo 9: *Investigating Ineffective Assistance*

You were recently admitted to the Bar of your state and are engaged in an active criminal law practice. As *pro bono* work, you take an occasional "innocence case," one in which you have serious doubts about whether someone was fairly convicted of a crime. One day, J.T. Booker comes to see you about his brother, John, who is on death row having been convicted of a brutal rape and murder. J.T. tells you that John could not have committed the rape or the murder because he was in another city at the time of the crime. J.T. is so sincere, and so convinced of his brother's innocence, that you decide to take the case. Suppose that you may want to pursue an ineffective assistance of claim with respect to trial counsel's performance. What steps would you take in order to decide whether ineffective assistance actually existed, and whether you should assert this claim? What types of evidence would be useful to you? How would you go about obtaining such evidence? How would you begin?

Exercise: *IAC Claim*

Defendant Larry Hall was convicted at trial along with a codefendant, G., of the rape and murder of a young woman. The crime was one of a series of similar, seemingly-random abductions, rapes, and grisly murders of young women which took place during 1981 and 1982. Hall's defense at trial—which was apparently not credited by the jury—was strictly one of factual innocence. Hall was sentenced to death. His conviction and death sentence were affirmed on direct appeal.

Hall has now sought postconviction relief in state court, arguing that he is entitled to a new trial because of the ineffective assistance of his trial counsel, Kyle LaBomba (which he did not raise in his direct appeal since LaBomba was also his appellate counsel and failed to question his own ineffectiveness). The postconviction court denied Hall the opportunity for an evidentiary hearing on his claim of LaBomba's ineffectiveness, concluding that he did not make a sufficient showing of arguable ineffectiveness to justify such a hearing. Hall has appealed this decision to a state appellate court, arguing that he is entitled to a hearing. Attached to his appeal papers are affidavits from a number of psychiatrists which claim that he was psychotic and "psychologically adrift" at the time of the rape and murder for which he was sentenced to death and, further, that he was under the influence of the co-defendant, Linda Sanders, who initiated all of the crimes and "possessed a Charles Manson-like persona, subjugating Hall to her will."

Hall argues that LaBomba was ineffective in that he failed to raise any psychiatric defenses at trial. More important, Hall argues in his appeal papers that LaBomba failed even to obtain any psychiatric evaluation of Hall to assess whether or not such a defense might be tenable. It is Hall's argument that he is at least entitled to an evidentiary hearing at which he should be given an opportunity to show that LaBomba was constitutionally ineffective in failing to investigate and raise psychiatric defenses to these charges.

Half of you will be assigned to the defense, half to the prosecution. Prepare a brief (1 to 2 pages) outline of the arguments which support your side of the issue on appeal whether Hall should be entitled to such an evidentiary hearing on LaBomba's ineffectiveness.

D. Conflicts of Interest

In *Strickland*, the Court stated that when an attorney represents clients with conflicting interests, a limited presumption of incompetence can arise. *Cuyler* squarely presents that issue.

Cuyler v. Sullivan

446 U.S. 335 (1980).

MR. JUSTICE POWELL delivered the opinion of the Court.

Issue { The question presented is whether a state prisoner may obtain a federal writ of habeas corpus by showing that his retained defense counsel represented potentially conflicting interests.

Hear It

You can hear the oral argument in *Cuyler* at http://www.oyez.org/cases/1970-1979/1979/1979_78_1832.

Respondent John Sullivan was indicted with Gregory Carchidi and Anthony DiPasquale for the first-degree murders of John Gorey and Rita Janda. The victims, a labor official and his companion, were shot to death in Gorey's second-story office at the Philadelphia headquarters of Teamsters' Local 107. Francis McGrath, a janitor, saw the three defendants in the building just before the shooting. They appeared to be awaiting someone, and they encouraged McGrath to do his work on another day. McGrath ignored their suggestions. Shortly afterward, Gorey arrived and went to his office. McGrath then heard what sounded like firecrackers exploding in rapid succession. Carchidi, who was in the room where McGrath was working, abruptly directed McGrath to leave the building and to say nothing. McGrath hastily complied. When he returned to the building about 15 minutes later, the defendants were gone. The victims' bodies were discovered the next morning.

Two privately retained lawyers, G. Fred DiBona and A. Charles Peruto, represented all three defendants throughout the state proceedings that followed the indictment. Sullivan accepted representation from the two lawyers retained by his codefendants because he could not afford to pay his own lawyer. At no time did Sullivan or his lawyers object to the multiple representation. Sullivan was the first defendant to come to trial. The evidence against him was entirely circumstantial, consisting primarily of McGrath's testimony. At the close of the Commonwealth's case, the defense rested without presenting any evidence. The jury found Sullivan guilty and fixed his penalty at life imprisonment. The Pennsylvania Supreme Court affirmed his conviction by an equally divided vote. Sullivan's codefendants, Carchidi and DiPasquale, were acquitted at separate trials. In subsequent postconviction proceedings, a federal district court denied Sullivan's request for habeas corpus relief, but the Third Circuit Court of Appeals reversed, finding a conflict of interest sufficient to raise Sixth Amendment concerns.

The *Holloway* Court established that where counsel has brought the issue of potential conflict to a trial court's attention and the trial court failed properly to respond to the motion, e.g. by failing to either grant it or to ascertain the potentiality of a conflict at an appropriate hearing, in contrast to ordinary ineffectiveness inquiries, reversal of a defendant's conviction is "automatic," even in the absence of a demonstration of prejudice. As the Supreme Court subsequently reiterated this rule: "*Holloway* creates an automatic reversal rule where defense counsel is forced to represent codefendants over his timely objection, unless the trial court has determined that there is no conflict." *Mickens v. Taylor*, 535 U.S. 162, 168 (2002).

We come to Sullivan's claim that he was denied the effective assistance of counsel guaranteed by the Sixth Amendment because his lawyers had a conflict of interest. In *Holloway v. Arkansas*, 435 U.S. 475 (1978), a single public defender represented three defendants at the same trial. The trial court refused to consider the appointment of separate counsel despite the defense lawyer's timely and repeated assertions that the interests of his clients conflicted. This Court recognized that a lawyer forced to represent codefendants whose interests conflict cannot provide the adequate legal assistance required by the Sixth Amendment. Given the trial court's failure to respond to timely objections, however, the Court did not consider whether the alleged conflict actually existed. It simply held that the trial court's error unconstitutionally endangered the right to counsel.

American Bar Association Standards for Criminal Justice Defense Function Standard 4–1.7(d) (4th ed. 2015) provides as follows:

> Except where necessary to secure counsel for preliminary matters such as initial hearings or applications for bail, a defense counsel (or multiple counsel associated in practice) should not undertake to represent more than one client in the same criminal case. When there is not yet a criminal case, such multiple representation should be engaged in only when, after careful investigation and consideration, it is clear either that no conflict is likely to develop at any stage of the matter, or that multiple representation will be advantageous to each of the clients represented and that foreseeable conflicts can be waived.

Holloway requires state trial courts to investigate timely objections to multiple representation. But nothing in our precedents suggests that the Sixth Amendment requires state courts themselves to initiate inquiries into the propriety of multiple representation in every case. Defense counsel have an ethical obligation to avoid conflicting representations and to advise the court promptly when a conflict of interest arises during the course of trial. Absent special circumstances, therefore, trial courts may assume either that multiple representation entails no conflict or that the lawyer and his clients knowingly accept such risk of conflict as may exist. Unless the trial court knows or reasonably should know that a particular conflict exists, the court need not initiate an inquiry.

Holloway reaffirmed that multiple representation does not violate the Sixth Amendment unless it gives rise to a conflict of interest. Since a possible conflict inheres in almost every instance of multiple representation, a defendant who objects to multiple representation must have the opportunity to show that potential conflicts impermissibly imperil his right to a fair trial. But unless the trial court fails to afford such an opportunity, a reviewing court cannot presume that the possibility for conflict has resulted in ineffective assistance of counsel. Such a presumption would preclude multiple representation even in cases where " 'a common defense gives strength against a common attack.' "

In order to establish a violation of the Sixth Amendment, a defendant who raised no objection at trial must demonstrate that an actual conflict of interest adversely affected his lawyer's performance. In *Glasser v. United States*, 315 U.S. 60 (1942), for example, the record showed that defense counsel failed to cross-examine a prosecution witness whose testimony linked Glasser with the crime and failed to resist the presentation of arguably inadmissible evidence. The Court found that both omissions resulted from counsel's desire to diminish the jury's perception of a codefendant's guilt. Indeed, the evidence of counsel's "struggle to serve two masters could not seriously be doubted." Since this actual conflict of interest impaired Glasser's defense, the Court reversed his conviction.

Glasser established that unconstitutional multiple representation is never harmless error. Once the Court concluded that Glasser's lawyer had an actual conflict of interest, it refused "to indulge in nice calculations as to the amount of prejudice" attributable to the conflict. The conflict itself demonstrated a denial of the "right to have the effective assistance of counsel." Thus, a defendant who shows that a conflict of interest actually affected the adequacy of his representation need not demonstrate prejudice in order to obtain relief. But until a defendant shows that his counsel actively represented conflicting interests, he has not established the constitutional predicate for his claim of ineffective assistance.

The Court of Appeals granted Sullivan relief because he had shown that the multiple representation in this case involved a possible conflict of interest. We hold that the possibility of conflict is insufficient to impugn a criminal conviction. In order to demonstrate a violation of his Sixth Amendment rights, a defendant must establish that an actual conflict of interest adversely affected his lawyer's performance. Sullivan believes he should prevail even under this standard. He emphasizes Peruto's admission that the decision to rest Sullivan's defense reflected a reluctance to expose witnesses who later might have testified for the other defendants. The petitioner, on the other hand, points to DiBona's contrary testimony and to evidence that Sullivan himself wished to avoid taking the stand. Since the Court of Appeals did not weigh these conflicting contentions under the proper legal standard, its judgment is vacated and the case is remanded for further proceedings consistent with this opinion.

MR. JUSTICE BRENNAN, concurring in the result.

Upon discovery of joint representation, the duty of the trial court is to ensure that the defendants have not unwittingly given up their constitutional right to effective counsel. This is necessary since it is usually the case that defendants will not know what their rights are or how to raise them. Had the trial record in the present case shown that respondent made a knowing and intelligent choice of joint representation, I could accept the Court's standard for a postconviction determination as to whether respondent in fact was denied effective assistance. Here, however, where there is no evidence that the court advised respondent about the potential for conflict or that respondent made a knowing and intelligent choice to forgo his right to separate counsel, I believe that respondent, who has shown a significant possibility of conflict, is entitled to a presumption that his representation in fact suffered.

MR. JUSTICE MARSHALL, concurring in part and dissenting in part.

If "the possibility of the inconsistent interests of the clients was brought home to the court" by means of an objection at trial, the court may not require joint representation. But if no objection was made at trial, the appropriate inquiry is whether a conflict actually existed during the course of the representation. Because it is the simultaneous representation of conflicting interests against which the Sixth Amendment protects a defendant, he need go no further than to show the existence of an actual conflict. An actual conflict of interests negates the unimpaired loyalty a defendant is constitutionally entitled to expect and receive from his attorney. In the present case Peruto's testimony, if credited by the court, would be sufficient to make out a case of ineffective assistance by reason of a conflict of interests under even a restrictive reading of the Court's standard.

Points for Discussion

a. Disqualification Motions

It has become increasingly common for prosecutors to file pretrial motions to disqualify defense counsel. Such motions may be aimed at preventing counsel from engaging in the simultaneous representation of all or any one or more of multiple codefendants. Trial courts hearing such motions have the inherent judicial authority to oversee the conduct of the Bar, including the power to grant or deny such motions to disqualify. Typically, trial courts considering such motions in criminal cases look for guidance both to Sixth Amendment law and to applicable lawyer ethics code provisions relating to impermissible conflicts of interests.

b. Representation By Law Firm Partners

In *Burger v. Kemp*, 483 U.S. 776 (1987), petitioner was convicted of capital murder and sentenced to death. Petitioner claimed that his lawyer had a conflict of interest because his law partner represented petitioner's coindictee. Although the Supreme Court assumed that "two law partners are considered as one attorney," the Court refused to presume ineffective assistance. "We presume prejudice only if the defendant demonstrates that counsel 'actively represented conflicting interests' and that 'an actual conflict of interest adversely affected his lawyer's performance.'" The Court found that petitioner was unable to satisfy this standard:

> Petitioner argues that the joint representation adversely affected the quality of the counsel he received in two ways: Leaphart did not negotiate a plea agreement resulting in a life sentence, and he failed to take advantage of petitioner's lesser culpability when compared with his coindictee Stevens. We find that neither argument provides a basis for relief.
>
> The notion that the prosecutor would have been receptive to a plea bargain is completely unsupported in the record. The evidence of both defendants' guilt, including their confessions, and eyewitness and tangible evidence, was overwhelming and uncontradicted; the prosecutor had no need for petitioner's eyewitness testimony to persuade the jury to convict Stevens and to sentence him to death. Mr. Burger tried to

negotiate a plea with the district attorney for a life sentence. He flatly refused to even discuss it in any terms.

The argument that his partner's representation of Stevens inhibited Leaphart from arguing petitioner's lesser culpability because such reliance would be prejudicial to Stevens is also unsupported. Because the trials were separate, Leaphart would have had no particular reason for concern about the possible impact of the tactics in petitioner's trial on the outcome of Stevens' trial.

c. More on *Mickens*

In *Mickens v. Taylor,* 535 U.S. 162 (2002), involving defense counsel who had been representing his client's victim at the time of the victim's death, Justice Scalia added for the 5-to-4 majority that reversal need not be automatic every time a trial court fails to inquire into a potential conflict:

> The rule applied when the trial judge is not aware of the conflict (and thus not obligated to inquire) is that prejudice will be presumed only if the conflict has significantly affected counsel's performance—thereby rendering the verdict unreliable, even though *Strickland* prejudice cannot be shown. The trial court's awareness of a potential conflict neither renders it more likely that counsel's performance was significantly affected nor in any other way renders the verdict unreliable. Since this was not a case in which (as in *Holloway*) counsel protested his inability simultaneously to represent multiple defendants; and since the trial court's failure to make the *Sullivan*-mandated inquiry does not reduce the petitioner's burden of proof; it was at least necessary, to void the conviction, for petitioner to establish that the conflict of interest adversely affected his counsel's performance.

Suppose that, in *Mickens*, the attorney had informed the trial judge of his prior representation of Hall, stated that he was conflicted, asked to be replaced, and the trial judge dismissed the request without further inquiry. Would automatic reversal be required in that case?

d. Waiver of Conflicts

In *Wheat v. United States,* 486 U.S. 153 (1988), defendant Wheat was charged with participating in a drug distribution conspiracy. Also charged were Gomez-Barajas and Bravo, who were represented by attorney Iredale. Gomez-Barajas was tried and acquitted on drug charges overlapping with those against Wheat. To avoid a trial on other charges, Gomez-Barajas offered to plead guilty to tax evasion and illegal importation of merchandise. At the commencement of Wheat's trial, the plea had not been accepted and could have been withdrawn. Bravo decided to plead guilty to one count of transporting marijuana. After the plea was accepted, Iredale notified the court that he had been asked to defend Wheat. When the

Government objected because of a possible conflict of interest, the trial court refused to allow the representation. Wheat's conviction was upheld on appeal:

> A defendant may not insist on retaining an attorney who has a previous or ongoing relationship with an opposing party, even when the opposing party is the Government. Where a court justifiably finds an actual conflict of interest, it may decline a proffer of waiver, and insist that defendants be separately represented. The court must be allowed substantial latitude in refusing waivers of conflicts of interest not only in those rare cases where an actual conflict may be demonstrated before trial, but in the more common cases where a potential for conflict exists which may or may not burgeon into an actual conflict as the trial progresses.

e. Sex With Clients

In *Commonwealth v. Stote*, 456 Mass. 213, 922 N.E.2d 768 (2010), the Supreme Judicial Court of Massachusetts concluded that no unconstitutional conflict of interest existed where defense counsel at trial was discovered to have had an intimate relationship with an assistant district attorney (ADA) in the appellate division of the prosecutor's office, and a previous intimate relationship with the actual trial prosecutor. The court found that no *actual* conflict of interest existed with respect to the ongoing relationship as both defense counsel and the ADA swore that no confidential information about defendant was disclosed, and there was nothing in the record to suggest otherwise. The ADA added, moreover, that she had no involvement in the Commonwealth's appeal and knew nothing about the case, and this averment was corroborated by the trial prosecutor. Moreover, the court found that no conflict of interest existed with respect to defense counsel's prior relationship, which had ended seventeen years before trial, noting that "the trial judge pointed out that defense counsel 'had no hesitation whatsoever in lambasting the trial prosecutor for her alleged transgressions at trial' and concluded that 'he vigorously represented the defendant both at trial and on appeal.'"

Do these conclusions make sense to you? Does the fact that defense counsel "lambasted" the prosecutor at trial, for example, really indicate the absence of a conflict? What if defense counsel and the trial prosecutor were married or simply living together? Would that or should that make a difference? Should the defendant at least have been informed of that fact? What do you think?

Hypo 1: *Conflicted Partners*

A codefendant in a Baltimore heroin distribution prosecution, Jones, was represented by Denholm. Another codefendant, Wise, was represented by Salkin, Denholm's law partner. Just prior to trial, Wise agreed to plead guilty and to testify against her codefendants in exchange for a suspended sentence. The trial judge then issued a "gag order," ordering Salkin not to talk to his partner, Denholm, about the case as Salkin's client's interests now differed from the interests of Denholm's client. Dehholm objected to the issuance of the order, noting that if Salkin weren't his partner, he could talk to him about his client's testimony. His objections were overruled. At trial, Wise did testify against Jones. Her testimony about Jones' involvement in the heroin distribution scheme differed from the story she had told Denholm when she was a codefendant (that Jones was not involved), however Denholm did not try to impeach her on the basis of prior inconsistent statements. Jones was convicted and argued on appeal that Denholm had an impermissible conflict of interest due to the participation of his law partner in the proceedings. Do you agree? What arguments can appellate counsel make to support this argument? In any event, how could or should the trial court have handled this matter better to avoid any potential conflict of interest? *See Austin v. State*, 327 Md. 375, 609 A.2d 728 (Md. Ct. App.1992).

Hypo 2: *Retained Counsel & Ineffectiveness*

Should a *non-indigent* defendant be able to complain that his or her retained counsel was "ineffective?" As a general rule, non-indigent defendants have the right to choose the counsel they prefer (subject, of course, to their ability to pay the attorney's fees and the attorney's willingness to take the case). If the non-indigent chooses poorly and counsel commits prejudicial error, should that conviction be reversed for ineffectiveness?

Hypo 3: *Lump Sum Fees & Conflicts*

Has defense counsel rendered ineffective assistance of counsel as a result of a conflict of interest when he was paid a lump sum amount for his representation of a client rather than on an hourly basis? Defendant argued that this compensation agreement created an inherent and irreconcilable conflict of interest because both counsel's compensation and the costs for investigative and expert services were covered by a lump sum fee. Defendant asserted that this circumstance created a financial disincentive for counsel to adequately investigate and prepare his case. What do you think? *See People v. Doolin*, 45 Cal.4th 390, 87 Cal. Rptr.3d 209, 198 P.3d 11 (2009).

E. The Griffin-Douglas Doctrine

In *Griffin v. Illinois*, 351 U.S. 12 (1956), the Supreme Court concluded that an indigent prisoner appealing from conviction in state court had a Fourteenth Amendment right (under both the due process and equal protection clauses) to a free transcript of the trial proceedings where such transcripts were often a practical necessity for securing an appeal. In a plurality opinion, writing for four justices, Justice Black concluded that "there can be no equal justice where the kind of trial a man [*sic*] gets depends on the amount of money he has. Destitute defendants must be afforded as adequate appellate review as defendants who have money enough to buy transcripts."

Thereafter, the Court held in *Douglas v. California*, 372 U.S. 353 (1963), a companion case to *Gideon*, that indigent convicted defendants have a Fourteenth Amendment right (under both the due process and equal protection clauses) to the assistance of counsel on a first appeal where the state has granted them the right to appeal (as opposed to those instances where entitlement to appeal is only discretionary). Justice Douglas opined that "where the merits of the one and only appeal an indigent has as of right are decided without benefit of counsel, we think an unconstitutional line has been drawn between rich and poor."

Food for Thought

As then-Justice Rehnquist acknowledged in *Ross v. Moffitt*, indigent defendants are "somewhat handicapped' as compared to more affluent defendants by that decision, requiring only an "adequate"—but not an *equal*—opportunity to present one's claims. Does the Constitution require that the government address and relieve such handicaps?

Subsequently, the Court declined to extend this so-called "*Griffin-Douglas* Doctrine" so as to require a Fourteenth Amendment entitlement to counsel by indigents in discretionary state appeals and applications for review to the Supreme Court, holding that "the duty of the State under our cases is not to duplicate the legal arsenal that may be privately retained by a criminal defendant in a continuing effort to reverse his conviction, but only to assure the indigent defendant an adequate opportunity to present his claims fairly in the context of the State's appellate process." *Ross v. Moffitt*, 417 U.S. 600, 616 (1974).

The Supreme Court's 2005 decision in *Halbert v. Michigan* made it clear, however, that *Ross* did not supplant the Court's *Griffin-Douglas* commitment to equal justice for rich and poor:

Halbert v. Michigan

545 U.S. 605 (2005).

Hear It

You can hear the oral argument in *Halbert* at http://www.oyez.org/cases/2000-2009/2004/2004_03_10198.

JUSTICE GINSBURG delivered the opinion of the Court.

In 1994, Michigan voters approved a proposal amending the State Constitution to provide that "an appeal by an accused who pleads guilty or nolo contendere shall be by leave of the court." Thereafter, "several Michigan state judges began to deny appointed appellate counsel to indigents" convicted by plea. Rejecting challenges based on the Equal Protection and Due Process Clauses of the Fourteenth Amendment to the Federal Constitution, the Michigan Supreme Court upheld this practice.

Petitioner Antonio Dwayne Halbert, convicted on his plea of <u>nolo contendere</u>, sought the appointment of counsel to assist him in applying for leave to appeal to the Michigan Court of Appeals. The state trial court and the Court of Appeals denied Halbert's requests for appointed counsel, and the Michigan Supreme Court declined review.

Michigan Court of Appeals review of an application for leave to appeal, Halbert contends, ranks as a first-tier appellate proceeding requiring appointment of counsel under *Douglas v. California*, 372 U.S. 353 (1963). Michigan urges that appeal to the State Court of Appeals is discretionary and, for an appeal of that order, *Ross v. Moffitt*, 417 U.S. 600 (1974), holds counsel need not be appointed. Today, we conclude that Halbert's case is properly ranked with *Douglas* rather than *Ross*. Accordingly, we hold that the Due Process and Equal Protection Clauses require the appointment of counsel for defendants, convicted on their pleas, who seek access to first-tier review in the Michigan Court of Appeals.

The Federal Constitution imposes on the States no obligation to provide appellate review of criminal convictions. Having provided such an avenue, however, a State may not "bolt the door to equal justice" to indigent defendants. *Griffin* held that, when a State conditions an appeal from a conviction on the provision of a trial transcript, the State must furnish free transcripts to indigent defendants who seek to appeal. *Douglas* relied on *Griffin's* reasoning to hold that, in first

Griffen Rule

appeals as of right, States must appoint counsel to represent indigent defendants. *Ross* held, however, that a State need not appoint counsel to aid a poor person in discretionary appeals to the State's highest court, or in petitioning for review in this Court.

Cases on appeal barriers encountered by persons unable to pay their own way, we have observed, "cannot be resolved by resort to easy slogans or pigeonhole analysis." Our decisions in point reflect "both equal protection and due process concerns." "The equal protection concern relates to the legitimacy of fencing out would-be appellants based solely on their inability to pay core costs," while "the due process concern homes in on the essential fairness of the state-ordered proceedings."

Two considerations were key to our decision in *Douglas* that a State is required to appoint counsel for an indigent defendant's first-tier appeal as of right. First, such an appeal entails an adjudication on the "merits." Second, first-tier review differs from subsequent appellate stages "at which the claims have once been presented by appellate counsel and passed upon by an appellate court."

In *Ross*, we explained why the rationale of *Douglas* did not extend to the appointment of counsel for an indigent seeking to pursue a second-tier discretionary appeal to the North Carolina Supreme Court or, thereafter, certiorari review in this Court. The North Carolina Supreme Court, in common with this Court we perceived, does not sit as an error-correction instance. Principal criteria for state high court review, we noted, included "whether the subject matter of the appeal has significant public interest, whether the cause involves legal principles of major significance to the jurisprudence of the State, and whether the decision below is in probable conflict" with the court's precedent. Further, we pointed out, a defendant who had already benefitted from counsel's aid in a first-tier appeal as of right would have, "at the very least, a transcript or other record of trial proceedings, a brief on his behalf in the Court of Appeals setting forth his claims of error, and in many cases an opinion by the Court of Appeals disposing of his case."

Halbert's case is framed by these two prior decisions of this Court concerning state-funded appellate counsel, *Douglas* and *Ross*. The question before us is essentially one of classification: With which of those decisions should the instant case be aligned? We hold that *Douglas* provides the controlling instruction. Two aspects of the Michigan Court of Appeals' process following plea-based convictions lead us to that conclusion. First, in determining how to dispose of an application for leave to appeal, Michigan's intermediate appellate court looks to the merits of the claims made in the application. Second, indigent defendants pursuing first-tier review in the Court of Appeals are generally ill equipped to represent themselves.

A defendant who pleads guilty or nolo contendere in a Michigan court does not thereby forfeit all opportunity for appellate review. Although he relinquishes access to an appeal as of right, he is entitled to apply for leave to appeal, and that entitlement is officially conveyed to him. Of critical importance, the tribunal to which he addresses his application, the Michigan Court of Appeals, unlike the Michigan Supreme Court, sits as an error-correction instance.

Whether formally categorized as the decision of an appeal or the disposal of a leave application, the Court of Appeals' ruling on a plea-convicted defendant's claims provides the first, and likely the only, direct review the defendant's conviction and sentence will receive. Parties like Halbert, however, are disarmed in their endeavor to gain first-tier review. As the Court in *Ross* emphasized, a defendant seeking State Supreme Court review following a first-tier appeal as of right earlier had the assistance of appellate counsel. The attorney appointed to serve at the intermediate appellate court level will have reviewed the trial court record, researched the legal issues, and prepared a brief reflecting that review and research. The defendant seeking second-tier review may also be armed with an opinion of the intermediate appellate court addressing the issues counsel raised. A first-tier review applicant, forced to act *pro se*, will face a record unreviewed by appellate counsel, and will be equipped with no attorney's brief prepared for, or reasoned opinion by, a court of review.

Persons in Halbert's situation are particularly handicapped as self-representatives. "Approximately 70% of indigent defendants represented by appointed counsel plead guilty, and 70% of those convicted are incarcerated." "Sixty-eight percent of the state prison population did not complete high school, and many lack the most basic literacy skills." "Seven out of ten inmates fall in the lowest two out of five levels of literacy—marked by an inability to do such basic tasks as write a brief letter to explain an error on a credit card bill, use a bus schedule, or state in writing an argument made in a lengthy newspaper article." Many, Halbert among them, have learning disabilities and mental impairments.

Navigating the appellate process without a lawyer's assistance is a perilous endeavor for a layperson, and well beyond the competence of individuals, like Halbert, who have little education, learning disabilities, and mental impairments. Appeals by defendants convicted on their pleas may involve "myriad and often complicated" substantive issues, and may be "no less complex than other appeals." One who pleads guilty or nolo contendere may still raise on appeal "constitutional defects that are irrelevant to his factual guilt, double jeopardy claims requiring no further factual record, jurisdictional defects, challenges to the sufficiency of the evidence at the preliminary examination, preserved entrapment claims, mental competency claims, factual basis claims, claims that the state had no right to proceed in the first place, including claims that a defendant was charged under an inapplicable statute, and claims of ineffective assistance of counsel."

While the State has a legitimate interest in reducing the workload of its judiciary, providing indigents with appellate counsel will yield applications easier to comprehend. Michigan's Court of Appeals would still have recourse to summary denials of leave applications in cases not warranting further review. And when a defendant's case presents no genuinely arguable issue, appointed counsel may so inform the court.

For the reasons stated, we vacate the judgment of the Michigan Court of Appeals and remand the case for further proceedings not inconsistent with this opinion.

JUSTICE THOMAS, with whom JUSTICE SCALIA joins, and with whom the CHIEF JUSTICE joins in part, dissenting.

The majority holds that Michigan's system is constitutionally inadequate. It finds that all plea-convicted indigent defendants have the right to appellate counsel when seeking leave to appeal. *Douglas*, however, does not support extending the right to counsel to any form of discretionary review, as *Ross v. Moffitt*, and later cases make clear. Moreover, Michigan has not engaged in the sort of invidious discrimination against indigent defendants that *Douglas* condemns. Michigan has done no more than recognize the undeniable difference between defendants who plead guilty and those who maintain their innocence, in an attempt to divert resources from largely frivolous appeals to more meritorious ones. The majority substitutes its own policy preference for that of Michigan voters, and it does so based on an untenable reading of *Douglas*.

Food for Thought

Do you agree with dissenting Justice Thomas? Is the Court in essence ordering the State to pay for the appointment of counsel in a class of largely frivolous appeals? Remember these would-be appellants have pleaded guilty (or nolo) previously, often as the result of an advantageous plea agreement. Should the State have to bear the cost of these largely frivolous appeals?

Today the Court confers on defendants convicted by plea a right nowhere to be found in the Constitution or this Court's cases. It does so at the expense of defendants whose claims are, on average, likely more meritorious. I respectfully dissent.

* * *

One of the most significant applications of the *Griffin-Douglas* Doctrine in the criminal justice system involves the question of what assistance—other than defense counsel—the government must provide to indigent defendants.

Ake v. Oklahoma

470 U.S. 68 (1985).

JUSTICE MARSHALL delivered the opinion of the Court.

The issue in this case is whether the Constitution requires that an indigent defendant have access to the psychiatric examination and assistance necessary to prepare an effective defense based on his mental condition, when his sanity at the time of the offense is seriously in question.

Late in 1979, Glen Burton Ake was arrested and charged with murdering a couple and wounding their two children. His behavior at arraignment, and in other prearraignment incidents at the jail, was so bizarre that the trial judge, *sua sponte*, ordered him to be examined by a psychiatrist "for the purpose of advising with the Court as to his impressions of whether the Defendant may need an extended period of mental observation." The examining psychiatrist reported: "At times Ake appears to be frankly delusional. He claims to be the 'sword of vengeance' of the Lord and that he will sit at the left hand of God in heaven." He diagnosed Ake as a probable paranoid schizophrenic and recommended a prolonged psychiatric evaluation to determine whether Ake was competent to stand trial.

In March, Ake was committed to a state hospital to be examined with respect to his "present sanity," i.e., his competency to stand trial. On April 10, less than six months after the incidents for which Ake was indicted, the chief forensic psychiatrist at the state hospital informed the court that Ake was not competent to stand trial. The court then held a competency hearing, at which a psychiatrist testified:

> "Ake is a psychotic. His psychiatric diagnosis was that of paranoid schizophrenia—chronic, with exacerbation, that is with current upset, and that in addition he is dangerous. Because of the severity of his mental illness and because of the intensities of his rage, his poor control, his delusions, he requires a maximum security facility within—I believe—the State Psychiatric Hospital system."

The court found Ake to be a "mentally ill person in need of care and treatment" and incompetent to stand trial, and ordered him committed to the state mental hospital.

Six weeks later, the chief forensic psychiatrist informed the court that Ake had become competent to stand trial. At the time, Ake was receiving 200 milligrams of Thorazine, an antipsychotic drug, three times daily, and the psychiatrist indicated that, if Ake continued to receive that dosage, his condition would remain stable. The State then resumed proceedings against Ake.

At a pretrial conference in June, Ake's attorney informed the court that his client would raise an insanity defense. To enable him to prepare and present such a defense adequately, the attorney stated, a psychiatrist would have to examine Ake with respect to his mental condition at the time of the offense. During Ake's 3-month stay at the state hospital, no inquiry had been made into his sanity at the time of the offense, and, as an indigent, Ake could not afford to pay for a psychiatrist. Counsel asked the court either to arrange to have a psychiatrist perform the examination, or to provide funds to allow the defense to arrange one. The trial judge rejected counsel's argument that the Federal Constitution requires that an indigent defendant receive the assistance of a psychiatrist when that assistance is necessary to the defense, and he denied the motion for a psychiatric evaluation at state expense.

Ake was tried for two counts of murder in the first degree, a crime punishable by death in Oklahoma, and for two counts of shooting with intent to kill. At the guilt phase of trial, his sole defense was insanity. Although defense counsel called to the stand and questioned each of the psychiatrists who had examined Ake at the state hospital, none testified about his mental state at the time of the offense because none had examined him on that point. The prosecution, in turn, asked each of these psychiatrists whether he had performed or seen the results of any examination diagnosing Ake's mental state at the time of the offense, and each doctor replied that he had not. As a result, there was no expert testimony for either side on Ake's sanity at the time of the offense. The jurors were then instructed that Ake could be found not guilty by reason of insanity if he did not have the ability to distinguish right from wrong at the time of the alleged offense. They were further told that Ake was to be presumed sane at the time of the crime unless he presented evidence sufficient to raise a reasonable doubt about his sanity at that time. If he raised such a doubt in their minds, the jurors were informed, the burden of proof shifted to the State to prove sanity beyond a reasonable doubt. The jury rejected Ake's insanity defense and returned a verdict of guilty on all counts.

At the sentencing proceeding, the State asked for the death penalty. No new evidence was presented. The prosecutor relied significantly on the testimony of the state psychiatrists who had examined Ake, and who had testified at the guilt phase that Ake was dangerous to society, to establish the likelihood of his future dangerous behavior. Ake had no expert witness to rebut this testimony or to introduce on his behalf evidence in mitigation of his punishment. The jury sentenced Ake to death on each of the two murder counts, and to 500 years' imprisonment on each of the two counts of shooting with intent to kill.

The Oklahoma Court of Criminal Appeals upheld Ake's conviction on appeal. We hold that when a defendant has made a preliminary showing that his sanity at the time of the offense is likely to be a significant factor at trial, the Constitution requires that a State provide access to a psychiatrist's assistance on this issue if the defendant cannot otherwise afford one.

This Court has long recognized that when a State brings its judicial power to bear on an indigent defendant in a criminal proceeding, it must take steps to assure that the defendant has a fair opportunity to present his defense. This elementary principle, grounded in significant part on the Fourteenth Amendment's due process guarantee of fundamental fairness, derives from the belief that justice cannot be equal where, simply as a result of his poverty, a defendant is denied the opportunity to participate meaningfully in a judicial proceeding in which his liberty is at stake. In recognition of this right, this Court held almost 30 years ago that once a State offers to criminal defendants the opportunity to appeal their cases, it must provide a trial transcript to an indigent defendant if the transcript is necessary to a decision on the merits of the appeal. *Griffin v. Illinois*, 351 U.S. 12 (1956). Since then, this Court has held that an indigent defendant may not be required to pay a fee before filing a notice of appeal of his conviction, that an indigent defendant is entitled to the assistance of counsel at trial, and on his first direct appeal as of right, and that such assistance must be effective.

Meaningful access to justice has been the consistent theme of these cases. We recognized long ago that mere access to the courthouse doors does not by itself assure a proper functioning of the adversary process, and that a criminal trial is fundamentally unfair if the State proceeds against an indigent defendant without making certain that he has access to the raw materials integral to the building of an effective defense. Thus, while the Court has not held that a State must purchase for the indigent defendant all the assistance that his wealthier counterpart might buy, it has often reaffirmed that fundamental fairness entitles indigent defendants to "an adequate opportunity to present their claims fairly within the adversary system." To implement this principle, we have focused on identifying the "basic tools of an adequate defense or appeal," and we have required that such tools be provided to those defendants who cannot afford to pay for them.

To say that these basic tools must be provided is, of course, merely to begin our inquiry. In this case we must decide whether, and under what conditions, the participation of a psychiatrist is important enough to preparation of a defense to require the State to provide an indigent defendant with access to competent psychiatric assistance in preparing the defense. Three factors are relevant to this determination. The first is the private interest that will be affected by the action of the State. The second is the governmental interest that will be affected if the safeguard is to be provided. The third is the probable value of the additional or substitute procedural safeguards that are sought, and the risk of an erroneous deprivation of the affected interest if those safeguards are not provided.

The private interest in the accuracy of a criminal proceeding that places an individual's life or liberty at risk is almost uniquely compelling. Indeed, the host of safeguards fashioned by this Court over the years to diminish the risk of erroneous conviction stands as a testament to that concern. The interest of the individual in the outcome of the State's effort to overcome the presumption of innocence is obvious and weighs heavily in our analysis.

We consider, next, the interest of the State. Oklahoma asserts that to provide Ake with psychiatric assistance on the record before us would result in a staggering burden to the State. We are unpersuaded by this assertion. Many States, as well as the Federal Government, currently make psychiatric assistance available to indigent defendants, and they have not found the financial burden so great as to preclude this assistance. This is especially so when the obligation of the State is limited to provision of one competent psychiatrist, as it is in many States, and as we limit the right we recognize today. At the same time, it is difficult to identify any interest of the State, other than that in its economy, that weighs against recognition of this right. The State's interest in prevailing at trial—unlike that of a private litigant—is necessarily tempered by its interest in the fair and accurate adjudication of criminal cases. Thus, also unlike a private litigant, a State may not legitimately assert an interest in maintenance of a strategic advantage over the defense, if the result of that advantage is to cast a pall on the accuracy of the verdict obtained. We therefore conclude that the governmental interest in denying Ake the assistance of a psychiatrist is not substantial, in light of the compelling interest of both the State and the individual in accurate dispositions.

Last, we inquire into the probable value of the psychiatric assistance sought, and the risk of error in the proceeding if such assistance is not offered. We begin by considering the pivotal role that psychiatry has come to play in criminal proceedings. More than 40 States, as well as the Federal Government, have decided either through legislation or judicial decision that indigent defendants are entitled, under certain circumstances, to the assistance of a psychiatrist's expertise. These statutes and court decisions reflect a reality that we recognize today, namely, that when the State has made the defendant's mental condition relevant to his criminal culpability and to the punishment he might suffer, the assistance of a psychiatrist may well be crucial to the defendant's ability to marshal his defense. In this role, psychiatrists gather facts, through professional examination, interviews, and elsewhere, that they will share with the judge or jury; they analyze the information gathered and from it draw plausible conclusions about the defendant's mental condition, and about the effects of any disorder on behavior; and they offer opinions about how the defendant's mental condition might have affected his behavior at the time in question.

Psychiatry is not an exact science, and psychiatrists disagree widely and frequently on what constitutes mental illness, on the appropriate diagnosis to be attached to given behavior and symptoms, on cure and treatment, and on likelihood of future dangerousness. Perhaps because there often is no single, accurate psychiatric conclusion on legal insanity in a given case, juries remain the primary fact-finders on this issue, and they must resolve differences in opinion within the psychiatric profession on the basis of the evidence offered by each party. When jurors make this determination about issues that inevitably are complex and foreign, the testimony of psychiatrists can be crucial and "a virtual necessity if an insanity plea is to have any chance of success." In so saying, we neither approve nor disapprove the widespread reliance on psychiatrists but instead recognize the unfairness of a contrary holding in light of the evolving practice.

Food for Thought

In this day and age when it may appear that no two psychological experts ever hold the same viewpoint, what accounts for the lower courts' reluctance to provide such services? The obvious answer is the slippery slope. If you provide a psychiatrist, then won't you need to provide investigators, and medical examiners, and accident reconstruction professionals, and ballistics experts, and DNA specialists, and jury consultants, etc., etc. When have you left the realm of "basic tools' and simply provided a "defense consultant" (as Justice Rehnquist worries in his omitted dissent). At a time when it stretches governmental units' budgets simply to provide indigents with appointed counsel, where would the money come from for such "extravagances?"

The foregoing leads inexorably to the conclusion that, without the assistance of a psychiatrist to conduct a professional examination on issues relevant to the defense, to help determine whether the insanity defense is viable, to present testimony, and to assist in preparing the cross-examination of a State's psychiatric witnesses, the risk of an inaccurate resolution of sanity issues is extremely high. With such assistance, the defendant is fairly able to present at least enough information to the jury, in a meaningful manner, as to permit it to make a sensible determination.

We therefore hold that when a defendant demonstrates to the trial judge that his sanity at the time of the offense is to be a significant factor at trial, the State must, at a minimum, assure the defendant access to a competent psychiatrist who will conduct an appropriate examination and assist in evaluation, preparation, and presentation of the defense. This is not to say, of course, that the indigent defendant has a constitutional right to choose a psychiatrist of his personal liking or to receive funds to hire his own. Our concern is that the indigent defendant have access to a competent psychiatrist for the purpose we have discussed, and as in the case of the provision of counsel we leave to the States the decision on how to implement this right.

Ake also was denied the means of presenting evidence to rebut the State's evidence of his future dangerousness. The foregoing discussion compels a similar conclusion in the context of a capital sentencing proceeding, when the State presents psychiatric evidence of the defendant's future dangerousness. We have repeatedly recognized the defendant's compelling interest in fair adjudication at the sentencing phase of a capital case. The State, too, has a profound interest in assuring that its ultimate sanction is not erroneously imposed, and we do not see why monetary considerations should be more persuasive in this context than at trial.

We turn now to apply these standards to the facts of this case. On the record before us, it is clear that Ake's mental state at the time of the offense was a substantial factor in his defense, and that the trial court was on notice of that fact when the request for a court-appointed psychiatrist was made. In addition, Ake's future dangerousness was a significant factor at the sentencing phase. The state psychiatrist who treated Ake at the state mental hospital testified at the guilt phase that, because of his mental illness, Ake posed a threat of continuing criminal violence. This testimony raised the issue of Ake's future dangerousness, which is an aggravating factor under Oklahoma's capital sentencing scheme, and on which the prosecutor relied at sentencing. We therefore conclude that Ake also was entitled to the assistance of a psychiatrist on this issue and that the denial of that assistance deprived him of due process.

Accordingly, we reverse and remand for a new trial.

Point for Discussion

Volunteer Psychologist Insufficient

In *McWilliams v. Dunn*, 137 S.Ct. 1790 (2017), a 5-to-4 majority of the Supreme Court held that Alabama failed to meet its obligations under *Ake v. Oklahoma* to provide a capital murder defendant, McWilliams, with access to a mental health expert to assist in the evaluation, preparation, and presentation of his defense at sentencing. Alabama argued that the State was exempted from its obligations under *Ake* because McWilliams already had the assistance of a psychologist from the University of Alabama who had volunteered to help defense counsel "in her spare time." Justice Breyer ruled for the majority that "even if the episodic assistance of an outside volunteer could relieve the State of its constitutional duty to ensure an indigent defendant access to meaningful expert assistance, no lower court has held or suggested that that psychologist was available to help, or might have helped, McWilliams at the judicial sentencing proceeding, the proceeding here at issue. Alabama does not refer to any specific record facts that indicate that she was available to the defense at this time."

"No one denies that the conditions that trigger application of *Ake* are present," the majority added, as "McWilliams is and was an 'indigent defendant,' his 'mental condition' was 'relevant to the punishment he might suffer, and that 'mental condition,' i.e., his 'sanity at the time of the offense,' was 'seriously in question.'" Consequently, the Constitution, as interpreted in *Ake*, required the State to provide McWilliams with "access to a competent psychiatrist who will conduct an appropriate examination and assist in evaluation, preparation, and presentation of the defense."

Hypo 1: *Additional Assistance*

Defendant James Kelly was convicted of the robbery, rape and murder of a college student who was working as a pizza delivery person and who had delivered a pizza to Kelly's girlfriend's apartment. He was sentenced to death. On appeal, Kelly contended that the trial judge erred by denying his pretrial request for provision of a private investigator and other experts. The trial judge had concluded that *Ake* does not give a defendant a constitutional right to any expert other than a psychiatrist. Kelly argued that, although he had consensual sex with the victim, he did not kill her, and that a private investigator would have enabled him to find key (unnamed) witnesses who would have helped to confirm his story. Moreover, he argued that he should have been provided with: (1) a forensic expert to assess the truthfulness of the prosecution's forensic experts (who "matched" his DNA with DNA found in the victim's vagina and on the victim's underwear and jeans); and (2) a medical expert to "go over" the medical examiner's report. Do you think that the trial court's ruling was correct? *See Rogers v. Oklahoma*, 890 P.2d 959 (Okla. Cr. App. 1995).

Hypo 2: *Transcript of Co-Defendant's Trial*

Should a defendant have the right under the *Griffin-Douglas* Doctrine to be provided with a free copy of his *co-defendant's* trial transcript when the two of them have had separate trials but the facts all arose out of the same incident? *See State v. Scott*, 131 Hawai'i 333, 319 P.3d 252 (2013).

Executive Summary

Right to Counsel. People have a right to the assistance of counsel for their defense at all critical stages of the proceedings when they are charged with a criminal offense, and if they are indigent and cannot afford counsel, one will be appointed for them.

Indigent Appointments. Indigent criminal defendants are only entitled to appointment of counsel when they will receive a punishment of at least one day in jail, whether or not that sentence is suspended.

Waiver of Right to Counsel. A waiver of the right to counsel must be knowing and intelligent.

Right to Proceed *Pro Se*. Competent criminal defendants have the right to waive the assistance of counsel and to represent themselves at trial (deemed "proceeding *pro se*").

Standby Counsel. Standby counsel may be appointed to assist a *pro se* criminal defendant in his or her defense, but counsel must endeavor to preserve the *pro se* defendant's actual control over the case, and is not allowed to destroy the jury's perception that the defendant is representing himself or herself.

Major Themes

a. Indigent Representation Unequal—Although indigent criminal defendants are entitled to appointed counsel, they do not have the right to counsel of their choice, nor representation at every point in the proceedings, nor the full array of resources available to someone who can afford to retain his or her own attorney.

b. Ineffectiveness Difficult to Establish—Although criminal defendants are entitled to receive the effective assistance of counsel, ineffectiveness under the *Strickland* two-part test is extremely difficult to establish, and very few convictions are reversed on this basis.

Ineffective Assistance of Counsel. To obtain a reversal of a conviction on grounds of ineffective assistance under the seminal *Strickland* decision, a convicted defendant must show *both* that defense counsel's performance was deficient in that it fell below an objective standard of reasonableness *and* that counsel's deficient performance was prejudicial in that there was a reasonable probability that, absent counsel's errors, the fact-finder would have had a reasonable doubt respecting his or her guilt.

Conflicts of Interest. In order to establish ineffectiveness based upon defense counsel's conflict of interest, a defendant who raised no objection at trial must demonstrate that an actual conflict of interest adversely affected his or her lawyer's performance.

Other Assistance Beyond Counsel. An indigent criminal defendant has a right under the Fourteenth Amendment to assistance other than representation by a lawyer when that assistance constitutes a basic tool of

Test Your Knowledge

To assess your understanding of the material in this chapter, click here to take a quiz.

an adequate defense or appeal, such as access to a psychological expert where defendant's sanity will be a significant issue at trial.

For More Information

• AMERICAN BAR ASSOCIATION, *GIDEON'S BROKEN PROMISE: AMERICA'S CONTINUING QUEST FOR EQUAL JUSTICE* (2004).

• MARY SUE BACKUS & PAUL MARCUS, THE RIGHT TO COUNSEL IN CRIMINAL CASES: A NATIONAL CRISIS (2006).

• JOHN M. BURKOFF & NANCY M. BURKOFF, INEFFECTIVE ASSISTANCE OF COUNSEL (Thomson Reuters/West, annual editions).

• DAVID COLE, NO EQUAL JUSTICE (1999).

• David Harris, *The Constitution and Truth Seeking: A New Theory on Expert Services for Indigent Defendants*, 83 J. CRIM. L. & C. 469 (1992).

• Bruce R. Jacob, *Memories of and Reflections About Gideon v. Wainwright*, 33 STETSON L. REV. 181 (2003).

• Janet Moore, *The Antidemocratic Sixth Amendment*, 91 Wash. L. Rev. 1705 (2016).

• Anne Bowen Poulin, *The Role of Standby Counsel in Criminal Cases: In the Twilight Zone of the Criminal Justice System*, 75 N.Y.U. L. REV. 676 (2000).

• John Rappaport, *The Structural Function of the Sixth Amendment Right to Counsel of Choice*, 2016 Sup. Ct. Rev. 117 (2016).

• Abbe Smith, *The Difference in Criminal Defense and the Difference It Makes*, 11 WASH.U. J.L.& POL'Y 83 (2003).

• JAMES TOMKOVICZ, THE RIGHT TO THE ASSISTANCE OF COUNSEL (Greenwood Press 2002).

• RUSSELL L. WEAVER, JOHN M. BURKOFF, CATHERINE HANCOCK & STEVEN I. FRIEDLAND, PRINCIPLES OF CRIMINAL PROCEDURE Ch. 3 (6th ed. 2018).

CHAPTER **4**

Arrest, Search & Seizure

A. Search Warrants

1. The Warrant Preference

The Supreme Court has instructed law enforcement officers and lower courts that it has a strong "preference" that warrants should be used even where a warrantless search would otherwise be constitutional. As the Court explained in a key 1984 decision:

> Because a search warrant "provides the detached scrutiny of a neutral magistrate, which is a more reliable safeguard against improper searches than the hurried judgment of a law enforcement officer 'engaged in the often competitive enterprise of ferreting out crime,' " we have expressed a strong preference for warrants and declared that "in a doubtful or marginal case a search under a warrant may be sustainable where one without it may fail."

United States v. Leon, 468 U.S. 897, 913-14 (1984), *quoting United States v. Chadwick*, 433 U.S. 1, 9 (1977) (*Chadwick quoting Johnson v. United States*, 333 U.S. 10, 14 (1948)), and *United States v. Ventresca*, 380 U.S. 102, 106 (1965).

Food for Thought

It is easy enough to point out that we want neutral magistrates—not the officers themselves—to make the probable cause determination necessary prior to a search or seizure. But why do you think that is the case? Don't we trust police officers? Should we?

2. The Warrant Requirement

The Supreme Court has also long established that a warrant "requirement" is—at least as a matter of theory—one of the first principles of its Fourth Amendment jurisprudence. As the Court explained in *Thompson v. Louisiana*, 469 U.S. 17, 19–20 (1984), *quoting Katz v. United States*, 389 U.S. 347, 357 (1967):

In a long line of cases, this Court has stressed that "searches conducted outside the judicial process, without prior approval by judge or magistrate, are per se unreasonable under the Fourth Amendment-subject only to a few specifically established and well delineated exceptions." In all cases outside the exceptions to the warrant requirement the Fourth Amendment requires the interposition of a neutral and detached magistrate between the police and the "persons, houses, papers and effects" of the citizen.

Practice Pointer

Despite the fact that the warrant requirement is and remains such a firm theoretical fixture of Fourth Amendment law, the truth of the matter is that, in actual practice, the number of searches justified under one of the "few specifically established and well delineated exceptions" to the warrant requirement far outnumber the number of searches actually undertaken with a warrant. In short, while only a relatively few exceptions to the warrant requirement exist, most searches fall within these exceptional categories. As a result, a more useful and practical way to view this rule of law is to use the following rule of practice, even if it puts the cart before the horse: if a search is not justified by one of the warrant requirement "exceptions," then a search warrant must be obtained.

Why are warrants required? The Court answered this question in *Skinner v. Railway Labor Executives' Ass'n*, 489 U.S. 602, 621–22 (1989) as follows:

An essential purpose of a warrant requirement is to protect privacy interests by assuring citizens subject to a search or seizure that such intrusions are not the random or arbitrary acts of government agents.   A warrant assures the citizen that the intrusion is authorized by law, and that it is narrowly limited in its objectives and scope. A warrant also provides the detached and neutral scrutiny of a neutral magistrate, and thus ensures an objective determination whether an intrusion is justified in any given case.

3. Obtaining Warrants

In most jurisdictions, any law enforcement or prosecuting officer is authorized to apply for a search warrant simply by taking an application for a search warrant to a magistrate authorized by law to issue warrants. Typically, the application must include an attachment of one or more written affidavits. In such affidavits, the affiant must have sworn under oath to facts sufficient to establish probable cause to believe both that the items to be listed for seizure in the warrant are

See It

What does a search warrant look like? Take a look at a blank federal search warrant. *See* http://www.uscourts.gov/sites/default/files/ao093.pdf
What does a search warrant application look like? Take a look at a blank federal search warrant application. *See* http://www.uscourts.gov/forms/law-enforcement-grand-jury-and-prosecution-forms/application-search-warrant

in fact evidence of specified criminal activity, and that these items are presently located at the premises for which the search warrant is being sought.

In addition, under F.R.Cr.P. 41(d)(3), "a magistrate judge may issue a warrant based on information communicated by telephone or other reliable electronic means." Many states now have similar court rule provisions.

Exercise: *Preparing Affidavit*

You are an FBI Special Agent working in New York City. You have recently been contacted by e-mail by a confidential informant (CI), who has not revealed his or her identity to you, but who sent you information by e-mail six months ago identifying by name and address a person the CI said was selling sexually explicit images of children over the internet. (This is a federal crime. See FYI at right.). A subsequent investigation of that individual by your office revealed that he was indeed engaged in such criminal activity and criminal charges have been filed against him. In the message you have just received, the CI has stated as follows:

18 U.S.C. § 2252(A) provides, inter alia, that "any person who—(1) knowingly transports or ships using any means or facility of interstate or foreign commerce or in or affecting interstate or foreign commerce by any means including by computer or mails, any visual depiction, if—

(A) the producing of such visual depiction involves the use of a minor engaging in sexually explicit conduct; and (b) such visual depiction is of such conduct; (2) knowingly receives, or distributes, any visual depiction using any means or facility of interstate or foreign commerce or that has been mailed, or has been shipped or transported in or affecting interstate or foreign commerce or through the mails, contain any visual depiction that has been mailed, or has been shipped or transported using any means or facility of interstate or foreign commerce or in or affecting interstate or foreign commerce, or which was produced using materials which have been mailed or so shipped or transported, by any means including by computer, if—(i) the producing of such visual depiction involves the use of a minor engaging in sexually explicit conduct; and (ii) such visual depiction is of such conduct; Shall be punished as provided in subsection (b) of this section."

I've got another scoop for you guys. In the past week, I've downloaded 67 GIF image files from a guy calling himself Nick9795 who is operating on USOL, the "United States OnLine" computer service. I paid Nick9795 $19.95 twice to gain access to these files. All of the pictures were of young children (boys and girls) engaged in gross sex acts with grown women. I hacked around in the USOL files and I think that Nick9795 is a guy named Gary Durham who lives in Oswego. GO GET HIM!!!

You have located four people named Gary Durham who live in Oswego, New York, and have placed a "dialed number recorder" (DNR) (a device which records outgoing phone numbers) on each of their home telephone lines. The DNR on one of the phone lines, a line belonging to Gary Durham of 234 Ash Street in Oswego, indicates numerous phone calls have been placed in the last three months to telephone numbers associated with USOL dial-in services. Accordingly, you have decided to obtain a search warrant to search 234 Ash Street for child pornography.

Go Online

For information about the FBI's Violent Crimes Against Children/ Online Predators Program, *see* https://www.fbi.gov/investigate/ violent-crime/cac

You have tried to find out both the identity of "Nick 9795" and the frequency of his or her usage of USOL services. However, you have contacted USOL and they have refused to give you that information, citing customer privacy concerns. You have decided, accordingly, that you need to obtain a search warrant to search USOL's files in order to seize the file of "Nick9795."

Your class will be divided in half. The first group should prepare an affidavit based on the information set forth above to attempt to support the issuance of a search warrant for the Gary Durham residence in Oswego.

The second group should prepare an affidavit based on the information set forth above which will support the issuance of a search warrant for the "Nick9795" file at the offices of USOL.

(If, in preparing your affidavit, you decide that you do not possess sufficient information to support the issuance of a search warrant, you should include all the relevant information that you do possess in your affidavit, but add a separate page at the end of this assignment discussing what additional investigative techniques you would use in order to turn up additional information which would be sufficient to support the issuance of such a search warrant.)

4. Challenging Warrants

After a search has been made pursuant to a warrant, defense counsel can subsequently challenge the lawfulness of the search based upon the insufficiency of the supporting affidavit in two different ways. <u>First</u>, defense counsel can argue that the supporting affidavit *on its face* did not establish sufficient probable cause to support issuance of the warrant (and, hence, that the evidence seized pursuant to execution of the warrant must be suppressed as the fruits of an unconstitutional search). <u>Second,</u> defense counsel can try to challenge the accuracy or veracity of the statements in the affidavit which on their face establish probable cause. However, as the following Supreme Court decision makes clear, it is very difficult for counsel to win such a challenge, to "*go behind*" the warrant.

Franks v. Delaware

438 U.S. 154 (1978).

MR. JUSTICE BLACKMUN delivered the opinion of the Court.

This case presents an important and longstanding issue of Fourth Amendment law. Does a defendant in a criminal proceeding ever have the right, under the Fourth and Fourteenth Amendments, subsequent to the ex parte issuance of a search warrant, to challenge the truthfulness of factual statements made in an affidavit supporting the warrant?

In the present case the Supreme Court of Delaware held, as a matter of first impression for it, that a defendant under no circumstances may so challenge the veracity of a sworn statement used by police to procure a search warrant. We reverse, and we hold that, where the defendant makes a substantial preliminary showing that a false statement knowingly and intentionally, or with reckless disregard for the truth, was included by the affiant in the warrant affidavit, and if the allegedly false statement is necessary to the finding of probable cause, the Fourth Amendment requires that a hearing be held at the defendant's request. In the event that at that hearing the allegation of perjury or reckless disregard is established by the defendant by a preponderance of the evidence, and, with the affidavit's false material set to one side, the

Food for Thought

Why do you think that the Delaware Supreme Court ruled below that a defendant could *never* "go behind" a search warrant affidavit? *Never!* Doesn't such a ruling mean that a search warrant could be issued based entirely upon lies and/or conjecture? How do the majority and dissenting Justices deal with this issue?

affidavit's remaining content is insufficient to establish probable cause, the search warrant must be voided and the fruits of the search excluded to the same extent as if probable cause was lacking on the face of the affidavit.

Whether the Fourth and Fourteenth Amendments, and the derivative exclusionary rule ever mandate that a defendant be permitted to attack the veracity of a warrant affidavit after the warrant has been issued and executed, is a question that encounters conflicting values. The bulwark of Fourth Amendment protection, of course, is the Warrant Clause, requiring that, absent certain exceptions, police obtain a warrant from a neutral and disinterested magistrate before embarking upon a search. In deciding today that, in certain circumstances, a challenge to a warrant's veracity must be permitted, we derive our ground from language of the Warrant Clause itself, which surely takes the affiant's good faith as its premise: "No Warrants shall issue, but upon probable cause, supported by Oath or affirmation." Judge Frankel, in *United States v. Halsey*, 257 F. Supp. 1002, 1005 (S.D.N.Y. 1966), aff'd, Docket No. 31369 (CA2, June 12, 1967) (unreported), put the matter simply: "When the Fourth Amendment demands a factual showing sufficient to comprise 'probable cause,' the obvious assumption is that there will be a *truthful* showing" (emphasis in original). This does not mean "truthful" in the sense that every fact recited in the warrant affidavit is necessarily correct, for probable cause may be founded upon hearsay and upon information received from informants, as well as upon information within the affiant's own knowledge that sometimes must be garnered hastily. But surely it is to be "truthful" in the sense that the information put forth is believed or appropriately accepted by the affiant as true. Because it is the magistrate who must determine independently whether there is probable cause, it would be an unthinkable imposition upon his authority if a warrant affidavit, revealed after the fact to contain a deliberately or recklessly false statement, were to stand beyond impeachment.

In saying this, however, one must give cognizance to competing values that lead us to impose limitations. They perhaps can be best addressed by noting the arguments of respondent and others against allowing veracity challenges. First, respondent argues that the exclusionary rule is not a personal constitutional right, but only a judicially created remedy extended where its benefit as a deterrent promises to outweigh the societal cost of its use; that the Court has declined to apply the exclusionary rule when illegally seized evidence is used to impeach the credibility of a defendant's testimony, is used in a grand jury proceeding, or is used in a civil trial; and that the Court similarly has restricted application of the Fourth Amendment exclusionary rule in federal habeas corpus review of a state conviction. Respondent argues that applying the exclusionary rule to another situation-the deterrence of deliberate or reckless untruthfulness in a warrant affidavit-is not justified for many of the same reasons that led to the above restrictions; interfering with a criminal conviction in order to deter official misconduct is a burden too great to impose on society.

Second, respondent argues that a citizen's privacy interests are adequately protected by a requirement that applicants for a warrant submit a sworn affidavit and by the magistrate's independent determination of sufficiency based on the face of the affidavit.

Third, it is argued that the magistrate already is equipped to conduct a fairly vigorous inquiry into the accuracy of the factual affidavit supporting a warrant application. He may question the affiant, or summon other persons to give testimony at the warrant proceeding. The incremental gain from a post-search adversary proceeding, it is said, would not be great.

Fourth, it is argued that it would unwisely diminish the solemnity and moment of the magistrate's proceeding to make his inquiry into probable cause reviewable in regard to veracity. The less final, and less deference paid to, the magistrate's determination of veracity, the less initiative will he use in that task.

Fifth, it is argued that permitting a post-search evidentiary hearing on issues of veracity would confuse the pressing issue of guilt or innocence with the collateral question as to whether there had been official misconduct in the drafting of the affidavit.

Sixth and finally, it is argued that a post-search veracity challenge is inappropriate because the accuracy of an affidavit in large part is beyond the control of the affiant. An affidavit may properly be based on hearsay, on fleeting observations, and on tips received from unnamed informants whose identity often will be properly protected from revelation under *McCray v. Illinois*, 386 U.S. 300 (1967).

None of these considerations is trivial. Indeed, because of them, the rule announced today has a limited scope, both in regard to when exclusion of the seized evidence is mandated, and when a hearing on allegations of misstatements must be accorded. But neither do the considerations cited by respondent and others have a fully controlling weight; we conclude that they are insufficient to justify an absolute ban on post-search impeachment of veracity. On this side of the balance, also, there are pressing considerations:

First, a flat ban on impeachment of veracity could denude the probable-cause requirement of all real meaning. The requirement that a warrant not issue "but upon probable cause, supported by Oath or affirmation," would be reduced to a nullity if a police officer was able to use deliberately falsified allegations to demonstrate probable cause, and, having misled the magistrate, then was able to remain confident that the ploy was worthwhile.

Second, the hearing before the magistrate not always will suffice to discourage lawless or reckless misconduct. The pre-search proceeding is necessarily ex parte, since the subject of the search cannot be tipped off to the application for a warrant lest he destroy or remove evidence. The usual reliance of our legal system on adversary proceedings itself should be an indication that an ex parte inquiry is likely to be less vigorous.

Third, the alternative sanctions of a perjury prosecution, administrative discipline, contempt, or a civil suit are not likely to fill the gap.

Fourth, allowing an evidentiary hearing, after a suitable preliminary proffer of material falsity, would not diminish the importance and solemnity of the warrant-issuing process. Our reluctance today to extend the rule of exclusion beyond instances of deliberate misstatements, and those of reckless disregard, leaves a broad field where the magistrate is the sole protection of a citizen's Fourth Amendment rights, namely, in instances where police have been merely negligent in checking or recording the facts relevant to a probable-cause determination.

Fifth, the claim that a post-search hearing will confuse the issue of the defendant's guilt with the issue of the State's possible misbehavior is footless. The hearing will not be in the presence of the jury. An issue extraneous to guilt already is examined in any probable-cause determination or review of probable cause.

Sixth and finally, as to the argument that the exclusionary rule should not be extended to a "new" area, we cannot regard any such extension really to be at issue here. Despite the deep skepticism of Members of this Court as to the wisdom of extending the exclusionary rule to collateral areas, such as civil or grand jury proceedings, the Court has not questioned, in the absence of a more efficacious sanction, the continued application of the rule to suppress evidence from the State's case where a

Food for Thought

Does the result of this balancing-of-interests analysis make sense to you? Would you have reached a different conclusion" Why?

Fourth Amendment violation has been substantial and deliberate. We see no principled basis for distinguishing between the question of the sufficiency of an affidavit, which also is subject to a post-search reexamination, and the question of its integrity.

In sum, and to repeat with some embellishment what we stated at the beginning of this opinion: There is, of course, a presumption of validity with respect to the affidavit supporting the search warrant. To mandate an evidentiary hearing, the challenger's attack must be more than conclusory and must be supported by more than a mere desire to cross-examine. There must be allegations of deliberate falsehood or of reckless disregard for the truth, and those allegations must be accompanied by an offer of proof. They should point out specifically the portion of the warrant affidavit that is claimed to be false; and they should be accompanied by a statement of supporting reasons. Allegations of negligence or innocent mistake are insufficient. The deliberate falsity or reckless disregard whose impeachment is permitted today is only that of the affiant, not of any nongovernmental informant. Finally, if these requirements are met, and if, when material that is the subject of the alleged falsity or reckless disregard is set to one side, there remains sufficient content in the warrant affidavit to support a finding of probable cause, no hearing is required. On the other hand, if the remaining content is insufficient, the defendant is entitled, under the Fourth and Fourteenth Amendments, to his hearing. Whether he will prevail at that hearing is, of course, another issue.

Because of Delaware's absolute rule, its courts did not have occasion to consider the proffer put forward by petitioner Franks. The judgment of the Supreme Court of Delaware is reversed.

MR. JUSTICE REHNQUIST, with whom THE CHIEF JUSTICE joins, dissenting.

If the function of the warrant requirement is to obtain the determination of a neutral magistrate as to whether sufficient grounds have been urged to support the issuance of a warrant, that function is fulfilled at the time the magistrate concludes that the requirement has been met. Like any other determination of a magistrate, of a court, or of countless other fact-finding tribunals, the decision may be incorrect as a matter of law. Even if correct, some inaccurate or falsified information may have gone into the making of the determination. But unless we are to exalt as the *ne plus ultra* of our system of criminal justice the absolute correctness of every factual determination made along the tortuous route from the filing of the complaint or the issuance of an indictment to the final determination that a judgment of conviction was properly obtained, we shall lose perspective as to the purposes of the system as well as of the warrant requirement of the Fourth and Fourteenth Amendments.

> ### Take Note
>
> Don't miss the point made by the majority that even if an affidavit averment is shown to have been a deliberate, out-and-out lie on the part of the affiant, the warrant is still not necessarily defective. If a sufficient offer of proof is made by the defendant that the affidavit in question contains deliberately or recklessly-made misstatements or fails to include such omissions, the subsequent procedure is that the court holding a *Franks* hearing must consider the affidavit, redacted to strike the appropriate material and to add the appropriate omitted material, and consider whether or not the affidavit—as so redacted—establishes sufficient probable cause to search the specified premises for the specified objects of the search. If it does, then despite whatever lies that may have been included, the search warrant is still good and the exclusionary rule inapplicable. If probable cause does not exist in the affidavit as redacted, the warrant is defective and the exclusionary rule applies to all evidence derived from its execution.

> ### Food for Thought
>
> Do you agree with then-Justice Rehnquist? Isn't there some virtue in finality, even if the issuing magistrate got it wrong only because he or she was misled?

Point for Discussion

Omission of Information

The *Franks* test for determining when defense counsel may successfully "go behind" statements in a warrant affidavit also applies to an affiant's reckless or intentional *omission* of material information from an affidavit. If the affiant knows-and intentionally or recklessly withholds-information from an affidavit which would have cast doubt upon the existence of probable cause had it been considered by the issuing magistrate, the search warrant is defective and the fruits of its execution may be suppressed.

Hypo 1: *Omitted Information About Search Target's Incarceration*

A drive-by shooting occurred in Santa Maria, California. Shots were fired from a vehicle into an occupied home, striking and injuring a young boy. Informants told the police that the occupants were formerly associated with the Tangas gang and that the shooting was a reaction to their disassociation from the gang. Police officers obtained a list of names of alleged Tangas members believed to be closely associated with the suspected shooters. Based on this and other information, an officer obtained a "multiple location gang association warrant," authorizing a search of seven individuals' homes based upon the belief that these individuals might be harboring weapons or evidence related to the shooting. The warrant affidavit failed to disclose, however, that Javier Bravo, Jr., one of the seven individuals, was at that time and for over six months, incarcerated in the California prison system and therefore not only was he not present in the Bravo home when the warrant was executed, but he could not have been involved in the shooting or the storage of weapons used in it. Assuming that evidence of criminal activity was seized in the execution of that warrant and criminal charges brought against one of the occupants of the Bravo home, could that occupant suppress the evidence based upon the omission of this information relating to Bravo's incarceration from the warrant application? Does it matter that the officer who prepared the affidavit did not know that Bravo was in custody? Should it matter? See *Bravo v. City of Santa Maria*, 665 F.3d 1076 (9th Cir. 2011).

Hypo 2: *Powder Not Crack Cocaine*

Eugenio Negron sold crack cocaine to an undercover police officer. After he was arrested, Negron agreed to cooperate with the police and told them that he had recently bought fifty grams of "drugs" from a person he knew only as "Fat Back," who resided at 50 Putnam Circle. Based on this information, officers obtained a warrant to search that address and discovered 17.4 kilograms of *powder* cocaine. Fat Back (who turned out to be Jimmy Rosario) was arrested and now seeks to suppress the seized cocaine, arguing that the affidavit used to obtain the search warrant was inaccurate as the affiant averred that Negron had bought 50 grams of "crack cocaine" from Rosario, when Negron later testified that he bought 50 grams of powder cocaine from him. The officer who prepared the affidavit conceded that he had simply assumed that the purchase was of crack cocaine because Negron had been arrested carrying crack cocaine. Is this misstatement sufficient to support suppression of the cocaine seized under *Franks*? *See United States v. Rosario*, 810 F. Supp.2d 375 (D. Mass. 2011).

Exercise: *Motion to Suppress Based on Bad Affidavit*

Take home and review one of the affidavits prepared previously in the Chapter 4(A)(3) Exercise. You are now defense counsel representing Durham after the search pursuant to a search warrant based upon this affidavit has taken place (and has produced evidence that the U.S. Attorney's Office seeks to use against Durham in a federal criminal prosecution). Assuming that the warrant issued based solely upon this affidavit (and ignoring any standing issues that might be present), prepare a Brief in Support of Defendant Durham's Motion to Suppress (of no more than 5 pages in length) contending that the affidavit was either insufficient to support the warrant on its face and/or that it was recklessly or intentionally misleading within the meaning of *Franks*.

5. The Particularity Requirement

The Fourth Amendment expressly requires that "no Warrants shall issue, but upon probable cause, and particularly describing the place to be searched, and the persons or things to be seized." The Supreme Court has made clear that "the uniformly applied rule is that a search conducted pursuant to a warrant that fails to conform to the particularity requirement of the Fourth Amendment is unconstitutional." *Massachusetts v. Sheppard*, 468 U.S. 981, 988 n. 5 (1984).

To answer the question just *how* particular a description of the place to be searched must be to satisfy the particularity requirement, the Supreme Court has adopted the following test: "It is enough if the description is such that the officer with a search warrant can with reasonable effort ascertain and identify the place intended." *Steele v. U.S. No. 1*, 267 U.S. 498, 503 (1925). As to the things to be seized, the Supreme Court has stated that if the language in a search warrant description is so imprecise as to have an "indiscriminate sweep," the search warrant is, accordingly, "constitutionally intolerable." *Stanford v. Texas*, 379 U.S. 476, 486 (1965).

United States v. Grubbs

547 U.S. 90 (2006).

JUSTICE SCALIA delivered the opinion of the Court.

Federal law enforcement officers obtained a search warrant for respondent's house on the basis of an affidavit explaining that the warrant would be executed only after a controlled delivery of contraband to that location. We address two challenges to the constitutionality of this anticipatory warrant.

Hear It

You can hear the oral argument in *Grubbs* at http://www.oyez.org/cases/2000-2009/2005/2005_04_1414.

Respondent Jeffrey Grubbs purchased a videotape containing child pornography from a Web site operated by an undercover postal inspector. Officers from the Postal Inspection Service arranged a controlled delivery of a package containing the videotape to Grubbs' residence. A postal inspector submitted a search warrant application to a Magistrate Judge for the Eastern District of California, accompanied by an affidavit describing the proposed operation in detail. The affidavit stated:

> "Execution of this search warrant will not occur unless and until the parcel has been received by a person(s) and has been physically taken into the residence. At that time, and not before, this search warrant will be executed by me and other United States Postal inspectors, with appropriate assistance from other law enforcement officers in accordance with this warrant's command."

In addition to describing this triggering condition, the affidavit referred to two attachments, which described Grubbs' residence and the items officers would seize. These attachments, but not the body of the affidavit, were incorporated into the requested warrant. The affidavit concluded: "Based upon the foregoing facts, I respectfully submit there exists probable cause to believe that the items set forth in Attachment B to this affidavit and the search warrant, will be found at Grubbs' residence, which residence is further described at Attachment A."

The Magistrate Judge issued the warrant as requested. Two days later, an undercover postal inspector delivered the package. Grubbs' wife signed for it and took the unopened package inside. The inspectors detained Grubbs as he left his home a few minutes later, then entered the house and commenced the search. Roughly 30 minutes into the search, Grubbs was provided with a copy of the warrant, which included both attachments but not the supporting affidavit that explained when the warrant would be executed. Grubbs consented to interrogation by the postal inspectors and admitted ordering the videotape. He was placed under arrest, and various items were seized, including the videotape. After moving unsuccessfully to suppress evidence seized during the search of his residence, Grubbs pleaded guilty to one count of receiving a visual depiction of a minor engaged in sexually explicit conduct, but reserved his right to appeal the denial of his motion to suppress. The Court of Appeals for the Ninth Circuit reversed.

An anticipatory warrant is "a warrant based upon an affidavit showing probable cause that at some future time (but not presently) certain evidence of crime will be located at a specified place." Most anticipatory warrants subject their execution to some condition precedent other than the mere passage of time-a so-called "triggering condition." The affidavit at issue here, for instance, explained that "execution of the search warrant will not occur unless and until the parcel containing child pornography has been received by a person(s) and has been physically taken into the residence." If the government were to execute an anticipatory warrant before the triggering condition occurred, there would be no reason to believe the item described in the warrant could be found at the searched location; by definition, the triggering condition which establishes probable cause has not yet been satisfied when the warrant is issued. Grubbs argues that for this reason anticipatory warrants contravene the Fourth Amendment's provision that "no Warrants shall issue, but upon probable cause."

We reject this view, as has every Court of Appeals to confront the issue. Probable cause exists when "there is a fair probability that contraband or evidence of a crime will be found in a particular place." Because the probable-cause requirement looks to whether evidence will be found when the search is conducted, all warrants are, in a sense, "anticipatory." In the typical case where the police seek permission to search a house for an item they believe is already located there, the magistrate's determination that there is probable cause for the search amounts to a prediction that the item will still be there when the warrant is executed.

Anticipatory warrants are, therefore, no different in principle from ordinary warrants. They require the magistrate to determine (1) that it is now probable that (2) contraband, evidence of a crime, or a fugitive will be on the described premises (3) when the warrant is executed. It should be

Take Note

Despite the unanimity in Courts of Appeals decisions on this point, *Grubbs* is notable because it is the *first* Supreme Court decision to expressly hold anticipatory warrants to be constitutional in the appropriate circumstances.

noted, however, that where the anticipatory warrant places a condition (other than the mere passage of time) upon its execution, the first of these determinations goes not merely to what will probably be found if the condition is met. (If that were the extent of the probability determination, an anticipatory warrant could be issued for every house in the country, authorizing search and seizure if contraband should be delivered-though for any single location there is no likelihood that contraband will be delivered.) Rather, the probability determination for a conditioned anticipatory warrant looks also to the likelihood that the condition will occur, and thus that a proper object of seizure will be on the described premises. In other words, for a conditioned anticipatory warrant to comply with the Fourth Amendment's requirement of probable cause, two prerequisites of probability must be satisfied. It must be true not only that if the triggering condition occurs "there is a fair probability that contraband or evidence of a crime will be found in a particular place," but also that there is probable cause to believe the triggering condition will occur. The supporting affidavit must provide the magistrate with sufficient information to evaluate both aspects of the probable-cause determination.

In this case, the occurrence of the triggering condition—successful delivery of the videotape to Grubbs' residence—would plainly establish probable cause for the search. In addition, the affidavit established probable cause to believe the triggering condition would be satisfied. Although it is possible that Grubbs could have refused delivery of the videotape he had ordered, that was unlikely. The Magistrate therefore "had a 'substantial basis for . . . concluding' that probable cause existed."

Take Note

Note the risk that exists when law enforcement officers obtain an anticipatory warrant, i.e. that the triggering condition upon which the warrant is based must *actually* occur; if it doesn't, the warrant is defective and unconstitutional.

The Ninth Circuit invalidated the anticipatory search warrant at issue here because the warrant failed to specify the triggering condition. The Fourth Amendment's particularity requirement, it held, "applies with full force to the conditions precedent to an anticipatory search warrant."

The Fourth Amendment, however, does not set forth some general "particularity requirement." It specifies only two matters that must be "particularly described" in the warrant: "the place to be searched" and "the persons or things to be seized." We have previously rejected efforts to expand the scope of this provision to embrace unenumerated matters.

Because the Fourth Amendment does not require that the triggering condition for an anticipatory search warrant be set forth in the warrant itself, the Court of Appeals erred in invalidating the warrant at issue here. The judgment of the Court of Appeals is reversed, and the case is remanded for further proceedings consistent with this opinion.

JUSTICE ALITO took no part in the consideration or decision of this case. JUSTICE SOUTER, with whom JUSTICE STEVENS and JUSTICE GINSBURG join, concurring in part and concurring in the judgment.

The Court notes that a warrant's failure to specify the place to be searched and the objects sought violates an express textual requirement of the Fourth Amendment, whereas the text says nothing about a condition placed by the issuing magistrate on the authorization to search (here, delivery of the package of contraband). That textual difference is, however, no authority for neglecting to specify the point or contingency intended by the magistrate to trigger authorization, and the government should beware of banking on the terms of a warrant without such specification. The notation of a starting date was an established feature even of the objectionable 18th-century writs of assistance.

Practice Pointer

Even though the *Grubbs* decision holds that the Fourth Amendment does not require that the triggering condition in an anticipatory warrant be particularized in the warrant itself (as opposed to the affidavit, where it needs to be included in order to establish prospective probable cause), it nonetheless *should* be included as a matter of good practice. That's the dissenters' real concern, namely that an anticipatory warrant that doesn't particularize the triggering condition will end up being executed by officers who don't realize that there is such a condition and they might execute the warrant before the condition takes place, thus rendering the warrant defective.

An issuing magistrate's failure to mention that condition can lead to several untoward consequences with constitutional significance. To begin with, a warrant that fails to tell the truth about what a magistrate authorized cannot inform the police officer's responsibility to respect the limits of authorization, a failing assuming real significance when the warrant is not executed by the official who applied for it and happens to know the unstated condition. The peril is that if an officer simply takes such a warrant on its face and makes the ostensibly authorized search before the unstated condition has been met, the search will be held unreasonable.

Hypo 1: *Which Apartment?*

The police had probable cause to believe that Daniels had made purchases of narcotics at 105 Wayne Avenue, but they were unsure in which apartment at that address he made the buys. A magistrate issued a warrant to search the apartment at 105 Wayne Avenue to which Daniels has "possession, custody, control or access," and further provided that "the search warrant for the premises will be executed if and only if the following specifically described events which give rise to probable cause actually occur so as to protect against premature execution of the search warrant, namely: (1) that Allen Daniels is secured outside 105 Wayne Avenue and (2) that a search of Allen Daniels reveals documentation or keys which identify the specific apartment inside 105 Wayne Avenue to which Allen Daniels has possession, custody, control, or access, or if he divulges such information to the officers executing the search warrant for his person. In the event that the officers are unable to identify the apartment utilized by Allen Daniels through the abovementioned means, this premises warrant will not be executed." After the conditions were satisfied, the police executed the warrant. Did this warrant describe the apartment with sufficient particularity to satisfy the requirements of the Fourth Amendment? *See State v. Marshall*, 199 N.J. 602, 974 A.2d 1038 (2009).

Hypo 2: *Particularity & John Doe's DNA*

Following a serious sex crime (forcible rape), although police did not know the name of the perpetrator of the crime, they were able to isolate and identify his DNA from sperm found on the victim. Shortly before the statute of limitations expired, although the police were still unable to identify the perpetrator, they applied for a "John Doe" arrest warrant based on the perpetrator's DNA profile. Shortly thereafter, a police lab technician was able to match John Doe's DNA to that of a man found in a police data base. The particularity requirement applies in the same fashion to arrest as to search warrants. Was it satisfied here, by a John Doe warrant that identified a suspect not by name, but only by his DNA profile? *See People v. Robinson*, 47 Cal.4th 1104, 104 Cal.Rptr.3d 727, 224 P.3d 55 (2010).

Hypo 3: *Seizing Safes*

Pursuant to a warrant authorizing them to search for stolen and forged checks, the police searched defendant's home. During the search, they found two locked safes capable of holding checks. Police seized the safes and transported them to the police station. When they were opened, they were found to contain methamphetamine. Defendant filed a motion to suppress on the basis that the safes were not particularly described in the search warrant and, hence, they could not be seized in order to be searched back at the police station. Is this a good argument? What if the safes had been unlocked or open when the police officers searched the home? Could they have been searched at that time? *See State v. Powell*, 306 S.W.3d 761 (Tex. Crim. App. 2010).

If executing officers mistakenly search the wrong search premises, i.e. a place not particularly described in the search warrant, that does not necessarily mean that the search is unconstitutional (or that the fruits of the search must be suppressed).

Maryland v. Garrison

480 U.S. 79 (1987).

JUSTICE STEVENS delivered the opinion of the Court.

Baltimore police officers obtained and executed a warrant to search the person of Lawrence McWebb and "the premises known as 2036 Park Avenue third floor apartment." When the police applied for the warrant and when they conducted the search pursuant to the warrant, they reasonably believed that there was only one apartment on the premises described in the warrant. In fact, the third floor was divided into two apartments, one occupied by McWebb and one by respondent Garrison. Before the officers executing the warrant became aware that they were in a separate apartment occupied by respondent, they had discovered the contraband that provided the basis for respondent's conviction for violating Maryland's Controlled Substances Act. The question presented is whether the seizure of that contraband was prohibited by the Fourth Amendment.

There is no question that the warrant was valid and was supported by probable cause. The trial court found, and the two appellate courts did not dispute, that after making a reasonable investigation, including a verification of information obtained from a reliable informant, an exterior examination of the three-story building at 2036 Park Avenue, and an inquiry of the utility company, the officer who obtained the warrant reasonably concluded that there was only one apartment on the third floor and that it was occupied by McWebb. Only after respondent's apartment had been entered and heroin, cash, and drug paraphernalia had been found did any of the officers realize that the third floor contained two apartments. As soon as they became aware of that fact, the search was discontinued. All of the officers reasonably believed that they were searching McWebb's apartment. No further search of respondent's apartment was made.

The manifest purpose of the particularity requirement was to prevent general searches. By limiting the authorization to search to the specific areas and things for which there is probable cause to search, the requirement ensures that the search will be carefully tailored to its justifications, and will not take on the character of the wide-ranging exploratory searches the Framers intended to prohibit. Thus, the scope of a lawful search is "defined by the object of the search and the places in which there is probable cause to believe that it may be found. Just as probable cause to believe that a stolen lawnmower may be found in a garage will not support a warrant to search an upstairs bedroom, probable cause to believe that undocumented aliens are being transported in a van will not justify a warrantless search of a suitcase."

Food for Thought

The police did not have probable cause to search Garrison's apartment. Was it really appropriate to interpret the Particularity Clause in such a way that its constitutional privacy protections are no longer present just because a police officer has made a mistake? What do you think?

In this case there is no claim that the "persons or things to be seized" were inadequately described or that there was no probable cause to believe that those things might be found in "the place to be searched" as it was described in the warrant. With the benefit of hindsight, however, we now know that the description of that place was broader than appropriate because it was based on the mistaken belief that there was only one apartment on the third floor of the building at 2036 Park Avenue. The question is whether that factual mistake invalidated a warrant that undoubtedly would have been valid if it had reflected a completely accurate understanding of the building's floor plan.

Plainly, if the officers had known, or even if they should have known, that there were two separate dwelling units on the third floor of 2036 Park Avenue, they would have been obligated to exclude respondent's apartment from the scope of the requested warrant. But we must judge the constitutionality of their conduct in light of the information available to them at the time they acted. Those items of evidence that emerge after the warrant is issued have no bearing on whether or not a warrant was validly issued. Just as the discovery of contraband cannot validate a warrant invalid when issued, so is it equally clear that the discovery of facts demonstrating that a valid warrant was unnecessarily broad does not retroactively invalidate the warrant. The validity of the warrant must be assessed on the basis of the information that the officers disclosed, or had a duty to discover and to disclose, to the issuing Magistrate. On the basis of that information, we agree with the conclusion of all three Maryland courts that the warrant, insofar as it authorized a search that turned out to be ambiguous in scope, was valid when it issued.

The question whether the execution of the warrant violated respondent's constitutional right to be secure in his home is somewhat less clear. If the officers had known, or should have known, that the third floor contained two apartments before they entered the living quarters on the third floor, and thus had been aware of the error in the warrant, they would have been obligated to limit their search to McWebb's apartment. Moreover, as the officers recognized, they were required to discontinue the search of respondent's apartment as soon as they discovered that there were two separate units on the third floor and therefore were put on notice of the risk that they might be in a unit erroneously included within the terms of the warrant. The officers' conduct and the limits of the search were based on the information available as the search proceeded. While the purposes justifying a police search strictly limit the permissible extent of the search, the Court has also recognized the need to allow some latitude for honest mistakes that are made by officers in the dangerous and difficult process of making arrests and executing search warrants. The objective facts available to the officers at the time suggested no distinction between McWebb's apartment and the third-floor premises.

Food for Thought

Shouldn't police officers *always* be on notice that there may be multiple units in an apartment building? The majority acknowledges that this would have been a different case if the executing officers *knew* there were actually two apartments on the third floor. But *shouldn't* they have realized this? Is this the sort of case where we should be concerned about police perjury? Do you suspect that the officers *really* knew they were in the wrong apartment? (But why would they want to search the wrong apartment?) Should we charge the police with taking more care to check out whether they are in the correct premises in multi-unit buildings?

For that reason, the officers properly responded to the command contained in a valid warrant even if the warrant is interpreted as authorizing a search limited to McWebb's apartment rather than the entire third floor. Prior to the officers' discovery of the factual mistake, they perceived McWebb's apartment and the third-floor premises as one and the same; therefore their execution of the warrant reasonably included the entire third floor.[13]

The judgment of the Court of Appeals is reversed.

---

[13] We expressly distinguish the facts of this case from a situation in which the police know there are two apartments on a certain floor of a building, and have probable cause to believe that drugs are being sold out of that floor, but do not know in which of the two apartments the illegal transactions are taking place. A search pursuant to a warrant authorizing a search of the entire floor under those circumstances would present quite different issues from the ones before us in this case.

JUSTICE BLACKMUN, with whom JUSTICE BRENNAN and JUSTICE MARSHALL join, dissenting.

Even if one accepts the majority's view that there is no Fourth Amendment violation where the officers' mistake is reasonable, it is questionable whether that standard was met in this case. The place at issue here is a small multiple-occupancy building. Such forms of habitation are now common in this country, particularly in neighborhoods with changing populations and of declining affluence. Accordingly, any analysis of the "reasonableness" of the officers' behavior here must be done with this context in mind. In the Court's view, the "objective facts" did not put the officers on notice that they were dealing with two separate apartments on the third floor until the moment, considerably into the search after they had rummaged through a dresser and a closet in respondent's apartment and had discovered evidence incriminating him, when they realized their "mistake." The Court appears to base its conclusion that the officers' error here was reasonable on the fact that neither McWebb nor respondent ever told the officers during the search that they lived in separate apartments.

In my view, however, the "objective facts" should have made the officers aware that there were two different apartments on the third floor well before they discovered the incriminating evidence in respondent's apartment. Before McWebb happened to drive up while the search party was preparing to execute the warrant, one of the officers, Detective Shea, somewhat disguised as a construction worker, was already on the porch of the row house and was seeking to gain access to the locked first-floor door that permitted entrance into the building. From this vantage point he had time to observe the seven mailboxes and bells; indeed, he rang all seven bells, apparently in an effort to summon some resident to open the front door to the search party. A reasonable officer in Detective Shea's position, already aware that this was a multiunit building and now armed with further knowledge of the number of units in the structure, would have conducted at that time more investigation to specify the exact location of McWebb's apartment before proceeding further. For example, he might have questioned another resident of the building.

A reasonable officer would have realized the mistake in the warrant during the moments following the officers' entrance to the third floor. In the open doorway to his apartment, they encountered respondent, clad in pajamas and wearing a half-body cast as a result of a recent spinal operation. It appears that respondent, together with McWebb and the passenger from McWebb's car, were shepherded into McWebb's apartment across the vestibule from his own. Once again, the officers were curiously silent. The informant had not led the officers to believe that anyone other than McWebb lived in the third-floor apartment; the search party had McWebb, the person targeted by the search warrant, in custody when it gained access to the vestibule; yet when they met respondent on the third floor, they simply asked him who he was but never where he lived. Had they done so, it is likely that they would have discovered the mistake in the warrant before they began their search.

Finally and most importantly, even if the officers had learned nothing from respondent, they should have realized the error in the warrant from their initial security sweep. Once on the third floor, the officers first fanned out through the rooms to conduct a preliminary check for other occupants who might pose a danger to them. As the map of the third floor demonstrates, the two apartments were almost a mirror image of each other-each had a bathroom, a kitchen, a living room, and a bedroom. Given the somewhat symmetrical layout of the apartments, it is difficult to imagine that, in the initial security sweep, a reasonable officer would not have discerned that two apartments were on the third floor, realized his mistake, and then confined the ensuing search to McWebb's residence.

Points for Discussion

a. Particularity and Affidavits

When faced with a challenge at a suppression hearing to the particularity of the description contained in a search warrant, courts generally look both to the actual descriptive language in the warrant itself and to the description contained in any accompanying affidavits, if such affidavits are physically attached to the warrant (and thus available to the executing officers for their consultation) and incorporated by suitable words of reference. Where there has been no such incorporation by reference, however, a warrant that does not otherwise satisfy the particularity requirement is unconstitutional. *See Groh v. Ramirez*, 540 U.S. 551 (2004).

b. Errors in Description

An error in the description of the place to be searched or the things to be seized in a search warrant does not render the warrant defective provided that other descriptive information in the warrant establishes with reasonable certainty the place to be searched or the things to be seized. *See, e.g., United States v. Brobst*, 558 F.3d 982, 992 (9th Cir. 2009) ("31 Driftwood Lane, Woods Bay, Montana" instead of "32877 Driftwood Lane, Bigfork, Montana" error OK where both the mailbox and the sign on the tree in front of the searched residence bore the search target's name); *United States v. Hang Le-Thy Tran*, 433 F.3d 472, 479-81 (6th Cir. 2006) ("937 28th Street S.W." instead of "931 28th Street S.W." error OK where executing officers knew correct address and mistake was typographic error); *People v. Amador*, 24 Cal.4th 387, 100 Cal.Rptr.2d 617, 621-25, 9 P.3d 993 (2000) ("two story single family residence located at 10817 Leland, Santa Fe Springs, County of Los Angeles" instead of correct one-story residence at 10811 Leland held not to constitute defective warrant where the executing officer knew the correct house and it had been shown to him by the informant); *State v. Grant*, 52 So.3d 149, 151-54 (La. Ct. App. 5 Cir. 2010) (434 Ocean Ave. instead of 474 Ocean Ave. and description of premises to be searched as a wooden structure with a tan door instead of stucco concrete structure with a white door errors held OK where "there was no reasonable probability that the wrong residence would be searched"); *People v DeWitt*, 107 A.D.3d 1452, 1452-53, 967 N.Y.S.2d 547 (2013) (error in listing particularly-described vehicle under the heading "Persons" instead of "Vehicles" held OK).

c. Badly-Described Items & Properly-Described Items

Where an item to be seized has not been particularly described, a search warrant which has otherwise been lawfully obtained and executed remains constitutional with respect to any remaining items to be seized that have been properly described in the warrant. *See, e.g., State v. Tucker*, 133 N.H. 204, 575 A.2d 810, 813-15 (1990) (Opinion of former Justice Souter before he was appointed to the Supreme Court) ("it is not apparent why the public interest in prosecuting crime should be taxed by suppressing any evidence beyond that obtained under the ostensible authority of the warrant's unduly general element"). In addition, those items not "particularly described" may be seizable under the plain view doctrine.

d. Overbreadth in Description

The Supreme Court has upheld the seizure of a sawed off shotgun pursuant to a warrant description of "all firearms," even though the executing officers knew that the shooting under investigation was committed with a different "black sawed off shotgun with a pistol grip." As the Court reasoned, "even if the scope of the warrant were overbroad in authorizing a search for all guns when there was information only about a specific one, that specific one was a sawed-off shotgun with a pistol grip, owned by a known gang member, who had just fired the weapon five times in public in an attempt to murder another person. Under these circumstances-set forth in the warrant-it would not have been unreasonable for an officer to conclude that there was a 'fair probability' that the sawed-off shotgun was not the only firearm Bowen owned. And it certainly would have been reasonable for an officer to assume that Bowen's sawed-off shotgun was illegal. Evidence of one crime is not always evidence of several, but given Bowen's possession of one illegal gun, his gang membership, his willingness to use the gun to kill someone, and his concern about the police, a reasonable officer could conclude that there would be additional illegal guns among others that Bowen owned." *Messerschmidt v. Millender*, 565 U.S. 535, 548-49 (2012).

Hypo 1: *Searches of Multi-Unit Buildings*

Law enforcement officers had probable cause to believe that defendant Will Nelson Clark was dealing drugs from inside a multi-unit building at 1015 Fairfield Avenue and also from the front porch of that building. Accordingly, they obtained a search warrant to search the entire premises of that building, including "any and all persons present at this location during execution of said search warrant, all rooms, contents of those rooms, including any computers and hard drives of same, hallways, stairways, storage areas, basement, attic areas, closets, any and all locked and secured areas, locked safes or containers and porches to said address." In one of the downstairs apartments belonging to defendant Clark, executing officers seized a quantity of drugs, which subsequently tested as cocaine base, approximately $1703 in cash, and various items of drug paraphernalia. Was this a valid search? *See United States v. Clark,* 638 F.3d 89 (2d Cir. 2011).

Hypo 2: *A Search For "Ladies' Costume Jewelry"*

A search warrant authorized executing officers to seize, *inter alia,* "lady's [sic] costume jewelry" from Jose Garcia-Perlera's apartment. The police possessed probable cause to believe that Garcia-Perlera had broken into and ransacked a victim's home, stealing money, a laptop computer, and multiple items of costume jewelry. Was this warrant sufficiently particular to justify the seizure of jewelry in the apartment, even non-costume jewelry? What do you think? *See Garcia-Perlera v. State,* 197 Md.App. 534, 14 A.3d 1164 (2011).

Hypo 3: *Searches of Computers*

Based on probable cause to believe that Payton was selling narcotics, a warrant was issued for the search of his home. The warrant particularly described "sales ledgers showing narcotics transactions such as pay/owe sheets", as well as "financial records of the person(s) in control of the residence or premises, bank accounts, loan applications, and income and expense records," but it did not explicitly authorize the search of computers. During the search, the police found no evidence relating to narcotics, but they did find a computer that was on with the screen saver activated. An officer moved the mouse and observed what he believed to be child pornography. The police then seized the computer on the grounds that they had the right to check it for records relating to drug transactions, and that they found the child pornography in "plain view" when they did. Payton claimed that, without specific authorization, the police had no right to examine his computer. Is he right? Did the search warrant authorize the officers to look at information on Payton's computer? Would it have made a difference if the officers had specified in their search warrant application that the records they were seeking might be in hard copy or electronic form? *See United States v. Payton*, 573 F.3d 859 (9th Cir. 2009).

Go Online

In the last couple of decades, searches and seizures of computers have posed a number of extremely complicated legal questions for courts and prosecutors and defense attorneys, as well. The law continues to develop on this subject, probably no faster than computer technology itself continues to develop. You might be interested in taking a look at the Justice Department's snapshot view of the developing law in this area. *See* Computer Crime and Intellectual Property Section, Criminal Division, U.S. Dept. of Justice, "Searching and Seizing Computers and Obtaining Electronic Evidence in Criminal Investigations" (Office of Legal Education, Executive Office for United States Attorneys 2009), http://www.justice. gov/criminal/cybercrime/docs/ssmanual2009.pdf. See also Office of the Attorney General, Memorandum: "Intake and Charging Policy for Computer Crime Matters" (September 11, 2014), https://www.justice.gov/criminal-ccips/file/904941/download.

Hypo 4: *Warrants to Hack Computers*

The Government applied for a search warrant targeting a computer allegedly used to violate federal bank fraud, identity theft, and computer security laws. Unknown persons were alleged to have committed these crimes using a particular email account via an unknown computer at an unknown location. The search was to be accomplished by contacting the Target Computer via a counterfeit email address, and then surreptitiously installing software designed not only to extract certain stored electronic records but also to generate user photographs and location information over a 30-day period. In other words, the Government sought a warrant "to hack" a computer suspected of criminal use. Does this application for a warrant raise particularity issues? Should this warrant application be granted? If a warrant application was denied on this basis, how else could the Government ever find this computer? *See In re Warrant to Search a Target Computer at Premises Unknown*, 958 F. Supp.2d 753 (S.D. Tex. 2013).

Hypo 5: *Searches of Data Files on Phones*

Law enforcement officers obtained a search warrant to search for "any or all files" on defendant's cell phone that constituted the offense of public indecency. Do you think that this description of the items to be seized was sufficiently particular to withstand constitutional scrutiny? Would there or should there be any data files that could not or should not be searched using this description? What do you think? *See* United States v. Winn, 79 F. Supp.3d 904 (S.D. Il. 2015).

Hypo 6: *Searches of Photographic Files on Phones*

Law enforcement officers obtained a search warrant to search defendant's iPhone for evidence of communications that would link him and another suspect to a shooting that occurred in the Hyde Park section of Boston. During the course of that search, the Government searched not only his contact lists and text messages, but also his photograph files. Defense counsel argues that photographs found in that search that linked defendant to the shooting had to be suppressed because there was no probable cause to search the iPhone's photograph files. Was defense counsel correct? If not, is there any limit to the data which the Government could lawfully search on that phone? Should there be? *See Com. v. Dorelas*, 473 Mass. 496, 43 N.E.3d 306, 313-314 (2016).

Hypo 7: *Forcing Manufacturers to Enable Government to Search Phones*

Assuming that Government agents have probable cause to suspect that data relevant to the commission of a crime is contained in data stored in a "locked" smartphone, should the Government have the right to force the phones' manufacturer to "unlock" that phone and "let them in?" Does it or should it matter that the Government has obtained a search warrant for the phone? See, e.g., *In re Apple, Inc.*, 149 F.Supp.3d 341 (E.D.N.Y. 2016). Does it or should it make a difference that the Government may be able to unlock that phone without the manufacturer's assistance, e.g. by employing a "hacker?" *See, e.g.*, Katie Benner & Eric Lichtblau, "U.S. Says It Has Unlocked iPhone Without Apple," New York Times p. A1 (March 28, 2016).

Hypo 8: *Particularity & Roving Wiretaps*

Federal and New Jersey law each contain a "roving wiretap" provision that allows law enforcement officers, under certain circumstances, to intercept communications on newly-discovered telephone facilities used by a wiretap target, without first returning to the judge who issued the wiretap warrant. A criminal defendant challenged this roving wiretap provision, claiming that because it does not require law enforcement to identify a telephone facility with particularity and get court approval in advance, it violates both the Fourth Amendment and New Jersey constitutional law. Does it? What do you think? If a search target moved from one house to another, should a search warrant for the target in the first, particularized house, automatically move to the next house, without having to go back to the issuing judge for approval? *See State v. Feliciano*, 224 N.J. 351, 132 A.3d 1245 (2016).

6. Warrant Execution

Wilson v. Arkansas

514 U.S. 927 (1995).

JUSTICE THOMAS delivered the opinion of the Court.

At the time of the framing, the common law of search and seizure recognized a law enforcement officer's authority to break open the doors of a dwelling, but generally indicated that he first ought to announce his presence and authority. In this case, we hold that this common-law "knock and announce" principle forms a part of the reasonableness inquiry under the Fourth Amendment.

Hear It

You can hear the oral argument in *Wilson* at http://www.oyez.org/cases/1990-1999/1994/1994_94_5707.

During November and December 1992, petitioner Sharlene Wilson made a series of narcotics sales to an informant acting at the direction of the Arkansas State Police. In late November, the informant purchased marijuana and methamphetamine at the home that petitioner shared with Bryson Jacobs. On December 30, the informant telephoned petitioner at her home and arranged to meet her at a local store to buy some marijuana. According to testimony presented below, petitioner produced a semiautomatic pistol at this meeting and waved it in the informant's face, threatening to kill her if she turned out to be working for the police. Petitioner then sold the informant a bag of marijuana.

The next day, police officers applied for and obtained warrants to search petitioner's home and to arrest both petitioner and Jacobs. Affidavits filed in support of the warrants set forth the details of the narcotics transactions and stated that Jacobs had previously been convicted of arson and firebombing. The search was conducted later that afternoon. Police officers found the main door to petitioner's home open. While opening an unlocked screen door and entering the residence, they identified themselves as police officers and stated that they had a warrant. Once inside the home, the officers seized marijuana, methamphetamine, valium, narcotics paraphernalia, a gun, and ammunition. They also found petitioner in the bathroom, flushing marijuana down the toilet. Petitioner and Jacobs were arrested and charged with delivery of marijuana, delivery of methamphetamine, possession of drug paraphernalia, and possession of marijuana.

Before trial, petitioner filed a motion to suppress the evidence seized during the search. Petitioner asserted that the search was invalid on various grounds, including that the officers had failed to "knock and announce" before entering her home. The trial court summarily denied the suppression motion. After a jury trial, petitioner was convicted of all charges and sentenced to 32 years in prison. The Arkansas Supreme Court affirmed, finding "no authority for petitioner's theory that the knock and announce principle is required by the Fourth Amendment." We granted certiorari to resolve the conflict among the lower courts as to whether the common-law knock-and-announce principle forms a part of the Fourth Amendment reasonableness inquiry. We hold that it does, and accordingly reverse and remand.

The Fourth Amendment to the Constitution protects "the right of the people to be secure in their persons, houses, papers, and effects, against unreasonable searches and seizures." In evaluating the scope of this right, we have looked to the traditional protections against unreasonable searches and seizures afforded by the common law at the time of the framing. An examination of the common law of search and seizure leaves no doubt that the reasonableness of a search of a dwelling may depend in part on whether law enforcement officers announced their presence and authority prior to entering.

Although the common law generally protected a man's house as "his castle of defense and asylum," common-law courts long have held that "when the King is party, the sheriff (if the doors be not open) may break the party's house, either to arrest him, or to do other execution of the King's process, if otherwise he cannot enter." To this rule, however, common-law courts appended an important qualification:

"But before he breaks it, he ought to signify the cause of his coming, and to make request to open doors, for the law without a default in the owner abhors the destruction or breaking of any house (which is for the habitation and safety of man) by which great damage and inconvenience might ensue to the party, when no default is in him; for perhaps he did not know of the process, of which, if he had notice, it is to be presumed that he would obey it."

Several prominent founding-era commentators agreed on this basic principle. According to Sir Matthew Hale, the "constant practice" at common law was that "the officer may break open the door, if he be sure the offender is there, if after acquainting them of the business, and demanding the prisoner, he refuses to open the door." William Hawkins propounded a similar principle: "the law doth never allow" an officer to break open the door of a dwelling "but in cases of necessity," that is, unless he "first signify to those in the house the cause of his coming, and request them to give him admittance." Sir William Blackstone stated simply that the sheriff may "justify breaking open doors, if the possession be not quietly delivered."

The common-law knock-and-announce principle was woven quickly into the fabric of early American law. Most of the States that ratified the Fourth Amendment had enacted constitutional provisions or statutes generally incorporating English common law, and a few States had enacted statutes specifically embracing the common-law view that the breaking of the door of a dwelling was permitted once admittance was refused.

Our own cases have acknowledged that the common law principle of announcement is "embedded in Anglo-American law," but we have never squarely held that this principle is an element of the reasonableness inquiry under the Fourth Amendment. We now so hold. Given the longstanding common-law endorsement of the practice of announcement, we have little doubt that the Framers of the Fourth Amendment thought that the method of an officer's entry into a dwelling was among the factors to be considered in assessing the reasonableness of a search or seizure.

This is not to say, of course, that every entry must be preceded by an announcement. The Fourth

Take Note

Aside from the common law history recounted by Justice Thomas, it is useful to understand just why entries without the sort of notice required by the knock and announce doctrine are problematic as a matter of common sense in addition to common law. As the Wisconsin Supreme Court made the point, "the knock and announce rule has three primary justifications. First, it serves to protect the safety of police officers and others by warning the occupants of the officers' entrance. Second, it protects the occupants' limited privacy interests when the police already have a warrant. Third, it helps prevent the physical destruction of property." *State v. Stevens*, 511 N.W.2d 591, 594 (Wis. 1994), *cert. denied*, 515 U.S. 1102 (1995).

Amendment's flexible requirement of reasonableness should not be read to mandate a rigid rule of announcement that ignores countervailing law enforcement interests. As even petitioner concedes, the common-law principle of announcement was never stated as an inflexible rule requiring announcement under all circumstances.

Because the common-law rule was justified in part by the belief that announcement generally would avoid "the destruction or breaking of any house by which great damage and inconvenience might ensue," courts acknowledged that the presumption in favor of announcement would yield under circumstances presenting a threat of physical violence. And courts have indicated that unannounced entry may be justified where police officers have reason to believe that evidence would likely be destroyed if advance notice were given.

We need not attempt a comprehensive catalog of the relevant countervailing factors here. For now, we leave to the lower courts the task of determining the circumstances under which an unannounced entry is reasonable under the Fourth Amendment. We simply hold that although a search or seizure of a dwelling might be constitutionally defective if police officers enter without prior announcement, law enforcement interests may also establish the reasonableness of an unannounced entry.

Take Note

It is important to recognize that the knock and announce doctrine consists of *three* separate and independent elements: (a) announcement of the presence of the police (their "identity"); (b) announcement of the police purpose (*e.g.*, "We've got a warrant to search your apartment!"); and (c) delay prior to entry sufficient to permit the occupants to open the door. Failure by an executing officer to comply sufficiently with *any one* of these three requirements renders the warrant execution defective.

Respondent contends that the judgment below should be affirmed because the unannounced entry in this case was justified for two reasons. First, respondent argues that police officers reasonably believed that a prior announcement would have placed them in peril, given their knowledge that petitioner had threatened a government informant with a semiautomatic weapon and that Mr. Jacobs had previously been convicted of arson and firebombing. Second, respondent suggests that prior announcement would have produced an unreasonable risk that petitioner would destroy easily disposable narcotics evidence.

These considerations may well provide the necessary justification for the unannounced entry in this case. Because the Arkansas Supreme Court did not address their sufficiency, however, we remand to allow the state courts to make any necessary findings of fact and to make the determination of reasonableness in the first instance. The judgment of the Arkansas Supreme Court is reversed.

Points for Discussion

a. No Federal Exclusionary Remedy

As discussed in more detail in Chapter 8, the federal exclusionary rule does not apply in these situations. In *Hudson v. Michigan*, 547 U.S. 586 (2006), police waited only three to five seconds after knocking on a suspect's door before entering to execute a search warrant. Although the Court held that the police violated the "knock and announce" requirement, a majority of the Court, significantly, held that the evidence should not be excluded because the federal exclusionary rule does not apply to knock and announce violations.

b. State Exclusionary Rules

Some states, however, continue to apply an exclusionary rule in cases involving knock and announce violations pursuant to their own state constitutions. *See, e.g., State v. Rodriguez*, 399 N.J.Super. 192, 203, 943 A.2d 901, 908 (App. Div. 2008) ("Although conclusive as to the application of the Fourth Amendment, even if by the barest of margins, Hudson by no means governs the application of our state constitution to a knock and announce violation."); *State v. Jean-Paul*, 2013-NMCA-032, 295 P.3d 1072, 1076-77 (N.M. Ct. App. 2013) ("the remedy for any violation of Article II, Section 10's knock-and-announce requirement continues to be suppression of the evidence"); *State v. Majors*, 318 S.W.3d 850, 858-59 (Tenn. 2010) ("except in certain exigent circumstances, failure to comply with the rule in Tennessee is grounds for excluding any evidence seized under the search warrant.").

c. How Loud is Loud Enough?

The announcement of identity and purpose need not be shouted, but it must be loud enough to be reasonably audible by the occupants of the search premises. *Compare United States v. Spriggs*, 996 F.2d 320, 322-23 (D.C. Cir.), *cert. denied*, 510 U.S. 938 (1993) (announcement held appropriate where it was "'slightly above a normal tone of voice'—and thus apparently sufficient to alert the residents of the apartment") *with People v. Ortiz*, 569 N.W.2d 653, 658-59 (Mich. Ct. App. 1997) (announcement held constitutionally deficient where "five persons within earshot and in varying positions could not hear' it; "the notice given by the police was not reasonably calculated to provide notice to the occupants under the circumstances and was therefore inadequate").

Richards v. Wisconsin

520 U.S. 385 (1997).

JUSTICE STEVENS delivered the opinion of the Court.

In *Wilson v. Arkansas*, we held that the Fourth Amendment incorporates the common law requirement that police officers entering a dwelling must knock on the door and announce

Hear It

You can hear the oral argument in *Richards* at http://www.oyez.org/cases/1990-1999/1996/1996_96_5955.

their identity and purpose before attempting forcible entry. At the same time, we recognized that the "flexible requirement of reasonableness should not be read to mandate a rigid rule of announcement that ignores countervailing law enforcement interests" and left "to the lower courts the task of determining the circumstances under which an unannounced entry is reasonable under the Fourth Amendment."

In this case, the Wisconsin Supreme Court concluded that police officers are never required to knock and announce their presence when executing a search warrant in a felony drug investigation. We disagree with the court's conclusion that the Fourth Amendment permits a blanket exception to the knock-and-announce requirement for this entire category of criminal activity.

On December 31, 1991, police officers in Madison, Wisconsin obtained a warrant to search Steiney Richards' hotel room for drugs and related paraphernalia. The search warrant was the culmination of an investigation that had uncovered substantial evidence that Richards was one of several individuals dealing drugs out of hotel rooms in Madison. The police requested a warrant that would have given advance authorization for a "no-knock" entry into the hotel room, but the magistrate explicitly deleted those portions of the warrant.

The officers arrived at the hotel room at 3:40 a.m. Officer Pharo, dressed as a maintenance man, led the team. With him were several plainclothes officers and at least one man in uniform. Officer Pharo knocked on Richards' door and, responding to the query from inside the room, stated that he was a maintenance man. With the chain still on the door, Richards cracked it open. Although there is some dispute as to what occurred next, Richards acknowledges that when he opened the door he saw the man in uniform standing behind Officer Pharo. He quickly slammed the door closed and, after waiting two or three seconds, the officers began kicking and ramming the door to gain entry to the locked room. At trial, the officers testified that they identified themselves as police while they were kicking the door in. When they finally did break into the room, the officers caught Richards trying to escape through the window. They also found cash and cocaine hidden in plastic bags above the bathroom ceiling tiles.

Richards sought to have the evidence from his hotel room suppressed on the ground that the officers had failed to knock and announce their presence prior to forcing entry into the room. The trial court denied the motion. The Wisconsin Supreme Court affirmed, concluding that exigent circumstances justifying a no-knock entry are always present in felony drug cases.

We recognized in *Wilson* that the knock-and-announce requirement could give way "under circumstances presenting a threat of physical violence," or "where police officers have reason to believe that evidence would likely be destroyed if advance notice were given." It is indisputable that felony drug investigations may frequently involve both of these circumstances. The question we must resolve is whether this fact justifies dispensing with case-by-case evaluation of the manner in which a search was executed.

The Wisconsin court explained its blanket exception as necessitated by the special circumstances of today's drug culture, and the State asserted at oral argument that the blanket exception was reasonable in "felony drug cases because of the convergence in a violent and dangerous form of commerce of weapons and the destruction of drugs." But creating exceptions to the knock-and-announce rule based on the "culture" surrounding a general category of criminal behavior presents at least two serious concerns.

First, the exception contains considerable overgeneralization. For example, while drug investigation frequently does pose special risks to officer safety and the preservation of evidence, not every drug investigation will pose these risks to a substantial degree.

A second difficulty with permitting a criminal-category exception to the knock-and-announce requirement is that the reasons for creating an exception in one category can, relatively easily, be applied to others. Armed bank robbers, for example, are, by definition, likely to have weapons, and the fruits of their crime may be destroyed without too much difficulty. If a per se exception were allowed for each category of criminal investigation that included a considerable-albeit hypothetical-risk of danger to officers or destruction of evidence, the knock-and-announce element of the Fourth Amendment's reasonableness requirement would be meaningless.

Thus, the fact that felony drug investigations may frequently present circumstances warranting a no-knock entry cannot remove from the neutral scrutiny of a reviewing court the reasonableness of the police decision not to knock and announce in a particular case. Instead, in each case, it is the duty of a court confronted with the question to determine whether the facts and circumstances of the particular entry justified dispensing with the knock-and-announce requirement.

In order to justify a "no-knock" entry, the police must have a reasonable suspicion that knocking and announcing their presence, under the particular circumstances, would be dangerous or futile, or that it would inhibit the effective investigation of the crime by, for example, allowing the destruction of evidence. This standard—as opposed to a probable cause requirement— strikes the appropriate balance between the legitimate law enforcement concerns at issue in the execution of search warrants and the individual privacy interests affected by no-knock entries. This showing is not high, but the police should be required to make it whenever the reasonableness of a no-knock entry is challenged.

Take Note

The *Richards* decision is important because it makes it clear that exigency-based exceptions (involving danger or destruction of evidence) to the knock-and-announce doctrine are not "automatic" (so called *per se* or "blanket" exceptions), i.e. exigency must be established individually in each particular case. But *Richards* is also important because it establishes the actual standard to be met by executing officers before exigency is recognized as an exception, namely a "*reasonable suspicion*" standard. Is this standard too low?

Although we reject the Wisconsin court's blanket exception to the knock-and-announce requirement, we conclude that the officers' no-knock entry into Richards' hotel room did not violate the Fourth Amendment. The circumstances in this case show that the officers had a reasonable suspicion that Richards might destroy evidence if given further opportunity to do so.

The judge who heard testimony at Richards' suppression hearing concluded that it was reasonable for the officers executing the warrant to believe that Richards knew, after opening the door to his hotel room the first time, that the men seeking entry to his room were the police. Once the officers reasonably believed that Richards knew who they were, the court concluded, it was reasonable for them to force entry immediately given the disposable nature of the drugs.

In arguing that the officers' entry was unreasonable, Richards places great emphasis on the fact that the magistrate who signed the search warrant for his hotel room deleted the portions of the proposed warrant that would have given the officers permission to execute a no-knock entry. But this fact does not alter the reasonableness of the officers' decision, which must be evaluated as of the time they entered the hotel room. At the time the officers obtained the warrant, they did not have evidence sufficient, in the judgment of the magistrate, to justify a no-knock warrant. Of course, the magistrate could not have anticipated in every particular the circumstances that would confront the officers when they arrived at Richards' hotel room.[4] These actual circumstances—petitioner's apparent recognition of the officers

---

[4] A number of States give magistrate judges the authority to issue "no-knock" warrants if the officers demonstrate ahead of time a reasonable suspicion that entry without prior announcement will be

combined with the easily disposable nature of the drugs—justified the officers' ultimate decision to enter without first announcing their presence and authority.

Accordingly, although we reject the blanket exception to the knock-and-announce requirement for felony drug investigations, the judgment of the Wisconsin Supreme Court is affirmed.

Point for Discussion

Futile Gestures

Note that the *Richards* decision includes a reference not only to danger and evidentiary destruction exceptions to the knock and announce requirement, but also refers to situations where announcing (and/or delaying) would be "futile." Although not cited expressly by the Court, there are a number of lower court decisions which hold that the knock and announce doctrine is excused where the giving of notice would be a "futile (or useless) gesture." *See, e.g., United States v. Metz*, 608 F.2d 147 (5th Cir. 1979), *cert. denied*, 449 U.S. 821 (1980) (failure to knock and announce held reasonable where one occupant was in police custody and yelled to other occupants inside that the police were standing outside); *People v. Uhler*, 256 Cal. Rptr. 336 (Cal. Ct. App. 1989) (failure to delay after knock and announce held reasonable where occupants saw the executing officer through the screen door); *State v. Kelley*, 265 Neb. 563, 658 N.W.2d 279, 285-90 (2003) ("the deputies could reasonably infer that it would have been futile to knock and announce their identity and purpose for a substantial period of time given that Kelley's wife looked out the window and proceeded away from the directly adjacent door rather than responding to the deputies' knocking"). Indeed, the *Richards* case itself is, in application, at least in part, a "futile gesture" case as Richards had already seen a uniformed police officer in the hallway and slammed the door shut for that reason. (It is also an exigency-based, evidentiary-destruction exception case.)

Hypo 1: *Entry After Anonymous Tip*

Police officers received an anonymous uncorroborated tip that a house contained a methamphetamine lab and firearms. Based on that tip, they obtained a warrant to search the house. Must the police knock and announce themselves before entering the residence? *See Doran v. Eckold*, 409 F.3d 958 (8th Cir. 2005).

---

appropriate in a particular context. The practice of allowing magistrates to issue no-knock warrants seems entirely reasonable when sufficient cause to do so can be demonstrated ahead of time. But, as the facts of this case demonstrate, a magistrate's decision not to authorize a no-knock entry should not be interpreted to remove the officers' authority to exercise independent judgment concerning the wisdom of a no-knock entry at the time the warrant is being executed.

Hypo 2: *Entry After Surveillance Evidence*

Would your answer to Hypo 1 be affected by the fact that, before conducting the search, the police staked out the house and obtained additional evidence suggesting:

A. A certainty that a methamphetamine lab existed on the premises?

B. A certainty that firearms were present on the premises?

C. The presence of individuals with criminal records evidencing their prior commission of violent felonies?

Hypo 3: What Was Being Flushed?

Law enforcement officers executing a search warrant for narcotics broke down the door and entered forcibly after no one answered their announcement. As the officers entered, they heard a toilet running. They found 500 grams of crack cocaine in the residence, including some in the toilet. Do you think that the sound of a toilet flushing always justifies a forcible entry, i.e. that an occupant might be trying to destroy evidence? Does it matter that the officers did not actually hear the toilet running until after they entered? *See United States v. Williams*, 79 F. Supp.3d 888 (S.D. Ill. 2015).

Points for Discussion

a. Detention During Execution of Warrant

In *Ybarra v. Illinois*, 444 U.S. 85 (1979), the Supreme Court struck down an Illinois statute that authorized law enforcement officers to detain and search any person found on premises being searched pursuant to a search warrant. "The 'narrow scope' of the *Terry* exception does not permit a frisk for weapons on less than reasonable belief or suspicion directed at the person to be frisked, even though that person happens to be on premises where an authorized narcotics search is taking place."

Nevertheless, in *Michigan v. Summers*, 452 U.S. 692 (1981), the Court upheld police detention of the occupant of a house while a search warrant for the house was being executed. The Court held that the "limited intrusion on the personal security" of the person detained was justified "by such substantial law enforcement interests" that the seizure could be made on articulable suspicion not amounting to probable cause.

In *Muehler v. Mena*, 544 U.S. 93 (2005), the Court ruled that—in the proper circumstances—an individual detained while a search warrant is being executed may be held for a period of 2 to 3 hours, and also may be handcuffed during that period. As Chief Justice Rehnquist explained for a majority of the Court:

> This was no ordinary search. The governmental interests in not only detaining, but using handcuffs, are at their maximum when, as here, a warrant authorizes a search for weapons and a wanted gang member resides on the premises. In such inherently dangerous situations, the use of handcuffs minimizes the risk of harm to both officers and occupants. Though this safety risk inherent in executing a search warrant for weapons was sufficient to justify the use of handcuffs, the need to detain multiple occupants made the use of handcuffs all the more reasonable.

Subsequently, in *Los Angeles County, California v. Rettele*, 550 U.S. 609 (2007), the Court upheld as reasonable the detention of two occupants of a house being searched (mistakenly as the police officers were in the wrong house) pursuant to search warrant. These occupants, a man and a woman, Rettele and Sadler, had been sleeping naked when the officers burst in. They were then made to stand naked at gunpoint for a few minutes with their hands up before being allowed to dress. The Court ruled as follows:

> In executing a search warrant officers may take reasonable action to secure the premises and to ensure their own safety and the efficacy of the search. The test of reasonableness under the Fourth Amendment is an objective one. Unreasonable actions include the use of excessive force or restraints that cause unnecessary pain or are imposed for a prolonged and unnecessary period of time.

> The orders by the police to the occupants, in the context of this lawful search, were permissible, and perhaps necessary, to protect the safety of the deputies. Blankets and bedding can conceal a weapon, and one of the suspects was known to own a firearm, factors which underscore this point. The Constitution does not require an officer to ignore the possibility that an armed suspect may sleep with a weapon within reach.

> The deputies needed a moment to secure the room and ensure that other persons were not close by or did not present a danger. Deputies were not required to turn their backs to allow Rettele and Sadler to

retrieve clothing or to cover themselves with the sheets. This is not to say, of course, that the deputies were free to force Retelle and Sadler to remain motionless and standing for any longer than necessary. But there is no accusation that the detention here was prolonged. The deputies left the home less than 15 minutes after arriving.

The Fourth Amendment allows warrants to issue on probable cause, a ✓ standard well short of absolute certainly. Valid warrants will issue to search the innocent, and people like Rettele and Sadler unfortunately bear the cost. Officers executing search warrants on occasion enter a house when residents are engaged in private activity; and the resulting frustration, embarrassment, and humiliation may be real, as was true here. When officers execute a valid warrant and act in a reasonable manner to protect themselves from harm, however, the Fourth Amendment is not violated.

b. Proximity of Detention to Search Premises

In *Bailey v. United States*, 568 U.S. 186 (2013), the Supreme Court ruled that "detentions incident to the execution of a search warrant are reasonable under the Fourth Amendment because the limited intrusion on personal liberty is outweighed by the special law enforcement interests at stake." But, the Court added, "once an individual has left the immediate vicinity of a premises to be searched, however, detentions must be justified by some other rationale." The *Bailey* Court ruled unconstitutional the stop of vehicle and a search of its occupants who had been seen five minutes earlier, exiting an apartment which was about to be searched. The stop took place about a mile away from the apartment. The Court found this sort of detention more intrusive than a detention at the scene of the search:

Hear It

You can listen to the oral argument before the Supreme Court in the *Bailey* case at http://www.oyez.org/cases/2010-2019/2012/2012_11_770.

> Where officers arrest an individual away from his home, there is an additional level of intrusiveness. A public detention, even if merely incident to a search, will resemble a full-fledged arrest. As demonstrated here, detention beyond the immediate vicinity can involve an initial detention away from the scene and a second detention at the residence. In between, the individual will suffer the additional indignity of a compelled transfer back to the premises, giving all the appearances of an arrest. The detention here was more intrusive than a usual detention at the search scene. Bailey's car was stopped; he was ordered to step out and was detained in full public view; he was handcuffed, transported in a marked patrol car, and detained further outside the apartment. These facts illustrate that detention away from a premises where police are already present often will be more intrusive than detentions at the scene.

Hence, the types of detentions held reasonable in *Summers* must be limited to the "immediate vicinity" of the search, which the search in *Bailey* was not:

> Limiting the rule in *Summers* to the area in which an occupant poses a real threat to the safe and efficient execution of a search warrant ensures that the scope of the detention incident to a search is confined to its underlying justification. Once an occupant is beyond the immediate vicinity of the premises to be searched, the search-related law enforcement interests are diminished and the intrusiveness of the detention is more severe.

> Here, petitioner was detained at a point beyond any reasonable understanding of the immediate vicinity of the premises in question; and so this case presents neither the necessity nor the occasion to further define the meaning of immediate vicinity. In closer cases courts can consider a number of factors to determine whether an occupant was detained within the immediate vicinity of the premises to be searched, including the lawful limits of the premises, whether the occupant was within the line of sight of his dwelling, the ease of reentry from the occupant's location, and other relevant factors.

Hypo: *Stop of Car Away From Search Premises So As Not To Alert Occupants*

Local police officers obtained a search warrant to search an apartment at 117 Selman for narcotics. Before announcing and entering, they surveilled the location from a distance for a few minutes, and, while there, observed Daryl Nelson, who they knew lived in that apartment, arrive and a few minutes later, depart in a car. The officers quickly contacted nearby DEA agents who stopped Nelson's vehicle about one mile away from his apartment. One of the executing officers testified he wanted the vehicle stop made far enough away from the residence so that no other possible target would be alerted to the police presence and impending search. After the stop, Nelson eventually consented to a search of the car, and a bag of marijuana was found. Was the search warrant for narcotics in Nelson's apartment a sufficient basis for stopping him in his car one mile away? Can the bag of marijuana found in the car be suppressed? *State v. Nelson*, 215 So.3d 389 (La. Ct. App. 2 Cir. 2017).

c. Time Limits for Execution

A search warrant must be executed within the time period prescribed by the issuing magistrate, not to exceed the period established for execution of a search warrant in the applicable jurisdiction. This time limit, established by statute or court rule, is most commonly 10 days, although states have set limits as various as 2 to 60 days. *See, e.g.,* Fed. R. Crim. P. 41(e)(2)(A) (i) (federal time period not to exceed 14 days.)

d. Nighttime Execution

Most jurisdictions require law enforcement officers applying for a search warrant to be executed during the nighttime to make a special showing of necessity to search at that time. See, e.g., Fed. R. Crim. P. 41(e)(2)(A)(ii) ("The warrant must command the officer to execute the warrant during the daytime, unless the judge for good cause expressly authorizes execution at another time."). In about half of these jurisdictions, however, law enforcement failures to follow nighttime search requirements have been held not to constitute error of a constitutional dimension. Although three justices of the Supreme Court held in 1974 that this requirement is a federal constitutional requirement, *Gooding v. United States,* 416 U.S. 430 (1974), this proposition has never been accepted by a majority of the Court.

Global View

The Brazilian Constitution of 1988, tit. II, chapt. I, art. 5 (XI), provides that homes may not be entered except by court order "during the day except in the event of 'flagrante delicto' or disaster, or to give help." Would this sort of provision be preferable to the U.S. Constitution's silence on this subject?

Hypo: *Nighttime Searches for Narcotics*

Police officers received numerous anonymous tips on a narcotics tip line that Todd Zeller, living at 114 24th Street South in Fargo, North Dakota, was selling methamphetamine from his home. They sent an undercover agent to the area and he made a "controlled buy" of meth from Zeller in the vicinity of that residence. The police then obtained a search warrant to search 114 24th Street South authorizing a nighttime search, and the warrant was executed at 4:00 am. Nighttime searches in North Dakota are only permitted when police demonstrate "reasonable cause" to search at night. The detective seeking the warrant included a special request for nighttime service authorization "to allow officers the ability to get closer to the residence before being detected under the cover of darkness." The affidavit also stated, "entry of law enforcement in this manner will be safer to those inside as well as the law enforcement officers executing the search warrant." Was this nighttime search justified? *See State v. Zeller,* 845 N.W.2d 6 (N.D. 2014).

United States v. Banks

540 U.S. 31 (2003).

JUSTICE SOUTER delivered the opinion of the Court.

Officers executing a warrant to search for cocaine in respondent Banks's apartment knocked and announced their authority. The question is whether their 15-to-20-second wait before a forcible entry satisfied the Fourth Amendment. We hold that it did.

Hear It

You can hear the oral argument in *Banks* at http://www.oyez.org/cases/2000-2009/2003/2003_02_473.

With information that Banks was selling cocaine at home, North Las Vegas Police Department officers and Federal Bureau of Investigation agents got a warrant to search his two-bedroom apartment. As soon as they arrived there, about 2 o'clock on a Wednesday afternoon, officers posted in front called out "police search warrant" and rapped hard enough on the door to be heard by officers at the back door. There was no indication whether anyone was home, and after waiting for 15 to 20 seconds with no answer, the officers broke open the front door with a battering ram. Banks was in the shower and testified that he heard nothing until the crash of the door, which brought him out dripping to confront the police. The search produced weapons, crack cocaine, and other evidence of drug dealing.

In response to drug and firearms charges, Banks moved to suppress evidence, arguing that the officers executing the search warrant waited an unreasonably short time before forcing entry, and so violated the Fourth Amendment. The District Court denied the motion, and Banks pleaded guilty, reserving his right to challenge the search on appeal. The Ninth Circuit Court of Appeals reversed in a 2-to-1 panel opinion.

We granted certiorari to consider how to go about applying the standard of reasonableness to the length of time police with a warrant must wait before entering without permission after knocking and announcing their intent in a felony case. We now reverse.

There has never been a dispute that these officers were obliged to knock and announce their intentions when executing the search warrant, an obligation they concededly honored. The Fourth Amendment says nothing specific about formalities in exercising a warrant's authorization, speaking to the manner of searching as well as to the legitimacy of searching at all simply in terms of the right to be "secure against unreasonable searches and seizures." Although the notion of reasonable execution must therefore be fleshed out, we have done that case by case, largely avoiding categories and protocols for searches. Instead, we have treated reasonableness as a function of the facts of cases so various that no template is likely to produce sounder results than examining the totality of circumstances in a given case; it is too hard to invent categories without giving short shrift to details that turn out to be important in a given instance, and without inflating marginal ones. We have, however, pointed out factual considerations of unusual, albeit not dispositive, significance.

Since most people keep their doors locked, entering without knocking will normally do some damage, a circumstance too common to require a heightened justification when a reasonable suspicion of exigency already justifies an unwarned entry. We have accordingly held that police in exigent circumstances may damage premises so far as necessary for a no-knock entrance without demonstrating the suspected risk in any more detail than the law demands for an unannounced intrusion simply by lifting the latch. Either way, it is enough that the officers had a reasonable suspicion of exigent circumstances.

This case turns on the significance of exigency revealed by circumstances known to the officers. Here the Government claims that a risk of losing evidence arose shortly after knocking and announcing. Although the police concededly arrived at Banks's door without reasonable suspicion of facts justifying a no-knock entry, they argue that announcing their presence started the clock running toward the moment of apprehension that Banks would flush away the easily disposable cocaine, prompted by knowing the police would soon be coming in.

Banks does not, of course, deny that exigency may develop in the period beginning when officers with a warrant knock to be admitted, and the issue comes down to whether it was reasonable to suspect imminent loss of evidence after the 15 to 20 seconds the officers waited prior to forcing their way. Though we agree with the dissenting opinion below that this call is a close one, we think that after 15 or 20 seconds without a response, police could fairly suspect that cocaine would be gone if they were reticent any longer. Courts of Appeals have, indeed, routinely held similar wait times to be reasonable in drug cases with similar facts including easily disposable evidence (and some courts have found even shorter ones to be reasonable enough).

A look at Banks's counterarguments shows why these courts reached sensible results, for each of his reasons for saying that 15 to 20 seconds was too brief rests on a mistake about the relevant enquiry: the fact that he was actually in the shower and did not hear the officers is not to the point, and the same is true of the claim that it might have taken him longer than 20 seconds if he had heard the knock and headed straight for the door. As for the shower, it is enough to say that the facts known to the police are what count in judging reasonable waiting time, and there is no indication that the police knew that Banks was in the shower and thus unaware of an impending search that he would otherwise have tried to frustrate.

And the argument that 15 to 20 seconds was too short for Banks to have come to the door ignores the very risk that justified prompt entry. True, if the officers were to justify their timing here by claiming that Banks's failure to admit them fairly suggested a refusal to let them in, Banks could at least argue that no such suspicion can arise until an occupant has had time to get to the door, a time that will vary with the size of the establishment, perhaps five seconds to open a motel room door, or several minutes to move through a townhouse. In this case, however, the police claim exigent need to enter, and the crucial fact in examining their actions is not time to reach the door but the particular exigency claimed. On the record here, what matters is the opportunity to get rid of cocaine, which a prudent dealer will keep near a commode or kitchen sink. The significant circumstances include the arrival of the police during the day, when anyone inside would probably have been up and around, and the sufficiency of 15 to 20 seconds for getting to the bathroom or the kitchen to start flushing cocaine down the drain. That is, when circumstances are exigent because a pusher may be near the point of putting his drugs beyond reach, it is imminent disposal, not travel time to the entrance, that governs when the police may reasonably enter; since the bathroom and kitchen are usually in the interior of a dwelling, not the front hall, there is no reason generally to peg the travel time to the location of the door, and no reliable basis for giving the proprietor of a mansion a longer wait than the resident of a bungalow, or an apartment like Banks's. And 15 to 20 seconds does not seem an unrealistic guess about the time someone would need to get in a position to rid his quarters of cocaine.

Once the exigency had matured, of course, the officers were not bound to learn anything more or wait any longer before going in, even though their entry entailed some harm to the building. The exigent need of law enforcement trumps a resident's interest in avoiding all property damage. One point in making an officer knock and announce, then, is to give a person inside the chance to save his door. That is why, in the case with no reason to suspect an immediate risk of frustration or futility in waiting at all, the reasonable wait time may well be longer when police make a forced entry, since they ought to be more certain the occupant has had time to answer the door. It is hard to be more definite than that. Suffice it to say that the need to damage property in the course of getting in is a good reason to require more patience than it would be reasonable to expect if the door were open. Police seeking a stolen piano may be able to spend more time to make sure they really need the battering ram.

The judgment of the Court of Appeals is reversed.

Food for Thought

How often do you think that police officers actually execute search warrants to look for stolen pianos, or anything else so large that it cannot be destroyed or hidden relatively quickly?

After the *Banks* decision, do you think that executing officers will *ever* really be required to delay more than 15 seconds? Can you answer your door in 15 seconds even when you're in the shower when they knock, and still hold on to your towel?

Go Online

But *see, e.g.,* "From antifreeze to a baby grand piano, police bust stolen merchandise ring," CTV News Toronto, June 27, 2014, http://toronto.ctvnews.ca/from-antifreeze-to-a-baby-grand-piano-police-bust-stolen-merchandise-ring-1.1889829. Do you suppose that searches for grand pianos happen more commonly in Canada?

Points for Discussion

a. Statutory vs. Constitutional Knock-and-Announce Requirements

Some states, like Florida, for example, have enacted knock-and-announce rules by statute rather than through judicial decision based upon the federal or state constitutions. In states like Florida, what then is the effect of the *Hudson* decision holding that the federal exclusionary rule does not apply, i.e. does it supplant the exclusionary rule that applies pursuant to a violation of the state knock-and-announce statute? *See State v. Cable*, 51 So.3d 434 (Fla. 2010).

b. When Is Destructive Behavior By Executing Officers Excessive?

In *United States v. Ramirez*, 523 U.S. 65, 71 (1998), the Supreme Court held that "excessive or unnecessary destruction of property in the course of a search may violate the Fourth Amendment, even though the entry itself is lawful and the fruits of the search are not subject to suppression." *See also, e.g., Ginter v. Stallcup*, 869 F.2d 384, 389 (8th Cir.1989) (there is a "Fourth Amendment right to be free from an unnecessarily destructive search and seizure. Thus, any destruction caused by law enforcement officers in the execution of a search or an arrest warrant must be necessary to effectively execute that warrant."); *Gurski v. New Jersey State Police Dept.*, 242 N.J.Super. 148, 576 A.2d 292, 299 (1990) ("No police officer in the course of executing a warrant can or should, without justification or sufficient reason, destroy private property, take or use any personal property of another without permission, or use abusive language.").

c. Excessive Force in Making Seizures

In *County of Los Angeles v. Mendez*, 137 S.Ct. 1539 (2017), a unanimous Supreme Court ruled that the operative question in excessive force cases is whether the totality of the circumstances justifies a particular sort of search or seizure. The reasonableness of the use of force is evaluated under an 'objective' inquiry that pays 'careful attention to the facts and circumstances of each particular case.' And 'the "reasonableness" of a particular use of force must be judged from the perspective of a reasonable officer on the scene, rather than with the 20/20 vision of hindsight.' That inquiry is dispositive: When an officer carries out a seizure that is reasonable, taking into account all relevant circumstances, there is no valid excessive force claim.

The *Mendez* Court affirmed a lower court determination that deputies executing a search warrant did not act with excessive force when, after making a warrantless entry into a shack located behind the premises, they shot two individuals when one of them picked up what turned out to be a BB gun. The Court also reversed the Ninth Circuit Court of Appeals' holding that the officers were nonetheless liable for damages because the officers intentionally or recklessly "provoked" the violent confrontation. As the Court reasoned,

> the basic problem with the provocation rule is that it fails to stop there. Instead, the rule provides a novel and unsupported path to liability in cases in which the use of force was reasonable. Specifically, it instructs courts to look back in time to see if there was a different Fourth Amendment violation that is somehow tied to the eventual use of force. That distinct violation, rather than the forceful seizure itself, may then serve as the foundation of the plaintiff's excessive force claim.

> This approach mistakenly conflates distinct Fourth Amendment claims. Contrary to this approach, the objective reasonableness analysis must be conducted separately for each search or seizure that is alleged to be unconstitutional. An excessive force claim is a claim that a law enforcement officer carried out an unreasonable seizure through a use of force that was not justified under the relevant circumstances. It is not a claim that an officer used reasonable force after committing a distinct Fourth Amendment violation such as an unreasonable entry.

> By conflating excessive force claims with other Fourth Amendment claims, the provocation rule permits excessive force claims that cannot succeed on their own terms. That is precisely how the rule operated in this case. The District Court found (and the Ninth Circuit did not dispute) that the use of force by the deputies was reasonable. However, respondents were still able to recover damages because the deputies committed a separate constitutional violation (the warrantless entry into the shack) that in some sense set the table for the use of force. That is wrong.

d. When Can Executing Officers Kill Animals Living on the Search Premises?

The Ninth Circuit Court of Appeals has held that the intentional killing of three dogs, two of them "guard dogs" on search premises, one of them a Rottweiler, during the execution of a search warrants on a Hells Angels clubhouse and residences was not justified under the Fourth Amendment:

> Reasonableness is the touchstone of any seizure under the Fourth Amendment. Thus, to comply with the Fourth Amendment, the seizure-in this case, shooting and death-of the dogs must have been reasonable under the circumstances. We look to the totality of the circumstances to determine whether the destruction of property was reasonably necessary to effectuate the performance of the law enforcement officer's duties. To determine whether the shooting of the dogs was reasonable, we balance "the nature and quality of the intrusion on the individual's Fourth Amendment interests against the countervailing governmental interests at stake."

> Here, the intrusion was severe. We have recognized that dogs are more than just a personal effect. The emotional attachment to a family's dog is not comparable to a possessory interest in furniture. The seizures were unreasonable, in violation of the Fourth Amendment. Most important, both entry teams had a week to plan the execution of the entry. Despite advance knowledge of the presence of two guard dogs, the full extent of the plan to protect the entry team from the dogs was to either "isolate" or shoot the dogs. The officers had no specific plan for isolating the dogs.

> The contention that shooting the dogs was necessary to preserve stealth is unpersuasive. It was the officers' own method of entry that compromised their ability to effectuate a quiet entry. All of the above considerations support the conclusion that the officers violated the plaintiffs' Fourth Amendment rights by unnecessarily shooting the dogs.

San Jose Chapter of Hells Angels Motorcycle Club v. City of San Jose, 402 F.3d 962 (9th Cir. 2005), cert. denied, 546 U.S. 1061 (2005).

Do you think that the Ninth Circuit was correct? Did these dogs pose a danger to the executing officers and/or to the successful completion of the search that justified the officers' actions? This case was a civil rights action brought against the city of San Jose for damages occasioned by the shooting of the dogs and other property damage that occurred during the raids. San Jose ultimately settled the case by paying $990,000, $530,000 of which was payment of the plaintiffs' attorneys' fees.

Some executing officers have executed no-knock warrants while using so-called "flash-bang" devices (also called "stun grenades"). These devices produce an intense flash of light and a loud noise to briefly distract the occupants of search premises. The flash momentarily activates photoreceptor cells in peoples' eyes, making vision difficult for a few seconds. The blast causes a temporary loss of hearing and balance. Most courts find the use of such flash-bang devices unreasonable where the executing officers neither possess a no-knock warrant nor face unexpected dangers upon entry.

See It

What does execution of a search warrant with a flash-bang device actually look and sound like? See for yourself at https://www.youtube.com/watch?v=s4VJaNVHa88.

Hypo 1: *Flash-Bang Device in Driveway*

Defendant Rockford argued that an entry into his and his parents' home to execute a search warrant was unconstitutional due to the executing officers' use of a flash-bang device outside in the driveway just prior to their knock, announce, delay, and entry by use of a battering ram. Defendant's mother, who was inside the home, testified that she mistook the sound of the flash-bang device for a problem with her furnace, that she did not hear knocking on the door before hearing the sound of the battering ram and seeing officers in her home, and that she was "scared to death" to encounter a police officer pointing a gun at her. Is this a violation of the knock-and announce doctrine? Does it matter, do you think, that the police may have made so much noise that no occupant could ever have heard their knock and announcement? *State v. Rockford*, 213 N.J. 424, 64 A.3d 514 (2013).

Hypo 2: *When Must a Search End?*

Police officers were lawfully inside defendant's home which he shared with his mother when they saw what they thought were three long guns near a staircase. Knowing that defendant's mother was a convicted felon and, thus, prohibited from possessing firearms, they obtained a warrant to search the home for prohibited weapons. Early in their search, the executing officers learned that the guns near the staircase were in fact

"BB" guns. Nonetheless the officers continued the search and ultimately discovered cocaine. Can the cocaine be suppressed? Was it discovered during the lawful execution of a search warrant? What do you think? *State v. Schulz*, 164 N.H. 217, 55 A.3d 933 (2012).

B. Protected Fourth Amendment Interests

The Fourth Amendment provides protection only from governmental "searches" and "seizures." For more than a century after the Fourth Amendment was adopted, there was little doubt regarding the meaning of the term "search." Those who suffered through the colonial period, and those who formulated and ratified the Fourth Amendment, were well aware of the British practices that led to demands for constitutional protections against "unreasonable searches and seizures." Colonial officials had conducted actual physical searches of "persons, houses, papers, and effects," and the Court fashioned a definition of "search" that focused on whether the government's intrusion constituted a physical "trespass" into a "constitutionally protected area."

By the early twentieth century, the development of new communications and electronic surveillance technologies allowed the government to perform intrusions that did not require a physical trespass. As long as the Court maintained its original definition of a "search," no Fourth Amendment protection could be provided for conversations inside a home or office that could be monitored by devices that required no physical entry into these structures. This lack of protection is exemplified in *Olmstead v. United States*, 277 U.S. 438 (1928), in which a closely divided Court held that capturing conversations with wiretaps did not constitute a trespassory "search," and that intangible conversations could not be "seized" as "effects" because they were "secured by the sense of hearing only." The *Olmstead* dissenters recognized that meaningful Fourth Amendment protection would require the Court to expand the "search" and "seizure" definitions beyond its rhetoric anchored in the material world of trespass. For example, Justice Brandeis's dissent noted that a private telephone communication deserved no less Fourth Amendment protection than a sealed letter, given the Framers' commitment to protect "Americans in their beliefs, their thoughts, their emotions, and their sensations." In his view, the Fourth Amendment protects "the right to be let alone," and "every unjustifiable intrusion upon privacy, whatever the means employed," constitutes a violation of the Fourth Amendment.

For over 30 years after *Olmstead*, the Court continued to link privacy interests to trespassory intrusions. In *Goldman v. United States,* 316 U.S. 129 (1942), the Court held that no trespass occurred when agents placed a "detectaphone" device against a common wall to amplify the sound waves of conversations coming from an adjoining office. Justice Murphy's dissent criticized the failure of the trespass theory to cope with advancing surveillance technology: "Science has brought forth far more effective devices for the invasion of a person's privacy than the direct and obvious methods of oppression which were detested by our forebears and which inspired the Fourth Amendment. Whether the search of private quarters is accomplished by placing on the outer walls of the sanctum a detectaphone that transmits to the outside listener the intimate details of a private conversation, or by new methods of photography that penetrate walls or overcome distances, the privacy of the citizen is equally invaded by agents of the Government and intimate personal matters are laid bare to view." Finally, in *Silverman v. United States,* 365 U.S. 505 (1961), the Court recognized *sub* silentio that intangible conversations could be "seized," and held that agents committed a trespass by inserting a "spike mike" a few inches into the common wall of a house in order to listen to conversations. Douglas's concurrence emphasized that this technical trespass was not a principled basis for justifying Fourth Amendment protection of conversations in *Silverman* while denying it in *Goldman* and *Olmstead*. Only a few years after *Silverman*, the *Katz* case overruled *Goldman* and *Olmstead*, and established a new doctrine designed to address the need for privacy protections from non-physical government surveillance.

1. Development of the Reasonable Expectation of Privacy Test

Consider how the *Katz* Court's new approach to regulating government searches and seizures of conversations may be applied to other methods of information gathering.

Katz v. United States

389 U.S. 347 (1967).

MR. JUSTICE STEWART delivered the opinion of the Court.

[Katz was convicted of transmitting wagering information by telephone. He made calls from a set of telephone booths near his apartment, and the phone company put one of the telephones out of order at the FBI's request. Then agents placed a listening and recording device on top of and between the other booths.

When Katz left his apartment, one agent signaled another agent who ran to the booths and turned on the device. The agents obtained six recordings, averaging about three minutes each, and preserved only Katz's end of the conversations, which were introduced at trial. The lower court assumed that the recordings did not violate the Fourth Amendment because "there was no physical entrance into the area occupied by" Katz.]

Katz has strenuously argued that the booth was a "constitutionally protected area." The Government has maintained with equal vigor that it was not. But this effort to decide whether or not a given "area," viewed in the abstract, is "constitutionally protected" deflects attention from the problem presented by this case. For the Fourth Amendment protects people, not places. What a person knowingly exposes to the public, even in his own home or office, is not a subject of Fourth Amendment protection. See *Lewis v. United States*, 385 U.S. 206 (1966). But what he seeks to preserve as private, even in an area accessible to the public, may be constitutionally protected.

The Government stresses that the telephone booth from which Katz made his calls was constructed partly of glass, so that he was as visible after he entered it as he would have been if he had remained outside. But what he sought to exclude when he entered the booth was not the intruding eye—it was the uninvited ear. He did not shed his right to do so simply because he made his calls from a place where he might be seen. No less than an individual in a business office, in a friend's apartment, or in a taxicab, a person in a telephone booth may rely upon the protection of the Fourth Amendment. [One who occupies it, shuts the door behind him, and pays the toll that permits him to place a call is surely entitled to assume that the words he utters into the mouthpiece will not be broadcast to the world.] To read the Constitution more narrowly is to ignore the vital role that the public telephone has come to play in private communication.

Food for Thought

How could the Court respond to the argument that Katz knowingly exposed his conversation to anyone working for the telephone company who could have listened to his call?

The Government contends, however, that the activities of its agents in this case should not be tested by Fourth Amendment requirements, for the surveillance technique they employed involved no physical penetration of the telephone booth from which the petitioner placed his calls. It is true that the absence of such penetration was at one time thought to foreclose further Fourth Amendment inquiry, for that Amendment was thought to limit only searches and seizures of tangible property. But although a closely divided Court supposed in *Olmstead v. United States*, 277 U.S. 438 (1928), that surveillance without any trespass and without the seizure of any material object fell outside the ambit of the Constitution, we have since departed from the narrow view on which that decision rested. Indeed, we have expressly held that the Fourth Amendment governs not only the seizure of tangible items, but extends as well to the recording of oral statements overheard without any "technical trespass." *Silverman v. United States*, 365 U.S. 505, 511 (1961). Once it is recognized that the Fourth Amendment protects people—and not simply "areas"—against unreasonable searches and seizures it becomes clear that the reach of that Amendment cannot turn upon the presence or absence of a physical intrusion into any given enclosure.

We conclude that the underpinnings of *Olmstead* and *Goldman* have been so eroded by our subsequent decisions that the "trespass" doctrine can no longer be regarded as controlling. The Government's activities in electronically listening to and recording Katz's words violated the privacy upon which he justifiably relied while using the telephone booth and thus constituted a "search and seizure" within the meaning of the Fourth Amendment. The fact that the electronic device employed to achieve that end did not happen to penetrate the wall of the booth can have no constitutional significance.

Practice Pointer

In the merits brief for *Katz*, defense counsel argued that the Fourth Amendment provided absolute protection for conversations, echoing the position of the *Olmstead* dissent by Justice Brandeis. But in the reply brief and at oral argument, defense counsel argued instead that the warrant procedure was both feasible and required for lawful electronic surveillance of Katz's speech in the phone booth.

The question remaining for decision is whether the search and seizure conducted in this case complied with constitutional standards. It is clear that this surveillance was so narrowly circumscribed that a duly authorized magistrate could constitutionally have authorized, with appropriate safeguards, the very limited search and seizure that the Government asserts, in fact, took place. The Government urges that because its agents did no more here than they might properly have done with prior judicial sanction, we should retroactively validate their conduct. That we cannot do. The inescapable fact is that in this case, restraint was imposed by the agents themselves, not by a judicial officer. They were not required, before commencing their search, to present their estimate of probable cause for detached scrutiny by a neutral magistrate. They were not compelled, during the conduct of the search itself, to observe precise limits established in advance by a specific court order.

The Government urges the creation of a new exception in this case. It argues that surveillance of a telephone booth should be exempted from the usual requirement of advance authorization by a magistrate upon a showing of probable cause. We cannot agree. Omission of such authorization "bypasses the safeguards provided by an objective predetermination of probable cause. And bypassing a neutral predetermination of the scope of a search leaves individuals secure from Fourth Amendment violations 'only in the discretion of the police.'" *Beck v. Ohio*, 379 U.S. 89, 96, 97 (1964).

These considerations do not vanish when the search in question is transferred from the setting of a home, an office, or a hotel room to that of a telephone booth. Wherever a man may be, he is entitled to know that he will remain free from unreasonable searches and seizures. The government agents here ignored a procedure that we hold to be a constitutional precondition of the kind of electronic surveillance involved in this case. Because the surveillance here failed to meet that condition, and because it led to the petitioner's conviction, the judgment must be reversed. *It is so ordered.*

> **FYI**
>
> After *Olmstead*, Congress enacted a federal anti-wiretapping statute, which the Court interpreted in *Nardone v. United States*, 302 U.S. 379 (1937) as prohibiting the testimony of federal agents about illegally wiretapped conversations. But violations of federal and state wiretapping laws were widespread in later years. Following *Katz*, Congress enacted Title III of the Omnibus Crime Control and Safe Streets Act of 1968 to define the procedures for obtaining a wiretapping warrant, relying on the requirements for such warrants described in *Katz* and *Berger v. New York*, 388 U.S. 41 (1967).

MR. JUSTICE HARLAN, concurring.

As the Court's opinion states, "the Fourth Amendment protects people, not places." The question, however, is what protection it affords to those people. Generally the answer to that question requires reference to a "place." My understanding of the rule that has emerged from prior decisions is that there is a twofold requirement, first that a person have exhibited an actual (subjective) expectation of privacy and, second, that the expectation be one that society is prepared to recognize as "reasonable." Thus a man's home is, for most purposes, a place where he expects privacy, but objects, activities, or statements that he exposes to the "plain view" of outsiders are not "protected" because no intention to keep them to himself has been exhibited. On the other hand, conversations in the open would not be protected against being overheard, for the expectation of privacy under the circumstances would be unreasonable. The critical fact in this case is that "one who occupies it, (a telephone booth) shuts the door behind him, and pays the toll that permits him to place a call is surely entitled to assume" that his conversation is not being intercepted. The point is not that the booth is "accessible to the public" at other times, but that it is a temporarily private place whose momentary occupants' expectations of freedom from intrusion are recognized as reasonable.

Points for Discussion

a. Reasonable Expectation of Privacy (REOP) v. Physical Trespass

Following *Katz*, the Court approved Justice Harlan's formula—requiring a subjective manifestation of an expectation of privacy that is objectively reasonable—as the expression of *Katz's* holding. Although most post-*Katz* decisions have defined the concept of "reasonable expectations of privacy" (REOP), the Court has emphasized that the *Katz* test was "*added to*, not *substituted for*" the physi-

> **Food for Thought**
>
> An overnight guest has a REOP in a dwelling. But only people with a "property or possessory interest" in a car may challenge a police search of the car. These people include the owner or driver but not a mere passenger. Are these rulings consistent with *Katz*?

cal trespass test. This is because "for most of our history the Fourth Amendment was understood to embody a particular concern for government trespass upon the areas ("persons, houses, papers, and effects") it enumerates. *Katz* did not repudiate that understanding" or "erode the principle 'that when the Government does engage in physical intrusion of a constitutionally protected area in order to obtain information, that information may constitute a violation of the Fourth Amendment.'" *United States v. Jones*, 565 U.S. 400, 405, 406 (2012). Thus, aside from *Olmstead* and *Goldman*, pre-*Katz* precedents defining "constitutionally protected areas" remained good law after *Katz*. The *Katz* opinion alluded to such precedents when noting the Fourth Amendment protection for people occupying a business office, a friend's apartment, a taxi cab, a home, or a hotel room. *Compare Lanza v. New York*, 370 U.S. 139, 143 (1962). What language in the *Katz* Court's opinion—and in Justice Harlan's concurrence—points to the future coexistence of the *Katz* and trespass tests? What would be the consequences of reading *Katz* differently as a replacement for trespass theory?

b. Privacy in the Home

The Court's precedents repeatedly endorse the principle that, "At the very core" of the Fourth Amendment "stands the right of a man to retreat into his own home and there be free from unreasonable governmental intrusion." *Silverman v. United States*, 365 U.S. 505, 515 (1961). In the post-*Katz* era, the Fourth Amendment's protection of the home from trespassory intrusions has been extended to encompass intangible intrusions to obtain "information from the interior of the home" that "could not otherwise [be] obtained without physical intrusion into a constitutionally protected area." *Kyllo v. United States*, 533 U.S. 27, 34 (2001). Even before *Katz*, the Court recognized that "a person can have a legally sufficient interest in a place other than his own home" and that the "arcane distinctions" of property and tort law (between "guests, licensees, invitees and the like") do not control. *Rakas v. Illinois*, 439 U.S. 128, 142 (1978). In *Minnesota v. Olson*, 495 U.S. 91, 98 (1990), the Court held that overnight guests in a home have REOP protection, reasoning that this rule "merely recognizes the everyday expectations of privacy that we all share," and validates "a longstanding social custom that serves functions recognized as valuable by society." The shelter and security of the host's home make it "a temporarily private place" for the guest as a "momentary occupant" whose expectations of freedom from intrusion are recognized as reasonable." But one who is merely "present with the consent of the householder" may not claim Fourth Amendment protection, such as ✗ *Wrong* visitors to a home who have no previous relationship with the homeowner and no purpose for their brief visit other than an illegal business transaction. *See Minnesota v. Carter*, 525 U.S. 83, 90 (1998). Does the *Olson* reasoning apply to a social guest who is a long-term acquaintance who has visited a home numerous times without staying overnight? If a tenant has not paid rent for several months but is still living in an apartment, when does she lose her REOP in that home? Note that the REOP rules for homes and cars are different under *Rakas*, which recognizes a REOP only ✗ *Wrong* for people with a "property or possessory interest" in a car. These people include the car's owner and anyone who drives with the owner's permission, but not mere passengers. Is this holding consistent with Katz?

c. Undercover Agents and Informants — *Before Katz*

The *Katz* opinion cited *Lewis v. United States*, 385 U.S. 206 (1966), as a case involving an unprotected disclosure where "a person knowingly exposed information to the public in his own home or office." The *Lewis* Court held that the defendant had no privacy interest in the incriminating conversations he had with an undercover police officer, whom he had invited into his home to buy drugs. This invitation "converted" the home into a "commercial center to which outsiders are invited for purposes of unlawful business," and the agent did not "see, hear, or take anything in the home that was not intended by the defendant." Similarly, in *Hoffa v. United States*, 385 U.S. 293 (1966), a plurality held that a defendant had no privacy interest in incriminating conversations in his hotel suite with an informant, when those conversations were "directed to" the informant or "knowingly carried on in his presence." The plurality declined to protect the "misplaced confidence" of the *Lewis* and *Hoffa* defendants that their associates "would not reveal their wrongdoing" by talking to government agents.

The Court later affirmed the continuing validity of both rulings in *United States v. White*, 401 U.S. 745 (1971). The informant in *White* wore a wire with a radio transmitter that allowed agents to both monitor and record his conversations with the defendant, which occurred in the defendant's home and other locations. The Court reasoned that the electronic surveillance should be equated with the non-electronic reporting of the informants in *Lewis* and *Hoffa*, and that an expectation of privacy from electronic surveillance would be unreasonable because anyone "contemplating illegal activities must realize and risk that his companions may be reporting to the police." Justice Harlan, joined by four justices, dissented and reasoned as follows:

UNLESS IN A PHONE BOOTH?

The impact of the practice of third-party bugging, must, I think, be considered such as to undermine that confidence and sense of security in dealing with one another that is characteristic of individual relationships between citizens in a free society. It goes beyond the impact on privacy occasioned by the ordinary type of "informer" investigation upheld in *Lewis* and *Hoffa*. The argument of the plurality opinion, to the effect that it is irrelevant whether secrets are revealed by the mere tattletale or the transistor, ignores the differences occasioned by third-party monitoring and recording which insures full and accurate disclosure of all that is said, free of the possibility of error and oversight that inheres in human reporting. The interest the plurality fails to protect is the expectation of the ordinary citizen, who has never engaged in illegal conduct in his life, that he may carry on his private discourse freely, openly, and spontaneously without measuring his every word against the connotations it might carry when instantaneously heard by others unknown to him and unfamiliar with his situation or analyzed in a cold, formal record played days, months, or years after the conversation. Interposition of a warrant requirement is designed not to shield "wrongdoers," but to secure a measure of privacy and a sense of personal security throughout our society.

d. Private Search Doctrine

The *Katz* Court referred approvingly to *Ex parte Jackson*, 96 U.S. 727 (1877), holding that letters and packages in the mail are protected by a REOP. In post-*Katz* cases, however, the Court recognized the "private search" doctrine, which governs the scenario in which a private actor opens an incriminating package and then turns it over to a government agent. Here no violation of REOP occurs unless the agent's subsequent intrusion is more extensive than that of the private actor. Such an intrusion requires a warrant. *Compare Walter v. United States*, 447 U.S. 649 (1980) (violation of REOP when private actor held film up to the light and agent later viewed the film on a projector); *United States v. Jacobsen*, 466 U.S. 109 (1984) (no violation of REOP when agent imitated all the search steps of FedEx employee who found white powder inside a package, even when agent also performed field test to determine powder was cocaine). The private search doctrine has been applied by lower courts to searches of computers, so that no warrant is required for an agent who stays within the scope of a prior actor's search.

Hypo 1: *Backpacks & Safety Deposit Boxes*

A safety deposit box is one of the most secure and private ways to protect property against the police or others. But few individuals keep all of their valuables in safety deposit boxes. Suppose that a law student brings her backpack to class. If the backpack remains zipped, does she have a reasonable expectation of privacy in the contents of the backpack? If so, does the reasonable expectation of privacy continue to exist when the student leaves the classroom for five minutes? Would it matter that the backpack is unzipped?

Hypo 2: *House Party*

Assume that Larry is a law student who decides to hold a party for all the students in his law school, their spouses or significant others, and friends. A total of 200 people actually attend the party. During the course of the evening, there is a constant flow of people in and out of Larry's home. Assume that Larry leaves marijuana cigarettes on the coffee table in his living room for the enjoyment of his guests, and that marijuana is an illegal drug. Does Larry have a reasonable expectation of privacy regarding the marijuana cigarettes on his coffee table?

Hypo 3: *Government Manipulation or Erosion of Privacy Expectations*

In *Smith v. Maryland*, 442 U.S. 735, 740 n.5 (1979), the Court observed that "if the Government were suddenly to announce on nationwide television that all homes henceforth would be subject to warrantless entry, individuals might not in fact entertain any actual expectation of privacy regarding their homes, papers and effects. But where an individual's subjective expectations have been 'conditioned' by influences alien to well-recognized Fourth Amendment freedoms, those subjective expectations obviously could play no meaningful role in ascertaining what the scope of Fourth Amendment protection was." However, even in the absence of such obvious government manipulation of privacy expectations of the citizenry, some forms of privacy erosion may lessen the collective social expectations of privacy in ways that would be accepted by the Court. If the government announces that it will place aural monitoring devices on public property outside each home and monitor all conversations in every house 24 hours a day, what reasoning could the Court use to find that this surveillance would violate reasonable expectations of privacy? See Anthony G. Amsterdam, Perspectives on the Fourth Amendment, 58 MINN. L. REV. 349 (1974). What less intrusive type of aural monitoring might be accepted by the Court as not violating a protected privacy interest?

Hypo 4: British Camera System

In 2002, the government in Great Britain installed approximately 4.2 million surveillance cameras in public places to watch and monitor the populace, with one camera for every 15 people. This system allows the government, for example, to monitor each person in London with 300 cameras each day. Following the London subway bombings in July 2005, the police made arrests based on information provided by the camera system. Cities such as Baltimore, Chicago, and New Orleans have received federal grants to install surveillance cameras, although some studies show that the use of cameras is less likely to have a deterrent effect on crime than the placement of additional officers on the streets and the improvement of public lighting in high-crime areas. Assume that a citizen's group sues one of these cities because of a concern about the loss of privacy in public spaces. Can it be argued that the use of a camera system violates the reasonable expectations of privacy of the residents of the city?

e. Protection for Curtilage, Not for Open Fields

After Katz , the Court sometimes found it necessary to address the impact of REOP theory on precedents from the *Olmstead* era. In *Oliver v. United States, 466 U.S. 170 (1984),* the Court affirmed the pre-*Katz* precedent that distinguished between protected curtilage land (immediately surrounding and associated with a dwelling or protected structure) and the unprotected land that lies beyond the curtilage, the so-called "open fields." *See Hester v. United States*, 265 U.S. 57 (1924). This distinction accorded with *Katz's* privacy analysis because the curtilage traditionally was viewed as "part of the home itself for Fourth Amendment purposes," given its association with "intimate activity" and "the privacies of life." Therefore, an expectation of privacy in the curtilage could be deemed reasonable, whereas a trespassory intrusion and visual surveillance of the open fields land was not, for these reasons:

> In assessing the degree to which a search infringes upon individual privacy, the Court has given weight to such factors as the intention of the Framers of the Fourth Amendment, the uses to which the individual has put a location, and our societal understanding that certain areas deserve the most scrupulous protection from government invasion. The Amendment reflects the recognition of the Framers that certain enclaves should be free from arbitrary government interference. For example, the Court since the enactment of the Fourth Amendment has stressed "the overriding respect for the sanctity of the home that has been embedded in our traditions since the origins of the Republic." In contrast, open fields do

not provide the setting for those intimate activities that the Amendment is intended to shelter from government interference or surveillance. There is no societal interest in protecting the privacy of those activities, such as the cultivation of crops, that occur in open fields. Moreover, as a practical matter these lands usually are accessible to the public and the police in ways that a home, an office, or commercial structure would not be. It is not generally true that fences or "No Trespassing" signs effectively bar the public from viewing open fields in rural areas. For these reasons, the asserted expectation of privacy in open fields is not an expectation "that society recognizes as reasonable."

Notably, the *Oliver* Court rejected the proposal that REOP theory should be used to expand Fourth Amendment protection to "secluded" open fields in which an owner attempted to deter trespassers from entry with No Trespassing signs and fences. Instead, *Oliver* maintained the traditional dichotomy between curtilage and "open fields" as consistent with *Katz*. In drawing the boundary between the protected curtilage and unprotected open fields, the Court approved of the traditional case-by-case factors used by lower courts in pre-*Katz* cases. Later in *United States v. Dunn*, 480 U.S. 294 (1987), the Court recognized that these four factors typically provide the basis for lower courts to resolve curtilage questions: "[1] the proximity of the area claimed to be curtilage to the home; [2] whether the area is included within an enclosure surrounding the home; [3] the nature of the uses to which the area is put; and [4] the steps taken by the resident to protect the area from observation by people passing by."

Another pre-*Katz* feature of the curtilage doctrine was the recognition of lower courts that based on customs and social norms, a homeowner is deemed to have conferred an invitation or "implied license" to members of the public to make a limited entry upon the curtilage of his or her dwelling. As the Court described that license in *Florida v. Jardines*, 569 U.S. 1 (2013), this implied license "typically permits a visitor to approach the home by the front path, knock promptly, wait briefly to be received, and then (absent invitation to linger longer) leave." Similarly, "a police officer not armed with a warrant may approach a home and knock, precisely because that is 'no more than any private citizen might do,'" as recognized in *Kentucky v. King*, 131 S.Ct. 1849 (2011). Given the precedents recognizing the curtilage as a "constitutionally protected area," however, *Jardines* emphasized that the Fourth Amendment prohibits physical intrusions upon the curtilage "to engage in conduct not explicitly or implicitly permitted by the homeowner." Therefore, the Court held that police officers violated that prohibition when they brought a trained drug-sniffing dog to the defendant's front porch "in the hopes of discovering incriminating evidence." The Court found it unnecessary to decide whether this police conduct violated the defendant's REOP in his curtilage and home. Instead, the Court relied on "the Fourth Amendment's property-rights baseline" in determining that "the background social norms that invite a visitor to the front door do not invite [any visitor] there to conduct a search."

Since "the officers learned what they learned only by physically intruding on Jardines' property to gather evidence," this fact was "enough to establish that a search occurred" and that a warrant was required. Later in *Carrol v. Carman*, 135 S.Ct. 348 (2014), the Court recognized that lower courts have taken different approaches to resolving the question whether there are any circumstances under which police may approach other entries to a home for a "knock and talk" (without a forensic narcotics dog).

Hypo: *Cluttered Yard*

When Officer May observes Zeb's home from the sidewalk, she notices that no defined pathway leads to the front door, and that the yard is filled with obstructions, including stacked wood, a rusting truck, a wheelbarrow, garden tools, and bags of soil. The trees on the property have thick foliage that makes it impossible for Officer May to see into the windows of the house from the sidewalk. She decides to walk into the yard, and after she scrambles around the obstructions, she reaches a small clear area at the back of the yard, peers into the nearest window, and notices marijuana plants inside the house. Does her conduct violate Zeb's reasonable expectation of privacy under *Oliver* and *Dunn*? Assume instead that Officer May sees that there is a clear pathway to Zeb's front door and that a driveway leads from the street to a carport at the back of the yard. So she walks down the driveway to the carport, peers into the window, and then notices the marijuana plants. How does the analysis of the curtilage issue change? Compare *Washington v. Ross*, 91 Wash. App. 814, 959 P.2d 1188 (1998); *Commonwealth v. Dixon*, 482 S.E.3d 886 (Ky. 2015).

---

2. Post-*Katz* Decisions Developing the Third Party Doctrine to Defeat REOP Claims

When *Katz* was decided, some commentators thought that the ruling signaled the Court's willingness to deal with the problem of advancing surveillance technology, especially given the breadth of the "reasonable expectation of privacy" concept, and the Court's declaration that, "wherever a man may be, he is entitled to know that he will remain free from unreasonable searches and seizures." Paradoxically, the Court has chosen repeatedly to construe the REOP test narrowly by relying on two expansive concepts in order to find privacy expectations to be unreasonable. The *Smith* case remains influential today because of its "voluntary conveyance" and "knowing exposure" rationales for finding expectations of privacy to be unreasonable.

Smith v. Maryland

442 U.S. 735 (1979).

MR. JUSTICE BLACKMUN delivered the opinion of the Court.

[The police suspected Smith of robbing a victim who received subsequent threatening and obscene phone calls from the perpetrator. Smith fit the victim's description and his car was seen at the crime scene and noticed repeatedly in the victim's neighborhood. So the police asked the telephone company to install a pen register to record numbers dialed from Smith's home telephone, as the company did not keep records for local calls. That same day, the pen register recorded one call made from Smith's home telephone to the victim, and the police obtained a search warrant and discovered evidence at his home. Smith argued that the installation of the pen register was a "search" under *Katz* and lost in the lower courts.]

[handwritten margin note: NOT IN ORDINARY COURSE OF BUSINESS]

> **See It**
>
> See http://s3-media2.fl.yelpcdn.com/bphoto/5Tyw352fdlXJt1aqUUTYQw/l.jpg for a photo of a pen register device.

Smith obviously cannot claim that his "property" was invaded or that police intruded into a "constitutionally protected area." His claim is that, notwithstanding the absence of a trespass, the State, as did the Government in *Katz*, infringed a "legitimate expectation of privacy" that he held. Yet a pen register differs significantly from the listening device in *Katz*, for pen registers do not acquire the *contents* of communications. Given a pen register's limited capabilities, therefore, Smith's argument rests upon a claim that he had a "legitimate expectation of privacy" regarding the numbers he dialed on his phone.

We doubt that people in general entertain any actual expectation of privacy in the numbers they dial. All telephone users realize that they must "convey" phone numbers to the telephone company, and that the phone company has the facilities for recording this information.

This Court consistently has held that a person has no legitimate expectation of privacy in information he voluntarily turns over to third parties. In *United States v. Miller*, 425 U.S. 435, 442 (1976), for example, the Court held that a bank depositor has no "legitimate 'expectation of privacy'" in financial information "voluntarily conveyed to banks and exposed to their employees in the ordinary course of business." Because the depositor assumed the risk of disclosure, the Court held that it would be unreasonable for him to expect his financial records to remain private. When he used his phone, Smith voluntarily conveyed numerical information to the telephone company and "exposed" that information to its equipment in the ordinary course of business. In so doing, Smith assumed the risk that the company would reveal to police the numbers he dialed.

The installation of the pen register, consequently, was not a "search," and no warrant was required. The judgment of the Maryland Court of Appeals is affirmed. *It is so ordered.*

JUSTICE STEWART, with whom JUSTICE BRENNAN joins, dissenting.

The information captured by such surveillance emanated from private conduct within a person's home or office—locations that without question are entitled to constitutional protection. Further, that information is an integral part of the telephonic communication that under *Katz* is entitled to constitutional protection, whether or not it is captured by a trespass into such an area. The numbers dialed from a private telephone are not without "content." I doubt there are any who would be happy to have broadcast to the world a list of the local or long distance numbers they have called. It easily could reveal the identities of the persons and places called, and thus reveal the most intimate details of a person's life.

JUSTICE MARSHALL, with whom JUSTICE BRENNAN joins, dissenting.

Privacy is not a discrete commodity, possessed absolutely or not at all. Those who disclose certain facts to a bank or phone company for a limited business purpose need not assume that this information will be released to other persons for other purposes. The Court determines that individuals who convey information to third parties have "assumed the risk" of disclosure to the government. This analysis is misconceived in two critical respects. Implicit in the concept of assumption of risk is some notion of choice. By contrast here, unless a person is prepared to forgo use of what for many has become a personal or professional necessity, he cannot help but accept the risk of surveillance. More fundamentally, to make risk analysis dispositive in assessing the reasonableness of privacy expectations would allow the government to define the scope of Fourth Amendment protection. Whether privacy expectations are legitimate within the meaning of *Katz* depends not on the risks an individual can be presumed to accept when imparting information to third parties, but on the risks he should be forced to assume in a free and open society. The prospect of unregulated government monitoring will undoubtedly prove disturbing even to those with nothing illicit to hide, and I am unwilling to insulate use of pen registers from independent judicial review.

Points for Discussion

a. Precedent for *Smith*'s Third Party Doctrine

In *Miller v. United States*, 425 U.S. 435 (1976), the Court tied the concepts of voluntary conveyance and knowing exposure to the declaration in the *Katz* opinion that, "What a person knowingly exposes to the public, even in his own home or office, is not a subject of Fourth Amendment protection." The federal agents in *Miller* obtained copies of the defendant's checks and bank records by means of subpoenas to banks where he had accounts. In rejecting the defendant's REOP argument, the *Miller* Court emphasized one rationale that went unmentioned in *Smith*, which was that the lack of REOP in bank records "was assumed by Congress" when enacting the Bank Secrecy Act of 1970 that required the banks to maintain the records. A similar rationale appeared in *Couch v. United States*, 409 U.S. 322, 335 (1973), to justify the rejection of the defendant's proposal that an "accountant-client" privilege should be recognized to support her REOP in documents held by her accountant on her behalf. The Court opined that "there can be little expectation of privacy where records are handed to an accountant, knowing that mandatory disclosure of much of the information therein is required in an income tax return."

b. *Smith*'s Application to Electronic Information

When the Court's precedents rejecting REOP claims in the 1980s and 1990s invoked *Smith* in a wide variety of contexts, it appeared that even the remote prospect of "exposure" could be sufficient for the government to rebut a REOP claim under *Katz*. But as advancing technology gave rise to new surveillance tools to capture electronic information, some judges questioned the usefulness of *Smith* as authority for resolving novel privacy questions in the internet era. *See, e.g., United States v. Jones*, 565 U.S. 400, 411, 417 (2012) (Sotomayor, J., concurring). Consider what support for judicial limitations on *Smith*'s third party doctrine may be found in the REOP cases that follow. If *Smith* is "ill suited" for resolving REOP issues in the digital age, then what interpretation of *Katz* should take its place?

c. NSA Surveillance

In the wake of Edward Snowden's revelations in 2013, two suits were filed to challenge the constitutionality of the NSA's bulk telephony metadata surveillance program through which the government obtained the records of millions of domestic subscribers from internet service providers. The user data did not include the content of calls, but did include the phone numbers of callers and recipients, location data, and the time and duration of calls. Neither suit led to the finding that the NSA's program violated the Fourth Amendment. Other suits have challenged the NSA's PRISM program, which allows the government to investigate non-U.S. persons outside the country by obtaining from internet service providers (ISPs) the target's telephone and internet data, including emails, videos, voice chat, photos, and social networking data. Lower courts have upheld the "reasonableness" of the PRISM program based on the compelling interest in national security.

Hypo: *Are Text Messages Different?*

Suppose that police investigators suspect that someone is involved in criminal activity, so they subpoena his text messages on his cell phone from his internet service provider. Does *Smith v. Maryland* suggest that there is no REOP in the text messages, and thus, that no Fourth Amendment violation occurs when police subpoena and read the messages? After all, the text messages were sent through a third party. Can it be argued, on the other hand, that the warrantless police seizure of text messages is fundamentally different from the seizure of the dialed telephone numbers that are recorded by the pen register. Can text messages be analogized to ordinary mail sent through the post office, which is protected by *Katz*, so that the sender can assume that the messages will be read only by the recipient and not the carrier? *See Love v. State*, 2016 WL 7131259, ___ S.W.3d ___ (Tex. Ct. Crim. App. 2016).

United States v. Knotts

460 U.S. 276 (1983).

JUSTICE REHNQUIST delivered the opinion of the Court.

[Police officers suspected that Knotts' co-defendant Petschen could lead them to the site of a drug lab. So the officers arranged for a radio transmitter to be placed inside a five-gallon drum of chloroform that Petschen bought and placed in a car. The officers followed the car but were not able to maintain continual visual surveillance, and they had to rely on the signals of the tracking beeper, which ultimately led them to a secluded cabin, which was owned and occupied by Knotts. The officers obtained a search warrant based on that discovery and found a drug lab in the cabin. The five-gallon drum was outside the cabin. Knotts argued that the use of the tracking beeper violated his reasonable expectation of privacy.]

A person traveling in an automobile on public thoroughfares has no reasonable expectation of privacy in his movements from one place to another. When Petschen traveled over the public streets he voluntarily conveyed to anyone who wanted to look the fact that he was traveling over particular roads in a particular direction, the fact of whatever stops he made, and the fact of his final destination when he exited from public roads onto private property.

As the owner of the cabin and surrounding premises to which Petschen drove, Knotts undoubtedly had the traditional expectation of privacy within a dwelling place insofar as the cabin was concerned. But no such expectation of privacy extended to the visual observation of the automobile arriving on his premises after leaving a public highway, nor to movements of objects such as the drum of chloroform outside the cabin in the "open fields."

Visual surveillance from public places along the car's route or adjoining Knotts' premises would have sufficed to reveal all of these facts to the police. The fact that the officers in this case relied not only on visual surveillance but also on the use of the beeper does not alter the situation. Nothing in the Fourth Amendment prohibited the police from augmenting their sensory faculties with such enhancement as science and technology afforded them in this case.

We have recently had occasion to deal with another claim which was [a] factual counterpart of Knotts' assertions here. In *Smith v. Maryland*, 442 U.S. 735, 745 (1979), we said: "Smith voluntarily conveyed numerical information to the telephone company and 'exposed' that information to its equipment. In so doing, Smith assumed the risk that the company would reveal to police the numbers he dialed." Knotts does not actually quarrel with this analysis, though he expresses the generalized view that that the result of the holding sought by the Government would be that "twenty-four hour surveillance of any citizen of this country will be possible, without judicial knowledge or supervision." If such dragnet type law enforcement practices as Knotts envisions should eventually occur, there will be time enough then to determine whether different constitutional principles may be applicable.

Nothing in this record indicates that the beeper signal was received or relied upon after it had indicated that the drum had ended its automotive journey at rest on Knotts' land. There is no indication that the beeper was used in any way to reveal information as to the movement of the drum within the cabin, or in any way that would not have been visible to the naked eye from outside the cabin.

There was neither a "search" nor a "seizure" within the contemplation of the Fourth Amendment. The judgment of the Court of Appeals is therefore *Reversed*.

Points for Discussion

a. Tracking Objects into Dwellings

In *United States v. Karo*, 468 U.S. 705 (1984), the Court held that the use of a tracking beeper violated a homeowner's reasonable expectation of privacy because police continued to monitor the location of the beeper until after it was taken inside a dwelling, and thereby were able to know when the bottle (containing the beeper) was moved to another location. The Court reasoned that a search occurs when the Government "surreptitiously employs an electronic device to obtain information that it could not have obtained by observation from outside the curtilage of the house. The beeper tells the agent that a particular article is actually located at a particular time in the private residence and is in the possession of the person or persons whose residence is being watched." Thus, the beeper reveals "a critical fact about the interior of the premises" that the Government "could not have obtained without a warrant." By contrast, the beeper in *Knotts* "told the authorities nothing about the interior of Knotts' cabin." The information obtained in *Knotts* was "voluntarily conveyed to anyone who wanted to look," whereas in *Karo*, "the monitoring indicated that the beeper was inside the house, a fact that could not have been visually verified."

b. GPS Surveillance

Most lower courts relied on *Knotts* to reject claims by defendants for a REOP from GPS surveillance when the Court decided to address this issue in a case in which the police officers had installed a GPS tracking device on the undercarriage of the defendant's car. Instead of resolving the REOP question in *United States v. Jones*, 565 U.S. 400 (2012), the Court surprised observers by producing a narrow holding that revived the old trespass test, and did not address the cases in which police engage in GPS surveillance solely by electronic means. In relying on trespass theory to invalidate the warrantless attachment of the device—and its use to monitor the defendant's car on public streets—the Court reasoned as follows:

> The Government physically occupied private property for the purpose of obtaining information. We have no doubt that such a physical intrusion would have been considered a "search" within the meaning of the Fourth Amendment when it was adopted. *Entick v. Carrington*, 95 Eng. Rep. 807 (C.P. 1765). The text of the Fourth Amendment reflects its close connection to property, since otherwise it would have referred simply to "the right of the people to be secure against unreasonable searches and seizures"; the phrase "in their persons, houses, papers, and effects" would have been superfluous. The Government contends that the *Katz* standard shows that no search occurred here, since Jones had no "reasonable expectation of privacy" in the area of the Jeep accessed by Government agents (its underbody) and in the locations of the Jeep on the public roads, which were visible to all. But we need not address the Government's contentions, because Jones's Fourth Amendment rights do not rise or fall with the *Katz* formulation. We must "assure preservation of that degree of privacy against government that existed when the Fourth Amendment was adopted." *Kyllo v. United States*, 533 U.S. 27, 34 (2001). For most of our history the Fourth Amendment was understood to embody a particular concern for government trespass upon the areas ("persons, houses, papers, and effects") it enumerates. *Katz* did not repudiate that understanding [or] erode the principle "that, when the Government does engage in physical intrusion of a constitutionally protected area in order to obtain information, that intrusion may constitute a violation of the Fourth Amendment." *United States v. Knotts*, 460 U.S. 276, 286

(1983) (Brennan, J., concurring). What we apply is an 18th-century guarantee against unreasonable searches, which we believe must provide *at a minimum* the degree of protection it afforded when it was adopted. We do not make trespass the exclusive test. Situations involving merely the transmission of electronic signals without trespass would *remain* subject to *Katz* analysis. It may be that achieving the same result [achieved here] through electronic means, without an accompanying trespass, is an unconstitutional invasion of privacy, but the present case does not require us to answer that question.

Hypo: *Mosaic Theory*

The D.C. Circuit decision below in Jones held that the defendant had a REOP from the Government's use of GPS surveillance to monitor his movements. In constructing arguments to explain why Knotts was not controlling, the court alluded to the term "mosaic theory" to describe the insight that the exposure of "the whole of one's movements" during prolonged surveillance "is not actually exposed to the public," and that this whole reveals more "than does the sum of its parts," namely "an intimate picture" of the person's life. *United States v. Maynard*, 615 F.3d 544, 558, 562 (D.C. Cir. 2010). The four Justices who concurred in the Jones result took a different position. They would have found that although the defendant's REOP was violated by the long-term monitoring of the movements of his car, the use of GPS surveillance for a shorter period of time would not necessarily violate his REOP. What arguments can be made on both sides of the REOP issue regarding the use of GPS surveillance? What precedents will be used by each side in this debate?

California v. Ciraolo

476 U.S. 207 (1986).

CHIEF JUSTICE BURGER delivered the opinion of the Court.

[Police officers received an anonymous tip that marijuana was growing in Ciraolo's garden, but they discovered that they could not observe the interior of the yard from the vantage point of the sidewalk, given the ten-foot fence enclosing the yard. So they obtained the use of an airplane to fly in navigable airspace at 1,000 feet over Ciraolo's house and backyard. Their aerial view allowed them to see marijuana plants in the garden and they obtained a search warrant based on that information. Ciraolo argued that the aerial surveillance violated his reasonable expectation of privacy but his suppression motion was denied. The state appellate court reversed his conviction, finding that the flyover was not a routine patrol but was undertaken in order to inspect Ciraolo's curtilage, and thus, the flyover was a direct intrusion into the sanctity of the home.]

The State argues that Ciraolo has "knowingly exposed" his backyard to aerial observation, because all that was seen was visible to the naked eye from any aircraft flying overhead. The State analogizes its mode of observation to a knothole or opening in a fence; if there is an opening, the police may look. Ciraolo contends he has done all that can reasonably be expected to tell the world he wishes to maintain the privacy of his garden within the curtilage without covering his yard. Such covering, he argues, would defeat its purpose as an outside living area; he asserts he has not "knowingly" exposed himself to aerial views.

That the area is within the curtilage does not itself bar all police observation. The Fourth Amendment protection of the home has never been extended to require law enforcement officers to shield their eyes when passing by a home on public thoroughfares. Nor does the mere fact that an individual has taken measures to restrict some views of his activities preclude an officer's observations from a public vantage point where he has a right to be and which renders the activities clearly visible. *E.g. United States v. Knotts*, 460 U.S. 276 (1983). "What a person knowingly exposes to the public, even in his own home or office, is not a subject of Fourth Amendment protection. *Katz v. United States*, 389 U.S. 347, 351 (1967). Any member of the public flying in this airspace who glanced down could have seen everything that these officers observed. Ciraolo's expectation that his garden was protected from such observation is unreasonable and is not an expectation that society is prepared to honor. The Fourth Amendment simply does not require the police traveling in the public airways at this altitude to obtain a warrant in order to observe what is visible to the naked eye. *Reversed.*

Justice Powell, with whom Justice Brennan, Justice Marshall, and Justice Blackmun join, dissenting.

Our decisions have made clear that the *Katz* inquiry often must be decided by "reference to a 'place,'" and that a home is a place in which a subjective expectation of privacy virtually always will be legitimate. *United States v. Karo*, 468 U.S 705, 713-715 (1984). "At the very core of the Fourth Amendment stands the right of a person to retreat into his own home and there be free from unreasonable governmental intrusion." *Silverman v. United States*, 365 U.S. 505, 511 (1961).

The Court finds support for its conclusion in *United States v. Knotts*, 460 U.S. 276 (1983), but its reasoning is flawed. First, the actual risk to privacy from commercial or pleasure aircraft is virtually nonexistent, as travelers normally obtain at most a fleeting, anonymous, and nondiscriminating glimpse of the landscape and buildings over which they pass. The risk that a passenger on a plane might observe private activities, and might connect those activities with particular people, is simply too trivial to protect against. People do not "'knowingly expose'" their residential yards "'to the public'" merely by failing to build barriers that prevent aerial surveillance. The activities under surveillance in *Knotts* took place on public streets, not in private homes. The activity in this case, by contrast, took place within the private area immediately adjacent to a home. Here, police conducted an overflight at low altitude solely for the purpose of discovering evidence of crime within a private enclave into which they were constitutionally forbidden to intrude at ground level without a warrant. We have consistently afforded heightened protection to a person's right to be left alone in the privacy of his house. The Court fails to enforce that right or to give any weight to the longstanding presumption that warrantless intrusions into the home are unreasonable. I dissent.

Point for Discussion

Limits on Flyovers

In a companion case, *Dow Chemical Co. v. United States*, 476 U.S. 227 (1986), the Court rejected the defendant's asserted REOP claim when agents took photographs of the "business curtilage" of a chemical plant during a flyover at 1200 feet. The Court reasoned, first, that the camera was a "conventional, albeit precise, commercial camera commonly used in mapmaking." It was not "some unique sensory device that, for example, could penetrate the walls of buildings and record conversations in Dow's plants, offices or laboratories." The Government conceded, and the Court agreed, that "surveillance of private property by using highly sophisticated surveillance equipment not generally available to the public, such as satellite technology, might be constitutionally proscribed absent a warrant." Second, the Court observed that the photographs were "not so revealing of intimate details as to raise constitutional concerns." A plurality of the Court extended *Ciraolo's* reasoning

Food for Thought

The FAA's current rules require commercial drones to fly below 400 feet during the daytime within the operator's line of sight. Within 10 years there may be tens of thousands of *7,000,000 IN 2020* drones in the air. What influence will this development have on the judicial resolution of the question whether to recognize a REOP from surveillance from police drones. Drone-related legislation has been enacted in more than 30 states and many statutes create prohibitions that apply to the use of surveillance drones by law enforcement entities. One typical exception is the scenario in which a warrant is obtained based on probable cause. What other exceptions would be likely to be endorsed in these statutes? Or allowed based on a lack of REOP?

HELICOPTER

in *Florida v. Riley*, 488 U.S. 445 (1989), in which an officer used a helicopter flyover at 400 feet to look down through the holes in the roof of a greenhouse in the defendant's curtilage. This naked-eye observation of the marijuana plants did not violate the defendant's REOP because "any member of the public could legally have been flying over Riley's property in a helicopter at the altitude of 400 feet and could have observed Riley's greenhouse." The Court noted that helicopters are not bound by the limits of navigable airspace imposed on airplanes, and there was no "intimation" either that the helicopter interfered with use of the curtilage or that "intimate details" were observed.

California v. Greenwood

486 U.S. 35 (1988).

JUSTICE WHITE delivered the opinion of the Court.

The issue is whether the Fourth Amendment prohibits the warrantless search and seizure of garbage left for collection outside the curtilage of a home. We conclude, in accordance with the vast majority of lower courts that have addressed the issue, that it does not.

[When a police officer received a tip indicating that Greenwood might be engaged in narcotics trafficking at his house, she obtained the cooperation of the trash collector, who agreed to pick up the plastic garbage bags left on the curb in front of Greenwood's house, and then turn them over to the officer. When she searched through the trash, she found items related to narcotics use. This information was used to obtain a search warrant for Greenwood's home. When the warrant

Go Online

The garbage search presented the Court with another technique that coincided with the development of other surveillance strategies during the era of the "war on drugs." For a chronology of the history of the "war on drugs" in the United States, assembled by the PBS Frontline program, see http://www.pbs.org/wgbh/pages/frontline/shows/drugs/cron/

was executed, drugs were seized and Greenwood and others were arrested. Then the next month, the police officer obtained the garbage again using the same method. A second search warrant was obtained based on the evidence of narcotics use in the second set of garbage bags. Once again the search of Greenwood's house led to the seizure of drugs and the second arrest of Greenwood and others.]

The warrantless search and seizure of the garbage bags left at the curb outside the Greenwood house would violate the Fourth Amendment only if the respondents manifested a subjective expectation of privacy in their garbage that KATZ society accepts as objectively reasonable. Respondents assert that they had, and exhibited, an expectation of privacy with respect to the trash that was searched by the police: The trash, which was placed on the street for collection at a fixed time, was contained in opaque plastic bags, which the garbage collector was expected to pick up, mingle with the trash of others, and deposit at the garbage dump. The trash was only temporarily on the street, and there was little likelihood that it would be inspected by anyone.

Here, we conclude that respondents exposed their garbage to the public sufficiently to defeat their claim to Fourth Amendment protection. It is common knowledge that plastic garbage bags left on or at the side of a public street are readily accessible to animals, children, scavengers, snoops, and other members of the public. Moreover, defendants placed their refuse at the curb for the express purpose of conveying it to a third party, the trash collector, who might himself have sorted through defendants' trash or permitted others, such as the police, to do so. Having deposited their garbage "in an area particularly suited for public inspection and, in a manner of speaking, public consumption, for the express purpose of having strangers take it," defendants could have had no reasonable expectation of privacy in the inculpatory items that they discarded.

Furthermore, the police cannot reasonably be expected to avert their eyes from evidence of criminal activity that could have been observed by any member of the public. We held in *Smith v. Maryland*, 442 U.S. 735 (1979), that the police did not violate the Fourth Amendment by causing a pen register to be installed at the telephone company's offices to record the telephone numbers dialed by a criminal suspect. An individual has no legitimate expectation of privacy in the numbers dialed on his telephone, we reasoned, because he voluntarily conveys those numbers to the telephone company [and] "a person has no legitimate expectation of privacy in information he voluntarily turns over to third parties."

JUSTICE BRENNAN, with whom JUSTICE MARSHALL joins, dissenting:

A trash bag is "a common repository for one's personal effects" and is "inevitably associated with the expectation of privacy." A single bag of trash testifies eloquently to the eating, reading, and recreational habits of the person who produced it. A search of trash, like a search of the bedroom, can relate intimate details about sexual practices, health, and personal hygiene. Like rifling through desk drawers or intercepting phone calls, rummaging through trash can divulge the target's financial and professional status, political affiliations and inclinations, private thoughts, personal relationships, and romantic interests. It cannot be doubted that a sealed trash bag harbors telling evidence of the "intimate activity associated with the 'sanctity of a man's home and the privacies of life,'" which the Fourth Amendment is designed to protect. The mere *possibility* that unwelcome meddlers might open and rummage through the containers does not negate the expectation of privacy in their contents any more than the possibility of a burglary negates an expectation of privacy in the home; or the possibility of a private intrusion negates an expectation of privacy in an unopened package; or the possibility that an operator will listen in on a telephone conversation negates an expectation of privacy in the words spoken on the telephone.

Nor is it dispositive that "defendants placed their refuse at the curb for the express purpose of conveying it to a third party, who might himself have sorted through the trash or permitted others, such as the police, to do so." Even the voluntary relinquishment of possession or control over an effect does not necessarily amount to a relinquishment of a privacy expectation in it. Were it otherwise, a letter or package would lose all Fourth Amendment protection when placed in a mailbox or other depository with the "express purpose" of entrusting it to the postal officer or a private carrier. Yet, it has been clear for at least 110 years that the possibility of such an intrusion does not justify a warrantless search by police in the first instance. *See Ex Parte Jackson*, 96 U.S. 727 (1878).

Point for Discussion

Luggage Surveillance

In Bond v. United States, 529 U.S. 334 (2000), the government invoked both *Smith* rationales in an attempt to defeat a bus passenger's claim that the "luggage squeeze" surveillance method violated a reasonable expectation of privacy. In *Bond*, a border patrol agent implemented this search method by walking down the aisle of a bus and squeezing each piece of soft luggage stored in the luggage bins above the passenger seats. Inside the defendant's canvas bag, the agent felt a "brick-like" object, and a search of the bag revealed a "brick" of methamphetamine wrapped in duct tape. The *Bond* Court concluded that the tactile intrusion of the "luggage squeeze" and the visual intrusion of flyover surveillance were not analogous: "Physically invasive inspection is simply more intrusive than purely visual inspection. When a bus passenger places a bag in an overhead bin, he expects that other passengers or bus employees may move it for one reason or another. Thus, a bus passenger clearly expects that his bag may be handled. He does not expect that other passengers or bus employees will, as a matter of course, feel the bag in an exploratory manner. But this is exactly what the agent did here. We therefore hold that the agent's physical manipulation of petitioner's bag violated the Fourth Amendment." The *Bond* dissenters would have relied on *Smith's* rationales—conveyance to a third party and knowing exposure—to reject the *Bond* defendant's asserted expectation of privacy. What policy reasons may explain the *Bond* Court's refusal to extend these rationales to permit warrantless luggage squeezes?

* * *

Aside from the doctrines of the *Smith* progeny cases, the other important doctrine for rejecting REOP arguments in the 1980s and 1990s was the Court's holding that a "canine sniff" is a *sui generis* investigative method that does not qualify as a "search." Given the broad rationales underlying this doctrine, are there any principled limits that can be imposed on the use of the canine sniff in any surveillance context?

United States v. Place

462 U.S. 696 (1983).

JUSTICE O'CONNOR delivered the opinion of the Court.

DEA agents, suspicious of Place's behavior, seized his luggage and subjected it to a canine sniff. In deciding whether the seizure was permissible, the Court was called on to decide whether the sniff constituted a search within the meaning of the Fourth Amendment.

The Fourth Amendment "protects people from unreasonable government intrusions into their legitimate expectations of privacy." We have affirmed that a person possesses a privacy interest in the contents of personal luggage that is protected by the Fourth Amendment. A "canine sniff" by a well-trained narcotics detection dog, however, does not require opening the luggage. It does not expose noncontraband items that otherwise would remain hidden from public view, as does, for example, an officer's rummaging through the contents of the luggage. Thus, the manner in which information is obtained through this investigative technique is much less intrusive than a typical search. Moreover, the sniff discloses only the presence or absence of narcotics, a contraband item. Thus, despite the fact that the sniff tells the authorities something about the contents of the luggage, the information obtained is limited. This limited disclosure also ensures that the owner of the property is not subjected to the embarrassment and inconvenience entailed in less discriminate and more intrusive investigative methods.

In these respects, the canine sniff is *sui generis*. We are aware of no other investigative procedure that is so limited both in the manner in which the information is obtained and in the content of the information revealed by the procedure. Therefore, we conclude that the particular course of investigation that the agents intended to pursue here—exposure of respondent's luggage, which was located in a public place, to a trained canine—did not constitute a "search" within the meaning of the Fourth Amendment.

Point for Discussion

Traffic Stops

The Court observed in *Indianapolis v. Edmond*, 531 U.S. 32 (2000), that "the fact that officers walk a narcotics-detection dog around the exterior" of a car "does not establish a 'search.'" In *Illinois v. Caballes*, 543 U.S. 405 (2005), the Court held that "conducting a dog sniff would not change the character of a traffic stop that is lawful at its inception and otherwise executed in a reasonable manner." The Court rejected the defendant's argument that error rates "call into question the premise that drug-detection dogs will alert only to contraband." The *Caballes* dissenters disagreed, and emphasized that empirical evidence demonstrates "that the dog that alerts hundreds of times will be wrong dozens of times." They called for reconsideration of *Place* and urged that canine sniffs should be treated as a "search" when used during car stops for traffic crimes. In *Rodriguez v. United States*, 135 S.Ct. 1609 (2015), the Court followed up on dicta in *Caballes* noting that a traffic stop would become unlawful if the dog sniff prolonged its duration beyond "the time reasonable required" to issue a ticket. The officer's stop in *Rodriquez* was held to be unlawful for that reason.

3. Seeds of Doctrinal Change

More than 30 years after *Katz*, a Court majority recognized that a new approach to privacy was needed. Most of the *Katz* jurisprudence defined privacy expectations as unreasonable, as illustrated by the *Smith* and *Place* lines of precedent. The Internet era posed new threats to privacy from advancing technology, but the Court's pre-Internet interpretations of *Katz* had not been constructed with an awareness of those threats. However, the ruling in *Kyllo* (2001) signaled the Court's willingness to take on the project of addressing the "power of technology to shrink the realm of guaranteed privacy." *Kyllo* relied on REOP reasoning to protect "information regarding the interior of the home" from being obtained by the use of some types of sense-enhancing technology. Then the Court took the unusual step of relying on trespass theory to hold that the Government engaged in impermissible physical intrusions when agents installed a GPS tracking device on an automobile in *Jones* (2012) and brought a narcotics-detection to the front porch of a home to sniff the front door in *Jardines* (2013). These trespass rulings established protections that *Katz* REOP precedents arguably might not support, just as *Katz*'s REOP theory initially was used to establish broader protections than trespass theory would allow.

Kyllo v. United States

533 U.S. 27 (2001).

JUSTICE SCALIA delivered the opinion of the Court.

An agent at the Department of Interior suspected that Kyllo was growing marijuana plants inside his home that was part of a triplex. Such a growing operation usually requires high-intensity lamps. So agents used an Agema Thermovision 210 thermal imager to scan the home in order to detect and measure the heat inside that

Hear It

Listen to the oral argument before the Supreme Court in the *Kyllo* case at http://www.oyez.org/cas es/2000-2009/2000/2000_99_8508

was emitted as infrared radiation. This device operated like a video camera showing heat images in shades of black, gray, and white. When the agents performed the scan at night from their car across the street from Kyllo's home, the garage roof and one side wall appeared to be relatively hot compared to the rest of the home, and substantially warmer than the other homes in the triplex. Based on the information from the scan and other evidence, the agents obtained a search warrant and discovered more than 100 marijuana plants inside the home. The lower courts rejected Kyllo's claim that the warrantless use of the thermal imager to scan his home violated his reasonable expectation of privacy.

This case presents the question whether the use of a thermal-imaging device aimed at a private home from a public street to detect relative amounts of heat within the home constitutes a "search" within the meaning of the Fourth Amendment. "At the very core" of the Fourth Amendment "stands the right of a man to retreat into his own home and there be free from unreasonable governmental intrusion." *Silverman v. United States*, 365 U.S. 505 (1961). With few exceptions, the question whether a warrantless search of a home is reasonable and hence constitutional must be answered no.

The permissibility of ordinary visual surveillance of a home used to be clear because, well into the twentieth century, our Fourth Amendment jurisprudence was tied to common-law trespass. We have since decoupled violation of a person's Fourth Amendment rights from trespassory violation of his property, but the lawfulness of warrantless visual surveillance of a home has still been preserved. We have previously reserved judgment as to how much technological enhancement of ordinary perception from such a vantage point, if any, is too much. The question we confront today is what limits there are upon this power of technology to shrink the realm of guaranteed privacy.

The *Katz* test—whether the individual has an expectation of privacy that society is prepared to recognize as reasonable—often has been criticized as circular, and hence subjective and unpredictable. But in the case of the search of the interior of homes, there is a ready criterion, with roots deep in the common law, of the minimal expectation of privacy that *exists*, and that is acknowledged to be *reasonable*. To withdraw protection of this minimum expectation would be to permit police technology to erode the privacy guaranteed by the Fourth Amendment. We think that obtaining by sense-enhancing technology any information regarding the interior of the home that could not otherwise have been obtained without physical "intrusion into a constitutionally protected area," *Silverman*, 365 U.S. at 512, constitutes a search—at least where (as here) the technology in question is not in general public use. This assures preservation of that degree of privacy against government that existed when the Fourth Amendment was adopted. On the basis of this criterion, the information obtained by the thermal imager in this case was the product of a search.

The Government maintains, however, that the thermal imaging must be upheld because it detected "only heat radiating from the external surface of the house." But just as a thermal imager captures only heat emanating from a house, so also a powerful directional microphone picks up only sound emanating from a house—and a satellite capable of scanning from many miles away would pick up only visible light emanating from a house. We rejected such a mechanical interpretation of the Fourth Amendment in *Katz*, where the eavesdropping device picked up only sound waves that reached the exterior of the phone booth. Reversing that approach would leave the homeowner at the mercy of advancing technology—including imaging technology that could discern all human activity in the home. While the technology used in the present case was relatively crude, the rule we adopt must take account of more sophisticated systems that are already in use or in development.

Take Note

The *Kyllo* opinion cited three examples of sophisticated technology projects described on the website of the National Law Enforcement and Corrections Technology Center. They included a "Radar-Based Through-the-Wall Surveillance System," "Handheld Ultrasound Through the Wall Surveillance," and a "Radar Flashlight" to permit the detection of individuals "through interior building walls." For current projects, see https://justnet.org/About_NLECTC.html.

The Government also contends that the thermal imaging was constitutional because it did not "detect private activities occurring in private areas." The Fourth Amendment's protection of the home has never been tied to measurement of the quality or quantity of information obtained. There is no exception to the warrant requirement for the officer who barely cracks open the front door and sees nothing but the nonintimate rug on the vestibule floor. In the home, *all* details are intimate details, because the entire area is held safe from prying government eyes. Limiting the prohibition of thermal imaging to "intimate details" would not only be wrong in principle; it would be impractical in application. To begin with, there is no necessary connection between the sophistication of the surveillance equipment and the "intimacy" of the details that it observes. It might disclose, for example, at what hour each night the lady of the house takes her daily sauna and bath—a detail that many would consider "intimate"; and a much more sophisticated system might detect nothing more intimate than the fact that someone left a closet light on. We would have to develop a jurisprudence specifying which home activities are "intimate"

> **Take Note**
>
> Justice Scalia's opinion noted that it is irrelevant whether neighbors or passersby may be able to detect heat emanating from a home, because "[t]he fact that equivalent information could sometimes be obtained by other means does not make lawful the use of means that violate the Fourth Amendment." Moreover, at the time of the heat scan by the agents, "no outside observer could have discerned the relative heat of Kyllo's home without thermal imaging" because it was nighttime.

and which are not. No police officer would be able to know *in advance* whether his through-the-wall surveillance picks up "intimate" details—and thus would be unable to know in advance whether it is constitutional.

We have said that the Fourth Amendment draws "a firm line at the entrance to the house." *Payton v. New York*, 445 U.S. 573, 590 (1980). That line must be not only firm but also bright—which requires clear specification of those methods of surveillance that require a warrant. We must take the long view, from the original meaning of the Fourth Amendment forward. Where, as here, the Government uses a device that is not in general public use, to explore details of the home that would previously have been unknowable without physical intrusion, the surveillance is a "search" and is presumptively unreasonable without a warrant.

HELD

The judgment of the Court of Appeals is reversed; the case is remanded for further proceedings consistent with this opinion. *It is so ordered.*

JUSTICE STEVENS, with whom THE CHIEF JUSTICE, JUSTICE O'CONNOR, and JUSTICE KENNEDY join, dissenting.

This case involves nothing more than off-the-wall surveillance by law enforcement officers to gather information exposed to the general public from the outside of a home. The ordinary use of the senses might enable a neighbor or passerby to notice the heat emanating from a building. Additionally, any member of the public might notice that one part of a house is warmer than another part or a nearby building if, for example, rainwater evaporates or snow melts at different rates across its surfaces. The notion that heat emissions from the outside of a dwelling are a private matter implicating the protections of the Fourth Amendment is not only unprecedented but also quite difficult to take seriously. Heat waves, like aromas that are generated in a kitchen, or in a laboratory or opium den, enter the public domain if and when they leave a building. A subjective expectation that they would remain private is not only implausible but also surely not "one that society is prepared to recognize as reasonable."

Just as "the police cannot reasonably be expected to avert their eyes from evidence of criminal activity that could have been observed by any member of the public," *Greenwood v. California*, 486 U.S. 35, 41 (1988), so too public officials should not have to avert their senses or their equipment from detecting emissions in the public domain such as excessive heat, traces of smoke, suspicious odors, odorless gases, airborne particulates, or radioactive emissions, any of which could identify hazards to the community. On the other hand, the countervailing privacy interest is at best trivial. Homes generally are insulated to keep heat in, rather than to prevent the detection of heat going out, and it does not seem that society will suffer from a rule requiring the rare homeowner who both intends to engage in uncommon activities that produce extraordinary amounts of heat, and wishes to conceal that production from outsiders, to make sure that the surrounding area is well insulated.

The Court has unfortunately failed to heed the tried and true counsel of judicial restraint and has endeavored to craft an all-encompassing rule for the future. It would be far wiser to give legislatures an unimpeded opportunity to grapple with these emerging issues rather than to shackle them with prematurely devised constitutional restraints. I respectfully dissent.

Hypo: *Sense-Enhancing Devices*

Assume that a police agent stands on the sidewalk, points a "powerful directional microphone" at a front window of the house, and eavesdrops on conversations in the living room. The government argues that no REOP protects the homeowner from this surveillance because the microphone can be purchased for $100 at any retail store that sells electronics, and therefore, this device is in "general public use" under *Kyllo*. How should the Court rule? As an alternate scenario, assume that the FBI obtains the assistance of an internet service provider in remotely activating the microphone and transmitter in the homeowner's cell phone, which is on a table in the living room. Then FBI agents use this microphone to eavesdrop on the conversations of people in the living room who happen be standing near the cell phone. What result under *Kyllo*?

The Court's first decision regarding Fourth Amendment protection for cell phone privacy was unanimous in rejecting government arguments that sought to justify warrantless searches of cell phones seized incident to arrest. The government did not deny that cell phones were protected by *Katz*. But a decision in the government's favor would have effectively negated such protection for arrested persons. The government argued that cell phones are no different from all other objects that police are entitled to search categorically under *United States v. Robinson*, 414 U.S. 218 (1973), when discovered on an arrestee's person or within an arrestee's reach. For example, the arresting officer in *Robinson* made a valid search incident to arrest when searching a cigarette package in an arrestee's pocket and finding drugs. In the opinion below, the Court explained the many reasons that cell phone privacy is not subject to this traditional exception to the warrant requirement. At least in the context of physical seizures of arrestees' cell phones by police officers, the Court concluded that officers must either get a search warrant or prove that exigent circumstances justified a warrantless search.

Riley v. California

134 S.Ct. 2473 (2014).

CHIEF JUSTICE ROBERTS delivered the opinion of the Court.

These two cases raise a common question: whether the police may, without a warrant, search digital information on a cell phone seized from an individual who has been arrested.

In the first case, petitioner David Riley was stopped by a police officer for driving with expired registration tags. In the course of the stop, the officer learned that Riley's license had been suspended. The officer impounded Riley's car, pursuant to department policy, and another officer conducted an inventory search of the car. Riley was arrested for possession of concealed and loaded firearms when that search turned up two handguns under the car's hood. An officer searched Riley incident to the arrest and found items associated with the "Bloods" street gang. He also seized a cell phone from Riley's pocket. The phone was a "smart phone," a cell phone with a broad range of other functions based on advanced computing capability, large storage capacity, and Internet connectivity. The officer accessed the phone and noticed that some words (presumably in text messages or a contacts list) were preceded by the letters "CK"—a label that, he believed, stood for "Crip Killers," a slang term for members of the Bloods gang. At the police station about two hours after the arrest, a detective specializing in gangs further examined the contents of the phone. The detective testified that he "went through" Riley's phone "looking for evidence, because gang members will often video themselves with guns or take pictures of themselves with the guns." Although there was "a lot of stuff" on the phone, particular files that "caught the detective's eye" included videos of young men sparring while someone yelled encouragement using the moniker "Blood." The police also found photographs of Riley standing in front of a car they suspected had been involved in a shooting a few weeks earlier. Riley was charged in connection with that earlier shooting, with firing at an occupied vehicle, assault with a semiautomatic firearm, and attempted murder. The State alleged that Riley had committed those crimes for the benefit of a criminal street gang, an aggravating factor that carries an enhanced sentence. Prior to trial, Riley moved to suppress all evidence that the police had obtained from his cell phone. The trial court rejected that motion. Riley was convicted on all three counts. The California Court of Appeal affirmed. The California Supreme Court denied Riley's petition for review and we granted certiorari.

In the second case, a police officer performing routine surveillance observed respondent Brima Wurie make an apparent drug sale from a car. Officers subsequently arrested Wurie. At the station, the officers seized two cell phones from Wurie's person. The one at issue here was a "flip phone." Five to ten minutes after arriving at the station, the officers noticed that the phone was repeatedly receiving calls from a source identified as "my house" on the phone's external screen. They opened the phone and saw a photograph of a woman and a baby set as the phone's wallpaper. They pressed one button on the phone to access its call log, then another button to determine the phone number associated with the "my house" label. They next used an online phone directory to trace that phone number to an apartment building. When the officers went to the building, they saw Wurie's name on a mailbox and observed through a window a woman who resembled the woman in the photograph on Wurie's phone. They secured the apartment while obtaining a search warrant and, upon later executing the warrant, found and seized 215 grams of crack cocaine, marijuana, drug paraphernalia, a firearm and ammunition, and cash. Wurie was charged with distributing crack cocaine, possessing crack cocaine with intent to distribute, and being a felon in possession of a firearm and ammunition. He moved to suppress the evidence from the search of the apartment. The District Court denied the motion and Wurie was convicted. A divided panel of the First Circuit reversed and vacated Wurie's convictions. We granted certiorari.

These cases require us to decide how the search incident to arrest doctrine applies to modern cell phones, which are now such a pervasive and insistent part of daily life that the proverbial visitor from Mars might conclude they were an important feature of human anatomy. A smart phone of the sort taken from Riley was unheard of ten years ago; a significant majority of American adults now own such phones. Even less sophisticated phones like Wurie's have been around for less than 15 years. Both phones are based on technology nearly inconceivable just a few decades ago, when *United States v. Robinson*, 414 U.S. 218 (1973), was decided. Absent more precise guidance from the founding era, we generally determine whether to exempt a given type of search from the warrant requirement "by assessing, on the one hand, the degree to which it intrudes upon an individual's privacy and, on the other, the degree to which it is needed for the promotion of legitimate governmental interests." *Wyoming v. Houghton*, 526 U. S. 295, 300 (1999).

Robinson regarded any privacy interests retained by an individual after arrest as significantly diminished by the fact of the arrest itself. Cell phones, however, place vast quantities of personal information literally in the hands of individuals. A search of the information on a cell phone bears little resemblance to the type of brief physical search considered in *Robinson*. We therefore decline to extend *Robinson* to searches of data on cell phones, and hold instead that officers must generally secure a warrant before conducting such a search.

Digital data stored on a cell phone cannot be used as a weapon to harm an arresting officer or to effectuate the arrestee's escape. Law enforcement officers remain free to examine the physical aspects of a phone to ensure that it will not be used as a weapon—say, to determine whether there is a razor blade hidden between the phone and its case. Once an officer has secured a phone and eliminated any potential physical threats, data on the phone can endanger no one. Perhaps the same might have been said of the cigarette pack seized from Robinson's pocket. The officer in *Robinson* testified that he could not identify the objects in the cigarette pack but knew they were not cigarettes. Given that, a further search was a reasonable protective measure. No such unknowns exist with respect to digital data. The officers who searched Wurie's cell phone "knew exactly what they would find therein: data. They also knew that the data could not harm them."

Both Riley and Wurie concede that officers could have seized and secured their cell phones to prevent destruction of evidence while seeking a warrant. See *Illinois v. McArthur*, 531 U. S. 326, 331 (2001); *Chadwick, supra*, at 13. Once law enforcement officers have secured a cell phone, there is no longer any risk that the arrestee himself will be able to delete incriminating data from the phone. To the extent that law enforcement still has specific concerns about the potential loss of evidence in a particular case, there are targeted ways to address those concerns. If "the police are truly confronted with a 'now or never' situation,"—for example, circumstances suggesting that a defendant's phone will be the target of an imminent remote-wipe attempt—they may be able to rely on exigent circumstances to search the phone immediately. *Missouri v. McNeely*, 133 S. Ct. 1552 1562 (2013) (quoting *Roaden v. Kentucky*, 413 U. S. 496, 505 (1973)).

Not every search "is acceptable solely because a person is in custody." *Maryland v. King*, 133 S. Ct. 1958, 1979 (2013). To the contrary, when "privacy-related ✓ concerns are weighty enough" a "search may require a warrant, notwithstanding the diminished expectations of privacy of the arrestee."

The United States asserts that a search of all data stored on a cell phone is "materially indistinguishable" from searches of physical items. Modern cell phones, as a category, implicate privacy concerns far beyond those implicated by the search of a cigarette pack, a wallet, or a purse. A conclusion that inspecting the contents of an arrestee's pockets works no substantial additional intrusion on privacy beyond the arrest itself may make sense as applied to physical items, but any extension of that reasoning to digital data has to rest on its own bottom. Cell phones differ in both a quantitative and a qualitative sense from other objects that might be kept on an arrestee's person. The term "cell phone" is itself misleading shorthand; many of these devices are in fact minicomputers that also happen to have the capacity to be used as a telephone. They could just as easily be called cameras, video players, rolodexes, calendars, tape recorders, libraries, diaries, albums, televisions, maps, or newspapers. One of the most notable distinguishing features of modern cell phones is their immense storage capacity. Before cell phones, a search of a person was limited by physical realities and tended as a general matter to constitute only a narrow intrusion on privacy. Most people cannot lug around every piece of mail they have received for the past several months, every picture they have taken, or every book or article they have read—nor would they have any reason to attempt to do so. And if they did, they would have to drag behind them a trunk rather than a container the size of the cigarette package in *Robinson*.

But the possible intrusion on privacy is not physically limited in the same way when it comes to cell phones. The current top-selling smart phone has a standard capacity of 16 gigabytes (and is available with up to 64 gigabytes). Sixteen gigabytes translates to millions of pages of text, thousands of pictures, or hundreds of videos. Cell phones couple that capacity with the ability to store many different types of information: Even the most basic phones that sell for less than $20 might hold photographs, picture messages, text messages, Internet browsing history, a calendar, a thousand-entry phone book, and so on. We expect that the gulf between physical practicability and digital capacity will only continue to widen in the future.

The storage capacity of cell phones has several interrelated consequences for privacy. First, a cell phone collects in one place many distinct types of information—an address, a note, a prescription, a bank statement, a video—that reveal much more in combination than any isolated record. Second, a cell phone's capacity allows even just one type of information to convey far more than previously possible. The sum of an individual's private life can be reconstructed through a thousand photographs labeled with dates, locations, and descriptions; the same cannot be said of a photograph or two of loved ones tucked into a wallet. Third, the data on a phone can date back to the purchase of the phone, or even earlier. A person might carry in his pocket a slip of paper reminding him to call Mr. Jones; he would not carry a record of all his communications with Mr. Jones for the past several months, as would routinely be kept on a phone.

Finally, there is an element of pervasiveness that characterizes cell phones but not physical records. Prior to the digital age, people did not typically carry a cache of sensitive personal information with them as they went about their day. Now it is the person who is not carrying a cell phone, with all that it contains, who is the exception. According to one poll, nearly three-quarters of smart phone users report being within five feet of their phones most of the time, with 12% admitting that they even use their phones in the shower. A decade ago police officers searching an arrestee might have occasionally stumbled across a highly personal item such as a diary. But those discoveries were likely to be few and far between. Today, by contrast, it is no exaggeration to say that many of the more than 90% of American adults who own a cell phone keep on their person a digital record of nearly every aspect of their lives—from the mundane to the intimate. Allowing the police to scrutinize such records on a routine basis is quite different from allowing them to search a personal item or two in the occasional case.

Although the data stored on a cell phone is distinguished from physical records by quantity alone, certain types of data are also qualitatively different. An Internet search and browsing history, for example, can be found on an Internet-enabled phone and could reveal an individual's private interests or concerns—perhaps a search for certain symptoms of disease, coupled with frequent visits to WebMD. Data on a cell phone can also reveal where a person has been. Historic location information is a standard feature on many smart phones and can reconstruct someone's specific movements down to the minute, not only around town but also within a particular building. See *United States v. Jones*, 132 S. Ct. 945 (2012) (Sotomayor, J., concurring) ("GPS monitoring generates a precise, comprehensive record of a person's public movements that reflects a wealth of detail about her familial, political, professional, religious, and sexual associations.").

Mobile application software on a cell phone, or "apps," offer a range of tools for managing detailed information about all aspects of a person's life. There are apps for Democratic Party news and Republican Party news; apps for alcohol, drug, and gambling addictions; apps for sharing prayer requests; apps for tracking pregnancy symptoms; apps for planning your budget; apps for every conceivable hobby or pastime; apps for improving your romantic life. There are popular apps for buying or selling just about anything, and the records of such transactions may be accessible on the phone indefinitely. There are over a million apps available in each of the two major app stores; the phrase "there's an app for that" is now part of the popular lexicon. The average smart phone user has installed 33 apps, which together can form a revealing montage of the user's life.

In 1926, Learned Hand observed (in an opinion quoted in *Chimel*) that it is "a totally different thing to search a man's pockets and use against him what they contain, from ransacking his house for everything which may incriminate him." *United States v. Kirschenblatt*, 16 F. 2d 202, 203 (CA2). If his pockets contain a cell phone, that is no longer true. A cell phone search would typically expose to the government far *more* than the most exhaustive search of a house: A phone not only contains in digital form many sensitive records previously found in the home; it also contains a broad array of private information never found in a home in any form—unless the phone is.

To further complicate the scope of the privacy interests at stake, the data a user views on many modern cell phones may not in fact be stored on the device itself. Treating a cell phone as a container whose contents may be searched incident to an arrest is a bit strained as an initial matter. But the analogy crumbles entirely when a cell phone is used to access data located elsewhere, at the tap of a screen. That is what cell phones, with increasing frequency, are designed to do by taking advantage of "cloud computing." Cloud computing is the capacity of Internet-connected devices to display data stored on remote servers rather than on the device itself. Cell phone users often may not know whether particular information is stored on the device or in the cloud, and it generally makes little difference. Moreover, the same type of data may be stored locally on the device for one user and in the cloud for another.

Call Log

We reject the suggestion that officers should always be able to search a phone's call log. The Government relies on *Smith v. Maryland*, 442 U. S. 735 (1979), which held that no warrant was required to use a pen register at telephone company premises to identify numbers dialed by a particular caller. That case, however, concluded that the use of a pen register was not a "search" under the Fourth Amendment. There is no dispute here that the officers engaged in a search of Wurie's cell phone. Moreover, call logs typically contain more than just phone numbers; they include any identifying information that an individual might add, such as the label "my house" in Wurie's case.

California suggested that officers could search cell phone data if they could have obtained the same information from a pre-digital counterpart. But the fact that a search in the pre-digital era could have turned up a photograph or two in a wallet does not justify a search of thousands of photos in a digital gallery. The fact that someone could have tucked a paper bank statement in a pocket does not justify a search of every bank statement from the last five years. Such an analogue test would allow law enforcement to search a range of items contained on a phone, even though people would be unlikely to carry such a variety of information in physical form. In Riley's case, it is implausible that he would have strolled around with video tapes, photo albums, and an address book all crammed into his pockets. But because each of those items has a pre-digital analogue, police would be able to search a phone for all of those items—a significant diminution of privacy. In addition, an analogue test would launch courts on a difficult line-drawing expedition to determine which digital files are comparable to physical records. Is an e-mail equivalent to a letter? Is a voicemail equivalent to a phone message slip? It is not clear how officers could make these kinds of decisions before conducting a search, or how courts would apply the proposed rule after the fact.

We cannot deny that our decision will have an impact on the ability of law enforcement to combat crime. Cell phones have become important tools in facilitating coordination and communication among members of criminal enterprises, and can provide valuable incriminating information about dangerous criminals. Privacy comes at a cost. Our holding is not that the information on a cell phone is immune from search; it is instead that a warrant is generally required before such a search, even when a cell phone is seized incident to arrest. Our cases have recognized that the warrant requirement is "an important working part of our machinery of government," not merely "an inconvenience to be somehow 'weighed' against the claims of police efficiency." *Coolidge v. New Hampshire*, 403 U. S. 443, 481 (1971). Recent technological advances similar to those discussed here have made the process of obtaining a warrant itself more efficient. See *McNeely*, 133 S. Ct. at 1561 (Roberts, C. J., concurring and dissenting) ("police officers can e-mail warrant requests to judges' iPads and judges have signed such warrants and e-mailed them back to officers in less than 15 minutes").

[The Court went on to discuss the applicability of various exceptions to the warrant requirement, including the exigent circumstances exception and the search incident to legal arrest exception, both of which were rejected.]

Our cases have recognized that the Fourth Amendment was the founding generation's response to the reviled "general warrants" and "writs of assistance" of the colonial era, which allowed British officers to rummage through homes in an unrestrained search for evidence of criminal activity. Opposition to such searches was in fact one of the driving forces behind the Revolution itself. 10 Works of John Adams 247–248 (C. Adams ed. 1856). Modern cellphones are not just another technological convenience. With all they contain and all they may reveal, they hold for many Americans "the privacies of life." The fact that technology now allows an individual to carry such information in his hand does not make the information any less worthy of the protection for which the Founders fought. Our answer to the question of what police must do before searching a cell phone seized incident to an arrest is accordingly simple—get a warrant.

Points for Discussion

a. CSLI Data and Clouds

The Supreme Court soon will decide whether police may obtain "cell site location information" (CSLI) data from internet service providers (ISPs) without a warrant. This case raises the question whether Smith's third party search doctrine can justify the rejection of the claim of cell phone owners to possess a REOP in such data. *See Carpenter v. United States*, 819 F.3d 880 (6th Cir. 2016), cert. granted, 137 S.Ct. 2211 (2017). In the typical litigation regarding CSLI data, government agents obtain an order directing an ISP to provide data that reveals the movement of the defendant's cell phone. Although the lower courts are divided on the REOP issue, most federal courts have upheld such orders, which do not require probable cause.

Since 2008, the advent of cloud computing has posed new REOP issues. Arguably, the application of the third party doctrine would result in the rejection of a REOP in cloud data when a service agreement gives the cloud service provider the right of access to cloud data. Notably, however, the Riley Court observed that cell phone users "often may not know whether particular information is stored on their devices or in the cloud."

b. Sources of Protection for Electronic Communications

In 2014, the Missouri state constitution was amended as the result of a popular referendum to add "electronic communications and data" to the textual reference to protection for "persons, houses, papers, and effects." In 2015, the California legislature enacted the Electronic Communications Privacy Act, which requires a warrant for "all digital content, location information, metadata, and access to devices like cell phones."

Hypo 1: *Police Device to Track Cell Phones*

Federal and state law enforcement officials are now using a device known as a "stingray" or "ISMI catcher," which can imitate a cell phone tower and thereby interact with all nearby cell phones. Using radio waves, the stingray downloads the identifying data (IMSI or ESN) from all of the connected cell phones without going through the service provider. The stingray device can pinpoint the house in which a cell phone is located, even when no one is using the phone to make a call or obtain access to the internet. When stingray surveillance occurs, service to the connected cell phone is disrupted and it cannot be used. In order to obtain a stingray device from the manufacturer, a police department must sign a non-disclosure agreement, which is why the prevalence of stingray use remained secret until media revelations in 2014. Does the use of a stingray device constitute a "search" of the cell phones that are forced to connect to it? Does it matter whether the cell phone is in public or in a private home? If so, should the warrant requirement apply to stingray usage? How should a court respond if a prosecutor or police officer refuses to disclose evidence of stingray use, either to defense counsel or to the court, during court proceedings? *See United States v. Lambis*, 197 F.Supp.3d 606 (S.D.N.Y. 2016); *United States v. Patrick*, 842 F.3d 540 (7th Cir. 2016).

Hypo 2: *License Plate Tracking*

The DEA has accumulated a database based on information received from "license plate reader" cameras located on major highways, including cameras operated by state and local law enforcement. The data provides information about the location and movement of vehicles in real time, and has resulted in the storage of hundreds of millions of records that can be accessed by police nationwide for their investigations. Initially, the DEA program focused on camera data from highways in states along the U.S. border, but the program was expanded to other states, and the DEA does not disclose the locations of the highway cameras used to collect the data. Although the data in the original program was preserved in the DEA database for two years, the data is saved now for only three months. Previously unknown details about the program were revealed in records obtained by the ACLU by means of a Freedom of Information Act request and shared with the media. Does this data gathering violate the REOP of motorists regarding their movements? If so, what kind of judicial supervision of the program should be required under the Fourth Amendment?

Hypo 3: *Facial Recognition Technology*

Some of the images obtained from "license plate reader" cameras (described in the prior Hypo) make it possible to identify drivers and passengers accurately, and the DEA's database includes such photos of vehicle occupants. Does a Fourth Amendment "search" occur when these photos are taken? Or does it occur when the photos are entered into a "facial recognition" database so that they can be compared to other facial images (such as those on Facebook, in blog posts, or in other internet sources) for purposes of "facial recognition tracking"?

c. Probable Cause

Probable cause is an integral part of the Fourth Amendment's prohibition against unreasonable searches and seizures: "no Warrants shall issue, but upon probable cause, supported by Oath or affirmation." When the police obtain a warrant, the warrant must be based on probable cause. In addition, some exceptions to the warrant requirement also require probable cause (i.e., the automobile exception). *Marshall v. Barlows, Inc.*, 436 U.S. 307 (1978); *United States v. Leon,*

468 U.S. 897 (1984). What must be "probable?" When the police want to conduct a search, probable cause requires proof of two things: that the fruits, instrumentalities or evidence of crime exist, and that they can be found at the place to be searched. When the police want to arrest, probable cause requires proof that a crime was committed and that the person to be arrested committed it.

Applied literally, "probable cause" requires that something be "more probable than not." However, the courts have not applied the probable cause requirement literally. In *Draper v. United States*, 358 U.S. 307 (1959), the Court defined probable cause in the following way: "In dealing with probable cause, as the very name implies, we deal with probabilities. These are not technical; they are the factual and practical considerations of everyday life on which reasonable and prudent men, not legal technicians, act." Probable cause exists where "the facts and circumstances within the arresting officers' knowledge and of which they had reasonably trustworthy information are sufficient in themselves to warrant a man of reasonable caution in the belief that 'an offense has been or is being committed.'" *Carroll v. United States*, 267 U.S. 132 (1925).

> **FYI**
>
> Why was the probable cause requirement included in the Fourth Amendment? Dissenting in *Marshall v. Barlow's, Inc.*, 436 U.S. 307 (1978), Mr. Justice Stevens explained: "Since the general warrant, not the warrantless search, was the immediate evil at which the Fourth Amendment was directed, it is not surprising that the Framers placed precise limits on its issuance. The requirement that a warrant only issue on a showing of particularized probable cause was the means adopted to circumscribe the warrant power." *See also United States v. Leon*, 468 U.S. 897 (1984) (Stevens, J., concurring) ("In the Framers' minds the paradigm of an abusive search was the execution of a warrant not based on probable cause."). So, not only must a warrant particularly describe the place to be searched and the things to be seized, but it must be based on probable cause to believe that the searched for items can be found at the place to be searched.

Carroll v. United States

267 U.S. 132 (1925).

MR. CHIEF JUSTICE TAFT, delivered the opinion of the Court.

Section 25, title 2, of the National Prohibition Act, passed to enforce the Eighteenth Amendment, makes it unlawful to have or possess any liquor intended for use in violating the act.

Grand Rapids is about 152 miles from Detroit. Detroit and its neighborhood along the Detroit river, which is the international boundary, is one of the most active centers for introducing illegally into this country spirituous liquors for distribution into the interior. Prohibition agents were engaged in a regular patrol along the important highways from Detroit to Grand Rapids to stop and seize liquor carried in automobiles. They <u>knew</u> or <u>had convincing evidence to believe</u> that the Carroll boys, as they called them, were so-called "bootleggers" in Grand Rapids; i.e., that they were engaged in plying the unlawful trade of selling liquor in that city. The officers soon after noted their going from Grand Rapids half way to Detroit, and attempted to follow them to that city to see where they went, but they escaped observation. Two months later the officers suddenly met the same men on their way westward presumably from Detroit. They were in the same automobile they had been in the night when they tried to furnish the whisky to the officers. They were coming from the direction of the great source of supply for their stock to Grand Rapids, where they plied their trade. That the officers, when they saw the defendants, believed that they were carrying liquor, we can have no doubt, and we think it is equally clear that they had reasonable cause for thinking so. Emphasis is put by defendants' counsel on the statement made by one of the officers that they were not looking for defendants at the particular time when they appeared. As soon as they appeared, the officers were entitled to use their reasoning faculties upon all the facts of which they had previous knowledge in respect to the defendants.

In light of these authorities, and this record, it is clear the officers here had justification for the search and seizure. This is to say that the facts and circumstances within their knowledge and of which they had reasonably trustworthy information were sufficient in themselves to warrant a man of reasonable caution in the belief that intoxicating liquor was being transported in the automobile which they stopped and searched.

The judgment is affirmed.

The separate opinion of MR. JUSTICE MCREYNOLDS.

While quietly driving an ordinary automobile along a much frequented public road, plaintiffs in error were arrested by federal officers without a warrant and upon mere suspicion. The facts known by the officers who arrested plaintiffs in error were wholly insufficient to create a reasonable belief that they were transporting liquor contrary to law. The negotiation concerning three cases of whisky on September 29th was the only circumstance which could have subjected plaintiffs in error to any reasonable suspicion. No whisky was delivered, and it is not certain that they ever intended to deliver any. The arrest came 2 ½ months after the negotiation. Every act in the meantime is consistent with complete innocence. Has it come about that merely because a man once agreed to deliver whisky, but did not, he may be arrested whenever thereafter he ventures to drive an automobile on the road to Detroit!

Point for Discussion

Probable Cause for Possession

In *Maryland v. Pringle*, 540 U.S. 366 (2003), a police officer stopped a vehicle for a speeding violation and found cocaine between the back seat and the arm rest. When all three passengers denied ownership, the officer arrested all three. The Court held that the officer had probable cause to arrest all of them despite their denials. Later, after being given a *Miranda* warning, Pringle admitted that the cocaine belonged to him and that he planned to sell it. When the admission was used against him at trial, Pringle appealed claiming that the admission was the illegal fruit of an unlawful arrest. The Court held that the officer had probable cause to arrest all three passengers: "We think it an entirely reasonable inference from these facts that any or all three of the occupants had knowledge of, and exercised dominion and control over, the cocaine. Thus a reasonable officer could conclude that there was probable cause to believe Pringle committed the crime of possession of cocaine, either solely or jointly."

Hypo 1: *Applying the Probable Cause Requirement*

Suppose that there is a street in your city where a large number of drug transactions occur. A significant percentage (in excess of 50%) of people on that street are either drug pushers or are drug users who are purchasing drugs. Given these facts, do the police have "probable cause" to believe that everyone they find on the street is in possession of drugs? As a result, would the police have probable cause to arrest those that they find suspiciously "hanging-out" on a street corner? What about a little old lady walking down the street pulling a shopping cart? If the police do not have probable cause as to everyone, how does the character of the street affect the probable cause determination in an individual case?

Hypo 2: *Refusing Consent*

Suppose that a police officer validly stops a motorist for a traffic violation (a burnt out taillight). After issuing the motorist a citation, the officer asks the motorist for permission to search the motorist's trunk, but the motorist refuses. The officer, who honestly believes that any law-abiding citizen would graciously consent to a search request, believes that the motorist has "something to hide. Otherwise, he would have given consent." Does the motorist's refusal give the officer probable cause to believe that the car contains contraband?

Hypo 3: *Retracting Consent*

Defendant is stopped at a valid roadblock established to check driver's licenses. After checking defendant's driver's license and registration, the officer requests permission to search the car. The officer does so based on a "hunch" that the odor of a deodorizing agent emanating from the car might indicate the presence of narcotics. When defendant opens the trunk, the officer sees a "heavily taped" cardboard box. When the officer presses on the box, defendant puts a briefcase on top of the box, closes the trunk, and states that the search is over. Based upon the circumstances, the officer thinks that he has probable cause to believe that defendant is in possession of narcotics. Does the officer have probable cause to search the box? *See State v. Zelinske*, 108 N.M. 784, 779 P.2d 97 (App. 1989).

Hypo 4: *The "Pot Odor"*

When a police officer validly stops an automobile, he smells a marijuana scent emanating from the vehicle. Does the officer have probable cause to arrest the driver? *See State v. Grande*, 164 Wash.2d 135, 187 P.3d 248 (2008). Would it matter whether the state has a medical marijuana statute that allows individuals to possess marijuana for therapeutic medical reasons? *See State v. Senna*, 79 A.3d 45 (Vt. 2013).

Hypo 5: *Defining Probable Cause*

Shortly before midnight, a police officer stops Digiovanni's car on an interstate highway because the officer believes that it is traveling too close to the car in front. When the officer asks the driver for his driver's license and registration, the driver provides a rental contract along with a Massachusetts driver's license. During this process, the officer, relying on his experience, concludes that the driver is involved in drug trafficking. He bases this conclusion on several factors: two shirts hanging in the rear passenger compartment and a hygiene bag on the back seat and the fact that the interior of the car is clean. The officer believes that non-drug traffickers on vacation would pack the shirts in a clothing bag. The officer views the cleanness of the car as suspicious because "it is indicative of nonstop driving." The officer views the rental contract as indicative of drug trafficking activity because the car was rented at Fort Lauderdale International Airport the previous day and was to be dropped off at Logan International Airport in Boston, at a cost of $438. The officer views this car rental as "implausible." Does the officer possess probable cause to believe that the driver is in possession of illegal drugs? *See United States v. Digiovanni*, 650 F.3d 498 (4th Cir. 2011).

Hypo 6: *More on Defining Probable Cause*

In the prior problem, assume that the driver is ordered to exit the car, and the officer asks questions concerning his travel plans. The driver states that he is traveling from Florida, where he spent the weekend with family, to Boston (where he lives), with a stop at his sister's residence in New York to pick up "some paintings and whatnot." The officer then asks the driver if he has any luggage in the car and if everything in the car belongs to him. The driver responds in the affirmative and says "oh boy" as he tosses his cigarette over the guardrail. The officer finds this remark "extremely suspicious," and asks the driver what is the matter, to which he replies, "it's just so hot." The officer then asks the driver if there is any marijuana in the car. The driver replies, "no sir. I never smoked marijuana in my life. It puts me to sleep." The officer asks the driver if there is any cocaine, heroin or methamphetamine in the car. The officer follows up with, "are you sure?," to which the driver replies, "I'm positive." Does the officer have probable cause to search the vehicle? How does the driver's nonsensical response (that he had "never" smoked marijuana because it puts him to sleep) enter into the analysis? See *United States v. Digiovanni*, 650 F.3d 498 (4th Cir. 2011).

Hypo 7: *Public Telephones and Drug Transactions*

A police detective knows that drug transactions are often arranged using public telephones, and that a particular public phone is frequently used for this purpose. One night, he sees a car parked near the phone, and also sees a man exit the car, make a short phone call, and then drive off. The officer follows the car which parks by the side of the road a short distance away. Another car pulls up nearby, a man leaves the other car and enters the first car, the two drive around the block, and the man (from the other car) exits and returns to his original vehicle. Although the officer does not witness an exchange of drugs or money during these events, he believes (based on his experience) that a drug transaction has taken place. Does the officer have probable cause to stop and search either or both vehicles? *See Commonwealth v. Levy*, 76 Mass. App. Ct. 617, 924 N.E.2d 771 (2010).

Hypo 8: *Computers Images of Child Pornography*

A police officer finds McArthur masturbating in a public place, and arrests him for public indecency. In inventorying the contents of McArthur's wallet at the police station, the police find child pornography. Based on the photograph, and McArthur's conduct in public, the police apply for a warrant to search his home. Suppose that you are the judge assigned to hear the case. Is there probable cause to believe that McArthur has child pornography in his home? *See United States v. McArthur,* 573 F.3d 608 (8th Cir. 2009); *State v. Byrne,* 972 A.2d 633 (R.I. 2009). Would your analysis be affected by the fact that McArthur has previously been convicted of committing two sex offenses (one involving sodomy on a minor), and has failed to register as a sex offender?

Spinelli v. United States

393 U.S. 410 (1969).

MR. JUSTICE HARLAN delivered the opinion of the Court.

William Spinelli was convicted of traveling to St. Louis, Missouri, from a nearby Illinois suburb with the intention of conducting gambling activities proscribed by Missouri law. Believing it desirable that the principles of *Aguilar v. Texas*, 378 U.S. 108 (1964), should be further explicated, we granted certiorari.

In *Aguilar*, a search warrant issued upon an affidavit of police officers who swore only that they had "received reliable information from a credible person and do believe" that narcotics were being illegally stored on the described premises. Recognizing that the constitutional requirement of probable cause can be satisfied by hearsay information, this Court held the affidavit inadequate for two reasons. First, the application failed to set forth any of the "underlying circumstances" necessary to enable the magistrate independently to judge the validity of the informant's conclusion that the narcotics were where he said they were. Second, the affiant-officers did not attempt to support their claim that their informant was "credible" or his information "reliable." The Government is, however, quite right in saying that the FBI affidavit in the present case is more ample than that in *Aguilar*. Not only does it contain a report from an anonymous informant, but it also contains a report of an independent FBI investigation which is said to corroborate the informant's tip. We are then, required to delineate the manner in which *Aguilar*'s two-pronged test should be applied in these circumstances.

In essence, the affidavit contained the following allegations:

1. The FBI had kept track of Spinelli's movements on five days during the month of August 1965. On four of these occasions, Spinelli was seen crossing one of two bridges leading from Illinois into St. Louis, Missouri, between 11 a.m. and 12:15 p.m. On four of the five days, Spinelli was also seen parking his car in a lot used by residents of an apartment house at 1108 Indian Circle Drive in St. Louis, between 3:30 p.m. and 4:45 p.m.[6] On one day, Spinelli was followed further and seen to enter a particular apartment in the building.

2. An FBI check with the telephone company revealed that this apartment contained two telephones listed under the name of Grace P. Hagen, and carrying the numbers WYdown 4–0029 and WYdown 4–0136.

3. The application stated that "William Spinelli is known to this affiant and to federal law enforcement agents and local law enforcement agents as a bookmaker, an associate of bookmakers, a gambler, and an associate of gamblers."

4. Finally it was stated that the FBI "has been informed by a confidential reliable informant that William Spinelli is operating a handbook and accepting wagers and disseminating wagering information by means of the telephones which have been assigned the numbers WYdown 4–0029 and WYdown 4–0136."

The last item mentioned, detailing the informant's tip, has a fundamental place in this warrant application. Without it, probable cause could not be established. The first two items reflect only innocent-seeming activity and data. Spinelli's travels to and from the apartment building and his entry into a particular apartment on one occasion could hardly be taken as bespeaking gambling activity; and there is surely nothing unusual about an apartment containing two separate telephones. Many a householder indulges himself in this petty luxury. Finally, the allegation that Spinelli was "known" to the affiant and to other federal and local law enforcement officers as a gambler and an associate of gamblers is but a bald and unilluminating assertion of suspicion that is entitled to no weight in appraising the magistrate's decision.

---

[6] No report was made as to Spinelli's movements during the period between his arrival in St. Louis at noon and his arrival at the parking lot in the late afternoon. Evidence at trial indicated that Spinelli frequented the offices of his stockbroker during this period.

So much indeed the Government does not deny. Rather, the Government claims that the informant's tip gives a suspicious color to the FBI's reports detailing Spinelli's innocent-seeming conduct and that, conversely, the FBI's surveillance corroborates the informant's tip, thereby entitling it to more weight. It is true, of course, that the magistrate is obligated to render a judgment based upon a common-sense reading of the entire affidavit. We believe, however, that the "totality of circumstances" approach taken by the Court of Appeals paints with too broad a brush. Where, as here, the informer's tip is a necessary element in a finding of probable cause, its proper weight must be determined by a more precise analysis.

The informer's report must first be measured against *Aguilar*'s standards so that its probative value can be assessed. If the tip is found inadequate under *Aguilar*, the other allegations which corroborate the information contained in the hearsay report should then be considered. At this stage as well, however, the standards enunciated in *Aguilar* must inform the magistrate's decision. He must ask: Can it fairly be said that the tip, even when certain parts of it have been corroborated by independent sources, is as trustworthy as a tip which would pass *Aguilar*'s tests without independent corroboration? *Aguilar* establishes that probable cause must be determined by a "neutral and detached magistrate," and not by "the officer engaged in the often competitive enterprise of ferreting out crime." A magistrate cannot properly discharge his constitutional duty if he relies on an informer's tip which—even when partially corroborated—is not as reliable as one which passes *Aguilar*'s requirements when standing alone.

Applying these principles to the present case, we first consider the weight to be given the informer's tip when it is considered apart from the rest of the affidavit. It is clear that a Commissioner could not credit it without abdicating his constitutional function. Though the affiant swore that his confidant was "reliable," he offered the magistrate no reason in support of this conclusion. Perhaps even more important is the fact that *Aguilar*'s other test has not been satisfied. The tip does not contain a sufficient statement of the underlying circumstances from which the informer concluded that Spinelli was running a bookmaking operation. We are not told how the FBI's source received his information—it is not alleged that the informant personally observed Spinelli at work or that he had ever placed a bet with him. Moreover, if the informant came by the information indirectly, he did not explain why his sources were reliable. In the absence of a statement detailing the manner in which the information was gathered, it is especially important that the tip describe the accused's criminal activity in sufficient detail that the magistrate may know that he is relying on something more substantial than a casual rumor circulating in the underworld or an accusation based merely on an individual's general reputation.

The detail provided by the informant in *Draper v. United States*, 358 U.S. 307 (1959), provides a suitable benchmark. While Hereford, the Government's informer in that case did not state the way in which he had obtained his information, he reported that Draper had gone to Chicago the day before by train and that he would return to Denver by train with three ounces of heroin on one of two specified mornings. Moreover, Hereford went on to describe, with minute particularity, the clothes that Draper would be wearing upon his arrival at the Denver station. A magistrate, when confronted with such detail, could reasonably infer that the informant had gained his information in a reliable way.[7] Such an inference cannot be made in the present case. Here, the only facts supplied were that Spinelli was using two specified telephones and that these phones were being used in gambling operations. This meager report could easily have been obtained from an offhand remark heard at a neighborhood bar.

Nor do we believe that the patent doubts *Aguilar* raises as to the report's reliability are adequately resolved by a consideration of the allegations detailing the FBI's independent investigative efforts. At most, these allegations indicated that Spinelli could have used the telephones specified by the informant for some purpose. This cannot by itself be said to support both the inference that the informer was generally trustworthy and that he had made his charge against Spinelli on the basis of information obtained in a reliable way. Once again, *Draper* provides a relevant comparison. Independent police work in that case corroborated much more than one small detail that had been provided by the informant. There, the police, upon meeting the inbound Denver train on the second morning specified by informer Hereford, saw a man whose dress corresponded precisely to Hereford's detailed description. It was then apparent that the informant had not been fabricating his report out of whole cloth; since the report was of the sort which in common experience may be recognized as having been obtained in a reliable way, it was perfectly clear that probable cause had been established.

We conclude that the informant's tip—even when corroborated to the extent indicated—was not sufficient to provide the basis for a finding of probable cause. This is not to say that the tip was so insubstantial that it could not properly have counted in the magistrate's determination. Rather, it needed some further support. When we look to the other parts of the application, however, we find nothing alleged which would permit the suspicions engendered by the informant's report to ripen into a judgment that a crime was probably being committed.

The judgment of the Court of Appeals is *reversed*.

MR. JUSTICE WHITE, concurring.

The informant claimed the business involved gambling. Since his specific information about Spinelli using two phones with particular numbers had been

---

[7] While *Draper* involved the question whether the police had probable cause for an arrest without a warrant, the analysis required for this question is basically similar to that demanded when a magistrate considers whether a search warrant should issue.

verified, did not his allegation about gambling thereby become sufficiently more believable if the *Draper* principle is given any scope at all? I would think so, particularly since information from the informant which was verified was not neutral, irrelevant information but was material to proving the gambling allegation: two phones with different numbers in an apartment used away from home indicates a business use in an operation, like bookmaking, where multiple phones are needed. The *Draper* approach would reasonably justify the issuance of a warrant in this case, particularly since the police had some awareness of Spinelli's past activities. The majority, however, while seemingly embracing *Draper*, confines that case to its own facts. I join the opinion of the Court and the judgment of reversal.

MR. JUSTICE BLACK, dissenting.

The affidavit given the magistrate was more than ample to show probable cause of the petitioner's guilt. The affidavit meticulously set out facts sufficient to show the following:

1. The petitioner had been shown going to and coming from a room in an apartment which contained two telephones listed under the name of another person. Nothing indicates that the apartment was of that large and luxurious type which could only be occupied by a person to whom it would be a "petty luxury" to have two separate telephones, with different numbers, both listed under the name of a person who did not live there.

2. The petitioner's car had been observed parked in the apartment's parking lot. This fact was highly relevant in showing that the petitioner was extremely interested in some enterprise which was located in the apartment.

3. The FBI had been informed by a reliable informant that the petitioner was accepting wagering information by telephones—the particular telephones located in the apartment the defendant had been repeatedly visiting. Unless the Court, going beyond the requirements of the Fourth Amendment, wishes to require magistrates to hold trials before issuing warrants, it is not necessary to have the affiant explain "the underlying circumstances from which the informer concluded that Spinelli was running a bookmaking operation."

4. The petitioner was known by federal and local law enforcement agents as a bookmaker and an associate of gamblers. Although the statement is hearsay that might not be admissible in a regular trial, everyone knows, unless he shuts his eyes to the realities of life, that this is a relevant fact which, together with other circumstances, might indicate a factual probability that gambling is taking place.

The foregoing facts should be enough to constitute probable cause for anyone who does not believe that the only way to obtain a search warrant is to prove beyond a reasonable doubt that a defendant is guilty. Even *Aguilar* cannot support the contrary result.

MR. JUSTICE FORTAS, dissenting.

A policeman's affidavit should not be judged as an entry in an essay contest. A policeman's affidavit is entitled to common-sense evaluation. The judgment of the Court of Appeals for the Eighth Circuit should be affirmed.

Make the Connection

Although *Spinelli* made clear that the police could use hearsay testimony in a probable cause hearing, the Court placed limits on the use of such testimony by imposing the *Aguilar-Spinelli* test. Ordinarily, when the police seek a warrant, they do so based on the testimony or affidavits of police officers. However, informants are an integral part of the investigative process, and are often relied on by police in their affidavits and testimony. The difficulty is that the testimony of informants is often used in a "hearsay" way (hearsay being defined as an out-of-court statement offered to prove the truth of the matter asserted in the statement). In criminal and civil trials, the use of hearsay is usually prohibited except when the statement fits into one of the many exceptions to the hearsay rule. By contrast, hearsay is usually admissible in a probable cause hearing. In *Draper v. United States*, 358 U.S. 307 (1959), the Court rejected petitioner's contention that "because hearsay is not legally competent evidence in a criminal trial, it could not legally have been considered, but should have been put out of mind" in deciding whether probable cause existed to arrest petitioner. The Court justified its holding by stating that there "is a large difference between the two things to be proved, guilt and probable cause, as well as between the tribunals which determine them, and therefore a like difference in the quanta and modes of proof required to establish them."

Food for Thought

The *Spinelli* decision discusses the decision in *Draper v. United States*. Is it clear to you why probable cause existed in *Draper*, but not in *Spinelli*? What additional facts would have been needed to establish probable cause in *Spinelli* under the *Draper* precedent?

Hypo 1: *Corroboration of an Informer's Tip*

A veteran informer warns police that a suspect is going to make a cocaine delivery by a particular route. The tip provides the race and age of the suspect, as well as his name, and information regarding the suspect's vehicle, license plate number, the time of day and route that the suspect will take (going from Vermont to Pennsylvania). A police officer stakes out the route. When the officer observes a car and driver matching the description, he follows it. Under the *Aguilar-Spinelli* standards, does the officer have probable cause to stop and search the vehicle? *See State v. Robinson*, 185 Vt. 232, 969 A.2d 127 (2009).

Hypo 2: *The Repairman's Phone Call*

A landlord calls a repairman to fix a problem at a rental home. The repairman observes marijuana and other suspicious items in the house, lying in plain view, and calls the police. Based on the repairman's phone call, do the police have probable cause to obtain a warrant under the *Aguilar-Spinelli* standards if the repairman has not previously given a tip? *See State v. Eisfeldt*, 163 Wash.2d 628, 185 P.3d 580 (2008).

Hypo 3: *The Eyewitness Report*

A woman is sweeping the front porch of her home when she sees a man walk onto a neighbor's porch and peer in the front door. The man then stops at another house and disappears. The woman later sees the man standing at a nearby bus stop where he has taken off his shirt and is using it to cover a television set. He is pacing nervously and is trying to hitchhike while waiting for the bus to arrive. The woman calls the police, tells them about the man's activities and location, and reports her suspicions of burglary. Officer Freeman, a twenty year veteran, arrives five minutes later. He asks the man for identification which he cannot produce. When the officer asks about the television set, the man states that he bought the television set from someone in the neighborhood for $100. A "pat down" search for weapons reveals that the man (who is wearing only an undershirt) has brown wool gloves in his back pocket. While the man is being questioned, the woman makes herself known to the officers as the woman who called the police. The man is then arrested and searched. Did the officer have probable cause to arrest the man? Would it matter that, after the arrest, the owners of a house one block south of the woman's house report that their house has been burglarized and that a television set (the one found in the man's possession) has been stolen? *See People v. Quintero*, 657 P.2d 948 (Colo., En Banc, 1973).

Illinois v. Gates

462 U.S. 213 (1983).

JUSTICE REHNQUIST delivered the opinion of the Court.

Bloomingdale, Ill, is a suburb of Chicago located in DuPage County. On May 3, 1978, the Bloomingdale Police Department received by mail an anonymous handwritten letter which read as follows:

> "This letter is to inform you that you have a couple in your town who strictly make their living on selling drugs. They are Sue and Lance Gates, they live on Greenway, off Bloomingdale Rd. in the condominiums. Most of their buys are done in Florida. Sue his wife drives their car to Florida, where she leaves it to be loaded up with drugs, then Lance flies down and drives it back. Sue flies back after she drops the car off in Florida. May 3 she is driving down there again and Lance will be flying down in a few days to drive it back. At the time Lance drives the car back he has the trunk loaded with over $100,000.00 in drugs. Presently they have over $100,000.00 worth of drugs in their basement.
>
> They brag about the fact they never have to work, and make their entire living on pushers. I guarantee if you watch them carefully you will make a big catch. They are friends with some big drugs dealers, who visit their house often.
>
> Lance & Susan Gates
>
> Greenway
>
> in Condominiums"

The letter was referred by the Chief of Police of the Bloomingdale Police Department to Detective Mader, who decided to pursue the tip. Mader learned, from the office of the Illinois Secretary of State, that an Illinois driver's license had been issued to one Lance Gates, residing at a stated address in Bloomingdale. He contacted a confidential informant, whose examination of certain financial records revealed a more recent address for the Gates, and he also learned from a police officer assigned to O'Hare Airport that "L. Gates" had made a reservation on Eastern Airlines flight 245 to West Palm Beach, Fla., scheduled to depart from Chicago on May 5 at 4:15 p.m.

Mader then made arrangements with an agent of the Drug Enforcement Administration for surveillance of the May 5 Eastern Airlines flight. The agent later reported to Mader that Gates had boarded the flight, and that federal agents in Florida had observed him arrive in West Palm Beach and take a taxi to the nearby Holiday Inn. They also reported that Gates went to a room registered to one Susan Gates and that, at 7:00 a.m. the next morning, Gates and an unidentified woman left the motel in a Mercury bearing Illinois license plates and drove northbound on an interstate frequently used by travelers to the Chicago area. In addition, the DEA agent informed Mader that the license plate number on the Mercury registered to a Hornet station wagon owned by Gates. The agent also advised Mader that the driving time between West Palm Beach and Bloomingdale was approximately 22 to 24 hours.

Mader signed an affidavit setting forth the foregoing facts, and submitted it to a judge of the Circuit Court of DuPage County, together with a copy of the anonymous letter. The judge thereupon issued a search warrant for the Gates' residence and for their automobile. The judge, in deciding to issue the warrant, could have determined that the *modus operandi* of the Gates had been substantially corroborated. As the anonymous letter predicted, Lance Gates had flown from Chicago to West Palm Beach late in the afternoon of May 5th, had checked into a hotel room registered in the name of his wife, and, at 7:00 a.m. the following morning, had headed north, accompanied by an unidentified woman, out of West Palm Beach on an interstate highway used by travelers from South Florida to Chicago in an automobile bearing a license plate issued to him.

At 5:15 a.m. on May 7th, only 36 hours after he had flown out of Chicago, Lance Gates, and his wife, returned to their home in Bloomingdale, driving the car in which they had left West Palm Beach some 22 hours earlier. The Bloomingdale police were awaiting them, searched the trunk of the Mercury, and uncovered approximately 350 pounds of marijuana. A search of the Gates' home revealed marijuana, weapons, and other contraband. The Illinois Circuit Court ordered suppression of all these items, on the ground that the affidavit submitted to the Circuit Judge failed to support the necessary determination of probable cause to believe that the Gates' automobile and home contained the contraband in question. The Illinois Appellate Court and the Supreme Court of Illinois affirmed.

The Illinois Supreme Court concluded—and we agree—that, standing alone, the anonymous letter sent to the Bloomingdale Police Department would not provide the basis for a magistrate's determination that there was probable cause to believe contraband would be found in the Gates' car and home. The letter provides virtually nothing from which one might conclude that its author is either honest or his information reliable; likewise, the letter gives absolutely no indication of the basis for the writer's predictions regarding the Gates' criminal activities. Something more was required, then, before a magistrate could conclude that there was probable cause to believe that contraband would be found in the Gates' home and car.

The Illinois Supreme Court also properly recognized that Detective Mader's affidavit might be capable of supplementing the anonymous letter with information sufficient to permit a determination of probable cause. In holding that the affidavit in fact did not contain sufficient additional information to sustain a determination of probable cause, the Illinois court applied a "two-pronged test," derived from our decision in *Spinelli v. United States*. The court understood *Spinelli* as requiring that the anonymous letter satisfy each of two independent requirements before it could be relied on. The letter, as supplemented by Mader's affidavit, first had to adequately reveal the "basis of knowledge" of the letter writer—the particular means by which he came by the information given in his report. Second, it had to provide facts sufficiently establishing either the "veracity" of the affiant's informant, or, alternatively, the "reliability" of the informant's report in this particular case.

The Illinois court, alluding to an elaborate set of legal rules that have developed among various lower courts to enforce the "two-pronged test,"[8] found that the test had not been satisfied. First, the "veracity" prong was not satisfied because, "there was simply no basis for concluding that the anonymous person who wrote the letter to the Bloomingdale Police Department was credible." The court indicated that corroboration by police of details contained in the letter might never satisfy the "veracity" prong, and in any event, could not do so if only "innocent" details are corroborated. In addition, the letter gave no indication of the basis of its writer's knowledge of the Gates' activities. The court understood *Spinelli* as permitting the detail contained in a tip to be used to infer that the informant had a reliable basis for his statements, but it thought that the anonymous letter failed to provide sufficient detail to permit such an inference. Thus, it concluded that no showing of probable cause had been made.

We agree that an informant's "veracity," "reliability" and "basis of knowledge" are all highly relevant in determining the value of his report. We do not agree, however, that these elements should be understood as entirely separate and independent requirements to be rigidly exacted in every case. Rather they should be understood simply as closely intertwined issues that may usefully illuminate the commonsense, practical question whether there is "probable cause" to believe that contraband or evidence is located in a particular place.

This totality of the circumstances approach is far more consistent with our prior treatment of probable cause than is any rigid demand that specific "tests" be satisfied by every informant's tip. Perhaps the central teaching of our decisions bearing on the probable cause standard is that it is a "practical, nontechnical conception." *Brinegar v. United States*, 338 U.S. 160, 176 (1949). These are not technical; they are the factual and practical considerations of everyday life on

---

[8] The "veracity" prong of the *Spinelli* test has two "spurs"—the informant's "credibility" and the "reliability" of his information. Both the "basis of knowledge" prong and the "veracity" prong are treated as entirely separate requirements, which must be independently satisfied in every case in order to sustain a determination of probable cause. Some ancillary doctrines are relied on to satisfy certain of the foregoing requirements. For example, the "self-verifying detail" of a tip may satisfy the "basis of knowledge" requirement, although not the "credibility" spur of the "veracity" prong. Conversely, corroboration would seem not capable of supporting the "basis of knowledge" prong, but only the "veracity" prong.

which reasonable and prudent men, not legal technicians, act." Our observation in *United States v. Cortez*, 449 U.S. 411, 418 621 (1981), regarding "particularized suspicion," is also applicable to the probable cause standard:

> The process does not deal with hard certainties, but with probabilities. Long before the law of probabilities was articulated as such, practical people formulated certain common-sense conclusions about human behavior; jurors as fact finders are permitted to do the same—and so are law enforcement officers. Finally, the evidence thus collected must be seen and weighed not in terms of library analysis by scholars, but as understood by those versed in the field of law enforcement.

As these comments illustrate, probable cause is a fluid concept—turning on the assessment of probabilities in particular factual contexts—not readily, or even usefully, reduced to a neat set of legal rules. Informants' tips doubtless come in many shapes and sizes from many different types of persons. As we said in *Adams v. Williams*, 407 U.S. 143, 147 (1972), "Informants' tips, like all other clues and evidence coming to a policeman on the scene may vary greatly in their value and reliability." Rigid legal rules are ill-suited to an area of such diversity. "One simple rule will not cover every situation."

Moreover, the "two-pronged test" directs analysis into two largely independent channels—the informant's "veracity" or "reliability" and his "basis of knowledge." There are persuasive arguments against according these two elements such independent status. Instead, they are better understood as relevant considerations in the totality of circumstances analysis that traditionally has guided probable cause determinations: a deficiency in one may be compensated for, in determining the overall reliability of a tip, by a strong showing as to the other, or by some other indicia of reliability.

If, for example, a particular informant is known for the unusual reliability of his predictions of certain types of criminal activities in a locality, his failure, in a particular case, to thoroughly set forth the basis of his knowledge surely should not serve as an absolute bar to a finding of probable cause based on his tip. Likewise, if an unquestionably honest citizen comes forward with a report of criminal activity—which if fabricated would subject him to criminal liability—we have found rigorous scrutiny of the basis of his knowledge unnecessary. Conversely, even if we entertain some doubt as to an informant's motives, his explicit and detailed description of alleged wrongdoing, along with a statement that the event was observed first-hand, entitles his tip to greater weight than might otherwise be the case. Unlike a totality of circumstances analysis, which permits a balanced assessment of the relative weights of all the various indicia of reliability (and unreliability) attending an informant's tip, the "two-pronged test" has encouraged an excessively technical dissection of informants' tips, with undue attention being focused on isolated issues that cannot sensibly be divorced from the other facts presented to the magistrate.

Finely-tuned standards such as proof beyond a reasonable doubt or by a preponderance of the evidence, useful in formal trials, have no place in the magistrate's decision. While an effort to fix some general, numerically precise degree of certainty corresponding to "probable cause" may not be helpful, it is clear that "only the probability, and not a prima facie showing, of criminal activity is the standard of probable cause."

We also have recognized that affidavits "are normally drafted by nonlawyers in the midst and haste of a criminal investigation. Technical requirements of elaborate specificity once exacted under common law pleading have no proper place in this area." Likewise, search and arrest warrants long have been issued by persons who are neither lawyers nor judges, and who certainly do not remain abreast of each judicial refinement of the nature of "probable cause." The rigorous inquiry into the *Spinelli* prongs and the complex superstructure of evidentiary and analytical rules that some have seen implicit in our *Spinelli* decision, cannot be reconciled with the fact that many warrants are—quite properly—issued on the basis of nontechnical, common-sense judgments of laymen applying a standard less demanding than those used in more formal legal proceedings. Given the informal, often hurried context in which it must be applied, the "built-in subtleties" of the "two-pronged test" are particularly unlikely to assist magistrates in determining probable cause.

We have repeatedly said that after-the-fact scrutiny by courts of the sufficiency of an affidavit should not take the form of *de novo* review. A magistrate's "determination of probable cause should be paid great deference by reviewing courts." "A grudging or negative attitude by reviewing courts toward warrants," is inconsistent with the Fourth Amendment's strong preference for searches conducted pursuant to a warrant, "courts should not invalidate warrants by interpreting affidavits in a hyper technical, rather than a commonsense, manner."

If the affidavits submitted by police officers are subjected to the type of scrutiny some courts have deemed appropriate, police might well resort to warrantless searches, with the hope of relying on consent or some other exception to the warrant clause that might develop at the time of the search. In addition, the possession of a warrant by officers conducting an arrest or search greatly reduces the perception of unlawful or intrusive police conduct, by assuring "the individual whose property is searched or seized of the lawful authority of the executing officer, his need to search, and the limits of his power to search." Reflecting this preference for the warrant process, the traditional standard for review of an issuing magistrate's probable cause determination has been that so long as the magistrate had a "substantial basis for concluding" that a search would uncover evidence of wrongdoing, the Fourth Amendment requires no more. We think reaffirmation of this standard better serves the purpose of encouraging recourse to the warrant procedure and is more consistent with our traditional deference to the probable cause determinations of magistrates than is the "two-pronged test."

Finally, the direction taken by decisions following *Spinelli* poorly serves "the most basic function of any government": "to provide for the security of the individual and of his property." The strictures that inevitably accompany the "two-pronged test" cannot avoid seriously impeding the task of law enforcement. If that test must be rigorously applied in every case, anonymous tips seldom would be of greatly diminished value in police work. Ordinary citizens, like ordinary witnesses, generally do not provide extensive recitations of the basis of their everyday observations. Likewise, the veracity of persons supplying anonymous tips is by hypothesis largely unknown, and unknowable. As a result, anonymous tips seldom could survive a rigorous application of either of the *Spinelli* prongs. Yet, such tips, particularly when supplemented by independent police investigation, frequently contribute to the solution of otherwise "perfect crimes." While a conscientious assessment of the basis for crediting such tips is required by the Fourth Amendment, a standard that leaves virtually no place for anonymous citizen informants is not.

For all these reasons, we conclude that it is wiser to abandon the "two-pronged test" established by our decisions in *Aguilar* and *Spinelli*. In its place we reaffirm the totality of the circumstances analysis that traditionally has informed probable cause determinations. The task of the issuing magistrate is simply to make a practical, common-sense decision whether, given all the circumstances set forth in the affidavit before him, including the "veracity" and "basis of knowledge" of persons supplying hearsay information, there is a fair probability that contraband or evidence of a crime will be found in a particular place. And the duty of a reviewing court is simply to ensure that the magistrate had a "substantial basis for concluding" that probable cause existed. We are convinced that this flexible, easily applied standard will better achieve the accommodation of public and private interests that the Fourth Amendment requires than does the approach that has developed from *Aguilar* and *Spinelli*.

Our earlier cases illustrate the limits beyond which a magistrate may not venture in issuing a warrant. A sworn statement of an affiant that "he has cause to suspect and does believe that" liquor illegally brought into the United States is located on certain premises will not do. *Nathanson v. United States*, 290 U.S. 41 (1933). The affidavit must provide the magistrate with a substantial basis for determining the existence of probable cause, and the wholly conclusory statement at issue in *Nathanson* failed to meet this requirement. An officer's statement that "affiants have received reliable information from a credible person and believe" that heroin is stored in a home, is likewise inadequate. *Aguilar v. Texas*, 378 U.S. 108 (1964). As in *Nathanson*, this is a mere conclusory statement that gives the magistrate virtually no basis at all for making a judgment regarding probable cause. Sufficient information must be presented to the magistrate to allow that official to determine probable cause; his action cannot be a mere ratification of the bare conclusions of others. In order to ensure that such an abdication of the magistrate's duty does not occur, courts must continue to conscientiously review the sufficiency of affidavits on which warrants are issued. But when we move beyond the "bare bones" affidavits present in cases such as *Nathanson* and *Aguilar*, this area simply does not lend itself to a prescribed set of rules, like that which had developed from *Spinelli*. Instead, the flexible, common-sense standard articulated in prior precedent better serves the purposes of the Fourth Amendment's probable cause requirement.

Nothing in our opinion in any way lessens the authority of the magistrate to draw such reasonable inferences as he will from the material supplied to him by applicants for a warrant; indeed, he is freer than under the regime of *Aguilar* and *Spinelli* to draw such inferences, or to refuse to draw them if he is so minded.

Justice Brennan's criticism seems to be that magistrates should be restricted in their authority to make probable cause determinations by the standards laid down in *Aguilar* and *Spinelli*, and that such findings "should not be authorized unless there is some assurance that the information on which they are based has been obtained in a reliable way by an honest or credible person." However, under our opinion magistrates remain perfectly free to exact such assurances as they deem necessary, as well as those required by this opinion, in making probable cause determinations. Justice Brennan would apparently prefer that magistrates be restricted in their findings of probable cause by the development of an elaborate body of case law dealing with the *Spinelli* test That such a labyrinthine body of judicial refinement bears any relationship to familiar definitions of probable cause is hard to imagine. Probable cause deals "with probabilities. These are not technical; they are the factual and practical considerations of everyday life on which reasonable and prudent men, not legal technicians, act."

Justice Brennan's dissent suggests that "words such as 'practical,' 'nontechnical,' and 'common sense,' are but code words for an overly-permissive attitude towards police practices in derogation of the rights secured by the Fourth Amendment." "Fidelity" to the commands of the Constitution suggests balanced judgment rather than exhortation. The highest "fidelity" is achieved neither by the judge who instinctively goes furthest in upholding even the most bizarre claim of individual constitutional rights, any more than it is achieved by a judge who instinctively goes furthest in accepting the most restrictive claims of governmental authorities. The task of this Court, as of other courts, is to "hold the balance true," and we think we have done that in this case.

Our decisions applying the totality of circumstances analysis outlined above have consistently recognized the value of corroboration of details of an informant's tip by independent police work. In *Jones v. United States, supra,* 362 U.S., at 269 we held that an affidavit relying on hearsay "is not to be deemed insufficient on that score, so long as a substantial basis for crediting the hearsay is presented." We went on to say that even in making a warrantless arrest an officer "may rely upon information received through an informant, rather than upon his direct observations, so long as the informant's statement is reasonably corroborated by other matters within the officer's knowledge." Likewise, we recognized the probative value of corroborative efforts of police officials in *Aguilar*—the source of the "two-pronged test"—by observing that if the police had made some effort to corroborate the informant's report at issue, "an entirely different case" would have been presented.

Our decision in *Draper v. United States,* 358 U.S. 307 (1959), however, is the classic case on the value of corroborative efforts of police officials. The showing of probable cause in the present case was fully as compelling as that in *Draper*. Even standing alone, the facts obtained through the independent investigation of Mader and the DEA at least suggested that the Gates were involved in drug trafficking. In addition to being a popular vacation site, Florida is well-known as a source of narcotics and other illegal drugs. Lance Gates' flight to Palm Beach, his brief, overnight stay in a motel, and apparent immediate return north to Chicago in the family car, conveniently awaiting him in West Palm Beach, is as suggestive of a pre-arranged drug run, as it is of an ordinary vacation trip.

In addition, the magistrate could rely on the anonymous letter, which had been corroborated in major part by Mader's efforts—just as had occurred in *Draper*. The Illinois court reasoned that *Draper* involved an informant who had given reliable information on previous occasions, while the honesty and reliability of the anonymous informant in this case were unknown to the Bloomingdale police. While this distinction might be an apt one at the time the police department received the anonymous letter, it became far less significant after Mader's independent investigative work occurred. The corroboration of the letter's predictions that the Gates' car would be in Florida, that Lance Gates would fly to Florida in the next day or so, and that he would drive the car north toward Bloomingdale all indicated, albeit not with certainty, that the informant's other assertions also were true. "Because an informant is right about some things, he is more probably right about other facts"—including the claim regarding the Gates' illegal activity. This may well not be the type of "reliability" or "veracity" necessary to satisfy some views of the "veracity prong" of *Spinelli*, but we think it suffices for the practical, common-sense judgment called for in making a probable cause determination. It is enough, for purposes of assessing probable cause, that "corroboration through other sources of information reduced the chances of a reckless or prevaricating tale," thus providing "a substantial basis for crediting the hearsay."

Finally, the anonymous letter contained a range of details relating not just to easily obtained facts and conditions existing at the time of the tip, but to future actions of third parties ordinarily not easily predicted. The letter writer's accurate information as to the travel plans of each of the Gates was of a character likely obtained only from the Gates themselves, or from someone familiar with their not entirely ordinary travel plans. If the informant had access to accurate information of this type a magistrate could properly conclude that it was not unlikely that he also had access to reliable information of the Gates' alleged illegal activities.[9] Of course, the Gates' travel plans might have been learned from a talkative neighbor or travel agent; under the "two-pronged test" developed from *Spinelli*, the character of the details in the anonymous letter might well not permit a sufficiently clear inference regarding the letter writer's "basis of knowledge." But probable cause does not demand the certainty we associate with formal trials. It is enough that there was a fair probability that the writer of the anonymous letter had obtained his entire story either from the Gates or someone they trusted. And corroboration of major portions of the letter's predictions provides just this probability. It is apparent, therefore, that the judge issuing the warrant had a "substantial basis for concluding" that probable cause to search the Gates' home and car existed. The judgment of the Supreme Court of Illinois therefore must be

Reversed.

JUSTICE WHITE, concurring in the judgment.

I agree that the warrant should be upheld, but under the *Aguilar-Spinelli* framework. The Gates' activity was quite suspicious. Lance Gates' flight to Palm Beach, an area known to be a source of narcotics, the brief overnight stay in a motel, and apparent immediate return North, suggest a pattern that trained law-enforcement officers have recognized as indicative of illicit drug-dealing activity. Even had the corroboration related only to completely innocuous activities, this would not preclude the issuance of a valid warrant. The critical issue is not whether the activities observed by the police are innocent or suspicious. The proper focus should be on whether the actions of the suspects, whatever their nature, give rise to an inference that the informant is credible and that he obtained his information in a reliable manner.

---

[9] The dissent seizes on one inaccuracy in the anonymous informant's letter—its statement that Sue Gates would fly from Florida to Illinois, when in fact she drove—and argues that the probative value of the entire tip was undermined by this allegedly "material mistake." The dissent apparently adopts the rather implausible notion that persons dealing in drugs always stay at home, apparently out of fear that to leave might risk intrusion by criminals. The magistrate's determination that there might be drugs or evidence of criminal activity in the Gates' home was well-supported by the less speculative theory that if the informant could predict with considerable accuracy the somewhat unusual travel plans of the Gates, he probably also had a reliable basis for his statements that the Gates' kept a large quantity of drugs in their home and frequently were visited by other drug traffickers there.

In *Draper*, the fact that the informer was able to predict, two days in advance, the exact clothing Draper would be wearing dispelled the possibility that his tip was just based on rumor or "an off-hand remark heard at a neighborhood bar." Probably Draper had planned in advance to wear these specific clothes so that an accomplice could identify him. A clear inference could therefore be drawn that the informant was either involved in the criminal scheme himself or that he otherwise had access to reliable, inside information.

As in *Draper*, the police investigation in the present case satisfactorily demonstrated that the informant's tip was as trustworthy as one that would alone satisfy the Aguilar tests. The tip predicted that Sue Gates would drive to Florida, that Lance Gates would fly there a few days after May 3, and that Lance would then drive the car back. After the police corroborated these facts, the magistrate could reasonably have inferred, as he apparently did, that the informant, who had specific knowledge of these unusual travel plans, did not make up his story and that he obtained his information in a reliable way.

It is not at all necessary to overrule *Aguilar-Spinelli* in order to reverse the judgment below. I am reluctant to approve any standard that does not expressly require, as a prerequisite to issuance of a warrant, some showing of facts from which an inference may be drawn that the informant is credible and that his information was obtained in a reliable way. The Court is correctly concerned with the fact that some lower courts have been applying *Aguilar-Spinelli* in an unduly rigid manner. I believe that with clarification of the rule of corroborating information, the lower courts are fully able to properly interpret *Aguilar-Spinelli* and avoid such unduly-rigid applications. It may prove to be the case that the only profitable instruction we can provide to magistrates is to rely on common sense. But the question whether a particular anonymous tip provides the basis for issuance of a warrant will often be a difficult one, and I would at least attempt to provide more precise guidance by clarifying *Aguilar-Spinelli* and the relationship of those cases with *Draper* before totally abdicating our responsibility in this area.

JUSTICE BRENNAN, with whom JUSTICE MARSHALL joins, dissenting.

Although I believe that the warrant is invalid even under the newly announced "totality of the circumstances" test, I write separately to dissent from the Court's unjustified and ill-advised rejection of the two-prong test for evaluating the validity of a warrant based on hearsay announced in *Aguilar* and refined in *Spinelli*.

In recognition of the judiciary's role as the only effective guardian of Fourth Amendment rights, this Court has developed a set of coherent rules governing a magistrate's consideration of a warrant application and the showings that are necessary to support a finding of probable cause. A neutral and detached magistrate, and not the police, should determine whether there is probable cause to support the issuance of a warrant. In order to emphasize the magistrate's role as an independent arbiter of probable cause and to insure that searches or seizures are not effected on less than probable cause, the Court has insisted that police officers provide magistrates with the underlying facts and circumstances that support the officers' conclusions.

The use of hearsay to support the issuance of a warrant presents special problems because informants, unlike police officers, are not regarded as presumptively reliable or honest. Moreover, the basis for an informant's conclusions is not always clear from an affidavit that merely reports those conclusions. If the conclusory allegations of a police officer are insufficient to support a finding of probable cause, surely the conclusory allegations of an informant should a fortiori be insufficient.

Properly understood, *Spinelli* stands for the proposition that corroboration of certain details in a tip may be sufficient to satisfy the veracity, but not the basis of knowledge, prong of *Aguilar*. *Spinelli* also suggests that in some limited circumstances considerable detail in an informant's tip may be adequate to satisfy the basis of knowledge prong of *Aguilar*. The rules drawn from the cases advance an important underlying substantive value: Findings of probable cause, and attendant intrusions, should not be authorized unless there is some assurance that the information on which they are based has been obtained in a reliable way by an honest or credible person. As applied to police officers, the rules focus on the way in which the information was acquired. As applied to informants, the rules focus both on the honesty or credibility of the informant and on the reliability of the way in which the information was acquired. An evaluation of affidavits based on hearsay involves a more difficult inquiry. This suggests a need to structure the inquiry in an effort to insure greater accuracy. The standards announced in *Aguilar,* as refined by *Spinelli*, fulfill that need. The standards inform the police of what information they have to provide and magistrates of what information they should demand. The standards also inform magistrates of the subsidiary findings they must make in order to arrive at an ultimate finding of probable cause. *Spinelli* directs the magistrate's attention to the possibility that the presence of self-verifying detail might satisfy *Aguilar*'s basis of knowledge prong and that corroboration of the details of a tip might satisfy *Aguilar*'s veracity prong. *Aguilar* and *Spinelli* assure the magistrate's role as an independent arbiter of probable cause, insure greater accuracy in probable cause determinations, and advance the substantive value identified above.

Both *Aguilar* and *Spinelli* dealt with tips from informants known at least to the police. And surely there is even more reason to subject anonymous informants' tips to the tests established by *Aguilar* and *Spinelli*. By definition nothing is known about an anonymous informant's identity, honesty, or reliability. Nor is there any basis for assuming that the information provided by an anonymous informant has been obtained in a reliable way. If we are unwilling to accept conclusory allegations from the police, who are presumptively reliable, or from informants who are known, at least to the police, there cannot possibly be any rational basis for accepting conclusory allegations from anonymous informants.

Police corroboration of the details of the tip might establish the reliability of the informant under *Aguilar's* veracity prong, as refined in *Spinelli*, and the details in the tip might be sufficient to qualify under the "self-verifying detail" test established by *Spinelli* as a means of satisfying *Aguilar's* basis of knowledge prong. The *Aguilar* and *Spinelli* tests must be applied to anonymous informants' tips, however, if we are to continue to insure that findings of probable cause, and attendant intrusions, are based on information provided by an honest or credible person who has acquired the information in a reliable way.

In light of the important purposes served by *Aguilar* and *Spinelli*, I would not reject the standards they establish. If anything, I simply would make more clear that *Spinelli*, properly understood, does not depart in any fundamental way from the test established by *Aguilar*.

One can concede that probable cause is a "practical, nontechnical" concept without betraying the values that *Aguilar* and *Spinelli* reflect. *Aguilar* and *Spinelli* require the police to provide magistrates with certain crucial information. They also provide structure for magistrates' probable cause inquiries. Once a magistrate has determined that he has information before him that he can reasonably say has been obtained in a reliable way by a credible person, he has ample room to use his common sense and to apply a practical, nontechnical conception of probable cause.

The Court insists that the *Aguilar-Spinelli* standards must be abandoned because they are inconsistent with the fact that non-lawyers frequently serve as magistrates. To the contrary, the standards help to structure probable cause inquiries and, properly interpreted, may actually help a non-lawyer magistrate in making a probable cause determination. Of particular concern to all Americans must be that the Court gives virtually no consideration to the value of insuring that findings of probable cause are based on information that a magistrate can reasonably say has been obtained in a reliable way by an honest or credible person. Words such as "practical," "nontechnical," and "commonsense" are but code words for an overly permissive attitude towards police practices in derogation of the rights secured by the Fourth Amendment. Everyone shares the Court's concern over the horrors of drug trafficking, but under our Constitution only measures consistent with the Fourth Amendment may be employed by government to cure this evil.

By replacing *Aguilar* and *Spinelli* with a test that provides no assurance that magistrates, rather than the police, or informants, will make determinations of probable cause; imposes no structure on magistrates' probable cause inquiries; and invites the possibility that intrusions may be justified on less than reliable information from an honest or credible person, today's decision threatens to "obliterate one of the most fundamental distinctions between our form of government, where officers are under the law, and the police-state where they are the law."

JUSTICE STEVENS, with whom JUSTICE BRENNAN joins, dissenting.

The fact that Lance and Sue Gates made a 22-hour nonstop drive from West Palm Beach, Florida, to Bloomingdale, Illinois, only a few hours after Lance had flown to Florida provided persuasive evidence that they were engaged in illicit activity. That fact, however, was not known to the magistrate when he issued the warrant to search their home. What the magistrate did know at that time was that the anonymous informant had not been completely accurate in his or her predictions. The informant had indicated that "Sue drives their car to Florida *where she leaves it to be loaded up with drugs. Sue flies back after she drops the car off in Florida.*" Yet Detective Mader's affidavit reported that she "left the West Palm Beach area driving the Mercury northbound."

The discrepancy between the informant's predictions and the facts known to Detective Mader is significant for three reasons. First, it cast doubt on the informant's hypothesis that the Gates already had "over $100,000 worth of drugs in their basement." The informant had predicted an itinerary that always kept one spouse in Bloomingdale, suggesting that the Gates did not want to leave their home unguarded because something valuable was hidden within. That inference obviously could not be drawn when it was known that the pair was actually together over a thousand miles from home. Second, the discrepancy made the Gates' conduct seem substantially less unusual than the informant had predicted it would be. It would have been odd if, as predicted, Sue had driven down to Florida on Wednesday, left the car, and flown right back to Illinois. But the mere facts that Sue was in West Palm Beach with the car,[10] that she was joined by her husband at the Holiday Inn on Friday,[11] and that the couple drove north together the next morning[12] are neither unusual nor

---

[10] The anonymous note suggested that she was going down on Wednesday, but for all the officers knew she had been in Florida for a month.

[11] Lance does not appear to have behaved suspiciously in flying down to Florida. He made a reservation in his own name and gave an accurate home phone number to the airlines. And Detective Mader's affidavit does not report that he did any of the other things drug couriers are notorious for doing, such as paying for the ticket in cash, dressing casually, looking pale and nervous, improperly filling out baggage tags, carrying American Tourister luggage, not carrying any luggage, or changing airlines en route.

[12] Detective Mader's affidavit hinted darkly that the couple had set out upon "that interstate highway commonly used by travelers to the Chicago area." But the same highway is also commonly used by travelers to Disney World, Sea World, and Ringling Brothers and Barnum and Bailey Circus World. It is also the road to Cocoa Beach, Cape Canaveral, and Washington, D.C. I would venture that each year dozens of perfectly innocent people fly to Florida, meet a waiting spouse, and drive off together in the family car.

probative of criminal activity. Third, the fact that the anonymous letter contained a material mistake undermines the reasonableness of relying on it as a basis for making a forcible entry into a private home.

Of course, the activities in this case did not stop when the magistrate issued the warrant. The Gates drove all night to Bloomingdale, the officers searched the car and found 400 pounds of marijuana, and then they searched the house. However, none of these subsequent events may be considered in evaluating the warrant, and the search of the house was legal only if the warrant was valid. I cannot accept the Court's casual conclusion that, before the Gates arrived in Bloomingdale, there was probable cause to justify a valid entry and search of a private home. No one knows who the informant in this case was, or what motivated him or her to write the note. Given that the note's predictions were faulty in one significant respect, and were corroborated by nothing except ordinary innocent activity, I must surmise that the Court's evaluation of the warrant's validity has been colored by subsequent events.

Points for Discussion

a. Analyzing *Gates*

Does *Gates* abandon the *Aguilar-Spinelli* two-part test? What does the Court suggest in *Gates*? In thinking about this issue, consider *Massachusetts v. Upton*, 466 U.S. 727 (1984), decided the following year. That case also involved an anonymous tip, but the Massachusetts Supreme Judicial Court narrowly construed *Gates* and reversed Upton's conviction. The U.S. Supreme Court summarized the Massachusetts court's decision as follows: "The Massachusetts court apparently viewed *Gates* as merely adding a new wrinkle to the *Aguilar-Spinelli* two-pronged test: where an informant's veracity and/or basis of knowledge are not sufficiently clear, substantial corroboration of the tip may save an otherwise invalid warrant." The U.S. Supreme Court reversed: "In *Gates*, we did not merely refine or qualify the 'two-pronged test.' We rejected it as hyper technical and divorced from 'the factual and practical considerations of everyday life on which reasonable and prudent men, not legal technicians, act.' " "We conclude that it is wiser to abandon the 'two-pronged test' established by our decisions in *Aguilar* and *Spinelli*. In its place we reaffirm the totality-of-the-circumstances analysis that traditionally has informed probable-cause determinations."

b. Informer's Privilege

If a defendant whose home was searched wants to challenge the probable cause determination, he might seek to discover the names of all informants relied on by the police. In *McCray v. Illinois*, 386 U.S. 300 (1967), petitioner was arrested for possession of narcotics and moved to suppress the evidence. Since the arrest was based on an informant's tip, petitioner sought to learn the informant's identity. The trial court denied the motion for disclosure, and the Court upheld the denial: "The informer is a vital part of society's defensive arsenal. We have repeatedly made clear that federal officers need not disclose an informer's identity in applying for an arrest or search warrant."

In *Roviaro v. United States*, 353 U.S. 53 (1957), defendant was convicted under the Narcotic Drugs Import and Export Act. Again, the government refused to reveal the identity of an informant. Although the Court suggested that the decision to disclose should be made on a case-by-case basis, it held that the identity should have been revealed in that case:

The scope of the privilege is limited by its underlying purpose. Thus, where the disclosure of the contents of a communication will not tend to reveal the identity of an informer, the contents are not privileged. Likewise, once the identity of the informer has been disclosed to those who would have cause to resent the communication, the privilege is no longer applicable. A further limitation on the applicability of the privilege arises from the fundamental requirements of fairness. Where the disclosure of an informer's identity, or of the contents of his communication, is relevant and helpful to the defense of an accused, or is essential to a fair determination of a cause, the privilege must give way. In these situations the trial court may require disclosure and, if the Government withholds the information, dismiss the action.

Food for Thought

In *Draper,* the Court emphasized that the informers' tip included great detail, and the police officer confirmed that detail. In *Gates,* there was also considerable detail in the tip, but were the police able to confirm the validity of the tip? Were there respects in which the tip was inaccurate? Should the inaccuracies be regarded as significant?

Food for Thought

Even if the Court could conclude that the Gates went to West Palm Beach to purchase more illegal drugs, was there probable cause to search their home? After all, the tip could be construed as suggesting that they always left someone at home to guard it. If, on this occasion, both flew to Florida and drove back, does that suggest that they might be out of drugs at home?

The problem is one that calls for balancing the public interest in protecting the flow of information against the individual's right to prepare his defense. Whether a proper balance renders nondisclosure erroneous must depend on the particular circumstances of each case, taking into consideration the crime charged, the possible defenses, the possible significance of the informer's testimony, and other relevant factors. The circumstances demonstrate that John Doe's possible testimony was highly relevant and might have been helpful to the defense. So far as petitioner knew, he and John Doe were alone and unobserved during the crucial occurrence for which he was indicted. Unless petitioner waived his constitutional right not to take the stand in his own defense, John Doe was his one material witness. His testimony might have disclosed an entrapment. He might have thrown doubt upon petitioner's identity or on the identity of the package. He was the only witness who might have testified to petitioner's possible lack of knowledge of the contents of the package that he "transported" from the tree to John Doe's car. The desirability of calling John Doe as a witness, or at least interviewing him in preparation for trial, was a matter for the accused rather than the Government to decide. Finally, the Government's use against petitioner of his conversation with John Doe while riding in Doe's car particularly emphasizes the unfairness of the nondisclosure in this case. The only person, other than petitioner himself, who could controvert, explain or amplify Bryson's report of this important conversation was John Doe. Contradiction or amplification might have borne upon petitioner's knowledge of the contents of the package or might have tended to show an entrapment.

c. Drug Detection Dogs and Probable Cause.

In *Florida v. Harris*, 568 U.S. 237 (2013), the Court addressed the question of whether an "alert" by a drug-detection dog during a traffic stop provides probable cause to search a vehicle. In that case, a canine alerted at the driver's side door handle (suggesting that he smelled drugs there). In the ensuring search, the officer did not find any of the drugs that the dog was trained to detect (methamphetamine, marijuana, cocaine, heroin, and ecstasy), but did find 200 pseudoephedrine pills, 8,000 matches, a bottle of hydrochloric acid, two containers of antifreeze, and a coffee filter full of iodine crystals—all ingredients used in making methamphetamine. The officer then gave the driver a *Miranda* warning and he admitted to cooking meth at his home. The officer then arrested the driver for possession of pseudoephedrine for use in making meth. After the driver was released, the officer stopped him again, and the dog again alerted to the same door handle. This time, the officer discovered nothing of interest. At his trial, defendant moved to suppress evidence obtained from the first stop on the basis on the basis that the dog alert was unreliable because the dog had allegedly made two false positives on defendant's truck, and therefore did not provide the officer with probable cause to search the truck. The Court disagreed, noting that a dog's reliability should not be determined based on the dog's performance in actual traffic stops which can be deceiving because, if the dog failed to alert when drugs were present, nobody would know that drugs had been present. Conversely, if the dog alerted to vehicles in which the officer found no narcotics, "the dog may not have made a mistake at all. The dog may have detected substances that were too well hidden or present in quantities too small for the officer to locate. Or the dog may have smelled the residual odor of drugs previously in the vehicle or on the driver's person. Field data thus may markedly overstate a dog's real false positives." As a result, the Court held that a dog's reliability must be determined based on his performance in training exercises: "If a bona fide organization has certified a dog after testing his reliability in a controlled setting, a court can presume (subject to any conflicting evidence) that the dog's alert provides probable cause to search. The same is true, even in the absence of formal certification, if the dog has recently and successfully completed a training program that evaluated his proficiency in locating drugs." Given this particular dog's performance in training, the Court concluded that probable cause existed when the officer searched defendant's car. Two years earlier, the dog had successfully completed a 120-hour program in narcotics detection, and separately obtained a certification from an independent company. The Sheriff's Office required continuing training for the dog and his handler, and both satisfactorily completed another 40-hour training program one year earlier. Also, the handler worked with the dog four hours per week on exercises designed to keep his skills sharp. Throughout, the dog always performed at the highest level.

Food for Thought

In analyzing the *Gates* facts, the Court emphasized that the Gates left Palm Beach heading North on a highway that leads to Chicago, and that they drove all night. Was it appropriate for the Court to consider the fact that they drove all night since that fact could not have been known at the time that the warrant was issued? Although the Court could consider the fact that the Gates were headed North, how many options does one have from Palm Beach? Is it possible to go very far East, or very far South or West? Moreover, might the Gates have flown to West Palm Beach and driven to a nearby beach resort to the North? The highway did lead North, and therefore could take one to Chicago, but could the road also take one to virtually anywhere else in the United States?

Food for Thought

In light of the *Gates* holding, would *Spinelli* be decided the same way today? In other words, applying the *Gates* "totality of the circumstances" test, rather than the two-pronged *Aguilar-Spinelli* test, would the Court be inclined to find that probable cause existed on the *Spinelli* facts?

Hypo 1: *Establishing Probable Cause*

A police detective, an eleven-year veteran with training and experience in narcotics investigations, learns from a confidential informant that there is "a dark skinned Hispanic male who is selling heroin" in varying amounts and prices in the city. The informant states that the heroin dealer walks with a pronounced limp, and that he can be reached at either of two telephone numbers. He also states that, if someone calls the dealer to purchase drugs, he will ask "how much" and then provide a location where he will meet a purchaser to exchange money for heroin. The dealer will arrive at the location either in a white Toyota sedan or a "sharp looking" green Audi sedan with tinted windows and after-market wheels. When asked where the dealer keeps the drugs, the informant is unsure. If you are asked to advise the detective about how to proceed with the investigation, what would you advise? *See Commonwealth v. Escalera*, 462 Mass. 636, 970 N.E.2d 319 (2012).

Hypo 2: *The Tip*

The police receive an anonymous phone "tip" which states that a house is rented to Gary Moore; that Keith Umfleet has drugs stored in the refrigerator at the house; that Moore and Umfleet are eating a meal and afterwards plan to travel to Illinois to dispose of the drugs; that the parties own a red Volkswagen which they might drive to Illinois; that there is an incinerator located in the back of the apartment. After receiving the call, a police officer verifies that the house is rented and lived-in by Moore; that a red Volkswagen is parked outside; that there is an incinerator in the back of the apartment. The officer knows that Umfleet has a reputation as a previously arrested drug trafficker. Following the verification, the police stake out the house. While they do not see either Moore or Umfleet, they do see David Hill, a known drug user, walk "in and about the house." The officers also see an orange car pull into the parking lot, begin to look for a parking place, but drive off "in a very big hurry" when the driver spots the police. After a few hours, several officers go to the door of the house. The officers knock on the door, announce that the occupants are under arrest for the possession of controlled substances and advise them of their rights. One officer then opens the refrigerator and removes a white plastic bag of drugs from the lower compartment of the refrigerator. The bag is a white zipper top plastic bag about eight by ten inches in size containing glass bottles. Did the police have "probable cause" to believe that the occupants of the apartment were in possession of drugs? What arguments might be made on behalf of the police? How might the occupants respond? Do not concern yourself with the question of whether, even if probable cause existed, the police could enter the house without a warrant. *See State v. Wiley*, 522 S.W.2d 281 (Mo., En Banc, 1975).

Hypo 3: *Child Abuse Informant*

At around 6:30 p.m., an anonymous tipster calls a child abuse hotline. She identifies Kendra D'Andrea and Willie Jordan as partners, provides D'Andrea's residential address, and identifies Jordan's employer by name. She informs the hotline that she received a message on her mobile phone containing photographs of D'Andrea and Jordan performing sexual acts on D'Andrea's eight-year-old daughter with her genitalia exposed. Based solely on the tip, do the police have probable cause to obtain a search warrant to search the residence? If not, what steps should they take to establish probable cause? *See United States v. D'Andrea*, 648 F.3d 1 (1st Cir. 2011).

Hypo 4: *The Cocaine Seller*

A police officer receives a tip about a black male named "Greg" who sells cocaine. The tip states that the seller drives a gold colored Mercedes to deliver the narcotics, and that he sells drugs only during the evening hours. The informant also supplies the officer with Greg's cellular and home phone numbers, and the location where a narcotics sale will be made. The officer investigates the residence and learns that a man named "Gregory Wallace" has registered to vote at that location. Further investigation reveals Greg's date of birth and driver's license number. At this point, do the police have probable cause to search the house? Would you reach a different conclusion if the police saw the informant enter the house to buy drugs, exit the house, and then they see Greg exit the house walking towards the informant with what appears to be drugs? *See Commonwealth v. Wallace*, 42 A.3d 1040 (Pa. 2012).

Hypo 5: *More on Cocaine Sellers*

Suppose that police receive an anonymous tip suggesting that a man by the name of Steve Clark, a white male, approximately 6' to 6'2" in height and weighing approximately 170-195 lbs., who goes by "Steve," packages and distributes cocaine from 4242 Salmon Street in Philadelphia, and makes deliveries of cocaine in a white Pontiac Grand Am with a black roof, Pennsylvania license number FRG–5450. If the police go to that address, confirm that someone named "Steve Clark" lives there, find a Pontiac which matches that description bearing the stated license plate number, and see a man matching "Steve's" description leave the house, do they have probable cause to obtain a warrant to search the house? Do they need additional evidence? If so, what do they need? *See Commonwealth v. Clark*, 28 A.3d 1284 (Pa. 2011).

Hypo 6: *The Stash House*

Police receive an anonymous tip regarding a "narcotics stash house" and have the house under surveillance when they see an unidentified male arrive and enter the house. A few minutes later, the man leaves the house with a large white box that he places inside his truck. Police follow the truck which pulls over to the curb at a nearby street. The driver exits with the white box, walks over to a white GMC Envoy, and hands the box to a second unknown male (Cervantes). Cervantes drives his GMC Envoy to a nearby liquor store where he makes a purchase and drives away. Does the officer have probable cause to stop and search Cervantes's vehicle? *See United States v. Cervantes*, 678 F.3d 798 (9th Cir. 2012).

Hypo 7: *The Tip*

After the police arrest a high-ranking member of the West Hell Gang for possession of narcotics, he tells an officer that he knows where they can find some illegal guns. The gang is known for violence and is alleged to have been involved in the commission of several homicides and other shootings. The informant, who has recently been released on parole, believes and hopes that, by providing the information, the police will "go easier" on him. He then gives the police a precise address, tells them the guns can be found in an abandoned car under the front seat. The officers know that this particular informant has never provided the police with information in the past. Does the tip, offered under such circumstances, provide the police with probable cause to believe that illegal guns can be found in the vehicle? *See Harris v. O'Hare*, 770 F.3d 224 (2d Cir. 2014).

D. Warrantless Searches and Seizures

Despite the preference for a warrant, the courts have established numerous exceptions to the warrant requirement. As we shall see, the courts distinguish between warrantless arrests and warrantless searches. Even though warrantless arrests are generally permissible, warrantless searches are disfavored and are *"per se* unreasonable subject only to a few specifically established and well-delineated exceptions." *Katz v. United States*, 389 U.S. 347, 357 (1967). In this section, we examine the exceptions and the justifications that underlie them.

1. Plain View Exception

The "plain view" exception is an often-used exception to the warrant requirement. When the police are conducting a lawful search, and are in a place where they have the right to be, this exception allows them to seize items that they find in plain view. However, there have been debates about the limits of the exception.

Horton v. California

496 U.S. 128 (1990).

JUSTICE STEVENS delivered the opinion of the Court.

Pursuant to a warrant, an experienced police officer (Sergeant LaRault) searched Petitioner's home for the proceeds of a robbery. The officer did not find the stolen property. He did discover weapons in plain view and seized them. Specifically, he seized an Uzi machine gun, a .38-caliber revolver, two stun guns, a handcuff key, a San Jose Coin Club advertising brochure the victim was the Treasurer of the Club, and a few items of clothing identified by the victim. LaRault testified that while he was searching for the stolen [3] rings, he also was interested in finding other evidence connecting petitioner to the robbery. Thus, the seized evidence was not discovered "inadvertently."

The "plain-view" doctrine is often considered an exception to the general rule that warrantless searches are presumptively unreasonable, but this characterization overlooks the important difference between searches and seizures. If an article is already in plain view, neither its observation nor its seizure would involve any invasion of privacy. A seizure of the article, however, would obviously invade the owner's possessory interest. If "plain view" justifies an exception from an otherwise applicable warrant requirement, therefore, it must be an exception that is addressed to the concerns that are implicated by seizures rather than by searches.

In *Coolidge v. New Hampshire*, 403 U. S. 443, 481 (1971, Justice Stewart described two limitations on the plain view doctrine that he found implicit in its rationale: First, "plain view *alone* is never enough to justify the warrantless seizure of evidence," and second, "the discovery of evidence in plain view must be inadvertent." Justice Stewart's analysis of the "plain-view" doctrine did not command a majority, and a plurality of the Court has since made clear that the discussion is "not a binding precedent."

An essential predicate to any valid warrantless seizure of incriminating evidence is that the officer did not violate the Fourth Amendment in arriving at the place from which the evidence could be plainly viewed. There are, moreover, two additional conditions that must be satisfied to justify the warrantless seizure. First, not only must the item be in plain view; its incriminating character must also be "immediately apparent." Second, not only must the officer be lawfully located in a place from which the object can be plainly seen, but he or she must also have a lawful right of access to the object itself.

Justice Stewart concluded that the inadvertence requirement was necessary to avoid a violation of the express constitutional requirement that a valid warrant must particularly describe the things to be seized. He explained: "The requirement of a warrant to seize imposes no inconvenience whatever, or at least none which is constitutionally cognizable in a legal system that regards warrantless searches as '*per se* unreasonable' in the absence of 'exigent circumstances.' If the initial intrusion is bottomed upon a warrant that fails to mention a particular object, though the police know its location and intend to seize it, then there is a violation of the express constitutional requirement of "Warrants particularly describing the things to be seized.""

We find two flaws in this reasoning. First, evenhanded law enforcement is best achieved by the application of objective standards of conduct, rather than standards that depend upon the subjective state of mind of the officer. The fact that an officer is interested in an item of evidence and fully expects to find it in the course of a search should not invalidate its seizure if the search is confined in area and duration by the terms of a warrant or a valid exception to the warrant requirement. If the officer has knowledge approaching certainty that the item will be found, we see no reason why he or she would deliberately omit a particular description of the item to be seized from the application for a search warrant. Specification of the additional item could only permit the officer ✓ to expand the scope of the search. On the other hand, if he or she has a valid warrant to search for one item and merely a suspicion concerning the second, whether or not it amounts to probable cause, we fail to see why that suspicion should immunize the second item from seizure if it is found during a lawful search for the first.

Second, the suggestion that the inadvertence requirement is necessary to prevent the police from conducting general searches, or from converting specific warrants into general warrants, is not persuasive because that interest is already served by the requirements that no warrant issue unless it "particularly describes the place to be searched and the persons or things to be seized," and that a warrantless search be circumscribed by the exigencies which justify its initiation. Scrupulous adherence to these requirements serves the interests in limiting the area and duration of the search that the inadvertence requirement inadequately protects. Once those commands have been satisfied and the officer has a lawful right of access, however, no additional Fourth Amendment interest is furthered by requiring that the discovery of evidence be inadvertent. If the scope of the search exceeds that permitted by the terms of a validly issued warrant or the character of the relevant exception from the warrant requirement, the subsequent seizure is unconstitutional without more.

In this case, the scope of the search was not enlarged in the slightest by the omission of any reference to the weapons in the warrant. Indeed, if the three rings and other items named in the warrant had been found at the outset—or if petitioner had them in his possession and had responded to the warrant by producing them immediately—no search for weapons could have taken place.

The seizure of an object in plain view does not involve an intrusion on privacy. If the interest in privacy has been invaded, the violation must have occurred before the object came into plain view and there is no need for an inadvertence limitation on seizures to condemn it. The prohibition against general searches and general warrants serves primarily as a protection against unjustified intrusions on privacy. But reliance on privacy concerns that support that prohibition is misplaced when the inquiry concerns the scope of an exception that merely authorizes an officer with a lawful right of access to an item to seize it without a warrant.

In this case the items seized from petitioner's home were discovered during a lawful search authorized by a valid warrant. When they were discovered, it was immediately apparent to the officer that they constituted incriminating evidence. He had probable cause, not only to obtain a warrant to search for the stolen property, but also to believe that the weapons and handguns had been used in the crime he was investigating. The search was authorized by the warrant; the seizure was authorized by the "plain-view" doctrine. The judgment is affirmed.

It is so ordered.

JUSTICE BRENNAN, with whom JUSTICE MARSHALL joins, dissenting.

The inadvertent discovery requirement is essential if we are to take seriously the Fourth Amendment's protection of possessory interests as well as privacy interests. If an officer enters a house pursuant to a warrant to search for evidence of one crime when he is really interested only in seizing evidence relating to another crime, for which he does not have a warrant, his search is "pretextual" and the fruits of that search should be suppressed. Similarly, an officer might use an exception to the generally applicable warrant requirement, such as "hot pursuit," as a pretext to enter a home to seize items he knows he will find in plain view. Such conduct would be a deliberate attempt to circumvent the constitutional requirement of a warrant "particularly describing the place to be searched, and the persons or things to be seized," and cannot be condoned.

Points for Discussion

a. Immediately Apparent Requirement

In order for the plain view exception to apply, the criminal nature of the thing observed must be "immediately apparent." In *Minnesota v. Dickerson*, 508 U.S. 366 (1993), police officers stopped Dickerson and forced him to submit to a frisk. The frisk revealed no weapons, but the officer found a small lump in respondent's nylon jacket. The officer examined the lump with his fingers. By sliding the lump, the officer determined that it was crack cocaine in cellophane. The officer then reached into respondent's pocket and retrieved a small plastic bag containing one fifth of one gram of crack cocaine. Respondent was arrested and charged with possession of a controlled substance. The Court held that the seizure was invalid: "If a police officer lawfully pats down a suspect's outer clothing and feels an object whose contour or mass makes its identity immediately apparent, there has been no invasion of the suspect's privacy beyond that already authorized by the officer's search for weapons; if the object is contraband, its warrantless seizure would be justified by the same practical considerations that inhere in the plain-view context. Here, the officer determined that the lump was contraband only after 'squeezing, sliding and otherwise manipulating the contents of the defendant's pocket'—a pocket which the officer already knew contained no weapon. The officer's exploration of respondent's pocket after having concluded that it contained no weapon was unrelated to 'the sole justification of the search under *Terry*: the protection of the police officer and others nearby.' "

> The plain view exception is frequently applied in situations like the one involved in *Horton*: a police officer has lawfully entered a house and finds evidence in plain view. The officer uses the exception to justify the seizure of the evidence. Illustrative is the holding in *Washington v. Chrisman*, 455 U.S. 1 (1982), in which a university police officer arrested a student for carrying a half-gallon bottle of gin on campus (state law prohibited the possession of alcoholic beverages by individuals under 21). After the student was handcuffed, the officer asked the student for identification which the student was unable to produce. The student then asked for permission to return to his dormitory room to retrieve his identification, and the officer accompanied the student to the room. At the room, the officer observed what appeared to be a pipe and marijuana seeds in plain view and seized them. The seizure was upheld.

b. Narcotics Balloon

In *Texas v. Brown*, 460 U.S. 730 (1983), Brown was stopped at a driver's license checkpoint, and was found holding an opaque, green party balloon between his two middle fingers. The balloon was knotted about one half inch from the tip. When Brown reached across the passenger seat and opened the glove compartment, the officer noticed that the compartment contained several small plastic vials, quantities of loose white powder, and an open bag of party balloons. The officer reached into the car and picked up the green balloon which seemed to contain a powdery substance within the tied-off portion of the balloon. Subsequent analysis revealed that the balloon contained heroin. The Court concluded that the heroin was "immediately apparent": "Officer Maples possessed probable cause to believe that the balloon in Brown's hand contained an illicit substance. Maples testified that he was aware, both from his participation in previous narcotics arrests and from discussions with other officers, that balloons tied in the manner of the one possessed by Brown were frequently used to carry narcotics. This testimony was corroborated by that of a police department chemist who noted that it was "common" for balloons to be used in packaging narcotics. In addition, Maples was able to observe the contents of the glove compartment of Brown's car, which revealed further suggestions that Brown was engaged in activities that might involve possession of illicit substances. The fact that Maples could not see through the opaque fabric of the balloon is all but irrelevant: the distinctive character of the balloon itself spoke volumes as to its contents—particularly to the trained eye of the officer." Justice Stevens concurred: "The balloon could be one of those rare single-purpose containers which 'by their very nature cannot support any reasonable expectation of privacy because their contents can be inferred from their outward appearance.' "

Take Note

If an officer needs to move an object to determine whether it is "incriminating," the plain view doctrine does not apply. In *Arizona v. Hicks*, 480 U.S. 321 (1987), a bullet was fired through the floor of respondent's apartment, striking and injuring a man in the apartment below. When police officers entered respondent's apartment to search for the shooter, for other victims, and for weapons, one of the officers noticed expensive stereo components which seemed out of place in the squalid apartment. Suspecting that they were stolen, the officer moved some of the components so that he could read and record their serial numbers. The serial numbers allowed him to determine that the turntable had been stolen in an armed robbery. The Court concluded that the "moving" of the stereo equipment to view the serial numbers could not be justified under the plain view exception: "Inspecting those parts of the turntable that came into view during the search would not have constituted an independent search, because it would have produced no additional invasion of respondent's privacy interest. But taking action, the objectives of the authorized intrusion, which exposed to view concealed portions of the apartment or its contents, did produce a new invasion of respondent's privacy unjustified by the exigent circumstance that validated the entry. A search is a search, even if it happens to disclose nothing but the bottom of a turntable. 'The "plain view" doctrine may not be used to extend a general exploratory search from one object to another until something incriminating at last emerges.'" Justice Powell dissented: "The majority's unrelated to distinction between 'looking' at a suspicious object in plain view and 'moving' it even a few inches trivializes the Fourth Amendment." Justice O'Connor also dissented: "If police officers have a reasonable, articulable suspicion that an object they come across during the course of a lawful search is evidence of crime, they may make a cursory examination of the object to verify their suspicion. The additional intrusion caused by an inspection of an item in plain view for its serial number is minuscule."

Food for Thought

Rambo Royster is walking down a public street smoking a marijuana joint. A police officer sees Royster and the joint. Does the plain view doctrine come into play in a situation like this? If so, how?

Hypo 1: *Marijuana on the Window Sill*

A police officer is walking down a public sidewalk when he observes three marijuana plants growing on the window sill inside a townhouse. Does the plain view exception apply? May the officer use the plain view doctrine to enter the house and seize the plants? If not, how does the exception apply?

Hypo 2: *"Plain Smell" Doctrine?*

 yes

Is there a "plain smell" doctrine analogous to the "plain view" doctrine? Suppose that a police officer stops a car that is traveling at excessive speed. When the occupant of the car rolls down the window, the officer smells marijuana smoke emanating from the window. Would the "plain smell" doctrine justify a search of the car? Might the officer be able to justify the search on other grounds?

Hypo 3: *Computers and Plain View*

The police have reason to believe that defendant is a child pornographer, and obtain a warrant to search his home for books and magazines containing child pornography. On entering defendant's house, the police find a computer that is linked to the internet. Because many pornographers now use the internet to obtain pictures of children, the police seize the computer on the theory that it reflects "evidence" of child pornography found in "plain view." Is the seizure valid? After the seizure, can the police enter the hard drive of the computer and search for evidence of child pornography?

Hypo 4: *More on Computers and Plain View*

Suppose that, in the prior problem, the police have probable cause to believe that defendant is using his computer to seek out and download child pornography, and particularly describe the computer as an item to be seized under the warrant. Following the seizure, as the police are going through defendant's computer files, they find a file titled "Bookmaking." Can the police search the "bookmaking" file on the assumption that it was found in "plain view" during the computer search, and is plainly evident of illegality? Does it matter whether the police are generally searching through the entire computer, or only examining files with titles suggesting that they might contain child pornography? *See United States v. Galpin*, 720 F.3d 436 (2d Cir. 2013).

Hypo 5: *Plain View During a "Knock and Talk"*

Suppose that the police believe that defendant (Fisher) is operating a meth lab out of his home. Lacking probable cause to obtain a warrant, the officers decide to go to Fisher's house and conduct a "knock and talk." In other words, they plan to knock on Fisher's door, talk to him a bit, and see if he will consent to a search of the house. During the "knock and talk," the officer (who is standing at Fisher's front door) happens to see meth-related items (e.g., pseudoephedrine) lying just inside the door on the coffee table. Does the "plain view" doctrine apply to the items? Does the officer have the right to enter the house and seize the items without a warrant? *See McClish v. Nugent*, 483 F.3d 1231 (11th Cir. 2007); *State v. Fisher*, 283 Kan. 272, 154 P.3d 455 (2007). Would the validity of a "knock and talk" be affected by the fact that a number of police officers come to defendant's door at the same time, and refuse to allow him to re-enter the house even though he is barefoot, bare-chested, and the weather is cold and stormy. *See Keenom v. State*, 349 Ark. 381, 80 S.W.3d 743 (2002).

Hypo 6: *Plain View and the Dog Killing*

The police respond to a frantic call from a woman who claims that her neighbor is shooting at her dog. When the police arrive, defendant admits that he killed a dog, but claims that it was one of his own dogs, and that the police will "never find it." From where they are standing on the sidewalk, the police can see that a patch of ground on defendant's property, near his residence (20 feet away), has been dug up, and they can also see a dog collar lying on top of the dirt. Can the fresh dirt, and the dog bones buried beneath it, be regarded as being in plain view? Are the police required to obtain a warrant in order to dig up and examine what is under the dirt? *See State v. Goulet*, 21 A.3d 302 (R.I. 2011).

Hypo 7: *More on Plain View*

The police are called to a residence that has been burglarized, and they notice that a window has been broken, presumably to effect entry. The owner asks the officers to do a sweep of the house in order to ensure that no intruder remains on the premises. The police take a dog with them. The dog "alerts" to a door in a way (barking) which suggests that there is a human behind the door. When the police open the door, they do not find a human. However, the dog sticks his nose into a plastic bag revealing to the officers the existence of marijuana. Can the officers seize the evidence under the plain view doctrine? Should the dog's actions be regarded as equivalent to the officer's decision to move the turntable (in order to ascertain serial numbers) in *Hicks*? Or should the dog's instinctive reactions be regarded as different for Fourth Amendment purposes? *See State v. Miller*, 367 N.C. 702, 766 S.E.2d 289 (2014).

2. Search Incident to Legal Arrest

The search incident to legal arrest exception is one of the oldest and most well-established exceptions to the warrant requirement. It provides that, when the police make a legal arrest, they have the right to make a search incident to that arrest.

Take Note

An arrest is the most serious form of seizure, and it occurs when the police take a suspect into custody in order to bring charges.

Until 1976, there was uncertainty about the requirements for an arrest. Could an arrest be based solely on probable cause? Or, as under the search prong of the Fourth Amendment, is a warrant required?

United States v. Watson

423 U.S. 411 (1976).

MR. JUSTICE WHITE delivered the opinion of the Court.

Based on information received from an informant, a federal postal inspector had reason to believe that Watson was in possession of credit cards stolen from the U.S. mail. The informant arranged to meet Watson in a restaurant. On the informant's signal (which indicated that Watson was in possession of the cards), federal inspectors closed in and arrested Watson for possession of stolen mail. After the arrest, Watson consented to a search of his car which revealed two more stolen credit cards. The court of appeals held that Watson's arrest was unconstitutional because the inspector acted without a warrant and granted Watson's motion to suppress the credit cards.

Under the Fourth Amendment, the people are to be "secure in their persons, houses, papers, and effects, against unreasonable searches and seizures, and no Warrants shall issue, but upon probable cause." The statute under which Watson was arrested represents a judgment by Congress that it is not unreasonable under the Fourth Amendment for postal inspectors to arrest without a warrant provided they have probable cause to do so. This was not an isolated or quixotic judgment of the legislative branch. Other federal law enforcement officers have been expressly authorized by statute for many years to make felony arrests on probable cause but without a warrant. This is true of United States marshals, and of agents of the Federal Bureau of Investigation, the Drug Enforcement Administration, the Secret Service, and the Customs Service.

There is nothing in the Court's prior cases indicating that under the Fourth Amendment a warrant is required to make a valid arrest for a felony. Indeed, the relevant prior decisions are uniformly to the contrary. "The usual rule is that a police officer may arrest without warrant one believed by the officer upon reasonable cause to have been guilty of a felony." *Carroll v. United States*, 267 U.S. 132, 156 (1925).

Cases construing the Fourth Amendment thus reflect the ancient common-law rule that a peace officer was permitted to arrest without a warrant for a misdemeanor or felony committed in his presence as well as for a felony not committed in his presence if there was reasonable ground for making the arrest. 10 Halsbury's Laws of England 344–345 (3d ed. 1955). This has also been the prevailing rule under state constitutions and statutes.

Because the common-law rule authorizing arrests without a warrant generally prevailed in the States, it is important for present purposes to note that in 1792 Congress invested United States marshals and their deputies with "the same powers in executing the laws of the United States, as sheriffs and their deputies in the several states have by law, in executing the laws of their respective states." The Second Congress thus saw no inconsistency between the Fourth Amendment and legislation giving United States marshals the same power as local peace officers to arrest for a felony without a warrant. This provision equating the power of federal marshals with those of local sheriffs was several times re-enacted and is today § 570 of Title 28 of the United States Code.

The balance struck by the common law in generally authorizing felony arrests on probable cause, but without a warrant, has survived substantially intact. It appears in almost all of the States in the form of express statutory authorization. The American Law Institute's model arrest statute authorizes an officer to take a person into custody if the officer has reasonable cause to believe that the person to be arrested has committed a felony, or has committed a misdemeanor or petty misdemeanor in his presence. The commentary to this section said: "The Code thus adopts the traditional and almost universal standard for arrest without a warrant."

This is the rule Congress has long directed its principal law enforcement officers to follow. Congress has plainly decided against conditioning warrantless arrest power on proof of exigent circumstances. Law enforcement officers may find it wise to seek arrest warrants where practicable to do so, and their judgments about probable cause may be more readily accepted where backed by a warrant issued by a magistrate. But we decline to transform this judicial preference into a constitutional rule when the judgment of the Nation and Congress has for so long been to authorize warrantless public arrests on probable cause rather than to encumber criminal prosecutions with endless litigation with respect to the existence of exigent circumstances, whether it was practicable to get a warrant, whether the suspect was about to flee, and the like.

Watson's arrest did not violate the Fourth Amendment, and the Court of Appeals erred in holding to the contrary.

MR. JUSTICE POWELL, concurring.

The historical momentum for acceptance of warrantless arrests, already strong at the adoption of the Fourth Amendment, has gained strength during the ensuing two centuries. Both the judiciary and the legislative bodies of this Nation repeatedly have placed their imprimaturs upon the practice and law enforcement agencies have developed their investigative and arrest procedures upon an assumption that warrantless arrests were valid so long as based upon probable cause.

A constitutional rule permitting felony arrests only with a warrant or in exigent circumstances could severely hamper effective law enforcement. Good police practice often requires postponing an arrest, even after probable cause has been established, in order to place the suspect under surveillance or otherwise develop further evidence necessary to prove guilt to a jury. Additional investigative work could imperil the entire prosecution. Should the officers fail to obtain a warrant initially, and later be required by unforeseen circumstances to arrest immediately with no chance to procure a last-minute warrant, they would risk a court decision that the subsequent exigency did not excuse their failure to get a warrant in the interim since they first developed probable cause. If the officers attempted to meet such a contingency by procuring a warrant as soon as they had probable cause and then merely held it during their subsequent investigation, they would risk a court decision that the warrant had grown stale by the time it was used. Law enforcement personnel caught in this squeeze could ensure validity of their arrests only by obtaining a warrant and arresting as soon as probable cause existed, thereby foreclosing the possibility of gathering vital additional evidence from the suspect's continued actions.

MR. JUSTICE MARSHALL, with whom MR. JUSTICE BRENNAN joins, dissenting.

The Court relies on the English common-law rule of arrest and the many state and federal statutes following it. The substance of the ancient common-law rule provides no support for the far-reaching modern rule that the Court fashions on its model. A felony at common law and a felony today bear only slight resemblance. At common law, "No crime was considered a felony which did not occasion a total forfeiture of the offender's lands or goods or both." Today, "Any offense punishable by death or imprisonment for a term exceeding one year is a felony." 18 U.S.C. § 1.

This difference reflects more than changing notions of penology. Only the most serious crimes were felonies at common law, and many crimes now classified as felonies under federal or state law were treated as misdemeanors. To make an arrest for any of these crimes at common law, the police officer was required to obtain a warrant, unless the crime was committed in his presence. Since many of these same crimes are commonly classified as felonies today, a warrant is no longer needed to make such arrests. The balance struck by the common law decreed that only in the most serious of cases could the warrant be dispensed with. This balance is not recognized when the common-law rule is unthinkingly transposed to our present classifications of criminal offenses. The Court relies on the numerous state and federal statutes codifying the common-law rule. The mere existence of statutes or practice, even of long standing, is no defense to an unconstitutional practice.

A warrant is required in search situations not because of some high regard for property, but because of our regard for the individual, and his interest in his possessions and person. There can be no less invasion of privacy when the individual himself, rather than his property, is searched and seized. An unjustified arrest that forces the individual temporarily to forfeit his right to control his person and movements and interrupts the course of his daily business may be more intrusive than an unjustified search. "Being arrested and held by the police, even if for a few hours, is for most persons, awesome and frightening." ALI, Model Code of Pre-arraignment Procedure, Commentary 290–291 (1975).

A warrant requirement for arrests would, of course, minimize the possibility that such an intrusion would occur on less than probable cause. For this reason, a warrant is required for searches. Surely there is no reason to place greater trust in the partisan assessment of a police officer that there is probable cause for an arrest than in his determination that probable cause exists for a search.

The concern that the warrant requirement would unduly burden law enforcement interests are wholly illusory. "It is the standard practice of the Federal Bureau of Investigation to obtain a warrant before making an arrest." The Government's assertion that a warrant requirement would impose an intolerable burden stems from the specious supposition that procurement of an arrest warrant would be necessary as soon as probable cause ripens. There is no requirement that a search ✓ warrant be obtained the moment police have probable cause to search. Police would not have to cut their investigation short the moment they obtain probable cause to arrest, nor would undercover agents be forced suddenly to terminate their work and forfeit their covers. Moreover, if in the course of the continued police investigation exigent circumstances develop that demand an immediate arrest, the arrest may be made without fear of unconstitutionality, so long as the exigency was unanticipated and not used to avoid the arrest warrant requirement.

I respectfully dissent.

More than two decades after *Watson*, the Court addressed the legality of warrantless misdemeanor arrests in *Atwater v. City of Lago Vista*, 532 U.S. 318 (2001). Atwater was subjected to a full custodial arrest for a misdemeanor seatbelt violation punishable only by a fine. In upholding the arrest, the Court noted that early English statutes allowed the police to make warrantless misdemeanor arrests "for all sorts of relatively minor offenses unaccompanied by violence." Similar statutes existed in the District of Columbia and all 50 states, and the Court concluded that "the fact that many of the original States with such constitutional limitations continued to grant their own peace officers broad warrantless misdemeanor arrest authority undermines Atwater's contention that the founding generation meant to bar federal law enforcement officers from exercising the same authority." The Court found that there had been "two centuries of uninterrupted (and largely unchallenged) state and federal practice permitting warrantless arrests for misdemeanors not amounting to or involving breach of the peace." Justice O'Connor dissented noting that "justifying a full arrest by the same quantum of evidence that justifies a traffic stop defies any sense of proportionality and is in serious tension with the Fourth Amendment's proscription of unreasonable seizures." She noted that a "custodial arrest exacts an obvious toll on an individual's liberty and privacy, even when the period of custody is relatively brief." In her view, "the penalty that may attach to any particular offense seems to provide the clearest and most consistent indication of the State's interest in arresting individuals suspected of committing that offense." Since the state imposed only a fine for driving without a seatbelt, "the State's interest in taking a person suspected of committing that offense into custody is surely limited, at best."

Points for Discussion

a. The Impact of State Law

In *Virginia v. Moore*, 553 U.S. 164 (2008), the Court rejected the idea that a police officer violates the Fourth Amendment by making an arrest based on probable cause but prohibited by state law (state law precluded a custodial arrest for driving on a suspended license unless the driver refuses to desist or the officer reasonably believes that the driver is likely to disregard a summons, or is likely to harm himself or others). In *Moore*, when the police conducted a search incident to arrest, they turned up cocaine. The Court noted that there was nothing to indicate that the Fourth Amendment "was intended to incorporate subsequently enacted statutes." "When an officer has probable cause to believe a person committed even a minor crime in his presence, the balancing of private and public interests is not in doubt. The arrest is constitutionally reasonable. The Fourth Amendment's meaning did not change with local law enforcement practices-even practices set by rule and state restrictions do not alter the Fourth Amendment's protections."

b. Arrests at Private Residences

In *Payton v. New York*, 445 U.S. 573 (1980), the Court struck down a New York law which authorized police officers to enter private residences without warrants, by force if necessary, to make a routine felony arrest: "The Fourth Amendment has drawn a firm line at the entrance to the house. Absent exigent circumstances, that threshold may not reasonably be crossed without a warrant. An arrest warrant requirement may afford less protection than a search warrant requirement, but it will suffice to interpose the magistrate's determination of probable cause between the zealous officer and the citizen. If there is sufficient evidence of a citizen's participation in a felony to persuade a judicial officer that his arrest is justified, it is constitutionally reasonable to require him to open his doors to the officers of the law. An arrest warrant founded on probable cause implicitly carries with it the limited authority to enter a dwelling in which the suspect lives when there is reason to believe the suspect is within." Mr. Justice White dissented: "Warrantless arrest entries were firmly accepted at common law." In *Steagald v. United States*, 451 U.S. 204 (1981), the Court held that a law enforcement officer may not search for the subject of an arrest warrant in the home of a third party without first obtaining a search warrant. *See also Minnesota v. Olson*, 495 U.S. 91 (1990). Suppose that the police conduct a "knock and talk" at defendant's house at his front door, and they develop probable cause to arrest him. Can they make a cross-threshhold arrest? *See United States v. Allen*, 813 F.3d 76 (2nd Cir. 2016).

Take Note

What if a traffic arrest is used as the pretext for a car search? In *Arkansas v. Sullivan*, 532 U.S. 769 (2001), an officer stopped Sullivan for speeding as well as for having an improperly tinted windshield. After reviewing Sullivan's license, the officer realized that he was aware of "intelligence on Sullivan regarding narcotics." While Sullivan was trying unsuccessfully to locate his registration and insurance papers, the officer noticed a rusted roofing hatchet on the car's floorboard. The officer then arrested Sullivan for speeding, driving without registration and insurance documentation, carrying a weapon (the roofing hatchet), and improper window tinting. The officer then searched the car and found a substance that appeared to be methamphetamine as well as drug paraphernalia. Sullivan was charged with various state-law drug offenses, unlawful possession of a weapon, and speeding, and moved to suppress the evidence on the basis that his arrest was merely a "pretext and sham to search" him. The Court rejected the challenge noting that "subjective intentions play no role in ordinary, probable-cause Fourth Amendment analysis."

FYI

In *Tennessee v. Garner*, 471 U.S. 1 (1985), the Court held that the Constitution prohibits the use of deadly force to make an arrest in most instances: "The use of deadly force is a self-defeating way of apprehending a suspect and so setting the criminal justice mechanism in motion. If successful, it guarantees that that mechanism will not be set in motion. While the meaningful threat of deadly force might be thought to lead to the arrest of more live suspects by discouraging escape attempts, the presently available evidence does not support this thesis." The Court did hold that deadly force is permissible when the suspect "poses a threat of serious physical harm either to the officer or to others." In *Garner*, the suspect's youth, slightness, and lack of a weapon suggested that he did not pose a threat of physical danger to himself or others. As a result, the use of deadly force was deemed inappropriate. Justice O'Connor dissented: "The public interest involved in the use of deadly force as a last resort to apprehend a fleeing burglary suspect relates primarily to the serious nature of the crime. Household burglaries not only represent the illegal entry into a person's home, but also 'pose real risk of serious harm to others.' If apprehension is not immediate, it is likely that the suspect will not be caught." In *Scott v. Harris*, 550 U.S. 372 (2007), the Court held that a police officer could attempt to stop a fleeing motorist (who refused to yield to pursuing police) by ramming the motorist's car from behind even though the ramming ultimately rendered the motorist a paraplegic. The Court rejected the notion that the officer had used deadly force in contravention of the Court's holding in *Garner.*

c. Stated Basis for Arrest

In *Devenpeck v. Alford,* 543 U.S. 146 (2004), a police officer possessed probable cause to believe that defendant had been impersonating a police officer. However, when the officer realized that defendant had a tape recorder and was recording their conversation, the officer decided to arrest defendant for violating the Washington Privacy Act, Wash. Rev.Code § 9.73.030 (1994). When the charges were dismissed, defendant filed suit under 42 U.S.C. § 1983, and also filed a state cause of action for unlawful arrest and imprisonment. The Court refused to accept the proposition that the probable-cause inquiry is confined to the facts actually invoked at the time of arrest, and that (in addition) the offense supported by these known facts must be "closely related" to the offense that the officer invoked. The Court emphasized that the officer had probable cause to arrest defendant for impersonating a police officer, and chose not to charge for that offense solely because of a departmental policy against "stacking" charges. "We have consistently rejected a conception of the Fourth Amendment that would produce such haphazard results." "Subjective intent of the arresting officer, *however* it is determined (and of course subjective intent is *always* determined by objective means), is simply no basis for invalidating an arrest. Those are lawfully arrested whom the facts known to the arresting officers give probable cause to arrest."

FYI

What if a material-witness arrest warrant is used as a pretext? In *Ashcroft v. al–Kidd,* 563 U.S. 731 (2011), plaintiff claimed that Attorney General Ashcroft had misused a material-witness warrant. Under federal law, a judge may order the arrest of a person whose testimony is regarded as "material in a criminal proceeding if it is shown that it may become impracticable to secure the presence of the person by subpoena." 18 U.S.C. § 3144. Abdullah al-Kidd (who was detained for 16 days and was under supervised revised relief for 14 months) sued, complaining that then-Attorney General John Ashcroft authorized federal officials to detain individuals with suspected ties to terrorist organizations. He contended that federal officials did not intend to call most of these individuals as witnesses, but instead detained them because of suspected terrorist ties because he lacked sufficient evidence to actually charge them with crimes. The Court held that "Fourth Amendment reasonableness 'is predominantly an objective inquiry,' and that the question is whether 'the circumstances, viewed objectively, justify the challenged action.' " If so, the governmental actor's subject intent is irrelevant. Since al-Kidd conceded that individualized suspicion supported the issuance of the material-witness arrest warrant, and did not assert that his arrest would have been unconstitutional absent the alleged pretextual use of the warrant, the Court found no Fourth Amendment violation, and concluded that there was no need to address the question of whether Ashcroft was entitled to qualified immunity. In *Alicea v. Thomas*, 815 F.3d 283 (7th Cir. 2016), the court held that the police acted unreasonably in ordering a dog to attack a burglary suspect.

Hypo 1: *"Knock and Talk" Arrest Under Payton*

Under *Payton, supra*, a police officer cannot arrest an individual at a private residence without a warrant. However, in *United States v. Santana*, 427 U.S. 38 (1976), the Court held that a suspect who was outside her home, and therefore knowingly exposed herself to "public view," and then retreated into the house, could be arrested without a warrant. Suppose that the police decide to conduct a "knock and talk" at Jane's house. While the police have probable cause to believe that Jane is a drug dealer, they do not have a warrant for her arrest and do not have a warrant to search the house. In response to the police knock, Jane opens the door and steps out onto the porch. Has Jane knowingly exposed herself to public view so that she can be arrested without a warrant? What if the police ask her to step outside and she does? *See McClish v. Nugent*, 483 F.3d 1231 (11th Cir. 2007).

Hypo 2: *Tasers and Unreasonable Force*

An 11-year-old girl, J.N., had been driving an ATV through the streets with another young passenger. J.N. had run several stop signs and was otherwise driving dangerously. When a police officer spotted J.N., he used his overhead lights and a siren to signal to J.N. to stop. J.N. responded by trying to escape on the ATV, and later abandoned the ATV to flee on foot. The officer chased J.N. on foot and finally caught up with her. According to J.N., she was never aggressive or threatening towards the officer, and she had already stopped attempting to flee, when she was tased. According to the officer, she was still trying to resist arrest. All agree that the officer used his taser multiple times against J.N. Given the circumstances, did the officer use excessive force against J.N.? *See Russell v. Virg-In*, 258 P.3d 795 (Alaska 2011).

* * *

Once a legal arrest occurs, the police are allowed to make a search incident to arrest. While the right to search is clear enough, the scope of the search can be open to debate.

Riley v. California

134 S.Ct. 2473 (2014).

CHIEF JUSTICE ROBERTS delivered the opinion of the Court.

In the first case, petitioner David Riley was stopped by a police officer for driving with expired registration tags. In the course of the stop, the officer learned that Riley's license had been suspended. The officer impounded Riley's car, pursuant to department policy, and another officer conducted an inventory search of the car. Riley was arrested for possession of concealed and loaded firearms when that search turned up two handguns under the car's hood. An officer searched Riley incident to the arrest and found items associated with the "Bloods" street gang. He also seized a cell phone from Riley's pocket. The phone was a "smart phone," a cell phone with a broad range of other functions based on advanced computing capability, large storage capacity, and Internet connectivity. The officer accessed the phone and noticed that some words (presumably in text messages or a contacts list) were preceded by the letters "CK"—a label that, he believed, stood for "Crip Killers," a slang term for members of the Bloods gang. At the police station about two hours after the arrest, a detective specializing in gangs further examined the contents of the phone. The detective testified that he "went through" Riley's phone "looking for evidence, because gang members will often video themselves with guns or take pictures of themselves with the guns." Particular files that "caught the detective's eye" included videos of young men sparring while someone yelled encouragement using the moniker "Blood." The police also found photographs of Riley standing in front of a car they suspected had been involved in a shooting a few weeks earlier. Riley was charged in connection with that earlier shooting, with firing at an occupied vehicle, assault with a semiautomatic firearm, and attempted murder. The State alleged that Riley had committed those crimes for the benefit of a criminal street gang, an aggravating factor that carries an enhanced sentence. Prior to trial, Riley moved to suppress all evidence that the police had obtained from his cell phone. The trial court rejected that motion. Riley was convicted. The California Court of Appeal affirmed. The California Supreme Court denied Riley's petition for review and we granted certiorari.

In the second case, a police officer observed respondent Brima Wurie make an apparent drug sale from a car. Officers subsequently arrested Wurie. At the station, the officers seized two cell phones from Wurie's person. The one at issue was a "flip phone." The officers noticed that the phone was repeatedly receiving calls from a source identified as "my house" on the phone's external screen. They opened the phone and saw a photograph of a woman and a baby set as the phone's wallpaper. They pressed one button to access its call log, then another button to determine the phone number associated with the "my house" label. They next used an online phone directory to trace that phone number to an apartment building. When the officers went to the building, they saw Wurie's name on a mailbox and observed through a window a woman who resembled the woman in the photograph on Wurie's phone. They secured the apartment while obtaining a search warrant and, upon executing the warrant, found and seized 215 grams of crack cocaine, marijuana, drug paraphernalia, a firearm and ammunition, and cash. Wurie was charged with distributing crack cocaine, possessing crack cocaine with intent to distribute, and being a felon in possession of a firearm and ammunition. He moved to suppress. The District Court denied the motion and Wurie was convicted. A divided panel of the First Circuit reversed and vacated Wurie's convictions. We granted certiorari.

"The ultimate touchstone of the Fourth Amendment is 'reasonableness.' " *Brigham City v. Stuart*, 547 U. S. 398, 403 (2006). "Where a search is undertaken by law enforcement officials to discover evidence of criminal wrongdoing, reasonableness generally requires the obtaining of a judicial warrant." *Vernonia School Dist. 47J v. Acton*, 515 U. S. 646, 653 (1995). A warrant ensures that the inferences to support a search are "drawn by a neutral and detached magistrate instead of being judged by the officer engaged in the often competitive enterprise of ferreting out crime." *Johnson v. United States*, 333 U. S. 10, 14 (1948). In the absence of a warrant, a search is reasonable only if it falls within a specific exception to the warrant requirement. See *Kentucky v. King*, 563 U.S. 452131 S. Ct. 1849 (2011).

The cases before us concern the reasonableness of a warrantless search incident to a lawful arrest. In 1914, this Court first acknowledged in dictum "the right on the part of the Government, always recognized under English and American law, to search the person of the accused when legally arrested to discover and seize the fruits or evidences of crime." *Weeks v. United States*, 232 U. S. 383, 392. Since that time, it has been well accepted that such a search constitutes an exception to the warrant requirement. The label "exception" is something of a misnomer as warrantless searches incident to arrest occur with far greater frequency than searches conducted pursuant to a warrant.

Although the existence of the exception for such searches has been recognized for a century, its scope has been debated for nearly as long. See *Arizona v. Gant*, 556 U. S. 332, 350 (2009). That debate has focused on the extent to which officers may search property found on or near the arrestee.

Three related precedents set forth the rules governing such searches. The first, *Chimel v. California*, 395 U. S. 752 (1969), laid the groundwork for most of the existing search incident to arrest doctrine. Police officers in that case arrested Chimel inside his home and proceeded to search his entire three-bedroom house, including the attic and garage. In particular rooms, they also looked through the contents of drawers. The Court crafted the following rule for assessing the reasonableness of a search incident to arrest: "When an arrest is made, it is reasonable for the arresting officer to search the person arrested in order to remove any weapons that the latter might seek to use in order to resist arrest or effect his escape. Otherwise, the officer's safety might well be endangered, and the arrest itself frustrated. In addition, it is entirely reasonable for the arresting officer to search for and seize any evidence on the arrestee's person in order to prevent its concealment or destruction. There is ample justification, therefore, for a search of the arrestee's person and the area 'within his immediate control'—construing that phrase to mean the area from within which he might gain possession of a weapon or destructible evidence." The extensive warrantless search of Chimel's home did not fit within this exception, because it was not needed to protect officer safety or to preserve evidence. Four years later, in *United States v. Robinson*, 414 U. S. 218 (1973), the Court applied *Chimel* in the context of a search of the arrestee's person. A police officer had arrested Robinson for driving with a revoked license. The officer conducted a patdown search and felt an object that he could not identify in Robinson's coat pocket. He removed the object, which turned out to be a crumpled cigarette package, and opened it. Inside were 14 capsules of heroin. This Court held that "the authority to search the person incident to a lawful custodial arrest, while based upon the need to disarm and to discover evidence, does not depend on what a court may later decide was the probability in a particular arrest situation that weapons or evidence would in fact be found upon the person of the suspect." A "custodial arrest of a suspect based on probable cause is a reasonable intrusion under the Fourth Amendment; that intrusion being lawful, a search incident to the arrest requires no additional justification." Thus the search of Robinson was reasonable even though there was no concern about the loss of evidence, and the arresting officer had no specific concern that Robinson might be armed. The Court did not draw a line between a search of Robinson's person and a further examination of the cigarette pack found during that search. "Having in the course of a lawful search come upon the crumpled package of cigarettes, the officer was entitled to inspect it." *Gant* concluded that *Chimel* could authorize police to search a vehicle "only when the arrestee is unsecured and within reaching distance of the passenger compartment at the time of the search." *Gant* added, however, an independent exception for a warrantless search of a vehicle's passenger compartment "when it is 'reasonable to believe evidence relevant to the crime of arrest might be found in the vehicle.'"

These cases require us to decide how the search incident to arrest doctrine applies to modern cell phones, which are now such a pervasive and insistent part of daily life that the proverbial visitor from Mars might conclude they were an important feature of human anatomy. A smart phone of the sort taken from Riley was unheard of ten years ago; a significant majority of American adults now own such phones. Even less sophisticated phones like Wurie's have been around for less than 15 years. Both phones are based on technology nearly inconceivable just a few decades ago, when *Chimel* and *Robinson* were decided. Absent more precise guidance from the founding era, we generally determine whether to exempt a given type of search from the warrant requirement "by assessing, on the one hand, the degree to which it intrudes upon an individual's privacy and, on the other, the degree to which it is needed for the promotion of legitimate governmental interests." *Wyoming v. Houghton*, 526 U. S. 295, 300 (1999).

While *Robinson's* categorical rule strikes the appropriate balance in the context of physical objects, neither of its rationales has much force with respect to digital content on cell phones. The two risks identified in *Chimel*—harm to officers and destruction of evidence—are present in all custodial arrests. There are no comparable risks when the search is of digital data. *Robinson* regarded any privacy interests retained by an individual after arrest as significantly diminished by the fact of the arrest itself. Cell phones, however, place vast quantities of personal information literally in the hands of individuals. A search of the information on a cell phone bears little resemblance to the type of brief physical search considered in *Robinson*. We therefore decline to extend *Robinson* to searches of data on cell phones, and hold that officers must generally secure a warrant before conducting such a search.

We do not overlook *Robinson's* admonition that searches of a person incident to arrest, "while based upon the need to disarm and to discover evidence," are reasonable regardless of "the probability in a particular arrest situation that weapons or evidence would in fact be found." Rather than requiring "case-by-case adjudication," we ask instead whether application of the search incident to arrest doctrine to this particular category of effects would "untether the rule from the justifications underlying the *Chimel* exception," *Gant, supra*, at 343. Digital data stored on a cell phone cannot be used as a weapon to harm an arresting officer or to effectuate the arrestee's escape. Law enforcement officers remain free to examine the physical aspects of a phone to ensure that it will not be used as a weapon—say, to determine whether there is a razor blade hidden between the phone and its case. Once an officer has secured a phone and eliminated any potential physical threats, data on the phone can endanger no one. Perhaps the same might have been said of the cigarette pack seized from Robinson's pocket. The officer in *Robinson* testified that he could not identify the objects in the cigarette pack but knew they were not cigarettes. Given that, a further search was a reasonable protective measure. No such unknowns exist with respect to digital data. The officers who searched Wurie's cell phone "knew exactly what they would find therein: data. They also knew that the data could not harm them."

The United States and California suggest that a search of cell phone data might help ensure officer safety in more indirect ways, for example by alerting officers that confederates of the arrestee are headed to the scene. There is undoubtedly a strong government interest in warning officers about such possibilities, but neither offers evidence to suggest that their concerns are based on actual experience. The proposed consideration would also represent a broadening of *Chimel's* concern that an *arrestee himself* might grab a weapon and use it against an officer "to resist arrest or effect his escape." Any such threats from outside the arrest scene do not "lurk in all custodial arrests." *Chadwick*, 433 U. S., at 14–15. Accordingly, the interest in protecting officer safety does not justify dispensing with the warrant requirement across the board. To the extent dangers to arresting officers may be implicated in a particular case, they are better addressed through consideration of case-specific exceptions to the warrant requirement, such as the one for exigent circumstances. See, *e.g., Warden, Md. Penitentiary v. Hayden*, 387 U. S. 294 (1967).

Both Riley and Wurie concede that officers could have seized and secured their cell phones to prevent destruction of evidence while seeking a warrant. See *Illinois v. McArthur*, 531 U. S. 326 (2001); *Chadwick, supra*, at 13. Once law enforcement officers have secured a cell phone, there is no longer any risk that the arrestee will be able to delete incriminating data from the phone. Information on a cell phone may be vulnerable to two types of evidence destruction unique to digital data—remote wiping and data encryption. Remote wiping occurs when a phone, connected to a wireless network, receives a signal that erases stored data. This can happen when a third party sends a remote signal or when a phone is preprogrammed to delete data upon entering or leaving certain geographic areas (so-called "geofencing"). Encryption is a security feature that some modern cell phones use in addition to password protection. When such phones lock, data becomes protected by sophisticated encryption that renders a phone all but "unbreakable" unless police know the password. These broader concerns about the loss of evidence are distinct from *Chimel's* focus on a defendant who responds to arrest by trying to conceal or destroy evidence within his reach. With respect to remote wiping, the Government's primary concern turns on the actions of third parties who are not present at the scene of arrest. Data encryption is even further afield. There, the Government focuses on the ordinary operation of a phone's security features, apart from *any* active attempt by a defendant or his associates to conceal or destroy evidence upon arrest. We have been given little reason to believe that either problem is prevalent. The briefing reveals only anecdotal examples of remote wiping triggered by an arrest. Similarly, the opportunities for officers to search a password-protected phone before data becomes encrypted are quite limited. Law enforcement officers are very unlikely to come upon such a phone in an unlocked state because most phones lock at the touch of a button or, as a default, after some very short period of inactivity.

In situations in which an arrest might trigger a remote-wipe attempt or an officer discovers an unlocked phone, the need to effect the arrest, secure the scene, and tend to other pressing matters means that law enforcement officers may well not be able to turn their attention to a cell phone right away. Cell phone data would be vulnerable to remote wiping from the time an individual anticipates arrest to the time any eventual search of the phone is completed, which might be at the station house hours later. Likewise, an officer who seizes a phone in an unlocked state might not be able to begin his search in the short time remaining before the phone locks and data becomes encrypted. Law enforcement is not without specific means to address the threat. Remote wiping can be prevented by disconnecting a phone from the network. Law enforcement officers can turn the phone off or remove its battery. If they are concerned about encryption or other potential problems, they can leave a phone powered on and place it in an enclosure that isolates the phone from radio waves. Such devices are commonly called "Faraday bags." They are essentially sandwich bags made of aluminum foil: cheap, lightweight, and easy to use. They may not be a complete answer to the problem, but at least for now they provide a reasonable response. In fact, a number of law enforcement agencies around the country already encourage the use of Faraday bags.

To the extent that law enforcement still has specific concerns about the potential loss of evidence in a particular case, there remain more targeted ways to address those concerns. If "the police are truly confronted with a 'now or never' situation,"—for example, circumstances suggesting that a defendant's phone will be the target of an imminent remote-wipe attempt—they may be able to rely on exigent circumstances to search the phone immediately. *Missouri v. McNeely*, 133 S. Ct. 1552(2013). If officers happen to seize a phone in an unlocked state, they may be able to disable a phone's automatic-lock feature in order to prevent the phone from locking and encrypting data. Such a preventive measure could be analyzed under the principles set forth in our decision in *McArthur*, 531 U. S. 326, which approved officers' reasonable steps to secure a scene to preserve evidence while they awaited a warrant. Not every search "is acceptable solely because a person is in custody." *Maryland v. King*, 133 S. Ct. 1958, 1979 (2013).

The United States asserts that a search of data stored on a cell phone is "materially indistinguishable" from searches of physical items. Modern cell phones, as a category, implicate privacy concerns far beyond those implicated by the search of a cigarette pack, a wallet, or a purse. A conclusion that inspecting the contents of an arrestee's pockets works no substantial additional intrusion on privacy beyond the arrest itself may make sense as applied to physical items, but any extension of that reasoning to digital data has to rest on its own bottom. Cell phones differ in both a quantitative and a qualitative sense from other objects that might be kept on an arrestee's person. The term "cell phone" is itself misleading; many of these devices are in fact minicomputers that also have the capacity to be used as a telephone. They could just as easily be called cameras, video players, rolodexes, calendars, tape recorders, libraries, diaries, albums, televisions, maps, or newspapers. One of the most notable distinguishing features of modern cell phones is their immense storage capacity. Before cell phones, a search of a person was limited by physical realities and tended as a general matter to constitute only a narrow intrusion on privacy. Most people cannot lug around every piece of mail they have received for the past several months, every picture they have taken, or every book or article they have read—nor would they have any reason to attempt to do so. If they did, they would have to drag behind them a trunk rather than a container the size of the cigarette package in *Robinson*. But the possible intrusion on privacy is not physically limited in the same way when it comes to cell phones. The current top-selling smart phone has a standard capacity of 16 gigabytes (and is available with up to 64 gigabytes). Sixteen gigabytes translates to millions of pages of text, thousands of pictures, or hundreds of videos. Cell phones couple that capacity with the ability to store many different types of information: Even the most basic phones that sell for less than $20 might hold photographs, picture messages, text messages, Internet browsing history, a calendar, a thousand-entry phone book, and so on. The gulf between physical practicability and digital capacity will only continue to widen in the future.

The storage capacity of cell phones has several interrelated consequences for privacy. First, a cell phone collects in one place many distinct types of information—an address, a note, a prescription, a bank statement, a video—that reveal much more in combination than any isolated record. Second, a cell phone's capacity allows even just one type of information to convey far more than previously possible. The sum of an individual's private life can be reconstructed through a thousand photographs labeled with dates, locations, and descriptions; the same cannot be said of a photograph or two of loved ones tucked into a wallet. Third, the data on a phone can date back to the purchase of the phone, or even earlier. A person might carry in his pocket a slip of paper reminding him to call Mr. Jones; he would not carry a record of all his communications with Mr. Jones for the past several months, as would routinely be kept on a phone.

Finally, there is an element of pervasiveness that characterizes cell phones but not physical records. Prior to the digital age, people did not typically carry a cache of sensitive personal information with them as they went about their day. Now it is the person who is not carrying a cell phone who is the exception. Nearly three-quarters of smart phone users report being within five feet of their phones most of the time, with 12% admitting that they even use their phones in the shower. A decade ago police officers searching an arrestee might have occasionally stumbled across a highly personal item such as a diary. Today, many of the more than 90% of American adults who own a cell phone keep on their person a digital record of nearly every aspect of their lives—from the mundane to the intimate. Allowing the police to scrutinize such records on a routine basis is quite different from allowing them to search a personal item or two in the occasional case.

The data stored on a cell phone is also qualitatively different. An Internet search and browsing history, for example, can be found on an Internet-enabled phone and could reveal an individual's private interests or concerns—perhaps a search for certain symptoms of disease, coupled with frequent visits to WebMD. Data on a cell phone can also reveal where a person has been. Historic location information is a standard feature on many smart phones and can reconstruct someone's specific movements down to the minute, not only around town but also within a particular building. See *United States v. Jones*, 132 S. Ct. 945 (2012) (Sotomayor, J., concurring) ("GPS monitoring generates a precise, comprehensive record of a person's public movements that reflects a wealth of detail about her familial, political, professional, religious, and sexual associations.").

Mobile application software on a cell phone, or "apps," offer a range of tools for managing detailed information about all aspects of a person's life. There are apps for Democratic Party news and Republican Party news; apps for alcohol, drug, and gambling addictions; apps for sharing prayer requests; apps for tracking pregnancy symptoms; apps for planning your budget; apps for every conceivable hobby or pastime; apps for improving your romantic life. There are popular apps for buying or selling just about anything, and the records of such transactions may be accessible on the phone indefinitely. There are over a million apps available in each of the two major app stores; the phrase "there's an app for that" is now part of the popular lexicon. The average smart phone user has installed 33 apps, which together can form a revealing montage of the user's life.

In 1926, Learned Hand observed that it is "a totally different thing to search a man's pockets and use against him what they contain, from ransacking his house for everything which may incriminate him." *United States v. Kirschenblatt*, 16 F. 2d 202, 203 (CA2). If his pockets contain a cell phone, that is no longer true. A cell phone search would typically expose to the government far *more* than the most exhaustive search of a house: A phone not only contains in digital form many sensitive records previously found in the home; it also contains a broad array of private information never found in a home in any form—unless the phone is.

To further complicate the scope of the privacy interests at stake, the data a user views on many modern cell phones may not in fact be stored on the device itself. Treating a cell phone as a container whose contents may be searched incident to an arrest is a bit strained. But the analogy crumbles when a cell phone is used to access data located elsewhere, at the tap of a screen. That is what cell phones, with increasing frequency, are designed to do by taking advantage of "cloud computing." Cloud computing is the capacity of Internet-connected devices to display data stored on remote servers rather than on the device itself. Cell phone users often may not know whether particular information is stored on the device or in the cloud, and it generally makes little difference. Moreover, the same type of data may be stored on the device for one user and in the cloud for another. The United States concedes that the search incident to arrest exception may not be stretched to cover a search of files accessed remotely—a search of files stored in the cloud. Such a search would be like finding a key in a suspect's pocket and arguing that it allowed law enforcement to unlock and search a house. Officers searching a phone's data would not typically know whether the information they are viewing was stored locally at the time of the arrest or has been pulled from the cloud.

The Government suggests that officers could disconnect a phone from the network before searching the device. Alternatively, the Government proposes that law enforcement agencies "develop protocols to address" concerns raised by cloud computing. Probably a good idea, but the Founders did not fight a revolution to gain the right to government agency protocols. The possibility that a search might extend well beyond papers and effects in the physical proximity of an arrestee is yet another reason that the privacy interests here dwarf those in *Robinson*.

The United States and California offer various fallback options for permitting warrantless cell phone searches under certain circumstances. The United States proposes that the *Gant* standard be imported from the vehicle context, allowing a warrantless search of an arrestee's cell phone whenever it is reasonable to believe that the phone contains evidence of the crime of arrest. But Gant relied on "circumstances unique to the vehicle context" to endorse a search solely for the purpose of gathering evidence. Justice Scalia's *Thornton* opinion, on which *Gant* was based, explained that those unique circumstances are "a reduced expectation of privacy" and "heightened law enforcement needs" when it comes to motor vehicles. For reasons that we have explained, cell phone searches bear neither of those characteristics. A *Gant* standard would prove no practical limit when it comes to cell phone searches. In the vehicle context, *Gant* generally protects against searches for evidence of past crimes. In the cell phone context, it is reasonable to expect that incriminating information will be found on a phone regardless of when the crime occurred. Similarly, in the vehicle context *Gant* restricts broad searches resulting from minor crimes such as traffic violations. That would not necessarily be true for cell phones. It would be a particularly inexperienced or unimaginative law enforcement officer who could not come up with several reasons to suppose evidence of just about any crime could be found on a cell phone. Even an individual pulled over for something as basic as speeding might well have locational data dispositive of guilt on his phone. An individual pulled over for reckless driving might have evidence on the phone that shows whether he was texting while driving. The sources of potential pertinent information are virtually unlimited, so applying the *Gant* standard to cell phones would in effect give "police officers unbridled discretion to rummage at will among a person's private effects."

The United States also proposes a rule that would restrict the scope of a cell phone search to those areas of the phone where an officer reasonably believes that information relevant to the crime, the arrestee's identity, or officer safety will be discovered. This approach would again impose few meaningful constraints. The proposed categories would sweep in a great deal of information, and officers would not always be able to discern in advance what information would be found where.

We also reject the suggestion that officers should always be able to search a phone's call log. The Government relies on *Smith v. Maryland*, 442 U. S. 735 (1979), which held that no warrant was required to use a pen register at telephone company premises to identify numbers dialed by a particular caller. That case, however, concluded that the use of a pen register was not a "search" under the Fourth Amendment. There is no dispute here that the officers engaged in a search of Wurie's cell phone. Moreover, call logs typically contain more than just phone numbers; they include any identifying information that an individual might add, such as the label "my house" in Wurie's case.

California suggested that officers could search cell phone data if they could have obtained the same information from a pre-digital counterpart. But the fact that a search in the pre-digital era could have turned up a photograph or two in a wallet does not justify a search of thousands of photos in a digital gallery. The fact that someone could have tucked a paper bank statement in a pocket does not justify a search of every bank statement from the last five years. Such an analogue test would allow law enforcement to search a range of items contained on a phone, even though people would be unlikely to carry such a variety of information in physical form. In Riley's case, it is implausible that he would have strolled around with video tapes, photo albums, and an address book all crammed into his pockets. But because each of those items has a pre-digital analogue, police would be able to search a phone for all of those items—a significant diminution of privacy. In addition, an analogue test would launch courts on a difficult line-drawing expedition to determine which digital files are comparable to physical records. Is an e-mail equivalent to a letter? Is a voicemail equivalent to a phone message slip? It is not clear how officers could make these kinds of decisions before conducting a search, or how courts would apply the proposed rule after the fact.

We cannot deny that our decision will have an impact on the ability of law enforcement to combat crime. Cell phones have become important tools in facilitating coordination and communication among members of criminal enterprises, and can provide valuable incriminating information about dangerous criminals. Privacy comes at a cost. Our holding is not that the information on a cell phone is immune from search; it is that a warrant is generally required before such a search, even when a cell phone is seized incident to arrest. Our cases have recognized that the warrant requirement is "an important working part of our machinery of government," not merely "an inconvenience to be somehow 'weighed' against the claims of police efficiency." *Coolidge v. New Hampshire*, 403 U. S. 443, 481 (1971). Recent technological advances similar to those discussed here have, in addition, made the process of obtaining a warrant itself more efficient. See *McNeely*, 133 S. Ct. at 1561 (Roberts, C. J., concurring in part and dissenting in part) ("police officers can e-mail warrant requests to judges' iPads and judges have signed such warrants and e-mailed them back to officers in less than 15 minutes").

Even though the search incident to arrest exception does not apply to cell phones, other case-specific exceptions may still justify a warrantless search of a particular phone. "One well-recognized exception applies when " 'the exigencies of the situation' make the needs of law enforcement so compelling that a warrantless search is objectively reasonable under the Fourth Amendment." *Kentucky v. King*, 5131 S. Ct. at 1856. Such exigencies could include the need to prevent the imminent destruction of evidence in individual cases, to pursue a fleeing suspect, and to assist persons who are seriously injured or are threatened with imminent injury. In light of the exigent circumstances exception, there is no reason to believe that law enforcement officers will not be able to address some of the more extreme hypotheticals that have been suggested: a suspect texting an accomplice who, it is feared, is preparing to detonate a bomb, or a child abductor who may have information about the child's location on his cell phone. Such fact-specific threats may justify a warrantless search of cell phone data. The exigent circumstances exception requires a court to examine whether an emergency justified a warrantless search in each particular case.

Our cases have recognized that the Fourth Amendment was the founding generation's response to the reviled "general warrants" and "writs of assistance" of the colonial era, which allowed British officers to rummage through homes in an unrestrained search for evidence of criminal activity. Opposition to such searches was in fact one of the driving forces behind the Revolution itself. 10 Works of John Adams 247–248 (C. Adams ed. 1856). Modern cellphones are not just another technological convenience. With all they contain and all they may reveal, they hold for many Americans "the privacies of life." The fact that technology now allows an individual to carry such information in his hand does not make the information any less worthy of the protection for which the Founders fought. Our answer to the question of what police must do before searching a cell phone seized incident to an arrest is accordingly simple—get a warrant.

We reverse the judgment of the California Court of Appeal in No. 13–132 and remand the case for further proceedings not inconsistent with this opinion. We affirm the judgment of the First Circuit in No. 13–212.

It is so ordered.

JUSTICE ALITO, concurring in part and concurring in the judgment.

I am not convinced that the ancient rule on searches incident to arrest is based exclusively (or primarily) on the need to protect the safety of arresting officers and the need to prevent the destruction of evidence. When pre-*Weeks* authorities discussed the rule, what was mentioned was the need to obtain probative evidence. *Chimel's* reasoning is questionable.

We should not mechanically apply the rule used in the predigital era to the search of a cell phone. Many cell phones now in use are capable of storing and accessing a quantity of information, some highly personal, that no person would ever have had on his person in hard-copy form. This calls for a new balancing of law enforcement and privacy interests. The Court strikes this balance in favor of privacy interests with respect to all cell phones and all information found in them, and this approach leads to anomalies. For example, the Court's broad holding favors information in digital form over information in hard-copy form. Suppose that two suspects are arrested. Suspect number one has in his pocket a monthly bill for his land-line phone, and the bill lists an incriminating call to a long-distance number. He also has in his a wallet a few snapshots, and one of these is incriminating. Suspect number two has in his pocket a cell phone, the call log of which shows a call to the same incriminating number. In addition, a number of photos are stored in the memory of the cell phone, and one of these is incriminating. Under established law, the police may seize and examine the phone bill and the snapshots in the wallet without obtaining a warrant, but under the Court's holding today, the information stored in the cell phone is out. While the Court's approach leads to anomalies, I do not see a workable alternative. Law enforcement officers need clear rules regarding searches incident to arrest, and it would take many cases and many years for the courts to develop more nuanced rules. During that time, the nature of the electronic devices that ordinary Americans carry on their persons would continue to change.

I would reconsider the question presented here if either Congress or state legislatures, after assessing the legitimate needs of law enforcement and the privacy interests of cell phone owners, enact legislation that draws reasonable distinctions based on categories of information or perhaps other variables. Many forms of modern technology are making it easier and easier for both government and private entities to amass a wealth of information about the lives of ordinary

Americans, and any ordinary Americans are choosing to make public much information that was seldom revealed to outsiders just a few decades ago. It would be unfortunate if privacy protection in the 21st century were left primarily to the federal courts using the blunt instrument of the Fourth Amendment. Legislatures, elected by the people, are in a better position than we are to assess and respond to the changes that have already occurred and those that almost certainly will take place in the future.

Hypo 1: *The Contemporaneousness Requirement*

Four police officers enter a hotel room (legally) to arrest a suspect. After the police handcuff her, and move her to the hallway outside the room, two officers re-enter the room and search it. The search extends to the dresser drawer and the suspect's purse (which was lying on the bed). In the drawer and in the purse, the police find contraband. Suppose that you represent the suspect, how can you argue that this search does not fit within the scope of the search incident to arrest exception? How might the state respond to these arguments? How would you expect the court to rule? See *People v. Perry,* 47 Ill.2d 402, 266 N.E.2d 330 (1971).

Hypo 2: *The Limits of Contemporaneousness*

Police, investigating Gorup on suspicion of dealing narcotics, arrested him outside of his apartment under an outstanding arrest warrant. The officers decide to enter the apartment to conduct a search incident to illegal arrest. During this time, Gorup remains outside the apartment with his hands cuffed behind his back. Over the next thirty minutes, the officers examine the adjoining room, including a "small black zippered case" that they find on a table about five feet inside of the doorway. Should the search be upheld under the search incident to legal arrest exception? See *State v. Gorup,* 279 Neb. 841, 782 N.W.2d 16 (2010).

Arizona v. Gant

556 U.S. 332 (2009).

JUSTICE STEVENS delivered the opinion of the Court.

Acting on an anonymous tip that the residence at 2524 North Walnut Avenue was being used to sell drugs, Tucson police officers Griffith and Reed knocked on the front door and asked to speak to the owner. Gant answered the door and, after identifying himself, stated that he expected the owner to return later. The officers left the residence and conducted a records check, which revealed that Gant's driver's license had been suspended and there was an outstanding warrant for his arrest for driving with a suspended license.

When the officers returned to the house that evening, they found a man near the back of the house and a woman in a car parked in front of it. After a third officer arrived, they arrested the man for providing a false name and the woman for possessing drug paraphernalia. Both arrestees were handcuffed and secured in separate patrol cars when Gant arrived. The officers recognized his car as it entered the driveway, and Officer Griffith confirmed that Gant was the driver by shining a flashlight into the car as it drove by him. Gant parked at the end of the driveway, got out of his car, and shut the door. Griffith, called to Gant, and they approached each other, meeting 10-to-12 feet from Gant's car. Griffith immediately arrested Gant and handcuffed him.

Because the other arrestees were secured in the only patrol cars at the scene, Griffith called for backup. When two more officers arrived, they locked Gant in the backseat of their vehicle. After Gant had been handcuffed and placed in the back of a patrol car, two officers searched his car: One of them found a gun, and the other discovered a bag of cocaine in the pocket of a jacket on the backseat.

Gant was charged with two offenses—possession of a narcotic drug for sale and possession of drug paraphernalia (i.e., the plastic bag in which the cocaine was found). He moved to suppress the evidence seized from his car on the ground that the warrantless search violated the Fourth Amendment. Among other things, Gant argued that *New York v. Belton,* 453 U. S. 454 (1981) did not authorize the search of his vehicle because he posed no threat to the officers after he was handcuffed in the patrol car and because he was arrested for a traffic offense for which no evidence could be found in his vehicle. When asked at the suppression hearing why the search was conducted, Officer Griffith responded: "Because the law says we can do it."

The trial court held that the search was permissible as a search incident to arrest. A jury found Gant guilty on both drug counts, and he was sentenced to a 3-year term of imprisonment. The Arizona Supreme Court reversed and we granted the State's petition for certiorari.

Our analysis begins, as it should in every case addressing the reasonableness of a warrantless search, with the basic rule that "searches conducted outside the judicial process, without prior approval by judge or magistrate, are *per se* unreasonable under the Fourth Amendment—subject only to a few specifically established and well-delineated exceptions." *Katz v. United States*, 389 U. S. 347, 357 (1967). Among the exceptions to the warrant requirement is a search incident to a lawful arrest. The exception derives from interests in officer safety and evidence preservation that are typically implicated in arrest situations. See *United States v. Robinson, Chimel v. California*, 395 U. S. 752 (1969).

In *Belton*, we considered *Chimel's* application to the automobile context. A lone police officer stopped a speeding car in which Belton was one of four occupants. While asking for the driver's license and registration, the officer smelled burnt marijuana and observed an envelope on the car floor marked "Supergold"—a name he associated with marijuana. Thus having probable cause to believe the occupants had committed a drug offense, the officer ordered them out of the vehicle, placed them under arrest, and patted them down. Without handcuffing the arrestees,[1] the officer "split them up into four separate areas of the Thruway so they would not be in physical touching area of each other" and searched the vehicle, including the pocket of a jacket on the backseat, in which he found cocaine.

We granted certiorari because "courts had found no workable definition of 'the area within the immediate control of the arrestee' when that area arguably includes the interior of an automobile." We held that when an officer lawfully arrests "the occupant of an automobile, he may, as a contemporaneous incident of that arrest, search the passenger compartment of the automobile" and any containers therein. That holding was based in large part on our assumption "that articles inside the relatively narrow compass of the passenger compartment of an automobile are in fact generally, even if not inevitably, within 'the area into which an arrestee might reach.' "

Our opinion has been widely understood to allow a vehicle search incident to the arrest of a recent occupant even if there is no possibility the arrestee could gain access to the vehicle at the time of the search. Under this broad reading of *Belton*, a vehicle search would be authorized incident to every arrest of a recent occupant notwithstanding that in most cases the vehicle's passenger compartment will not be within the arrestee's reach at the time of the search. To read *Belton* as authorizing a vehicle search incident to every recent occupant's arrest would thus untether

---

[1] The officer was unable to handcuff the occupants because he had only one set of handcuffs.

the rule from the justifications underlying the *Chimel* exception—a result clearly incompatible with our statement in *Belton* that it "in no way alters the fundamental principles established in the *Chimel* case regarding the basic scope of searches incident to lawful custodial arrests." Accordingly, we reject this reading of *Belton* and hold that the *Chimel* rationale authorizes police to search a vehicle incident to a recent occupant's arrest only when the arrestee is unsecured and within reaching distance of the passenger compartment at the time of the search.[2]

[handwritten margin note: One way.]

We also conclude that circumstances unique to the vehicle context justify a search incident to a lawful arrest when it is "reasonable to believe evidence relevant to the crime of arrest might be found in the vehicle." *Thornton v. United States*, 541 U. S. 615 (2004). In many cases, as when a recent occupant is arrested for a traffic violation, there will be no reasonable basis to believe the vehicle contains relevant evidence. But in others, including *Belton* and *Thornton*, the offense of arrest will supply a basis for searching the passenger compartment of an arrestee's vehicle and any containers therein.

[handwritten margin note: 2nd way — Reasonable suspicion.]

Neither the possibility of access nor the likelihood of discovering offense-related evidence authorized the search in this case. Unlike in *Belton*, which involved a single officer confronted with four unsecured arrestees, the five officers in this case outnumbered the three arrestees, all of whom had been handcuffed and secured in separate patrol cars before the officers searched Gant's car. Under those circumstances, Gant clearly was not within reaching distance of his car at the time of the search. An evidentiary basis for the search was also lacking. Whereas Belton and Thornton were arrested for drug offenses, Gant was arrested for driving with a suspended license—an offense for which police could not expect to find evidence in the passenger compartment of Gant's car. Because police could not reasonably have believed either that Gant could have accessed his car at the time of the search or that evidence of the offense for which he was arrested might have been found therein, the search in this case was unreasonable.

The State argues that *Belton* searches are reasonable regardless of the possibility of access in a given case because that expansive rule correctly balances law enforcement interests, including the interest in a bright-line rule, with an arrestee's limited privacy interest in his vehicle. We reject the State's argument. First, the State seriously undervalues the privacy interests at stake. Although we have recognized that a motorist's privacy interest in his vehicle is less substantial than in his home, the former interest is nevertheless important and deserving of constitutional protection. It is particularly significant that *Belton* searches authorize police officers to search not just the passenger compartment but every

---

[2] Because officers have many means of ensuring the safe arrest of vehicle occupants, it will be the rare case in which an officer is unable to fully effectuate an arrest so that a real possibility of access to the arrestees vehicle remains. But in such a case a search incident to arrest is reasonable under the Fourth Amendment.

purse, briefcase, or other container within that space. A rule that gives police the power to conduct such a search whenever an individual is caught committing a traffic offense, when there is no basis for believing evidence of the offense might be found in the vehicle, creates a serious and recurring threat to the privacy of countless individuals. Indeed, the character of that threat implicates the central concern underlying the Fourth Amendment—the concern about giving police officers unbridled discretion to rummage at will among a person's private effects.

At the same time as it undervalues these privacy concerns, the State exaggerates the clarity that its reading of *Belton* provides. Courts that have read *Belton* expansively are at odds regarding how close in time to the arrest and how proximate to the arrestee's vehicle an officer's first contact with the arrestee must be to bring the encounter within *Belton's* purview and whether a search is reasonable when it commences or continues after the arrestee has been removed from the scene. The rule has thus generated a great deal of uncertainty, particularly for a rule touted as providing a "bright line."

A broad reading of *Belton* is also unnecessary to protect law enforcement safety and evidentiary interests. *Belton* and *Thornton* permit an officer to conduct a vehicle search when an arrestee is within reaching distance of the vehicle or it is reasonable to believe the vehicle contains evidence of the offense of arrest. Other established exceptions to the warrant requirement authorize a vehicle search under additional circumstances when safety or evidentiary concerns demand. For instance, *Michigan v. Long*, 463 U. S. 1032 (1983), permits an officer to search a vehicle's passenger compartment when he has reasonable suspicion that an individual, whether or not the arrestee, is "dangerous", might access the vehicle to "gain immediate control of weapons." If there is probable cause to believe a vehicle contains evidence of criminal activity, *United States v. Ross*, 456 U. S. 798 (1982), authorizes a search of any area of the vehicle in which the evidence might be found. *Ross* allows searches for evidence relevant to offenses other than the offense of arrest, and the scope of the search authorized is broader. Finally, there may be still other circumstances in which safety or evidentiary interests would justify a search. Cf. *Maryland v. Buie*, 494 U. S. 325 (1990).

These exceptions together ensure that officers may search a vehicle when genuine safety or evidentiary concerns encountered during the arrest of a vehicle's recent occupant justify a search. Construing *Belton* broadly to allow vehicle searches incident to any arrest would serve no purpose except to provide a police entitlement, and it is anathema to the Fourth Amendment to permit a warrantless search on that basis. For these reasons, we are unpersuaded by the State's arguments that a broad reading of *Belton* would meaningfully further law enforcement interests and justify a substantial intrusion on individuals' privacy.[3]

---

[3] At least eight States have reached the same conclusion. Vermont, New Jersey, New Mexico, Nevada,

Our dissenting colleagues argue that *stare decisis* requires adherence to a broad reading of *Belton* even though the justifications for searching a vehicle incident to arrest are in most cases absent. We have never relied on *stare decisis* to justify the continuance of an unconstitutional police practice. The safety and evidentiary interests that supported the search in *Belton* simply are not present in this case. Indeed, it is hard to imagine two cases that are factually more distinct, as *Belton* involved one officer confronted by four unsecured arrestees suspected of committing a drug offense and this case involves several officers confronted with a securely detained arrestee apprehended for driving with a suspended license. Although it appears that the State's reading of *Belton* has been widely taught in police academies and that law enforcement officers have relied on the rule in conducting vehicle searches during the past 28 years,[6] many of these searches were not justified by the reasons underlying the *Chimel* exception. Countless individuals guilty of nothing more serious than a traffic violation have had their constitutional right to the security of their private effects violated as a result. The fact that the law enforcement community may view the State's version of the *Belton* rule as an entitlement does not establish the sort of reliance interest that could outweigh the countervailing interest that all individuals share in having their constitutional rights fully protected. If it is clear that a practice is unlawful, individuals' interest in its discontinuance clearly outweighs any law enforcement "entitlement" to its persistence. *Stare decisis* does not require us to approve routine constitutional violations.

Police may search a vehicle incident to a recent occupant's arrest only if the arrestee is within reaching distance of the passenger compartment at the time of the search or it is reasonable to believe the vehicle contains evidence of the offense of arrest. When these justifications are absent, a search of an arrestee's vehicle will be unreasonable unless police obtain a warrant or show that another exception to the warrant requirement applies. The Arizona Supreme Court correctly held that this case involved an unreasonable search. Accordingly, the judgment of the State Supreme Court is affirmed.

It is so ordered.

JUSTICE SCALIA, concurring.

When an arrest is made in connection with a roadside stop, police virtually always have a less intrusive and more effective means of ensuring their safety— and a means that is virtually always employed: ordering the arrestee away from

---

Pennsylvania, New York, Oregon, and Wyoming have declined to follow a broad reading of Belton under their state constitutions. And a Massachusetts statute provides that a search incident to arrest may be made only for the purposes of seizing weapons or evidence of the offense of arrest.

[1] Because a broad reading of *Belton* has been widely accepted, the doctrine of qualified immunity will shield officers from liability for searches conducted in reasonable reliance on that understanding.

the vehicle, patting him down in the open, handcuffing him, and placing him in the squad car. Law enforcement officers face a risk of being shot whenever they pull a car over. But that risk is at its height at the time of the initial confrontation; and it is *not at all* reduced by allowing a search of the stopped vehicle after the driver has been arrested and placed in the squad car. The government had failed to provide a single instance in which a formerly restrained arrestee escaped to retrieve a weapon from his own vehicle.

We are speaking here only of a rule automatically permitting a search when the driver or an occupant is arrested. Where no arrest is made, we have held that officers may search the car if they reasonably believe "the suspect is dangerous and may gain immediate control of weapons." *Michigan v. Long*, 463 U. S. 1032, 1049 (1983). In the no-arrest case, the possibility of access to weapons in the vehicle always exists, since the driver or passenger will be allowed to return to the vehicle when the interrogation is completed.

In my view we should simply abandon the *Belton-Thornton* charade of officer safety and overrule those cases. I would hold that a vehicle search incident to arrest is *ipso facto* "reasonable" only when the object of the search is evidence of the crime for which the arrest was made, or of another crime that the officer has probable cause to believe occurred. Because respondent was arrested for driving without a license (a crime for which no evidence could be expected to be found in the vehicle), I would hold in the present case that the search was unlawful.

JUSTICE BREYER, dissenting.

Principles of *stare decisis* must apply, and those who wish this Court to change a well-established legal precedent—where, as here, there has been considerable reliance on the legal rule in question—bear a heavy burden. I have not found that burden met. I consequently join Justice Alito's dissenting opinion with the exception of Part II–E.

JUSTICE ALITO, with whom THE CHIEF JUSTICE and JUSTICE KENNEDY join, and with whom JUSTICE BREYER joins except as to Part II–E, dissenting.

Although the Court refuses to acknowledge that it is overruling *Belton* and *Thornton*, there can be no doubt that it does so.

II

The Court has said that a constitutional precedent should be followed unless there is a "special justification" for its abandonment.

The *Belton* rule was adopted for the express purpose of providing a test that would be relatively easy for police officers and judges to apply. The first part of the

Court's new rule—which permits the search of a vehicle's passenger compartment if it is within an arrestee's reach at the time of the search—reintroduces the same sort of case-by-case, fact-specific decision making that the *Belton* rule was adopted to avoid. As *Belton* illustrated, there are cases in which it is unclear whether an arrestee could retrieve a weapon or evidence in the passenger compartment of a car. Even more serious problems will also result from the second part of the Court's new rule, which requires officers making roadside arrests to determine whether there is reason to believe that the vehicle contains evidence of the crime of arrest. What this rule permits in a variety of situations is entirely unclear.

E

Belton represented only a modest—and quite defensible—extension of *Chimel* which concluded that there are only two justifications for a warrantless search incident to arrest-officer safety and the preservation of evidence—the Court stated that such a search must be confined to "the arrestee's person" and "the area from within which he might gain possession of a weapon or destructible evidence."

Unfortunately, *Chimel* did not say whether "the area from within which an arrestee might gain possession of a weapon or destructible evidence" is to be measured at the time of the arrest or at the time of the search, but unless the *Chimel* rule was meant to be a specialty rule, applicable to only a few unusual cases, the Court must have intended for this area to be measured at the time of arrest.

This is so because the Court can hardly have failed to appreciate the following two facts. First, in the great majority of cases, an officer making an arrest is able to handcuff the arrestee and remove him to a secure place before conducting a search incident to the arrest. Second, because it is safer for an arresting officer to secure an arrestee before searching, it is likely that this is what arresting officers do in the great majority of cases. Thus, if the area within an arrestee's reach were assessed, not at the time of arrest, but at the time of the search, the *Chimel* rule would rarely come into play.

Moreover, if the applicability of the *Chimel* rule turned on whether an arresting officer chooses to secure an arrestee prior to conducting a search, rather than searching first and securing the arrestee later, the rule would "create a perverse incentive for an arresting officer to prolong the period during which the arrestee is kept in an area where he could pose a danger to the officer." *United States v. Abdul-Saboor*, 85 F. 3d 664, 669 (CADC 1996). If this is the law, the D. C. Circuit observed, "the law would truly be, as Mr. Bumble said, 'a ass.' " *Ibid.*

The *Belton* Court reasoned that articles in the passenger compartment of a car are "generally, even if not inevitably" within an arrestee's reach. This is undoubtedly true at the time of the arrest of a person who is seated in a car but plainly not true when the person has been removed from the car and placed in handcuffs.

Accordingly, the *Belton* Court must have proceeded on the assumption that the *Chimel* rule was to be applied at the time of arrest. Viewing *Chimel* as having focused on the time of arrest, *Belton*'s only new step was to eliminate the need to decide on a case-by-case basis whether a particular person seated in a car actually could have reached the part of the passenger compartment where a weapon or evidence was hidden.

Hypo 1: *Defining Gant's Scope*

A police officer arrests a motorist for driving without a driver's license, as well as for driving with expired license plates. Instead of handcuffing the driver, and placing him in the backseat of the nearby police car, the officer decides to conduct a patdown of the motorist next to the motorist's vehicle. While the motorist is spreadeagled next to his vehicle, the officer conducts a "search incident to legal arrest" of the vehicle. The search turns up an unlicensed handgun under the front seat. At a subsequent suppression hearing, the state argues that the motorist had not yet been fully subdued, and therefore might have re-entered the vehicle and gained access to a weapon. Under *Gant*, can the search be justified as incident to a legal arrest? Is there another way to justify the search?

Hypo 2: *Search Incident and Other Occupants*

In his dissent, Justice Alito notes that the police might (in some cases) arrest one person who is traveling in a car, but not everyone. As a result, following the arrest, some of the former occupants of the car will re-enter it. Should the officers have the right to search the vehicle in order to make sure that it does not contain a weapon that the other occupants will be able to access? On what basis?

Food for Thought

Does *Gant*'s holding extend to non-vehicle searches? Return to the hypothetical discussed earlier: police officers arrest a suspect in a hotel room. They handcuff the arrestee and move her to the hall outside the room where she is guarded by two police officers. A third officer then re-enters the room and conducts a search. After *Gant*, can the room search be justified under the search incident to legal arrest doctrine?

Hypo 3: *The Wallet*

A warrant is issued for a man's arrest for his failure to appear at a criminal hearing. When the police locate the man, he is sitting in a truck and is ordered to exit the vehicle. As the man does, he leaves his wallet on the seat of the truck. As the officer arrests the man, he does a search incident to legal arrest of the man. May the officer also retrieve and examine the wallet on the theory that the man had it on him when he was placed under arrest? Even though the officer knows the man, can the officer justify examining the wallet in order to "verify" the man's identity? See *State v. Hargis,* 756 S.E. 2d 529 (Ga. 2014).

Hypo 4: *Searching the Motorist's Person*

If a police officer validly arrests the driver of a vehicle, may the officer search the arrestee's person for drugs or weapons, or does *Gant* preclude such a search as well?

Hypo 5: *Probable Cause to Search the Vehicle*

Taylor's automobile rear-ends an SUV occupied by three deputy U.S. marshalls. One of the deputies alights and asks Taylor for his insurance information. The card that he produces has expired. While they are talking, Taylor suddenly indicates that he has to use the bathroom and urinates on a nearby tree. Based on this behavior, as well as the smell of alcohol on Taylor's breath and his unusual swaying back and forth, the deputy suspects that Taylor has been drinking. One of the other deputies calls the police who arrive shortly thereafter. After speaking with Taylor, the police also conclude that Taylor is intoxicated based on his slurred speech, his swaying from side to side, the odor of alcohol coming from his person, the way he fumbles with his wallet while searching for his driver's license, and his statement that he consumed two beers about two hours earlier. The officer administers standard field sobriety tests which appellee fails. The police arrest Taylor for driving under the influence, place him in handcuffs, and put him in a patrol car for transport. Following the arrest, the officer searches the passenger compartment of Taylor's truck, looking for a current insurance card and evidence of alcohol consumption. Was the search valid? See *United States v. Taylor,* 49 A.3d 818, 821 (D.C.2012).

Hypo 6: *More on Probable Cause*

A police officer is searching for a man, for whom a warrant has been issued, when he happens on another man who is acting in a way that the officer thinks is "curious": the man has something in his hand that he is manipulating. When the man spots the officer, he turns and begin to walk in the other direction carrying what appears to be a hamburger wrapper. The officer stops the man and runs a warrants check on him. The check reveals an outstanding warrant for the man and the officer tells him that he is under arrest. When the man drops the hamburger wrapper, and begins grinding it with his foot, the officer notices a baggie with pills under it. Under *Gant*, after finding the man in possession of illegal pills, does the officer have probable cause to search the man's truck (located nearby)? See *People v. Crum*, 312 P.3d 186 (Colo. 2013).

Hypo 7: *DUI Arrests and Probable Cause*

Suppose that a police officer has probable cause to arrest a driver for DUI, and executes the arrest. May the office assume that drunk drivers probably have open containers in their vehicles, and therefore search the vehicle? *See Taylor v. State*, 137 A.3d 1029 (Md. 2016). Suppose that a police officer lawfully stops a motorist for a defective taillight. When the officer approaches the vehicle, he notices an open container of alcohol in the center console. The officer arrests the driver for having an open alcoholic container in the vehicle. May the officer search the vehicle on the theory that those who have open alcoholic beverage containers in a car often have cups as well (because, when they drink, they put the alcohol in cups because they do not wish to be observed drinking from an open container of alcohol)? *See United States v. Nash*, 100 A.3d 157 (D.C. App. 2014).

3. Booking Searches

When the police "book" a suspect, and place the suspect in jail, the police usually conduct a so-called "detention search" or "booking search." This type of search was upheld in *Illinois v. Lafayette*, 462 U.S. 640 (1983), in which respondent was arrested for disturbing the peace after fighting with the manager of a theater. The search occurred in the booking room where the police found ten amphetamine pills inside a cigarette case in respondent's shoulder bag. The Court concluded that it "is entirely proper for police to remove and list or inventory property found on the person or in the possession of an arrested person who is to be jailed. A range of governmental interests support an inventory process. It is not unheard of for persons employed in police activities to steal property taken from arrested persons; similarly, arrested persons have been known to make false claims regarding what was taken from their possession at the stationhouse. A standardized procedure for making a list or inventory as soon as reasonable after reaching the stationhouse not only deters false claims but also inhibits theft or careless handling of articles taken from the arrested person. Arrested persons have also been known to injure themselves—or others—with belts, knives, drugs or other items on their person while being detained. Dangerous instrumentalities—such as razor blades, bombs, or weapons—can be concealed in innocent-looking articles taken from the arrestee's possession. Examining all the items removed from the arrestee's person or possession and listing or inventorying them is an entirely reasonable administrative procedure. It is immaterial whether the police actually fear any particular package or container; the need to protect against such risks arises independent of a particular officer's subjective concerns. Finally, inspection of an arrestee's personal property may assist the police in ascertaining or verifying his identity. In short, every consideration of orderly police administration benefiting both police and the public points toward the appropriateness of the examination of respondent's shoulder bag prior to his incarceration." In *United States v. Edwards*, 415 U.S. 800 (1974), the Court upheld a booking search that took place nearly ten hours after a defendant's arrest: "searches and seizures that could be made on the spot at the time of arrest may legally be conducted later when the accused arrives at the place of detention."

Florence v. Board of Chosen Freeholders of the County of Burlington

132 S.Ct. 1510 (2012).

JUSTICE KENNEDY delivered the opinion of the Court, except as to Part IV.[2]

Correctional officials have a legitimate interest, indeed a responsibility, to ensure that jails are not made less secure by reason of what new detainees may carry in on their bodies. Facility personnel, other inmates, and the new detainee himself or herself may be in danger if these threats are introduced into the jail population. The term "jail" is used here in a broad sense to include prisons and

---

[2] Justice Thomas joins all but Part IV of the opinion.

other detention facilities. The specific measures being challenged involve whether every detainee who will be admitted to the general population may be required to undergo a close visual inspection while undressed. In addressing this type of constitutional claim courts must defer to the judgment of correctional officials unless the record contains substantial evidence showing their policies are an unnecessary or un-justified response to problems of jail security. That necessary showing has not been made in this case.

I

Seven years before the incidents at issue, petitioner Albert Florence was arrested after fleeing from police officers in Essex County, New Jersey. He was charged with obstruction of justice and use of a deadly weapon. Petitioner entered a plea of guilty to two lesser offenses and was sentenced to pay a fine in monthly installments. After he fell behind on his payments and failed to appear at an enforcement hearing, a bench warrant was issued for his arrest. He paid the outstanding balance less than a week later; but, for some unexplained reason, the warrant remained in a statewide computer database. Two years later, in New Jersey, petitioner and his wife were stopped in their automobile by a state trooper. Based on the outstanding warrant, the officer arrested petitioner and took him to the Burlington County Detention Center. He was held there for six days and then transferred to the Essex County Correctional Facility.

Burlington County jail procedures required every arrestee to shower with a delousing agent. Officers would check arrestees for scars, marks, gang tattoos, and contraband as they disrobed. Petitioner claims he was also instructed to open his mouth, lift his tongue, hold out his arms, turn around, and lift his genitals. Petitioner shared a cell with at least one other person and interacted with other inmates following his admission to the jail.

The Essex County Correctional Facility, where petitioner was taken after six days, is the largest county jail in New Jersey. It admits more than 25,000 inmates each year and houses about 1,000 gang members at any given time. All arriving detainees passed through a metal detector and waited in a group holding cell for a more thorough search. When they left the holding cell, they were instructed to remove their clothing while an officer looked for body markings, wounds, and contraband. Without touching the detainees, an officer looked at their ears, nose, mouth, hair, scalp, fingers, hands, arms, armpits, and other body openings. This policy applied regardless of the circumstances of the arrest, the suspected offense, or the detainee's behavior, demeanor, or criminal history. Petitioner alleges he was required to lift his genitals, turn around, and cough in a squatting position. After a mandatory shower, during which his clothes were inspected, petitioner was admitted to the facility. He was released the next day, when the charges against him were dismissed.

Petitioner sued the governmental entities that operated the jails, one of the wardens, and certain other defendants. Seeking relief under 42 U. S. C. §1983 for violations of his Fourth and Fourteenth Amendment rights, petitioner maintained that officials could conduct this kind of search only if they had reason to suspect a particular inmate of concealing a weapon, drugs, or other contraband. The District Court concluded that any policy of "strip searching" nonindictable offenders without reasonable suspicion violated the Fourth Amendment. The United States Court of Appeals for the Third Circuit reversed. This Court granted certiorari.

The term "strip search" is imprecise. It may refer simply to the instruction to remove clothing while an officer observes from a distance of, say, five feet or more; it may mean a visual inspection from a closer, more uncomfortable distance; it may include directing detainees to shake their heads or to run their hands through their hair to dislodge what might be hidden there; or it may involve instructions to raise arms, to display foot insteps, to expose the back of the ears, to move or spread the buttocks or genital areas, or to cough in a squatting position. In the instant case, the term does not include any touching of unclothed areas by the inspecting officer. There are no allegations that the detainees here were touched in any way as part of the searches.

II

The difficulties of operating a detention center must not be underestimated by the courts. *Turner v. Safley*, 482 U. S. 78 (1987). Jails (in the stricter sense of the term, excluding prison facilities) admit more than 13 million inmates a year. The largest facilities process hundreds of people every day; smaller jails may be crowded on weekend nights, after a large police operation, or because of detainees arriving from other jurisdictions. Maintaining safety and order at these institutions requires the expertise of correctional officials, who must have substantial discretion to devise reasonable solutions to the problems they face. The Court has confirmed the importance of deference to correctional officials and explained that a regulation impinging on an inmate's constitutional rights must be upheld "if it is reasonably related to legitimate penological interests." *Turner, supra*, at 89. *Bell v. Wolfish*, 441 U. S. 520 (1979) addressed a rule requiring pretrial detainees in any correctional facility run by the Federal Bureau of Prisons "to expose their body cavities for visual inspection as a part of a strip search conducted after every contact visit with a person from outside the institution." Inmates at the federal Metropolitan Correctional Center in New York City argued there was no security justification for these searches. Officers searched guests before they entered the visiting room, and the inmates were under constant surveillance during the visit. There had been but one instance in which an inmate attempted to sneak contraband back into the facility. The Court nonetheless upheld the search policy. It deferred to the judgment of correctional officials that the inspections served not only to discover but also to deter the smuggling of weapons, drugs, and other prohibited items inside. The Court explained that there is no mechanical way to determine whether intrusions on an inmate's privacy are reasonable. The need for a particular search must be balanced against the resulting invasion of personal rights. Policies designed to keep contraband out of jails and prisons have been upheld in cases decided since *Bell*. In *Block v. Rutherford*, 468 U. S. 576 (1984), for example, the Court concluded that the Los Angeles County Jail could ban all contact visits because of the threat they posed.

There were "many justifications" for imposing a general ban rather than trying to carve out exceptions for certain detainees. It would be "a difficult if not impossible task" to identify "inmates who have propensities for violence, escape, or drug smuggling." This is made "even more difficult by the brevity of detention and the constantly changing nature of the inmate population." The Court has recognized that deterring the possession of contraband depends in part on the ability to conduct searches without predictable exceptions. Inmates would adapt to any pattern or loopholes they discovered in the search protocol and then undermine the security of the institution.

These cases establish that correctional officials must be permitted to devise reasonable search policies to detect and deter the possession of contraband in their facilities. See *Bell*, 441 U. S., at 546. The task of determining whether a policy is reasonably related to legitimate security interests is "peculiarly within the province and professional expertise of corrections officials." *Id.*, at 548. "In the absence of substantial evidence to indicate that the officials have exaggerated their response to these considerations courts should ordinarily defer to their expert judgment in such matters." *Block, supra*, at 584–585.

In many jails, officials seek to improve security by requiring some kind of strip search of everyone who is to be detained. These procedures have been used in different places throughout the country. Persons arrested for minor offenses may be among the detainees processed at these facilities. This is, in part, a consequence of the exercise of state authority that was the subject of *Atwater v. Lago Vista*, 532 U. S. 318 (2001).

III

The question is whether undoubted security imperatives involved in jail supervision override the assertion that some detainees must be exempt from the more invasive search procedures at issue absent reasonable suspicion of a concealed weapon or other contraband. The Court has held that deference must be given to the officials in charge of the jail unless there is "substantial evidence" demonstrating their response to the situation is exaggerated. Petitioner has not met this standard, and the record provides full justifications for the procedures used.

Correctional officials have a significant interest in conducting a thorough search as a standard part of the intake process. The admission of inmates creates numerous risks for facility staff, for the existing detainee population, and for a new detainee himself or herself. The danger of introducing lice or contagious infections, for example, is well documented. Persons just arrested may have wounds or other injuries requiring immediate medical attention. It may be difficult to identify and treat these problems until detainees remove their clothes for a visual inspection. Jails and prisons also face grave threats posed by the increasing number of gang members who go through the intake process. The groups recruit new members by force, engage in assaults against staff, and give other inmates a reason to arm themselves. Fights among feuding gangs can be deadly, and the officers who must maintain order are put in harm's way. These considerations provide a reasonable basis to justify a visual inspection for certain tattoos and other signs of gang affiliation as part of the intake process. The identification and isolation of gang members before they are admitted protects everyone in the facility.

Detecting contraband concealed by new detainees, furthermore, is a most serious responsibility. Weapons, drugs, and alcohol all disrupt the safe operation of a jail. Correctional officers have had to confront arrestees concealing knives, scissors, razor blades, glass shards, and other prohibited items on their person, including in their body cavities. They have also found crack, heroin, and marijuana. The use of drugs can embolden inmates in aggression toward officers or each other; and, even apart from their use, the trade in these substances can lead to violent confrontations.

There are many other kinds of contraband. The textbook definition of the term covers any unauthorized item. Everyday items can undermine security if introduced into a detention facility: "Lighters and matches are fire and arson risks or potential weapons. Cell phones are used to orchestrate violence and criminality both within and without jailhouse walls. Pills and medications enhance suicide risks. Chewing gum can block locking devices; hairpins can open handcuffs; wigs can conceal drugs and weapons." New Jersey Wardens Brief 8–9. Something as simple as an overlooked pen can pose a significant danger. Inmates commit more than 10,000 assaults on correctional staff every year and many more among themselves.

Contraband creates additional problems because scarce items, including currency, have value in a jail's culture and underground economy. Correctional officials inform us "the competition for such goods begets violence, extortion, and disorder." Gangs exacerbate the problem. They "orchestrate thefts, commit assaults, and approach inmates in packs to take the contraband from the weak." This puts the entire facility, including detainees being held for a brief term for a minor offense, at risk. Gangs do coerce inmates who have access to the outside world, such as people serving their time on the weekends, to sneak things into the jail. These inmates, who might be thought to pose the least risk, have been caught smuggling prohibited items into jail. Concealing contraband often takes little time and effort. It might be done as an officer approaches a suspect's car or during a brief commotion in a group holding cell. Something small might be tucked or taped under an armpit, behind an ear, between the buttocks, in the instep of a foot, or inside the mouth or some other body cavity.

It is not surprising that correctional officials have sought to perform thorough searches at intake for disease, gang affiliation, and contraband. Jails are often crowded, unsanitary, and dangerous places. There is a substantial interest in preventing any new inmate, either of his own will or as a result of coercion, from putting all who live or work at these institutions at even greater risk when he is admitted to the general population.

Petitioner maintains there is little benefit to conducting these more invasive steps on a new detainee who has not been arrested for a serious crime or for any offense involving a weapon or drugs. In his view these detainees should be exempt from this process unless they give officers a particular reason to suspect them of hiding contraband. It is reasonable, however, for correctional officials to conclude this standard would be unworkable. The seriousness of an offense is a poor predictor of who has contraband and that it would be difficult in practice to determine whether individual detainees fall within the proposed exemption.

People detained for minor offenses can turn out to be the most devious and dangerous criminals. Hours after the Oklahoma City bombing, Timothy McVeigh was stopped by a state trooper who noticed he was driving without a license plate. Police stopped serial killer Joel Rifkin for the same reason. One of the terrorists involved in the September 11 attacks was stopped and ticketed for speeding just two days before hijacking Flight 93. Reasonable correctional officials could conclude these uncertainties mean they must conduct the same thorough search of everyone who will be admitted to their facilities. Experience shows that people arrested for minor offenses have tried to smuggle prohibited items into jail, sometimes by using their rectal cavities or genitals for the concealment. They may have some of the same incentives as a serious criminal to hide contraband. A detainee might risk carrying cash, cigarettes, or a penknife to survive in jail. Others may make a quick decision to hide unlawful substances to avoid getting in more trouble at the time of their arrest. Officers at the Atlantic County Correctional Facility, for example, discovered that a man arrested for driving under the influence had "2 dime bags of weed, 1 pack of rolling papers, 20 matches, and 5 sleeping pills" taped under his scrotum. A person booked on a misdemeanor charge of disorderly conduct in Washington State managed to hide a lighter, tobacco, tattoo needles, and other prohibited items in his rectal cavity. San Francisco officials have discovered contraband hidden in body cavities of people arrested for trespassing, public nuisance, and shoplifting. There have been similar incidents at jails throughout the country.

Even if people arrested for a minor offense do not themselves wish to introduce contraband into a jail, they may be coerced into doing so by others. This could happen any time detainees are held in the same area, including in a van on the way to the station or in the holding cell of the jail. If a person arrested and detained for unpaid traffic citations is not subject to the same search as others, this will be well known to other detainees with jail experience. A hardened criminal or gang member can, in just a few minutes, approach the person and coerce him into hiding the fruits of a crime, a weapon, or some other contraband. Exempting people arrested for minor offenses from a standard search protocol thus may put them at greater risk and result in more contraband being brought into the detention facility. This is a substantial reason not to mandate the exception petitioner seeks as a matter of constitutional law.

It also may be difficult, as a practical matter, to classify inmates by their current and prior offenses before the intake search. Jails can be even more dangerous than prisons because officials know so little about the people they admit at the outset. An arrestee may be carrying a false ID or lie about his identity. The officers who conduct an initial search often do not have access to criminal history records. And those records can be inaccurate or incomplete. Petitioner's rap sheet is an example. It did not reflect his previous arrest for possession of a deadly weapon. In the absence of reliable information it would be illogical to require officers to assume the arrestees in front of them do not pose a risk of smuggling something into the facility. The laborious administration of prisons would become less effective, and likely less fair and evenhanded, were the practical problems inevitable from the rules suggested by petitioner to be imposed as a constitutional mandate. Even if they had accurate information about a detainee's current and prior arrests, officers, under petitioner's proposed regime, would encounter serious implementation difficulties. They would be required, in a few minutes, to determine whether any of the underlying offenses were serious enough to authorize the more invasive search protocol. Other possible classifications based on characteristics of individual detainees also might prove to be unworkable or even give rise to charges of discriminatory application. Most officers would not be well equipped to make any of these legal determinations during the pressures of the intake process. To avoid liability, officers might be inclined not to conduct a thorough search in any close case, thus creating unnecessary risk for the entire jail population.

One of the central principles in *Atwater* applies with equal force here. Officers who interact with those suspected of violating the law have an "essential interest in readily administrable rules." The restrictions suggested by petitioner would limit the intrusion on the privacy of some detainees but at the risk of increased danger to everyone in the facility, including the less serious offenders themselves.

IV

This case does not require the Court to rule on the types of searches that would be reasonable in instances where, for example, a detainee will be held without assignment to the general jail population and without substantial contact with other detainees. The accommodations provided in these situations may diminish the need to conduct some aspects of the searches at issue. Petitioner's *amici* raise concerns about instances of officers engaging in intentional humiliation and other abusive practices. There also may be legitimate concerns about the invasiveness of searches that involve the touching of detainees. These issues are not implicated on the facts of this case, and it is unnecessary to consider them here.

V

The search procedures at the Burlington County Detention Center and the Essex County Correctional Facility struck a reasonable balance between inmate privacy and the needs of the institutions. The Fourth and Fourteenth Amendments do not require adoption of the framework of rules petitioner proposes. The judgment of the Court of Appeals for the Third Circuit is affirmed.

It is so ordered.

CHIEF JUSTICE ROBERTS, concurring.

The Court makes a persuasive case for the general applicability of the rule it announces. The Court is nonetheless wise to leave open the possibility of exceptions, to ensure that we do "not embarrass the future."

JUSTICE ALITO, concurring.

Most of those arrested for minor offenses are not dangerous, and most are released from custody prior to or at the time of their initial appearance. In some cases, the charges are dropped or arrestees are released either on their own recognizance or on minimal bail. Few are sentenced to incarceration. For these persons, admission to the general jail population, with the concomitant humiliation of a strip search, may not be reasonable, particularly if an alternative procedure is feasible. For example, the Federal Bureau of Prisons (BOP) segregates temporary detainees who are minor offenders from the general population.[1] The Court does not address whether it is always reasonable, without regard to the offense or the reason for detention, to strip search an arrestee before the arrestee's detention has been reviewed by a judicial officer.

---

[1] According to BOP policy, prison and jail officials cannot subject persons arrested for misdemeanor or civil contempt offenses to visual body-cavity searches without their consent or without reasonable suspicion that they are concealing contraband. Those who are not searched must be housed separately from inmates in the general population.

JUSTICE BREYER, with whom JUSTICE GINSBURG, JUSTICE SOTOMAYOR, and JUSTICE KAGAN join, dissenting.

This case is limited to strip searches of those arrestees entering a jail's general population, and involve close observation of the private areas of a person's body and for that reason constitute a far more serious invasion of that person's privacy. Such a search of an individual arrested for a minor offense that does not involve drugs or violence—say a traffic offense, a regulatory offense, an essentially civil matter, or any other such misdemeanor—is an "unreasonable search" forbidden by the Fourth Amendment, unless prison authorities have reasonable suspicion to believe that the individual possesses drugs or other contraband.

Those confined in prison retain basic constitutional rights. In *Bell v. Wolfish*, the Court said:"The test of reasonableness under the Fourth Amendment is not capable of precise definition or mechanical application. In each case it requires a balancing of the need for the particular search against the invasion of personal rights that the search entails. Courts must consider the scope of the particular intrusion, the manner in which it is conducted, the justification for initiating it, and the place in which it is conducted."

A strip search that involves a stranger peering without consent at a naked individual, and in particular at the most private portions of that person's body, is a serious invasion of privacy. Even when carried out in a respectful manner, and even absent any physical touching, such searches are inherently harmful, humiliating, and degrading. The harm to privacy interests would seem particularly acute where the person searched may well have no expectation of being subject to such a search, say, because she had simply received a traffic ticket for failing to buckle a seatbelt, because he had not previously paid a civil fine, or because she had been arrested for a minor trespass.

I recognize: that managing a jail or prison is an "inordinately difficult undertaking," that prison regulations that interfere with important constitutional interests are generally valid as long as they are "reasonably related to legitimate penological interests," that finding injuries and preventing the spread of disease, minimizing the threat of gang violence, and detecting contraband are "legitimate penological interests," and that we normally defer to the expertise of jail and prison

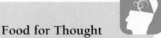

Food for Thought

Suppose that you are the legal adviser to your city which does not routinely strip search everyone who is incarcerated in the city jail. Following the decision in *Florence*, city officials are debating whether they *should* routinely strip search those who are incarcerated, and have asked you for advice. How would you advise them? Are there less intrusive alternatives that would be preferable?

administrators in such matters. Nonetheless, the "particular" invasion of interests, must be "reasonably related" to the justifying "penological interest" and the need must not be "exaggerated." I have found no convincing reason indicating that, in the absence of reasonable suspicion, involuntary strip searches of those arrested for minor offenses are necessary in order to further the penal interests mentioned. And there are strong reasons to believe they are not justified.

The lack of justification for such a strip search is less obvious but no less real in respect to the detection of contraband. Neither the majority's opinion nor the briefs set forth any clear example of an instance in which contraband was smuggled into the general jail population during intake that could not have been discovered if the jail was employing a reasonable suspicion standard. In an appropriate case, it remains open for the Court to consider whether it would be reasonable to admit an arrestee for a minor offense to the general jail population, and to subject her to the "humiliation of a strip search," prior to any review by a judicial officer.

Hypo 1: *Booking Searches and Non-Incarceration*

Suppose that a truck driver is stopped because his truck emits excess smoke. In checking the driver's license, a state trooper learns that there are two warrants for the driver's arrest (one for failure to appear on a misdemeanor charge and the other for failure to pay a $25 fine for possession of marijuana). The trooper arrests the driver and takes him to the city jail. Jail procedures require complete processing of all arrestees, including a property inventory, whether or not the arrestee is able to post bail when the arrestee arrives at jail. On the driver's behalf, he argues that any evidence found during the booking search should be excluded since the driver planned to immediately post bail. Does the state have a valid response to these arguments? See *Zehrung v. State*, 569 P.2d 189 (Alaska 1977).

Food for Thought

Everett Hoffman is arrested. At the station, the police want to search his backpack. Hoffman objects claiming that the police can serve their interest in "preservation of the defendant's property and protection of police from claims of lost or stolen property" by sealing the backpack in a plastic bag or box and placing it in a secure locker. Do the police have to accept Hoffman's suggestion or should they be allowed to search the backpack? What arguments can be made on Hoffman's behalf? How might the police respond to those arguments?

Maryland v. King

569 U.S. 435 (2013).

JUSTICE KENNEDY delivered the opinion of the Court.

In 2003 a man concealing his face and armed with a gun broke into a woman's home in Maryland. He raped her. The police were unable to identify or apprehend the assailant, but they did obtain a sample of the perpetrator's DNA. In 2009 Alonzo King was arrested in Maryland, and charged with assault for menacing a group of people with a shotgun. As part of a routine booking procedure for serious offenses, his DNA sample was taken by applying a cotton swab or filter paper—known as a buccal swab—to the inside of his cheeks. The DNA was found to match the DNA taken from the rape victim. King was tried and convicted for the rape. The Court of Appeals of Maryland ruled that the DNA taken when King was booked for the 2009 charge was an unlawful seizure and set the rape conviction aside. This Court granted certiorari.

DNA technology is one of the most significant scientific advancements. Law enforcement, the defense bar, and the courts have acknowledged DNA testing's 'unparalleled ability both to exonerate the wrongly convicted and to identify the guilty.' The current standard for forensic DNA testing relies on an analysis of the chromosomes located within the nucleus of all human cells. 'DNA material is composed of 'coding' and 'noncoding' regions. The coding regions are known as *genes* and contain the information necessary for a cell to make proteins. Non-protein-coding regions are not related directly to making proteins, and have been referred to as 'junk' DNA.' The adjective 'junk' may mislead for this is the DNA region used with near certainty to identify a person. The term indicates that this particular noncoding region, while useful and even dispositive for purposes like identity, does not show more far-reaching and complex characteristics like genetic traits. Many of the patterns found in DNA are shared among all people, so forensic analysis focuses on 'repeated DNA sequences scattered throughout the human genome,' known as 'short tandem repeats' (STRs). The alternative possibilities for the size and frequency of these STRs at any given point along a strand of DNA are known as 'alleles,' and multiple alleles are analyzed in order to ensure that a DNA profile matches only one individual. STR analysis makes it 'possible to determine whether a biological tissue matches a suspect with near certainty.' *Osborne, supra*, at 62.

The Act authorizes Maryland law enforcement authorities to collect DNA samples from 'an individual who is charged with a crime of violence or an attempt to commit a crime of violence; or burglary or an attempt to commit burglary.' Md. Pub. Saf. Code Ann. §2-504(a)(3)(I) (Lexis 2011). Maryland law defines a crime of violence to include murder, rape, first-degree assault, kidnaping, arson, sexual assault, and a variety of other serious crimes. A DNA sample may not be processed or placed in a database before the individual is arraigned (unless the individual consents). A judicial officer ensures that there is probable cause to detain the arrestee on a qualifying serious offense. If 'all qualifying criminal charges are determined to be unsupported by probable cause the DNA sample shall be immediately destroyed.' DNA samples are also destroyed if 'a criminal action begun against the individual does not result in a conviction,' 'the conviction is finally reversed or vacated and no new trial is permitted,' or 'the individual is granted an unconditional pardon.' The Act also limits the information added to a DNA database and how it may be used. Specifically, no purpose other than identification is permissible: 'A person may not willfully test a DNA sample for information that does not relate to the identification of individuals as specified in this subtitle.' Tests for familial matches are also prohibited. The officers involved in taking and analyzing respondent's DNA sample complied with the Act.

Authorized by Congress and supervised by the Federal Bureau of Investigation, the Combined DNA Index System (CODIS) connects DNA laboratories at the local, state, and national level. Since its authorization in 1994, the CODIS system has grown to include all 50 States and a number of federal agencies. CODIS collects DNA profiles provided by local laboratories taken from arrestees, convicted offenders, and forensic evidence found at crime scenes. To participate in CODIS, a local laboratory must sign a memorandum of understanding agreeing to adhere to quality standards and submit to audits to evaluate compliance with the federal standards for scientifically rigorous DNA testing. One of the most significant aspects of CODIS is the standardization of the points of comparison in DNA analysis. The CODIS database is based on 13 loci at which the STR alleles are noted and compared. These loci make possible extreme accuracy in matching individual samples, with a 'random match probability of approximately 1 in 100 trillion (assuming unrelated individuals).' The CODIS loci are from the non-protein coding junk regions of DNA, and 'are not known to have any association with a genetic disease or any other genetic predisposition. Thus, the information in the database is only useful for human identity testing.' STR information is recorded only as a 'string of numbers'; and the DNA identification is accompanied only by information denoting the laboratory and the analyst responsible for the submission. In short, CODIS sets uniform national standards for DNA matching and then facilitates connections between local law enforcement agencies who can share more specific information about matched STR profiles.

All 50 States require the collection of DNA from felony convicts, and respondent does not dispute the validity of that practice. Twenty-eight States and the Federal Government have adopted laws authorizing the collection of DNA from some or all arrestees. Although those statutes vary in their particulars, their similarity means that this case implicates more than the specific Maryland law.

The framework for deciding the issue is well established. Using a buccal swab on the inner tissues of a person's cheek in order to obtain DNA samples is a search. A buccal swab is a far more gentle process than a venipuncture to draw blood. It involves but a light touch on the inside of the cheek; and although it can be deemed a search within the body of the arrestee, it requires no 'surgical intrusions beneath the skin.'

'As the text of the Fourth Amendment indicates, the ultimate measure of the constitutionality of a governmental search is 'reasonableness.'' *Vernonia School Dist. 47J v. Acton*, 515 U. S. 646, 652 (1995). In giving content to the inquiry whether an intrusion is reasonable, the Court has preferred 'some quantum of individualized suspicion as a prerequisite to a constitutional search or seizure. But the Fourth Amendment imposes no irreducible requirement of such suspicion.' *United States v. Martinez-Fuerte*, 428 U. S. 543, 560 (1976). In some circumstances, such as 'when faced with special law enforcement needs, diminished expectations of privacy, minimal intrusions, or the like, the Court has found that certain general, or individual, circumstances may render a warrantless search or seizure reasonable.' *Illinois v. McArthur*, 531 U. S. 326, 330 (2001). Those circumstances diminish the need for a warrant.

The Maryland DNA Collection Act provides that all arrestees charged with serious crimes must furnish the sample on a buccal swab. The arrestee is already in valid police custody for a serious offense supported by probable cause. The DNA collection is not subject to the judgment of officers whose perspective might be 'colored by their primary involvement in 'the often competitive enterprise of ferreting out crime.'' *Terry, supra*, at 12 (quoting *Johnson v. United States*, 333 U. S. 10, 14 (1948)). 'Both the circumstances justifying toxicological testing and the permissible limits of such intrusions are defined narrowly and specifically in the regulations that authorize them. In light of the standardized nature of the tests and the minimal discretion vested in those charged with administering the program, there are virtually no facts for a neutral magistrate to evaluate.' *Skinner, supra*, at 622. Here, the search falls within the category of cases this Court has analyzed by reference to the proposition that the 'touchstone of the Fourth Amendment is reasonableness, not individualized suspicion.' *Samson, supra*, at 855, n. 4.

Urgent government interests are not a license for indiscriminate police behavior. To say that no warrant is required is merely to acknowledge that 'rather than employing a *per se* rule of unreasonableness, we balance the privacy-related and law enforcement-related concerns to determine if the intrusion was reasonable.' *McArthur, supra*, at 331. This application of 'traditional standards of reasonableness' requires a court to weigh 'the promotion of legitimate governmental interests' against 'the degree to which the search intrudes upon an individual's privacy.' *Wyoming v. Houghton*, 526 U. S. 295, 300 (1999).

The legitimate government interest served by the Maryland DNA Collection Act is one that is well established: the need for law enforcement officers in a safe and accurate way to process and identify the persons and possessions they must take into custody. It is beyond dispute that 'probable cause provides legal justification for arresting a person suspected of crime, and for a brief period of detention to take the administrative steps incident to arrest.' *Gerstein v. Pugh*, 420 U. S. 103, 113 (1975). Also uncontested is the 'right on the part of the Government to search the person of the accused when legally arrested.' *Weeks v. United States*, 232 U. S. 383, 392 (1914). The 'routine administrative procedures at a police station house incident to booking and jailing the suspect' derive from different origins and have different constitutional justifications than, say, the search of a place. The interests are further different when an individual is formally processed into police custody. Then 'the law is in the act of subjecting the body of the accused to its physical dominion.' *People v. Chiagles*, 237 N. Y. 193, 197, 142 N. E. 583, 584 (1923) (Cardozo, J.). When probable cause exists to remove an individual from the normal channels of society and hold him in legal custody, DNA identification plays a critical role in serving those interests.

First, 'in every criminal case, it is known and must be known who has been arrested and who is being tried.' *Hiibel v. Sixth Judicial Dist. Court of Nev., Humboldt Cty.*, 542 U. S. 177, 191 (2004). 'A perpetrator will take unusual steps to conceal not only his conduct, but also his identity. Disguises used while committing a crime may be supplemented or replaced by changed names, and even changed physical features.' *Jones v. Murray*, 962 F. 2d 302, 307 (CA4 1992). An 'arrestee may be carrying a false ID or lie about his identity,' and 'criminal history records can be inaccurate or incomplete.' *Florence v. Board of Chosen Freeholders of County of Burlington*, 132 S. Ct. 1510, 1521 (2012). A suspect's criminal history is a critical part of his identity. It is a common occurrence that 'people detained for minor offenses turn out to be the most devious and dangerous criminals. Police already use routine and accepted means as varied as comparing the suspect's booking photograph to sketch artists' depictions of persons of interest, showing his mugshot to potential witnesses, and of course making a computerized comparison of the arrestee's fingerprints against electronic databases of known criminals and unsolved crimes. The only difference between DNA analysis and the accepted use of fingerprint databases is the unparalleled accuracy DNA provides. DNA collected from arrestees is an irrefutable identification of the person from whom it was taken. In this respect the use of DNA is no different than matching an arrestee's face to a wanted poster of a previously unidentified suspect; or matching tattoos to known gang symbols to reveal a criminal affiliation; or matching the arrestee's fingerprints to those recovered from a crime scene.

Second, law enforcement officers bear a responsibility for ensuring that the custody of an arrestee does not create inordinate 'risks for facility staff, for the existing detainee population, and for a new detainee.' *Florence, supra,* at 1518. 'Knowledge of identity may inform an officer that a suspect is wanted for another offense, or has a record of violence or mental disorder. On the other hand, knowing identity may help clear a suspect and allow the police to concentrate their efforts elsewhere.

Third, 'the Government has a substantial interest in ensuring that persons accused of crimes are available for trials.' *Bell v. Wolfish,* 441 U. S. 520, 534 (1979). A person who is arrested for one offense but knows that he has yet to answer for some past crime may be more inclined to flee the instant charges. A defendant who had committed a prior sexual assault might be inclined to flee on a burglary charge, knowing that a DNA sample would be taken from him after his conviction on the burglary charge that would tie him to the more serious charge of rape. A detainee who absconds from custody presents a risk to law enforcement officers, other detainees, victims of previous crimes, witnesses, and society at large.

Fourth, an arrestee's past conduct is essential to an assessment of the danger he poses to the public, and this will inform a court's determination whether the individual should be released on bail. Knowing that the defendant is wanted for a previous violent crime based on DNA identification is especially probative of the court's consideration of 'the danger of the defendant to the alleged victim, another person, or the community.' Even when release is permitted, the background identity of the suspect is necessary for determining what conditions must be met before release is allowed. The facts of this case are illustrative. When the DNA report linked him to the prior rape, it would be relevant to the conditions of his release. Even if an arrestee is released on bail, development of DNA identification revealing the defendant's unknown violent past can and should lead to the revocation of his conditional release.

Finally, in the interests of justice, the identification of an arrestee as the perpetrator of some heinous crime may have the salutary effect of freeing a person wrongfully imprisoned for the same offense. 'Prompt DNA testing would speed up apprehension of criminals before they commit additional crimes, and prevent the grotesque detention of innocent people.' J. Dwyer, P. Neufeld, & B. Scheck, Actual Innocence 245 (2000).

The Court has recognized that the 'governmental interests underlying a station-house search of the arrestee's person and possessions may in some circumstances be even greater than those supporting a search immediately following arrest.' *Lafayette,* 462 U. S., at 645. Thus, the Court has been reluctant to circumscribe the authority of the police to conduct reasonable booking searches.

DNA identification represents an important advance in the techniques used by law enforcement to serve legitimate police concerns. Law enforcement agencies routinely have used scientific advancements in their standard procedures for the identification of arrestees. 'Police had been using photography to capture the faces of criminals almost since its invention.' S. Cole, Suspect Identities 20 (2001). Perhaps the most direct historical analogue to the DNA technology used to identify respondent is fingerprinting. DNA identification is an advanced technique superior to fingerprinting in many ways. A suspect who has changed his facial features to evade photographic identification or even one who has undertaken the more arduous task of altering his fingerprints cannot escape the revealing power of his DNA. Respondent's primary objection is that DNA identification is not as fast as fingerprinting. Prior to 1999, the processing of fingerprint submissions was largely a manual, labor-intensive process, taking weeks or months to process a single submission.' The question of how long it takes to process identifying information obtained from a valid search goes only to the efficacy of the search for its purpose of prompt identification, not the constitutionality of the search. Even so, the delay in processing DNA from arrestees is being reduced by rapid technical advances. Actual release of a serious offender as a routine matter takes weeks or months in any event.

Courts have confirmed that the Fourth Amendment allows police to take certain routine 'administrative steps incident to arrest—i.e., booking, photographing, and fingerprinting.' *McLaughlin,* 500 U. S., at 58. DNA identification of arrestees is 'no more than an extension of methods of identification long used in dealing with persons under arrest.' *Kelly,* 55 F. 2d, at 69. In the balance of reasonableness required by the Fourth Amendment, the Court must give great weight both to the significant government interest at stake in the identification of arrestees and to the unmatched potential of DNA identification to serve that interest.

The intrusion of a cheek swab to obtain a DNA sample is a minimal one. A significant government interest does not alone suffice to justify a search. The government interest must outweigh the degree to which the search invades an individual's legitimate expectations of privacy. The expectations of privacy of an individual taken into police custody 'necessarily are of a diminished scope.' *Bell,* 441 U. S., at 557. 'Both the person and the property in his immediate possession may be searched at the station house.' *United States v. Edwards,* 415 U. S. 800, 803 (1974). A search of the detainee's person when he is booked into custody may 'involve a relatively extensive exploration.' *Robinson,* 414 U. S., at 227. This is not to suggest that any search is acceptable solely because a person is in custody. Some searches, such as invasive surgery, or a search of the arrestee's home, involve either greater intrusions or higher expectations of privacy than are present in this case. A buccal swab involves an even more brief and still minimal intrusion. A gentle rub along the inside of the cheek does not break the skin, and it 'involves virtually no risk, trauma, or pain.' Nothing suggests that a buccal swab poses any physical danger whatsoever. A swab of this nature does not increase the indignity already attendant to normal incidents of arrest.

The processing of respondent's DNA sample's 13 CODIS loci did not intrude on respondent's privacy in a way that would make his DNA identification unconstitutional. The CODIS loci come from noncoding parts of the DNA that do not reveal the genetic traits of the arrestee. Even if non-coding alleles could provide some information, law enforcement officers analyze DNA for the sole purpose of generating a unique identifying number against which future samples may be matched. If future police analyze samples to determine, for instance, an arrestee's predisposition for a particular disease or other hereditary factors not relevant to identity, that case would present additional privacy concerns not present here. The Act provides statutory protections that guard against further invasion of privacy. The Act requires that 'only DNA records that directly relate to the identification of individuals shall be collected and stored.' The Court need not speculate about the risks posed 'by a system that did not contain comparable security provisions.'

DNA identification of arrestees is a reasonable search that can be considered part of a routine booking procedure. The judgment of the Court of Appeals of Maryland is reversed.

It is so ordered.

JUSTICE SCALIA, with whom JUSTICE GINSBURG, JUSTICE SOTOMAYOR, and JUSTICE KAGAN join, dissenting.

While we have permitted searches without individualized suspicion, 'in none of these cases did we indicate approval of a search whose primary purpose was to detect evidence of ordinary criminal wrongdoing.' *Indianapolis v. Edmond*, 531 U. S. 32, 38 (2000). The Court elaborates at length the ways that the search here served the special purpose of 'identifying' King. If the purpose of this Act is to assess 'whether King should be released on bail,' why would it *possibly* forbid the DNA testing process to *begin* until King was arraigned? The truth is that this search had nothing to do with establishing King's identity. King's DNA sample was not received by the Maryland State Police's Forensic Sciences Division until two weeks after his arrest. It sat in that office two months after it was received, and nearly three since King's arrest. The data from the tests were not available for several more weeks when the test results were entered into Maryland's DNA database, *together with information identifying the person from whom the sample was taken.* Meanwhile, bail had been set, King had engaged in discovery, and he had requested a speedy trial.

It was not until four months after King's arrest that the forwarded sample transmitted (*without* identifying information) from the Maryland DNA database to the Federal Bureau of Investigation's national database was matched with a sample taken from the scene of an unrelated crime years earlier. King could not have been *identified* by this match. The FBI's DNA database consists of two distinct collections. The one to which King's DNA was submitted consists of DNA samples taken from known convicts or arrestees. The other collection consists of samples taken from crime scenes; the 'Unsolved Crimes Collection.' The Convict and Arrestee Collection contains only the DNA profile itself, the name of the agency that submitted it, the laboratory personnel who analyzed it, and an identification number for the specimen. If one wanted to identify someone in custody using his DNA, the logical thing to do would be to compare that DNA against the Convict and Arrestee Collection. But that is not what was done. And that is because this search had nothing to do with identification.

The Maryland Act has a section helpfully entitled 'Purpose of collecting and testing DNA samples.' Md. Pub. Saf. Code Ann. §2-505. That provision lists five purposes for which DNA samples may be tested. The Court's imagined purpose is not among them. Instead, the law provides that DNA samples are collected and tested, as a matter of Maryland law, 'as part of an official investigation into a crime.' The attorney general of Maryland remarked that he 'looked forward to the opportunity to defend this important crime-fighting tool,' and praised the DNA database for helping to 'bring to justice violent perpetrators.'

Food for Thought

Justice Scalia's dissent suggests the fear that states will expand their DNA testing to cover even minor offenses. Recall, when we studied arrest principles, we saw that individuals could be subjected to custodial arrest for relatively minor offenses (*e.g.,* failure to wear seat belts). Would the Maryland law be constitutional if it applied to *all* arrestees?

Today's judgment will have the beneficial effect of solving more crimes; so would the taking of DNA samples from anyone who flies on an airplane. I doubt that the proud men who wrote the charter of our liberties would have been so eager to open their mouths for royal inspection.

Hypo 1: *Other Possible DNA Collections*

What if states decided to collect and store information related to all arrestees genetic traits, and medical tendencies. Would the *King* decision allow the states to use DNA for these purposes? Are there justifications for doing so?

CHAPTER 4 *Arrest, Search & Seizure*

Hypo 2: *More on DNA Testing of Arrestees*

In *King*, the Maryland statute provided for DNA testing only after a judicial officer has made a probable cause determination, and the arrestee has been charged with a crime. Would a DNA testing law be constitutional if it provided for DNA testing as soon as "immediately practicable" after a suspect is arrested? In other words, it required testing before a judicial officer determined that the state had probable cause to arrest the suspect? Does *King* suggest that the state has a valid interest in ascertaining the identity of those who have been arrested for a crime, but not yet charged? *See People v. Buza*, 180 Cal. Rptr. 3d 753, 231 Cal. App.4th 1446 (Cal. App. 2014).

4. Automobile Exception

The automobile exception is one of the oldest exceptions to the warrant requirement. It provides that, when the police have probable cause to believe that an automobile contains the fruits, instrumentalities or evidence of crime, they may search the vehicle without a warrant.

California v. Carney

471 U.S. 386 (1985).

CHIEF JUSTICE BURGER delivered the opinion of the Court.

On May 31, 1979, Drug Enforcement Agency Agent Robert Williams watched respondent, Charles Carney, approach a youth in downtown San Diego. The youth accompanied Carney to a Dodge Mini Motor Home parked in a nearby lot. Carney and the youth closed the window shades in the motor home. Agent Williams had previously received uncorroborated information that the same motor home was used by another person who was exchanging marihuana for sex. Williams, with assistance from other agents, kept the motor home under surveillance for the entire one and one-quarter hours that Carney and the youth remained inside. When the youth left the motor home, the agents followed and stopped him. The youth told the agents that he had received marijuana in return for allowing Carney sexual contacts.

At the agents' request, the youth returned to the motor home and knocked on its door; Carney stepped out. The agents identified themselves as law enforcement officers. Without a warrant or consent, one agent entered the motor home and observed marihuana, plastic bags, and a scale of the kind used in weighing drugs on a table. Agent Williams took Carney into custody and took possession of the motor home. A subsequent search of the motor home at the police station revealed additional marihuana in the cupboards and refrigerator. Respondent was convicted of possession of marihuana for sale. The California Supreme Court reversed the conviction. We granted certiorari. We reverse. → *convicted.*

There are exceptions to the general rule that a warrant must be secured before a search is undertaken; one is the so-called "automobile exception" at issue in this case. This exception to the warrant requirement was first set forth by the Court 60 years ago in *Carroll v. United States*, 267 U.S. 132 (1925). There, the Court recognized that the privacy interests in an automobile are constitutionally protected; however, it held that the ready mobility of the automobile justifies a lesser degree of protection of those interests. Our later cases have made clear that ready mobility is not the only basis for the exception. "Besides the element of mobility, less rigorous warrant requirements govern because the expectation of privacy with respect to one's automobile is significantly less than that relating to one's home or office."

Even in cases where an automobile was not immediately mobile, the lesser expectation of privacy resulting from its use as a readily mobile vehicle justified application of the vehicular exception. In some cases, the configuration of the vehicle contributed to the lower expectations of privacy; for example, we held in *Cardwell v. Lewis, supra*, 417 U.S., at 590, that, because the passenger compartment of a standard automobile is relatively open to plain view, there are lesser expectations of privacy. But even when enclosed "repository" areas have been involved, we have concluded that the lesser expectations of privacy warrant application of the exception. We have applied the exception in the context of a locked car trunk, a sealed package in a car trunk, a closed compartment under the dashboard, the interior of a vehicle's upholstery, or sealed packages inside a covered pickup truck.

These reduced expectations of privacy derive not from the fact that the area to be searched is in plain view, but from the pervasive regulation of vehicles capable of traveling on the public highways. As we explained in *South Dakota v. Opperman*, 428 U.S. 364 (1976), an inventory search case: "Automobiles, unlike homes, are subjected to pervasive and continuing governmental regulation and controls, including periodic inspection and licensing requirements. As an everyday occurrence, police stop and examine vehicles when license plates or inspection stickers have expired, or if other violations, such as exhaust fumes or excessive noise, are noted, or if headlights or other safety equipment are not in proper working order."

The public is fully aware that it is accorded less privacy in its automobiles because of this compelling governmental need for regulation. In short, the pervasive schemes of regulation, which necessarily lead to reduced expectations of privacy, and the exigencies attendant to ready mobility justify searches without prior recourse to the authority of a magistrate so long as the overriding standard of probable cause is met.

When a vehicle is being used on the highways, or if it is readily capable of such use and is found stationary in a place not regularly used for residential purposes—temporary or otherwise—the two justifications for the vehicle exception come into play. First, the vehicle is obviously readily mobile by the turn of an ignition key, if not actually moving. Second, there is a reduced expectation of privacy stemming from its use as a licensed motor vehicle subject to a range of police regulation inapplicable to a fixed dwelling. At least in these circumstances, the overriding societal interests in effective law enforcement justify an immediate search before the vehicle and its occupants become unavailable.

While it is true that respondent's vehicle possessed some, if not many of the attributes of a home, it is equally clear that the vehicle falls clearly within the scope of the exception. Respondent's motor home was readily mobile. Absent the prompt search and seizure, it could readily have been moved beyond the reach of the police. Furthermore, the vehicle was licensed to "operate on public streets; was serviced in public places; and was subject to extensive regulation and inspection." *Rakas v. Illinois*, 439 U.S. 128, 154 (1978) (Powell, J., concurring). And the vehicle was so situated that an objective observer would conclude that it was being used not as a residence, but as a vehicle.

Respondent urges us to distinguish his vehicle from other vehicles because it was capable of functioning as a home. In our increasingly mobile society, many vehicles used for transportation can be and are being used not only for transportation but for shelter, *i.e.*, as a "home" or "residence." To distinguish between respondent's motor home and an ordinary sedan for purposes of the vehicle exception would require that we apply the exception depending upon the size of the vehicle and the quality of its appointments. Moreover, to fail to apply the exception to vehicles such as a motor home ignores the fact that a motor home lends itself easily to use as an instrument of illicit drug traffic and other illegal activity. In *United States v. Ross*, 456 U.S., at 822, we declined to distinguish between "worthy" and "unworthy" containers, noting that "the central purpose of the Fourth Amendment forecloses such a distinction." We decline today to distinguish between "worthy" and "unworthy" vehicles which are either on the public roads and highways, or situated such that it is reasonable to conclude that the vehicle is not being used as a residence.

Our application of the vehicle exception has never turned on the other uses to which a vehicle might be put. The exception has historically turned on the ready mobility of the vehicle, and on the presence of the vehicle in a setting that objectively indicates that the vehicle is being used for transportation.[17] These

---

[17] We need not pass on the application of the vehicle exception to a motor home that is situated in a way or place that indicates that it is being used as a residence. Among the factors that might be relevant in determining whether a warrant would be required in such a circumstance is its location, whether the vehicle is readily mobile or elevated on blocks, whether the vehicle is licensed, whether it is connected to utilities, and whether it has convenient access to a public road.

two requirements for application of the exception ensure that law enforcement officials are not unnecessarily hamstrung in their efforts to detect and prosecute criminal activity, and that the legitimate privacy interests of the public are protected. Applying the vehicle exception in these circumstances allows the essential purposes served by the exception to be fulfilled, while assuring that the exception will acknowledge legitimate privacy interests.

This search was not unreasonable; it was plainly one that the magistrate could authorize if presented with these facts. The DEA agents had fresh, direct, uncontradicted evidence that the respondent was distributing a controlled substance from the vehicle, apart from evidence of other possible offenses. The agents thus had abundant probable cause to enter and search the vehicle for evidence of a crime notwithstanding its possible use as a dwelling place.

The judgment of the California Supreme Court is *reversed*.

JUSTICE STEVENS, with whom JUSTICE BRENNAN and JUSTICE MARSHALL join, dissenting.

It is hardly unrealistic to expect experienced law enforcement officers to obtain a search warrant when one can easily be secured. The ascendancy of the warrant requirement in our system of justice must not be bullied aside by extravagant claims of necessity. Inherent mobility is not a sufficient justification for the fashioning of an exception to the warrant requirement, especially in the face of heightened expectations of privacy in the location searched. Motor homes, by their common use and construction, afford their owners a substantial and legitimate expectation of privacy when they dwell within. When a motor home is parked in a location that is removed from the public highway, society is prepared to recognize that the expectations of privacy within it are not unlike the expectations one has in a fixed dwelling. Such places may only be searched with a warrant based upon probable cause. Warrantless searches of motor homes are only reasonable when the motor home is traveling on the public streets or highways, or when exigent circumstances otherwise require an immediate search without the expenditure of time necessary to obtain a warrant. In this case, the motor

Take Note

No exigent circumstances are needed for police to rely on the "automobile exception," only probable cause. In *Maryland v. Dyson*, 527 U.S. 465 (1999), the police had probable cause to believe that a vehicle contained illegal drugs, and they searched it without a warrant even though there was time to obtain one. The Maryland Court of Special Appeals invalidated the search on the basis that there were no exigent circumstances justifying the warrantless search. The United States Supreme Court reversed, noting that automobiles should be treated differently than homes, and that only probable cause is required to invoke the automobile exception.

home was parked in an off-the-street lot only a few blocks from the courthouse in downtown San Diego where dozens of magistrates were available to entertain a warrant application.[18] The officers plainly had probable cause to arrest the respondent and search the motor home, and it is inexplicable why they eschewed the safe harbor of a warrant. The motor home in this case was designed to accommodate a breadth of ordinary everyday living.

The State contends that officers in the field will have an impossible task determining whether or not other vehicles contain mobile living quarters. Surely the exteriors of these vehicles contain clues about their different functions which could alert officers in the field to the necessity of a warrant. A motor home is usually the functional equivalent of a hotel room, a vacation and retirement home, or a hunting and fishing cabin. The highest and most legitimate expectations of privacy associated with these temporary abodes should command the respect of this Court. A warrantless search of living quarters in a motor home is "presumptively unreasonable absent exigent circumstances."

Point for Discussion

Delayed Automobile Searches

Arguably, if the search of an automobile is delayed, the police have time to obtain a warrant and should be required to do so. However, in *Chambers v. Maroney,* 399 U.S. 42 (1970), the Court upheld a delayed search. Petitioner was riding in an automobile at the time of his arrest, but the vehicle was searched later at the police station rather than at the scene. The Court held that: "For constitutional purposes, we see no difference between on the one hand seizing and holding a car before presenting the probable cause issue to a magistrate and on the other hand carrying out an immediate search without a warrant. Given probable cause to search, either course is reasonable under the Fourth Amendment. The blue station wagon could have been searched on the spot when it was stopped since there was prob-

Food for Thought

The Oregon Supreme Court has construed the Oregon Constitution as precluding use of the "automobile exception" to permit a warrantless search of a defendant's vehicle when the vehicle is parked, immobile, and unoccupied at the time that the police encounter it in connection with a crime. The court held that the "constitution requires a warrant so that a disinterested branch of government—the judicial branch—and not the branch that conducts the search—the executive branch—makes the decision as to whether there is probable cause to search." The court went on to note that a neutral magistrate's evaluation of probable cause continued to be a desired goal, and the court did not anticipate that the police would rely on the automobile exception when advances in technology permitted quick and efficient electronic issuance of warrants. Is the Oregon approach preferable to the *Dyson* court's per se rule? See *State v. Kurokawa-Lasciak,* 351 Or. 179, 263 P.3d 336 (2011).

---

[18] In addition, a telephonic warrant was only 20 cents and the nearest phone booth away.

able cause to search and it was a fleeting target for a search. The probable-cause factor still obtained at the station house and so did the mobility of the car. In that event there is little to choose in terms of practical consequences between an immediate search without a warrant and the car's immobilization until a warrant is obtained."

In *United States v. Johns*, 469 U.S. 478 (1985), the police stopped and searched a vehicle based on probable cause. The police removed packages from the vehicle, and searched the packages several days later. The Court upheld the search: "We do not think that delay in the execution of the warrantless search is necessarily unreasonable. We do not suggest that police officers may indefinitely retain possession of a vehicle and its contents before they complete a vehicle search. Respondents have not even alleged, much less proved, that the delay in the search of packages adversely affected legitimate interests protected by the Fourth Amendment." Justice Brennan dissented: "A warrantless search occurring three days after seizure of a package found in an automobile violates the Fourth Amendment. There is simply no justification for departing from the Fourth Amendment warrant requirement under the circumstances of this case; no exigency precluded reasonable efforts to obtain a warrant prior to the search of the packages in the warehouse."

Food for Thought

In light of later decisions, would you expect the *Coolidge* case to be decided the same way if it arose today? In *Coolidge v. New Hampshire*, 403 U.S. 443 (1971), petitioner was arrested for murder at his home. His car, which was sitting on the front driveway, was impounded and towed to the police station. The car was searched two days later, as well as a year later. Evidence obtained from the search was admitted at petitioner's trial. In a plurality opinion, the Court held that the trial court erred in admitting the evidence: "The police had known for some time of the probable role of the Pontiac car in the crime. Coolidge was aware that he was a suspect, but he had been extremely cooperative throughout the investigation, and there was no indication that he meant to flee. He had already had ample opportunity to destroy any evidence he thought incriminating. There is no suggestion that, on the night in question, the car was being used for any illegal purpose, and it was regularly parked in the driveway of his house. The opportunity for search was thus hardly "fleeting." The objects that the police are assumed to have had probable cause to search for in the car were neither stolen nor contraband nor dangerous. The word "automobile" is not a talisman in whose presence the Fourth Amendment fades away and disappears. In short, by no possible stretch of the legal imagination can this be made into a case where "it is not practicable to secure a warrant," and the "automobile exception," despite its label, is simply irrelevant." Is the *Coolidge* reasoning still good law?

Hypo 1: *The Staged Accident*

The police have probable cause to make a warrantless search of an automobile for illegal drugs. However, because the owner is part of a drug ring, the police are reluctant to make a forcible search for fear of tipping off other members of the ring. Instead, the police stage a phony automobile accident (that causes minor damage) using an undercover police officer who appears to be drunk, and who is purportedly "arrested" at the scene of the accident. The real suspects are told to leave the keys in the vehicle and sit in the back of a police cruiser. After the suspects are seated in the cruiser, a "thief" (really a police operative) steals the vehicle. The police then search the vehicle and return it to the suspects. Did the police conduct a permissible automobile search? See *United States v. Alverez-Tejeda*, 491 F.3d 1013 (9th Cir. 2007).

Hypo 2: *The Drug Investigation*

Possessing probable cause to believe that defendant is a drug pusher, police obtain a valid warrant to search his house. As the police arrive at the house, the suspected pusher arrives in his car. In addition to searching the house (which did not reveal evidence of illegal drug activity), the police wish to search the vehicle. Based on the fact that the police had probable cause to believe that defendant was a drug pusher, and that he had drugs in his house (a belief that turned out to be inaccurate), did they have probable cause to believe that he had illegal drugs in his car? Would your analysis be different if, during the search of the house, the suspect's girl friend informed police that defendant deals drugs out of his car? See *Commonwealth v. Fernandez*, 458 Mass. 137, 934 N.E.2d 810 (2010).

Hypo 3: *The Detached Camper*

A police officer, who observed "suspicious" behavior from a detached camper, comes closer in order to "observe" what is happening. As she does, she smells a strong odor of marijuana, leading the officer to believe that she has probable cause to believe that marijuana can be found in the vehicle. However, the camper is not hooked up to a vehicle, is in fact hooked up to an electrical outlet, and has its "stabilizing legs" extended and firmly in place. Can the officer search the vehicle without a warrant under the automobile exception? In other words, does that exception apply to a detached camper? See *State v. Otto*, 840 N.W.2d 589 (N.D. 2013).

California v. Acevedo

500 U.S. 565 (1991).

JUSTICE BLACKMUN delivered the opinion of the Court.

On October 28, 1987, Officer Coleman of the Santa Ana, Cal., Police Department received a telephone call from a federal drug enforcement agent in Hawaii. The agent informed Coleman that he had seized a package containing marijuana which was to have been delivered to the Federal Express Office in Santa Ana and which was addressed to J.R. Daza at 805 West Stevens Avenue in that city. The agent arranged to send the package to Coleman instead. Coleman then was to take the package to the Federal Express office and arrest the person who arrived to claim it. Coleman received the package on October 29, verified its contents, and took it to the Senior Operations Manager at the Federal Express office. At about 10:30 a.m. on October 30, a man, who identified himself as Jamie Daza, arrived to claim the package. He accepted it and drove to his apartment on West Stevens. He carried the package into the apartment.

At 11:45 a.m., officers observed Daza leave the apartment and drop the box and paper that had contained the marijuana into a trash bin. Coleman at that point left the scene to get a search warrant. About 12:05 p.m., the officers saw Richard St. George leave the apartment carrying a blue knapsack which appeared to be half full. The officers stopped him as he was driving off, searched the knapsack, and found 1 ½ pounds of marijuana.

At 12:30 p.m., respondent Charles Steven Acevedo arrived. He entered Daza's apartment, stayed for about 10 minutes, and reappeared carrying a brown paper bag that looked full. The officers noticed that the bag was the size of one of the wrapped marijuana packages sent from Hawaii. Acevedo walked to a silver Honda in the parking lot. He placed the bag in the trunk of the car and started to drive away. Fearing the loss of evidence, officers in a marked police car stopped him. They opened the trunk and the bag, and found marijuana.

Respondent was charged with possession of marijuana for sale. When his motion to suppress was denied, he pleaded guilty but appealed the denial of his suppression motion. The California Court of Appeal's concluded that the marijuana should have been suppressed. We granted certiorari to reexamine the law applicable to a closed container in an automobile, a subject that has troubled courts and law enforcement officers since it was first considered in *United States v. Chadwick*, 433 U.S. 1 (1977).

In *United States v. Ross*, 456 U.S. 798 (1982), we held that a warrantless search of an automobile could include a search of a container or package found inside the car when such a search was supported by probable cause. The warrantless search of Ross' car occurred after an informant told the police that he had seen Ross complete a drug transaction using drugs stored in the trunk of his car. The police stopped the car, searched it, and discovered in the trunk a brown paper bag containing drugs. We decided that the search of Ross' car was not unreasonable under the Fourth Amendment: "The scope of a warrantless search based on probable cause is no narrower—and no broader—than the scope of a search authorized by a warrant supported by probable cause." Thus, "if probable cause justifies the search of a lawfully stopped vehicle, it justifies the search of every part of the vehicle and its contents that may conceal the object of the search." In *Ross*, we clarified the scope of the *Carroll* doctrine as properly including a "probing search" of compartments and containers within the automobile so long as the search is supported by probable cause.

Ross distinguished the *Carroll* doctrine from the separate rule that governed the search of closed containers. The Court had announced this separate rule, unique to luggage and other closed packages, bags, and containers, in *United States v. Chadwick*, 433 U.S. 1 (1977). In *Chadwick*, federal narcotics agents had probable cause to believe that a 200-pound double-locked footlocker contained marijuana. The agents tracked the locker as the defendants removed it from a train and carried it through the station to a waiting car. As soon as the defendants lifted the locker into the trunk of the car, the agents arrested them, seized the locker, and searched it. In this Court, the United States did not contend that the locker's brief contact with the automobile's trunk sufficed to make the *Carroll* doctrine applicable. Rather, the United States urged that the search of movable luggage could be considered analogous to the search of an automobile. The Court rejected this argument because, it reasoned, a person expects more privacy in his luggage and personal effects than he does in his automobile. Moreover, it concluded that as "may often not be the case when automobiles are seized," secure storage facilities are usually available when the police seize luggage.

In *Arkansas v. Sanders*, 442 U.S. 753 (1979), the Court extended *Chadwick*'s rule to apply to a suitcase actually being transported in the trunk of a car. In *Sanders*, the police had probable cause to believe a suitcase contained marijuana. They watched as defendant placed the suitcase in the trunk of a taxi and was driven away. The police pursued the taxi for several blocks, stopped it, found the suitcase in the trunk, and searched it. *Sanders* stressed the heightened privacy expectation in personal luggage and concluded that the presence of luggage in an automobile did not diminish the owner's expectation of privacy in his personal items.

In *Ross*, the Court endeavored to distinguish *Carroll*, which governed the *Ross* automobile search, and *Chadwick*, which governed the *Sanders* automobile search. It held that the *Carroll* doctrine covered searches of automobiles when the police had probable cause to search an entire vehicle, but that the *Chadwick* doctrine governed searches of luggage when the officers had probable cause to search only a container within the vehicle. Thus, in a *Ross* situation, the police could conduct a reasonable search under the Fourth Amendment without obtaining a warrant, whereas in a *Sanders* situation, the police had to obtain a warrant before they searched. *Ross* held that closed containers encountered by the police during a warrantless search of a car pursuant to the automobile exception could also be searched. Thus, Ross took the critical step of saying that closed containers in cars could be searched without a warrant because of their presence within the automobile. Despite the protection that *Sanders* purported to extend to closed containers, the privacy interest in those closed containers yielded to the broad scope of an automobile search.

The facts in this case closely resemble the facts in *Ross*. In *Ross*, the police had probable cause to believe that drugs were stored in the trunk of a particular car. Here, the police had probable cause to believe that respondent was carrying marijuana in a bag in his car's trunk. Furthermore, in *Ross*, as here, the drugs in the trunk were contained in a brown paper bag.

Ross rejected *Chadwick*'s distinction between containers and cars. It concluded that the expectation of privacy in one's vehicle is equal to one's expectation of privacy in the container, and noted that "the privacy interests in a car's trunk or glove compartment may be no less than those in a movable container." It also recognized that it was arguable that the same exigent circumstances that permit a warrantless search of an automobile would justify the warrantless search of a movable container. In deference to the rule of *Chadwick* and *Sanders*, however, the Court put that question to one side.

We see no principled distinction in terms of either the privacy expectation or the exigent circumstances between the paper bag found by the police in *Ross* and the paper bag found by the police here. Furthermore, by attempting to distinguish between a container for which the police are specifically searching and a container which they come across in a car, we have provided only minimal protection for privacy and have impeded effective law enforcement.

The line between probable cause to search a vehicle and probable cause to search a package in that vehicle is not always clear, and separate rules that govern the two objects to be searched may enable the police to broaden their power to make warrantless searches and disserve privacy interests. If the police know that they may open a bag only if they are actually searching the entire car, they may search more extensively than they otherwise would in order to establish the general probable cause required by *Ross*.

To the extent that the *Chadwick-Sanders* rule protects privacy, its protection is minimal. Law enforcement officers may seize a container and hold it until they obtain a search warrant. "Since the police, by hypothesis, have probable cause to seize the property, we can assume that a warrant will be routinely forthcoming in the overwhelming majority of cases.".

Finally, the search of a paper bag intrudes far less on individual privacy than does the incursion sanctioned long ago in *Carroll*. In that case, prohibition agents slashed the upholstery of the automobile. This Court nonetheless found their search to be reasonable under the Fourth Amendment. If destroying the interior of an automobile is not unreasonable, we cannot conclude that looking inside a closed container is. In light of the minimal protection to privacy afforded by the *Chadwick-Sanders* rule, and our serious doubt whether that rule substantially serves privacy interests, we now hold that the Fourth Amendment does not compel separate treatment for an automobile search that extends only to a container within the vehicle.

The *Chadwick-Sanders* rule not only has failed to protect privacy but also has confused courts and police officers and impeded effective law enforcement. The discrepancy between the two rules has led to confusion for law enforcement officers. For example, when an officer, who has developed probable cause to believe that a vehicle contains drugs, begins to search the vehicle and immediately discovers a closed container, which rule applies? Defendant will argue that the fact that the officer first chose to search the container indicates that his probable cause extended only to the container and that *Chadwick* and *Sanders* therefore require a warrant. On the other hand, the fact that the officer first chose to search in the most obvious location should not restrict the propriety of the search. The *Chadwick* rule, as applied in *Sanders*, has devolved into an anomaly such that the more likely the police are to discover drugs in a container, the less authority they have to search it. We have noted the virtue of providing " 'clear and unequivocal' guidelines to the law enforcement profession." The *Chadwick-Sanders* rule is the antithesis of a " 'clear and unequivocal' guideline."

The *Chadwick* dissenters predicted that the container rule would have "the perverse result of allowing fortuitous circumstances to control the outcome" of various searches. The rule was so confusing that within two years after *Chadwick*, this Court found it necessary to expound on the meaning of that decision and explain its application to luggage in general. It is better to adopt one clear-cut rule to govern automobile searches and eliminate the warrant requirement for closed containers set forth in *Sanders*. The interpretation of the *Carroll* doctrine set forth in *Ross* now applies to all searches of containers found in an automobile. In other words, the police may search without a warrant if their search is supported by probable cause.

Our holding today neither extends the *Carroll* doctrine nor broadens the scope of the permissible automobile search. It remains a "cardinal principle that 'searches conducted outside the judicial process, without prior approval by judge or magistrate, are *per se* unreasonable under the Fourth Amendment—subject only to a few specifically established and well-delineated exceptions.' " We held in *Ross*: "The exception recognized in *Carroll* is unquestionably one that is 'specifically established and well delineated.' "

We therefore interpret *Carroll* as providing one rule to govern all automobile searches. The police may search an automobile and the containers within it where they have probable cause to believe contraband or evidence is contained.

JUSTICE STEVENS, with whom JUSTICE MARSHALL joins, dissenting.

In *Chadwick*, we held that the privacy interest in luggage is "substantially greater than in an automobile." Indeed, luggage is specifically intended to safeguard the privacy of personal effects, unlike an automobile, "whose primary function is transportation." We then held that the mobility of luggage did not justify creating an additional exception to the Warrant Clause. Unlike an automobile, luggage can easily be seized and detained pending judicial approval of a search. Once the police have luggage "under their exclusive control, there is not the slightest danger that the luggage or its contents could be removed before a valid search warrant could be obtained. It is unreasonable to undertake the additional and greater intrusion of a search without a warrant".

To the extent there was any "anomaly" in our prior jurisprudence, the Court has "cured" it at the expense of creating a more serious paradox. For surely it is anomalous to prohibit a search of a briefcase while the owner is carrying it exposed on a public street yet to permit a search once the owner has placed the briefcase in the locked trunk of his car. One's privacy interest in one's luggage can certainly not be diminished by one's removing it from a public thoroughfare and placing it—out of sight—in a privately owned vehicle. Nor is the danger that evidence will escape increased if the luggage is in a car rather than on the street. In either location, if the police have probable cause, they are authorized to seize the luggage and to detain it until they obtain judicial approval for a search. Even if the warrant requirement does inconvenience the police to some extent, that fact does not distinguish this constitutional requirement from any other procedural protection secured by the Bill of Rights. It is merely a part of the price that our society must pay in order to preserve its freedom.

Hypo 1: *Scope of the Automobile Exception*

Does the automobile exception authorize a broader search or a more narrow one? Does the answer to this question depend on circumstances? Consider the following facts in which the police have probable cause to believe that a suspect is carrying drugs: a) in his glove compartment; b) in the trunk of his car; c) in the left front wheel well; d) in the engine compartment; e) somewhere in the vehicle. Where may the police search in each of these situations?

Food for Thought

Suppose that the police have probable cause to believe that a woman in this criminal procedure class is carrying heroin in her purse. Absent exigent circumstances, may the police make a warrantless search of the purse when the woman is outside her vehicle? Does the situation change when she enters the vehicle with the purse?

Hypo 2: *The Marijuana Odor*

Just before midnight, Trooper Larsen notices that a vehicle driven by Tibbles has a defective taillight. When he approaches the car, he detects a strong marijuana odor. Although Tibbles produces a valid driver's license, he cannot find his vehicle registration. Larsen then asks Tibbles to step out of his vehicle, and Tibbles complies. The trooper then informs Tibbles that he could smell marijuana and Tibbles replies that he does not have any in his possession. Trooper Larsen then searches Tibbles's person, but does not find either marijuana or drug paraphernalia. In response to the trooper's questioning, Tibbles denies smoking marijuana that day. Does the officer have probable cause to search the vehicle? See *State v. Tibbles*, 169 Wash.2d 364, 236 P.3d 885 (En Banc 2010).

5. Inventory Exception

There is also an "inventory" exception to the warrant requirement. The most common inventory search occurs when the police impound a vehicle. The following case analyzes this type of search.

Colorado v. Bertine

479 U.S. 367 (1987).

CHIEF JUSTICE REHNQUIST delivered the opinion of the Court.

A police officer in Boulder, Colorado, arrested respondent Steven Lee Bertine for driving while under the influence of alcohol. After Bertine was taken into custody and before the arrival of a tow truck to take Bertine's van to an impoundment lot,[19] a backup officer inventoried the contents of the van. The officer opened a closed backpack in which he found controlled substances, cocaine paraphernalia, and a large amount of cash. Bertine was subsequently charged with driving while under the

---

[19] Section 7–7–2(a)(4) of the Boulder Revised Code authorizes police officers to impound vehicles when drivers are taken into custody. * * *

influence of alcohol, unlawful possession of cocaine with intent to dispense, sell, and distribute, and unlawful possession of methaqualone. We are asked to decide whether the Fourth Amendment prohibits the State from proving these charges with the evidence discovered during the inventory of Bertine's van. We hold that it does not.

The backup officer inventoried the van in accordance with local police procedures, which require a detailed inspection and inventory of impounded vehicles. He found the backpack directly behind the frontseat of the van. Inside the pack, the officer observed a nylon bag containing metal canisters. Opening the canisters, the officer discovered that they contained cocaine, methaqualone tablets, cocaine paraphernalia, and $700 in cash. In an outside zippered pouch of the backpack, he also found $210 in cash in a sealed envelope. After completing the inventory of the van, the officer had the van towed to an impound lot and brought the backpack, money, and contraband to the police station.

The Supreme Court of Colorado affirmed a lower court ruling granting Bertine's motion to suppress. The Colorado Supreme Court recognized that in *South Dakota v. Opperman*, 428 U.S. 364 (1976), we held inventory searches of automobiles to be consistent with the Fourth Amendment, and in *Illinois v. Lafayette*, 462 U.S. 640 (1983), we had held that the inventory search of personal effects of an arrestee at a police station was also permissible under that Amendment. The Supreme Court of Colorado felt, that our decisions holding searches of closed trunks and suitcases to violate the Fourth Amendment, meant that *Opperman* and *Lafayette* did not govern this case. We granted certiorari.

Inventory searches are now a well-defined exception to the warrant requirement of the Fourth Amendment. An inventory search may be "reasonable" under the Fourth Amendment even though it is not conducted pursuant to a warrant based upon probable cause. In *Opperman*, this Court assessed the reasonableness of an inventory search of the glove compartment in an abandoned automobile impounded by the police. We found that inventory procedures serve to protect an owner's property while it is in the custody of the police, to insure against claims of lost, stolen, or vandalized property, and to guard the police from danger. In light of these strong governmental interests and the diminished expectation of privacy in an automobile, we upheld the search. We observed that our cases accorded deference to police caretaking procedures designed to secure and protect vehicles and their contents within police custody.

In the present case, as in *Opperman* and *Lafayette*, there was no showing that the police, who were following standardized procedures, acted in bad faith or for the sole purpose of investigation. In addition, the governmental interests justifying the inventory searches in *Opperman* and *Lafayette* are nearly the same as those which obtain here. In each case, the police were potentially responsible for the property taken into their custody. By securing the property, the police protected the property from unauthorized interference. Knowledge of the precise nature of the property helped guard against claims of theft, vandalism, or negligence. Such knowledge also helped to avert any danger to police or others that may have been posed by the property.

The Supreme Court of Colorado opined that *Lafayette* was not controlling because there was no danger of introducing contraband or weapons into a jail facility. *Lafayette*, however, did not suggest that the station-house setting of the inventory search was critical to our holding in that case. Both in the present case and in *Lafayette*, the common governmental interests described above were served by the inventory searches.

The Supreme Court of Colorado also expressed the view that the search in this case was unreasonable because Bertine's van was towed to a secure, lighted facility and because Bertine himself could have been offered the opportunity to make other arrangements for the safekeeping of his property. But the security of the storage facility does not completely eliminate the need for inventorying; the police may still wish to protect themselves or the owners of the lot against false claims of theft or dangerous instrumentalities. While giving Bertine an opportunity to make alternative arrangements would undoubtedly have been possible, reasonable police regulations relating to inventory procedures administered in good faith satisfy the Fourth Amendment, even though courts might as a matter of hindsight be able to devise equally reasonable rules requiring a different procedure.[20]

The Supreme Court of Colorado thought it necessary to require that police, before inventorying a container, weigh the strength of the individual's privacy interest in the container against the possibility that the container might serve as a repository for dangerous or valuable items. We think that such a requirement is contrary to our decisions: "When a legitimate search is under way, and when its purpose and its limits have been precisely defined, nice distinctions between closets, drawers, and containers, in the case of a home, or between glove compartments, upholstered seats, trunks, and wrapped packages, in the case of a vehicle, must give way to the interest in the prompt and efficient completion of the task at hand." *United States v. Ross*, 456 U.S., at 821.

We reaffirm these principles here: "a single familiar standard is essential to guide police officers who have only limited time and expertise to reflect on and balance the social and individual interests involved in the specific circumstances they confront." *Lafayette, supra*, 462 U.S., at 648.

Bertine argues that the inventory search of his van was unconstitutional because departmental regulations gave the police officers discretion to choose between impounding his van and parking and locking it in a public parking place.

---

[20] The trial court found that the Police Department's procedures mandated the opening of closed containers and the listing of their contents. Our decisions have always adhered to the requirement that inventories be conducted according to standardized criteria. * * *

Nothing in *Opperman* or *Lafayette* prohibits the exercise of police discretion so long as that discretion is exercised according to standard criteria and on the basis of something other than suspicion of evidence of criminal activity. Here, the discretion afforded the Boulder police was exercised in light of standardized criteria, related to the feasibility and appropriateness of parking and locking a vehicle rather than impounding it.[21] There was no showing that the police chose to impound Bertine's van in order to investigate suspected criminal activity.

While both *Opperman* and *Lafayette* are distinguishable from the present case, we think that the principles enunciated in those cases govern the present one. The judgment of the Supreme Court of Colorado is therefore

Reversed.

JUSTICE BLACKMUN, with whom JUSTICE POWELL and JUSTICE O'CONNOR join, concurring.

Absence of discretion ensures that inventory searches will not be used as a purposeful and general means of discovering evidence of crime. It is permissible for police officers to open closed containers in an inventory search only if they are following standard police procedures that mandate the opening of such containers in every impounded vehicle. The Police Department's standard procedures did mandate the opening of closed containers and the listing of their contents.

JUSTICE MARSHALL, with whom JUSTICE BRENNAN joins, dissenting.

No standardized criteria limit a Boulder police officer's discretion. According to a departmental directive, after placing a driver under arrest, an officer has three options for disposing of the vehicle. First, he can allow a third party to take custody. Second, the officer or the driver (depending on the nature of the arrest) may take the car to the nearest public parking facility, lock it, and take the keys. Finally, the officer can do what was done in this case: impound the vehicle, and search and inventory its contents, including closed containers.

Under the first option, the police have no occasion to search the automobile. Under the "park and lock" option, "closed containers that give no indication of containing either valuables or a weapon may not be opened and the contents searched (*i.e.*, inventoried)." Only if the police choose the third option are they entitled to search closed containers in the vehicle. Where the vehicle is not itself

---

[21] Boulder Police Department procedures establish several conditions that must be met before an officer may pursue the park-and-lock alternative. For example, police may not park and lock the vehicle where there is reasonable risk of damage or vandalism to the vehicle or where the approval of the arrestee cannot be obtained. Not only do such conditions circumscribe the discretion of individual officers, but they also protect the vehicle and its contents and minimize claims of property loss.

evidence of a crime, as in this case, the police apparently have totally unbridled discretion as to which procedure to use. Consistent with this conclusion, Officer Reichenbach testified that such decisions were left to the discretion of the officer on the scene.

Once a Boulder police officer has made this initial discretionary decision to impound a vehicle, he is given little guidance as to which areas to search and what sort of items to inventory. The arresting officer testified at the suppression hearing as to what items would be inventoried: "That would I think be very individualistic as far as what an officer may or may not go into." In application, these so-called procedures left the breadth of the "inventory" to the whim of the individual officer.

Inventory searches are not subject to the warrant requirement because they are conducted by the government as part of a "community caretaking" function, "totally divorced from the detection, investigation, or acquisition of evidence relating to the violation of a criminal statute." *Cady v. Dombrowski*, 413 U.S., at 441. Standardized procedures are necessary to ensure that this narrow exception is not improperly used to justify, after the fact, a warrantless investigative foray. Accordingly, to invalidate a search that is conducted without established procedures, it is not necessary to establish that the police actually acted in bad faith, or that the inventory was in fact a "pretext." Boulder's discretionary scheme is unreasonable because of the " 'grave danger' of abuse of discretion."

The Court greatly overstates the justifications for the inventory exception to the Fourth Amendment. *Opperman* relied on three governmental interests to justify the inventory search of an unlocked glove compartment in an automobile. The majority finds that "nearly the same" interests obtain in this case. The use of secure impoundment facilities effectively eliminates this concern.[22] As to false claims, "inventories are not a completely effective means of discouraging false claims, since there remains the possibility of accompanying such claims with an assertion that an item was stolen prior to the inventory or was intentionally omitted from the police records." Officer Reichenbach's inventory in this case would not have protected the police against claims lodged by respondent, false or otherwise. Indeed, the trial court's characterization of the inventory as "slip-shod" is the height of understatement. The third interest—protecting the police from potential danger—failed to receive the endorsement of a majority of the Court in *Opperman*. There is nothing in the nature of the offense for which respondent was arrested that suggests he was likely to be carrying weapons, explosives, or other dangerous items. Moreover, opening closed containers to inventory the contents can only increase the risk. "No sane individual inspects for booby-traps by simply

---

[22] Respondent's vehicle was taken to a lighted, private storage lot with a locked 6-foot fence. The lot was patrolled by private security officers and police, and nothing had ever been stolen from a vehicle in the lot.

opening the container." Thus, only the government's interest in protecting the owner's property actually justifies an inventory search of an impounded vehicle. I fail to see how preservation can even be asserted as a justification for the search in this case. The owner was "present to make other arrangements for the safekeeping of his belongings," yet the police made no attempt to ascertain whether in fact he wanted them to "safeguard" his property. Since respondent was charged with a traffic offense, he was unlikely to remain in custody for more than a few hours. He might well have been willing to leave his valuables unattended in the locked van for such a short period of time.

The Court completely ignores respondent's expectation of privacy in his backpack. Whatever his expectation of privacy in his automobile generally, our prior decisions clearly establish that he retained a reasonable expectation of privacy in the backpack and its contents. Indeed, the Boulder police officer who conducted the inventory acknowledged that backpacks commonly serve as repositories for personal effects. Thus, even if the governmental interests in this case were the same as those in *Opperman*, they would nonetheless be outweighed by respondent's comparatively greater expectation of privacy in his luggage.

Point for Discussion

Departmental Policies

In *Florida v. Wells*, 495 U.S. 1 (1990), Wells was arrested for driving under the influence and his car was impounded. An inventory search at the impoundment facility revealed two marijuana cigarettes. It also turned up a locked suitcase which was found to contain a considerable quantity of marijuana. The record contained no evidence of any Highway Patrol policy on the opening of closed containers during inventory searches. The Court upheld the Florida Supreme Court's decision to exclude the evidence: "An inventory search must not be a ruse for a general rummaging in order to discover incriminating evidence. There is no reason to insist that inventory searches be conducted in a totally mechanical 'all or nothing' fashion. A police officer may be allowed latitude to determine whether a particular container should or should not be opened in light of the nature of the search and characteristics of the container itself. While policies of opening all containers or of opening no containers are unquestionably permissible, it would be equally permissible to allow the opening of closed containers whose contents officers are unable to ascertain from examining the containers' exteriors. The Florida Highway Patrol had no policy whatever with respect to the opening of closed containers encountered during an inventory search. Absent such a policy, the instant search was not sufficiently regulated to satisfy the Fourth Amendment."

Take Note

In order for an inventory search to be legal, the vehicle must have been legally impounded. Rules vary regarding the circumstances under which an impoundment is permitted. In *Cardwell v. Commonwealth*, 639 S.W.2d 549 (Ky.App.1982), defendant burglarized a home and stole guns and knives. Fleeing the scene, defendant was involved in an automobile accident and taken to a hospital, his car was left by the side of the road. Although defendant told the police that his father would retrieve the car, the officer towed the vehicle since it protruded onto the road and constituted a hazard. Because the trunk's lock was broken, the officer searched the trunk to remove valuables and found two shotguns and a rifle marked with the name of the burglary victim. The officer then went to the victim's house where he found evidence of a break-in. When the officer returned to the car, he found one of the burglary victim's knives. Cardwell was arrested at the hospital where he later confessed to the crimes. The Court concluded that the impoundment was proper: "The vehicle was a safety hazard and had to be removed from the scene as soon as possible because of its damaged condition, its close proximity to the roadway, and its location on a curve with short visibility. These circumstances cause other motorists to be distracted, to look and gawk out of concerns for rendering aid or curiosity. It impedes traffic flow and constitutes a hazard upon the highway. The arrangement whereby his father would come from Louisville would create several hours delay while the vehicle was abandoned and exposed to the public on the roadway. The officer acted properly by ordering the impoundment and removal by a local wrecker. With the vehicle impounded and in a position to be removed from the scene, the trooper innocently discovered the fruits of the appellant's crimes. Finding the trunk lid loose, without a lock, the trooper did what we would expect a peace officer to do under like circumstances: to protect property as well as citizens. Keep in mind, the appellant was not present. He was on his way to the hospital by ambulance." In *Florida v. White*, 526 U.S. 559 (1999), the police had probable cause to believe that a vehicle contained contraband. They seized the vehicle and subjected it to an inventory search. The Court held that the police do not need a warrant to seize an automobile from a public place when they have probable cause to believe that it contains forfeitable contraband.

Food for Thought

At 3:00 a.m., a police officer spots a heavily loaded car in a residential area. May the police officer pull the motorist over and inventory the contents of the car? Why? Why not?

Hypo 1: *Proof Requirements*

Do the police need either probable cause or reasonable suspicion in order to conduct an inventory search?

Food for Thought

Some state supreme courts restrict the availability of inventory searches under their state constitutions. *Wagner v. Commonwealth*, 581 S.W.2d 352 (Ky. 1979), involved a rape that occurred in Wagner's car. Shortly after the rape, the police apprehended Wagner and allowed him to lock and secure his car. However, when the victim pointed to her scarves and a spot of blood on the seat which she said was her blood. the police took Wagner to police headquarters for questioning and impounded his car. After Wagner was formally arrested, the police conducted an "inventory" search of his car "looking for evidence." The Kentucky Supreme Court invalidated the impoundment and the inventory search:

> "A vehicle may be impounded without a warrant in only four situations: 1) The owner or permissive user consents to the impoundment; 2)The vehicle, if not removed, constitutes a danger to other persons or property or the public safety[23] and the owner or permissive user cannot reasonably arrange for alternate means of removal; 3) The police have probable cause to believe both that the vehicle constitutes an instrumentality or fruit of a crime and that absent immediate impoundment the vehicle will be removed by a third party; or 4) The police have probable cause to believe that the vehicle contains evidence of a crime and that absent immediate impoundment the evidence will be lost or destroyed.

> So long as the only potential danger that might ensue from non-impoundment is danger to the safety of the vehicle and its contents no public interest exists to justify impoundment of the vehicle without the consent of its owner or permissive user. The driver, even though in police custody, is competent to decide whether to park the vehicle in a "bad" neighborhood and risk damage through vandalism or allow the police to take custody. Only when the vehicle if not removed poses a danger to other persons, property or the public safety does there exist a public interest to justify impoundment if the owner or permissive user is unable to reasonably arrange for a third party to provide for the vehicle's removal.

> Mere legal custody of an automobile by law enforcement officials does not automatically create a right to rummage about its interior. A routine police inventory of the contents of an impounded vehicle constitutes a substantial invasion of the zone of privacy of its owner or permissive user. It is an invasion additional to the intrusion upon his privacy interests occasioned by the impoundment itself.

---

[23] An illegally parked vehicle would constitute a danger to public safety under this exception to the warrant requirement and could be impounded.

Such an inventory is impermissible unless the owner or permissive user consents or substantial necessities grounded upon public safety justify the search.

If a vehicle is legally impounded and its owner or permissive user is present or otherwise known at the time the vehicle is seized no such need is ordinarily manifest. If the owner or permissive user does not consent to the routine inventory he will assume the risk that items obtained in the vehicle will be lost or stolen. The police merely lock up the vehicle and leave it in place until the owner or permissive user makes suitable arrangements for its removal. Concomitant with this right to prevent a routine inventory is the owner's or permissive user's right to have a representative present during any inventory that is authorized and his right to limit the inventory to only specific portions of the vehicle.

If the police have probable cause, they can prevent the removal of the vehicle until a reasonable time has elapsed in which a warrant can be secured. Because the vehicle is in police custody there is no danger that any evidence it contains will be lost or stolen and hence no necessity to depart from the warrant requirement. If a warrant cannot be obtained no inventory can be undertaken unless the owner or permissive user consents. In this case the owner-driver of the seized vehicle was at police headquarters at the time of impoundment. Because neither a search warrant nor his consent was obtained prior rummaging through the interior of the car constituted an illegal search even though the car had been lawfully impounded. The evidence will be suppressed."

In *Commonwealth v. Lagenella*, 83 A.3d 94 (Pa. 2013), the Pennsylvania Supreme Court interpreted Pennsylvania law as providing that a car that has been left legally parked following an arrest may not be impounded and inventoried when it does not present a danger to efficient or safe traffic flow or otherwise endanger the public. Are these state court approaches preferable?

Hypo 2: *The Permissibility of Impoundment*

Defendant is stopped for "reckless" driving after police officers observe him driving in excess of the speed limit and weaving in and out of traffic. Defendant pulls over into a legal parking spot. Because of the dangerous nature of his conduct, the police officer decides to arrest him. May the police have defendant's car towed to a police impound lot and conduct an inventory search? Should it matter whether the city or the police department have a policy on whether, and when, vehicles should be impounded and towed to impoundment lots? See *Baxter v. State*, 238 P.3d 934 (Okla. Crim. App. 2010).

Hypo 3: *Departmental Policies*

Ford was arrested and jailed for driving on a suspended driver's license. Since Ford's vehicle was obstructing traffic, the police officer called a tow truck to remove it. In conformity with Charleston Police Department "policy," the officer conducted an inventory search of the vehicle before releasing it to the custody of the tow truck driver. The search yielded a sawed-off shotgun, with a barrel length of 9 ½ inches and an overall length of 17 ½ inches. Subsequent investigation revealed that this weapon was not registered, and Ford was charged with violating the National Firearms Act. Ford challenges the inventory search on the basis that it was "a guise to justify a criminal investigatory search." Ford points to the fact that the Department had no written policies regarding inventory searches, but rather only "customary" policies followed in doing such searches. Must a departmental policy be in writing to satisfy *Bertine*? On behalf of Ford, how can you argue that the policy must be in writing? How might the state respond? See *United States v. Ford*, 986 F.2d 57 (4th Cir.1993), and *Clark v. Commonwealth*, 868 S.W.2d 101 (Ky.App.1993).

Hypo 4: *More on Impoundment*

A drug store was robbed of money and restricted drugs. The next morning, two police officers see an automobile make a quick turn at an intersection and travel past them in the opposite direction. The officers follow the car which speeds up and disappears. Shortly thereafter the officers see Helm walking on the sidewalk and stop him. After learning Helm's name, the officers ask him about the location of the car that he was driving. Helm replies, "What car?" When the police run a computer check and determine that there is an outstanding robbery warrant for Helm's arrest, they arrest him and take him to jail where a search reveals a single car key. Afterwards, the officers return to the area and find a 1978 silver Monte Carlo with a warm motor less than a block from the place of arrest. The key operates the ignition. Clothing and paraphernalia are observed lying in the back seat. The officers tow the vehicle for "safekeeping" based on police policy, as well as because they had no way to contact the owner and the vehicle was in a high crime area. The officers search the trunk, which did not contain a lock, and find a paper bag containing money and bottles of restricted drugs from the recently robbed drug store. Was the vehicle properly impounded? See *Helm v. Commonwealth*, 813 S.W.2d 816 (1991).

Hypo 5: *Inventorying the Locked Bag*

A police officer, who finds Vanya trespassing on school property, decides to drive the boy home in his police cruiser. As part of his standard procedure, the officer frisks the boy before placing him in the cruiser. During the frisk, the officer uncovers a 4 inch by 5 inch hard item, with a 90 degree angle, in the small of the boy's back. The boy reacts hostilely when the officer touches it. The object turns out to be a locked bag. The officer eventually opens the bag and finds money and marijuana. The police department's inventory policy provides, "Any container or article found on an arrestee's person or carried by him shall be opened and its contents inventoried." The juvenile argues that the policy is impermissibly vague because it "is silent with respect to locked containers versus closed containers." Was it permissible for the police to open the locked container? Does it matter whether they found a key to the bag, or whether they were forced to damage the bag in order to open it? See *Commonwealth v. Vanya V*, 75 Mass. App. Ct. 370, 914 N.E.2d 339 (2009).

6. Consent

The consent exception is not really an "exception" to the warrant requirement. Any constitutional right can be waived, and citizens can waive their Fourth Amendment right to be free from governmental searches and seizures. The courts have struggled to determine what constitutes "consent."

Schneckloth v. Bustamonte

412 U.S. 218 (1973).

MR. JUSTICE STEWART delivered the opinion of the Court.

While on routine patrol in Sunnyvale, California, at approximately 2:40 in the morning, Police Officer James Rand stopped an automobile when he observed that one headlight and its license plate light were burned out. Six men were in the vehicle. Joe Alcala and respondent, Robert Bustamonte, were in the front seat with Joe Gonzales, the driver. Three older men were seated in the rear. When Gonzales could not produce a driver's license, Rand asked if any of the other five had any evidence of identification. Only Alcala produced a license, and he explained that the car was his brother's. After the six occupants had stepped out of the car at the officer's request and after two additional policemen arrived, Officer Rand asked

Alcala if he could search the car. Alcala replied, "Sure, go ahead." Prior to the search no one was threatened with arrest and, according to Officer Rand's uncontradicted testimony, it "was all very congenial at this time." Gonzales testified that Alcala actually helped in the search of the car, by opening the trunk and glove compartment. In Gonzales' words: "The police officer asked Joe (Alcala), he goes, 'Does the trunk open?' And Joe said, 'Yes.' He went to the car and got the keys and opened up the trunk." Wadded up under the left rear seat, the police officers found three checks that had been stolen from a car wash. The trial judge denied the motion to suppress, and the checks were admitted in evidence at Bustamonte's trial. He was convicted.

A search authorized by consent is wholly valid but the State has the burden of proving that the consent was, in fact, freely and voluntarily given. *Bumper v. North Carolina*, 391 U.S. 543, 548. The precise question in this case, then, is what must the prosecution prove to demonstrate that a consent was "voluntarily" given. The most extensive judicial exposition of the meaning of "voluntariness" has been developed in those cases in which the Court has had to determine the "voluntariness" of a defendant's confession for purposes of the Fourteenth Amendment. The significant fact about all of these decisions is that none of them turned on the presence or absence of a single controlling criterion; each reflected a careful scrutiny of all the surrounding circumstances. In none of them did the Court rule that the Due Process Clause required the prosecution to prove as part of its initial burden that the defendant knew he had a right to refuse to answer the questions that were put. While the state of the accused's mind, and the failure of the police to advise the accused of his rights, were certainly factors to be evaluated in assessing the "voluntariness" of an accused's responses, they were not in and of themselves determinative.

The question whether a consent to a search was in fact "voluntary" or was the product of duress or coercion, express or implied, is a question of fact to be determined from the totality of all the circumstances. While knowledge of the right to refuse consent is one factor to be taken into account, the government need not establish such knowledge as the *sine qua non* of an effective consent. As with police questioning, two competing concerns must be accommodated in determining the meaning of a "voluntary" consent—the legitimate need for such searches and the equally important requirement of assuring the absence of coercion.

In situations where the police have some evidence of illicit activity, but lack probable cause to arrest or search, a search authorized by a valid consent may be the only means of obtaining important and reliable evidence. In the present case, while the police had reason to stop the car for traffic violations, the State does not contend that there was probable cause to search the vehicle or that the search was incident to a valid arrest of any of the occupants. Yet, the search yielded tangible evidence that served as a basis for a prosecution, and provided some assurance that others, wholly innocent of the crime, were not mistakenly brought to trial. In those cases where there is probable cause to arrest or search, but where the police lack a warrant, a consent search may still be valuable. If the search is conducted and proves fruitless, that in itself may convince the police that an arrest with its possible stigma and embarrassment is unnecessary, or that a far more extensive search pursuant to a warrant is not justified. In short, a search pursuant to consent may result in considerably less inconvenience for the subject of the search, and, properly conducted, is a constitutionally permissible and wholly legitimate aspect of effective police activity.

But the Fourth and Fourteenth Amendments require that a consent not be coerced, by explicit or implicit means, by implied threat or covert force. For, no matter how subtly the coercion was applied, the resulting "consent" would be no more than a pretext for the unjustified police intrusion against which the Fourth Amendment is directed.

The problem of reconciling the recognized legitimacy of consent searches with the requirement that they be free from any aspect of official coercion cannot be resolved by any infallible touchstone. To approve such searches without the most careful scrutiny would sanction the possibility of official coercion; to place artificial restrictions upon such searches would jeopardize their basic validity. Just as was true with confessions, the requirement of a "voluntary" consent reflects a fair accommodation of the constitutional requirements involved. In examining all the surrounding circumstances to determine if in fact the consent to search was coerced, account must be taken of subtly coercive police questions, as well as the possibly vulnerable subjective state of the person who consents. Those searches that are the product of police coercion can thus be filtered out without undermining the continuing validity of consent searches. In sum, there is no reason for us to depart in the area of consent searches, from the traditional definition of "voluntariness."

The approach of the Court of Appeals, that the State must affirmatively prove that the subject of the search knew that he had a right to refuse consent, would, in practice, create serious doubt whether consent searches could be conducted. There might be rare cases where it could be proved that a person in fact affirmatively knew of his right to refuse—such as a case where he announced to the police that if he didn't sign the consent form, "you police are going to get a search warrant;" or a case where by prior experience and training a person had clearly and convincingly demonstrated such knowledge. But more commonly where there was no evidence of any coercion, explicit or implicit, the prosecution would be unable to demonstrate that the subject of the search in fact had known of his right to refuse consent. The very object of the inquiry—the nature of a person's subjective understanding—underlines the difficulty of the prosecution's burden. Any defendant who was the subject of a search authorized solely by his consent could effectively frustrate the introduction into evidence of the fruits of that search by simply failing to testify that he in fact knew he could refuse to consent. And the near impossibility of meeting this prosecutorial burden suggests why this Court has never accepted any such litmus-paper test of voluntariness.

One alternative that would go far toward proving that the subject of a search did know he had a right to refuse consent would be to advise him of that right before eliciting his consent. That suggestion has been almost universally repudiated by both federal and state courts, and rightly so. It would be thoroughly impractical to impose on the normal consent search the detailed requirements of an effective warning. Consent searches are part of the standard investigatory techniques of law enforcement agencies. They normally occur on the highway, or in a person's home or office, and under informal and unstructured conditions. The circumstances that prompt the initial request to search may develop quickly or be a logical extension of investigative police questioning. The police may seek to investigate further suspicious circumstances or to follow up leads developed in questioning persons at the scene of a crime. These situations are a far cry from the structured atmosphere of a trial where, assisted by counsel, a defendant is informed of his trial rights. While surely a closer question, these situations are still immeasurably, far removed from "custodial interrogation" where, in *Miranda v. Arizona*, we found that the Constitution required certain now familiar warnings as a prerequisite to police interrogation. Consequently, we cannot accept the position that proof of knowledge of the right to refuse consent is a necessary prerequisite to demonstrating a "voluntary" consent. Rather it is only by analyzing all the circumstances of an individual consent that it can be ascertained whether in fact it was voluntary or coerced. It is this careful sifting of the unique facts and circumstances of each case that is evidenced in our prior decisions involving consent searches.

It is argued that to establish a "waiver" the State must demonstrate "an intentional relinquishment or abandonment of a known right or privilege." Our cases do not reflect an uncritical demand for a knowing and intelligent waiver in every situation where a person has failed to invoke a constitutional protection. Almost without exception, the requirement of a knowing and intelligent waiver has been applied only to those rights which the Constitution guarantees to a criminal defendant in order to preserve a fair trial. Hence, the standard of a knowing and intelligent waiver has most often been applied to test the validity of a waiver of counsel, either at trial, or upon a guilty plea. The Court has also applied the criteria to assess the effectiveness of a waiver of other trial rights such as the right to confrontation, to a jury trial, and to a speedy trial, and the right to be free from twice being placed in jeopardy. Guilty pleas have been carefully scrutinized to determine whether the accused knew and understood all the rights to which he would be entitled at trial, and that he had intentionally chosen to forgo them. The Court has evaluated the knowing and intelligent nature of the waiver of trial rights in trial-type situations, such as the waiver of the privilege against compulsory self-incrimination before an administrative agency or a congressional committee, or the waiver of counsel in a juvenile proceeding. The guarantees afforded a criminal defendant at trial also protect him at certain stages before the actual trial, and any alleged waiver must meet the strict standard of an intentional relinquishment of a "known" right. But the "trial" guarantees that have been applied to the "pretrial" stage of the criminal process are similarly designed to protect the fairness of the trial itself.

There is a vast difference between those rights that protect a fair criminal trial and the rights guaranteed under the Fourth Amendment. Nothing, either in the purposes behind requiring a "knowing" and "intelligent" waiver of trial rights, or in the practical application of such a requirement suggests that it ought to be extended to the constitutional guarantee against unreasonable searches and seizures. A strict standard of waiver has been applied to those rights guaranteed to a criminal defendant to insure that he will be accorded the greatest possible opportunity to utilize every facet of the constitutional model of a fair criminal trial. Any trial conducted in derogation of that model leaves open the possibility that the trial reached an unfair result precisely because all the protections specified in the Constitution were not provided. A prime example is the right to counsel. Without that right, a wholly innocent accused faces the real and substantial danger that simply because of his lack of legal expertise he may be convicted. The Constitution requires that every effort be made to see to it that a defendant in a criminal case has not unknowingly relinquished the basic protections that the Framers thought indispensable to a fair trial.

The protections of the Fourth Amendment are of a wholly different order, and have nothing whatever to do with promoting the fair ascertainment of truth at a criminal trial. Rather, as Mr. Justice Frankfurter put it in *Wolf v. Colorado*, 338 U.S. 25, 27, the Fourth Amendment protects the "security of one's privacy against arbitrary intrusion by the police." Nor can it even be said that a search, as opposed to an eventual trial, is somehow "unfair" if a person consents to a search. While the Fourth and Fourteenth Amendments limit the circumstances under which the police can conduct a search, there is nothing constitutionally suspect in a person's voluntarily allowing a search. The actual conduct of the search may be precisely the same as if the police had obtained a warrant. Unlike those constitutional guarantees that protect a defendant at trial, it cannot be said every reasonable presumption ought to be indulged against voluntary relinquishment. The community has a real interest in encouraging consent, for the resulting search may yield necessary evidence for the solution and prosecution of crime, evidence that may insure that a wholly innocent person is not wrongly charged with a criminal offense.

It would be next to impossible to apply to a consent search the standard of "an intentional relinquishment or abandonment of a known right or privilege." There must be examination into the knowing and understanding nature of the waiver, an examination that was designed for a trial judge in the structured atmosphere of a courtroom. It would be unrealistic to expect that in the informal, unstructured context of a consent search, a policeman, upon pain of tainting the evidence obtained, could make the detailed type of examination demanded. If for this reason a diluted form of "waiver" were found acceptable, that would itself be ample recognition of the fact that there is no universal standard that must be applied in every situation where a person forgoes a constitutional right.[24]

In short, there is nothing in the purposes or application of the waiver requirements of *Johnson v. Zerbst* that justifies, much less compels, the easy equation of a knowing waiver with a consent search. To make such an equation is to generalize from the broad rhetoric of some of our decisions, and to ignore the substance of the differing constitutional guarantees.

Much of what has already been said disposes of the argument that *Miranda* requires the conclusion that knowledge of a right to refuse is an indispensable element of a valid consent. In *Miranda* the Court found that the techniques of police questioning and the nature of custodial surroundings produce an inherently coercive situation. The Court concluded that "unless adequate protective devices are employed to dispel the compulsion inherent in custodial surroundings, no statement obtained from the defendant can truly be the product of his free choice." And at another point the Court noted that "without proper safeguards the process of in-custody interrogation of persons suspected or accused of crime contains inherently compelling pressures which work to undermine the individual's will to resist and to compel him to speak where he would not otherwise do so freely."

---

[24] It seems clear that even a limited view of the demands of "an intentional relinquishment or abandonment of a known right or privilege" standard would inevitably lead to a requirement of detailed warnings before any consent search—a requirement all but universally rejected. As the Court stated in *Miranda* with respect to the privilege against compulsory self-incrimination: "We will not pause to inquire in individual cases whether the defendant was aware of his rights without a warning being given. Assessments of the knowledge the defendant possessed, based on information as to his age, education, intelligence, or prior contact with authorities, can never be more than speculation; a warning is a clear-cut fact." *Miranda v. Arizona*, 384 U.S., at 468–469.

In this case, there is no evidence of any inherently coercive tactics—either from the nature of the police questioning or the environment in which it took place. Indeed, since consent searches will normally occur on a person's own familiar territory, the specter of incommunicado police interrogation in some remote station house is simply inapposite. There is no reason to believe, under circumstances such as are present here, that the response to a policeman's question is presumptively coerced; and there is, therefore, no reason to reject the traditional test for determining the voluntariness of a person's response. *Miranda*, of course, did not reach investigative questioning of a person not in custody, which is most directly analogous to the situation of a consent search, and it assuredly did not indicate that such questioning ought to be deemed inherently coercive.

It is also argued that the failure to require the Government to establish knowledge as a prerequisite to a valid consent, will relegate the Fourth Amendment to the special province of "the sophisticated versus the knowledgeable and the privileged." We cannot agree. The traditional definition of voluntariness has always taken into account evidence of minimal schooling, low intelligence, and the lack of any effective warnings to a person of his rights; and the voluntariness of any statement taken under those conditions has been carefully scrutinized to determine whether it was in fact voluntarily given.

Take Note

What is the scope of a search when a person gives consent? In *Florida v. Jimeno*, 500 U.S. 248 (1991), believing that respondent was carrying narcotics, a police officer asked for permission to search his car. Respondent consented, stating that he had nothing to hide. The officer found a folded brown paper bag containing a kilogram of cocaine on the floorboard. The trial court held that the consent did not extend to the paper bag, and the Court reversed: "Respondent granted Officer Trujillo permission to search his car, and did not place any explicit limitation on the scope of the search. It was objectively reasonable for the police to conclude that the general consent to search respondent's car included consent to search containers within that car which might bear drugs including the paper bag lying on the car's floor." Justice Marshall dissented: "An individual has a heightened expectation of privacy in the contents of a closed container. It follows that an individual's consent to a search of the interior of his car cannot necessarily be understood as extending to containers in the car."

Our decision today is narrow. We hold only that when the subject of a search is not in custody and the State attempts to justify a search on the basis of his consent, the Fourth and Fourteenth Amendments require that it demonstrate that the consent was in fact voluntarily given, and not the result of duress or coercion, express or implied. Voluntariness is a question of fact to be determined from all the circumstances, and while the subject's knowledge of a right to refuse is a factor to be taken into account, the prosecution is not required to demonstrate such knowledge as a prerequisite to establishing a voluntary consent.

Rule

The judgment must be *reversed*.

MR. JUSTICE BRENNAN, dissenting.

It wholly escapes me how our citizens can meaningfully be said to have waived something as precious as a constitutional guarantee without ever being aware of its existence. The Court's conclusion is supported neither by "linguistics," nor by "epistemology," nor by "common sense."

MR. JUSTICE MARSHALL, dissenting.

This Court has always scrutinized with great care claims that a person has foregone the opportunity to assert constitutional rights. Consent searches are permitted, not because such an exception to the requirements of probable cause and warrant is essential to proper law enforcement, but because we permit our citizens to choose whether or not they wish to exercise their constitutional rights. Our prior decisions simply do not support the view that a meaningful choice has been made solely because no coercion was brought to bear on the subject. I am at a loss to understand why consent "cannot be taken literally to mean a 'knowing' choice." I have difficulty in comprehending how a decision made without knowledge of available alternatives can be treated as a choice at all.

If consent to search means that a person has chosen to forgo his right to exclude the police from the place they seek to search, it follows that his consent cannot be considered a meaningful choice unless he knew that he could in fact exclude the police. I can think of no other situation in which we would say that a person agreed to some course of action if he convinced us that he did not know that there was some other course he might have pursued. I would therefore hold, at a minimum, that the prosecution may not rely on a purported consent to search if the subject of the search did not know that he could refuse to give consent.

If one accepts this view, the question then is a simple one: must the Government show that the subject knew of his rights, or must the subject show that he lacked such knowledge? Any fair allocation of the burden would require that it be placed on the prosecution. If the burden is placed on the defendant, all the subject can do is to testify that he did not know of his rights. I doubt that many trial judges will find for the defendant on the basis of that testimony. Precisely because the evidence is very hard to come by, courts have traditionally been reluctant to require a party to prove negatives such as the lack of knowledge.

There are several ways by which the subject's knowledge of his rights may be shown. The subject may affirmatively demonstrate such knowledge by his responses at the time the search took place. Where the person giving consent is someone other than the defendant, the prosecution may require him to testify under oath. Denials of knowledge may be disproved by establishing that the subject had, in the recent past, demonstrated his knowledge of his rights, for example, by refusing entry when it was requested by the police. The prior experience or training of the subject might in some cases support an inference that he knew of his right to exclude the police.

The burden on the prosecutor would disappear, of course, if the police, at the time they requested consent to search, also told the subject that he had a right to refuse consent and that his decision to refuse would be respected. The Court contends that if an officer paused to inform the subject of his rights, the informality of the exchange would be destroyed. I doubt that a simple statement by an officer of an individual's right to refuse consent would do much except to alert the subject to a fact that he surely is entitled to know. For many years the agents of the Federal Bureau of Investigation have routinely informed subjects of their right to refuse when they request consent to search. The information can be given without disrupting the casual flow of events. Nothing disastrous would happen if the police, before requesting consent, informed the subject that he had a right to refuse consent and that his refusal would be respected. When the Court speaks of practicality, what it really is talking of is the continued ability of the police to capitalize on the ignorance of citizens so as to accomplish by subterfuge what they could not achieve by relying only on the knowing relinquishment of constitutional rights.

I believe that "under many circumstances a reasonable person might read an officer's 'May I' as the courteous expression of a demand backed by force of law." Consent is ordinarily given as acquiescence in an implicit claim of authority to search. Permitting searches in such circumstances, without any assurance at all that the subject of the search knew that, by his consent, he was relinquishing his constitutional rights, is something that I cannot believe is sanctioned by the Constitution.

Point for Discussion

Duty to Advise

In *Ohio v. Robinette*, 519 U.S. 33 (1996), Robinette was lawfully stopped for speeding on an interstate highway and given a verbal warning. The officer then asked Robinette whether he was carrying contraband. When Robinette answered in the negative, the officer asked for and obtained permission to search Robinette's car. The search revealed a small amount of marijuana and a contraband pill. The Court held that the officer was not required to tell Robinette that he was "free to go" before asking for consent to search the vehicle: "The Fourth Amendment test for a valid consent to search is that the consent be voluntary, and 'voluntariness is a question of fact to be determined from all the circumstances.'" Justice Stevens dissented: "When the officer had completed his task of either arresting or reprimanding the driver of the speeding car, his continued detention of that person constituted an illegal seizure. Because Robinette's consent to the search was the product of an unlawful detention, 'the consent was tainted by the illegality and was ineffective to justify the search.'"

In Justice Stevens' view, had the officer told Robinette that he was "free to go", this warning would have terminated the seizure and rendered the consent valid.

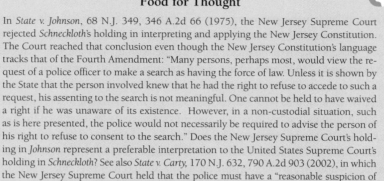

Food for Thought

In *State v. Johnson*, 68 N.J. 349, 346 A.2d 66 (1975), the New Jersey Supreme Court rejected *Schneckloth*'s holding in interpreting and applying the New Jersey Constitution. The Court reached that conclusion even though the New Jersey Constitution's language tracks that of the Fourth Amendment: "Many persons, perhaps most, would view the request of a police officer to make a search as having the force of law. Unless it is shown by the State that the person involved knew that he had the right to refuse to accede to such a request, his assenting to the search is not meaningful. One cannot be held to have waived a right if he was unaware of its existence. However, in a non-custodial situation, such as is here presented, the police would not necessarily be required to advise the person of his right to refuse to consent to the search." Does the New Jersey Supreme Court's holding in *Johnson* represent a preferable interpretation to the United States Supreme Court's holding in *Schneckloth*? See also *State v. Carty*, 170 N.J. 632, 790 A.2d 903 (2002), in which the New Jersey Supreme Court held that the police must have a "reasonable suspicion of criminal activity" before seeking a motorist's consent to search, and must also specifically inform the motorist of his right to refuse the consent. Is such a rule desirable? Should the police be required to have a "reasonable suspicion of criminal activity," or for that matter "probable cause," before requesting consent to search? In *State v. Budd*, 185 Wash.2d 566, 374 P.3d 137 (En banc, 2016), the Washington Supreme Court held that, when police execute a "knock and talk" at a suspect's house, and request permission to search the house, they are required to advise the suspect of his/her right to refuse consent.

Hypo 1: *What Constitutes Consent?*

After *Schneckloth*, when will consent be invalid? A narcotics detective received a tip from a known narcotics user that unknown persons were smoking opium in the Europe Hotel. At the hotel, the detective smelled a strong odor of burning opium coming from Room #1. The officers knocked on the door and a voice inside asked who was there. "Lieutenant Belland," was the reply. There was a slight delay, some "shuffling or noise" in the room and then the defendant opened the door. The officer said, "I want to talk to you." She then, as he describes it, "stepped back acquiescently and admitted us." The officer then said, "I want to talk to you about the opium smell in this room." She denied that there was such a smell. Then he said, "I want you to consider yourself under arrest because we are going to search the room." The search turned up opium and a smoking apparatus, the latter being warm from recent use. Did defendant "consent" to the officers entry and search? Based on *Schneckloth*, how might defendant argue that she did not consent? How might the prosecution respond to that argument? How should the court rule? *See Johnson v. United States*, 333 U.S. 10 (1948).

Hypo 2: *Police Misrepresentations & Consent*

Petitioner lived with his grandmother, a 66-year-old widowed black woman, in a house located in a rural area at the end of an isolated road. Four white law enforcement officers went to the house and found the grandmother there with some young children. One of the officers stated "I have a warrant to search your house." The grandmother responded, "Go ahead," and opened the door. In the kitchen, the officers found a rifle that was later used as evidence against petitioner. Did the grandmother consent? Should it matter that the officers did not have a warrant? Would it matter whether the police had probable cause to obtain a warrant? Should it matter how the grandmother responded? Suppose that she had stated: a) "You don't need a warrant. I'd be happy to let you search"; b) "Well, if you have a warrant, I guess I'll have to let you search"; c) "I have no objection to you searching my house. You can look in any room or drawer in my house that you desire." In which of these situations does a valid consent exist? *See Bumper v. State of North Carolina,* 391 U.S. 543 (1968). Police discover "a little weed" on Pitts. At the time, Pitts is under arrest outside of his sister's house where he lives. Following the arrest, the police ask the sister for permission to search the house, explaining that she has the right to refuse consent. However, they also tell her that they will seek a warrant if she refuses to give consent, and will leave an officer to secure the house while the warrant is obtained. The sister, fearful that her son will return home and see the police, consents to the search. Was the consent coerced? See *State v. Pitts,* 978 A.2d 14, 2009 Vt. 51.

Hypo 3: *The Nature of the Misrepresentation*

Suppose that an undercover narcotics agent, after misrepresenting himself as a drug purchaser, is invited into John Preston's home to make a purchase. After the deal is consummated, the agent arrests Preston. At Preston's trial, the prosecution seeks to admit the purchase. Preston moves to suppress claiming that, because he did not realize that the agent was with law enforcement, his consent was not valid. Should the motion be granted? *See Lewis v. United States,* 385 U.S. 206 (1966).

Hypo 4: *More on the Nature of the Misrepresentation*

A detective receives information from a federal agent suggesting that defendant purchased child pornography over the Internet. The detective speaks to defendant's credit card company and is informed that there is a disputed charge on defendant's account, that the account was closed, and that a new card was issued. The detective then obtains defendant's new credit card number and computer screen name, and goes to defendant's residence under the guise of interviewing him about "possible fraudulent charges made on his credit card." Defendant agrees to discuss the fraud and provides his credit card number to the detective who sees that it matches the one used to subscribe to a kiddie porn web site. The detective then asks defendant for permission to search his computer in regard to the fraudulent credit card charges. Defendant consents, and the detective inserts a forensic preview program into the computer and begins searching for kiddie porn rather than for fraudulent credit card charges. Was the consent to search valid when defendant was misled regarding the purpose of the search? See *People v. Prinzing*, 233 Ill.2d 587, 335 Ill.Dec. 643, 907 N.E.2d 87 (Ill. 2009).

Hypo 5: *The Scope of Consent*

Police stopped defendant's vehicle because of "excessively tinted" windows. When the officer noticed fresh undercoating on the car, he asked for and obtained permission to search. When the officer pulled up some non-factory carpeting on the floor, and noticed a small cut or hole in the floorboard, the officer took a crowbar and pried open the gas tank where he found cocaine. Did defendant's consent justify the officer's use of the crowbar? Does it matter that the car was returned to defendant in a "materially different" condition with an effect on its "structural integrity?" Was the officer required to obtain additional permission before using the crowbar? See *People v. Gomez*, 5 N.Y.3d 416, 805 N.Y.S.2d 24, 838 N.E.2d 1271 (2005).

Hypo 6: *More on the Scope of Consent*

If an individual consents to a search, how far does the consent extend? For example, if an individual consents to a search of his cell phone, does that consent give the officer the right to answer an incoming phone call? *See United States v. Lopez-Cruz*, 730 F.3d 803 (9th Cir. 2013). Also, suppose that a police officer stops a car for speeding. After inquiring whether there are any drugs or weapons in the vehicle, and receiving a negative answer, the officer asks for and obtains permission to search the vehicle. During the search, the officer finds a gift-wrapped box in the trunk. Is the officer required to obtain additional consent to open the box? *See State v. Howell*, 284 Neb. 559, 822 N.W.2d 391 (2012). A police officer stops a woman for speeding, and asks for and obtains permission to search the trunk of the vehicle. The officer finds a letter that seems to have been sent by a court. May the officer open the letter and read it? *See Winfield v. Trottier*, 710 F.3d 49 (2d Cir. 2013). Likewise, suppose that the police are investigating the disappearance of a man's live-in girlfriend, and ask for permission to enter and "look around" their shared house. In the house, they find the keys to the girlfriend's car. Does the consent to "look around" include the right to open the car trunk (where the girlfriend's dead body was found)? *See State v. Bruce*, 412 S.C. 504, 772 S.E.2d 753 (S.C. 2015).

Hypo 7: *"Knock and Talk" Consent*

An informant tells police that Lucas (a 25-year-old college graduate) is growing marijuana in his home. Two plain clothes detectives visit Lucas, police badges visible, to conduct a "knock and talk." When Lucas opens the door, they identify themselves as detectives, and Lucas invites them into the house where they smell burnt marijuana. One detective tells Lucas that he has heard there is marijuana in the house and that he will only write a citation if Lucas possesses drug paraphernalia or more than a small amount of marijuana for personal use. The other detective notices a marijuana pipe on a shelf in plain view and asks if Lucas has any similar items. Lucas produces a box containing rolling papers, marijuana pipes, and marijuana residue, but denies that he has other drug-related items. The tone of this exchange is conversational, the detectives do not threaten arrest, and the detectives do not draw their weapons. Lucas does not appear to be intoxicated. After more police detectives arrive, one detective asks Lucas to sign a consent form to allow a search of his house. Lucas hesitates. The detective explains that probable cause exists to obtain a search warrant based on the marijuana pipe that was found in plain view, the marijuana aroma, the drug paraphernalia, and the information provided by the informant. When Lucas does not sign the form, the detectives conduct a protective sweep to secure the house in anticipation of obtaining a search warrant. At that point, Lucas says, "What do I have to sign?" The detective verbally reviews the consent form, informs Lucas of his right to refuse permission, and orally advises Lucas of his right to stop the search at any time. Lucas signs the consent form. The form provides that the detectives may search his residence for illegal controlled substances, drug paraphernalia, and "other material or records pertaining to narcotics." Was the consent valid? See *United States v. Lucas*, 640 F.3d 168 (6th Cir. 2011). Suppose that, during the search, the detectives find marijuana plants, each separately potted and named. The detectives then notice a laptop computer in the living room of the house. Near the laptop, a detective observes a handwritten marijuana plant "grow chart" with a numbered list of the named marijuana plants found earlier in the bedroom closet, as well as height measurements, pot sizes, and notes. The chart is accompanied by a "to-do" list. Based on his training and experience, the detective knows that marijuana growers commonly keep similar data and digital photographs on computers and upload the information to the Internet. The detective asks Lucas whether the computer is password-protected, and Lucas responds that it is not. When the detective accesses the laptop, he finds images of child pornography. Did Lucas' consent extend to the laptop? See *United States v. Lucas*, 640 F.3d 168 (6th Cir. 2011).

Hypo 8: *Collecting DNA*

Defendant is a suspect in a series of residential burglaries from which genetic material has been collected. When defendant is stopped for a traffic violation, his eyes are bloodshot and watery. Defendant performs sobriety tests and consents to a PAS breath test that requires him to place his mouth over the plastic tip of a PAS device and blow into it. Defendant is let go after passing all tests, but instead of discarding the mouthpiece of the PAS device, the police preserve it for DNA testing. The DNA profile links defendant to two burglaries. A DNA sample obtained after defendant's arrest matches genetic material recovered from five of the burglaries. Was defendant's consent valid? *See People v. Thomas*, 200 Cal.App.4th 338, 132 Cal.Rptr.3d 714 (2011).

Hypo 9: *Consent and the Passenger*

When a police officer makes a valid stop of an automobile, he obtains consent from the driver to search the vehicle. During the search, the officer comes upon a briefcase. A passenger in the vehicle asserts ownership of the briefcase, and asks the officer "Got a warrant for that?" Assume that the driver validly consented to the search of the vehicle, does the passenger's question constitute a revocation of consent regarding the briefcase, or was the meaning of the question ambiguous? Faced with the question, is the officer required to clarify whether the passenger is challenging the consent to search? See *State v. Wantland*, 2014 WI 58, 848 N.W.2d 810 (2014).

Hypo 10: *The Burglar's Consent*

A burglar breaks into a home. While the burglar is in the house, the police knock at the door. The burglar, being rather bold, opens the door. The police, assuming that the burglar is the owner of the house (or, otherwise, he wouldn't have opened the door) tell the burglar that they would like to search the house and ask for permission to do so. The burglar responds that he doesn't object to the search, but that he is just leaving for an urgent appointment. The burglar (whom the police still assume is the owner of the house) agrees to the search provided that two conditions are met: the burglar is free to leave for his appointment, and the police agree to lock up the house as they leave. If the police search the home and find illegal narcotics, can the evidence be admitted against the owner? On behalf of the owner, what arguments might you make? How might the state respond to those arguments? Does the following case affect your analysis?

Illinois v. Rodriguez

497 U.S. 177 (1990).

JUSTICE SCALIA delivered the opinion of the Court.

On July 26, 1985, police were summoned to the residence of Dorothy Jackson in Chicago. They were met by Ms. Jackson's daughter, Gail Fischer, who showed signs of a severe beating. She told officers that she had been assaulted by respondent Edward Rodriguez earlier that day in an apartment on South California. Fischer stated that Rodriguez was asleep in the apartment, and she consented to travel there with the police in order to unlock the door with her key so that the officers could enter and arrest him. Fischer several times referred to the apartment on South California as "our" apartment, and said that she had clothes and furniture there. It is unclear whether she indicated that she currently lived at the apartment, or only that she used to live there.

Police officers drove to the apartment accompanied by Fischer. They did not obtain an arrest warrant for Rodriguez, nor did they seek a search warrant. Fischer unlocked the door with her key and gave the officers permission to enter. They moved through the door into the living room, where they observed in plain view drug paraphernalia and containers filled with white powder that they believed (correctly) to be cocaine. They proceeded to the bedroom, where they found Rodriguez asleep and discovered additional containers of white powder in two open attache cases. The officers arrested Rodriguez and seized the drugs and related paraphernalia. Rodriguez was charged with possession of a controlled substance with intent to deliver. The trial court's decision to grant Rodriguez's motion to suppress was affirmed on appeal.

The Fourth Amendment generally prohibits the warrantless entry of a person's home, whether to make an arrest or to search for specific objects. The prohibition does not apply, however, to situations in which voluntary consent has been obtained, either from the individual whose property is searched, or from a third party who possesses common authority over the premises. The State of Illinois contends that that exception applies in the present case.

As we stated in *United States v. Matlock*, 415 U.S. 164 (1974), "common authority" rests "on mutual use of the property by persons generally having joint access or control for most purposes." The burden of establishing that common authority rests upon the State. That burden was not sustained. Although Fischer, with her two small children, had lived with Rodriguez, she had moved out almost a month before the search, and had gone to live with her mother. She took her and her children's clothing with her, though leaving behind some furniture and household effects. After July 1 she sometimes spent the night at Rodriguez's apartment, but never invited her friends there, and never went there herself when he was not home. Her name was not on the lease nor did she contribute to the rent. She had a key to the apartment, which she had taken without Rodriguez's knowledge (though she testified that Rodriguez had given her the key). On these facts the State has not established that Fischer had "joint access or control for most purposes."

Respondent asserts that permitting a reasonable belief of common authority to validate an entry would cause a defendant's Fourth Amendment rights to be "vicariously waived." We disagree. What Rodriguez is assured by the Fourth Amendment is not that no government search of his house will occur unless he consents; but that no such search will occur that is "unreasonable." There are various elements that can make a search of a person's house "reasonable"—one of which is the consent of the person or his cotenant. The essence of respondent's argument is that we should impose upon this element a requirement that we have not imposed upon other elements that regularly compel government officers to exercise judgment regarding the facts: namely, the requirement that their judgment be not only responsible but correct.

The fundamental objective that alone validates all unconsented government searches is, of course, the seizure of persons who have committed or are about to commit crimes, or of evidence related to crimes. But "reasonableness," with respect to this necessary element, does not demand that the government be factually correct in its assessment that that is what a search will produce. Warrants need only be supported by "probable cause," which demands no more than a proper "assessment of probabilities in particular factual contexts." *Illinois v. Gates*, 462 U.S. 213, 232 (1983). If a magistrate, based upon seemingly reliable but factually inaccurate information, issues a warrant for the search of a house in which the sought-after felon is not present, has never been present, and was never likely to have been present, the owner of that house suffers one of the inconveniences we all expose ourselves to as the cost of living in a safe society; he does not suffer a violation of the Fourth Amendment.

Another element often required in order to render an unconsented search "reasonable" is that the officer be authorized by a valid warrant. We have not held that "reasonableness" precludes error with respect to those factual judgments that law enforcement officials are expected to make. For example, in *Maryland v. Garrison*, we held the search unquestionably was objectively understandable and reasonable. The objective facts available to the officers at the time suggested no distinction between the suspect's apartment and the third-floor premises.

In order to satisfy the "reasonableness" requirement of the Fourth Amendment, what is generally demanded of the many factual determinations that must regularly be made by agents of the government—whether the magistrate issuing a warrant, the police officer executing a warrant, or the police officer conducting a search or seizure under one of the exceptions to the warrant requirement—is not that they always be correct, but that they be reasonable. As we put it in *Brinegar v. United States*, 338 U.S. 160, 176 (1949): "Because many situations which confront officers in the course of executing their duties are more or less ambiguous, room must be allowed for some mistakes on their part. But the mistakes must be those of reasonable men, acting on facts leading sensibly to their conclusions of probability."

We see no reason to depart from this general rule with respect to the authority to consent to a search. Whether the basis for such authority exists is the sort of recurring factual question to which law enforcement officials must be expected to apply their judgment; and all the Fourth Amendment requires is that they answer it reasonably. The Constitution is no more violated when officers enter without a warrant because they reasonably (though erroneously) believe that the person who has consented to their entry is a resident of the premises, than it is violated when they enter without a warrant because they reasonably (though erroneously) believe they are in pursuit of a violent felon who is about to escape.

What we hold today does not suggest that law enforcement officers may always accept a person's invitation to enter premises. Even when the invitation is accompanied by an explicit assertion that the person lives there, the surrounding circumstances could conceivably be such that a reasonable person would doubt its truth and not act upon it without further inquiry. As with other factual determinations bearing upon search and seizure, determination of consent to enter must "be judged against an objective standard: would the facts available to the officer at the moment 'warrant a man of reasonable caution in the belief' " that the consenting party had authority over the premises? If not, then warrantless entry without further inquiry is unlawful unless authority actually exists. But if so, the search is valid.

The Appellate Court found it unnecessary to determine whether the officers reasonably believed that Fischer had the authority to consent. We remand for consideration of that question.

So ordered.

JUSTICE MARSHALL, with whom JUSTICE BRENNAN and JUSTICE STEVENS join, dissenting.

A departure from the warrant requirement is not justified simply because an officer reasonably believes a third party has consented to a search of the defendant's home. Third-party consent searches are not based on an exigency and serve no compelling social goal. Police officers, when faced with the choice of relying on consent by a third party or securing a warrant, should secure a warrant and must therefore accept the risk of error should they instead choose to rely on consent.

Food for Thought

In light of the holding in *Rodriguez,* reconsider Hypo 10, *supra,* before *Rodriguez,* entitled "The Burglar's Consent."

Third-party consent limits a person's ability to challenge the reasonableness of the search only because that person voluntarily has relinquished some of his expectation of privacy by sharing access or control over his property with another person. A search conducted pursuant to an officer's reasonable but mistaken belief that a third party had authority to consent is thus on an entirely different constitutional footing from one based on the consent of a third party who in fact has such authority. Even if the officers reasonably believed that Fischer had authority to consent, she did not, and Rodriguez's expectation of privacy was therefore undiminished. Rodriguez accordingly can challenge the warrantless intrusion into his home as a violation of the Fourth Amendment.

Hypo 1: *The Sister's Consent*

School officials discover that a laptop computer is missing. Since the computer is equipped with tracking software, the police are able to trace the computer to a particular address. Police officers go to that address, a single-family dwelling, and enter the vestibule without ringing the doorbell or announcing their presence, and knock on an inner door separating the vestibule from the rest of the home. A woman (the suspect's sister), who heard the officers enter, welcomes the officers saying "Thank God you're all here." When asked whether the suspect is at home, she answers affirmatively, explaining that her brother has been "acting up" and cursing at her mother, and that she "was going to call the police anyway." The sister directs the officers upstairs, to a bedroom where they encounter a young man with a laptop. When asked whether it is his laptop, the young man answers that it is not. At this point, the suspect enters the room and says, "That's my laptop." The suspect moves to suppress evidence obtained by the police at his residence, arguing that the sister's consent was insufficient, and that it did not extend to entry into the suspect's bedroom. Should the evidence be suppressed? *See In re Leroy*, 16 N.Y.3d 243, 919 N.Y.S.2d 484, 944 N.E.2d 1123 (2011).

Hypo 2: *Supervisors and Employees*

May a supervisor consent to a search of an employee's desk? Appellee was arrested for petty larceny. The police suspected that he stashed some of the loot in a drawer in his office. With the consent of appellee's supervisor, the police search the desk (which was used only by defendant and was not shared with anyone else). The police find the loot in the drawer. Is a supervisor entitled to consent to the search of an employee's desk under these circumstances? What arguments might be made on behalf of appellee? How might the government respond to these arguments? *See United States v. Blok*, 188 F.2d 1019, 88 U.S.App.D.C. 326 (D.C.Cir.1951).

Hypo 3: *More on Supervisors and Employees*

At the U.S. Mint in D.C., there was a loud noise that sounded like an explosion. An investigation reveals that a firecracker or other explosive had gone off. In an effort to find other fireworks possessed by Mint employees, the Captain of the security guard decides to search all employee lockers. In Donato's locker, he finds a bag of quarters. Donato is charged with embezzlement. Did the security guard, acting on behalf of Donato's employer, need Donato's consent to search the locker? Would it matter whether Mint regulations expressly state that "No mint lockers in mint institutions shall be considered to be private lockers," that all employee lockers are subject to inspection and will be regularly inspected by Mint security guards for sanitation purposes, and that Mint security guards have a master key that opens all employee lockers? See *United States v. Donato*, 269 F.Supp. 921 (E.D.Pa. 1967); see also United States v. Oliver, 630 F.3d 397 (5th Cir. 2011); *United States v. Purcell*, 526 F.3d 953 (6th Cir. 2008).

Hypo 4: *The Scope of Third Party Consent*

Stabile lived with Debbie Deetz, who believed that she was married to him (she was not), in a house secured by a mortgage and home equity credit line in the name of Stabile's brother. Stabile defaulted on the loans and tried to mask his default by passing counterfeit checks. When police officers sought to question Stabile about counterfeiting checks, he was not at home. Deetz invited the agents into the house. The officers asked Deetz for consent to search the house, provided her with a consent form, and informed her that she could refuse consent. Deetz reviewed the form for thirty minutes and signed so that she could find out about Stabile's financial practices. The agents then searched the house led by Deetz who provided the agents with documents and showed the agents several computers. Next to one computer, the agents found check stock, check writing software, photocopies of checks, copies of previously-passed fraudulent checks, two printers, and checks with an alias. The agents then disconnected the hard drives. When one officer had difficulty removing a hard drive, Deetz voluntarily provided the officer with a screwdriver from Stabile's toolbox. The officers left with six hard drives. Stabile claims at trial that Deetz did not have authority to consent to a seizure of the computer. Is Stabile correct? See *United States v. Stabile*, 633 F.3d 219 (3rd Cir. 2011).

Hypo 5: *Third Party Consent - Take Three*

Police, responding to a 9-1-1 call, find Hernandez' girlfriend (Elizabeth Romero), bruised, beaten, and visibly shaken. She tells police that Hernandez beat her and held her against her will until she escaped. She informs the police that she has been living with Hernandez for two weeks and that her personal belongings are in his apartment. She states that Hernandez has "lots of guns" and has stated that he "is not going to jail." When Hernandez appears, and spies the officers, he quickly walks into the corridor that leads to his apartment. When the police call Hernandez's cell phone, he denies that he is in his apartment and responds "with foul language" after the sergeant encourages him to meet with the deputies to "resolve the situation." Believing that Hernandez is in his apartment, the deputies cordon off the area. No effort is made to obtain a warrant. At that point, Romero gives the police consent to enter the apartment to search for Hernandez. Romero states that there is one locked room in the apartment that she is not permitted to enter. The police find that the door to that room is locked. As part of a "protective sweep," an officer forces the locked door open. Did the officers act properly in entering the apartment and forcing the door? See *Hernandez v. State*, 98 So.3d 702 (Fl. App. 2012).

Hypo 6: *The Juvenile Center Director*

A juvenile is living at a transitional family center with his mother. When the director spots him with a gun, the director notifies the police and gives consent for the police to search his room. The director has a master key that opens every door in the shelter, and staff members have a master key that opens every resident's room. Members of the shelter's staff have the right to enter any room "for professional business purposes (maintenance, room inspections, etc.)," but only with the knowledge of the director. If a "business professional," such as a repair person or exterminator, requires entry to a resident's room, he or she must be escorted by a staff member, with the director's approval. Shelter staff may conduct "room checks" at any time without warning to monitor compliance with the shelter's "Good Housekeeping Standard" and other rules and regulations, including those affecting health and safety. The manual has a "zero tolerance policy in regards to violent acts committed by residents" and the possession of any weapon: "any resident in possession of a weapon will be terminated immediately." The shelter "reserves the right to contact the Police should the situation warrant," but the manual does not state that the shelter director or a staff member may consent to a police search of a resident's room. Before entering the room, the police speak with the director and review the manual. Their entry is proceeded by the director who announces that she is conducting a room search. The search turns up the gun. The juvenile moves to suppress on the theory that the director lacked authority to consent to the search. Should the gun be suppressed? See *Commonwealth v. Porter*, 456 Mass. 254, 923 N.E.2d 36 (2010).

Georgia v. Randolph

547 U.S. 103 (2006).

JUSTICE SOUTER delivered the opinion of the Court.

The Fourth Amendment recognizes a valid warrantless entry and search of premises when police obtain the voluntary consent of an occupant who shares, or is reasonably believed to share, authority over the area in common with a co-occupant who later objects to the use of evidence so obtained. *Illinois v. Rodriguez*, 497 U.S. 177 (1990); *United States v. Matlock*, 415 U.S. 164 (1974). The question here is whether such an evidentiary seizure is likewise lawful with the permission of one occupant when the other, who later seeks to suppress the evidence, is present at the scene and expressly refuses to consent.

Respondent Scott Randolph and his wife, Janet, separated in May 2001, when she left the marital residence in Georgia, and went to stay with her parents, taking their son and some belongings. In July, she returned to the house with the child, though the record does not reveal whether her object was reconciliation or retrieval of remaining possessions. On the morning of July 6, she complained to the police that after a domestic dispute her husband took their son away, and when officers reached the house she told them that her husband was a cocaine user whose habit had caused financial troubles. After the police arrived, Scott Randolph returned and explained that he had removed the child to a neighbor's house out of concern that his wife might take the boy out of the country again; he denied cocaine use, and countered that it was in fact his wife who abused drugs and alcohol.

One of the officers, Sergeant Murray, went with Janet Randolph to reclaim the child, and when they returned she not only renewed her complaints about her husband's drug use, but also volunteered that there were "items of drug evidence" in the house. Sergeant Murray asked Scott Randolph for permission to search the house, which he unequivocally refused. The sergeant turned to Janet Randolph for consent to search, which she readily gave. She led the officer upstairs to a bedroom that she identified as Scott's, where the sergeant noticed a drinking straw with a powdery residue he suspected was cocaine. He then left the house to get an evidence bag from his car and to call the district attorney's office, who instructed him to stop the search and apply for a warrant. When Sergeant Murray returned to the house, Janet Randolph withdrew her consent. The police took the straw to the police station, along with the Randolphs. After getting a search warrant, they returned to the house and seized further evidence of drug use, on the basis of which Scott Randolph was indicted for possession of cocaine. He moved to suppress the evidence, as products of a warrantless search of his house unauthorized by his wife's consent over his express refusal. The trial court denied the motion. The Court of Appeals of Georgia reversed, and was sustained by the State Supreme Court. We granted certiorari and affirm.

To the Fourth Amendment rule ordinarily prohibiting the warrantless entry of a person's house as unreasonable *per se*, one "jealously and carefully drawn" exception recognizes the validity of searches with the voluntary consent of an individual possessing authority. None of our co-occupant consent-to-search cases has presented the further fact of a second occupant physically present and refusing permission to search, and later moving to suppress evidence so obtained.[2] The significance of such a refusal turns on the underpinnings of the co-occupant consent rule, as recognized since *Matlock*.

The defendant in that case was arrested in the yard of a house where he lived with a Mrs. Graff and several of her relatives, and was detained in a squad car parked nearby. When the police went to the door, Mrs. Graff admitted them and consented to a search of the house. We said that "the consent of one who possesses common authority over premises or effects is valid as against the absent, nonconsenting person with whom that authority is shared." Consistent with our prior understanding that Fourth Amendment rights are not limited by the law of property, we explained that the third party's "common authority" is not synonymous with a technical property interest:

> "The authority which justified the third-party consent does not rest upon the law of property, with its attendant historical and legal refinement, but rests rather on mutual use of the property by persons generally having joint access or control for most purposes, so that it is reasonable to recognize that any of the co-inhabitants has the right to permit the inspection in his own right and that the others have assumed the risk that one of their number might permit the common area to be searched."

---

[2] Mindful of the multiplicity of living arrangements, we do not mean to suggest that the rule to be applied to them is varied.

The constant element in assessing Fourth Amendment reasonableness in the consent cases is the great significance given to widely shared social expectations, which are naturally enough influenced by the law of property, but not controlled by its rules. *Matlock* not only holds that a solitary co-inhabitant may sometimes consent to a search of shared premises, but stands for the proposition that the reasonableness of such a search is in significant part a function of commonly held understanding about the authority that co-inhabitants may exercise in ways that affect each other's interests.

When someone comes to the door of a domestic dwelling with a baby at her hip, as Mrs. Graff did, she shows that she belongs there, and that fact standing alone is enough to tell a law enforcement officer or any other visitor that if she occupies the place along with others, she probably lives there subject to the assumption tenants usually make about their common authority when they share quarters. They understand that any one of them may admit visitors, with the consequence that a guest obnoxious to one may nevertheless be admitted in his absence by another. As *Matlock* put it, shared tenancy is understood to include an "assumption of risk," on which police officers are entitled to rely, and although some group living together might make an exceptional arrangement that no one could admit a guest without the agreement of all, the chance of such an eccentric scheme is too remote to expect visitors to investigate a particular household's rules before accepting an invitation to come in. So, *Matlock* relied on what was usual and placed no burden on the police to eliminate the possibility of atypical arrangements, in the absence of reason to doubt that the regular scheme was in place.

It is easy to imagine different facts on which, if known, no common authority could sensibly be suspected. A landlord or a hotel manager calls up no customary understanding of authority to admit guests without the consent of the current occupant. See *Chapman v. United States*, supra (landlord); *Stoner v. California*, 376 U.S. 483 (1964) (hotel manager). A tenant in the ordinary course does not take rented premises subject to any formal or informal agreement that the landlord may let visitors into the dwelling, and a hotel guest customarily has no reason to expect the manager to allow anyone but his own employees into his room. In these circumstances, neither state-law property rights, nor common contractual arrangements, nor any other source points to a common understanding of authority to admit third parties generally without the consent of a person occupying the premises. When it comes to searching through bureau drawers, there will be instances in which even a person clearly belonging on premises as an occupant may lack any perceived authority to consent; "a child of eight might well be considered to have the power to consent to the police crossing the threshold into that part of the house where any caller, such as a pollster or salesman, might well be admitted," 4 LaFave 8.4(c), at 207 (4th ed. 2004), but no one would reasonably expect such a child to be in a position to authorize anyone to rummage through his parents' bedroom.

A caller standing at the door of shared premises would have no confidence that one occupant's invitation was a sufficiently good reason to enter when a fellow tenant stood there saying, "stay out." Without some very good reason, no sensible person would go inside under those conditions. Fear for the safety of the occupant issuing the invitation, or of someone else inside, would be thought to justify entry, but the justification then would be the personal risk, the threats to life or limb, not the disputed invitation.

The visitor's reticence would show not timidity but a realization that when people living together disagree over the use of their common quarters, a resolution must come through voluntary accommodation, not by appeals to authority. Unless the people living together fall within some recognized hierarchy, like a household of parent and child or barracks housing military personnel of different grades, there is no societal understanding of superior and inferior, a fact reflected in a standard formulation of domestic property law, that "each cotenant has the right to use and enjoy the entire property as if he or she were the sole owner, limited only by the same right in the other cotenants." 7 R. Powell, Powell on Real Property 50.031, p. 50–14 (M. Wolf gen. ed. 2005). The law does not ask who has the better side of the conflict; it simply provides a right to any co-tenant, even the most unreasonable, to obtain a decree partitioning the property (when the relationship is one of co-ownership) and terminating the relationship. In sum, there is no common understanding that one co-tenant generally has a right or authority to prevail over the express wishes of another, whether the issue is the color of the curtains or invitations to outsiders.

Since the co-tenant wishing to open the door to a third party has no recognized authority in law or social practice to prevail over a present and objecting co-tenant, his disputed invitation, without more, gives a police officer no better claim to reasonableness in entering than the officer would have in the absence of any consent at all. We have, after all, lived our whole national history with an understanding of "the ancient adage that a man's home is his castle to the point that the poorest man may in his cottage bid defiance to all the forces of the Crown," *Miller v. United States*, 357 U.S. 301 (1958). Disputed permission is thus no match for this central value of the Fourth Amendment. We recognize the consenting tenant's interest as a citizen in bringing criminal activity to light. And we understand a co-tenant's legitimate self-interest in siding with the police to deflect suspicion raised by sharing quarters with a criminal.

But society can have the benefit of these interests without relying on a theory of consent that ignores an inhabitant's refusal to allow a warrantless search. The co-tenant acting on his own initiative may be able to deliver evidence to the police, and can tell the police what he knows, for use before a magistrate in getting a warrant.[6] The reliance on a co-tenant's information instead of disputed consent accords with the law's general partiality toward "police action taken under a warrant as against searches and seizures without one," *United States v. Lefkowitz,* 285 U.S. 452 (1932).

No question has been raised about the authority of the police to enter a dwelling to protect a resident from domestic violence; so long as they have good reason to believe such a threat exists. (And since the police would then be lawfully in the premises, there is no question that they could seize any evidence in plain view or take further action supported by any consequent probable cause) The undoubted right of the police to enter in order to protect a victim has nothing to do with the question in this case, whether a search with the consent of one co-tenant is good against another, standing at the door and expressly refusing consent.[7] None of the cases cited by the dissent support its improbable view that recognizing limits on merely evidentiary searches would compromise the capacity to protect a fearful occupant. We therefore hold that a warrantless search of a shared dwelling for evidence over the express refusal of consent by a physically present resident cannot be justified as reasonable as to him on the basis of consent given to the police by another resident.

To ask whether the consenting tenant has the right to admit the police when a physically present fellow tenant objects is not to question whether some property right may be divested by the mere objection of another. It is, rather, whether customary social understanding accords the consenting tenant authority powerful enough to prevail over the co-tenant's objection. If a potential defendant with self-interest in objecting is in fact at the door and objects, the co-tenant's permission does not suffice for a reasonable search, whereas the potential objector, nearby but not invited to take part in the threshold colloquy, loses out.

There is practical value in the simple clarity of complementary rules, one recognizing the co-tenant's permission when there is no fellow occupant on hand, the other according dispositive weight to the fellow occupant's contrary indication when he expresses it. It would needlessly limit the capacity of the police to respond if we were to hold that reasonableness required the police to take affirmative steps to find a potentially objecting co-tenant before acting on the permission they had already received. Every co-tenant consent case would turn into a test about the adequacy of the police's efforts to consult with a potential objector.

---

[6] The very exchange of information like this in front of the objecting inhabitant may render consent irrelevant by creating an exigency that justifies immediate action on the police's part; if the objecting tenant cannot be incapacitated from destroying easily disposable evidence during the time required to get a warrant, a fairly perceived need to act on the spot to preserve evidence may justify entry and search under the exigent circumstances exception .

[7] We understand the possibility that a battered individual will be afraid to express fear candidly, but this does not seem to be a reason to think such a person would invite the police into the dwelling to search for evidence against another.

This case invites a straightforward application of the rule that a physically present inhabitant's express refusal of consent to a police search is dispositive as to him, regardless of the consent of a fellow occupant. The State does not argue that she gave any indication to the police of a need for protection inside the house that might have justified entry into the portion of the premises where the police found the powdery straw. Nor does the State claim that the entry and search should be upheld under the rubric of exigent circumstances .

The judgment of the Supreme Court of Georgia is therefore affirmed.

It is so ordered.

JUSTICE ALITO took no part in the consideration or decision of this case.

JUSTICE STEVENS, concurring.

When the Fourth Amendment was adopted, given the then-prevailing dramatic differences between the property rights of the husband and the far lesser rights of the wife, only the consent of the husband would matter. Assuming that both spouses are competent, neither one is a master possessing the power to override the other's constitutional right to deny entry to their castle.

JUSTICE BREYER, concurring.

The "totality of the circumstances" do not justify abandoning the Fourth Amendment's traditional hostility to police entry into a home without a warrant. The risk of an ongoing crime or other exigent circumstance can make a critical difference. If a possible abuse victim invites a responding officer to enter a home or consents to the officer's entry request, that invitation (or consent) could reflect the victim's fear about being left alone with an abuser. In that context, an invitation (or consent) would provide a special reason for immediate, rather than later, police entry. Today's decision will not adversely affect ordinary law enforcement practices.

CHIEF JUSTICE ROBERTS, with whom JUSTICE SCALIA joins, dissenting.

The rule the majority fashions provides protection on a random and happenstance basis, protecting, for example, a co-occupant who happens to be at the front door when the other occupant consents to a search, but not one napping or watching television in the next room. The correct approach recognizes that the Fourth Amendment protects privacy. If an individual shares information, papers, or places with another, he assumes the risk that the other person will in turn share access to that information or those papers or places with the government. Co-occupants have "assumed the risk that one of their number might permit a common area to be searched." *United States v. Matlock*, 415 U.S. 164 (1974).

Just as Mrs. Randolph could walk upstairs, come down, and turn her husband's cocaine straw over to the police, she can consent to police entry and search of what is, after all, her home, too.

The majority assumes that an invited social guest who arrives at the door of a shared residence, and is greeted by a disagreeable co-occupant shouting "stay out," would simply go away. A relative or good friend of one of two feuding room-mates might well enter the apartment over the objection of the other roommate. A guest who came to celebrate an occupant's birthday, or one who had traveled some distance for a particular reason, might not readily turn away simply because of a roommate's objection. The nature of the place itself is also pertinent: Invitees may react one way if the feuding roommates share one room, differently if there are common areas from which the objecting roommate could readily be expected to absent himself. The possible scenarios are limitless, and slight variations in the fact pattern yield vastly different expectations about whether the invitee might be expected to enter or to go away. Such shifting expectations are not a promising foundation on which to ground a constitutional rule.

The normal Fourth Amendment rule is that items discovered in plain view are admissible if the officers were legitimately on the premises; if the entry and search were reasonable "as to" Mrs. Randolph, based on her consent, it is not clear why the cocaine straw should not be admissible "as to" Mr. Randolph, as discovered in plain view during a legitimate search.

The question presented often arises when innocent cotenants seek to disassociate or protect themselves from ongoing criminal activity. There will be many cases in which a consenting co-occupant's wish to have the police enter is overridden by an objection from another present co-occupant. What does the majority imagine will happen when the consenting co-occupant is concerned about the other's criminal activity, once the door clicks shut? The objecting co-occupant may pause briefly to decide whether to destroy any evidence of wrongdoing or to inflict retribution on the consenting co-occupant first, but there can be little doubt that he will attend to both in short order. The majority's rule forbids police from entering to assist with a domestic dispute if the abuser whose behavior prompted the request for police assistance objects. It is far from clear that an exception for emergency entries suffices to protect the safety of occupants in domestic disputes. I respectfully dissent.

JUSTICE SCALIA, dissenting.

The issue is what to do when there is a *conflict* between two equals. It does not follow that the spouse who *refuses* consent should be the winner of the contest. Given the usual patterns of domestic violence, how often can police be expected to encounter the situation in which a man urges them to enter the home while a woman simultaneously demands that they stay out? The most common practical effect of today's decision is to give men the power to stop women from allowing police into their homes.

JUSTICE THOMAS, dissenting.

When a citizen leads police officers into a home shared with her spouse to show them evidence relevant to their investigation no Fourth Amendment search has occurred.

a. Removed Co-Occupant

Randolph was qualified by the holding in *Fernandez v. California*, 134 S.Ct. 1126 (2014). The case was similar to *Randolph* in that a co-occupant objected to allowing the police to search a house. However, after the objecting co-occupant was arrested and removed from the apartment house by the police, the remaining occupant gave the police permission to enter and search. The removed co-occupant sought to suppress the results of the search. The court upheld the search:

> "This brings us to petitioner's argument that his objection, made at the threshold of the premises that the police wanted to search, remained effective until he changed his mind and withdrew his objection. This argument cannot be squared with the "widely shared social expectations" or "customary social usage" upon which *Randolph* was based. When the objecting occupant is standing at the threshold saying "stay out," a friend or visitor invited to enter by another occupant can expect at best an uncomfortable scene and at worst violence if he or she tries to brush past the objector. But when the objector is not on the scene (and especially when it is known that the objector will not return during the course of the visit), the friend or visitor is much more likely to accept the invitation to enter.
>
> Petitioner argues that an objection, once made, should last until it is withdrawn by the objector, but such a rule would be unreasonable. Suppose that a husband and wife owned a house as joint tenants and that the husband, after objecting to a search of the house, was convicted and sentenced to a 15-year prison term. Under petitioner's proposed rule, the wife would be unable to consent to a search of the house 10 years after the date on which her husband objected. We refuse to stretch *Randolph* to such strange lengths. Nor are we persuaded to hold that an objection lasts for a "reasonable" time. "It is certainly unusual for this Court to set forth precise time limits governing police action," and what interval of time would be reasonable in this context? A week? A month? A year? Ten years? Petitioner's rule would require the police and ultimately the courts to determine whether, after the passage of time, an objector still had "common authority" over the premises, and this would often be a tricky question. Suppose that an incarcerated objector and a consenting co-occupant were joint tenants on a lease. If the objector, after incarceration, stopped paying rent, would he still have "common authority," and

would his objection retain its force? Would it be enough that his name remained on the lease? Would the result be different if the objecting and consenting lessees had an oral month-to-month tenancy?

Another problem concerns the procedure needed to register a continuing objection. Would it be necessary for an occupant to object while police officers are at the door? Could a person like Randolph, suspecting that his estranged wife might invite the police to view his drug stash and paraphernalia, register an objection in advance? Could this be done by posting a sign in front of the house? Could a standing objection be registered by serving notice on the chief of police?

Finally, there is the question of the particular law enforcement officers who would be bound by an objection. Would this include just the officers who were present when the objection was made? Would it also apply to other officers working on the same investigation? Would it extend to officers who were unaware of the objection? How about officers assigned to different but arguably related cases? Would it be limited by law enforcement agency?

Justice Ginsburg, joined by two other justices, dissented "Even if shared tenancy were understood to entail the prospect of visits by unwanted social callers while the objecting resident was gone, that unwelcome visitor's license would hardly include free rein to rummage through the dwelling in search of evidence and contraband. In this case, the police could readily have obtained a warrant to search the shared residence. I would honor the Fourth Amendment's warrant requirement and hold that Fernandez' objection to the search did not become null upon his arrest and removal from the scene."

> **Food for Thought**
>
> How does the Court's decision apply to a defendant who happens to be asleep when his wife agrees to allow the police to enter their residence. Suppose that the defendant wakes up and immediately objects to the search. May the police continue with the search, or must they discontinue their efforts? How would you advise the police to act?

Hypo 1: *The Co-Occupant in the Patrol Car*

Defendant has been arrested, placed in handcuffs, and seated in the back of a patrol car. Suppose that the police ask defendant's wife for permission to search the house, and she consents. Defendant, who is within earshot and realizes what is going on, yells out an objection. May the police enter? *See United States v. Henderson* 536 F.3d 776 (7th Cir. 2008).

Food for Thought

Defendant, who was present when the police ask for permission to search her house for evidence of a meth lab, objects loudly. However, the husband pleads with the police to enter anyway because he fears that the meth chemicals are dangerous to his house, to him, and to their kids. May the police enter the house anyway? See, *e.g., United States v. Hendrix*, 595 F.2d 883 (D.C.Cir.1979).

Food for Thought

How would *Randolph* apply to a situation in which the police ask for permission to search an automobile, but one of the spouses objects while the other consents? Suppose that the driver consents while the passenger objects? Does the driver's consent carry more weight? Or, under *Randolph*, does the objection of one spouse preclude consent?

Hypo 2: *The Guest's Consent*

Believing that criminals are using a house to traffic narcotics, the police ask Chambers (who does not own the house, but is simply staying there with the permission of the owner) for permission to search the house for evidence of money laundering and drug trafficking. If Chambers consents, is the search valid if it reveals cocaine in the living room? What if the police find a boarded-up attic entryway, and Chambers consents to using a sledgehammer to dislodge the boards? In the attic, the police find nearly $1,000,000 in cash, more drugs, and ledgers. Did Chambers have the power to consent to a search of the boarded-up attic? If you represent the owner of the house, how would you argue that the search is invalid? How might the state respond? *See United States v. Arreguin*, 735 F.3d 1168 (9th Cir. 2013); *United States v. Ibarra*, 948 F.2d 903 (5th Cir.1991).

Hypo 3: *The Grandmother's Consent*

In *Bumpers, supra,* the police searched a grandmother's home looking for a rifle allegedly used by her grandson in committing a rape. If the grandmother owns the house, can she consent to a search of her grandson's bedroom? Does it matter whether the grandson is present and objecting? *See United States v. Peyton*, 745 F.3d 546 (D.C. Cir. 2014).

Hypo 4: *The Executive's Computer*

The police have reason to believe that a corporation's high-level executive is accessing child pornography from his office computer. The computer is owned by the company, but is protected by an individual log-in and password. However, the company's IT department has complete administrative access to all computers, uses a firewall to monitor employee's internet activity, and makes employees aware of the monitoring. Under these circumstances, does the CFO have the authority to consent to a police search of the executive's computer? *See United States v. Ziegler,* 474 F.3d 1184 (9th Cir. 2007).

Hypo 5: *Possession of Keys*

Defendant was arrested at a casino. While he is being taken away, he gives the keys to his vehicle to his girlfriend, and tells her: "lock it up and just wait for me." Despite the fact that the girlfriend possesses the keys to the vehicle, she does not believe that she has the authority to drive it because she is not listed on the rental agreement and is not insured. After repeated requests from the police, she consents to a search of the vehicle. Did she have the authority to consent? *See State v. Kurokawa-Lasciak,* 249 Or.App. 435, 278 P.3d 38 (2012).

Hypo 6: *The Overdue Rental Car*

Suppose that a man, who is driving a rental car, objects to a search of the vehicle. However, the rental car is overdue and the company has a right to repossess it. May the rental car company consent to a search of the car notwithstanding the driver's objections? *See United States v. Lumpkins,* 687 F.3d 1011 (8th Cir. 2012).

7. Administrative Inspections

A number of agencies regularly inspect buildings and worksites. Health inspectors enter restaurants to determine whether food preparation and service areas are clean, as well as to see whether food is being kept under healthy conditions. OSHA inspectors examine construction and factory sites to make sure that workers are employed in safe and healthy conditions. In some instances, administrative officials even seek to enter people's homes or yards (*e.g.*, child welfare officials enter a house looking for abused or neglected children).

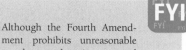

Although the Fourth Amendment prohibits unreasonable searches and seizures, and therefore seems to provide homeowners and businessmen with some protection against administrative prying, until the 1960s there was doubt about whether the Fourth Amendment applied to administrative inspections. The Fourth Amendment clearly applies when the police search homes or businesses for evidence of criminal activity. However, prior to the following decision, many believed that administrative inspections were fundamentally different than police searches, and were not therefore subject to Fourth Amendment requirements.

Camara v. Municipal Court

387 U.S. 523 (1967).

Mr. Justice White delivered the opinion of the Court.

Appellant Camara leased a ground floor apartment. City inspectors sought to inspect the apartment under § 503 of a San Francisco ordinance which authorized them to enter buildings "to perform any duty imposed upon them by the Municipal Code." When Camara refused to allow the inspectors to enter his apartment without a warrant, he was charged with violating § 507 of the ordinance which made it illegal to refuse to permit a lawful inspection.

The Fourth Amendment was designed to safeguard the privacy and security of individuals against arbitrary invasions by governmental officials. Except in certain carefully defined classes of cases, a search of private property without proper consent is "unreasonable" unless it has been authorized by a valid search warrant.

In *Frank v. State of Maryland*, 359 U.S. 360 (1959), this Court upheld the conviction of one who refused to permit a warrantless inspection of private premises for the purposes of locating and abating a suspected public nuisance. To the

Frank majority, municipal fire, health, and housing inspection programs "touch at most upon the periphery of the important interests safeguarded by the Fourteenth Amendment's protection against official intrusion," because the inspections are merely to determine whether physical conditions exist which do not comply with minimum standards prescribed in local regulatory ordinances. Since the inspector does not ask that the property owner open his doors to a search for "evidence of criminal action" which may be used to secure the owner's criminal conviction, historic interests of "self-protection" jointly protected by the Fourth and Fifth Amendments are said not to be involved, but only the less intense "right to be secure from intrusion into personal privacy."

A routine inspection of the physical condition of private property is a less hostile intrusion than the typical policeman's search for the fruits and instrumentalities of crime. But we cannot agree that the Fourth Amendment interests at stake in these inspection cases are merely "peripheral." It is surely anomalous to say that the individual and his private property are fully protected by the Fourth Amendment only when the individual is suspected of criminal behavior. Even the most law-abiding citizen has a very tangible interest in limiting the circumstances under which the sanctity of his home may be broken by official authority, for the possibility of criminal entry under the guise of official sanction is a serious threat to personal and family security. And even accepting *Frank*'s rather remarkable premise, inspections of the kind we are here considering do in fact jeopardize "self-protection" interests of the property owner. Like most regulatory laws, fire, health, and housing codes are enforced by criminal processes. In some cities, discovery of a violation by the inspector leads to a criminal complaint. Even in cities where discovery of a violation produces only an administrative compliance order, refusal to comply is a criminal offense, and the fact of compliance is verified by a second inspection, again without a warrant. Finally, refusal to permit an inspection is itself a crime, punishable by fine or even by jail sentence.

Appellee asserts that the warrant process could not function effectively in this field. The decision to inspect an entire municipal area is based upon legislative or administrative assessment of broad factors such as the area's age and condition. Unless the magistrate is to review such policy matters, he must issue a "rubber stamp" warrant which provides no protection at all to the property owner.

These arguments unduly discount the purposes behind the warrant machinery contemplated by the Fourth Amendment. When the inspector demands entry, the occupant has no way of knowing whether enforcement of the municipal code involved requires inspection of his premises, no way of knowing the lawful limits of the inspector's power to search, and no way of knowing whether the inspector himself is acting under proper authorization. These are questions which may be reviewed by a neutral magistrate without any reassessment of the basic agency decision to canvass an area. Yet, only by refusing entry and risking a criminal conviction can the occupant challenge the inspector's decision to search. And even if the occupant possesses sufficient fortitude to take this risk, he may never learn any more about the reason for the inspection than that the law generally allows housing inspectors to gain entry. The practical effect of this system is to leave the occupant subject to the discretion of the official in the field. This is the discretion to invade private property which we have consistently circumscribed by a requirement that a disinterested party warrant the need to search.

The final justification suggested for warrantless administrative searches is that the public interest demands such a rule: it is argued that the health and safety of entire urban populations is dependent upon enforcement of minimum fire, housing, and sanitation standards, and that the only effective means of enforcing such codes is by routine systematized inspection of all physical structures. But the question is not whether these inspections may be made, but whether they may ✓ be made without a warrant. In assessing whether the public interest demands creation of a general exception to the Fourth Amendment's warrant requirement, the question is not whether the public interest justifies the type of search in question, but whether the authority to search should be evidenced by a warrant, which in turn depends in part upon whether the burden of obtaining a warrant is likely to frustrate the governmental purpose behind the search. It has nowhere been urged that fire, health, and housing code inspection programs could not achieve their goals within the confines of a reasonable search warrant requirement.

We hold that administrative searches of the kind at issue here are signifi- ✦ cant intrusions upon the interests protected by the Fourth Amendment, that such searches when authorized and conducted without a warrant procedure lack the traditional safeguards which the Fourth Amendment guarantees to the individual, and that the reasons put forth in *Frank* and other cases for upholding these warrantless searches are insufficient to justify so substantial a weakening of the Fourth Amendment's protections. Because of the nature of the municipal programs under consideration, these conclusions must be the beginning, not the end, of our inquiry.

In cases in which the Fourth Amendment requires that a warrant to search be obtained, "probable cause" is the standard by which a particular decision to search is tested against the constitutional mandate of reasonableness. To apply this standard, it is obviously necessary to focus upon the governmental interest which allegedly justifies official intrusion upon the constitutionally protected interests of the private citizen. In a criminal investigation, the police may undertake to recover specific stolen or contraband goods. But that public interest would hardly justify a sweeping search of an entire city in the hope that these goods might be found. A search for goods, even with a warrant, is "reasonable" only when there is "probable cause" to believe that they will be uncovered in a particular dwelling.

The inspection programs at issue are aimed at securing city-wide compliance with minimum physical standards for private property. The primary governmental interest at stake is to prevent even the unintentional development of conditions which are hazardous to public health and safety. Because fires and epidemics may ravage large urban areas, because unsightly conditions adversely affect the economic values of neighboring structures, numerous courts have upheld the police power of municipalities to impose and enforce such minimum standards even upon existing structures. In determining whether a particular inspection is reasonable—and thus in determining whether there is probable cause to issue a warrant for that inspection—the need for the inspection must be weighed in terms of these reasonable goals of code enforcement.

There is unanimous agreement among those most familiar with this field that the only effective way to seek universal compliance with the minimum standards required by municipal codes is through routine periodic inspections of all structures. It is here that the probable cause debate is focused, for the agency's decision to conduct an area inspection is unavoidably based on its appraisal of conditions in the area as a whole, not on its knowledge of conditions in each particular building. Appellee contends that, if the probable cause standard is adopted, the area inspection will be eliminated as a means of seeking compliance with code standards and the reasonable goals of code enforcement will be dealt a crushing blow.

There can be no ready test for determining reasonableness other than by balancing the need to search against the invasion which the search entails. A number of persuasive factors combine to support the reasonableness of area code-enforcement inspections. First, such programs have a long history of judicial and public acceptance. Second, the public interest demands that all dangerous conditions be prevented or abated, yet it is doubtful that any other canvassing technique would achieve acceptable results. Many such conditions—faulty wiring—are not observable from outside the building and indeed may not be apparent to the inexpert occupant himself. Finally, because the inspections are neither personal in nature nor aimed at the discovery of evidence of crime, they involve a relatively limited invasion of the urban citizen's privacy.

"Probable cause" to issue a warrant to inspect must exist if reasonable legislative or administrative standards for conducting an area inspection are satisfied with respect to a particular dwelling. Such standards, which will vary with the municipal program being enforced, may be based upon the passage of time, the nature of the building (*e.g.*, a multifamily apartment house), or the condition of the entire area, but they will not necessarily depend upon specific knowledge of the condition of the particular dwelling. It has been suggested that so to vary the probable cause test from the standard applied in criminal cases would be to authorize a "synthetic search warrant" and thereby to lessen the overall protections of the Fourth Amendment. We do not agree. The warrant procedure is designed to guarantee that a decision to search private property is justified by a reasonable governmental interest. But reasonableness is still the ultimate standard. If a valid public interest justifies the intrusion contemplated, then there is probable cause to issue a suitably restricted search warrant. Such an approach neither endangers time-honored doctrines applicable to criminal investigations nor makes a nullity of the probable cause requirement in this area. It merely gives full recognition to the competing public and private interests here at stake and, in so doing, best fulfills the historic purpose behind the constitutional right to be free from unreasonable government invasions of privacy.

Since our holding emphasizes the controlling standard of reasonableness, nothing we say is intended to foreclose prompt inspections, even without a warrant, that the law has traditionally upheld in emergency situations. *See North American Cold Storage Co. v. City of Chicago*, 211 U.S. 306 (seizure of unwholesome food); *Jacobson v. Commonwealth of Massachusetts*, 197 U.S. 11 (compulsory smallpox vaccination); *Compagnie Francaise de Navigation a Vapeur v. Louisiana State Board of Health*, 186 U.S. 380 (health quarantine); *Kroplin v. Truax*, 119 Ohio St. 610, 165 N.E. 498 (summary destruction of tubercular cattle). On the other hand, in the case of most routine area inspections, there is no compelling urgency to inspect at a particular time or on a particular day. Moreover, most citizens allow inspections of their property without a warrant. *Consent* Thus, as a practical matter and in light of the Fourth Amendment's requirement that a warrant specify the property to be searched, it seems likely that warrants should normally be sought only after entry is refused unless there has been a citizen complaint or there is other satisfactory reason for securing immediate entry. Similarly, the requirement of a warrant procedure does not suggest any change in what seems to be the prevailing local policy, in most situations, of authorizing entry, but not entry by force, to inspect.

In this case, appellant has been charged with a crime for his refusal to permit housing inspectors to enter his leasehold without a warrant. There was no emergency demanding immediate access; in fact, the inspectors made three trips to the building in an attempt to obtain appellant's consent to search. Yet no warrant was obtained and thus appellant was unable to verify either the need for or the appropriate limits of the inspection. We therefore conclude that appellant had a constitutional right to insist that the inspectors obtain a warrant to search and that appellant may not constitutionally be convicted for refusing to consent to the inspection.

Judgment vacated and case remanded.

Hypo 1: *Applying Camara*

Although *Camara* involved a person's home, its holding extends to government inspections of business property. Suppose that you are an attorney for the Occupational Safety & Health Administration (OSHA). You just received a call from Ms. Grace Harlow, a workplace inspector, assigned to the inspection of poultry factories. Tomorrow morning, Ms. Harlow plans to visit the Ajax Poultry Co. (Ajax). She wants to know whether she needs to obtain a warrant before going to the factory, or whether she can just show up. How would you advise Ms. Harlow? Does *Camara* force an inspector to begin every day at a judge's office seeking a warrant authorizing the search of a business or home?

Hypo 2: *The Factory Owner's Response*

Now, assume that you represent Ajax rather than OSHA. You receive a call from Ajax's President Herb Deets indicating that a Ms. Harlow, an OSHA inspector, just "showed up" at Ajax's factory—unannounced and without a warrant. (OSHA's attorneys advised Ms. Harlow that a warrant was not necessary.) Mr. Deets wants to know whether he should allow the inspector to enter without a warrant. Mr. Deets feels that his plant is in compliance with OSHA regulations. However, OSHA regulations are so strict that an overzealous inspector can always find a violation of OSHA. Would it be advisable to give, or to refuse, consent? Advise Mr. Deets.

Hypo 3: *The Elevator Inspector and the Cocaine*

Suppose that an elevator inspector enters an office building to inspect an elevator. While there, he happens to notice crack cocaine lying in plain view. You are the lawyer for the agency for which the inspector works, and he calls you for advice. May the inspector seize the cocaine? Can he make arrests? If not, what can he do? How should he proceed?

City of Los Angeles v. Patel

135 S.Ct. 2443 (2015)

JUSTICE SOTOMAYOR delivered the opinion of the Court.

Los Angeles Municipal Code (LAMC) § 41.49 requires hotel operators to record

information about their guests, including: the guest's name and address; the number of people in each guest's party; the make, model, and license plate number of any guest's vehicle parked on hotel property; the guest's date and time of arrival and scheduled departure date; the room number assigned to the guest; the rate charged and amount collected for the room; and the method of payment. Guests without reservations, those who pay for their rooms with cash, and any guests who rent a room for less than 12 hours must present photographic identification at the time of check-in, and hotel operators are required to record the number and expiration date of that document. For those guests who check in using an electronic kiosk, the hotel's records must also contain the guest's credit card information. This information can be maintained in either electronic or paper form, but it must be "kept on the hotel premises in the guest reception or guest check-in area or in an office adjacent" thereto for a period of 90 days. Section 41.49(3)(a) states that hotel guest records "shall be made available to any officer of the Los Angeles ✓ Police Department for inspection," provided that "whenever possible, the inspection shall be conducted at a time and in a manner that minimizes any interference with the operation of the business." A hotel operator's failure to make his or her guest records available for police inspection is a misdemeanor punishable by up to six months in jail and a $1,000 fine.

Respondents, a group of motel operators along with a lodging association, sued the city of Los Angeles challenging the constitutionality of § 41.49(3)(a). They sought declaratory and injunctive relief. The District Court entered judgment in favor of the City. A divided panel of the Ninth Circuit affirmed. On rehearing en banc, the Court of Appeals reversed. We granted certiorari and now affirm.

§ 41.49(3)(a) is facially unconstitutional because it fails to provide hotel operators with an opportunity for precompliance review. The Court has repeatedly held that "searches conducted outside the judicial process, without prior approval by a judge or a magistrate are *per se* unreasonable subject only to a few specifically established and well-delineated exceptions." *Arizona v. Gant*, 556 U.S. 332, 338 (2009). This rule "applies to commercial premises as well as to homes." *Marshall v. Barlow's*, Inc., 436 U.S. 307, 312 (1978).

Search regimes where no warrant is ever required may be reasonable where "special needs make the warrant and probable-cause requirement impracticable," and where the "primary purpose" of the searches is "distinguishable from the general interest in crime control," *Indianapolis v. Edmond*, 531 U.S. 32, 44 (2000). Here, we assume that the searches authorized by § 41.49 serve a "special need" other than conducting criminal investigations: They ensure compliance with the recordkeeping requirement, which in turn deters criminals from operating on the hotels' premises. The Court has referred to this kind of search as an "administrative search." *Camara v. Municipal Court of City and County of San Francisco*, 387 U.S. 523, 534 (1967).

Absent consent, exigent circumstances, or the like, in order for an administrative search to be constitutional, the subject of the search must be afforded an opportunity to obtain precompliance review before a neutral decisionmaker. While the Court has never attempted to prescribe the exact form an opportunity for precompliance review must take, the City does not argue that § 41.49(3)(a) affords hotel operators any opportunity whatsoever. Section 41.49(3)(a) is, therefore, facially invalid. A hotel owner who refuses to give an officer access to his or her registry can be arrested on the spot. The Court has held that business owners cannot reasonably be put to this kind of choice. *Camara*, 387 U.S., at 533. Absent an opportunity for precompliance review, the ordinance creates an intolerable risk that searches authorized by it will exceed statutory limits, or be used as a pretext to harass hotel operators and their guests. Even if a hotel has been searched 10 times a day, every day, for three months, without any violation being found, the operator can only refuse to comply with an officer's demand to turn over the registry at his or her own peril.

We hold only that a hotel owner must be afforded an *opportunity* to have a neutral decisionmaker review an officer's demand to search the registry before he or she faces penalties for failing to comply. Actual review need only occur in those rare instances where a hotel operator objects to turning over the registry. Moreover, this opportunity can be provided without imposing onerous burdens on those charged with an administrative scheme's enforcement. The searches authorized by § 41.49(3)(a) would be constitutional if they were performed pursuant to an administrative subpoena. These subpoenas, which are typically a simple form, can be issued by the individual seeking the record—here, officers in the field—without probable cause that a regulation is being infringed. Issuing a subpoena will usually be the full extent of an officer's burden because "the great majority of businessmen can be expected in normal course to consent to inspection without warrant." *Barlow's, Inc.*, 436 U.S., at 316.

In those instances where a subpoenaed hotel operator believes that an attempted search is motivated by illicit purposes, respondents suggest it would be sufficient if he or she could move to quash the subpoena before any search takes place. A neutral decisionmaker, including an administrative law judge, would then review the subpoenaed party's objections before deciding whether the subpoena is enforceable. Given the limited grounds on which a motion to quash can be granted, such challenges will likely be rare. In the even rarer event that an officer reasonably suspects that a hotel operator may tamper with the registry while the motion to quash is pending, he or she can guard the registry until the required hearing can occur, which ought not take long. *Illinois v. McArthur,* 531 U.S. 326 (2001). A 2002 report by the Department of Justice "identified approximately 335 existing administrative subpoena authorities held by various federal executive branch entities." In most contexts, business owners can be afforded at least an opportunity to contest an administrative search's propriety without unduly compromising the government's ability to achieve its regulatory aims. Of course administrative subpoenas are only one way in which an opportunity for precompliance review can be made available. But whatever the precise form, the availability of precompliance review alters the dynamic between the officer and the hotel to be searched, and reduces the risk that officers will use these administrative searches as a pretext to harass business owners.

Respondents have not challenged those parts of § 41.49 that require hotel operators to maintain guest registries containing certain information. Even absent legislative action to create a procedure along the lines discussed above, police will not be prevented from obtaining access to these documents. Hotel operators remain free to consent to searches of their registries and police can compel them to turn them over if they have a proper administrative warrant—including one that was issued *ex parte*—or if some other exception to the warrant requirement applies, including exigent circumstances.

✓ The City contends that hotels are "closely regulated," and that the ordinance is facially valid under the more relaxed standard that applies to searches of this category of businesses. Over the past 45 years, the Court has identified only four industries that "have such a history of government oversight that no reasonable expectation of privacy could exist for a proprietor over the stock of such an enterprise," See *Barlow's, Inc.,* 436 U.S., at 313. Unlike

In *New York v. Burger,* 482 U.S. 691, the Court took the extraordinary step of upholding warrantless searches of automobile junkyards by the police. The Court viewed the junkyards as constituting "closely regulated businesses," and upheld the searches even thought they were being conducted by the police.

liquor sales, *Colonnade Catering Corp. v. United States,* 397 U.S. 72 (1970), firearms dealing, *United States v. Biswell,* 406 U.S. 311, 311–312 (1972), mining, *Donovan v. Dewey,* 452 U.S. 594 (1981), or running an automobile junkyard, *New York v. Burger,* 482 U.S. 691 (1987), nothing inherent in the operation of hotels poses a clear and significant risk to the public welfare. See, *e.g., id., at 709* ("Automobile junkyards and vehicle dismantlers provide the major market for stolen vehicles and vehicle parts"); *Dewey*, 452 U.S., at 602 (describing the mining industry as "among the most hazardous in the country"). "The clear import of our cases is that the closely regulated industry is the exception." *Barlow's, Inc.*, 436 U.S., at 313. To classify hotels as pervasively regulated would permit what has always been a narrow exception to swallow the rule. The City refrains from arguing that § 41.49 itself renders hotels closely regulated. Nor do any of the other regulations—regulations requiring hotels to maintain a license, collect taxes, conspicuously post their rates, and meet certain sanitary standards—establish a comprehensive scheme of regulation that distinguishes hotels from numerous other businesses. All businesses in Los Angeles need a license to operate. While some regulations apply to a smaller set of businesses, these can hardly be said to have created a "comprehensive" scheme that puts hotel owners on notice that their "property will be subject to periodic inspections undertaken for specific purposes." *Burger*, 482 U.S., at 705, n. 16. Instead, they are more akin to the widely applicable minimum wage and maximum hour rules that the Court rejected as a basis for deeming "the entirety of American interstate commerce" to be closely regulated in *Barlow's, Inc.* If such general regulations were sufficient to invoke the closely regulated industry exception, it would be hard to imagine a type of business that would not qualify.

Petitioner attempts to recast this hodgepodge of regulations as a comprehensive scheme by referring to a "centuries-old tradition" of warrantless searches of hotels. Laws obligating inns to provide suitable lodging to all paying guests are not the same as laws subjecting inns to warrantless searches. Petitioner asserts that "for a long time, hotel owners left their registers open to widespread inspection." Setting aside that modern hotel registries contain sensitive information, such as driver's licenses and credit card numbers for which there is no historic analog, the fact that some hotels chose to make registries accessible to the public has little bearing on whether government authorities could have viewed these documents on demand without a hotel's consent.

Even if hotels are pervasively regulated, § 41.49 would need to satisfy three additional criteria to be reasonable under the Fourth Amendment: (1) "There must be a 'substantial' government interest that informs the regulatory scheme pursuant to which the inspection is made"; (2) "the warrantless inspections must be 'necessary' to further the regulatory scheme"; and (3) "the statute's inspection program, in terms of the certainty and regularity of its application, must provide a constitutionally adequate substitute for a warrant." *Burger*, 482 U.S., at 702. Petitioner's interest in ensuring that hotels maintain accurate and complete registries might fulfill the first of these requirements, but § 41.49 fails the second and third prongs.

The City claims that affording hotel operators any opportunity for precompliance review would fatally undermine the scheme's efficacy by giving operators a chance to falsify their records. This argument could be made regarding any recordkeeping requirement. Nothing precludes an officer from conducting a surprise inspection by obtaining an *ex parte* warrant or, where an officer reasonably suspects the registry would be altered, from guarding the registry pending a hearing on a motion to quash. See *Barlow's, Inc.*, 436 U.S., at 319-20. While there are approximately 2,000 hotels in Los Angeles, there is no basis to believe that resort to such measures will be needed to conduct spot checks in the vast majority of them.

Section 41.49 is constitutionally deficient under the "certainty and regularity" prong of the closely regulated industries test because it fails sufficiently to constrain police officers' discretion as to which hotels to search and under what circumstances. While the Court has upheld inspection schemes of closely regulated industries that called for searches at least four times a year, or on a "regular basis," § 41.49 imposes no comparable standard.

For the foregoing reasons, we agree that § 41.49(3)(a) is facially invalid insofar as it fails to provide any opportunity for precompliance review before a hotel must give its guest registry to the police for inspection. Accordingly, the judgment of the Ninth Circuit is affirmed.

It is so ordered.

Justice Scalia, with whom The Chief Justice and Justice Thomas join, dissenting.

In determining whether a business is closely regulated, this Court has looked to factors including the duration of the regulatory tradition, *Colonnade Catering Corp. v. United States*, 397 U.S. 72 (1970), *Donovan v. Dewey*, 452 U.S. 594 (1981); the comprehensiveness of the regulatory regime, and the imposition of similar regulations by other jurisdictions. These factors shed light on the expectation of privacy the owner of a business may reasonably have, which in turn affects the reasonableness of a warrantless search. Governments have long subjected motels to unique public duties, and have established inspection regimes to ensure compliance. "Innkeepers are bound to take, not merely ordinary care, but uncommon care, of the goods, money, and baggage of their guests," as travelers "are obliged to rely almost implicitly on the good faith of inn holders, who might have frequent opportunities of associating with ruffians and pilferers." At the time of the founding, searches—indeed, warrantless searches—of inns and similar places of public accommodation were commonplace. The regulatory tradition governing motels is not only longstanding, but comprehensive. Los Angeles imposes an occupancy tax upon transients who stay in motels, and makes the motel owner responsible for collecting it. It authorizes city officials "to enter a motel during business hours" in order to "inspect and examine" them to determine whether these tax provisions have been complied with. It requires all motels to obtain a "Transient Occupancy Registration Certificate," which must be displayed on the premises. State law requires motels to "post in a conspicuous place a statement of rate or range of rates by the day for lodging," and forbids any charges in excess of those posted rates. Hotels must change bed linens between guests, and they must offer guests the option not to have towels and linens laundered daily. "Multiuse drinking utensils" may be placed in guest rooms only if they are "thoroughly washed and sanitized after each use" and "placed in protective bags." State authorities, like their municipal counterparts, "may at reasonable times enter and inspect any hotels, motels, or other public places" to ensure compliance. The regulatory regime is thus substantially *more* comprehensive than the regulations governing junkyards in *Burger*, where licensing, inventory-recording, and permit-posting requirements were found sufficient to qualify the industry as closely regulated. This evidence is surely enough to establish that "when a motel operator chooses to engage in this pervasively regulated business he does so with the knowledge that his business records will be subject to effective inspection." *United States v. Biswell*, 406 U.S. 311, 316 (1972).

Since we first concluded in *Colonnade Catering* that warrantless searches of closely regulated businesses are reasonable, we have only identified *one* industry as *not* closely regulated. Lower courts, have identified many more businesses as closely regulated: pharmacies, massage parlors, commercial-fishing operations, day-care facilities, nursing homes, jewelers, barbershops, and even rabbit dealers. Like automobile junkyards and catering companies that serve alcohol, many of these businesses are far from "intrinsically dangerous." The reason closely regulated industries may be searched without a warrant has nothing to do with the risk of harm they pose; rather, it has to do with the expectations of those who enter such a line of work. The City's ordinance easily satisfies the remaining *Burger* requirements: It furthers a substantial governmental interest, it is necessary to achieving that interest, and it provides an adequate substitute for a search warrant.

The private pain and public costs imposed by drug dealing, prostitution, and human trafficking are beyond contention, and motels provide an obvious haven for those who trade in human misery. Although law enforcement can enter a motel room without a warrant when exigent circumstances exist, the whole reason criminals use motel rooms is that they offer privacy and secrecy, so that police will never come to discover these exigencies. The recordkeeping requirement operates by *deterring* crime. Criminals, who depend on the anonymity that motels offer, will balk when confronted with a motel's demand that they produce identification. And a motel's evasion of the recordkeeping requirement fosters crime. In San Diego, for example, motel owners were indicted for collaborating with members of the Crips street gang in the prostitution of underage girls; the motel owners "set aside rooms apart from the rest of their legitimate customers where girls and women were housed, charged the gang members/pimps a higher rate for the rooms where 'dates' or 'tricks' took place, and warned the gang members of inquiries by law enforcement." The warrantless inspection requirement provides a necessary incentive for motels to maintain their registers thoroughly and accurately: They never know when law enforcement might drop by to inspect. Motel operators who conspire with drug dealers and procurers may demand precompliance judicial review simply as a pretext to buy time for making fraudulent entries in their guest registers.

The Court suggests that police could obtain an administrative subpoena to search a guest register and, if a motel moves to quash, the police could "guard the registry pending a hearing" on the motion. This proposal protects motels from ✓ government inspection of their registers by authorizing government agents to seize the registers or to upset guests by a prolonged police presence at the motel. The Court also notes that police can obtain an *ex parte* warrant before conducting a register inspection. Presumably such warrants could issue without probable cause of wrongdoing by a particular motel, otherwise, this would be no alternative at all. Even so, under this regime police would have to obtain an *ex parte* warrant before *every* inspection. That is because law enforcement would have no way of knowing ahead of time which motels would refuse consent to a search upon request; and if they wait to obtain a warrant until consent is refused, motels will have the opportunity to falsify their guest registers while the police jump through the procedural hoops required to obtain a warrant. It is plausible that the costs of this always-get-a-warrant "alternative" would be prohibitive for a police force in one of America's largest cities, juggling numerous law-enforcement priorities, and confronting more than 2,000 motels within its jurisdiction. To be sure, the fact that obtaining a warrant might be costly will not by itself render a warrantless search reasonable under the Fourth Amendment; but it can render a warrantless search *necessary* in the context of an administrative-search regime governing closely regulated businesses. The administrative search need only be reasonable.

Finally, the City's ordinance provides an adequate substitute for a warrant. Warrants "advise the owner of the scope and objects of the search, beyond which limits the inspector is not expected to proceed." *Barlow's*, 436 U.S., at 323. Ultimately, they aim to protect against "devolving almost unbridled discretion upon executive and administrative officers, particularly those in the field, as to when to search and whom to search." *Ibid.* Nothing in the ordinance authorizes law ✓ enforcement to enter a nonpublic part of the motel. Compare this to the statute upheld in *Colonnade Catering*, which provided that "the Secretary or his delegate may enter, in the daytime, any building or place where any articles or objects subject to tax are made, produced, or kept, so far as it may be necessary for the purpose of examining said articles or objects." The Los Angeles ordinance—which limits warrantless police searches to the pages of a guest register in a public part of a motel—circumscribes police discretion in much more exacting terms than the laws we have approved in our earlier cases. The Court claims that Los Angeles's ordinance confers too much discretion because it does not adequately limit the *frequency* of searches. But the warrantless police searches of a business "10 times a day, every day, for three months" that the Court envisions under Los Angeles's regime are entirely consistent with the regimes in *Dewey* and *Burger*; 10 times a day, every day, is "at least four times a year," and on a (much too) "regular basis."

An administrative, warrantless-search ordinance that narrowly limits the scope of searches to a single business record, that does not authorize entry upon premises not open to the public, and that is supported by the need to prevent fabrication of guest registers, is far afield from the laws at issue in the cases the Court relies upon. The Court concludes that such minor intrusions, permissible when the police are trying to tamp down the market in stolen auto parts, are "unreasonable" when police are instead attempting to stamp out the market in child sex slaves.

Even though *Camara* loosened the probable cause requirements for administrative searches, illegal inspections do occur. Sometimes, an agency obtains a warrant but the warrant was invalidly issued. In other cases, as in *Barlow*, the agency searches without a warrant when one is required. Or, as sometimes happens, the police conduct an illegal search and give the results to administrative officials.

Point for Discussion

Trucker Checkpoints

In *United States v. Parker*, 583 F.3d 1049 (8th Cir. 2009), the court held that interstate trucking is a closely regulated industry so that state officials can stop truckers at checkpoints and conduct random inquiries regarding compliance with state truck regulation laws. In *Parker*, a police officer made a random check of a truck that was pulling a trailer containing three vehicles: a 2001 Ford Excursion, a 1995 Nissan Quest, and a 2000 Chevrolet Silverado. The check was a "Level 1 inspection" under the North American Standard Inspection

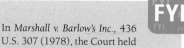

In *Marshall v. Barlow's Inc.*, 436 U.S. 307 (1978), the Court held that the Occupational Safety & Health Act, which authorized health and safety inspections of workplaces, did not authorize warrantless searches. The Court noted that virtually every business is subject to OSHA, and therefore an OSHA exception would eviscerate the Fourth Amendment warrant requirement. In addition, the Court concluded that there was less need and justification for warrantless inspections.

Program (NASIP) that involved a check of the driver's logbook, bills of lading, insurance, and license. During the stop, the officer determined that the driver did not have a commercial license, and that his logbook was not up-to-date, and ordered defendant not to proceed for the next 10 hours. Although the officer did not require defendant to remain with the truck, he did remain and ultimately consented to a search of vehicles that he was transporting (which were found to contain contraband drugs).

Hypo: *McCown Iron*

Occupational Safety and Health Administration (OSHA) officials have a long and complicated history with McCown Iron Works (McCown Iron), an iron foundry in Coeur d'Alene, Idaho. When OSHA attempted a few years ago, John McCown, CEO and principal owner, refused to permit inspectors to enter. OSHA aborted the attempted search. Later that year, in response to an employee complaint, OHSA made an unannounced visit to the foundry with a warrant. McCown Iron barred entry and was held in contempt of court. The next year, when OSHA sent letters of inquiry to McCown Iron, after receiving letters of complaint from McCown Iron employees, John McCown responded aggressively. In a letter to OSHA, McCown stated that: "You have wasted my time and taxpayer money without improving safety. This is the problem with OSHA. It makes you look like fools and wastes everyone's time and money. Why don't you try to help the employers by providing information about unsafe products and processes rather than acting like the Gestapo with secret informants and star courts." Despite the letters of inquiry, OSHA did not attempt to inspect McCown Iron.

A few months ago, OSHA sought a search warrant to inspect McCown Iron's foundry. In its application to a federal court, OSHA stated that McCown was selected pursuant to its General Schedule System (GSS) which outlines OSHA's search policies and assigns each industry a nationwide Standard Industrial Classification (SIC) Code. OSHA also complies lists which show each industry employer with a lost work day injury rate (LWDI) at or above the national LWDI rate for their industries.

From this list, inspection sites are selected randomly for each high rate industry. Based on the GSS, SIC and LWDI, a federal court issued a warrant. Suppose that you represent McCown Iron, and John McCown has called you for advice. The company would like to resist the subpoena. May it do so? On what grounds? Will McCown Iron suffer any special risks if it refuses to admit OSHA inspectors? How is OSHA likely to respond to McCown Iron's arguments, and how would you expect the court to rule?

8. Stop and Frisk

Although the "stop and frisk" exception is one of the more recent exceptions to the warrant requirement, it has reshaped Fourth Amendment law in important respects.

Terry v. State of Ohio

392 U.S. 1 (1968).

MR. CHIEF JUSTICE WARREN delivered the opinion of the Court.

Petitioner Terry was convicted of carrying a concealed weapon and sentenced to one to three years in the penitentiary. Following denial of a motion to suppress, the prosecution introduced in evidence two revolvers and a number of bullets seized from Terry and a codefendant by Cleveland Police Detective Martin McFadden. At the hearing on the motion to suppress this evidence, Officer McFadden testified that while he was patrolling in plain clothes in downtown Cleveland at approximately 2:30 in the afternoon, his attention was attracted by two men, Chilton and Terry, standing on the corner of Huron Road and Euclid Avenue. He had never seen the two men before, and he was unable to say precisely what first drew his eye to them. However, he testified that he had been a policeman for 39 years and a detective for 35 and that he had been assigned to patrol this vicinity of downtown Cleveland for shoplifters and pickpockets for 30 years. He explained that he had developed routine habits of observation over the years and that he would "stand and watch people or walk and watch people at many intervals of the day." "Now, in this case when I looked over they didn't look right to me at the time."

His interest aroused, Officer McFadden took up a post of observation in the entrance to a store 300 to 400 feet away from the two men. He saw one of the men leave the other one and walk southwest on Huron Road, past some stores. The man paused for a moment and looked in a store window, then walked on a short distance, turned around and walked back toward the corner, pausing once again to look in the same store window. He rejoined his companion at the corner, and the two conferred briefly. Then the second man went through the same series of motions, strolling down Huron Road, looking in the same window, walking on a short distance, turning back, peering in the store window again, and returning to confer with the first man at the corner. The two men repeated this ritual alternately between five and six times apiece—in all, roughly a dozen trips. At one point, while the two were standing together on the corner, a third man approached them and engaged them briefly in conversation. This man then left the two others and walked west. Chilton and Terry resumed their measured pacing, peering and conferring. After this had gone on for 10 to 12 minutes, the two men walked off together, heading west, following the path taken earlier by the third man.

By this time Officer McFadden had become thoroughly suspicious. After observing their elaborately casual and oft-repeated reconnaissance of the store window, he suspected the two men of "casing a job, a stick-up," and he considered it his duty as a police officer to investigate further. He feared "they may have a gun." Officer McFadden followed Chilton and Terry and saw them stop in front of Zucker's store to talk to the same man who had conferred with them earlier. Deciding that the situation was ripe for direct action, Officer McFadden approached the three men, identified himself as a police officer and asked for their names. At this point his knowledge was confined to what he had observed. He was not acquainted with any of the three men by name or by sight, and he had received no information concerning them from any other source. When the men "mumbled something" in response to his inquiries, Officer McFadden grabbed petitioner Terry, spun him around so that they were facing the other two, with Terry between McFadden and the others, and patted down the outside of his clothing. In the left breast pocket of Terry's overcoat Officer McFadden felt a pistol. He reached inside the overcoat, but was unable to remove the gun. At this point, keeping Terry between himself and the others, the officer ordered all three men to enter Zucker's store. As they went in, he removed Terry's overcoat completely, removed a .38-caliber revolver from the pocket and ordered all three men to face the wall with their hands raised. Officer McFadden proceeded to pat down the outer clothing of Chilton and the third man, Katz. He discovered another revolver in the outer pocket of Chilton's overcoat, but no weapons on Katz. The officer testified that he only patted the men down to see whether they had weapons, and that he did not put his hands beneath the outer garments of either Terry or Chilton until he felt their guns. He never placed his hands beneath Katz' outer garments. Officer McFadden seized Chilton's gun, asked the proprietor of the store to call a police wagon, and took all three men to the station, where Chilton and Terry were formally charged with carrying concealed weapons.

We granted certiorari to determine whether the admission of the revolvers in evidence violated petitioner's rights under the Fourth Amendment, made applicable to the States by the Fourteenth.

Petitioner was entitled to the protection of the Fourth Amendment as he walked down the street in Cleveland. The question is whether in all the circumstances of this on-the-street encounter, his right to personal security was violated by an unreasonable search and seizure. This question thrusts to the fore difficult and troublesome issues regarding a sensitive area of police activity. It is frequently argued that in dealing with the rapidly unfolding and often dangerous situations on city streets the police are in need of an escalating set of flexible responses, graduated in relation to the amount of information they possess. For this purpose it is urged that distinctions should be made between a "stop" and an "arrest" (or a "seizure" of a person), and between a "frisk" and a "search." Thus, it is argued, the police should be allowed to "stop" a person and detain him briefly for questioning upon suspicion that he may be connected with criminal activity. Upon suspicion that the person may be armed, the police should have the power to "frisk" him for weapons. If the "stop" and the "frisk" give rise to probable cause to believe that the suspect has committed a crime, then the police should be empowered to make a formal "arrest," and a full incident "search" of the person. This scheme is justified in part upon the notion that a "stop" and a "frisk" amount to a mere "minor inconvenience and petty indignity," which can properly be imposed upon the citizen in the interest of effective law enforcement on the basis of a police officer's suspicion.

The argument is made that the authority of the police must be strictly circumscribed by the law of arrest and search as it has developed to date in the traditional jurisprudence of the Fourth Amendment. It is contended with some force that there is not—and cannot be—a variety of police activity which does not depend solely upon the voluntary cooperation of the citizen and yet which stops short of an arrest based upon probable cause to make such an arrest. The heart of the Fourth Amendment, the argument runs, is a severe requirement of specific justification for any intrusion upon protected personal security, coupled with a highly developed system of judicial controls to enforce upon the agents of the State the commands of the Constitution. We approach the issues in this case mindful of the limitations of the judicial function in controlling the myriad daily situations in which policemen and citizens confront each other on the street.

We turn our attention to the quite narrow question posed by the facts before us: whether it is always unreasonable for a policeman to seize a person and subject him to a limited search for weapons unless there is probable cause for an arrest. Our first task is to establish at what point in this encounter the Fourth Amendment becomes relevant. We must decide whether and when Officer McFadden "seized" Terry and whether and when he conducted a "search." There is some suggestion in the use of such terms as "stop" and "frisk" that such police conduct is outside the purview of the Fourth Amendment because neither action rises to the level of a "search" or "seizure" within the meaning of the Constitution. We emphatically reject this notion. It is quite plain that the Fourth Amendment governs "seizures" of the person which do not eventuate in a trip to the station house and prosecution for crime—"arrests" in traditional terminology. Whenever a police officer accosts an individual and restrains his freedom to walk away, he has "seized" that person. And it is nothing less than sheer torture of the English language to suggest that a careful exploration of the outer surfaces of a person's clothing all over his or her body in an attempt to find weapons is not a "search." Moreover, it is simply fantastic to urge that such a procedure performed in public by a policeman while the citizen stands helpless, perhaps facing a wall with his hands raised, is a "petty indignity." It is a serious intrusion upon the sanctity of the person, which may inflict great indignity and arouse strong resentment, and it is not to be undertaken lightly.

The danger in the logic which proceeds upon distinctions between a "stop" and an "arrest," or "seizure" of the person, and between a "frisk" and a "search" is twofold. It seeks to isolate from constitutional scrutiny the initial stages of the contact between the policeman and the citizen. By suggesting a rigid all-or-nothing model of justification and regulation under the Amendment, it obscures the utility of limitations upon the scope, as well as the initiation, of police action as a means of constitutional regulation. This Court has held in the past that a search which is reasonable at its inception may violate the Fourth Amendment by virtue of its intolerable intensity and scope. The scope of the search must be "strictly tied to and justified by" the circumstances which rendered its initiation permissible.

The distinctions of classical "stop-and-frisk" theory thus serve to divert attention from the central inquiry under the Fourth Amendment—the reasonableness in all the circumstances of the particular governmental invasion of a citizen's personal security. "Search" and "seizure" are not talismans. We therefore reject the notions that the Fourth Amendment does not come into play at all as a limitation upon police conduct if the officers stop short of something called a "technical arrest" or a "full-blown search."

In this case there can be no question that Officer McFadden "seized" petitioner and subjected him to a "search" when he took hold of him and patted down the outer surfaces of his clothing. We must decide whether at that point it was reasonable for Officer McFadden to have interfered with petitioner's personal security as he did. And in determining whether the seizure and search were "unreasonable" our inquiry is a dual one—whether the officer's action was justified at its inception, and whether it was reasonably related in scope to the circumstances which justified the interference in the first place.

We do not retreat from our holdings that the police must, whenever practicable, obtain advance judicial approval of searches and seizures through the warrant procedure, or that in most instances failure to comply with the warrant requirement can only be excused by exigent circumstances. But we deal here with an entire rubric of police conduct—necessarily swift action predicated upon the on-the-spot observations of the officer on the beat—which historically has not been, and as a practical matter could not be, subjected to the warrant procedure. Instead, the conduct involved in this case must be tested by the Fourth Amendment's general proscription against unreasonable searches and seizures.

Nonetheless, the notions which underlie both the warrant procedure and the requirement of probable cause remain fully relevant in this context. In order to assess the reasonableness of Officer McFadden's conduct as a general proposition, it is necessary "first to focus upon the governmental interest which allegedly justifies official intrusion upon the constitutionally protected interests of the private citizen," for there is "no ready test for determining reasonableness other than by balancing the need to search (or seize) against the invasion which the search (or seizure) entails." *Camara v. Municipal Court*, 387 U.S. 523, 534–535 (1967). In justifying the particular intrusion the police officer must be able to point to specific and articulable facts which, taken together with rational inferences from those facts, reasonably warrant that intrusion. The scheme of the Fourth Amendment becomes meaningful only when it is assured that at some point the conduct of those charged with enforcing the laws can be subjected to the more detached, neutral scrutiny of a judge who must evaluate the reasonableness of a particular search or seizure in light of the particular circumstances. In making that assessment it is imperative that the facts be judged against an objective standard: would the facts available to the officer at the moment of the seizure or the search "warrant a man of reasonable caution in the belief" that the action taken was appropriate? Anything less would invite intrusions upon constitutionally guaranteed rights based on nothing more substantial than inarticulate hunches, a result this Court has consistently refused to sanction. Simple "good faith on the part of the arresting officer is not enough. If subjective good faith alone were the test, the protections of the Fourth Amendment would evaporate, and the people would be 'secure in their persons, houses, papers and effects,' only in the discretion of the police."

Applying these principles, we consider the nature and extent of the governmental interests involved. One general interest is that of effective crime prevention and detection; it is this interest which underlies the recognition that a police officer may in appropriate circumstances and in an appropriate manner approach a person for purposes of investigating possibly criminal behavior even though there is no probable cause to make an arrest. It was this legitimate investigative function Officer McFadden was discharging when he decided to approach petitioner and his companions after he had observed Terry, Chilton, and Katz go through a series of acts, each of them perhaps innocent in itself, but which taken together warranted further investigation. There is nothing unusual in two men standing together on a street corner, perhaps waiting for someone. Nor is there anything suspicious about people in such circumstances strolling up and down the street, singly or in pairs. Store windows are made to be looked in. But the story is quite different where, as here, two men hover about a street corner for an extended period of time, at the end of which it becomes apparent that they are not waiting for anyone or anything; where these men pace alternately along an identical route, pausing to stare in the same store window roughly 24 times; where each completion of this route is followed immediately by a conference between the two men on the corner; where they are joined in one of these conferences by a third man who leaves swiftly; and where the two men finally follow the third and rejoin him a couple of blocks away. It would have been poor police work indeed for an officer of 30 years' experience in the detection of thievery from stores in this same neighborhood to have failed to investigate this behavior further.

The crux of this case is not the propriety of Officer McFadden's taking steps to investigate petitioner's suspicious behavior, but whether there was justification for McFadden's invasion of Terry's personal security by searching him for weapons in the course of that investigation. We are concerned with more than the governmental interest in investigating crime; there is the more immediate interest of the police officer in taking steps to assure himself that the person with whom he is dealing is not armed with a weapon that could unexpectedly and fatally be used against him. Certainly it would be unreasonable to require that police officers take unnecessary risks in the performance of their duties. American criminals have a long tradition of armed violence, and every year in this country many law enforcement officers are killed in the line of duty, and thousands more are wounded. Virtually all of these deaths and a substantial portion of the injuries are inflicted with guns and knives.

We cannot blind ourselves to the need for law enforcement officers to protect themselves and other prospective victims of violence in situations where they may lack probable cause for an arrest. When an officer is justified in believing that the individual whose suspicious behavior he is investigating at close range is armed and presently dangerous to the officer or to others, it would appear to be clearly unreasonable to deny the officer the power to take necessary measures to determine whether the person is in fact carrying a weapon and to neutralize the threat of physical harm.

We must still consider the nature and quality of the intrusion on individual rights which must be accepted if police officers are to be conceded the right to search for weapons in situations where probable cause to arrest for crime is lacking. Even a limited search of the outer clothing for weapons constitutes a severe, though brief, intrusion upon cherished personal security, and it must surely be an annoying, frightening, and perhaps humiliating experience. Petitioner contends that such an intrusion is permissible only incident to a lawful arrest, either for a crime involving the possession of weapons or for a crime the commission of which led the officer to investigate in the first place. However, this argument must be closely examined.

Petitioner does not argue that a police officer should refrain from making any investigation of suspicious circumstances until such time as he has probable cause to make an arrest; nor does he deny that police officers in properly discharging their investigative function may find themselves confronting persons who might well be armed and dangerous. Moreover, he does not say that an officer is always unjustified in searching a suspect to discover weapons. Rather, he says it is unreasonable for the policeman to take that step until such time as the situation evolves to a point where there is probable cause to make an arrest. When that point has been reached, petitioner would concede the officer's right to conduct a search of the suspect for weapons, fruits or instrumentalities of the crime, or "mere" evidence, incident to the arrest.

There are two weaknesses in this line of reasoning. First, it fails to take account of traditional limitations upon the scope of searches, and thus recognizes no distinction in purpose, character, and extent between a search incident to an arrest and a limited search for weapons. The former, although justified in part by the acknowledged necessity to protect the arresting officer from assault with a concealed weapon, is also justified on other grounds, and can therefore involve a relatively extensive exploration of the person. A search for weapons in the absence of probable cause to arrest, however, must, like any other search, be strictly circumscribed by the exigencies which justify its initiation. Thus it must be limited to that which is necessary for the discovery of weapons which might be used to harm the officer or others nearby, and may realistically be characterized as something less than a "full" search, even though it remains a serious intrusion.

A second, and related, objection to petitioner's argument is that it assumes that the law of arrest has already worked out the balance between the particular interests involved here—the neutralization of danger to the policeman in the investigative circumstance and the sanctity of the individual. This is not so. An arrest is a wholly different kind of intrusion upon individual freedom from a limited search for weapons, and the interests each is designed to serve are likewise quite different. An arrest is the initial stage of a criminal prosecution. It is intended to vindicate society's interest in having its laws obeyed, and it is inevitably accompanied by future interference with the individual's freedom of movement, whether or not trial or conviction ultimately follows. The protective search for weapons, on the other hand, constitutes a brief, though far from inconsiderable, intrusion upon the sanctity of the person. It does not follow that because an officer may lawfully arrest a person only when he is apprised of facts sufficient to warrant a belief that the person has committed or is committing a crime, the officer is equally unjustified, absent that kind of evidence, in making any intrusions short of an arrest. Moreover, a perfectly reasonable apprehension of danger may arise long before the officer is possessed of adequate information to justify taking a person into custody for the purpose of prosecuting him for a crime.

Our evaluation of the proper balance that has to be struck in this type of case leads us to conclude that there must be a narrowly drawn authority to permit a reasonable search for weapons for the protection of the police officer, where he has reason to believe that he is dealing with an armed and dangerous individual, regardless of whether he has probable cause to arrest the individual for a crime. The officer need not be absolutely certain that the individual is armed; the issue is whether a reasonably prudent man in the circumstances would be warranted in the belief that his safety or that of others was in danger. And in determining whether the officer acted reasonably in such circumstances, due weight must be given, not to his inchoate and unparticularized suspicion or "hunch," but to the specific reasonable inferences which he is entitled to draw from the facts in light of his experience.

We must now examine the conduct of Officer McFadden in this case to determine whether his search and seizure of petitioner were reasonable, both at their inception and as conducted. He had observed Terry, together with Chilton and another man, acting in a manner he took to be preface to a "stick-up." We think on the facts and circumstances Officer McFadden detailed before the trial judge a reasonably prudent man would have been warranted in believing petitioner was armed and thus presented a threat to the officer's safety while he was investigating his suspicious behavior. The actions of Terry and Chilton were consistent with McFadden's hypothesis that these men were contemplating a daylight robbery—which would be likely to involve the use of weapons—and nothing in their conduct from the time he first noticed them until the time he confronted them and identified himself as a police officer gave him sufficient reason to negate that hypothesis. Although the trio had departed the original scene, there was nothing to indicate abandonment of an intent to commit a robbery. Thus, when Officer McFadden approached the three men gathered before Zucker's store he had observed enough to make it quite reasonable to fear that they were armed; and nothing in their response to his hailing them, identifying himself as a police officer, and asking their names served to dispel that reasonable belief. We cannot say his decision at that point to seize Terry and pat his clothing for weapons was the product of a volatile or inventive imagination, or was undertaken simply as an act of harassment; the record evidences the tempered act of a policeman who in the course of an investigation had to make a quick decision as to how to protect himself and others from possible danger, and took limited steps to do so.

The manner in which the seizure and search were conducted is as vital a part of the inquiry as whether they were warranted at all. We need not develop at length the limitations which the Fourth Amendment places upon a protective seizure and search for weapons. These limitations will have to be developed in the concrete factual circumstances of individual cases. Suffice it to note that such a search, unlike a search without a warrant incident to a lawful arrest, is not justified by any need to prevent the disappearance or destruction of evidence of crime. The sole justification of the search is the protection of the police officer and others nearby, and it must therefore be confined in scope to an intrusion reasonably designed to discover guns, knives, clubs, or other hidden instruments for the assault of the police officer.

The scope of the search in this case presents no serious problem in light of these standards. Officer McFadden patted down the outer clothing of petitioner and his two companions. He did not place his hands in their pockets or under the outer surface of their garments until he had felt weapons, and then he merely reached for and removed the guns. He never did invade Katz' person beyond the outer surfaces of his clothes, since he discovered nothing in his patdown which might have been a weapon. Officer McFadden confined his search strictly to what was minimally necessary to learn whether the men were armed and to disarm them once he discovered the weapons. He did not conduct a general exploratory search for whatever evidence of criminal activity he might find.

We conclude that the revolver seized from Terry was properly admitted in evidence against him. At the time he seized petitioner and searched him for weapons, Officer McFadden had reasonable grounds to believe that petitioner was armed and dangerous, and it was necessary for the protection of himself and others to take swift measures to discover the true facts and neutralize the threat of harm if it materialized. The policeman carefully restricted his search to what was appropriate to the discovery of the particular items which he sought. Each case of this sort will have to be decided on its own facts. We merely hold today that where a police officer observes unusual conduct which leads him reasonably to conclude in light of his experience that criminal activity may be afoot and that the persons with whom he is dealing may be armed and presently dangerous, where in the course of investigating this behavior he identifies himself as a policeman and makes reasonable inquiries, and where nothing in the initial stages of the encounter serves to dispel his reasonable fear for his own or others' safety, he is entitled for the protection of himself and others in the area to conduct a carefully limited search of the outer clothing of such persons in an attempt to discover weapons which might be used to assault him. Such a search is a reasonable search under the Fourth Amendment, and any weapons seized may properly be introduced in evidence against the person from whom they were taken.

Affirmed.

MR. JUSTICE HARLAN, concurring.

A limited frisk incident to a lawful stop must often be rapid and routine. There is no reason why an officer, rightfully but forcibly confronting a person suspected of a serious crime, should have to ask one question and take the risk that the answer might be a bullet.

MR. JUSTICE DOUGLAS, dissenting.

The infringement on personal liberty of any "seizure" of a person can only be "reasonable" under the Fourth Amendment if we require the police to possess "probable cause" before they seize him. Only that line draws a meaningful distinction between an officer's mere inkling and the presence of facts within the officer's personal knowledge which would convince a reasonable man that the person seized has committed, is committing, or is about to commit a particular crime. To give the police greater power than a magistrate is to take a long step down the totalitarian path. Perhaps such a step is desirable to cope with modern forms of lawlessness. But if it is taken, it should be the deliberate choice of the people through a constitutional amendment.

Points for Discussion

a. More on Frisks

In *Florida v. J.L.*, 529 U.S. 266 (2000), the police received an anonymous tip that a young black male wearing a plaid shirt at a bus stop was carrying a gun. At the stop, the police find three young black males, including one who is wearing a plaid shirt. Except for the tip, the officers have no reason to believe that any of the males is engaged in illegal conduct. The officers immediately frisk defendant, find a gun in his pocket, and charge him with carrying a concealed firearm. The Court invalidated the search: "All the police had to go on in this case was the bare report of an unknown, unaccountable informant who neither explained how he knew about the gun nor supplied any basis for believing he had inside information about J.L. An accurate description of a subject's readily observable location and appearance will help the police correctly identify the person whom the tipster means to accuse. Such a tip, however, does not show that the tipster has knowledge of concealed criminal activity. Reasonable suspicion here requires that a tip be reliable in its assertion of illegality, not just in its tendency to identify a determinate person." The Court also rejected the state's contention that *Terry* should encompass a "firearms exception" permitting police to stop and frisk individuals for firearms.

When is it permissible to search the passenger compartment of a car? In *Michigan v. Long*, 463 U.S. 1032 (1983), the police saw a car traveling "erratically" and at excessive speed. When the car turned down a side road and swerved into a shallow ditch, the officers stopped to investigate. Long (the driver) appeared to be "under the influence," and officers observed a large hunting knife on the floorboard of the driver's side of the car. The officers then subjected Long to a frisk that revealed no weapons, and searched his car where they found marijuana. The Court upheld Long's conviction for possession:

> Roadside encounters between police and suspects are especially hazardous, and danger may arise from the possible presence of weapons in the area surrounding a suspect. The search of the passenger compartment of an automobile, limited to those areas in which a weapon may be placed or hidden, is permissible if the police officer possesses a reasonable belief based on "specific and articulable facts which, taken together with the rational inferences from those facts, reasonably warrant" the officers in believing that the suspect is dangerous and the suspect may gain immediate control of weapons. The circumstances clearly justified the officers in their reasonable belief that Long posed a danger if he were permitted to reenter his vehicle. The hour was late and the area rural. Long was driving his automobile at excessive speed, and his car swerved into a ditch. The officers had to repeat their questions to Long, who appeared to be "under the influence" of some intoxicant. Long was not frisked until the officers observed that there was a large knife in the interior of the car into which Long was about to reenter. The search of the car was restricted to those areas to Long would have immediate control, and that could contain a weapon. The leather pouch containing marijuana could have contained a weapon. It is clear that the intrusion was "strictly circumscribed by the exigencies which justified its initiation." A *Terry* suspect in Long's position might break away from police control and retrieve a weapon from his automobile. In addition, if the suspect is not placed under arrest, he will be permitted to reenter his automobile, and he will then have access to any weapons inside. Or the suspect may be permitted to reenter the vehicle before the *Terry* investigation is over, and again, may have access to weapons.

b. The "Bulge"

In *Pennsylvania v. Mimms*, 434 U.S. 106 (1966), the police stopped a vehicle because it's license plane was expired. The officer approached the vehicle, asked the driver to step out, and also asked for the driver's license and registration. When the man exited the vehicle, the officer observed a "bulge" under the man's sports jacket, and decided to frisk him. In *Mimms*, the Court upheld the frisk. Even though the suspect was not acting suspiciously, the "bulge permitted the

 Food for Thought

Would *Michigan v. Long* (referred to in the immediately preceding FYI box) justify the police in conducting a frisk when the police did not find a weapon (or have reason to believe that the driver had one), but the driver appeared to be nervous, was uncooperative, and verbally belligerent? *See Frazier v. Commonwealth*, 406 S.W.3d 448 (Ky. 2013). Would a frisk be allowed if the officer, during the course of a lawful stop, observes bullets in the car's ashtray? *See State v. Santos*, 64 A.3d 314 (R.I. 2013).

officer to conclude that Mimms was armed and thus posed a serious and present danger to the safety of the officer. In these circumstances, any man of 'reasonable caution' would likely have conducted the 'pat down.'"

c. The Recovering Drug Addict

In *Sibron v. New York*, 392 U.S. 40 (1968), a police officer continuously observed Sibron from 4:00 p.m. until midnight, observing him in conversation with known drug addicts. The officer could not overhear these conversations, and did not see anything pass between Sibron and the addicts. Late evening, Sibron enters a restaurant and begins eating with several known addicts. At that point, the officer approaches Sibron and states "You know what I am after." Sibron mumbles something and thrusts has hand into his pocket. The officer immediately reaches into the same pocket and finds several envelopes containing heroin. The Court rejected the idea that "persons who talk to narcotics addicts are engaged in the criminal traffic in narcotics" and found that the officer did not fear that Sibron was going for a weapon when he stuck his hand in his pocket. Justice Black dissented: "When Sibron, who had been approaching and talking to addicts for eight hours, reached his hand quickly to his left coat pocket, he might well be reaching for a gun. A policeman under such circumstances has to act in a split second; delay may mean death for him."

d. The Seated Suspect

In *Adams v. Williams*, 407 U.S. 143 (1972), a police officer, working in a high crime area, received a tip that an individual seated in a nearby car was carrying narcotics and had a gun in his waistband. The officer approached the vehicle, tapped on the window, and asked the driver to open his door. When the driver rolled down his window instead, the officer reached into the vehicle and retrieved a fully loaded revolver from the suspect's waistband. The Court upheld the decision to reach into the vehicle. "Under these circumstances the policeman's action in reaching to the spot where the gun was thought to be hidden constituted a limited intrusion designed to insure his safety, and we conclude that it was reasonable. The loaded gun was therefore admissible at Williams' trial." Justice Marshall dissented, arguing that there was insufficient basis for a frisk.

Food for Thought

Was it really necessary for the Court to create the stop and frisk exception? Did Officer McFadden have probable cause to arrest Terry and his cohorts? Did he have probable cause to search them? Even if McFadden possessed probable cause to search, based on what you have studied thus far, could he have searched Terry without a warrant? Should Officer McFadden have been forced to wait until Terry and his cohorts "made their move?"

e. Frisking Passengers

In *Arizona v. Johnson*, 555 U.S. 323 (2009), police were on patrol one evening in a neighborhood associated with the Crips gang. When an officer stopped and approached a vehicle, she noticed that one of the passengers was wearing a blue bandana associated with the Crips gang and had a scanner. She regarded the scanner as suspicious because few people carry scanners unless they are engaged in criminal activity or are trying to avoid the police. The passenger provided his name and volunteered that he lived in a nearby city associated with the Crips gang, as well as the fact that he had served time in prison for burglary. The Court held that, when an officer validly stops a vehicle, and develops reason to believe that a passenger is armed and dangerous, then the officer may pat down the passenger. The Court found sufficient basis for the pat down in the *Johnson* case.

f. The N.Y.P.D. Decree

In 2013, a federal judge concluded that the N.Y.P.D.'s stop and frisk policy disproportionately targeted blacks and Hispanics, and ordered the N.Y.P.D. to order additional training, and develop a "remedial process." *See Floyd v. City of New York*, 959 F. Supp.2d 540 (S.D.N.Y. 2013). The decree seemed to be inconsistent with U.S. Supreme Court precedent. *See Rizzo v. Goode*, 423 U.S. 362 (1976). The court of appeals eventually overturned the decree and ordered the judge removed from the case. *See Ligon v. City of New York*, 736 F.3d 231 (2d Cir. 2013).

Hypo 1: *NRA Affliations*

A police officer stops a pickup truck for speeding on a public highway. As the officer approaches the truck, he notices a "National Rifle Association" sticker on the back window. Even though the officer does not otherwise have a basis for concluding that the driver is "armed" and "dangerous," can the officer conduct a stop and frisk on the basis of the sticker? *See Estep v. Dallas County*, 310 F.3d 353 (5th Cir. 2002). In that same vein, suppose that a University of Louisville nursing student blogs about the importance of a citizen's right to bear arms, but does not advocate for violent or illegal conduct. When nursing schools officials decide to dismiss the woman for blog comments that they regard as racist (the dismissal was later overturned by the courts), they want to subject her to a frisk before bringing her into the nursing school office. Based on the blog, and the woman's stated positions regarding the right to bear arms, can school officials assume that the woman is "armed and dangerous" and subject her to a stop and frisk? See Andrew Wolfson, *U of L Dismisses Student Over Blog Posts: Woman Files Lawsuit To Gain Restatement*, Courier-Journal, Mar. 14, 2009, at B–1, c. 1–5.

Hypo 2: *Guns and Drug Deals*

Suppose that the police have probable cause to believe that the driver of a vehicle has engaged in a drug deal. Do they have sufficient cause to frisk any passenger they find riding in the vehicle? *See State v. Lemert*, 843 N.W.2d 227 (Minn. 2014). What if the driver is wanted for commission of a violent crime (pistol whipping) and is a suspect in a shooting? If a solo officer attempts to arrest the driver, who is accompanied by three others, may he frisk the other three passengers? *See United States v. Howard*, 729 F.3rd 665 (7th Cir. 2013).

Hypo 3: *The Fleeing Suspect*

While police officers are patrolling in a heavy narcotics trafficking area, defendant flee when he sees them. The officers chase defendant, catch him, and subject him to a pat-down search for weapons. During the frisk, an officer squeezes the bag defendant is carrying and feels a heavy, hard object similar to the shape of a gun. The officer then opens the bag and discovers a .38-caliber handgun with five live rounds of ammunition. Did the officer act properly under the stop and frisk doctrine? *See Illinois v. Wardlow*, 528 U.S. 119 (2000) ; see also *Mackey v. State*, 124 So.3d 176 (Fl. 2013).

Hypo 4: *Retaliation Killings and Frisks*

Boston police are patrolling city streets in an area plagued by gunfire in recent weeks. The night before, an individual was shot, and two individuals were killed in a nearby neighborhood. When the police see two unfamiliar men standing on a street corner, they approach the men. When the men see the police, they begin to walk away. The officers follow the individuals and ask for their names, where they live, and what they are doing. One of the men states that he came to the area to visit a store on a particular street (no such store exists), and admits that he lives in the nearby area where the murders occurred the night before. Do the officers have sufficient cause to stop and frisk the suspects? *See Commonwealth v. Narcisse*, 73 Mass. App. Ct. 406, 898 N.E.2d 507 (2008).

Hypo 5: *The "One Plus" Rule*

Two police officers are patrolling in a high crime area one evening when they see a vehicle pull up to a gas station pump. When the driver does not leave the car, pump gas, or go into the convenience store, the officers regard the behavior as "unusual" and indicative of a drug transaction. When the vehicle leaves, the officers follow. The driver stops, exits, and walks over to a group of men who are talking and laughing. The officers recognize one of the men from prior drug arrests, but are unaware of whether he was convicted. The officers decide to approach the men, and see that one of the men is openly wearing a gun in a holster (legal under state law). Based on their training, the officers believe that where there is one gun, there usually is another (the "one plus" rule). Do the officers have sufficient cause to stop and frisk all the men? *See United States v. Black*, 707 F.3d 531 (4th Cir. 2013).

Hypo 6: *Taser Stops*

The police receive a call from an informant who states that a tall, black male is armed and selling drugs at a particular location. Reid, an experienced detective, goes to the scene and sees a group of men, including a taller man, near a black Honda. The informant had told the officer that the tall man had guns and drugs. As the officer approaches, the tall man moves to conceal the right side of his body from the officer before running away. The officer orders the man to stop, but he does not. Would it be reasonable to shoot Taser darts into the man in order to accomplish the stop? *See Reid v. State*, 428 Md. 289, 51 A.3d 597 (2012).

Hypo 7: *A Permissible Stop and Frisk?*

Plum, a 13-year police veteran is on routine patrol when he receives a police dispatch stating that an anonymous caller has reported a man with a handgun on a nearby street corner known for gang violence. The caller describes the individual as a tall, thin, dark-skinned male wearing a black jacket and a black and red cap. Plum arrives quickly, and sees three men standing on the corner. One of them is wearing a red jacket and a black and red cap. Except for the color of the jacket, the man matches the physical description relayed by the dispatcher. The man's jacket is open, and he is wearing a white tee-shirt. Plum recognizes the man from prior narcotics investigations, and recalls that he has arrested the man on drug charges. Although Plum has not known the man to carry weapons, he knows that it is common for guns to be carried in connection with narcotics offenses. Plum is also aware that the man lives in the area and is associated with a group involved in handguns and shootings. On seeing Plum, all three men begin to walk away. The suspect man seems quite nervous and moves his hand towards his waistband. Based on both the man's conduct, and the fact that he partially matches the anonymous caller's description of a man with a gun, Plum believes that the man might have a weapon concealed in his waistband. Plum directs the man to place his hands against a chain-link fence. Plum then lifts the man's tee-shirt and observes the top of a plastic bag (protruding above the waistband). Plum removes the bag and finds crack cocaine. Did Plum have adequate cause to conduct a stop and frisk? Was the scope of the frisk permissible? *See State v. Privott,* 203 N.J. 16, 999 A.2d 415 (2010).

Hypo 8: *The Gunfight and the Bullet-Riddled Car*

There was a gunfight in which a man was killed. A day later, police pull over a vehicle for an improper turn and demand identification. The officers know that Nolan (the passenger) is associated with a local gang. On approaching the driver's-side door, the arresting officer notices bullet holes in the car. After running data checks on the driver and the passenger, the officer notices that the homicide unit has put out a "locate" for Nolan. A "locate" means that an officer wishes to speak with the individual, but it does not give the officers authority to arrest the individual. At that point, the officer asks Nolan to get out of his car and stand near the back fender. Nolan goes past that area and sits on the curb. Nolan moves "very quickly" and grabs his waistband which was falling down, and the officer notices that there is something heavy in his pants. When asked if he has any weapons or other dangerous objects on his person, Nolan does not respond. Does the officer have sufficient cause to frisk Nolan? *See State v. Nolan,* 283 Neb. 50, 807 N.W.2d 520 (2012).

Hypo 9: *The Scope of a Stop and Frisk*

Suppose that a police officer has a valid basis for conducting a stop and frisk. During the course of the frisk, the officer feels a "hard object" in the suspect's left pants pocket which the officer believes might be a weapon. When he removes the object, he sees that it is a bundle of paper currency. Continuing the pat-down, the officer finds another hard object in the suspect's right pants pocket, and the suspect immediately tries to pull away when the officer touches it. The officer is uncertain what this other object may be. May the officer remove this other hard object from the suspect's pocket as well? *See United States v. Richardson*, 657 F.3d 521 (7th Cir. 2011); see also *United States v. I.E.V.*, 705 F.3d 430 (9th Cir. 2012).

Hypo 10: *Pretextual Stops*

When the driver of a late model convertible sees the police, he abruptly turns away and slides down, causing the police to become "suspicious" that the car is "a stolen vehicle." As the police follow, and run a registration check, the driver "reaches way down, as if to obtain an object or place an object under the right front seat." The movement causes the car to abruptly swerve across the center line, and the officers decide to conduct a traffic stop. The police admit that they did not stop the driver for a traffic offense, but rather because they were suspicious that the vehicle might be stolen and that the driver might have a weapon. As the officers approach the car, the driver "gets low in the seat" with his right arm positioned "low in his lap." At that point, the police order the driver to place his hands where they can see them and pull him from the car. The officers then frisk the driver and find an object in defendant's right jacket pocket which "felt like the butt of a small automatic." An officer then reaches into the pocket and finds only a "considerable sum of money folded in half," and a "plastic Baggi with a white powdery substance." Defendant is then placed under arrest for possession of a controlled substance. Did the police act properly? *See State v. Cotterman*, 544 S.W.2d 322 (Mo.App. 1976).

Hypo 11: *Pepper Spray*

A police officer, responding to a report of a domestic dispute, sees a man walking on the street near the site of the reported dispute. The officer does not know the man, and has no reason (other than the man's proximity to the dispute) to believe that he has been involved in the dispute. The officer shines a spotlight on the man, exits his car, and tells the man to "stop." The man states that he is going to his cousin's house, and continues walking. Since the man is "fumbling in his pockets," the officer fears that he has a gun, pulls his own, and twice orders the man to remove his hands from his pockets. When the man keeps on walking, the officer sprays him in the face with pepper spray. Under *Terry*, did the officer act appropriately in attempting to stop the man and in using the pepper spray to accomplish the stop? *See State v. Garcia*, 147 N.M. 134, 217 P.3d 1032 (2009).

Safford Unified School District #1 v. Redding

557 U.S. 364 (2009).

JUSTICE SOUTER delivered the opinion of the Court.

Savana Redding's mother filed suit against Safford Unified School District #1, and various school officials, for conducting a strip search in violation of Savana's Fourth Amendment rights. Petitioners moved for summary judgment, raising a defense of qualified immunity that the District Court for the District of Arizona granted. Following the two-step protocol for evaluating claims of qualified immunity, the Ninth Circuit held that the strip search was unjustified under the Fourth Amendment test for searches of children by school officials set out in *New Jersey v. T. L. O.*, 469 U. S. 325 (1985). The upshot was reversal of summary judgment as to Wilson, while affirming the judgments in favor of Schwallier, the school nurse, and Romero, the administrative assistant, since they had not acted as independent decisionmakers. We granted certiorari, and now affirm in part, reverse in part, and remand.

The Fourth Amendment "right of the people to be secure in their persons against unreasonable searches and seizures" generally requires a law enforcement officer to have probable cause for conducting a search. In *T. L. O.*, we recognized that the school setting "requires some modification of the level of suspicion of illicit activity needed to justify a search," and held that for searches by school officials "a careful balancing of governmental and private interests suggests that the public interest is best served by a Fourth Amendment standard of reasonableness that stops short of probable cause." We have thus applied a standard of reasonable suspicion to determine the legality of a school administrators search of a student, and have held that a school search "will be permissible in its scope when the measures adopted are reasonably related to the objectives of the search and not excessively intrusive in light of the age and sex of the student and the nature of the infraction."

A number of cases on probable cause have an implicit bearing on the reliable knowledge element of reasonable suspicion, as we have attempted to flesh out the knowledge component by looking to the degree to which known facts imply prohibited conduct, the specificity of the information received, and the reliability of its source. At the end of the day, we have realized that these factors cannot rigidly control, *Illinois v. Gates*, 462 U. S. 213 (1983), and the standards are "fluid concepts that take their substantive content from the particular contexts" in which they are being assessed. *Ornelas v. United States*, 517 U. S. 690, 696 (1996). Perhaps the best that can be said about the required knowledge component of probable cause for a law enforcement officer's evidence search is that it raise a "fair probability," *Gates*, 462 U. S., at 238, or a "substantial chance," of discovering evidence of criminal activity. The lesser standard for school searches could as readily be described as a moderate chance of finding evidence of wrong-doing.

In this case, the school's policies strictly prohibit the nonmedical use, possession, or sale of any drug on school grounds, including "any prescription or over-the-counter drug, except those for which permission to use in school has been granted pursuant to Board policy."[3]   A week before Savana was searched, another student, Jordan Romero (no relation of the school's administrative assistant), told the principal and Assistant Principal Wilson that "certain students were bringing drugs and weapons on campus," and that he had been sick after taking some pills that "he got from a classmate." On October 8, the same boy handed Wilson a white pill that he said Marissa Glines had given him. He told Wilson that students were planning to take the pills at lunch.

Wilson learned from Peggy Schwallier, the school nurse, that the pill was Ibuprofen 400 mg, available only by prescription. Wilson then called Marissa out

---

[3] The Court said in *New Jersey v. T. L. O.*, 469 U. S. 325 (1985), that standards of conduct for schools are for school administrators to determine without second-guessing by courts lacking the experience to appreciate what may be needed. There is no need to explain the imperative of keeping drugs out of schools, or to explain the reasons for the school's rule banning all drugs, no matter how benign, without advance permission. Teachers are not pharmacologists trained to identify pills and powders, and an effective drug ban has to be enforceable fast. The plenary ban makes sense, and there is no basis to claim that the search was unreasonable owing to some defect or shortcoming of the rule it was aimed at enforcing.

of class. Outside the classroom, Marissa's teacher handed Wilson the day planner, found within Marissa's reach, containing various contraband items. Wilson escorted Marissa back to his office.

In the presence of Helen Romero, Wilson requested Marissa to turn out her pockets and open her wallet. Marissa produced a blue pill, several white ones, and a razor blade. Wilson asked where the blue pill came from, and Marissa answered, "I guess it slipped in when she gave me the IBU 400s." When Wilson asked whom she meant, Marissa replied, "Savana Redding." Wilson then enquired about the day planner and its contents; Marissa denied knowing anything about them. Wilson did not ask Marissa any follow-up questions to determine whether there was any likelihood that Savana presently had pills: neither asking when Marissa received the pills from Savana nor where Savana might be hiding them.

Schwallier did not immediately recognize the blue pill, but information provided through a poison control hotline indicated that the pill was a 200-mg dose of an anti-inflammatory drug, generically called naproxen, available over the counter. At Wilson's direction, Marissa was then subjected to a search of her bra and underpants by Romero and Schwallier, as Savana was later on. The search revealed no additional pills.

It was at this juncture that Wilson called Savana into his office and showed her the day planner. Their conversation established that Savana and Marissa were on friendly terms: while she denied knowledge of the contraband, Savana admitted that the day planner was hers and that she had lent it to Marissa. Wilson had other reports of their friendship from staff members, who had identified Savana and Marissa as part of an unusually rowdy group at the school's opening dance in August, during which alcohol and cigarettes were found in the girl's bathroom. Wilson had reason to connect the girls with this contraband, for Wilson knew that Jordan Romero had told the principal that before the dance, he had been at a party at Savana's house where alcohol was served. Marissa's statement that the pills came from Savana was thus sufficiently plausible to warrant suspicion that Savana was involved in pill distribution.

This suspicion was enough to justify a search of Savana's backpack and outer clothing.[4] If a student is reasonably suspected of giving out contraband pills, she is reasonably suspected of carrying them on her person and in the carryall. The look into Savana's bag, in her presence and in the relative privacy of Wilson's office, was not excessively intrusive, any more than Romero's subsequent search of her outer clothing.

---

[4] There is no question here that justification for the school officials' search was required in accordance with the *T. L. O.* standard of reasonable suspicion, for it is common ground that Savana had a reasonable expectation of privacy covering the personal things she chose to carry in her backpack, and that Wilson's decision to look through it was a "search" within the meaning of the Fourth Amendment.

A strip search followed. Romero and Schwallier directed Savana to remove her clothes down to her underwear, and then "pull out" her bra and the elastic band on her underpants. Although Romero and Schwallier stated that they did not see anything when Savana followed their instructions, we would not define strip search and its Fourth Amendment consequences in a way that would guarantee litigation about who was looking and how much was seen. The very fact of Savana's pulling her underwear away from her body in the presence of the two officials who were able to see her necessarily exposed her breasts and pelvic area to some degree, and both subjective and reasonable societal expectations of personal privacy support the treatment of such a search as categorically distinct, requiring distinct elements of justification on the part of school authorities for going beyond a search of outer clothing and belongings.

Savana's subjective expectation of privacy against such a search is inherent in her account of it as embarrassing, frightening, and humiliating. The reasonableness of her expectation (required by the Fourth Amendment standard) is indicated by the consistent experiences of other young people similarly searched, whose adolescent vulnerability intensifies the patent intrusiveness of the exposure. The common reaction of these adolescents simply registers the obviously different meaning of a search exposing the body from the experience of nakedness or near undress in other school circumstances. Changing for gym is getting ready for play; exposing for a search is responding to an accusation reserved for suspected wrongdoers and fairly understood as so degrading that a number of communities have decided that strip searches in schools are never reasonable and have banned them no matter what the facts may be.

The indignity of the search does not, of course, outlaw it, but it does implicate the rule of reasonableness as stated in *T. L. O.*, that "the search as actually conducted be reasonably related in scope to the circumstances which justified the interference in the first place." The scope will be permissible, that is, when it is "not excessively intrusive in light of the age and sex of the student and the nature of the infraction."

Here, the content of the suspicion failed to match the degree of intrusion. Wilson knew beforehand that the pills were prescription-strength ibuprofen and over-the-counter naproxen, common pain relievers equivalent to two Advil, or one Aleve. He must have been aware of the nature and limited threat of the specific drugs he was searching for, and while just about anything can be taken in quantities that will do real harm, Wilson had no reason to suspect that large amounts of the drugs were being passed around, or that individual students were receiving great numbers of pills.

Nor could Wilson have suspected that Savana was hiding common painkillers in her underwear. Petitioners suggest that "students hide contraband in or under their clothing," and cite a smattering of cases of students with contraband in their underwear. But a reasonable search that extensive calls for suspicion that it will pay off. But nondangerous school contraband does not raise the specter of stashes in intimate places, and there is no evidence of any general practice among Safford Middle School students of hiding that sort of thing in underwear; neither Jordan nor Marissa suggested to Wilson that Savana was doing that, and the preceding search of Marissa that Wilson ordered yielded nothing. Wilson never even determined when Marissa had received the pills from Savana; if it had been a few days before, that would weigh heavily against any reasonable conclusion that Savana presently had the pills on her person, much less in her underwear.

In sum, what was missing from the suspected facts that pointed to Savana was any indication of danger to the students from the power of the drugs or their quantity, and any reason to suppose that Savana was carrying pills in her underwear. We think that the combination of these deficiencies was fatal to finding the search reasonable.

In so holding, we mean to cast no ill reflection on the assistant principal, for the record raises no doubt that his motive throughout was to eliminate drugs from his school and protect students from what Jordan Romero had gone through. Parents are known to overreact to protect their children from danger, and a school official with responsibility for safety may tend to do the same. The difference is that the Fourth Amendment places limits on the official, even with the high degree of deference that courts must pay to the educators professional judgment.

We do mean, though, to make it clear that the *T. L. O.* concern to limit a school search to reasonable scope requires the support of reasonable suspicion of danger or of resort to underwear for hiding evidence of wrongdoing before a search can reasonably make the quantum leap from outer clothes and backpacks to exposure of intimate parts. The meaning of such a search, and the degradation its subject may reasonably feel, place a search that intrusive in a category of its own demanding its own specific suspicions.

A school official searching a student is "entitled to qualified immunity where clearly established law does not show that the search violated the Fourth Amendment." *Pearson v. Callahan*, 555 U. S. 223 (2009). To be established clearly, however, there is no need that "the very action in question have previously been held unlawful." *Wilson v. Layne*, 526 U. S. 603, 615 (1999). Even as to action less than an outrage, "officials can still be on notice that their conduct violates established law in novel factual circumstances." *Hope v. Pelzer*, 536 U. S. 730, 741 (2002).

T. L. O. directed school officials to limit the intrusiveness of a search, "in light of the age and sex of the student and the nature of the infraction," and the intrusiveness of the strip search here cannot be seen as justifiably related to the circumstances. But the lower courts have reached divergent conclusions regarding how the *T. L. O.* standard applies to such searches. A number of judges have read *T. L. O.* as the en banc minority of the Ninth Circuit did here. Other courts considering qualified immunity for strip searches have read *T. L. O.* as "a series of abstractions, and a declaration of seeming deference to the judgments of school officials, on the other," which made it impossible "to establish clearly the contours of a Fourth Amendment right in the wide variety of possible school settings different from those involved in *T. L. O.*" itself.

The strip search of Savana Redding was unreasonable and a violation of the Fourth Amendment, but petitioners are nevertheless protected from liability through qualified immunity. Our conclusions do not resolve the question of the liability of Safford Unified School District #1 under *Monell v. New York City Dept. of Social Servs.*, 436 U. S. 658, 694 (1978). The judgment of the Ninth Circuit is therefore affirmed in part and reversed in part, and this case is remanded for consideration of the *Monell* claim.

It is so ordered.

Justice Stevens, with whom Justice Ginsburg joins, concurring in part and dissenting in part.

This is a case in which clearly established law meets clearly outrageous conduct. "It does not require a constitutional scholar to conclude that a nude search of a 13-year-old child is an invasion of constitutional rights of some magnitude." I disagree with the Court's decision to extend qualified immunity to the school official who authorized this unconstitutional search.

Justice Ginsburg, concurring in part and dissenting in part.

Assistant Principal Wilson's subjection of 13-year-old Savana Redding to a humiliating strip down search violated the Fourth Amendment. I join Justice Stevens in dissenting from the Courts acceptance of Wilson's qualified immunity plea.

Justice Thomas, concurring in the judgment in part and dissenting in part.

The search of Savana Redding did not violate the Fourth Amendment. Under *T. L. O.*, all petitioners, including the school district, are entitled to judgment as a matter of law in their favor.

Take Note

In *New Jersey v. T.L.O.*, 469 U.S. 325 (1985), a teacher found two girls smoking in a lavatory. Both girls were taken to the Principal's office where they met with the Assistant Vice Principal, Mr. Choplick. When T.L.O. denied that she had been smoking, Choplick demanded to see her purse where he found cigarettes, rolling papers, marijuana and a substantial number of one-dollar bills. Afterwards, T.L.O. confessed to selling marijuana. Based on the confession and the evidence found during the search, delinquency charges were brought against T.L.O. The Court upheld the search, holding that the Fourth Amendment applies to searches by public school officials, but finding that such officials have greater latitude: "Against the child's interest in privacy must be set the substantial interest of teachers and administrators in maintaining discipline in the classroom and on school grounds. The school setting requires some easing of the restrictions to which searches by public authorities are ordinarily subject. The warrant requirement, would unduly interfere with the maintenance of the swift and informal disciplinary procedures needed in the schools. The legality of a search of a student should depend simply on the reasonableness, under all the circumstances, of the search. Determining the reasonableness of any search involves a two-fold inquiry: first, one must consider whether the action was justified at its inception," and whether the search as actually conducted 'was reasonably related in scope to the circumstances which justified the interference in the first place.' Under ordinary circumstances, a search of a student by a teacher or other school official will be 'justified at its inception' when there are reasonable grounds for suspecting that the search will turn up evidence that the student has violated or is violating either the law or the rules of the school. Such a search will be permissible in its scope when the measures adopted are reasonably related to the objectives of the search and not excessively intrusive in light of the age and sex of the student and the nature of the infraction."

Food for Thought

In *Redding*, the school official suspected Savana of carrying prescription strength ibuprofen. Suppose that the school official had suspected Savana of carrying heroin or cocaine. Would that change in facts alter the analysis regarding the propriety of a strip search?

Hypo 1: *A Search for Weapons*

Would the search have been justified if the school official had suspected Savana of carrying detonator caps for explosives? Or are there less intrusive methods for searching for such weapons?

Hypo 2: *Canine Sniffs at Public Schools*

After determining that there is a "serious drug problem," involving 80-200 incidents per year, a school district adopts a policy authorizing the local police to enter the school to conduct random canine sniffs of student backpacks and lockers for evidence of contraband drugs. In adopting the policy, the district intended to "balance each student's right to privacy" with "the need to maintain an appropriate learning environment." However, the district was particularly concerned about the need "to protect the safety and health of the district's faculty, staff and students." The policy states that "once a drug detection dog has completed sniffing an area, the dog handler and drug detection dog will retire from the area." A student's possessions will only be searched if a drug dog has twice alerted on the same property. Is the search justifiable under *Safford? See Burlison v. Springfield Public Schools*, 708 F.3d 1034 (8th Cir. 2013).

Hypo 3: *Searching the Student's Truck*

After discovering that a student had left school without permission to obtain something from his truck, parked on a residential street outside school grounds, the principal summoned the student to the office and searched him for drugs. Although the student claimed that he had gone to the truck simply to retrieve his wallet, the principal suspected that he might have retrieved drugs. However, no drugs are found. Based on the available evidence, does the principal have adequate grounds to search the truck even though it is not located on school property? *See J.P. v. Millard Public Schools,* 285 Neb. 890, 830 N.W.2d 453 (Neb. 2013).

Hypo 4: *Checking the Cell Phone*

During his freshman year in high school, G.C. began to have disciplinary problems, including drug use, anger and depression. Later, he was warned for excessive tardiness, disciplined for fighting in the boys locker room, was caught with tobacco products at school, and confessed to being suicidal. A treatment counselor was very concerned and suggested that G.C. be committed to an institution. When G.C. violated the school's cell-phone policy by texting in class, a teacher confiscated the phone, and the principal read four text messages on the phone. The principal stated that he was worried because G.C. had engaged in angry outbursts. Was the phone search justifiable? See *G.C. v. Owensboro Public Schools*, 711 F.3d 623 (6th Cir. 2013).

* * *

In addition to authorizing a "frisk," *Terry* also authorizes the police to make an "investigative stop" which is a form of seizure. The Fourth Amendment prohibits not only unreasonable searches, but also unreasonable "seizures." The Court has recognized many different types of seizures ranging from an investigatory stop to an arrest. These seizures are subject to differing constitutional requirements.

United States v. Mendenhall

446 U.S. 544 (1980).

MR. JUSTICE STEWART announced the judgment of the Court and delivered an opinion, in which MR. JUSTICE REHNQUIST joined.

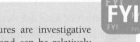

Most seizures are investigative in nature and can be relatively brief. Roadside stops usually fit this description. However, the police also "seize" individuals for fingerprinting, lineups or interrogation purposes. What constitutes a seizure? When are such seizures valid? Consider the following cases.

Respondent arrived at the Detroit Metropolitan Airport on a commercial airline flight from Los Angeles early in the morning on February 10, 1976. As she disembarked from the plane, she was observed by two agents of the DEA, who were present at the airport for the purpose of detecting unlawful traffic in narcotics. After observing the respondent's conduct, which appeared to the agents to be characteristic of persons unlawfully carrying narcotics, the agents approached her as she was walking through the concourse, identified themselves as federal agents, and asked to see her identification and airline ticket. Respondent produced her driver's license, which was in the name of Sylvia Mendenhall, and, in answer to a question of one of the agents, stated that she resided at the address appearing on the license. The airline ticket was issued in the name of "Annette Ford." When asked why the ticket bore a name different from her own, respondent stated that she "just felt like using that name." In response to a further question, respondent indicated that she had been in California only two days. Agent Anderson then identified himself as a federal narcotics agent and respondent "became quite shaken, extremely nervous. She had a hard time speaking."

After returning the airline ticket and driver's license to her, Agent Anderson asked respondent if she would accompany him to the airport DEA office for further questions. She did so, although the record does not indicate a verbal response to the request. The office, which was located up one flight of stairs about 50 feet from where the respondent had first been approached, consisted of a reception area adjoined by three other rooms. At the office the agent asked respondent if she would allow a search of her person and handbag and told her that she had the right to decline the search if she desired. She responded: "Go ahead." She then handed Agent Anderson her purse, which contained a receipt for an airline ticket that had been issued to "F. Bush" three days earlier for a flight from Pittsburgh through Chicago to Los Angeles. The agent asked whether this was the ticket that she had used for her flight to California, and respondent stated that it was.

A female police officer then arrived to search respondent's person. She asked the agents if respondent had consented to be searched. The agents said that she had, and respondent followed the policewoman into a private room. There the policewoman again asked respondent if she consented to the search, and respondent replied that she did. The policewoman explained that the search would require that respondent remove her clothing. Respondent stated that she had a plane to catch and was assured by the policewoman that if she were carrying no narcotics, there would be no problem. Respondent then began to disrobe without further comment. As respondent removed her clothing, she took from her undergarments two small packages, one of which appeared to contain heroin, and handed both to the policewoman. The agents then arrested respondent for possessing heroin. At her trial, respondent moved to suppress the heroin. The motion was denied.

The Government concedes that its agents had neither a warrant nor probable cause to believe that respondent was carrying narcotics when the agents conducted a search of respondent's person. It is the Government's position that the search was conducted pursuant to respondent's consent, and thus was excepted from the requirements of both a warrant and probable cause.

The Fourth Amendment's requirement that searches and seizures be founded upon an objective justification, governs all seizures of the person, "including seizures that involve only a brief detention short of traditional arrest." Accordingly, if respondent was "seized" when the DEA agents approached her on the concourse and asked questions of her, the agents' conduct in doing so was constitutional only if they reasonably suspected respondent of wrongdoing. But "obviously, not all personal intercourse between policemen and citizens involves 'seizures' of persons. Only when the officer, by means of physical force or show of authority, has in some way restrained the liberty of a citizen may we conclude that a 'seizure' has occurred."

A person is "seized" only when, by means of physical force or a show of authority, his freedom of movement is restrained. Only when such restraint is imposed is there any foundation whatever for invoking constitutional safeguards. The purpose of the Fourth Amendment is not to eliminate all contact between the police and the citizenry, but "to prevent arbitrary and oppressive interference by enforcement officials with the privacy and personal security of individuals." As long as the person to whom questions are put remains free to disregard the questions and walk away, there has been no intrusion upon that person's liberty or privacy as would under the Constitution require some particularized and objective justification.

Characterizing every street encounter between a citizen and the police as a "seizure," while not enhancing any interest secured by the Fourth Amendment, would impose wholly unrealistic restrictions upon a wide variety of legitimate law enforcement practices. The Court has acknowledged the need for police questioning as a tool in the effective enforcement of the criminal laws. "Without such investigation, those who were innocent might be falsely accused, those who were guilty might wholly escape prosecution, and many crimes would go unsolved. In short, the security of all would be diminished." *Schneckloth v. Bustamonte*, 412 U.S., at 225.

We conclude that a person has been "seized" within the meaning of the Fourth Amendment only if, in view of all of the circumstances surrounding the incident, a reasonable person would have believed that he was not free to leave.[8] Examples of circumstances that might indicate a seizure, even where the person did not attempt to leave, would be the threatening presence of several officers, the display of a weapon by an officer, some physical touching of the person of the citizen, or the use of language or tone of voice indicating that compliance with the officer's request might be compelled. In the absence of some such evidence, otherwise inoffensive contact between a member of the public and the police cannot, as a matter of law, amount to a seizure of that person.

---

[8] The subjective intention of the DEA agent to detain respondent, had she attempted to leave, is irrelevant except insofar as that may have been conveyed to the respondent.

On the facts of this case, no "seizure" occurred. The events took place in the public concourse. The agents wore no uniforms and displayed no weapons. They did not summon respondent to their presence, but instead approached her and identified themselves as federal agents. They requested, but did not demand to see respondent's identification and ticket. Such conduct without more, did not amount to an intrusion upon any constitutionally protected interest. Respondent was not seized simply by reason of the fact that the agents approached her, asked her if she would show them her ticket and identification, and posed to her a few questions. Nor was it enough that the person asking the questions was a law enforcement official. In short, nothing suggests that respondent had any objective reason to believe that she was not free to end the conversation in the concourse and proceed on her way, and for that reason we conclude that the agents' initial approach to her was not a seizure.

Our conclusion that no seizure occurred is not affected by the fact that respondent was not expressly told by the agents that she was free to decline to cooperate with their inquiry, for the voluntariness of her responses does not depend upon her having been so informed. We also reject the argument that the only inference to be drawn from the fact that respondent acted in a manner so contrary to her self-interest is that she was compelled to answer the agents' questions. It may happen that a person makes statements to law enforcement officials that he later regrets, but the issue in such cases is not whether the statement was self-protective, but rather whether it was made voluntarily.

Although we have concluded that the initial encounter between the DEA agents and respondent on the concourse at the Detroit Airport did not constitute an unlawful seizure, it is still arguable that respondent's Fourth Amendment protections were violated when she went from the concourse to the DEA office. Such a violation might in turn infect the subsequent search of the respondent's person.

Whether respondent's consent to accompany the agents was in fact voluntary or was the product of duress or coercion, express or implied, is to be determined by the totality of all the circumstances, and is a matter which the Government has the burden of proving. The Government's evidence showed that respondent was not told that she had to go to the office, but was simply asked if she would accompany the officers. There were neither threats nor any show of force. Respondent had been questioned only briefly, and her ticket and identification were returned to her before she was asked to accompany the officers.

It is argued that the incident would reasonably have appeared coercive to respondent, who was 22 years old and had not graduated from high school. It is additionally suggested that respondent, a female and a Negro, may have felt unusually threatened by the officers, who were white males. While these factors were not irrelevant, neither were they decisive, and the totality of the evidence in this case was plainly adequate to support the finding that respondent voluntarily consented to accompany the officers to the DEA office.

Because the search of respondent's person was not preceded by an impermissible seizure of her person, it cannot be contended that her apparent consent to the subsequent search was infected by an unlawful detention. There remains to be considered whether respondent's consent to the search was for any other reason invalid. The District Court found that the "consent was freely and voluntarily given." There was more than enough evidence to sustain that view. First, respondent, who was 22 years old and had an 11th-grade education, was plainly capable of a knowing consent. Second, it is especially significant that respondent was twice expressly told that she was free to decline to consent to the search, and only thereafter explicitly consented to it. Although the Constitution does not require "proof of knowledge of a right to refuse as the *sine qua non* of an effective consent to a search," such knowledge was highly relevant to the determination that there had been consent. Perhaps more important for present purposes, the fact that the officers themselves informed respondent that she was free to withhold her consent substantially lessened the probability that their conduct could reasonably have appeared to her to be coercive.

Respondent has argued that she did in fact resist the search, relying principally on the testimony that when she was told that the search would require the removal of her clothing, she stated to the female police officer that "she had a plane to catch." But the trial court was entitled to view the statement as simply an expression of concern that the search be conducted quickly. Respondent had twice unequivocally indicated her consent to the search, and when assured by the police officer that there would be no problem if nothing were turned up by the search, she began to undress without further comment.

Respondent also argued that because she was within the DEA office when she consented to the search, her consent may have resulted from the inherently coercive nature of those surroundings. But there is no evidence that she was in any way coerced. In response to the argument that the respondent would not voluntarily have consented to a search that was likely to disclose the narcotics that she carried, the question is not whether the respondent acted in her ultimate self-interest, but whether she acted voluntarily.[9]

---

[9] Respondent may have thought she was acting in her self-interest by voluntarily cooperating with the officers in the hope of receiving more lenient treatment.

We conclude that the District Court's determination that respondent consented to the search of her person "freely and voluntarily" was sustained by the evidence.

It is so ordered.

MR. JUSTICE WHITE, with whom MR. JUSTICE BRENNAN, MR. JUSTICE MARSHALL, and MR. JUSTICE STEVENS join, dissenting.

Mendenhall undoubtedly was "seized" within the meaning of the Fourth Amendment when the agents escorted her from the public area of the terminal to the DEA office for questioning and a strip-search of her person. Although Mendenhall was not told that she was under arrest, she in fact was not free to refuse to go to the DEA office and was not told that she was. Once inside the office, Ms. Mendenhall would not have been permitted to leave without submitting to a strip-search. The Court's conclusion that the "totality of evidence was plainly adequate" to support a finding of consent can only be based on the notion that consent can be assumed from the absence of proof that a suspect resisted police authority. This is a notion that we have squarely rejected. The Government cannot rely solely on acquiescence to the officers' wishes to establish the requisite consent. Because Ms. Mendenhall was being illegally detained at the time of the search of her person, her suppression motion should have been granted in the absence of evidence to dissipate the taint.

Points for Discussion

a. Seizures and Passengers

In *Brendlin v. California*, 551 U.S. 249 (2007), the Court held that when a police officer makes a traffic stop, the passenger of the vehicle (as well as the driver) is seized within the meaning of the Fourth Amendment. As a result, the passenger may challenge the constitutionality of the stop: "An officer who orders a car to pull over acts with an implicit claim of right based on fault of some sort, and a sensible person would not expect a police officer to allow people to come and go freely from the physical focal point of an investigation. If the likely wrongdoing is not the driving, the passenger will reasonably feel subject to suspicion owing to close association; but even when the wrongdoing is only bad driving, the passenger will expect to be subject to some scrutiny, and his attempt to leave the scene would be likely to prompt an objection from the officer that no passenger would feel free to leave in the first place. It is also reasonable for passengers to expect that a police officer at the scene of a crime, arrest, or investigation will not let people move around in ways that could jeopardize his safety."

b. Bus Sweeps

In *Florida v. Bostick*, 501 U.S. 429 (1991), two police officers, with badges, insignia and holstered pistols, boarded a bus bound from Miami to Atlanta during a stopover in Fort Lauderdale. Without any articulable suspicion, the officers picked out defendant passenger and asked to inspect his ticket and identification. The ticket matched the defendant's identification and both were immediately returned to him. The officers then explained their presence as narcotics agents, and requested consent to search his luggage. The police specifically advised defendant that he had the right to refuse consent, and they did not threaten him. The Court concluded that defendant had not been "seized" within the meaning of the Fourth Amendment, and that his consent was therefore valid: "When police attempt to question a person who is walking down the street or through an airport lobby, it makes sense to inquire whether a reasonable person would feel free to continue walking. But when the person is seated on a bus and has no desire to leave, the degree to which a reasonable person would feel that he or she could leave is not an accurate measure of the coercive effect of the encounter." Justice Marshall dissented: "Officers who conduct suspicionless, dragnet-style sweeps put passengers to the choice of cooperating or of exiting their buses and possibly being stranded in unfamiliar locations. It is exactly because this 'choice' is no 'choice' at all

Take Note

Following the decision in *Mendenhall*, the Court decided *Florida v. Royer*, 460 U.S. 491 (1983). *Royer* was factually similar to *Mendenhall* in that he was singled out because he fit a so-called "drug courier profile." He had purchased a one-way plane ticket to N.Y.C. and checked his bags with an identification tag that used a name that was different than his own. Two agents approached Royer, asked to speak to him, and also asked for his plane ticket and driver's license. The ticket bore the name "Holt." Royer then became nervous and the detectives informed Royer that he was under suspicion for transporting narcotics. Without returning Royer's license or ticket, the detectives asked him to accompany them to the DEA office located in the airport. Royer did not respond, but followed them. The detectives also had his luggage removed from the plane and brought to the room. When asked to consent to a search of his luggage, Royer produced a key and opened it. The search produced illegal drugs. The Court held that Royer, unlike Mendenhall, had been "seized" within the meaning of the Fourth Amendment, because the police retained his identification and plane ticket and removed his luggage from the airplane. The Court noted that "statements given during a period of illegal detention are inadmissible even though voluntarily given if they are the product of the illegal detention and not the result of an independent act of free will: "Because Royer was being illegally detained when he consented to the search of his luggage, the consent was tainted by the illegality and was ineffective to justify the search."

that police engage this technique. The police may continue to confront passengers without suspicion so long as they take simple steps, like advising the passengers confronted of their right to decline to be questioned, to dispel the aura of coercion and intimidation that pervades such encounters."

c. Factory Sweeps

In *Immigration and Naturalization Service v. Delgado*, 466 U.S. 210 (1984), under a warrant based on probable cause, the INS surveyed the work force at a plant looking for illegal aliens. Some agents positioned themselves near the buildings' exits, while other agents dispersed throughout the factory to question employees at their work stations. The agents displayed badges, carried walkie-talkies, and carried holstered weapons. The agents approached employees and, after identifying themselves, asked one to three questions relating to their citizenship. If an employee gave a credible reply that he was a United States citizen, the questioning ended, and the agent moved on to the next employee. If the employee gave an unsatisfactory response or admitted that he was an alien, the employee was asked to produce his immigration papers. During the survey, employees continued with their work and were free to walk about the factory. The Court rejected the employees' claim that they had been "seized": "When people are at work their freedom to move about has been meaningfully restricted, not by the actions of law enforcement officials, but by the workers' voluntary obligations to their employers. There is nothing to indicate that the stationing of agents near the factory doors showed the INS's intent to prevent people from leaving. The obvious purpose of the agents' presence at the factory doors was to insure that all persons in the factories were questioned. If mere questioning does not constitute a seizure when it occurs inside the factory, it is no more a seizure when it occurs at the exits. Respondents argue that the manner in which the surveys were conducted and the attendant disruption caused by the surveys created a psychological environment which made them reasonably afraid they were not free to leave. It was obvious from the beginning of the surveys that the INS agents were only questioning people. Persons who simply went about their business in the workplace were not detained in any way. While persons who attempted to flee or evade the agents may eventually have been detained for questioning, respondents did not do so and were not in fact detained. The manner in which respondents were questioned, given its obvious purpose, could hardly result in a reasonable fear that respondents were not free to continue working or to move about the factory. The encounters with the INS agents were classic

Food for Thought

Do you agree with the holding in *Mendenhall*? Would an ordinary person (one not schooled in criminal procedure), who is approached by the police in an airport, believe that she is "free to leave?" Could she respond to a police request by saying "Sorry, I'd love to chat with you, but I need to get a cup of coffee and don't really have time to chat. Perhaps next time." Or would the ordinary person more likely believe that she was required to submit to police questioning?

consensual encounters rather than Fourth Amendment seizures." Justice Brennan concurred in part and dissented in part: "It is fantastic to conclude that a reasonable person could ignore all that was occurring throughout the factory and, when the INS agents reached him, have the temerity to believe that he was at liberty to refuse to answer their questions and walk away. Respondents' testimony paints a frightening picture of people subjected to wholesale interrogation under conditions designed not to respect personal security and privacy, but rather to elicit prompt answers from completely intimidated workers. These tactics amounted to seizures of respondents under the Fourth Amendment."

Hypo 1: *Rethinking Mendenhall*

Given that Mendenhall must have known that she was carrying drugs in her clothes, how do you explain her decision to submit to a strip search? Was she acting voluntarily, or out of public spirit? Or did she not realize that she had the right to refuse?

Hypo 2: *Applying the Mendenhall Test*

On your way home from this class, a police cruiser follows you for three blocks when the officer turns on his lights and siren. Believing that the officer wants you to stop, you pull off the road. The officer pulls over behind you and approaches your car. Under *Mendenhall*, have you been seized?

Hypo 3: *More on Applying the Mendenhall Test*

A robbery occurs at the campus book store. Shortly afterwards, the police search the campus for the robbers as well as for evidence. About this time, you are walking across campus on your way to this class. A police officer approaches you and says: "A robbery has just occurred at the campus book store, I'm looking for witnesses, and would like to ask you a few questions." Have you been "seized" within the meaning of the Fourth Amendment? Would you conclude that you had been "seized" if the officer regarded you as a possible suspect rather than as a witness? Is the officer's subjective intent relevant? What arguments can you make in support of the position that you have been "seized"?

Hypo 4: *The Border Patrol Encounter*

At night, border patrol agents stop two cars in the northbound lane of a highway that runs perpendicular to the Mexican border. As part of the stop, the officers turn on the emergency lights on their vehicles, and leave them flashing throughout the duration of the stop. One of the agents is carrying a flashlight which he shines at a passing vehicle. The officer, who is quite tall (6'9"), does not motion for the car to stop, but notices what appear to be individuals hiding on the floorboard of the vehicle. The driver of the passing vehicle decides to stop about 15' beyond the officer, and is apprehended for smuggling illegal aliens. When the officer shined his flashlight at the passing vehicle, was there a "stop" or "seizure" within the meaning of the Fourth Amendment? *See United States v. Al Nasser*, 555 F.3d 722 (9th Cir. 2009).

Hypo 5: *When Does a Seizure End?*

Two police officers see two adults sitting near a tree. The officers consider their presence "unusual" because the park is usually frequented only by children and the elderly at that time of day. Suppose that the police approach the man and the woman, demand identification to check their identities against a police data base, and determine that there is a restraining order that prevents the man from coming within 100 feet of the woman. The police arrest the man, return the woman's identification, and begin the process of taking the man into custody. During the following minutes there is casual conversation between the police officers and the woman regarding the restraining order (the woman states that she is trying to reconcile with the man). At some point, the officer asks the woman whether she would mind if he searches her purse. The woman permits the search which reveals evidence of crystal meth. For purposes of determining whether the woman voluntarily consented to a search of her purse, was the woman seized when the officer initially approached her and asked to see her identification? Did the seizure terminate when the officer returned the identification? *See State v. Ashbaugh*, 349 Or. 297, 244 P.3d 360 (2010).

Food for Thought

Of course, the *Mendenhall* Court concluded that she was not "seized" within the meaning of the Fourth Amendment when the DEA agents approached her in the airport concourse. If there had been a seizure, the Court suggested that the initial seizure could have been justified based on a "reasonable suspicion" that Mendenhall was involved in criminal activity. Did the DEA agents have a reasonable suspicion regarding Mendenhall? What factors might have led the agents to believe that she was involved in criminal activity?

Hypo 6: *Drug Couriers?*

A police officer, assigned to a drug interdiction team, notices a green sport utility vehicle ("SUV") on an interstate highway. Based on his experience, the officer suspects that the SUV is a rental vehicle because it is new, clean, has no window tinting, and has no dealer insignia. The officer paces the vehicle and concludes that it is traveling at 75 mph in a 70 mph zone. The officer also observes a white van traveling approximately four car lengths in front of the SUV at the same speed, and he suspects, based on the same indicators, that it is a rental vehicle as well. Both vehicles display Texas license plates, a "source state" for narcotics entering the state. In the officer's experience, a tandem driving formation of rental vehicles suggests a possible narcotics transporting arrangement. He travels beside the van and observes that the rear seats are folded down and that the driver appears to be nervous. Does the officer have sufficient justification to initiate a traffic stop of both vehicles? *See United States v. Allen*, 705 F.3d 367 (8th Cir. 2013).

Hypo 7: *More on Evaluating "Reasonable Suspicion"*

A police officer is on routine evening patrol in a "high-drug" and "high-crime area" where "multiple shootings" and "countless drug arrests" have taken place when he notices two men standing next to a dumpster at a convenience store where "no trespassing signs" have been posted. As he approaches the store, the officer notices two men standing next to a pair of garbage dumpsters "toward the back" of the convenience store's side parking lot. The place where the men are standing is "not close" to the convenience store's front entrance. The men do not have shopping bags or any other items suggestive of recent purchases from the store. When the men see the officer, they "almost immediately" begin to walk away at a "fast pace," trying to "get away from the area." Although their path takes them past the convenience store's entrance, neither man attempts to enter the store. Suspecting that the men have been trespassing, the officer exits his vehicle and tells them that they are not free to go. Did the officer have a "reasonable suspicion" that the men were involved in criminal activity? *See United States v. Bumpers*, 705 F.3d 168 (4th Cir. 2013).

California v. Hodari D.

499 U.S. 621 (1991).

JUSTICE SCALIA delivered the opinion of the Court.

Late one evening, Officers Brian McColgin and Jerry Pertoso were on patrol in a high-crime area of Oakland, California. They were dressed in street clothes but wearing jackets with "Police" embossed on both front and back. As they rounded a corner, they saw four or five youths huddled around a small red car parked at the curb. When the youths saw the officers' car approaching they apparently panicked, and took flight. Respondent, Hodari D., and one companion ran west through an alley; the others fled south. The red car also headed south, at a high rate of speed.

The officers were suspicious and gave chase. McColgin remained in the car and continued south on 63rd Avenue; Pertoso left the car, ran back north along 63rd, then west on Foothill Boulevard, and turned south on 62nd Avenue. Hodari, meanwhile, emerged from the alley onto 62nd and ran north. Looking behind as he ran, he did not turn and see Pertoso until the officer was almost upon him, whereupon he tossed away what appeared to be a small rock. A moment later, Pertoso tackled Hodari, handcuffed him, and radioed for assistance. Hodari was found to be carrying $130 in cash and a pager; and the rock he had discarded was found to be crack cocaine. In the juvenile proceeding brought against him, Hodari moved to suppress the evidence relating to the cocaine. The court denied the motion.

The only issue is whether, at the time he dropped the drugs, Hodari had been "seized" within the meaning of the Fourth Amendment. If so, respondent argues, the drugs were the fruit of that seizure and the evidence concerning them was properly excluded. If not, the drugs were abandoned by Hodari and lawfully recovered by the police, and the evidence should have been admitted.

The Fourth Amendment's protection against "unreasonable seizures" includes seizure of the person. From the time of the founding to the present, the word "seizure" has meant a "taking possession." For most purposes at common law, the word connoted not merely grasping, or applying physical force to, the animate or inanimate object in question, but actually bringing it within physical control. A ship still fleeing, even though under attack, would not be considered to have been seized as a war prize. To constitute an arrest, however—the quintessential "seizure of the person" under our Fourth Amendment jurisprudence—the mere grasping or application of physical force with lawful authority, whether or not it succeeded in subduing the arrestee, was sufficient. As one commentator has described it: "There can be constructive detention, which will constitute an arrest, although the party is never actually brought within the physical control of the party making an arrest. This is accomplished by merely touching, however slightly, the body of the accused, by the party making the arrest and for that purpose, although he does not succeed in stopping or holding him even for an instant; as where the bailiff had tried to arrest one who fought him off by a fork, the court said, 'If the bailiff had touched him, that had been an arrest' " A. CORNELIUS, SEARCH AND SEIZURE 163 (2d ed. 1930).

To say that an arrest is effected by the slightest application of physical force, despite the arrestee's escape, is not to say that for Fourth Amendment purposes there is a continuing arrest during the period of fugitivity. If Pertoso had laid his hands upon Hodari to arrest him, but Hodari had broken away and had then cast away the cocaine, it would hardly be realistic to say that that disclosure had been made during the course of an arrest. The present case, is even further removed. It does not involve the application of any physical force; Hodari was untouched by Officer Pertoso at the time he discarded the cocaine. His defense relies instead upon the proposition that a seizure occurs "when the officer, by means of physical force or show of authority, has in some way restrained the liberty of a citizen." Hodari contends that Pertoso's pursuit qualified as a "show of authority" calling upon Hodari to halt. The question before us is whether, with respect to a show of authority as with respect to application of physical force, a seizure occurs even though the subject does not yield. We hold that it does not.

The language of the Fourth Amendment cannot sustain respondent's contention. The word "seizure" readily bears the meaning of a laying on of hands or application of physical force to restrain movement, even when it is ultimately unsuccessful. ("She seized the purse-snatcher, but he broke out of her grasp.") It does not remotely apply, however, to the prospect of a policeman yelling "Stop, in the name of the law!" at a fleeing form that continues to flee. That is no seizure. Nor can the result respondent wishes to achieve be produced—indirectly by suggesting that Pertoso's uncomplied—with show of authority was a common-law arrest, and then appealing to the principle that all common-law arrests are seizures. An arrest requires either physical force or, where that is absent, submission to the assertion of authority.

"Mere words will not constitute an arrest, while, on the other hand, no actual, physical touching is essential. The apparent inconsistency in the two parts of this statement is explained by the fact that an assertion of authority and purpose to arrest followed by submission of the arrestee constitutes an arrest. There can be no arrest without either touching or submission." Perkins, *The Law of Arrest*, 25 Iowa L.Rev. 201, 206 (1940).

We do not think it desirable, even as a policy matter, to stretch the Fourth Amendment beyond its words and beyond the meaning of arrest. Street pursuits always place the public at some risk, and compliance with police orders to stop should therefore be encouraged. Only a few of those orders will be without adequate basis, and since the addressee has no ready means of identifying the deficient ones it almost invariably is the responsible course to comply. Unlawful orders will not be deterred, by sanctioning through the exclusionary rule those of them that are not obeyed. Since policemen do not command "Stop!" expecting to be ignored, or give chase hoping to be outrun, it fully suffices to apply the deterrent to their genuine, successful seizures.

Respondent contends that his position is sustained by the *Mendenhall* test *United States v. Mendenhall*, 446 U.S. 544 (1980). That test says that a person has been seized "only if," not that he has been seized "whenever"; it states a necessary, but not a sufficient, condition for seizure—or, more precisely, for seizure effected through a "show of authority." *Mendenhall* establishes that the test for existence of a "show of authority" is an objective one: not whether the citizen perceived that he was being ordered to restrict his movement, but whether the officer's words and actions would have conveyed that to a reasonable person. Application of this objective test was the basis for our decision in the other case principally relied upon by respondent where we concluded that the police cruiser's slow following of the defendant did not convey the message that he was not free to disregard the police and go about his business. We did not address in *Chesternut*, however, the question whether, if the *Mendenhall* test was met—if the message that the defendant was not free to leave had been conveyed—a Fourth Amendment seizure would have occurred.

In sum, assuming that Pertoso's pursuit in the present case constituted a "show of authority" enjoining Hodari to halt, since Hodari did not comply with that injunction he was not seized until he was tackled. The cocaine abandoned while he was running was in this case not the fruit of a seizure, and his motion to exclude evidence of it was properly denied. We reverse the decision of the California Court of Appeal, and remand for further proceedings not inconsistent with this opinion.

It is so ordered.

JUSTICE STEVENS, with whom JUSTICE MARSHALL joins, dissenting.

The officer's show of force—taking the form of a head-on chase—adequately conveyed the message that respondent was not free to leave. Here, respondent attempted to end "the conversation" before it began and soon found himself literally "not free to leave" when confronted by an officer running toward him head-on who eventually tackled him to the ground. There was an interval of time between the moment that respondent saw the officer fast approaching and the moment when he was tackled, and thus brought under the control of the officer. The question is whether the Fourth Amendment was implicated at the earlier or the later moment.

The same issue would arise if the show of force took the form of a command to "freeze," a warning shot, or the sound of sirens accompanied by a patrol car's flashing lights. In these situations, there may be a significant time interval between the initiation of the officer's show of force and the complete submission by the citizen. The Court concludes that the timing of the seizure is governed by the citizen's reaction, rather than by the officer's conduct. One consequence of this conclusion is that the point at which the interaction between citizen and police officer becomes a seizure occurs, not when a reasonable citizen believes he or she is no longer free to go, but, rather, only after the officer exercises control over the citizen.

Interests in effective law enforcement and in personal liberty would be better served by adhering to a standard that "allows the police to determine in advance whether the conduct contemplated will implicate the Fourth Amendment." The range of possible responses to a police show of force, and the multitude of problems that may arise in determining whether, and at which moment, there has been "submission," can only create uncertainty and generate litigation. In some cases, of course, it is immediately apparent at which moment the suspect submitted to an officer's show of force.

The constitutionality of a police officer's show of force should be measured by the conditions that exist at the time of the officer's action. The character of the citizen's response should not govern the constitutionality of the officer's conduct. In the present case, if Officer Pertoso had succeeded in tackling respondent before he dropped the rock of cocaine, the rock unquestionably would have been excluded as the fruit of the officer's unlawful seizure. Under the Court's analysis, the exclusionary rule has no application because an attempt to make an unconstitutional seizure is beyond the coverage of the Fourth Amendment, no matter how outrageous or unreasonable the officer's conduct may be.

Points for Discussion

a. The Fleeing Motorist

A similar decision was rendered in *Hester v. United States*, 265 U.S. 57 (1924). During Prohibition, federal agents saw a moonshiner hand a customer a quart of whiskey. The agents tried to arrest both the moonshiner and the customer, but both fled. During the chase, both the moonshiner and the customer dropped various items of contraband. The police recovered the items and used them to convict the moonshiner of concealing alcohol in violation of federal law. The Court concluded that the items were properly admitted in evidence: "the defendant's own acts disclosed the contraband and there was no seizure in the sense of the law when the officers examined the contents of each after they had been abandoned."

b. The Police Cruiser

In *Michigan v. Chesternut*, 486 U.S. 567 (1988), police officers were engaged in routine patrol in a marked police cruiser. When respondent saw the patrol car nearing the corner where he stood, he turned and began to run. The cruiser followed respondent "to see where he was going." The cruiser quickly caught up with respondent, drove alongside him for a short distance, and saw him discard a number of packets. The officers retrieved the packets, found that they contained pills which appeared to be codeine, and arrested respondent for possession of narcotics. During an ensuing search, the police discovered another packet of pills, a packet containing heroin, and a hypodermic needle. The Court upheld respondent's conviction for possession of illegal narcotics: "Respondent was not seized before he discarded the packets containing the controlled substance. The police conduct would not have communicated to the reasonable person an attempt to capture or otherwise intrude upon respondent's freedom of movement. The record does not reflect that the police activated a siren or flashers; or that they commanded respondent to halt, or displayed any weapons; or that they operated the car in an aggressive manner to block respondent's course or otherwise control the direction or speed of his movement. While the very presence of a police car driving parallel to a running pedestrian could be somewhat intimidating, this kind of police presence does not, standing alone, constitute a seizure. The police therefore were not required to have "a particularized and objective basis for suspecting respondent of criminal activity," in order to pursue him."

Food for Thought

Suppose that the officer shot Hodari to prevent his escape. Hodari was seriously wounded, unable to run away, and immediately fell to the ground. Before the officer could get to Hodari, he discarded a chunk of rock cocaine. The officer retrieved the cocaine and then subdued Hodari. At what point was Hodari seized? Was the cocaine obtained as a result of the seizure or afterwards? See *Tennessee v. Garner*, 471 U.S. 1 (1985).

Hypo 1: *More on Fleeing Motorists*

Johnson stole an automobile and eluded police by traveling at high speeds. During this time, Johnson was followed by police cars with flashing lights. The chase ended when Johnson slammed into a police roadblock killing himself. The roadblock consisted of tractor-trailers placed across both lanes of a two-lane highway. The roadblock was "concealed" by the fact that it was around a bend in the road and was unilluminated. In addition, a police car, with its headlights on, had been placed between Johnson's oncoming vehicle and the truck, so that Johnson was "blinded." Johnson's heirs sued, claiming that the police had effected an unreasonable seizure in violation of the Fourth Amendment. In light of the holdings in *Mendenhall* and *Hodari D*, do you agree that Johnson was seized? If so, when did the seizure occur? What arguments might you make on behalf of Johnson's estate? How might the State respond? How should the Court rule? *See Brower v. County of Inyo*, 489 U.S. 593 (1989).

Hypo 2: *The Man and the Jacket*

Just after midnight, two police officers on routine patrol in a "high crime area" pull their marked vehicle alongside three young men who are walking. One officer explains to the men that they are "not in trouble," but that he would like to "talk to them" about some recent robberies. The officers then ask the men if they would agree to a pat-down for weapons. Two of the men reply that they have no objection, and one officer frisked them. The third man (Henson) also consented to a pat-down and placed his hands on the hood of the police car. However, before the officer could begin the frisk, the man started walking away. The officer then "grabbed the man's jacket," but the man "was able to wiggle out of it." The officer chased the man for about twenty yards until the man slipped and fell on the snow and the officer caught up with him. After a brief struggle, the officer places the man in handcuffs. When was the man seized for purposes of the Fourth Amendment? *See Henson v. United States*, 55 A.3d 859 (D.C. Ct. App. 2012).

Hypo 3: *The Searchlight and the Pedestrian*

A police officer is patrolling in a high-crime area when he sees an individual standing next to a parked car. The officer shines the patrol car spotlight on the individual, exits his car, walks briskly towards the individual, and asks whether the individual is on probation or parole. The individual does not resist or attempt to run away. Was the individual "seized" when the officer exited the vehicle? *See People v. Garry*, 156 Cal. App.4th 1100, 67 Cal.Rptr.3d 849 (2007).

Food for Thought

Suppose that there is a history of racial tension in a particular city, and that racial tensions in the area have been heightened by recent police shootings of African-American motorists. Around midnight, two white police officers approach an African-American man who is seated in his lawfully parked car in an effort to "find out what he is doing." Under the circumstances, has the man been seized? To what extent is the racial identity of the man, or the racial identity of the police officers, or the racial tensions, relevant to your answer? *See United States v. Washington*, 490 F.3d 765 (9th Cir. 2007).

Hypo 4: *The Smell of "Fresh Marijuana"*

After an anonymous tip that a woman and a man were smoking marijuana outside an apartment building, police officers proceeded to the location and found a properly parked vehicle with the windows down containing two people (a man and a woman) smoking cigarettes. The officers asked the passengers to exit the vehicle. One officer spoke to the man, and could detect the smell of marijuana. When the police called in a drug sniffing dog, the man admitted to possessing marijuana and showed the police where it could be found. Was the man "seized" within the meaning of the Fourth Amendment? If so, when did the seizure begin? *See State v. Joyce*, 159 N.H. 440, 986 A.2d 642 (2009).

* * *

Mendenhall makes clear that the police (or DEA agents or other governmental officials) can make an investigative stop when they have a reasonable suspicion that a suspect is involved in criminal activity. However, unlike a custodial arrest, an investigative stop is a much more limited intrusion on individual privacy. In *Florida v. Royer,* 460 U.S. 491 (1983), a case that was factually similar (although distinguishable) from *Mendenhall*, the Court noted that an "investigative detention must be temporary and last no longer than is necessary to effectuate the purpose of the stop," and should involve "the least intrusive means reasonably available to verify or dispel the officer's suspicion in a short period of time." The Court held that the agents were free to conduct an investigative stop against Royer because they had reason to believe that he was carrying illegal drugs. However, because the officers removed Royer to the DEA office, and removed his luggage from the plane, the Court concluded that the " detention to which he was then subjected was a more serious intrusion on his personal liberty than is allowable on mere suspicion of criminal activity." As a result, it required greater justification.

Points for Discussion

a. Defining Reasonable Suspicion

In *Fields v. Swenson*, 459 F.2d 1064 (8th Cir.1972), late at night, two police officers observed a station wagon at rest in an unlighted section of a parking lot near a hardware store. All nearby business establishments were closed. One of the officers was familiar with the area and had never seen the car before, but he recognized the license number as belonging to a David Montgomery, whom he knew as a suspect in some burglaries. At 11:40 p.m., the officers see three persons approach the car "carrying something." One enters the car's back seat while the other two walk away. When the car is driven away, the police follow for several blocks and see the occupant of the rear seat take off a red jacket. When the officers stopped the car, they observed a lady's handbag containing tools (hammers and other large tools) on the floor. The occupants of the car are then placed under arrest for "investigation of burglary and larceny" and possession of burglary tools. The Court concluded that the police had a sufficient basis for an investigative stop.

Take Note

In *United States v. Sokolow*, 490 U.S. 1 (1989), the Court held that "reasonable suspicion" involves "something more than an 'inchoate' and unparticularized suspicion or 'hunch,' " but "considerably less than proof of wrongdoing by a preponderance of the evidence." "Probable cause means 'a fair probability that contraband or evidence of a crime will be found,' and the level of suspicion required for a *Terry* stop is obviously less demanding than that for probable cause." In *United States v. Cortez*, 449 U.S. 411 (1981), the Court held that "reasonable suspicion" should be determined using a "totality of the circumstances" standard: "Based upon that whole picture the detaining officers must have a particularized and objective basis for suspecting the particular person stopped of criminal activity."

b. 911 Calls and Reasonable Suspicion

In *Navarette v. California*, 134 S.Ct. 1683 (2014), after a 911 caller reported that a vehicle had run her off the road, a police officer located the reported vehicle and executed a traffic stop. The Court held that the 911 call provided the officer with sufficient cause for the stop even though the tip was made anonymously, and there was no information regarding the informant's veracity or basis of knowledge. The Court found the tip "sufficiently reliable" for several reasons: "the caller claimed eyewitness knowledge of the alleged dangerous driving," adding "significant support" to "the tip's reliability," she reported "the incident soon after she was run off the road" (the Court regarded a "contemporaneous report" as "especially reliable"), and the caller used the 911 emergency system which permits the police to identify and trace callers, thereby providing "safeguards against making false reports with immunity." Therefore, the Court concluded that the tip provided the basis for concluding that the driver of the stopped vehicle was driving drunk or had been involved in "an isolated episode of past recklessness." Although the erratic driving might have been explainable as caused by an unruly child in the vehicle, the Court emphasized that reasonable suspicion "need not rule out the possibility of innocent conduct." Justice Scalia dissented, claiming that the Court's new rule suggests that "anonymous claims of a single instance of possibly careless or reckless driving, called in to 911, will support a traffic stop." He argued that the stop was not justified because the police knew nothing about the tipster, the conduct they observed was innocent, and the fact that the call was made to 911 was insufficient to assure reliability.

> **FYI**
>
> In *Alabama v. White*, 496 U.S. 325 (1990), the Court held that police could rely on an anonymous tip in developing "reasonable suspicion." "Reasonable suspicion, like probable cause, is dependent upon both the content of information possessed by police and its degree of reliability." In considering the totality of the circumstances, "if a tip has a relatively low degree of reliability, more information will be required to establish the requisite quantum of suspicion than would be required if the tip were more reliable."

c. Drug Courier Profiles

In recent years, narcotics agents have increasingly relied on so-called "drug courier profiles" to establish the basis for an investigative stop In *Mendenhall*, for example, detectives claimed that a profile focused their attention on Mendenhall:

> The agent testified that the respondent's behavior fit the so-called "drug courier profile"—an informally compiled abstract of characteristics thought typical of persons carrying illicit drugs. In this case the agents thought it relevant that (1) respondent was arriving on a flight from Los Angeles, a city believed by the agents to be the place of origin for much of the heroin brought to Detroit; (2) respondent was the last person to leave the plane, "appeared to be very nervous," and "completely scanned the whole area where the agents were standing"; (3) after leaving the plane respondent proceeded past the baggage area without claiming any luggage; and (4) respondent changed airlines for her flight out of Detroit.

Mendenhall engaged in behavior that the agents believed was designed to evade detection. She deplaned only after all other passengers had left the aircraft. Agent Anderson testified that drug couriers often disembark last in order to have a clear view of the terminal so that they more easily can detect government agents. Once inside the terminal, respondent scanned the entire gate area and walked "very, very slowly" toward the baggage area. When she arrived there, she claimed no baggage. Instead, she asked a skycap for directions to the Eastern Airlines ticket counter located in a different terminal. Although she carried an American Airlines ticket for a flight from Detroit to Pittsburgh, she asked for an Eastern Airlines ticket. An airline employee gave her an Eastern Airlines boarding pass. Agent Anderson testified that drug couriers frequently travel without baggage and change flights en route to avoid surveillance. On the basis of these observations, the agents stopped and questioned respondent.

In *United States v. Sokolow*, 490 U.S. 1 (1989), the Court upheld the use of so-called "drug courier profiles": "A court sitting to determine the existence of reasonable suspicion must require the agent to articulate the factors leading to that conclusion, but the fact that these factors may be set forth in a 'profile' does not somehow detract from their evidentiary significance as seen by a trained agent."

d. Mistakes and Reasonable Suspicion

In *Heien v. North Carolina*, 135 S.Ct. 530 (2014), a police officer stopped a vehicle because of a faulty brake light, and checked the driver's license and registration. While undertaking these tasks, the officer became suspicious because the driver was acting nervously. The officer asked for and obtained consent to search the vehicle and found cocaine during the ensuing search. Heien, who was charged with attempted trafficking in cocaine, moved to suppress the cocaine seized from the car on the basis that it did not violate state law to drive with only one working brake light. Therefore, so Heien argued, the stop was "objectively unreasonable," violated the Fourth Amendment, and the cocaine found during the stop should be suppressed. The Court disagreed. While the Court recognized that, in order to make a traffic stop, an officer must hold a "reasonable suspicion"—that is, "a particularized and objective basis for suspecting the particular person stopped" of breaking the law – the Court held that the "ultimate touchstone of the Fourth Amendment is reasonableness." The Court noted that "reasonable men make mistakes of law, too, and such mistakes are no less compatible with the concept of reasonable suspicion. Officers in the field must make factual assessments on the fly, and so deserve a margin of error. The Fourth Amendment tolerates only *reasonable* mistakes, and those mistakes—whether of fact or of law—must be *objectively* reasonable. Although the North Carolina statute at issue refers to '*a* stop lamp,' suggesting the need for only a single working brake light, it also provides that 'the stop lamp may be incorporated into a unit with one or more *other* rear lamps.' Another subsection of the same provision requires that vehicles 'have all originally equipped rear lamps or the equivalent in good working order,' arguably indicating that if a vehicle has multiple 'stop lamps,' all must be functional." The Court noted that there had been confusion in state court decisions construing the statute. Justice Sotomayor dissented, arguing that there "is nothing in our case law requiring us to hold that a reasonable mistake of law can justify a seizure under the Fourth Amendment, and quite a bit suggesting just the opposite."

e. Pretextual Stops

In *Whren v. United States*, 517 U.S. 806 (1996), two undercover police officers were patrolling in a "high drug area" when they saw respondent driving in an unusual manner and stopped him. Although respondent conceded that the officers had probable cause to stop him for traffic violations, he argued that it was a pretextual stop designed to search for drugs. The Court upheld the stop: "Prior cases foreclose any argument that the constitutional reasonableness of traffic stops depends on the actual motivations of the individual officers involved. The Constitution prohibits selective enforcement based on considerations such as race. But the constitutional basis for objecting to intentionally discriminatory application of laws is the Equal Protection Clause. Subjective intentions play no role in ordinary, probable-cause Fourth Amendment analysis."

Take Note

In *Muehler v. Mena*, 544 U.S. 93 (2005), during execution of a search warrant, the police handcuffed and detained an occupant of a house which they believed was occupied by a criminal gang. During the search, an officer asked the detainee about her immigration status, and the Court decided that this question did not constitute a separate seizure requiring reasonable suspicion, because "mere police questioning does not constitute a seizure." Instead, the Court emphasized that the duration of the questioning, not the content of the questioning, would be relevant to determine whether the detention was lawful. Compare *United States v. Stewart*, 473 F.3d 1265 (10th Cir. 2007) with *United States v. Mendez*, 467 F.3d 1162 (9th Cir. 2006).

f. Duration of Stop

In *United States v. Sharpe*, 470 U.S. 675 (1985), the Court rejected a court of appeals decision holding that investigative stops could not last longer than twenty minutes, noting that there is: "no rigid time limitation on *Terry* stops. While it is clear that 'the brevity of the invasion of the individual's Fourth Amendment interests is an important factor in determining whether the seizure is so minimally intrusive as to be justifiable on reasonable suspicion,' we need to consider the law enforcement purposes to be served by the stop as well as the time reasonably needed to effectuate those purposes." The Court went on: "In assessing whether a detention is too long to be justified as an investigative stop, it is appropriate to examine whether the police diligently pursued a means of investigation that was likely to confirm or dispel their suspicions quickly, during which time it was necessary to detain the defendant. A court making this assessment should consider whether the police are acting in a swiftly developing situation, and not indulge in unrealistic second-guessing. The question is not simply whether some other alternative was available, but whether the police acted unreasonably in failing to recognize or to pursue it."

g. Custodial Questioning

When may the police force a suspect to go to the police station for questioning? In *Dunaway v. New York*, 442 U.S. 200 (1979), the police viewed Dunaway as the prime suspect in a murder case, and decided to "pick him up" and "bring him in" for questioning. Dunaway was not told that he was under arrest, but the police stated that he would have been physically restrained had he attempted to leave. The Court held that probable cause was required. "The detention of petitioner was in important respects indistinguishable from a traditional arrest Any 'exception' that could cover a seizure as intrusive as that in this case would threaten to swallow the general rule that Fourth Amendment seizures are 'reasonable' only if based on probable cause."

h. Fingerprinting

In *Davis v. Mississippi*, 394 U.S. 721 (1969), Davis was convicted of rape and sentenced to life imprisonment based on fingerprints taken after a forced trip to the police station. The Court held that probable cause was required. Mr. Justice Stewart dissented: "Like the color of a man's eyes, his height, or his very physiognomy, the tips of his fingers are an inherent and unchanging characteristic of the man. We do not deal here with a confession wrongfully obtained or with property wrongfully seized. We deal, instead, with 'evidence' that can be identically reproduced and lawfully used at any subsequent trial." In *Hayes v. Florida*, 470 U.S. 811 (1985), in dicta, the Court suggested that a brief field detention for fingerprinting might be justified based only on a reasonable suspicion. "If there are articulable facts supporting a reasonable suspicion that a person has committed a criminal offense, that person may be stopped in order to identify him, to question him briefly, or to detain him briefly while attempting to obtain additional information."

Food for Thought

Consider the drug courier profile (referred to above) that DEA agents used to identify Mendenhall as a drug courier. Do you agree that Mendenhall's conduct was "suspicious?" In thinking about that issue, consider Justice White's dissent:

No aspects of Ms. Mendenhall's conduct, either alone or in combination, were sufficient to provide reasonable suspicion that she was engaged in criminal activity. The fact that Ms. Mendenhall was the last person to alight from a flight originating in Los Angeles was plainly insufficient to provide a basis for stopping her. Nor was the fact that her flight originated from a "major source city," for the mere proximity of a person to areas with a high incidence of drug activity or to persons known to be drug addicts, does not provide the necessary reasonable suspicion for an investigatory stop. The DEA agents' observations that Ms. Mendenhall claimed no luggage and changed airlines were also insufficient to provide reasonable suspicion. Unlike *Terry*, where "nothing in the suspects' conduct from the time the officer first noticed them until the time he confronted them and identified himself as a police officer gave him sufficient reason to negate his hypothesis" of criminal behavior. Ms. Mendenhall's subsequent conduct negated any reasonable inference that she was traveling a long distance without luggage or changing her ticket to a different airline to avoid detection. Agent Anderson testified that he heard the ticket agent tell Ms. Mendenhall that her ticket to Pittsburgh already was in order and that all she needed was a boarding pass for the flight. Thus it should have been plain to an experienced observer that Ms. Mendenhall's failure to claim luggage was attributable to the fact that she was already ticketed through to Pittsburgh on a different airline. Because Agent Anderson's suspicion that Ms. Mendenhall was transporting narcotics could be based only on "his inchoate and unparticularized suspicion or 'hunch,'" rather than "specific reasonable inferences which he is entitled to draw from the facts in light of his experience," he was not justified in "seizing" Ms. Mendenhall.

Food for Thought

Is there a "reasonable suspicion of criminal activity" when a suspect (1) pays $2,100 for two airplane tickets from a roll of $20 bills; (2) travels under a name that does not match the name under which his telephone number is listed; (3) his original destination is Miami, a source city for illicit drugs; (4) he stayed in Miami for only 48 hours, even though a round-trip flight from Honolulu to Miami takes 20 hours; (5) he appeared nervous during his trip; and (6) he checked none of his luggage? *See United States v. Sokolow*, 490 U.S. 1 (1989).

Hypo 1: *Automobile Profiles?*

Suppose that the police create a "drug courier" profile for suspects that transport drugs between Miami and New York City or Boston by automobile. The profile focuses on cars coming from a "source city" (Miami) using a major "drug highway" (I–95). Because so many drivers on this highway tend to exceed the speed limit, and because drug couriers are anxious about not being stopped, the profile includes a reference to drivers who are traveling at or below the speed limit. Do the police have a "reasonable suspicion" that anyone meeting this profile is a "drug courier?"

Food for Thought

After *Mendenhall* and *Royer*, do narcotics agents have clear guidance about how they may act in airport situations? Suppose that the officers had approached Royer in the airport, and sought to ask him some questions, but Royer had refused to answer them. In light of the holding in Royer, what may the officers do next?

Hypo 2: *More on Defining Reasonable Suspicion*

Recall the *Digiovanni* problem in which a police officer stopped a car for following another car too closely. Now consider whether, even if the facts do not provide the officer with probable cause to arrest Digiovanni for a drug crime, the facts provide the officer with at least "reasonable suspicion" to believe that Digiovanni is in possession of illegal drugs. Recall that the officer saw two shirts hanging in the rear passenger compartment and a hygiene bag on the back seat, and he noticed that the interior of the car was clean. The officer viewed these facts as suggestive of drug trafficking activity. The officer also testified that the rental contract also made him suspicious of drug trafficking activity. The rental contract indicated that the car was rented at Fort Lauderdale International Airport the previous day and was to be dropped off at Logan International Airport in Boston, at a cost of $438. The officer testified that Digiovanni's one-way, $438 car rental was "implausible." Does the officer have "reasonable suspicion" to continue the detention? If so, then what is the officer allowed to do? *See United States v. Digiovanni*, 650 F. 3d 498 (4th Cir. 2011). Consider whether you would reach a different conclusion about the existence of reasonable suspicion if the officer testified that he asked Digiovanni if he had any luggage in the car and if everything in the car belonged to him. Digiovanni responded in the affirmative to both questions. Then Digiovanni said, "Oh boy," as he tossed the cigarette he was smoking over the guardrail. The officer testified that he found this remark "extremely suspicious," because "now he is saying 'Oh boy' in response to my questioning." The officer then asked Digiovanni what was the matter, to which Digiovanni replied, "It's just so hot." Then the officer explained to Digiovanni that "people smuggle drugs and guns up and down I–95," and asked Digiovanni if there was any marijuana in the car. Digiovanni replied, "No sir. I never smoked marijuana in my life. It puts me to sleep." Next, the officer asked Digiovanni if there was any cocaine or heroin in the car, and Digiovanni responded in the negative. The officer also asked Digiovanni if there was any methamphetamine in the car, and Digiovanni indicated that there was not. When the officer followed up with, "Are you sure?," Digiovanni replied, "I'm positive." Under these circumstances, does the officer possess a reasonable suspicion that Digiovanni is involved in drug trafficking? If so, what is the officer allowed to do next? How does Digiovanni's nonsensical response (that he had "never" smoked marijuana because it puts him to sleep) enter into the analysis? *See United States v. Digiovanni,* 650 F.3d 498 (4th Cir. 2011).

Hypo 3: *The Suspicious Rental Car*

A police officer, traveling on an interstate highway, observes a driver who unsafely passes another car. The officer stops the driver who appears to be "extremely nervous" and does not maintain eye contact. The officer checks the driver's license and registration, as well as the rental car agreement. In talking to the driver, the officer learns that the car was rented in Las Vegas, Nevada (hundreds of miles away from the site of the stop in Kansas, and generally regarded by police as a "source city" for illegal drugs) the day before, that the driver is traveling to Indianapolis (also hundreds of miles away) because he has to be at work the following day, and that the driver plans to return the car to Las Vegas two days later. The officer believes that these travel plans are "bizarre." By this time, the officer has written a citation for the unlawful pass and given it to the driver. Does the officer have a reasonable suspicion that the driver is involved in criminal activity (over and above the unsafe pass)? If so, what may the officer do in order to verify (or dispel) his suspicions? See *United States v. White,* 584 F.3d 935 (10th Cir. 2009).

Hypo 4: *The Suspicious Driver*

Suppose that a police officer has reason to suspect that the driver of a lawfully stopped vehicle may be involved in drug trafficking. What steps may the officer take to dispel (or verify) his suspicion? If the officer has a drug sniffing dog with him, may he subject the vehicle and passengers to a drug sniff? If the officer does not happen to have a drug sniffing dog with him, can he order the driver to follow him to the state highway patrol office where a dog can conduct the sniff? The office is about 9 miles away. While the officer could have waited for the dog to be brought to the scene of the stop, he believed that the sniff would occur much more quickly if it were conducted at the office. Would his action be permissible?

Hypo 5: *Length of Stop*

Suppose that a police officer validly stops a suspect for a traffic violation. May the police officer extend the stop long enough to run a background check on the suspect to make sure who she is dealing with and to check for outstanding warrants? *See People v. Harris*, 228 Ill.2d 222, 319 Ill.Dec. 823, 886 N.E.2d 947 (2008). After the officer confirms the validity of the suspect's driver's license and the absence of outstanding warrants, the officer is writing a citation when another officer arrives and informs the first officer that the suspect is believed to be involved in drug activity. The first officer immediately stops writing the ticket, and goes to the suspect's car to question him about illegal drugs. After a very brief conversation, the suspect consents to a search of the vehicle which turns up illegal narcotics and illegal firearms. Did the officer act permissibly in prolonging the search to ask about drugs and request consent to search? Does it matter whether the officer had a "reasonable suspicion" on which to base the inquiry? *See United States v. Turvin*, 517 F.3d 1097 (9th Cir. 2008); *State v. Louthan*, 275 Neb. 101, 744 N.W.2d 454 (2008).

Hypo 6: *The Scope of the Stop*

One evening, an officer notices a van with illegal window tinting. The officer activates his lights and pulls the car over. When the van stops, the officer notices that there is a "lot of shaking," so he immediately walks to the driver's side door. The officer notices a man (Jackson), and he assumes that the man has switched seats because the female had been in the driver's seat when the officer first spotted the vehicle. The officer stated that, in his experience, such switching involves an attempt to hide or retrieve weapons. The driver admits that he switched places with the woman. When the officer asks the driver whether he has any weapons on him, the driver replies "no," and the officer finds no weapons in the ensuing pat-down. However, the officer notices that the driver is nervous and that his heart is beating fast. The officer then handcuffs the female passenger while he places the driver in the back seat of his patrol car. The driver is told that he is not under arrest. The officer then searches the front passenger compartment of the van for weapons and finds whiskey under the van's rear floorboard, and a small hatchet beside the driver's seat. The officer also removes the cover of the horn on the steering wheel after noticing that it looks out of position. There, he discovers Ziploc bags containing a rock-like substance that turns out to be cocaine. Did the officer act properly in stopping the vehicle, frisking the occupants, and in searching the vehicle? *See Jackson v. United States*, 56 A.3d 1206 (D.C. App. 2012).

Hypo 7: *The Gun Shells*

A police officer responds to an unverified 911 call from a children's clothing store. The officer knows that there is drug activity in the surrounding area and that there have been several burglaries in this particular mall. When he arrives, a security guard tells the officer that a man has attempted to steal some clothing. The guard identifies a male who is walking quickly away from the store. There are six to eight people in the direction the guard points, but Griffin is the only one who fit the guard's description of "the black man in the green jacket and jeans." The officer follows the man who continuously looks over his shoulder and walk away briskly. The officer tells the man to stop. When the man disobeys and continues to walk away, the officer grabs the man's wrists, and states that he is investigating a petty theft. Even though the man denies stealing anything, the officer frisks the man in order to ensure his own safety. During the frisk, the officer feels what he "believed to be" batteries in the man's pocket. The officer does not reach into the pocket, but does find "it odd that someone is carrying batteries," he asks the man, "Hey, what's in your pocket? Why do you have batteries?" Griffin responded that the items are shotgun shells. The officer then asks the man if he has ever been to prison, and the man answers "yes." When the officer states that it is illegal for felons to possess weapons or ammunition, the man flees. Did the police officer act properly in asking the man the additional questions? Did the questions unduly prolong the seizure? *See United States v. Griffin*, 696 F.3d 1354 (11th Cir. 2012).

Hypo 8: *The Knife*

While on routine patrol, two officers pull over defendant's vehicle because of a defective rear brake light. In addition to defendant, who is behind the wheel, there are four male occupants in the vehicle. According to one officer, the three passengers in the rear seat "were a little furtive," kept "looking behind," and "stiffened up" when the officers approached the vehicle. The other officer observed that the passengers "made furtive movements, and acted nervous." When asked for his license and registration, the driver complied with the request. An officer then asked if anyone in the vehicle had a weapon, and the passenger in the rear middle seat answered, "Yes, I have a knife." The officer directed the passenger to place the knife on the floor and to keep his hands in view. The passenger complied. The officers then ordered the occupants out of the vehicle and frisked each man as he exited the car. After the last passenger exited, one officer saw what appeared to be "a gun or some sort of weapon" wedged between the front passenger seat and the door of the vehicle. With the aid of a flashlight, the officer retrieved and inspected the item, an air pistol. Did the officers act properly? *See People v. Garcia,* 20 N.Y.3d 317, 983 N.E.2d 259, 959 N.Y.S.2d 464 (2012).

Hypo 9: *Frisking the Passenger*

A police officer, cruising in an unmarked cruiser in "a high crime area," observes a truck with license plates from another county. He follows the truck, believing that it might have come to Dayton to buy illegal drugs. He also runs a license check on the truck and learns that it is registered to someone who has a drug-related conviction, and for whom there is an outstanding arrest warrant. When the driver of the truck leaves the house several hours later, with another man (later identified as Gardner), the officer follows. When the truck stops at a gas station, the officer approaches the car, confirms the driver's identity (as the man for which there was a warrant), and places him under arrest. During the arrest, the officer notices that Gardner is moving inside the car, has his hand on the door handle, and appears to be ready to exit the vehicle. As the officer walks around the car, he sees Gardner rise from the seat and reach into his back pocket. The officer orders Gardner to place his hands on the dashboard. Gardner compiles. The officer then removes Gardner from the truck and handcuffs him (the officer is the only officer at the scene). The officer tells Gardner that he is not under arrest, but that he is being handcuffed for the officer's safety. The officer then pats Gardner down for weapons. Although he does not find one, he does find something that he suspects to be crack cocaine. The officer arrests Gardner and removes the contraband. Did the officer act properly? *See State v. Gardner,* 135 Ohio St.3d 99, 984 N.E.2d 1025 (2012).

United States v. Place

462 U.S. 696 (1983).

JUSTICE O'CONNOR delivered the opinion of the Court.

Respondent Place's behavior aroused the suspicions of law enforcement officers as he waited in line at the Miami International Airport to purchase a ticket to New York's LaGuardia Airport. As Place proceeded to the gate for his flight, agents approached him and requested his airline ticket and some identification. Place complied and consented to a search of the two suitcases he had checked. Because his flight was about to depart, however, the agents decided not to search the luggage.

Prompted by Place's parting remark that he had recognized that they were police, the agents inspected the address tags on the checked luggage and noted discrepancies in the street addresses. Further investigation revealed that neither address existed and that the telephone number Place had given the airline belonged to a third address on the same street. On the basis of their encounter with Place and this information, the agents called Drug Enforcement Administration (DEA) authorities in New York to relay their information about Place.

Two DEA agents waited for Place at the arrival gate at LaGuardia Airport in New York. There again, his behavior aroused the suspicion of the agents. After he claimed his two bags and called a limousine, the agents decided to approach him. They identified themselves as federal narcotics agents, to which Place responded that he knew they were "cops" and had spotted them as soon as he had deplaned. One of the agents informed Place that, based on their own observations and information obtained from the Miami authorities, they believed that he might be carrying narcotics. The agents requested and received identification from Place— a New Jersey driver's license, on which the agents later ran a computer check that disclosed no offenses, and his airline ticket receipt. When Place refused to consent to a search of his luggage, one of the agents told him that they were going to take the luggage to a federal judge to try to obtain a search warrant and that Place was free to accompany them. Place declined, but obtained from one of the agents telephone numbers at which the agents could be reached.

The agents then took the bags to Kennedy Airport, where they subjected the bags to a "sniff test" by a trained narcotics detection dog. The dog reacted positively to the smaller of the two bags but ambiguously to the larger bag. Approximately 90 minutes had elapsed since the seizure of respondent's luggage. Because it was late on a Friday afternoon, the agents retained the luggage until Monday morning, when they secured a search warrant from a magistrate for the smaller bag. Upon opening that bag, the agents discovered 1,125 grams of cocaine. Place was indicted for possession of cocaine with intent to distribute. The District Court denied Place's motion to suppress, but the court of appeals reversed.

The Court has viewed a seizure of personal property as *per se* unreasonable within the meaning of the Fourth Amendment unless it is accomplished pursuant to a judicial warrant issued upon probable cause and particularly describing the items to be seized. Where law enforcement authorities have probable cause to believe that a container holds contraband or evidence of a crime, but have not secured a warrant, the Court has interpreted the Amendment to permit seizure of the property, pending issuance of a warrant to examine its contents, if the exigencies of the circumstances demand it or some other recognized exception to the warrant requirement is present. For example, "objects such as weapons or contraband found in a public place may be seized by the police without a warrant," because, under these circumstances, the risk of the item's disappearance or use for its intended purpose before a warrant may be obtained outweighs the interest in possession.

The Government asks us to recognize the reasonableness under the Fourth Amendment of warrantless seizures of personal luggage from the custody of the owner on the basis of less than probable cause, for the purpose of pursuing a limited course of investigation, short of opening the luggage, that would quickly confirm or dispel the authorities' suspicion. Specifically, we are asked to apply the principles of *Terry* to permit seizures on the basis of reasonable, articulable suspicion, premised on objective facts, that the luggage contains contraband or evidence of a crime. In our view, such application is appropriate.

Where the authorities possess specific and articulable facts warranting a reasonable belief that a traveler's luggage contains narcotics, the governmental interest in seizing the luggage briefly to pursue further investigation is substantial. "The public has a compelling interest in detecting those who would traffic in deadly drugs for personal profit." In *Terry*, we described the governmental interests supporting the initial seizure of the person as "effective crime prevention and detection; it is this interest which underlies the recognition that a police officer may in appropriate circumstances and in an appropriate manner approach a person for purposes of investigating possibly criminal behavior even though there is no probable cause to make an arrest." Similarly, in *Michigan v. Summers* we identified three law enforcement interests that justified limited detention of the occupants of the premises during execution of a valid search warrant: "preventing flight in the event that incriminating evidence is found," "minimizing the risk of harm" both to the officers and the occupants, and "orderly completion of the search." The test is whether those interests are sufficiently "substantial," not whether they are independent of the interest in investigating crimes effectively and apprehending suspects. The context of a particular law enforcement practice may affect the determination whether a brief intrusion on Fourth Amendment interests on less than probable cause is essential to effective criminal investigation. Because of the inherently transient nature of drug courier activity at airports, allowing police to make brief investigative stops of persons at airports on reasonable suspicion of drug-trafficking substantially enhances the likelihood that police will be able to prevent the flow of narcotics into distribution channels.

Against this strong governmental interest, we must weigh the nature and extent of the intrusion upon the individual's Fourth Amendment rights when the police briefly detain luggage for limited investigative purposes. The intrusion on possessory interests occasioned by a seizure of one's personal effects can vary both in its nature and extent. The seizure may be made after the owner has relinquished control of the property to a third party or, as here, from the immediate custody and control of the owner. Moreover, the police may confine their investigation to an on-the-spot inquiry—for example, immediate exposure of the luggage to a trained narcotics detection dog—or transport the property to another location. Given the fact that seizures of property can vary in intrusiveness, some brief detentions of personal effects may be so minimally intrusive of Fourth Amendment interests that strong countervailing governmental interests will justify a seizure based only on specific articulable facts that the property contains contraband or evidence of a crime.

We conclude that when an officer's observations lead him reasonably to believe that a traveler is carrying luggage that contains narcotics, the principles of *Terry* and its progeny would permit the officer to detain the luggage briefly to investigate the circumstances that aroused his suspicion, provided that the investigative detention is properly limited in scope.

The purpose for which respondent's luggage was seized was to arrange its exposure to a narcotics detection dog. If this investigative procedure is itself a search requiring probable cause, the seizure of respondent's luggage for the purpose of subjecting it to the sniff test—no matter how brief—could not be justified on less than probable cause. A "canine sniff" by a well-trained narcotics detection dog, however, does not require opening the luggage. It does not expose noncontraband items that otherwise would remain hidden from public view, as does, for example, an officer's rummaging through the contents of the luggage. Thus, the manner in which information is obtained through this investigative technique is much less intrusive than a typical search. Moreover, the sniff discloses only the presence or absence of narcotics, a contraband item. Despite the fact that the sniff tells the authorities something about the contents of the luggage, the information obtained is limited. This limited disclosure also ensures that the owner of the property is not subjected to the embarrassment and inconvenience entailed in less discriminate and more intrusive investigative methods. We conclude that the particular course of investigation that the agents intended to pursue here—exposure of respondent's luggage, which was located in a public place, to a trained canine—did not constitute a "search" within the meaning of the Fourth Amendment.

There is no doubt that the agents made a "seizure" of Place's luggage for purposes of the Fourth Amendment when, following his refusal to consent to a search, the agent told Place that he was going to take the luggage to a federal judge to secure issuance of a warrant. We reject the Government's suggestion that the point at which probable cause for seizure of luggage from the person's presence becomes necessary is more distant than in the case of a *Terry* stop of the person himself. The premise of the Government's argument is that seizures of property are generally less intrusive than seizures of the person. While true in some circumstances, the precise type of detention we confront here is seizure of personal luggage from the immediate possession of the suspect for the purpose of arranging exposure to a narcotics detection dog. In the case of detention of luggage within the traveler's immediate possession, the police conduct intrudes on both the suspect's possessory interest in his luggage as well as his liberty interest in proceeding with his itinerary. The person whose luggage is detained is technically still free to continue his travels or carry out other personal activities pending release of the luggage. Moreover, he is not subjected to the coercive atmosphere of a custodial confinement or to the public indignity of being personally detained. Nevertheless, such a seizure can effectively restrain the person since he is subjected to the possible disruption of his travel plans in order to remain with his luggage or to arrange for its return. Therefore, when the police seize luggage from the suspect's custody, we think the limitations applicable to investigative detentions of the person should define the permissible scope of an investigative detention of the person's luggage on less than probable cause. Under this standard, it is clear that the police conduct here exceeded the permissible limits of a *Terry*-type investigative stop.

The length of the detention of Place's luggage precludes a conclusion that the seizure was reasonable in the absence of probable cause. The brevity of the invasion of the individual's Fourth Amendment interests is an important factor in determining whether the seizure is so minimally intrusive as to be justifiable on reasonable suspicion. Moreover, in assessing the effect of the length of the detention, we take into account whether the police diligently pursue their investigation. Here the New York agents knew the time of Place's scheduled arrival at LaGuardia, had ample time to arrange for their additional investigation, and thereby could have minimized the intrusion on respondent's Fourth Amendment interests. Although we decline to adopt any outside time limitation for a permissible *Terry* stop,[11] we have never approved a seizure of the person for the prolonged 90-minute period involved here and cannot do so on the facts presented by this case.

---

[11] Cf. ALI, Model Code of Pre-Arraignment Procedure § 110.2(1) (1975)(recommending a maximum of 20 minutes for a *Terry* stop).

Although the 90-minute detention of respondent's luggage is sufficient to render the seizure unreasonable, the violation was exacerbated by the failure of the agents to accurately inform respondent of the place to which they were transporting his luggage, of the length of time he might be dispossessed, and of what arrangements would be made for return of the luggage if the investigation dispelled the suspicion. The detention of respondent's luggage went beyond the narrow authority possessed by police to detain briefly luggage reasonably suspected to contain narcotics. Under all of the circumstances of this case, the seizure of respondent's luggage was unreasonable under the Fourth Amendment. Consequently, the evidence obtained from the subsequent search of his luggage was inadmissible, and Place's conviction must be reversed.

JUSTICE BRENNAN, with whom JUSTICE MARSHALL joins, concurring in the result.

The use of a balancing test in this case is inappropriate. First, the intrusion involved in this case is no longer the "narrow" one contemplated by the *Terry* line of cases. In addition, the intrusion involves not only the seizure of a person, but also the seizure of property. The Court today has employed a balancing test 'to swallow the general rule that seizures of property are "reasonable" only if based on probable cause.' " Justice Blackmun's concern over "an emerging tendency on the part of the Court to convert the *Terry* decision into a general statement that the Fourth Amendment requires only that any seizure be reasonable," is certainly justified.

Point for Discussion

Seizing Mail

In *United States v. Van Leeuwen*, 397 U.S. 249 (1970), respondent mailed two 12-pound packages at a post office in the State of Washington, near the Canadian border, declaring that the packages contained coins addressed to post office boxes in California and Tennessee. Each package was sent airmail registered and insured for $10,000, so

Food for Thought

In *Place*, suppose that you had been asked to advise the police about how to handle the Place investigation. What would you have advised them to do differently?

that they were not subject to discretionary inspection. When the postal clerk told police that he was suspicious of the packages, an officer noticed that the return address was a vacant housing area and that the license plates of respondent's car were from British Columbia. Further investigation revealed that the California address was under investigation for trafficking in illegal coins. Seattle customs was unable to reach Nashville until the following morning, but they then learned that the Tennessee address was being investigated for the same crime. A customs official in Seattle thereupon obtained a search warrant, and the packages were opened and inspected. Respondent was subsequently tried for illegally importing gold coins. The Court upheld the seizure: "No interest protected by the Fourth Amendment was invaded by forwarding the packages the following day rather than the day when they were deposited. The significant Fourth Amendment interest was in the privacy of this first-class mail; and that privacy was not disturbed or invaded until the approval of the magistrate was obtained. Given the nature of the mailings, their suspicious character, the fact that there were two packages going to separate destinations, the unavoidable delay in contacting the more distant of the two destinations, the distance between Mt. Vernon and Seattle—a 29-hour delay between the mailings and the service of the warrant cannot be said to be 'unreasonable' within the meaning of the Fourth Amendment."

Rodriguez v. United States

135 S.Ct. 1609 (2015).

JUSTICE GINSBURG delivered the opinion of the Court.

Just after midnight, police officer Morgan Struble observed a Mercury Mountaineer veer slowly onto the shoulder of Nebraska State Highway 275 for one or two seconds and then jerk back onto the road. Nebraska law prohibits driving on highway shoulders, and on that basis, Struble pulled the Mountaineer over. Struble is a K–9 officer with the Valley Police Department in Nebraska, and his dog Floyd was in his patrol car that night. Two men were in the Mountaineer: the driver, Denny Rodriguez, and a front-seat passenger, Scott Pollman. Struble approached the Mountaineer on the passenger's side. After Rodriguez identified himself, Struble asked him why he had driven onto the shoulder. Rodriguez replied that he had swerved to avoid a pothole. Struble then gathered Rodriguez's license, registration, and proof of insurance. Rodriguez decided to wait in his own vehicle. After running a records check on Rodriguez, Struble asked passenger Pollman for his driver's license and began to question him about where the two men were coming from and where they were going. Pollman replied that they had traveled to Omaha, Nebraska, to look at a Ford Mustang that was for sale and that they were returning to Norfolk, Nebraska. Struble returned again to his patrol car, where he completed a records check on Pollman, and called for a second officer. Struble then began writing a warning ticket for Rodriguez for driving on the shoulder of the road.

Struble returned to Rodriguez's vehicle a third time to issue the written warning. By 12:27 or 12:28 a.m., Struble had finished explaining the warning to Rodriguez, and had given back to Rodriguez and Pollman the documents obtained from them. Although justification for the traffic stop was "out of the way," Struble asked for permission to walk his dog around Rodriguez's vehicle. Rodriguez said no. Struble then instructed Rodriguez to turn off the ignition, exit the vehicle, and stand in front of the patrol car to wait for the second officer. Rodriguez complied. At 12:33 a.m., a deputy sheriff arrived. Struble retrieved his dog and led him twice around the Mountaineer. The dog alerted to the presence of drugs halfway through Struble's second pass. All told, seven or eight minutes had elapsed from the time Struble issued the written warning until the dog indicated the presence of drugs. A search of the vehicle revealed a large bag of methamphetamine.

Rodriguez was indicted on one count of possession with intent to distribute 50 grams or more of methamphetamine. He moved to suppress the evidence seized. The District Court denied Rodriguez's motion to suppress. The Eighth Circuit affirmed. We granted certiorari to resolve a division among lower courts on the question whether police routinely may extend an otherwise-completed traffic stop, absent reasonable suspicion, in order to conduct a dog sniff.

A seizure for a traffic violation justifies a police investigation of that violation. "A relatively brief encounter," a routine traffic stop is "more analogous to a so-called '*Terry* stop' than to a formal arrest." *Knowles v. Iowa*, 525 U.S. 113, 117 (1998). Like a *Terry* stop, the tolerable duration of police inquiries in the traffic-stop context is determined by the seizure's "mission"—to address the traffic violation that warranted the stop, and attend to related safety concerns. See also *United States v. Sharpe*, 470 U.S. 675 (1985); *Florida v. Royer*, 460 U.S. 491 (1983) (plurality opinion) ("The scope of the detention must be carefully tailored to its underlying justification."). Because addressing the infraction is the purpose of the stop, it may "last no longer than is necessary to effectuate that purpose." Authority for the seizure thus ends when tasks tied to the traffic infraction are—or reasonably should have been—completed. See *Sharpe*, 470 U.S., at 686.

Our decisions in *Caballes* and *Johnson* heed these constraints. In *Illinois v. Caballes*, 543 U.S. 405 (2005), we concluded that the Fourth Amendment tolerated certain unrelated investigations that did not lengthen the roadside detention. *Johnson*, 555 U.S., at 327–328 (questioning); *Caballes*, 543 U.S., at 406 (dog sniff). In *Caballes*, however, we cautioned that a traffic stop "can become unlawful if it is prolonged beyond the time reasonably required to complete the mission" of issuing a warning ticket. We repeated that admonition in *Johnson* : The seizure remains lawful only "so long as unrelated inquiries do not measurably extend the duration of the stop." An officer, in other words, may conduct certain unrelated checks during an otherwise lawful traffic stop. But he may not do so in a way that prolongs the stop, absent the reasonable suspicion ordinarily demanded to justify detaining an individual.

Beyond determining whether to issue a traffic ticket, an officer's mission includes "ordinary inquiries incident to the traffic stop." *Caballes*, 543 U.S., at 408.

Typically such inquiries involve checking the driver's license, determining whether there are outstanding warrants against the driver, and inspecting the automobile's registration and proof of insurance. These checks serve the same objective as enforcement of the traffic code: ensuring that vehicles on the road are operated safely and responsibly. See *Prouse,* 440 U.S., at 658–659.

A dog sniff, by contrast, is a measure aimed at "detecting evidence of ordinary criminal wrongdoing." *Indianapolis v. Edmond,* 531 U.S. 32, 40–41 (2000). See also *Florida v. Jardines,* 133 S.Ct. 1409 (2013). Candidly, the Government acknowledged that a dog sniff, unlike the routine measures just mentioned, is not an ordinary incident of a traffic stop. Lacking the same close connection to roadway safety as the ordinary inquiries, a dog sniff is not fairly characterized as part of the officer's traffic mission. In *Mimms,* we reasoned that the government's "legitimate and weighty" interest in officer safety outweighs the "*de minimis*" additional intrusion of requiring a driver, already lawfully stopped, to exit the vehicle. See also *Maryland v. Wilson,* 519 U.S. 408 (1997). The Eighth Circuit believed that the imposition here similarly could be offset by the Government's "strong interest in interdicting the flow of illegal drugs along the nation's highways."

Unlike a general interest in criminal enforcement, the government's safety interest stems from the mission of the stop itself. Traffic stops are "especially fraught with danger to police officers," *Johnson,* 555 U.S., at 330, so an officer may need to take certain negligibly burdensome precautions in order to complete his mission safely. On-scene investigation into other crimes, however, detours from that mission. So too do safety precautions taken in order to facilitate such detours. Even assuming that the imposition here was no more intrusive than the exit order in *Mimms,* the dog sniff could not be justified on the same basis. Highway and officer safety are interests different in kind from the Government's endeavor to detect crime in general or drug trafficking in particular.

The Government argues that an officer may "incrementally" prolong a stop to conduct a dog sniff so long as the officer is reasonably diligent in pursuing the traffic-related purpose of the stop, and the overall duration of the stop remains reasonable in relation to the duration of other traffic stops involving similar circumstances. The reasonableness of a seizure, however, depends on what the police in fact do. If an officer can complete traffic-based inquiries expeditiously, then that is the amount of "time reasonably required to complete the stop's mission." *Caballes,* 543 U.S., at 407. As we said in *Caballes,* a traffic stop "prolonged beyond" that point is "unlawful." The critical question is not whether the dog sniff occurs before or after the officer issues a ticket, but whether conducting the sniff "prolongs"—i.e., adds time to—"the stop."

The Magistrate Judge found that detention for the dog sniff in this case was not independently supported by individualized suspicion, and the District

Court adopted the Magistrate Judge's findings. The question whether reasonable suspicion of criminal activity justified detaining Rodriguez beyond completion of the traffic infraction investigation, therefore, remains open for Eighth Circuit consideration on remand.

For the reasons stated, the judgment of the United States Court of Appeals for the Eighth Circuit is vacated, and the case is remanded for further proceedings consistent with this opinion.

It is so ordered.

JUSTICE THOMAS, with whom JUSTICE ALITO joins, and with whom JUSTICE KENNEDY joins as to all but Part III, dissenting.

Because the stop was reasonably executed, no Fourth Amendment violation occurred.

I

Approximately 29 minutes passed from the time Officer Struble stopped Rodriguez until his narcotics-detection dog alerted to the presence of drugs. That amount of time is hardly out of the ordinary for a traffic stop by a single officer of a vehicle containing multiple occupants even when no dog sniff is involved. During that time, Officer Struble conducted the ordinary activities of a traffic stop—he approached the vehicle, questioned Rodriguez about the observed violation, asked Pollman about their travel plans, ran serial warrant checks on Rodriguez and Pollman, and issued a written warning to Rodriguez. The fact that Officer Struble waited until after he gave Rodriguez the warning to conduct the dog sniff does not alter this analysis. Because "the use of a well-trained narcotics-detection dog generally does not implicate legitimate privacy interests," "conducting a dog sniff would not change the character of a traffic stop that is lawful at its inception and otherwise executed in a reasonable manner."

II

Caballes expressly anticipated that a traffic stop could be *reasonably* prolonged for officers to engage in a dog sniff. We explained that no Fourth Amendment violation had occurred in *Caballes,* where the "duration of the stop was entirely justified by the traffic offense and the ordinary inquiries incident to such a stop," but suggested a different result might attend a case "involving a dog sniff that occurred during an *unreasonably* prolonged traffic stop." The dividing line was whether the overall duration of the stop exceeded "the time reasonably required to complete the mission," not whether the duration of the stop "in fact" exceeded the time necessary to complete the traffic-related inquiries.

The majority's approach draws an artificial line between dog sniffs and other common police practices. Lower courts have confirmed that warrant checks are a constitutionally permissible part of a traffic stop, and the majority finds no fault in these measures. Yet its reasoning suggests the opposite. Such warrant checks look more like they are directed to "detecting evidence of ordinary criminal wrongdoing" than to "ensuring that vehicles on the road are operated safely and responsibly." Perhaps the existence of an outstanding warrant might make a driver less likely to operate his vehicle safely and responsibly on the road, but the same could be said about a driver in possession of contraband. A driver confronted by the police in either case might try to flee or become violent toward the officer. The majority suggests that a warrant check is an ordinary inquiry incident to a traffic stop because it can be used "to determine whether the apparent traffic violator is wanted for one or more previous traffic offenses." But such checks are a "manifestation of the 'war on drugs' motivation so often underlying routine traffic stops," and thus are very much like the dog sniff in this case. "Asking questions is an essential part of police investigations." *Hiibel v. Sixth Judicial Dist. Court of Nev., Humboldt Cty.,* 542 U.S. 177, 185 (2004). The lower courts have upheld such questioning during routine traffic stops. The majority's reasoning appears to allow officers to engage in *some* questioning aimed at detecting evidence of ordinary criminal wrongdoing. But it is hard to see how such inquiries fall within the "seizure's 'mission' of addressing the traffic violation that warranted the stop," or "attending to related safety concerns." Its reasoning appears to come down to the principle that dogs are different.

A traffic stop based on reasonable suspicion, like all *Terry* stops, must be "justified at its inception" and "reasonably related in scope to the circumstances which justified the interference in the first place." *Hiibel,* 542 U.S., at 185. It also "cannot continue for an excessive period of time or resemble a traditional arrest." *Id.,* at 185–186. By contrast, a stop based on probable cause affords an officer considerably more leeway. In such seizures, an officer may engage in a warrantless arrest of the driver, a warrantless search incident to arrest of the driver, and a warrantless search incident to arrest of the vehicle if it is reasonable to believe evidence relevant to the crime of arrest might be found there. The *only* case involving a traffic stop based on probable cause that the majority cites is *Caballes.* But *Caballes* made clear that, in the context of a traffic stop supported by probable cause, "a dog sniff would not change the character of a traffic stop that is lawful at its inception and otherwise executed in a reasonable manner." Had Officer Struble arrested, handcuffed, and taken Rodriguez to the police station for his traffic violation, he would have complied with the Fourth Amendment. But because he made Rodriguez wait for seven or eight extra minutes until a dog arrived, he evidently committed a constitutional violation. Such a view of the Fourth Amendment makes little sense.

III

The Fourth Amendment permits an officer to conduct an investigative traffic stop when that officer has "a particularized and objective basis for suspecting the particular person stopped of criminal activity." Officer Struble testified that he first became suspicious that Rodriguez was engaged in criminal activity for a number of reasons. When he approached the vehicle, he smelled an "overwhelming odor of air freshener coming from the vehicle," which is, in his experience, "a common attempt to conceal an odor that people don't want to be smelled by the police." He observed that Rodriguez's passenger, Scott Pollman, appeared nervous. Pollman pulled his hat down low, puffed nervously on a cigarette, and refused to make eye contact with him. The officer thought he was "more nervous than your typical passenger" who "doesn't have anything to worry about because they didn't commit a traffic violation." Officer Struble's interactions with the vehicle's occupants only increased his suspicions. When he asked Rodriguez why he had driven onto the shoulder, Rodriguez claimed that he swerved to avoid a pothole. But that story could not be squared with Officer Struble's observation of the vehicle slowly driving off the road before being jerked back onto it. When Officer Struble asked Pollman where they were coming from and where they were going, Pollman told him they were traveling from Omaha, Nebraska, back to Norfolk, Nebraska, after looking at a vehicle they were considering purchasing. Pollman told the officer that he had neither seen pictures of the vehicle nor confirmed title before the trip. As Officer Struble explained, it "seemed suspicious" to him "to drive approximately two hours late at night to see a vehicle sight unseen to possibly buy it," and to go from Norfolk to Omaha to look at it because "usually people leave Omaha to go get vehicles, not the other way around" due to higher Omaha taxes. These facts, taken together, easily meet our standard for reasonable suspicion. Acts that, by themselves, might be innocent can, when taken together, give rise to reasonable suspicion. Officer Struble possessed probable cause to stop Rodriguez for driving on the shoulder, and he executed the subsequent stop in a reasonable manner.

JUSTICE ALITO, dissenting.

The Court refuses to address the real Fourth Amendment question: whether the stop was unreasonably prolonged. Instead, the Court latches onto the fact that Officer Struble delivered the warning prior to the dog sniff and proclaims that the authority to detain based on a traffic stop ends when a citation or warning is handed over to the driver. This holding is perverse since Officer Struble chose that sequence for the purpose of protecting his own safety and possibly the safety of others. Officer Struble could have conducted the dog sniff while one of the tasks that the Court regards as properly part of the traffic stop was still in progress, but that sequence would have entailed unnecessary risk. When occupants of a vehicle who know that their vehicle contains a large amount of illegal drugs see that a drug-sniffing dog has alerted for the presence of drugs, they will almost certainly realize that the police will then proceed to search the vehicle, discover the drugs, and make arrests. Thus, it is reasonable for an officer to believe that an alert will increase the risk that the occupants of the vehicle will attempt to flee or perhaps even attack the officer. In this case, Officer Struble was outnumbered at the scene, and he therefore called for backup and waited for the arrival of another officer before conducting the sniff. As a result, the sniff was not completed until seven or eight minutes after he delivered the warning. But Officer Struble could have proceeded with the dog sniff while he was waiting for the results of the records check on Pollman and before the arrival of the second officer. If he had chosen that riskier sequence of events, the dog sniff would have been completed before the point in time when, according to the Court, the authority to detain for the traffic stop ended. Thus, an action that would have been lawful had the officer made the *unreasonable* decision to risk his life became unlawful when the officer made the *reasonable* decision to wait a few minutes for backup. The rule is unlikely to have any appreciable effect on the length of future traffic stops. Most officers will learn the prescribed sequence of events even if they cannot fathom the reason for that requirement.

Point for Discussion

Length of Seizure

In *United States v. Sokolow*, 490 U.S. 1 (1989), believing that Sokolow was a drug courier, DEA agents approached him during a stopover in Los Angeles. Sokolow "appeared very nervous." Later that day, Sokolow arrived in Honolulu. He had not checked any luggage and proceeded directly to the street, and tried to hail a cab, where DEA agents approached him. One agent displayed his credentials, grabbed Sokolow by the arm, and moved him back onto the sidewalk. The agent asked Sokolow for his airline ticket and identification; Sokolow said that he had neither. He told the agents that his name was "Sokolow," but that he was traveling under his mother's maiden name, "Kray." Sokolow was escorted to the DEA office at the airport. There, his luggage was examined by a narcotics detector dog which alerted on Sokolow's brown shoulder bag. The agents arrested respondent and obtained a warrant to search the bag. They found no illicit drugs, but the bag did contain several suspicious documents indicating respondent's involvement in drug trafficking. The agents had the dog reexamine the remaining luggage, and this time the dog alerted on a medium-sized bag. Since it was too late for agents to obtain a second warrant, they allowed respondent to leave for the night, but kept his luggage. The next morning, the agents obtained a warrant and found 1,063 grams of cocaine inside the bag. The Court rejected the challenge: "Respondent points to the statement in *Royer*, that 'the investigative methods employed should be the least intrusive means reasonably available to verify or dispel the officer's suspicion in a short period of time.' That statement, however, was directed at the length of the investigative stop, not at whether the police had a less intrusive means to verify their suspicions before stopping Royer. The reasonableness of the officer's decision to stop a suspect does not turn on the availability of less intrusive investigatory techniques. Such a rule would unduly hamper the police's ability to make swift, on-the-spot decisions—here, respondent was about to get into a taxicab—and it would require courts to indulge in 'unrealistic second-guessing.' "

Hypo 1: *The Jacket*

Police detain a suspect at his home while they search the home. Because the weather is chilly, and the police intend to take defendant outside, the police unilaterally decide to provide the suspect with a jacket and they choose the jacket from his closet. Before the police hand the jacket to the suspect, may they "frisk" the jacket to make sure that it does not contain a weapon or evidence? How would you respond to defendant's argument that, since the police have chosen to place the jacket within the area of defendant's "immediate control," they may not also search it? *See State v. Peterson*, 110 P.3d 699 (Utah 2005).

Hypo 2: *The Express Delivery Package*

Police believe that Jefferson might be involved in illegal narcotics operations, and ask postal officials to alert them if Jefferson receives a package. When a package arrives for him (the package was sent the day before and was guaranteed for delivery within two days), the police instruct postal officials to hold it until the next day so that it can be inspected. The next day, the police subject the package to a canine sniff and the dog alerts. The package is delivered to Jefferson at 5 p.m. that same day, and he is arrested at that time. Was there a search of the package? If not, was the "seizure" (since delivery of the package was delayed) impermissible if it delayed delivery of the package beyond the guaranteed delivery time? *See United States v. Jefferson*, 566 F.3d 928 (9th Cir. 2009).

Hypo 3: *The Bus and the Suspicious Baggage*

Narcotics detectives are observing passengers exist a bus at a depot (passengers were required to exit while the bus was cleaned and refueled), and they examine the cargo hold of the bus. An officer becomes suspicious of a bag in the hold that has a computer generated destination tag for Dayton, Ohio, but a handwritten note indicating that the bag is headed for Indianapolis, IN. The officer has never seen a bag with a handwritten note that overrode the computer generated tag. The bag is outfitted with a strong after-market padlock. The officer has the bag removed from the bus and placed inside the bus terminal. When the passengers re-board the bus, three officers board as well, with an officer holding the bag and asking the owner of the bag to identify himself. When no one does, an officer asks each passenger individually whether he/she owns the bag. When Alvarez responds in the affirmative, he is asked to leave the bus and does. During the questioning that follows, Alvarez produces a claim ticket for the bag that corresponds to the name on the bag. The officer then handcuffs Alvarez in order to prevent him from fleeing, and takes him to a police office inside the station. In Alvarez's presence, the bag is subjected to a canine sniff and the dog alerts. The bag is taken to a police station where it is subjected to a scan that reveals the presence of cocaine. Were the police actions permissible under the Fourth Amendment? *See United States v. Alvarez-Manzo*, 570 F.3d 1070 (8th Cir. 2009).

Hypo 4: *The Briefcase and the Drug Tainted Money*

Because Fallon purchased a one-way train ticket with cash, just 72 hours prior to departure, police conclude that he satisfies a drug courier profile. Police meet Fallon at the train and ask him to accompany them to an office in the station. He does. During the subsequent questioning, when police ask Fallon whether he is carrying drugs or money, he begins sweating. At some point, when Fallon admits that he is carrying a large quantity of money, police take the briefcase and open it without permission. Inside, they find more than $100,000. The officers then call in a drug sniffing dog who alerts to the case, and the police seize the briefcase and the money. Did the officers act properly? If you had been advising the police, how would you have instructed them to proceed? *See United States v. Marrocco*, 578 F.3d 627 (7th Cir. 2009).

Hiibel v. Sixth Judicial District Court

542 U.S. 177 (2004).

JUSTICE KENNEDY delivered the opinion of the Court.

The sheriff's department in Humboldt County, Nevada, received an afternoon telephone call reporting an assault by a man in a red and silver GMC truck and dispatched an officer to investigate. When the officer arrived at the scene, he found the truck parked on the side of the road. A man was standing by the truck, and a young woman was sitting inside it. The officer observed skid marks in the gravel behind the vehicle, leading him to believe it had come to a sudden stop.

The officer approached the man and explained that he was investigating a report of a fight. The man appeared to be intoxicated. The officer asked him if he had "any identification on him," which we understand as a request to produce a driver's license or some other form of written identification. The man refused and asked why the officer wanted to see identification. The officer responded that he was conducting an investigation and needed to see some identification. The man became agitated and insisted he had done nothing wrong. The officer explained that he wanted to find out who the man was and what he was doing. After continued refusals to comply with the officer's request for identification, the man began to taunt the officer by placing his hands behind his back and telling the officer to arrest him and take him to jail. This routine kept up for several minutes: the officer asked for identification 11 times and was refused each time. After warning the man that he would be arrested if he continued to refuse to comply, the officer placed him under arrest.

The man, Larry Hiibel, was charged with "willfully resisting, delaying, or obstructing a public officer in discharging or attempting to discharge any legal duty of his office" in violation of Nev.Rev.Stat. (NRS) § 199.280 (2003). A Nevada statute defines the legal rights and duties of a police officer in the context of an investigative stop. Section 171.123 provides in relevant part: "1. Any peace officer may detain any person whom the officer encounters under circumstances which reasonably indicate that the person has committed, is committing or is about to commit a crime. . . . 3. The officer may detain the person pursuant to this section only to ascertain his identity and the suspicious circumstances surrounding his presence abroad. Any person so detained shall identify himself, but may not be compelled to answer any other inquiry of any peace officer." Hiibel was convicted and fined $250. The Supreme Court of Nevada affirmed. We granted certiorari.

NRS § 171.123(3) is an enactment sometimes referred to as a "stop and identify" statute. Stop and identify statutes often combine elements of traditional vagrancy laws with provisions intended to regulate police behavior in the course of investigatory stops. The statutes vary, but all permit an officer to ask or require a suspect to disclose his identity. A few States model their statutes on the Uniform Arrest Act, a model code that permits an officer to stop a person reasonably suspected of committing a crime and "demand of him his name, address, business abroad and whither he is going." Warner, *The Uniform Arrest Act*, 28 Va. L.Rev. 315, 344 (1942). Other statutes are based on the text of the Model Penal Code. The provision provides that a person who is loitering "under circumstances which justify suspicion that he may be engaged or about to engage in crime commits a violation if he refuses the request of a peace officer that he identify himself and give a reasonably credible account of the lawfulness of his conduct and purposes." In some States, a suspect's refusal to identify himself is a misdemeanor offense or civil violation; in others, it is a factor to be considered in whether the suspect has violated loitering laws. In other States, a suspect may decline to identify himself without penalty.

Stop and identify statutes have their roots in early English vagrancy laws that required suspected vagrants to face arrest unless they gave "a good Account of themselves," a power that itself reflected common-law rights of private persons to "arrest any suspicious night-walker, and detain him till he give a good account of himself." 2 W. Hawkins, Pleas of the Crown, ch. 13, § 6, p. 130. (6th ed. 1787). In recent decades, the Court has found constitutional infirmity in traditional vagrancy laws. In *Papachristou v. Jacksonville*, 405 U.S. 156 (1972), the Court held that a traditional vagrancy law was void for vagueness. Its broad scope and imprecise terms denied proper notice to potential offenders and permitted police officers to exercise unfettered discretion in the enforcement of the law.

The Court has recognized similar constitutional limitations on the scope and operation of stop and identify statutes. In *Brown v. Texas*, 443 U.S. 47 (1979), the Court invalidated a conviction for violating a Texas stop and identify statute on Fourth Amendment grounds. The Court ruled that the initial stop was not based on specific, objective facts establishing reasonable suspicion to believe the suspect was involved in criminal activity. Absent that factual basis for detaining the defendant, the Court held, the risk of "arbitrary and abusive police practices" was too great and the stop was impermissible. Later, the Court invalidated a modified stop and identify statute on vagueness grounds. In *Kolender v. Lawson*, 461 U.S. 352 (1983), a California law required a suspect to give an officer "credible and reliable" identification when asked to identify himself. The Court held that the statute was void because it provided no standard for determining what a suspect must do to comply with it, resulting in "virtually unrestrained power to arrest and charge persons with a violation."

Here there is no question that the initial stop was based on reasonable suspicion, satisfying the Fourth Amendment requirements noted in *Brown*. Further, the petitioner has not alleged that the statute is unconstitutionally vague. The Nevada statute is narrower and more precise. In contrast to *Kolender*, the Nevada Supreme Court has interpreted NRS § 171.123(3) to require only that a suspect disclose his name. The statute does not require a suspect to give the officer a driver's license or any other document. Provided that the suspect either states his name or communicates it to the officer by other means—a choice, we assume, that the suspect may make—the statute is satisfied and no violation occurs.

Hiibel argues that his conviction cannot stand because the officer's conduct violated his Fourth Amendment rights. We disagree. Beginning with *Terry v. Ohio*, 392 U.S. 1 (1968), the Court has recognized that a law enforcement officer's reasonable suspicion that a person may be involved in criminal activity permits the officer to stop the person for a brief time and take additional steps to investigate further. To ensure that the resulting seizure is constitutionally reasonable, a *Terry* stop must be limited. The officer's action must be "justified at its inception, and reasonably related in scope to the circumstances which justified the interference in the first place." The seizure cannot continue for an excessive period of time or resemble a traditional arrest.

Questions concerning a suspect's identity are a routine and accepted part of many *Terry* stops. Obtaining a suspect's name in the course of a *Terry* stop serves important government interests. Knowledge of identity may inform an officer that a suspect is wanted for another offense, or has a record of violence or mental disorder. On the other hand, knowing identity may help clear a suspect and allow the police to concentrate their efforts elsewhere. Identity may prove particularly important in cases such as this, where the police are investigating what appears to be a domestic assault. Officers called to investigate domestic disputes need to know whom they are dealing with in order to assess the situation, the threat to their own safety, and possible danger to the potential victim.

It has been an open question whether the suspect can be arrested and prosecuted for refusal to answer. The reasonableness of a seizure under the Fourth Amendment is determined "by balancing its intrusion on the individual's Fourth Amendment interests against its promotion of legitimate government interests." *Delaware v. Prouse*, 440 U.S. 648 (1979). The Nevada statute satisfies that standard. The request for identity has an immediate relation to the purpose, rationale, and practical demands of a *Terry* stop. The threat of criminal sanction helps ensure that the request for identity does not become a legal nullity. On the other hand, the Nevada statute does not alter the nature of the stop itself: it does not change its duration or its location.

Petitioner argues that the Nevada statute circumvents the probable cause requirement, in effect allowing an officer to arrest a person for being suspicious. Petitioner's concerns are met by the requirement that a *Terry* stop must be justified at its inception and "reasonably related in scope to the circumstances which justified" the initial stop. It is clear in this case that the request for identification was "reasonably related in scope to the circumstances which justified" the stop. The officer's request was a commonsense inquiry, not an effort to obtain an arrest for failure to identify after a *Terry* stop yielded insufficient evidence. The stop, the request, and the State's requirement of a response did not contravene the guarantees of the Fourth Amendment.

Petitioner further contends that his conviction violates the Fifth Amendment's prohibition on compelled self-incrimination. As we stated in *Kastigar v. United States*, 406 U.S. 441 (1972), the Fifth Amendment privilege against compulsory self-incrimination "protects against any disclosures that the witness reasonably believes could be used in a criminal prosecution or could lead to other evidence that might be so used." Petitioner's refusal to disclose his name was not based on any articulated real and appreciable fear that his name would be used to incriminate him, or that it "would furnish a link in the chain of evidence needed to prosecute" him. Petitioner refused to identify himself only because he thought his name was none of the officer's business. While we recognize petitioner's strong belief that he should not have to disclose his identity, the Fifth Amendment does not override the Nevada Legislature's judgment to the contrary absent a reasonable belief that the disclosure would tend to incriminate him.

The narrow scope of the disclosure requirement is important. One's identity is, by definition, unique; yet it is a universal characteristic. Answering a request to disclose a name is likely to be so insignificant in the scheme of things as to be incriminating only in unusual circumstances. In every criminal case, it is known and must be known who has been arrested and who is being tried. Even witnesses who plan to invoke the Fifth Amendment privilege answer when their names are called to take the stand. Still, a case may arise where there is a substantial allegation that furnishing identity at the time of a stop would have given the police a link in the chain of evidence needed to convict the individual of a separate offense. We need not resolve those questions here.

The judgment of the Nevada Supreme Court is

Affirmed.

JUSTICE STEVENS, dissenting.

Given that citizens are not required to respond to police officers' questions during a *Terry* stop, it is no surprise that petitioner assumed that he had a right not to disclose his identity. The Court reasons that we should not assume that the disclosure of petitioner's name would be used to incriminate him or that it would

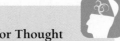

Food for Thought

In *Hibbel*, the Court emphasizes that Nevada only requires a suspect to state his name and does not require him/her to produce credible proof of identity (e.g., a driver's license). Would the result in this case have been different had Nevada required proof of identity as well?

furnish a link in a chain of evidence needed to prosecute him. But why else would an officer ask for it? And why else would the Nevada Legislature require its disclosure only when circumstances "reasonably indicate that the person has committed, is committing or is about to commit a crime"? If the Court is correct, then petitioner's refusal to cooperate did not impede the police investigation. The Nevada Legislature intended to provide its police officers with a useful law enforcement tool, and that the very existence of the statute demonstrates the value of the information it demands.

JUSTICE BREYER, with whom JUSTICE SOUTER and JUSTICE GINSBURG join, dissenting.

Can a State, in addition to requiring a stopped individual to answer "What's your name?" also require an answer to "What's your license number?" or "Where do you live?" Answers to any of these questions may, or may not, incriminate, depending upon the circumstances. A name will sometimes provide the police with "a link in the chain of evidence needed to convict the individual of a separate offense."

Food for Thought

A dissenting Justice Breyer inquired whether a state, "in addition to requiring a stopped individual to answer 'What's your name?,' " can also require an answer to "What's your license number?" or "Where do you live?" How would you answer Justice Breyer's questions?

Hypo 1: *Hibbel's Limits*

In light of the Court's holding, consider the validity of the following laws mentioned in the majority opinion:

A. The Uniform Arrest Act's provisions which allow a police officer to stop a person reasonably suspected of committing a crime and "demand of him his name, address, business abroad and whither he is going."

B. The Model Penal Code's provisions which state that a person who is loitering "under circumstances which justify suspicion that he may be engaged or about to engage in crime commits a violation if he refuses the request of a peace officer that he identify himself and gives a reasonably credible account of the lawfulness of his conduct and purposes."

C. The rule in some States that a suspect's refusal to identify himself is a misdemeanor offense or civil violation.

D. The rule in some states that a suspect's refusal to identify himself is a factor to be considered in whether the suspect has violated loitering laws.

Hypo 2: *More on Hiibel*

Following *Hibbel*, when can the police demand identification? Consider the following scenarios:

A) In an effort to be pro-active and "nip crime in the bud," a police officer decides to make routine stops of motorists to demand identification; B) At 3:00 am, a policeman sees a carload of teenagers driving in a residential neighborhood. The officer stops the teenagers to demand identification and information about their activities.

Hypo 3: *More on Requests for Identification*

Suppose that two police officers are on patrol in the middle of the afternoon, in an area that has been beset by a string of burglaries, when they see two men sitting on the front steps of a vacant building. The officers ask the men to justify their presence and to produce identification. Did the officers have sufficient cause to justify demanding that the men produce identification? *See Commonwealth v. Lyles*, 97 A.3d 298 (Penn. 2014).

Hypo 4: *The Men in the Alley*

Suppose that police are patrolling when they observe Brown and another man walking in opposite directions away from one another in an alley. The officers believe that the two have been together or were about to meet until the patrol car appeared. The officers stop one of the men, and ask him to identify himself and explain what he is doing. The other man disappears. The officer testifies that he stopped appellant because the situation "looked suspicious and we had never seen him in that area before." The area where appellant was stopped has a high incidence of drug traffic, but the officers did not suspect appellant of any specific misconduct, and did not have any reason to believe that he was armed. Appellant refused to identify himself and angrily asserted that the officers had no right to stop him. The man was then arrested under a state law which made it a crime for a person to refuse to give his name and address to an officer "who has lawfully stopped him and requested the information." Was the arrest for failure to produce identification legal and proper?

Hypo 5: *"Just Chilling"*

Detective Ragland, a 17-year veteran, exits a restaurant after eating lunch. As Ragland, in plain clothes, walks towards his unmarked vehicle, he notices a young male sitting in the driver's seat of an SUV. He also sees a second male in the passenger seat. The detective recognizes the second individual as Foster who he knows from a previous arrest for driving with a revoked license, as well as for a marijuana-related crime. The detective believes that Foster recognizes him as a police officer, and begins "shifting" his arms and "going haywire." However, the detective does not see Foster's hands, but only his upper body and upper arms. As the detective walks past the SUV, he asks "What are ya'll doing?" Foster replies that they are "just chilling." The detective then leaves the parking lot in his car, goes across the street to a bank parking lot, and continues to observe the SUV. He does not see anyone enter or leave the vehicle. He then calls the police department and is informed that Foster is under investigation for a drug related offense. The detective calls for assistance and returns to the parked SUV with the other officer. The officers use their vehicles to block the SUV, exit their cars, and separately approach both sides of the SUV with their guns drawn. The officers ask Foster and the driver to show their hands, and the two comply. The detective then asks the driver for identification, asks for the vehicle registration, and Foster opens the glove compartment to retrieve it. The moment the glove compartment opens, the detective sees a plastic bag containing a white powdery substance that he believes to be cocaine. Did the officers act properly in conducting this stop? *See United States v. Foster*, 634 F.3d 243 (4th Cir. 2011).

Hypo 6: *Warrant Checks on Pedestrians*

Shortly before midnight, a police officer on patrol sees three individuals exit an alleyway and begin walking down the middle of the street, side-by-side. One of the individuals is carrying a pit bull. The officer decides to question the individuals because they are walking in the middle of the street in violation of local law, and because there have been dog thefts in the area. The officer does not intend to cite the individuals, but he does intend to give them a verbal warning for walking in the street, to find out who they are, to find out why they are carrying the dog, and to determine whether the dog is stolen. The officer approaches the individuals, asks them to "hold up," and informs them that they are not permitted to walk in the middle of the street. He then talks to them about what they are doing with the dog. Satisfied with their explanations, he asks the individuals for their names. He immediately radios in a warrants check on each of them. Shortly thereafter, the dispatcher responds that there is an outstanding warrant for one of them (Burleson). The total duration of this initial encounter takes three to five minutes. After confirming Burleson's identity, the officer places him under arrest. At that point, Burleson admits that he has guns on him. Was the officer justified in extending the stop long enough to run a warrants check on the suspects? *See United States v. Burleson*, 657 F.3d 1040 (10th Cir. 2011).

Hypo 7: *The Encounter in the Park*

As police officers are riding bicycles through a park, they happen to notice a man and a woman sitting under a tree. Although the officers do not witness the two engaged in any criminal activity, they regard it as "unusual" that a middle-aged couple would be in the park at that time of day (when it was usually frequented only by children and the elderly). The officers approach the man and the woman, ask to see identification, and then run a computer check on their names. Did the encounter amount to a stop? Did the police act permissibly in requesting identification? *See State v. Ashbaugh*, 349 Or. 297, 244 P.3d 360 (2010).

Hypo 8: *Green Card*

A police officer spots a pickup truck speeding. As the truck passes, the driver brakes and both the driver and the passenger turn their heads away from the patrolman. The truck slows to the speed limit. When the officer follows the truck, the driver speeds up or slows down to lose him. The truck bears an out-of-state plate and the officer sees the truck "cross the center line several times." The officer decides to stop the vehicle because there are "indicators of someone impaired or doing suspicious activity." The officer asks the driver for his driver's license, the vehicle's registration, and proof of insurance. He also asks for identification from the front- and back-seat passengers. Two comply, but the third (Guijon) does not because he cannot speak English. When he is asked again in Spanish, he produces a Lawful Permanent Resident Card ("Green Card") in the name of Daniel Gaitan. Guijon appears "very nervous" and "was shaking" as he did so. The patrolman then checks with headquarters for outstanding warrants and finds that there are none. The officer then decides to call the Bureau of Immigration and Customs Enforcement (ICE) "to verify the status of the permanent resident card." The entire process takes a number of minutes. Did the officer act properly? Should it matter whether (a) the officer suspected Guijon's ID was false or altered, or belonged to someone else; (b) suspected that, regardless of the validity of the ID, the defendant or one of the others might have been in the country unlawfully; (c) checked with ICE as a matter of routine; or (d) he simply had a hunch? Did the officer act properly? Was the stop of excessive length? See *United States v. Guijon-Ortiz*, 660 F.3d 757 (4th Cir. 2011). If, after checking with ICE, the officer still has concerns regarding Guijon's status, may he take Guijon to the ICE office which is approximately 15 minutes away? Does it matter that he gave the driver and the other passenger permission to leave, and gave them contact information for Guijon? Can ICE officers question Guijon regarding his immigration status? *See United States v. Guijon-Ortiz*, 660 F.3d 757 (4th Cir. 2011).

Maryland v. Buie

494 U.S. 325 (1990).

Justice White delivered the opinion of the Court.

On February 3, 1986, two men committed an armed robbery of a Godfather's Pizza restaurant in Prince George's County, Maryland. One of the robbers was wearing a red running suit. That same day, Prince George's County police obtained arrest warrants for respondent Jerome Edward Buie and his suspected accomplice in the robbery, Lloyd Allen. Buie's house was placed under police surveillance. On February 5, the police executed the arrest warrant for Buie. They first had a police department secretary telephone Buie's house to verify that he was home. The secretary spoke to a female, then to Buie himself. Six or seven officers proceeded to Buie's house. Once inside, the officers fanned out through the first and second floors. Corporal James Rozar announced that he would "freeze" the basement so that no one could come up and surprise the officers. With his revolver drawn, Rozar twice shouted into the basement, ordering anyone down there to come out. When a voice asked who was calling, Rozar announced three times: "this is the police, show me your hands." Eventually, a pair of hands appeared around the bottom of the stairwell and Buie emerged from the basement. He was arrested, searched, and handcuffed. Thereafter, Detective Joseph Frolich entered the basement "in case there was someone else" down there. He noticed a red running suit lying in plain view on a stack of clothing and seized it. The trial court denied Buie's motion to suppress the running suit, but the Court of Appeals of Maryland reversed. We granted certiorari.

Until the point of Buie's arrest the police had the right, based on the authority of the arrest warrant, to search anywhere in the house that Buie might have been found, including the basement. If Detective Frolich's entry into the basement was lawful, the seizure of the red running suit, which was in plain view and which the officer had probable cause to believe was evidence of a crime, was also lawful under the Fourth Amendment. The issue is what level of justification the Fourth Amendment required before Detective Frolich could legally enter the basement to see if someone else was there.

The ingredients to apply the balance struck in *Terry* and *Long* are present in this case. Possessing an arrest warrant and probable cause to believe Buie was in his home, the officers were entitled to enter and to search anywhere in the house in which Buie might be found. Once he was found, however, the search for him was over, and there was no longer that particular justification for entering any rooms that had not yet been searched.

That Buie had an expectation of privacy in those remaining areas of his house does not mean such rooms were immune from entry. In *Terry* and *Long* we were concerned with the immediate interest of the police officers in taking steps to assure themselves that the persons with whom they were dealing were not armed with, or able to gain immediate control of, a weapon that could unexpectedly and fatally be used against them. In the instant case, there is an analogous interest in taking steps to assure that the house in which a suspect is being, or has just been, arrested is not harboring other persons who are dangerous and who could unexpectedly launch an attack. The risk of danger in the context of an arrest in the home is as great as, if not greater than, it is in an on-the-street or roadside investigatory encounter. A *Terry* or *Long* frisk occurs before a police-citizen confrontation has escalated to the point of arrest. A protective sweep, in contrast, occurs as an adjunct to the serious step of taking a person into custody for the purpose of prosecuting him for a crime. Unlike an encounter on the street or along a highway, an in-home arrest puts the officer at the disadvantage of being on his adversary's "turf." An ambush in a confined setting of unknown configuration is more to be feared than it is in open, more familiar surroundings.

We recognized in *Terry* that "even a limited search of the outer clothing for weapons constitutes a severe, though brief, intrusion upon cherished personal security, and it must surely be an annoying, frightening, and perhaps humiliating experience." But we permitted the intrusion, which was no more than necessary to protect the officer from harm. Nor do we here suggest that entering rooms not examined prior to the arrest is a *de minimis* intrusion that may be disregarded. We are quite sure that the arresting officers are permitted in such circumstances to take reasonable steps to ensure their safety after, and while making, the arrest. That interest is sufficient to outweigh the intrusion such procedures may entail.

A warrant was not required. As an incident to the arrest the officers could, as a precautionary matter and without probable cause or reasonable suspicion, look in closets and other spaces immediately adjoining the place of arrest from which an attack could be immediately launched. There must be articulable facts which, taken together with the rational inferences from those facts, would warrant a reasonably prudent officer in believing that the area to be swept harbors an individual posing a danger to those on the arrest scene. A protective sweep, aimed at protecting the arresting officers, if justified by the circumstances, is nevertheless not a full search of the premises, but may extend only to a cursory inspection of those spaces where a person may be found. The sweep lasts no longer than is necessary to dispel the reasonable suspicion of danger and in any event no longer than it takes to complete the arrest and depart the premises.

The Fourth Amendment permits a properly limited protective sweep in conjunction with an in-home arrest when the searching officer possesses a reasonable belief based on specific and articulable facts that the area to be swept harbors an individual posing a danger to those on the arrest scene. We therefore vacate the judgment below and remand this case to the Court of Appeals for further proceedings not inconsistent with this opinion.

It is so ordered.

JUSTICE STEVENS, concurring.

The fact that respondent offered no resistance when he emerged from the basement is inconsistent with the hypothesis that the danger of an attack by a hidden confederate persisted after the arrest. Moreover, Officer Rozar testified that he was not worried about any possible danger when he arrested Buie. Officer Frolich supplied no explanation for why he might have thought another person was in the basement. He said only that he "had no idea who lived there." But Officer Frolich participated in the 3-day prearrest surveillance of Buie's home. No reasonable suspicion of danger justified the entry into the basement. If the officers were concerned about safety, one would expect them to do what Officer Rozar did before the arrest: guard the basement door to prevent surprise attacks. Officer Frolich might reasonably have "looked in" the already open basement door to ensure that no accomplice had followed Buie to the stairwell. But Officer Frolich did not merely "look in" the basement; he entered it. That strategy is a surprising choice for an officer, worried about safety, who need not risk entering the stairwell at all.

JUSTICE BRENNAN, with whom JUSTICE MARSHALL joins, dissenting.

Terry "permitted only brief investigative stops and extremely limited searches based on reasonable suspicion." This Court more recently has applied the rationale underlying *Terry* to a wide variety of more intrusive searches and seizures, prompting my continued criticism of the "emerging tendency on the part of the Court to convert the *Terry* decision" from a narrow exception into one that "swallows the general rule that searches are 'reasonable' only if based on probable cause."

The majority offers no support for its assumption that the danger of ambush during planned home arrests approaches the danger of unavoidable "on-the-beat" confrontations in "the myriad daily situations in which policemen and citizens confront each other on the street." The Court's implicit judgment that a protective sweep constitutes a "minimally intrusive" search akin to that involved in *Terry* markedly undervalues the nature and scope of the privacy interests involved. A protective sweep would bring within police purview virtually all personal possessions within the house not hidden from view in a small enclosed space. Police officers searching for potential ambushers might enter every room including basements and attics; open up closets, lockers, chests, wardrobes, and cars; and peer under beds and behind furniture. The officers will view letters, documents, and personal effects that are on tables or desks or are visible inside open drawers; books, records, tapes, and pictures on shelves; and clothing, medicines, toiletries and other paraphernalia not carefully stored in dresser drawers or bathroom cupboards. While perhaps not a "full-blown" or "top-to-bottom" search, a protective sweep is much closer to it than to a "limited patdown for weapons" or a " 'frisk' of an automobile." The nature and scope of the intrusion sanctioned here are far greater than those upheld in *Terry* and *Long*. In light of the special sanctity of a private residence and the highly intrusive nature of a protective sweep, police officers must have probable cause to fear that their personal safety is threatened by a hidden confederate of an arrestee before they may sweep through the entire home. I would affirm the state court's decision to suppress the incriminating evidence. I respectfully dissent.

Points for Discussion

a. Securing the Premises

In *Illinois v. McArthur*, 531 U.S. 326 (2001), a woman asked police to accompany her to a trailer that she shared with her husband so that she could retrieve her belongings. As the woman was leaving, she told police that her husband, "had dope in there" and that she had seen him "slide some dope underneath the couch." The officer then asked Chuck (the husband) for permission to search the trailer and he refused. The officer then sent another officer to obtain a warrant, and told Chuck that he could not reenter the trailer unless accompanied by a police officer. Chuck reentered the trailer two or three times (to get cigarettes and make phone calls), and each time the officer stood just inside the door to see what Chuck did. A couple of hours later, when a warrant arrived, the police searched and found a marijuana pipe, a box for marijuana, and a small amount of marijuana. Chuck claimed that he was unlawfully seized when the officer refused to allow him

> **Take Note**
>
> In *Michigan v. Summers*, 452 U.S. 692 (1981), the occupant of a house was detained while a search warrant for the house was being executed. The Court held that the warrant made the occupant sufficiently suspicious to justify his temporary seizure: the "limited intrusion on the personal security" of the person detained was justified "by such substantial law enforcement interests" that the seizure could be made on articulable suspicion not amounting to probable cause. However, in *Bailey v. United States*, 568 U.S. 186 (2013), the Court held that the police did not have the authority to seize the occupant of a house, while executing a search warrant, when the occupant was some distance away from the premises to be searched and the only justification for the detention was to ensure the safety and efficacy of the search.

to enter the trailer unaccompanied. The Court disagreed: "We cannot say that the warrantless seizure was *per se* unreasonable. It involves a claim of specially pressing or urgent law enforcement need, *i.e.*, 'exigent circumstances.' Moreover, the restraint was tailored to that need, limited in time and scope, and avoided significant intrusion into the home itself. Rather than employing a *per se* rule of unreasonableness, we balance the privacy-related and law enforcement-related concerns to determine if the intrusion was reasonable, and hence lawful, in light of the following circumstances. First, the police had probable cause to believe that McArthur's trailer home contained evidence of a crime and contraband, namely, unlawful drugs. Second, the police had good reason to fear that, unless restrained, McArthur would destroy the drugs before they could return with a warrant. Third, the police made reasonable efforts to reconcile their law enforcement needs with the demands of personal privacy. They neither searched the trailer nor arrested McArthur before obtaining a warrant. Rather, they imposed a significantly less restrictive restraint, preventing McArthur only from entering the trailer unaccompanied. They left his home and his belongings intact—until a neutral Magistrate, finding probable cause, issued a warrant. Fourth, the police imposed the restraint for a limited period of time, namely, two hours. This time period was no longer than reasonably necessary for the police, acting with diligence, to obtain the warrant." Justice Stevens dissented. "Illinois has decided that the possession of less than 2.5 grams of marijuana is a class C misdemeanor" and therefore is not "a law enforcement priority in the State of Illinois." Balancing the need versus the intrusion, he concluded that the majority got "the balance wrong" given McArthur's interest in the sanctity of his home.

b. Relying on "Wanted Fliers" to Establish "Reasonable Suspicion"

In *United States v. Hensley*, 469 U.S. 221 (1985), following an armed robbery, an informant told police that Hensley had driven the getaway car. Based on this information, the officer issued a "wanted flyer" which stated that Hensley was wanted for investigation of an aggravated robbery, described Hensley, stated the date and location of the alleged robbery, and asked other departments to pick up and hold Hensley in the event he was located. The flyer also warned other departments to use caution and to consider Hensley armed and dangerous. Based on the flyer, officers from another department stopped Hensley. When the officers spotted a revolver in plain view, they arrested Hensley. A search revealed other weapons. Based on the weapons, Hensley was convicted of being a convicted felon in possession of firearms. The Court upheld the stop, noting that admissibility turns on whether the officers who issued the flyer possessed probable cause to make the arrest. It does not turn on whether those relying on the flyer were themselves aware of the specific facts which led their colleagues to seek their assistance. "Reliance on a flyer or bulletin justifies a stop to check identification, to pose questions to the person, or to detain the person briefly while attempting to obtain further information. If the flyer has been issued in the absence of a reasonable suspicion, then a stop in the objective reliance upon it violates the Fourth Amendment. Of course, the officers making the stop may have a good-faith defense to any civil suit."

c. Can an Officer Order the Driver and Passengers to Exit a Lawfully-Stopped Vehicle?

In *Pennsylvania v. Mimms*, 434 U.S. 106 (1977), the Court held that a police officer may as a matter of course order the driver of a lawfully stopped car to exit the vehicle. In *Maryland v. Wilson*, 519 U.S. 408 (1997), the Court extended this rule to passengers. In *Wilson*, an officer attempted to stop a speeding vehicle, but the driver refused to stop. During the pursuit, the officer noticed that there were three occupants in the car and that the two passengers turned to look at him several times, repeatedly ducking below sight level and then reappearing. As the officer approached the car on foot, the driver alighted and met him halfway. The driver was trembling and appeared extremely nervous, but nonetheless produced a valid driver's license. Hughes instructed him to return to the car and retrieve the rental documents, and he complied. During this encounter, Hughes noticed that the front-seat passenger (Wilson) was sweating and appeared extremely nervous. While the driver was looking for the rental papers, Hughes ordered Wilson out of the car. When Wilson exited the car, a quantity of crack cocaine fell to the ground. Wilson was then arrested and charged with possession of cocaine with intent to distribute. The Court held that the officer validly ordered Wilson to exit the vehicle Although there may be no reason to conclude that the passenger has committed an offense, the Court found that the "same weighty interest in officer safety is present regardless of whether the occupant of the stopped car is a driver or passenger." The Court went on to state that in: "1994 alone, there were 5,762 officer assaults and 11 officers killed during traffic pursuits and stops. The fact that there is more than one occupant of the vehicle increases the possible sources of harm to the officer." "The possibility of a violent encounter stems not from the ordinary reaction of a motorist stopped for a speeding violation, but from the fact that evidence of a more serious crime might be uncovered during the stop. The motivation of a passenger to employ violence to prevent apprehension of such a crime is every bit as great as that of the driver." Justice Stevens dissented: "If a police officer has an articulable suspicion of possible danger, the officer may order passengers to exit the vehicle as a defensive tactic without running afoul of the Fourth Amendment." Justice Kennedy also dissented: "Traffic stops, even for minor violations, can take upwards of 30 minutes. When an officer commands passengers innocent of any violation to leave the vehicle and stand by the side of the road in full view of the public, the seizure is serious, not trivial. The command to exit ought not to be given unless there are objective circumstances making it reasonable for the officer to issue the order."

d. *Rettele* and the Naked Occupants

In *Los Angeles County v. Rettele* 550 U.S. 609 (2007), police officers arrived to execute a search warrant at a house where they expected the occupants to be armed, and found two individuals (a man and a woman) of a different race than the suspects in bed. The officers ordered the individuals to stand up even though they were unclothed, and made them stand there for a few minutes before they allowed the individuals to dress. In fact, the officers were unaware that the actual suspects had moved out of the house three months earlier. The individuals brought suit under 42 U.S.C. § 1983, claiming that their Fourth Amendment right to be free from unreasonable searches and seizures had been violated. They claimed that a reasonable deputy would have stopped the search upon discovering that respondents were of a different race than the suspects and that a reasonable deputy would not have ordered respondents from their bed. The Court disagreed: "When the deputies ordered respondents from their bed, they had no way of knowing whether the African-American suspects were elsewhere in the house. The presence of some Caucasians in the residence did not eliminate the possibility that the suspects lived there as well. The deputies, who were searching a house where they believed a suspect might be armed, possessed authority to secure the premises before deciding whether to continue with the search. In executing a search warrant officers may take reasonable action to secure the premises and to ensure their own safety and the efficacy of the search. The orders by the police to the occupants, in the context of this lawful search, were permissible, and perhaps necessary, to protect the safety of the deputies. Blankets and bedding can conceal a weapon, and one of the suspects was known to own a firearm. The deputies needed a moment to secure the room and ensure that other persons were not close by or did not present a danger."

Hypo 1: *Protective Sweeps*

Police were investigating Gorup on suspicion of dealing narcotics from his apartment. When they learned that Gorup was subject to an outstanding arrest warrant for a previous drug violation, detectives decided to conduct a "knock-and-talk investigation." Once they arrived, the officers placed Gorup (who was standing outside his apartment) under arrest and handcuffed him. When the officers noticed that there were other individuals inside, they decided to conduct a "protective sweep" of the apartment. It was unclear whether the other individuals could see either the police or Gorup. Is a protective sweep permissible under these circumstances? Would it extend to a "small black zippered-type case" located on a table just inside the doorway? *See State v. Gorup*, 279 Neb. 841, 782 N.W.2d 16 (2010).

Hypo 2: *More on Knock and Talk*

Based on a tip from a confidential informant, police develop reason to believe that Basil is selling illegal drugs out of his house. In the course of the investigation, the police learn that "Basil" occupies the front bedroom in the basement apartment in which he resides. They also learn that he stays out late, sleeps late, usually departs from his apartment around noon, and has no known legal employment. The officers decide to go to Basil's home and conduct a "knock and talk." Three officers knock on the front door, and two more knock on the rear door after entering the fenced-in area of the yard. When a woman opens the back door, she mentions that there are other people in the apartment. At that point, officers Quinn and Salvetti pass through the apartment directly to the front bedroom. Quinn believes that this bedroom is occupied by "Basil." Quinn has his gun drawn on the theory that Basil "could come out with a firearm or a gun or pose a danger." In the bedroom, underneath the bed, Quinn discovers a Hi-Point .380 caliber pistol with a defaced serial number. This pistol provides the basis of the firearm count with which Hassock is charged. Can the entry into the apartment be justified as a protective sweep? *See United States v. Hassock*, 631 F.3d 79 (2d Cir. 2011).

Hypo 3: *The Scope of a Protective Sweep*

Having probable cause to believe that Manuel was involved in a robbery and murder at a shop, police arrested him outside of his hotel room, forced him to the ground, and handcuffed him. Because the door to the room was open, the police immediately conducted a protective sweep of the room. One officer lifted the mattress and box spring from the foot of the bed to see if anyone was under it. When he did so, he heard a "clunking" sound and could see a gun in the box spring. Was it permissible for the officer to lift the mattress and box spring as part of a protective sweep? *See State v. Manuel*, 229 Ariz. 1, 270 P.3d 828 (Ariz. 2011).

Hypo 4: *Helping the Co-Occupant*

After midnight, officers responded to a radio call that an individual had a gun at a residence. When they arrived, the officers saw Vaz, who stated that Simmons, his roommate, had displayed a handgun during a dispute. Vaz requested that the officers accompany him into the apartment so that he could retrieve his belongings. After entering, the officers conducted a protective sweep of the living room and kitchen, and then proceeded down a hallway to the rear of the apartment where the bedrooms were located. As they did, the officers had their guns drawn and announced their presence. When they reached Simmon's bedroom, the officers found the bedroom door open, the room dimly lit, and Simmons lying in his bed. One officer sees a shiny object, that he thinks might be the gun Vaz had described, on a table next to the bed. When Simmons gets up and approaches the doorway, the officers instruct him to show his hands. Simmons complies, and is taken out into the hallway. Were the officers justified in removing Simmons from the bedroom? *See United States v. Simmons*, 661 F.3d 151 (2d Cir. 2011).

Hypo 5: *The Permissibility of a Protective Sweep*

Suppose that the police go to a suspect's home to arrest him pursuant to a warrant. The warrant was issued because defendant failed to appear in court in response to charges of "disorderly conduct" (he played his stereo too loud late at night). The police are admitted to the house by the suspect's wife, and they call to him from the bottom of the stairs on the first floor, asking him to come downstairs. The suspect does come down, is handcuffed, and is taken to the kitchen. Before leaving, the police conduct a protective sweep of the upstairs. As you read *Buie*, is the protective sweep permissible? If not, why not? *See State v. McGrane*, 733 N.W.2d 671 (Iowa 2007). Suppose that the facts are the same except that the suspect is being arrested on drug charges, and the police have reason to believe that the suspect is dealing drugs out of his house. Does the nature of the charge alter the analysis? *See State v. McGrane*, 733 N.W.2d 671 (Iowa 2007).

Hypo 6: *Searching Under the Mattress*

FBI agents execute an arrest warrant for a man that they believe to be "armed and dangerous." While two agents seize the subject of the warrant, other officers conduct a protective sweep of the remainder of the house. In one room, they find two teenage boys who they handcuff. Since the officers intend to place the boys on the bed, they look under the bed to make sure that there are no weapons there. In doing so, they find an illegal firearm. Did the officer's act consistently with the scope of a protective sweep in looking under the bed? *See United States v. Bennett*, 555 F.3d 962 (11th Cir. 2009).

Hypo 7: *Security Sweep of the Barricaded Home*

A man barricades himself in his house with a shotgun during a standoff with police. Eventually, the SWAT team is called in and zaps the man with a stun gun, thereby allowing the police to apprehend him. The man and his girlfriend claim that no one else is in the house. May the police nonetheless conduct a security sweep to make sure that there is no one else inside who poses a threat to them? *See Commonwealth v. Robertson*, 275 Va. 559, 659 S.E.2d 321 (2008).

Hypo 8: *The Scope of a Protective Sweep*

A warrant authorized police to search the Aurora Tavern and the person of "Greg," a white male who worked at the tavern, for possession of controlled substances. Police officers go to the tavern to execute the warrant, announce their purpose, and advise all present that they are going to conduct a "cursory search for weapons." The officers pat down each of the 13 customers. In patting down Gregory, the officer feels what appears to be "a cigarette pack with objects in it." The officer retrieves the cigarette pack from Gregory's pants pocket. Inside the pack he finds tinfoil packets containing a brown powdery substance which later turns out to be heroin. Was the search of Gregory constitutional? What arguments might be made on behalf of the police? How might Gregory respond to these arguments? How should the Court rule? *See Ybarra v. Illinois*, 444 U.S. 85 (1979).

Hypo 9: *More on the Scope of a Protective Sweep*

Police officers have a warrant to arrest Johnson, but do not have a search warrant for his residence. An informant tells police that Johnson is staying in a particular house, is armed, and might have accomplices with him. The officers stake out the apartment. When Johnson's fiance emerges, she tells the police that Johnson is inside alone. When Johnson happens to step outside, leaving the door ajar, the police arrest him. While handcuffing Johnson, the officer notices that Hamilton is observing from a distance, and Johnson tells Hamilton "they got me." Hamilton disappears. When other officers arrive, an officer conducts a "security check" of the house, including the bedroom, bathroom, and kitchen to verify that there are no armed individuals who might threaten the officers. In the bedroom, the officer discovers and seizes a gun sitting on a dresser and two bags of heroin lying in an open drawer. Did the police act properly in entering the apartment? *See United States v. Henry,* 48 F.3d 1282, 310 U.S.App.D.C. 431 (D.C.Cir.1995).

Hypo 10: *The Investigation*

Police officers are "investigating gambling establishments" on complaints of noise and disorderly conduct. A man, who has "supplied reliable information" to police in the past, exits the building and tells the police that he bought alcohol at 56 Albany Street. The officers go to that address, enter without a warrant, and find themselves in a big room containing a pool table, barber chairs, a shoeshine stand and a showcase. An officer asks the owner whether he is selling drinks, and he denies it. Finding nothing incriminating, the officers search the bathrooms, a storage and wash room, before entering a large room at the back. In that room, the officers find a bar, two stools, a table with six chairs, and a refrigerator loaded with beer. On the bar are whisky bottles. No one is present. The officers place the owner under arrest for the illegal sale of alcohol, and search his person, finding two marijuana cigarettes. The events take 30 minutes. Did the police act properly in searching the establishment without a warrant? *See State v. Baker,* 112 N.J.Super. 351, 271 A.2d 435 (1970).

Delaware v. Prouse

440 U.S. 648 (1979).

MR. JUSTICE WHITE delivered the opinion of the Court.

A patrolman in a police cruiser stopped the automobile occupied by respondent. The patrolman smelled marihuana smoke as he was walking toward the stopped vehicle, and he seized marihuana in plain view on the car floor. At a hearing on respondent's motion to suppress, the patrolman testified that prior to stopping the vehicle he had observed neither traffic or equipment violations nor any suspicious activity, and that he made the stop only in order to check the driver's license and registration. The patrolman was not acting pursuant to any standards, guidelines, or procedures pertaining to document spot checks, promulgated by either his department or the State Attorney General. Characterizing the stop as "routine," the patrolman explained, "I saw the car in the area and wasn't answering any complaints, so I decided to pull them off." The trial court granted the motion to suppress.

The permissibility of a particular law enforcement practice is judged by balancing its intrusion on the individual's Fourth Amendment interests against its promotion of legitimate governmental interests. Implemented in this manner, the reasonableness standard usually requires, at a minimum, that the facts upon which an intrusion is based be capable of measurement against "an objective standard," whether this be probable cause or a less stringent test.

The State of Delaware urges that these stops are reasonable under the Fourth Amendment because the State's interest in the practice as a means of promoting public safety upon its roads more than outweighs the intrusion entailed. Although the record discloses no statistics concerning a lack of highway safety, we are aware of the danger to life and property posed by vehicular traffic and of the difficulties that even a cautious and an experienced driver may encounter. The States have a vital interest in ensuring that only those qualified to do so are permitted to operate motor vehicles, that these vehicles are fit for safe operation, and that licensing, registration, and vehicle inspection requirements are being observed. Automobile licenses are issued periodically to evidence that the drivers holding them are sufficiently familiar with the rules of the road and are physically qualified to operate a motor vehicle. The registration requirement and the related annual inspection requirement in Delaware are designed to keep dangerous automobiles off the road. Unquestionably, these provisions, properly administered, are essential elements in a highway safety program. Furthermore, we note that the State of Delaware requires a minimum amount of insurance coverage as a condition to automobile registration, implementing its legitimate interest in seeing to it that its citizens have protection when involved in a motor vehicle accident.

The question remains whether in the service of these important ends the discretionary spot check is a sufficiently productive mechanism to justify the intrusion upon Fourth Amendment interests which such stops entail. That question must be answered in the negative. Given the alternative mechanisms available, both those in use and those that might be adopted, we are unconvinced that the incremental contribution to highway safety of the random spot check justifies the practice under the Fourth Amendment.

The foremost method of enforcing traffic and vehicle safety regulations is acting upon observed violations. Vehicle stops for traffic violations occur countless times each day; and on these occasions, licenses and registration papers are subject to inspection and drivers without them will be ascertained. Furthermore, drivers without licenses are presumably the less safe drivers whose propensities may well exhibit themselves. Absent some empirical data to the contrary, it must be assumed that finding an unlicensed driver among those who commit traffic violations is a much more likely event than finding an unlicensed driver by choosing randomly from the entire universe of drivers. The contribution to highway safety made by discretionary stops selected from among drivers generally will therefore be marginal at best. Furthermore, we find it difficult to believe that the unlicensed driver would not be deterred by the possibility of being involved in a traffic violation or having some other experience calling for proof of his entitlement to drive but that he would be deterred by the possibility that he would be one of those chosen for a spot check. In terms of actually discovering unlicensed drivers or deterring them from driving, the spot check does not appear sufficiently productive to qualify as a reasonable law enforcement practice under the Fourth Amendment.

Much the same can be said about the safety aspects of automobiles as distinguished from drivers. Many violations of minimum vehicle-safety requirements are observable, and something can be done about them by the observing officer, directly and immediately. In Delaware, as elsewhere, vehicles must carry and display current license plates, which themselves evidence that the vehicle is properly registered; and, under Delaware law, to qualify for annual registration a vehicle must pass the annual safety inspection and be properly insured. It does not appear, therefore, that a stop of a Delaware-registered vehicle is necessary in order to ascertain compliance with the State's registration requirements; and, because there is nothing to show that a significant percentage of automobiles from other States do not also require license plates indicating current registration, there is no basis for concluding that stopping even out-of-state cars for document checks substantially promotes the State's interest.

The marginal contribution to roadway safety possibly resulting from a system of spot checks cannot justify subjecting every occupant of every vehicle on the roads to a seizure—limited in magnitude compared to other intrusions but nonetheless constitutionally cognizable—at the unbridled discretion of law enforcement officials. Stopping apparently safe drivers is necessary only because the danger presented by some drivers is not observable at the time of the stop. When there is not probable cause to believe that a driver is violating any one of the multitude of applicable traffic and equipment regulations—or other articulable basis amounting to reasonable suspicion that the driver is unlicensed or his vehicle unregistered— we cannot conceive of any legitimate basis upon which a patrolman could decide that stopping a particular driver for a spot check would be more productive than stopping any other driver. This kind of standardless and unconstrained discretion is the evil the Court has discerned when in previous cases it has insisted that the discretion of the official in the field be circumscribed, at least to some extent.

The "grave danger" of abuse of discretion does not disappear simply because the automobile is subject to state regulation resulting in numerous instances of police-citizen contact. There are certain "relatively unique circumstances" in which consent to regulatory restrictions is presumptively concurrent with participation in the regulated enterprise. Otherwise, regulatory inspections unaccompanied by any quantum of individualized, articulable suspicion must be undertaken pursuant to previously specified "neutral criteria."

An individual operating or traveling in an automobile does not lose all reasonable expectation of privacy simply because the automobile and its use are subject to government regulation. Automobile travel is a basic, pervasive, and often necessary mode of transportation to and from one's home, workplace, and leisure activities. Many people spend more hours each day traveling in cars than walking on the streets. Undoubtedly, many find a greater sense of security and privacy in traveling in an automobile than they do in exposing themselves by pedestrian or other modes of travel. Were the individual subject to unfettered governmental intrusion every time he entered an automobile, the security guaranteed by the Fourth Amendment would be seriously circumscribed.

Except in those situations in which there is at least articulable and reasonable suspicion that a motorist is unlicensed or that an automobile is not registered, or that either the vehicle or an occupant is otherwise subject to seizure for violation of law, stopping an automobile and detaining the driver in order to check his driver's license and the registration of the automobile are unreasonable under the Fourth Amendment.

MR. JUSTICE REHNQUIST, dissenting.

The State may require the licensing of those who drive on its highways and the registration of vehicles which are driven on those highways. If it may insist on these requirements, it obviously may take steps necessary to enforce compliance. The reasonableness of the enforcement measure chosen by the State is tested by weighing its intrusion on the motorists' Fourth Amendment interests against its promotion of the State's legitimate interests. The State's primary interest is in traffic safety, not in apprehending unlicensed motorists for the sake of apprehending unlicensed motorists. The whole point of enforcing motor vehicle safety regulations is to remove from the road the unlicensed driver before he demonstrates why he is unlicensed.

Point for Discussion

Defining Reasonable Suspicion

In *United States v. Cortez*, 449 U.S. 411 (1981), border patrol agents stopped a van which they suspected contained illegal aliens. The Court held that the suspicion was "reasonable":

> When used by trained law enforcement officers, objective facts, meaningless to the untrained, can be combined with permissible deductions from such facts to form a legitimate basis for suspicion of a particular person and for action on that suspicion. The officers knew that the area was a crossing point for illegal aliens. They knew that it was common for persons to lead aliens through the desert from the border to Highway 86, where they could—by prearrangement—be picked up by a vehicle. Based upon clues they had discovered in the 2-month period prior to the events at issue, they believed that one such guide, whom they designated "Chevron," had a particular pattern of operations. By piecing together the information at their disposal, the officers tentatively concluded that there was a reasonable likelihood that "Chevron" would attempt to lead a group of aliens on the night of Sunday, January 30–31. Someone with chevron-soled shoes had led several groups of aliens in the previous two months, yet it had been two weeks since the latest crossing. "Chevron," they deduced, was therefore due reasonably soon. "Chevron" tended to travel on clear weekend nights. Because it had rained on the Friday and Saturday nights of the weekend, Sunday was the only clear night of that weekend.
>
> The officers drew upon other objective facts known to them to deduce a time frame within which "Chevron" and the aliens were likely to arrive. They knew the time when sunset would occur; they knew about how long the trip would take. They were thus able to deduce that "Chevron" would likely arrive at the pickup point on Highway 86 in the time frame between 2 a.m. and 6 a.m. From objective facts, the officers also deduced the probable point on the highway—milepost 122—at which "Chevron" would likely rendezvous with a pickup vehicle. They deduced from the direction taken by the sets of "Chevron" footprints they had earlier discovered that the pickup vehicle would approach the aliens from, and return with them to, a point east of milepost 122. They therefore staked out a position east of milepost 122 and watched for vehicles that passed them going west and then, approximately one and a half hours later, [a van] passed them again, this time going east.
>
> From what they had observed about the previous groups guided by the person with "chevron" shoes, they deduced that "Chevron" would

lead a group of 8 to 20 aliens. They therefore focused their attention on enclosed vehicles of that passenger capacity. In a 4-hour period the officers observed only one vehicle meeting that description. And it is not surprising that when they stopped the vehicle on its return trip it contained "Chevron" and several illegal aliens.

The limited purpose of the stop in this case was to question the occupants of the vehicle about their citizenship and immigration status and the reasons for the round trip in a short timespan in a virtually deserted area. No search of the camper or any of its occupants occurred until after respondent Cortez voluntarily opened the back door of the camper. The intrusion upon privacy associated with this stop was limited and reasonable.

Hypo 1: *The Evasive Camper*

A federal agent observes a pickup truck with a camper shell traveling in tandem with another vehicle for 20 miles in an area near the coast known to be frequented by drug traffickers. The agent testifies that campers are often used to transport large quantities of marihuana. The pickup truck in question appears to be heavily loaded, and the windows are covered with a quilted bed-sheet material. When the officer begins following the vehicles in a marked police car, both vehicles take evasive actions and start speeding. Was there sufficient cause to stop the camper? *See United States v. Sharpe*, 470 U.S. 675 (1985).

Hypo 2: *"Reasonable Suspicion"*

In *Alabama v. White*, 496 U.S. 325 (1990), police receive an anonymous call stating that Vanessa White will be leaving Lynwood Apartments at a particular time in a brown Plymouth station wagon with the right taillight lens broken, that she will be going to Dobey's Motel, and that she will be carrying an ounce of cocaine in a brown attache case. Officers go to the apartments, find a brown Plymouth station wagon with a broken right taillight, observe respondent leave the building (carrying nothing in her hands) and enter the station wagon. They follow the vehicle as it drives the most direct route to Dobey's Motel. When the vehicle is stopped just short of the motel, the officer asks respondent to step to the rear of her car, where he informs her that she has been stopped because she is suspected of carrying cocaine. He asks if they may look for cocaine, and respondent consents. The officers find a locked brown attache case in the car, and, upon request, respondent provides the combination to the lock. The officers find cocaine in the attache case and place respondent under arrest. Did the police have reasonable suspicion for the stop?

Hypo 3: DMV Computer Checks and Reasonable Suspicion

A police officer, parked by the side of the road, runs the license plate numbers of passing motorists through a department of motor vehicles data base. When the search reveals that the license plate of a passing car has been suspended, the officer pulls the driver over. During the stop, the officer runs the driver's license through the same data base and finds that it is suspended as well. Also, the officer realizes that the driver is intoxicated. Was it permissible for the officer to run the driver's license plate through the data base without any suspicion of criminal activity? *See People v. Bushey*, 29 N.Y.3d 158, 75 N.E.3d 1165, 53 N.Y.S.3d 604 (2017).

Hypo 4: *Canine Sniffs*

Defendant was stopped for weaving across traffic lines. After checking defendant's license and registration, the officer gave defendant a "courtesy warning." The officer then asked defendant whether he was carrying narcotics. Defendant responded in the negative. When the officer asked for permission to search the vehicle, defendant refused. The officer immediately requested a drug canine unit and ran a criminal history check on defendant. About six minutes later, the canine unit arrived and reacted positively to defendant's vehicle. Did the officer act permissibly in detaining the motorist long enough to run a background check and bring in a canine unit? *See United States v. Boyce*, 351 F.3d 1102 (11th Cir.2003). *Henderson v. State*, 416 Md. 125, 5 A.3d 1072 (2010). Would you reach a different result if the officer had stopped the motorist based on a valid drug courier profile (suggesting that the suspect was transporting narcotics)? During a canine sniff, can the officer order the driver to roll up the windows of her vehicle and turn her ventilation system's blowers on high before a second officer conducts a canine sniff of the exterior of her truck? *See People v. Bartelt*, 241 Ill.2d 217, 349 Ill. Dec. 949, 948 N.E.2d 52 (2011).

Hypo 5: *Drug Couriers*

A state trooper, with 17 years experience, stopped an east bound vehicle bearing Indiana license plates in Texas, for speeding on a portion of I–30 that the officer knew as a "drug trafficking corridor" between Houston and Dallas, major drug distribution centers. The trooper approached the passenger side of the vehicle and asked for identification and the vehicle's registration. The trooper noticed that Pack appeared to be extremely nervous—he was breathing heavily, his hands were shaking, and his carotid artery was visibly pulsing. The trooper asked Williamson (the driver) to accompany him to the patrol car where he stated that he planned to issue her a warning for speeding. He then asked her about her travel history. She replied that she and Pack (her boyfriend) had been visiting her aunt in Houston who was ill. The trooper radioed dispatch and requested computer checks on Williamson's and Pack's licenses and criminal histories. The trooper then returned to the vehicle and asked Pack about the couple's travel history. Pack told the trooper that he and Williamson were coming from Dallas, where they had visited friends, and that they had stayed with some relatives in San Antonio. Pack said that he was not aware of any family Williamson might have in Texas or that were ill. Because of the circumstances, can the officer reasonably conclude that they are engaged in criminal drug activity and order a canine sniff? *See United States v. Pack*, 612 F.3d 341 (5th Cir. 2010); *see also People v. Devone*, 15 N.Y.3d 106, 905 N.Y.S.2d 101, 931 N.E.2d 70 (2010).

Hypo 6: *The Lost Motorist*

A police officer concludes that the driver of an automobile is lost, and stops the driver to offer help. As the officer approaches the vehicle, he spots a bomb in plain view in the backseat. How might you argue that the officer acted properly? How might the driver respond? Are there instances when the police should stop someone to offer help (*i.e.*, a bridge is out and an officer wants to stop the motorist to inform him of this fact)?

Food for Thought

In some areas, the police have instituted "good driving" programs designed to reward "good drivers." Under these programs, officers pull drivers over (using their sirens and lights), and present the drivers with gift certificates and coupons for prizes. The purpose of these programs is to encourage better driving. Are "good driving" programs constitutional? Suppose, for example, that an officer pulls a driver over to award a certificate, notices contraband in the car, and arrests the driver. Can the state use the evidence against the driver? How might you argue that the evidence should be suppressed? How might the state respond? Is a "good driving" program more likely to be constitutional if the police provide drivers with bumper stickers designed to signal their participation in the "good driver" program, and only pull over cars that have such stickers on their bumpers?

Hypo 7: *Stops for Completed Crimes*

A day after a business is robbed, the police learn the identity of the robber and issue a "wanted flyer." Relying on the flyer, an officer pulls defendant over with his revolver drawn, and orders Hensley and a passenger to step out of the car. The officer recognizes the passenger as a convicted felon. The officer then steps up to the open passenger door and observes the butt of a revolver protruding from underneath the passenger seat. The felon is then arrested. A search of the car uncovers a second handgun in the middle of the front seat and a third handgun in a bag in the back seat. After the discovery of these weapons, defendant is arrested, and moves to suppress arguing that a *Terry* stop can only be justified for a "crime in progress." If you represent the State, how might you respond to Hensley's argument? On behalf of Hensley, what flaws do you see in the State's position? *See United States v. Hensley*, 469 U.S. 221 (1985).

Hypo 8: *Driving Slowly*

A police officer on routine patrol observes a driver traveling at 48 mph in a 65 mph zone. Based solely on the speed of the vehicle, does the officer have reasonable suspicion to stop the car? Must there be additional evidence, such as erratic driving or unusual behavior by the driver, to justify a stop? *See State v. Rincon*, 122 Nev. 1170, 147 P.3d 233 (2006).

Hypo 9: *The Mistaken Stop*

A police officer stops a vehicle because it is registered to a woman with an outstanding warrant for her arrest. As he approaches the vehicle, he realizes that it is being driven by a man. Since the officer has already stopped the vehicle, he decides to ask the driver for his license and registration. Are the officer's actions permissible? *See People v. Cummings,* 6 N.E.3d 725 (Ill. 2014).

City of Indianapolis v. Edmond

531 U.S. 32 (2000).

JUSTICE O'CONNOR delivered the opinion of the Court.

In *Michigan Dept. of State Police v. Sitz,* 496 U.S. 444 (1990), and *United States v. Martinez-Fuerte,* 428 U.S. 543 (1976), we held that brief, suspicionless seizures at highway checkpoints for the purposes of combating drunk driving and intercepting illegal immigrants were constitutional. We now consider the constitutionality of a highway checkpoint program whose primary purpose is the discovery and interdiction of illegal narcotics.

In 1998, the city of Indianapolis began to operate vehicle checkpoints on Indianapolis roads in an effort to interdict unlawful drugs. The city conducted six such roadblocks between August and November that year, stopping 1,161 vehicles and arresting 104 motorists. Fifty-five arrests were for drug-related crimes, while 49 were for offenses unrelated to drugs. The overall "hit rate" of the program was approximately nine percent.

At each checkpoint location, the police stop a predetermined number of vehicles. Approximately 30 officers are stationed at the checkpoint. Pursuant to written directives issued by the chief of police, at least one officer approaches the vehicle, advises the driver that he or she is being stopped briefly at a drug checkpoint, and asks the driver to produce a license and registration. The officer also looks for signs of impairment and conducts an open-view examination of the vehicle from the outside. A narcotics-detection dog walks around the outside of each stopped vehicle.

Directives instruct the officers that they may conduct a search only by consent or based on the appropriate quantum of particularized suspicion. Officers must conduct each stop in the same manner until particularized suspicion develops, and the officers have no discretion to stop any vehicle out of sequence. The city agreed to operate the checkpoints in such a way as to ensure that the total duration of each stop, absent reasonable suspicion or probable cause, would be five minutes or less.

Checkpoint locations are selected weeks in advance based on such considerations as area crime statistics and traffic flow. The checkpoints are generally operated during daylight hours and are identified with lighted signs reading, "NARCOTICS CHECKPOINT ___ MILE AHEAD, NARCOTICS K-9 IN USE, BE PREPARED TO STOP." Once a group of cars has been stopped, other traffic proceeds without interruption until all the stopped cars have been processed or diverted for further processing. The average stop for a vehicle not subject to further processing lasts two to three minutes or less.

Respondents James Edmond and Joell Palmer were each stopped at a narcotics checkpoint in September 1998. Respondents then filed suit on behalf of themselves and the class of all motorists who had been stopped or were subject to being stopped in the future at the checkpoints. The trial court denied the motion for a preliminary injunction. A divided United States Court of Appeals for the Seventh Circuit reversed. We granted certiorari and affirm.

The Fourth Amendment requires that searches and seizures be reasonable. A search or seizure is ordinarily unreasonable in the absence of individualized suspicion of wrongdoing. While such suspicion is not an "irreducible" component of reasonableness, we have recognized only limited circumstances in which the usual rule does not apply. For example, we have upheld certain regimes of suspicionless searches where the program was designed to serve "special needs, beyond the normal need for law enforcement." *See, e.g., Vernonia School Dist. 47J v. Acton*, 515 U.S. 646 (1995) (random drug testing of student-athletes); *Treasury Employees v. Von Raab*, 489 U.S. 656 (1989) (drug tests for United States Customs Service employees seeking transfer or promotion to certain positions); *Skinner v. Railway Labor Executives' Assn.*, 489 U.S. 602 (1989) (drug and alcohol tests for railway employees involved in train accidents or found to be in violation of particular safety regulations). We have also allowed searches for certain administrative purposes without particularized suspicion of misconduct, provided that those searches are appropriately limited. *See, e.g., New York v. Burger*, 482 U.S. 691 (1987) (warrantless administrative inspection of premises of "closely regulated" business); *Michigan v. Tyler*, 436 U.S. 499 (1978) (administrative inspection of fire-damaged premises to determine cause of blaze); *Camara v. Municipal Court*, 387 U.S. 523 (1967) (administrative inspection to ensure compliance with city housing code).

We have also upheld brief, suspicionless seizures of motorists at a fixed Border Patrol checkpoint designed to intercept illegal aliens, and at a sobriety checkpoint aimed at removing drunk drivers from the road. In addition, in *Delaware v. Prouse,* 440 U.S. 648 (1979), we suggested that a similar type of roadblock with the purpose of verifying drivers' licenses and vehicle registrations would be permissible. In none of these cases, however, did we indicate approval of a checkpoint program whose primary purpose was to detect evidence of ordinary criminal wrongdoing.

In *Martinez-Fuerte, supra,* we entertained Fourth Amendment challenges to stops at two permanent immigration checkpoints located on major United States highways less than 100 miles from the Mexican border. We noted the "formidable law enforcement problems" posed by the northbound tide of illegal entrants into the United States. We found that the balance tipped in favor of the Government's interests in policing the Nation's borders, and emphasized the difficulty of effectively containing illegal immigration at the border itself. We also stressed the impracticality of the particularized study of a given car to discern whether it was transporting illegal aliens, as well as the relatively modest degree of intrusion entailed by the stops . Although the stops did not occur at the border itself, the checkpoints were located near the border and served a border control function made necessary by the difficulty of guarding the border's entire length.

In *Sitz, supra,* we evaluated the constitutionality of a Michigan highway sobriety checkpoint program involving brief suspicionless stops of motorists so that police officers could detect signs of intoxication and remove impaired drivers from the road. Motorists who exhibited signs of intoxication were diverted for a license and registration check and, if warranted, further sobriety tests. This checkpoint program was clearly aimed at reducing the immediate hazard posed by the presence of drunk drivers on the highways, and there was an obvious connection between the imperative of highway safety and the law enforcement practice at issue. The gravity of the drunk driving problem and the magnitude of the State's interest in getting drunk drivers off the road weighed heavily in our determination that the program was constitutional.

In *Prouse,* we invalidated a discretionary, suspicionless stop for a spot check of a motorist's driver's license and vehicle registration. We nonetheless acknowledged the States' "vital interest in ensuring that only those qualified to do so are permitted to operate motor vehicles, that these vehicles are fit for safe operation, and hence that licensing, registration, and vehicle inspection requirements are being observed." Accordingly, we suggested that "questioning of all oncoming traffic at roadblock-type stops" would be a lawful means of serving this interest in highway safety.

We indicated in *Prouse* that we considered the purposes of such a hypothetical roadblock to be distinct from a general purpose of investigating crime. The State proffered the additional interests of "the apprehension of stolen motor vehicles and of drivers under the influence of alcohol or narcotics" in its effort to justify the discretionary spot check. We attributed the entirety of the latter interest to the State's interest in roadway safety. The interest in apprehending stolen vehicles may be partly subsumed by the interest in roadway safety. We observed, however, that "the remaining governmental interest in controlling automobile thefts is not distinguishable from the general interest in crime control." Not only does the common thread of highway safety thus run through *Sitz* and *Prouse*, but *Prouse* itself reveals a difference in the Fourth Amendment significance of highway safety interests and the general interest in crime control.

A vehicle stop at a highway checkpoint effectuates a seizure within the meaning of the Fourth Amendment. The fact that officers walk a narcotics-detection dog around the exterior of each car at the Indianapolis checkpoints does not transform the seizure into a search. *See United States v. Place*, 462 U.S. 696 (1983). An exterior sniff of an automobile does not require entry into the car and is not designed to disclose any information other than the presence or absence of narcotics. A sniff by a dog that simply walks around a car is "much less intrusive than a typical search."

The Indianapolis checkpoint program unquestionably has the primary purpose of interdicting illegal narcotics. The parties refer to the checkpoints as "drug checkpoints" and as "being operated in an effort to interdict unlawful drugs in Indianapolis." We have never approved a checkpoint program whose primary purpose was to detect evidence of ordinary criminal wrongdoing. Rather, our checkpoint cases have recognized only limited exceptions to the general rule that a seizure must be accompanied by some measure of individualized suspicion. We suggested in *Prouse* that we would not credit the "general interest in crime control" as justification for a regime of suspicionless stops. Consistent with this suggestion, each of the checkpoint programs that we have approved was designed primarily to serve purposes closely related to the problems of policing the border or the necessity of ensuring roadway safety. Because the primary purpose of the Indianapolis narcotics checkpoint program is to uncover evidence of ordinary criminal wrongdoing, the program contravenes the Fourth Amendment.

Petitioners propose several ways in which the narcotics-detection purpose of the instant checkpoint program may resemble the primary purposes of the checkpoints in *Sitz* and *Martinez-Fuerte*. The checkpoints in those cases had the same ultimate purpose of arresting those suspected of committing crimes. Securing the border and apprehending drunk drivers are, of course, law enforcement activities, and law enforcement officers employ arrests and criminal prosecutions in pursuit of these goals. If we were to rest at this high level of generality, there would be little check on the ability of the authorities to construct roadblocks for almost any conceivable law enforcement purpose. The Fourth Amendment would do little to prevent such intrusions from becoming a routine part of American life.

Petitioners emphasize the severe and intractable nature of the drug problem as justification for the checkpoint program. There is no doubt that traffic in illegal narcotics creates social harms of the first magnitude. The law enforcement problems that the drug trade creates likewise remain daunting and complex, particularly in light of the myriad forms of spin-off crime that it spawns. The same can be said of various other illegal activities, if only to a lesser degree. But the gravity of the threat alone cannot be dispositive of questions concerning what means law enforcement officers may employ to pursue a given purpose. Rather, in determining whether individualized suspicion is required, we must consider the nature of the interests threatened and their connection to the particular law enforcement practices at issue. We are reluctant to recognize exceptions to the general rule of individualized suspicion where governmental authorities primarily pursue their general crime control ends.

Nor can the narcotics-interdiction purpose of the checkpoints be rationalized in terms of a highway safety concern similar to that present in *Sitz*. The detection and punishment of almost any criminal offense serves broadly the safety of the community, and our streets would no doubt be safer but for the scourge of illegal drugs. Only with respect to a smaller class of offenses, however, is society confronted with the type of immediate, vehicle-bound threat to life and limb that the sobriety checkpoint in *Sitz* was designed to eliminate.

Petitioners liken the anticontraband agenda of the Indianapolis checkpoints to the antismuggling purpose of the checkpoints in *Martinez-Fuerte*. Petitioners cite this Court's conclusion in *Martinez-Fuerte* that the flow of traffic was too heavy to permit "particularized study of a given car that would enable it to be identified as a possible carrier of illegal aliens," and claim that this logic has even more force here. The problem is that the same logic prevails any time a vehicle is employed to conceal contraband or other evidence of a crime. Further, the Indianapolis checkpoints are removed from the border context that was crucial in *Martinez-Fuerte*. We must look more closely at the nature of the public interests that such a regime is designed principally to serve.

The primary purpose of the Indianapolis checkpoints is to advance "the general interest in crime control." We decline to suspend the usual requirement of individualized suspicion where the police seek to employ a checkpoint primarily for the ordinary enterprise of investigating crimes. We cannot sanction stops justified only by the generalized and ever-present possibility that interrogation and inspection may reveal that a given motorist has committed some crime.

There are circumstances that may justify a law enforcement checkpoint where the primary purpose would otherwise, but for some emergency, relate to ordinary crime control. For example, the Fourth Amendment would almost certainly permit an appropriately tailored roadblock set up to thwart an imminent terrorist attack or to catch a dangerous criminal who is likely to flee by way of a particular route. The exigencies created by these scenarios are far removed from the circumstances under which authorities might simply stop cars as a matter of course to see if there just happens to be a felon leaving the jurisdiction. While we do not limit the purposes that may justify a checkpoint program to any rigid set of categories, we decline to approve a program whose primary purpose is ultimately indistinguishable from the general interest in crime control.

Petitioners argue that the Indianapolis checkpoint program is justified by lawful secondary purposes of keeping impaired motorists off the road and verifying licenses and registrations. If this were the case, law enforcement authorities would be able to establish checkpoints for virtually any purpose so long as they also included a license or sobriety check. We examine the evidence to determine the primary purpose of the checkpoint program. A program driven by an impermissible purpose may be proscribed while a program impelled by licit purposes is permitted, even though the challenged conduct may be outwardly similar. Our holding today does nothing to alter the constitutional status of the sobriety and border checkpoints that we approved in *Sitz* and *Martinez-Fuerte*, or of the type of traffic checkpoint that we suggested would be lawful in *Prouse*. Our holding also does not affect the validity of border searches or searches at places like airports and government buildings, where the need for such measures to ensure public safety can be particularly acute. Our holding also does not impair the ability of police officers to act appropriately upon information that they properly learn during a checkpoint stop justified by a lawful primary purpose, even where such action may result in the arrest of a motorist for an offense unrelated to that purpose. We caution that the purpose inquiry is to be conducted at the programmatic level and is not an invitation to probe the minds of individual officers acting at the scene.

Because the primary purpose of the Indianapolis checkpoint program is indistinguishable from the general interest in crime control, the checkpoints violate the Fourth Amendment. The judgment of the Court of Appeals is accordingly affirmed.

It is so ordered.

CHIEF JUSTICE REHNQUIST, with whom JUSTICE THOMAS joins, and with whom JUSTICE SCALIA joins as to Part I, dissenting.

This case follows naturally from *Martinez-Fuerte* and *Sitz* and it is constitutionally irrelevant that petitioners hoped to interdict drugs. The seizure is objectively reasonable as it lasts, on average, two to three minutes and does not involve a search. The checkpoints are clearly marked and operated by uniformed officers who are directed to stop every vehicle in the same manner. We have already held that a "sniff test" by a trained narcotics dog is not a "search" within the meaning of the Fourth Amendment. There is nothing to indicate that the sniff lengthens the stop. Finally, the checkpoints' success rate—49 arrests for offenses unrelated to drugs—confirms the State's legitimate interests in preventing drunken driving and ensuring the proper licensing of drivers and registration of their vehicles. The "special needs" doctrine, which has been used to uphold certain suspicionless searches performed for reasons unrelated to law enforcement, is an exception to the general rule that a search must be based on individualized suspicion of wrongdoing. *See, e.g., Skinner v. Railway Labor Executives' Assn.*, 489 U.S. 602 (1989) (drug test search).

Point for Discussion

Discretion to Suspend Roadblock

In *Commonwealth v. Worthy*, 598 Pa. 470, 957 A.2d 720 (2008), the court held that police could exercise discretion to suspend a DUI roadblock long enough to alleviate a traffic jam, and then resume the roadblock. The court sustained the suspension even though state guidelines required that every car be stopped. The court found "substantial compliance" with the

> In dicta, *Prouse* sanctioned roadside truck weigh-stations and inspection checkpoints. The Court recognized that some vehicles may be subjected to longer detention and more intrusive inspections than others.

guidelines, even though police suspended the roadblock three times to alleviate heavy traffic.

Take Note

In *Illinois v. Lidster*, 540 U.S. 419 (2004), after a bicyclist was struck and killed by a motorist late one evening, the police decided to establish a checkpoint at about the same time of night at the same location in an effort to locate potential witnesses to the incident. The roadblock slowed traffic and created lines of up to 15 cars in each lane. Each vehicle was stopped for 15-20 seconds, was given a flier related to the fatal hit and run accident, and asked for assistance in solving the crime. Lidster, one of the motorists stopped, was determined to be driving under the influence of alcohol. The Court rejected the idea that *Edmond* required the Court to find the check point unconstitutional: "The relevant public concern was grave. Police were investigating a crime that had resulted in a human death. The stop's objective was to help find the perpetrator of a specific and known crime, not of unknown crimes of a general sort. The stop advanced this grave public concern to a significant degree. The police approximately tailored their checkpoint stops to fit important criminal investigatory needs. The stops took place about one week after the hit-and-run accident, on the same highway near the location of the accident, and at about the same time of night. Police used the stops to obtain information from drivers, some of whom might well have been in the vicinity of the crime at the time it occurred. Most importantly, the stops interfered only minimally with liberty of the sort the Fourth Amendment seeks to protect. Each stop required only a brief wait in line—a very few minutes at most. Contact with the police lasted only a few seconds. Police contact consisted simply of a request for information and the distribution of a flyer. Viewed subjectively, the contact provided little reason for anxiety or alarm. The police stopped all vehicles systematically. And there is no allegation here that the police acted in a discriminatory or otherwise unlawful manner while questioning motorists during stops."

Food for Thought

On New Year's Eve, the police establish a sobriety checkpoint on a divided interstate highway about a mile beyond an exit. Approximately one-half mile beyond the exit is a large sign that reads: "Sobriety checkpoint one mile ahead. Prepare to stop." On seeing the sign, some drivers make a u-turn over the median and head in the opposite direction. (State law permits u-turns on divided highways provided that the driver makes the turn in a "careful and prudent" manner) Do the police have reasonable suspicion to stop drivers who make u-turns? What arguments might be made on behalf of the police? How might the driver respond to those arguments? Would it matter that the signs were placed just before the entrance to a rest area, and that there is no actual roadblock ahead. Would the police have "reasonable suspicion" to stop any car that enters the rest area? Now, suppose that (in addition) the police had stationed a patrol car in the median of the interstate to monitor the reactions of drivers, and stop cars that seem to make a hurried exit into the rest area. *See State v. Hedgcock*, 277 Neb. 805, 765 N.W.2d 469 (2009).

Hypo 1: *Sobriety Checkpoints with Drug Sniffing Dogs*

Suppose that the police establish sobriety checkpoints rather than drug interdiction checkpoints, and the stated goal of the checkpoints is simply to catch drunk drivers. However, during the sobriety checks, officers walk drug sniffing dogs around the cars. Is the procedure permissible if it is "primarily" justified as a sobriety check and does not lengthen the stop?

Hypo 2: *The "Terrorist" Plot*

Just weeks after the Madrid commuter rail bombings, the Massachusetts Bay Transit Authority (MBTA) received a tip suggesting that terrorists were plotting to attack a Boston rail station. Adjacent to the Sullivan MBTA subway station is a parking lot owned by the MBTA. One morning, an officer notices a white van with two occupants parked in the lot. The officer, who has been trained to identify terrorists, is concerned because it is unusual for vehicles to remain parked in the lot with occupants inside. From her experience, people use the lot to "park and ride," and they use a different lot to pick up or discharge passengers. Continuing to observe the vehicle, the officer realizes that that there are more than two men in the van, and that they are writing notes. Her terrorism training makes her suspicious that the van's occupants could be planning where to plant explosives. If the men had been working for the MBTA, she would have expected them to have checked-in at the station and to have displayed a work permit. The officer decides to investigate. Walking past the van, she sees that it has a paper license plate over a regular license plate, which her training taught her was suspicious. She also sees that the van has tinted windows, obscuring the view of the van's interior. She sees that there are more than five men sitting in the van, that no other vehicles in the lot have people sitting in them, that the men appear to be of Middle Eastern descent (with darker skin color). The officer then decides to approach the van, knock on the driver's side window, order everyone out, and ask them to identify themselves. The driver is of Mexican descent with a Texas driver's license, and the passengers have Brazilian passports with no indication of lawful entry into the United States. Did the officer act properly in approaching the van, demanding identification, and ordering the passengers out of the vehicle? *See United States v. Ramos*, 629 F.3d 60 (1st Cir. 2010).

Hypo 3: *The Anti-Poaching Checkpoint*

In order to combat poaching, park police are thinking about establishing vehicle checkpoints in order to question individuals about whether they intend to hunt or have hunted in the park (hunting is illegal). The checkpoint will be placed at park entrances and all vehicles will be stopped as they enter or leave the park. Rangers will post signs instructing drivers to prepare to stop, and the stops will be conducted by rangers in uniforms and reflective jackets. A ranger will approach the vehicle, identify himself as a park ranger, state that he is conducting a hunting checkpoint, and ask the driver, "have you been hunting?" If the driver responds that he or she was not hunting, the ranger will not search the vehicle. Questioning will last 15 to 25 seconds, and drivers will sometimes have to wait in line for about one minute before being questioned. You work as an attorney for the park service and have been asked for an opinion regarding the constitutionality of the proposed roadblock. What advice would you give? *See United States v. Fraire*, 575 F.3d 929 (9th Cir. 2009).

Hypo 4: *Neighborhood Safety Zones*

Because a particular neighborhood suffers from an exceptionally high crime rate, including murders and gun-related crimes, police designate it as a "neighborhood safety zone." The police wish to establish vehicle checkpoints over a five day period in order "to provide high police visibility, prevent and deter crime, safeguard officers and community members, and create safer neighborhoods." Under the program, the police will provide motorists with advance notice of the checkpoints, mark them with signs, barricades, lights, cones, and/or flares, and stop all vehicles entering the area, but will not stop pedestrians or vehicles leaving the area absent particularized suspicion. Officers will identify themselves and inquire whether the motorists have "legitimate reasons" for entering the area. Legitimate reasons include the fact that the motorist is (1) a resident; (2) is employed or on a commercial delivery; (3) is attending school or taking a child to school or day-care; (4) is related to a resident; (5) is elderly, disabled or seeking medical attention; and/or (6) is attempting to attend a verified organized civic, community, or religious event. If the motorist provides the officer with a legitimate reason, the officer will be authorized to request additional information sufficient to verify the motorist's stated reason for entry. Officers will deny entry to those motorists who do not have a legitimate reason for entry, who cannot substantiate their reason for entry, or who refuse to provide a legitimate reason. The police may not search a vehicle absent particularized suspicion. If you are counsel to the police department, how would you advise them regarding the constitutionality of the program? *See Mills v. District of Columbia*, 571 F.3d 1304 (D.C. Cir. 2009).

Food for Thought

How far can the "need" versus "intrusion" test be pushed? Suppose that, over the last five months, seven gruesome murders have been committed in Gainesville, Florida near the University of Florida campus. Even though the police have reason to believe that all of the murders were committed by a single person who lives in the area, they are not close to making an arrest and they believe that more murders will be committed in the near future. Desperate for information, the police establish roadblocks for the purpose of interviewing motorists. The police hope that one or more motorists will provide information that will lead to a break in the case. Given the "need" to find the murderer before another crime is committed, are the roadblocks constitutional? If the roadblocks prove unsuccessful, and another murder is committed, would the police be justified in making house-to-house searches in hopes of finding relevant evidence?

9. Border Searches

The government has always exercised broad authority to stop individuals seeking to enter the United States, to demand identification, and to search their persons and effects to make sure that contraband is not being smuggled. However, there are questions regarding the scope of governmental authority. Consider the following case.

United States v. Flores-Montano

541 U.S. 149 (2004).

CHIEF JUSTICE REHNQUIST delivered the opinion of the Court.

Respondent, driving a 1987 Ford Taurus station wagon, attempted to enter the United States at the Otay Mesa Port of Entry in southern California. A customs inspector conducted an inspection of the station wagon, and requested respondent to leave the vehicle. The vehicle was then taken to a secondary inspection station where a second customs inspector inspected the gas tank by tapping it, and noted that the tank sounded solid. The inspector requested a mechanic under contract with Customs to come to the border station to remove the tank. Within 20 to 30 minutes, the mechanic arrived. He raised the car on a hydraulic lift, loosened the straps and unscrewed the bolts holding the gas tank to the undercarriage of the vehicle, and then disconnected some hoses and electrical connections. After the gas tank was removed, the inspector hammered off bondo (a putty-like hardening substance used to seal openings) from the top of the gas tank. The inspector opened an access plate and found 37 kilograms of marijuana bricks. The process took 15 to 25 minutes.

A grand jury indicted respondent on one count of unlawfully importing marijuana, in violation of 21 U.S.C. § 952, and one count of possession of marijuana with intent to distribute, in violation of § 841(a)(1). The District Court held that reasonable suspicion was required to justify the search and granted respondent's motion to suppress. The Court of Appeals affirmed. We granted certiorari and now reverse.

The reasons that might support a requirement of some level of suspicion in the case of highly intrusive searches of the person—dignity and privacy interests of the person being searched—simply do not carry over to vehicles. Complex balancing tests to determine what is a "routine" search of a vehicle, as opposed to a more "intrusive" search of a person, have no place in border searches of vehicles.

The Government's interest in preventing the entry of unwanted persons and effects is at its zenith at the international border. Time and again, we have stated that "searches made at the border, pursuant to the longstanding right of the sovereign to protect itself by stopping and examining persons and property crossing into this country, are reasonable simply by virtue of the fact that they occur at the border." *United States v. Ramsey*, 431 U.S. 606 (1977). Congress, since the beginning of our Government, "has granted the Executive plenary authority to conduct routine searches and seizures at the border, without probable cause or a warrant, in order to regulate the collection of duties and to prevent the introduction of contraband into this country." *Montoya de Hernandez, supra*, at 537. The modern statute, 19 U.S.C. § 1581(a),[12] derived from a statute passed by the First Congress, and reflects the "impressive historical pedigree" of the Government's power and interest. It is axiomatic that the United States, as sovereign, has the inherent authority to protect, and a paramount interest in protecting, its territorial integrity.

Smugglers frequently attempt to penetrate our borders with contraband secreted in their automobiles' fuel tank. Over the past 5½ years, there have been 18,788 vehicle drug seizures at California ports of entry. Of those 18,788, gas tank drug seizures have accounted for 4,619 of the vehicle drug seizures, or approximately 25%. Instances of persons smuggled in and around gas tank compartments are discovered at San Ysidro and Otay Mesa at a rate averaging 1 approximately every 10 days.

Respondent urges that he has a privacy interest in his fuel tank, and that the suspicionless disassembly of his tank is an invasion of his privacy. We have noted that the expectation of privacy is less at the border than it is in the interior. *Montoya de Hernandez, supra*, at 538. We have long recognized that automobiles seeking entry into this country may be searched. It is difficult to imagine how the search of a gas tank, which should be solely a repository for fuel, could be more of an invasion of privacy than the search of the automobile's passenger compartment.

Second, respondent argues that the Fourth Amendment "protects property as well as privacy," *Soldal v. Cook County*, 506 U.S. 56 (1992), and that the disassembly and reassembly of his gas tank is a significant deprivation of his property interest because it may damage the vehicle. He cannot, truly contend that the procedure of removal, disassembly, and reassembly of the fuel tank has resulted in serious damage to, or destruction of, the property. In fiscal year 2003, 348 gas tank searches conducted along the southern border were negative (*i.e.*, no contraband was found), the gas tanks were reassembled, and the vehicles continued their entry into the United States without incident. Respondent cites not

---

[12] Section 1581(a) provides: "Any officer of the customs may at any time go on board any vehicle at any place in the United States or, as he may be authorized, within a customs-enforcement area established under the Anti-Smuggling Act, or at any other authorized place, without as well as within his district, and examine and examine, inspect, and search the vessel or vehicle and every part thereof and any person, trunk, package, or cargo on board, and to this end may hail and stop such vessel or vehicle, and use all necessary force to compel compliance."

a single accident involving the vehicle or motorist in the many thousands of gas tank disassemblies that have occurred at the border. A gas tank search involves a brief procedure that can be reversed without damaging the safety or operation of the vehicle. If damage to a vehicle were to occur, the motorist might be entitled to recovery. While the interference with a motorist's possessory interest is not insignificant when the Government removes, disassembles, and reassembles his gas tank, it nevertheless is justified by the Government's paramount interest in protecting the border.[3]

We conclude that the Government's authority to conduct suspicionless inspections at the border includes the authority to remove, disassemble, and reassemble a vehicle's fuel tank. While some searches of property are so destructive as to require a different result, this was not one of them. The judgment of the United States Court of Appeals for the Ninth Circuit is therefore reversed, and the case is remanded for further proceedings consistent with this opinion.

It is so ordered.

JUSTICE BREYER, concurring.

Customs keeps track of the border searches its agents conduct, including the reasons for the searches. This administrative process should help minimize concerns that gas tank searches might be undertaken in an abusive manner.

> **FYI**
>
> In *United States v. Martinez-Fuerte*, 428 U.S. 543 (1976), the Court upheld immigration roadblocks located within 100 miles of the United States border.

Point for Discussion

Roving Border Patrols

In *United States v. Brignoni-Ponce*, 422 U.S. 873 (1975), the Court held that a roving patrol of law enforcement officers could stop motorists near an international border to briefly inquire about their residence status provided that the officers "reasonably suspect that vehicles contain aliens who are illegally in the country." But what constitutes "reasonable suspicion" that vehicles contain illegal aliens? Near the Mexican border, is there sufficient cause if an officer spots someone of Hispanic descent driving a vehicle? What more should be required?

---

[3] Respondent also argued that he has a Fourth Amendment right not to be subject to delay at the international border and that the need for the use of specialized labor, as well as the hour actual delay here and the potential for even greater delay for reassembly are an invasion of that right. Respondent points to no cases indicating the Fourth Amendment shields entrants from inconvenience or delay at the international border. Delays of one to two hours at international borders are to be expected.

Take Note

Under 19 U.S.C. § 1583 customs officials are required to possess a "reasonable suspicion" of criminal activity before opening and reading private mail being sent to foreign countries. However, under 19 U.S.C. § 5317(b), individuals who send more than $10,000 in currency or negotiable instruments, are required to submit a declaration form, and customs officials are allowed to conduct suspicionless searches. In *United States v. Seljan*, 547 F.3d 993 (9th Cir. 2008), the court upheld the actions of customs officials who read a private letter contained in a packet subject to a § 5317(b) form.

Food for Thought

Following the holding in *Flores-Montano*, suppose that customs officials believe that an entrant is trying to smuggle illegal drugs into the U.S.? What powers may they exercise? Rip out the seats? Tear luggage apart? Strip searches? Body cavity searches?

Hypo 1: *Advising the Border Patrol*

A mile inside the U.S.-Mexico border, in an area with sand dunes and valleys, border patrol agents spot an SUV coming from the direction of the Mexican border. The vehicle is moving unusually fast for the terrain, is not bearing the required orange safety flag and recreational permit, is traveling in a straight path uncharacteristic of recreational use, and the entire rear portion of the vehicle is covered by a black tarp (often used by drug smugglers to cover their vehicles). The officers want advice about whether they can stop the vehicle using a tire deflation device designed to flatten all four of the vehicle's tires and effectively render it inoperable. Under the circumstances, how would you advise them given that the device will render the vehicle inoperable, and require great effort (obtaining and mounting four new tires) to render the vehicle operable again? Is it relevant that drug smugglers generally refuse to yield to lights or sirens and frequently engage in desperate attempts to escape apprehension (*e.g.*, crossing freeway medians, driving into oncoming traffic, and leading officers on high-speed pursuits) that sometimes cause death to innocent bystanders? *See United States v. Guzman-Padilla*, 573 F.3d 865 (9th Cir. 2009).

Food for Thought

As a general rule, customs officials have the right to search individuals and any baggage or containers that they are carrying with them. Suppose that an individual arrives at the U.S. border carrying a laptop. Do customs officials have the right to examine the electronic contents of the laptop to make sure that the individual is not carrying illegal material (e.g., child pornography) into the country? Can they copy the contents of the laptop for later review? Alternatively, can they seize the laptop for a few days to a week so that it can be sent to a laboratory for more detailed examination? A new Department of Homeland Security regulation seems to give DHS officials broad authority to do all of these things. *See* U.S. Department of Homeland Security, Privacy Impact Assessment for the Border Searches of Electronic Devices (2009) 1, 6 (2009) (hereafter Homeland Security Assessment), http://www.dhs.gov/xlibrary/assets/privacy/privacy_pia_cbp_laptop.pdf. Should a court require DHS to establish probable cause, or at least a "reasonable suspicion" of criminal activity, before reviewing the contents of a laptop or iphone? *See United States v. Cotterman*, 709 F.3d 952 (9th Cir. 2013). Would you view the situation differently if customs detained the laptop for seven days, and mistakenly damaged it rendering the information unusable? *See Kam-Almaz v. United States*, 682 F.3d 1364 (Fed. Cir. 2012).

Hypo 2: *Searching for Text Messages*

Assume that Shommo is traveling to the United States from a foreign country, and is carrying an iPhone. Customs officials, who find the iPhone in his possession, want to review defendant's text messages and Internet search history. You are the INS' counsel, and you receive a phone call inquiring whether it is permissible to do so. How would you advise the INS? Are such searches consistent with the justifications for allowing border searches? In deciding whether to examine a particular entrant's phone, could the INS take into account the entrant's ethnicity and country of origin? Would it matter that prior digital searches of computers and iPhones had uncovered digital pictures of high-level Al-Qaida officials and video clips of improvised explosive devices? See Joelle Tessler, *Lawmakers May Restrict Federal Agents' Searches of Laptops*, Courier-Journal, Dec. 14, 2008, at D–7, C 1–6. Does the *Riley* decision, *supra*, offer any guidance on this issue? *See United States v. Sanoonchi*, 48 F. Supp.3d 815 (D. Md. 2014). If cause should be required, suppose that ICE agents believe that a suspect may be shuttling illegal drugs between Columbia and the United States. Can ICE seize the suspect's laptop and gaming system and hold them for a week for electronic analysis? If the seizure is regarded as "non-routine," so that a "reasonable suspicion" of criminal activity should be required, would the following facts provide the required suspicion: the suspect made four trips to Colombia (a reputed drug capitol) in the prior five months; all of the trips were short (4-5 days); the suspect purchased the tickets with cash; the suspect did not know the last names of the people that he was visiting. *See United States v. Molina-Gomez*, 781 F.3d 13 (1st Cir. 2015).

Hypo 3: *More on Extended Border Searches*

In interviewing a suspected drug smuggler, Immigration and Customs Enforcement ("ICE") agents learn that he is involved in a larger drug trafficking organization, as well as that he plans to meet a white Toyota Tacoma, which would serve as a "load vehicle," and a white PT Cruiser, which would serve as a "scout vehicle." He is supposed to meet the cars on the California side of the border at which point he will be led to a separate drop-off location The smuggler shows the agents a picture of the PT Cruiser on his cell phone, from which ICE agents can decipher a license plate number, 6CHU366. The following morning, Villasenor is observed driving a white PT Cruiser with the same license plate number to a nearby U.S. border checkpoint. A narcotics detection dog sniffs the car but fails to alert and the driver and car are allowed entry. Shortly thereafter, ICE agent Torregrosa is driving near the border crossing when he spots the PT Cruiser, realizes that it is the vehicle that the smuggler referred to, and begins following it. Villasenor stops at a gas station, gets out while talking on his cell phone, but keeps looking at the border crossing. He then returns to his car and drives off without filling up. He then stops at another service station where he continues to talk on his phone and then drives off again. Torregrosa then stops the Cruiser. While a police officer (who assists the agent) writes Villasenor a ticket for failure to provide proof of insurance, Torregrosa calls in a drug sniffing dog. Forty-five minutes later, the dog arrives and alerts to the right rear panel on the car (the agents were unaware of the prior sniff). The agents look behind the panel and discover cocaine. Was the second dog sniff permissible? *See United States v. Villasenor,* 608 F.3d 467 (9th Cir. 2010).

10. Special Needs Searches

In a number of recent cases, the Court has established and developed a "special needs" exception to the warrant requirement. This exception, which especially applies in safety and administrative situations, allows the government to search or seize without probable cause and sometimes even without reasonable suspicion.

Take Note

A foundational decision is *Skinner v. Railway Labor Executives' Association*, 489 U.S. 602 (1989). In that case, the Court upheld Federal Railroad Administration (FRA) regulations mandating blood and urine tests of railroad employees involved in "major" train accidents, and authorizing railroads to administer breath and urine tests to employees who violate certain safety rules. The regulations were designed to combat the problem of drug and controlled substance abuse by railroad employees. The Court upheld the regulations, noting that the "governmental interest in ensuring the safety of the traveling public and of the employees themselves plainly justifies prohibiting covered employees from using alcohol or drugs on duty, or while subject to being called for duty." The Court emphasized that "Alcohol and other drugs are eliminated from the bloodstream at a constant rate, and blood and breath samples taken to measure whether these substances were in the bloodstream when a triggering event occurred must be obtained as soon as possible. The delay necessary to procure a warrant nevertheless may result in the destruction of valuable evidence." As a result, the Court concluded that the "Government interest in testing without a showing of individualized suspicion is compelling." Finally, the Court held that covered employees had a diminished expectation of privacy due to the nature of their jobs, and that "the privacy interests implicated by the search are minimal" because of the manner in which the tests were performed.

In *Bill v. Brewer*, 799 F.3d 1295 (9th Cir. 2015), following a crime, police investigators sought DNA from police officers in order to exclude them as possible contributors of DNA to the crime scene. Before the request, the officers were told that they had been excluded as possible suspects, and that any DNA that they contributed would not be entered into the Combined DNA Index System (CODIS). The court uphold a lower court order requiring the officers to provide the DNA evidence through buccal swabs. Although the court concluded that a warrant could be invalidated if it unduly intruded on personal privacy, the court concluded that this order was not unduly intrusive.

Board of Education of Independent School District No. 92 of Pottawatomie County v. Earls

536 U.S. 822 (2002).

JUSTICE THOMAS delivered the opinion of the Court.

Tecumseh, Oklahoma, is a rural community about 40 miles southeast of Oklahoma City. In 1998, the School District adopted the Student Activities Drug Testing Policy (Policy), which requires all middle and high school students to consent to drug testing in order to participate in any extracurricular activity. In practice, the Policy has been applied only to competitive extracurricular activities sanctioned by the Oklahoma Secondary Schools Activities Association, such as the Academic Team, Future Farmers of America, Future Homemakers of America, band, choir, pom pom, cheerleading, and athletics. Under the Policy, students are required to take a drug test before participating in an extracurricular activity, must submit to random drug testing while participating in that activity, and must agree to be tested at any time upon reasonable suspicion. The urinalysis tests are designed to detect only the use of illegal drugs, including amphetamines, marijuana, cocaine, opiates, and barbituates, not medical conditions or the presence of authorized prescription medications. Lindsay Earls was a member of the show choir, the marching band, the Academic Team, and the National Honor Society. Daniel James sought to participate in the Academic Team. Both challenged the Policy on Fourth Amendment grounds. The district court rejected respondents' claim and the court of appeals reversed. We granted certiorari.

Searches by public school officials, such as the collection of urine samples, implicate Fourth Amendment interests. *See Vernonia School Dist. 47J v. Acton*, 515 U. S. 646 (1995). We must therefore review the School District's Policy for "reasonableness," which is the touchstone of the constitutionality of a governmental search. Reasonableness usually requires a showing of probable cause. The probable-cause standard, however, "is peculiarly related to criminal investigations" and may be unsuited to determining the reasonableness of administrative searches where the "Government seeks to prevent the development of hazardous conditions." *Treasury Employees v. Von Raab*, 489 U. S. 656 (1989). A warrant and finding of probable cause are unnecessary in the public school context because such requirements "would unduly interfere with the maintenance of the swift and informal disciplinary procedures that are needed." *Vernonia, supra*, at 653.

Respondents argue that drug testing must be based at least on some level of individualized suspicion. We generally determine the reasonableness of a search by balancing the nature of the intrusion on the individual's privacy against the promotion of legitimate governmental interests. But we have long held that "the Fourth Amendment imposes no irreducible requirement of individualized suspicion." *United States v. Martinez-Fuerte*, 428 U. S. 543 (1976). "In certain limited circumstances, the Government's need to discover such latent or hidden conditions, or to prevent their development, is sufficiently compelling to justify the intrusion on privacy entailed by conducting such searches without any measure of individualized suspicion." *Von Raab, supra*, at 668. In the context of safety and administrative regulations, a search unsupported by probable cause may be reasonable "when 'special needs, beyond the normal need for law enforcement, make the warrant and probable-cause requirement impracticable.' " *Griffin v. Wisconsin*, 483 U. S. 868 (1987) (quoting T.L.O., supra, at 351 (Blackmun, J., concurring)).

This Court has previously held that "special needs" inhere in the public school context. While schoolchildren do not shed their constitutional rights when they enter the schoolhouse, "Fourth Amendment rights are different in public schools than elsewhere; the 'reasonableness' inquiry cannot disregard the schools' custodial and tutelary responsibility for children." In particular, a finding of individualized suspicion may not be necessary when a school conducts drug testing. In *Vernonia*, this Court held that the suspicionless drug testing of athletes was constitutional. The Court, however, did not simply authorize all school drug testing, but rather conducted a fact-specific balancing of the intrusion on the children's Fourth Amendment rights against the promotion of legitimate governmental interests. Applying *Vernonia* to this case, we conclude that Tecumseh's Policy is also constitutional.

We first consider the nature of the privacy interest allegedly compromised by the drug testing. A student's privacy interest is limited in a public school environment where the State is responsible for maintaining discipline, health, and safety. Schoolchildren are routinely required to submit to physical examinations and vaccinations against disease. Securing order in the school environment sometimes requires that students be subjected to greater controls than those appropriate for adults.

Respondents argue that because children participating in nonathletic extracurricular activities are not subject to regular physicals and communal undress, they have a stronger expectation of privacy than the athletes tested in *Vernonia*. This distinction was not essential to our decision in *Vernonia*, which depended primarily upon the school's custodial responsibility and authority. In any event, students who participate in competitive extracurricular activities voluntarily subject themselves to many of the same intrusions on their privacy as do athletes. Some of these clubs and activities require occasional off-campus travel and communal undress. All of them have their own rules and requirements for participating students that do not apply to the student body as a whole and a faculty sponsor monitors students for compliance with these rules. This regulation of extracurricular activities further diminishes the expectation of privacy among schoolchildren. We conclude that the students affected by this Policy have a limited expectation of privacy.

Next, we consider the character of the intrusion imposed by the Policy. Urination is "an excretory function traditionally shielded by great privacy." But the "degree of intrusion" on one's privacy caused by collecting a urine sample "depends upon the manner in which production of the urine sample is monitored." Under the Policy, a faculty monitor waits outside the closed restroom stall for the student to produce a sample and must "listen for the normal sounds of urination in order to guard against tampered specimens and to insure an accurate chain of custody." The monitor then pours the sample into two bottles that are sealed and placed into a mailing pouch along with a consent form signed by the student. This procedure is virtually identical to that reviewed in *Vernonia*, except that it additionally protects privacy by allowing male students to produce their samples behind a closed stall. Given that we considered the method of collection in *Vernonia* a "negligible" intrusion, the method here is even less problematic.

The Policy clearly requires that the test results be kept in confidential files separate from a student's other educational records and released to school personnel only on a "need to know" basis. Respondents contend that the intrusion on students' privacy is significant because the Policy fails to protect effectively against the disclosure of confidential information and, specifically, that the school "has been careless in protecting that information: for example, the Choir teacher looked at students' prescription drug lists and left them where other students could see them." But the choir teacher is someone with a "need to know," because during off-campus trips she needs to know what medications are taken by her students. In any event, there is no allegation that any other student did see such information. This one example of alleged carelessness hardly increases the character of the intrusion.

Moreover, the test results are not turned over to any law enforcement authority. Nor do the test results here lead to the imposition of discipline or have any academic consequences. The only consequence of a failed drug test is to limit the student's privilege of participating in extracurricular activities. Indeed, a student may test positive for drugs twice and still be allowed to participate in extracurricular activities. After the first positive test, the school contacts the student's parent or guardian for a meeting. The student may continue to participate in the activity if within five days of the meeting the student shows proof of receiving drug counseling and submits to a second drug test in two weeks. For the second positive test, the student is suspended from participation in all extracurricular activities for 14 days, must complete four hours of substance abuse counseling, and must submit to monthly drug tests. Only after a third positive test will the student be suspended from participating in any extracurricular activity for the remainder of the school year, or 88 school days, whichever is longer. Given the minimally intrusive nature of the sample collection and the limited uses to which the test results are put, we conclude that the invasion of students' privacy is not significant.

Finally, this Court must consider the nature and immediacy of the government's concerns and the efficacy of the Policy in meeting them. This Court has articulated the importance of the governmental concern in preventing drug use by schoolchildren. The drug abuse problem among our Nation's youth has hardly abated since *Vernonia* was decided in 1995. In fact, evidence suggests that it has only grown worse. As in *Vernonia*, "the necessity for the State to act is magnified by the fact that this evil is being visited not just upon individuals at large, but upon children for whom it has undertaken a special responsibility of care and direction." The health and safety risks identified in *Vernonia* apply with equal force to Tecumseh's children. Indeed, the nationwide drug epidemic makes the war against drugs a pressing concern in every school.

The School District in this case has presented specific evidence of drug use at Tecumseh schools. Teachers testified that they had seen students who appeared to be under the influence of drugs and that they had heard students speaking openly about using drugs. A drug dog found marijuana cigarettes near the school parking lot. Police officers once found drugs or drug paraphernalia in a car driven by a Future Farmers of America member. And the school board president reported that people in the community were calling the board to discuss the "drug situation." We decline to second-guess the finding that "the School District was faced with a 'drug problem' when it adopted the Policy."

Respondents argue that there is no "real and immediate interest" to justify a policy of drug testing nonathletes. We have recognized that "a demonstrated problem of drug abuse is not in all cases necessary to the validity of a testing regime," but that some showing does "shore up an assertion of special need for a suspicionless general search program." The School District has provided sufficient evidence to shore up the need for its drug testing program.

Furthermore, this Court has not required a particularized or pervasive drug problem before allowing the government to conduct suspicionless drug testing. In *Von Raab* the Court upheld the drug testing of customs officials on a purely preventive basis, without any documented history of drug use by such officials. In response to the lack of evidence relating to drug use, the Court noted that "drug abuse is one of the most serious problems confronting our society today," and that programs to prevent and detect drug use among customs officials could not be deemed unreasonable. Likewise, the need to prevent and deter the substantial harm of childhood drug use provides the necessary immediacy for a school testing policy. It would make little sense to require a school district to wait for a substantial portion of its students to begin using drugs before it was allowed to institute a drug testing program designed to deter drug use. Given the nationwide epidemic of drug use, and the evidence of increased drug use in Tecumseh schools, it was entirely reasonable for the School District to enact this particular drug testing policy.

Respondents argue that the testing of nonathletes does not implicate any safety concerns, and that safety is a "crucial factor" in applying the special needs framework. They contend that there must be "surpassing safety interests," or "extraordinary safety and national security hazards," in order to override the usual protections of the Fourth Amendment. Respondents are correct that safety factors into the special needs analysis, but the safety interest furthered by drug testing is undoubtedly substantial for all children, athletes and nonathletes alike. Drug use carries a variety of health risks for children, including death from overdose.

We reject the argument that drug testing must presumptively be based upon an individualized reasonable suspicion of wrongdoing because such a testing regime would be less intrusive. In this context, the Fourth Amendment does not require a finding of individualized suspicion, and we decline to impose such a requirement on schools attempting to prevent and detect drug use by students. Moreover, we question whether testing based on individualized suspicion would be less intrusive. Such a regime would place an additional burden on public school teachers who are already tasked with the difficult job of maintaining order and discipline and might unfairly target members of unpopular groups. The fear of lawsuits resulting from such targeted searches may chill enforcement of the program, rendering it ineffective in combating drug use. In any case, this Court has repeatedly stated that reasonableness under the Fourth Amendment does not require employing the least intrusive means, because "the logic of such elaborate less-restrictive-alternative arguments could raise insuperable barriers to the exercise of virtually all search-and-seizure powers." *Martinez-Fuerte*, 428 U. S., at 556–557, n. 12.

We find that testing students who participate in extracurricular activities is a reasonably effective means of addressing the School District's legitimate concerns in preventing, deterring, and detecting drug use. While in *Vernonia* there might have been a closer fit between the testing of athletes and the finding that the drug problem was "fueled by the 'role model' effect of athletes' drug use," such a finding was not essential to the holding. Drug testing of Tecumseh students who participate in extracurricular activities effectively serves the School District's interest in protecting the safety and health of its students.

Within the limits of the Fourth Amendment, local school boards must assess the desirability of drug testing schoolchildren. In upholding the constitutionality of the Policy, we express no opinion as to its wisdom. We hold only that Tecumseh's Policy is a reasonable means of furthering the School District's important interest in preventing and deterring drug use among its schoolchildren. We reverse the judgment of the Court of Appeals.

It is so ordered.

JUSTICE BREYER, concurring.

The drug problem in our Nation's schools is serious in terms of size, the kinds of drugs being used, and the consequences of that use both for our children and the rest of us. The program at issue here seeks to discourage demand for drugs by changing the school's environment in order to combat the single most important factor leading school children to take drugs, namely, peer pressure. It offers the adolescent a nonthreatening reason to decline his friend's drug-use invitations, namely, that he intends to play baseball, participate in debate, join the band, or engage in any one of half a dozen useful, interesting, and important activities.

Not everyone would agree with this Court's characterization of the privacy-related significance of urine sampling as "negligible." But the testing program avoids subjecting the entire school to testing and it preserves an option for a conscientious objector. He can refuse testing while paying a price (nonparticipation) that is serious, but less severe than expulsion from the school. I cannot know whether the school's drug testing program will work. But the Constitution does not prohibit the effort.

JUSTICE GINSBURG, with whom JUSTICE STEVENS, JUSTICE O'CONNOR, and JUSTICE SOUTER join, dissenting.

The testing program upheld today is not reasonable. Petitioners' policy targets for testing a student population least likely to be at risk from illicit drugs and their damaging effects. *Vernonia* cannot be read to endorse invasive and suspicionless drug testing of all students upon any evidence of drug use, solely because drugs jeopardize the life and health of those who use them. Many children, like many adults, engage in dangerous activities on their own time; that the children are enrolled in school scarcely allows government to monitor all such activities. If a student has a reasonable subjective expectation of privacy in the personal items she brings to school, surely she has a similar expectation regarding the chemical composition of her urine.

While extracurricular activities are "voluntary" in the sense that they are not required for graduation, participation in such activities is a key component of school life, essential in reality for students applying to college, and a significant contributor to the breadth and quality of the educational experience. Voluntary participation in athletics has a distinctly different dimension: Schools regulate student athletes discretely because competitive school sports by their nature require communal undress and, more important, expose students to physical risks that schools have a duty to mitigate. Schools cannot offer a program of competitive athletics without intimately

FYI

In *Griffin v. Wisconsin*, 483 U.S. 868 (1987), the Court upheld probationer searches conducted pursuant to a Wisconsin regulation permitting "any probation officer to search a probationer's home without a warrant as long as his supervisor approves and as long as there are 'reasonable grounds' to believe the presence of contraband." The Court held that a probation system presented a "special need" for the "exercise of supervision to assure that probation restrictions are in fact observed" and therefore the search was reasonable. Likewise, in *United States v. Knights*, 534 U.S. 112 (2001), when a judge imposed a similar restriction as a condition of probation, the Court upheld a search of the probationer's residence based on a reasonable suspicion that he was involved in criminal activity. The Court balanced the need for the search against the intrusion, and held that the search was justified. In assessing the intrusion, the Court held that probationers do not enjoy the same liberties as other citizens, "a court granting probation may impose reasonable conditions that deprive the offender of some freedoms enjoyed by law-abiding citizens," and that a probationer "is more likely than the ordinary citizen to violate the law." The Court held that the search could be justified based on a finding of reasonable suspicion that the probationer is involved in criminal activity.

affecting the privacy of students. Interscholastic athletics require close safety and health regulation; a school's choir, band, and academic team do not. Student athletes' expectations of privacy are necessarily attenuated. On "occasional out-of-town trips," students like Lindsay Earls "must sleep together in communal settings and use communal bathrooms." But those situations are hardly equivalent to the routine communal undress associated with athletics.

In this case, respondents allege that the School District handled personal information collected under the policy carelessly, with little regard for its confidentiality.

Vernonia initiated its drug testing policy in response to "a large segment of the student body, particularly those involved in interscholastic athletics, in a state of rebellion." Tecumseh, by contrast, repeatedly reported to the Federal Government that drug use was not a major problem. *Vernonia* emphasized that "the particular drugs screened by Vernonia's Policy have been demonstrated to pose substantial physical risks to athletes." Despite nightmarish images of colliding tubas, the great majority of students are engaged in activities that are not safety sensitive to an unusual degree. There is a difference between imperfect tailoring and no tailoring.

Nationwide, students who participate in extracurricular activities are significantly less likely to develop substance abuse problems than are their less-involved peers. Tecumseh's policy thus falls short doubly if deterrence is its aim: It invades the privacy of students who need deterrence least, and risks steering students at greatest risk for substance abuse away from extracurricular involvement that potentially may palliate drug problems.

It is a sad irony that the School District seeks to justify its edict by trumpeting "the schools' custodial and tutelary responsibility for children." "That schools are educating the young for citizenship is reason for scrupulous protection of Constitutional freedoms of the individual, if we are not to strangle the free mind at its source and teach youth to discount important principles of our government as mere platitudes." *West Virginia Bd. of Ed. v. Barnette*, 319 U.S. 624, 637 (1943).

Food for Thought

Following the favorable decision in this case, suppose that the Tecumseh school district decides to adopt a drug testing program applicable to all students, not just those involved in extra-curricular activities. Based on the Court's decision, and the evidence before the Court in the *Earls* case, would such a program be constitutional? Would it matter whether the program involved only "random" drug testing (10 students were chosen per week based on their names' position in the alphabet), or whether it involved an annual drug test of every student?

Hypo 1: *Direct Observation*

In an effort to ensure the integrity of the program referred to in the *Earls* case, could a school require that all urine samples be collected under the direct observation of school employees (rather than in a closed stall)?

Hypo 2: *Drug Interdiction Searches*

A public high school is thinking about adopting a drug interdiction policy which provides that it is designed to "balance each student's right to privacy" with "the need to maintain an appropriate learning environment." In particular, the policy would allow school administrators in conjunction with the police to screen student property using trained drug and weapons detection dogs. The policy permits dogs to sniff student lockers, desks, backpacks, and similar items. When the dogs are brought into a classroom, the students are asked to leave all items in the room, but to exit while the canine performs the sniff. The policy states that a student's possessions will only be searched if a drug dog has twice alerted on the same property. Suppose that the school has evidence suggesting that it frequently receives reports from students, parents, and teachers regarding the use of illegal and prescription drugs in the school, and that schools officials handle drug related incidents on average three or more times per week, leading them to believe that "there was and is a drug problem" at the high school. Can the search be upheld under the special needs exception? *See Burlison v. Springfield Public Schools*, 708 F.3d 1034 (8th Cir. 2013).

Hypo 3: *Searching the Student's Car*

After receiving a report of a student "under the influence," the assistant principal of a school meets with the student who admits to taking a "green pill" given to him by another student. After sending the student for medical care, the assistant principal confronts the other student (Best) and questions him. Best denies giving the first student any pill although he admits giving another student a "nutritional supplement" and a search reveals that he has several white pills of unknown composition on his person. The assistant principal then searches Best's car and finds drugs and drug paraphernalia. Was the assistant principal's search of the vehicle permissible under the Fourth Amendment? *See State v. Best*, 201 N.J. 100, 987 A.2d 605 (2010).

Hypo 4: *Advising the City*

The City of Mesa, Arizona, wishes to adopt a random drug testing program for firefighters in an effort to deter drug and alcohol use. In order to adopt a valid program, what findings must the City make in order to justify the program? How should the program be administered?

Hypo 5: *Terrorism and Football*

Florida's Tampa Sports Authority (TSA), concerned about the possibility of terrorists entering Raymond James Stadium, wants to conduct suspicionless pat-down searches of all individuals attending games at the Stadium. You are the attorney for the TSA. What must the TSA show in order to impose the pat-down search requirement? *See Johnston v. Tampa Sports Authority,* 442 F. Supp.2d 1257 (M.D. Fla. 2006).

Hypo 6: *Terrorism and Subways*

In response to subway attacks in other countries, the New York Police Department (NYPD) would like to implement a program of random, suspicionless, searches of items being carried by subway passengers. Suppose that you are the legal adviser to the NYPD. What must the NYPD show in order to create a valid "special needs" program involving such searches. For example, must it show that it is responding to a particular terrorist threat regarding its subway lines? Must it show that the program will be effective in deterring potential terrorists? Must the NYPD place warning signs at the entrances to subway stations warning riders that "by choosing to ride on the subway, they agree to consent to random searches of their persons and effects"? Must the program be random? *See MacWade v. Kelly,* 460 F.3d 260 (2d Cir. 2006).

Hypo 7: *Public School Teacher Drug Testing*

After two teachers are arrested for possession of illegal drugs, a school board decides to adopt a policy providing for random drug testing of teachers. The policy applies to all school board employees (including Board Members) and provides for testing under the following circumstances: (a) a job application; (b) reasonable suspicion of drug or alcohol use; (c) "routine" fitness-for-duty drug or alcohol testing; (d) "follow-up" drug or alcohol testing; (e) "post-accident testing." The Policy would provide that all supervisors and teachers must receive training on alcohol abuse and the use of controlled substances. The Policy also provides for random drug testing of at least ten (10%) percent of all employees annually. The policy provides that tested employees are subject to a urine test that includes testing for alcohol, amphetamines, cannabinoids, cocaine, phencyclidine and opiates or any other substance prohibited by statute. However, the testing also involves searches for the presence of benzodiazepines, barbiturates, propoxyphene, and methadone which include some commonly prescribed medications such as Xanax (alprazolam), and benzodiazepine. When a teacher reports for testing, only a nurse is in the testing room. After confirming the teacher's identity, the nurse breaks open a package that contains the sample cup and two vials. The teacher goes into the bathroom alone to produce the sample. Upon completion, the nurse splits the sample into two vials, with the first to be used for testing, and the second for confirmation, if necessary. The vials are then sealed and the teacher signs a form stating that the samples are hers. The teacher is then free to leave. Can the drug testing policy be justified on the basis that teachers serve "*in an in loco parentis*" capacity and are charged with the responsibility to secure order and to protect students from harm while in their custody." What about the argument that teachers should be unimpaired and mentally and physically able to respond promptly to any emergency of which they become aware? There have been situations in the schools which called for quick and decisive actions by a teacher, including when a bleeding student fell out of a chair; a student passed out in a classroom, a student who appeared to be "high" and almost fell, and occasions when a student suffered a seizure in the classroom. Is the policy valid? *See Smith County Education Association v. Smith County Board of Education*, 781 F.Supp.2d 604 (M.D. Tenn. 2011).

Hypo 8: *Drug Testing and Librarians*

May a city require drug testing of all applicants for all city jobs? Jane Foeburn is denied a job as a librarian on the basis that she refused to take a drug test. If hired, Foeburn would have retrieved items from the book drop and returned them to the shelves. In challenging the denial, Foeburn claims that the city is unable to establish a "special need" for subjecting librarians to drug tests. The city disagrees. Who is correct? How might the city justify the testing? *See Lanier v. Woodburn*, 518 F.3d 1147 (9th Cir. 2008). Could a city drug test all welfare recipients as a prerequisite to eligibility? Would it matter that the city's goal is to make sure that the children of needy families are receiving adequate parental care? *See Marchwinski v. Howard*, 309 F.3d 330 (6th Cir. 2002).

Hypo 9: *Breathalyzers Following Police Killings*

The N.Y.C. police department is considering adopting a policy requiring that all police officers who kill or injure citizens with their guns submit to an immediate breathalyzer test to determine the amount of alcohol in their systems. Under the proposed policy, the initial test would be administered on site via a portable machine. If that test produces a positive result, the officer would be transported to a police facility for a second test with a non-portable machine. Suppose that you are the legal adviser to the police department and you are asked to advise it regarding the constitutionality of the policy. How might you respond? Now, suppose that you are hired by the American Civil Liberties Union (ACLU) to assist it in commenting on the proposed policy, what concerns or objections might the ACLU raise? *See Lynch v. New York City*, 589 F.3d 94 (2d Cir. 2009).

Food for Thought

In *Maryland v. King*, 569 U.S. 435 (2013), the Court suggested that the technology of DNA testing is changing rapidly, and might evolve to the point where DNA can be analyzed very quickly. Suppose that it is now possible to analyze DNA samples in a matter of seconds, and the Transportation Security Administration (TSA) has decided that it would like to test the DNA of all airline passengers in order to more accurately determine the identity of those who are traveling. Can TSA mandate DNA screening, along with presumably checks against governmental DNA data bases, for all airline passengers?

Ferguson v. City of Charleston

532 U.S. 67 (2001).

JUSTICE STEVENS delivered the opinion of the Court.

We must decide whether a state hospital's performance of a diagnostic test to obtain evidence of a patient's criminal conduct for law enforcement purposes is an unreasonable search if the patient has not consented to the procedure. More narrowly, the question is whether the interest in using the threat of criminal sanctions to deter pregnant women from using cocaine can justify a departure from the general rule that an official nonconsensual search is unconstitutional if not authorized by a valid warrant.

In 1988, staff members at the public hospital operated in the city of Charleston by the Medical University of South Carolina (MUSC) became concerned about an increase in the use of cocaine by patients who were receiving prenatal treatment. MUSC began to order drug screens performed on urine samples from maternity patients who were suspected of using cocaine. If a patient tested positive, she was referred to the county substance abuse commission for counseling and treatment. The incidence of cocaine use among the patients at MUSC did not appear to change.

Four months later, Nurse Shirley Brown, case manager for the MUSC obstetrics department, heard that the police were arresting pregnant users of cocaine for child abuse.[6] Nurse Brown discussed the story with MUSC's general counsel who contacted Charleston's Solicitor to offer cooperation in prosecuting mothers whose children tested positive for drugs at birth. Solicitor Condon appointed a task force with representatives of MUSC, the police, the County Substance Abuse Commission and the Department of Social Services. Their deliberations led to MUSC's adoption of a document entitled "POLICY M–7," dealing with the subject of "Management of Drug Abuse During Pregnancy."

The first three pages of Policy M–7 set forth the procedure to be followed by the hospital staff to "identify/assist pregnant patients suspected of drug abuse." The first section, the "Identification of Drug Abusers," provided that a patient should be tested for cocaine through a urine drug screen if she met one or more of nine criteria.[7] It also stated that a chain of custody should be followed when obtaining and testing urine samples to make sure that the results could be used in subsequent criminal proceedings. The policy also provided for education and referral to a substance abuse clinic for patients who tested positive. It added the

---

[6] Under South Carolina law, a viable fetus has been regarded as a person and the ingestion of cocaine during the third trimester of pregnancy constitutes criminal child neglect.

[7] Those criteria were as follows: 1. No prenatal care; 2. Late prenatal care after 24 weeks gestation; 3. Incomplete prenatal care; 4. Abruptio placentae; 5. Intrauterine fetal death; 6. Preterm labor "of no obvious cause"; 7. IUGR intrauterine growth retardation "of no obvious cause"; 8. Previously known drug or alcohol abuse; 9. Unexplained congenital anomalies.

threat of law enforcement intervention which was regarded as essential to the program's success in getting women into treatment and keeping them there.

The threat of law enforcement involvement was set forth in two protocols, the first dealing with the identification of drug use during pregnancy, and the second with identification of drug use after labor. Under the latter protocol, the police were to be notified without delay and the patient promptly arrested. Under the former, after the initial positive drug test, the police were to be notified (and the patient arrested) only if the patient tested positive for cocaine a second time or if she missed an appointment with a substance abuse counselor. In 1990, the policy was modified to give the patient who tested positive during labor, like the patient who tested positive during a prenatal care visit, an opportunity to avoid arrest by consenting to substance abuse treatment.

The policy contained forms for the patients to sign, as well as procedures for the police to follow when a patient was arrested. The policy prescribed the precise offenses with which a woman could be charged. If the pregnancy was 27 weeks or less, the patient was to be charged with simple possession. If it was 28 weeks or more, she was to be charged with possession and distribution to a person under the age of 18, the fetus. If she delivered "while testing positive for illegal drugs," she was also to be charged with unlawful neglect of a child. Under the policy, the police were instructed to interrogate the arrestee in order "to ascertain the identity of the subject who provided illegal drugs to the suspect." The policy made no mention of any change in the prenatal care of such patients, nor did it prescribe any special treatment for the newborns.

Petitioners are women who received obstetrical care at MUSC and who were arrested after testing positive for cocaine. Respondents include the city of Charleston, law enforcement officials, and representatives of MUSC. Petitioners' challenged the validity of the policy under various theories, including the claim that warrantless and nonconsensual drug tests conducted for criminal investigatory purposes were unconstitutional searches. Lower courts found for respondents. We granted certiorari.

Because the hospital seeks to justify its authority to conduct drug tests and to turn the results over to law enforcement agents without the knowledge or consent of the patients, this case differs from the four previous cases in which we have considered whether comparable drug tests "fit within the closely guarded category of constitutionally permissible suspicionless searches." In three of those cases, we sustained drug tests for railway employees involved in train accidents, *Skinner v. Railway Labor Executives' Assn.*, 489 U.S. 602 (1989), for United States Customs Service employees seeking promotion to certain sensitive positions, *Treasury Employees v. Von Raab*, 489 U.S. 656 (1989), and for high school students participating in interscholastic sports, *Vernonia School Dist. 47J v. Acton*, 515 U.S. 646 (1995). In the fourth case, we struck down such testing for candidates for designated state offices as unreasonable. *Chandler v. Miller*, 520 U.S. 305 (1997).

Those cases balanced the intrusion on the individual's interest in privacy against the "special needs" that supported the program. The invasion of privacy in this case is far more substantial. In the previous four cases, there was no misunderstanding about the purpose of the test or the potential use of the test results, and there were protections against the dissemination of the results to third parties. The use of an adverse test result to disqualify one from eligibility for a particular benefit, such as a promotion or an opportunity to participate in an extracurricular activity, involves a less serious intrusion on privacy than the unauthorized dissemination of such results to third parties. The reasonable expectation of privacy enjoyed by the typical patient undergoing diagnostic tests in a hospital is that the results of those tests will not be shared with nonmedical personnel without her consent. In none of our prior cases was there any intrusion upon that kind of expectation.

The critical difference between those four drug-testing cases and this one lies in the nature of the "special need" asserted as justification for the warrantless searches. In the earlier cases, the "special need" was one divorced from the State's general interest in law enforcement. In this case, the central and indispensable feature of the policy was the use of law enforcement to coerce the patients into substance abuse treatment. This fact distinguishes this case from circumstances in which physicians or psychologists, in the course of ordinary medical procedures aimed at helping the patient herself, come across information that under rules of law or ethics is subject to reporting requirements.

Respondents argue that their ultimate purpose—protecting the health of both mother and child—is a beneficent one. In this case, a review of the M–7 policy reveals that the purpose served by the MUSC searches "is indistinguishable from the general interest in crime control." "It is clear that an initial and continuing focus of the policy was on the arrest and prosecution of drug-abusing mothers." The document codifying the policy incorporates the police's operational guidelines. It devotes its attention to the chain of custody, the range of possible criminal charges, and the logistics of police notification and arrests. Nowhere does the document discuss medical treatment for either mother or infant, aside from treatment for the mother's addiction.

Throughout the development and application of the policy, the Charleston prosecutors and police were extensively involved in the day-to-day administration of the policy. Police and prosecutors decided who would receive the reports of positive drug screens and what information would be included with those reports. Law enforcement officials helped determine the procedures to be followed when performing the screens. They had access to medical files on the women who tested positive, routinely attended the substance abuse team's meetings, and regularly received copies of team documents discussing the women's progress. Police took pains to coordinate the timing and circumstances of the arrests with MUSC staff.

While the ultimate goal of the program may well have been to get the women into substance abuse treatment and off of drugs, the immediate objective of the searches was to generate evidence for law enforcement purposes in order to reach that goal.[21]   The threat of law enforcement may ultimately have been intended as a means to an end, but the direct and primary purpose of MUSC's policy was to ensure the use of those means. This distinction is critical. Because law enforcement involvement always serves some broader social purpose or objective, virtually any nonconsensual suspicionless search could be immunized under the special needs doctrine by defining the search solely in terms of its ultimate, rather than immediate, purpose. Such an approach is inconsistent with the Fourth Amendment. Given the primary purpose of the Charleston program, which was to use the threat of arrest and prosecution in order to force women into treatment, and given the extensive involvement of law enforcement officials at every stage of the policy, this case simply does not fit within the closely guarded category of "special needs."[23]

The fact that positive test results were turned over to the police does not merely provide a basis for distinguishing our prior cases applying the "special needs" balancing approach to the determination of drug use. It also provides an affirmative reason for enforcing the strictures of the Fourth Amendment. While state hospital employees, like other citizens, may have a duty to provide the police with evidence of criminal conduct that they inadvertently acquire in the course of routine treatment, when they undertake to obtain such evidence from their patients *for the specific purpose of incriminating those patients*, they have a special obligation to make sure that the patients are fully informed about their constitutional rights, as standards of knowing waiver require.

Respondents motive was benign rather than punitive. Such a motive, however, cannot justify a departure from Fourth Amendment protections, given the pervasive involvement of law enforcement with the development and application of the MUSC policy. While drug abuse is a serious problem, "the gravity of the threat alone cannot be dispositive of questions concerning what means law enforcement officers may employ to pursue a given purpose." The Fourth Amendment's general prohibition against nonconsensual, warrantless, and suspicionless searches necessarily applies to such a policy.

The judgment of the Court of Appeals is reversed, and the case is remanded for further proceedings consistent with this opinion.

---

[21] This case differs from *New York v. Burger*, 482 U.S. 691 (1987), because the discovery of evidence of other violations would have been incidental to the purposes of the administrative search. This policy was specifically designed to gather evidence of violations of penal laws. This case also differs from the roadblock seizure cases which did not involve "intrusive search of the body or the home" and distinguished checkpoints from cases dealing with "special needs."

[23] It is difficult to argue that the program here was designed simply to save lives. *Amici* claim a near consensus in the medical community that programs of the sort at issue, by discouraging women who use drugs from seeking prenatal care, harm, rather than advance, the cause of prenatal health.

It is so ordered.

JUSTICE KENNEDY, concurring in the judgment.

None of our special needs precedents has sanctioned the routine inclusion of law enforcement, both in the design of the policy and in using arrests, either threatened or real, to implement the system designed for the special needs objectives. The traditional warrant and probable-cause requirements are waived on the explicit assumption that the evidence is not intended for law enforcement purposes. While the policy may well have served legitimate needs unrelated to law enforcement, it had as well a penal character with a far greater connection to law enforcement than other searches sustained under our special needs rationale. We recognize the legitimacy of the State's interest in fetal life and of the grave risk to the life and health of the fetus, and later the child, caused by cocaine ingestion. South Carolina can impose punishment upon an expectant mother who has so little regard for her own unborn that she risks causing lifelong damage and suffering.

An essential, distinguishing feature of the special needs cases is that the person searched has consented, though the usual voluntariness analysis is altered because adverse consequences, (e.g., dismissal from employment or disqualification from playing on a high school sports team), will follow from refusal. The consent, and the circumstances in which it was given, bear upon the reasonableness of the whole special needs program.

JUSTICE SCALIA, with whom THE CHIEF JUSTICE and JUSTICE THOMAS join as to Part II, dissenting.

The hospital's reporting of positive drug-test results to police is obviously not a search. At most it may be a "derivative use of the product of a past unlawful search," which "works no new Fourth Amendment wrong" and "presents a question, not of rights, but of remedies."

A search which has been consented to is not unreasonable. There is no contention that the urine samples were extracted forcibly. We have *never* held—or even suggested— that material which a person voluntarily entrusts to someone else cannot be given by that person to the police, and used for whatever evidence it may contain. There is no basis to "distinguish this case from circumstances in which physicians or psychologists, in the course of ordinary medical procedures aimed at helping the patient herself, come across information that is subject to reporting requirements.

Food for Thought

Suppose that you are the legal adviser to MUSC. Following the decision in this case, you are asked for advice about how to establish a constitutionally permissible program for expectant mothers. How would you advise MUSC to proceed?

Hypo 1: *Suspicionless Drug Testing of Welfare Recipients*

Suppose that your state legislature is considering the possibility of requiring welfare recipients, as a condition of receiving government-provided monetary assistance, to submit to suspicionless drug testing. Under the proposed law, when an individual applies for public assistance, he is notified that he will be required to submit to and pay for drug testing as a condition of receiving benefits. If the applicant submits to the drug testing and tests negative, the cost of the test will be reimbursed to the applicant through a one-time increase in benefits. If the applicant tests positive for controlled substances, he is ineligible to receive benefits for one year, but can reapply in six months if he completes a substance abuse treatment program and passes another drug test, both at his own expense. Although an adult applicant who fails the drug test is ineligible for benefits, the applicant's dependent child may still receive benefits so long as the adult designates an appropriate payee to receive the child's benefits. However, the individual who wishes to serve as the payee must also submit to and pass mandatory drug testing to receive benefits for the child. In addition to the mandatory drug test, applicants are required to sign a release acknowledging their consent to be tested. How would you advise the legislature? Is the law valid? *See Lebron v. Secretary,* 710 F.3d 1202 (11th Cir. 2013).

Hypo 2: *The Fire Department Program*

A city fire department adopts a program of random suspicionless drug testing in an effort to control drug and alcohol use among firemen. The Program requires testing of firefighters in four situations: (1) if the Department has reasonable suspicion to believe an individual firefighter has abused drugs or alcohol; (2) after a firefighter is involved in an accident on the job; (3) following a firefighter's return to duty or as a follow-up to "a determination that a covered member is in need of assistance"; and (4) "on an unannounced and random basis spread reasonably throughout the calendar year." Under the program, a computer would select the firefighters to be tested, and the Department would notify firefighters of their selection for random testing immediately before, during, or after work; the firefighters would be tested within thirty minutes of their notification, with allowance for travel time to the laboratory for collection. Once at the laboratory, firefighters would be permitted to use private bathroom stalls when providing urine samples, which are then inspected by a monitor for the proper color and temperature.

A laboratory would test the sample for the presence of marijuana, cocaine, opiates, amphetamines, and phencyclidine. The laboratory would initially test the specimens by using an immunoassay test that meets the requirements of the Food and Drug Administration for commercial distribution. The laboratory would then confirm all positive test results using the gas chromatography/mass spectrometry technique and report positive results to a Medical Review Officer (MRO), who would have a "detailed knowledge of possible alternate medical explanations." The MRO would review the results before giving the information to the Department's administrative official. Only confirmed tests would be reported to the Department as positive for a specific drug. Before verifying a positive result, however, the MRO must contact the firefighter on a confidential basis.

The Department would not release information in a firefighter's drug testing record outside the Department without the firefighter's consent. A firefighter whose test revealed a blood alcohol concentration in excess of that allowed under the Program or who tested positive for any of several specified drugs would be removed from all covered positions and would be evaluated by a substance abuse professional. The Department could discipline or terminate the employment of a firefighter who tested positive a second time or who refused to submit to a required test. According to section 8 of the Program, the primary purpose of the random testing component would be "to deter prohibited alcohol and controlled substance use and to detect prohibited use for the purpose of removing identified users from the safety-sensitive work force." That purpose would advance the City's goal of establishing "a work environment that is totally free of the harmful effects of drugs and the misuse of alcohol." Is the program constitutional?

Hypo 3: *Additional Factors*

In the prior problem, which of the following facts might be determinative regarding the constitutionality of the program:

A. The City asserts that it has a "special need" to test firefighters because they occupy safety-sensitive positions. The City alleges that random testing furthers this interest by deterring "prohibited alcohol and controlled substance use" and detecting "prohibited use for the purpose of removing identified users from the safety-sensitive work force."

B. The fact that the record is devoid of any evidence of even a single instance of drug use among the firefighters to be tested but also of any evidence of accidents, fatalities, injuries, or property damage that can be attributed to drug or alcohol use by the City's firefighters.

C. Can it be argued that it is reasonable to assume that anyone applying for a safety-sensitive position in a heavily regulated field of activity anticipates—and implicitly agrees to—a probing inquiry into the applicant's capacity to perform job-related duties.

Hypo 4: *Required Drug Testing by Juvenile Authorities*

John and Jane Doe's daughter was convicted in juvenile court of petty theft. Since the Does had a history of drug abuse, a court ordered juvenile authorities to conduct regular random drug tests of both John and Jane to make sure that they are not continuing to use drugs. Under the terms of the order, the results of the drug tests are to be shared with the court and the prosecutor. Can the court's order be justified under the special needs exception to the warrant requirement? *See State v. Doe*, 149 Idaho 353, 233 P.3d 1275 (2010).

Hypo 5: *The Conditional Release Program*

Norris is arrested for sexually abusing his stepdaughter, but is ultimately released under a conditional release program. Ky.Rev.Stat. Ann. § 431.064. Under that program persons awaiting trial may be freed if they agree to certain judicially-imposed conditions. To participate in the Program, Norris agreed that he would avoid contact with his stepdaughter and not use illegal drugs or consume alcoholic beverages. He also agreed that he would undergo random drug testing. Premier, a private corporation, conducts pretrial drug testing for the courts. Premier uses a "direct observation" method in obtaining urine samples for testing. Premier requires that a male lower his pants so that its employee may "directly observe the urine coming straight out of the body," and must "allow collector visibility of the participant's genitalia." Kentucky judges view the direct observation method as "essential." Is the testing regime valid? *See Norris v. Premier Integrity Solutions, Inc.*, 641 F.3d 695 (6th Cir. 2011).

Hypo 6: *Post-Conviction Testing*

Following defendant's conviction for a sex offense, the court granted the state's motion to compel defendant to submit to testing for sexually transmitted diseases. The court's stated purpose was to enable the victim of a criminal sexual act to determine if he or she has been, or will be, further victimized by contracting AIDS or other sexually transmitted diseases, and enable a victim to address his or her physical and medical condition in a meaningful way. Regarding defendant's privacy rights, the court noted that any test results could not be used against defendant in criminal proceedings and that, if the test results were positive, the victim has the right to discuss her physical and medical condition with medical providers, friends, family, and potential intimate partners. Is the court's order valid? *See State v. Handy,* 44 A.3d 776 (Vt. 2012).

11. Exigent Circumstances

The police can also dispense with a warrant when they are faced with "exigent circumstances." For example, there is a long line of cases which suggests that the police may make a warrantless entry into a home in order to prevent the imminent destruction of evidence. See, *e.g., Kentucky v. King,* 563 U.S. 452 (2011).

Likewise, it has always been assumed that the police perform a "community caretaking" function which may give them the authority to make a warrantless entry into a private place in order to protect lives or property. For example, when a police officer hears shots followed by cries for help from a nearby apartment, the officer can enter the apartment to render emergency help and assistance. *See McDonald v. United States,* 335 U.S. 451 (1948). Likewise, "a warrant is not required to break down a door to enter a burning home to rescue occupants or extinguish a fire, or to bring emergency aid to an injured person." *See Wayne v. United States,* 318 F.2d 205 (D.C.Cir.1963). Under what other circumstances may police search without a warrant? Consider the following cases.

Take Note

In *Warden v. Hayden,* 387 U.S. 294 (1967), the Court held that the police may make a warrantless entry into a home when they are in "hot pursuit" of a fleeing armed robber: "The exigencies of the situation made a warrantless entry and search imperative. The police were informed that an armed robbery had taken place, and that the suspect had entered the house less than five minutes before they reached it. The Fourth Amendment does not require police officers to delay in the course of an investigation if to do so would gravely endanger their lives or the lives of others." The Court held that the police were also allowed to search the home for weapons: "The permissible scope of a search must, therefore, at the least, be as broad as may reasonably be necessary to prevent the dangers that the suspect at large in the house may resist or escape. The officer who found the clothes in the washing machine knew that the robber was armed and he did not know that some weapons had been found at the time he opened the machine. In these circumstances the inference that he was in fact also looking for weapons is fully justified."

Michigan v. Fisher

558 U.S. 45 (2009).

PER CURIAM.

Police officers responded to a complaint of a disturbance near Allen Road in Brownstown, Michigan. Officer Goolsby testified that, as he and his partner approached the area, a couple directed them to a residence where a man was "going crazy." Upon their arrival, the officers found a household in considerable chaos: a pickup truck in the driveway with its front smashed, damaged fence posts along the side of the property, and three broken house windows, the glass still on the ground outside. The officers also noticed blood on the hood of the pickup and on clothes inside of it, as well as on one of the doors to the house. Through a window, the officers could see respondent, Jeremy Fisher, inside the house, screaming and throwing things. The back door was locked, and a couch had been placed to block the front door.

The officers knocked, but Fisher refused to answer. They saw that Fisher had a cut on his hand, and they asked him whether he needed medical attention. Fisher ignored these questions and demanded, with accompanying profanity, that the officers obtain a search warrant. Officer Goolsby then pushed the front door partway open and ventured into the house. Through the window of the open door he saw Fisher pointing a long gun at him. Officer Goolsby withdrew.

Fisher was charged under Michigan law with assault with a dangerous weapon and possession of a firearm during the commission of a felony. The trial court concluded that Goolsby violated the Fourth Amendment when he entered Fisher's house, and granted Fisher's motion to suppress Goolsby's statement that Fisher pointed a rifle at him. The Michigan Court of Appeals affirmed and the Michigan Supreme Court denied leave to appeal. Because the decision of the Michigan Court of Appeals is contrary to our Fourth Amendment case law, particularly *Brigham City v. Stuart*, 547 U.S. 398 (2006), we grant the State's petition for certiorari and reverse.

"The ultimate touchstone of the Fourth Amendment," we have often said, is "reasonableness." "Searches and seizures inside a home without a warrant are presumptively unreasonable," Groh v. Ramirez, 540 U.S. 551, 559 (2004), but that presumption can be overcome. For example, "the exigencies of the situation may make the needs of law enforcement so compelling that the warrantless search is objectively reasonable." *Mincey v. Arizona*, 437 U.S. 385, 393–394 (1978).

Brigham City v. Stuart, 547 U.S. 398 (2006) identified one such exigency: "the need to assist persons who are seriously injured or threatened with such injury." Thus, law enforcement officers "may enter a home without a warrant to render emergency assistance to an injured occupant or to protect an occupant from imminent injury." This "emergency aid exception" does not depend on the officers' subjective intent or the seriousness of any crime they are investigating when the emergency arises. It requires only "an objectively reasonable basis for believing," that "a person within the house is in need of immediate aid," *Mincey, supra*, at 392.

Brigham City illustrates the application of this standard. Police officers responded to a noise complaint in the early hours of the morning. "As they approached the house, they could hear an altercation occurring, some kind of fight." Following the tumult to the back of the house whence it came, the officers saw juveniles drinking beer in the backyard and a fight unfolding in the kitchen. They watched through the window as a juvenile broke free from the adults restraining him and punched another adult in the face, who recoiled to the sink, spitting blood. Under these circumstances, we found it "plainly reasonable" for the officers to enter the house and quell the violence, for they had "an objectively reasonable basis for believing both that the injured adult might need help and that the violence in the kitchen was just beginning."

A straightforward application of the emergency aid exception dictates that the officer's entry in this case was reasonable. As in *Brigham City*, the police officers here were responding to a report of a disturbance. Just as in *Brigham City*, when they arrived on the scene they encountered a tumultuous situation in the house-and they also found signs of a recent injury, perhaps from a car accident, outside. As in *Brigham City*, the officers could see violent behavior inside. Although Officer Goolsby and his partner did not see punches thrown, as did the officers in *Brigham City*, they did see Fisher screaming and throwing things. It would be objectively reasonable to believe that Fisher's projectiles might have a human target (perhaps a spouse or a child), or that Fisher would hurt himself in the course of his rage. We find it as plain here as we did in *Brigham City* that the officer's entry was reasonable under the Fourth Amendment.

The Michigan Court of Appeals, however, thought the situation "did not rise to a level of emergency justifying the warrantless intrusion into a residence." Although the court conceded that "there was evidence an injured person was on the premises," it found it significant that "the mere drops of blood did not signal a likely serious, life-threatening injury." The court added that the cut Officer Goolsby observed on Fisher's hand "likely explained the trail of blood" and that Fisher "was very much on his feet and apparently able to see to his own needs."

Officers do not need ironclad proof of "a likely serious, life-threatening" injury to invoke the emergency aid exception. The only injury police could confirm in *Brigham City* was the bloody lip they saw the juvenile inflict upon the adult. Fisher argues that the officers here could not have been motivated by a perceived need to provide medical assistance, since they never summoned emergency medical personnel. This would have no bearing, of course, upon their need to assure that Fisher was not endangering someone else in the house. Moreover, even if the failure to summon medical personnel conclusively established that Goolsby did not subjectively believe, when he entered the house, that Fisher or someone else was seriously injured (which is doubtful), the test is not what Goolsby believed, but whether there was "an objectively reasonable basis for believing" that medical assistance was needed, or persons were in danger, *Brigham City, supra*, at 406; *Mincey, supra*, at 392.

It was error for the Michigan Court of Appeals to replace that objective inquiry into appearances with its hindsight determination that there was in fact no emergency. It does not meet the needs of law enforcement or the demands of public safety to require officers to walk away from a situation like the one they encountered here. Only when an apparent threat has become an actual harm can officers rule out innocuous explanations for ominous circumstances. "The role of a peace officer includes preventing violence and restoring order, not simply rendering first aid to casualties." *Brigham City, supra*, at 406. It sufficed to invoke the emergency aid exception that it was reasonable to believe that Fisher had hurt himself (albeit nonfatally) and needed treatment that in his rage he was unable to provide, or that Fisher was about to hurt, or had already hurt, someone else.

The petition for certiorari is granted. The judgment of the Michigan Court of Appeals is reversed, and the case is remanded for further proceedings not inconsistent with this opinion.

It is so ordered.

JUSTICE STEVENS, with whom JUSTICE SOTOMAYOR joins, dissenting.

A warrantless entry is justified by the "need to protect or preserve life or avoid serious injury." *Mincey v. Arizona, supra,* at 392. The State bears the burden of proof on that factual issue. Goolsby was not sure about certain facts—such as whether Fisher had a cut on his hand-but he did remember that Fisher repeatedly swore at the officers and told them to get a warrant, and that Fisher was screaming and throwing things. Goolsby also testified that he saw "mere drops" of blood outside Fisher's home. Goolsby did not testify that he had any reason to believe that anyone else was in the house. The factual question was whether Goolsby had "an objectively reasonable basis for believing that Fisher was seriously injured or imminently threatened with such injury." The trial judge found the police decision to leave the scene and not return for several hours-without resolving any potentially dangerous situation and without calling for medical assistance-inconsistent with a reasonable belief that Fisher was in need of immediate aid. In sum, the one judge who heard Goolsby's testimony was not persuaded that Goolsby had an objectively reasonable basis for believing that entering Fisher's home was necessary to avoid serious injury. We ought not usurp the role of the fact finder when faced with a close question of the reasonableness of an officer's actions, particularly in a case tried in a state court.

In *United States v. Santana*, 427 U.S. 38 (1976), after an undercover drug buy, the police went to "Mom" Santana's home to arrest her (Santana had provided drugs to the seller), and found her standing in the doorway with a brown paper bag in her hand. When the officers shouted "police," and displayed their identification, Santana retreated into her house. The officers followed through the open door and caught her in the vestibule. As she tried to pull away, the bag tilted and "two bundles of glazed paper packets with a white powder" fell to the floor. The Court upheld the entry into the house: " 'Hot pursuit' means some sort of a chase, but it need not be an extended hue and cry 'in and about the public streets.' The fact that the pursuit here ended almost as soon as it began did not render it any the less a 'hot pursuit' sufficient to justify the warrantless entry into Santana's house. Once Santana saw the police, there was likewise a realistic expectation that any delay would result in destruction of evidence. Once she had been arrested the search, incident to that arrest, which produced the drugs and money was clearly justified."

Points for Discussion

a. More on the Emergency Exception

In *Ryburn v. Huff,* 565 U.S. 469 (2012), police officers responded to a call for distress from a high school, and learned that a student was rumored to have written a letter threatening to "shoot up" the school. Because of the threat, many parents had decided to keep their children at home. While interviewing students, the police learned that the student in question (Vincent) had been absent from school for two days and that he was frequently subjected to bullying. The officers had received training on targeted school violence and were aware that these characteristics are common among perpetrators of school shootings. As a result, the officers decided to interview the student at his home. When no one responded to a knock on the door, or to a phone call, the police called the mother's cell phone and learned that she and Vincent were inside the house. The mother and Vincent then came out of the house, but refused a police request to discuss the matter inside the house. When asked about whether there were any guns inside the house, the mother responded by "immediately turning around and running into the house." One of the officers, who was "scared because he didn't know what was in that house" and had "seen too many officers killed," entered the house behind her. Other officers, concerned for the first officer's safety, also entered the house. The officers ultimately concluded that the rumor was unfounded and left the house. The student and his family brought an action under 42 U.S.C. § 1983. The Court rejected the suit, concluding that a reasonable police officer could have construed *Brigham City* as allowing an officer to enter a residence if the officer has a reasonable basis for concluding that there is an imminent threat of violence. The Court noted that the district court found that the police had an objectively reasonable basis for reaching such a conclusion.

Take Note

In *Kentucky v. King*, 563 U.S. 452 (2011), the Court rejected the position, adopted by some courts, that the exigent circumstances exception did not apply when the police "deliberately created the exigent circumstances with the bad faith intent to avoid the warrant requirement." The police made a warrantless entry into a home after they heard the occupants attempting to destroy evidence (drugs). The case was complicated by the fact that the police chose to knock on the door of the residence and announce their presence. When they did, the occupants engaged in hurried activities suggesting that they were trying to destroy evidence. As a result, the Court was presented with the question of whether the police could invoke the exigent circumstances exception when their conduct precipitated the evidence destruction (a so-called "police created exigency"). The Court upheld the entry and search: "Where, as here, the police did not create the exigency by engaging or threatening to engage in conduct that violates the Fourth Amendment, warrantless entry to prevent the destruction of evidence is reasonable and thus allowed." The Court refused to focus on the subjective intentions of the police officers, choosing instead to focus on whether the police conduct was objectively justifiable. Even if the police have probable cause to obtain a warrant, they are not required to do so, but may proceed without a warrant so long as they do not violate the law. The Court held that the officers were entitled to knock on the door and announce their presence. If the occupants of the premises respond by attempting to destroy evidence, the police may make an immediate warrantless entry: "Occupants who choose not to stand on their constitutional rights but instead elect to attempt to destroy evidence have only themselves to blame for the warrantless exigent-circumstances search that may ensue."

Food for Thought

In *Evans v. Commonwealth*, 290 Va. 277, 776 S.E.2d 760 (2015), police officers are on patrol when they notice a marijuana smell emanating from an apartment. The officers stop, knock on the door, and explain their suspicions to a woman who opens the door. The woman denies that anyone is smoking marijuana and immediately slams the door. The officers then hear movement inside the apartment. Do exigent circumstances justify a warrantless entry into the apartment?

b. Homicide Scenes

In *Flippo v. West Virginia*, 528 U.S. 11 (1999), after Flippo's wife was found dead at a cabin in a state park, and Flippo was taken to a hospital (he claimed that he and his wife had been attacked), officers returned and searched the cabin where the two had been staying. In the cabin, they found photographs that were later used at Flippo's trial. The Court rejected the argument that the police had an automatic right to make a warrantless search of a "homicide crime scene."

c. Political Assassination

In *People v. Sirhan*, 7 Cal.3d 710, 102 Cal.Rptr. 385, 497 P.2d 1121 (1972), after Senator Robert Kennedy was murdered, the police took Sirhan Sirhan into custody, and searched his home where they found several items that were ultimately used against him (e.g., pages from his notebooks and an envelope). The court upheld the search: "The officers believed that there might be a conspiracy to assassinate political leaders in this country and that prompt action on their part was necessary. Their beliefs were entirely reasonable. The crime was one of enormous gravity. The victim was a major presidential candidate, and a crime of violence had already been committed against him. Although the officers did not have reasonable cause to believe that the house contained evidence of a conspiracy to assassinate prominent political leaders, the mere possibility that there might be such evidence in the house fully warranted the officers'

Food for Thought

Police receive a tip that there is "a dead body in apartment 618 of the Rhode Island Avenue Plaza." The police knock repeatedly and identify themselves as police officers. After ten minutes of knocking and identifying themselves, the police enter the apartment and find the body. Was it permissible for the police to enter without a warrant on the report of a "dead body?" How might the owner of the premises argue that the entry was improper? How might the state respond? What if the police had received a report of an "unconscious" rather than a "dead" body? *See Wayne v. United States*, 318 F.2d 205, 115 U.S.App.D.C. 234 (D.C.Cir.1963).

actions. It is not difficult to envisage what would have been the effect on this nation if several more political assassinations had followed that of Senator Kennedy. Today when assassinations of persons of prominence have repeatedly been committed in this country, it is essential that law enforcement officers be allowed to take fast action in their endeavors to combat such crimes."

Hypo 1: *The "Foaming" Driver*

The police find Dunavan in a disabled car foaming at the mouth and unable to talk. The police remove Dunavan, send him to the hospital, and search the car for identification. The search reveals a Social Security card, $961 in cash, a motel key, a car rental agreement and two locked briefcases. Fearing for Dunavan's safety, and hopeful that they can find medical information, the police enter Dunavan's motel room and find two small keys which fit the briefcases. While there, the police are told that Dunavan is a diabetic and that he keeps insulin in one of the briefcases. Both briefcases are opened. The first is full of money, banded with Green Hills Branch Bank bands (that bank had been robbed earlier that day), marked with red dye and smelling of gas. The dye and gas result from a bank anti-robbery device. In the second brief case, the police find insulin and a syringe, along with a lot more money marked like the money in the first case. Based on the evidence found in the two briefcases, the police charge Dunavan with the bank robbery. Dunavan moves to suppress the evidence. Can the police justify the search under the community caretaking exception? How might Dunavan argue that the exception does not apply? *See United States v. Dunavan*, 485 F.2d 201 (6th Cir. 1973).

Food for Thought

Police receive an anonymous telephone call from a payphone, indicating that a man is beating a woman in a nearby house, and that the neighbors can hear loud screams coming from the house. The police respond, but find that the house is all quiet. They knock on both the front door and the back door, but no one answers the door. Having a "gut feeling" that someone in the house is in need of assistance, the police enter the house where they find a woman who has been severely beaten. The woman is rushed to the hospital where she dies. Did the police have sufficient proof that someone was in need of immediate police assistance to justify entering the house without a warrant? *See Commonwealth v. Davido*, 106 A.3d 611 (Penn. 2014).

Hypo 2: *The Light in the Vacant House*

Police respond to a call indicating that the lights are on in a house which is believed to be vacant. The police enter the house, believing that a burglary might be in progress, in order to investigate. Inside, while conducting a protective sweep, the police discover marijuana plants growing in the basement. Can the entry and the search be justified under the community caretaking exception? *See United States v. McClain*, 430 F.3d 299 (6th Cir. 2005).

Food for Thought

On a winter evening, a police officer observes a jeep with its headlights on parked in a "pull off" adjacent to the westbound lane of travel, but facing east. The car is eight feet from the edge of the roadway. It is a dark, cold night and there is snow on the ground, but the road markings are visible. The officer believes that it is "unusual" to see a car parked in such a manner. In addition, the officer recently covered a fatal motor vehicle accident in which a vehicle parked similarly to the defendant's was a contributing factor, and he believes that the manner in which the Jeep is parked violates state law. The officer stops "to check things out." He pulls behind the Jeep and activates his cruiser's blue lights and spotlight in order to alert occupants of the vehicle and other motorists to his presence. He does not know whether the vehicle is occupied, whether an accident has occurred, or whether any potential occupants need assistance. When he approaches the Jeep, he observes two men in the front seat and asks the passenger to lower his window. The officer then smells the odor of marijuana emanating from the vehicle, and charges the occupants with possession of drugs. Was the officer justified in his actions? See *State v. Boutin*, 161 N.H. 139, 13 A.3d 334 (2010).

Hypo 3: *Sleeping in Residence*

A police officer receives an anonymous tip that two people "Big Boy" and "Amalia" are sleeping at a residence, that cocaine, money and a digital scale are next to them, and that the rear door to the residence is open. The officer goes to the residence, finds the door open, knocks, and announces his presence. After waiting 45 seconds and receiving no response, the officer enters the residence. He wants "to make sure that the occupants are not crime victims, are not injured, and have not been subject to a home invasion or robbery. After entry, the officer can see a bedroom directly to his left with the door open and two people inside who "appear to be sleeping." The officer enters the bedroom "just to see if he can wake the occupants" and again loudly announces himself as the police. Neither of the occupants responds. The officer physically shakes the man to wake him. In plain view, the officer sees cocaine, crack cocaine, marijuana and a digital scale. The officer arrests the man and seizes a gun from underneath the mattress on which the man was sleeping. Can the entry and search be justified under the "community caretaking" theory? Can it be justified on some other basis? *See State v. Pinkard*, 327 Wis.2d 346, 785 N.W.2d 592 (2010).

Food for Thought

When a police officer sees an individual commit a traffic violation, he turns on his lights and siren intending to pull the driver over. The driver flees. Eventually, the driver arrives at a residence, quickly exits the vehicle, and enters the home. Under the hot pursuit doctrine, is the officer entitled to make a warrantless entry into the house? Should it matter that there is no indication that the fleeing individual is dangerous, or is about to destroy evidence? See *Trent v. Wade*, 776 F.3d 368 (5th Cir. 2015).

Hypo 4: *Arrested at Home*

Police receive a 911 call from a neighbor indicating that the owners of a nearby house are at work and that a white male wearing a black jacket and carrying a red backpack has scaled their fence and entered their backyard. Officers, responding to the call, enter the backyard of the private home without a warrant (one scales the fence and another kicks open a padlocked gate). Before doing so, the officers see that a red backpack is lying against a porch in the backyard, and that a white male (wearing a black jacket) is present in the yard. However, they see no signs of forced entry into the house. When the officers order the man to get down on the ground, the man responds that he lives at the house. As it turns out, he does, but the officers verify that fact only after they arrest the man and search his backpack, finding an unloaded handgun. By that point, the officers have also learned that the man is a felon. Did the police act properly in entering the backyard, in seizing the man, and in searching his backpack? *See United States v. Struckman*, 603 F.3d 731 (9th Cir. 2010).

Hypo 5: *The Static 911 Call*

When a 911 dispatcher receives a phone call from a residence that contains nothing but static, the dispatcher tries unsuccessfully to return the call, and then sends two police officers to the residence to investigate. The officers arrive twenty-six minutes after the 911 call at the house which is located in a rural area on a secluded lot. When the officers arrive, the gate to the property is closed, but they walk through an opening next to the gate. They repeatedly knock on the front door and announce their presence, but they receive no response. The officers inspect the perimeter of the house and look into the windows, but see no signs of forced entry and they cannot see nor hear anyone inside. The officers then walk up an exterior staircase to a second-floor balcony. There, they find a closed but unlocked sliding glass door. Through the glass, they can see some electronics boxes near the door and they notice that the house looks disheveled. The officers open the sliding glass door and announce their presence. They receive no response. The officers enter through the door and conduct a sweep of the house "to ensure that no one was injured, unconscious, or deceased." During the search, they see drugs and drug paraphernalia in plain view. Did the officers act properly in entering the house? *See United States v. Martinez*, 643 F.3d 1292 (10th Cir. 2011).

Food for Thought

A woman, on returning to her apartment finds a bullet hole in a wall that she shares with her neighbor, and calls 911. The responding police knock on the neighbor's door, but nobody responds. May the police break into the adjoining apartment to make sure that everyone is ok? *See United States v. Timmann*, 741 F.3d 1170 (11th Cir. 2013).

Food for Thought

A woman is involved in an automobile collision which causes her car to roll over. Before the police arrive, the woman's husband arrives and drives her away. The police, worried that the woman may have been seriously injured because of the severity of the crash, decide to go to her home to make sure that she is ok. If nobody answers the door, may the police make a warrantless entry to check on the woman's well-being? *See State v. Saale*, 204 P.3d 1220 (Mont. 2009).

Hypo 6: *Flipping Off the Police Officer*

John and Judy were driving to the home of Judy's son with John in the passenger seat. As they approach an intersection, John sees a police officer using a radar device to track the speed of vehicles. John expresses his displeasure by reaching his right arm outside the passenger side window and extending his middle finger over the car's roof. Judy is not speeding or committing any other traffic violation. The officer follows with lights flashing. The officer claims that he initiated the stop because he felt that John was trying to get his attention, that there might be a problem in the car, and that he just wanted to "assure the safety of the passengers." The officer also indicated that he was concerned for the safety of the female driver because there might have been a "domestic dispute." Was the stop reasonable under the Fourth Amendment? *See Swartz v. Insogna*, 704 F.3d 105 (2d Cir. 2013).

Food for Thought

Vargas resided in a second-floor apartment. With his rent five days overdue, Vargas' landlord made several unsuccessful attempts to contact him by knocking on the door and leaving voice messages. Other tenants told the landlord that they had not seen Vargas for "several days" to "a week," that a bag of trash had been left on Vargas's front porch, and that Vargas's Jaguar convertible had not been moved. Ten days later, the landlord found Vargas's Jaguar still unmoved, covered in pollen, with its rear tires deflated, Vargas's mailbox was full, and the landlord's earlier letter had not been removed. The landlord again knocked on Vargas's door and called Vargas' phone without any response. At this point, the landlord called 9-1-1 and explained the situation. Police officers were dispatched to the scene for a "welfare check," and peered through a window but saw no one. With the landlord's help, the officers entered Vargas's apartment because they "had reasons to fear for his safety." Can the officers justify the entry under their "community caretaking" function? *See State v. Vargas*, 213 N.J. 301, 63 A.3d 175 (2013).

Hypo 7: *Offering Assistance*

Just after midnight, a police officer sees a vehicle pull off of the road and come to a stop on the shoulder of the road. In the area, there are only a few businesses, no houses, and only one traffic light. Believing that the driver needs assistance, the officer activates both his front-facing and rear-facing overhead red and blue lights to notify the driver that it is the police and not "some bad guy" who has pulled in behind him. The officer's sole reason for stopping is "to see if the driver had a problem or maybe was lost" and "to see if he needed assistance." The driver begins to drive away, but quickly stops. The officer stops the vehicle, notices a strong odor of alcohol coming from the vehicle, and notices that the driver's eyes are bloodshot and his speech slurred. Did the officer act properly in stopping the vehicle? *See Gonzales v. State*, 369 S.W.3d 851 (Tex. Crim. App. 2012).

Food for Thought

Suppose that anti-abortion protestors drive on city streets with trucks that depict large photos of aborted fetuses. Because of the potentially offensive nature of the material, the protestors cover the photos with tarps when going to and from protest sites. In addition, because of the potential for violence at protest sites, the protestors wear helmets and kevlar vests. A police officer on routine patrol happens to observe the trucks (covered by tarps) being driven by individuals with helmets and kevlar vests. Fearing a terrorist strike, the police officer decides to stop the trucks and search them. Did the officer act properly? See *Center for Bio-Ethical Reform, Inc. v. Springboro*, 477 F.3d 807 (6th Cir. 2007).

Take Note

In *Minnesota v. Olson*, 495 U.S. 91 (1990), following a robbery at a gasoline station, during which the station manager was fatally shot, the police apprehend the individual who actually killed the manager, but an accomplice escaped. Using information obtained from the get-away vehicle, police ascertained the name of the accomplice (Olson). The next day, the police received a tip which stated where Olson was staying and indicated that he was about to leave town. Police surrounded the residence, phoned, and asked Olson to come out. The detective heard a male voice say, "tell them I left." At that point, the police entered the house, with guns drawn, to arrest Olson. At the police station, Olson made an inculpatory statement. The Court concluded that the police did not have exigent circumstances for entering the house without a warrant: "Although a grave crime was involved, respondent 'was known not to be the murderer but thought to be the driver of the getaway car,' and the police had already recovered the murder weapon." The police knew that the women with the suspect were under no threat of danger. Police squads surrounded the house. The time was 3 p.m., Sunday. It was evident the suspect was going nowhere. If he came out of the house he would have been promptly apprehended."

In *Vale v. Louisiana*, 399 U.S. 30 (1970), officers possessed a warrant for Vale's arrest and had information that he was residing at a particular place. After surveilling the house, the officers observed a car drive up and sound the horn. Vale, who was known to the officers, came out of the house and had a brief conversation with the driver. After looking up and down the street, he returned to the house and reappeared a few minutes later. He again looked up and down the street, went to the car, and leaned through the window. The officers were convinced that a narcotics sale was taking place. They immediately drove toward Vale. As he saw them, he turned and walked quickly toward the house. The officers called for Vale to stop as he reached the front steps of the house. Once the officers subdued Vale, they told him that they were going to search the house. After entering, the officers made a cursory inspection to ascertain if anyone else was present. At that point, Mrs. Vale and James Vale, mother and brother of defendant, returned home carrying groceries and were informed of the arrest and impending search. The search of a rear bedroom revealed a quantity of narcotics. The Court held that the search could not be justified under the "exigent circumstances" exception: "The officers were not responding to an emergency. They were not in hot pursuit of a fleeing felon. The goods ultimately seized were not in the process of destruction. Nor were they about to be removed from the jurisdiction. The officers were able to procure two warrants for Vale's arrest. They also had information that he was residing at the address where they found him. There is thus no reason to suppose that it was impracticable for them to obtain a search warrant as well. We decline to hold that an arrest on the street can provide its own 'exigent circumstance' so as to justify a warrantless search of the arrestee's house." Mr. Justice Black dissented: "Vale's arrest took place near the house, and anyone observing from inside would surely have been alerted to destroy the stocks of contraband which the police believed Vale had left there. The police were faced with the choice of risking the immediate destruction of evidence or entering the house and conducting a search. I cannot say that their decision to search was unreasonable."

Hypo 8: *The Screams*

Early afternoon, police officers hear screams coming from a nearby hotel. An officer determines that the screams are coming from room #7, and knocks on that door. When a male voice inquires as to who is knocking, the officers answer "the police." After several repetitions of this exchange a woman opens the door. The woman and another woman, the lessee of the room, state that they do not know of any cause for the screams, and one woman states that she might have had a nightmare. The officers then hear the flushing of a toilet in the bathroom, and see defendant emerge from the bathroom in his undershorts. An officer immediately enters the bathroom, observes pieces of currency floating in the commode, and retrieves them. The officer then pulls the chain of the water closet and recovers additional pieces of currency which have floated to the surface. Did the officer have sufficient cause to enter the bathroom and observe the commode? *See United States v. Barone*, 330 F.2d 543 (2d Cir. 1964).

Food for Thought

Aware (based on a tip) that Hendrix is selling drugs from his house, two officers stake out the house while another officer telephones the residence. The telephoning officer asks for "Hendrix," receives an affirmative response, and warns him that the police are on their way to the house with a search warrant. The lights in the house go off, and there is a great deal of activity within the house for three or four minutes, then the lights come back on. Hendrix exits the residence, jumps in his Lincoln Continental, and drives away. An officer follows the Lincoln which travels a short distance and turns into a driveway on another street. Did the officer have adequate cause to stop Hendrix and search the vehicle? How would you argue the case for the State? How might Hendrix respond?

Food for Thought

In the prior Food for Thought, suppose that the officer did not stop the vehicle and search it, but rather simply followed it. He sees Hendrix stop and hurriedly exit. The officer goes to the car, peers in, and sees a set of scales commonly used for weighing cocaine, a lock box, a large suitcase, and a bottle of Inositol powder (used to dilute cocaine). The officer then enters the car, opens the suitcase and finds weapons inside. When he removes the scales and lock box from the back seat he observes a plastic bag of cocaine. A search warrant is subsequently obtained to open the lock box which contains a larger quantity of cocaine in plastic bags. Did the officer act properly? *See State v. Hendrix,* 782 S.W.2d 833 (Tenn.1989).

Hypo 9: *The Disturbance*

Just after midnight, two police officers respond to a disturbance call at an apartment where there is yelling, screaming, and the sounds of objects being thrown. When they knock, a woman opens the door, appearing to be "extremely distraught and highly intoxicated," stumbling as she walks, and speaking in a slurred manner. However, she does not seem to have any injuries. The woman denies that there has been domestic violence, and states that she threw things because she discovered that her boyfriend was seeing other women. She states further that he is not there and she does not know where he has gone. The woman does state that there are babies in the apartment. During these events, the woman repeatedly asks the police to leave. Eventually, the woman is more emphatic: "Get out of my f * * * ing house!" The police refuse to leave because there is evidence of "a disturbance," even though there are no signs of injury, and the officers feel that they should investigate in order to ensure the safety of any babies in the apartment, and should run a warrant check on the woman. While they remain, the police observe a small, burned marijuana cigarette and arrest the woman. The officers search further and find two baggies containing traces of a white powdery substance. Did the officers act properly in refusing to leave the residence under these circumstances? *See Miller v. State,* 393 S.W.3d 255 (Tex. Crim. App. 2012).

Hypo 10: *Applying the "Community Caretaking" Exception*

A police officer is on patrol when he spots a dirt bike on the side of the road. He writes down the bike's vehicle identification number, enters the VIN in a computer, and drives away. When he learns that the bike is stolen, he returns to the scene, but the bike is gone. Later that day, he spots the same bike being ridden by an unknown male. Later, when he spots the bike in the back of a house, he walks around to the front yard and notices that the front door is open. He also sees candlelight through a boarded-up window on the first floor. The officer believes that the house is abandoned because it is in a state of severe disrepair, the backyard is full of trash, there are "boards on the door and the windows," the yard is covered in weeds and generally untended, there is nothing covering the windows on the second floor, and the two first floor windows on the front of the house are boarded up with plywood, and the front door is unlocked and ajar. The officer walks in the front door without knocking or announcing his presence. Inside the house, the officer finds Harrison with a gun, scales, pills, and cocaine base on the table next to him. Harrison lives at another address, but pays the owner for the use of the house and has the key in his possession. Did the officer act properly in entering the house? *See United States v. Harrison*, 689 F.3d 301 (3rd Cir. 2012).

Hypo 11: *The 911 Call*

Early one morning, Infante called 911 to request that an ambulance be sent to his house. He explains that he just severed the tip of his finger and lacerated the side of his hand when a propane tank exploded. Infante affirms that he is home alone. Asked whether anything is still burning or smoldering, he replies, "No, it just went bang big time." Infante states that he is out of danger and is securing his home because he is going out. The dispatcher advises him that help is on the way, and broadcasts a regional "fire call and rescue" regarding "a propane explosion" at the address where a "male, by himself, has a large cut, and finger amputated." Infante decides not to wait for an ambulance and drives himself to the hospital. Nevertheless, the fire department responds and sees Infante driving with his warning lights on. When they persuade Infante to stop for medical assistance, the paramedics observe that Infante has superficial "shrapnel" wounds and a hand wrapped in a bloody towel. A paramedic unwraps the towel and provides medical assistance. Afterwards, Infante gets in his car and leaves. Firemen nevertheless proceed to the site of the explosion.

Finding no signs of an explosion on the outside, they call the 911 dispatcher who states that Infante indicated that the explosion had occurred inside from a butane lighter. From the window, the officers see blood inside the house. The firemen decide to enter the house to search for the source of the explosion, and to "make sure there were no other hazards to the homeowner or the public." By this time, about one hour had elapsed since the original 911 call. Following the trail of blood down the cellar stairs, they observed marijuana plants and plant growing equipment, and continue to search for the source of the explosion. They eventually find three pipe-bombs under an upside down hubcap. The officers immediately exit the house and call the police. Did the fireman act properly in entering the house under these circumstances? *See United States v. Infante*, 701 F.3d 386 (1st Cir. 2012).

Hypo 12: *Child Safety*

Lopez, an investigator with a state's Department of Family Services goes to investigate allegations of marijuana use at Turrubiate's home. Erin Guller, Turrubiate's girlfriend, and her six-month old child, also live there. When the investigator knocks, Turrubiate cracks the door open, and Lopez notices a strong odor of marijuana emanating from the home. Turrubiate claims that Guller and her child are not at home. Lopez immediately contacts his supervisor and the sheriff's department, and informs them that the home smells like marijuana. When Lopez returns with a police officer to investigate, and Turrubiate opens the door, Lopez again smells "a strong, fresh odor of marijuana" and determines that entry is required to "prevent the marijuana from being destroyed" while he obtains a warrant. As a result, Lopez and the officer forcibly enter the home, point a taser gun at Turribate, handcuff him, and place him on the floor. They then search Turribate and the surrounding area for weapons, finding marijuana in Turribate's backpack. Were there sufficient exigent circumstances to justify a warrantless entry into the home? Is it relevant that Turrubiate did not destroy the marijuana after Lopez's initial visit? *See Turrubiate v. State*, 399 S.W.3d 147 (Tex. Crim. App. 2013).

Hypo 13: *Gunshots*

Late one evening, police respond to a caller who reports hearing a series of gunshots. Over a dozen officers arrive, and they learn that a person has been shot in the leg and taken to the hospital. The officers remain in the neighborhood until about 4 a.m. Schmidt lives nearby in a house that shares a backyard with another duplex. The front and back of the duplexes are almost entirely enclosed by chain-link fences with "No Trespassing" signs, chain-link gates, and a wooden fence. About 1:00 a.m., an investigating officer approaches the duplex from the back alley. He notices bullet holes in a car parked on a concrete slab adjacent to the backyard and bullet holes in the duplex itself. He also notices a trail of about nine spent casings on the ground, including five casings right next to the duplex and one casing in the yard. The chain-link gate on the back alley side is open, and the officer, without a warrant, enters the backyard and pans the area with his flashlight. Does the officer have the right to enter the property in order to investigate? *See United States v. Schmidt*, 700 F.3d 934 (7th Cir. 2012).

Hypo 14: *More on Community Caretaking*

Suppose that the police are dispatched to a house based on a report of a need for medical care. When they arrive, they find a blood spattered door and find a man who is covered in blood. They arrange an ambulance to take the man to the hospital. After the ambulance departs, the officers go to the back door of the house where they find more blood, and a blood trail that leads to a nearby house. The officers find blood on the door of that residence, and they hear loud noises coming from inside. The officers then call for backup. When the backup arrives, they enter the home to check on the residents. Seeing blood on the stairs, the officers continue upstairs where they find a door covered in blood. The officers demand entry and find a marijuana plant. Can the officers' actions be justified under the community caretaking doctrine? *See State v. Matalonis*, 2016 WI 7, 875 N.W.2d 567 (2016).

Food for Thought

During a bank robbery, a GPS device is inserted into a bag of stolen money. Tracking the GPS, the police receive tracking information suggesting that the tracker is somewhere on a block where 92 vehicles are located. May the police block off the road, question the owners of all vehicles on the street, and bring in a tracking device to determine which vehicle has the GPS device? *See United States v. Paetsch*, 782 F.3d 1162 (10th Cir. 2015).

Food for Thought

Receiving a report from a landlord that he was unable to awaken defendant, who was unresponsive, the police enter the apartment to make sure that defendant is okay. After they enter, he wakes up and appears to be fine. Must they police leave or can they investigate further? What if they do not investigate further, but do see contraband lying in plain view. *See State v. Neighbors*, 328 P.3d 1081 (Kan. 2014).

Rochin v. California

342 U.S. 165 (1952).

MR. JUSTICE FRANKFURTER delivered the opinion of the Court.

Having "information that petitioner was selling narcotics," deputy sheriffs of the County of Los Angeles, went to the two-story dwelling house in which Rochin lived. Finding the outside door open, they entered and then forced open the door to Rochin's room on the second floor. Inside they found petitioner sitting partly dressed on the side of the bed, upon which his wife was lying. On a "night stand" beside the bed the deputies spied two capsules. When asked "Whose stuff is this?" Rochin seized the capsules and put them in his mouth. A struggle ensued during which the officers attempted to extract the capsules. The force they applied proved unavailing against Rochin's resistance. He was handcuffed and taken to a hospital. At the direction of one of the officers a doctor forced an emetic solution through a tube into Rochin's stomach against his will. This "stomach pumping" produced vomiting. In the vomited matter were found two capsules which proved to contain morphine.

Regard for the requirements of the Due Process Clause "inescapably imposes upon this Court an exercise of judgment upon the whole course of the proceedings (resulting in a conviction) in order to ascertain whether they offend those canons of decency and fairness which express the notions of justice of English-speaking peoples even toward those charged with the most heinous offenses."

These standards of justice are not authoritatively formulated anywhere as though they were specifics. Due process of law is a summarized constitutional guarantee of respect for those personal immunities which, as Mr. Justice Cardozo twice wrote for the Court, are "so rooted in the traditions and conscience of our people as to be ranked as fundamental", or are "implicit in the concept of ordered liberty". *Palko v. State of Connecticut*, 302 U.S. 319.

The vague contours of the Due Process Clause do not leave judges at large. We may not draw on our merely personal and private notions and disregard the limits that bind judges in their judicial function. Even though the concept of due process of law is not final and fixed, these limits are derived from considerations that are fused in the whole nature of or judicial process. *See* CARDOZO, THE NATURE OF THE JUDICIAL PROCESS; THE GROWTH OF THE LAW; THE PARADOXES OF LEGAL SCIENCE. These are considerations deeply rooted in reason and in the compelling traditions of the legal profession. The Due Process Clause places upon this Court the duty of exercising a judgment, within the narrow confines of judicial power in reviewing State convictions, upon interests of society pushing in opposite directions.

Due process of law thus conceived is not to be derided as resort to a revival of "natural law." To believe that this judicial exercise of judgment could be avoided by freezing "due process of law" at some fixed stage of time or thought is to suggest that the most important aspect of constitutional adjudication is a function for inanimate machines and not for judges, for whom the independence safeguarded by Article III of the Constitution was designed and who are presumably guided by established standards of judicial behavior.

Applying these general considerations to the present case, we are compelled to conclude that the proceedings by which this conviction was obtained do more than offend some fastidious squeamishness or private sentimentalism about combating crime too energetically. This is conduct that shocks the conscience. Illegally breaking into the privacy of the petitioner, the struggle to open his mouth and remove what was there, the forcible extraction of his stomach's contents—this course of proceeding by agents of government to obtain evidence is bound to offend even hardened sensibilities. They are methods too close to the rack and the screw to permit of constitutional differentiation.

On the facts of this case the conviction of the petitioner has been obtained by methods that offend the Due Process Clause. The judgment below must be reversed.

Reversed.

MR. JUSTICE BLACK, concurring.

If the Due Process Clause does vest this Court with such unlimited power to invalidate laws, I am still in doubt as to why we should consider only the notions of English-speaking peoples to determine what are immutable and fundamental principles of justice. One may well ask what avenues of investigation are open to discover "canons" of conduct so universally favored that this Court should write them into the Constitution? All we are told is that the discovery must be made by an "evaluation based on a disinterested inquiry pursued in the spirit of science, on a balanced order of facts."

Mr. JUSTICE DOUGLAS, concurring.

The evidence obtained from this accused's stomach would be admissible in the majority of states where the question has been raised. Yet the Court now says that the rule which the majority of the states have fashioned violates the "decencies of civilized conduct." To that I cannot agree. It is a rule formulated by responsible courts with judges as sensitive as we are to the proper standards for law administration.

Birchfield v. North Dakota

136 S.Ct. 2160 (2016).

JUSTICE ALITO delivered the opinion of the Court.

Drunk drivers take a grisly toll on the Nation's roads, claiming thousands of lives, injuring many more victims, and inflicting billions of dollars in property damage every year. Early laws made it illegal to drive while intoxicated but did not provide a statistical definition of intoxication. As a result, prosecutors normally had to present testimony that the defendant was showing outward signs of intoxication, like imbalance or slurred speech. Later, States and adopted laws providing that driving with a 0.10% BAC or higher was *per se* illegal.

Enforcement of laws of this type requires the measurement of BAC. One way of doing this is to analyze a sample of a driver's blood directly. A technician with medical training uses a syringe to draw a blood sample from the veins of the subject, who must remain still during the procedure, and then the sample is shipped to a separate laboratory for measurement of its alcohol concentration. Many States prohibit drawing blood from a driver who resists 'to avoid violent confrontations.' The most common and economical method of calculating BAC is by means of a machine that measures the amount of alcohol in a person's breath. The subject would inflate a small balloon, and then the test analyst would release this captured breath into the machine, which forced it through a chemical solution that reacted to the presence of alcohol by changing color. The test could observe the amount of breath required to produce the color change and calculate the subject's breath alcohol concentration and by extension, BAC, from this figure. Today, such devices can detect the presence of alcohol more quickly and accurately, typically using infrared technology rather than a chemical reaction. These machines are very reliable.

Measurement of BAC based on a breath test requires the cooperation of the person being tested. Typically the test subject must blow air into the device 'for a period of several seconds' to produce an adequate breath sample, and the process is sometimes repeated so that analysts can compare multiple samples to ensure the device's accuracy. Modern breath test machines are designed to capture so-called 'deep lung' or alveolar air. Most evidentiary breath tests do not occur next to the vehicle, at the side of the road, but in a police station, where the controlled environment is especially conducive to reliable testing, or in some cases in the officer's patrol vehicle or in special mobile testing facilities.

Cooperation of the test subject is necessary when a breath test is administered and highly preferable when a blood sample is taken. 'Implied consent' laws were enacted to achieve this result. Today, all 50 States have adopted implied consent laws that require motorists, as a condition of operating a motor vehicle within the State, to consent to BAC testing if they are arrested or otherwise detained on suspicion of a drunk-driving offense. Suspension or revocation of the motorist's driver's license remains the legal consequence of refusal. In addition, evidence of the motorist's refusal is admitted as evidence of likely intoxication in a drunk-driving prosecution.

In recent decades, the States and the Federal Government have toughened drunk-driving laws, and those efforts have corresponded to a dramatic decrease in alcohol-related fatalities. One legal change has been further lowering the BAC standard from 0.10% to 0.08%. In addition, many States now impose increased penalties for recidivists and drivers with a BAC level that exceeds a higher threshold. But, if the penalty for driving with a greatly elevated BAC or for repeat violations exceeds the penalty for refusing to submit to testing, motorists who fear conviction for the more severely punished offenses have an incentive to reject testing. In some States, the refusal rate is high. To combat the problem of test refusal, some States have begun to enact laws making it a crime to refuse to undergo testing. The Federal Government encourages this approach as a means for overcoming the incentive that drunk drivers have to refuse a test.

The Fourth Amendment prohibits 'unreasonable searches,' and our cases establish that the taking of a blood sample or the administration of a breath test is a search. See *Skinner v. Railway Labor Executives' Assn.*, 489 U. S. 602 (1989); *Schmerber v. California*, 384 U. S. 757 (1966). 'This Court has inferred that a warrant must usually be secured' subject to a number of exceptions. We have previously had occasion to examine whether one such exception-- for 'exigent circumstances'--applies in drunk-driving investigations. The exigent circumstances exception allows a warrantless search when an emergency leaves police insufficient time to seek a warrant. It permits the warrantless entry of private property when there is a need to provide urgent aid to those inside, when police are in hot pursuit of a fleeing suspect, and when police fear the imminent destruction of evidence. In *Schmerber v. California*, we held that drunk driving *may* present such an exigency. There, an officer directed hospital personnel to take a blood sample from a driver who was receiving treatment for car crash injuries. The Court concluded that the officer 'might reasonably have believed that he was confronted with an emergency' that left no time to seek a warrant because 'the percentage of alcohol in the blood begins to diminish shortly after drinking stops.' Where time had already been lost taking the driver to the hospital and investigating the accident, the Court found no Fourth Amendment violation even though the warrantless blood draw took place over the driver's objection.

The natural dissipation of alcohol from the bloodstream does not *always* constitute an exigency justifying the warrantless taking of a blood sample. That was the holding of *Missouri v. McNeely*, 133 S.Ct. 1552 (2013), where the State of Missouri was seeking a *per se* rule that 'whenever an officer has probable cause to believe an individual has been driving under the influence of alcohol, exigent circumstances will necessarily exist because BAC evidence is inherently evanescent.' We disagreed. We refused to 'depart from careful case-by-case assessment of exigency and adopt the categorical rule proposed by the State.' But the Court pointedly did not address any potential justification for warrantless testing of drunk-driving suspects except for the exception for exigent circumstances.

In the cases before us, the drivers were searched or told that they were required to submit to a search after being placed under arrest for drunk driving. We therefore consider how the search-incident-to-arrest doctrine applies to breath and blood tests incident to such arrests. Blood and breath tests to measure blood alcohol concentration are not as new as searches of cell phones, but the founding era does not provide any definitive guidance as to whether they should be allowed incident to arrest. Lacking such guidance, we examine 'the degree to which they intrude upon an individual's privacy and the degree to which they are needed for the promotion of legitimate governmental interests.'

Breath tests do not 'implicate significant privacy concerns.' *Skinner*, 489 U.S., at 626. The physical intrusion is almost negligible. Breath tests 'do not require piercing the skin' and entail 'a minimum of inconvenience.' The effort is no more demanding than blowing up a party balloon. [Petitioner] Bernard argues that the process is nevertheless a significant intrusion because the arrestee must insert the mouthpiece of the machine into his or her mouth. But there is nothing painful or strange about this requirement. Nor is the test a significant intrusion because it 'does not capture an ordinary exhalation of the kind that routinely is exposed to the public' but instead 'requires a sample of 'alveolar' (deep lung) air.' The air that humans exhale is not part of their bodies. Exhalation is a natural process—one that is necessary for life. Humans cannot hold their breath for more than a few minutes, and all the air that is breathed into a breath analyzing machine, including deep lung air, sooner or later would be exhaled even without the test.

We have upheld warrantless searches involving physical intrusions that were at least as significant as that entailed in the administration of a breath test. Just recently we described the process of collecting a DNA sample by rubbing a swab on the inside of a person's cheek as a 'negligible' intrusion. *Maryland v. King*, 133 S.Ct. 1958 (2013). We have also upheld scraping underneath a suspect's fingernails to find evidence of a crime, calling that a 'very limited intrusion.' *Cupp v. Murphy*, 412 U. S. 291 (1973). A breath test is no more intrusive than either of these procedures. Breath tests are capable of revealing only one bit of information, the amount of alcohol in the subject's breath. In this respect, they contrast sharply with the sample of cells collected by the swab in *King*. The DNA obtained in that case put into the possession of law enforcement authorities a sample from which a wealth of additional, highly personal information could potentially be obtained. A breath test results in a BAC reading on a machine, nothing more. No sample of anything is left in the possession of the police. Finally, participation in a breath test is not an experience that is likely to cause any great enhancement in the embarrassment that is inherent in any arrest. Such tests are normally administered in private at a police station, in a patrol car, or in a mobile testing facility, out of public view. Moreover, once under arrest, the individual's expectation of privacy is necessarily diminished. For all these reasons, a breath test does not 'implicate significant privacy concerns.'

Blood tests are a different matter. They 'require piercing the skin' and extract a part of the subject's body. While humans exhale air from their lungs many times per minute, humans do not continually shed blood. People voluntarily submit to the taking of blood samples as part of a physical examination, and the process involves little pain or risk. Nevertheless, the process is not one they relish. It is significantly more intrusive than blowing into a tube. In addition, a blood test, unlike a breath test, places in the hands of law enforcement authorities a sample that can be preserved and from which it is possible to extract information beyond a simple BAC reading. Even if the law enforcement agency is precluded from testing the blood for any purpose other than to measure BAC, the potential remains and may result in anxiety for the person tested.

The States and the Federal Government have a 'paramount interest in preserving the safety of public highways.' Alcohol consumption is a leading cause of traffic fatalities and injuries. Our cases have long recognized the 'carnage' and 'slaughter' caused by drunk drivers. Justice Sotomayor's partial dissent suggests that States' interests in fighting drunk driving are satisfied once suspected drunk drivers are arrested, since such arrests take intoxicated drivers off the roads where they might do harm. Of course States are not solely concerned with neutralizing the threat posed by a drunk driver. They also have a compelling interest in creating effective 'deterrents to drunken driving' so individuals make responsible decisions and do not become a threat to others in the first place. To deter potential drunk drivers and thereby reduce alcohol-related injuries, the States and the Federal Government make it a crime to refuse to submit to a BAC test to provide an incentive to cooperate in such cases.

If a search warrant were required for every search incident to arrest that does not involve exigent circumstances, the courts would be swamped. Even if we arbitrarily singled out BAC tests incident to arrest for this special treatment, the impact would be considerable. In many jurisdictions, judicial officers have the authority to issue warrants only within their own districts, and in rural areas, some districts may have only a small number of judicial officers.

Search warrants protect privacy in two main ways. First, they ensure that a search is not carried out unless a neutral magistrate makes an independent determination that there is probable cause to believe that evidence will be found. Second, if the magistrate finds probable cause, the warrant limits the intrusion on privacy by specifying the scope of the search--that is, the area that can be searched and the items that can be sought. The facts that establish probable cause are largely the same from one drunk-driving stop to the next and consist largely of the officer's own characterization of his or her observations--that there was a strong odor of alcohol, that the motorist wobbled when attempting to stand, that the motorist paused when reciting the alphabet or counting backwards, and so on. A magistrate would be in a poor position to challenge such characterizations. As for the second function served by search warrants--delineating the scope of a search--the scope of the warrant would simply be a BAC test of the arrestee. For these reasons, requiring the police to obtain a warrant in every case would impose a substantial burden but no commensurate benefit.

Petitioner Birchfield identifies 19 strategies that he claims would be at least as effective as implied consent laws, including high-visibility sobriety checkpoints, installing ignition interlocks on repeat offenders' cars that would disable their operation when the driver's breath reveals a sufficiently high alcohol concentration, and alcohol treatment programs. But the cited report describes many of these measures, such as checkpoints, as significantly more costly than test refusal penalties. Others, such as ignition interlocks, target only a segment of the drunk-driver population. Still others, such as treatment programs, are already in widespread use. Moreover, BAC test refusal penalties would be *more* effective if the consequences for refusal were made more severe, including through the addition of criminal penalties.

Having assessed the effect of BAC tests on privacy interests and the need for such tests, we conclude that the Fourth Amendment permits warrantless breath tests incident to arrests for drunk driving. The impact of breath tests on privacy is slight, and the need for BAC testing is great. Blood tests are significantly more intrusive, and their reasonableness must be judged in light of the availability of the less invasive alternative of a breath test. Respondents have offered no satisfactory justification for demanding the more intrusive alternative without a warrant. Breath tests have been common for many years. Their results are admissible in court and are widely credited by juries, and respondents do not dispute their accuracy or utility. One advantage of blood tests is their ability to detect not just alcohol but also other substances that can impair a driver's ability to operate a car safely. A breath test cannot do this, but police have other measures at their disposal when they have reason to believe that a motorist may be under the influence of some other substance (for example, if a breath test indicates that a clearly impaired motorist has little if any alcohol in his blood). Nothing prevents the police from seeking a warrant for a blood test when there is sufficient time to do so in the particular circumstances or from relying on the exigent circumstances exception to the warrant requirement when there is not.

A blood test requires less driver participation than a breath test. In order for a technician to take a blood sample, all that is needed is for the subject to remain still, either voluntarily or by being immobilized. Thus, it is possible to extract a blood sample from a subject who forcibly resists, but many States prefer not to take this step because of the risk of dangerous altercations between police officers and arrestees in rural areas where the arresting officer may not have backup. Only in cases involving an accident that results in death or serious injury may blood be taken from arrestees who resist. It is true that a blood test, unlike a breath test, may be administered to a person who is unconscious (perhaps as a result of a crash) or who is unable to do what is needed to take a breath test due to profound intoxication or injuries. But we have no reason to believe that such situations are common in drunk-driving arrests, and when they arise, the police may apply for a warrant if need be. A breath test may also be ineffective if an arrestee deliberately attempts to prevent an accurate reading by failing to blow into the tube for the requisite length of time or with the necessary force. But courts have held that such conduct qualifies as a refusal to undergo testing, and it may be prosecuted as such. Again, a warrant for a blood test may be sought. Because breath tests are significantly less intrusive than blood tests and in most cases amply serve law enforcement interests, we conclude that a breath test, but not a blood test, may be administered as a search incident to a lawful arrest for drunk driving. As in all cases involving reasonable searches incident to arrest, a warrant is not needed in this situation.

Having concluded that the search incident to arrest doctrine does not justify the warrantless taking of a blood sample, we must address whether such tests are justified based on the driver's legally implied consent to submit to them. A search is reasonable when the subject consents, and that sometimes consent to a search may be fairly inferred from context. Our prior opinions have referred approvingly to implied-consent laws that impose civil penalties and evidentiary consequences on motorists who refuse to comply. Petitioners do not question the constitutionality of those laws. It is another matter, however, for a State not only to insist upon an intrusive blood test, but also to impose criminal penalties on the refusal to submit to such a test. There must be a limit to the consequences to which motorists may be deemed to have consented by virtue of a decision to drive on public roads.

North Dakota emphasizes that its law makes refusal a misdemeanor and suggests that laws punishing refusal more severely would present a different issue. We conclude that motorists cannot be deemed to have consented to submit to a blood test on pain of committing a criminal offense.

Petitioner Birchfield was criminally prosecuted for refusing a warrantless blood draw, and therefore the search he refused cannot be justified as a search incident to his arrest or on the basis of implied consent. There is no indication that a breath test would have failed to satisfy the State's interests in acquiring evidence to enforce its drunk-driving laws. North Dakota has not presented any information to suggest that the exigent circumstances exception would have justified a warrantless search. Bernard was criminally prosecuted for refusing a warrantless breath test. That test *was* a permissible search incident to Bernard's arrest for drunk driving. Accordingly, the Fourth Amendment did not require officers to obtain a warrant prior to demanding the test, and Bernard had no right to refuse it. Beylund submitted to a blood test after police told him that the law required his submission, and his license was then suspended and he was fined. Because voluntariness must be 'determined from the totality of all the circumstances,' we leave it to the state court to reevaluate Beylund's consent given the partial inaccuracy of the officer's advisory.

We accordingly reverse the judgment of the North Dakota Supreme Court in No. 14-1468 and remand the case for further proceedings. We affirm the judgment of the Minnesota Supreme Court in No. 14-1470. And we vacate the judgment in No. 14-1507 and remand.

It is so ordered.

JUSTICE SOTOMAYOR, with whom JUSTICE GINSBURG joins, concurring in part and dissenting in part.

Neither the Court nor the States provide any evidence to suggest that, in the normal course of affairs, obtaining a warrant and conducting a breath test will exceed the allotted 2-hour window. Neither has demonstrated that requiring police to obtain warrants for breath tests would impose a sufficiently significant burden on state resources to justify the elimination of the Fourth Amendment's warrant requirement. Assuming that North Dakota police officers would need to obtain a warrant for every drunk-driving arrest tomorrow, each of the State's 82 judges and magistrate judges would need to issue fewer than two extra warrants per week. But States only need to obtain warrants for drivers who refuse testing and a significant majority of drivers voluntarily consent to breath tests. Mere convenience in investigating drunk driving cannot itself justify an exception to the warrant requirement.

JUSTICE THOMAS, concurring in judgment in part and dissenting in part.

The tests revealing the BAC of a driver suspected of driving drunk are constitutional under the exigent-circumstances exception to the warrant requirement.

Points for Discussion

a. Fingernail Scrapings

In *Cupp v. Murphy*, 412 U.S. 291 (1973), Murphy's wife died by strangulation at her home with abrasions and lacerations on her throat, but no indication of a break-in. When Murphy, who did not live with his wife, agreed to come to the police station for questioning, the police noticed a dark spot on his finger. Suspecting that the spot might be dried blood, and aware that strangulation often leaves evidence under the assailant's fingernails, the police requested permission to take a sample of the spot. When Murphy refused, and was seen trying to remove the blood, the police took the sample without a warrant. The samples were found to include fabric from the victim's nightgown as well as traces of her skin and blood. The Court upheld the search: "Murphy was motivated to attempt to destroy what evidence he could without attracting further attention. Considering the existence of probable cause, the very limited intrusion undertaken incident to the station house detention, and the ready destructibility of the evidence, we cannot say that this search violated the Fourth and Fourteenth Amendments." Mr. Justice Marshall concurred: "If the Fourth Amendment permits a stop-and-frisk, it also permits fingernail scrapings in the circumstances of this case." Mr. Justice Douglas dissented in part: "Scraping a man's fingernails is an invasion of that privacy and it is tolerable, constitutionally speaking, only if there is a warrant for a search or seizure issued by a magistrate on a showing of 'probable cause' that the suspect had committed the crime. Murphy could have been detained while one was sought; and that detention would have preserved the perishable evidence the police sought."

b. Seizure for Breathalyzer Test

In *Welsh v. Wisconsin*, 466 U.S. 740 (1984), the police received reports indicating that Welsh had been driving under the influence. When Welsh's stepdaughter answered the door of his home, the police entered and proceeded upstairs to Welsh's bedroom where they found him lying naked in bed. The police arrested Welsh and took him to the police station where he refused to submit to a breathalyzer test. The Court concluded that the police acted improperly:

> Before the government may invade the sanctity of the home, the burden is on the government to demonstrate exigent circumstances that overcome the presumption of unreasonableness that attaches to all warrantless home entries. When the government's interest is only to arrest for a minor offense, that presumption of unreasonableness is difficult to rebut, and the government usually should be allowed to make such arrests only with a warrant issued upon

In *United States v. Smith*, 470 F.2d 377 (D.C.Cir.1972), defendant was charged with assault with intent to commit rape against a six year-old girl who was raped and left bleeding. The police then asked defendant to undergo a benzidine test "to see if there was a show of blood". The mechanics of the test were outlined, and defendant was advised that if the test results were positive he would be charged with the offense; if negative, he would be released. Defendant replied that "he had no fear about the test because he knew it would be negative." The test was performed and there was a positive reaction. The court held that the test results had been properly admitted: "The search was reasonable since it was necessary to conduct the test as promptly as possible because of the ease with which the evidence could be destroyed by a thorough washing. The simplicity of the test makes it unnecessary to have it conducted by a physician. It is a chemical test not a medical test and was properly administered by a trained police technician."

probable cause by a neutral and detached magistrate. The claim of hot pursuit is unconvincing because there was no immediate or continuous pursuit of the petitioner from the scene of a crime. Moreover, because the petitioner had already arrived home, and had abandoned his car at the scene of the accident, there was little remaining threat to the public safety. The only potential emergency claimed by the State was the need to ascertain the petitioner's blood-alcohol level. The similarity to other cases involving the imminent destruction of evidence is not sufficient. The State of Wisconsin has chosen to classify the first offense for driving while intoxicated as a noncriminal, civil forfeiture offense for which no imprisonment is possible. Given this expression of the State's interest, a warrantless home arrest cannot be upheld simply because evidence of the petitioner's blood-alcohol level might have dissipated while the police obtained a warrant.

Justice White dissented: "A test under which the existence of exigent circumstances turns on the perceived gravity of the crime would significantly hamper law enforcement and burden courts with pointless litigation concerning the nature and gradation of various crimes. Nevertheless, this Court has long recognized the compelling state interest in highway safety."

Food for Thought

Suppose that police officers are watching a warehouse and observe a worker carrying bundles from the warehouse to a large bonfire and throwing them into the blaze. As a result, the officers have probable cause to believe that the bundles contain marijuana. Because there is only one person carrying the bundles, the officers believe it will take hours to completely destroy the drugs. During that time the officers likely could obtain a warrant. Must the officers sit idly by and watch the destruction of evidence while they wait for a warrant? Would it matter, as in a drunk driving case, that the ever-diminishing quantity of drugs may have an impact on the severity of the crime and the length of the sentence?

Hypo 1: *Surgical Bullet Removal*

During a robbery of a shop, the assailant is wounded and flees. Twenty minutes later, police find defendant eight blocks from the robbery scene suffering from a gunshot wound to the chest. He tells police that he was shot when a man tried to rob him. When defendant arrives at the emergency room, the victim of the robbery sees defendant, and exclaims "that's the man that shot me." The police decide that defendant's story of himself being a robbery victim is untrue. Since the bullet in defendant's stomach constitutes evidence, the state seeks an order forcing him to undergo surgery to remove the bullet (lodged under his left collarbone). Defendant objects to the procedure which would take 45 minutes and involve a three to four percent chance of temporary nerve damage, a one percent chance of permanent nerve damage, and a one-tenth of one percent chance of death. The surgeon states that a general anesthetic would be desirable for medical reasons, and that the risks described above derive from the anesthetic. In light of *Rochin* and *Schmerber*, may a court order defendant to undergo the surgical procedure under a general anesthetic for removal of the bullet lodged in his chest? What arguments might you make on defendant's behalf? How might the state respond? *See Winston v. Lee*, 470 U.S. 753 (1985).

Hypo 2: *Searching the Pregnant Woman*

Defendant is arrested at home on a warrant charging her with selling cocaine. During the arrest, the officers see paraphernalia used in the heating and administering of heroin (*e.g.*, hypodermic needles, an eyedropper, water, copper wire, a "cooker" (a burned bottle cap with a wad of cotton) and white residue). Two policewomen take defendant (clad only in a nightgown and underpants) into the bathroom to search her, and tell her to strip, bend over, and spread her buttocks. It is difficult for defendant to bend over because she is seven months pregnant. The police women then look into her privates and find nothing. Because of cramped quarters and poor lighting in the bathroom, the officers decide that defendant should be searched a second time at the station. The detectives have information from a "reliable informer" that defendant is known to carry heroin in her vagina. At the station, defendant is again forced to disrobe and bend over (this time leaning on a chair), and a policewomen uses rubber gloves to spread her buttocks. Are such procedures permissible? *See United States v. McCauley*, 385 F.Supp. 193 (E.D.Wis.1974).

Hypo 3: *Abdominal Surgery*

When a hand-held metal detector suggests the presence of metal on a prison inmate, prison guards subject the inmate to a search and eventually to a strip search. When the search reveals nothing, the inmate is subjected to an x-ray that seems to reveal the presence of a foreign object in his stomach. Under such circumstances, are prison officials allowed to subject the inmate to abdominal surgery to determine the nature of the object? Would the surgery be permissible if the inmate had undergone two bowel movements neither of which revealed a foreign object? *See Sanchez v. Pereira-Castillo*, 590 F.3d 31 (1st Cir. 2009).

Hypo 4: *Swabbing the Arrestee's Private Parts*

At 2:30 a.m., responding to a distress call, police find a highly distressed naked woman (D.L.) who claims to have been forced to engage in oral sex with a "fat white guy" in his twenties, with "short, dark hair wearing no shirt, black pants and smelling of alcohol." D.L.'s face is injured, bruised and bloody, she has bruises to her stomach and back, and she has scrape marks on her arms and legs. The officers go to the scene of the alleged crime (a garage), and "observe that two chairs have been knocked over outside the access door and that there is female clothing, including a bra, a shirt and a woman's shoe as well as condom wrappers strewn about on the ground as though a struggle had occurred." They also see a pair of jeans hanging off, a "make-shift bed on the floor of the garage," and "blood on the floor adjacent to the bed." Based on the statements of D.L., along with the evidence in the garage, the officers determine that they "have probable cause to believe that a criminal-sexual-conduct crime has occurred and that the suspect is inside a nearby house possibly destroying evidence." They arrest the man, place him in the back of a squad car, and notice that he has numerous scratches on his chest, stomach, back, arms, as well as blood on his hands, his shirt inside-out, and his pants and belt undone. The officers then swab respondent's hands to take a sample of the blood because they fear that it will be washed or rubbed off. Can the swabbing be justified under the exigent circumstances doctrine? *See State v. Lussier,* 770 N.W.2d 581 (Minn. App. 2009).

Hypo 5: *Probing for Cocaine*

After receiving a tip that Gray is in possession of crack cocaine, police arrest him based on a warrant. Gray is taken to jail where a strip search is conducted, but Gray is "not fully cooperative." The police then do an extensive, two-hour search of Gray's vehicle, which also turns up nothing. Gray is then taken out of the general population and strip-searched a second time. As a part of his strip search, he is instructed to squat, pull his buttocks apart, and cough, in order to dislodge anything that may be concealed in the anus. Gray will only "slightly bend at the knees and give a faint cough." In addition, the police conduct a second search of the scene where they stopped Gray, and jail personnel conduct strip searches of all inmates who were in Gray's holding cell with him. None of these searches turns up any drugs or other contraband. At this point, the police present Gray with some options: Gary can undergo a third strip search; he can be placed in a cell with a waterless toilet; or he can consent to a rectal x-ray examination. Gray refuses to consent to any of these options. Based on all of these events and their education, training, and experience, police believe that the "only place" Gray could be concealing the crack cocaine is in his rectum. Suppose that you are the judge assigned to hear the request for a warrant. The affidavit states that police suspect Gray of concealing crack cocaine in his "anal cavity," and request the right to examine this cavity using "recognized medical procedures." Should you grant the request? *See United States v. Gray,* 669 F.3d 556 (5th Cir. 2012).

Hypo 6: *More on Probing for Cocaine*

In the prior problem, suppose that you have granted the request for a warrant, and the police decide to subject Gray to an x-ray. Gray is uncooperative with the x-ray technician, and the technician is unable to "get a good picture with the portable x-ray." The technician tries again with a stationary x-ray machine, but Gray will not lie still and will not stay "where he is told." Eventually, the x-ray technician obtains a useable picture, and notices something that he thinks could either be a gas pocket or a foreign object. The police then subject Gray to a digital exam. Have the police acted properly under the circumstances? If the digital exam is inconclusive, can the police undertake a proctoscopic examination of Gray's rectum? Essentially, what they want to do is to inset an illuminated tube up the anal canal and into the rectum, fill the rectum with air, causing the rectum walls to distend so that they can be examined. In order to administer the exam, medical personnel will subject Gray to two sedatives (Versed and Etomidate) that will be administered intravenously. Doctors believe that the risks associated with the sedatives are low, and Gray's cardiovascular status will be monitored throughout the examination. The sedatives carry with them a risk of respiratory depression or arrest. Proctoscopy also has associated risks, including pain and potential anal bleeding or perforation, and are not usually conducted on uncooperative patients. Is the procedure permissible? Should police first resort to other procedures (e.g., watch and wait, or an enema) that would not require sedation? *See United States v. Gray*, 669 F.3d 556 (5th Cir. 2012).

Hypo 7: *Cutting the Baggie Off*

After receiving a report indicating that Edwards had brandished a firearm, police officers locate Edwards on a residential street and detain him. Since Edwards did not make any movements characteristic of someone who is armed, or who is engaged in a drug transaction, the officers are not "too worried." Once a search warrant is issued for Edwards' arrest, the officers request a police van to transport Edwards to the station. While they are waiting for the van, the officers subject Edwards to a pat-down search that reveals nothing. When the van arrives, the officers decide to search Edwards a second time before placing him in the van. While three male officers surround Edwards, one officer unfastens

Edwards' belt, loosens it, and pulls Edwards' pants and underwear six or seven inches away from his body. The officers direct a flashlight beam inside both the front and the back of Edwards' underwear, and they notice a plastic sandwich baggie tied in a knot around Edwards' penis that appears to contain smaller blue ziplock baggies which contain "a white rocklike substance." Based on his training and experience, the officer concludes that the baggie and its contents are consistent with the packaging or distribution of a controlled substance. May the officers cut the baggie off of Edwards' penis with a knife? *See United States v. Edwards*, 666 F.3d 877 (4th Cir. 2011).

Executive Summary

Warrant Requirement. The failure to obtain a search warrant is unreasonable under the Fourth Amendment unless the searching officers are acting pursuant to one or more of the recognized exceptions to the Warrant Requirement.

Affidavits. Search warrants are usually obtained from a neutral magistrate who must find probable cause to exist based on the information presented to the court in sworn (usually written) affidavits.

Defective Warrants. A search warrant is defective if it is not supported by probable cause set out in a supporting affidavit "on it's face." A search warrant can also be challenged as defective by "going behind" the affidavit and establishing that the affiant included false information necessary to establish probable cause (or omitted information necessary to establish probable cause) recklessly or intentionally. Challenges to the supporting affidavits take place in pre-trial "*Franks* hearings."

Major Themes

a. Warrants Uncommon - Although there is a constitutional warrant preference and a constitutional warrant requirement, in actuality, the overwhelming majority of searches and seizures occur—lawfully—without a warrant, pursuant to one of the recognized exceptions to the warrant requirement.

b. Coexisting Tests for Recognition of Protected Interests - Before 1967, the Supreme Court used the physical trespass test and provided Fourth Amendment protection only when a government surveillance method constituted a physical intrusion into a constitutionally protected area. In 1967, the Court endorsed a supplementary test in *Katz* to be used for determining whether Fourth Amendment protection should be recognized in scenarios that did not satisfy the physical trespass requirement. Under *Katz*, a person must exhibit an actual subjective expectation of privacy, and that expectation objectively must be recognized by society as reasonable. The Court continues to employ both tests today.

Particularity. Search warrants must particularly describe the place to be searched and the things to be seized. The description must be detailed enough to insure that the executing officers can reasonably ascertain and identify the place to be searched and the things to be seized. A search warrant lacking in particularity is unconstitutionally defective.

Search of Wrong Premises. The mistaken search of the wrong premises with a search warrant is not unconstitutional if the executing officers did not know or should not have known that the premises described in the warrant were described too broadly, and where the officers leave immediately when they learn that they are in the wrong place.

Knock and Announce Requirement. In the absence of exigent circumstances, officers executing a search warrant must (a) announce their presence at the search premises; (b) announce their purpose, i.e. that they have a warrant; and (c) delay prior to entry for a sufficient time to permit the occupants to open the door. Typically, a delay of 15 to 20 seconds will suffice. "No-knock" entries are permitted, however, where the police have a specific reasonable suspicion that knocking and announcing would be dangerous, futile, or could lead to the destruction of evidence. In any event, the federal exclusionary rule does not apply to knock-and-announce violations.

Protection of Privacy in the Home. A reasonable expectation of privacy has been recognized in a dwelling and the curtilage land around it. This protection extends to conversations inside a home, to information that a monitored tracking

c. Complexity of *Katz* Test—In assessing whether an expectation of privacy is reasonable under *Katz*, the Court has considered a variety of factors. Some precedents find that no reasonable expectation exists when a defendant voluntarily conveys information to a third party or knowingly exposes the information to the public. Other precedents reach the same result when a government search technique discloses only limited information and requires no exposure of possessions. The dog sniff precedents focus the question whether the government surveillance method produces information that would previously have been unknowable without a physical intrusion, or whether relevant common law history supports a social consensus about privacy values.

d. The Probable Cause Requirement—The Fourth Amendment requires that all warrants be based (among other things) on probable cause, and some exceptions to the warrant requirement (e.g., the automobile exception) also require probable cause. "Probable cause" is not a technical term, but instead involves a commonsense determination regarding whether reasonable cause exists to believe that the fruits, instrumentalities or evidence of crime can be found at the place to be searched, or that the person to be arrested committed a crime.

e. The Warrant Preference—Although the courts impose a warrant "preference," meaning that warrantless searches are presumptively unconstitutional, the Fourth Amendment does not require a warrant as a precondition for a valid search. The Fourth Amendment requires only that searches be "reasonable."

f. Exceptions to the Warrant Requirement—Despite the warrant preference, there are multiple exceptions to the warrant requirement. Indeed, there are so many exceptions that they almost swallow the warrant preference.

beeper has been tracked inside the home, to heat emanating from a home as captured in a thermal imaging device from outside the home, and to other information regarding the interior of a home that could not otherwise have been obtained without a physical intrusion.

Protected Privacy Interests Outside the Home. A reasonable expectation of privacy (REOP) interest has been recognized in conversations in a public telephone booth obtained by a recording device outside the booth, and in a bus passenger's luggage placed in overhead rack and squeezed to determine its contents. Otherwise, outside the home, the Court has somewhat narrowly construed the REOP test.

Constitutionally Protected Areas and Physical Trespass Intrusions. Both a home and the curtilage land around it are constitutionally protected areas. The curtilage is protected against the physical intrusion of a government agent's entry and visual surveillance on the ground, and also against the use of a narcotics-detection dog. Conversations in the home are protected from recording with a device that involves a physical intrusion. While a person's movement by car on public streets is generally not protected against monitoring by a GPS device, it is protected when the device is attached to the car by means of a physical intrusion.

Lack of Protection of Privacy Interests. Even in the protected area of the home, there is no Fourth Amendment protection from the recording of conversations by a government informant. Similarly, curtilage is protected only from physical entry on the ground, not from aerial surveillance from a helicopter or airplane flying in navigable air space. Open fields are not a constitutionally protected area, nor is there a reasonable expectation of privacy from a government agent's entry and visual surveillance of open fields. There is no REOP protection from a search of garbage placed on a curb in front of a dwelling. Similarly, a narcotics-detection dog may sniff luggage in a public place or sniff the exterior of an automobile during a roadblock or traffic stop. Nor is there a valid privacy expectation for freedom from surveillance by means of a tracking beeper to monitor a person's movement by car on public streets.

Modern Approaches to Privacy. Based on the *Jones* case, the Court still uses the old physical trespass test in deciding whether the government has engaged in a search. In addition, the Court seems somewhat more sympathetic to finding the existence of a search when the police use technologies to spy on citizens.

The Importance of Probable Cause. Probable cause is an integral part of the Fourth Amendment's prohibition against unreasonable searches and seizures. In order to obtain a warrant to search, among other things, a magistrate must find probable cause to believe that the fruits instrumentalities or evidence of crime can be found at the place to be searched. For an arrest warrant, there must be probable cause to believe that a crime has been committed and that the person to be arrested committed it. Some exceptions to the warrant requirement also require proof of probable cause.

The Meaning of Probable Cause. Applied literally, "probable cause" requires that something be "more probable than not." However, the courts have rarely applied the probable cause requirement literally. The U.S. Supreme Court has indicated that the probable cause determination is not "technical," but instead deals with "probabilities" and the "factual and practical considerations of everyday life on which reasonable and prudent men, not legal technicians, act." The question is whether there are sufficient "facts and circumstances" to lead a reasonable person to conclude that there is "reasonably trustworthy information" to support the conclusions reached.

The *Aguilar-Spinelli* Test. In *Spinelli v. United States*, 393 U.S. 410 (1969), the Court imposed a two-prong test for evaluating whether an informant's tip provided the police with probable cause. That test, called the *Aguilar-Spinelli* test because it was partly based on the holding in *Aguilar v. Texas*, 378 U.S. 108 (1964), provides that, in order for the police to rely on an informant's tip, that must find that the tip must set forth the "underlying circumstances" necessary to evaluate the factual accuracy of the tip, and must contain information suggesting that the informant is "credible" and "reliable."

The *Draper* Case. In *Draper v. United States*, 358 U.S. 307 (1959), the Court relaxed the "basis of information prong of the *Aguilar-Spinelli* test. In that case, although the police had information regarding the informant's credibility (he had given correct information to the police in the past), he failed to state how he had obtained his information. However, the tip did contain a degree of detail, and the police were able to verify that detail, so the Court concluded that probable cause existed: "Independent police work case corroborated much more than one small detail."

***Gates'* Modification of the *Aguilar-Spinelli* Test.** In *Illinois v. Gates*, 462 U.S. 213 (1983), the Court modified the *Aguilar-Spinelli* test. That case involved a tip from an anonymous information so that neither prong of the test was satisfied. Although the Court suggested that an informant's "veracity," "reliability" and "basis of knowledge" are all "highly relevant in determining the value of his report," the Court concluded that they should be used simply to "illuminate the commonsense, practical question whether there is 'probable cause' to believe that contraband or evidence is located in a particular place." In other words, the Court did not regard the probable cause determination as "technical, but as sweeping in the factual and practical considerations of everyday life on which reasonable and prudent men, not legal technicians, act." In *Gates*, the Court concluded that probable cause existed even though neither prong of the *Aguilar-Spinelli* test was satisfied. Instead, the Court looked at the "totality of circumstances" and simply considered the *Aguilar-Spinelli* test as part of that analysis.

Probable Cause and Canine Drug-Sniffing. In *Florida v. Harris,* 568 U.S. 237 (2013), the Court concluded that the police could establish probable cause based on the "alert" of a drug-detection dog. In that case, although the dog had allegedly misfired during a couple of traffic stops, he had certified as reliable during his training, and the Court concluded that the training records were sufficient, in and of themselves, to prove the dog's reliability. The Court discounted the alleged misfires during the traffic stops.

The Warrant Preference and Warrantless Searches. Despite the preference for a warrant, the courts have established numerous exceptions to the warrant requirement. The courts distinguish between warrantless arrests and warrantless searches. Even though warrantless arrests are generally permissible, warrantless searches are disfavored and are "*per se* unreasonable subject only to a few specifically established and well-delineated exceptions." *Katz v. United States*, 389 U.S. 347, 357 (1967).

Plain View Exception. The "plain view" exception is an often-used exception to the warrant requirement. When the police are conducting a lawful search, and are in a place where they have the right to be, this exception allows them to seize items that they find in plain view. To be in plain view, the criminal nature of the item must be "immediately apparent." An item is not in "plain view" if the police must move it to determine its contraband status, but drugs hidden in an opaque balloon (of a type commonly used to carry drugs) are considered to be in "plain view."

Search Incident to Legal Arrest Exception. The search incident to legal arrest exception is one of the oldest and most well-established exceptions to the warrant requirement. It provides that, when the police make a legal arrest, they have the right to make a search incident to that arrest. The police can only search the area within the individual's "immediate control."

Requirement for a Valid Arrest. An arrest is the most serious form of seizure, and it occurs when the police take a suspect into custody. The requirements for a valid arrest were articulated in *United States v. Watson*, 423 U.S. 411 (1976). In that case, the Court indicated that a peace officer is "permitted to arrest without a warrant for a misdemeanor or felony committed in his presence as well as for a felony not committed in his presence if there was reasonable ground for making the arrest." In *Atwater v. City of Lago Vista*, 532 U.S. 318 (2001), the Court held that police can make warrantless misdemeanor arrests "for all sorts of relatively minor offenses unaccompanied by violence." In evaluating the validity of an arrest, the courts should not delve into the arresting officer's subjective intentions.

Arrests in Special Situations. In *Payton v. New York*, 445 U.S. 573 (1980), the Court held that, absent exigent circumstances, the police may not arrest an individual at home without a warrant. In *Steagald v. United States*, 451 U.S. 204 (1981), the Court held that a law enforcement officer may not search for the subject of an arrest warrant in the home of a third party without first obtaining a search warrant. See also *Minnesota v. Olson*, 495 U.S. 91 (1990).

Using Deadly Force to Effect an Arrest. In *Tennessee v. Garner*, 471 U.S. 1 (1985), the Court held that the Constitution prohibits the use of deadly force to make an arrest except when the arrestee "poses a threat of serious physical harm either to the officer or to others." In *Garner*, the suspect's youth, slightness, and lack of a weapon suggested that he did not pose a threat of physical danger to himself or others. In *Scott v. Harris*, 550 U.S. 372 (2007), the Court held that a police officer could attempt to stop a fleeing motorist (who refused to yield to pursuing police) by ramming the motorist's car from behind even though the ramming ultimately rendered the motorist a paraplegic. The Court rejected the notion that the officer had used deadly force in contravention of the Court's holding in *Garner*.

Search Incident to Arrest of Automobiles. In *Arizona v. Gant*, 556 U.S. 332 (2009), the Court redefined the search incident to arrest exception as applied to someone who is arrested while driving in an automobile. In a prior case, *New York v. Belton*, 453 U.S. 454 (1981), the Court had held that when an officer lawfully arrests "the occupant of an automobile, he may, as a contemporaneous incident of that arrest, search the passenger compartment of the automobile" and any containers therein." *Gant* overruled *Belton* and held that the police may only search a car when the arrestee is unsecured and within reaching distance of the passenger compartment at the time of the search, or when it is "reasonable to believe evidence relevant to the crime of arrest might be found in the vehicle."

Cell Phone Searches Incident to Arrest. In *Riley v. California*, 134 U.S. 2473 (2014), because of the privacy implications, the Court held that the police do not have *carte blanche* to go through the contents of a cell phone incident to arrest. The Court concluded that "a warrant is generally required before such a search, even when a cell phone is seized incident to arrest." "Even though the search incident to arrest exception does not apply to cell phones, other case-specific exceptions may still justify a warrantless search of a particular phone.

Such exigencies could include the need to prevent the imminent destruction of evidence in individual cases, to pursue a fleeing suspect, and to assist persons who are seriously injured or who are threatened with imminent injury."

Booking Search Exception. Before jail or prison officials actually admit an individual to the inmate population, they will usually conduct a "booking search" for weapons or contraband that the individual may be carrying. In *Florence v. Board of Chosen Freeholders of the County of Burlington*, 566 U.S. 318 (2012), the Court concluded that jail or prison officials also have the right to impose strip searches as part of these booking procedures. In *Maryland v. King*, 569 U.S. 435 (2013), the Court held that jail and prison officials could also require those incarcerated to submit to DNA analysis in order to verify their identities.

The Automobile Exception. The automobile exception is one of the oldest exceptions to the warrant requirement. It provides that, when the police have probable cause to believe that an automobile contains the fruits, instrumentalities or evidence of crime, they may search the vehicle without a warrant. The exception is justified by the mobility of vehicles (the circumstances giving rise to probably cause can arise unexpectedly, and vehicles can quickly disappear), as well as the fact that they are accompanied by a "diminished expectation of privacy." The scope of an automobile search allows the police to search anywhere in the vehicle that they have probable cause to believe that the fruits, instrumentalities or evidence of crime can be found. The exception includes the right to open closed containers if the police have probable cause to believe that contraband can be found in those containers.

Inventory Exception. There is also an "inventory" exception to the warrant requirement. The most common inventory search occurs when the police impound a vehicle. Inventory searches serve to protect an owner's property while it is in the custody of the police, to insure against claims of lost, stolen, or vandalized property, and to guard the police from danger. An inventory search can extend to the entire vehicle. However, courts will sometimes focus on whether the jurisdiction has established policies or procedures regarding when vehicles can be impounded, and the scope of inventory searches.

Consent Searches. The consent exception is not really an "exception" to the warrant requirement. Any constitutional right can be waived, and citizens can waive their Fourth Amendment right to be free from governmental searches and seizures. The courts have struggled to determine what constitutes "consent." The question is whether the consent was voluntarily given or whether it was coerced. Issues of consent are determined by considering the totality of circumstances. Although an individual can consent even though an individual is unaware of the right to refuse consent, unawareness is a relevant consideration in the analysis.

Authority to Consent. Ordinarily, one would assume that only those who own or possess property would have the authority to consent to a search of that property. However, in *Illinois v. Rodriguez*, 497 U.S. 177 (1990), the Court held that a woman's consent to search an apartment was valid even though she did not live in the apartment (she used to live there and had a key without the owner's knowledge), if the police acted reasonably in relying on her purported consent: "The Constitution is no more violated when officers enter without a warrant because they reasonably (though erroneously) believe that the person who has consented to their entry is a resident of the premises, than it is violated when they enter without a warrant because they reasonably (though erroneously) believe they are in pursuit of a violent felon who is about to escape."

Objecting Co-Tenants. In *Georgia v. Randolph*, 547 U.S. 103 (2006), a wife granted the police consent to search their home in the presence of her objecting husband. The Court held that, even though both spouses would ordinarily be entitled to consent to a search since they have common authority over the premises, "shared social expectations" would not permit entry when one spouse was present and objecting" "A caller standing at the door of shared premises would have no confidence that one occupant's invitation was a sufficiently good reason to enter when a fellow tenant stood there saying, 'stay out.'" In the Court's subsequent decision in *Fernandez v. California*, 134 S.Ct. 1126 (2014), the Court held that the other tenant had the authority to consent after the objecting tenant was removed from the premises (in that case, he was removed under arrest by the police).

The Administrative Inspection Exception. In *Camara v. Municipal Court*, 387 U.S. 523 (1967), the Court held that administrative inspections are subject to the Fourth Amendment's requirement of a warrant based on probable cause. However, the Court redefined the concept of "probable cause" by providing that the agency only need prove the existence of a reasonable administrative inspection plan, and show showed that it is time to search the particular premises under that plan, in order to establish probable cause to obtain a warrant. In a number of cases, the Court has held that certain "highly regulated industries" (e.g., firearms and liquor sellers) can be subjected to warrantless searches.

Stop and Frisk Exception. In *Terry v. State of Ohio*, 392 U.S. 1 (1968), the Court articulated the "stop and frisk" exception to the warrant requirement. In doing so, the Court balanced the "governmental interest" or "need" against the level of intrusion on the individual, and held that when "a police officer observes unusual conduct which leads him reasonably to conclude in light of his experience that criminal activity may be afoot and that the persons with whom he is dealing may be armed and presently dangerous, where in the course of investigating this behavior he identifies himself as a policeman and makes reasonable inquiries, and where nothing in the initial stages of the encounter serves to dispel his reasonable fear for his own or others' safety, he is entitled for the protection of himself and others in the area to conduct a carefully limited search of the outer clothing of such persons in an attempt to discover weapons which might be used to assault him."

Strip Searches of High School Students. In *Safford Unified School District v. Redding*, 557 U.S. 364 (2009), although the Court held that school officials could search a high school student's backpack in an effort to find prescription strength Ibuprofen, but could not subject her to a strip search: "The meaning of such a search, and the degradation its subject may reasonably feel, place a search that intrusive in a category of its own demanding its own specific suspicions."

Other Investigative Stops. In addition to authorizing a "stop and frisk," in appropriate situations, *Terry* also authorizes the police to make "investigative stops" which are a form of seizure. The Court has recognized many different types of seizures ranging from an investigatory stop to an arrest. These seizures are subject to differing constitutional requirements. Most seizures are investigative in nature and can be relatively brief. Roadside stops usually fit this description. However, the police also "seize" individuals for fingerprinting, lineups or interrogation purposes.

Investigative Stops. In *United States v. Mendenhall*, 446 U.S. 544 (1980), the Court held that the police may make investigative stops when they have a reasonable suspicion to believe that a suspect is involved in criminal activity. Balancing the need for the search against the level of intrusion, the Court justified these stops on the basis that they are generally of relatively brief duration and relatively less intrusive.

Defining an Investigative Stop. In *Mendenhall*, the Court held that an investigative stop occurs when a reasonable person in the suspect's position would not feel free to leave. However, if the suspect resists or flees, *California v. Hodari D.*, 499 U.S. 621 (1991), held that there is an investigative seizure "when the officer, by means of physical force or show of authority, has in some way restrained the liberty of a citizen." By contrast, if the police wish to force an individual to go to the police station for questioning, or to participate in a lineup or to be fingerprinted, probable cause (rather than reasonable suspicion) is required. In *United States v. Place*, 462 U.S. 696 (1983), the Court held that the police exceeded the scope of a permissible investigative stop when they detained Place's luggage for 45 minutes (to allow a drug sniffing dog to be brought up) and then detained the luggage for 48 hours in order to obtain a warrant (after the dog alerted to it): "The length of the detention of Place's luggage precludes a conclusion that the seizure was reasonable in the absence of probable cause."

The Scope of Different Types of Seizures. The Court has made it clear that an investigative stop can be justified based on a reasonable suspicion because it "must be temporary and last no longer than is necessary to effectuate the purpose of the stop."

Demanding Identification. In *Hiibel v. Sixth Judicial District Court*, 542 U.S. 177 (2004), the Court held that the police may demand identification from individuals in certain situations: "It is clear in this case that the request for identification was 'reasonably related in scope to the circumstances which justified' the stop. The officer's request was a commonsense inquiry, not an effort to obtain an arrest for failure to identify after a *Terry* stop yielded insufficient evidence. The stop, the request, and the State's requirement of a response did not contravene the guarantees of the Fourth Amendment."

Protective Sweeps. In various cases, the Court has held that the police may conduct protective sweeps of homes to make sure that there are no threats to their safety. For example, when the police execute an arrest warrant, they may take steps to ensure "that the house in which a suspect is being, or has just been, arrested is not harboring other persons who are dangerous and who could unexpectedly launch an attack." The permitted sweep is "not a full search of the premises, but only a cursory inspection of those spaces where a person may be found. The sweep lasts no longer than is necessary to dispel the reasonable suspicion of danger and in any event no longer than it takes to complete the arrest and depart the premises." The Court has allowed the police to temporarily detain the occupant of a home while executing a warrant to search the home.

Police Stops of Automobiles. In *Delaware v. Prouse*, 440 U.S. 648 (1979), the Court held that the police may not stop motorists simply to check their driver's license and registration absent a reasonable suspicion that they are involved in criminal activity. The Court concluded that the primary method for enforcing traffic and vehicle safety regulations is by responding to observed violations of traffic laws. The Court was concerned about abuse of discretion if police officers were free to pull drivers over at will.

Roadblock Checkpoints. In *Michigan Dept. of State Police v. Sitz*, 496 U.S. 444 (1990), and *United States v. Martinez-Fuerte*, 428 U.S. 543 (1976), the Court upheld brief, suspicionless seizures at highway checkpoints for the purposes of combating drunk driving and intercepting illegal immigrants. However, in *City of Indianapolis v. Edmond*, 531 U.S. 32 (2000), the Court invalidated a drug interdiction checkpoint, holding that it had "never approved a checkpoint program whose primary purpose was to detect evidence of ordinary criminal wrongdoing." In *Illinois v. Lidster*, 540 U.S. 419 (2004), the Court upheld a checkpoint designed to locate potential witnesses to a fatal accident involving a bicyclist: "The stops took place about one week after the hit-and-run accident, on the same highway near the location of the accident, and at about the same time of night. Police used the stops to obtain information from drivers, some of whom might well have been in the vicinity of the crime at the time it occurred."

The Border Exception. The government has always exercised broad authority to stop individuals seeking to enter the United States, to demand identification, and to search their persons and effects to make sure that contraband is not being smuggled. For example, in *United States v. Flores-Montano*, 541 U.S. 149 (2004), the Court held that border patrol agents could dismantle an automobile's gas tank to determine whether illegal drugs were being carried in the trunk.

Special Needs Searches. In a number of recent cases, the Court has developed a "special needs" exception to the warrant requirement. This exception, which especially applies in safety and administrative cases, allows the government to search or seize without probable cause and sometimes even without reasonable suspicion. For example, in *Skinner v. Railway Labor Executives' Association*, 489 U.S. 602 (1989), the Court upheld Federal Railroad Administration (FRA) regulations that required blood and urine tests of railroad employees involved in "major" train accidents, and authorizing railroads to administer breath and urine tests to employees who violate certain safety rules. In *Board of Education v. Earls*, 536 U.S. 822 (2002), the Court upheld mandatory drug testing for students involved in extracurricular activities. However, in *Ferguson v. City of Charleston*, 532 U.S. 67 (2001), the Court struck down a hospital's prenatal urine testing program that tested maternity patients for usage of illegal drugs and turned the results over to the police for prosecution. Although the patients agreed to the test, they were unaware that the results would be turned over to the police. The Court struck the program down: "The reasonable expectation of privacy enjoyed by the typical patient undergoing diagnostic tests in a hospital is that the results of those tests will not be shared with nonmedical personnel without her consent. In none of our prior cases was there any intrusion upon that kind of expectation."

Exigent Circumstances. The police can also dispense with a warrant when they are faced with "exigent circumstances." For example, there is a long line of cases which suggests that the police may make a warrantless entry into a home in order to prevent the imminent destruction of evidence. In addition, the police are regarded as having a "community caretaking" function, and are sometimes allowed to make warrantless entry into buildings when there is "an objectively reasonable basis for believing," that "a person within the house is in need of immediate aid."

Due Process Limitations. In *Rochin v. California*, 342 U.S. 165 (1952), the Court held that the police could not forcibly extract evidence from an individual's stomach (the police believed that Rochin had swallowed morphine to prevent the police from seizing it) by forcing emetic solution into his stomach. The Court concluded that the police conduct "shocks the conscience." In general, although the police do not need a warrant to force someone to take a breath test, designed to determine whether a driver is intoxicated, a warrant is generally now required for blood draws designed to test the level of alcohol in a driver's blood.

Test Your Knowledge

To assess your understanding of the material in this chapter, click here to take a quiz.

For More Information

- JOHN BURKOFF, SEARCH WARRANT LAW DESKBOOK (semi-annual editions) (Thomson Reuters)

- THOMAS K. CLANCY, THE FOURTH AMENDMENT: ITS HISTORY AND INTERPRETATION. (2d ed. 2013).

- Andrew Guthrie Ferguson, *The "Smart" Fourth Amendment*, 102 Cornell L. Rev. 547 (2017).

- Brandon Garrett & Seth Stoughton, *A Tactical Fourth Amendment*, 103 Va. L. Rev. 211 (2017).

- Orin S. Kerr, *The Effect of Legislation on Fourth Amendment Protection,* 115 Mich. L. Rev. 1117 (2017).

- ORIN KERR, *The Fourth Amendment and the Global Internet*, 67 STAN. L. REV. 285 (2015).

- WAYNE LAFAVE, SEARCH AND SEIZURE: A TREATISE ON THE FOURTH AMENDMENT (5th ed.) (Thomson Reuters) (2012).

- Christopher Slobogin, *Policing as Administration*, 165 U. Pa. L. Rev. 91 (2016).

- Russell L. Weaver, John M. Burkoff, Catherine Hancock & Steven I. Friedland, Principles of Criminal Procedure Ch. 4 (6th ed. 2018).

CHAPTER 5

Entrapment

By the time the Supreme Court recognized the criminal law defense of entrapment for defendants in federal cases, the defense had been recognized by state courts for over 50 years and was supported by federal court precedents. However, in its earliest entrapment decision in *Sorrells v. United States* (1932), the Supreme Court was split regarding the definition and scope of the defense, and the same division marked the Court's opinion in *Sherman v. United States* (1958). In both rulings, the "subjective" test was affirmed by a Court majority and the "objective" test was favored by a minority. Notably, the subjective test produces a narrower defense and requires the assessment of a jury. If a defendant produces some evidence of "inducement" by a government agent, then the defendant will receive a jury instruction posing the question whether the prosecution can prove beyond a reasonable doubt that the defendant was "predisposed" to commit the crime. Federal courts are required to use the subjective test, which is also used by a majority of state courts. By contrast, the objective test is used by a minority of state courts. It requires a judge to determine as a matter of law whether the particular government inducement to which the defendant was exposed would have created a substantial risk that a crime would be committed by a person who normally would avoid crime. A small number of courts have recognized the potential value of a Due Process defense to protect "predisposed" defendants from entrapment strategies that rise to the level of "outrageous government conduct." But the Supreme Court has declined to recognize that defense.

A. The Entrapment Defense

1. Early Foundations: Debate Over Subjective Test v. Objective Test

The subjective test for the entrapment defense was established in *Sorrells v. United States* (1932) and reaffirmed in *Sherman v. United States* (1958). Consider the priorities expressed in the *Sherman* majority's defense of the subjective test, and compare the views of the concurring justices who favor the objective test.

What reasons may explain why the subjective test is sufficiently controversial to provoke resistance among the state courts that adhere to the objective test instead?

Sherman v. United States

356 U.S. 369 (1958).

MR. CHIEF JUSTICE WARREN delivered the opinion of the Court.

[After Kalchinian was arrested for narcotics crimes, he agreed to act as a government informer and to identify others who could be persuaded to sell him drugs.] In late August 1951, he first met petitioner at a doctor's office where both were being treated to be cured of narcotics addiction. Several accidental meetings followed, either at the doctor's office or at the pharmacy where both filled their prescriptions from the doctor. From mere greetings, conversation progressed to a discussion of mutual experiences and problems, including their attempts to overcome addiction to narcotics. Finally Kalchinian asked petitioner if he knew of a good source of narcotics. He asked petitioner to supply him with a source because he was not responding to treatment and was suffering withdrawal symptoms. From the first, petitioner tried to avoid the issue. Not until after a number of repetitions of the request, predicated on Kalchinian's presumed suffering, did petitioner finally acquiesce. Several times thereafter he obtained a quantity of narcotics which he shared with Kalchinian. Each time petitioner told Kalchinian that the total cost of narcotics he obtained was twenty-five dollars and that Kalchinian owed him fifteen dollars. The informer thus bore the cost of his share of the narcotics plus the taxi and other expenses necessary to obtain the drug. After several such sales Kalchinian informed agents of the Bureau of Narcotics that he had another seller for them. On three occasions during November 1951 Government agents observed petitioner give narcotics to Kalchinian in return for money supplied by the Government.

At the trial the factual issue was whether the informer had convinced an otherwise unwilling person to commit a criminal act or whether petitioner was already predisposed to commit the act and exhibited only the natural hesitancy of one acquainted with the narcotics trade. The issue of entrapment went to the jury, and a conviction resulted. Petitioner was sentenced to imprisonment for ten years. The Court of Appeals for the Second Circuit affirmed.

In *Sorrells v. United States*, 287 U.S. 435 (1932), this Court firmly recognized the defense of entrapment in the federal courts. The intervening years have in no way detracted from the principles underlying that decision. Criminal activity is such that stealth and strategy are necessary weapons in the arsenal of the police officer. However, "A different question is presented when the criminal design originates with the officials of the government, and they implant in the mind of an innocent person the disposition to commit the alleged offense and induce its commission in order that they may prosecute." The stealth and strategy become as objectionable police methods as the coerced confession and the unlawful search. Congress could not have intended that its statutes were to be enforced by tempting innocent persons into violations.

However, the fact that government agents "merely afford opportunities or facilities for the commission of the offense does not" constitute entrapment. Entrapment occurs only when the criminal conduct was "the product of the creative activity" of law enforcement officials. To determine whether entrapment has been established, a line must be drawn between the trap for the unwary innocent and the trap for the unwary criminal.

We conclude from the evidence that entrapment was established as a matter of law. It is patently clear that petitioner was induced by Kalchinian. In Kalchinian's own words we are told of the accidental, yet recurring, meetings, the ensuing conversations concerning mutual experiences in regard to narcotics addiction, and then of Kalchinian's resort to sympathy. One request was not enough, for Kalchinian tells us that additional ones were necessary to overcome, first, petitioner's refusal, then his evasiveness, and then his hesitancy in order to achieve capitulation. Kalchinian not only procured a source of narcotics but apparently also induced petitioner to return to the habit. Finally, assured of a catch, Kalchinian informed the authorities so that they could close the net. Although he was not being paid, Kalchinian was an active government informer who had but recently been the instigator of at least two other prosecutions. Undoubtedly the impetus for such achievements was the fact that Kalchinian was himself under criminal charges for illegally selling narcotics and had not yet been sentenced. It makes no difference that the sales for which petitioner was convicted occurred after a series of sales. They were not independent acts subsequent to the inducement but part of a course of conduct which was the product of the inducement.

The Government sought to overcome the defense of entrapment by claiming that petitioner evinced a "ready complaisance" to accede to Kalchinian's request. Aside from a record of past convictions, the Government's case is unsupported. There is no evidence that petitioner himself was in the trade. When his apartment was searched after arrest, no narcotics were found. There is no significant evidence that petitioner even made a profit on

Take Note

Kalchinian ultimately received a suspended sentence in 1952, after the federal prosecutor informed the judge that Kalchinian had fulfilled his agreement to cooperate with the Government.

any sale to Kalchinian. The Government's characterization of petitioner's hesitancy to Kalchinian's request as the natural wariness of the criminal cannot fill the evidentiary void.

The Government sought to show that petitioner was ready and willing to sell narcotics should the opportunity present itself, based on petitioner's record of two past narcotics convictions. In 1942 petitioner was convicted of illegally selling narcotics; in 1946 he was convicted of illegally possessing them. However, a nine-year-old sales conviction and a five-year-old possession conviction are insufficient to prove petitioner had a readiness to sell narcotics at the time Kalchinian approached him, particularly when we must assume from the record he was trying to overcome the narcotics habit at the time.

The case at bar illustrates an evil which the defense of entrapment is designed to overcome. The government informer entices someone attempting to avoid narcotics not only into carrying out an illegal sale but also into returning to the habit of use. Selecting the proper time, the informer then tells the government agent. The set-up is accepted by the agent without even a question as to the manner in which the informer encountered the seller. Thus the Government plays on the weaknesses of an innocent party and beguiles him into committing crimes which he otherwise would not have attempted. Law enforcement does not require methods such as this.

Food for Thought

One way to prove predisposition is to demonstrate a defendant's ready response to an inducement. What types of evidence may provide proof of such readiness that is synonymous with predisposition, as indicated in the *Sherman* opinion? Why did the Court conclude that the evidence was insufficient in *Sherman* to justify the jury's finding of predisposition, so that a finding of entrapment was required as a matter of law?

Food for Thought

The *Sherman* majority assumed that if the Government could have shown the defendant's predisposition, then the same successful scheme to set him up would not be "an evil" that required the remedy of acquittal based on the entrapment defense. What arguments could be used to justify this view? What arguments could be used to criticize it?

The judgment of the Court of Appeals is reversed and the case is remanded to the District Court with instructions to dismiss the indictment.

MR. JUSTICE FRANKFURTER, whom MR. JUSTICE DOUGLAS, MR. JUSTICE HARLAN, and MR. JUSTICE BRENNAN join, concurring in the result.

Today's opinion accepts without re-examination the theory espoused in

Sorrells. It is surely sheer fiction to suggest that a conviction cannot be had when a defendant has been entrapped by government officers or informers because "Congress could not have intended that its statutes were to be enforced by tempting innocent persons into violations." The courts refuse to convict an entrapped defendant, not because his conduct falls outside the proscription of the statute, but because, even if his guilt be admitted, the methods employed on behalf of the Government to bring about conviction cannot be countenanced. As Mr. Justice Holmes said in *Olmstead v. United States*, 277 U.S. 438, 470 (1925) (dissenting), in another connection, "For my part I think it a less evil that some criminals should escape than that the government should play an ignoble part." Public confidence in the fair and honorable administration of justice, upon which ultimately depends the rule of law, is the transcending value at stake.

The crucial question is whether the police conduct revealed in the particular case falls below standards for the proper use of governmental power. Of course in every case of this kind the intention that the particular crime be committed originates with the police, and without their inducement the crime would not have occurred. But it is perfectly clear that where the police in effect simply furnished the opportunity for the commission of the crime, that this is not enough to enable the defendant to escape conviction.

Make the Connection

Justice Holmes dissented in *Olmstead* from the Court's ruling that no Fourth Amendment "search" occurred when agents inserted wiretaps into telephone wires, given the lack of "actual physical invasion" into a "constitutionally protected area." He observed the federal agents in *Olmstead* violated a state criminal law, and that "the Government should not itself foster and pay for other crimes, when they are the means by which the evidence is to be obtained."

The intention referred to, therefore, must be a predisposition to commit, whenever the opportunity should arise, crimes of the kind solicited, and in proof of such a predisposition evidence has often been admitted to show the defendant's reputation, criminal activities, and prior disposition. The danger of prejudice in such a situation, when the issue of entrapment must be submitted to the jury, is evident. The defendant must run the substantial risk that, in spite of instructions, the jury will allow a criminal record or bad reputation to weigh in its determination of guilt of the specific offense of which he stands charged. Furthermore, a test that looks to the character and predisposition of the defendant rather than the conduct of the police loses sight of the underlying reason for the defense of entrapment. No matter what the defendant's past record and present inclinations to criminality, certain police conduct to ensnare him into further crime is not to be tolerated by an advanced society. Permissible police activity does not vary according to the particular defendant concerned; surely if two suspects have been solicited at the same time in the same manner, one should not go to jail simply because he has been convicted before and is said to have a criminal disposition. Appeals to sympathy, friendship, the possibility of exorbitant gain, and so forth, can no more be tolerated when directed against a past offender than against an ordinary law-abiding citizen. Past crimes do not forever outlaw the criminal and open him to police practices, aimed at securing his repeated conviction, from which the ordinary citizen is protected. The whole ameliorative hopes of modern penology and prison administration strongly counsel against such a view.

This does not mean that the police may not act so as to detect those engaged in criminal conduct and ready and willing to commit further crimes should the occasion arise. It does mean that in holding out inducements they should act in such a manner as is likely to induce to the commission of crime only these persons and not others who would normally avoid crime and through self-struggle resist ordinary temptations. This test shifts attention from the record and predisposition of the particular defendant to the conduct of the police and the likelihood, objectively considered, that it would entrap only those ready and willing to commit crime.

What's That?

Justice Frankfurter's reference to the "ameliorative hopes of modern penology" is an allusion to the consensus of criminal justice reformers in the *Sherman* era that rehabilitation was the primary purpose of punishment. This view found expression in the practice of sentencing defendants to "indeterminate" prison terms, with release made contingent upon a prisoner's successful rehabilitation as determined by corrections officials. *Compare* Francis A. Allen, The Decline of the Rehabilitative Ideal (1981).

It is as objective a test as the subject matter permits and draws directly on the fundamental intuition that led in the first instance to the outlawing of "entrapment" as a prosecutorial instrument. The power of government is abused and directed to an end for which it was not constituted when employed to bring about the downfall of those who, left to themselves, might well have obeyed the law. Human nature is weak enough and sufficiently beset by temptations without government adding to them and generating crime.

What police conduct is to be condemned, because likely to induce those not otherwise ready and willing to commit crime, must be picked out from case to case as new situations arise involving different crimes and new methods of detection. Particularly reprehensible in the present case was the use of repeated requests to overcome petitioner's hesitancy, coupled with appeals to sympathy based on mutual experiences with narcotics addiction. Evidence of the setting in which the inducement took place is of course highly relevant in judging its likely effect, and the court should also consider the nature of the crime involved, its secrecy and difficulty of detection, and the manner in which the particular criminal business is usually carried on.

It is the province of the court and not the jury to protect the government from the prostitution of the criminal law. Only the court can do this with the degree of certainty that the wise administration of criminal justice demands.

Food for Thought

The *Sherman* case involved the use of a decoy addict to prosecute sales of illegal narcotics and *Sorrells* involved a sting to prosecute the sale of contraband alcohol. What other crimes have been prosecuted through the use of decoy and sting operations during the 20th century? What crimes have been targeted with such operations during more recent years?

Points for Discussion

a. What Is an Inducement?

Most courts recognize that an inducement requires more than "the fact that government agents initiated contact with the defendant and offered an ordinary opportunity to commit a crime." *United States v. Mayfield*, 771 F.3d 417, 431 (7th Cir. 2014) (en banc). In this context, the term "ordinary" means "something close to what unfolds when a sting operation mirrors the customary execution of the crime charged." For an inducement to exist, "Something more is required, either in terms of the character and degree of the government's persistence or persuasion, or the nature of the enticement or reward."

An inducement has been described as "a special incentive" that "can consist of anything that materially alters the balance of risks and rewards bearing on a defendant's decision whether to commit the offense, so as to increase the likelihood that he will engage in the particular criminal conduct." *United States v. Poehlman*, 217 F.3d 692, 698 (9th Cir. 2000). Typically, an inducement involves "excessive pressure by the government or the government's taking advantage of an alternative, non-criminal type of motive." *Jacobson v. United States*, 503 U.S. 540, 550 (1992). For example, an inducement may take the form of a plea based on friendship or need, or it may offer positive incentives, such as "promises of reward," or negative incentives, such as "threats, coercive tactics, or harassment." Even "very subtle government pressure, if skillfully applied, can amount to inducement," such as the establishment of a "friendly relationship" as in *Sherman*, followed by a plea for empathy with a suffering friend. *Poehlman*, 217 F.3d at 698, 701–702.

b. Proving Predisposition

The Government may use one of several general approaches to demonstrate a defendant's predisposition, including proving: 1) "an existing course of criminal conduct similar to the crime for which the defendant is charged"; 2) "an already formed design on the part of the accused to commit the crime for which he is charged"; or 3) the defendant's "willingness to commit the crime" as shown by his or her "ready response to the inducement." *United States v. Brunshtein*, 344 F.3d 91, 101 (2d Cir. 2003). Since *Sherman*, courts have looked to a wide variety of "factors" in assessing jury findings of predisposition. As enumerated in *United States v. Dion*, 762 F.2d 674 (8th Cir. 1985), *rev'd on other grounds*, 476 U.S. 734 (1986), those factors have included: (1) "the circumstances surrounding the illegal conduct"; (2) "the state of mind of a defendant before government agents make any suggestion that he shall commit a crime"; (3) "the defendant's reputation"; (4) "the conduct of the defendant during the negotiations with the undercover agent"; (5) "whether the defendant has refused to commit similar acts on other occasions"; (6) "the nature of the crime charged"; and (7) "the degree of coercion present in the instigation law officers have contributed to the transaction" relative to the "defendant's criminal background." Examples of additional "factors" include: (8) "whether the defendant engaged in the criminal activity for profit"; (9) "whether the defendant evidenced a reluctance to commit the offense that was overcome by government persuasion"; and (10) "the nature of the inducement or persuasion by the government." *United States v. Pillado,* 656 F.3d 754, 766 (7th Cir. 2011). Not until *Jacobson* (1992) did the Supreme Court clarify predisposition analysis by explicating the *Sorrells* admonition that government agents should not "implant in the mind" of the defendant "the disposition to commit the alleged offense" and then "induce its commission."

c. Persistent Split Over Test

Food for Thought

Suppose that Anne regularly sells cocaine to close friends but not to others because she is afraid of getting caught. When an undercover agent offers to buy drugs at the going rate from Anne, she rejects his offer. But when the agent offers Anne four times the normal price, she agrees to sell. If Anne is convicted and brings an appeal based on the entrapment defense, would she have a better chance of success in a jurisdiction using the "subjective" test or the "objective" test?

In advocating for the objective test, the concurring justices in *Sherman* adhered to the position of the *Sorrells* dissenters, including Justice Brandeis, whose earlier advocacy of the objective test in *Casey v. United States*, 276 U.S. 413, 423 (1928) (dissenting), prefigured the views of its defenders in *Sorrells* and *Sherman*: "The government may not provoke or create a crime and then punish the criminal, its creature. If such a one is guilty, it is because he yielded to the temptation presented by the officers. It does not follow that the court must suffer a detective-made criminal to be punished. To permit that would be tantamount to a ratification by the government of the officers' unauthorized and unjustifiable conduct."

Four years after *Sherman*, the Model Penal Code endorsed the objective test for the entrapment defense by requiring acquittal under the following circumstances: "A public law enforcement official or person acting in cooperation with such an official perpetrates an entrapment if for the purpose of obtaining evidence of the commission of an offense, he induces or encourages another person to engage in conduct constituting such offense by employing methods of persuasion or inducement that create a substantial risk that such an offense will be committed by persons other than those who are ready to commit it." Model Penal Code § 2.13. How does this provision resemble the objective test as it is characterized in Justice Frankfurter's concurring opinion in *Sherman*?

Food for Thought

The persistent debate over the competing tests has produced "substantial volatility" in state entrapment doctrines. Some state courts and legislatures have switched back and forth between the subjective and objective tests (or vice versa), and some states have adopted "an amalgamated approach." Joseph A. Colquitt, *Rethinking Entrapment*, 41 Am. Crim. L. Rev. 1389, 1402 (2004). What policy concerns may help to explain the continuing resistance to the dominance of the subjective test? Why might judicial adoption of the objective test serve as a lightning rod for legislative criticism and provoke the enactment of a statutory subjective test?

Hypo 1: *Wartime Experiences*

In *Sorrells*, an undercover agent joined a group of defendant's friends during their visit to defendant's home, and repeatedly asked defendant to sell him some whisky. Defendant brushed off these requests. When the agent learned that defendant was a World War I veteran, the agent identified himself as a veteran, and conversed about their wartime experiences. Then when the agent made a third request for whisky, defendant left his house and returned with a half-gallon jug that he sold to the agent for five dollars. Defendant was convicted of crimes under the National Prohibition Act after the trial judge refused to give a jury instruction on entrapment. Was there sufficient inducement to apply the entrapment defense? How might the government attempt to prove the defendant's predisposition at the new trial? *Compare Sorrells v. United States*, 287 U.S. 435 (1932).

Hypo 2: *Entrapment Instruction?*

Upon receiving information that some members of the San Antonio Police Department were willing to commit crimes in exchange for money, FBI agents created a reverse-sting operation using an undercover agent who posed as a drug dealer named Page. He offered to pay officers $2,500 in exchange for their services in providing "security" during illegal drug transactions. Sally was a sergeant who heard about Page's operation and told him that she wanted to participate. After Sally provided "security" for several transactions, Page asked her whether she knew any other officers who might want to provide security. When Sally told Zeno, one of the new police cadets, about the lucrative opportunity available in Page's operation, Zeno told Sally, "I want in." After Zeno received $2,500 from Page for providing security during one transaction, Zeno was arrested along with the other officers involved in Page's sting. At Zeno's trial for drug crimes, his defense counsel sought an entrapment instruction, arguing that: 1) Sally's acts in recruiting Zeno should be attributed to the Government; and 2) that there was sufficient evidence of Sally's inducement of Zeno, because she was his superior officer and he was frightened of her. The trial judge denied the instruction. Should the appellate court affirm that ruling? *Compare* United States v. Gutierrez, 343 F.3d 415 (5th Cir. 2003).

Hypo 3: *Decoy Addict*

Undercover agents noticed Stan because he appeared to be a narcotics addict suffering from withdrawal. He was pale, twitching, shaking, and vomiting as the agents approached him. The agents decided to use Stan as a decoy. When the agents gave Stan $50 and asked him to buy drugs for them, the man led the agents to a nearby intersection where he expected to find drug sellers. Finding no sellers at the intersection, Stan called out to a passing stranger, Ricardo, saying, "I need a fix, I need your help, I'm really hurting. Please, just find me someone who can sell me something right away." Ricardo told Stan that he was sorry to see Stan in such terrible shape, and that he had heard some people say that drug sellers sometimes came to a nearby park. So Ricardo and Stan walked to the park, with the agents trailing them at a distance. At the park, Stan collapsed on a bench, while Ricardo took Stan's $50 and approached a woman who appeared to be selling drugs. Ricardo bought the drugs for Stan and when he gave them to Stan, Ricardo was arrested and charged with drug crimes. Ricardo's defense counsel asks for an entrapment instruction at trial. Was there sufficient evidence of inducement? *Compare Bradley v. Duncan,* 315 F.3d 1091 (9th Cir. 2002).

2. Modern Developments

The *Jacobson* case was a milestone in entrapment law because it shifted the emphasis of the predisposition concept—from the examination of the defendant's response to the assessment of whether the defendant would have committed the crime without the government's involvement.

Jacobson v. United States

503 U.S. 540 (1992).

JUSTICE WHITE delivered the opinion of the Court, in which JUSTICE BLACKMUN, JUSTICE STEVENS, JUSTICE SOUTER and JUSTICE THOMAS, joined.

Because the Government overstepped the line between setting a trap for the "unwary innocent" and the "unwary criminal," *Sherman v. United States,* 356 U.S. 369, 372 (1958), and as a matter of law failed to establish that petitioner was independently predisposed to commit the crime for which he was arrested, we reverse the Court of Appeals' judgment affirming his conviction.

In February 1984, petitioner, a 56-year-old veteran-turned-farmer, who supported his elderly father in Nebraska, ordered two magazines and a brochure from a California adult bookstore. The magazines, entitled Bare Boys I and Bare Boys II, contained photographs of nude preteen and teenage boys. The contents of the magazines startled petitioner, who testified that he had expected to receive photographs of "young men 18 years or older." The young men depicted in the magazines were not engaged in sexual activity, and petitioner's receipt of the magazines was legal under both federal and Nebraska law. Within three months, the law with respect to child pornography changed; Congress passed the Act illegalizing the receipt through the mails of sexually explicit depictions of children. In the very month that the new provision became law, postal inspectors found petitioner's name on the mailing list of the California bookstore that had mailed him Bare Boys I and II. There followed over the next 2 ½ years repeated efforts by two Government agencies, through five fictitious organizations and a bogus pen pal, to explore petitioner's willingness to break the new law by ordering sexually explicit photographs of children through the mail.

The Government began its efforts in January 1985 when a postal inspector sent petitioner a letter supposedly from the American Hedonist Society, which in fact was a fictitious organization. The letter included a membership application and stated the Society's doctrine: that members had the "right to read what we desire, the right to discuss similar interests with those who share our philosophy, and finally that we have the right to seek pleasure without restrictions being placed on us by outdated puritan morality." Petitioner enrolled in the organization and returned a sexual attitude questionnaire that asked him to rank on a scale of one to four his enjoyment of various sexual materials, with one being "really enjoy," two being "enjoy,"

Take Note

The *Jacobson* defendant was targeted by the Postal Service's Operation Looking Glass, a "reverse-sting" which resulted in 161 arrests and 147 convictions. Only the *Jacobson* prosecution led to a ruling that upheld the entrapment defense. By the time the Supreme Court decided his case in 1992, five years had passed since Jacobson's arrest in 1987 and he "had completed his sentence." Joseph A. Colquitt, *Rethinking Entrapment*, 41 Am. Crim. L. Rev. 1389, 1391, 1414 (2004). Jacobson received a three-year prison sentence that was suspended to 250 hours of community service and two years of probation.

three being "somewhat enjoy," and four being "do not enjoy." Petitioner ranked the entry "pre-teen sex" as a two, but indicated that he was opposed to pedophilia.

For a time, the Government left petitioner alone. But then a new "prohibited mailing specialist" in the Postal Service found petitioner's name in a file, and in May 1986, petitioner received a solicitation from a second fictitious consumer research company, "Midlands Data Research," seeking a response from those who "believe in the joys of sex and the complete awareness of those lusty and youthful lads and lasses of the neophite [sic] age." The letter never explained whether "neophite" referred to minors or young adults. Petitioner responded: "Please feel free to send me more information, I am interested in teenage sexuality. Please keep my name confidential."

Petitioner then heard from yet another Government creation, "Heartland Institute for a New Tomorrow" (HINT), which proclaimed that it was "an organization founded to protect and promote sexual freedom and freedom of choice. We believe that arbitrarily imposed legislative sanctions restricting your sexual freedom should be rescinded through the legislative process." The letter also enclosed a second survey. Petitioner indicated that his interest in "preteen sex-homosexual" material was above average, but not high. In response to another question, petitioner wrote: "Not only sexual expression but freedom of the press is under attack. We must be ever vigilant to counter attack right wing fundamentalists who are determined to curtail our freedoms." HINT replied, portraying itself as a lobbying organization seeking to repeal "all statutes which regulate sexual activities, except those laws which deal with violent behavior, such as rape. HINT is also lobbying to eliminate any legal definition of 'the age of consent.'" HINT also provided computer matching of group members with similar survey responses; and, although petitioner was supplied with a list of potential "pen pals," he did not initiate any correspondence.

Nevertheless, the Government's "prohibited mailing specialist" began writing to petitioner, using the pseudonym "Carl Long." The letters employed a tactic known as "mirroring," which the inspector described as "reflecting whatever the interests are of the person we are writing to." Petitioner responded at first, indicating that his interest was primarily in "male-male items." Inspector "Long" wrote back:

> "My interests too are primarily male-male items. Are you satisfied with the type of VCR tapes available? Personally, I like the amateur stuff better if its [sic] well produced as it can get more kinky and also seems more real. I think the actors enjoy it more."

Petitioner responded:

> "As far as my likes are concerned, I like good looking young guys (in their late teens and early 20's) doing their thing together."

Petitioner's letters to "Long" made no reference to child pornography. After writing two letters, petitioner discontinued the correspondence.

By March 1987, 34 months had passed since the Government obtained petitioner's name from the mailing list of the California bookstore, and 26 months had passed since the Postal Service had commenced its mailings to petitioner. Although petitioner had responded to surveys and letters, the Government had no evidence that petitioner had ever intentionally possessed or been exposed to child pornography. At this point, the Postal Service wrote to petitioner as the "Far Eastern Trading Company Ltd." The letter began:

> "As many of you know, much hysterical nonsense has appeared in the American media concerning 'pornography' and what must be done to stop it from coming across your borders. This brief letter does not allow us to give much comment; however, why is your government spending millions of dollars to exercise international censorship while tons of

drugs, which makes yours the world's most crime ridden country, are passed through easily."

The letter went on to say:

"We have devised a method of getting these to you without prying eyes of U.S. Customs seizing your mail. After consultations with American solicitors, we have been advised that once we have posted our material through your system, it cannot be opened for any inspection without authorization of a judge."

The letter invited petitioner to send for more information. It also asked petitioner to sign an affirmation that he was "not a law enforcement officer or agent of the U.S. Government acting in an undercover capacity for the purpose of entrapping Far Eastern Trading Company, its agents or customers." Petitioner responded. A catalog was sent, and petitioner ordered Boys Who Love Boys, a pornographic magazine depicting young boys engaged in various sexual activities. Petitioner was arrested after a controlled delivery of a photocopy of the magazine.

When petitioner was asked at trial why he placed such an order, he explained that the Government had succeeded in piquing his curiosity: "Well, the statement was made of all the trouble and the hysteria over pornography and I wanted to see what the material was. It didn't describe the—I didn't know for sure what kind of sexual action they were referring to in the Canadian letter."

In petitioner's home, the Government found the Bare Boys magazines and materials that the Government had sent to him in the course of its protracted investigation, but no other materials that would indicate that petitioner collected, or was actively interested in, child pornography.

Petitioner was indicted for violating 18 U.S.C. § 2252(a)(2)(A). [This provision in the Child Protection Act of 1984 prohibits the conduct of "knowingly receiving any visual depiction" that has been mailed "if the producing of such visual depiction involves the use of a minor engaging in sexually explicit conduct and such visual depiction is of such conduct."] The trial court instructed the jury on the petitioner's entrapment defense, and petitioner was convicted.

There can be no dispute about the evils of child pornography or the difficulties that laws and law enforcement have encountered in eliminating it. Likewise, there can be no dispute that the Government may use undercover agents to enforce the law. "It is well settled that the fact that officers or employees of the Government merely afford opportunities or facilities for the commission of the offense does not defeat the prosecution. Artifice and stratagem may be employed to catch those engaged in criminal enterprises." *Sorrells v. United States*, 287 U.S. 435, 441 (1932).

In their zeal to enforce the law, however, Government agents may not originate a criminal design, implant in an innocent person's mind the disposition to commit a criminal act, and then induce commission of the crime so that the Government may prosecute. Where the Government has induced an individual to break the law and the defense of entrapment is at issue, as it was in this case, the prosecution must prove beyond reasonable doubt that the defendant was disposed to commit the criminal act prior to first being approached by Government agents.

Where the defendant is simply provided with the opportunity to commit a crime, the entrapment defense is of little use because the ready commission of the criminal act amply demonstrates the defendant's predisposition. Had the agents in this case simply offered petitioner the opportunity to order child pornography through the mails, and petitioner—who must be presumed to know the law—had promptly availed himself of this criminal opportunity, it is unlikely that his entrapment defense would have warranted a jury instruction.

But that is not what happened here. By the time petitioner finally placed his order, he had already been the target of 26 months of repeated mailings and communications from Government agents and fictitious organizations. Therefore, although he had become predisposed to break the law by May 1987, it is our view that the Government did not prove that this predisposition was independent and not the product of the attention that the Government had directed at petitioner since January 1985.

The prosecution's evidence of predisposition falls into two categories: evidence developed prior to the Postal Service's mail campaign, and that developed during the course of the investigation. The sole piece of pre-investigation evidence is petitioner's 1984 order and receipt of the Bare Boys magazines. But this is scant if any proof of petitioner's predisposition to commit an illegal act, the criminal character of which a defendant is presumed to know. It may indicate a predisposition to view sexually oriented photographs that are responsive to his sexual tastes; but evidence that merely indicates a generic inclination to act within a broad range, not all of which is criminal, is of little probative value in establishing predisposition.

Take Note

Justice White noted that "the proposition that the accused must be predisposed prior to contact with law enforcement officers is so firmly established that the Government conceded the point at oral argument." What the Government argued was that "the evidence it developed during the course of its investigation" was probative in demonstrating petitioner's predisposed "state of mind prior to the commencement of the Government's investigation."

Furthermore, petitioner was acting within the law at the time he received these magazines. Evidence of predisposition to do what once was lawful is not, by itself, sufficient to show predisposition to do what is now illegal, for there is a common understanding that most people obey the law even when they disapprove of it. Hence, the fact that petitioner legally ordered and received the Bare Boys magazines does little to further the Government's burden of proving that petitioner was predisposed to commit a criminal act. This is particularly true given petitioner's unchallenged testimony that he did not know until they arrived that the magazines would depict minors.

The prosecution's evidence gathered during the investigation also fails to carry the Government's burden. Petitioner's responses to the many communications prior to the ultimate criminal act were at most indicative of certain personal inclinations, including a predisposition to view photographs of preteen sex and a willingness to promote a given agenda by supporting lobbying organizations. Even so, petitioner's responses hardly support an inference that he would commit the crime of receiving child pornography through the mails. Furthermore, a person's inclinations and "fantasies are his own and beyond the reach of government." *Stanley v. Georgia*, 394 U.S. 552, 565 (1969).

On the other hand, the strong arguable inference is that, by waving the banner of individual rights and disparaging the legitimacy and constitutionality of efforts to restrict the availability of sexually explicit materials, the Government not only excited petitioner's interest in sexually explicit materials banned by law but also exerted substantial pressure on petitioner to obtain and read such material as part of a fight against censorship and the infringement of individual rights. For instance, HINT described itself as "an organization founded to protect and promote sexual freedom and freedom of choice" and stated that "the most appropriate means to accomplish its objectives is to promote honest dialogue among concerned individuals and to continue its lobbying efforts with State Legislators." Mailings from the equally fictitious American Hedonist Society, and the correspondence from the nonexistent Carl Long, endorsed these themes.

Similarly, the mailing from the Far Eastern Trading Company in the spring of 1987 raised the spectre of censorship while suggesting that petitioner ought to be allowed to do what he had been solicited to do. The Postal Service solicitation described the concern about child pornography as "hysterical nonsense," decried "international censorship," and assured petitioner, based on consultation with "American solicitors," that an order that had been posted could not be opened for inspection without authorization of a judge.

Petitioner's ready response to these solicitations cannot be enough to establish beyond reasonable doubt that he was predisposed, prior to the Government acts intended to create predisposition, to commit the crime of receiving child pornography through the mails. The evidence that petitioner was ready and willing to commit the offense came only after the Government had devoted 2 ½ years to convincing him that he had or should have the right to engage in the very behavior proscribed by law. Rational jurors could not say beyond a reasonable doubt that petitioner possessed the requisite predisposition prior to the Government's investigation and that it existed independent of the Government's many and varied approaches to petitioner. As was explained in *Sherman*, where entrapment was found as a matter of law, "the Government may not play on the weaknesses of an innocent party and beguile him into committing crimes which he otherwise would not have attempted."

Food for Thought

At what point did the Government's repeated inducements create the petitioner's predisposition? What action can government agents take in a child pornography sting operation in order to avoid the creation of predisposition, thereby preserving their ability to show that a targeted person was "independently predisposed to commit the crime" at the time of the first government contact?

When the Government's quest for convictions leads to the apprehension of an otherwise law-abiding citizen who, if left to his own devices, likely would have never run afoul of the law, the courts should intervene. Because we conclude that this is such a case and that the prosecution failed, as a matter of law, to adduce evidence to support the jury verdict that petitioner was predisposed, independent of the Government's acts and beyond a reasonable doubt, to violate the law, we reverse the Court of Appeals' judgment affirming the conviction of Keith Jacobson.

JUSTICE O'CONNOR, with whom THE CHIEF JUSTICE and JUSTICE KENNEDY join, and with whom JUSTICE SCALIA joins except as to Part II, dissenting.

Government agents admittedly did not offer Mr. Jacobson the chance to buy child pornography right away. Instead, they first sent questionnaires in order to make sure that he was generally interested in the subject matter. Indeed, a "cold call" in such a business would not only risk rebuff and suspicion, but might also shock and offend the uninitiated, or expose minors to suggestive materials. Mr. Jacobson's responses to the questionnaires gave the investigators reason to think he would be interested in photographs depicting preteen sex.

The Court, however, concludes that a reasonable jury could not have found Mr. Jacobson to be predisposed beyond a reasonable doubt on the basis of his responses to the Government's catalogs, even though it admits that, by that time he was predisposed to commit the crime. The Government, the Court holds, failed to provide evidence that Mr. Jacobson's obvious predisposition at the time of the crime "was independent and not the product of the attention that the Government had directed at petitioner." In so holding, I believe the Court fails to acknowledge the reasonableness of the jury's inference from the evidence, and introduces a new requirement that Government sting operations have a reasonable suspicion of illegal activity before contacting a suspect.

Make the Connection

In arguing that a reasonable suspicion requirement (drawn from Fourth Amendment doctrine) was implied in the Court's opinion, Justice O'Connor's dissent relied on this logic: If the Court's holding requires that the Government possess "sufficient evidence of a defendant's predisposition before it ever seeks to contact him," then "the Government must have a reasonable suspicion of criminal activity before it begins an investigation." However, the *Jacobson* decision was not interpreted subsequently as imposing such a reasonable suspicion requirement.

The crux of the Court's concern is that the Government went too far and "abused" the "'processes of detection and enforcement'" by luring an innocent person to violate the law. Consequently, the Court holds that the Government failed to prove beyond a reasonable doubt that Mr. Jacobson was predisposed to commit the crime. It was, however, the jury's task, as the conscience of the community, to decide whether Mr. Jacobson was a willing participant in the criminal activity here or an innocent dupe. Because I believe there was sufficient evidence to uphold the jury's verdict, I respectfully dissent.

Points for Discussion

a. *Jacobson's* Significance

Justice White noted in *Jacobson* that the 1980 Attorney General's Guidelines on FBI Undercover Operations limit the offering of an inducement to these two scenarios: 1) When "there is a reasonable indication, based on information developed through informants or other means, that the subject is engaging, has engaged, or is likely to engage in illegal activity of a similar type"; or 2) When "the opportunity for illegal activity has been structured so that there is reason for believing that persons drawn to the opportunity, or brought to it, are predisposed to engage in the contemplated illegal activity."

One year after *Jacobson*, an FBI bulletin provided the following advice to agents from an instructor at the FBI Academy:

> First, while reasonable suspicion is not legally necessary to initiate an undercover investigation, officers should nonetheless be prepared to articulate a legitimate law enforcement purpose for beginning such an investigation. Second, they should, to the extent possible, avoid using persistent or coercive techniques, and instead, merely create an opportunity or provide the facilities for the target to commit the crime. Third, officers should document and be prepared to articulate the factors demonstrating a defendant was disposed to commit the criminal act prior to government contact.

Paul Marcus, *Presenting, Back from the [Almost] Dead, the Entrapment Defense*, 47 Fla. L. Rev. 205, 237 (1995) (quoting Thomas V. Kukura, *Undercover Investigations and the Entrapment Defense*, FBI L. Enforcement Bull., April 1993, at 32).

b. Interpretations of *Jacobson*

In *United States v. Gendron*, 18 F.3d 955 (1st Cir. 1994) (Breyer, J.), the court viewed the government's inability to prove the requisite type of predisposition in *Jacobson* as attributable to the government's use of inducements that were not "ordinary" but "special" in three respects:

Food for Thought

Professor Marcus argues that although *Jacobson* did not alter the elements of the entrapment defense, the decision was significant because the of the Court's emphasis on the need for appellate courts to engage in "more careful review of evidence concerning government activity and the defendant's state of mind." What are the benefits of "more careful" judicial scrutiny of cases in which the jury has rejected the entrapment defense? Does the FBI Bulletin from 1993 suggest that *Jacobson* encouraged more careful design of sting operations by government agents?

> First, the solicitations reflected a psychologically "graduated" set of responses to Jacobson's own noncriminal responses, beginning with innocent lures and progressing to frank offers. Second, the government's soliciting letters sometimes depicted their senders as "free speech" lobbying organizations and fighters for the "right to read what we desire"; they asked Jacobson to "fight against censorship and the infringement of individual rights." Third, the government's effort to provide an "opportunity" to buy child pornography stretched out over two and a half years. Thus, the government's evidence did not show how Jacobson would have acted had he been faced with an ordinary "opportunity" to commit the crime rather than a "special" inducement.

A more complex interpretation of *Jacobson* appeared in *United States v. Hollingsworth*, 27 F.3d 1196, 1200 (7th Cir. 1994) (en banc):

We do not suggest that *Jacobson* adds a new element to the entrapment defense—"readiness" or "ability" or "dangerousness" on top of inducement and, most important, predisposition. (An inducement is significant chiefly as evidence bearing on predisposition; the greater the inducement, the weaker the inference that in yielding to it the defendant demonstrated that he was predisposed to commit the crime in question.) Rather, the Court clarified the meaning of predisposition. Predisposition is not a purely mental state, the state of being willing to swallow the government's bait. It has positional as well as dispositional force. The dictionary definitions of the word include "tendency" as well as "inclination." The defendant must be so situated by reason of previous training or experience or occupation or acquaintances that it is likely that if the government had not induced him to commit the crime some criminal would have done so; only then does a sting or other arranged crime take a dangerous person out of circulation. However, if the defendant had the idea for the crime all worked out and lacked merely the present means to commit it, and if the government had not supplied them someone else very well might have, then that would be a case in which the government had merely furnished the opportunity to commit the crime to someone already predisposed to commit it.

Hollingsworth's "positional predisposition" approach has been viewed as an interpretation of *Jacobson's* instruction "to ask what the defendant would have done without governmental involvement," by looking "not only to the defendant's mental state ('his disposition') but also to whether the defendant was able and likely, based on experience, training, and contacts, to actually commit the crime (his 'position')." *United States v. Knox*, 112 F.3d 802, 807 (5th Cir. 1997).

Some courts have rejected the "positional predisposition" doctrine on the ground that it is not expressly supported in *Jacobson's* reasoning. *See United States v. Cromitie*, 727 F.3d 194, 217 (2d Cir. 2013); *United States v. Thickstun*, 110 F.3d 1394, 1398 (9th Cir. 1997). These courts also cite the objections advanced by the *Hollingsworth* dissent:

> The *Hollingsworth* majority has changed the "ready" defendant from one who is inclined, feeling or exhibiting no reluctance, to one on the point of acting. Its holding will benefit not only the pathetic incompetents of the criminal world but also the very competent criminal who is sufficiently studied in his way of doing business so as to appear not too organized. The most problematic application

of the new rule will come when a sting operation attracts a very willing but also not very well organized or inept first offender. A defendant's prior arrests and convictions, as well as his previous associations with drug traffickers, are strong indications of predisposition. Without that past record, however, would the neophyte's quick reply to an agent's invitation to "talk business" count as predisposition? Would his agreement to distribute drugs show a willingness, but not a readiness? There is, of course, no constitutional requirement that the Congress punish only activity that *is immediately* dangerous.

Hypo 1: *Special Teacher*

Mark's wife sought a divorce when she discovered that Mark liked cross-dressing. He became lonely and depressed and started to visit "alternative lifestyle" discussion groups on the internet, looking for a female companion. Mark got a positive reaction from Shari, who told him that she thought cross-dressing was OK. When they exchanged emails, Mark described his status as a divorced father with two sons, and Shari shared her own biography as a mother of twin twelve-year-old daughters—her "sweethearts." Mark told Shari that he was "looking for a long-term relationship leading to marriage," and that he believed in strong family values and would treat Shari's children as his own. Shari told Mark that she was "looking for someone who understands us and does not let society's views stand in the way." When Shari told Mark that she was "looking for a special man teacher" for her sweethearts, Mark assured Shari that he would "teach her children proper morals and give support to them where it is needed." Ultimately, Shari asked Mark what he would teach her sweethearts "as a first lesson," if he were their "special man teacher." She advised him that, "If I disagree with something, I'll just say so. I do like to watch, though. I hope you don't think I'm too weird." Then Mark finally realized that Shari wanted him to play sex instructor, and he agreed to be a "special teacher" for her daughters. But he also kept saying that he wanted a relationship with her. After six months of exchanging emails, Shari invited Mark to her home. When he arrived, he discovered that Shari was an FBI agent whose assignment was to catch pedophiles on the internet. Mark was charged with the federal crime of attempted lewd acts with a minor. How will Mark's defense counsel argue that the necessary inducement evidence exists in this case? What arguments will defense counsel make to rebut the government's argument that Mark was predisposed? *Compare United States v. Poehlman*, 217 F.3d 692 (9th Cir. 2000).

Hypo 2: *Terrorist Designs*

Hussain is a Pakistani national who was paid to work undercover for the FBI in the Hudson River Valley with the goal of locating "disaffected Muslims who might be harboring terrorist designs on the United States." When attending a mosque in Newburgh, he portrayed himself as a wealthy businessman. Hussain then cultivated a friendship with Cromitie, an impoverished man who worshipped at the mosque and worked a night shift at Walmart. Cromitie's father was from Afghanistan. When Hussain asked Cromitie whether he would like to travel to Afghanistan, Cromitie said that he would, and added that he wanted to "do something to America," and to "die like a martyr and go to Paradise." The FBI instructed Hussain to tell Cromitie that he was a representative of a terrorist group in Pakistan (JeM). In response, Cromitie said that he wanted to join JeM. In September, Hussain mentioned to Cromitie that military planes flew from the nearby Newburgh Airport to take arms and ammunition to Afghanistan and Iraq. In response, Cromitie expressed his frustration with the United States, "taking down our Islamic countries" and disrespecting Muslims. Hussain asked Cromitie if he had ever thought of "doing something here in the U.S." and confided to Cromitie that he could obtain guns and rockets. In December, Hussain said, "Let's pick a target," and Cromitie said that he'd "like to get a synagogue." Later, Cromitie told Hussain that he was hard up for money, and Hussain said he could give Cromitie $250,000, that Hussain would train Cromitie how to use a rocket launcher, and that JeM would provide a missile. Hussain bought Cromitie a camera and drove him to the airport and to a synagogue to conduct

See It

A documentary film entitled, "The Newburgh Sting" (2014), portrays the entrapment story in the *Cromitie* case described here and can be viewed at the HBO website.

surveillance. In May, Hussain drove Cromitie to a warehouse where three fake bombs and two fake missiles were stored. They put the bombs in Hussain's car and drove to a synagogue where the FBI arrested Cromitie. At his trial for terrorism crimes, the jury rejected Cromitie's entrapment defense. What arguments will the prosecutor and defense counsel make on appeal regarding the defense claim that the evidence established entrapment as a matter of law? *Compare United States v. Cromitie*, 727 F.3d 194 (2d Cir. 2013).

B. Due Process and "Outrageous Government Conduct"

In the post-*Sherman* era, some federal circuit courts have recognized the need for a Due Process doctrine that could be used to reverse the conviction of a predisposed defendant who is apprehended by means of a police operation that rises to the level of "outrageous government conduct." However, the Supreme Court failed to endorse such a doctrine when the opportunity to do so arose in two cases in the 1970s. These precedents have had a chilling effect on the viability of a Due Process defense in some federal circuits today. The opinions in *United States v. Russell* (1973) and *Hampton v. United States* (1976) illustrate the Court's debates concerning the difficulties of identifying the characteristics of police operations that would justify the finding of a Due Process violation.

United States v. Russell

411 U.S. 423 (1973).

MR. JUSTICE REHQUIST delivered the opinion of the Court.

[Russell was convicted of drug crimes by a jury that received an entrapment instruction but rejected his defense.] The Court of Appeals reversed the conviction solely for the reason that an undercover agent supplied an essential chemical for manufacturing the methamphetamine which formed the basis of Russell's conviction. The court concluded that as a matter of law, "a defense to a criminal charge may be founded upon an intolerable degree of governmental participation in the criminal enterprise." We reverse that judgment.

A federal agent offered to supply Russell and the Connolly brothers with the chemical phenyl-2-propanone (P2P), a necessary ingredient for making methamphetamine, in exchange for receiving half of the drug they produced. They accepted his offer and also agreed to show him their meth lab and to give him a meth sample. At their lab, the agent saw an empty bottle of P2P. Two days later, he brought a 100-gram bottle of P2P to the lab. One of the Connollys added it to a flask, while Russell cut up aluminum foil pieces and put them in the flask. A few foil pieces fell on the ground and the agent picked them up and added them. The next day, Russell delivered the promised batches of meth to the agent. One month later, the agent returned to the lab to find out whether the trio was still interested in their "business arrangement." One of the Connollys told the agent that he had obtained two bottles of P2P that he was still using. Soon thereafter, the agent executed a search warrant and found the two bottles at the lab.

On appeal, Russell conceded that the jury could have found him predisposed to commit the offenses, but argued that on the facts presented there was entrapment as a matter of law. The Court of Appeals agreed and expanded the traditional notion of entrapment to mandate dismissal based on a new defense that was held to rest on either of two alternative theories. One theory is based on district court decisions which have found entrapment, regardless of predisposition, whenever the government supplies contraband to the defendants. The second theory is based on a decision that reversed a conviction because a government investigator was so enmeshed in the criminal activity that the prosecution of the defendants was held to be repugnant to the American criminal justice system. *Greene v. United States*, 454 F.3d 783 (9th Cir. 1971). The court below held that these two rationales constitute the same defense, and "both theories are premised on fundamental concepts of due process and evince the reluctance of the judiciary to countenance 'overzealous law enforcement.'" 459 F.3d at 674 (quoting *Sherman v. United States*, 356 U.S. 369, 381 (1958) (Frankfurter, J., concurring)).

In the instant case, defendant asks us to reconsider the theory of the entrapment defense and his contention is that the defense should rest on constitutional grounds. He argues that the level of the agent's involvement in the manufacture of the methamphetamine was so high that a criminal prosecution for the drug's manufacture violates the fundamental principles of due process. Defendant would have the Court adopt a rigid constitutional rule that would preclude any prosecution when it is shown that the criminal conduct would not have been possible had not an undercover agent "supplied an indispensable means to the commission of the crime that could not have been obtained otherwise, through legal or illegal channels." Even if we were to surmount the difficulties attending the notion that due process of law can be embodied in fixed rules, the rule he proposes would not appear to be of significant benefit to him. On the record presented, it appears that he cannot fit within the terms of the very rule he proposes.

The record discloses that although P2P was difficult to obtain, it was by no means impossible. Defendants admitted making the drug both before and after those batches made with the P2P supplied by the agent. He testified that he saw an empty bottle labeled phenyl-2-propanone on his first visit to the laboratory, and when it was searched, two additional bottles labeled P2P were seized. Thus, the facts amply demonstrate that the P2P used in the illicit manufacture of methamphetamine not only *could* have been obtained without the intervention of the agent but was in fact obtained by these defendants.

While we may be presented with a situation in which the conduct of law enforcement agents is so outrageous that due process principles would absolutely bar the government from invoking judicial processes to obtain a conviction, the instant case is not of that breed. The agent's contribution of P2P to the criminal enterprise already in process was scarcely objectionable. The chemical is by itself a harmless substance and its possession is legal.

The illicit manufacture of drugs is not a sporadic, isolated criminal incident, but a continuing, though illegal, business enterprise. In order to obtain convic-

In 1980, P2P was listed as a controlled substance. Would the *Russell* Court have reached a different result if P2P had been a controlled substance in 1973?

tions for illegally manufacturing drugs, the gathering of evidence of past unlawful conduct frequently proves to be an all but impossible task. Thus in drug-related offenses law enforcement personnel have turned to one of the only practicable means of detection: the infiltration of drug rings and a limited participation in their unlawful present practices. Such infiltration is a recognized and permissible means of investigation; if that be so, then the supply of some item of value that the drug ring requires must, as a general rule, also be permissible. For an agent will not be taken into the confidence of the illegal entrepreneurs unless he has something of value to offer them. Law enforcement tactics such as this can hardly be said to violate "fundamental fairness" or [to be] "shocking to the universal sense of justice."

Defendant also urges, as an alternative, that we broaden the non-constitutional defense of entrapment in order to sustain the judgment of the Court of Appeals. He argues that the views of the minority in *Sorrells v. United States*, 287 U.S. 435 (1932) and *Sherman* should be adopted by law. We decline to overrule these cases. Since the defense is not of a constitutional dimension, Congress may address itself to the question and adopt any substantive definition of the defense that it may find desirable. The defense of entrapment was not intended to give the federal judiciary a "chancellor's foot" veto over law enforcement practices of which it did not approve. We think that the decision of the Court of Appeals in this case quite unnecessarily introduces an unmanageably subjective standard which is contrary to the holdings of this Court in *Sorrells* and *Sherman*. The Court of Appeals was wrong, we believe, when it sought to broaden the principle laid down in [those cases]. Its judgment is therefore reversed.

What's That?

A "chancellor's foot veto" stands for inequitable variability in court decisions. The term was coined by John Selden, a 17th-century barrister, who said, "One Chancellor has a long foot, another a short foot, a third an indifferent foot; 'tis the same thing in the Chancellor's conscience."

Mr. Justice Douglas, with whom Mr. Justice Brennan concurs, dissenting.

My view is that of Mr. Justice Frankfurter stated in *Sherman v. United States*, 356 U.S. 378 (1958) (concurring in result). In my view, the fact that the chemical ingredient supplied by the federal agent might have been obtained from other sources is quite irrelevant. Supplying the chemical ingredient used in the manufacture of this batch of "speed" made the United States an active participant in the unlawful activity. Federal agents play a debased role when they become the instigators of the crime, or partners in its commission, or the creative brain behind the illegal scheme. That is what the federal agent did here when he furnished the accused with one of the chemical ingredients needed to manufacture the unlawful drug.

Mr. Justice Stewart, with whom Mr. Justice Brennan and Mr. Justice Marshall join, dissenting.

In my view, the objective approach to entrapment advanced by the minority in *Sorrells* and *Sherman* is the only one truly consistent with the underlying rationale of the defense. This does not mean that the Government's use of undercover activity, strategy, or deception is necessarily unlawful. But when the agents' involvement in criminal activities goes beyond the mere offering of such an opportunity and when their conduct is of a kind that could induce or instigate the commission of a crime by one not ready and willing to commit it, then—regardless of the character or propensities of the particular person induced—I think entrapment has occurred. In that situation, the Government has engaged in the impermissible manufacturing of crime, and the federal courts should bar the prosecution in order to preserve the institutional integrity of the system of federal criminal justice. It is the Government's duty to prevent crime, not to promote it. Here, the Government's agent asked that the illegal drug be produced for him, solved his quarry's practical problems

Food for Thought

Why did the *Russell* dissenters prefer to support the defendant's second argument that the objective test should be adopted for the entrapment defense in federal cases, instead of supporting the defendant's first argument based on Due Process?

with the assurance that he could provide the one essential ingredient that was difficult to obtain, furnished that element as he had promised, and bought the finished product from the defendant—all so that the defendant could be prosecuted for producing and selling the very drug for which the agent had asked and for which he had provided the necessary component. Under the objective approach that I would follow, this defendant was entrapped, regardless of his predisposition or "innocence."

Hampton v. United States

425 U.S. 484 (1976).

MR. JUSTICE REHNQUIST announced the judgment of the Court in an opinion in which THE CHIEF JUSTICE and MR. JUSTICE WHITE join.

According to the government's witnesses, when Hampton noticed needle marks in Hutton's arms, Hampton said that he needed money and knew where he could get some heroin to sell. Hampton did not realize that Hutton was a DEA informant. Hutton offered to find a buyer for the heroin so that Hampton could sell it. Then Hutton called another DEA agent to set up a meeting for the "buy." At the meeting with Hampton and Hutton, two DEA agents posed as narcotics dealers. Hampton brought a tinfoil packet of heroin and the agents paid him $145 after testing the heroin and pronouncing it "okay." Hampton offered to sell them more heroin, and the agents arranged for another "buy." This time when Hutton and Hampton arrived at the meeting, Hampton produced a tinfoil packet of heroin and asked for $500. Then he was arrested. At his trial, Hampton testified to an entirely different story. He admitted telling Hutton that he was short of cash, and claimed that Hutton's response was to propose that he could obtain a non-narcotic counterfeit drug from a pharmacist friend. The drug would produce the same reaction as heroin, so he and Hampton could make money by selling it to gullible acquaintances. At both meetings with the agents, Hampton believed that they were being duped into buying fake heroin. Hampton testified that it was Hutton who had supplied the drugs that Hampton sold to the agents, and that Hampton never realized that it was real heroin. At his trial, Hampton sought a non-standard jury instruction that provided: "The defendant asserts that he was the victim of entrapment. If you find that the narcotics were supplied to him by an informer in the employ of or acting on behalf of the government, then you must acquit the defendant because the law as a matter of policy forbids his conviction in such a case, and you need not consider the predisposition of the defendant to commit the defense charged." The trial judge denied the instruction and Hampton was convicted. The Court of Appeals affirmed the conviction, relying on *Russell*.

Defendant correctly recognizes that his case does not qualify as one involving "entrapment" at all. He instead relies on the language in *United States v. Russell*, 411 U.S. 423, 431 (1974), that "we may some day be presented with a situation in which the conduct of law enforcement agents is so outrageous that due process principles would absolutely bar the government from invoking judicial processes to obtain a conviction." Defendant's case is different from Russell's but the difference is one of degree not of kind. In *Russell* the ingredient supplied by the Government agent was a legal drug which the defendants demonstrably could have obtained from other sources besides the Government. Here the drug which the

Government informant allegedly supplied to defendant both was illegal and constituted the *corpus delicti* for the sale of which he was convicted. The Government obviously played a more significant role in enabling him to sell contraband in this case than it did in *Russell*.

But in each case the Government agents were acting in concert with the defendant, and in each case either the jury found or the defendant conceded that he was predisposed to commit the crime for which he was convicted. The remedy of the criminal defendant with respect to the acts of Government agents, which, far from being resisted, are encouraged by him, lies solely in the defense of entrapment. Defendant's conceded predisposition rendered this defense unavailable to him.

It's Latin to Me

The term *"corpus delicti"* means "body of crime," and it stands for the principle that in order for a person to be convicted of a crime, it must be proved that the crime actually occurred."

To sustain defendant's contention here would run directly contrary to our statement in *Russell* that the defense of entrapment is not intended "to give the federal judiciary a 'chancellor's foot' veto over law enforcement practices of which it did not approve."

The limitations of the Due Process Clause of the Fifth Amendment come into play only when the Government activity in question violates some protected right of the *defendant*. Here, the police, the Government informant, and the defendant acted in concert with one another. If the police engage in illegal activity in concert with a defendant beyond the scope of their duties, the remedy lies not in freeing the equally culpable defendant, but in prosecuting the police under the applicable provisions of state or federal law. But the police conduct here no more deprived defendant of any right secured to him by the United States Constitution than did the police conduct in *Russell* deprive Russell of any rights. *Affirmed.*

MR. JUSTICE POWELL, with whom MR. JUSTICE BLACKMUN joins, concurring in the judgment.

Defendant Hampton contends that the Government's supplying of contraband to one later prosecuted for trafficking in contraband constitutes a *per se* denial of due process. As I do not accept this proposition, I concur in the judgment of the Court. I am not able to join the plurality opinion, as it would unnecessarily reach and decide difficult questions not before us.

Hampton would distinguish *Russell* on the ground that here contraband itself was supplied by the Government, while the phenyl-2-propanone P2P supplied in

Russell was not contraband. Given the characteristics of P2P, this is a distinction without a difference and *Russell* disposes of this case. But the plurality does not stop there. In discussing Hampton's Due Process contention, it enunciates a *per se* rule: "The remedy of the criminal defendant with respect to the acts of Government agents, which, far from being resisted, are encouraged by him, lies *solely* in the defense of entrapment." The plurality thus says that the concept of fundamental fairness inherent in the guarantee of due process would never prevent the conviction of a predisposed defendant, regardless of the outrageousness of police behavior in light of the surrounding circumstances. I do not understand *Russell* or earlier cases delineating the defense of entrapment to have gone so far, and there was no need for them to do so. Nor have we had occasion yet to confront Government over-involvement in areas outside the realm of contraband offenses. *Cf. United States v. Archer*, 486 F.2d 670 (2d Cir. 1973). I am unwilling to conclude that an analysis other than one limited to predisposition would never be appropriate under due process principles.

Take Note

In *United States v. Archer*, 486 F.2d 670, 676–77 (2d Cir.1973), the court found it unnecessary to decide whether "outrageous government conduct" occurred because the conviction could be reversed on other grounds. The federal agents in *Archer* acquired evidence of a state prosecutor's acceptance of a bribe by "lying to New York police officers and committing perjury before New York judges and grand jurors." The court noted that the federal agents' operation displayed an "arrogant disregard for the sanctity of the state judicial and police processes," which was "substantially more offensive" than "common cases where government agents induce the sale of narcotics in order to make drug arrests."

Mr. Justice Brennan, with whom Mr. Justice Stewart and Mr. Justice Marshall concur, dissenting.

Defendant's claims in this case allege a course of police conduct that would plainly be held to constitute entrapment as a matter of law under the objective test, and I think that reversal of defendant's conviction also is compelled for those who follow the "subjective" approach to the defense of entrapment. In addition, I agree with Mr. Justice Powell that *Russell* does not foreclose imposition of a bar to conviction—based on due process principles—where the conduct of law enforcement authorities is sufficiently offensive, even though the individuals entitled to invoke such a defense might be "predisposed." In my view, the police activity in this case was beyond permissible limits.

Two facts sufficiently distinguish this case from *Russell*. First, the chemical supplied in that case was not contraband. In contrast, defendant claims that the very narcotic he is accused of selling was supplied by an agent of the government.

Second, the defendant in *Russell* "was an active participant in an illegal drug manufacturing enterprise which began before the Government agent appeared on the scene and continued after the Government agent had left the scene." In contrast, the two sales for which defendant was convicted were allegedly instigated by Government agents and completed by the Government's purchase. The beginning and end of this crime thus coincided exactly with the Government's entry into and withdrawal from the criminal activity in this case, while the Government was not similarly involved in Russell's crime.

Where the Government's agent deliberately sets up the accused by supplying him with contraband and then bringing him to another agent as a potential purchaser, the Government's role has passed the point of toleration. The Government is doing nothing less than buying contraband from itself through an intermediary and jailing the intermediary. There is little, if any, law enforcement interest promoted by such conduct; plainly it is not designed to discover ongoing drug traffic. That the accused is "predisposed" cannot possibly justify the action of government officials in purposefully creating the crime. No one would suggest that the police could round up and jail all "predisposed" individuals, yet that is precisely what set-ups like the instant one are intended to accomplish. Thus, this case is nothing less than an instance of "the Government seeking to punish for an alleged offense which is the product of the creative activity of its own officials." *Sorrells v. United States*, 287 U.S. 435, 451(1932).

Food for Thought

One problem for federal judges is how to articulate a Due Process concept of outrageous government conduct that does not simply mimic the standards of the objective test. As one judge noted, "the language used in both *Russell* and *Hampton* indicates that no such back-door reincarnation of the objective approach was intended." *United States v. Twigg*, 588 F.2d 373, 385 (3d Cir. 1978) (Adams, J., dissenting). What approaches to Due Process are expressed in the opinions in *Hampton*?

Points for Discussion

a. Need for Due Process Defense

The need for a Due Process defense for predisposed defendants was expressed in the Second Circuit's observation in *Archer* that it would be "unthinkable, for example, to permit government agents to instigate robberies and beatings merely to gather evidence to convict other members of a gang of hoodlums." Consider the similar policy judgment reflected in the Tenth Circuit's version of the "outrageous governmental conduct" defense that requires a defendant to bear the burden of proving either "(1) excessive government involvement in the creation of the crime, or (2) significant governmental coercion to induce the crime." *United States v. Pedraza*, 27 F.3d 1515, 1521 (10th Cir. 1994). Could defense counsel in *Russell* and *Hampton* argue that the facts of those cases met this Tenth Circuit standard? What counter-arguments would a prosecutor make regarding that question?

b. Rarely Successful Defense

The Supreme Court's reasoning in *Russell* and *Hampton* persuaded the Sixth and Seventh Circuits to reject the establishment of a Due Process defense based on "outrageous government conduct." The First, Fourth, and Eleventh Circuits have recognized the potential existence of the defense, but have never reversed a conviction based on a defendant's Due Process claim. The Tenth Circuit has granted such relief only once. *See United States v. Dyke*, 718 F.3d 1281, 1285 (10th Cir. 2013). Even when courts have established criteria for the Due Process defense and encounter frequent claims, it is typical to see the "doctrine of outrageous police conduct" described as one that "must be sparingly applied and used only in the most egregious situations." *State v. Markwart*, 329 P.3d 108, 115 (Wash. App. 2014). Government operations that have been upheld as insufficiently outrageous include these examples: 1) agents purchasing "lewd table dances with public funds to gain evidence of violation of liquor rules"; 2) agents creating "a phony job recruiting center and soliciting the purchase of marijuana from a potential job applicant"; 3) agents selling "illegally imported bobcat hides and providing false forms intended to show that the hides were legal." *Id.* One repeatedly quoted perspective is that "the banner of outrageous misconduct is often raised but seldom saluted." *United States v. Santana*, 6 F.3d 1, 4 (1st Cir. 1993).

c. Articulation of Due Process Criteria

Some state courts that use the subjective test for entrapment have established criteria for the assessment of Due Process claims. One example appears in *State v. Lively*, 130 Wash.2d 1, 921 P.2d 1035 (1996), which explains Due Process analysis as follows:

> In determining whether police conduct violates Due Process, this court has held that the conduct must be so shocking that it violates fundamental fairness. A Due Process claim based on outrageous conduct requires more than a mere demonstration of flagrant police conduct. Dismissal based on outrageous conduct is reserved for only the most egregious circumstances. While some courts have limited the outrageous conduct defense to a "slim category of cases in which the police have been brutal, employing physical or psychological coercion against the defendant," other courts recognize the violation of Due Process standards in cases

where the government conduct is so integrally involved in the offense that the government agents direct the crime from beginning to end, or where the crime is fabricated by the police to obtain a defendant's conviction, rather than to protect the public from criminal behavior.

We agree with those courts which hold that in reviewing a defense of outrageous government conduct, the court should evaluate the conduct based on the "totality of the circumstances." There are several factors to consider when determining whether police conduct offends Due Process: whether the police conduct instigated a crime or merely infiltrated ongoing criminal activity; whether the defendant's reluctance to commit a crime was overcome by pleas of sympathy, promises of excessive profits, or persistent solicitation; whether the government controls the criminal activity or simply allows for the criminal activity to occur; whether the police motive was to prevent crime or protect the public; and whether the government conduct itself amounted to criminal activity or conduct "repugnant to a sense of justice."

Food for Thought

How could defense counsel in *Russell* and *Hampton* argue that the facts of those cases satisfied the Due Process criteria described in *Lively*? What counter-arguments would a prosecutor make regarding the facts of each case?

Hypo 1: *Fencing Operation*

In an attempt to uncover information about illegal activity, the police set up an undercover operation and accept stolen property from people who steal the property or know that it is stolen. Then the police resell it to others who know the property is stolen. Because of the fencing operation, the police are able to crack a major theft ring. Eventually, the police shut down the operation and make a number of arrests for burglary, possession of stolen property, receiving stolen property, and other related crimes. Defendants claim that the government violated Due Process by establishing and operating the fencing operation. Did the government embroil itself to an intolerable degree in the criminal enterprise? *Compare State v. Brooks*, 30 Wash. App. 280, 633 P.2d 1345 (1981).

Hypo 2: *Child Prostitution Sting*

Recognizing that child sexual abuse is a major problem, the police recruit young boys to work as prostitutes. The boys are encouraged to cooperate with the "johns" and to place themselves in revealing situations. At the appropriate point, the police break in and arrest the "john." Given the compelling nature of the child abuse problem, is this sting operation justifiable, or would it violate Due Process? *Compare State v. Jessup*, 31 Wash. App. 304, 641 P.2d 1185 (1982).

Hypo 3: *Plan to Marry*

As part of an undercover drug investigation, Koby Desai, an informant for the Seattle Police Department, arranged a cocaine purchase from the target, Amy Lively, by an undercover detective named David. A week later, Desai arranged for David to purchase more cocaine from Lively at Desai's apartment. Lively was arrested and charged with drug crimes. At her trial, Lively raised both the entrapment defense and the Due Process defense of "outrageous government conduct." She testified that she started drinking alcohol and using cocaine at age fourteen. She eventually admitted herself into a detoxification program, and began attending Alcoholics Anonymous/Narcotics Anonymous (AA/NA) meetings. Later, she had an alcoholic relapse and entered a 28-day inpatient detoxification program. At this point, she had never sold or offered to sell drugs. She also testified that she was not using drugs at the time of the offenses and had not used cocaine for several years. When Desai began working as a police informant, the police provided him with an apartment, including utilities, a car, and other living expenses. Desai began attending AA/NA meetings, where he met Lively, following the completion of her inpatient treatment program. Desai's attendance was approved by the drug squad of the Seattle Police Department. At trial, Lively testified that: 1) she had tried to kill herself after completing the program and was emotionally distraught; 2) Desai asked her out on a date and she started a sexual relationship with him because he was supportive and emotionally responsive; (3) she moved in with Desai and they made plans to marry; he promised to assist her in obtaining a divorce, and to fly her friends to California for the wedding; 4) about this time, Desai told Lively that he had a friend David, the undercover detective, who wanted to buy cocaine, and Desai asked her to obtain the drugs for David; 5) Desai's requests continued for two weeks before Lively finally agreed to obtain cocaine for David. Desai admitted lying repeatedly to Lively, but stated that he thought it was all right to lie to maintain his cover story. Assume that the trial judge instructs the jury on the entrapment defense but the jury rejects Lively's defense based on predisposition. On appeal, what arguments can defense counsel make regarding the Due Process defense, in order to persuade the court to reverse the conviction? *Compare* State v. Lively, 130 Wash.2d 1, 921 P.2d 1035 (1996) (en banc).

Hypo 4: *Phony Stash House*

Explain the arguments to be made on both sides regarding the viability of the Due Process defense of outrageous government conduct in a Ninth Circuit case with the following facts: "The government sent a paid confidential informant (CI) to Phoenix with instructions to recruit random persons to help rob a non-existent cocaine stash house. Following orders, CI went to bars in "a bad part of town" and looked for people who seemed to him like "bad guys." CI had not been told to seek out people already engaged in criminal activity or even persons engaged in suspicious conduct. Rather, he trolled for targets in bars and eventually encountered Simpson, who expressed a willingness to join in the robbery. CI introduced Simpson to his handler, Agent Z, who posed as a disgruntled former drug courier. Simpson asserted that he had criminal experience and introduced Z to Black. Agent Z fed details about the imaginary

See It

In 2014, USA Today launched an investigative series regarding the ATF sting operations in which targeted individuals were enticed by the prospect of large payments to steal drugs from a phony stash house supposedly operated by a Mexican drug ring. One of these operations led to the prosecution described in Hypo #4. Several indictments have been dismissed in similar prosecutions based on the Due Process defense of outrageous government conduct.

target (including the number of kilos of cocaine to be found in the imaginary stash house), and encouraged them to be sure to bring guns along while performing their government-created mission. When the defendants met with Agent Z in preparation for the robbery, he led them to a warehouse where they were arrested." *Compare United States v. Black, 750 F.3d 1053 (9th Cir. 2014)* (Reinhardt, J.) (dissenting from denial of rehearing en banc).

Executive Summary

Subjective Test for Entrapment. Assuming that a defendant produces some evidence of government inducement, the question is whether the government can show beyond a reasonable doubt that the defendant was predisposed to commit the crime.

Inducement. An inducement occurs when the government creates an opportunity plus a special incentive of some kind for the defendant to commit a crime.

Predisposition. The government must show that the defendant was predisposed to commit the crime before the inducement occurred, assuming that sufficient evidence of inducement exists. To prove disposition, the government may show that the defendant engaged in a similar existing course of conduct, or had an already formed design to commit the crime, or responded readily to the inducement.

Objective Test for Entrapment. A court using this test will rule in favor of a defendant, as a matter of law, when the type of inducement offered by the government was one that was likely to induce ordinary people, who would normally avoid crime, to yield to the inducement.

Major Themes

a. Split over Test for Entrapment Defense—The federal courts have followed the subjective test since the Supreme Court endorsed it in *Sherman*. However, a minority of states use the objective test because of the various weaknesses of the subjective test, including its toleration for government entrapment of predisposed defendants.

b. Split over Due Process Defense—The Supreme Court and some federal courts have declined to recognize this defense. However, other federal circuit courts have recognized the defense in order to allow predisposed defendants to argue that some inducements and government conduct are too outrageous to be tolerable as a matter of Due Process.

Due Process or Outrageous Government Conduct Defense. Courts that recognize the Due Process defense have pointed to a variety of factors that supply criteria for the inquiry whether government conduct is so shocking that it violates fundamental fairness. Such factors include the use of physical or psychological coercion, or the government direction of a crime from its initiation through to its conclusion. However, the federal and state courts that recognize the defense have rarely upheld the defense and reversed a conviction.

Test Your Knowledge

To assess your understanding of the material in this chapter, click here to take a quiz.

For More Information

• Joseph A. Colquitt, *Rethinking Entrapment*, 41 AM. CRIM. L. REV. 1389 (2004).

• Wayne R. LaFave, CRIMINAL LAW § 9.8, at 529-550 (5th ed. 2010).

• Paul Marcus, *Presenting Back from the [Almost] Dead, The Entrapment Defense*, 47 FLA. L. REV. 205 (1995).

• RUSSELL L. WEAVER, JOHN M. BURKOFF, CATHERINE HANCOCK & STEVE FRIEDLAND, PRINCIPLES OF CRIMINAL PROCEDURE Ch. 6 (6th ed. 2018).

• AMERICAN LAW INSTITUTE, MODEL PENAL CODE AND COMMENTARIES, Part I, § 2.13, Comments at 405-420 (1980).

CHAPTER **6**

Police Interrogations &
Confessions

A. Pre-*Miranda* Doctrines

Prior to the landmark decision in *Miranda v. Arizona* in 1966, the Supreme Court used three doctrines to regulate police interrogations. Beginning in 1936, the Court began applying the Due Process Clause of the Fourteenth Amendment as a source of standards governing the admissibility of confessions in state courts; the same analysis came to be used for the Fifth Amendment Due Process standards in federal courts. The Court also developed the non-constitutional *McNabb-Mallory* doctrine to exclude some confessions under its supervisory powers to create evidence rules for federal courts. Finally, in 1964 the Court relied on Sixth Amendment right-to-counsel doctrine to limit post-indictment interrogations by undercover government agents.

Take Note

The doctrines established in the Court's Due Process and Sixth Amendment confession precedents remain good law today. However, the modern scope of each doctrine has been influenced in significant ways by *Miranda* doctrine, which delineates the rights of persons interrogated in police custody, and thereby serves to protect the exercise of the Fifth Amendment privilege against self-incrimination.

1. Pre-*Miranda* Due Process

Brown v. Mississippi

297 U.S. 278 (1936).

MR. CHIEF JUSTICE HUGHES delivered the opinion of the Court.

The violent acts used to procure the confessions of three African-American defendants were admitted at trial by the white sheriff and white men who helped him. After arrest, one defendant was "hanged by a rope to the limb of a tree" three times, "tied to a tree and whipped," and then released, "suffering intense pain and agony." A day or two later, the same man was arrested again, "severely whipped," and told that the whipping would continue "until he confessed" to murder, which he did. When the two other defendants were arrested and taken to jail, they were made to strip, "and they were laid over chairs and their backs were cut to pieces with a leather strap with buckles on it." They were told that the whipping would continue until they confessed. When they did confess, they "changed or adjusted their confession in all particulars of detail so as to conform to the demands of their torturers." The two-day trial began the day after the arraignment when the defendants received appointed counsel; the defendants testified that their confessions were false, but they were convicted of murder and sentenced to death. They challenged their convictions on Due Process grounds.

The question is whether convictions, which rest solely upon confessions shown to have been extorted by brutality and violence, are consistent with the due process of law required by the Fourteenth Amendment. The state stresses that "exemption from compulsory self-incrimination in the courts of the states is not secured by any part of the Federal Constitution," and that "the privilege against self-incrimination may be withdrawn and the accused put upon the stand as a witness for the state." But the question of the right of the state to withdraw the privilege against self-incrimination is not here involved. The compulsion to which the Fifth Amendment refers is that of the processes of justice by which the accused may be called as a witness and required to testify. Compulsion by torture to extort a confession is a different matter.

The state is free to regulate the procedure of its courts in accordance with its own conceptions of policy, unless in so doing it "offends some principle of justice so rooted in the traditions and conscience of our people as to be ranked as fundamental." The freedom of the state in establishing its policy is limited by the requirement of due process of law. Because a state may dispense with a jury trial, it does not follow that it may substitute trial by ordeal. The rack and torture chamber may not be substituted for the witness stand. The state may not permit an accused to be hurried to conviction under mob domination—where the whole proceeding is but a mask—without supplying corrective process. *Moore v. Dempsey*, 261 U.S. 86 (1923). The state may not deny to the accused the aid of counsel. *Powell v. Alabama*, 287 U.S. 45 (1932). Nor may a state, through the action of its officers, contrive a conviction through the pretense of a trial which "deprives a defendant of liberty through a deliberate deception of court and jury by the presentation of testimony known to be perjured." *Mooney v. Holohan*, 294 U.S. 103, 112 (1935). The trial equally is a mere pretense where the state authorities have contrived a conviction resting solely upon confessions obtained by violence. The due process clause requires that government action "shall be consistent with the fundamental principles of liberty and justice which lie at the base of all our civil and political institutions." *Hebert v. Louisiana*, 272 U.S. 312 (1926). It would be difficult to conceive of methods more revolting to the sense of justice than those taken to procure the confessions of these defendants, and the use of the confessions thus obtained as the basis for conviction and sentence was a clear denial of due process.

Point for Discussion

Language of Voluntariness

Over time, the Court used Due Process doctrine to hold that only "voluntary" confessions are admissible, produced by the "free will" of the defendant. The Court would reject statements that involved police "coercion," including inducements, threats, or deceptive stratagems. *See, e.g., Spano v. New York*, 360 U.S. 315 (1959) (involuntary confession obtained by tricks of lying police officer); *Lynumn v. Illinois*, 372 U.S. 528 (1963) (involuntary confession obtained by threat that defendant's children could be taken away from her if she did not cooperate).

Take Note

The purposes of the Due Process ban on involuntary confessions overlapped with the purpose of common law evidence doctrine that prohibits the admission of such evidence. The evidence doctrine was intended to insure the inadmissibility of "presumptively false evidence," whereas an additional purpose of the Due Process doctrine was to prevent unfairness "in the use of evidence whether true or false." *Lisenba v. California*, 314 U.S. 219, 236 (1941).

During the thirty years between *Brown* and *Miranda*, the Court relied on Due Process doctrine to invalidate confessions in more than twenty cases, while upholding confessions in less than half that number. Most of these decisions revealed sharp disagreements among the justices concerning the interpretation of the "voluntariness" concept. Over time, the Court expanded this concept to encompass various types of psychologically coercive interrogation strategies, and came to focus upon the customs of *incommunicado* police questioning as the ultimate source of the coercion problem. The concept of voluntariness continued to evolve in Due Process decisions after *Miranda*.

small sample

Haynes v. Washington

373 U.S. 503 (1963).

MR. JUSTICE GOLDBERG delivered the opinion of the Court.

Haynes was arrested at night for robbing a gas station; he was taken to the police station and booked for "investigation" on the "small book," which meant that he was not allowed to make phone calls or to have visitors. During the interrogation that night, Haynes asked to call an attorney and to call his wife, but the police refused these requests, telling him that "he might make a call if he confessed." The next day, the police continued to reject his requests to call his wife during interrogation, while telling Haynes that after he "made a statement and cooperated with" the police, they "would see to it" that he could call his wife. Then during a third interrogation in the prosecutor's office, Haynes made further requests to call his wife, which were rejected again. He made incriminating statements during all three interrogations, and his second and third statements were transcribed. Haynes signed the second statement but refused to sign the third one, telling the prosecutor that "all the promises of all the officers I had talked to had not been fulfilled and so I would sign nothing under any conditions until I was allowed to call my wife to see about legal counsel." After he appeared at a preliminary hearing on the day after arrest, Haynes was returned to jail and held incommunicado while the police made repeated efforts to obtain his signature on the third statement. He was not allowed to call his wife until "some five or seven days after his arrest." The signed statement was admitted at his trial, and he was convicted of robbery; he argued that this statement was involuntary under Due Process standards.

It is uncontroverted that Haynes was not taken before a magistrate and granted a preliminary hearing until he had acceded to demands that he give and sign the written statement. Nor is there any indication that prior to signing the written confession, or even thereafter, Haynes was advised by authorities of his right to remain silent, warned that his answers might be used against him, or told of his rights respecting consultation with an attorney. Whether the confession was obtained by coercion or improper inducement can be determined only by an examination of all of the attendant circumstances. Haynes' undisputed testimony as to the making and signing of the challenged confession permits no doubt that it was obtained under a totality of circumstances evidencing an involuntary written admission of guilt. Haynes was alone in the hands of the police, with no one to advise or aid him, and he had "no reason not to believe that the police had ample power to carry out their threats," to continue, for a much longer period if need be, the incommunicado detention—as in fact was actually done. Confronted with the express threat of continued incommunicado detention and induced by the promise of communication with and access to family, Haynes understandably chose to make and sign the damning written statement.

We cannot blind ourselves to what experience unmistakably teaches: that even apart from the express threat, the basic techniques present here—the secret and incommunicado detention and interrogation—are devices adapted and used to extort confessions from suspects. The line between proper and permissible police conduct and techniques and methods offensive to due process is, at best, a difficult one to draw, particularly in cases such as this where it is necessary to make fine judgments as to the effect of psychologically coercive pressures and inducements on the mind and will of an accused. We are here impelled to the conclusion, from all of the facts presented, that the bounds of due process have been exceeded. History amply shows that confessions have often been extorted to save law enforcement officials the trouble and effort of obtaining valid and independent evidence; the coercive devices used here were designed to obtain admissions to complete a case in which there had already been obtained, by proper investigative efforts, competent evidence sufficient to sustain a conviction. The procedures here are no less constitutionally impermissible, and perhaps more unwarranted because so unnecessary.

Official overzealousness of the type which vitiates a conviction has only deleterious effects. Here it has put the State to the substantial additional expense of prosecuting the case through the appellate courts and will require even a greater expenditure in the event of retrial, as is likely. But it is the deprivation of the protected rights themselves which is fundamental and the most regrettable, not only because of the effect on the individual defendant, but because of the effect on our system of law and justice. Whether there is involved the brutal "third degree," or the more subtle, but no less offensive, methods here obtaining, official misconduct cannot but breed disrespect for law, as well as for those charged with its enforcement.

MR. JUSTICE CLARK, with whom MR. JUSTICE HARLAN, MR. JUSTICE STEWART and MR. JUSTICE WHITE, join, dissenting.

Haynes is neither youthful nor lacking in experience in law breaking. He is married and was a skilled sheet-metal worker temporarily unemployed. He had served time. He cannot be placed in the category of those types of people with whom our Due Process cases have ordinarily dealt, such as the mentally subnormal accused, the youthful offender, or the naive and impressionable defendant. There is no contention of physical abuse, no extended or repeated interrogation, no deprivation of sleep or food, no use of psychiatric techniques, and no threat of mob violence. In light of his age, intelligence and experience with the police, the comparative absence of any coercive circumstances, and the fact that he never evidenced a will to deny his guilt, his written confession was not involuntary.

FYI

The Court's Due Process precedents often relied on the defendant's special vulnerability to police coercion, based on physical and mental attributes and life experiences. In *Spano v. New York*, 360 U.S. 315 (1959), the Court relied on a "totality of circumstances" analysis to invalidate a confession, including the defendant's attributes: "Spano was a foreign-born man of 25 with no past history of law violation. He had progressed only one-half year into high school and he had a history of emotional instability. He had suffered a cerebral concussion, and was found unacceptable for military service primarily because of psychiatric disorder. He had also failed the Army's intelligence test. He was subjected to questioning from early evening into the night by fifteen police officers, prosecutors, and others for virtually eight straight hours before he confessed. The questioners persisted in the face of his repeated refusals to answer on the advice of his attorney, and they ignored his reasonable requests to contact his retained attorney. The use of Bruno, a police cadet and 'childhood friend' of Spano's is another factor which deserves mention because Bruno's was the one face visible to Spano in which he could put some trust. The police officers instructed Bruno falsely to state that his job was in jeopardy unless Spano confessed, and that loss of his job would be disastrous to his three children, his wife and his unborn child. Spano ultimately yielded to his false friend's entreaties. We conclude that Spano's will was overborne by official pressure, fatigue and sympathy falsely aroused after considering all the facts."

Points for Discussion

a. Inherent Coercion and Alternatives to Due Process

In *Stein v. New York,* 346 U.S. 156 (1953), the Court opined that some defendants might be especially resistant to police coercion, reasoning that, "What would be overpowering to the weak of will or mind might be utterly ineffective against an experienced criminal." However, *Stein* recognized that the defendant's attributes might be irrelevant in some cases, such as when "physical violence or threat of it invalidates confessions and is universally condemned by law," so "there is no need to weigh or measure its effects on the will of the individual victim." Another decision that focused on the inherently coercive nature of an interrogation strategy was *Ashcraft v. Tennessee,* 322 U.S. 143 (1944), where the Court determined that 36 hours of "third degree" interrogation inevitably would produce an involuntary confession.

Take Note

A number of justices were dissatisfied with the Due Process "totality" doctrine because it failed to provide clear, predictable, and uniform guidelines as to the boundaries of acceptable police conduct during interrogations. Moreover, the difficulties of defining "voluntariness" were magnified, as one justice observed, because "the trial on the issue of coercion is seldom helpful," as police "usually testify one way, the accused another," and the secrecy of interrogations gives defendants "little chance to prove coercion at trial." *Crooker v. California,* 357 U.S. 433 (1958) (Douglas, J., dissenting).

b. The Movement Towards *Per Se* Rules

The creation of *per se* rules for interrogations offered the promise of clearer guidelines for police and greater protections from coercion for interrogated people. One such rule was proposed by some justices in *Spano* who endorsed a *per se* Due Process right for an indicted defendant who asks for counsel during interrogation to be allowed to consult with counsel. *See Spano,* 360 U.S. at 324 (Douglas, J., concurring, joined by Justices Black and Brennan).

Hypo 1: *Interrogation of Juvenile*

Robert Gallegos, a 14-year-old boy, is arrested for assault, and when the victim dies from his injuries, Gallegos becomes a potential defendant in a homicide prosecution. During his detention in a juvenile facility, his mother attempts to visit him; but is told that she must wait at least three days until the next visiting day occurs on a Monday, or wait six more days and visit on the next Thursday. By the time she visits Gallegos on a Thursday, he has signed a confession. He is detained incommunicado during this entire period. Before his confession, police tell Gallegos that he may ask to have his parents or an attorney present during the interrogation, but he does not make this request. Police also warn him that he does not have to make a statement and that he faces the possibility of a murder charge. His mother is informed by police that Gallegos has a right to counsel, but she did not obtain a lawyer for him. Gallegos later testifies that he was not threatened by the police and not questioned for long periods of time. Do the circumstances of his interrogation violate Due Process? *See Gallegos v. Colorado*, 370 U.S. 49 (1962).

2. The *McNabb-Mallory* Rule

During the post-*Brown* era, the Court supplemented the Due Process doctrine with the *McNabb-Mallory* rule that applied only in the federal courts. In *McNabb v. United States*, 318 U.S. 332 (1943), the Court created an exclusionary rule to enforce the command of 18 U.S.C. § 595, which requires that a federal officer who arrests any person must "take the defendant before the nearest judicial officer having jurisdiction for a hearing, commitment, or taking bail for trial."

Take Note

The Court repeatedly rejected the argument that the *McNabb-Mallory* rule should be incorporated into Due Process doctrine and applied to the states, but some state courts chose to incorporate the rule into their own state law on their own. *McNabb* and *Mallory* rested on the Supreme Court's supervisory authority over the federal courts.

The *McNabb* rule allowed courts to exclude confessions obtained in a suspicious context, where a federal officer delayed an arrestee's appearance in court so as to perform interrogation before counsel could be appointed. The *McNabb* Court acknowledged that, "Congress has not explicitly forbidden the use of evidence" procured in this way, but declared that the admission of such a confession "would stultify the policy" of that of § 595.

In *Mallory v. United States*, 354 U.S. 449 (1957), the Court created an exclusionary rule to enforce the mandate of Rule 5(a) of the Federal Rules of Criminal Procedure, which requires arraignment of federal arrestees without "unnecessary delay." The *Mallory* Court reasoned that the purpose of this requirement was to insure that a person "may be advised of his rights" by a judicial officer "as quickly as possible" after arrest. Therefore, a court should invalidate a confession in a case such as *Mallory*, where the officers delayed arraignment for over four hours, used that time to procure a confession at police headquarters, and refrained from informing the arrestee "of his right to counsel," his right "to a preliminary examination before a magistrate," his right "to keep silent," and his right to know that "any statement made by him may be used against him." The *McNabb-Mallory* rule expressed the Court's concern that arrestees could be interrogated while remaining ignorant of their rights, as long as information about those rights was communicated only by judges at a hearing that came too late for arrestees to learn of those rights and exercise them.

FYI

In effect, the *McNabb-Mallory* doctrine was based on the assumption that the exclusion of some confessions would have a deterrent effect on police decisions to delay the access of arrestees to hearings and consultations with counsel.

In *Corley v. United States*, 556 U.S. 303 (2009), the Court determined that Congress narrowed the *McNabb-Mallory* rule in Title II of the Omnibus Crime Control and Safe Streets Act of 1968, but did not eliminate it. That statute provides in § 3501(c) that a confession made by a federal defendant under arrest "shall not be inadmissible solely because of delay in bringing such person before a magistrate judge if such confession is made voluntarily within six hours of arrest." This six-hour period may be extended if further delay is "reasonable considering the means of transportation and the distance to be traveled to the nearest available magistrate." For confessions that occur more than six hours after arrest, the *McNabb-Mallory* doctrine applies for determinations whether there was "unnecessary" delay that requires exclusion of the confession from evidence.

3. Pre-*Miranda* Sixth Amendment Right to Counsel

After the Sixth Amendment right to counsel was incorporated into Due Process and applied to the states in 1963, two different approaches to regulating police interrogations appeared the next year. One approach is discussed in the following case which imposed a ban on the admission of a confession elicited surreptitiously from an indicted defendant by an undercover government agent or informant.

Massiah v. United States

377 U.S. 201 (1964).

MR. JUSTICE STEWART delivered the opinion of the Court.

Massiah was indicted for violating the federal narcotics laws. He retained a lawyer, pleaded not guilty, and was released on bail. While he was free on bail a federal agent succeeded by surreptitious means in listening to incriminating conversations with a co-defendant who had agreed to hide a radio transmitter under his car seat to broadcast the conversations to the agent. These statements were introduced at Massiah's trial and he was convicted. He argued that his Sixth Amendment rights were violated by the agent's deliberate elicitation of his statements, after indictment and in the absence of his counsel.

Some justices opined in *Spano* that a confession is inadmissible when it is deliberately elicited by the police after the defendant has been indicted, and therefore is clearly entitled to a lawyer's help. A Constitution which guarantees a defendant the aid of counsel at a public trial could surely vouchsafe no less to an indicted defendant under interrogation by the police in a completely extrajudicial proceeding. Anything less might deny a defendant "effective representation by counsel at the only stage when legal aid and advice would help him." Since *Spano*, the New York courts have followed this rule: "Any secret interrogation of the defendant, from and after the finding of the indictment, without the protection afforded by the presence of counsel, contravenes the basic dictates of fairness in the conduct of criminal causes and the fundamental rights of person charged with crime." This view no more than reflects a constitutional principle established as long ago as *Powell v. Alabama*, 287 U.S. 45 (1932), *where the Court* noted that "during perhaps the most critical period of the proceedings from the time of their arraignment until the beginning of their trial, when consultation, thorough-going investigation and preparation are vitally important, the defendants are as much entitled to the aid of counsel during that period as at the trial itself."

We hold that Massiah was denied the basic protections of the Sixth Amendment when there was used against him at his trial evidence of his own incriminating words, which federal agents had deliberately elicited from him after he had been indicted and in the absence of his counsel. It is true that in the *Spano* case the defendant was interrogated in a police station, while here the damaging testimony was elicited from the defendant without his knowledge while he was free on bail. But "if such a rule is to have any efficacy it must apply to indirect and surreptitious interrogations as well as those conducted in the jailhouse."

We do not question that in this case it was entirely proper to continue an investigation of the suspected criminal activities of the defendant and his alleged confederates, even though the defendant had already been indicted. All that we hold is that the defendant's own incriminating statements could not constitutionally be used by the prosecution as evidence against him at his trial on the narcotics charge.

MR. JUSTICE WHITE, with whom MR. JUSTICE CLARK and MR. JUSTICE HARLAN join, dissenting.

I am unable to see how this case presents an unconstitutional interference with Massiah's right to counsel. Massiah was not prevented from consulting with counsel as often as he wished. No meetings with counsel were disturbed or spied upon. Preparation for trial was in no way obstructed. It is unsound to say that because Massiah had a right to counsel's aid before and during the trial, his out-of-court conversations and admissions must be excluded if obtained without counsel's consent or presence. The right to counsel has never meant as much before. Had there been no prior arrangements between Massiah's co-defendant and the police, his testimony would be readily admissible at Massiah's trial. But because the co-defendant had been cooperating with the police prior to his meeting with Massiah, his evidence is somehow transformed into inadmissible evidence despite the fact that the hazard to Massiah remains precisely the same—the defection of a confederate in crime.

Point for Discussion

The Sixth Amendment and Pre-Indictment Arrestees

Take Note

Escobedo's extension of the Sixth Amendment to the pre-indictment phase of an investigation was retracted in *Kirby v. Illinois*, 406 U.S. 682 (1972), which held that the right to counsel applies only to "critical stages" of a prosecution that occur after the commencement of "adversarial judicial proceedings." The event of arrest does not qualify as this type of proceeding. After *Kirby*, *Escobedo*'s Sixth Amendment rationale became untenable. The Court formally recognized this point in *Oregon v. Elstad*, 470 U.S. 298 (1985), and given the fact that *Miranda*'s Fifth Amendment rules had supplanted *Escobedo*'s holding, the *Elstad* Court decided to reinterpret *Escobedo* retrospectively as a Fifth Amendment decision.

Soon after *Massiah*, the Court extended the right to counsel to arrestees who were not yet indicted. In *Escobedo v. Illinois*, 378 U.S. 478 (1964), the Court held that the police violated the Sixth Amendment because the police investigation had "begun to focus on" the defendant in custody as "a particular suspect," the police had not "effectively warned" the defendant of "the right to remain silent," the defendant had "requested and been denied an opportunity to consult with his lawyer," and the police had elicited incriminating statements from him during questioning. Escobedo was repeatedly refused access to his lawyer even after the lawyer arrived at the police station, although they did come "into each other's view for a few moments." *Escobedo* reasoned that the right to counsel for indicted defendants was necessary both at trial and during the "completely extrajudicial proceeding" of police interrogation, and that it "should make no difference" that defendant had not yet been indicted. For the "right to use counsel at the formal trial" would be "a very hollow thing" if "for all practical purposes, the conviction is already assured" by pre-indictment interrogation of an arrestee. *Escobedo* acknowledged that the police need to use interrogations to investigate "an unsolved crime," but concluded that once the police "process shifts from investigatory to accusatory" so that the purpose of that process "is to elicit a confession," then the "adversary system begins to operate" for Sixth Amendment purposes.

The *Massiah* Court's prohibition on the elicitation of statements from indicted defendants was consistent with the alignment of the Sixth Amendment right to counsel with adversary judicial proceedings. Unlike *Escobedo*, the *Massiah* decision was not made redundant by *Miranda*. *Massiah* rights apply to indicted persons who are not in custody, and to indicted persons who are questioned surreptitiously by government agents, whereas *Miranda* rights do not apply to persons in either category. The post-*Miranda* cases interpreting *Massiah* rights are presented later in this chapter.

B. The Fifth Amendment and *Miranda*

The Court's recognition of the shortcomings of Due Process doctrine led to the articulation of Fifth Amendment protections for interrogated persons in custody.

Miranda v. Arizona

384 U.S. 436 (1966).

Mr. Chief Justice Warren delivered the opinion of the Court.

The question is whether the Fifth Amendment privilege "is fully applicable during a period of custodial interrogation." More specifically, we deal with the admissibility of statements obtained from an individual who is subjected to custodial police interrogation and the necessity for procedures which assure that the individual is accorded his privilege under the Fifth Amendment not to be compelled to incriminate himself or herself. The modern practice of in-custody interrogation is psychologically rather than physically oriented. Interrogation still takes place in privacy. Privacy results in secrecy and this in turn results in a gap in our knowledge as to what in fact goes on in the interrogation rooms. A valuable source of information about present police practices, however, may be found in various police manuals and texts which document procedures employed with success in the past. These texts are used by law enforcement agencies themselves as guides. The officers are told by the manuals that the "principal psychological factor contributing to a successful interrogation is privacy—being alone with the person under interrogation." The efficacy of this tactic has been explained as follows:

> "If at all practicable, the interrogation should take place in the investigator's office or at least in a room of his choice. In his own home he may be confident, indignant, or recalcitrant. He is more keenly aware of his rights and more reluctant to tell of his indiscretions of criminal behavior within the walls of his home. Moreover his family and other friends are nearby, their presence lending moral support. In his office, the investigator possesses all the advantages. The atmosphere suggests the invincibility of the forces of the law."

The manuals instruct the police to display an air of confidence in the suspect's guilt and from outward appearance to maintain only an interest in confirming certain details. The interrogator should direct his comments toward the reasons why the subject committed the act, rather than court failure by asking the subject whether he did it. The officers are instructed to minimize the moral seriousness of the offense, to cast blame on the victim or on society. These tactics are designed to put the subject in a psychological state where his story is but an elaboration of what the police purport to know already—that he is guilty. Explanations to the contrary are dismissed and discouraged. The texts thus stress that the major qualities an interrogator should possess are patience and perseverance: "The investigator will encounter many situations where the sheer weight of his personality will be the deciding factor. Where emotional appeals and tricks are employed to no avail, he must rely on an oppressive atmosphere of dogged persistence. He must interrogate steadily and without relent, leaving the subject no prospect of surcease. He must dominate his subject and overwhelm him with his inexorable will to obtain the truth. He should interrogate for a spell of several hours pausing only for the subject's necessities in acknowledgment of the need to avoid a charge of duress that can be technically substantiated. In a serious case, the interrogation may continue for days, with the required intervals for food and sleep, but with no respite from the atmosphere of domination. It is possible in this way to induce the subject to talk without resorting to duress or coercion."

The manuals suggest that the suspect be offered legal excuses for his actions in order to obtain an initial admission of guilt. Where there is a suspected revenge-killing, for example, the interrogator may say: "Joe, you probably didn't go out looking for this fellow with the purpose of shooting him. My guess is, however, that you expected something from him and that's why you carried a gun—for your own protection. You knew him for what he was, no good. Then when you met him he probably started using foul, abusive language and he gave some indication that he was about to pull a gun on you, and that's when you had to act to save your own life. That's about it, isn't it, Joe?" Having then obtained the admission of shooting, the interrogator is advised to refer to circumstantial evidence which negates the self-defense explanation. This should enable him to secure the entire story. One text notes that "Even if he fails to do so, the inconsistency between the subject's original denial of the shooting and his present admission of at least doing the shooting will serve to deprive him of a self-defense 'out' at the time of trial."

When the techniques described above prove unavailing, the texts recommend they be alternated with a show of some hostility. One ploy often used has been termed the "friendly-unfriendly" or the "Mutt and Jeff" act: "In this technique, two agents are employed. Mutt, the relentless investigator, who knows the subject is guilty and is not going to waste any time. He's sent a dozen men away for this crime and he's going to send the subject away for the full term. Jeff, on the other hand, is obviously a kindhearted man. He disapproves of Mutt and his tactics and will arrange to get him off the case if the subject will cooperate. He can't hold Mutt off for very long. The subject would be wise to make a quick decision. The technique is applied by having both investigators present while Mutt acts out his role. Jeff may stand by quietly and demur at some of Mutt's tactics. When Jeff makes his plea for cooperation, Mutt is not present in the room."

The interrogators sometimes are instructed to induce a confession out of trickery. In the identification situation, the interrogator may take a break in his questioning to place the subject among a group of men in a line-up. "The witness or complainant (previously coached, if necessary) studies the line-up and confidently points out the subject as the guilty party." Then the questioning resumes "as though there were now no doubt about the guilt of the subject." A variation on this technique is called the "reverse line-up": "The accused is placed in a line up, but this time he is identified by several fictitious witnesses or victims who associated him with different offenses. It is expected that the subject will become desperate and confess to the offense under investigation in order to escape from the false accusations."

The manuals also contain instructions for police on how to handle the individual who refuses to discuss the matter entirely, or who asks for an attorney or relatives. The examiner is to concede him the right to remain silent. "This usually has a very undermining effect. First of all, he is disappointed in his expectation of an unfavorable reaction on the part of the interrogator. Secondly, a concession of this right to remain silent impresses the subject with the apparent fairness of his interrogator." After this psychological conditioning, however, the officer is told to point out the incriminating significance of the suspect's refusal to talk:

> "Joe, you have a right to remain silent. That's your privilege and I'm the last person in the world who'll try to take it away from you. If that's the

way you want to leave this, O.K. But let me ask you this. Suppose you were in my shoes and I were in yours and you called me in to ask me about this and I told you, 'I don't want to answer any of your questions.' You'd think I had something to hide, and you'd probably be right in thinking that. That's exactly what I'll have to think about you, and so will everybody else. So let's sit here and talk this whole thing over."

Few will persist in their initial refusal to talk, it is said, if this monologue is employed correctly. In the event that the subject wishes to speak to a relative or an attorney, the following advice is tendered: "The interrogator should respond by suggesting that the subject first tell the truth to the interrogator himself rather than get anyone else involved in the matter. If the request is for an attorney, the interrogator may suggest that the subject save himself or his family the expense of any such professional service, particularly if he is innocent of the offense under investigation. The interrogator may also add, 'Joe, I'm only looking for the truth, and if you're telling the truth, that's it. You can handle this by yourself.'"

From these representative samples of interrogation techniques, the setting prescribed by the manuals and observed in practice becomes clear. In essence, it is this: To be alone with the subject is essential to prevent distraction and to deprive him of any outside support. The aura of confidence in his guilt undermines his will to resist. To obtain a confession, the interrogator must "patiently maneuver himself or his quarry into a position from which the desired objective may be attained." When normal procedures fail to produce the needed result, the police may resort to deceptive stratagems such as giving false legal advice. It is important to keep the subject off balance, for example, by trading on his insecurity about himself or his surroundings. The police then persuade, trick, or cajole him out of exercising his constitutional rights. Even without employing brutality, the "third degree" or the specific stratagems described here, the very fact of custodial interrogation exacts a heavy toll on individual liberty and trades on the weakness of individuals.

In the four cases before us, we concern ourselves primarily with this interrogation atmosphere and the evils it can bring. In these cases, we might not find the defendants' statements to have been involuntary in traditional terms. However, in each of the cases, defendant was thrust into an unfamiliar atmosphere and run through menacing police interrogation procedures. To be sure, the records do not evince overt physical coercion or patent psychological ploys. The fact remains that in none of these cases did the officers undertake to afford appropriate safeguards at the outset of the interrogation to insure that the statements were truly the product of free choice.

It is obvious that such an interrogation environment is created for no purpose other than to subjugate the individual to the will of his examiner. This atmosphere carries its own badge of intimidation. To be sure, this is not physical intimidation, but it is equally destructive of human dignity. The current practice of incommunicado interrogation is at odds with one of our Nation's most cherished principles—that the individual may not be compelled to incriminate himself. Unless adequate protective devices are employed to dispel the compulsion inherent in custodial surroundings, no statement obtained from the defendant can truly be the product of his free choice. From the foregoing, we can readily perceive an intimate connection between the privilege against self-incrimination and police custodial questioning.

The privilege against self-incrimination—the essential mainstay of our adversary system—is founded on a complex of values. All these policies point to one overriding thought: the constitutional foundation underlying the privilege is the respect a government—state or federal—must accord to the dignity and integrity of its citizens. To maintain a "fair state-individual balance," to require the government "to shoulder the entire load," to respect the inviolability of the human personality, our accusatory system of criminal justice demands that the government seeking to punish an individual produce the evidence against him by its own independent labors, rather than by the cruel, simple expedient of compelling it from his own mouth. In sum, the privilege is fulfilled only when the person is guaranteed the right "to remain silent unless he chooses to speak in the unfettered exercise of his own will." *Malloy v. Hogan,* 378 U.S. 1, 8 (1964).

All the principles embodied in the privilege apply to informal compulsion exerted by law-enforcement officers during in-custody questioning. An individual swept from familiar surroundings into police custody, surrounded by antagonistic forces, and subjected to the techniques of persuasion described above cannot be otherwise than under compulsion to speak. As a practical matter, the compulsion to speak in the isolated setting of the police station may well be greater than in courts or other official investigations, where there are often impartial observers to guard against intimidation or trickery.

There can be no doubt that the Fifth Amendment privilege is available outside of criminal court proceedings and serves to protect persons in all settings in which their freedom of action is curtailed in any significant way from being compelled to incriminate themselves. We have concluded that without proper safeguards the process of in-custody interrogation of persons suspected or accused of crime contains inherently compelling pressures which work to undermine the individual's will to resist and to compel him to speak where he would not otherwise do so freely. In order to combat these pressures and to permit a full opportunity to exercise the privilege against self-incrimination, the accused must be adequately and effectively apprised of his rights and the exercise of those rights must be fully honored. It is impossible for us to foresee the potential alternatives for protecting the privilege which might be devised by Congress or the States in the exercise of their creative rule-making capacities. Our decision in no way creates a constitutional straitjacket which will handicap sound efforts at reform, nor is it intended to have this effect. We encourage Congress and the States to continue their laudable search for increasingly effective ways of protecting the rights of the individual while promoting efficient enforcement of our criminal laws. However, unless we are shown other procedures which are at least as effective in apprising accused persons of their right of silence and in assuring a continuous opportunity to exercise it, the following safeguards must be observed.

First, at the outset, if a person in custody is to be subjected to interrogation, he must first be informed in clear and unequivocal terms that he has the right to remain silent. For those unaware of the privilege, the warning is needed simply to make them aware of it—the threshold requirement for an intelligent decision as to its exercise. More important, such a warning is an absolute prerequisite in overcoming the inherent pressures of the interrogation atmosphere. The warning will show the individual that his interrogators are prepared to recognize his privilege should he choose to exercise it. The Fifth Amendment privilege is so fundamental to our system of constitutional rule and the expedient of giving an adequate warning as to the availability of the privilege so simple, we will not pause to inquire in individual cases whether the defendant was aware of his rights without a warning being given.

Second, the warning of the right to remain silent must be accompanied by the explanation that anything said can and will be used against the individual in court. This warning is needed in order to make him aware not only of the privilege, but also of the consequences of forgoing it. It is only through an awareness of these consequences that there can be any assurance of real understanding and intelligent exercise of the privilege. Moreover, this warning may serve to make the individual more acutely aware that he is faced with a phase of the adversary system—that he is not in the presence of persons acting solely in his interest.

Third, the right to have counsel present at the interrogation is indispensable to the protection of the Fifth Amendment privilege under the system we delineate today. A once-stated warning, delivered by those who will conduct the interrogation, cannot itself suffice to that end among those who most require knowledge of their rights. Even preliminary advice given to the accused by his own attorney can be swiftly overcome by the secret interrogation process. Thus, the need for counsel to protect the Fifth Amendment privilege comprehends not merely a right to consult with counsel prior to questioning, but also to have counsel present during any questioning if the defendant so desires. An individual need not make a pre-interrogation request for a lawyer. While such request affirmatively secures his right to have one, his failure to ask for a lawyer does not constitute a waiver. No effective waiver of the right to counsel during interrogation can be recognized unless specifically made after the warnings have been given. The accused who does not know his rights and therefore does not make a request may be the person who most needs counsel. Accordingly we hold that an individual held for interrogation must be clearly informed that he has the right to consult with a lawyer and to have the lawyer with him during interrogation under the system for protecting the privilege we delineate today. As with the warnings of the right to remain silent and that anything stated can be used in evidence against him, this warning is an absolute prerequisite to interrogation.

Fourth, if an individual indicates that he wishes the assistance of counsel before any interrogation occurs, the authorities cannot rationally ignore his request on the basis that the individual does not have or cannot afford a retained attorney. The privilege against self-incrimination secured by the Constitution applies to all individuals. The need for counsel in order to protect the privilege exists for the indigent as well as the affluent. The vast majority of confession cases with which we have dealt involve those unable to retain counsel. Therefore, it is necessary to warn an interrogated person that if he is indigent a lawyer will be appointed to represent him. Without this additional warning, the admonition of the right to consult with counsel would often be understood as meaning only that he can consult with a lawyer if he has one or has the funds to obtain one. The warning of a right to counsel would be hollow if not couched in terms that would convey to the indigent the knowledge that he too has a right to have counsel present. As with the warnings of the right to remain silent and of the general right to counsel, only by effective and express explanation to the indigent of this right can there be assurance that he was truly in a position to exercise it.

Fifth, once warnings have been given, the subsequent procedure is clear. If the individual indicates in any manner, at any time prior to or during questioning, that he wishes to remain silent, the interrogation must cease. At this point he has shown that he intends to exercise his Fifth Amendment privilege; any statement taken after the person invokes his privilege cannot be other than the product of compulsion, subtle or otherwise. Without the right to cut off questioning, the setting of in-custody interrogation operates on the individual to overcome free choice in producing a statement after the privilege has been once invoked. If the individual states that he wants an attorney, the interrogation must cease until an attorney is present. At that time, the individual must have an opportunity to confer with the attorney and to have him present during any subsequent questioning. If the individual cannot obtain an attorney and he indicates that he wants one before speaking to police, they must respect his decision to remain silent. This does not mean that each police station must have a "station house lawyer" present at all times to advise prisoners. It does mean that if police authorities conclude that they will not provide counsel during a reasonable period of time in which investigation in the field is carried out, they may refrain from doing so without violating the person's Fifth Amendment privilege so long as they do not question him during that time.

Sixth, if the interrogation continues without the presence of an attorney and a statement is taken, a heavy burden rests on the government to demonstrate that the defendant knowingly and intelligently waived his privilege against self-incrimination and his right to retained or appointed counsel. An express statement that the individual is willing to make a statement and does not want an attorney followed closely by a statement could constitute a waiver. But a valid waiver will not be presumed simply from the silence of the accused after warnings are given or simply from the fact that a confession was in fact eventually obtained. The fact of lengthy interrogation or incommunicado incarceration before a statement is made is strong evidence that the accused did not validly waive his rights because the fact that the individual eventually made a statement is consistent with the conclusion that the compelling influence of the interrogation finally forced him to do so. Moreover, any evidence that the accused was threatened, tricked, or cajoled into a waiver will, of course, show that the defendant did not voluntarily waive his privilege.

Finally, no distinction can be drawn between statements which are direct confessions and statements which amount to "admissions" of part or all of an offense. The privilege against self-incrimination does not distinguish degrees of incrimination. Similarly, no distinction may be drawn between inculpatory statements and statements alleged to be merely "exculpatory." If a statement were in fact truly exculpatory it would never be used by the prosecution. When an individual is in custody on probable cause, the police may seek out evidence in the field to be used at trial against him. Such investigation may include inquiry of persons not under restraint. General on-the-scene questioning as to facts surrounding a crime or other general questioning of citizens in the fact-finding process is not affected by our holding.

We hold that when an individual is taken into custody or otherwise deprived of his freedom by the authorities in any significant way and is subjected to questioning, the privilege against self-incrimination is jeopardized. Procedural safeguards must be employed to protect the privilege and in the absence of other fully effective measures, the following measures are required. He must be warned prior to any questioning that he has the right to remain silent, that anything he says can be used against him in a court of law, that he has the right to the presence of an attorney, and that if he cannot afford an attorney one will be appointed for him prior to any questioning if he so desires. Opportunity to exercise these rights must be afforded to him throughout the interrogation. After such warnings have been given, and such opportunity afforded him, the individual may knowingly and intelligently waive these rights and agree to answer questions or make a statement. But unless and until such warnings and waiver are demonstrated by the prosecution at trial, no evidence obtained as a result of interrogation can be used against him.

A recurrent argument made is that society's need for interrogation outweighs the privilege. But the Constitution has prescribed the rights of the individual when it provided in the Fifth Amendment that an individual cannot be compelled to be a witness against himself. That right cannot be abridged. Our decision does not in any way preclude police from carrying out their traditional investigatory functions. Although confessions may play an important role in some convictions, the cases before us present graphic examples of the overstatement of the "need" for confessions because even after police officers obtained "considerable" independent evidence against each defendant, they still conducted interrogations.

It is urged that an unfettered right to detention for interrogation should be allowed because it will often redound to the benefit of the person questioned. But the person who has committed no offense will be better able to clear himself after warnings with counsel present than without. Custodial interrogation, does not necessarily afford the innocent an opportunity to clear themselves. A serious consequence of the present practice is that many arrests "for investigation" subject large numbers of innocent persons to detention and interrogation. In one case here, police held four persons in jail for five days until one defendant confessed, although the police stated later that there was "no evidence to connect them with any crime."

Over the years the Federal Bureau of Investigation has compiled an exemplary record of effective law enforcement while advising any suspect or arrested person, at the outset of an interview, that he is not required to make a statement, that any statement may be used against him in court, that the individual may obtain the services of an attorney of his own choice and, more recently, that he has a right to free counsel if he is unable to pay. The practice of the FBI can readily be emulated by state and local enforcement agencies.

Judicial solutions to problems of constitutional dimension have evolved decade by decade. As courts have been presented with the need to enforce constitutional rights, they have found means of doing so. Where rights secured by the Constitution are involved, there can be no rule making or legislation which would abrogate them.

MR. JUSTICE CLARK, dissenting.

I would continue to follow the Due Process rule. I would consider whether the police officer prior to custodial interrogation added the warning that the suspect might have counsel present at the interrogation and the warning that a court would appoint one at his request if he was too poor to employ counsel. In the absence of warnings, the burden would be on the State to prove that counsel was knowingly and intelligently waived or that in the totality of the circumstances, including the failure to give the necessary warnings, the confession was clearly voluntary.

MR. JUSTICE HARLAN, whom MR. JUSTICE STEWART and MR. JUSTICE WHITE join, dissenting.

The new rules are not designed to guard against police brutality or other unmistakably banned forms of coercion. Those who use third-degree tactics and deny them in court are equally able and destined to lie as skillfully about warnings and waivers. Rather, the thrust of the new rules is to negate all pressures, to reinforce the nervous or ignorant suspect, and ultimately to discourage any confession at all. What the Court largely ignores is that its rules impair, if they will not eventually serve wholly to frustrate, an instrument of law enforcement that has long and quite reasonably been thought worth the price paid for it. The Court's new code would markedly decrease the number of confessions. To warn the suspect that he may remain silent and remind him that his confession may be used in court are minor obstructions. To require also an express waiver by the suspect and an end to questioning whenever he demurs must heavily handicap questioning. To suggest or provide counsel for the suspect simply invites the end of the interrogation.

How much harm this decision will inflict on law enforcement cannot be predicted with accuracy. We know that some crimes cannot be solved without confessions, that expert testimony attests to their importance in crime control, and that the Court is taking a real risk with society's welfare in imposing its new regime on the country. While passing over the costs and risks of its experiment, the Court portrays the evils of normal police questioning in exaggerated terms. Interrogation is no doubt often inconvenient and unpleasant for the suspect. However, it is no less so for a man to be arrested and jailed, to have his house searched, or to stand trial in court, yet all this may properly happen to the most innocent given probable cause, a warrant, or an indictment. Society has always paid a stiff price for law and order, and peaceful interrogation is not one of the dark moments of the law.

MR. JUSTICE WHITE, with whom MR. JUSTICE HARLAN and MR. JUSTICE STWEART join, dissenting.

Even if some confessions are coerced and present judicial procedures are believed to be inadequate to identify the confessions that are coerced and those that are not, it would still not be essential to impose the rule that the Court has now fashioned. Transcripts or observers could be required, specific time limits, tailored to fit the cause, could be imposed, or other devices could be utilized to reduce the chances that otherwise indiscernible coercion will produce an inadmissible confession. By considering any answers to any interrogation to be compelled and by escalating the requirements to prove waiver, the Court, for all practical purposes, forbids interrogation except in the presence of counsel. Instead of confining itself to protection of the right against compelled self-incrimination the Court has created a limited Fifth Amendment right to counsel—or, as the Court expresses it, a "need for counsel to protect the Fifth Amendment privilege."

There is every reason to believe that a good many criminal defendants who otherwise would have been convicted will now under this new version of the Fifth Amendment, either not be tried at all or will be acquitted if the State's evidence, minus the confession, is put to the test of litigation. Today's decision leaves open such questions as whether the accused was in custody, whether his statements were spontaneous or the product of interrogation, and whether the accused has effectively waived his rights, all of which are certain to prove productive of uncertainty during investigation and litigation during prosecution.

> **FYI**
>
> Prior to *Miranda*, the Court sometimes referred to certain trial rights and procedures as "safeguards" that protect the right to a fair trial. For example, the Court described its judge-made exclusionary rule in *Brown* as one of the "procedural safeguards of due process" for the pre-trial stage of a criminal prosecution. *Chambers v. Florida*, 309 U.S. 227, 238 (1940). Later the Court identified the theory underlying Due Process doctrine as "a compound of two influences": the idea that the right to a fair trial with "procedural safeguards" should be viewed as an antidote to inquisitorial procedures like police interrogation; and the idea that the Fourteenth Amendment prohibition on coercion and the Fifth Amendment prohibition on compulsion are linked together. *Gallegos v. Colorado*, 370 U.S. 49, 55 (1962). The *Miranda* Court continued to use the Due Process metaphor of "safeguards" in fashioning new methods for effectuating the Fifth Amendment privilege, and subsequent decisions reveal differing perspectives concerning the consequences of the labeling of *Miranda's* requirements as "prophylactic safeguards." *Compare Withrow v. Williams*, 507 U.S. 680 (1993) with *United States v. Patane*, 542 U.S. 630 (2004) (plurality opinion).

> ### Take Note
>
> More than 30 years after *Miranda*, the Court addressed the constitutionality of 18 U.S.C. § 3501, which provided that confessions are admissible in federal courts if they are voluntarily given. In *Dickerson v. United States*, 530 U.S. 428 (2000), the Court held that § 3501 is unconstitutional. The Court noted that the *Miranda* opinion "is replete with statements indicating that the majority thought it was announcing a constitutional rule," and concluded that, "Congress may not legislatively supersede our decisions interpreting and applying the Constitution." However, the *Dickerson* Court declined to hold that "the *Miranda* warnings are required by the Constitution, in the sense that nothing else will suffice to satisfy constitutional requirements." Instead, the Court found that, "the *Miranda* decision was based on the assumption that 'something more than the Due Process totality test was necessary' to prevent involuntary custodial confessions. Therefore, the totality test of § 3501 "cannot be sustained if *Miranda* is to remain the law." The *Dickerson* Court found no justification for overruling *Miranda* because the decision "has become embedded in routine police practice to the point where the warnings have become part of our national culture" and because principles of *stare decisis* "weigh heavily against overruling it."

Points for Discussion

a. *Miranda* Violations and Civil Damage Actions

In *Chavez v. Martinez*, 538 U.S. 760 (2003), Martinez alleged that he was coercively interrogated in violation of *Miranda*. Since he was never prosecuted, he could not seek suppression of his statements at trial; instead, he brought a civil suit under 42 U.S.C. § 1983 and claimed that the officer's actions violated his Fifth Amendment privilege, as well as his Due Process right to be free from coercive questioning. The *Chavez* Court concluded that Martinez could not establish a violation of his Fifth Amendment rights because the privilege only prevents a defendant from being "compelled in any criminal case to be a witness against himself." This right could not have been violated since "Martinez was never prosecuted for a crime."

b. *Miranda* and Habeas Review

In *Withrow v. Williams*, 507 U.S. 680 (1993), the Court held that even when a defendant has received a "full and fair chance to litigate" a *Miranda* claim in state court, the doctrine of *Stone v. Powell*, 428 U.S. 465 (1976), does not bar habeas review of that claim. However, *Miranda* habeas claims are subject to the requirements of the Antiterrorism and Effective Death Penalty Act of 1996 (AEDPA), so that a defendant must show that the state-court ruling on the *Miranda* claim "was contrary to, or involved an unreasonable application of, clearly established" federal law as determined by the Supreme Court precedents under 28 U.S.C. § 2254(d)(1).

> **Food for Thought**
>
> Consider the fact that the *Miranda* Court relied extensively on police interrogation manuals to support its decision. The curious thing about the decision is that the decision almost ignores the facts of the cases before it. If techniques like the "Mutt and Jeff" treatment were not used against Miranda, why did they receive so much attention in the Court's opinion?

> **Food for Thought**
>
> Arguably, *Miranda* is a pro-prosecution ruling as well as a pro-defendant ruling. Prosecutors are critical of the decision which they regard as "highly technical" and as sometimes mandating the exclusion of valuable evidence based on police violations of rules that may be difficult to interpret and easy to violate in good faith. On the other hand, it is not clear that the warning provides as much protection for suspects as the Court might have hoped. The warning is sometimes administered in a very perfunctory manner, and, in any event, does not eliminate the inherent coerciveness of the custodial interrogation situation. A suspect may still be isolated from the outside world in a police-dominated environment. Moreover, although suspects may receive the warning, they may not be familiar with the rules of evidence or the fact that seemingly innocent statements can be incriminating. Moreover, once a *Miranda* warning has been given, any resulting confession is much more likely to be regarded as voluntary and therefore admissible. So, are the *Miranda* warnings a panacea for the confessions problem?

> ### Hypo: *Alternatives to Miranda*
>
> Justice White's dissent proposed that specific alternatives, such as transcripts or observers, could serve as substitutes for the *Miranda* remedies. Subsequently, as technology has improved, and become considerably cheaper, it is possible to tape record all confessions. Would transcripts, observers or cameras be preferable to the *Miranda* warnings?

C. *Miranda's* Application

In extending the privilege against self-incrimination to custodial interrogations, *Miranda* raised a host of questions regarding the scope of its requirements, and years of litigation have been required to define such terms as "custody," "interrogation," "adequate warnings," "voluntary, knowing and intelligent" waiver, "unambiguous invocations" of the rights to silence and counsel, and post-invocation "initiation" that nullifies an invocation.

1. Custody

The duty to give *Miranda* warnings arises only when the police interrogate a person who is in "custody." The concepts of "custody" and "interrogation" are distinct and must coexist during "custodial interrogation" in order to give rise to *Miranda* rights and duties. In *Thompson v. Keohane*, 516 U.S. 99 (1995), while the Court did not provide a precise definition of the term "custody," it did state that "the court must apply an objective test to resolve the ultimate inquiry: was there a formal arrest or restraint on freedom of movement of the degree associated with a formal arrest."

Stansbury v. California

511 U.S. 318 (1994).

PER CURIAM.

The initial determination of custody depends on the objective circumstances of the interrogation, not on the subjective views harbored by either the interrogating officers or the person being questioned. In *Beckwith v. United States*, 425 U.S. 341 (1976), for example, the defendant, without being advised of his *Miranda* rights, made incriminating statements to Government agents during an interview in a private home. He later asked that *Miranda* "be extended to cover interrogation in non-custodial circumstances after a police investigation has focused on the suspect." We found his argument unpersuasive, explaining that it "was the compulsive aspect of custodial interrogation, and not the strength or content of the government's suspicions at the time the questioning was conducted, which led the Court to impose the *Miranda* requirements with regard to custodial questioning."

In *Berkemer v. McCarty*, 468 U.S. 420 (1984), we reaffirmed *Beckwith*. *Berkemer* concerned the roadside questioning of a motorist detained in a traffic stop. We decided that the motorist was not in custody for purposes of *Miranda* even though the traffic officer "apparently decided as soon as the motorist stepped out of his car that the motorist would be taken into custody and charged with a traffic offense." The reason was that the officer "never communicated his intention to" the motorist during the relevant questioning. Under *Miranda* "a policeman's unarticulated plan has no bearing on the question whether a suspect was 'in custody' at a particular time"; rather, "the only relevant inquiry is how a reasonable man in the suspect's shoes would have understood his situation."

It is well settled, then, that a police officer's subjective view that the individual under questioning is a suspect, if undisclosed, does not bear upon the question whether the individual is in custody for purposes of *Miranda*. The same principle obtains if an officer's undisclosed assessment is that the person being questioned is not a suspect. In either instance, one cannot expect the person under interrogation to probe the officer's innermost thoughts. Save as they are communicated or otherwise manifested to the person being questioned, an officer's evolving but unarticulated suspicions do not affect the objective circumstances of an interrogation or interview, and thus cannot affect the *Miranda* custody inquiry.

An officer's knowledge or beliefs may bear upon the custody issue if they are conveyed, by word or deed, to the individual being questioned. Those beliefs are relevant to the extent they would affect how a reasonable person in the position of the individual being questioned would gauge the breadth of his or her "freedom of action." Even a clear statement from an officer that the person under interrogation is a prime suspect is not, in itself, dispositive of the custody issue, for some suspects are free to come and go until the police decide to make an arrest. The weight and pertinence of any communications regarding the officer's degree of suspicion will depend upon the facts and circumstances of the particular case.

We think it appropriate for the California Supreme Court to consider this question of custody in the first instance. We therefore reverse its judgment and remand the case for further proceedings not inconsistent with this opinion.

Points for Discussion

a. Routine Traffic Stops

Stansbury relied on *Berkemer v. McCarty*, 468 U.S. 420 (1984), a case which held that "routine" traffic stops do not create custody for purposes of *Miranda:* "Two features of an ordinary traffic stop mitigate the danger that a person questioned will be induced "to speak where he would not otherwise do so freely." First, detention of a motorist pursuant to a traffic stop is presumptively temporary and brief. A motorist's expectations are that he will be obliged to spend a short period of time answering questions and waiting while the officer checks his license and registration, that he may then be given a citation, but that in the end he most likely will be allowed to continue on his way. In this respect, questioning incident to an ordinary traffic stop is quite different from station house interrogation, which frequently is prolonged, and in which the detainee often is aware that questioning will continue until he provides his interrogators the answers they seek. Second, circumstances associated with the typical traffic stop are not such that the motorist feels completely at the mercy of the police. To be sure, the aura of authority surrounding an armed, uniformed officer and the knowledge that the officer has some discretion in deciding whether to issue a citation, in combination, exert some pressure on the detainee to respond to questions. But the typical traffic stop is public, at least to some degree. This exposure to public view both reduces the ability of an unscrupulous policeman to

Take Note

The *Stansbury* Court refers to the perspective of the "reasonable person in the suspect's shoes," and the defendant's personal characteristics may or may not be relevant to that "perspective." In *Yarborough v. Alvarado*, 541 U.S. 652 (2004), the Court explained that the "objective" aspect of the "reasonable person" standard is meant to further the clarity of the custody test, so that police officers do not have "to make guesses" about a person's subjective experiences before deciding how they may interrogate a person. The Court acknowledged that "the line between permissible objective facts and impermissible subjective experiences can be indistinct in some cases." However, the Court held that a person's "prior history with law enforcement" is irrelevant to the custody inquiry, reasoning as follows: "In most cases, police officers will not know a suspect's interrogation history. Even if they do, the relationship between a suspect's past experiences and the likelihood a reasonable person with that experience would feel free to leave often will be speculative. Suspects with prior law enforcement experience may understand police procedures and reasonably feel free to leave unless told otherwise. On the other hand, they may view past as prologue and expect another in a string of arrests. We do not ask police officers to consider these contingent psychological factors when deciding when suspects should be advised of their *Miranda* rights. The inquiry turns too much on the suspect's subjective state of mind and not enough on the "objective circumstances of the interrogation."

use illegitimate means to elicit self-incriminating statements and diminishes the motorist's fear that, if he does not cooperate, he will be subjected to abuse. The fact that the detained motorist typically is confronted by only one or at most two officers further mutes his sense of vulnerability. In short, the atmosphere surrounding an ordinary traffic stop is substantially less "police dominated" than that surrounding the kinds of interrogation at issue in *Miranda* itself, and in the subsequent cases in which we have applied *Miranda*."

b. Voluntary Interview

Stansbury also relied on *Oregon v. Mathiason*, 429 U.S. 492 (1977), in which the Court held that a voluntary interview at the police station may not qualify as "custody" if the interview does not involve a "restraint on freedom of movement of the degree associated with a formal arrest." Several factors led the Court to conclude that the interview in that case was non-custodial: "Mathiason came voluntarily to the police station, where he was immediately informed that he was not under arrest. At the close of a half-hour interview Mathiason did in fact leave the police station without hindrance. A noncustodial situation is not converted to one simply because the questioning took place in a coercive environment. Any interview of one suspected of a crime by a police officer will have coercive aspects to it. But the requirement of *Miranda* warnings is not to be imposed simply because the questioning takes place in the station house, or because the questioned person is one whom the police suspect." Justice Marshall dissented, arguing that *Miranda* "requires us to distinguish situations that resemble the 'coercive aspects' of custodial interrogation from those that more nearly resemble 'general on-the-scene questioning or other general questioning of citizens in the fact-finding process.' " He emphasized that Mathiason was interrogated in "private" and "unfamiliar surroundings," while being subjected to "deceptive strategems" condemned in *Miranda*. Justice Stevens dissented on the ground that a parolee like Mathiason "should always be warned" during a police interview because a "parolee is technically in legal custody continuously until his sentence has been served."

c. Custody and Inmates

In *Mathis v. United States*, 391 U.S. 1 (1968), the Court held that a state prison inmate should have received *Miranda* warnings when he was interrogated by an IRS agent in an isolated prison location regarding potential violations of the tax code. The Court reasoned that even "routine" tax investigations can lead to criminal prosecutions, and that nothing in *Miranda* "calls for a curtailment of the warnings based on the reason why the person is in custody." However, in *Maryland v. Shatzer*, 559 U.S. 98 (2010), the Court held that the mere fact of imprisonment does not establish the existence of custody for *Miranda* purposes. During the time when inmates are neither interrogated nor "isolated with their accusers," but living instead in the "accustomed surroundings" of the "general prison population," the fact of incarceration alone "does not create the coercive pressures identified in *Miranda*." However, *Shatzer* held that *Miranda* warnings must be given to inmates in "interrogative custody." However, each time that Shatzer was interrogated, he received *Miranda* warnings.

In *Howes v. Fields,* 565 U.S. 499 (2012), the Court held that courts must examine the totality of circumstances on a case-by-case basis in determining whether an inmate is in custody for *Miranda* purposes: "We have declined to accord talismanic power to the freedom-of-movement inquiry, and instead have asked whether the relevant environment presents the same inherently coercive pressures as the type of station house questioning at issue in *Miranda*." *Howes* concluded that the inmate was not in custody because he was interrogated in a conference room in which he was "not physically restrained or threatened," and was "told at the outset of the interrogation," and reminded later, "that he could leave and go back to his cell whenever he wanted." He was offered "food and water," and "the door to the conference room was sometimes left open." He never asked to go back to his cell. Justice Ginsburg's *Howes* dissent proposed that custody should be found to exist when an inmate is "subjected to 'incommunicado interrogation' " in a "police-dominated atmosphere," and placed "against his will" in an "inherently stressful situation," with his "freedom of action" "curtailed in any significant way." She noted that: "The deputies were armed, and they questioned the inmate in isolation for between five to seven hours into the early morning hours. He was not given his evening medications. Even though the inmate was told that he was free to return to his cell, he did not ask to do so because he believed, with good reason, that they would not have allowed him to leave. The officers had ignored his repeated statements that he did not want to speak to them."

d. Juvenile Justice

In *J.D.B.* the Court focused on whether a child's age is a subjective factor that is relevant to the determination of custody: "Neither officers nor courts can reasonably evaluate the effect of objective circumstances that are specific to children," such as the schoolhouse setting of an interrogation, "without accounting for the age of the child subjected to those circumstances." *J.D.B.* distinguished *Alvarado*: "Precisely because childhood yields objective conclusions—among others, that children are "most susceptible to influence" and 'outside pressures'—considering age in the custody analysis in no way involves a determination of how youth "subjectively affects the mindset" of any particular child." *J.D.B.* acknowledged that a child's age would not necessarily be "a determinative, or even a significant, factor in every case." But the Court rejected the State's argument that a child's age should never be relevant to the custody determination, because such a rule would "ignore the very real differences between children and adults" and would "deny children the full scope of the procedural safeguards that *Miranda* guarantees to adults."

Hypo 1: *Stansbury Facts*

Assume that four police officers go to Stansbury's home near midnight, and ask him to accompany them to the police station for questioning as a possible witness in a homicide investigation. They offer him the choice of riding in the patrol car or driving himself to the station, and Stansbury chooses to accept the ride. In order to reach the interview room in the jail area of the station, Stansbury is forced to pass through a locked parking garage door and a locked jail entrance, both of which are locked from both the inside and the outside, and he is subjected to a pat-down search. Stansbury is not restrained in the interview room, and two police officers are present. Oliver, the interviewing officer, tels Stansbury that he is being questioned as a witness, and that he is not "under arrest". After 30 minutes of questioning, Oliver decides to give Stansbury the *Miranda* warnings when Stansbury mentions a potentially incriminating fact. Was Stansbury in custody before Oliver gave him the warnings? *Compare People v. Stansbury*, 9 Cal.4th 824, 38 Cal.Rptr.2d 394, 889 P.2d 588 (Ca. 1995) and *People v. Elmarr*, 181 P.3d 1157 (Colo. 2008); *State v. Muntean*, 189 Vt. 50, 12 A.3d 518 (2010); *State v. Waring*, 364 N.C. 443, 701 S.E.2d 615 (2010); *United States v. Ambrose*, 668 F.3d 943 (7th Cir. 2012).

Food for Thought

A Fourth Amendment "seizure" occurs when an individual is subjected either to an investigative stop based on reasonable suspicion, or to a custodial arrest based on probable cause. Assume that a motorist dutifully stops at a police roadblock set up to catch drunk drivers. Is the motorist in custody for purposes of *Miranda*? If the motorist is not in custody, what circumstances might arise at the roadblock to justify a finding of custody so as to require *Miranda* warnings?

Hypo 2: *More on Traffic Stops*

Which of the following facts would you deem sufficient to transform a "traffic stop" into a "custodial interrogation?" Would it be enough if the officer asks a stopped driver to sit in the front seat of his police car, and the driver agrees to do so (while the officer sits in the driver's seat of the same car)? Suppose another police officer arrives, and stands outside of the passenger window of the stopped motorist's car? Does the situation change significantly if one of the officers tells the stopped driver that he is aware that she was recently arrested for possession of illegal drugs, and that he suspects her of being in possession of drugs? *See State v. Landis, 281 Neb. 139, 794 N.W.2d 151 (2011)*; see also *People v. Thomas, 51 Cal.4th 449, 121 Ca. Rptr.3d 521, 247 P.3d 886 (2011)*.

Hypo 3: *Home Interviews*

What circumstances might transform a home interview into a custodial interrogation? Suppose that the questioning officer makes clear that the suspect is not under arrest, that the officer "just wants to talk," and that the suspect will not be arrested that day regardless of what he says. Is there "custody" if the officer suggests that the interview should take place in a quiet area, and the officer and the suspect move to a storage room (where they will not be heard by others) and close the door? *See United States v. Craighead, 539 F.3d 1073 (9th Cir. 2008)*; *see also Mumford v. People, 270 P.3d 953 (Colo. 2012)*. Would your view be different if seven police officers, all displaying guns, arrive to execute a search warrant at a woman's house, and order her to sit on the couch. Would it matter whether the police told the woman that she was not under arrest? *See State v. Mangual, 85 A.3d 627 (Conn. 2014)*. Suppose that a nine year old of limited intelligence is suspected of having murdered his infant brother. A police officer indicates a desire to talk to the boy. Sitting at the dining room table, at the family home, with the father present, the officer asks the boy "what happened?" in a conversational tone. Was the boy in custody? How does the boy's age enter into the analysis of custody and coercion issues? *See In re DLH, Jr., 32 N.E.3d 1075 (Ill. 2015)*.

Hypo 4: *Hospital Interview*

Jamison was taken to the emergency room where he tells a police officer, Maurice, that he was shot by a stranger who ran away. Maurice asks Jamison for the location of the shooting and arranges for a detective to come to the hospital to investigate. Maurice follows Jamison to a treatment room, where Jamison lays on a gurney while attending nurses cut away his clothing and treat the entrance and exit wounds on his leg. Maurice places bags on Jamison's hands, which is routine procedure to preserve evidence on the hands of shooting victims. After noticing that there are no bullet holes in Jamison's clothing, Officer Maurice asks him to recount what happened during the shooting, and Jamison admits that he shot himself with an illegal handgun. Was Jamison in custody and entitled to *Miranda* warnings? *See United States v. Jamison,* 509 F.3d 623 (4th Cir. 2007).

Food for Thought

The *J.B.D.* decision, discussed *supra*, discusses the idea that courts might be more inclined to find that a juvenile is in custody even though it might not find that an adult is in custody under similar circumstances. Let's think a bit about how the holding in *J.B.D.* might be applied. Suppose that a high school student, who is suspected of having given prescription pain killers to a fellow student, is sent to the principal's office. As he enters the officer, is the student now in "custody?" Would your view be different if the principal has called the police, waits until the police arrive, and then calls the student in for an interview? Does the age of the student matter? Would you be more likely to find "custody" when a middle school student is called to the principal's office than when a high school student is called? See *N.C. v. Commonwealth,* 396 S.W.2d 852 (Ky. 2013); *State v. Pearson,* 804 N.W.2d 260 (Iowa 2011).

Hypo 5: *More on Custody*

The police have a warrant to arrest McKenna for child molestation. Before making the arrest, they decide to speak with him to see whether he has an alibi defense (*e.g.,* he was out of the country at the time of the alleged molestation). The police drive to McKenna's restaurant, and ask whether he is willing to speak with them about a "private" matter. McKenna agrees to do so. For over an hour, while the police and McKenna are strolling outside of McKenna's restaurant, they discuss the allegations. At one point, McKenna indicates an intention to enter some woods. The interrogation officer tells McKenna that they need to stay in eyesight of an officer who is watching the interrogation from a nearby police car. Was McKenna in custody for purposes of *Miranda*? If so, when did the custody begin? *See State v. McKenna,* 166 N.H. 671, 103 A.3d 756 (2014).

Hypo 6: *Custody at the Border?*

An individual, who has been flagged for further scrutiny, arrives at the U.S. border. After some brief questioning, he is referred for "secondary questioning" which takes place in a small (10' x 10') room, lasts for two hours, and is focused on the belief that he is engaged in drug smuggling. Under these circumstances, was defendant in "custody" so that a *Miranda* warning is required? By contrast, is there "interrogation" when the suspect is asked only "routine" immigration questions at the border? *See United States v. Molina-Gomez*, 781 F.3d 13 (1st Cir. 2015).

Hypo 7: *Custody During Street Encounters?*

Suppose that federal agents receive a tip from a gun dealer that an individual is purchasing guns for others (a federal crime). The officers follow the individual when he leaves the shop, and stop him for committing various traffic infractions. Knowing that the suspect has just purchased guns and ammunition, the officers approach the vehicle with their guns drawn. After a few minutes, they holster their guns, and tell him that he is not "under arrest." The officers speak to the suspect for a few minutes without administering a *Miranda* warning, and he makes incriminating statements. Was the suspect "in custody" for purposes of *Miranda*? *See United States v. Ortiz*, 781 F.3d 221 (5th Cir. 2015).

Hypo 8: *Barricaded Suspect*

Police officers have probable cause to believe that Mack shot and wounded his wife and daughter, and have a warrant for his arrest. Mack barricades himself in a motel room with hostages and weapons. The agents surround Mack's room. When Mack does not respond to police requests to give himself up, communicated to him by bullhorn, the police bring in an FBI hostage negotiator who calls Mack on the telephone. For three hours, the FBI agent converses with Mack without giving him *Miranda* warnings. At Mack's trial, the prosecution seeks to introduce Mack's statements to the FBI agent. Was Mack in "custody" during the hostage negotiation and entitled to *Miranda* warnings? *See United States v. Mesa*, 638 F.2d 582 (3d Cir. 1980).

2. Interrogation

In order for *Miranda* to apply, not only must the suspect be in "custody," there must also be "interrogation." Just as the courts have struggled to define the term "custody," they have also struggled to define the term "interrogation."

Rhode Island v. Innis

446 U.S. 291 (1980).

Mr. Justice Stewart delivered the opinion of the Court.

A taxi driver was robbed shortly after midnight by a man with a sawed-off shotgun; the driver identified Innis as the robber from a photo array, and reported that he had dropped Innis off in the Mount Pleasant section of Providence. Five days earlier, another Providence taxi driver had been killed by a man with a shotgun. Around 4:30 a.m., Patrolman Lovell was cruising in a patrol car when he spotted Innis standing in the street. Lovell arrested Innis, who was unarmed, and advised him of his *Miranda* rights. Lovell and Innis waited in the patrol car and Lovell did not converse with Innis. A sergeant soon arrived and read Innis the *Miranda* warnings; minutes later Captain Leyden arrived with other officers and advised Innis again of his *Miranda* rights. Innis stated that he understood those rights and wanted to speak with a lawyer. Captain Leyden then directed that Innis should be placed in a "caged wagon," a four-door police car with a wire screen mesh between the front and rear seats, and be driven to the central police station. Three officers were assigned to accompany Innis to the police station. Captain Leyden then instructed the officers not to question Innis or intimidate or coerce him in any way.

While en route to the station, Patrolman Gleckman initiated a conversation with Patrolman McKenna concerning the missing shotgun. Gleckman testified: "I was talking with Patrolman McKenna stating that I frequent this area while on patrol and that because a school for handicapped children is located nearby, there's a lot of handicapped children running around in this area, and God forbid one of them might find a weapon with shells and they might hurt themselves." Patrolman McKenna testified: "I more or less concurred with Gleckman that it was a safety factor and that we should continue to search for the weapon." Patrolman Williams testified that he heard Gleckman say, "it would be too bad if the little—I believe he said a girl—would pick up the gun, maybe kill herself." Innis then interrupted the conversation, stating that the officers should turn the car around so he could show them where the gun was located. At the time, they had traveled no more than a mile, a trip encompassing only a few minutes. The police vehicle then returned to the scene of the arrest where a search for the shotgun was in progress. There, Captain Leyden again advised Innis of his *Miranda* rights and Innis replied that he understood those rights but that he "wanted to get the gun out of the way because of the kids in the area in the school." Innis then led the police to a nearby field, where he pointed out the shotgun under some rocks by the side of the road. The gun and his statements were introduced at his trial for kidnaping, robbery, and murder, and Innis was convicted of these crimes. He argued that the gun and statements were inadmissible because of improper police interrogation after he invoked his right to counsel under *Miranda*.

The starting point for defining "interrogation" is *Miranda* where the Court observed that "by custodial interrogation, we mean questioning initiated by law enforcement officers after a person has been taken into custody or otherwise deprived of his freedom of action in any significant way." This passage might suggest that the *Miranda* rules were to apply only to those police interrogation practices that involve express questioning of a defendant while in custody.

We do not, however, construe *Miranda* so narrowly. The concern of *Miranda* was that the "interrogation environment" created by the interplay of interrogation and custody would "subjugate the individual to the will of his examiner" and thereby undermine the privilege against compulsory self-incrimination. The police practices that evoked this concern included several that did not involve express questioning. For example, one of the practices was the use of line-ups in which a coached witness would pick the defendant as the perpetrator. This was designed to establish that the defendant was in fact guilty as a predicate for further interrogation. A variation on this theme was the so-called "reverse line-up" in which a defendant would be identified by coached witnesses as the perpetrator of a fictitious crime, with the object of inducing him to confess to the actual crime of which he was suspected in order to escape the false prosecution. *Miranda* also included in its survey of interrogation practices the use of psychological ploys, such as to "posit" "the guilt of the subject," to "minimize the moral seriousness of the offense," and "to cast blame on the victim or on society." It is clear that these techniques of persuasion, no less than express questioning, were thought, in a custodial setting, to amount to interrogation. This is not to say that all statements obtained by the police after a person has been taken into custody are to be considered the product of interrogation. As *Miranda* noted: "Volunteered statements of any kind are not barred by the Fifth Amendment." The special procedural safeguards outlined in *Miranda* are required not where a suspect is simply taken into custody, but rather where a suspect in custody is subjected to interrogation. 'Interrogation,' as conceptualized in *Miranda*, must reflect a measure of compulsion above and beyond that inherent in custody itself."

We conclude that the *Miranda* safeguards come into play whenever a person in custody is subjected to either express questioning or its functional equivalent. That is to say, the term "interrogation" refers also to any words or actions on the part of the police (other than those normally attendant to arrest and custody) that the police should know are reasonably likely to elicit an incriminating response from the suspect. The latter portion of this definition focuses primarily upon the perceptions of the suspect, rather than the intent of the police. This focus reflects the fact that the *Miranda* safeguards were designed to vest a suspect in custody with an added measure of protection against coercive police practices, without regard to objective proof of the underlying intent of the police.

Turning to the present case, we conclude that Innis was not "interrogated" within the meaning of *Miranda*. The conversation between Gleckman and McKenna included no express questioning of Innis. Rather, that conversation was, at least in form, nothing more than a dialogue between the two officers to which no response from Innis was invited. Moreover, it cannot be fairly concluded that Innis was subjected to the "functional equivalent" of questioning. It cannot be said that Gleckman and McKenna should have known that their conversation was reasonably likely to elicit an incriminating response from Innis. There is nothing in the record to suggest that the officers were aware that Innis was peculiarly susceptible to an appeal to his conscience concerning the safety of handicapped children. Nor is there anything to suggest that the police knew that he was unusually disoriented or upset at the time of his arrest.

The case thus boils down to whether, in the context of a brief conversation, the officers should have known that Innis would suddenly be moved to make a self-incriminating response. Given the fact that the entire conversation appears to have consisted of no more than a few off hand remarks, we cannot say that the officers should have known that it was reasonably likely that Innis would so respond. This is not a case where the police carried on a lengthy harangue in the presence of the suspect. Nor does the record support the contention by Innis that, under the circumstances, the officers' comments were particularly "evocative." It is our view, therefore, that Innis was not subjected by the police to words or actions that the police should have known were reasonably likely to elicit an incriminating response from him.

MR. JUSTICE MARSHALL, with whom MR. JUSTICE BRENNAN joins, dissenting.

I agree with the Court's definition of "interrogation" within the meaning of *Miranda*. I am utterly at a loss, however, to understand how this objective standard as applied to the facts before us can rationally lead to the conclusion that there was no interrogation. If the statements had been addressed to Innis, it would be impossible to draw such a conclusion. The simple message of the "talking back and forth" between Gleckman and McKenna was that they had to find the shotgun to avert a child's death. One can scarcely imagine a stronger appeal to the conscience of a suspect—any suspect—than the assertion that if the weapon is not found an innocent person will be hurt or killed. Not just any innocent person, but an innocent child—a little girl—a helpless, handicapped little girl on her way to school. The notion that such an appeal could not be expected to have any effect unless the suspect were known to have some special interest in handicapped children verges on the ludicrous. The appeal to a suspect to confess for the sake of others, to "display some evidence of decency and honor," is a classic interrogation technique. See, e.g., F. Inbau & J. Reid, Criminal Interrogation and Confessions 60–62 (2d ed. 1967). This is not a case where police officers speaking among themselves are accidentally overheard by a suspect. These officers were "talking back and forth" in close quarters with the handcuffed suspect, traveling past the very place where they believed the weapon was located. They knew respondent would hear their conversation, and they are chargeable with knowledge of and responsibility for the pressures to speak which they created.

Points for Discussion

a. Public Safety Exception

In *New York v. Quarles*, 467 U.S. 649 (1984), the Court held that police officers may sometimes withhold the *Miranda* warnings until after they ask an arrestee questions that are "necessary to secure their own safety or the safety of the public." In *Quarles*, police received information from a rape victim, describing the clothing and height of her assailant, and reporting that the man had just entered a nearby supermarket carrying a gun. When the officers entered the store, a man matching the victim's description turned and ran. The officers pursued and caught the man, after losing sight of him briefly. When they stopped him at gunpoint and frisked him, the police discovered that the man was wearing an empty shoulder holster. One officer handcuffed the man in the presence of three other officers, and then asked the man about the location of the gun. When the man nodded in the direction of some empty cartons and said, "Over there," the police located the gun and then recited the *Miranda* warnings. *Quarles* held that the gun and the statement about its location should be admissible at his trial for criminal possession of the weapon, under a "public safety" exception to *Miranda*, reasoning as follows: "The police, in the act of apprehending a suspect, were confronted with the immediate necessity of ascertaining the whereabouts of a gun which they had every reason to believe the suspect had just removed from his empty holster and discarded in the supermarket. So long as the gun was concealed somewhere in the supermarket, it posed more than one danger to the public safety: an accomplice might use it, a customer or employee might come upon it. If the police are required to recite the *Miranda* warnings before asking the whereabouts of the gun, suspects in Quarles' position might well be deterred from responding. Procedural safeguards which deter a suspect from responding were deemed acceptable in *Miranda* in order to protect the Fifth Amendment privilege; when the primary social cost of those added protections is the possibility of fewer convictions, the *Miranda* majority was willing to bear that cost. Here, had *Miranda* warnings deterred Quarles from responding to the question about the whereabouts of the gun, the police could not have insured that further danger to the public did not result from the concealment of the gun in a public area. The officer asked only the question necessary to locate the missing gun before advising Quarles of his rights. The exception which we recognize today, far from complicating the thought processes and the on-the-scene judgments of police officers, will simply free them to follow their legitimate instincts when confronting situations presenting a danger to the public safety."

b. Undercover Agent Exception

In *Illinois v. Perkins*, 496 U.S. 292 (1990), the Court held that when an undercover agent questions a suspect in custody, such questioning does not qualify as "interrogation" under *Miranda*, reasoning as follows: "Conversations between suspects and undercover agents do not implicate the concerns underlying *Miranda*.

> **FYI**
>
> The *Quarles* dissenters argued against the public safety exception, contending that the police had not shown a danger to public safety. They emphasized that *Miranda* was not based on a cost-benefit analysis, and that "society's need for interrogation" cannot "outweigh" the privilege against self-incrimination. In addition, the dissenters viewed the Court's claim that the "public was at risk" as "speculative": "Before the interrogation, Quarles had been 'reduced to a condition of physical powerlessness' and he was not believed to have an accomplice. When the questioning began, the arresting officers were sufficiently confident of their safety to put away their guns. Based on the interrogating officer's testimony that 'the situation was under control', the lower court found that 'nothing suggests that any of the officers was concerned for his own physical safety.' The conclusion that neither Quarles nor his missing gun posed a threat to the public's safety is amply supported by evidence that no customers or employees were wandering about the store, and Quarles' arrest took place during the middle of the night when the store was deserted except for clerks at the checkout counter. The police could easily have cordoned off the store and searched for the missing gun. Had they done so, they would have found the gun quickly because they were well aware that Quarles had discarded his weapon somewhere near the scene of the arrest."

The essential ingredients of a "police-dominated atmosphere" and compulsion are not present when an incarcerated person speaks freely to someone whom he believes to be a fellow inmate. Coercion is determined from the perspective of the suspect. It is the premise of *Miranda* that the danger of coercion results from the interaction of custody and official interrogation. Questioning by captors, who appear to control the suspect's fate, may create mutually reinforcing pressures that the Court has assumed will weaken the suspect's will, but where a suspect does not know that he is conversing with a government agent, these pressures do not exist. When the suspect has no reason to think that the listeners have official power over him, it should not be assumed that his words are motivated by the reaction he expects from his listeners. "When the agent carries neither badge nor gun and wears not 'police blue,' but the same prison gray" as the suspect, there is no 'interplay between police interrogation and police custody.' The use of undercover agents is a recognized law enforcement technique, often employed in the prison context to detect violence against correctional officials or inmates, as well as for the purposes of gathering evidence here."

The "routine booking question" exception derives from the *Miranda* Court's observation that police questions that are "normally attendant to arrest and custody" do not qualify as "interrogation." In *Pennsylvania v. Muniz*, 496 U.S. 582 (1990), the Court noted that "routine booking questions" typically are asked to secure "the biographical data necessary to complete booking or pretrial services," and held that an intoxicated driver could be asked booking questions about his or her "name, address, height, weight, eye color, date of birth, and current age." The government conceded that a sixth question for the driver was not a "routine booking question": "Do you know what the date was of your sixth birthday?" The Court concluded that this question violated the Fifth Amendment because it called for a "testimonial response": it called for defendant to "explicitly or implicitly relate a factual assertion or disclose information," and it subjected defendant to the "cruel trilemma" of "self-accusation, perjury, or contempt."

Food for Thought

In *Innis*, suppose that there had been a school for handicapped children in the vicinity of the defendant's arrest, and the police knew that Innis had a handicapped daughter who was six years old. After the officer made his remark about a handicapped girl killing herself, he states, "You know, I saw that happen once. It was just terrible. The little girl blew her own head right off." Would these facts alter the result in *Innis*?

Hypo 1: *Stolen Furs*

Defendant is arrested for the murder of a woman and the theft of her furs. After defendant invokes his right to remain silent, and is placed in a cell, the police place the stolen furs about a foot away from the cell. At this point, defendant makes several incriminating statements. Was defendant subjected to "interrogation" within the meaning of *Miranda*? *See People v. Ferro*, 63 N.Y.2d 316, 472 N.E.2d 13, 482 N.Y.S.2d 237 (1984).

Hypo 2: *Playing Audio Tapes*

Vallar is arrested at home for drug conspiracy, and taken to the police station, but is not given a *Miranda* warning. The police do not question Vallar, but they do make him listen to audio tapes of conversations between two of Vallar's friends implicating Vallar in the conspiracy. Vallar listens silently and says nothing. Then a detective gives Vallar a *Miranda* warning, and Vallar says, "OK, I will waive my rights," signs a waiver form, and makes incriminating statements during the subsequent interrogation. Did the playing of the audio tapes constitute interrogation under *Innis*? *See United States v. Vallar*, 635 F.3d 271 (7th Cir. 2011).

Hypo 3: *Creating an Evocative Situation*

A man is arrested for killing his son, is given a *Miranda* warning, and invokes his rights. When the man's wife is brought in for questioning, she asks to speak to her husband. The police grant the request, but keep a police officer in the room for security reasons. The man objects to his wife's presence, as well as to the presence of a tape recorder. Even though the man continuously asks his wife to remain silent, she makes several incriminating statements. Does placing the wife in the room with her husband, amount to interrogation? *See Arizona v. Mauro*, 481 U.S. 520 (1987).

Hypo 4: *The Blabbermouth*

A suspect in a stabbing incident is taken to the police station where the investigating detective tells the suspect that he has spoken with the arresting officer (the suspect made incriminating statements to the arresting officer). The suspect responds "I told it to him 14 times." The detective responds, "OK, do you want to tell it to me?" Did the officer's statement involve "interrogation" so that a *Miranda* warning was required? Should it matter that the detective knew that the suspect tended to be a "blabbermouth?" *See State v. Juranek,* 844 N.W.2d 791 (Neb. 2014).

Food for Thought

From reading the note about *Quarles,* do you have a clear understanding regarding when the public safety exception applies (and, equally importantly,) when it does not apply? Part of the difficulty is that most matters that involve the police implicate "public safety." Moreover, the facts of *Quarles* were not particularly compelling in terms of establishing the need to act in the public interest (the effort to locate a lost weapon). One can think of a variety of scenarios where the "public interest" might be more compelling (e.g., murder, robbery, rape), especially when the perpetrator is on the loose. As a result, if the exception is broadly applied, it has the potential to dramatically undercut the *Miranda* requirement. Can you think of criteria that courts could use to decide which situations are compelling enough to justify dispensing with the *Miranda* warning?

Hypo 5: *Meaning of Quarles and Its Application*

In which of the following situations would you apply the public safety exception:

A. Suppose that there are a series of murders in a community. Although the police are unable to locate the murderer, they have identified several suspects. Given the heinous nature of the crimes, if the police question each of the suspects without giving *Miranda* warnings, should a court rely on the *Quarles* public safety exception to find that the incriminating statements of one suspect are admissible?

B. A teenage boy has mysteriously disappeared. The police have probable cause to believe that Rubio has kidnapped the boy so they bring him to the stationhouse for questioning. Would the public safety exception justify the police in dispensing with a *Miranda* warning when they interrogate Rubio? *See United States v. Vega Rubio,* 2011 WL 220033 (D. Nev. 2011); *People v. Davis,* 208 P.2d 78 (Cal. 2009).

C. Suppose that the police discover an unexploded bomb near Times Square in N.Y.C. An investigation reveals that Shahzad may have planted the bomb. Shahzad is apprehended as he is trying to board a flight at JFK airport. If the police are fearful that Shahzad is part of a terrorist network, that is planning to commit other crimes, may they interrogate him without giving him a *Miranda* warning? *See In re Terrorist Bombings of U.S. Embassies in East Africa*, 552 P.3d 93 (2d Cir. 2008); *United States v. Hasan*, 747 F. Supp.2d 642 (E.D. Va. 2010).

D. Responding to a 911 call about suspicious activity, the police find a man in a rural area with blood on his hunting coveralls. The man provides identification, and states that he is walking for his health and is wearing coveralls because of the cold. When the police ask the man about the blood, he invokes his right to remain silent. If the police fear that the blood relates to a homicide, may they question the man without providing him with a *Miranda* warning? *See People v. Doll*, 998 N.E.2d 384 (N.Y. 2013).

Hypo 6: *"Routine Booking Questions?"*

The police arrest Denise for stealing morphine tablets from a pharmacy. After Denise is given a *Miranda* warning, she states that she wants to remain silent, and is turned over to jail personnel. However, a police detective listens to the answers that Denise gives during the booking process. Some of the questions on a medical questionnaire inquire about drug use in order to help the facility decide whether the arrestee should be placed in jail or in a medical facility. Denise admits that she took one morphine tablet that day, and states that she has used morphine within the last 72 hours. Can these questions be regarded as "routine booking questions?" *See State v. Denney*, 152 Wash. App. 665, 218 P.3d 633 (2009).

Hypo 7: *Border Crossing*

When Calzada's plane arrives at JFK airport from the Dominican Republic, a Customs & Border Patrol (CBP) officer notices that her name is in a database of people that are subject to outstanding arrest warrants. She is escorted to a conference room for questioning to determine whether she should be admitted to the United States. In reviewing Calzada's passport documents, the officer notices that there is a passport application by someone of the exact same name with a photograph of a woman who looks nothing like Calzada. As she is questioned, Calzada admits that she is traveling under a false name, and is charged with identity theft and misuse of a passport. The prosecution admits that Calzada was not given a *Miranda* warning, but argues that there should be an exception for "routine border crossing" inquiries designed to determine whether a person may be admitted to the United States. How should the court rule? *See United States v. FNU LNU, 653 F.3d 144 (2d Cir. 2011).*

3. Adequate Warnings

When custodial interrogation takes place, the prosecution must prove that an adequate set of *Miranda* warnings were given before interrogation occurred. *Tague v. Louisiana, 444 U.S. 469 (1980).* To be adequate, warnings must "reasonably convey" the substance of the mandated warning. Warnings may be inadequate if they are incomplete or provide misleading information about a suspect's rights. Warnings can also be inadequate if they are "non-functional" in that the police fail to warn at the outset of an interrogation, and then deliver "midstream" warnings and continue the interrogation. If a court determines that the *Miranda* warnings were inadequate, then post-warning incriminating statements will be inadmissible. Thus, a claim that warnings were "inadequate" is distinct from a claim that an invalid waiver was obtained after adequate warnings were provided.

Florida v. Powell

559 U.S. 50 (2010).

JUSTICE GINSBURG delivered the opinion of the Court.

On August 10, 2004, law enforcement officers in Tampa, Florida, seeking to apprehend respondent Kevin Powell in connection with a robbery investigation, entered an apartment rented by Powell's girlfriend. After spotting Powell coming from a bedroom, the officers searched the room and discovered a loaded nine-millimeter handgun under the bed. The officers arrested Powell and transported him to the Tampa Police headquarters. Once there, and before asking Powell any questions, the officers read Powell the standard Tampa Police Department Consent and Release Form 310. The form states: "You have the right to remain silent. If you give up the right to remain silent, anything you say can be used against you in court. You have the right to talk to a lawyer before answering any of our questions. If you cannot afford to hire a lawyer, one will be appointed for you without cost and before any questioning. You have the right to use any of these rights at any time you want during this interview." Acknowledging that he had been informed of his rights, that he "understood them," and that he was "willing to talk" to the officers, Powell signed the form. He then admitted that he owned the handgun found in the apartment. Powell knew he was prohibited from possessing a gun because he had previously been convicted of a felony, but said he had nevertheless purchased and carried the firearm for his protection.

Powell was charged with possession of a weapon by a prohibited possessor. Contending that the *Miranda* warnings were deficient because they did not adequately convey his right to the presence of an attorney during questioning, he moved to suppress his inculpatory statements. The trial court denied the motion and convicted Powell of the charge. The Florida Supreme Court found that the advice Powell received was misleading because it suggested that Powell could "only consult with an attorney before questioning" and did not convey Powell's entitlement to counsel's presence throughout the interrogation. We granted certiorari and reverse.

To give force to the Constitution's protection against compelled self-incrimination, the Court established in *Miranda* "certain procedural safeguards that require police to advise criminal suspects of their rights under the Fifth and Fourteenth Amendments before commencing custodial interrogation." *Duckworth v. Eagan*, 492 U.S. 195, 201 (1989). Intent on "giving concrete constitutional guidelines for law enforcement agencies and courts to follow," *Miranda* prescribed the following four now-familiar warnings: "A suspect must be warned prior to an questioning that he has the right to remain silent, that anything he says can be used against him in a court of law, that he has the right to the presence of an attorney, and that if he cannot afford an attorney one will be appointed for him prior to any questioning if he so desires."

Miranda's third warning addresses our concern that "the circumstances surrounding in-custody interrogation can operate very quickly to overbear the will of one merely made aware of his privilege to remain silent by his interrogators." Responsive to that concern, as "an absolute prerequisite to interrogation," an individual held for questioning "must be clearly informed that he has the right to consult with a lawyer and to have the lawyer with him during interrogation." The question before us is whether the warnings Powell received satisfied this requirement.

The four warnings are invariable, but this Court has not dictated the words in which the essential information must be conveyed. *See California v. Prysock,* 453

U.S. 355 (1981) *(per curiam).* In determining whether police officers adequately conveyed the four warnings, reviewing courts are not required to examine the words "as if construing a will or defining the terms of an easement. The inquiry is simply whether the warnings reasonably 'convey to a suspect his rights as required by *Miranda.*' " *Duckworth,* 492 U.S. at 203 (quoting *Prysock,* 453 U.S. at 361).

[handwritten marginal note: *state defferance*]

Prysock and *Duckworth* inform our judgment. In *Prysock,* an officer informed the suspect of, *inter alia,* his right to a lawyer's presence during questioning and his right to counsel appointed at no cost. The Court of Appeals held the advice inadequate because it lacked an express statement that the appointment of an attorney would occur prior to the impending interrogation. We reversed. "Nothing in the warnings," we observed, "suggested a limitation on the right to the presence of appointed counsel different from the clearly conveyed rights to a lawyer in general, including the right to a lawyer before the suspect is questioned, while he is being questioned, and all during the questioning."

In *Duckworth,* we upheld advice that communicated the right to have an attorney present during the interrogation and the right to an appointed attorney, but also informed the suspect that the lawyer would be appointed "if and when the suspect goes to court." The Court of Appeals "thought the 'if and when you go to court' language suggested that only those accused who can afford an attorney have the right to have one present before answering any questions." We thought otherwise. Under the relevant state law, we noted, "counsel is appointed at a defendant's initial appearance in court." The "if and when you go to court" advice, we said, "simply anticipated" a question the suspect might be expected to ask after receiving *Miranda* warnings, *i.e.,* "*when* will he obtain counsel." We held that the warnings, "in their totality, satisfied *Miranda.*"

We reach the same conclusion in this case. The officers did not "entirely omit," any information *Miranda* required them to impart. They informed Powell that he had "the right to talk to a lawyer before answering any of their questions" and "the right to use any of his rights at any time he wanted during the interview." The first statement communicated that Powell could consult with a lawyer before answering any particular question, and the second statement confirmed that he could exercise that right while the interrogation was underway. In combination, the two warnings reasonably conveyed Powell's right to have an attorney present, not only at the outset of interrogation, but at all times.

To reach the opposite conclusion, *i.e.,* that the attorney would not be present throughout the interrogation, the suspect would have to imagine an unlikely scenario: To consult counsel, he would be obliged to exit and reenter the interrogation room between each query. A reasonable suspect in a custodial setting who has just been read his rights would not come to the counterintuitive conclusion that he is obligated, or allowed, to hop in and out of the holding area to seek his attorney's advice. Instead, the suspect would likely assume that he must stay put in the interrogation room and that his lawyer would be there with him the entire time.

The Florida Supreme Court found the warning misleading because it believed the language suggested Powell could consult with an attorney only before the interrogation started. In context, the term "before" merely conveyed when Powell's right to an attorney became effective—namely, before he answered any questions at all. Nothing in the words used indicated that counsel's presence would be restricted after the questioning commenced. Instead, the warning communicated that the right to counsel carried forward to and through the interrogation: Powell could seek his attorney's advice before responding to "*any* of the officers' questions" and "*at any time during* the interview." Although the warnings were not the *clearest possible* formulation of *Miranda*'s right-to-counsel advisement, they were sufficiently comprehensive and comprehensible when given a commonsense reading.

Powell points out that law enforcement agencies, hoping to obtain uninformed waivers, will be tempted to end-run *Miranda* by amending their warnings to introduce ambiguity. But as the United States explained as *amicus curiae*, "law enforcement agencies have little reason to assume the litigation risk of experimenting with novel *Miranda* formulations," instead, it is "desirable police practice" and "in law enforcement's own interest" to state warnings with maximum clarity. For these reasons, "all federal law enforcement agencies explicitly advise suspects of the full contours of each *Miranda* right, including the right to the presence of counsel during questioning." The standard warnings used by the Federal Bureau of Investigation are exemplary. They provide, in relevant part: "you have the right to talk to a lawyer for advice before we ask you any questions. you have the right to have a lawyer with you during questioning." This advice is admirably informative, but we decline to declare its precise formulation necessary to meet *Miranda*'s requirements. Different words were used in the advice Powell received, but they communicated the same essential message.

For the reasons stated, the judgment of the Supreme Court of Florida is reversed, and the case is remanded for further proceedings not inconsistent with this opinion.

It is so ordered.

JUSTICE STEVENS, with whom JUSTICE BREYER joins, dissenting.

In this case, the form regularly used by the Tampa police warned Powell only of the right to consult with a lawyer before questioning. The warning did not say anything about the right to have counsel present during interrogation. Although we have never required "rigidity in the *form* of the required warnings," *California v. Prysock,* 453 U.S. 355, 359 (1981) *(per curiam),* this is the first time the Court has approved a warning which, if given its natural reading, entirely omitted an essential element of a suspect's rights.

When the relevant clause is given its most natural reading, it communicated that Powell could exercise the previously listed rights at any time. Yet the only previously listed right was the "right to talk to a lawyer *before* answering any of the officers' questions." This warning did not reasonably convey the right to talk to a lawyer *after* answering some questions, much less implicitly inform Powell of his right to have a lawyer with him at all times during interrogation. Unlike the *Duckworth* warning, Powell's warning entirely failed to inform him of the separate and distinct right "to have counsel present during any questioning."

Food for Thought

Assume that a suspect receives a version of the warnings that is identical to those received by the *Powell* defendant, except that the so-called "catchall" warning ("You have the right to use any of these rights at any time you want during this interview") is *not* included in the language of the warnings. Would the Court still be inclined to find that the warnings are sufficient? *See United States v. Warren,* 642 F.3d 182 (3d Cir. 2011).

Hypo 1: *When A Suspect Knows the Warnings*

A police officer arrests defendant for a drug crime, and attempts to advise her regarding her *Miranda* rights. As the officer states, "You have the right to remain silent," the woman interrupts and tells the officer, "I know my rights, you don't have to tell me any more." The officer then asks the woman whether she is willing to waive her rights and identify her source of drugs, and the woman immediately says yes, and names Dan (a drug dealer) as her source. The prosecutor wants to introduce Jane's statement at her trial. Is this statement inadmissible because of inadequate *Miranda* warnings? *See United States v. Patane,* 542 U.S. 630 (2004).

Hypo 2: *The "Anything You Say" Warning*

Suppose that a police officer gives the following warning: "You have the right to remain silent, the right to the presence of an attorney if you so wish, you are not required to answer any questions and if you decide to answer questions you can stop and do so, and if you cannot afford an attorney one will be appointed before you answer any questions." How can Jane's counsel argue that these *Miranda* warnings are inadequate? *See United States v. Tillman*, 963 F.2d 137 (6th Cir. 1992). *Compare United States v. Rogers*, 659 F.3d 74 (1st Cir. 2011); *United States v. Moore*, 670 F.3d 222 (2d Cir. 2012).

Hypo 3: *Post-Waiver Break and Later Interrogation*

A police officer gives Larry a *Miranda* warning, and obtains a valid waiver. In response to questioning, Larry then makes a statement denying any involvement in a homicide. Larry is returned to his cell. The next morning, the same officer drives Larry from the jail to his first appearance hearing. The officer says to Larry, "if you have anything to say, now is the time to do it, because once we get to the hearing it will be too late." Larry makes an incriminating statement. Is this statement admissible, or were the police required to give him a new *Miranda* warning? *See United States v. Pruden*, 398 F.3d 241 (3d Cir. 2005).

Hypo 4: *"You Don't Need a Lawyer Present"*

Don is taken into custody and given a *Miranda* warning. When the officer asks Don whether he understands his rights, Don says, "Yes." Then the officer asks Don, "Do you want to make a statement now without a lawyer being present?" Don responds by asking her, "If I say yes, we're going to discuss the incident, right? Would I be setting myself up if we discuss the case without my lawyer?" The officer replies, "If we discuss any matters outside of the case, you don't need a lawyer present at all, period. When we discuss the case, when I ask you something specifically, or if you tell me something specifically, you have a right to have a lawyer present here. What you are doing here is giving up a right to have a lawyer present to tell me your side. You don't have to do that." Don responds, "All right. I know what you are saying." Then the officer says, "You understand that you do have rights. Do you want to make a statement at this time without a lawyer present?" Don says, "Yes," and makes incriminating statements. Did the officer violate *Miranda*? *See State v. Luckett*, 413 Md. 360, 993 A.2d 25 (2010).

Missouri v. Seibert

542 U.S. 600 (2004).

JUSTICE SOUTER announced the judgment of the Court and delivered an opinion, in which JUSTICE STEVENS, JUSTICE GINSBURG, and JUSTICE BREYER join.

A police officer testified that he made a "conscious decision" to withhold *Miranda* warnings from Seibert when interrogating her at the station, using an interrogation technique that he had been taught, to "question first, then give the warnings, and then repeat the question" until "I get the answer that the suspect has already provided once." Seibert made incriminating statements about her knowledge that her sons burned her mobile home with the expectation that an unrelated teenager living with the family would not be rescued from the fire. The initial interrogation lasted for 30 to 40 minutes, and then stopped for 20 minutes; then the same officer gave Seibert the *Miranda* warnings and she signed a waiver. During the interrogation that followed, the officer obtained incriminating statements that repeated the information in the pre-warnings statement. The pre-warning statement was suppressed at Seibert's trial, but the post-warning statement was admitted and Seibert was convicted of murder.

This case tests a police protocol for custodial interrogation that calls for giving no warnings of the rights to silence and counsel until interrogation has produced a confession. Then the interrogating officer follows it with *Miranda* warnings and leads the suspect to cover the same ground a second time. Because this midstream recitation of warnings following an interrogation and unwarned confession could not effectively comply with *Miranda's* constitutional requirement, we hold that a statement repeated after a warning in such circumstances is inadmissible.

The technique of interrogating in successive, unwarned and warned phases raises a new challenge to *Miranda*. One officer testified that the strategy of withholding *Miranda* warnings until after interrogating and drawing out a confession was promoted not only by his own department, but by a national police training organization and other departments in which he had worked. The Police Law Institute instructs that "officers may conduct a two-stage interrogation so that at any point during the pre-*Miranda* interrogation, usually after arrestees have confessed, officers may then read the *Miranda* warnings and ask for a waiver. If the arrestees waive their *Miranda* rights, officers will be able to repeat any subsequent incriminating statements later in court." Police Law Institute, Illinois Police Law Manual 83 (Jan. 2001–Dec. 2003).

The threshold issue when interrogators question first and warn later is whether it would be reasonable to find that in these circumstances the warnings could function "effectively" as *Miranda* requires. Could the warnings effectively advise the suspect that he had a real choice about giving an admissible statement or that he could choose to stop talking if he had talked earlier? For unless the warnings could place a suspect who has just been interrogated in a position to make such informed choices, there is no practical justification for accepting the formal warnings as compliance with *Miranda*, or for treating the second stage of interrogation as distinct from the first, unwarned and inadmissible segment.

By any objective measure, it is likely that if the interrogators employ the technique of withholding warnings until after interrogation succeeds in eliciting a confession, the warnings will be ineffective in preparing the suspect for successive interrogation, close in time and similar in content. Upon hearing warnings only in the aftermath of interrogation and just after making a confession, a suspect would hardly think he had a genuine right to remain silent, let alone persist in so believing once the police began to lead him over the same ground again. A more likely reaction on a suspect's part would be perplexity about the reason for discussing rights at that point. What is worse, telling a suspect that "anything you say can and will be used against you," without expressly excepting the statement just given, could lead to an entirely reasonable inference that what he has just said will be used, with subsequent silence being of no avail. Thus, when *Miranda* warnings are inserted in the midst of coordinated and continuing interrogation, they are likely to mislead and "deprive a defendant of knowledge essential to his ability to understand the nature of his rights and the consequences of abandoning them." By the same token, it would ordinarily be unrealistic to treat two spates of integrated and proximately conducted questioning as independent interrogations subject to independent evaluation simply because *Miranda* warnings formally punctuate them in the middle.

The State argues that a confession repeated at the end of an interrogation sequence envisioned in a question-first strategy is admissible on the authority of *Oregon v. Elstad*, 470 U.S. 298 (1985). In *Elstad*, the police went to the young suspect's house to take him into custody on a charge of burglary. Before the arrest, one officer spoke with the suspect's mother, while the other one joined the suspect in a "brief stop in the living room", where the officer said he "felt" the young man was involved in a burglary. The suspect acknowledged he had been at the scene. The Court assumed that the officer's initial failure to warn was an "oversight" that "may have been the result of confusion as to whether the brief exchange qualified as 'custodial interrogation'." At the outset of a later and systematic station house interrogation going well beyond the scope of the laconic prior admission, the suspect was given *Miranda* warnings and made a full confession. It is fair to read *Elstad* as treating the living room conversation as a good-faith *Miranda* mistake that was open to correction by careful warnings before systematic questioning.

At the opposite extreme are the facts here, which by any objective measure reveal a police strategy adapted to undermine the *Miranda* warnings. The unwarned interrogation was conducted in the station house, and the questioning was systematic, exhaustive, and managed with psychological skill. The warned phase of questioning proceeded after a pause of only 15 to 20 minutes, in the same place as the unwarned segment. When the same officer who had conducted the first phase recited the *Miranda* warnings, he said nothing to counter the probable misimpression that the advice that anything Seibert said could be used against her also applied to the details of the inculpatory statement previously elicited. In particular, the police did not advise that her prior statement could not be used. Nothing was said or done to dispel the oddity of warning about legal rights to silence and counsel right after the police had led her through a systematic inter-rogation. The impression that the further questioning was a mere continuation of the earlier questions and responses was fostered by references back to the confes-sion already given. It would have been reasonable to regard the two sessions as parts of a continuum, in which it would have been unnatural to refuse to repeat at the second stage what had been said before. These circumstances must be seen as challenging the comprehensibility and efficacy of the *Miranda* warnings to the point that a reasonable person in the suspect's shoes would not have understood them to convey a message that she retained a choice about continuing to talk. Because the question-first tactic effectively threatens to thwart *Miranda's* purpose of reducing the risk that a coerced confession would be admitted, and because the facts here do not reasonably support a conclusion that the warnings given could have served their purpose, Seibert's post warning statements are inadmissible. The judgment of the Supreme Court of Missouri is affirmed.

Justice O'Connor, with whom The Chief Justice, Justice Scalia and Justice Thomas join, dissenting.

We have previously rejected a theory that is indistinguishable from the one today's plurality adopts. In *Elstad*, we refused to recognize the "psychological impact of the suspect's conviction that he has let the cat out of the bag" because we refused to "endow those 'psychological effects' with 'constitutional implications.'" To do so would "effectively immunize a suspect who responds to pre-warning questions from the consequences of his subsequent informed waiver," an immunity that "comes at a high cost to legitimate law enforcement activity." I would analyze the two-step interrogation procedure under the voluntary waiver standard of *Elstad* and leave this analysis for the Missouri courts to conduct on remand.

Some lower courts follow the approach advocated by Justice Kennedy's concurring opinion in *Seibert* because he supplied the fifth vote for the result. His opinion reasoned as follows: "*Miranda's* clarity is one of its strengths, and a multifactor test that applies to every two-stage interrogation may undermine that clarity. If the deliberate two-step strategy has been used, postwarning statements that are related to the substance of prewarning statements must be excluded unless curative measures are taken before the postwarning statement is made. Curative measures should ensure that a reasonable person in the suspect's situation would understand the import and effect of the *Miranda* warning and the *Miranda* waiver. For example, a substantial break in time and circumstances between the prewarning statement and the *Miranda* warning may suffice in most circumstances, as it allows the accused to distinguish between the two contexts and appreciate that the interrogation has taken a new turn. An additional warning that explains the likely inadmissibility of the prewarning custodial statement may be sufficient. No curative steps were taken in this case, however, and so the prewarning statements are inadmissible and the conviction cannot stand."

Point for Discussion

Seibert Dissenters and Involuntary Waiver

The *Seibert* dissenters rejected the *Seibert* plurality's interpretation of *Elstad* as a precedent that posed no barrier to creation of the inadequate warnings doctrine. This is because *Elstad* opined that, "A subsequent administration of mid-interrogation *Miranda* warnings to a suspect who has given a prior unwarned statement ordinarily should suffice to remove the conditions namely, the initial lack of warnings that made the earlier statement inadmissible." If the *Seibert* dissenters had prevailed, they would have relied on *Elstad* to reject the defendant's claim that the midstream warnings did not reasonably convey the *Miranda* rights. The dissenters would have required the defendant to show on remand that her waiver was not "voluntary" based on a showing of "actual coercion", defined under *Elstad* as "physical violence or other deliberate means calculated to break the suspect's will."

Food for Thought

Defendant is arrested for robbery and brought to the station in the morning. No *Miranda* warnings are given, but he makes no incriminating statements during questioning. Then defendant is given a polygraph exam without warnings, and the officers tell him that he "failed" the polygraph. In the afternoon, defendant is taken to court and a magistrate gives him the *Miranda* warning. Upon his return to the police station, the officers obtain a waiver from defendant, and then he makes his first incriminating statements. Under Kennedy's test, will the trial court find that the magistrate's warnings failed to reasonably convey the *Miranda* rights? How will the analysis change if the trial court uses the *Seibert* plurality's test? See *Martinez v. State*, 272 S.W.3d 615 (Tex. Crim. App. 2008).

Hypo 1: *"Question First" Approach and Good Faith*

In *Seibert* the police admitted that they were trained to use the "question-first" approach – to withhold the *Miranda* warnings deliberately until after an arrestee confesses. Assume that in a future midstream-warnings case, the police testify that they did not intentionally use the "question-first" strategy, but that they acted in good faith when they failed to give the initial warnings. What factors might a reviewing court consider in determining whether the police conduct resembles the "good faith mistake" of the police in *Elstad* or the conduct of the police in *Seibert*? See *Kelly v. State*, 997 N.E.2d 1045 (Ind. 2013).

Hypo 2: *After the Autopsy*

Bob's two-year-old son is found dead. Officer Jules learns from the autopsy doctor that the only way the child could have died was by smothering or suffocation, and that the child had rib fractures. Jules takes Bob into custody and questions him for three hours. During the first hour, Bob makes no incriminating statements. After a short break, Jules informs Bob about the autopsy report, and questions Bob who admits that he covered the child's mouth to stop his crying. After another break, Jules gives Bob the *Miranda* warnings and Bob signs a waiver of rights. Further questioning produces Bob's admission that he covered the child's mouth for two minutes. Assume that the prosecutor does not seek the admission of any unwarned statements made during the first or second hour of questioning, but does seek admission of an incriminating statement during the third hour. Is that statement admissible under *Seibert*? See *State v. Navy*, 386 S.C. 294, 688 S.E.2d 838 (2010).

Hypo 3: *Central Booking Interview Program*

A prosecutor directs that indigent defendants be subjected to preliminary custodial interrogation before arraignment. In the jurisdiction, arraignment occurs only after an arrestee's paperwork is completed by the police, the Criminal Justice Agency has interviewed the arrestee in order to make a recommendation concerning bail, the criminal complaint has been drafted, and the district attorney delivers the relevant paperwork to the court. Thereafter, the case is docketed, and the next available appearance is scheduled for the defendant. Under the prosecutor's direction, indigent defendants who are "administratively ready" for arraignment are diverted to an interrogation room where prosecutors read from a prepared script which informs defendant of "the charges" he or she will face when he "goes to court," and that "in a few minutes," you will be read your rights and "given an opportunity to explain what you did at that date, time, and place." Then the following is recited by a prosecutor: "If you have an alibi, give us as much information as you can, including the names of any people you were with. If your version of the events that day is different from what we have heard, this is your opportunity to tell us your story. If there is something you would like us to investigate concerning this incident, if you tell us about it, we will look into it. Even if you have already spoken to someone else, you do not have to talk to me. This will be the only opportunity you will have to talk to me before you go to court on these charges." Then the defendant is read the *Miranda* warnings. Defendants who have retained counsel are allowed to proceed directly to arraignment. Only indigent defendants who cannot retain an attorney are diverted to the interrogation room. However, diversion is based on subjective criteria. Does the program violate *Seibert? See Brief of Amicus Curiae NYCLU et al., People v. Polhill*, N. Y. Sup. Ct., App. Div., 2d Dept., Index Nos. 10–1680, 10–03763; 10–04786; *People v. Perez*, 946 N.Y.S.2d 835, 2012 N.Y. Slip Op. 22103 (2012).

4. Waiver

Even when the *Miranda* warnings are given, the prosecution must prove by a preponderance of the evidence that the suspect "voluntarily, knowingly and intelligently" waived the *Miranda* rights. In *Moran v. Burbine*, 475 U.S. 412 (1986), the Court summarized the waiver requirement as follows: "The inquiry has two distinct dimensions. First, the relinquishment of the right must have been voluntary in the sense that it was the product of a free and deliberate choice rather than intimidation, coercion, or deception. Second, the waiver must have been made knowingly and intelligently, with a full awareness of both the nature of the right being abandoned and the consequences of the decision to abandon it. Only if the 'totality of the circumstances surrounding the interrogation' reveal both an uncoerced choice and the requisite level of comprehension may a court properly conclude that the *Miranda* rights have been waived."

Berghuis v. Thompkins

560 U.S. 370 (2010).

JUSTICE KENNEDY delivered the opinion of the Court.

On January 10, 2000, a shooting occurred outside a mall in Southfield, Michigan. Among the victims was Samuel Morris, who died from multiple gunshot wounds. The other victim, Frederick France, recovered from his injuries and later testified. Thompkins, who was a suspect, fled. About one year later he was found in Ohio and arrested there.

Two Southfield police officers traveled to Ohio to interrogate Thompkins, then awaiting transfer to Michigan. The interrogation began around 1:30 p.m. and lasted about three hours. The interrogation was conducted in a room that was 8 by 10 feet, and Thompkins sat in a chair that resembled a school desk. At the beginning of the interrogation, one of the officers, Detective Helgert, presented Thompkins with a form derived from the *Miranda* rule. It stated:

NOTIFICATION OF CONSTITUTIONAL RIGHTS AND STATEMENT

1. You have the right to remain silent.

2. Anything you say can and will be used against you in a court of law.

3. You have a right to talk to a lawyer before answering any questions and you have the right to have a lawyer present with you while you are answering any questions.

4. If you cannot afford to hire a lawyer, one will be appointed to represent you before any questioning, if you wish one.

5. You have the right to decide at any time before or during questioning to use your right to remain silent and your right to talk with a lawyer while you are being questioned.

Helgert asked Thompkins to read the fifth warning out loud. Thompkins complied. Helgert later said this was to ensure that Thompkins could read, and Helgert concluded that Thompkins understood English. Helgert then read the other four *Miranda* warnings out loud and asked Thompkins to sign the form to demonstrate that he understood his rights. Thompkins declined to sign the form. The record contains conflicting evidence about whether Thompkins then verbally confirmed that he understood the rights listed on the form.

At no point during the interrogation did Thompkins say that he wanted to remain silent, that he did not want to talk with the police, or that he wanted an attorney. Thompkins was "largely" silent during the interrogation, which lasted about three hours. He did give a few limited verbal responses such as "yeah," "no," or "I don't know." On occasion he communicated by nodding his head. Thompkins also said that he "didn't want a peppermint" that was offered to him by the police and that the chair he was "sitting in was hard."

About 2 hours and 45 minutes into the interrogation, Helgert asked Thompkins, "Do you believe in God?" Thompkins made eye contact with Helgert and said "Yes," as his eyes "welled up with tears." Helgert asked, "Do you pray to God?" Thompkins said "Yes." Helgert asked, "Do you pray to God to forgive you for shooting that boy down?" Thompkins answered "Yes" and looked away. Thompkins refused to make a written confession, and the interrogation ended about 15 minutes later.

Thompkins was charged with first-degree murder, assault with intent to commit murder, and certain firearms offenses. He moved to suppress the statements made during the interrogation. He argued that he had not waived his right to remain silent, and that his inculpatory statements were inadmissible. The trial court denied the motion. The jury found Thompkins guilty on all counts and sentenced him to life in prison without parole. The state courts rejected his *Miranda* claim, as did the District Court. The Sixth Circuit reversed and we granted certiorari.

All concede that the warning given in this case was in full compliance with *Miranda's* requirements. The dispute centers on the response—or nonresponse—from the suspect. Even absent the accused's invocation of the right to remain silent, the accused's statement during a custodial interrogation is inadmissible at trial unless the prosecution can establish that the accused "in fact knowingly and voluntarily waived *Miranda* rights" when making the statement. *North Carolina v. Butler*, 441 U.S. 369, 373 (1979). The waiver inquiry "has two distinct dimensions": waiver must be "voluntary in the sense that it was the product of a free and deliberate choice rather than intimidation, coercion, or deception," and "made with a full awareness of both the nature of the right being abandoned and the consequences of the decision to abandon it." *Moran v. Burbine*, 475 U.S. 412, 421 (1986).

Some language in *Miranda* could be read to indicate that waivers are difficult to establish absent an explicit written waiver or a formal, express oral statement. *Miranda* said "a valid waiver will not be presumed simply from the silence of the accused after warnings are given or simply from the fact that a confession was in fact eventually obtained." In addition, *Miranda* stated that "a heavy burden rests on the government to demonstrate that the defendant knowingly and intelligently waived his privilege against self-incrimination and his right to retained or appointed counsel."

Decisions since *Miranda* demonstrate that waivers can be established even absent formal or express statements of waiver that would be expected in, say, a judicial hearing to determine if a guilty plea has been properly entered. The purpose of *Miranda* is to ensure that an accused is advised of and understands the right to remain silent and the right to counsel. Thus, "our cases have reduced the impact of *Miranda* on legitimate law enforcement while reaffirming the decision's core ruling that unwarned statements may not be used as evidence in the prosecution's case in chief." *Dickerson v. United States*, 530 U.S. 428, 443–444 (2000).

One of the first cases to decide the meaning and import of *Miranda* with respect to waiver was *Butler*, which interpreted the *Miranda* language concerning the "heavy burden" to show waiver in accord with usual principles of determining waiver, which can include waiver implied from all the circumstances. In a later case, the Court stated that this "heavy burden" is not more than the burden to establish waiver by a preponderance of the evidence. *Colorado v. Connelly*, 479 U.S. 157, 168 (1986).

The prosecution does not need to show that a waiver of *Miranda* rights was express. An "implicit waiver" of the "right to remain silent" is sufficient to admit a suspect's statement into evidence. *Butler* made clear that a waiver of *Miranda* rights may be implied through "the defendant's silence, coupled with an understanding of his rights and a course of conduct indicating waiver." *Butler* therefore "retreated" from the "language and tenor of the *Miranda* opinion," which "suggested that the Court would require that a waiver be 'specifically made.' " *Connecticut v. Barrett*, 479 U.S. 523, 531–532 (1987) (Brennan, J., concurring in judgment).

If the State establishes that a *Miranda* warning was given and the accused made an uncoerced statement, this showing, standing alone, is insufficient to demonstrate "a valid waiver" of *Miranda* rights. The prosecution must make the additional showing that the accused understood these rights. Where the prosecution shows that a *Miranda* warning was given and that it was understood by the accused, an accused's uncoerced statement establishes an implied waiver of the right to remain silent.

Although *Miranda* imposes on the police a rule that is both formalistic and practical when it prevents them from interrogating suspects without first providing them with a *Miranda* warning, it does not impose a formalistic waiver procedure that a suspect must follow to relinquish those rights. As a general proposition, the law can presume that an individual who, with a full understanding of his or her rights, acts in a manner inconsistent with their exercise has made a deliberate choice to relinquish the protection those rights afford. As *Butler* recognized, *Miranda* rights can therefore be waived through means less formal than a typical waiver on the record in a courtroom, given the practical constraints and necessities of interrogation and the fact that *Miranda*'s main protection lies in advising defendants of their rights.

The record shows that Thompkins waived his right to remain silent. First, there is no contention that Thompkins did not understand his rights; and it follows that he knew what he gave up when he spoke. Thompkins received a written copy of the *Miranda* warnings; Detective Helgert determined that Thompkins could read and understand English; and Thompkins was given time to read the warnings. Thompkins, furthermore, read aloud the fifth warning. He was thus aware that his right to remain silent would not dissipate after a certain amount of time and that police would have to honor his right to be silent and his right to counsel during the whole course of interrogation. Those rights, the warning made clear, could be asserted at any time. Second, Thompkins's answer to Detective Helgert's question about whether Thompkins prayed to God for forgiveness for shooting the victim is a "course of conduct indicating waiver" of the right to remain silent. If Thompkins wanted to remain silent, he could have said nothing in response to Helgert's questions, or he could have unambiguously invoked his *Miranda* rights and ended the interrogation. The fact that Thompkins made a statement about three hours after receiving a *Miranda* warning does not overcome the fact that he engaged in a course of conduct indicating waiver. Police are not required to rewarn suspects from time to time. Waiver is confirmed by the fact that Thompkins had given sporadic answers to questions throughout the interrogation. Third, there is no evidence that Thompkins's statement was coerced. Thompkins does not claim that police threatened or injured him during the interrogation or that he was in any way fearful. The interrogation was conducted in a standard-sized room in the middle of the afternoon. The fact that Helgert's question referred to Thompkins's religious beliefs did not render Thompkins's statement involuntary. In these circumstances, Thompkins knowingly and voluntarily made a statement to police, so he waived his right to remain silent.

Thompkins argues that, even if his answer to Detective Helgert could constitute a waiver of his right to remain silent, the police were not allowed to question him until they obtained a waiver first. *Butler* held that courts can infer a waiver of *Miranda* rights "from the actions and words of the person interrogated." The *Miranda* rule and its requirements are met if a suspect receives adequate *Miranda* warnings, understands them, and has an opportunity to invoke the rights before giving any answers or admissions. Any waiver, express or implied, may be contradicted by an invocation at any time. If the right to counsel or the right to remain silent is invoked at any point during questioning, further interrogation must cease.

Interrogation provides the suspect with additional information that can put his or her decision to waive, or not to invoke, into perspective. When the suspect knows that *Miranda* rights can be invoked at any time, he or she has the opportunity to reassess his or her immediate and long-term interests. Cooperation with the police may result in more favorable treatment for the suspect; the apprehension of accomplices; the prevention of continuing injury and fear; beginning steps towards relief or solace for the victims; and the beginning of the suspect's own return to the law and the social order it seeks to protect.

In order for an accused's statement to be admissible at trial, police must have given the accused a *Miranda* warning. If that condition is established, the court can proceed to consider whether there has been an express or implied waiver of *Miranda* rights. In making its ruling on the admissibility of a statement made during custodial questioning, the trial court considers whether there is evidence to support the conclusion that, from the whole course of questioning, an express or implied waiver has been established. Thus, after giving a *Miranda* warning, police may interrogate a suspect who has neither invoked nor waived his or her *Miranda* rights. It follows the police were not required to obtain a waiver of Thompkins's *Miranda* rights before commencing the interrogation.

The judgment of the Court of Appeals is reversed, and the case is remanded with instructions to deny the petition.

It is so ordered.

Justice Sotomayor, with whom Justice Stevens, Justice Ginsburg, and Justice Breyer join, dissenting.

The Court concludes that a criminal suspect waives his right to remain silent if, after sitting tacit and uncommunicative through nearly three hours of police interrogation, he utters a few one-word responses. This proposition marks a substantial retreat from the protection against compelled self-incrimination that *Miranda* has long provided during custodial interrogation.

The State did not satisfy its "heavy burden" in proving waiver. *See, e.g., Tague v. Louisiana,* 444 U.S. 469, 470–471 (1980) *(per curiam).* We have affirmed that a court may not presume waiver from a suspect's silence or from the mere fact that a confession was eventually obtained. *Butler* made clear that the prosecution bears a substantial burden in establishing an implied waiver. *Miranda* "unequivocally said mere silence is not enough." We reiterated that "courts must presume that a defendant did not waive his rights; the prosecution's burden is great." It is undisputed here that Thompkins never expressly waived his right to remain silent. His refusal to sign even an acknowledgment that he understood his *Miranda* rights evinces, if anything, an intent not to waive those rights. That Thompkins did not make the inculpatory statements at issue until after approximately 2 hours and 45 minutes of interrogation serves as "strong evidence" against waiver.

Thompkins' "actions and words" preceding the inculpatory statements do not evidence a "course of conduct indicating waiver" sufficient to carry the prosecution's burden. Although Thompkins "sporadically" participated in the interview, the opinion and the record are silent as to the subject matter or context of even a single question to which Thompkins purportedly responded, other than the exchange about God and the statements respecting the peppermint and the chair. It is objectively unreasonable under our clearly established precedents to conclude the prosecution met its "heavy burden" of proof on a record consisting of three one-word answers, following 2 hours and 45 minutes of silence punctuated by a few largely nonverbal responses to unidentified questions. When waiver is inferred during a custodial interrogation, there are sound reasons to require evidence beyond inculpatory statements themselves. *Miranda* and our cases are premised on the idea that custodial interrogation is inherently coercive. Requiring proof of a course of conduct beyond the inculpatory statements themselves is critical to ensuring that those statements are voluntary admissions and not the dubious product of an overborne will.

> ### Food for Thought
>
> Assume that you are the law clerk for a state supreme court justice who tells you that the court is considering whether to reject *Moran*. Your judge asks for your analysis of the possible alternative rules that could be adopted instead of the rules endorsed by the court. Describe the possible duties that might be imposed on police to inform an interrogated person that his attorney (either his previously retained attorney or one obtained for him by friends or family) is trying to contact him. Explain how the state court could resolve the problems that are likely to arise if such a duty is created, including the problems mentioned by the *Moran* majority. Compare *Commonwealth v. Mavredakis*, 430 Mass. 848, 725 N.E.2d 169 (2000); *People v. Bender*, 452 Mich. 594, 551 N.W.2d 71 (1996); *State v. Stoddard*, 206 Conn. 157, 537 A.2d 446 (1988).

> ### Take Note
>
> In *Colorado v. Spring*, 479 U.S. 564 (1987), the Court rejected defendant's argument that his written waiver was invalid because ATF agents did not tell him that they planned to question him not only about a federal firearms violation, but also about an unrelated homicide. After questioning defendant about the firearms crime, the agents asked him if he had a criminal record. He admitted that he had a juvenile record involving a shooting, and then the agents asked if he had ever shot anyone else. The defendant "mumbled" that "I shot another guy once," and then provided no further information. The Court found that defendant's waiver was voluntary because the non-disclosure of possible topics did not raise "any of the traditional indicia of coercion," and did not constitute the type of "police trickery and deception" that was condemned in *Miranda*. The Court concluded that defendant's waiver was knowing and intelligent because there was no allegation that he "failed to understand" the warning, or that he "misunderstood the consequences of speaking freely"

to the police. The Court emphasized that defendant received a complete set of *Miranda* warnings before he signed the waiver, including the warning that "anything you say may be used against you." Noting that "there is no qualification of this broad and explicit warning," the Court held that defendant's "awareness of all the possible subjects of questioning in advance of interrogation" is not relevant to determining whether his waiver was voluntary, knowing, and intelligent.

Points for Discussion

a. Conditional Waivers with Limited Invocations

In *Connecticut v. Barrett*, 479 U.S. 523 (1987), defendant was arrested for sexual assault and given *Miranda* warnings. Defendant stated that "he would not give the police any written statements but that he had no problem in talking about the incident." Then he made incriminating statements. Thirty minutes later, the police gave him warnings again and this time defendant said that he would not make a written statement unless his attorney was present, but had "no problem" talking about the crime, and he made a second oral statement. He also made a third oral statement that was tape-recorded after he received additional warnings, and after he stated again that he had no problem with talking but would not put anything in writing until his attorney arrived. The Court upheld the admissibility of all three statements: "Barrett's limited requests for counsel were accompanied by affirmative announcements of his willingness to speak the authorities. Barrett made clear his intentions, and they were honored by police. To conclude that he invoked his right to counsel for all purposes requires a disregard of the ordinary meaning of his statement. We reject the contention that Barrett's distinction between oral and written statements indicates an understanding of the consequences so incomplete that we should deem his limited invocation of the right to counsel effective for all purposes. The warnings made clear to Barrett that 'If you talk to any police officers, anything you say can and will be used against you in court.' We have never embraced the theory that a defendant's ignorance of the full consequences of his decisions vitiates their voluntariness."

b. Efforts by Counsel to Contact a Custodial Defendant

In *Moran v. Burbine*, 475 U.S. 412 (1986) defendant was in custody when his sister retained a lawyer for him, and the lawyer telephoned the police in an effort to contact defendant prior to his interrogation. The lawyer was told that Burbine was not going to be interrogated because the police "were through with him for the night." However, police officers did interrogate Burbine an hour later without telling him about the lawyer's phone call. After receiving warnings, he waived his rights and made incriminating statements. The Court held that the waiver was valid because Burbine made a "voluntary decision to speak" with "full awareness and comprehension" of his rights: "Events occurring outside of the presence of the suspect and entirely unknown to him surely can have no bearing on the capacity to comprehend and knowingly relinquish a constitutional right. Although the 'deliberate or reckless' withholding of information is objectionable as a matter of ethics, such conduct is only relevant to the constitutional validity of a waiver if it deprives a defendant of knowledge essential to his ability to understand the nature of his rights and the consequences of abandoning them. We are not prepared to adopt a rule requiring that police inform a suspect of an attorney's efforts to reach him. While such a rule might add marginally to *Miranda's* goal of dispelling the compulsion inherent in custodial interrogation, overriding practical considerations counsel against its adoption. The proposed rule would have the inevitable consequence of muddying *Miranda's* otherwise relatively clear waters." Justice Stevens dissented, joined by two other justices, emphasizing that the police violated the ABA Standards for Criminal Justice, arguing that there should be "no constitutional distinction," between "a deceptive misstatement and the concealment by the police of the critical fact that an attorney retained by the accused or his family has offered assistance, either by telephone or in person."

Food for Thought

How do you explain the fact that defendant was willing to make an oral statement, but completely unwilling to make an oral statement, without the presence of an attorney? Is it possible that defendant did not understand that oral admissions can be as damaging as written admissions? Is there another explanation for his aversion to written statements?

c. Mental Illness and Voluntary Waiver

In *Colorado v. Connelly*, 479 U.S. 157 (1986), the Court rejected defendant's argument that his waiver of *Miranda* rights was not "voluntary" because he was mentally ill at the time of the interrogation. When Connelly approached a police officer and spontaneously confessed to murder, the officer gave him *Miranda* warnings. In answering the officer's questions, Connelly stated that he understood his rights, denied that he had been drinking or taking drugs, and admitted that he had been a patient in several mental hospitals. The officer "perceived no indication whatsoever" that defendant was "suffering from any kind of mental illness" and so Connelly was interrogated after waiving his *Miranda* rights. The next day Connelly told his appointed counsel that "voices" had ordered him to make a confession, and expert testimony at trial showed that he was suffering from chronic schizophrenia. The Court held that there was no evidence of "police overreaching" or "official coercion" to nullify the "voluntariness" of Connelly's waiver, and it found that the interrogation did not violate Due Process "voluntariness" standards. The Due Process ruling in the case is presented in Part E, *infra*.

Hypo 1: *Applying Davis*

A homicide suspect is read a *Miranda* warning, and asked whether he wishes to waive his rights. The man responds "I don't want to talk right now," but states that he would be willing to "write it down." Has the man invoked his right to remain silent? See *State v. Piatnitsky*, 325 P.3d 167 (Wash. 2014). Suppose that instead the man states that "If you can bring me a lawyer that way I can tell you everything that I know and everything that I need to tell you and have someone to represent me." Has the man invoked his right to counsel? *See People v. Sauceda-Contreras*, 282 P.2d 379 (Cal. 2012).

Hypo 2: *Blurted-Out Confession*

Assume that Mike is in custody in an interrogation room with a police officer who tells Mike that he has been arrested for the crime of bank robbery. After the officer gives the *Miranda* warnings, Mike says, "I did it. I robbed the bank." If Mike does makes this incriminating statement after receiving *Miranda* warnings, and then tells Kira, "I don't really understand my rights very well, and I'm not willing to sign a waiver form," has there been a waiver? May the officer ask whether Mike wishes to waive his rights without violating *Berghuis*? *Compare United States v. Plugh*, 576 F.3d 135 (2d Cir. 2009).

Food for Thought

Assume that defendant is in under arrest for bank robbery and is given the *Miranda* warnings. When the officer asks whether he wishes to waive his rights, Mike says that he wants to know: 1) what the police will do if he says he wants to remain silent or that he wants to talk to a lawyer, 2) whether police are required to let him actually talk to a lawyer before interrogation if he says he wants to do that, and 3) whether the officer thinks it is a good idea for him to talk to a lawyer now. How would a prosecutor advise the officer to respond to these questions, in order to maximize the chance that she will be able to obtain a valid waiver from Mike?

Hypo 3: *Capacity for Knowing and Intelligent Waiver*

Garner's lawyer argues that his waiver was not "knowing and intelligent" because of his borderline IQ and the results of the "Grisso test" which show that he has a low capacity for understanding the concepts involved in a *Miranda* waiver. Should Garner's mental capacity bear on whether he has made a knowing and intelligent waiver? Or should the court hold that Garner must show that there was "some observable indication" to the interrogating police officer that he was incapable of understanding the *Miranda* warnings at the time of the waiver? *See Garner v. Mitchell*, 557 F.3d 257 (6th Cir. 2009).

Food for Thought

Assume that you are a prosecutor. You are asked by the police chief to draw up some guidelines for obtaining waivers from people who are juveniles, who may be intoxicated, who may have language problems, or who may suffer from mental illness. What guidelines would you suggest in order to insure that valid waivers be obtained from these persons?

Hypo 4: *Prior "Field Checks" and Waiver*

Hector, a 17 year-old high school dropout, has been approached repeatedly on the street by police officers conducting "field checks" that involve questioning and frisking without *Miranda* warnings. During these encounters, Hector always cooperated and answered all questions. One day, Officer Smith (who conducted a number of the field checks), placed Hector in cuffs, took him inside his home, recited the *Miranda* warnings, and told Hector, "Just show us where the drugs are so we don't have to mess up everything in your house." Hector tells Smith, "I can show you where the drugs are," and does so. The prosecution wants to use this statement at Hector's trial for drug possession. Did Hector waive his *Miranda* rights? *Compare United States v. Gonzalez*, 719 F. Supp. 2d 167 (D. Mass. 2010).

Food for Thought

Defendant is arrested for burglarizing a neighbor's apartment. At the time of the arrest, the police ask defendant whether he wants to speak with them. Defendant replies "No. You know everything anyway." At that point, the police give defendant a *Miranda* warning and inquire whether he wishes to speak with them. The defendant agrees to talk with the police and makes incriminating statements. Did the police fail to respect defendant's invocation of his right to remain silent? *See State v. Johansen,* 2014 Me. 132, 105 A.3d 433 (2014).

Hypo 5: *Anticipatory Invocation*

Suppose that defendant, who is the prime suspect in a murder that was committed in Philadelphia, is apprehended by juvenile authorities in Florida. A public defender in Philadelphia, at the request of defendant's father, sends him a form to sign which purports to invoke his *Miranda* rights, including both the right to remain silent and the right to counsel. Defendant signs the form and hands it to the authorities in Florida. Six days later, after defendant is extradited back to Philadelphia where he is given a *Miranda* warning, waives his rights, and confesses to the murder. Was the anticipatory invocation of the *Miranda* warning valid against the subsequent waiver of rights? *See Commonwealth v. Bland,* 631 Pa. 644, 115 A.3d 854 (Pa. 2015).

Hypo 6: *Unequivocal Invocation?*

Suppose that a suspect is arrested and read a *Miranda* warning. At that point, the suspect says "I got a lawyer." A conversation ensues in which she (the arrestee) tells the officer the name of the lawyer and the location of his office. The officer then says "do you want to use the lawyer or do you want to talk to me?" and the suspect responds "I could use him." At that point, the officer says "I don't know whether we can get him over here at this moment," and re-asks whether she wants to talk to the officer now. At that point, the suspect states "I'll talk with you." Did the officer act properly under *Miranda*? *See Downey v. State,* 144 So.3d 146 (Miss. 2014).

Hypo 7: *More on Invocation*

Before a juvenile is taken into custody by the police, his father admonishes him to request a lawyer before speaking. When the police bring the juvenile into an interrogation room, the following conversation occurs: "There wouldn't be any possible way that I could have a—a lawyer present while we do this?" Det. Woods: "Well, uh, what I'll do is, um—" Sessoms: "Yeah, that's what my dad asked me to ask you guys ... uh, give me a lawyer." The officers then tell Sessoms that his accomplices have already told them what happened, and that the only way to tell his side of the story is to speak to the officers then and there, without an attorney. Only after talking with him, softening him up, and warning him regarding the "risks" of speaking with counsel, did the detectives read Sessoms his *Miranda* rights. At that point, Sessoms agreed to talk and made incriminating statements. Was Sessoms' request for counsel unequivocal? *See Sessoms v. Grounds,* 768 F.3d 882 (9th Cir. 2014).

Food for Thought

After a suspect is given a *Miranda* warning, he tells police to call his girlfriend to obtain the contact information for his lawyer and "get him down here." Is the suspect's invocation sufficiently unambiguous? *See State v. Philpot,* 299 Ga. 206, 787 S.E.2d 181 (2016).

Hypo 8: *"I Ain't Signing Shit Without My Attorney"*

After a suspect was read a *Miranda* warning, he was asked to sign a form authorizing a search of his house. He responded: "I ain't signing shit without my attorney." Has the suspect made a "clear and unequivocal" invocation of his right to an attorney? Could a reasonable police officer conclude that he was willing to speak to the officers, but that he was unwilling to sign the consent to search form? *See State v. Holman,* 502 S.W.3d 621 (Mo., en banc, 2016).

5. Invocations of *Miranda* Rights

The threshold issue in invocation litigation is whether the defendant effectively communicated an invocation to the interrogating officer after warnings. If so, then the officer must cut off questioning immediately without further waiver-seeking or interrogation.

> If a person in custody receives *Miranda* warnings and "invokes" either the Fifth Amendment right to remain silent, or the "Fifth Amendment right to counsel," *Miranda* requires the police to cease questioning immediately. *Miranda* assumed that once a person is notified of her rights, she can be expected to notify the interrogating officer that she wishes to exercise these rights. In the absence of such notice, the officer may assume that she does not wish to exercise them and may seek and obtain a waiver.

Davis v. United States

512 U.S. 452 (1994).

JUSTICE O'CONNOR delivered the opinion of the Court.

Navy authorities suspected Davis of murder. After receiving *Miranda* warnings, Davis waived his right to remain silent and his right to counsel, both orally and in writing. After an hour and a half of questioning, Davis said, "Maybe I should talk to a lawyer." The interrogating officer testified that he responded by telling Davis "that if he wants a lawyer, then we will stop any questioning with him, that we weren't going to pursue the matter unless we have it clarified is he asking for a lawyer or is he just making a comment about a lawyer, and he said, 'No, I'm not asking for a lawyer,' and 'I don't want a lawyer.' " After a short break, the officers reminded Davis of his rights to silence and to counsel. The questioning continued for another hour until Davis stated, "I think I want a lawyer before I say anything else." Then the questioning ceased. Davis sought to suppress his statements on the theory that he invoked his right to counsel when he said, "Maybe I should talk to a lawyer"; therefore, the subsequent comments by the officer violated the *Miranda* duty to cut off questioning, and statements made by Davis after these comments were inadmissible. The trial court rejected this argument; Davis was convicted of murder and appealed on *Miranda* grounds.

If a suspect requests counsel at any time during an interview, he is not subject to further questioning, and this rule requires courts to "determine whether the accused actually invoked his right to counsel." *Smith v. Illinois*, 469 U.S. 91, 98 1984. To avoid difficulties of proof and to provide guidance to officers conducting interrogations, this is an objective inquiry. If a suspect makes a reference to an attorney that is ambiguous or equivocal in that a reasonable officer in light of the circumstances would have understood only that the suspect might be invoking the right to counsel, our precedents do not require the cessation of questioning.

Rather, the suspect must unambiguously request counsel. "A statement either is an assertion of the right to counsel or it is not." *Smith*, 469 U.S. at 7–98. Although a suspect need not "speak with the discrimination of an Oxford don," he must articulate his desire to have counsel present sufficiently clearly that a reasonable police officer in the circumstances would understand the statement to be a request for an attorney. If the statement fails to meet the requisite level of clarity, the officers need not stop questioning the suspect. When officers reasonably do not know whether or not the suspect wants a lawyer, a cessation of questioning would needlessly prevent them from questioning when the suspect did not wish to have a lawyer present.

We recognize that requiring a clear assertion of the right to counsel might disadvantage some suspects—who because of fear, intimidation, lack of linguistic skills, or a variety of other reasons—will not articulate their right to counsel although they actually want to have a lawyer present. But if we were to require questioning to cease based on an ambiguous invocation, officers would be forced to make difficult judgment calls with the threat of suppression if they guess wrong. When a suspect makes an ambiguous or equivocal statement it will often be good police practice for the officers to clarify whether or not he actually wants an attorney, in order to help protect the rights of the suspect and to minimize the chance of a confession being suppressed. But we decline to adopt a rule requiring officers to ask clarifying questions.

The courts below found that the remark to the agents was not a request for counsel, and we see no reason to disturb that conclusion. The agents therefore were not required to stop questioning Davis, though it was entirely proper for them to clarify whether he wanted a lawyer. Because there is no ground for the suppression of his statements, the judgment of the Court of Military Appeals is

Affirmed.

JUSTICE SOUTER, with whom JUSTICES BLACKMUN, STEVENS and GINSBURG join, concurring in the judgment.

A rule barring government agents from further interrogation until they determine whether a suspect's ambiguous statement was meant as a request for counsel assures that a suspect's choice whether or not to deal with police through counsel will be "scrupulously honored" under *Miranda*. Moreover, this rule would relieve the officer for any responsibility for guessing "whether in fact the suspect wants a lawyer even though he hasn't said so" by assuring that the "judgment call" will be made by the party most competent to resolve the ambiguity, the individual suspect. I am not persuaded that even ambiguous statements require an end to all police questioning. The costs to society of losing confessions would be hard to bear where the suspect, if asked for his choice, would have chosen to continue. Here Davis's invocation was ambiguous and the officers properly confined their questions to verifying whether he meant to ask for a lawyer and so no *Miranda* violation occurred.

Points for Discussion

a. Timing of Invocation

Neither *Miranda* nor *Davis* address the issue of whether *Miranda* rights can be invoked even before the *Miranda* warnings are communicated to a person. Some lower courts recognize the validity of pre-warning invocations of the right to counsel by those in custody and assume that the unambiguous invocation requirement should apply to them. *See, e.g., Carr v. State*, 934 N.E.2d 1096 (Ind. 2010). However, other courts have relied on dicta from *McNeil v. Wisconsin*, 501 U.S. 171 (1991), as disallowing the "anticipatory invocation" of the *Miranda* right to counsel by anyone other than a person in custody. *See, e.g., State v. Hurst*, 151 Idaho 430, 258 P.3d 950 (Ct. App. 2011). *Compare State v. Davis*, 350 Or. 440, 256 P.3d 1075 (2011) (En Banc).

b. Incriminating Silence?

In *Harris v. New York*, 401 U.S. 222 (1971), the Court held that a defendant's statement, obtained in violation of *Miranda*, is admissible for purposes of impeaching the defendant's credibility at trial. The police violated *Miranda* by failing to give the defendant warnings, and so

Take Note

In *Berghuis v. Thompkins*, 560 U.S. 370 (2010), the Court applied the unambiguous invocation rule of *Davis*, referred to as the "clear statement" requirement, to invocations of the right to remain silent. The Court stated: "There is good reason to require an accused who wants to invoke his or her right to remain silent to do so unambiguously. A requirement of an unambiguous invocation of *Miranda* rights results in an objective inquiry that "avoids difficulties of proof and provides guidance to officers" on how to proceed in the face of ambiguity. If an ambiguous act, omission, or statement could require police to end the interrogation, police would be required to make difficult decisions about an accused's unclear intent and face the consequence of suppression 'if they guess wrong,' would place a significant burden on society's interest in prosecuting criminal activity, and would add only 'marginally to *Miranda*'s goal of dispelling the compulsion inherent in custodial interrogation.' " The dissenters argued that in "the 16 years since *Davis* was decided, ample evidence has accrued that criminal suspects often use equivocal or colloquial language in attempting to invoke their right to silence."

his incriminating statement about selling heroin was a "fruit" of the violation that was inadmissible in the prosecution's case in chief. The *Harris* defendant took the stand in order to testify that he sold baking powder rather than heroin, thus rebutting the testimony of a government witness that the substance sold was heroin. The prosecutor was allowed to cross-examine the defendant using the inadmissible statement to police, and the *Harris* Court validated this impeachment use of the otherwise inadmissible evidence. The Court reasoned that "the impeachment process undoubtedly provided valuable aid to the jury in assessing the defendant's credibility" and opined that "the shield provided by *Miranda*" should not be "perverted into a license to use perjury by way of defense, free from the risk of confrontation with prior inconsistent utterances." The *Harris* dissenters argued that the Court's rule would "seriously undermine" *Miranda's* objective of "deterring" unconstitutional police practices. But the Court declared that "the benefits" of the impeachment process "should not be lost" merely "because of the speculative possibility that impermissible police conduct will be encouraged thereby." As in *Tucker*, the *Harris* Court expressed confidence that sufficient deterrence of *Miranda* violations would be provided by making *Miranda*-defective statements "unavailable to the prosecution in its case in chief."

In *Doyle v. Ohio*, 426 U.S. 610 (1976), the Court held that it is a Due Process violation for a prosecutor to use the fact of the defendant's silence in response to *Miranda* warnings to impeach defendant's testimony at trial. The Court noted that "every post-arrest silence is insolubly ambiguous because of what the State is required to advise the person arrested," namely, the right to remain silent under *Miranda*. Therefore, an arrestee's "silence in the wake of the *Miranda* warnings may be nothing more than the arrestee's exercise of the *Miranda* rights." Although "the *Miranda* warnings contain no express assurance that silence will carry no penalty, the Court concluded that such an assurance "is implicit" and so it would violate the fairness concerns of Due Process "to allow the arrested person's silence to be used to impeach an explanation subsequently offered at trial."

The Court's later precedents consistently upheld the impeachment use of a person's silence in other contexts where such silence was not a response to the *Miranda* warnings. In *Jenkins v. Anderson*, 447 U.S. 231 (1980), the Court held that no violation occurred when the defendant's silence *before* arrest was used for impeachment purposes. This holding was justified on the grounds that "no governmental action" like *Miranda* warnings "induced the defendant to remain silent before arrest." The dissenters argued that pre-arrest silence is unlikely to be probative of the falsity of a defendant's trial testimony. Similarly, in *Fletcher v. Weir*, 455 U.S. 603 (1982), the Court found no *Doyle* violation where a defendant's silence *after* arrest occurred *before* warnings were given. *See also Brecht v. Abrahamson*, 507 U.S. 619 (1993). Even when a prosecutor commits a *Doyle* violation during cross-examination, the violation can be cured if the trial judge sustains a subsequent objection and instructs the jury to "ignore the prosecutor's question". See *Greer v. Miller*, 483 U.S. 756 (1987).

However, in *Salinas v. Texas,* 570 U.S. 178 (2013), the police sought to use defendant's conduct as evidence against him. In a non-custodial interview, during which defendant was not read the *Miranda* warnings, when defendant was asked whether his shotgun "would match the shells recovered at the scene of the murder," defendant declined to answer, "looked down at the floor, shuffled his feet, bit his bottom lip, clenched his hands in his lap, and began to tighten up." At trial, the prosecution sought to offer testimony regarding defendant's conduct. "We have before us no allegation that petitioner's failure to assert the privilege was involuntary, and it would have been a simple matter for him to say that he was not answering the officer's question on Fifth Amendment grounds. Because he failed to do so, the prosecution's use of his noncustodial silence did not violate the Fifth Amendment. Our cases establish that a defendant normally does not invoke the privilege by remaining silent. We have also repeatedly held that the express invocation requirement applies even when an official has reason to suspect that the answer to his question would incriminate the witness."

Hypo 1: *Name of Attorney*

Worth was arrested, given *Miranda* warnings, and stated that he wanted his lawyer but could not recall the lawyer's name. The officer later asks Worth, "Have you come up with the name yet?" When he says "no," the officer asks, "What do you want to do?", and Worth says, "I guess I'll talk to you." The officer asks, "Even without an attorney?" Worth says, "OK," and then signs a waiver, making incriminating statements. Did Worth unambiguously invoke his right to counsel? *See Wedgeworth v. State,* 374 Ark. 373, 288 S.W.3d 234 (2008).

Hypo 2: *Clarifying Invocation*

Sid is arrested for burglary, taken to the police station, and given *Miranda* warnings. The officer then states, "Do you want to talk to me?" Sid replies, "I got nothin' to say." The officer states, "So that's a no?" Sid says nothing. The officer says, "I just need a yes or a no—so do you want to give your side of the story, yes or no?" Sid replies, "Okay, yes." The officer says, "Yes—meaning you want to answer questions?" Sid states, "Ah, perhaps. I'm not gonna say anything." The officer says, "Well, you can stop any time you want." Sid says, "Okay." Then the officer asks questions about the burglary and Sid makes incriminating statements. Did Sid invoke his rights and did the police respond appropriately? *See State v. Szpyrka,* 220 Ariz. 59, 202 P.3d 5324 (App. 2008).

Hypo 3: *"I Am Doing My Right"*

An interrogation begins with casual conversation with police detectives, but the detectives eventually read *Miranda* warnings and state, "Do you understand the rights that I have explained to you? Yes or no?" Manzo states "I'm doing my right." A detective asks, "Okay, but do you understand them?" Manzo states, "I'm doing my right." Then the detective says, "OK—do you understand what he just read to you? I'm not asking you to tell me anything. I'm just asking do you understand what I told you?" Manzo replies, "Yes, I understand." A detective then says, "Okay. The point I made earlier is that I don't think you pulled the trigger, so I don't think you need to go down for life. Okay? You got your act together now, you got a job. You're staying clean, your girlfriend says you ain't doing dope. You're not hanging out down in the hood." Manzo then makes incriminating statements. Did Martin unambiguously invoke his right to remain silent? *See People v. Manzo*, 192 Cal.App.4th 366, 121 Cal.Rptr.3d 207 (2011).

Hypo 4: *Echoing the Rights*

After Harden is informed of his rights, and while the officer is attempting to obtain a written acknowledgement, Harden says, "You said I could have a lawyer. I can't afford no lawyer," and the officer responds, "Well, you know, that's all stuff that could be worked out—my question to you, do you want to get this off your back; I can tell you've got a lot of pressure on you right now." If Harden makes incriminating statements, did he unambiguously invoke his right to counsel? *See Harden v. State*, 59 So.3d 594 (Miss. 2011).

Hypo 5: *Shaking Head*

After Clarke is arrested, and taken to the police station, he is given a *Miranda* warning. Clarke is then given a waiver form, told to read it, and the detective reviews verbally each of the rights described on the form. The detective then asks Clarke, "Do you want to discuss the charges?

Clarke asks, "What happens if I don't speak to you?" The detective replies, "Nothing." Clarke says, "I just want to go home." The detective asks, "You just want to go home? So you don't want to speak?" At that point, Clarke shakes his head in a negative fashion. The detective then says, "OK." But the detective says, "When I said that 'nothing' would happen, that does not exclude us from charging you and detaining you here. You'll either be bailed, or you'll go to court in the morning to answer the charges. So it doesn't mean you'll get to walk out of here and go home now." If Clarke makes incriminating statements, can he argue that he unambiguously invoked his right to silence? *See Commonwealth v. Clarke*, 461 Mass. 336, 960 N.E.2d 306 (2012).

Hypo 6: *Can We Get Him Down Here Now?*

In *People v. Kutlak,* 364 P.3d 199 (Colo. 2016), defendant was in custody and had been given a *Miranda* warning. He then stated that he had a personal lawyer and asked "Can you get him down here now, or ....?" The officer responded that it might be difficult to get the lawyer there now, and asked defendant whether he wanted to continue with the interrogation, stating "It's entirely up to you." Defendant then stated that he would "take a dice roll" and continued with the interrogation. The court concluded that defendant did not clearly and unambiguously request counsel.

Hypo 7: *Request to Speak to Uncle*

Suppose that defendant is given a *Miranda* warning, and repeatedly asserts that he wishes to talk to his uncle before talking to the police. Does his request to speak to his uncle constitute the equivalent of a request to remain silent? *See State v. Maltese*, 222 N.J. 525, 120 A.3d 197 (2015).

6. Waiver-Seeking After Invocation

Once a suspect invokes either his *Miranda* rights, if there is a subsequent attempt to seek a waiver, the question is whether the waiver is valid. The Court has recognized that an invocation does not necessarily provide permanent immunity from interrogation. Instead, the validity of a subsequent interrogation depends on whether a person reinvokes the right to silence or the right to counsel. Later opportunities for officers to obtain waivers may arise after each type of invocation, but for different reasons, as demonstrated by the cases that follow.

Michigan v. Mosley

423 U.S. 96 (1975).

MR. JUSTICE STEWART delivered the opinion of the Court.

Mosley was arrested in the afternoon based on a tip that he had participated in two robberies at bars in Detroit. Detective Cowie brought Mosley to the Robbery Bureau on the fourth floor of the police headquarters, and gave him *Miranda* warnings. Mosley signed a "rights notification" form and then he said he did not want to answer any questions about the robberies. Cowie ceased the questioning, and took Mosley to a ninth-floor cell block. A few hours later, Detective Hill brought Mosley from the cell block to the fifth-floor office of the Homicide Bureau for questioning about the fatal shooting of Williams, who had been killed during an attempted holdup at a different bar. Hill read and explained the *Miranda* warnings to Mosley, and this time Mosley waived his rights. When Hill told Mosley that another man had implicated Mosley in the Williams homicide, Mosley made incriminating statements during the 15 minute interrogation that followed. These statements were admitted at Mosley's murder trial and he was convicted.

The issue is whether the conduct of the Detroit police that led to Mosley's incriminating statement violated *Miranda*. Resolution of the question turns almost entirely on the interpretation of a single passage in the *Miranda* opinion: "Once warnings have been given, the subsequent procedure is clear. If the individual indicates in any manner, at any time prior to or during questioning, that he wishes to remain silent, the interrogation must cease. At this point he has shown that he intends to exercise his Fifth Amendment privilege; any statement taken after the person invokes his privilege cannot be other than the product of compulsion, subtle or otherwise. Without the right to cut off questioning, the setting of in-custody interrogation operates on the individual to overcome free choice in producing a statement after the privilege has been once invoked."

This passage could be literally read to mean that a person who has invoked his "right to silence" can never again be subjected to custodial interrogation by any police officer at any time or place on any subject. Another possible construction of the passage would characterize "any statement taken after the person invokes his privilege" as inadmissible, even if it were volunteered by the person in custody. Or the passage could be interpreted to require only the immediate cessation of questioning, and to permit a resumption of interrogation after a momentary respite. It is evident that any of these possible literal interpretations would lead to absurd and unintended results. To permit the continuation of custodial interrogation after a momentary cessation would clearly frustrate the purposes of *Miranda* by allowing repeated rounds of questioning to undermine the will of the person being questioned. At the other extreme, a blanket prohibition against the taking of voluntary statements or a permanent immunity from further interrogation, regardless of the circumstances, would transform the *Miranda* safeguards into wholly irrational obstacles to legitimate police investigative activity, and deprive suspects of an opportunity to make informed and intelligent assessments of their interests. Moreover, *Miranda* prescribes different consequences for different kinds of invocations: an invocation of silence does not trigger the requirement of a lawyer's presence before interrogation can occur, but if "the individual states that he wants an attorney," then "the interrogation must cease until an attorney is present."

A reasonable and faithful interpretation of the *Miranda* opinion must rest on the intention of the Court to adopt "fully effective means to notify the person of his right of silence and to assure that the exercise of the right will be scrupulously honored." The critical safeguard is a person's "right to cut off questioning." Through the exercise of his option to terminate questioning he can control the time at which questioning occurs, the subjects discussed, and the duration of the interrogation. The requirement that law enforcement authorities must respect a person's exercise of that option counteracts the coercive pressures of the custodial setting.

A review of the circumstances leading to Mosley's confession reveals that his "right to cut off questioning" was scrupulously honored in this case. Before his initial interrogation, Mosley received warnings, orally acknowledged that he understood them, and signed a notification-of-rights form. When Mosley stated that he did not want to discuss the robberies, Detective Cowie immediately ceased the interrogation and did not try either to resume the questioning or in any way to persuade Mosley to reconsider his position. After an interval of more than two hours, Mosley was questioned by another police officer at another location about an unrelated holdup murder. He was given full and complete *Miranda* warnings at the outset of the second interrogation. The subsequent questioning did not undercut Mosley's previous decision not to answer Detective Cowie's inquiries. Detective Hill did not resume the interrogation about the robberies, but instead focused exclusively on the homicide, a crime different in nature and in time and place of occurrence from the robberies. The questioning of Mosley about an unrelated homicide was quite consistent with a reasonable interpretation of Mosley's earlier refusal to answer any questions about the robberies. For these reasons, we conclude that the admission in evidence of Mosley's incriminating statement did not violate the principles of *Miranda*.

Mr. Justice Brennan, with whom Mr. Justice Marshall joins, dissenting.

Miranda is not to be read to impose an absolute ban on resumption of questioning "at any time or place on any subject," or "to permit a resumption of interrogation after a momentary respite." *Miranda's* terms, however, are not so uncompromising as to preclude the fashioning of guidelines to govern this case. Michigan law requires that the suspect be arraigned before a judicial officer "without unnecessary delay," certainly not a burdensome requirement. Alternatively, a requirement that resumption of questioning should await appointment and arrival of counsel for the suspect would be an acceptable and readily satisfied precondition to resumption. The Court expediently bypasses this alternative in its search for circumstances where renewed questioning would be permissible. Today's decision virtually empties *Miranda* of principle, for plainly the decision encourages police asked to cease interrogation to continue the suspect's detention until the police station's coercive atmosphere does its work and the suspect responds to resumed questioning.

Hypo 1: *Waiver Seeking About Same Crime*

Assume that Kevin is arrested for theft, and after he receives *Miranda* warnings from an officer, he invokes the right to remain silent. Two hours later, the same officer comes to Kevin's cell, gives him the *Miranda* warnings again, and asks Kevin if he is willing to sign a waiver and talk about the theft. If Kevin now signs the waiver and makes incriminating statements, are they admissible? Would it matter if the officer waited only twenty minutes before coming back? *Compare Commonwealth v. Callendar*, 81 Mass. App. Ct. 153, 960 N.E.2d 910 (2012); *State v. Bauldwin*, 283 Neb. 678, 811 N.W.2d 267 (2012). Would it matter whether the same officer returned, or whether it was a different officer? *See United States v. Oquendo-Rivas,* 750 F.3d 12 (1st Cir. 2014). Suppose that the suspect reinitiates contact by asking "what happens next?," to which the officer replies that he intends to obtain a search warrant. Has the officer reinitiated the interrogation? *See State v. McKnight,* 319 P.3d 298 (Haw. 2013).

Hypo 2: *New Evidence*

Assume that when the officer in the prior hypo came to Kevin's cell two hours after Kevin's invocation of the right to remain silent, her justification for returning to seek a waiver was based on her discovery of new evidence about the same crime. She wanted to find out if Kevin was interested in hearing about the new evidence in order to reconsider his decision to remain silent. Would this change the arguments as to whether the officer violated *Miranda* when she returned and obtained the waiver from Kevin? Would it matter whether the officer mentioned the existence of new evidence at the time she gave Kevin the new *Miranda* warnings, before he signed the waiver? *Compare United States v. Guerra,* 237 F. Supp. 2d 795 (E.D. Mich. 2003).

Hypo 3: *No Additional Warnings*

When the officer in the prior hypo returned to seek a waiver from Kevin two hours after his invocation of the right to remain silent, she does not give Kevin the *Miranda* warnings again. Instead, she says, "Kevin, you remember me. Now that two hours have passed, I'm wondering whether you have changed your mind about remaining silent, and whether you are now willing to waive your rights and talk to me?" Assume that Kevin signs the waiver and makes incriminating statements. How does the officer's failure to provide the *Miranda* warnings again change the arguments as to whether she violated *Miranda*? *Compare State v. Hartley,* 103 N.J. 252, 511 A.2d 80 (1986).

Hypo 4: *Repeated Requests for Waiver*

Assume that the officer in the prior hypo failed to obtain a signed waiver after two hours because Kevin invoked the right to silence a second time. Assume that every two hours during the next 12 hours, the officer returns like clockwork to Kevin's cell, gives him the *Miranda* warnings again, and seeks a waiver from Kevin concerning the theft crime. Each time, Kevin invokes the right to remain silent again, and the officer leaves. Then the officer returns one more time to Kevin's cell, gives him *Miranda* warnings and seeks a waiver. This time Kevin signs the waiver and makes incriminating statements. On these facts, how would defense counsel argue that the officer violated *Miranda*? *Compare United States v. Barone*, 968 F.2d 1378 (1st Cir. 1992).

Hypo 5: *Invocation of Silence with Conditions*

Border patrol agents in San Diego arrested several occupants of a house for the crime of smuggling illegal immigrants into the country. An officer asks Jerry, one of the people arrested, whether he is willing to waive his rights, so that he can be questioned about his own citizenship and about other people in the house. Jerry says, "I'll make a statement about my citizenship, but I won't talk about other people." The agent says, "No, we want to talk about both your citizenship and that of the other people." Jerry responds, "I will only talk about my citizenship." Then the agent asks Jerry questions about his citizenship and about the people in the house and Jerry answers all the questions. Did the agent violate *Miranda* and *Mosley* by ignoring Jerry's attempt to invoke his right to silence on the subject of the people in the house? *See United States v. Soliz*, 129 F.3d 499 (9th Cir. 1997).

Food for Thought

The *Mosley* Court observes "that when the *Miranda* opinion described the need to assure an arrestee that the exercise of the right to silence will be scrupulously honored," the "critical safeguard" that will achieve that assurance is an arrested person's "right to cut off questioning." However, the *Miranda* warnings do not inform an arrestee that such a *Miranda* "right" exists, or that the beneficial consequence of an invocation is that it gives rise to the police duty to cut off questioning. What additional information would be useful for arrestees to understand concerning the operation of their invocation rights and the implementation of *Mosley* power by police officers? Would it be desirable to add such requirements?

Edwards v. Arizona

451 U.S. 477 (1981).

JUSTICE WHITE delivered the opinion of the Court.

Edwards was arrested for theft and homicide crimes and was given *Miranda* warnings at the police station. Edwards said that he understood his rights and would submit to questioning. Then he was told that another suspect had implicated him, and he denied involvement in the crimes, gave a taped statement presenting an alibi defense, and said he wanted to "make a deal." One interrogating officer replied that he had no authority to do that, and gave Edwards the telephone number of the county prosecutor. Edwards made the call but hung up after a few moments and declared, "I want an attorney before making a deal." At that point, questioning ceased and Edwards was taken to jail. The next morning, two detectives asked to see Edwards, and the guard told Edwards that "he had" to talk to them, even though Edwards told the guard that he did not want to talk to anyone. The detectives told Edwards that they wanted to question him, and gave him *Miranda* warnings. Edwards said that he was willing to talk, but first he wanted to hear the taped statement of the alleged suspect who had implicated him. After listening to the statement for several minutes, Edwards agreed to make a statement as long as it was not recorded. When the detectives explained that they could testify in court about any unrecorded statement he made, Edwards replied, "I'll tell you anything you want to know, but I don't want it on tape." He made incriminating statements that were admitted at the trial that led to his conviction.

Although we have held that after initially being advised of his *Miranda* rights, the accused may himself validly waive his rights and respond to interrogation, the Court has strongly indicated that additional safeguards are necessary when the accused asks for counsel; and we now hold that when an accused has invoked his right to have counsel present during custodial interrogation, a valid waiver of that right cannot be established by showing only that he responded to further police-initiated custodial interrogation even if he has been advised of his rights. We further hold that an accused, having expressed his desire to deal with the police only through counsel, is not subject to further interrogation by the authorities until counsel has been made available to him, unless the accused himself initiates further communication, exchanges, or conversations with the police. *Miranda* itself indicated that the assertion of the right to counsel was a significant event and that once exercised by the accused, "the interrogation must cease until an attorney is present." Our later cases have maintained that view. In *Michigan v. Mosley*, 423 U.S. 96 (1975), the Court noted that *Miranda* had distinguished between the procedural safeguards triggered by a request to remain silent and a request for an attorney and required that interrogation cease until an attorney was present only if the individual stated that he wanted counsel.

Had Edwards initiated the meeting with the detectives, nothing would prohibit them from merely listening to his volunteered statements and using them against him at the trial. Absent interrogation, there would have been no infringement of the right that Edwards invoked. Here, the officers conducting the first interrogation ceased their questions when Edwards requested counsel as he had been advised he had the right to do. But without making counsel available to Edwards, the police returned to him the next day. This was not at his suggestion or request. Indeed, Edwards informed the detention officer that he did not want to talk to anyone. At the meeting, the detectives told Edwards that they wanted to talk to him and again advised him of his *Miranda* rights. Edwards stated that he would talk, but what prompted this action does not appear. He listened at his own request to part of the taped statement made by one of his alleged accomplices and then made an incriminating statement, which was used against him at his trial. We think it clear that Edwards was subjected to custodial interrogation within the meaning of *Innis*, and that this occurred at the instance of the authorities. His statement made without access to counsel, did not amount to a valid waiver and hence was inadmissible.

The concept of a defendant's "initiation" that operates as a retraction of an invocation was defined in *Oregon v. Bradshaw*, 462 U.S. 1039 (1983), in which the defendant was arrested for furnishing liquor to a juvenile who died in a car accident. After defendant was given *Miranda* warnings, he denied involvement in the accident and invoked his right to counsel. The police officer cut off questioning. Soon thereafter, the following happened as "Bradshaw was being transferred to the county jail, some ten to fifteen miles away, Bradshaw inquired of a police officer, 'Well, what is going to happen to me now?' The officer answered by saying 'You do not have to talk to me. You have requested an attorney and I don't want you talking to me unless you so desire because anything you say—because—since you have requested an attorney, you know, it has to be at your own free will.' Bradshaw said he understood. There followed a discussion between Bradshaw and the officer concerning where Bradshaw was being taken and the offense with which he would be charged. The officer suggested that Bradshaw might help himself by taking a polygraph examination. Bradshaw agreed to do so, and he made incriminating statements during the examination the next day, after receiving warnings and waiving his rights during the polygraph procedure." The Court concluded that Bradshaw "initiated" the further conversation. While there are some types of inquiries (e.g., a request for a drink of water or a request to use a telephone) that are "so routine that they cannot be fairly said to represent a desire on the part of an accused to open up a more generalized discussion relating directly or indirectly to the investigation," the Court believed that "Bradshaw's question as to what was going to happen to him evinced a willingness and a desire for a generalized discussion about the investigation; it was not merely a necessary inquiry arising out of the incidents of the custodial relationship." In addition, the Court concluded that Bradshaw validly waived his rights. Justice Marshall, joined by three other justices, dissented, arguing that Bradshaw's question, which "came only minutes after invocation," was "a normal reaction to being taken from the police station and placed in a police car, obviously for transport to some destination." As a result, the dissent contended that it did not qualify as "initiation."

Points for Discussion

a. *Edwards* Invocation and Different Crimes

In *Arizona v. Roberson*, 486 U.S. 675 (1988), Roberson was arrested for burglary, given *Miranda* warnings, and invoked his right to counsel. Three days later, Roberson was still in custody when a different police officer, who was unaware of the earlier invocation, gave Roberson a new *Miranda* warning and sought to interrogate him about a different burglary. Roberson waived his rights and made incriminating statements about the other burglary. The Court interpreted *Edwards* as precluding the police from seeking a waiver regarding different crimes after invocation of the right to counsel: "Roberson's unwillingness to answer any questions without the advice of counsel indicated that he did not feel sufficiently comfortable with the pressures of custodial interrogation to answer questions without an attorney. This discomfort is precisely the state of mind that *Edwards* presumes to persist unless the suspect himself initiates further conversation about the investigation. *Edwards* laid down a rule designed to protect an accused from being badgered by police officers. After a person invokes the right to consult counsel, any further interrogation without counsel having been provided will surely exacerbate whatever compulsion to speak the suspect may be feeling. Police are free to inform the suspect of the facts of the second investigation as long as such communication does not constitute interrogation. We attach no significance to the fact that the officer who conducted the second interrogation did not know that respondent had made a request for counsel." Justice Kennedy, joined by Chief Justice Rehnquist, dissented, arguing that the Court's extension of *Edwards* to bar waiver-seeking for "separate and independent investigations" will deprive law enforcement of a useful investigative technique "routinely used to resolve major crimes." "When a person is arrested, his name and fingerprints are checked, and police frequently discover that this person "is wanted for questioning" for unrelated crimes. No *Edwards* protection is necessary from such questioning after invocation of counsel because 'the danger of badgering is minimal.' " The *Roberson* dissenters emphasized that *Mosley* supports the use of fresh *Miranda* warnings as sufficient protection before police engage in waiver-seeking and interrogation about a different crime; the warnings show a suspect that police respect his right to invoke, and to remind him that he may invoke his rights again.

b. Attempted Questioning after Consultation with Counsel

In *Minnick v. Mississippi*, 498 U.S. 146 (1990), defendant was arrested in San Diego for a murder committed in Mississippi. After he received *Miranda* warnings from the agents, he refused to sign a waiver and stated, "Come back Monday when I have a lawyer." The agents cut off questioning, and an appointed attorney met with defendant, warned him not to talk to anybody, and promised to get a court order to stop police interrogation. Three days later, a Mississippi sheriff came to question Minnick, and the jailer told Minnick that he must talk to the sheriff. After receiving *Miranda* warnings, Minnick again refused to sign a waiver, but he started to talk to the sheriff "about how everybody was back in the county jail and what everybody was doing, and what the sheriff had heard from his Mama or his brother, Tracy, and several different other questions pertaining to such things as how the escape went down at the county jail." Minnick made further incriminating statements, which were admitted at his murder trial; he was convicted and received the death penalty. The Court rejected the argument that after a defendant invokes the right to counsel, and consults with counsel, the police no longer have a duty to cut off questioning, and may renew the attempt to seek a waiver: "When counsel is requested, interrogation must cease, and officials may not reinitiate interrogation without counsel present, whether or not the accused has consulted with his attorney. Minnick testified that though he resisted, he was required to submit to both the interviews. The compulsion to submit to interrogation followed his unequivocal request during the FBI interview that questioning cease until counsel was present. We decline to remove protection from police-initiated questioning based on isolated consultations with counsel who is absent when the interrogation resumes." Justice Scalia dissented, joined by Chief Justice Rehnquist, arguing that after consultation with counsel, a suspect would have a heightened awareness of his or her rights, especially of the right to remain silent, so that any police-initiated waiver and confession could no longer be presumed to be based on the suspect's ignorance of rights or on police coercion. Scalia concluded that the decision was unjustified because it "makes it impossible" for police to ask a prisoner who invokes and consults counsel whether "he has changed his mind" about waiving his rights.

Take Note

In *Maryland v. Shatzer*, 559 U.S. 98 (2010), the Court held that after a person in custody invokes the right to counsel, the *Edwards* prohibition on waiver-seeking will expire 14 days after the person's release from custody: "It may be envisioned that once a suspect invokes his *Miranda* right to counsel, the police will release the suspect briefly (to end the *Edwards* presumption) and then promptly bring him back into custody for reinterrogation. But once the suspect has been out of custody long enough (14 days) to eliminate its coercive effect, there will be nothing to gain by such gamesmanship." On the facts of *Shatzer*, the Court concluded that a break in custody occurred when the inmate defendant invoked his *Edwards* right during a custodial interrogation in prison concerning a prior crime in the outside world, and then was released back into the general inmate population. Therefore, his invocation expired 14 days after that event.

Hypo 1: *Refusal to Honor the Invocation*

Suppose that Ted is given *Miranda* warnings during interrogation and invokes his right to counsel under *Edwards* by saying, "I want a lawyer now." The interrogating officers ignore Ted's invocation and continues to interrogate. Ted refuses to sign a waiver and repeatedly invokes his right to counsel during a three-hour interrogation during which he makes no incriminating statements. He is taken back to the jail. Five hours later he is brought back to the interrogation room for more questioning. Before he is given more warnings, Ted says, "What is going to happen to me now?" The police officer responds by saying, "We're going to resume our interrogation." At this point Ted makes incriminating statements. Did the police violate *Miranda*? *See Hill v. Brigano*, 199 F.3d 833 (6th Cir. 1999).

Hypo 2: *One Arrestee Speaking for Two*

Amy and her boyfriend Bo were arrested for burglary and placed in different interview rooms. Each received *Miranda* warnings and each invoked the right to counsel. They were taken to the courthouse for arraignment in the same police car. During the ride, Amy was silent, but Bo declared, "Take us to the station, let us talk together in private, and then we'll talk about the burglary." So the police returned to the station and Amy and Bo were allowed to speak privately. When the officers entered the room later, Amy was silent but Bo stated, "We're ready to talk, but we have to speak to you together." An officer recited the *Miranda* warnings again to Bo and Amy, asked them whether they understood their rights and were willing to waive them, and then gave Bo a waiver form, which Bo signed. Amy did not sign the form and remained silent. During the interrogation, Bo made incriminating statements. Amy made only one incriminating statement and was otherwise silent. Did the interrogation violate the *Miranda* rights of either Bo or Amy? *See United States v. Lafferty*, 503 F.3d 293 (3d Cir. 2007).

Hypo 3: *Initiation After Edwards Violation*

Although Dorsey was given *Miranda* warnings, and invoked his right to counsel, police detectives continued to interrogate him. When he tried to invoke his right to counsel several more times, the officers disparaged his request and continued to interrogate him. During thirteen hours of questioning, continuing through the night, Dorsey did not make any incriminating statements. He repeatedly told the officers that he needed sleep, and was taken to his cell at 8:00 a.m., but informed him that questioning would continue when he awoke. A few hours passed without interrogation after Dorsey woke up. At that point, Dorsey asked a guard if he could speak to one of the detectives, and then he told the detective that he was willing to talk. The interrogation continued without new *Miranda* warnings, and Dorsey made incriminating statements. Are the statements admissible? *See Dorsey v. United States*, 2 A.3d 222 (D.C. Ct. App. 2010). *Compare Ex parte Williams*, 31 So.3d 670 (Ala. 2009).

Hypo 4: *"Tell the Story to Me"*

After Phil is arrested for the crime of robbery, detectives take him to a police interrogation room, recite the *Miranda* warnings, and obtain a waiver of rights. For 45 minutes, one detective engages in general chat with Phil about his personal life, in order to put Phil at ease. When the other detective returns, he shouts that the robbery was a terrible crime and that Phil should confess. Phil responds, "I have changed my mind about talking and want to see an attorney immediately." At that point, the second detective leaves. The first detective then states, "Since you have invoked the right to counsel, I cannot speak to you. If you decide that you want to tell your story, you can do that. However, you must first affirm that you are willing to speak without counsel. I want to get your side of the story, but that is totally up to you." Did the detectives violate *Edwards*? *Compare Phillips v. State*, 425 Md. 210, 40 A.3d 25 (2012).

Hypo 5: *Arrestee in Jail*

Elliott was arrested for violating parole based on a tip that he had committed a robbery, and received a *Miranda* warning. The arresting officer wanted to interrogate Elliott, but Elliott invoked his right to counsel. The questioning ended and Elliott was placed in a cell. Three days later, he was in that cell when Cheryl, his parole officer, arrived at the jail to serve Elliott with parole-violation charges. Before meeting with Elliott, Cheryl met with the arresting officer, received the police report, and learned about the tip concerning the robbery. She then went to Elliott's cell, served him with the parole violation charges, and asked him to tell her about the robbery. Elliott made incriminating statements. Are these statements admissible at his robbery trial? *See People v. Elliott*, 295 Mich. App. 623, 815 N.W.2d 575 (2012).

7. *Miranda* in International Contexts

When statements are elicited during overseas interrogations by foreign police in the absence of *Miranda* warnings, they must be suppressed "whenever United States law enforcement agents actively participate in questioning conducted by foreign authorities." Although the mere presence of U.S. agents at such an interrogation does not constitute the active or substantial participation, the "coordination and direction of an investigation or interrogation by U.S. agents does." See *United States v. Abu Ali*, 528 F.3d 210 (4th Cir. 2008). When *Miranda* applies to the interrogation of a foreign national overseas, the U.S. agents must inform the person of his *Miranda* rights, including the right to consult counsel, and they must stop questioning when that right is invoked. However, the following warning may be used to describe the arrestee's actual access to counsel: "Whether you can retain a lawyer, or have a lawyer appointed for you, and whether you can consult with a lawyer and have a lawyer present during questioning are matters that depend on local law, and we cannot advise you on such matters. If local authorities permit you to obtain counsel (retained or appointed) and to consult with a lawyer at this time, you may attempt to obtain and consult with an attorney before speaking with us. Similarly, if local authorities permit you to have a lawyer present during questioning by local authorities, your lawyer may attend any questioning by us." See *In re Terrorist Bombings of U.S. Embassies in East Africa*, 552 F.3d 93 (2d Cir. 2008).

D. Post-*Miranda* Sixth Amendment Law

For more than a decade after *Miranda*, the Court did not decide a confession case on Sixth Amendment grounds, and did not address questions relating to the relationship between the *Miranda* and *Massiah* rights to counsel. Although *Massiah* established Sixth Amendment protection for indicted defendants questioned by undercover agents, that decision did not explain how the protection would apply (if at all) during police questioning. In 1977 the Court provided that explanation, when it used the *Massiah* doctrine to resolve a controversial case, and embarked upon the process of articulating the differences between *Massiah* and *Miranda* rights.

Brewer v. Williams

430 U.S. 387 (1977).

MR. JUSTICE STEWART delivered the opinion of the Court.

When an arrest warrant was issued for Williams in Des Moines for the crime of abduction, he was in Davenport. He sought the advice of a Des Moines attorney, who advised Williams to turn himself in to the Davenport police. Then Williams waited for the Des Moines police to pick him up. When Williams was arraigned in Davenport, he consulted with the local counsel who was appointed for him. Williams received *Miranda* warnings from the police who arrested him, from the magistrate during arraignment, and from Detective Leaming when the Des Moines police arrived to pick up Williams. But he never received a waiver form, and Detective Leaming never sought an oral waiver or provided additional warnings during the 160-mile car trip to Des Moines. When Detective Leaming arrived in Davenport and heard about the police agreement that Williams would not be questioned during the trip, Leaming rejected the request of counsel to accompany Williams. The incriminating statements that Williams made during the trip were admitted at his murder trial. The Court found it unnecessary to reach the *Miranda* issues.

When the ride began, the detective and his prisoner embarked on a wide-ranging conversation covering a variety of topics, including the subject of religion. Leaming knew that Williams was a former mental patient and was deeply religious. Not long after leaving Davenport and reaching the interstate highway, Leaming delivered what has been referred to as the "Christian burial speech." Addressing Williams as "Reverend," the detective said: "I want to give you something to think about while we're traveling down the road. I want you to observe the weather conditions, it's raining, it's sleeting, it's freezing, driving is very treacherous, visibility is poor, it's going to be dark early this evening. They are predicting several inches of snow for tonight, and you are the only person that knows where this little girl's body is, that you yourself have only been there once, and if you get a snow on top of it you yourself may be unable to find it. Since we will be going right past the area on the way into Des Moines, I feel that we could stop and locate the body, that the parents of this little girl should be entitled to a Christian burial for the little girl who was snatched away from them on Christmas Eve and murdered. I feel we should stop and locate it on the way in rather than waiting until morning and trying to come back out after a snow storm and possibly not being able to find it at all." Leaming then stated: "I do not want you to answer me. I don't want to discuss it any further. Just think about it as we're riding down the road." After the car traveled another 100 miles, Williams made incriminating statements and told the officers how to find the body.

There can be no doubt that judicial proceedings had been initiated against Williams before the start of the automobile ride from Davenport to Des Moines. A warrant had been issued for his arrest, he had been arraigned on that warrant before a judge in a Davenport courtroom, and he had been committed by the court to confinement in jail.

There can be no serious doubt that Leaming deliberately and designedly set out to elicit information from Williams just as surely as and perhaps more effectively than if he had formally interrogated him. The clear rule of *Massiah* is that once adversary proceedings have commenced against an individual, he has a right to legal representation when the government interrogates him.

The prosecutor argued that Williams waived his Sixth Amendment right to counsel. It was incumbent upon the State to prove "an intentional relinquishment or abandonment of a known right or privilege." *Johnson v. Zerbst*, 304 U.S. 458, 464 (1938). The record falls far short of sustaining the state's burden. Williams had been informed of and appeared to understand his right to counsel. But waiver requires not merely comprehension but relinquishment, and Williams' consistent reliance upon the advice of counsel in dealing with the authorities refutes any suggestion that he waived that right. Williams was advised not to make any statements before seeing his counsel in Des Moines, and was assured that the police had agreed not to question him. His statements while in the car "When I get to Des Moines and see my lawyer, I am going to tell you the whole story," were the clearest expressions by Williams himself that he desired the presence of an attorney before any interrogation took place. Even before making these statements, Williams had effectively asserted his right to counsel by having secured attorneys at both ends of the automobile trip, both of whom had made clear to the police that no interrogation was to occur during the journey. Williams knew of that agreement and, particularly in view of his consistent reliance on counsel, there is no basis for concluding that he disavowed it.

Despite Williams' express and implicit assertions of his right to counsel, Leaming proceeded to elicit incriminating statements from Williams. Leaming did not preface this effort by telling Williams that he had a right to the presence of a lawyer, and made no effort at all to ascertain whether Williams wished to relinquish that right. The circumstances thus provide no reasonable basis for finding that Williams waived his right to the assistance of counsel.

MR. CHIEF JUSTICE BURGER, dissenting.

It is clear that Williams made a valid waiver of his Fifth Amendment right to silence and his Sixth Amendment right to counsel when he led police to the body. The fundamental purpose of the Sixth Amendment is to safeguard the fairness of the trial and the integrity of the factfinding process. It appears suppression is mandated here for no other reason than the Court's general impression that it may have a beneficial effect on future police conduct.

MR. JUSTICE WHITE, with whom MR. JUSTICE BLACKMUN and MR. JUSTICE REHNQUIST join, dissenting.

Waiver is shown whenever the facts establish that an accused knew of a right and intended to relinquish it. Such waiver, even if not express, was plainly shown here. The officers' conduct did not jeopardize the fairness of the defendant's trial or in any way risk the conviction of an innocent man, the risk against which the Sixth Amendment guarantee of assistance of counsel is designed to protect.

When Williams was retried for murder, his statements about the location of the body were inadmissible, but the prosecutor relied on the "inevitable discovery" exception to the exclusionary rule to support the admission of location of the victim's body and condition. In *Nix v. Williams*, 467 U.S. 431 (1984), the Court upheld the conviction of Williams, and ruled that the prosecutor made a sufficient showing that the police would have "inevitably" discovered the location of the body by following the police search procedures that were underway at the time, so the *Massiah* violation could be ignored.

Take Note

The Court has identified a short list of events that qualify as "adversary judicial criminal proceedings," including a "formal charge, preliminary hearing, indictment, information, or arraignment." *Rothgery v. Gillespie County*, 554 U.S. 191, 198 (2008). Some of these events involve the defendant's appearance before a judicial officer, and other events involve only the participation of a prosecutor. If the Court decides to expand the *Rothgery* list in a future case, an event or procedure that involves neither element is unlikely to qualify as an "adversary judicial proceeding."

Points for Discussion

a. Contrasting "Deliberate Elicitation" with "Interrogation"

Following *Brewer*, the Court emphasized that the "deliberate elicitation" concept is central to the *Massiah* doctrine, and is distinct from *Miranda's* "interrogation" concept. *Brewer* does not compare the two concepts, but *Brewer* was decided before *Innis* established the modern definition of "interrogation." However, *Brewer* explained deliberate elicitation by noting that the detective "purposely sought" to isolate the defendant "from his lawyers to obtain as much incriminating information as possible", and that the detective conceded "as much" at trial. In *Fellers v. United States*, 540 U.S. 519 (2004), the Court justified a finding of deliberate elicitation in simpler terms, noting that when the police officers arrived at the defendant's home, "they informed him that their purpose in coming was to discuss his involvement in the distribution of methamphetamine and his association with certain charged co-conspirators." Therefore, the "ensuing discussion" violated the defendant's right to counsel because it occurred "after he had been indicted, outside the presence of counsel, and in the absence of any waiver of his Sixth Amendment rights".

b. Comparing *Innis* and *Brewer*

Innis emphasized that the concepts of "interrogation" and "deliberate elicitation" are not interchangeable, but then the Court used the *Brewer* facts to shape the definition of "interrogation" in *Innis*. For example, *Innis* states that "this is not a case in which the police carried on a lengthy harangue in the presence of a suspect," that the officers "were not aware that the defendant was peculiarly susceptible to an appeal to his conscience," that the officers' remarks in *Innis* were not "particularly evocative," and that their conversation "was nothing more than a dialogue between the two officers to which no response was invited." Surely not coincidentally, the scenario in *Brewer* presented the "perfect opposite" of *Innis* in these four respects. *Innis* implied that a finding of "interrogation" would have been justified in *Brewer* if the case had been decided on the basis of *Miranda* rather than *Massiah*.

Take Note

The *Massiah* right is more limited than the *Miranda* right because the Sixth Amendment right to counsel is "offense specific." Notably, *Brewer* held that after the defendant's Sixth Amendment right attached at his arraignment on an abduction charge, police violated that right by deliberately eliciting statements from him concerning an uncharged murder. However, in *Texas v. Cobb*, 532 U.S. 162 (2001), the Court interpreted *Massiah* as allowing police to question an indicted defendant about uncharged offenses that are "factually related" to the charged "offense," and imported the definition of "offense" from double jeopardy precedent into *Massiah* doctrine. Compare *Blockburger v. United States*, 284 U.S. 299, 304 (1932). Thus, under *Cobb*, police may question an indicted defendant about any uncharged offense that requires proof of a fact not required by the definition of the charged offense. The *Cobb* dissenters argued that police should be prohibited from deliberately eliciting information about uncharged offenses that are "closely related to" or "inextricably intertwined" with the charged offense. They predicted that the *Cobb* rule would operate to "remove a significant portion" of *Massiah's* protection because prosecutors can so easily "spin out a series of offenses from a single criminal transaction."

Food for Thought

Is *Brewer's* analysis of the Sixth Amendment right to counsel consistent with *Massiah's* analysis? (*Massiah* appears at the end of Part A in this chapter.) Explain the differences you see, as well as the ambiguities and potential similarities of each analysis.

Hypo: *"Deliberate Elicitation" and Comments Not Directed at Defendant*

Suppose that, instead of making the "Christian Burial Speech" to Williams, Detective Leaming and the other officer make a few off-hand remarks to each other. Leaming says, "They are predicting several inches of snow for tonight." The other officer replies, "Yes, and I sure hope that the people who are searching for the victim's body will be able to find it so that she can receive a proper Christian burial." Suddenly, Williams blurts out the location of the body. Would the Court still be inclined to find that Leaming "deliberately elicited" incriminating statements from Brewer? If the case had been decided under *Miranda*, rather than under the Sixth Amendment, would the Court be inclined to find that Leaming's words were "reasonably likely to elicit an incriminating response?" Would it matter if Leaming had also stated the following to the other officer: "I am so afraid that the body of that little girl is out there somewhere in the snow where no one can find her on Christmas Eve, and that her grieving parents will never be able to give her a Christian burial."

> ### Food for Thought
>
> A statute requires a child protective services agency to inform the police department when their investigators have reasonable cause to believe that child sexual abuse has occurred, and also requires them to determine the scope of potential risks to the child when the investigators learn of allegations of child sexual abuse. As part of this process, agency officials conduct interviews with alleged abusers, but are not allowed to ask suspected abusers whether they have been charged with a crime or whether they have counsel. In addition, they do not administer *Miranda* warnings. Should incriminating statements made to agency investigators be inadmissible at an abuser's trial? See *State v. Oliveira*, 961 A.2d 299 (R.I. 2008).

Kuhlmann v. Wilson

477 U.S. 436 (1986).

JUSTICE POWELL announced the judgment of the Court and delivered the opinion of the Court.

Kuhlmann was arraigned on charges of robbery and murder and placed in a cell with Lee, a prisoner who had agreed to act as a police informant. Lee agreed to listen to Kuhlmann's conversations and report his remarks to Detective Cullen, who wished to discover the identities of Kuhlmann's confederates. Cullen told Lee not to ask any questions, but simply to "keep his ears open." Kuhlmann first spoke to Lee about the crimes after he noticed that their cellblock window overlooked the taxi garage where the crimes had occurred. He said, "someone's messing with me," and told Lee the same story about the robbery that he gave the police at the time of his arrest. Lee advised Kuhlmann that his explanation "didn't sound too good," but Kuhlmann did not alter his story immediately. After a few days, Kuhlmann received a visit from his brother, who mentioned that members of his family were upset because they believed that Kuhlmann was guilty of murder. After the visit, Kuhlmann admitted to Lee that he and two other men had planned and carried out the robbery and murder. Lee reported Kuhlmann's statements to Detective Cullen, and gave Cullen the notes that he had written surreptitiously while sharing the cell with Kuhlmann.

The trial court found that Cullen had instructed Lee "to ask no questions of Kuhlmann about the crime but merely to listen as to what Kuhlmann might say in his presence." The court determined that Lee obeyed these instructions, that he "at no time asked any questions with respect to the crime," and that he "only listened to Kuhlmann and made notes regarding what he had to say." The trial court also found that Kuhlmann's statements to Lee were "spontaneous" and "unsolicited."

The primary concern of the *Massiah* precedents is secret interrogation by investigatory techniques that are the equivalent of direct police interrogation. Since "the Sixth Amendment is not violated whenever—by luck or happenstance—the State obtains incriminating statements from the accused after the right to counsel has attached," a defendant does not make out a violation of that right simply by showing that an informant, either through prior arrangement or voluntarily, reported his incriminating statements to the police. *Maine v. Moulton*, 474 U.S. 159, 176 (1985). Rather, defendant must demonstrate that the police and their informant took some action, beyond merely listening, that was designed deliberately to elicit incriminating remarks. Cullen instructed Lee only to listen to Kuhlmann and Lee followed these instructions; "at no time did he ask any questions" of Kuhlmann concerning the pending charges and he "only listened" to Kuhlmann's statements. The only remark made by Lee was his comment that Kuhlmann's initial version of his participation in the crimes "didn't sound too good."

[The Court concluded that based on the state court's findings on the record there was no "deliberate elicitation" by Lee that violated the Sixth Amendment. The Court also noted that the record provided no information concerning the fact that Kuhlmann was placed in a cell overlooking the crime scene.]

JUSTICE BRENNAN, with whom JUSTICE MARSHALL joins, dissenting.

Under *Massiah* it is irrelevant whether the informant asks pointed questions about the crime or "merely engages in general conversation about it." Lee encouraged Kuhlmann to talk about his crime by conversing with him on the subject over the course of several days and by telling him that his exculpatory story would not convince anyone without more work. A disturbing visit from his brother, rather than a conversation with the informant, seems to have been the catalyst for Kuhlmann's confession. But the deliberate-elicitation standard requires consideration of the entire course of government behavior. Here the State intentionally created a situation in which it was foreseeable that Kuhlmann would make incriminating statements without the assistance of counsel—it assigned him to a cell overlooking the scene of the crime and designated a secret informant to be his cellmate. The informant, while avoiding direct questions, nonetheless developed a relationship of cellmate camaraderie with Kuhlmann and encouraged him to talk about his crime. Clearly the State's actions had a sufficient nexus with Kuhlmann's admission of guilt to constitute deliberate elicitation.

After *Massiah*, it was necessary for the Court to define the factors that make an informant a government "agent." The Court held that there must be an agency relationship between the informant and the government, and that such a relationship can be prompted by extensive "police involvement with the informant." Relevant factors can include promises of rewards, requests to obtain incriminating evidence, placement of the informant in a position to obtain such evidence, and initiation of a pre-existing plan to secure it. When a government agent has not "directed or steered" an informant toward the defendant, a court may decide that the informant did not achieve the status of "agent" and was merely "an entrepreneur who hoped to sell information to the government." See *State v. Swinton*, 268 Conn. 781, 847 A.2d 921 (2004). Some courts use a bright line test to define an "agent" which provides that an informant becomes a government agent "only when the informant has been instructed by the police to get information about the particular defendant." Other courts employ a case-by-case approach, requiring only "some evidence that an agreement, express or implied, between the individual and a government official existed at the time the elicitation took place." One court observed that, "To hold otherwise would allow the State to accomplish 'with a wink and a nod' what it cannot do overtly." See *Ayers v. Hudson*, 623 F.3d 301 (6th Cir. 2010).

Points for Discussion

a. When Informant Violates Instructions to "Listen and Don't Ask Questions"

The informant in *Massiah* deliberately elicited information from his co-defendant by "inducing Massiah to enter the informant's car and talk about the case." In later cases, government agents instructed informants "not to question" the target defendant and "not to initiate any conversations" about the charged crime. However, in *United States v. Henry*, 447 U.S. 264 (1980), when a disobedient informant violated these instructions by "stimulating" conversations with the defendant in order to elicit information, the Court found that he had engaged in "deliberate elicitation" that was attributable to the government. *Henry* left open the question whether it would violate *Massiah* for the government to place an informant "in close proximity" to defendant, as long as the informant "makes no effort to stimulate conversations about the crime charged." *Kuhlmann* provided a negative answer to that question.

b. Knowing Exploitation of the Opportunity to Confront the Accused Without Counsel

In *Maine v. Moulton*, 474 U.S. 159 (1985), the informant was a co-defendant who received a proposal from Moulton to meet "to plan their defense." The government supplied the informant with a wire that would transmit conversations to a listening agent. Although instructed "not to question" Moulton, the informant asked Moulton to remind him about the details of the crime, thereby "deliberately eliciting" Moulton's statements. The prosecutor argued that no *Massiah* violation occurred because Moulton proposed the meeting, not the informant. In rejecting that argument, the Court held that the informant's "wired" presence involved a "knowing exploitation by the State of an opportunity to confront the accused without counsel being present," which it equated with the "intentional creation of the opportunity to circumvent the right to counsel." No *Massiah* violation occurs where agents obtain a statement "by luck or happenstance," but the *Moulton* scenario did not fit that category.

c. Continuing Investigations After Indictment

The *Massiah* Court observed that it was "entirely proper to continue investigating the suspected criminal activities of the defendant," so that admissible evidence unrelated to the charged offense might be obtained and used in prosecutions for other crimes. In *Maine v. Moulton*, 474 U.S. 159 (1985), the Court rejected a prosecutor's proposal to restrict *Massiah* by allowing government agents to deliberately elicit statements about a charged offense whenever the government puts forward a "legitimate reason" to do so that goes beyond the simple need to investigate the charged crime. *Moulton* reasoned that it would be too difficult for courts to define the parameters of a "legitimate reason" and predicted that the proposed limitation would invite "abuse by law enforcement personnel in the form of fabricated investigations and would risk the evisceration" of *Massiah* rights.

Take Note

In *Kansas v. Ventris*, 556 U.S. 586 (2009), the Court held that an informant's inadmissible testimony about an indicted defendant's statements could be used to impeach defendant's inconsistent testimony at trial, even though they were obtained in violation of *Massiah*. The Court held that *Massiah* is violated when impermissible deliberate elicitation occurs. *Ventris* concerned "the scope of the remedy for a violation that has already occurred." In the Court's view, the exclusion of *Massiah*-defective statements from the prosecutor's case in chief provides police with a "significant incentive" to comply with *Massiah*. *Ventris* concluded that the mere "speculative possibility" that police might violate *Massiah* in order to uncover impeachment evidence did not "trump the costs of allowing perjurious statements to go unchallenged." The *Ventris* dissenters argued that the "use of ill-gotten evidence during any phase of a criminal prosecution does damage to the adversarial process—the fairness of which the Sixth Amendment was designed to protect." They also emphasized that the admission of *Massiah*-defective evidence at trial was identified explicitly by the *Massiah* Court as a Sixth Amendment harm.

Food for Thought

Kuhlmann emphasized that the informant merely "listened" to the defendant and did not "ask questions" about the crime. Even though the informant did make one potentially evocative remark to the defendant, telling him that his story to the police "didn't sound too good," the Court did not view that comment as significant. What arguments could have been made by the prosecutor in *Kuhlmann* to explain why this remark was not sufficient to constitute "deliberate elicitation"?

Hypo 1 *Developing the Evidence*

Suppose that you are a defense attorney who has been appointed to represent a defendant like Kuhlmann who has made incriminating statements to an informant prisoner in the defendant's cell block. What types of evidence might convince a court to exclude the defendant's statements based on a *Massiah* violation? Explain how you would go about obtaining such evidence.

Hypo 2: *Handing Letter to Officer*

When David was indicted, the police were informed that he had requested and received counsel. However, Detective Flores, who was unaware of David's indictment and of counsel, had David brought to a large open area in the jail. When Detective Flores introduced himself as a police officer, David handed him a folded letter and said, "I've been waiting to talk to somebody." The letter contained incriminating statements which were admitted at David's trial. Did Officer Flores violate *Massiah* by "deliberately eliciting" information from David? *See State v. Maldonado*, 259 S.W.3d 184 (Tex. Crim. App. 2008).

Hypo 3: *Whereabouts of Witness*

Baker, who was charged with assaulting a man who threatened his girlfriend (Jen), was released on bail. Detective Ed thought that Baker might be trying to "hide" Jen from being interviewed by the prosecutor. When Ed went looking for Jen, Ed could not find her but he did find Baker. So he asked Baker, "Do you know the whereabouts of Jen?" Baker replied, "She is out for lunch with friends." Later Detective Ed discovered that Baker was lying and that Jen had taken a trip to Germany. At Baker's trial, Detective

Ed testified about the lie, and the prosecutor urged the jury to infer that Baker's lie showed that he was attempting to conceal the location of a witness, which indicated his "consciousness of guilt." Did Detective Ed violate *Massiah* by "deliberately eliciting" information from Baker when asking the question about the whereabouts of Jen? *See Baker v. State*, 157 Md.App. 600, 853 A.2d 796 (2004).

Patterson v. Illinois

487 U.S. 285 (1988).

JUSTICE WHITE delivered the opinion of the Court.

Patterson was arrested for battery and mob action and was suspected of murder. He was given *Miranda* warnings and he answered questions about the battery and mob action crimes, but denied knowing about the murder. The next day he was indicted for murder, taken from the lockup, and told that because he was now indicted, he was being transferred to another jail. When Patterson started to make incriminating statements, Officer Gresham interrupted him, gave him a *Miranda* form, and read the warnings aloud as Patterson read along with him. Patterson signed a waiver form and made incriminating statements to Gresham; during a later interview with a prosecutor, he received *Miranda* warnings again, waived his rights again, and made further incriminating statements.

Patterson's principal claim is that questioning him without counsel present violated the Sixth Amendment because he did not validly waive his right to have counsel present during the interviews. In the past, this Court has held that a waiver of the Sixth Amendment right to counsel is valid only when it reflects "an intentional relinquishment or abandonment of a known right or privilege." *Johnson v. Zerbst, supra*, at 464. In a case arising under the Fifth Amendment, we described this requirement as "a full awareness of both the nature of the right being abandoned and the consequences of the decision to abandon it." *Moran v. Burbine*, 475 U.S. 412, 421 (1986). Whichever of these formulations is used, the key inquiry in a case such as this one must be: Was the accused, who waived his Sixth Amendment rights during postindictment questioning, made sufficiently aware of his right to have counsel present during the questioning, and of the possible consequences of a decision to forgo the aid of counsel? In this case, we are convinced that by admonishing Patterson with the *Miranda* warnings, the state has met this burden and that petitioner's waiver of his right to counsel at the questioning was valid.

First, the *Miranda* warnings given Patterson made him aware of his right to have counsel present during the questioning. Second, the *Miranda* warnings also served to make Patterson aware of the consequences of a decision by him to waive his Sixth Amendment rights during postindictment questioning. He knew that any statement that he made could be used against him in subsequent criminal proceedings. This is the ultimate adverse consequence petitioner could have suffered by virtue of his choice to make uncounseled admissions to the authorities. This warning also sufficed to let him know what a lawyer could "do for him" during the postindictment questioning: namely, advise petitioner to refrain from making any such statements.

We reject the argument that a waiver of an accused's Sixth Amendment right to counsel should be "more difficult" to effectuate than waiver of a suspect's Fifth Amendment rights. We have never suggested that one right is "superior" or "greater" than the other. Instead, we have taken a more pragmatic approach to the waiver question—asking what purposes a lawyer can serve at the particular stage of the proceedings in question, and what assistance he could provide to an accused at that stage—to determine the scope of the Sixth Amendment right to counsel, and the type of warnings and procedures that should be required before a waiver of that right will be recognized.

Applying this approach, it is our view that whatever warnings suffice for *Miranda*'s purposes will also be sufficient in the context of postindictment questioning. The State's decision to take an additional step and commence formal adversarial proceedings against the accused does not substantially increase the value of counsel to the accused at questioning, or expand the limited purpose that an attorney serves when the accused is questioned by authorities. Because the role of counsel at questioning is relatively simple and limited, we see no problem in having a waiver procedure at that stage which is likewise simple and limited. So long as the accused is made aware of the "dangers and disadvantages of self-representation" during post-indictment questioning by use of the *Miranda* warnings, his waiver of his Sixth Amendment right to counsel at such questioning is "knowing and intelligent."

JUSTICE BLACKMUN, dissenting.

After formal adversary proceedings against a defendant have been commenced, the Sixth Amendment mandates that the defendant not be "subject to further interrogation by the authorities until counsel has been made available to him, unless the accused initiates further communication, exchanges, or conversations with the police." The Sixth Amendment does not allow the prosecution to take undue advantage of any gap between the commencement of the adversary process and the time at which counsel is appointed for a defendant.

JUSTICE STEVENS, with whom JUSTICE BRENNAN and JUSTICE MARSHALL join, dissenting.

To say that the *Miranda* warnings lay a sufficient basis for accepting a waiver of the Sixth Amendment right to counsel because they make clear to an accused that a lawyer could advise him to refrain from making any incriminating statements is a gross understatement of the disadvantage of proceeding without a lawyer and an understatement of what a defendant must understand to give a knowing waiver. The *Miranda* warnings do not inform the accused that a lawyer might examine the indictment for legal sufficiency or that a lawyer is likely to be considerably more skillful at negotiating a plea bargain and that such negotiations may be most fruitful if initiated prior to any interrogation. The warnings do not even go so far as to explain to the accused the nature of the charges pending against him—advice that a court would insist upon before allowing a defendant to enter a guilty plea with or without the presence of an attorney. After indictment the adversary relationship between the state and the accused has solidified, so it inescapably follows that a prosecutor may not conduct private interviews with a charged defendant. Even the *Miranda* warnings themselves are a species of legal advice that is improper when given by the prosecutor or his or her agents, the police after indictment.

Point for Discussion

Request for Appointment of Counsel at Arraignment

In *Montejo v. Louisiana*, 556 U.S. 778 (2009), the Court overruled *Michigan v. Jackson*, 475 U.S. 625 (1986), which held that police officers were prohibited under the Sixth Amendment from initiating an interrogation once a defendant makes a post-adversarial proceeding assertion of his right to counsel. Defendant argued that the Court should extend the *Jackson* rule to a preliminary hearing at which defendant made no explicit request for counsel because under state law counsel was automatically appointed. Instead, the Court determined that *Montejo* illustrated why the *Jackson* rule was unworkable. According to *Montejo, Jackson* was based on an analogy to the *Edwards* prohibition on waiver-seeking after invocation of the Fifth Amendment *Miranda* right to counsel, which prohibition is "designed to prevent police from badgering a defendant into waiving his previously asserted *Miranda* rights." Logically, when a defendant has not requested counsel, he has no need to be protected against "badgering." The Court noted that *Jackson* "is only two decades old," and "eliminating it would not upset expectations." Finally, the Court concluded that the *Jackson* Court did not recognize how "the marginal benefits" of its holding are "dwarfed" by "substantial costs" to the "truth-seeking process and the criminal justice system."

Justice Stevens' *Montejo* dissent, joined by three other justices, illustrates the values that underlie the *Jackson* rule. The dissenters emphasized that *Montejo* "flagrantly misrepresents *Jackson's* underlying rationale," which it described as "to 'protect the unaided layman at critical confrontations with his adversary,' by giving him 'the right to rely on counsel as a "medium" between himself and the State.' *Jackson* concluded that arraigned defendants are entitled to 'at least as much protection' during interrogation as the Fifth Amendment affords unindicted suspects, and *Jackson* is firmly rooted in the unique protections afforded to the attorney-client relationship by the Sixth Amendment." The *Montejo* dissenters would have found that Montejo did not need an extension of the *Jackson* rule because the police officers violated his Sixth Amendment rights by seeking a waiver after counsel was automatically appointed at his preliminary hearing, and the police questioned him "without notice to, and outside the presence of, his lawyer" and "the Sixth Amendment is violated when the State obtains incriminating statements by knowingly circumventing the accused's right to have counsel present in a confrontation between the accused and a state agent." *Maine v. Moulton*, 474 U.S. 159, 176 (1985).

Food for Thought

In *Patterson,* the officer told defendant about his indictment. The Court reserved the question whether "an accused must be told that he has been indicted before a post-indictment Sixth Amendment waiver will be valid," noting that "the desirability of so informing the accused" is "a matter that can be reasonably debated." After *Patterson*, the consensus of lower courts is that the "failure to inform the defendant that he has been charged with the crime with respect to which he is making a statement does not vitiate an otherwise valid *Miranda* warning given at the interview where the statement was made." What arguments can be made on both sides of this issue? See *Johnson v. State*, 851 N.E.2d 372 (Ind.App. 2006).

Hypo: Effect of Warnings

Franco was indicted for murder but was not taken into custody. The next day, Franco retained a lawyer to represent himself, and she advised him not to talk to anyone without her. The lawyer also spoke to the prosecutor and Detective York to inform them of her representation. A few days later, Franco was arrested by Officer Howard who Franco told that he had hired a lawyer, and he placed a phone call to the lawyer. When the lawyer tried calling Franco's cell phone, she got no answer. Then she called the prosecutor, Detective York, and Officer Howard, but she got no answer and none of them returned her calls. In the interim, Officer Howard interrogated Franco after giving him *Miranda* warnings, obtained a waiver, and obtained incriminating statements. Should Franco's statements be regarded as admissible under *Patterson* because he received the *Miranda* warnings? *See State v. Franco*, 133 P.3d 164 (Kan. App. 2006).

Food for Thought

The *Patterson* Court declared that "as a general matter" the *Miranda* warnings will "sufficiently apprise" a person of Sixth Amendment rights. But the Court also observed that there will be cases where a valid *Miranda* waiver "will not suffice for Sixth Amendment purposes" because "the Sixth Amendment's protection of the attorney-client relationship extends beyond *Miranda's* protection of the right to counsel." What scenarios may fit this category of cases?

E. Post-*Miranda* Due Process Law

In the post-*Miranda* era, defendants continue to challenge their confessions based on police violations of Due Process. For those defendants who do not have viable *Miranda* or *Massiah* claims, a Due Process claim may be the only basis for arguing that their statements to police are inadmissible at trial. These defendants may lack *Miranda* arguments when they waive their rights, when they confess while not in "custody," when they are interrogated by secret agents, and when they face impeachment on the stand with *Miranda*-defective statements. Even defendants who qualify for *Massiah* rights may lose them through waivers provided to police interrogators. The Court's modern Due Process precedents continues to rely on a "totality" test, which now incorporates the factor of police compliance with *Miranda*. As in the pre-*Miranda* era, the Court remains divided about the meaning of coercion and about the appropriate interpretation of the "involuntariness" standard.

Mincey v. Arizona

437 U.S. 385 (1978).

MR. JUSTICE STEWART delivered the opinion of the Court.

Mincey was wounded during an exchange of fire with officers entering his house to arrest him for narcotics crimes; he was taken to the hospital and treated in intensive care. An officer died in the shootout, and that evening, Detective Hust came to interrogate Mincey about the shooting. Hust gave *Miranda* warnings to Mincey and told him that he was under arrest. Mincey could not talk because of the tube in his mouth, and so he wrote out his answers to Hust's questions. The interrogation lasted until almost midnight, and Hust repeatedly violated *Miranda* by ignoring Mincey's repeated invocations of the right to counsel. However, Mincey took the stand at his murder trial, and so his *Miranda*-defective statements could be used to impeach his testimony under *Harris*. Mincey's statements were admitted and he was convicted, despite his counsel's argument that his hospital statements were inadmissible for impeachment purposes because they were involuntary under Due Process standards.

If Mincey's statements were not "product of a rational intellect and a free will," his conviction cannot stand. This Court is under a duty to make an independent evaluation of the record. Mincey had been seriously wounded and had arrived at the hospital "depressed almost to the point of coma," according to his physician. He complained to Detective Hust that the pain in his leg was "unbearable." He was evidently confused and unable to think clearly because some of his written answers were not entirely coherent. Finally, while Mincey was being questioned he was lying on his back on a hospital bed, encumbered by tubes, needles, and breathing apparatus. He was at "the complete mercy" of Detective Hust, unable to escape or resist the thrust of Hust's interrogations. In this debilitated and helpless condition, Mincey clearly expressed his wish not to be interrogated. As soon as Hust's questions turned to the details of the afternoon's events, Mincey wrote: "This is all I can say without a lawyer." Hust nonetheless continued to question him, and a nurse who was present suggested it would be best if Mincey answered. Hust ignored Mincey's second request for a lawyer and his third request made immediately thereafter. But despite Mincey's entreaties to be let alone, Hust ceased the interrogation only during intervals when Mincey lost consciousness or received medical treatment, and after each such interruption returned relentlessly to his task.

There were not present in this case some of the gross abuses that have led the Court in other cases to find confessions involuntary, such as beatings, or "truth serums." But "the blood of the accused is not the only hallmark of an unconstitutional inquisition." It is apparent from the record that Mincey's statements were involuntary. Mincey was weakened by pain and shock, isolated from family, friends, and legal counsel, and barely conscious, and his will was simply overborne. Due process of law requires that statements obtained as these were cannot be used in any way against a defendant at his trial.

Mr. Justice Rehnquist dissenting in part:

The Court ignores entirely some evidence of voluntariness. Mincey's nurse "testified that she had not given Mincey any medication and that he was alert and able to understand the officer's questions. She said that Mincey was in moderate pain but was very cooperative with everyone. The interrogating officer testified that Mincey did not appear to be under the influence of drugs and that his answers were generally responsive to the questions." While the interviews took place over a three-hour time span, they were not "very long; probably not more than an hour total for everything." Hust would leave the room whenever Mincey received medical treatment "or if it looked like he was getting a little bit exhausted." According to Hust, Mincey never "lost consciousness at any time." It was the testimony of both Detective Hust and Nurse Graham "that neither mental or physical force nor abuse was used on Mincey. Nor were any promises made." Mincey did not claim that he felt compelled by Detective Hust to answer the questions propounded. The trial court was entitled to conclude that notwithstanding Mincey's medical condition, his statements were admissible.

Colorado v. Connelly

479 U.S. 157 (1986).

CHIEF JUSTICE REHNQUIST delivered the opinion of the Court.

Connelly approached an officer in Denver and said without prompting that he had killed someone. The officer gave him *Miranda* warnings, and Connelly said he understood his rights and wanted to talk. In response to the officer's questions, Connelly denied that he had been taking drugs or drinking, but mentioned that he had been a patient in several mental hospitals. He told the officer he wanted to talk because his conscience had been bothering him. A detective gave *Miranda* warnings to Connelly again, and then asked him "what he had on his mind." Connelly told the officers that he killed a woman in November 1982 and he took the officers to the location of the killing. The officers did not perceive that Connelly was suffering from mental illness when he confessed. But after Connelly was held overnight, he became disoriented during an interview with the public defender the next morning and explained that "God's voice" told him to go to Denver and either confess to the murder or commit suicide. Experts at Connelly's preliminary hearing testified that he was suffering from chronic schizophrenia and was in a psychotic state at least as of the day before he confessed. Connelly argued that he did not confess voluntarily of his own "free will" but his confession was admitted at his trial and he was convicted of murder.

The Due Process cases since *Brown* have focused upon the crucial element of police overreaching. Absent police conduct causally related to the confession, there is simply no basis for concluding that any state actor has deprived a criminal defendant of due process of law. We do not agree that a defendant's mental condition, by itself and apart from its relation to official coercion, should ever dispose of the inquiry into constitutional "voluntariness." Connelly relies on *Blackburn v. Alabama*, 361 U.S. 199 (1960), and *Townsend v. Sain*, 372 U.S. 293 (1963), for the proposition that the "deficient mental condition of the defendants in those cases was sufficient to render their confessions involuntary." In *Blackburn*, the Court found that the petitioner was probably insane at the time of his confession and the police learned during the interrogation that he had a history of mental problems. The police exploited this weakness with coercive tactics and these tactics supported a finding that the confession was involuntary. *Townsend* presented a similar instance of police wrongdoing. In that case, a police physician had given Townsend a drug with truth-serum properties. These two cases demonstrate that while mental condition is surely relevant to an individual's susceptibility to police coercion, mere examination of the confessant's state of mind can never conclude the due process inquiry. The purpose of excluding evidence seized in violation of the Constitution is to substantially deter future violations of the Constitution. Only if we were to establish a brand new constitutional right—the right of a criminal defendant to confess to his crime only when totally rational and properly motivated—could respondent's present claim be sustained. We hold that coercive police activity is a necessary predicate to the finding that a confession is not "voluntary" within the meaning of the Due Process Clause of the Fourteenth Amendment. We also conclude that the taking of respondent's statements, and their admission into evidence, constitute no violation of that Clause.

JUSTICE BRENNAN, with whom JUSTICE MARSHALL joins, dissenting.

The Court's failure to recognize all forms of involuntariness or coercion as antithetical to due process reflects a refusal to acknowledge free will as a value of constitutional consequence. While police overreaching has been an element of every confession case to date, the Court has made clear that ensuring that a confession is a product of free will is an independent concern in our Due Process cases. No physical evidence links the defendant to the alleged crime. Police did not identify the alleged victim's body as the woman named by the defendant. Mr. Connelly identified the alleged scene of the crime, but it has not been verified that the unidentified body was found there or that a crime actually occurred there. There is not a shred of competent evidence in this record linking the defendant to the charged homicide. There is only Mr. Connelly's confession. Minimum standards of due process should require that the trial court find substantial indicia of reliability, on the basis of evidence extrinsic to the confession itself, before admitting the confession of a mentally ill person into evidence. To hold otherwise allows the State to imprison and possibly to execute a mentally ill defendant based solely upon an inherently unreliable confession. The dissent also noted that the officer and the detective were both aware of Connelly's five hospitalizations in mental institutions and this should be sufficient knowledge about Connelly's mental incapacity to render it "involuntary."

Arizona v. Fulminante

499 U.S. 279 (1991).

JUSTICE WHITE delivered the opinion of the Court.

Fulminante was serving a sentence for a firearms crime, and Sarivola was serving a short sentence for extortion, when they became friends and "came to spend several hours a day together" in a federal prison in New York. Sarivola was a former police officer with organized crime experience in loansharking, and as a paid informant for the FBI he was "masquerading" in prison as an organized crime figure. When he asked Fulminante about a prison rumor that Fulminante had killed a child in Arizona, Fulminante repeatedly denied the allegation. When Sarivola passed this information to an FBI agent, he was instructed to "find out more." Sarivola learned more one evening as he and Fulminante walked together around the prison track. Sarivola said that he knew Fulminante was "starting to get some tough treatment and whatnot" from other inmates because of the rumor. Sarivola offered to protect Fulminante from his fellow inmates, but told him, "You have to tell me about it,' you know. I mean, in other words, 'For me to give you any help." Fulminante then made incriminating statements to Sarivola, which were admitted at Fulminante's murder trial; Fulminante was convicted, and argued on appeal that his statements were involuntary under Due Process standards.

In applying the totality of the circumstances test to determine that the confession to Sarivola was coerced, the state supreme court focused on a number of relevant facts. First, the court noted that "because Fulminante was an alleged child murderer, he was in danger of physical harm at the hands of other inmates." Using his knowledge of these threats of receiving "rough treatment from the guys", Sarivola offered to protect Fulminante in exchange for a confession to the crime, and "in response to Sarivola's offer of protection, Fulminante confessed." The state court declared: "The confession was obtained as a direct result of extreme coercion and was tendered in the belief that the defendant's life was in jeopardy if he did not confess. This is a true coerced confession in every sense of the word." The Court noted that Fulminante dropped out of school in the fourth grade, that he is short in stature and slight of build, that he requested protective custody when he was in prison in his mid-twenties, and that he was once admitted to a psychiatric hospital in prison because he was unable to cope with the isolation. We normally give great deference to the factual findings of the state court and we agree that Fulminante's confession was coerced. A finding of coercion need not depend upon actual violence by a government agent; a credible threat is sufficient. "Coercion can be mental as well as physical, and the blood of the accused is not the only hallmark of an unconstitutional inquisition." *Blackburn v. Alabama,* 361 U.S. 199, 206 (1960). As in *Payne v. Arkansas,* 356 U.S. 560 (1958), where the Court found that a confession was coerced because the interrogating police officer had promised that if the accused confessed, the officer would protect the accused from an angry mob outside the jailhouse door, so too here, it was fear of physical violence, absent protection from his friend (and Government agent) Sarivola, which motivated Fulminante to confess. Given the credible threat of physical violence, we agree that Fulminante's will was overborne in such a way as to render his confession the product of coercion.

The dissenting opinion of CHIEF JUSTICE REHNQUIST, with whom JUSTICES O'CONNOR, KENNEDY, and SOUTER join:

Fulminante was no stranger to the criminal justice system: He had six prior felony convictions and had been imprisoned on three prior occasions. I am at a loss to see how the state supreme court found the confession involuntary. Since Fulminante was unaware that Sarivola was an FBI informant, there existed none of "the danger of coercion resulting from the interaction of custody and official interrogation." The conversations between Sarivola and Fulminante were not lengthy, and the defendant was free at all times to leave Sarivola's company. Sarivola at no time threatened him or demanded that he confess; he simply requested that he speak the truth about the matter. Fulminante was an experienced habitué of prisons, and presumably able to fend for himself. In concluding on these facts that Fulminante's confession was involuntary, the Court today embraces a more expansive definition of that term than is warranted by any of our decided cases.

Practice Pointer

Before *Miranda*, some states allowed a jury to determine the "voluntariness" of a confession at trial, but the Court invalidated this procedure in *Jackson v. Denno*, 378 U.S. 368 (1964). The Court held that a pre-trial judicial hearing is required to determine voluntariness because a jury cannot be expected to produce a fair and reliable finding on this question during the trial on the issue of guilt. The prosecutor bears the burden of proving that a confession does not violate Due Process by a preponderance of the evidence. *See Lego v. Twomey*, 404 U.S. 477 (1972).

Take Note

If a confession is admitted at trial, and is later held to be unconstitutional under Due Process standards, its admission may be found to be harmless error only if the prosecution shows that it was harmless beyond a reasonable doubt.

Point for Discussion

Harmless Error

Fulminante held that the admission of the defendant's confession made to an undercover agent was not harmless in that case; the Court also advised judges to "exercise extreme caution" before finding that the admission of a confession was harmless error, given "the risk that a given confession is unreliable, coupled with the profound impact that the confession has upon the jury."

Food for Thought

Assume that you are a legal adviser to the local police department. The police chief wants to know whether, in light of the Court's Due Process decisions, police interrogators may continue to use the "Mutt and Jeff" technique described in the *Miranda* opinion. Consider the pro and con arguments that may be made, and explain the advice that you will provide.

Hypo 1: *"You're Going Home"*

Brown went voluntarily to the police station to be interviewed by detectives regarding an assault crime. After a few minutes, Brown denied involvement, but asked the detectives, "But if I were involved, then what would the consequences be?" One detective replied: "I'm not going to sit here and tell you what a judge is going to do, and I can't tell you what the penalties are. I can't promise you anything or tell you anything. What I can tell you is that, no matter what you tell me or say to me, you're going home. If you tell me the assault happened, I'm not going to place you in handcuffs and arrest you. You're going home today." At this point, the other detective stated, "If you killed somebody, then you're not going home." When Brown looked startled, the detective said, "But no one has died. Just ignore me." During the next 40 minutes, both officers sought to persuade Brown to admit involvement. Finally, when Brown did make incriminating statements, one detective said, "Well, I hope you realize that I can't let you leave after what you just told us." Brown replied, "Yes, I know. And I'm in big trouble." Did the officers violate Brown's right to Due Process during the interrogation? *Compare Brown v. State*, 290 Ga. 865, 725 S.E.2d 320 (2012).

Food for Thought

To what extent should a suspect's vulnerabilities enter into the analysis? Suppose that an arrestee suffers from alcohol withdrawal and mental health problems. Would it be inappropriate for the questioning officer to focus on emotionally provocative topics and to ask leading questions? *See State v. Hoppe*, 661 N.W.2d 407 (Wis. 2003). What if the suspect has an IQ of 65. Suppose that the police ask leading questions that, while not technically coercive, require "yes" or "no" answers, all of which assume the defendant's guilt. Because of the suspect's limited intelligence, he does not challenge the fairness of the questions. *See United States v. Preston*, 2014 WL 18762669 (9th Cir.).

Hypo 2: *Lengthy Interrogations*

Now, let's think about how the courts might apply the due process test today. In which of the following situations would you conclude that police interrogation has violated the due process clause?

A. A 17 year old (Doody) is bought in for questioning on a homicide charge, is read a *Miranda* warning, and agrees to speak to the police. It is 9:00 p.m. at night and the police question Doody until 10:00 a.m. the next morning. During this time, the police repeatedly tell Doody that he "must" answer their questions, and that the questioning will continue until "we get some answers." *See Doody v. Schriro,* 548 F.3d 847 (9th Cir. 2008); vacated sub. nom. Doody v. Ryan, 562 U.S. 956 (2010), remanded sub. nom. *Doody v. Ryan,* 649 F.3d 986 (9th Cir. 2011); see also *Moore v. State,* 30 A.3d 945 (Md. App. 2011).

B. In the prior problem, suppose that the police did not tell Doody that he "must" respond, or that he would be forced to stay until "we get some answers," but they keep him at the police station for 55 hours. He is not continuously questioned, and has access to his father. At the end of the 55 hours, when he is not being questioned, he volunteers the fact that he committed the homicide. *See Carter v. Thompson,* 690 F.3d 837 (7th Cir. 2012).

Hypo 3: *Due Process and Threats*

Now, let's think about how the due process test might apply when the police make threats against a suspect. In all situations, assume that the suspect has waived his *Miranda* rights. Consider the following situations and decide whether there is a due process violation:

A. Police are interrogating a man regarding possible sexual molestation of his children. At one point, the police tell the man that they will seek a court order removing the children from the home unless he agrees to cooperate with them. At that point, the man makes incriminating statements. *See Stanton v. Commonwealth,* 349 S.W.3d 914 (Ky. 2011).

B. Suppose that the police arrange a fake lineup (the "witness" is actually a police officer) at which the witness "identifies" the suspect as the perpetrator of the crime, and then the suspect makes incriminating statements. *See State v. Patton,* 826 A.2d 783 (N.J. Super. 2003); *Whittington v. State,* 809 A.2d 721 (Md. App. 2002).

C. Suppose that a baby was badly injured under suspicious circumstances and would probably die. The father is in custody and the mother is at the child's bedside. When the man refuses to talk to the police, the police state that they intend to arrest the wife and bring her to the station for questioning. At that point, the man makes incriminating statements. *See People v. Thomas*, 985 N.Y.S.2d 193, 8 N.E.3d 308 (N.Y. App. 2014).

D. Suppose that Bond, who is black, is being questioned regarding a possible homicide. He makes incriminating statements after the questioning officer urges Bond not to subject himself to the "racist whims" of a rural jury pool composed of "white people, Hispanic people, and others not from your part of the hood." *See Bond v. State*, 9 N.E. 3d 134 (Ind. 2014).

E. A man is being investigated for sexual assault. During the interrogation, the man makes incriminating statements after he is told that he will likely be deported from the U.S. if he does not tell the truth. *See People v. Ramadon*, 314 P.3d 836 (Colo. 2013).

Hypo 4: *Due Process, Promises and Representations*

Which of the following statements would constitute due process violations (assume, again, that *Miranda* warnings were given and rights were waived) if the suspect makes incriminating statements:

A. Suppose that the police suggest that the district attorney might "go lighter" in terms of punishment recommendations if a suspect "comes clean." *Harper v. State*, 722 So.2d 1267 (Miss. App. 1998); *State v. Polk*, 812 N.W.2d 670 (Iowa 2012).

B. Suppose that a man is being investigated for child sexual abuse. During the interrogation, the police tell the man that the victim's family doesn't want to "get him in trouble. They just want an apology." When the man does confess, and gives a letter of apology, the police seek to use both as evidence against him. *See Hill v. State*, 12 A.3d 1193 (Md. 2011).

C. An officer tells a suspect about some of the charges that will be brought against him, but refuses to detail all of them unless the suspect "comes clean." *See State v. Pyles*, 90 A.3d 1228 (N.H. 2014).

D. Before a suspect makes incriminating statements, the police conceal the fact that the a warrant has been issued for his arrest, and assure him that he is not a "target" of their investigation. *See United States v. Boskic*, 545 F.3d 69 (1st Cir. 2008).

E. *Promises Regarding Girlfriend.* During an interrogation, it becomes clear that a suspect is deeply concerned about the possible consequences to his girlfriend who was an accomplice to the crime. As a result, the police make a number of references to her during the subsequent interrogation. For example, they suggest that they don't need to dig deeper once they have nailed the culprit, and that these charges could be very disruptive to her life. Defendant makes incriminating statements thinking that he will gain a benefit for his girlfriend. However, the police make it clear that they are not empowered to make any deals regarding her, but the suspect seems convinced that his incriminating statements will help her get off. If the suspect makes incriminating statements, should they be regarded as coerced? *See United States v. Hufstetler*, 782 F.3d 19 (1st Cir. 2015).

F. *Promises of Leniency.* During an interrogation, a police officer tells a suspect that "if he tells the truth and is honest, we are not going to charge you with anything. You'll have your life, maybe you'll go into the Marines ... and you'll chalk this up to a very scary time in your life." Perez then states that he has "some information," and he then confesses his involvement in a robbery during which Perez's accomplice killed the victim. Do the promises of leniency render the confession involuntary? What if the police promise a homeless woman leniency and also tell her that it will help her and her children find housing? *See People v. Perez*, 243 Cal.App.4th 863, 196 Cal.Rptr.3d 871 (2016); *Sharp v. Rohling*, 793 F.3d 1216 (10th Cir. 2015).

Executive Summary

The Due Process Test. In 1936, the Court recognized the Due Process Clause of the Fourteenth Amendment as a source for standards governing the admissibility of confessions in state courts; the same analysis came to be used for the Fifth Amendment Due Process standards applied in federal courts. The seminal case is *Brown v. Mississippi*, 297 U.S. 278 (1936), in which defendants were hung by their necks and beaten until they confessed. The Court found a due process violation: "It would be difficult to conceive of methods more revolting to the sense of justice than those taken to procure the confessions of these defendants, and the use of the confessions thus obtained as the basis for conviction and sentence was a clear denial of due process."

Due Process Standards. The vocabulary, and rules of evidence, came to be incorporated into Due Process law, as illustrated by the requirements that only "voluntary" confessions are admissible, produced by the "free will" of the defendant, rather than police "coercion" that includes inducements, threats, or deceptive stratagems.

From *Brown* to *Miranda*. During the thirty years between *Brown* and *Miranda*, the Court relied on Due Process doctrine to invalidate confessions in more than twenty cases, while upholding confessions in less than half that number. Most of these decisions reveal sharp disagreements among the justices concerning the interpretation of the "voluntariness" concept. Over time, the Court expanded this concept to encompass various types of psychologically coercive interrogation strategies, and came to focus upon the customs of *incommunicado* police questioning as the ultimate source of the coercion problem.

Defendant's Attributes. The Court's Due Process precedents often relied on the defendant's special vulnerability to police coercion, based on physical and mental attributes and life experiences.

Dissatisfaction with the Due Process Voluntariness Test. A number of justices were dissatisfied with the Due Process voluntariness test

Major Themes

a. The Search for a Panacea—For nearly a century, the courts have struggled with how to ensure that confessions are voluntary rather than coerced. In attempting to deal with these problems, courts have used various approaches for protecting suspects, including the Due Process voluntariness test, the *McNabb-Mallory* rule, the Sixth Amendment right to counsel, and the Fifth Amendment privilege against self-incrimination.

b. Modern Approaches—While none of the Court's approaches have been entirely satisfactory, the courts continue to regularly use all of the approaches except for the *McNabb-Mallory* test. Thus, courts will sometimes reject confessions under Due Process, under the Sixth Amendment right to counsel, and under the Fifth Amendment privilege against self-incrimination.

c. Differing Approaches—The various approaches have differing requirements. For example, for due process analysis, the focus is on whether a confession was "voluntary" or "coerced." Due process concerns can arise at any point in the criminal process. By contrast, the Fifth Amendment privilege against self-incrimination (as reflected in *Miranda*) focuses on whether a suspect who is being subjected to "custodial interrogation" has been given a *Miranda* warning, and whether the suspect validly waived his rights. The Sixth Amendment right to counsel only applies once adversarial proceedings have commenced, and focuses on whether defendant was provided with, or waived, counsel.

because it failed to provide clear, predictable, and uniform guidelines regarding the boundaries of acceptable police conduct during interrogations. Moreover, the difficulties of defining "voluntariness" were magnified, as one justice observed, because "the trial on the issue of coercion is seldom helpful," as police "usually testify one way, the accused another," and the secrecy of interrogations gives defendants "little chance to prove coercion at trial." *Crooker v. California*, 357 U.S. 433 (1958) (Douglas, J., dissenting).

The *McNabb-Mallory* Rule. During the post-*Brown* era, the Court supplemented the Due Process doctrine with the *McNabb-Mallory* rule that applied only in the federal courts. The Court repeatedly rejected the argument that this rule should be incorporated into Due Process doctrine and applied to the states, but some state courts chose to incorporate the rule into their own state law on their own. *McNabb* and *Mallory* rested on the Supreme Court's supervisory authority over the federal courts. In *McNabb v. United States*, 318 U.S. 332 (1943), the Court created an exclusionary rule to enforce the command of 18 U.S.C. § 595, which requires that a federal officer who arrests any person must "take the defendant before the nearest judicial officer having jurisdiction for a hearing, commitment, or taking bail for trial." *McNabb-Mallory* was partially overruled by congressional enactment.

The Sixth Amendment Right to Counsel. In *Massiah v. United States*, 377 U.S. 201 (1964), the Court applied the Sixth Amendment right to counsel to exclude a confession. The confession was extracted by surreptitious means from a defendant who had been indicted. Ater *Massiah*, the Court extended the right to counsel to arrestees who were not yet indicted. In *Escobedo v. Illinois*, 378 U.S. 478 (1964), the Court held that the police violated the Sixth Amendment because the police investigation had "begun to focus on" the defendant in custody as "a particular suspect," the police had not "effectively warned" the defendant of "the right to remain silent," the defendant had "requested and been denied an opportunity to consult with his lawyer," and the police had elicited incriminating statements from him during questioning. While *Massiah* remains good law today, *Escobedo* is no longer good law.

The Fifth Amendment and *Miranda*. In the Court's landmark decision in *Miranda v. Arizona*, 384 U.S. 436 (1966), the Court began applying the Fifth Amendment privilege to interrogations. Historically, the privilege had been applied at trial, but had not been applied to stationhouse interrogations. The Court expressed concern that police manuals suggested sophisticated tactics for evoking confessions from defendants, and provided the prophylactic remedy of requiring the police to give suspects the *Miranda* warning: "He must be warned prior to any questioning that he has the right to remain silent, that anything he says can be used against him in a court of law, that he has the right to the presence of an attorney, and that if he cannot afford an attorney one will be appointed for him prior to any questioning if he so desires." The right to counsel is a Fifth Amendment (rather than a Sixth Amendment) right to counsel. In other words, the right is imposed in order to protect the individual against compelled self-incrimination.

Miranda Applies to Custodial Interrogations. *Miranda* does not apply to all interrogations, but only to "custodial interrogations." "Custody" is something more than a mere seizure (when a reasonable person would not feel free to leave) and is more akin to an arrest. "Interrogation" involves either explicit questioning or its functional equivalent (questioning that is reasonably likely to elicit an incriminating response.)

Miranda Procedures. Once the warnings have been given, if the individual indicates, prior to or during questioning, that he wishes to remain silent, the interrogation must cease. If the individual states that he wants an attorney, the interrogation must cease until an attorney is present. If the individual cannot obtain an attorney and he indicates that he wants one before speaking to police, they must respect his decision to remain silent. If the interrogation continues without the presence of an attorney and a statement is taken, a heavy burden rests on the government to demonstrate that the defendant knowingly and intelligently waived his privilege against self-incrimination and his right to retained or appointed counsel.

Public Safety Exception. In *New York v. Quarles*, 467 U.S. 649 (1984), the Court held that police officers may sometimes withhold the *Miranda* warnings until after they ask an arrestee questions that are "necessary to secure their own safety or the safety of the public." The exception has remained relatively undefined and unapplied.

Routine Booking Question Exception. The *Miranda* Court observed that police questions that are "normally attendant to arrest and custody" do not qualify as "interrogation." In *Pennsylvania v. Muniz*, 496 U.S. 582 (1990), the Court noted that "routine booking questions" typically are asked to secure "the biographical data necessary to complete booking or pretrial services," and held that an intoxicated driver could be asked booking questions about his or her "name, address, height, weight, eye color, date of birth, and current age." The government conceded that a sixth question for the driver was not a "routine booking question": "Do you know what the date was of your sixth birthday?" The Court concluded that this question violated the Fifth Amendment because it called for a "testimonial response": it called for defendant to "explicitly or implicitly relate a factual assertion or disclose information," and make mental calculations that revealed his level of intoxication and it therefore subjected defendant to the "cruel trilemma" of "self-accusation, perjury, or contempt."

The Adequacy of *Miranda* Warnings. The *Miranda* warnings must "reasonably convey" the substance of the mandated warning. Warnings may be inadequate if they are incomplete or provide misleading information about a suspect's rights. Warnings can also be inadequate if they are "non-functional" in that the police fail to warn at the outset of an interrogation, and then deliver "midstream" warnings and continue the interrogation. If a court determines that the *Miranda* warnings were inadequate, then post-warning incriminating statements will be inadmissible. Thus, a claim that warnings were "inadequate" is distinct from a claim that an invalid waiver was obtained after adequate warnings were provided.

Waivers of *Miranda* Rights. The prosecution has the burden of proving that *Miranda* rights have been waived. The waiver inquiry "has two distinct dimensions": the waiver must be "voluntary in the sense that it was the product of a free and deliberate choice rather than intimidation, coercion, or deception," and must be "made with a full awareness of both the nature of the right being abandoned and the consequences of the decision to abandon it." A waiver will not be presumed from silence. However, waivers do not have to be formal or express. Even if a suspect neither invokes nor waives his rights, and is largely silent, he can implicitly waive his rights through limited responses such as nodding his head. However, the prosecution must still establish that the suspect understood his rights. The prosecution need not inform the suspect of the topics about which he/she will be questioned.

Police Conduct Following Invocation of Rights. If a suspect invokes either the right to remain silent, or the right to counsel, all questioning must cease. However, if a suspect makes a reference to an attorney that is ambiguous or equivocal, so that a reasonable officer in light of the circumstances would have understood only that the suspect might be invoking the right to counsel, the police need not terminate questioning. The suspect must unambiguously request counsel.

Waiver-Seeking After Invocation. The court has held that, once an individual invokes his right to remain silent, that invocation does not preclude all future questioning. In one case, after the police respected the suspect's invocation of rights, another police officer came to the suspect's cell a few hours later and gave a new warning. The Court held that the subsequent waiver was valid. However, when an individual invokes the right to counsel, the police may not seek a further waiver unless the suspect initiates the conversation. However, in *Maryland v. Shatzer*, 559 U.S. 98 (2010), the Court held that after a person in custody invokes the right to counsel, the prohibition on waiver-seeking will expire 14 days after the person's release from custody.

Post-*Miranda* Sixth Amendment Law. For more than a decade after *Miranda*, the Court did not decide a confession case on Sixth Amendment grounds, and did not address questions relating to the relationship between the *Miranda* and *Massiah* rights to counsel. However, in *Brewer v. Williams*, 430 U.S. 387 (1977), the Court made it clear that the Sixth Amendment right to counsel continues to apply to interrogations, but only after adversarial proceedings have commenced. In *Brewer*, the Court concluded that the police had "deliberately elicited" a confession from a suspect.

Attachment of the Sixth Amendment Right to Counsel. The Court has identified a short list of events that qualify as "adversary judicial criminal proceedings," including a "formal charge, preliminary hearing, indictment, information, or arraignment." *Rothgery v. Gillespie County*, 554 U.S. 191, 198 (2008). Some of these events involve the defendant's appearance before a judicial officer, and other events involve only the participation of a prosecutor.

Sixth Amendment Right to Counsel Is "Offense Specific." In *Texas v. Cobb*, 532 U.S. 162 (2001), the Court interpreted *Massiah* as allowing police to question an indicted defendant about uncharged offenses that are "factually related" to the charged "offense," and imported the definition of "offense" from double jeopardy precedent into *Massiah* doctrine. Thus, under *Cobb*, police may question an indicted defendant about any uncharged offense that requires proof of a fact not required by the definition of the charged offense.

Post-*Miranda* Due Process Law. In the post-*Miranda* era, defendants continue to challenge their confessions based on police violations of Due Process; for those defendants who do not have viable *Miranda* or *Massiah* claims, a Due Process claim may be the only basis for arguing that their statements to police are inadmissible at trial. These defendants lack *Miranda* arguments if they confess while not in "custody," when they are interrogated by secret agents, and when they face impeachment on the stand with *Miranda*-defective statements. Even defendants who qualify for *Massiah* rights may lose them through waivers provided to police interrogators. The Court's modern Due Process precedents continue to rely on a "totality" test, which now incorporates the factor of police compliance with *Miranda*. As in the pre-*Miranda* era, the Court remains divided about the meaning of coercion and about the appropriate interpretation of the "voluntariness" standard.

Test Your Knowledge

To assess your understanding of the material in this chapter, click here to take a quiz.

For More Information

• MARK E. CAMMACK & NORMAN M. GARLAND, ADVANCED CRIMINAL PROCEDURE (2006).

• WAYNE R. LAFAVE, JEROLD H. ISRAEL, NANCY J. KING & ORIN S. KERR, CRIMINAL PROCEDURE (5th ed. 2009).

• JEROLD H. ISRAEL & WAYNE R. LAFAVE, CRIMINAL PROCEDURE: CONSTITUTIONAL LIMITATIONS (8th ed. 2006).

• RUSSELL L. WEAVER, JOHN M. BURKOFF, CATHERINE HANCOCK & STEVEN I. FRIEDLAND, PRINCIPLES OF CRIMINAL PROCEDURE Ch. 5 (6th ed. 2018).

CHAPTER 7

Identification Procedures

A. The Nature and Constitutional Implications of Identification Processes

Eyewitness identification may be a particularly potent form of evidence in a criminal proceeding. Inherent in such evidentiary methods, however, are significant reliability risks. Accurate identification depends upon perception and recall that are free of distortion. A multiplicity of factors, individually or collectively, may operate under a given set of circumstances to impair either process. The ability to perceive may be skewed by physical realities such as distance, observation time, light and the field or content of activity. Stereotypes and cultural assumptions also may interfere with perceptual acuity. Even accurate perception may be undermined by suggestive questioning, faded memory and mental tendencies to convert assumption or expectation into reality.

Make the Connection

Like searches, seizures and custodial interrogation, identification procedures constitute a basic methodology for building a criminal case. Compulsory generation of an identifying characteristic, such as a writing exemplar, voice sample or fingerprint, could be understood as a seizure or self-incrimination. However, case law establishes that unlike searches and seizures, identification processes are not governed by the Fourth Amendment. Nor do they implicate the Fifth Amendment guarantee against self-incrimination.

1. The Problem: The Unreliability of Eyewitness Identification

Many believe "that the human brain operates more or less as a mechanical recording device" so that individuals record their memories as if "on a memory tape." Frederic D. Woocher—Note, Did Your Eyes Deceive You? Expert Psychological Testimony on the Unreliability of Eyewitness Identification. *29 Stan. L. Rev. 969, 971–89 (1977)*. Under this view, when a person wishes to recall a memory, he/she "simply selects the appropriate memory tape and plays it back, producing a faithful recounting of the original perception." *Id.* In fact, memory does not function in that way at all. When people perceive events, they frequently pay attention to only a limited number of environmental stimuli. Even as to those stimuli that they actually observe, "or pay attention to," "the representation of an event stored in memory undergoes constant change; some details are added or altered unconsciously to conform the original memory representation to new information about the event, while others simply are forgotten." *Id.* Likewise, there can be distortion when a memory is retrieved.

Part of the problem stems from the fact that individuals can only perceive a limited number of stimuli at any one time, and therefore they develop "unconscious strategies to aid in the selectivity of perceptual processes and ultimately to concentrate attention on the most necessary and useful details." *Id.* However, these "perceptual shortcuts and strategies," while generally useful and effective in daily life, can "lead to inaccurate perceptions when the eye must make the fine distinctions necessary to observe and recognize faces accurately." *Id.* In most cases, individuals are not aware of these shortcuts or the fact that they create perceptual inaccuracies. The net effect is that even trained observers have difficulty recounting the physical characteristics of individuals that they encounter. Lay witnesses have even more difficulty, and frequently cannot be precise in their recollections of faces.

Witnesses can also be imprecise in their estimates of how much time passed during a sudden event, such as a crime. When individuals are involved in "sudden action-packed events such as crimes, people almost always overestimate the length of time involved because the flurry of activity leads them to conclude that a significant amount of time has passed." *Id.* Time simply elapses more slowly "when the observer is caught in an anxiety-producing situation." *Id.*

Eyewitness perceptual inaccuracies can be caused by a variety of factors. For one thing, crimes are often "brief, fast-moving events; the victim and witnesses consequently will have difficulty getting a sufficiently good 'look' to allow them to process enough visual features of the event and the offender to make a reliable subsequent recognition." *Id.* Such perceptual difficulties are likely to arise when a "crime occurs suddenly, and the witness is thus unprepared to focus perceptual attention on the important features of the event." *Id.* A second factor that creates perceptual inaccuracies is anxiety. Although "victim's will sometimes assert that 'I was so frightened that his face is etched in my memory forever,' " the evidence shows "that perceptual abilities actually decrease significantly when the observer is in a fearful or anxiety-provoking situation." *Id.* Indeed, extreme anxiety can cause a witness to shut off "in order to block out and avoid recognition of stimuli that might produce anxiety." *Id.* Perceptual inaccuracies are also caused by stereotypes: "a victim may unwittingly distort her perception of an assailant to include physical features that the victim associates with the personality traits typified by the criminal's behavior." *Id.* Further, individuals have greater difficulty identifying people who are of a different race than their own.

Even if an individual clearly saw a crime perpetrator's characteristics, his/her later descriptions are likely to be inaccurate. Frequently, eyewitnesses are asked to give verbal descriptions of the perpetrator of crimes, but verbal descriptions can be imprecise and potentially inaccurate. While police investigators may push for detailed, precise and complete descriptions of the perpetrator, eyewitnesses rarely retain that level of detail. Moreover, memories tends to deteriorate over time. "Because of a psychological need to reduce uncertainty and eliminate inconsistencies, witnesses have a tendency not only to fill any gaps in memory by adding extraneous details but also to change mental representations unconsciously so that they 'all make sense.' " *Id.* In other words, memory is an "active" rather than a "static" process so that one's perception of events can change over time, and can be affected by media reports, mug shots, or event the process of observing a defendant in a lineup.

Eyewitness identifications can also be influenced by social psychological factors. When confronted with a lineup, a witness is likely to assume that the police believe that the criminal is in the lineup, and may feel that he is expected to pick the participant who most resembles the perpetrator—even if the eyewitness is not 100% sure that the identification is accurate. Plus, if the eyewitness is a victim, he/she may have hostility towards the perpetrator. These psychological factors can make eyewitnesses particularly susceptible to police suggestion which can exist by virtue of the way that the police have arranged the lineup (e.g., is the suspected perpetrator physically similar to, or different than, the other participants, or does the suspected perpetrator have one distinctive physical characteristic that the other suspects do not possess?), as well as by the police officer's voice intonation or other gestures. *Id.* Suggestiveness can also be created when the police arrange a photo display in advance of an actual lineup. If suggestiveness encourages the eyewitness to pick an individual out of the lineup, it is quite likely that the eyewitness will pick the same individual out of an actual lineup, and identify that person at trial.

Point for Discussion

Characteristics of Voice

Critical to the distinction between methods of seizure and identification is the concept of privacy. Referencing *Katz v. United States*, the Supreme Court has held that no reasonable expectation of privacy exists in publicly exposed traits. As a result, in *United States v. Dionisio*, 410 U.S. 1, 14 (1973), the Court rejected defendant's argument that disclosure of his voice implicated Fourth Amendment interests, observing that: "the physical characteristics of a person's voice, its tone and manner, as opposed to the content of a specific conversation, are constantly exposed to the public. Like a man's facial characteristics, or handwriting, his voice is repeatedly produced for others to hear. No person can have a reasonable expectation that others will not know the sound of his voice any more than he can reasonably expect that his face will be a mystery to the world."

Take Note

Although acknowledging that identification procedures elicit incriminating information, the Court has has also held that they do not implicate the Fifth Amendment. In rejecting a privilege against self-incrimination claim in the context of identification procedures, the Court characterized such evidence as nontestimonial. For example, in *Gilbert v. California*, 388 U.S. 263, 266–67 (1967), it held that: "the taking of handwriting exemplars did not violate petitioner's Fifth Amendment privilege against self-incrimination. The privilege reaches only compulsion of 'an accused's communications, whatever form they might take, and the compulsion of responses which are also communications.' One's voice and handwriting are, of course, means of communication. It by no means follows, however, that every compulsion of an accused to use his voice or write (compels) a communication within the cover of the privilege. A mere handwriting exemplar, in contrast to the content of what is written, like the voice or body itself, is an identifying physical characteristic outside its protection."

Despite the general irrelevance of the Fourth and Fifth Amendments to identifications (although Fourth Amendment interests may be implicated when a person is seized for purposes of obtaining identification, *Hayes v. Florida*, 470 U.S. 811 (1985)), identification procedures are not without significant constitutional protection. Like other criminal investigative methods, identification processes may implicate due process. Case law also has established that the right to counsel may attach to identification proceedings. Contrasted with the pervasive applicability of the due process clause, however, Sixth Amendment protection is limited to identification procedures employed "at or after the time that adversarial judicial proceedings have been initiated." *Kirby v. Illinois*, 406 U.S. 682, 688 (1972) (plurality opinion).

Hypo: *Display of Platinum Teeth*

Suppose that defendant has teeth that are made of platinum. Because the victim of an assault claims that his assailant had special teeth, the judge orders defendant to reveal his teeth to the witness and the jury. Defendant objects on the basis that the display of his teeth would constitute self-incrimination. He also claims that he will be unduly prejudiced because the platinum teeth make him look "particularly fierce," and therefore will encourage the jury to convict him of the crime. Can defendant be required to exhibit his teeth? *See State v. Gonzalez*, 359 Wisc.2d 1, 856 N.W.2d 850 (2014).

B. The Sixth Amendment

The right to counsel in an identification context is dependent upon whether the proceeding occurs at a stage of the process that is critical enough that counsel's presence "is necessary to preserve the defendant's basic right to a fair trial." *United States v. Wade*, 388 U.S. 218, 227 (1967). Seminal case law reflects the Court's sense that post-indictment line-ups not only satisfy the "critical stage" requirement but also present profound risks to a fair trial.

United States v. Wade

388 U.S. 218 (1967).

Mr. Justice Brennan delivered the opinion of the Court.

The federally insured bank in Eustace, Texas, was robbed on September 21, 1964. A man with a small strip of tape on each side of his face entered the bank, pointed a pistol at the female cashier and the vice president, the only persons in the bank at the time, and forced them to fill a pillowcase with the bank's money. The man then drove away with an accomplice who had been waiting in a stolen car outside the bank. An indictment was returned against respondent, Wade, and two others for conspiring to rob the bank, and against Wade and the accomplice for the robbery itself. Wade was arrested and counsel was appointed to represent him. Fifteen days later an FBI agent, without notice to Wade's lawyer, arranged to have the two bank employees observe a lineup made up of Wade and five or six other prisoners conducted in a courtroom of the local county courthouse. Each person in the line wore strips of tape as allegedly worn by the robber and upon direction each said something like "put the money in the bag," the words allegedly uttered by the robber. Both bank employees identified Wade as the bank robber.

At trial the two employees, when asked on direct examination if the robber was in the courtroom, pointed to Wade. The prior lineup identification was then elicited from both employees on cross-examination. Wade was convicted.

Neither the lineup itself nor anything shown by this record that Wade was required to do in the lineup violated his privilege against self-incrimination. The privilege "protects an accused only from being compelled to testify against himself, or otherwise provide the State with evidence of a testimonial or communicative nature."

The fact that the lineup involved no violation of Wade's privilege against self-incrimination does not, however, dispose of his contention that the courtroom identifications should have been excluded because the lineup was conducted without notice to and in the absence of his counsel. It is urged that the assistance of counsel at the lineup was indispensable to protect Wade's most basic right as a criminal defendant—his right to a fair trial at which the witnesses against him might be meaningfully cross-examined.

The Government characterizes the lineup as a mere preparatory step in the gathering of the prosecution's evidence, not different—for Sixth Amendment purposes—from various other preparatory steps, such as systematized or scientific analyzing of the accused's fingerprints, blood sample, clothing, hair, and the like. We think there are differences which preclude such stages being characterized as critical stages at which the accused has the right to the presence of his counsel. Knowledge of the techniques of science and technology is sufficiently available, and the variables in techniques few enough, that the accused has the opportunity for a meaningful confrontation of the Government's case at trial through the ordinary processes of cross-examination of the Government's expert witnesses and the presentation of the evidence of his own experts. The denial of a right to have his counsel present at such analyses does not therefore violate the Sixth Amendment; they are not critical stages since there is minimal risk that his counsel's absence at such stages might derogate from his right to a fair trial.

But the confrontation compelled by the State between the accused and the victim or witnesses to a crime to elicit identification evidence is peculiarly riddled with innumerable dangers and variable factors which might seriously, even crucially, derogate from a fair trial. The vagaries of eyewitness identification are well-known; the annals of criminal law are rife with instances of mistaken identification. Mr. Justice Frankfurter once said: "What is the worth of identification testimony even when uncontradicted? The identification of strangers is proverbially untrustworthy. The hazards of such testimony are established by a formidable number of instances in the records of English and American trials. These instances are recent—not due to the brutalities of ancient criminal procedure." A major factor contributing to the high incidence of miscarriage of justice from mistaken identification has been the degree of suggestion inherent in the manner in which the prosecution presents the suspect to witnesses for pretrial identification. Suggestion can be created intentionally or unintentionally in many subtle ways. The dangers for the suspect are particularly grave when the witness' opportunity for observation was insubstantial, and thus his susceptibility to suggestion the greatest. Moreover, "it is a matter of common experience that, once a witness has picked out the accused at the line-up, he is not likely to go back on his word later on, so that in practice the issue of identity may (in the absence of other relevant evidence) for all practical purposes be determined there and then, before the trial."

The pretrial confrontation for purpose of identification may take the form of a lineup, also known as an "identification parade" or "showup," as in the present case, or presentation of the suspect alone to the witness. Risks of suggestion attend either form of confrontation and increase the dangers inhering in eyewitness identification. But as with secret interrogations, there is serious difficulty in depicting what transpires at lineups and other forms of identification confrontations. "Privacy results in secrecy and this in turn results in a gap in our knowledge as to what in fact goes on." The defense can seldom reconstruct the manner and mode of lineup identification for judge or jury at trial. Those participating in a lineup with the accused may often be police officers; in any event, the participants' names are rarely recorded or divulged at trial. The impediments to an objective observation are increased when the victim is the witness. Lineups are prevalent in rape and robbery prosecutions and present a particular hazard that a victim's understandable outrage may excite vengeful or spiteful motives. In any event, neither witnesses nor lineup participants are apt to be alert for conditions prejudicial to the suspect. If they were, it would likely be of scant benefit to the suspect since neither witnesses nor lineup participants are likely to be schooled in the detection of suggestive influences. Improper influences may go undetected by a suspect, guilty or not, who experiences the emotional tension which we might expect in one being confronted with potential accusers. Even when he does observe abuse, if he has a criminal record he may be reluctant to take the stand and open the admission of prior convictions. Moreover any protestations by the suspect of the fairness of the lineup made at trial are likely to be in vain; the jury's choice is between the accused's unsupported version and that of the police officers. In short, the accused's inability effectively to reconstruct at trial any unfairness that occurred at the lineup may deprive him of his only opportunity meaningfully to attack the credibility of the witness' courtroom identification.

The potential for improper influence is illustrated by the circumstances surrounding the prior identifications in the three cases we decide today. In the present case, the testimony of the identifying witnesses elicited on cross-examination revealed that those witnesses were taken to the courthouse to await assembly of the lineup. The courtroom faced a hallway observable to the witnesses through an open door. The cashier testified that she saw Wade "standing in the hall" within sight of an FBI agent. Five or six other prisoners later appeared in the hall. The vice president testified that he saw a person in the hall in the custody of the agent who "resembled the person that we identified as the one that had entered the bank."

The vice of suggestion created by the identification in *Stovall v. Denno*, 388 U.S. 293, 302 (1967), was the presentation to the witness of the suspect alone handcuffed to police officers. It is hard to imagine a situation more clearly conveying the suggestion to the witness that the one presented is believed guilty by the police.

The few cases that have surfaced reveal the existence of a process attended with hazards of serious unfairness to the criminal accused and strongly suggest the plight of the more numerous defendants who are unable to ferret out suggestive influences in the secrecy of the confrontation. We do not assume that these risks are the result of police procedures intentionally designed to prejudice an accused. Rather we assume they derive from the dangers inherent in eyewitness identification and the suggestibility inherent in the context of the pretrial identification. Williams & Hammelmann, in one of the most comprehensive studies of such forms of identification, said, "The fact that the police have, in a given case, little or no doubt that the man put up for identification has committed the offense, and that their chief pre-occupation is with the problem of getting sufficient proof, because he has not 'come clean,' involves a danger that this persuasion may communicate itself even in a doubtful case to the witness in some way." Williams & Hammelmann, *Identification Parades*, Part I, (1963) Crim.L.Rev. 479, 483

Insofar as the accused's conviction may rest on a courtroom identification in fact the fruit of a suspect pretrial identification which the accused is helpless to subject to effective scrutiny at trial, the accused is deprived of that right of cross-examination which is an essential safeguard to his right to confront the witnesses against him. Even though cross-examination is a precious safeguard to a fair trial, it cannot be viewed as an absolute assurance of accuracy and reliability. In the present context, where so many variables and pitfalls exist, the first line of defense must be the prevention of unfairness and the lessening of the hazards of eyewitness identification at the lineup itself. The trial which might determine the accused's fate may well not be that in the courtroom but at the pretrial confrontation, with the State aligned against the accused, the witness the sole jury, and the accused unprotected against the overreaching, intentional or unintentional, and with little or no effective appeal from the judgment there rendered by the witness—"that's the man."

Since it appears that there is grave potential for prejudice, intentional or not, in the pretrial lineup, which may not be capable of reconstruction at trial, and since presence of counsel itself can often avert prejudice and assure a meaningful confrontation at trial, there can be little doubt that for Wade the postindictment lineup was a critical stage of the prosecution at which he was "as much entitled to such of counsel as at the trial itself." Thus both Wade and his counsel should have been notified of the impending lineup, and counsel's presence should have been a requisite to conduct of the lineup, absent an "intelligent waiver." No substantial countervailing policy considerations have been advanced against the requirement of the presence of counsel. Concern is expressed that the requirement will forestall prompt identifications and result in obstruction. As for the first, in the two cases in which the right to counsel is today held to apply, counsel had already been appointed and no argument is made that notice to counsel would have prejudicially delayed the confrontations. Moreover, we leave open the question whether the presence of substitute counsel might suffice where notification and presence of the suspect's own counsel would result in prejudicial delay. To refuse to recognize the right to counsel for fear that counsel will obstruct the course of justice is contrary to the basic assumptions upon which this Court has operated in Sixth Amendment cases. We rejected similar logic in *Miranda* concerning presence of counsel during custodial interrogation.

In our view counsel can hardly impede legitimate law enforcement; on the contrary, law enforcement may be assisted by preventing the infiltration of taint in the prosecution's identification evidence. That result cannot help the guilty avoid conviction but can only help assure that the right man has been brought to justice.

Legislative or other regulations, such as those of local police departments, which eliminate the risks of abuse and unintentional suggestion at lineup proceedings and the impediments to meaningful confrontation at trial may also remove the basis for regarding the stage as "critical." But neither Congress nor the federal authorities have seen fit to provide a solution. What we hold today "in no way creates a constitutional straitjacket which will handicap sound efforts at reform, nor is it intended to have this effect."

We come now to the question whether the denial of Wade's motion to strike the courtroom identification by the bank witnesses at trial because of the absence of his counsel at the lineup required the grant of a new trial at which such evidence is to be excluded. We do not think this disposition can be justified without first giving the Government the opportunity to establish by clear and convincing evidence that the in-court identifications were based upon observations of the suspect other than the lineup identification. Where the admissibility of evidence of the lineup identification itself is not involved, a *per se* rule of exclusion of courtroom identification would be unjustified. A rule limited solely to the exclusion of testimony concerning identification at the lineup itself, without regard to admissibility of the courtroom identification, would render the right to counsel an empty one. The lineup is most often used to crystallize the witnesses' identification of the defendant for future reference. We have already noted that the lineup identification will have that effect. The State may then rest upon the witnesses' unequivocal courtroom identifications, and not mention the pretrial identification as part of the State's case at trial. Counsel is then in the predicament in which Wade's counsel found himself—realizing that possible unfairness at the lineup may be the sole means of attack upon the unequivocal courtroom identification, and having to probe in the dark in an attempt to discover and reveal unfairness, while bolstering the government witness' courtroom identification by bringing out and dwelling upon his prior identification. Since counsel's presence at the lineup would equip him to attack not only the lineup identification but the courtroom identification as well, limiting the impact of violation of the right to counsel to exclusion of evidence only of identification at the lineup itself disregards a critical element of that right.

It follows that the proper test to be applied in these situations is "Whether, granting establishment of the primary illegality, the evidence to which instant objection is made has been come at by exploitation of that illegality or instead by means sufficiently distinguishable to be purged of the primary taint." Application of this requires consideration of various factors; for example, the prior opportunity to observe the alleged criminal act, the existence of any discrepancy between any pre-lineup description and the defendant's actual description, any identification prior to lineup of another person, the identification by picture of the defendant prior to the lineup, failure to identify the defendant on a prior occasion, and the lapse of time between the alleged act and the lineup identification. It is also relevant to consider facts which, despite the absence of counsel, are disclosed concerning the conduct of the lineup.

On the record before us we cannot make the determination whether the in-court identifications had an independent origin. We therefore vacate the conviction pending a hearing to determine whether the in-court identifications had an independent source, or whether, in any event, the introduction of the evidence was harmless error, and for the District Court to reinstate the conviction or order a new trial, as may be proper.

MR. JUSTICE BLACK, dissenting in part and concurring in part.

The Government forced Wade to stand in a lineup, wear strips on his face, and speak certain words, in order to make it possible for government witnesses to identify him as a criminal. Being forced by the Government to help convict himself and to supply evidence against himself by talking outside the courtroom is equally violative of his constitutional right not to be compelled to be a witness against himself. The assistance of counsel at the lineup is also necessary to protect the defendant's in-custody assertion of his privilege against self-incrimination, for counsel may advise the defendant not to participate in the lineup or to participate only under certain conditions.

MR. JUSTICE WHITE, whom MR. JUSTICE HARLAN and MR. JUSTICE STEWART join, dissenting in part and concurring in part.

The premise for the Court's rule is not the general unreliability of eyewitness identifications nor the difficulties inherent in observation, recall, and recognition. The Court assumes a narrower evil as the basis for its rule—improper police suggestion which contributes to erroneous identifications. I do not share this pervasive distrust of all official investigations. None of the materials the Court relies upon supports it.

It may be asked, what possible state interest militates against requiring the presence of defense counsel at lineups? After all, he *may* do some good, he *may* upgrade the quality of identification evidence in state courts and he can scarcely do any harm. Absent some reliably established constitutional violation, the processes by which the States enforce their criminal laws are their own prerogative.

I would not require counsel's presence at pretrial identification procedures. Some counsel may advise their clients to refuse to make any movements or to speak any words in a lineup or even to appear in one. The impact on truthful factfinding is obvious. Others will not only observe what occurs and develop possibility for later cross-examination but will hover over witnesses and begin their cross-examination then, menacing truthful factfinding as thoroughly as the Court fears the police now do. Certainly there is an implicit invitation to counsel to suggest rules for the lineup and to manage and produce it as best he can. I doubt that the Court's new rule, absent some clearly defined limits on counsel's role, will measurably contribute to more reliable pretrial identifications. The State is entitled to investigate and develop its case outside the presence of defense counsel. This includes the right to have private conversations with identification witnesses.

MR. JUSTICE FORTAS with whom THE CHIEF JUSTICE and MR. JUSTICE DOUGLAS join, concurring in part and dissenting in part.

The accused may not be compelled in a lineup to speak the words uttered by the person who committed the crime. It is more than passive, mute assistance to the eyes of the victim or of witnesses. It is the kind of volitional act—the kind of forced cooperation by the accused—which is within the historical perimeter of the privilege against compelled self-incrimination. I agree that the accused must be advised of and given the right to counsel before a lineup—and I join part of the Court's opinion.

Take Note

Crucial to *Wade's* outcome was the Court's recognition that lineups could be managed or manipulated in innumerable ways. The logical extension of that understanding is that identification methods which are a function of scientific review, such as fingerprinting, blood sampling, and hair, fiber or DNA analysis, do not trigger the right to counsel. Given the standardization of analysis characterizing such testing, *Wade* stressed "that the accused has the opportunity for a meaningful confrontation of the Government's case at trial through the ordinary processes of cross-examination of the Government's expert witnesses and the presentation of the evidence of his own experts." Such analysis and distinction illuminates an overarching concern with the right to counsel not independently but as a means of facilitating a fair trial when other protections would be inadequate. Elaborating on this theme, the Court in *Gilbert v. California*, 388 U.S. 263, 266 (1967), concluded that "The taking of handwriting exemplars was not a 'critical' stage of the criminal proceedings entitling petitioner to the assistance of counsel. Putting aside the fact that the exemplars were taken before the indictment and appointment of counsel, there is minimal risk that the absence of counsel might derogate from his right to a fair trial. If an unrepresentative exemplar is taken, this can be brought out and corrected through the adversary process at trial since the accused can make an unlimited number of additional exemplars for analysis and comparison by government and defense handwriting experts. Thus, "the accused has the opportunity for a meaningful confrontation of the State's case at trial through the ordinary processes of cross-examination of the State's expert handwriting witnesses and the presentation of the evidence of his own handwriting experts."

Point for Discussion

Pre-Charge Showup

In *Kirby v. Illinois*, 406 U.S. 682 (1972), the Court was asked to extend the exclusionary rule to identification testimony (a showup) that took place *before* the defendant had been indicted or otherwise formally charged with any criminal offense. The Court refused: "A person's Sixth and Fourteenth Amendment right to counsel attaches only at or after the time that adversary judicial proceedings have been initiated against him. The initiation of judicial criminal proceedings is far from a mere formalism. It is the starting point of our whole system of adversary criminal justice. It is only then that the government has committed itself to prosecute, and only then that the adverse positions of government and defendant have solidified. It is then that a defendant finds himself faced with the prosecutorial forces of organized society, and immersed in the intricacies of substantive and procedural criminal law." Mr. Justice Brennan dissented: "Counsel is required at confrontations because "the dangers inherent in eyewitness identification and the suggestibility inherent in the context of the pretrial identification," mean that protection must be afforded to the "most basic right of a criminal defendant—his right to a fair trial at which the witnesses against him might be meaningfully cross-examined." Hence, "the initiation of adversary judicial criminal proceedings," is completely irrelevant. There inhere in a confrontation for identification conducted after arrest the identical hazards to a fair trial that inhere in such a confrontation conducted 'after the onset of formal prosecutional proceedings.' "

Food for Thought

In *Rothgery v. Gillespie County*, 554 U.S. 191 (2008), the Court reaffirmed the idea "that the right to counsel guaranteed by the Sixth Amendment applies when adversary proceedings commence." The Court held that the adversary process can commence with "the initiation of adversary judicial criminal proceedings-whether by way of formal charge, preliminary hearing, indictment, information, or arraignment," as well as by "the first appearance before a judicial officer at which a defendant is told of the formal accusation against him and restrictions are imposed on his liberty." The Court relied on *Brewer v. Williams*, 430 U.S. 387, 398 (1977), and *Michigan v. Jackson*, 475 U.S. 625, 629 (1986). The Court went on to hold that the right attaches whether or not a public prosecutor is aware of the initial proceeding.

Hypo 1: *The Need for Counsel*

Is counsel really necessary in a lineup situation? Why isn't it possible for the suspect to "observe" and "report" to his/her attorney regarding circumstances at the lineup? Based on such observations, would it be possible for the attorney to cross-examine witnesses at trial?

Food for Thought

You have been hired to represent a suspect who is going to be placed in a lineup. After *Wade*, you know that you have to be concerned about the possibility of "suggestiveness" during the lineup. How is suggestiveness created? In other words, when you go to the lineup, what sorts of problems should you be looking for?

Food for Thought

You attend the actual lineup and find that it is unduly suggestive. What is your role? Do you object?

Hypo 2: *The Basis for a Challenge*

If the lineup is suggestive, but you were present, you probably won't be able to challenge the result of the identification on Sixth Amendment right to counsel grounds. So, on what basis do you challenge it?

Hypo 3: *Pre-Adversarial Proceedings Lineups*

Suppose that a lineup occurs before the suspect has been indicted or formally charged, and the suspect is forced to appear without the benefit of counsel. The suspect is identified by the witness, and the suspect is ultimately indicted. You have been appointed to represent him. After *Wade*, you know that you cannot object to the pre-trial identification (or, for that matter, to an in-court identification by the same witness) on Sixth Amendment right to counsel grounds. On what basis might you object if you felt that the process was tainted?

United States v. Ash

413 U.S. 300 (1973).

MR. JUSTICE BLACKMUN delivered the opinion of the Court.

On the morning of August 26, 1965, a man with a stocking mask entered a bank in Washington, D.C., and began waving a pistol. He ordered an employee to hang up the telephone and instructed all others present not to move. Seconds later a second man, also wearing a stocking mask, entered the bank, scooped up money from tellers' drawers into a bag, and left. The gunman followed, and both men escaped through an alley. The robbery lasted three or four minutes.

A Government informer, Clarence McFarland, told authorities that he had discussed the robbery with Charles J. Ash, Jr., the respondent here. Acting on this information, an FBI agent, in February 1966, showed five black-and-white mug shots of Negro males of generally the same age, height, and weight, one of which was of Ash, to four witnesses. All four made uncertain identifications of Ash's picture. At this time Ash was not in custody and had not been charged. On April 1, 1966, an indictment was returned charging Ash and a codefendant, John L. Bailey, in five counts related to this bank robbery.

In preparing for trial, the prosecutor decided to use a photographic display to determine whether the witnesses he planned to call would be able to make in-court identifications. Shortly before the trial, an FBI agent and the prosecutor showed five color photographs to the four witnesses who previously had tentatively identified the black-and-white photograph of Ash. Three of the witnesses selected the picture of Ash, but one was unable to make any selection. None of the witnesses selected the picture of Bailey which was in the group. This post-indictment identification provides the basis for respondent Ash's claim that he was denied the right to counsel at a "critical stage" of the prosecution.

The Government argued in *Wade* that if counsel was required at a lineup, the same forceful considerations would mandate counsel at other preparatory steps in the "gathering of the prosecution's evidence," such as, for particular example, the taking of fingerprints or blood samples.

The Court concluded that there were differences. Rather than distinguishing these situations from the lineup in terms of the need for counsel to assure an equal confrontation at the time, the Court recognized that there were times when the subsequent trial would cure a one-sided confrontation between prosecuting authorities and the uncounseled defendant. In other words, such stages were not "critical." Referring to fingerprints, hair, clothing, and other blood samples, the Court explained: "Knowledge of the techniques of science and technology is sufficiently available, and the variables in techniques few enough, that the accused has the opportunity for a meaningful confrontation of the Government's case at trial through the ordinary processes of cross-examination of the Government's expert witnesses and the presentation of the evidence of his own experts."

The structure of *Wade*, viewed in light of the careful limitation of the Court's language to "confrontations," makes it clear that lack of scientific precision and inability to reconstruct an event are not the tests for requiring counsel in the first instance. These are, instead, the tests to determine whether confrontation with counsel at trial can serve as a substitute for counsel at the pretrial confrontation. If accurate reconstruction is possible, the risks inherent in any confrontation still remain, but the opportunity to cure defects at trial causes the confrontation to cease to be "critical."

A substantial departure from the historical test would be necessary if the Sixth Amendment were interpreted to give Ash a right to counsel at the photographic identification in this case. Since the accused himself is not present at the time of the photographic display, and asserts no right to be present, no possibility arises that the accused might be misled by his lack of familiarity with the law or overpowered by his professional adversary. Similarly, the counsel guarantee would not be used to produce equality in a trial-like adversary confrontation. Rather, the guarantee was used by the Court of Appeals to produce confrontation at an event that previously was not analogous to an adversary trial.

Even if we were willing to view the counsel guarantee in broad terms as a generalized protection of the adversary process, we would be unwilling to go so far as to extend the right to a portion of the prosecutor's trial-preparation interviews with witnesses. Although photography is relatively new, the interviewing of witnesses before trial is a procedure that predates the Sixth Amendment. In England in the 16th and 17th centuries counsel regularly interviewed witnesses before trial. The traditional counterbalance in the American adversary system for these interviews arises from the equal ability of defense counsel to seek and interview witnesses himself.

That adversary mechanism remains as effective for a photographic display as for other parts of pretrial interviews. No greater limitations are placed on defense counsel in constructing displays, seeking witnesses, and conducting photographic identifications than those applicable to the prosecution. Selection of the picture of a person other than the accused, or the inability of a witness to make any selection, will be useful to the defense in precisely the same manner that the selection of a picture of the defendant would be useful to the prosecution. In this very case, for example, the initial tender of the photographic display was by Bailey's counsel, who sought to demonstrate that the witness had failed to make a photographic identification. Although we do not suggest that equality of access to photographs removes all potential for abuse, it does remove any inequality in the adversary process itself and thereby fully satisfies the historical spirit of the Sixth Amendment's counsel guarantee.

The argument has been advanced that requiring counsel might compel the police to observe more scientific procedures or might encourage them to utilize corporeal rather than photographic displays. This Court has recognized that improved procedures can minimize the dangers of suggestion. Pretrial photographic identifications, however, are hardly unique in offering possibilities for the actions of the prosecutor unfairly to prejudice the accused. Evidence favorable to the accused may be withheld; testimony of witnesses may be manipulated; the results of laboratory tests may be contrived. In many ways the prosecutor, by accident or by design, may improperly subvert the trial. The primary safeguard against abuses of this kind is the ethical responsibility of the prosecutor, who, as so often has been said, may "strike hard blows" but not "foul ones." If that safeguard fails, review remains available under due process standards.

We are not persuaded that the risks inherent in the use of photographic displays are so pernicious that an extraordinary system of safeguards is required. We hold, then, that the Sixth Amendment does not grant the right to counsel at photographic displays conducted by the Government for the purpose of allowing a witness to attempt an identification of the offender.

MR. JUSTICE STEWART, concurring in the judgment.

A photographic identification is quite different from a lineup, for there are substantially fewer possibilities of impermissible suggestion when photographs are used, and those unfair influences can be readily reconstructed at trial. It is true that defendant's photograph may be markedly different from the others displayed, but this unfairness can be demonstrated at trial from a comparison of the photographs used or from the witness' description of the display. Similarly, it is possible that the photographs could be arranged in a suggestive manner, or that by comment or gesture the prosecuting authorities might single out the defendant's picture. But these are the kinds of overt influence that a witness can easily recount and that would serve to impeach the identification testimony. In short, there are few possibilities for unfair suggestiveness—and those rather blatant and easily reconstructed. Accordingly, an accused would not be foreclosed from an effective cross-examination of an identification witness simply because his counsel was not present at the photographic display. For this reason, a photographic display cannot fairly be considered a "critical stage" of the prosecution.

MR. JUSTICE BRENNAN, with whom MR. JUSTICE DOUGLAS and MR. JUSTICE MARSHALL join, dissenting.

The "dangers of mistaken identification set forth in *Wade* are applicable in large measure to photographic as well as corporeal identifications." To the extent that misidentification may be attributable to a witness' faulty memory or perception, or inadequate opportunity for detailed observation during the crime, the risks are obviously as great at a photographic display as at a lineup. "Because of the inherent limitations of photography, which presents its subject in two dimensions rather than the three dimensions of reality, a photographic identification, even when properly obtained, is clearly inferior to a properly obtained corporeal identification." In this sense at least, the dangers of misidentification are even greater at a photographic display than at a lineup.

As in the lineup situation, the possibilities for impermissible suggestion in the context of a photographic display are manifold. Such suggestion, intentional or unintentional, may derive from three possible sources. First, the photographs themselves might tend to suggest which of the pictures is that of the suspect. For example, differences in age, pose, or other physical characteristics of the persons represented, and variations in the mounting, background, lighting, or markings of the photographs all might have the effect of singling out the accused. Second, impermissible suggestion may inhere in the manner in which the photographs are displayed to the witness. If the photographs are arranged in an asymmetrical pattern, or if they are displayed in a time sequence that tends to emphasize a particular photograph, "any identification of the photograph which stands out from the rest is no more reliable than an identification of a single photograph, exhibited alone."

Third, gestures or comments of the prosecutor at the time of the display may lead an otherwise uncertain witness to select the "correct" photograph. "Regardless of how the initial misidentification comes about, the witness is apt to retain in his memory the image of the photograph rather than of the person actually seen." As a result, "the issue of identity may in the absence of other relevant evidence for all practical purposes be determined there and then, before the trial."

Moreover, as with lineups, the defense can "seldom reconstruct" at trial the mode and manner of photographic identification. Preservation of the photographs affords little protection to the unrepresented accused. For, although retention of the photographs may mitigate the dangers of misidentification due to the suggestiveness of the photographs themselves, it cannot in any sense reveal to defense counsel the more subtle, and therefore more dangerous, suggestiveness that might derive from the manner in which the photographs were displayed or any accompanying comments or gestures. The accused cannot rely upon the witnesses themselves to expose these latter sources of suggestion, for the witnesses are not "apt to be alert for conditions prejudicial to the suspect. And if they were, it would likely be of scant benefit to the suspect" since the witnesses are hardly "likely to be schooled in the detection of suggestive influences."

Finally, the accused is not even present at the photographic identification, thereby reducing the likelihood that irregularities in the procedures will ever come to light. The difficulties of reconstructing at trial an uncounseled photographic display are at least equal to, and possibly greater than, those involved in reconstructing an uncounseled lineup.

This Court's decisions suggest that a "stage" of the prosecution must be deemed "critical" for the purposes of the Sixth Amendment if it is one at which the presence of counsel is necessary "to protect the fairness of the trial itself." To exclude counsel from a pretrial proceeding at which his presence might be necessary to assure the fairness of the subsequent trial would, in practical effect, render the Sixth Amendment guarantee virtually meaningless, for it would "deny a defendant 'effective representation by counsel at the only stage when legal aid and advice would help him.'"

Wade envisioned counsel's function at the lineup to be primarily that of a trained observer, able to detect the existence of any suggestive influences and capable of understanding the legal implications of the events that transpire. Having witnessed the proceedings, counsel would then be in a position effectively to reconstruct at trial any unfairness that occurred at the lineup, thereby preserving the accused's fundamental right to a fair trial on the issue of identification.

There simply is no meaningful difference, in terms of the need for attendance of counsel, between corporeal and photographic identifications. And applying established and well-reasoned Sixth Amendment principles, I can only conclude that a pretrial photographic display, like a pretrial lineup, is a "critical stage" of the prosecution at which the accused is constitutionally entitled to the presence of counsel.

Point for Discussion

Wade's Vitality

Post-*Ash* law establishes the continuing vitality of *Wade* in post-charging circumstances. In *Moore v. Illinois,* 434 U.S. 220, 224 (1977), the Court reiterated the basic premise that counsel must be present for a showup or one-on-one confrontation. The *Wade-Ash-Moore* line of decisions indicates that the right of counsel extends only to post-charging procedures requiring the presence and identification of the defendant. Prior to charging, counsel is not required even at a line-up or show-up. The distinction between pre-charging and post-charging circumstances is rooted in Sixth Amendment text that references "criminal prosecutions." In reviewing arguments for extending the *Wade* rule to pre-charging circumstances, the Court in *Kirby v. Illinois* reiterated the significance of actual judicial criminal proceedings rather than police investigations.

Hypo: *More on Photographic Displays*

In conducting a photographic identification, should it matter whether the photographs are presented simultaneously or in succession? Suppose that a witness is simultaneously shown photos of eleven different individuals, and is told to look at the photographs and to make an identification "if she can." She does, pointing out defendant as the culprit. Does due process require that the photographs be shown sequentially? Does it matter whether the police comment, positively or negatively, as the witness makes comments on the suspects? *See Commonwealth v. Thomas*, 476 Mass. 451, 68 N.E.3d 1161 (Mass. 2017).

C. Due Process Considerations

Even though the Sixth Amendment may not govern an identification proceeding, because of its timing or circumstance, constitutional review is not necessarily precluded. As a guarantor of procedural fairness, due process claims may be asserted in any investigative or adjudicative context. Due process review imposes upon claimants a significant task of demonstrating that identification methods were "unnecessarily suggestive and conducive to mistaken identification." *Stovall v. Denno*, 388 U.S. 293, 302 (1967). Unlike *Gilbert* and *Wade*, which referenced the Sixth Amendment's relevance to defendants identified in person, the companion case of *Stovall v. Denno* concerned a pre-indictment one-on-one identification. The *Stovall* decision represents the seminal articulation of due process principles governing identification procedures.

In *Stovall v. Denno*, 388 U.S. 293 (1967), Dr. Paul Behrendt was stabbed to death in the kitchen of his home. During the murder, Behrendt's wife was stabbed 11 times. She was hospitalized for major surgery to save her life. The police, without affording petitioner time to retain counsel, arranged with her surgeon to bring petitioner to her hospital room about noon, the day after the surgery. Petitioner was handcuffed to one of five police officers who, with two members of the staff of the District Attorney, brought him to the hospital room. Petitioner was the only Negro in the room. Mrs. Behrendt identified him from her hospital bed after being asked by an officer whether he "was the man" and after petitioner repeated at the direction of an officer a "few words for voice identification." None of the witnesses could recall the words that were used. Mrs. Behrendt and the officers testified at the trial to her identification of the petitioner in the hospital room, and she also made an in-court identification of petitioner in the courtroom.

Petitioner claimed that the in-hospital identification was unconstitutionally obtained. The Court disagreed: "A claimed violation of due process of law in the conduct of a confrontation depends on the totality of the circumstances surrounding it, and the record in the present case reveals that the showing of Stovall to Mrs. Behrendt in an immediate hospital confrontation was imperative." The Court quoted from the court of appeals' opinion: "Here was the only person in the world who could possibly exonerate Stovall. Her words, and only her words, 'He is not the man' could have resulted in freedom for Stovall. The hospital was not far distant from the courthouse and jail. No one knew how long Mrs. Behrendt might live. Faced with the responsibility of identifying the attacker, with the need for immediate action and with the knowledge that Mrs. Behrendt could not visit the jail, the police followed the only feasible procedure and took Stovall to the hospital room. Under these circumstances, the usual police station line-up was out of the question." *See also Simmons v. United States*, 390 U.S. 377, 384 (1968) (although the identification process included repetitive use of the suspect's picture, the Court found that there was a need for swift police action to determine whether police "were on the right track" and that the risk of misidentification was insignificant). A year later, in *Foster v. California*, the Court determined that an identification procedure was so suggestive, and reliability so undermined, that due process was denied.

Foster v. California

394 U.S. 440 (1969).

MR. JUSTICE FORTAS delivered the opinion of the Court.

Petitioner was charged by information with the armed robbery of a Western Union office. The day after the robbery one of the robbers, Clay, surrendered to the police and implicated Foster and Grice. Except for the robbers themselves, the only witness to the crime was Joseph David, the late-night manager of the Western Union office. After Foster had been arrested, David was called to the police station to view a lineup. There were three men in the lineup. One was petitioner. He is a tall man—close to six feet in height. The other two men were short—five feet, five or six inches. Petitioner wore a leather jacket which David said was similar to the one he had seen underneath the coveralls worn by the robber. After seeing this lineup, David could not positively identify petitioner as the robber. He "thought" he was the man, but he was not sure. David then asked to speak to petitioner, and petitioner was brought into an office and sat across from David at a table. Except for prosecuting officials there was no one else in the room. Even after this one-to-one confrontation David still was uncertain whether petitioner was one of the robbers: "truthfully—I was not sure," he testified at trial. A week or 10 days later, the police arranged for David to view a second lineup. There were five men in that lineup. Petitioner was the only person in the second lineup who had appeared in the first lineup. This time David was "convinced" petitioner was the man. At trial, David testified to his identification of petitioner in the lineups. He also repeated his identification of petitioner in the courtroom. The only other evidence against petitioner which concerned the particular robbery with which he was charged was the testimony of the alleged accomplice Clay.

This case presents a compelling example of unfair lineup procedures. In the first lineup arranged by the police, petitioner stood out from the other two men by the contrast of his height and by the fact that he was wearing a leather jacket similar to that worn by the robber. When this did not lead to positive identification, the police permitted a one-to-one confrontation between petitioner and the witness. This Court pointed out in Stovall that "the practice of showing suspects singly to persons for the purpose of identification, and not as part of a lineup, has been widely condemned." Even after this the witness' identification of petitioner was tentative. So some days later another lineup was arranged. Petitioner was the only person in this lineup who had also participated in the first lineup. This finally produced a definite identification.

The suggestive elements in this identification procedure made it all but inevitable that David would identify petitioner whether or not he was in fact "the man." In effect, the police repeatedly said to the witness, *This* is the man." This procedure so undermined the reliability of the eyewitness identification as to violate due process.

Point for Discussion

Irreparable Misidentification

Determining whether an identification procedure is "impermissible," even if suggestive, requires attention to concerns that compete with and may supersede optimum integrity and regularity. The *Simmons* Court referenced reliability and terminal prejudice factors as a potential offset to suggestive procedures. In *Neil v. Biggers*, the Court stressed that "irreparable misidentification" was "the primary evil to be avoided."

Neil v. Biggers

409 U.S. 188 (1972).

Mr. Justice Powell delivered the opinion of the Court.

Respondent was convicted of rape and was sentenced to 20 years' imprisonment. The State's evidence consisted in part of testimony concerning a station-house identification of respondent by the victim. The Tennessee Supreme Court affirmed. On certiorari, the judgment of the Tennessee Supreme Court was affirmed by an equally divided Court. Respondent then brought a federal habeas corpus action raising several claims.

The District Court held that the claims were not barred and, after a hearing, held in an unreported opinion that the station-house identification procedure was so suggestive as to violate due process. The Court of Appeals affirmed. We granted certiorari to decide whether the identification procedure violated due process.

The victim testified at trial that on the evening of January 22, 1965, a youth with a butcher knife grabbed her in the doorway to her kitchen:

"A. He grabbed me from behind, and grappled—twisted me on the floor. Threw me down on the floor.

"Q. And there was no light in that kitchen?

"A. Not in the kitchen.

"Q. So you couldn't have seen him then?

"A. Yet, I could see him, when I looked up in his face.

"Q. In the dark?

"A. He was right in the doorway—it was enough light from the bedroom shining through. Yes, I could see who he was.

"Q. You could see? No light? And you could see him and know him then?

"A. Yes."

When the victim screamed, her 12-year-old daughter came out of her bedroom and also began to scream. The assailant directed the victim to "tell her [the daughter] to shut up, or I'll kill you both." She did so, and was then walked at knifepoint about two blocks along a railroad track, taken into a woods, and raped there. She testified that "the moon was shining brightly, full moon." After the rape, the assailant ran off, and she returned home, the whole incident having taken between 15 minutes and half an hour.

She then gave the police what the trial court characterized as "only a very general description," describing him as "being fat and flabby with smooth skin, bushy hair and a youthful voice." Additionally, she testified at the habeas corpus hearing that she had described her assailant as being between 16 and 18 years old and between five feet ten inches and six feet tall, as weighing between 180 and 200 pounds, and as having a dark brown complexion. This testimony was substantially corroborated by that of a police officer who was testifying from his notes.

On several occasions over the course of the next seven months, she viewed suspects in her home or at the police station, some in lineups and others in show-ups, and was shown between 30 and 40 photographs. She told the police that a man pictured in one of the photographs had features similar to those of her assailant, but identified none of the suspects. On August 17, the police called her to the station to view respondent, who was being detained on another charge. In an effort to construct a suitable lineup, the police checked the city jail and the city juvenile home. Finding no one at either place fitting respondent's unusual physical description, they conducted a showup instead.

The showup consisted of two detectives walking respondent past the victim. At the victim's request, the police directed respondent to say "shut up or I'll kill you." The testimony was not altogether clear as to whether the victim first identified him and then asked that he repeat the words or made her identification after he had spoken. In any event, the victim testified that she had "no doubt" about her identification.

We turn to the central question, whether under the "totality of the circumstances" the identification was reliable even though the confrontation procedure was suggestive. The factors to be considered in evaluating the likelihood of misidentification include the opportunity of the witness to view the criminal at the time of the crime, the witness' degree of attention, the accuracy of the witness' prior description of the criminal, the level of certainty demonstrated by the witness at the confrontation, and the length of time between the crime and the confrontation. Applying these factors, we disagree with the District Court's conclusion.

The District Court focused unduly on the relative reliability of a lineup as opposed to a showup, the issue on which expert testimony was taken at the evidentiary hearing.

We find that the District Court's conclusions on the critical facts are unsupported by the record and clearly erroneous. The victim spent a considerable period of time with her assailant, up to half an hour. She was with him under adequate artificial light in her house and under a full moon outdoors, and at least twice, once in the house and later in the woods, faced him directly and intimately. She was no casual observer, but rather the victim of one of the most personally humiliating of all crimes. Her description to the police, which included the assailant's approximate age, height, weight, complexion, skin texture, build, and voice, might not have satisfied Proust but was more than ordinarily thorough. She had "no doubt" that respondent was the person who raped her. In the nature of the crime, there are rarely witnesses to a rape other than the victim, who often has a limited opportunity of observation. The victim here, a practical nurse by profession, had an unusual opportunity to observe and identify her assailant. She testified at the habeas corpus hearing that there was something about his face "I don't think I could ever forget."

Take Note

Biggers stressed that, even if an identification procedure is unnecessarily suggestive, the due process inquiry does not end. *Stovall* intimated that suggestiveness itself might be sufficient to make an identification inadmissible. *Stovall v. Denno*, 388 U.S. 293, 302 (1967). *Biggers* previewed a redirection of case law, emphasizing that suggestiveness is merely a factor, and that due process inquiry will be driven primarily by considerations of reliability.

There was, to be sure, a lapse of seven months between the rape and the confrontation. This would be a seriously negative factor in most cases. Here, however, the testimony is undisputed that the victim made no previous identification at any of the showups, lineups, or photographic showings. Her record for reliability was thus a good one, as she had previously resisted whatever suggestiveness inheres in a showup. Weighing all the factors, we find no substantial likelihood of misidentification. The evidence was properly allowed to go to the jury.

Manson v. Brathwaite

432 U.S. 98 (1977).

MR. JUSTICE BLACKMUN delivered the opinion of the Court.

Jimmy Glover, a trooper of the Connecticut State Police, in 1970 was assigned to the Narcotics Division in an undercover capacity. On May 5 of that year, about 7:45 p.m., and while there was still daylight, Glover and Henry Brown, an informant, went to an apartment building at 201 Westland, in Hartford, for the purpose of purchasing narcotics from "Dickie Boy" Cicero, a known narcotics dealer. Cicero lived on the third floor of that apartment building. Glover and Brown entered the building, observed by back-up Officers D'Onofrio and Gaffey, and proceeded to the third floor. Glover knocked at the door of one of the two apartments served by the stairway. The area was illuminated by natural light from a window in the third floor hallway. The door was opened 12 to 18 inches in response to the knock. Glover observed a man standing at the door and, behind him, a woman. Brown identified himself. Glover then asked for "two things" of narcotics. The man at the door held out his hand, and Glover gave him two $10 bills. The door closed. Soon the man returned and handed Glover two glassine bags. While the door was open, Glover stood within two feet of the person from whom he made the purchase and observed his face. Five to seven minutes elapsed from the time the door first opened until it closed the second time.

Glover and Brown then left the building about eight minutes after their arrival. Glover drove to headquarters where he described the seller to D'Onofrio and Gaffey. Glover at that time did not know the identity of the seller. He described him as being "a colored man, approximately five feet eleven inches tall, dark complexion, black hair, short Afro style, high cheekbones, and of heavy build. He was wearing at the time blue pants and a plaid shirt." D'Onofrio, suspecting from this description that respondent might be the seller, obtained a photograph of respondent from the Records Division of the Hartford Police Department. He left it at Glover's office. D'Onofrio was not acquainted with respondent personally but did know him by sight and had seen him "several times" prior to May 5. Glover, when alone, viewed the photograph for the first time upon his return to headquarters on May 7; he identified the person shown as the one from whom he had purchased the narcotics.

Respondent was charged, in a two-count information, with possession and sale of heroin. At trial, the photograph from which Glover had identified respondent was received in evidence without objection on the part of the defense. Glover testified that, although he had not seen respondent in the eight months that had elapsed since the sale, "there was no doubt whatsoever" in his mind that the person shown on the photograph was respondent. Glover also made a positive in-court identification without objection. No explanation was offered by the prosecution for the failure to utilize a photographic array or to conduct a lineup.

The jury found respondent guilty on both counts and was affirmed by the Connecticut Supreme Court. Thereafter, respondent filed a petition for habeas corpus, which the court of appeals granted. The court felt that evidence as to the photograph should have been excluded, regardless of reliability, because the examination of the single photograph was unnecessary and suggestive. In the court's view, the evidence was unreliable in any event.

Petitioner acknowledges that "the procedure was suggestive because only one photograph was used and unnecessary" because there was no emergency or exigent circumstance. The respondent proposes a *per se* rule of exclusion that he claims is dictated by the demands of the Fourteenth Amendment's guarantee of due process.

Since the decision in *Biggers*, the Courts of Appeals appear to have developed at least two approaches to such evidence. The first, or *per se* approach focuses on the procedures employed and requires exclusion of the out-of-court identification evidence, without regard to reliability, whenever it has been obtained through unnecessarily suggestive confrontation procedures. The justifications advanced are the elimination of evidence of uncertain reliability, deterrence of the police and prosecutors, and "assurance against the awful risks of misidentification."

The second, or more lenient, approach is one that continues to rely on the totality of the circumstances. It permits the admission of the confrontation evidence if, despite the suggestive aspect, the out-of-court identification possesses certain features of reliability. Its adherents feel that the *per se* approach is not mandated by the Due Process Clause of the Fourteenth Amendment. This second approach, in contrast, is ad hoc and serves to limit the societal costs imposed by a sanction that excludes relevant evidence from consideration and evaluation by the trier of fact.

There are, of course, several interests to be considered and taken into account. The driving force behind our prior holdings was concern with the problems of eyewitness identification. Usually the witness must testify about an encounter with a total stranger under circumstances of emergency or emotional stress. The witness' recollection of the stranger can be distorted easily by the circumstances or by later actions of the police. Thus, *Wade* and its companion cases reflect the concern that the jury not hear eyewitness testimony unless that evidence has aspects of reliability. Both approaches are responsive to this concern. The *per se* rule, however, goes too far since its application automatically and peremptorily, and without consideration of alleviating factors, keeps evidence from the jury that is reliable and relevant.

The second factor is deterrence. Although the *per se* approach has the more significant deterrent effect, the totality approach also has an influence on police behavior. The police will guard against unnecessarily suggestive procedures under the totality rule, as well as the *per se* one, for fear that their actions will lead to the exclusion of identifications as unreliable.

The third factor is the effect on the administration of justice. Here the *per se* approach suffers serious drawbacks. Since it denies the trier reliable evidence, it may result, on occasion, in the guilty going free. Also, because of its rigidity, the *per se* approach may make error by the trial judge more likely than the totality approach. And in those cases in which the admission of identification evidence is error under the *per se* approach but not under the totality approach—cases in which the identification is reliable despite an unnecessarily suggestive identification procedure-reversal is a Draconian sanction. Certainly, inflexible rules of exclusion that may frustrate rather than promote justice have not been viewed recently by this Court with unlimited enthusiasm.

It is true that *Biggers* referred to the pre-*Stovall* character of the confrontation in that case. But that observation was only one factor in the judgmental process. It does not translate into a holding that post-*Stovall* confrontation evidence automatically is to be excluded.

We conclude that reliability is the linchpin in determining the admissibility of identification testimony for both pre-and post-*Stovall* confrontations. The factors to be considered are set out in *Biggers*. These include the opportunity of the witness to view the criminal at the time of the crime, the witness' degree of attention, the accuracy of his prior description of the criminal, the level of certainty demonstrated at the confrontation, and the time between the crime and the confrontation. Against these factors is to be weighed the corrupting effect of the suggestive identification itself.

We turn, then, to the facts of this case and apply the analysis:

1. *The opportunity to view.* Glover testified that for two to three minutes he stood at the apartment door, within two feet of the respondent. The door opened twice, and each time the man stood at the door. The moments passed, the conversation took place, and payment was made. Glover looked directly at his vendor. It was near sunset, to be sure, but the sun had not yet set, so it was not dark or even dusk or twilight. Natural light from outside entered the hallway through a window. There was natural light, as well, from inside the apartment.

2. *The degree of attention.* Glover was not a casual or passing observer, as is often the case with eyewitness identification. Trooper Glover was a trained police officer on duty—and specialized and dangerous duty—when he called at the third floor of 201 Westland in Hartford on May 5, 1970. Glover was a Negro and unlikely to perceive only general features of "hundreds of Hartford black males." It is true that Glover's duty was that of ferreting out narcotics offenders and that he would be expected in his work to produce results. But it is also true that, as a specially trained, assigned, and experienced officer, he could be expected to pay scrupulous attention to detail, for he knew that subsequently he would have to find and arrest his vendor. In addition, he knew that his claimed observations would be subject later to close scrutiny and examination at any trial.

3. *The accuracy of the description.* Glover's description was given to D'Onofrio within minutes after the transaction. It included the vendor's race, height, build, the color and style of his hair, and the high cheekbone facial feature. It also included clothing the vendor wore. No claim has been made that respondent did not possess the physical characteristics so described. D'Onofrio reacted positively at once. Two days later, when Glover was alone, he viewed the photograph D'Onofrio and identified its subject as the narcotics seller.

4. *The witness' level of certainty.* There is no dispute that the photograph in question was that of respondent. Glover, in response to a question whether the photograph was that of the person from whom he made the purchase, testified: "There is no question whatsoever." This positive assurance was repeated.

5. *The time between the crime and the confrontation.* Glover's description of his vendor was given to D'Onofrio within minutes of the crime. The photographic identification took place only two days later. We do not have here the passage of weeks or months between the crime and the viewing of the photograph.

These indicators of Glover's ability to make an accurate identification are hardly outweighed by the corrupting effect of the challenged identification. Although identifications arising from single-photograph displays may be viewed in general with suspicion, we find in the instant case little pressure on the witness to acquiesce in the suggestion that such a display entails. D'Onofrio left the photograph at Glover's office and was not present when Glover first viewed it two days after the event. There thus was little urgency and Glover could view the photograph at his leisure. Since Glover examined the photograph alone, there was no coercive pressure to make an identification arising from the presence of another. The identification was made in circumstances allowing care and reflection.

Although it plays no part in our analysis, this assurance as to the reliability of the identification is hardly undermined by the facts that respondent was arrested in the very apartment where the sale had taken place, and that he acknowledged his frequent visits to that apartment.

Surely, we cannot say that under the circumstances of this case there is "a very substantial likelihood of irreparable misidentification." Such evidence is for the jury to weigh. We are content to rely upon the good sense and judgment of American juries, for evidence with some element of untrustworthiness is customary grist for the jury mill. Juries are not so susceptible that they cannot measure intelligently the weight of identification testimony that has some questionable feature.

Of course, it would have been better had D'Onofrio presented Glover with a photographic array including "so far as practicable a reasonable number of persons similar to any person then suspected whose likeness is included in the array." The use of that procedure would have enhanced the force of the identification and would have avoided the risk that the evidence would be excluded as unreliable. But we are not disposed to view D'Onofrio's failure as one of constitutional dimension to be enforced by a rigorous and unbending exclusionary rule. The defect, if there be one, goes to weight and not to substance.

The criteria laid down in *Biggers* are to be applied in determining the admissibility of evidence offered by the prosecution concerning a post-*Stovall* identification, and those criteria are satisfactorily met and complied with here.

The judgment of the Court of Appeals is reversed.

MR. JUSTICE STEVENS, concurring.

The Court's decision to fashion new rules to minimize the danger of convicting the innocent on the basis of unreliable eyewitness testimony can be performed "more effectively by the legislative process than by a somewhat clumsy judicial fiat." The Federal Constitution does not foreclose experimentation by the States in the development of such rules.

MR. JUSTICE MARSHALL, with whom MR. JUSTICE BRENNAN joins, dissenting.

The Court wrongly evaluates the impact of the *Biggers* factors. First, the Court acknowledges that one of the factors, deterrence of police use of unnecessarily suggestive identification procedures, favors the *per se* rule. Indeed, it does so heavily, for such a rule would make it unquestionably clear to the police they must never use a suggestive procedure when a fairer alternative is available. I have no doubt that conduct would quickly conform to the rule. Second, the Court gives passing consideration to the dangers of eyewitness identification recognized in the *Wade* trilogy. The dangers of mistaken identification are too great to permit unnecessarily suggestive identifications. Finally, the Court errs in its assessment of the relative impact of the two approaches on the administration of justice. The Court relies most heavily on this factor, finding that "reversal is a Draconian sanction" in cases where the identification is reliable despite an unnecessarily suggestive procedure used to obtain it. Relying on little more than a strong distaste for "inflexible rules of exclusion," the Court rejects the *per se* test.

In so doing, the Court disregards two significant distinctions between the *per se* rule advocated in this case and the exclusionary remedies for certain other constitutional violations. First, the *per se* rule here is not "inflexible." Where evidence is suppressed as the fruit of an unlawful search, it may well be forever lost to the prosecution. Identification evidence, however, can by its very nature be readily and effectively reproduced. The in-court identification, permitted under

Wade and *Simmons* if it has a source independent of an uncounseled or suggestive procedure, is one example. Similarly, when a prosecuting attorney learns that there has been a suggestive confrontation, he can easily arrange another lineup conducted under scrupulously fair conditions. Second, other exclusionary rules have been criticized for preventing jury consideration of relevant and usually reliable evidence in order to serve an interest unrelated to guilt or innocence, such as discouraging illegal searches or denial of counsel. Suggestively obtained eyewitness testimony is excluded, in contrast, precisely because of its unreliability and concomitant irrelevance. Its exclusion both protects the integrity of the truth-seeking function of the trial and discourages police use of needlessly inaccurate and ineffective investigatory methods.

Indeed, impermissibly suggestive identifications are not merely worthless law enforcement tools. They pose a grave threat to society at large in a more direct way than most governmental disobedience of the law. For if the police and the public erroneously conclude, on the basis of an unnecessarily suggestive confrontation, that the right man has been caught and convicted, the real outlaw must still remain at large. Law enforcement has failed in its primary function and has left society unprotected from the depredations of an active criminal. The Court's totality test will allow seriously unreliable and misleading evidence to be put before juries. Equally important, it will allow dangerous criminals to remain on the streets while citizens assume that police action has given them protection. According to my calculus, all three of the factors upon which the Court relies point to acceptance of the *per se* approach.

Despite my strong disagreement with the Court over the proper standards to be applied in this case, I am pleased that its application of the totality test does recognize the continuing vitality of *Stovall*. In assessing the reliability of the identification, the Court mandates weighing "the corrupting effect of the suggestive identification itself" against the "indicators of a witness' ability to make an accurate identification." The Court holds, as *Neil v. Biggers* failed to, that a due process identification inquiry must take account of the suggestiveness of a confrontation and the likelihood that it led to misidentification, as recognized in *Stovall* and *Wade*. Thus, even if a witness did have an otherwise adequate opportunity to view a criminal, the later use of a highly suggestive identification procedure can render his testimony inadmissible. Assuming applicability of the totality test enunciated by the Court, the facts of the present case require that result.

I consider first the opportunity that Officer Glover had to view the suspect. Careful review of the record shows that he could see the heroin seller only for the time it took to speak three sentences of four or five short words, to hand over some money, and later after the door reopened, to receive the drugs in return. The entire face-to-face transaction could have taken as little as 15 or 20 seconds. During this time, Glover's attention was not focused exclusively on the seller's face. He observed that the door was opened 12 to 18 inches, that there was a window in the room behind the door, and that there was a woman standing behind the man. Glover was, also concentrating on the details of the transaction—he must have looked away from the seller's face to hand him the money and receive the drugs. The observation thus may have been as brief as 5 or 10 seconds.

Glover was a police officer trained in and attentive to the need for making accurate identifications. Nevertheless, both common sense and scholarly study indicate that while a trained observer such as a police officer "is somewhat less likely to make an erroneous identification than the average untrained observer, the mere fact that he has been trained is no guarantee that he is correct in a specific case. His identification testimony should be scrutinized just as carefully as that of the normal witness." Moreover, "identifications made by policemen in highly competitive activities, such as undercover narcotic agents, should be scrutinized with special care." Yet it is just such a searching inquiry that the Court fails to make here.

Another factor on which the Court relies—the witness' degree of certainty in making the identification—is worthless as an indicator that he is correct. Even if Glover had been unsure initially about his identification of respondent's picture, by the time he was called at trial to present a key piece of evidence for the State that paid his salary, it is impossible to imagine his responding negatively to such questions as "is there any doubt in your mind whatsoever" that the identification was correct. As the Court noted in *Wade*: "It is a matter of common experience that, once a witness has picked out the accused at the pretrial confrontation, he is not likely to go back on his word later on." The Court finds that because the identification procedure took place two days after the crime, its reliability is enhanced. While such temporal proximity makes the identification more reliable than one occurring months later, the greatest memory loss occurs within hours after an event. After that, the drop-off continues much more slowly. Thus, the reliability of an identification is increased only if it was made within several hours of the crime. If the time gap is any greater, reliability necessarily decreases.

Finally, the Court makes much of the fact that Glover gave a description of the seller to D'Onofrio shortly after the incident. Despite the Court's assertion that because "Glover himself was a Negro and unlikely to perceive only general features of 'hundreds of Hartford black males,' as the Court of Appeals stated," the description given by Glover was actually no more than a general summary of the seller's appearance. We may discount entirely the seller's clothing, for that was of no significance. Indeed, to the extent that Glover noticed clothes, his attention was diverted from the seller's face. Glover merely described vaguely the seller's height, skin color, hairstyle, and build. He did say that the seller had "high cheek-bones," but there is no other mention of facial features, nor even an estimate of age. Conspicuously absent is any indication that the seller was a native of the West Indies, certainly something which a member of the black community could immediately recognize from both appearance and accent.

The evidence of Glover's ability to make an accurate identification is far weaker than the Court finds. The procedure used to identify respondent was both extraordinarily suggestive and strongly conducive to error. In dismissing "the corrupting effect of the suggestive identification" procedure, the Court virtually grants the police license to convict the innocent. By displaying a single photo-graph of respondent to the witness Glover under the circumstances in this record almost everything that could have been done wrong was done wrong.

In the first place, there was no need to use a photograph at all. Because photos are static, two-dimensional, and often outdated, they are "clearly inferior in reliability" to corporeal procedures.

Worse still than the failure to use an easily available corporeal identification was the display to Glover of only a single picture, rather than a photo array. With good reason, such single-suspect procedures have "been widely condemned." They give no assurance that the witness can identify the criminal from among a number of persons of similar appearance, surely the strongest evidence that there was no misidentification.

The use of a single picture (or the display of a single live suspect) is a grave error because it dramatically suggests to the witness that the person shown must be the culprit. Why else would the police choose the person? It is deeply ingrained in human nature to agree with the expressed opinions of others—particularly others who should be more knowledgeable—when making a difficult decision. In this case, the pressure was not limited to that inherent in the display of a single photograph. Glover, the identifying witness, was a state police officer on special assignment. He knew that D'Onofrio, an experienced Hartford narcotics detective, presumably familiar with local drug operations, believed respondent to be the seller. There was at work, then, both loyalty to another police officer and deference to a better-informed colleague. Finally, there was Glover's knowledge that without an identification and arrest, government funds used to buy heroin had been wasted.

The Court discounts this overwhelming evidence of suggestiveness. It reasons that because D'Onofrio was not present when Glover viewed the photograph, there was "little pressure on the witness to acquiesce in the suggestion." That conclusion blinks psychological reality. There is no doubt that even in D'Onofrio's absence, a clear and powerful message was telegraphed to Glover as he looked at respondent's photograph. He was emphatically told that "*this* is the man," and he responded by identifying respondent then and at trial "whether or not he was in fact 'the man.' " There was "a very substantial likelihood of misidentification" of respondent Brathwaite. The suggestive display of respondent's photograph to the witness Glover likely erased any independent memory that Glover had retained of the seller from his barely adequate opportunity to observe the criminal.

Take Note

Review of identification procedures has been characterized by less demanding criteria than those governing confessions. Even if found reliable, an involuntary confession is inadmissible. *Jackson v. Denno*, 378 U.S. 368, 376 (1964). Relevant case law, when involuntary confessions were concerned, reflects not only an inclination to exclude such evidence but an insistence upon excusing the jury when arguments on admissibility are heard. Although the impact of an inadmissible identification may be as profound as that of a confession, the admissibility question may be resolved with the jury present. *Watkins v. Sowders*, 449 U.S. 341, 349 (1981). Beyond finding reliability an offset to suggestiveness, the Court also may reference an independent source of identification or harmless error as a factor that supports admissibility.

Food for Thought

Recall the earlier problem in which a lineup occurs before the suspect has been indicted or formally charged, and the suspect is forced to appear without the benefit of counsel. When the suspect is identified by the witness, and the suspect is ultimately indicted, you are appointed to represent him. You object that neither identification should be permitted. Now you need to develop proof to support your objection. What type of proof would be convincing and probative? How would you develop it?

Hypo #1: *Bail Hearing Identification*

Shortly after noon, the victim awakened from a nap to find a man holding a knife in the doorway to her bedroom. The man entered the bedroom, threw her face down on the bed, and choked her until she was quiet. After covering his face with a bandana, the intruder partially undressed the victim, forced her to commit oral sodomy, raped her, and left. When police arrived, the victim gave them a description of her assailant. Although she did not know who he was and had seen his face for only 10 to 15 seconds during the attack, she thought he was the same man who had made offensive remarks to her in a neighborhood bar the night before. In the week that followed, police showed the victim two groups of photographs. From the first group of 200 she picked about 30 men who resembled her assailant in height, weight, and build. From the second group of 10, she picked two or three. One of these was petitioner. Police arrested petitioner at his apartment and held him overnight pending a preliminary hearing. The next morning, a policeman accompanied the victim to court for the hearing. The policeman told her she was going to view a suspect and should identify him if she could. He also asked her to sign a complaint that named petitioner as her assailant. At the hearing, petitioner's name was called and he was led before the bench. The judge told petitioner that he was charged with rape and deviate sexual behavior. The judge then called the victim, who had been in the courtroom waiting for the case to be called, to come before the bench. The State's Attorney stated that police had found evidence linking petitioner with the offenses charged. He asked the victim whether she saw her assailant in the courtroom, and she pointed at petitioner. At trial, the victim testified on direct examination that she had identified petitioner as her assailant at the preliminary hearing. She also testified that petitioner was the man who had raped her. Was petitioner's right to counsel, or his right to due process, violated by the pretrial identification? Should the witness be allowed to make an in-court identification of petitioner or to testify regarding the pre-trial identification? What arguments might be made on the defendant's behalf? How might the state respond to those arguments? *See Moore v. Illinois*, 434 U.S. 220 (1977).

Food for Thought

As we have seen, even though a defendant cannot object to a prior photographic identification on Sixth Amendment right to counsel grounds, he might be able to raise a due process objection. If you are appointed to represent a defendant confronted by this situation, what types of evidence might help you establish a due process violation? How might you develop the evidence?

Hypo #2: *More on Show Ups*

Police officers are observing a night club because rival gangs tend to congregate there, and problems sometimes develop. The police observe several men run out of the club, and then a BMW pulls up with a driver and passenger who are covered in blood. The police then seal off the club and order all male patrons to submit to a "show up" with the former BMW occupants. The process takes forty minutes. Palacios is identified as one of the perpetrators during the show up. Although the results of the show up are admitted at Palacios trial (at which he was convicted), the surviving BMW occupant (the other died on the night of the incident) was unable to identify Palacios as one of the perpetrators. Nevertheless, Palacios is convicted. In subjecting the males to the show up, were they "seized" within the meaning of the Fourth Amendment? If so, was the seizure permissible? Was the show up permissible and admissible at trial? *See Palacios v. Burge*, 589 F.3d 556 (2d Cir. 2009).

Hypo #3: *More on Identification Admissibility*

During the night, two men (Clark and Henderson) forcefully enter an apartment to collect money owed to Clark. While Harper (the victim) and Clark go to a different room to discuss the situation, the other man (Henderson) points a gun at Womble and tells him, "Don't move, stay right here, you're not involved in this." Womble testifies that he "got a look at" the stranger, but not "a real good look." Womble did overhear Clark and Harper arguing in the other room. Harper said, "do what you got to do," after which Womble heard a gunshot. Womble then walks into the room, sees Clark holding a handgun, offers to get Clark the $160, and urges him not to shoot Harper again. As Clark leaves, he warns Womble, "Don't rat me out, I know where you live." Harper dies from the gunshot wound. When approached by the police, Womble initially lies regarding being able to identify the perpetrator. He later admits that he lied because he "didn't want to get involved" for fear that they will retaliate against his elderly father. Womble leads the investigators to Clark, who eventually gives a statement about his involvement and identifies the person who accompanied him as Henderson. The officers then ask Womble to view a photographic array that involves seven "filler" photos and a photo of Henderson. The eight photos all depict headshots of white men between the ages of twenty-eight and thirty-five, with short hair, goatees, and similar facial features. Womble quickly eliminates five of the photos. He then reviews the remaining three, discounts one more, and says that he "isn't 100 percent sure of the final two pictures." Officers MacNair and Ruiz believe that Womble is holding back based on fear. Ruiz said Womble was "nervous, upset about his father." In an effort to calm Womble, MacNair "tells him to focus, calm down, relax and that any type of protection that he needs, any threats against him would be put to rest by the Police Department." Ruiz adds, "just do what you have to do, and we'll be out of here." In response, Womble says that he "can make an identification." The entire exchange lasts less than one minute. Then Officer McNair reshuffles the eight photos and again displays them to Womble sequentially. This time, when Womble sees defendant's photo, he slams his hand on the table and exclaims, "that's the guy." From start to finish, the entire process takes fifteen minutes. Womble does not recant his identification, but testifies that he felt as though Detective McNair was "nudging" him to choose defendant's photo, and "that there was pressure" to make a choice. Should the results of the photo identification be admitted at trial? Why or why not? *See State v. Henderson*, 208 N.J. 208, 27 A.3d 872 (N.J. 2011).

Food for Thought

A police officer responds to a burglary in progress, reportedly involving two black men and one white man. When he arrives at the house, the officer sees that the door has been forced open and that there are no lights on inside the house. He also sees that there is a staircase to the second floor that faces away from the front door towards the rear sliding-glass door. The base of the staircase is fifteen feet away and the sliding glass door is another three feet away. After hearing movement upstairs, the officer yells "police," and then he hears two individuals run down the stairs and bolt out the sliding glass door. Each man glances at the officer, but only for a brief "second." One is a "heavyset white male of medium complexion, and the other is a black male, not as heavy, with cornrows in his hair, light skin color, wearing a black jacket." Suppose that other police officers (who came to provide backup) apprehend several men a few minutes later, and the initial police officer identifies them based on the initial encounter. If you represent the defendant, how would you challenge the officer's identification of the man? *See Byrd v. State*, 25 A.3d 761 (Del. 2011).

Hypo #4: *More on the Byrd Problem*

Now, let's add a few facts to the prior problem. While the events are in progress, a third officer arrives on the scene, notices a black male (who turns out to be Denzel Butler) and an older woman (Butler's mother) standing in front of the house adjacent to the crime scene property, and decides to talk to Butler and his mother. Butler tells the officer that, earlier in the day, he saw three men in the street. He spoke briefly to one of the men with whom he had attended high school. Would your conclusion in the prior problem be different if the officer's testimony was supported by Butler's testimony and identification? *See Byrd v. State*, 25 A.3d 761 (Del. 2011).

Hypo # 5: *In-Court Identifications*

Do in-court identifications present special difficulties for defendants, especially when the witness has not previously been asked to make an out-of-court identification? After all, when the witness makes the identification, the defendant is likely to be sitting at the defense table, and therefore there is a suggestion of guilt because the state has decided to prosecute the defendant. The advantage of an in-court identification is that there is no prior suggestive out-of-court identification. Should courts be particularly wary of first-time in-court identifications? See *Commonwealth v. Crayton*, 21 N.E.3d 157 (Mass. Sup. Jud. Ct., Middlesex, 2015). What steps, if any, could a trial court take to overcome the suggestiveness inherent in an in-court identification?

Hypo # 6: *More on In-Court Identifications*

Would it matter if there had been a prior inconclusive out-of court identification? Suppose that a man is the only eyewitness to a murder. However, he had only a fleeting opportunity to view the perpetrator. He is shown a non-suggestive photographic display and fails to make an identification. However, he does suggest that defendant might be the perpetrator, and asks to see a side view of him (at the scene of the crime, the eyewitness had only a side view of the murderer). However, none is available. At trial, under oath, the eyewitness is asked whether he sees the perpetrator in the courtroom. The eyewitness immediately identifies defendant who is sitting with defense counsel. The defense objects that the identification is unduly suggestive under the circumstances, especially given the fact that defendant is sitting at the defense table, and obviously has been singled out for prosecution, and given the prior failure to make an identification. Should the in-court identification be admissible? Should any additional proof be required of the prosecution? *See Commonwealth v. Collins*, 21 N.E.3d 528 (Mass. 2014).

Hypo # 7: *Witness Identifications and Videos*

Suppose that the culprit of a crime is captured on video committing the crime, but the video is a bit fuzzy. A police detective circulates a picture of the culprit to other police officers, and one is able to identify the culprit as defendant. At trial, should the fellow officer be able to testify regarding the identity of the culprit? Or should the judge leave it to the jury to view the video itself, compare the image on the video to defendant, and make its own determination regarding whether defendant is the culprit? *See People v. Thompson*, 49 N.E.3d 393 (2016).

Hypo # 8: *The Man in the Mask*

A man, while wearing a ski mask, exposes himself to a young girl. Before the police ask the girl to identify the man in a showup, they tell her that they caught the man, and they dress him in a jacket similar to that worn by the culprit. She admits on cross-examination that she did not see the culprit's face at the scene of the crime, but claims that she can identify the jacket on the suspect as the one worn by the culprit. At the show-up, she is unable to identify the suspect's face but does identify the suspect based on the jacket. Is the girl's identification admissible? *See State v. Jones*, 224 N.J. 70, 128 A.3d 1096 (2016).

Perry v. New Hampshire

565 U.S. 338 (2012).

JUSTICE GINSBURG delivered the opinion of the Court.

In our system of justice, fair trial for persons charged with criminal offenses is secured by the Sixth Amendment, which guarantees to defendants the right to counsel, compulsory process to obtain defense witnesses, and the opportunity to cross-examine witnesses for the prosecution. Those safeguards apart, admission of evidence in state trials is ordinarily governed by state law, and the reliability of relevant testimony typically falls within the province of the jury to determine. This Court has recognized, in addition, a due process check on the admission of eyewitness identification, applicable when the police have arranged suggestive circumstances leading the witness to identify a particular person as the perpetrator of a crime. An identification infected by improper police influence is not automatically excluded. Instead, the trial judge must screen the evidence for reliability pretrial. If there is "a very substantial likelihood of irreparable misidentification," *Simmons v. United States,* 390 U.S. 377, 384 (1968), the judge must disallow presentation of the evidence at trial. But if the indicia of reliability are strong enough to outweigh the corrupting effect of the police-arranged suggestive circumstances, the identification evidence ordinarily will be admitted, and the jury will ultimately determine its worth.

We have not extended pretrial screening for reliability to cases in which the suggestive circumstances were not arranged by law enforcement officers. Petitioner requests that we do so because of the grave risk that mistaken identification will yield a miscarriage of justice. Our decisions, however, turn on the presence of state action and aim to deter police from rigging identification procedures, for example, at a lineup, showup, or photograph array. When no improper law enforcement activity is involved, it suffices to test reliability through the rights and opportunities generally designed for that purpose, notably, the presence of counsel at postindictment lineups, vigorous cross-examination, protective rules of evidence, and jury instructions on both the fallibility of eyewitness identification and the requirement that guilt be proved beyond a reasonable doubt.

Around 3 a.m. on August 15, 2008, Joffre Ullon called the Nashua, New Hampshire, Police Department and reported that an African-American male was trying to break into cars parked in the lot of Ullon's apartment building. Officer Nicole Clay responded to the call. Upon arriving at the parking lot, Clay heard what "sounded like a metal bat hitting the ground." She then saw petitioner Perry standing between two cars. Perry walked toward Clay, holding two car-stereo amplifiers in his hands. A metal bat lay on the ground behind him. Clay asked Perry where the amplifiers came from. "I found them on the ground," Perry responded. Meanwhile, Ullon's wife, Nubia Blandon, woke her neighbor, Alex Clavijo, and told him she had just seen someone break into his car. Clavijo immediately went downstairs to the parking lot to inspect the car. He first observed that one of the rear windows had been shattered. On further inspection, he discovered that the speakers and amplifiers from his car stereo were missing, as were his bat and wrench. Clavijo then approached Clay and told her about Blandon's alert and his own subsequent observations.

By this time, another officer had arrived at the scene. Clay asked Perry to stay in the parking lot with that officer, while she and Clavijo went to talk to Blandon. Clay and Clavijo then entered the apartment building and took the stairs to the fourth floor, where Blandon's and Clavijo's apartments were located. They met Blandon in the hallway just outside the open door to her apartment.

Asked to describe what she had seen, Blandon stated that, around 2:30 a.m., she saw from her kitchen window a tall, African-American man roaming the parking lot and looking into cars. Eventually, the man circled Clavijo's car, opened the trunk, and removed a large box.[2]

Clay asked Blandon for a more specific description of the man. Blandon pointed to her kitchen window and said the person she saw breaking into Clavijo's car was standing in the parking lot, next to the police officer. Perry's arrest followed this identification. About a month later, the police showed Blandon a photographic array that included a picture of Perry and asked her to point out the man who had broken into Clavijo's car. Blandon was unable to identify Perry.

Perry was charged in New Hampshire state court with one count of theft by unauthorized taking and one count of criminal mischief. He moved to suppress

---

[2] The box, which Clay found on the ground near where she first encountered Perry, contained car-stereo speakers.

Blandon's identification on the ground that admitting it at trial would violate due process. Blandon witnessed what amounted to a one-person showup in the parking lot, Perry asserted, which all but guaranteed that she would identify him as the culprit.

The New Hampshire Superior Court denied the motion. We granted certiorari to resolve a division of opinion on the question whether the Due Process Clause requires a trial judge to conduct a preliminary assessment of the reliability of an eyewitness identification made under suggestive circumstances not arranged by the police.

The Constitution protects a defendant against a conviction based on evidence of questionable reliability, not by prohibiting introduction of the evidence, but by affording the defendant means to persuade the jury that the evidence should be discounted as unworthy of credit. Constitutional safeguards available to defendants to counter the State's evidence include the Sixth Amendment rights to counsel, *Gideon v. Wainwright,* 372 U.S. 335 (1963); compulsory process, *Taylor v. Illinois,* 484 U.S. 400 (1988); and confrontation plus cross-examination of witnesses, *Delaware v. Fensterer,* 474 U.S. 15 (1985) *(per curiam).* Apart from these guarantees, state and federal statutes and rules ordinarily govern the admissibility of evidence, and juries are assigned the task of determining the reliability of the evidence presented at trial. See *Kansas v. Ventris,* 556 U.S. 586 (2009). Only when evidence "is so extremely unfair that its admission violates fundamental conceptions of justice," have we imposed a constraint tied to the Due Process Clause. See, *e.g., Napue v. Illinois,* 360 U.S. 264, 269 (1959).

Contending that the Due Process Clause is implicated here, Perry relies on a series of decisions involving police-arranged identification procedures. In *Stovall v. Denno,* 388 U.S. 293 (1967), a witness identified the defendant as her assailant after police officers brought the defendant to the witness' hospital room. Although the police-arranged showup was undeniably suggestive, the Court held that no due process violation occurred. Crucial to the Court's decision was the procedure's necessity: The witness was the only person who could identify or exonerate the defendant; the witness could not leave her hospital room; and it was uncertain whether she would live to identify the defendant in more neutral circumstances. A year later, in *Simmons v. United States,* 390 U.S. 377 (1968), the Court held that when a witness identifies the defendant in a police-organized photo lineup, the identification should be suppressed only where "the photographic identification procedure was so unnecessarily suggestive as to give rise to a very substantial likelihood of irreparable misidentification." The Court rejected the defendant's due process challenge to admission of the identification. In contrast, the Court held in *Foster v. California,* 394 U.S. 440 (1969), that due process required the exclusion of an eyewitness identification obtained through police-arranged procedures that "made it all but inevitable that the witness would identify the defendant."

Synthesizing previous decisions, we set forth in *Neil v. Biggers*, 409 U.S. 188 (1972), and reiterated in *Manson v. Brathwaite*, 432 U.S. 98 (1977), the approach appropriately used to determine whether the Due Process Clause requires suppression of an eyewitness identification tainted by police arrangement. The Court emphasized, first, that due process concerns arise only when law enforcement officers use an identification procedure that is both suggestive and unnecessary. Even when the police use such a procedure, suppression of the resulting identification is not the inevitable consequence. A rule requiring automatic exclusion, the Court reasoned, would "go too far," for it would "keep evidence from the jury that is reliable and relevant," and "may result, on occasion, in the guilty going free." The Court held that the Due Process Clause requires courts to assess, on a case-by-case basis, whether improper police conduct created a "substantial likelihood of misidentification." "Reliability [of the eyewitness identification] is the linchpin" of that evaluation, the Court stated in *Brathwaite*. Where the "indicators of a witness' ability to make an accurate identification" are "outweighed by the corrupting effect" of law enforcement suggestion, the identification should be suppressed. Otherwise, the evidence (if admissible in all other respects) should be submitted to the jury.[5]

Applying this "totality of the circumstances" approach, the Court held in *Biggers* that law enforcement's use of an unnecessarily suggestive showup did not require suppression of the victim's identification of her assailant. Notwithstanding the improper procedure, the victim's identification was reliable: She saw her assailant for a considerable period of time under adequate light, provided police with a detailed description of her attacker long before the showup, and had "no doubt" that the defendant was the person she had seen. Similarly, the Court concluded in *Brathwaite* that police use of an unnecessarily suggestive photo array did not require exclusion of the resulting identification. The witness, an undercover police officer, viewed the defendant in good light for several minutes, provided a thorough description of the suspect, and was certain of his identification. Hence, the "indicators of the witness' ability to make an accurate identification were hardly outweighed by the corrupting effect of the challenged identification."

Perry concedes that, in contrast to every case in the *Stovall* line, law enforcement officials did not arrange the suggestive circumstances surrounding Blandon's identification. The rationale underlying our decisions, Perry asserts, supports a rule requiring trial judges to prescreen eyewitness evidence for reliability any time an identification is made under suggestive circumstances. We disagree. Perry's argument depends, in large part, on the Court's statement in *Brathwaite* that "reliability is the linchpin in determining the admissibility of identification testimony."

---

[5] Among "factors to be considered" in evaluating a witness' "ability to make an accurate identification," the Court listed: "the opportunity of the witness to view the criminal at the time of the crime, the witness' degree of attention, the accuracy of his prior description of the criminal, the level of certainty demonstrated at the confrontation, and the time between the crime and the confrontation." *Manson v. Brathwaite*, 432 U.S. 98 (1977) (citing *Neil v. Biggers*, 409 U.S. 188, 199–200 (1972)).

If reliability is the linchpin of admissibility under the Due Process Clause, Perry maintains, it should make no difference whether law enforcement was responsible for creating the suggestive circumstances that marred the identification.

Perry has removed our statement in *Brathwaite* from its mooring. The *Brathwaite* Court's reference to reliability appears in a portion of the opinion concerning the appropriate remedy *when the police use an unnecessarily suggestive identification procedure*. The Court adopted a judicial screen for reliability as a course preferable to a *per se* rule requiring exclusion of identification evidence whenever law enforcement officers employ an improper procedure. The due process check for reliability comes into play only after the defendant establishes improper police conduct. The very purpose of the check is to avoid depriving the jury of identification evidence that is reliable, *notwithstanding* improper police conduct. A primary aim of excluding identification evidence obtained under unnecessarily suggestive circumstances is to deter law enforcement use of improper lineups, showups, and photo arrays in the first place. Alerted to the prospect that identification evidence improperly obtained may be excluded, police officers will "guard against unnecessarily suggestive procedures." This deterrence rationale is inapposite in cases, like Perry's, in which the police engaged in no improper conduct. *Coleman v. Alabama*, 399 U.S. 1 (1970), another decision in the *Stovall* line, similarly shows that the Court has linked the due process check, not to suspicion of eyewitness testimony generally, but only to improper police arrangement of the circumstances surrounding an identification. The defendants in *Coleman* contended that a witness' in-court identifications violated due process, because a pretrial stationhouse lineup was "so unduly prejudicial and conducive to irreparable misidentification as fatally to taint the later identifications." The Court rejected this argument. No due process violation occurred, the plurality explained, because nothing "the police said or did prompted the witness' virtually spontaneous identification of the defendants." True, Coleman was the only person in the lineup wearing a hat, the plurality noted, but "nothing in the record showed that he was required to do so."

Perry and the dissent place significant weight on *United States v. Wade*, 388 U.S. 218 (1967), describing it as a decision not anchored to improper police conduct. In fact, the risk of police rigging was the very danger to which the Court responded in *Wade* when it recognized a defendant's right to counsel at postindictment, police-organized identification procedures. "The confrontation *compelled by the State* between the accused and the victim or witnesses," the Court began, "is peculiarly riddled with innumerable dangers and variable factors which might seriously, even crucially, derogate from a fair trial." "A major factor contributing to the high incidence of miscarriage of justice from mistaken identification," the Court continued, "has been the degree of suggestion inherent in the manner in which *the prosecution* presents the suspect to witnesses for pretrial identification." To illustrate the improper suggestion it was concerned about, the Court pointed to police-designed lineups where "all in the lineup but the suspect were known to the identifying witness, the other participants in the lineup were grossly dissimilar in appearance to the suspect, only the suspect was required to wear distinctive clothing which the culprit allegedly wore, the witness is told by the police that they have caught the culprit after which the defendant is brought before the witness alone or is viewed in jail, the suspect is pointed out before or during a lineup, the participants in the lineup are asked to try on an article of clothing which fits only the suspect." Beyond genuine debate, then, prevention of unfair police practices prompted the Court to extend a defendant's right to counsel to cover postindictment lineups and showups.

Perry's argument would open the door to judicial preview, under the banner of due process, of most, if not all, eyewitness identifications. External suggestion is hardly the only factor that casts doubt on the trustworthiness of an eyewitness' testimony. Many other factors bear on "the likelihood of misidentification"—for example, the passage of time between exposure to and identification of the defendant, whether the witness was under stress when he first encountered the suspect, how much time the witness had to observe the suspect, how far the witness was from the suspect, whether the suspect carried a weapon, and the race of the suspect and the witness. There is no reason why an identification made by an eyewitness with poor vision, for example, or one who harbors a grudge against the defendant, should be regarded as inherently more reliable, less of a "threat to the fairness of trial," than the identification Blandon made in this case. To embrace Perry's view would thus entail a vast enlargement of the reach of due process as a constraint on the admission of evidence.

Perry maintains that the Court can limit the due process check he proposes to identifications made under "suggestive circumstances." Even if we could rationally distinguish suggestiveness from other factors bearing on the reliability of eyewitness evidence, Perry's limitation would still involve trial courts, routinely, in preliminary examinations. Most eyewitness identifications involve some element of suggestion. Indeed, all in-court identifications do. Out-of-court identifications volunteered by witnesses are also likely to involve suggestive circumstances. For example, suppose a witness identifies the defendant to police officers after seeing a photograph of the defendant in the press captioned "theft suspect," or hearing a radio report implicating the defendant in the crime. Or suppose the witness knew that the defendant ran with the wrong crowd and saw him on the day and in the vicinity of the crime. Any of these circumstances might have "suggested" to the witness that the defendant was the person the witness observed committing the crime.

Perry maintains that eyewitness identifications are a uniquely unreliable form of evidence. We do not doubt either the importance or the fallibility of eyewitness identifications. Indeed, in recognizing that defendants have a constitutional right to counsel at postindictment police lineups, we observed that "the annals of criminal law are rife with instances of mistaken identification." *Wade,* 388 U.S. at 228[.] We have concluded in other contexts, however, that the potential unreliability of a type of evidence does not alone render its introduction at the defendant's trial fundamentally unfair. See, *e.g., Ventris,* 556 U.S. at 594. We reach a similar conclusion here: The fallibility of eyewitness evidence does not, without the taint of improper state conduct, warrant a due process rule requiring a trial court to screen such evidence for reliability before allowing the jury to assess its creditworthiness.

Our unwillingness to enlarge the domain of due process rests, in large part, on our recognition that the jury, not the judge, traditionally determines the reliability of evidence. We also take account of other safeguards built into our adversary system that caution juries against placing undue weight on eyewitness testimony of questionable reliability. These protections include the defendant's Sixth Amendment right to confront the eyewitness. See *Maryland v. Craig,* 497 U.S. 836, 845 (1990). Another is the defendant's right to the effective assistance of an attorney, who can expose the flaws in the eyewitness' testimony during cross-examination and focus the jury's attention on the fallibility of such testimony during opening and closing arguments. Eyewitness-specific jury instructions, which many federal and state courts have adopted, likewise warn the jury to take care in appraising identification evidence. State and federal rules of evidence, moreover, permit trial judges to exclude relevant evidence if its probative value is substantially outweighed by its prejudicial impact or potential for misleading the jury. See, *e.g.,* Fed. Rule Evid. 403. In appropriate cases, some States also permit defendants to present expert testimony on the hazards of eyewitness identification evidence.

Many of the safeguards just noted were at work at Perry's trial. During her opening statement, Perry's court-appointed attorney cautioned the jury about the vulnerability of Blandon's identification. While cross-examining Blandon and Officer Clay, Perry's attorney constantly brought up the weaknesses of Blandon's identification. Perry's counsel reminded the jury of these frailties during her summation. After closing arguments, the trial court read the jury a lengthy instruction on identification testimony and the factors the jury should consider when evaluating it. The court also instructed the jury that the defendant's guilt must be proved beyond a reasonable doubt, and specifically cautioned that "one of the things the State must prove beyond a reasonable doubt is the identification of the defendant as the person who committed the offense."

Given the safeguards generally applicable in criminal trials, protections availed of by the defense in Perry's case, we hold that the introduction of Blandon's eyewitness testimony, without a preliminary judicial assessment of its reliability, did not render Perry's trial fundamentally unfair.

For the foregoing reasons, we agree with the New Hampshire courts' appraisal of our decisions. Finding no convincing reason to alter our precedent, we hold that the Due Process Clause does not require a preliminary judicial inquiry into the reliability of an eyewitness identification when the identification was not procured under unnecessarily suggestive circumstances arranged by law enforcement. Accordingly, the judgment of the New Hampshire Supreme Court is

Affirmed.

Justice Thomas, concurring.

The *Stovall* line of cases is premised on a "substantive due process" right to "fundamental fairness." Those cases are wrongly decided because the Fourteenth Amendment's Due Process Clause is not a "secret repository of substantive guarantees against 'unfairness.'" *BMW of North America, Inc. v. Gore,* 517 U.S. 559 (1996) (Scalia, J., dissenting). I would limit the Court's suggestive eyewitness identification cases to the precise circumstances that they involved.

Justice Sotomayor, dissenting.

This Court has long recognized that eyewitness identifications' unique confluence of features—their unreliability, susceptibility to suggestion, powerful impact on the jury, and resistance to the ordinary tests of the adversarial process—can undermine the fairness of a trial. Our cases thus establish a clear rule: The admission at trial of out-of-court eyewitness identifications derived from impermissibly suggestive circumstances that pose a very substantial likelihood of misidentification violates due process. The Court today announces that that rule does not even "come into play" unless the suggestive circumstances are improperly "police-arranged." Our due process concern, however, arises not from the act of suggestion, but rather from the corrosive effects of suggestion on the reliability of the resulting identification. The Court's holding enshrines a murky distinction—between suggestive confrontations intentionally orchestrated by the police and, as here, those inadvertently caused by police actions—that will sow confusion. It ignores our precedents' acute sensitivity to the hazards of intentional and unintentional suggestion alike and unmoors our rule from the very interest it protects, inviting arbitrary results. And it recasts the driving force of our decisions as an interest in police deterrence, rather than reliability.

The "driving force" behind *Wade, Gilbert,* and *Stovall* was "the Court's concern with the problems of eyewitness identification"—specifically, "the concern that the jury not hear eyewitness testimony unless that evidence has aspects of reliability." *Manson v. Brathwaite,* 432 U.S. 98, 111 (1977). We have pointed to the "formidable" number of "miscarriages of justice from mistaken identification" in the annals of criminal law. *Wade,* 388 U.S. at 228. We have warned of the "vagaries" and "proverbially untrustworthy" nature of eyewitness identifications. And we have singled out a "major factor contributing" to that proverbial unreliability: "the suggestibility inherent in the context of the pretrial identification." Our precedents make no distinction between intentional and unintentional suggestion. To the contrary, they explicitly state that "suggestion can be created intentionally or unintentionally in many subtle ways." *Moore v. Illinois,* 434 U.S. 220 (1977). The implication is that even police acting with the best of intentions can inadvertently signal "that's the man." *Wade,* 388 U.S. at 236.

In *Wade,* we noted that the "potential for improper influence [in pretrial confrontations] is illustrated by the circumstances." In underscoring the hazards, we made no mention of whether the encounter had been arranged; indeed, the facts suggest that it was not. More generally, our precedents focus not on the act of suggestion, but on suggestion's "corrupting effect" on reliability. *Brathwaite,* 432 U.S. at 114. Eyewitness evidence derived from suggestive circumstances is uniquely resistant to the ordinary tests of the adversary process. An eyewitness who has made an identification often becomes convinced of its accuracy. "*Regardless of how the initial misidentification comes about,* the witness thereafter is apt to retain in his memory the image of the photograph rather than of the person actually seen, reducing the trustworthiness of subsequent courtroom identification." *Simmons v. United States,* 390 U.S. 377, 383 (1968). Suggestion bolsters that confidence.

At trial, an eyewitness' artificially inflated confidence in an identification's accuracy complicates the jury's task of assessing witness credibility and reliability. It also impairs the defendant's ability to attack the eyewitness' credibility. That in turn jeopardizes the defendant's basic right to subject his accuser to meaningful cross-examination. See *Wade,* 388 U.S. at 235. The end result of suggestion, whether intentional or unintentional, is to fortify testimony bearing directly on guilt that juries find extremely convincing and are hesitant to discredit.

Consistent with our focus on reliability, we have declined to adopt a *per se* rule excluding all suggestive identifications. Instead, "reliability is the linchpin" in deciding admissibility. *Brathwaite,* 432 U.S. at 114. To protect that evidentiary interest, we have applied a two-step inquiry: First, the defendant has the burden of showing that the eyewitness identification was derived through "impermissibly suggestive" means. *Simmons,* 390 U.S. at 384. Second, if the defendant meets that burden, courts consider whether the identification was reliable under the totality of the circumstances. That step entails considering the witness' opportunity to view the perpetrator, degree of attention, accuracy of description, level of certainty, and the time between the crime and pretrial confrontation, then weighing such factors against the "corrupting effect of the suggestive identification." *Brathwaite,* 432 U.S. at 108, 114. Most identifications will be admissible. The standard of "fairness as required by the Due Process Clause" demands that a subset of the most unreliable identifications—those carrying a "very substantial likelihood of misidentification"—will be excluded. *Biggers,* 409 U.S. at 198.

The majority today categorically exempts all eyewitness identifications derived from suggestive circumstances that were not police-manipulated—however suggestive, and however unreliable—from our due process check. Police intent is now paramount. The opinion suggests that the police must arrange an identification "procedure," regardless of whether they "intend the arranged procedure to be suggestive." Elsewhere, it indicates that the police must arrange the "suggestive circumstances" that lead the witness to identify the accused. Still elsewhere it refers to "improper" police conduct, connoting bad faith. Does police "arrangement" relate to the procedure, the suggestiveness, or both? If it relates to the procedure, do suggestive preprocedure encounters no longer raise the same concerns? If the police need not "intend the arranged procedure to be suggestive," what makes the police action "improper"? Does that mean that good-faith, unintentional police suggestiveness in a police-arranged lineup can be "impermissibly suggestive"? If no, the majority runs headlong into *Wade.* If yes, on what basis—if not deterrence—does it distinguish unintentional police suggestiveness in an accidental confrontation?

The arrangement-focused inquiry will sow needless confusion. If the police had called Perry and Blandon to the police station for interviews, and Blandon saw Perry being questioned, would that be sufficiently "improper police arrangement"? If Perry had voluntarily come to the police station, would that change the result? Today's opinion renders the applicability of our ordinary inquiry contingent on a murky line-drawing exercise. Whereas our two-step inquiry focuses on overall reliability—and could account for the spontaneity of the witness' identification and degree of police manipulation under the totality of the circumstances—today's opinion forecloses that assessment by establishing a new and inflexible step zero.

The vast majority of eyewitness identifications that the State uses in criminal prosecutions are obtained in lineup, showup, and photograph displays arranged by the police. Our precedents reflect that practical reality. It is also beside the point. Our due process concerns were not predicated on the source of suggestiveness. Rather, "it is the likelihood of misidentification which violates a defendant's right to due process," *Biggers,* 409 U.S. at 198. Whether the police have created the suggestive circumstances intentionally or inadvertently, the resulting identification raises the same due process concerns. The arrangement-focused inquiry thus untethers our doctrine from the very " 'evidentiary interest' " it was designed to protect, inviting arbitrary results.

The majority's approach lies in tension with our precedents. Whereas we previously disclaimed the crabbed view of suggestiveness as "the result of police procedures intentionally designed to prejudice an accused," *Wade,* 388 U.S. at 235, the majority's focus on police rigging and improper conduct will revive it. Whereas our precedents were sensitive to intentional and unintentional suggestiveness alike, today's decision narrows our concern to intentionally orchestrated suggestive confrontations. We once described the "primary evil to be avoided" as the likelihood of misidentification. *Biggers,* 409 U.S. at 198. Today's decision means that even if that primary evil is at its apex, we need not avoid it at all so long as the suggestive circumstances do not stem from improper police arrangement.

The majority insists that our precedents "aim to deter police from rigging identification procedures," so our rule should be limited to applications that advance that "primary aim" and "key premise." That mischaracterizes our cases. First, we noted the "driving force" behind *Wade* and its companion cases—"the concern that the jury not hear eyewitness testimony unless that evidence has aspects of reliability." In addition to deterrence, we also noted a "third factor"—"the effect on the administration of justice"—describing the *per se* rule as having serious drawbacks on this front. In *Coleman,* we held that no due process violation occurred because the in-court identification appeared to be "entirely based upon observations at the time of the assault and not at all induced by the conduct of the lineup," and thus could not be said to stem from an identification procedure "so impermissibly suggestive as to give rise to a very substantial likelihood of irreparable misidentification."

The majority emphasizes that we should rely on the jury to determine the reliability of evidence. But jurors find eyewitness evidence unusually powerful and their ability to assess credibility is hindered by a witness' false confidence in the accuracy of his or her identification. That disability in no way depends on the intent behind the suggestive circumstances. The majority also suggests that applying our rule beyond police-arranged suggestive circumstances would entail a heavy practical burden, requiring courts to engage in "preliminary judicial inquiry" into "most, if not all, eyewitness identifications." But that is inaccurate. The burden of showing "impermissibly suggestive" circumstances is the defendant's, so the objection falls to the defendant to raise. Today's decision nonetheless precludes even the possibility that an unintended confrontation will meet that bar, mandating summary dismissal of every such claim at the threshold.

Finally, the majority questions how to "rationally distinguish suggestiveness from other factors bearing on the reliability of eyewitness evidence," such as "poor vision" or a prior "grudge," and more broadly, how to distinguish eyewitness evidence from other kinds of arguably unreliable evidence. Our precedents, however, did just that. The majority points to no other type of evidence that shares the rare confluence of characteristics that makes eyewitness evidence a unique threat to the fairness of trial. Jailhouse informants, unreliable as they may be, are not similarly resistant to the traditional tools of the adversarial process and, if anything, are met with particular skepticism by juries.

The empirical evidence demonstrates that eyewitness misidentification is "the single greatest cause of wrongful convictions in this country."[3] Researchers have found that a staggering 76% of the first 250 convictions overturned due to DNA evidence since 1989 involved eyewitness misidentification. Study after study demonstrates that eyewitness recollections are highly susceptible to distortion by postevent information or social cues; that jurors routinely overestimate the accuracy of eyewitness identifications; that jurors place the greatest weight on eyewitness confidence in assessing identifications even though confidence is a poor gauge of accuracy; and that suggestiveness can stem from sources beyond police-orchestrated procedures. The majority today nevertheless adopts an artificially narrow conception of the dangers of suggestive identifications at a time when our concerns should have deepened.

Hypo # 1: *The Ex-Girlfriend and the Pregnant Wife*

JC received a late evening call from his ex-girlfriend, Cecilia Chen. JC stated that he was happily married and expecting a child. Defendant told him that she had recently broken up with her boyfriend, and wondered "how things might have turned out" had they remained together. Chen cried during the conversation. Several days later, Helen (JC's wife), who was 5 months pregnant, received a phone call asking for JC. The caller explained that she was calling about a mortgage with Bank of America (the Kims had no such mortgage). The caller ID listed "Foley's Liquor Store"—located nearby. Helen went back to sleep but was awakened by the sound of knocking on the front door. When she responded, she saw a young woman she did not know. The woman explained that her car had broken down and asked to use a phone. Helen offered the woman a cell phone, but the woman said she needed to use the bathroom. Helen let the woman enter the house and noticed a computer cord sticking out of her left sleeve. Helen then called JC to tell him about the strange phone call and the woman. While they were speaking, the woman returned from the bathroom, grabbed Helen, and stabbed her with a kitchen knife in the shoulder. JC called 9-1-1. Helen fought back. The woman also tried to use the computer cord to choke Helen. Eventually, Helen disarmed her attacker. As Helen was about to strike her, the woman said, "Don't do anything to hurt your baby." Helen froze and the woman ran off.

---

[3]*State v. Henderson,* 208 N.J. 208, 231, 27 A.3d 872, 885 (2011).

When the police responded, Helen described her assailant as an Asian or Filipino woman, about 5'4", wearing a black jacket, gray hood, dark pants, brown boots, and black gloves. Helen added that her attacker was about twenty to twenty-five years old, weighed between 110 and 120 pounds, and wore black frame glasses and a gray scarf. The police were unable to locate the attacker, but recovered a pair of black-rimmed glasses, a steak knife, and a computer cord. The neighbor provided a similar description to the police within two hours of the attack. In a signed statement, the neighbor stated, "I didn't see her face except for a second when she turned."

Helen, who was unable to sleep after the incident, drew a picture of her assailant. When JC saw the picture, he stated that "it looked a little familiar." JC then accessed Chen's personal website and showed Helen five to ten pictures of Chen on the computer. When she saw one particular picture, Helen "just jumped" and was "ninety percent positive" that Chen was her attacker. Helen said she was not completely certain because Chen was smiling and not wearing glasses in the picture, unlike her assailant. In response, Helen's sister, who was also present, drew eyeglasses onto printed copies of two of the pictures. Helen testified that she looked at the photos about five more times during the first month after the attack. The Kims brought copies of the photos to the police station later in the day. Helen also worked with a police sketch artist who drew a composite sketch. She later testified that the sketch did not completely resemble her attacker. Nearly twenty-two months after the attack, the police presented a photo array to Helen and the neighbor for the first time. Detective Clancy used the photo array was a "concern" that the website pictures might have prejudiced Helen. Helen selected defendant's picture as did the neighbor. At trial, defense counsel argued that Helen's identification was based on seeing photos that her husband showed her rather than on her memory of the attack. The prosecution argued that "the procedure followed by the police was not impermissibly suggestive." Should the identifications be admitted? Do defendant's arguments go only to the weight of the identifications rather than their admissibility. Does the identification satisfy the *Biggers* criteria? *See State v. Chen*, 208 N.J. 307, 27 A.3d 930 (N.J. 2011).

Hypo # 2: More on Private Suggestive Identifications

Suppose that a man (the victim) runs into an old acquaintance in a bar. The man recognizes the acquaintance from having played youth football with him. A couple of hours later, the man is attacked by someone that he recognizes as the acquaintance. The man goes on the Internet, finds a My Space picture of the acquaintance, and gives it to the police. The police construct a photo display of possible suspects, which includes the picture that the victim found on the Internet, and asks the victim whether he can identify his assailant. The man picks the acquaintance out of the display. Should the identification be excluded on due process grounds? *See State v. Johnson,* 312 Conn. 687, 94 A.3d 1173 (2014).

Executive Summary

Concerns Regarding Eyewitness Identification Techniques. Although eyewitness identifications constitute a particularly potent form of evidence in criminal proceedings, such evidence involves significant reliability risks. A reliable identification depends upon both accurate perception and recall, matters that can be distorted by many factors, including distance, observation time, light, the field or content of activity, stereotypes, cultural assumptions, suggestive questioning, faded memory and mental tendencies that tend to convert assumption or expectation into reality.

The Fourth Amendment and Personal Traits. In *United States v. Dionisio,* 410 U.S. 1, 14 (1973), observed that an individual's personal traits receive no special protection under the Fourth Amendment: "the physical characteristics of a person's voice, its tone and manner, as opposed to the content

Major Themes

a. Concerns Regarding Eyewitness Identification Techniques—Although eyewitness identifications may be a particularly potent form of evidence in criminal proceedings, such evidence presents significant reliability risks. Even though an accurate identification depends upon accurate perception and recall, many factors can distort both perception and recall.

b. The Right to Counsel and Identification Procedures—The right to counsel attaches to some identification proceedings that are employed "at or after the time that adversarial judicial proceedings have been initiated." There is "grave potential for prejudice, intentional or not, in the pretrial lineup, which may not be capable of reconstruction at trial, and since presence of counsel itself can often avert prejudice and assure a meaningful confrontation at trial, the postindictment lineup was a critical stage of the prosecution" at which a defendant is entitled to counsel.

of a specific conversation, are constantly exposed to the public. Like a man's facial characteristics, or handwriting, his voice is repeatedly produced for others to hear. No person can have a reasonable expectation that others will not know the sound of his voice any more than he can reasonably expect that his face will be a mystery to the world."

The Fifth Amendment and Identification Procedures. Personal traits are also not protected against disclosure by the privilege against self-incrimination because they are regarded as nontestimonial. In *Gilbert v. California*, 388 U.S. 263, 266–67 (1967), the Court stated that "the taking of handwriting exemplars did not violate petitioner's Fifth Amendment privilege against self-incrimination. The privilege reaches only compulsion of 'an accused's communications, whatever form they might take, and the compulsion of responses which are also communications and not 'compulsion which makes a suspect or accused the source of real or physical evidence.' One's voice and handwriting are, of course, means of communication. It by no means follows, however, that every compulsion of an accused to use his voice or write (compels) a communication within the privilege. A mere handwriting exemplar, in contrast to the content of what is written, like the voice or body itself, is an identifying physical characteristic outside its protection."

Right to Counsel and Identification Procedures. Case law has established that the right to counsel may attach to identification proceedings. Contrasted with the pervasive applicability of the

c. Right to Counsel Inapplicable to Pre-Adversarial Identification Proceedings—Courts have refused to extend the exclusionary rule to identifications (e.g., a showup or lineup) that take place *before* the defendant has been indicted or otherwise formally charged with a criminal offense. The courts have also refused to extend the right to counsel to pretrial identification procedures involving photographic displays.

d. Due Process and Pre-Adversarial Process Identifications—As a guarantor of procedural fairness, due process claims may be asserted in any investigative or adjudicative context. The focus is on whether the identification methods used were "unnecessarily suggestive and conducive to mistaken identification." However, even if an identification is suggestive, the ultimate question is whether it is "reliable." That issue is to be determined by considering a variety of factors, including the "opportunity of the witness to view the criminal at the time of the crime, the witness' degree of attention, the accuracy of the witness' prior description of the criminal, the level of certainty demonstrated by the witness at the confrontation, and the length of time between the crime and the confrontation."

e. Suggestiveness in the Absence of State Action—Courts need not pre-screen cases for reliability when the suggestive circumstances of a pre-trial identification were not arranged by law enforcement officers, but by private individuals independently of state action. Rather, the Court concluded that the identification's reliability could be tested "through the rights and opportunities generally designed for that purpose, notably, the presence of counsel at postindictment lineups, vigorous cross-examination, protective rules of evidence, and jury instructions on both the fallibility of eyewitness identification and the requirement that guilt be proved beyond a reasonable doubt."

due process clause, however, Sixth Amendment protection is limited to identification procedures employed "at or after the time that adversarial judicial proceedings have been initiated." *Kirby v. Illinois*, 406 U.S. 682, 688 (1972) (plurality opinion).

Identifications and "Critical Stage" Analysis. The right to counsel in an identification context is dependent upon whether the identification occurs at a stage of the process that is critical enough that counsel's presence "is necessary to preserve the defendant's basic right to a fair trial." *United States v. Wade*, 388 U.S. 218, 227 (1967). Seminal case law reflects the Court's sense that post-indictment line-ups not only satisfy the "critical stage" requirement but also present profound risks to a fair trial.

f. Eyewitness Identifications— Such identifications involve a significant risk of irreparable mistaken identification.

g. Identifications After Commencement of Adversarial Proceedings—After the commencement of adversarial proceedings, criminal defendants have the right to the assistance of counsel.

h. Suggestive Circumstances— Even when an identification is made under suggestive circumstances, it will not be excluded from evidence if the identification is deemed to be "reliable."

Possibility for Irreparable Mistaken Identification. In *United States v. Wade*, the Court held that the Sixth Amendment right to counsel applies to post-adversarial proceedings because of the possibility of irreparable mistaken identification, and counsel's presence is needed to give counsel the opportunity to meaningfully cross-examine witnesses. The Court concluded that there is "grave potential for prejudice, intentional or not, in the pretrial lineup, which may not be capable of reconstruction at trial, and since presence of counsel itself can often avert prejudice and assure a meaningful confrontation at trial, the postindictment lineup was a critical stage of the prosecution" at which a defendant is entitled to counsel.

i. Variety of Factors—In determining whether an identification is reliable, courts consider a variety of factors, including the: "opportunity of the witness to view the criminal at the time of the crime, the witness' degree of attention, the accuracy of the witness' prior description of the criminal, the level of certainty demonstrated by the witness at the confrontation, and the length of time between the crime and the confrontation."

Right to Counsel Inapplicable to Pre-Adversarial Identification Proceedings. In *Kirby v. Illinois*, 406 U.S. 682 (1972), the Court declined to extend the exclusionary rule to identification testimony (a showup) that took place *before* the defendant had been indicted or otherwise formally charged with any criminal offense. The Court held: "The initiation of judicial criminal proceedings is far from a mere formalism. It is the starting point of our whole system of adversary criminal justice. For it is only then that the government has committed itself to prosecute, and only then that the adverse positions of government and defendant have solidified. It is then that a defendant finds himself faced with the prosecutorial forces of organized society, and immersed in the intricacies of substantive and procedural criminal law."

Defining the Commencement of Adversarial Proceedings. In *Rothgery v. Gillespie County*, 554 U.S. 191 (2008), the Court reaffirmed the idea "that the right to counsel guaranteed by the Sixth Amendment applies when adversary proceedings commence." The Court held that the adversary process can commence with "the initiation of adversary judicial criminal proceedings-whether by way of formal charge, preliminary hearing, indictment, information, or arraignment," as well as by "the first appearance before a judicial officer at which a defendant is told of the formal accusation against him and restrictions are imposed on his liberty."

The Right to Counsel and Photographic Displays. The courts have refused to extend the right to counsel to pre-trial identification procedures involving photographic displays. The Court concluded that it was "not persuaded that the risks inherent in the use of photographic displays are so pernicious that an extraordinary system of safeguards is required."

Due Process and Pre-Adversarial Process Identifications. As a guarantor of procedural fairness, due process claims may be asserted in any investigative or adjudicative context. The standards of review requires a demonstration that the identification methods used were "unnecessarily suggestive and conducive to mistaken identification." *Stovall v. Denno*, 388 U.S. 293, 302 (1967). In *Foster v. California*, 394 U.S. 440 (1969), the Court suppressed an identification that was deemed to be so suggestive that it "so undermined the reliability of the eyewitness identification as to violate due process."

The Focus on Reliability. In *Neil v. Biggers*, 409 U.S. 188 (1972), the Court concluded that the possibility of "irreparable mistaken identification" is the "primary evil sought to be avoided." The focus is on whether, even if an identification is suggestive, is it reliable? That issue is to be determined by considering a variety of factors, including "opportunity of the witness to view the criminal at the time of the crime, the witness' degree of attention,

Test Your Knowledge

To assess your understanding of the material in this chapter, click here to take a quiz.

the accuracy of the witness' prior description of the criminal, the level of certainty demonstrated by the witness at the confrontation, and the length of time between the crime and the confrontation."

Suggestiveness in the Absence of State Action. In *Perry v. New Hampshire,* 565 U.S. 228 (2012), the Court held that courts need not pre-screen cases for reliability when the suggestive circumstances of a pre-trial identification were not arranged by law enforcement officers, but rather by private individuals independently of state action. Rather, the Court concluded that the identification's reliability could be tested "through the rights and opportunities generally designed for that purpose, notably, the presence of counsel at postindictment line-ups, vigorous cross-examination, protective rules of evidence, and jury instructions on both the fallibility of eyewitness identification and the requirement that guilt be proved beyond a reasonable doubt."

For More Information

• MARK E. CAMMACK & NORMAN M. GARLAND, ADVANCED CRIMINAL PROCEDURE (2006).

• WAYNE R. LAFAVE, JEROLD H. ISRAEL, NANCY J. KING & ORIN S. KERR, CRIMINAL PROCEDURE (5th ed. 2009).

• JEROLD H. ISRAEL & WAYNE R. LAFAVE, CRIMINAL PROCEDURE: CONSTITUTIONAL LIMITATIONS (8th ed. 2006).

• RUSSELL L. WEAVER, JOHN M. BURKOFF, CATHERINE HANCOCK, JANET HOEFFEL, STEVE FRIEDLAND & STEPHEN SINGER, PRINCIPLES OF CRIMINAL PROCEDURE (6th ed. 2018).

CHAPTER 8

The Exclusionary Rule

The exclusionary evidence rule precludes the state from using evidence seized in violation of a defendant's constitutional rights to convict the defendant of a crime.

A. The Exclusionary Rule's Application to Federal and State Proceedings

Although the United States Supreme Court's 1914 decision in *Weeks v. United States*, 232 U.S. 383 (1914), held that the exclusionary rule applies in federal court proceedings, that decision failed to extend the rule to state court proceedings.

> **Make the Connection**
>
> Is the exclusionary rule only applied to violations of Fourth Amendment rights? A. No. Although the rule is frequently applied when the police conduct an illegal search or seizure, it is also applied to violations of other constitutional rights (*e.g.*, evidence obtained from unconstitutional lineups and interrogations).

Wolf v. Colorado

338 U.S. 25 (1949).

MR. JUSTICE FRANKFURTER delivered the opinion of the Court.

The security of one's privacy against arbitrary intrusion by the police—which is at the core of the Fourth Amendment—is basic to a free society. It is therefore implicit in "the concept of ordered liberty" and enforceable against the States through the Due Process Clause. The knock at the door, whether by day or by night, as a prelude to a search, without authority of law but solely on the authority of the police, did not need the commentary of recent history to be condemned as inconsistent with the conception of human rights enshrined in the history and the basic constitutional documents of English-speaking peoples.

Accordingly, we have no hesitation in saying that were a State affirmatively to sanction such police incursion into privacy it would run counter to the guaranty of the Fourteenth Amendment. But the ways of enforcing such a basic right raise questions of a different order. How such arbitrary conduct should be checked, what remedies against it should be afforded, the means by which the right should be made effective, are all questions that are not to be so dogmatically answered as to preclude the varying solutions which spring from an allowable range of judgment on issues not susceptible of quantitative solution.

In *Weeks v. United States*, 232 U.S. 383 (1914), this Court held that in a federal prosecution the Fourth Amendment barred the use of evidence secured through an illegal search and seizure. This ruling was not derived from the explicit requirements of the Fourth Amendment. The decision was a matter of judicial implication. Since then it has been frequently applied and we stoutly adhere to it. But the question is whether the basic right to protection against arbitrary intrusion by the police demands the exclusion of logically relevant evidence obtained by an unreasonable search and seizure because, in a federal prosecution for a federal crime, it would be excluded. One would suppose this to be an issue to which men with complete devotion to the protection of the right of privacy might give different answers. When we find that in fact most of the English-speaking world does not regard as vital to such protection the exclusion of evidence thus obtained, we must hesitate to treat this remedy as an essential ingredient of the right. The contrariety of views of the States is particularly impressive. I. Before the *Weeks* decision 27 States had passed on the admissibility of evidence obtained by unlawful search and seizure. (a) Of these, 26 States opposed the *Weeks* doctrine. (b) Of these, 1 State anticipated the *Weeks* doctrine. II. Since the *Weeks* decision 47 States have passed on the *Weeks* doctrine. (a) Of these, 20 passed on it for the first time. (1) Of the foregoing States, 6 followed the *Weeks* doctrine. (2) Of the foregoing States, 14 rejected the *Weeks* doctrine. (b) Of these, 26 States reviewed prior decisions contrary to the *Weeks* doctrine. (1) Of these, 10 States have followed *Weeks*, overruling or distinguishing their prior decisions. (2) Of these, 16 States adhered to their prior decisions against *Weeks*. (c) Of these, 1 State adhered to its prior formulation of the *Weeks* doctrine. III. As of today 30 States reject the *Weeks* doctrine, 17 States are in agreement with it. IV. Of 10 jurisdictions within the United Kingdom and the British Commonwealth of Nations which have passed on the question, none has held evidence obtained by illegal search and seizure inadmissible.

The jurisdictions which have rejected the *Weeks* doctrine have not left the right to privacy without other means of protection.[1] Indeed, the exclusion of

---

[1] The common law provides actions for damages against the searching officer; against one who procures the issuance of a warrant maliciously and without probable cause; against a magistrate who has acted without jurisdiction in issuing a warrant; and against persons assisting in the execution of an illegal search. One may also without liability use force to resist an unlawful search. Statutory sanctions provide for the punishment of one maliciously procuring a search warrant or willfully exceeding his authority in exercising it. Some statutes more broadly penalize unlawful searches. Virginia also makes punishable one who issues a general search warrant or a warrant unsupported by affidavit. A few States have provided statutory civil remedies. And in one State, misuse of a search warrant may be an abuse of process punishable as contempt of court.

evidence is a remedy which directly serves only to protect those upon whose person or premises something incriminating has been found. We cannot, therefore, regard it as a departure from basic standards to remand such persons, together with those who emerge scatheless from a search, to the remedies of private action and such protection as the internal discipline of the police, under the eyes of an alert public opinion, may afford. Granting that in practice the exclusion of evidence may be an effective way of deterring unreasonable searches, it is not for this Court to condemn as falling below the minimal standards assured by the Due Process Clause a State's reliance upon other methods which, if consistently enforced, would be equally effective. We cannot brush aside the experience of States which deem the incidence of such conduct by the police too slight to call for a deterrent remedy not by way of disciplinary measures but by overriding the relevant rules of evidence. There are, moreover, reasons for excluding evidence unreasonably obtained by the federal police which are less compelling in the case of police under State or local authority. The public opinion of a community can far more effectively be exerted against oppressive conduct on the part of police directly responsible to the community itself than can local opinion, sporadically aroused, be brought to bear upon remote authority pervasively exerted throughout the country.

We hold, therefore, that in a prosecution in a State court for a State crime the Fourteenth Amendment does not forbid the admission of evidence obtained by an unreasonable search and seizure.

Affirmed.

MR. JUSTICE BLACK, concurring.

The federal exclusionary rule is not a command of the Fourth Amendment but is a judicially created rule of evidence which Congress might negate.

MR. JUSTICE RUTLEDGE, dissenting.

I reject the conclusion that the mandate embodied in the Fourth Amendment, although binding on the states, does not carry with it the one sanction—exclusion of evidence taken in violation of the Amendment's terms—failure to observe which means that "the protection of the 4th Amendment might as well be stricken from the Constitution." *Weeks v. United States*, 232 U.S. 383. The Amendment without the sanction is a dead letter. Twenty-nine years ago this Court, speaking through Justice Holmes, refused to permit the Government to subpoena documentary evidence which it had stolen, copied and then returned, for the reason that such a procedure "reduces the Fourth Amendment to a form of words." *Silverthorne Lumber Co. v. United States*, 251 U.S. 385, 392. But the version of the Fourth Amendment today held applicable to the states hardly rises to the dignity of a form of words; at best it is a pale and frayed carbon copy of the original, bearing little resemblance to the Amendment the fulfillment of whose command I had heretofore thought to be "an indispensable need for a democratic society." The view that the Fourth Amendment itself forbids the introduction of evidence illegally obtained in federal prosecutions is one of long standing and firmly established. It is too late in my judgment to question it now.

Mr. Justice Murphy, with whom Mr. Justice Rutledge joins, dissenting.

There is but one alternative to the rule of exclusion. That is no sanction at all. This has been perfectly clear since 1914, when a unanimous Court decided *Weeks*. "If letters and private documents can be seized and held and used in evidence against a citizen accused of an offense," we said, "the protection of the 4th Amendment, declaring his right to be secure against such searches and seizures, is of no value, and might as well be stricken from the Constitution." "It would reduce the Fourth Amendment to a form of words." Holmes, J., for the Court, in *Silverthorne Lumber Co. v. United States*, 251 U.S. 385.

Today the Court wipes those statements from the books with this bland citation of "other remedies." Little need be said concerning the possibilities of criminal prosecution. Self-scrutiny is a lofty ideal, but its exaltation reaches new heights if we expect a District Attorney to prosecute himself or his associates for well-meaning violations of the search and seizure clause during a raid the District Attorney or his associates have ordered. A trespass action for damages is a venerable means of securing reparation for unauthorized invasion of the home. But what an illusory remedy this is, if by "remedy" we mean a positive deterrent to police and prosecutors tempted to violate the Fourth Amendment. The measure of damages is simply the extent of the injury to physical property. If the officer searches with care, he can avoid all but nominal damages. Are punitive damages possible? Perhaps. But a few states permit none, whatever the circumstances. In those that do, the plaintiff must show malice, and surely it is not unreasonable to assume that one in honest pursuit of crime bears no malice toward the search victim. If that burden is carried, recovery may be defeated by the rule that there must be physical damages before punitive damages may be awarded. In addition, some states limit punitive damages to the actual expenses of litigation. Others demand some arbitrary ratio between actual and punitive damages. Even assuming the ill will of the officer, his reasonable grounds for belief that the home he searched harbored evidence of crime is admissible in mitigation of punitive damages. The bad reputation of the plaintiff is likewise admissible. If the evidence seized was actually used at a trial, that fact has been held a complete justification of the search, and a defense against the trespass action. And even if the plaintiff hurdles all these obstacles, and gains a substantial verdict, the individual officer's finances may well make the judgment useless—for the municipality, of course, is not liable without its consent. Is it surprising that there is so little in the books concerning trespass actions for violation of the search and seizure clause?

One remedy exists to deter violations of the search and seizure clause. That is the rule which excludes illegally obtained evidence. Only by exclusion can we impress upon the zealous prosecutor that violation of the Constitution will do him no good. Only when that point is driven home can the prosecutor be expected to emphasize the importance of observing constitutional demands in his instructions to the police. If proof of the efficacy of the federal rule were needed, there is testimony in abundance in the recruit training programs and in-service courses provided the police in states which follow the federal rule. This is an area in which judicial action has positive effect upon the breach of law; and that without judicial action, there are simply no effective sanctions presently available. Today's decision will do inestimable harm to the cause of fair police methods in our cities and states. Even more important, it must have tragic effect upon public respect for our judiciary. The Court now allows what is indeed shabby business: lawlessness by officers of the law. Since the evidence admitted was secured in violation of the Fourth Amendment, the judgment should be reversed.

Points for Discussion

a. Section 1983 Actions

Are there other, more effective, remedies for Fourth Amendment violations? For example, would the § 1983 remedy provide an effective deterrent for police misconduct? That statute provides as follows: "Every person who, under color of any statute, ordinance, regulation, custom or usage, of any State or Territory, subjects, or causes to be subjected, any citizen of the United States or other person within the jurisdiction thereof to the deprivation of any rights, privileges, or immunities secured by the Constitution and laws, shall be liable to the party injured in an action at law, suit in equity, or other proper proceeding for redress." It is difficult to recover under § 1983 when the governing law is uncertain. *Monroe v. Pape,* 365 U.S. 167 (1961), construed § 1983 as applicable to suits against individual governmental officials. However, in *Pierson v. Ray,* 386 U.S. 547 (1967), the Court held that police officers are protected by qualified immunity "if they act in good faith and with probable cause in making an arrest under a statute that they believe to be valid." In *Gomez v. Toledo,* 446 U.S. 635 (1980), the Court held that defendant has the burden of proving qualified immunity in a 1983 action.

Food for Thought

Since § 1983 actions are generally unavailable when the offending official is a federal agent or employee, suits against such officials are often based directly on the Constitution itself. These so-called *"Bivens"* actions, named for the holding in *Bivens v. Six Unknown Named Agents,* 403 U.S. 388 (1971), are claims based directly on the Fourth Amendment itself: "It is well settled that where legal rights have been invaded, and a federal statute provides for general right to sue for such invasion, federal courts may use any available remedy to make good the wrong done." In *Carlson v. Green*, 446 U.S. 14 (1980), the Court held that the availability of relief under the Federal Tort Claims Act did not bar a *Bivens* action. Finally, in *Anderson v. Creighton*, 483 U.S. 635 (1987), the Court imposed a good faith defense in *Bivens* actions which provided that "a federal law enforcement officer may not be held personally liable for money damages if a reasonable officer could have believed that the search comported with the Fourth Amendment." Do *Bivens* actions against federal officials, coupled with § 1983 actions against state officials, provide an effective remedy?

b. The Possibility of Injunctive Relief

The injunctive remedy might seem particularly appropriate when the police have engaged in a pattern of misconduct. However, in *Rizzo v. Goode*, 423 U.S. 362 (1976), the Court imposed significant barriers to injunctive relief against police officials. That case involved a claim that the police had engaged in an "assertedly pervasive pattern of illegal and unconstitutional mistreatment" against "minority citizens in particular and against all Philadelphia residents in general." Plaintiffs presented 250 witnesses who described some 40-odd incidents. The trial court ordered petitioners to draft "a comprehensive program for dealing adequately with civilian complaints", for its approval. The Supreme Court concluded that injunctive relief was inappropriate:

We doubt whether an Art. III case or controversy exists. In *O'Shea v. Littleton*, 414 U.S. 488 (1974), plaintiffs alleged that a county magistrate and judge, had embarked on a continuing, intentional practice of racially discriminatory bond setting, sentencing, and assessing of jury fees. No specific instances involving the individual respondents were set forth in the prayer for injunctive relief. Even though some of the named respondents had in fact "suffered from the alleged unconstitutional practices," the Court concluded that "past exposure to illegal conduct does not in itself show a present case or controversy regarding injunctive relief, however, if unaccompanied by any continuing, present adverse effects." The Court further recognized that while "past wrongs are evidence bearing on whether there is a real and immediate threat of repeated injury", the attempt to anticipate under what circumstances the respondents there would be made to appear in the future before petitioners "takes us into the area of speculation and conjecture." These observations apply here with even more force, for the individual respondents' claim to "real and immediate" injury rests not upon what the named petitioners might do to them in the future such as set a bond on the basis of race but upon what one of a small, unnamed minority of policemen might do to them in the future because of that unknown policeman's perception of departmental disciplinary procedures. This hypothesis is even more attenuated than those allegations of future injury found insufficient in *O'Shea* to warrant invocation of federal jurisdiction. Thus, insofar as the individual respondents were concerned, we think they lacked the requisite "personal stake in the outcome"; *i.e.*, the order overhauling police disciplinary procedures. Considerations of federalism are additional factors weighing against the granting of relief. The District Court's injunctive order here, significantly revising the internal procedures of the Philadelphia police department, was indisputably a sharp limitation on the department's "latitude in the 'dispatch of its own internal affairs.' " Principles of federalism also have applicability where injunctive relief is sought, not against the judicial branch of the state government, but against those in charge of an executive branch of an agency of state or local governments such as petitioners here.

c. *Bivens* Actions.

In *Ziglar v. Abbasi*, 137 S.Ct. 1843 (2017), the Court limited *Bivens'* scope. Following the 9/11 terrorist attacks, the U.S. Government took hundreds of illegal aliens into custody, and allegedly subjected them to harsh prison conditions (*e.g.*, lights were left on in detainees' cells 24 hours a day, the cells were tiny, detainees were not given basic hygiene procedures, were allowed virtually no exercise or recreation, and were subjected to physical abuse). Plaintiffs sued, not only under *Bivens*, but under a federal statute. The Court noted that it had become cautious regarding the extension of *Bivens'* actions because of separation of powers concerns. Indeed, the Court has refused to expand *Bivens* for over thirty years in a variety of contexts. The Court held that, in "most instances, the Legislature is in the better position to decide whether the public interest would be served by imposing a new substantive legal liability," and that such remedy should not be available if there are "special factors counseling hesitation in the absence of affirmative action by Congress." The Court expressed concern regarding the impact of such suits on Government employees who are sued personally, as well as the projected costs and consequences to the Government itself when the tort and monetary liability mechanisms of the legal system are used to bring about the proper formulation and implementation of public policies." The Court noted that a *Bivens* action is not "a proper vehicle for altering an entity's policy," or for holding officers responsible for the acts of their subordinates. The Court went on to note that, to use a *Bivens* action in that context, "the discovery and litigation process would either border upon or directly implicate the discussion and deliberations that led to the formation of the policy in question," and they have shown deference to what the Executive Branch has determined is "essential to national security." The Court held that the detainees had other means for challenging the conditions of their confinement.

Hypo 1: *The Serial Murderer*

Serial murders are committed in the New Orleans area. The police search for the murderer, trying to find him before he kills again. Weeks pass, more murders occur, and still the murderer has not been found. The police suspect Yoplait of the crimes, but do not have probable cause to arrest him. In a desperate attempt to solve the crime and prevent further murders, the police illegally search Yoplait's apartment (the police lack both a search warrant and probable cause), and find conclusive evidence of Yoplait's involvement in the murders (Yoplait liked to keep gory pictures of the people he killed). Suppose that, under *Wolf*, the exclusionary rule does not apply in state court proceedings. Does Yoplait have adequate alternative remedies available to him? Consider the following possibilities:

A. Suppose that Yoplait brings a civil suit against the police officers claiming that the police officers trespassed, as well as that they converted his property. If Yoplait prevails, is a jury likely to award him substantial damages?

B. Of course, it is possible for the jury to award punitive damages. Is the jury likely to award punitive damages against the police in a case like this?

C. Public opinion can provide a powerful deterrent to police misconduct. Is the public likely to rise up in outrage over the illegal search?

D. Is the prosecutor likely to criminally prosecute the police for this illegal search (or, for that matter, is the police disciplinary board likely to bring disciplinary charges)?

Hypo 2: *More on the Serial Murderer*

In thinking about the prior hypo, would you answer the questions differently if the evidence showed a pervasive pattern of police misconduct? Suppose that there is evidence that New Orleans police routinely violate citizens' civil rights by illegally stopping motorists, "roughing them up," and illegally searching cars. Suppose that a motorist brings a civil suit against the police officers claiming intentional violations of his rights (e.g., assault, battery, kidnapping). Consider the following avenues for relief: a) damages in a tort action; b) punitive damages; c) public opinion; d) criminal prosecution of the offending police. Are any of these remedies likely to provide an effective deterrent to misconduct?

Hypo 3: *The Innocent Suspect*

Now, let's consider one more scenario. Suppose that the police intentionally search someone's home without a warrant or probable cause. Would it matter that the subject of the search was innocent, and that the police were completely mistaken about the subject's involvement in criminal activity? For example, suppose that the police illegally search a medical doctor's home believing that he is involved in illicit drug trafficking. The police are in error about this fact because, while listening to a wiretap, they *thought* they heard a reference to the doctor. Are the following remedies likely to be effective for this violation: a) Civil suit for damages? b) Punitive damages? c) Public opinion? d) Criminal prosecution? e) Disciplinary sanctions?

Mapp v. Ohio

367 U.S. 643 (1961).

MR. JUSTICE CLARK delivered the opinion of the Court.

Appellant was convicted of possession of lewd and lascivious books, pictures, and photographs in violation of Ohio law. The Supreme Court of Ohio upheld the conviction though "based upon evidence seized during an unlawful search of defendant's home."

The State says that even if the search were made without authority, or otherwise unreasonably, it is not prevented from using the unconstitutionally seized evidence at trial, citing *Wolf v. People of State of Colorado.*, 338 U.S. 25 (1949). Prior to the *Wolf* case, almost two-thirds of the States were opposed to the use of the exclusionary rule, now, despite *Wolf*, more than half of those since passing upon it, by their own legislative or judicial decision, have wholly or partly adopted or adhered to the *Weeks* rule. Significantly, among those now following the rule is California, which, according to its highest court, was "compelled to reach that conclusion because other remedies have completely failed to secure compliance with the constitutional provisions." *People v. Cahan*, 1955, 44 Cal.2d 434, 282 P.2d 905. *Wolf* concluded that "other means of protection" have been afforded "the right to privacy." The experience of California that such other remedies have been worthless and futile is buttressed by the experience of other States. The obvious futility of relegating the Fourth Amendment to the protection of other remedies has been recognized by this Court since *Wolf*. Likewise, time has set its face against what *Wolf* called the "weighty testimony" of *People v. Defore*, 1926,

242 N.Y. 13, 150 N.E. 585. There Justice (then Judge) Cardozo, rejecting adoption of the *Weeks* exclusionary rule in New York, said that "the Federal rule as it stands is either too strict or too lax." The force of that reasoning has been largely vitiated by later decisions of this Court.

It plainly appears that the factual considerations supporting the failure of the *Wolf* Court to include the *Weeks* exclusionary rule when it recognized the enforceability of the right to privacy against the States in 1949, while not basically relevant to the constitutional consideration, could not, in any analysis, now be deemed controlling.

Today we again examine *Wolf's* constitutional documentation of the right to privacy free from unreasonable state intrusion, and close the only courtroom door remaining open to evidence secured by official lawlessness in flagrant abuse of that basic right, reserved to all persons as a specific guarantee against that very same unlawful conduct. We hold that all evidence obtained by searches and seizures in violation of the Constitution is, by that same authority, inadmissible in a state court.

Since the Fourth Amendment's right of privacy has been declared enforceable against the States through the Due Process Clause of the Fourteenth, it is enforceable by the same sanction of exclusion as is used against the Federal Government. Were it otherwise, the assurance against unreasonable federal searches and seizures would be "a form of words", valueless and undeserving of mention in a perpetual charter of inestimable human liberties and the freedom from state invasions of privacy would be so ephemeral and so neatly severed from its conceptual nexus with the freedom from all brutish means of coercing evidence as not to merit this Court's high regard as a freedom "implicit in the concept of ordered liberty." At the time that the Court held in *Wolf* that the Amendment was applicable to the States through the Due Process Clause, cases had steadfastly held that as to federal officers the Fourth Amendment included the exclusion of the evidence seized in violation of its provisions. In extending the substantive protections of due process to all constitutionally unreasonable searches—state or federal—it was logically and constitutionally necessary that the exclusion doctrine—an essential part of the right to privacy—be also insisted upon as an essential ingredient of the right newly recognized by the *Wolf* case. The admission of the new constitutional right could not consistently tolerate denial of its most important constitutional privilege, namely, the exclusion of the evidence which an accused had been forced to give by reason of the unlawful seizure. To hold otherwise is to grant the right but in reality to withhold its privilege and enjoyment. Only last year the Court itself recognized that the purpose of the exclusionary rule "is to deter—to compel respect for the constitutional guaranty in the only effectively available way—by removing the incentive to disregard it." *Elkins v. United States,* 364 U.S. 206, 217 (1960).

We are aware of no restraint, similar to that rejected today, conditioning the enforcement of any other basic constitutional right. The right to privacy, no less important than any other right carefully and particularly reserved to the people, would stand in marked contrast to all other rights declared as "basic to a free society." This Court has not hesitated to enforce as strictly against the States the rights of free speech and of a free press, the rights to notice and to a fair, public trial, including the right not to be convicted by use of a coerced confession, however logically relevant it be, and without regard to its reliability. Nothing could be more certain than that when a coerced confession is involved, "the relevant rules of evidence" are overridden without regard to "the incidence of such conduct by the police." Why should not the same rule apply to what is tantamount to coerced testimony by way of unconstitutional seizure of goods, papers, effect, documents, etc.? As to the Federal Government, the Fourth and Fifth Amendments and, as to the States, the freedom from unconscionable invasions of privacy and the freedom from convictions based upon coerced confessions do enjoy an "intimate relation" in their perpetuation of "principles of humanity and civil liberty secured only after years of struggle." *Bram v. United States,* 1897, 168 U.S. 532. They express "supplementing phases of the same constitutional purpose—to maintain inviolate large areas of personal privacy." *Feldman v. United States,* 1944, 322 U.S. 487. The philosophy of each Amendment and of each freedom is complementary to, although not dependent upon, that of the other in its sphere of influence—the very least that together they assure in either sphere is that no man is to be convicted on unconstitutional evidence.

Our holding that the exclusionary rule is an essential part of both the Fourth and Fourteenth Amendments is not only the logical dictate of prior cases, it also makes very good sense. There is no war between the Constitution and common sense. Presently, a federal prosecutor may make no use of evidence illegally seized, but a State's attorney across the street may, although he supposedly is operating under the enforceable prohibitions of the same Amendment. Thus the State, by admitting evidence unlawfully seized, serves to encourage disobedience to the Federal Constitution which it is bound to uphold. In non-exclusionary States, federal officers, being human, were invited to and did step across the street to the State's attorney with their unconstitutionally seized evidence. Prosecution on the basis of that evidence was then had in a state court in utter disregard of the enforceable Fourth Amendment. If the fruits of an unconstitutional search had been inadmissible in both state and federal courts, this inducement to evasion would have been sooner eliminated. Federal-state cooperation in the solution of crime under constitutional standards will be promoted, if only by recognition of their now mutual obligation to respect the same fundamental criteria in their approaches. Denying shortcuts to only one of two cooperating law enforcement agencies tends naturally to breed legitimate suspicion of "working arrangements" whose results are equally tainted.

There are those who say, as did Justice (then Judge) Cardozo, that under our constitutional exclusionary doctrine "the criminal is to go free because the constable has blundered." *People v. Defore,* 242 N.Y. at page 21, 150 N.E. at page 587. In some cases this will undoubtedly be the result. But, as was said in *Elkins,* "there is another consideration—the imperative of judicial integrity." The criminal goes free, if he must, but it is the law that sets him free. Nothing can destroy a government more quickly than its failure to observe its own laws, or worse, its disregard of the charter of its own existence. As Mr. Justice Brandeis, dissenting, said in *Olmstead v. United States,* 1928, 277 U.S. 438: "Our government is the potent, the omnipresent teacher. For good or for ill, it teaches the whole people by its example. If the government becomes a lawbreaker, it breeds contempt for law; it invites every man to become a law unto himself; it invites anarchy." Nor can it lightly be assumed that, as a practical matter, adoption of the exclusionary rule fetters law enforcement. In *Elkins v. United States,* 364 U.S. at page 218, the Court noted that "The federal courts have operated under the exclusionary rule of *Weeks* for almost half a century; yet it has not been suggested either that the Federal Bureau of Investigation has thereby been rendered ineffective, or that the administration of criminal justice in the federal courts has thereby been disrupted. Moreover, the experience of the states is impressive. The movement towards the rule of exclusion has been halting but seemingly inexorable."

The ignoble shortcut to conviction left open to the State tends to destroy the entire system of constitutional restraints on which the liberties of the people rest. Having recognized that the right to privacy embodied in the Fourth Amendment is enforceable against the States, and that the right to be secure against rude invasions of privacy by state officers is constitutional in origin, we can no longer permit that right to remain an empty promise. Because it is enforceable in the same manner and to like effect as other basic rights secured by the Due Process Clause, we can no longer permit it to be revocable at the whim of any police officer who chooses to suspend its enjoyment. Our decision, founded on reason and truth, gives to the individual no more than that which the Constitution guarantees him, to the police officer no less than that to which honest law enforcement is entitled, and, to the courts, that judicial integrity so necessary in the true administration of justice.

The judgment of the Supreme Court of Ohio is reversed and the cause remanded for further proceedings not inconsistent with this opinion.

Reversed and remanded.

MR. JUSTICE BLACK, concurring.

The Fourth Amendment, standing alone, would not be enough to bar the introduction into evidence against an accused of papers and effects seized from him in violation of its commands. For the Fourth Amendment does not itself contain any provision expressly precluding the use of such evidence, and I am extremely doubtful that such a provision could properly be inferred from nothing more than the basic command against unreasonable searches and seizures. When the Fourth Amendment's ban against unreasonable searches and seizures is considered together with the Fifth Amendment's ban against compelled self-incrimination, a constitutional basis emerges which not only justifies but actually requires the exclusionary rule. In *Boyd v. United States*, the Court declared itself "unable to perceive that the seizure of a man's private books and papers to be used in evidence against him is substantially different from compelling him to be a witness against himself."

MR. JUSTICE DOUGLAS, concurring.

The facts of this case show—as would few other cases—the casual arrogance of those who have the untrammeled power to invade one's home and to seize one's person.

MR. JUSTICE HARLAN, whom MR. JUSTICE FRANKFURTER and MR. JUSTICE WHITTAKER join, dissenting.

I would not impose upon the States this federal exclusionary remedy. It is said that "the factual grounds upon which *Wolf* was based" have since changed, in that more States now follow the *Weeks* exclusionary rule. While that is true, one-half of the States still adhere to the common-law non-exclusionary rule. The preservation of a proper balance between state and federal responsibility in the administration of criminal justice demands patience on the part of those who might like to see things move faster. Problems of criminal law enforcement vary widely from State to State. One State may conclude that the need for embracing the *Weeks* rule is pressing because other remedies are unavailable or inadequate to secure compliance with the substantive Constitutional principle involved. Another, though equally solicitous of Constitutional rights, may choose to pursue one purpose at a time, allowing all evidence relevant to guilt to be brought into a criminal trial, and dealing with Constitutional infractions by other means. This Court should continue to forbear from fettering the States with an adamant rule in criminal law enforcement.

In *Weeks*, in implementing the Fourth Amendment, we occupied the position of a tribunal having the ultimate responsibility for developing the standards and procedures of judicial administration within the judicial system over which it presides. Here we review state procedures whose measure is to be taken not against the specific substantive commands of the Fourth Amendment but under the flexible contours of the Due Process Clause. I do not believe that the Fourteenth Amendment empowers this Court to mold state remedies effectuating the right to freedom from "arbitrary intrusion by the police."

In requiring exclusion of an involuntary statement of an accused, we are concerned not with an appropriate remedy for what the police have done, but with something which is regarded as going to the heart of our concepts of fairness in judicial procedure. "Ours is the accusatorial as opposed to the inquisitorial system." *Watts v. State of Indiana*, 338 U.S. 49. The trial defense to which an accused is entitled should not be rendered an empty formality by reason of statements wrung from him, for then "a prisoner has been made the deluded instrument of his own conviction." 2 Hawkins, Pleas of the Crown (8th ed., 1824), c. 46, § 34. The coerced confession analogy works strongly against what the Court does today. This Court can increase respect for the Constitution only if it rigidly respects the limitations which the Constitution places upon it, and respects as well the principles inherent in its own processes. In the present case we exceed both, and our voice becomes only a voice of power, not of reason.

Point for Discussion

The Exclusionary Rule in Forfeiture Proceedings

In *One 1958 Plymouth Sedan v. Commonwealth of Pennsylvania*, 380 U.S. 693 (1965), the Court applied the exclusionary rule to a forfeiture proceeding because of the "quasi-criminal" nature of that proceeding. That case involved the forfeiture of an automobile found to be carrying liquor without Pennsylvania tax seals.

Food for Thought

Consider then Chief Justice Burger's dissent in *Bivens v. Six Unknown Named Agents*, 403 U.S. 388 (1971):

Rejection of evidence does nothing to punish the wrong-doing official, while it may, and likely will, release the wrong-doing defendant. It deprives society of its remedy against one lawbreaker because he has been pursued by another. It protects one against whom incriminating evidence is discovered, but does nothing to protect innocent persons who are the victims of illegal but fruitless searches.

Instead of continuing to enforce the suppression doctrine inflexibly, rigidly, and mechanically, we should discontinue what the experience of over half a century has shown neither deters errant officers nor affords a remedy to the totally innocent victims of official misconduct. I do not propose that we abandon the suppression doctrine until some meaningful alternative can be developed. The public interest would be poorly served if law enforcement officials were suddenly to gain the impression that all constitutional restraints on police had somehow been removed—that an open season on "criminals" had been declared. The problems of both error and deliberate misconduct by law enforcement officials call for a workable remedy. Private damage actions against individual police officers concededly have not adequately met this requirement.

An entirely different remedy is necessary but it is beyond judicial power. Congress should develop an administrative or quasi-judicial remedy against the government itself to afford compensation and restitution for persons whose Fourth Amendment rights have been violated. The venerable doctrine of respondeat superior in our tort law provides an entirely appropriate conceptual basis for this remedy. Such a statutory scheme would have the added advantage of providing some remedy to the completely innocent persons who are sometimes the victims of illegal police conduct—something that the suppression doctrine, of course, can never accomplish. A simple structure would suffice. Congress could enact a statute along the following lines: (a) a waiver of sovereign immunity as to the illegal acts of law enforcement officials committed in the performance of assigned duties; (b) the creation of a cause of action for damages sustained by any person aggrieved by conduct of governmental agents in violation of the Fourth Amendment or statutes regulating official conduct; (c) the creation of a tribunal, quasi judicial in nature or perhaps patterned after the United States Court of Claims to adjudicate all claims under the statute; (d) a provision that this statutory remedy is in lieu of the exclusion of evidence; and (e) a provision directing that no evidence, otherwise admissible, shall be excluded from any criminal proceeding because of violation of the Fourth Amendment.

I doubt that lawyers serving on such a tribunal would be swayed either by undue sympathy for officers or by the prejudice against "criminals" that has sometimes moved lay jurors to deny claims. In addition to awarding damages, the record of the police conduct would become a relevant part of an officer's personnel file so that the need for additional training or disciplinary action could be identified or his future usefulness as a public official evaluated. Finally, appellate judicial review could be made available on much the same basis that it is now provided as to district courts and regulatory agencies. This would leave to the courts the ultimate responsibility for determining and articulating standards.

Once the constitutional validity of such a statute is established, it can reasonably be assumed that the States would develop their own remedial systems on the federal model. Steps along these lines would move our system toward more responsible law enforcement on the one hand and away from the irrational and drastic results of the suppression doctrine on the other.

Does Chief Justice Burger's proposal make sense? Is it a better alternative?

B. Modern Decisions Construing the Scope of the Exclusionary Rule

Because of the perceived "costs" associated with the exclusionary rule (*i.e.*, the loss of evidence, the reversal of convictions, and difficulty of convicting without suppressed evidence), some police and law enforcement officials have pressed for limitations on the exclusionary rule. One suggested limitation involves the so-called "good faith" exception to the exclusionary rule. That exception was considered in the following case.

United States v. Leon

468 U.S. 897 (1984).

JUSTICE WHITE delivered the opinion of the Court.

This case presents the question whether the Fourth Amendment exclusionary rule should be modified so as not to bar the use in the prosecution's case in chief of evidence obtained by officers acting in reasonable reliance on a search warrant issued by a detached and neutral magistrate but ultimately found to be unsupported by probable cause.

The Fourth Amendment contains no provision expressly precluding the use of evidence obtained in violation of its commands, and an examination of its origin and purposes makes clear that the use of fruits of a past unlawful search or seizure "works no new Fourth Amendment wrong." *United States v. Calandra,* 414 U.S. 338 (1974). The wrong condemned by the Amendment is "fully accomplished" by the unlawful search or seizure itself, and the exclusionary rule is neither intended nor able to "cure the invasion of the defendant's rights which he has already suffered." *Stone v. Powell,* 428 U.S. 465, 540 (1976) (White, J., dissenting). The rule thus operates as "a judicially created remedy designed to safeguard Fourth Amendment rights generally through its deterrent effect, rather than a personal constitutional right of the party aggrieved." *United States v. Calandra,* 414 U.S. at 348.

Whether the exclusionary sanction is appropriately imposed in a particular case is "an issue separate from the question whether the Fourth Amendment rights of the party seeking to invoke the rule were violated by police conduct." Only the former question is currently before us, and it must be resolved by weighing the costs and benefits of preventing the use in the prosecution's case in chief of inherently trustworthy tangible evidence obtained in reliance on a search warrant issued by a detached and neutral magistrate that ultimately is found to be defective.

The substantial social costs exacted by the exclusionary rule have long been a source of concern. "Unbending application of the exclusionary sanction to enforce ideals of governmental rectitude would impede unacceptably the truth-finding functions of judge and jury." *United States v. Payner,* 447 U.S. 727 (1980). An objectionable collateral consequence of this interference is that some guilty defendants may go free or receive reduced sentences as a result of favorable plea bargains.[6] Particularly when law enforcement officers have acted in objective

---

[6] One study suggests that the rule results in the nonprosecution or nonconviction of between 0.6% and 2.35% of individuals arrested for felonies. The estimates are higher for particular crimes the prosecution of which depends heavily on physical evidence. Thus, the cumulative loss of felony drug charges is probably in the range of 2.8% to 7.1%. Many researchers have concluded that the impact of the

good faith or their transgressions have been minor, the magnitude of the benefit conferred on such guilty defendants offends basic concepts of the criminal justice system. Indiscriminate application of the exclusionary rule may well "generate disrespect for the law and administration of justice." "As with any remedial device, the application of the rule has been restricted to those areas where its remedial objectives are thought most efficaciously served." *United States v. Calandra,* 414 U.S., at 348.

Close attention to those remedial objectives has characterized our recent decisions concerning the scope of the Fourth Amendment exclusionary rule. The Court has not seriously questioned, "in the absence of a more efficacious sanction, the continued application of the rule to suppress evidence from the prosecution's case where a Fourth Amendment violation has been substantial and deliberate." *Franks v. Delaware,* 438 U.S. 154 (1978). Nevertheless, the balancing approach "forcefully suggests that the exclusionary rule be modified to permit the introduction of evidence obtained in the reasonable good-faith belief that a search or seizure was in accord with the Fourth Amendment." *Illinois v. Gates,* 462 U.S. 213, 255 (1983) (White, J., concurring).

In *Stone v. Powell,* the Court emphasized the costs of the exclusionary rule, expressed its view that limiting the circumstances under which Fourth Amendment claims could be raised in federal habeas corpus proceedings would not reduce the rule's deterrent effect, and held that a state prisoner who has been afforded a full and fair opportunity to litigate a Fourth Amendment claim may not obtain federal habeas relief on the ground that unlawfully obtained evidence had been introduced at his trial. Proposed extensions of the exclusionary rule to proceedings other than the criminal trial itself have been evaluated and rejected under the same analytic approach. In *Calandra,* we declined to allow grand jury witnesses to refuse to answer questions based on evidence obtained from an unlawful search or seizure since "any incremental deterrent effect which might be achieved by extending the rule to grand jury proceedings is uncertain at best." Similarly, in *United States v. Janis,* 428 U.S. 433 (1976), we permitted the use in federal civil proceedings of evidence illegally seized by state officials since the likelihood of deterring police misconduct through such an extension of the exclusionary rule was insufficient to outweigh its substantial social costs. In so doing, we declared that, "if the exclusionary rule does not result in appreciable deterrence, then, clearly, its use in the instant situation is unwarranted."

---

exclusionary rule is insubstantial, but the small percentages with which they deal mask a large absolute number of felons who are released. "Any rule of evidence that denies the jury access to clearly probative and reliable evidence must bear a heavy burden of justification, and must be carefully limited to the circumstances in which it will pay its way by deterring official unlawlessness." *Illinois v. Gates,* 462 U.S. 213, 257 (1983) (White, J., concurring). Because the rule can have no substantial deterrent effect in the sorts of situations under consideration in this case, we conclude that it cannot pay its way in those situations.

It does not follow from the emphasis on the exclusionary rule's deterrent value that "anything which deters illegal searches is thereby commanded by the Fourth Amendment." In determining whether persons aggrieved solely by the introduction of damaging evidence unlawfully obtained from their co-conspirators or co-defendants could seek suppression, for example, we found that the additional benefits of such an extension of the exclusionary rule would not outweigh its costs. Standing to invoke the rule has thus been limited to cases in which the prosecution seeks to use the fruits of an illegal search or seizure against the victim of police misconduct.

Even defendants with standing to challenge the introduction in their criminal trials of unlawfully obtained evidence cannot prevent every conceivable use of such evidence. Evidence obtained in violation of the Fourth Amendment and inadmissible in the prosecution's case in chief may be used to impeach a defendant's direct testimony. A similar assessment of the "incremental furthering" of the ends of the exclusionary rule led us to conclude in *United States v. Havens,* 446 U.S. 620 (1980), that evidence may be used to impeach statements made by a defendant in response to "proper cross-examination reasonably suggested by the defendant's direct examination."

When considering the use of evidence obtained in violation of the Fourth Amendment in the prosecution's case in chief, moreover, we have declined to adopt a *per se* or "but for" rule that would render inadmissible any evidence that came to light through a chain of causation that began with an illegal arrest. We also have held that a witness' testimony may be admitted even when his identity was discovered in an unconstitutional search. The perception underlying these decisions—that the connection between police misconduct and evidence of crime may be sufficiently attenuated to permit the use of that evidence at trial—is a product of considerations relating to the exclusionary rule and the constitutional principles it is designed to protect.[7] In view of this purpose, an assessment of the flagrancy of the police misconduct constitutes an important step in the calculus.

We have not recognized any form of good-faith exception to the Fourth Amendment exclusionary rule. But the balancing approach that has evolved during the years of experience with the rule provides strong support for the modification currently urged upon us.

Because a search warrant "provides the detached scrutiny of a neutral magistrate, which is a more reliable safeguard against improper searches than the hurried judgment of a law enforcement officer 'engaged in the often competitive

---

[7] Where there is a close causal connection between the illegal seizure and the confession, not only is exclusion of the evidence more likely to deter similar police misconduct in the future, but use of the evidence is more likely to compromise the integrity of the courts." *Dunaway v. New York* 442 U.S. 200, 217–218 (1979).

enterprise of ferreting out crime,' " we have expressed a strong preference for warrants and declared that "in a doubtful or marginal case a search under a warrant may be sustainable where without one it would fall." *United States v. Ventresca,* 380 U.S. 102 (1965). Reasonable minds frequently may differ on the question whether a particular affidavit establishes probable cause, and the preference for warrants is most appropriately effectuated by according "great deference" to a magistrate's determination.

Deference to the magistrate, however, is not boundless. The deference accorded to a magistrate's finding of probable cause does not preclude inquiry into the knowing or reckless falsity of the affidavit on which that determination was based. The courts must also insist that the magistrate purport to "perform his 'neutral and detached' function and not serve merely as a rubber stamp for the police." A magistrate failing to "manifest that neutrality and detachment demanded of a judicial officer when presented with a warrant application" and who acts instead as "an adjunct law enforcement officer" cannot provide valid authorization for an otherwise unconstitutional search. Reviewing courts will not defer to a warrant based on an affidavit that does not "provide the magistrate with a substantial basis for determining the existence of probable cause." Even if the warrant application was supported by more than a "bare bones" affidavit, a reviewing court may properly conclude that, notwithstanding the deference that magistrates deserve, the warrant was invalid because the magistrate's probable-cause determination reflected an improper analysis of the totality of the circumstances, or because the form of the warrant was improper in some respect.

Only in the first of these three situations, however, has the Court set forth a rationale for suppressing evidence obtained pursuant to a search warrant; in the other areas, it has simply excluded such evidence without considering whether Fourth Amendment interests will be advanced. To the extent that proponents of exclusion rely on its behavioral effects on judges and magistrates in these areas, their reliance is misplaced. First, the exclusionary rule is designed to deter police misconduct rather than to punish the errors of judges and magistrates. Second, there exists no evidence suggesting that judges and magistrates are inclined to ignore or subvert the Fourth Amendment or that lawlessness among these actors requires application of the extreme sanction of exclusion. Third, we discern no basis for believing that exclusion of evidence seized pursuant to a warrant will have a significant deterrent effect on the issuing judge or magistrate. Many of the factors that indicate that the exclusionary rule cannot provide an effective "special" or "general" deterrent for individual offending law enforcement officers apply as well to judges or magistrates. To the extent that the rule is thought to operate as a "systemic" deterrent on a wider audience, it clearly can have no such effect on individuals empowered to issue search warrants. Judges and magistrates are not adjuncts to the law enforcement team; as neutral judicial officers, they have no stake in the outcome of particular criminal prosecutions. The threat of exclusion cannot be expected significantly to deter them. Imposition of the exclusionary sanction is not necessary meaningfully to inform judicial officers of their errors, and we cannot conclude that admitting evidence obtained pursuant to a warrant while at the same time declaring that the warrant was somehow defective will in any way reduce judicial officers' professional incentives to comply with the Fourth Amendment, encourage them to repeat their mistakes, or lead to the granting of all colorable warrant requests.[18]

If exclusion of evidence obtained pursuant to a subsequently invalidated warrant is to have any deterrent effect, it must alter the behavior of individual law enforcement officers or the policies of their departments. One could argue that applying the exclusionary rule in cases where the police failed to demonstrate probable cause in the warrant application deters future inadequate presentations or "magistrate shopping" and thus promotes the ends of the Fourth Amendment. Suppressing evidence obtained pursuant to a technically defective warrant supported by probable cause also might encourage officers to scrutinize more closely the form of the warrant and to point out suspected judicial errors. We find such arguments speculative and conclude that suppression of evidence obtained pursuant to a warrant should be ordered only in those unusual cases in which exclusion will further the purposes of the exclusionary rule.

We have frequently questioned whether the exclusionary rule can have any deterrent effect when the offending officers acted in the objectively reasonable belief that their conduct did not violate the Fourth Amendment. Even assuming that the rule effectively deters some police misconduct and provides incentives for the law enforcement profession as a whole to conduct itself in accord with the Fourth Amendment, it cannot be expected, and should not be applied, to deter objectively reasonable law enforcement activity. This is particularly true when an officer acting with objective good faith has obtained a search warrant from a judge or magistrate and acted within its scope. In most such cases, there is no police illegality and thus nothing to deter. It is the magistrate's responsibility to determine whether the officer's allegations establish probable cause and, if so, to issue a warrant comporting in form with the requirements of the Fourth Amendment. In the ordinary case, an officer cannot be expected to question the magistrate's probable-cause determination or his judgment that the form of the warrant is technically sufficient. Penalizing the officer for the magistrate's error, rather than his own, cannot logically contribute to the deterrence of Fourth Amendment violations.[22]

---

[18] If a magistrate serves merely as a "rubber stamp" for the police or is unable to exercise mature judgment, closer supervision or removal provides a more effective remedy than the exclusionary rule.

[22] When a Fourth Amendment violation has occurred because the police have reasonably relied on a warrant issued by a detached and neutral magistrate but ultimately found to be defective, "the integrity of the courts is not implicated." *Illinois v. Gates,* 462 U.S., at 259, n.14 (White, J., concurring.)

We conclude that the marginal or nonexistent benefits produced by suppressing evidence obtained in objectively reasonable reliance on a subsequently invalidated search warrant cannot justify the substantial costs of exclusion. We do not suggest that exclusion is always inappropriate in cases where an officer has obtained a warrant and abided by its terms. "Searches pursuant to a warrant will rarely require any deep inquiry into reasonableness" for "a warrant issued by a magistrate normally suffices to establish" that a law enforcement officer has "acted in good faith in conducting the search." *United States v. Ross,* 456 U.S. 798 (1982). Nevertheless, the officer's reliance on the magistrate's probable-cause determination and on the technical sufficiency of the warrant he issues must be objectively reasonable,[23] and it is clear that in some circumstances the officer[24] will have no reasonable grounds for believing that the warrant was properly issued.

Suppression therefore remains an appropriate remedy if the magistrate or judge in issuing a warrant was misled by information in an affidavit that the affiant knew was false or would have known was false except for his reckless disregard of the truth. The exception will also not apply where the issuing magistrate wholly abandoned his judicial role in the manner condemned in *Lo–Ji Sales, Inc. v. New York,* 442 U.S. 319 (1979); in such circumstances, no reasonably well trained officer should rely on the warrant. Nor would an officer manifest objective good faith in relying on a warrant based on an affidavit "so lacking in indicia of probable cause as to render official belief in its existence entirely unreasonable." Finally, depending on the circumstances of the particular case, a warrant may be so facially deficient—*i.e.,* in failing to particularize the place to be searched or the things to be seized—that the executing officers cannot reasonably presume it to be valid.

In limiting the suppression remedy, we leave untouched the probable-cause standard and the various requirements for a valid warrant. The good-faith exception, turning as it does on objective reasonableness, should not be difficult to apply in practice. When officers have acted pursuant to a warrant, the prosecution should ordinarily be able to establish objective good faith without a substantial expenditure of judicial time.

Nor are we persuaded that application of a good-faith exception to searches conducted pursuant to warrants will preclude review of the constitutionality of

---

[23] We eschew inquiries into the subjective beliefs of law enforcement officers who seize evidence pursuant to a subsequently invalidated warrant. Our good-faith inquiry is confined to the objectively ascertainable question whether a reasonably well trained officer would have known that the search was illegal despite the magistrate's authorization. In making this determination, all of the circumstances—including whether the warrant application had previously been rejected by a different magistrate—may be considered.

[24] We consider the objective reasonableness, not only of the officers who executed a warrant, but also of the officers who obtained it or who provided information material to the probable-cause determination. Nothing suggests that an officer could obtain a warrant on the basis of a "bare bones" affidavit and then rely on colleagues who are ignorant of the circumstances under which the warrant was obtained to conduct the search.

the search or seizure, deny needed guidance from the courts, or freeze Fourth Amendment law in its present state.[25] There is no need for courts to adopt the inflexible practice of always deciding whether the officers' conduct manifested objective good faith before turning to the question whether the Fourth Amendment has been violated. If resolution of a particular Fourth Amendment question is necessary to guide future action by law enforcement officers and magistrates, nothing will prevent reviewing courts from deciding that question before turning to the good-faith issue. Indeed, it frequently will be difficult to determine whether the officers acted reasonably without resolving the Fourth Amendment issue. Even if the Fourth Amendment question is not one of broad import, reviewing courts could decide in particular cases that magistrates under their supervision need to be informed of their errors and so evaluate the officers' good faith only after finding a violation. In other circumstances, those courts could reject suppression motions posing no important Fourth Amendment questions by turning immediately to a consideration of the officers' good faith.

When the principles we have enunciated today are applied to the facts of this case, the judgment of the Court of Appeals cannot stand. Leon has contended that no reasonably well trained police officer could have believed that there existed probable cause to search his house. Officer Rombach's application for a warrant clearly was supported by much more than a "bare bones" affidavit. The affidavit related the results of an extensive investigation and provided evidence sufficient to create disagreement among thoughtful and competent judges as to the existence of probable cause. Under these circumstances, the officers' reliance on the magistrate's determination of probable cause was objectively reasonable, and application of the extreme sanction of exclusion is inappropriate.

Accordingly, the judgment of the Court of Appeals is

Reversed.

JUSTICE BRENNAN, with whom JUSTICE MARSHALL joins, dissenting.

I have witnessed the Court's gradual but determined strangulation of the exclusionary rule. It now appears that the Court's victory over the Fourth Amendment is complete. Today the Court sanctions the use in the prosecution's case in chief of illegally obtained evidence against the individual whose rights have been violated.

The language of deterrence and of cost/benefit analysis creates an illusion of technical precision and ineluctability. When the Court's analysis is examined

---

[25] Although the exception might discourage presentation of insubstantial suppression motions, the magnitude of the benefit conferred on defendants by a successful motion makes it unlikely that litigation of colorable claims will be substantially diminished.

carefully, it is clear that we have not been treated to an honest assessment of the merits of the exclusionary rule, but have instead been drawn into a curious world where the "costs" of excluding illegally obtained evidence loom to exaggerated heights and where the "benefits" of such exclusion are made to disappear with a mere wave of the hand.

The Court treats the exclusionary rule as merely a "judicially created remedy designed to safeguard Fourth Amendment rights through its deterrent effect, rather than a personal constitutional right." The Fourth Amendment, like other provisions of the Bill of Rights, restrains the power of the government as a whole. The judiciary is responsible, no less than the executive, for ensuring that constitutional rights are respected. Because seizures are executed principally to secure evidence, and because such evidence generally has utility in our legal system only in the context of a trial, the admission of illegally obtained evidence implicates the same constitutional concerns as the initial seizure of that evidence. By admitting unlawfully seized evidence, the judiciary becomes a part of what is a single governmental action prohibited by the terms of the Amendment. The right to be free from the initial invasion of privacy and the right of exclusion are coordinate components of the central embracing right to be free from unreasonable searches and seizures. From *Weeks to Olmstead*, the Court plainly understood that the exclusion of illegally obtained evidence was compelled not by judicially fashioned remedial purposes, but rather by a direct constitutional command.

The deterrence theory is both misguided and unworkable. First, the Court has frequently bewailed the "cost" of excluding reliable evidence. The Amendment directly contemplates that some reliable and incriminating evidence will be lost to the government; therefore, it is not the exclusionary rule, but the Amendment itself that has imposed this cost. The entire enterprise of attempting to assess the benefits and costs of the exclusionary rule in various contexts is a virtually impossible task for the judiciary to perform honestly or accurately. To the extent empirical data are available regarding the general costs and benefits of the exclusionary rule, such data have shown that the costs are not as substantial as critics have asserted, and that while the exclusionary rule may well have certain deterrent effects, it is extremely difficult to determine with any degree of precision whether the incidence of unlawful conduct by police is now lower than it was prior to *Mapp*. The Court has sought to turn this uncertainty to its advantage by casting the burden of proof upon proponents of the rule.

In this case, the affidavit filed by the police officers failed to provide a basis on which a neutral and detached magistrate could conclude that there was probable cause to issue the warrant. The application for a warrant was based on information supplied by a confidential informant of unproven reliability that was over five months old. Although the police conducted an independent investigation, the additional information failed to corroborate the details of the tip and was "as consistent with innocence as with guilt." The warrant, therefore, should never have issued. Stripped of the authority of the warrant, the conduct of these officers was plainly unconstitutional—it amounted to nothing less than a naked invasion of the privacy of respondents' homes without the requisite justification demanded by the Fourth Amendment. It was necessary that the evidence be suppressed.

The tenor of the Court's opinion suggests that this order somehow imposed a grave and presumably unjustifiable cost on society. Such a suggestion, however, is a gross exaggeration. Since the bulk of the evidence seized was plainly admissible, the Government would clearly still be able to present a strong case to the jury following the court's suppression order.

The Court suggests that society has been asked to pay a high price—in terms either of setting guilty persons free or of impeding the proper functioning of trials—as a result of excluding relevant physical evidence in cases where the police, in conducting searches and seizing evidence, have made only an "objectively reasonable" mistake concerning the constitutionality of their actions. But what evidence is there to support such a claim? The Court points to none, and recent studies have demonstrated that the "costs" of the exclusionary rule—calculated in terms of dropped prosecutions and lost convictions—are quite low. Federal and state prosecutors very rarely drop cases because of potential search and seizure problems. A 1979 study reported that only 0.4% of all cases actually declined for prosecution by federal prosecutors were declined primarily because of illegal search problems. The study shows that only 0.2% of all felony arrests are declined for prosecution because of potential exclusionary rule problems.[11] Of course, these data describe only the costs attributable to the exclusion of evidence in all cases; the costs due to the exclusion of evidence in the narrower category of cases where police have made objectively reasonable mistakes must necessarily be even smaller. The Court ignores this distinction and mistakenly weighs the aggregated costs of exclusion in all cases, irrespective of the circumstances that led to exclusion, against the potential benefits associated with only those cases in which evidence is excluded because police reasonably but mistakenly believe that their conduct does not violate the Fourth Amendment. When such faulty scales are used, it is little wonder that the balance tips in favor of restricting the application of the rule.

The key to the Court's holding is the belief that the prospective deterrent effect of the exclusionary rule operates only in those situations in which police officers, when deciding whether to go forward with some particular search, have reason to know that their planned conduct will violate the requirements

---

[11] A recent National Institute of Justice NIJ study showed that 4.8% of all cases that were declined for prosecution by California prosecutors were rejected because of illegally seized evidence — only 0.8% of all arrests. The number of prosecutions that are dismissed or result in acquittals in cases where evidence has been excluded—the data show that the Court's assessment of the rule's costs has been exaggerated.

of the Fourth Amendment. The Court's argument captures only one comparatively minor element of the generally acknowledged deterrent purposes of the exclusionary rule. To be sure, the rule operates to deter future misconduct by individual officers who have had evidence suppressed in their own cases. What the Court overlooks is that the deterrence rationale is not designed to be a form of "punishment" of individual police officers for their failures to obey the restraints imposed by the Fourth Amendment. Instead, the chief deterrent function of the rule is its tendency to promote institutional compliance with Fourth Amendment requirements on the part of law enforcement agencies generally. "The exclusionary rule encourages those who formulate law enforcement policies, and the officers who implement them, to incorporate Fourth Amendment ideals into their value system." *Stone v. Powell*, 428 U.S., at 492. It is only through such an institution wide mechanism that information concerning Fourth Amendment standards can be effectively communicated to rank-and-file officers.

If the overall educational effect of the exclusionary rule is considered, application of the rule to even those situations in which individual police officers have acted on the basis of a reasonable but mistaken belief that their conduct was authorized can still be expected to have a considerable long-term deterrent effect. If evidence is consistently excluded in these circumstances, police departments will surely be prompted to instruct their officers to devote greater care and attention to providing sufficient information to establish probable cause when applying for a warrant, and to review with some attention the form of the warrant that they have been issued, rather than automatically assuming that whatever document the magistrate has signed will necessarily comport with Fourth Amendment requirements.

After today's decisions, that institutional incentive will be lost. The Court's "reasonable mistake" exception to the exclusionary rule will tend to put a premium on police ignorance of the law. Armed with the assurance provided by today's decisions that evidence will always be admissible whenever an officer has "reasonably" relied upon a warrant, police departments will be encouraged to train officers that if a warrant has simply been signed, it is reasonable, without more, to rely on it.

Moreover, the good-faith exception will encourage police to provide only the bare minimum of information in future warrant applications. The police will now know that if they can secure a warrant, so long as the circumstances of its issuance are not "entirely unreasonable," all police conduct pursuant to that warrant will be protected from further judicial review. The long-run effect unquestionably will be to undermine the integrity of the warrant process.

Given the relaxed standard for assessing probable cause established just last Term in *Illinois v. Gates*, 462 U.S. 213 (1983), the Court's newly fashioned good-faith exception, when applied in the warrant context, will rarely, if ever, offer any greater flexibility for police than the *Gates* standard already supplies.

When the public demands that those in government increase their efforts to combat crime, it is all too easy for those government officials to seek expedient solutions. The relaxation of Fourth Amendment standards seems a tempting, cost-less means of meeting the public's demand for better law enforcement. In the long run, however, we as a society pay a heavy price for such expediency. Once lost, rights are difficult to recover.

Justice Stevens, concurring in the judgment in No. 82–963, and dissenting in No. 82–1771.

The exclusionary rule is designed to prevent violations of the Fourth Amend-ment. Today's decisions do grave damage to that deterrent function. Under the majority's new rule, even when the police know their warrant application is probably insufficient, they retain an incentive to submit it to a magistrate, on the chance that he may take the bait. No longer must they hesitate and seek additional evidence in doubtful cases.

The Court is correct that the exclusionary rule cannot deter when the author-ities have no reason to know that their conduct is unconstitutional. But when probable cause is lacking, a reasonable person would not believe there is a fair likelihood that a search will produce evidence of a crime. Under such circum-stances well-trained professionals must know that they are violating the Constitu-tion. The Court's approach encourages the police to seek a warrant, even if they know the existence of probable cause is doubtful, can only lead to an increased number of constitutional violations.

The Court's decision tarnishes the role of the judiciary in enforcing the Con-stitution. Courts simply cannot escape their responsibility for redressing constitu-tional violations if they admit evidence obtained through unreasonable searches and seizures, since the entire point of police conduct that violates the Fourth Amendment is to obtain evidence for use at trial. It is true that the exclusionary rule exerts a high price—the loss of probative evidence of guilt. But that price is one courts have often been required to pay to serve important social goals. That price is also one the Fourth Amendment requires us to pay, assuming as we must that the Framers intended that its strictures "shall not be violated." We could facilitate the process of administering justice by ignoring the entire Bill of Rights—but it is the very purpose of a Bill of Rights to identify values that may not be sacrificed to expediency. In a just society those who govern, as well as those who are governed, must obey the law.

Food for Thought

About one-third of the states have rejected the good faith exception to the exclusionary rule under their own state constitutions. In construing the New Jersey Constitution, for example, the New Jersey Supreme Court rejected *Leon's* reasoning. In *State v. Novembrino*, 105 N.J. 95, 519 A.2d 820 (1987), the court offered the following reasons: "The exclusionary rule's function is not merely to deter police misconduct. The rule also serves as the indispensable mechanism for vindicating the constitutional right to be free from unreasonable searches. Because the good-faith exception would tend to undermine the constitutionally-guaranteed standard of probable cause, and in the process disrupt the highly effective procedures employed by our criminal justice system to accommodate that constitutional guarantee without impairing law enforcement, we decline to recognize a good-faith exception to the exclusionary rule. We see no need in New Jersey to experiment with the fundamental rights protected by the fourth-amendment counterpart of our State Constitution." Consider also *State v. Marsala*, 216 Conn. 150, 579 A.2d 58 (1990), another state court decision rejecting *Leon*: "A good faith exception to the exclusionary rule would have several negative effects. First, the good faith exception would encourage some police officers to expend less effort in establishing the necessary probable cause and more effort in locating a judge who might be less exacting than some others when ruling on whether an affidavit has established the requisite level of probable cause. Second, the "exception implicitly tells magistrates that they need not take much care in reviewing warrant applications, since their mistakes will from now on have virtually no consequence." Finally, it is unlikely "that overburdened trial and appellate courts will take the time and effort to write advisory opinions on search and seizure law when they can just as easily admit the evidence under the good faith exception." The exclusionary rule is not designed to "punish" anyone. It is designed to deter future police misconduct and ensure institutional compliance with the warrant issuing requirements of our state constitution. The relevant inquiry, therefore, is whether the sanction of the exclusionary rule is appropriate in cases where the officer in question believed that he was doing everything correctly, but in fact had not supplied the issuing authority with information sufficient to meet the constitutional requirement of probable cause. If evidence is consistently excluded, police departments will surely be prompted to instruct their officers to devote greater care and attention to providing sufficient information to establish probable cause when applying for a warrant, and to review with some attention the form of the warrant that they have been issued, rather than automatically assuming that whatever document the magistrate has signed will necessarily comport with Fourth Amendment requirements." Do you agree with these state court decisions?

In *Malley v. Briggs*, 475 U.S. 335 (1986), a police officer unconstitutionally arrested plaintiffs by presenting a judge with a complaint and a supporting affidavit which failed to establish probable cause. Plaintiffs sued the officers for damages. The Court held that the officers were protected by qualified immunity, but only if they acted "reasonably": "The question in this case is whether a reasonably well-trained officer in petitioner's position would have known that his affidavit failed to establish probable cause and that he should not have applied for the warrant. If such was the case, the officer's application for a warrant was not objectively reasonable, because it created the unnecessary danger of an unlawful arrest." Does the possibility of a civil suit sufficiently deter police misconduct?

In *Groh v. Ramirez*, 540 U.S. 551 (2004), the Court concluded that Bureau of Alcohol, Tobacco and Firearm (ATF) agents did not act reasonably when they executed a search warrant. The warrant failed to provide an adequate description of the place to be searched, and the Court concluded that the officers who executed the warrant were not entitled to qualified immunity. The Court concluded that the warrant was so "facially deficient" that the officers could not presume it to be valid. However, courts are often deferential to judgments made by the police, especially when they have relied on a warrant issued by a magistrate, and courts are therefore reluctant to impose damage awards. *See Messerschmidt v. Millender*, 565 U.S. 535 (2012).

Points for Discussion

a. Good Faith and "Technical Errors"

Massachusetts v. Sheppard, 468 U.S. 981 (1984) was a "companion case" to *Leon* and was handed down at the same time. In *Sheppard*, the Court extended *Leon* to a case involving a warrant invalidated because of a technical error on the part of the issuing judge: "Suppressing evidence because the judge failed to make all the necessary clerical corrections despite his assurances that such changes would be made will not serve the deterrent function that the exclusionary rule was designed to achieve."

b. Good Faith Reliance on an Invalid Statute

In *Illinois v. Krull*, 480 U.S. 340 (1987), the Court extended the good faith exception to situations when the police acted in objectively reasonable reliance upon a statute authorizing warrantless administrative searches, but where the statute was ultimately found to violate the Fourth Amendment: "The application of the exclusionary rule to suppress evidence obtained by an officer acting in objectively reasonable reliance on a statute would have as little deterrent effect on the officer's actions as would the exclusion of evidence when an officer acts in objectively reasonable reliance on a warrant. Unless a statute is clearly unconstitutional, an officer cannot be expected to question the judgment of the legislature that passed the law. If the statute is subsequently declared unconstitutional, excluding evidence obtained pursuant to it prior to such a judicial declaration will not deter future Fourth Amendment violations by an officer who has simply fulfilled his responsibility to enforce the statute as written." Justice O'Connor dissented: "Statutes authorizing unreasonable searches were the core concern of the Framers of the Fourth Amendment. Both the history of the Fourth Amendment and this Court's later interpretations of it, support application of the exclusionary rule to this situation."

c. Reliance on Prior Precedent

In *Davis v. United States*, 564 U.S. 229 (2011), the police conducted a search in reliance on U.S. Supreme Court precedent. However, that precedent (*New York v. Belton*), which allowed police to routinely search the interior of a vehicle as part of a search incident to legal arrest, was overruled by a later decision (*State v. Gant*). The Court again focused on the deterrence rationale, and held that the costs of excluding the evidence outweighed the potential benefits: "The question in this case is whether to apply the exclusionary rule when the police conduct a search in objectively reasonable reliance on binding judicial precedent. The officers who conducted the search did not violate Davis's Fourth Amendment rights deliberately, recklessly, or with gross negligence. Nor does this case involve any 'recurring or systemic negligence' on the part of law enforcement. The police acted in strict compliance with binding precedent, and their behavior was not wrongful. Unless the exclusionary rule is to become a strict-liability regime, it can have no application in this case. We have 'never applied' the exclusionary rule to suppress evidence obtained as a result of nonculpable, innocent police conduct. All that exclusion would deter in this case is conscientious police work. When binding appellate precedent specifically *authorizes* a particular police practice, well-trained officers will and should use that tool to fulfill their crime-detection and public-safety responsibilities."

d. Bookkeeping Errors

In *Herring v. United States*, 555 U.S. 135 (2009), a police officer made an arrest, based on an outstanding arrest warrant, but the warrant was invalid due to a negligent bookkeeping error by another police employee. The arrest led to information that Herring was in possession of illegal drugs, and a firearm (which was prohibited since he was a convicted felon). Focusing on the deterrence rationale for exclusion, and the cost-benefit test, the Court held that the evidence need not be excluded. The Court emphasized that it has generally applied the remedy of exclusion to flagrant misconduct: "To trigger the exclusionary rule, police conduct must be sufficiently deliberate that exclusion can meaningfully deter it, and sufficiently culpable that such deterrence is worth the price paid by the justice system." The Court concluded that the bookkeeping error did not rise to that level, and was not "so objectively culpable as to require exclusion." Exclusion might have been justified if the police had been "reckless in maintaining a warrant system, or knowingly made false entries to lay the groundwork for future false

Food for Thought

Reread *Mapp v. Ohio*. Does your reading suggest that the exclusionary rule is premised solely on principles of deterrence, or does it suggest that the rule is based on other considerations as well (e.g., the "imperative" of judicial integrity, or the Fourth Amendment itself—in other words, that the rule is "constitutionally required")?

arrests." Justice Ginsburg, joined by three other justices, dissented, arguing that exclusion is needed to discourage police error and to protect innocent individuals against improper arrest: "Negligent recordkeeping errors by law enforcement threaten individual liberty, are susceptible to deterrence by the exclusionary rule, and cannot be remedied effectively through other means."

Food for Thought

Would *Leon's* logic suggest that the good faith exception should apply when an officer makes a warrantless search in "good faith" (not in reliance on an invalid statute or prior judicial precedent)? For example, the officer believes that he has probable cause to search a vehicle, and therefore can invoke the automobile exception to the warrant requirement, but he is wrong in concluding that probable cause exists. Does *Leon's* rationale extend to warrantless searches of this type?

Hypo 1: *Application of the Good Faith Exception*

Suppose that the police receive information implicating a suspect in the theft of a police vehicle. They apply for a search warrant authorizing them to obtain a sample of the suspect's hair as well as a buccal swab. However, the search warrant application does not state that the police have hair samples or other evidence from the car against which the samples that would be taken from the suspect can be compared. Moreover, although the affidavit indicates that the police have probable cause to believe that defendant has committed a crime, the warrant does not specifically indicate which crime. There is a potential implication of a car theft because the warrant application refers to informants who implicated the suspect in that theft. Should the good faith exception apply in this situation if a reviewing court determines that the warrant application was not supported by probable cause? *See State v. Powell*, 299 Kan. 690, 325 P.3d 1162 (2014).

Hypo 2: *More on Application of the Good Faith Exception*

Suppose that the police obtain a search warrant for a suspect's computer in order to search for evidence of child pornography. They do so based on confirmation of his computer address with his ISP and proof that his computer accessed child pornography some nine months earlier.

Later, a court concludes that the evidence of prior access was "stale," and therefore probable cause did not exist for issuance of the warrant. The court emphasizes that there is a difference between someone who accidentally access a child porn website, and does not click on an image, and someone who seeks out that website and downloads computer images. While one might expect the intentional downloader to hoard the images that he downloaded, no similar conclusion can be drawn regarding someone who accidentally accessed the website and downloaded nothing. Despite the absence of probable cause, should the search be upheld under the good faith exception? *See United States v. Raymonda*, 780 F.3d 105 (2nd Cir. 2015).

Hudson v. Michigan

547 U.S. 586 (2006).

JUSTICE SCALIA delivered the opinion of the Court, except as to Part IV.

When the police arrived to execute a warrant, they announced their presence, but waited only a short time—perhaps "three to five seconds"—before turning the knob of the unlocked front door and entering Hudson's home. Hudson moved to suppress all the inculpatory evidence drugs and a loaded gun, arguing that the premature entry violated his Fourth Amendment rights. The evidence was admitted and Hudson's appeal was rejected. We granted certiorari.

The common-law principle that law enforcement officers must announce their presence and provide residents an opportunity to open the door is an ancient one. See *Wilson v. Arkansas,* 514 U.S. 927 (1995). Since 1917, this traditional protection has been part of federal statutory law and is currently codified at 18 U.S.C. § 3109. *Wilson* concluded that it was also a command of the Fourth Amendment. It is not necessary to knock and announce when "circumstances present a threat of physical violence," or if there is "reason to believe that evidence would likely be destroyed if advance notice were given," or if knocking and announcing would be "futile," *Richards v. Wisconsin,* 520 U.S. 385 (1997). We require only that police "have a reasonable suspicion under the particular circumstances" that one of these grounds for failing to knock and announce exists, and we have acknowledged that "this showing is not high."

When the knock-and-announce rule does apply, it is not easy to determine precisely what officers must do. How many seconds' wait are too few? Our "reasonable wait time" standard, see *United States v. Banks,* 540 U.S. 31 (2003), is necessarily vague. *Banks* (a drug case, like this one) held that the proper measure was not how long it would take the resident to reach the door, but how long it would take to dispose of the suspected drugs—but that such a time (15 to 20 seconds in that case) would necessarily be extended when, for instance, the suspected contraband was not easily concealed. If our *ex post* evaluation is subject to such calculations, it is unsurprising that, *ex ante,* police officers about to encounter someone who may try to harm them will be uncertain how long to wait.

Michigan has conceded that the entry was a knock-and-announce violation. The issue here is remedy. Suppression of evidence has always been our last resort, not our first impulse. The exclusionary rule generates "substantial social costs," *United States v. Leon,* 468 U.S. 897 (1984), which sometimes include setting the guilty free and the dangerous at large. We have therefore been "cautious against expanding" it, and "have repeatedly emphasized that the rule's 'costly toll' upon truth-seeking and law enforcement objectives presents a high obstacle for those urging its application," *Pennsylvania Bd. of Probation and Parole v. Scott,* 524 U.S. 357 (1998). We have rejected "indiscriminate application" of the rule, and have held it to be applicable only "where its remedial objectives are thought most efficaciously served,"—that is, "where its deterrence benefits outweigh its 'substantial social costs,' " *Scott, supra,* at 363 (quoting *Leon, supra,* at 907).

We did not always speak so guardedly. Dicta in *Mapp* suggested wide scope for the exclusionary rule. But we have long since rejected that approach. In *Leon,* we explained that "whether the exclusionary sanction is appropriately imposed in a particular case, is 'an issue separate from the question whether the Fourth Amendment rights of the party seeking to invoke the rule were violated by police conduct.' "

Exclusion may not be premised on the mere fact that a constitutional violation was a "but-for" cause of obtaining evidence. But-for causality is only a necessary, not a sufficient, condition for suppression. In this case, the constitutional violation of an illegal *manner* of entry was *not* a but-for cause. Whether that preliminary misstep had occurred *or not,* the police would have executed the warrant they had obtained, and would have discovered the gun and drugs inside the house. We have declined to "hold that all evidence is 'fruit of the poisonous tree' simply because it would not have come to light *but for* the illegal actions of the police. Rather, the more apt question in such a case is 'whether, granting establishment of the primary illegality, the evidence to which instant objection is made has been come at by exploitation of that illegality or instead by means sufficiently distinguishable to be purged of the primary taint.' " *Wong Sun v. United States,* 371 U.S. 471 (1963) (quoting J. Maguire, Evidence of Guilt 221 (1959)).

Attenuation can occur when the causal connection is remote. Attenuation also occurs when, even given a direct causal connection, the interest protected by the constitutional guarantee that has been violated would not be served by suppression of the evidence obtained. "The penalties visited upon the Government, and in turn upon the public, because its officers have violated the law must bear some relation to the purposes which the law is to serve." In *New York v. Harris,* 495 U.S. 14 (1990), where an illegal warrantless arrest was made in Harris' house, we held that "suppressing Harris' statement taken outside the house would not serve the purpose of the rule that made Harris' in-house arrest illegal. The warrant requirement for an arrest in the home is imposed to protect the home, and anything incriminating the police gathered from arresting Harris in his home, rather than elsewhere, has been excluded, as it should have been; the purpose of the rule has thereby been vindicated."

Cases excluding the fruits of unlawful warrantless searches say nothing about the appropriateness of exclusion to vindicate the interests protected by the knock-and-announce requirement. Until a valid warrant has issued, citizens are entitled to shield "their persons, houses, papers, and effects," U.S. Const., Amdt. 4, from the government's scrutiny. Exclusion of the evidence obtained by a warrantless search vindicates that entitlement. The interests protected by the knock-and-announce requirement are quite different—and do not include the shielding of potential evidence from the government's eyes.

One of those interests is the protection of human life and limb, because an unannounced entry may provoke violence in supposed self-defense by the surprised resident. Another interest is the protection of property. The knock and announce rule gives individuals "the opportunity to comply with the law and to avoid the destruction of property occasioned by a forcible entry." *Richards,* 520 U.S., at 393. Thirdly, the knock-and-announce rule protects those elements of privacy and dignity that can be destroyed by a sudden entrance. "The brief interlude between announcement and entry with a warrant may be the opportunity that an individual has to pull on clothes or get out of bed." In other words, it assures the opportunity to collect oneself before answering the door.

What the knock-and-announce rule has never protected, however, is one's interest in preventing the government from seeing or taking evidence described in a warrant. Since the interests that *were* violated in this case have nothing to do with the seizure of the evidence, the exclusionary rule is inapplicable.

Quite apart from the requirement of unattenuated causation, the exclusionary rule has never been applied except "where its deterrence benefits outweigh its 'substantial social costs,' " *Scott,* 524 U.S., at 363. The costs here are considerable. In addition to the grave adverse consequence that exclusion of relevant incriminating evidence always entails (viz., the risk of releasing dangerous criminals into society), imposing that massive remedy for a knock-and-announce violation would generate a constant flood of alleged failures to observe the rule, and claims that any asserted *Richards* justification for a no-knock entry had inadequate support. The cost of entering this lottery would be small, but the jackpot enormous: suppression of all evidence, amounting in many cases to a get-out-of-jail-free card. Courts would experience the reality that "the exclusionary rule frequently requires extensive litigation to determine whether particular evidence must be excluded." *Scott, supra,* at 366. Unlike the warrant or *Miranda* requirements, compliance with which is readily determined, what constituted a "reasonable wait time" in a particular case (or, for that matter, how many seconds the police in fact waited), or whether there was "reasonable suspicion" of the sort that would invoke the *Richards* exceptions, is difficult for the trial court to determine and even more difficult for an appellate court to review.

Another consequence of the incongruent remedy Hudson proposes would be police officers' refraining from timely entry after knocking and announcing. The amount of time they must wait is necessarily uncertain. If the consequences of running afoul of the rule were so massive, officers would be inclined to wait longer than the law requires—producing preventable violence against officers in some cases, and the destruction of evidence in many others. We deemed these consequences severe enough to produce our unanimous agreement that a mere "reasonable suspicion" that knocking and announcing "under the particular circumstances, would be dangerous or futile, or that it would inhibit the effective investigation of the crime," will cause the requirement to yield. *Richards, supra,* at 394.

Next to these "substantial social costs" we must consider the deterrence benefits, existence of which is a necessary condition for exclusion. *United States v. Calandra,* 414 U.S. 338, 350 (1974) The value of deterrence depends upon the strength of the incentive to commit the forbidden act. Viewed from this perspective, deterrence of knock-and-announce violations is not worth a lot. Violation of the warrant requirement sometimes produces incriminating evidence that could not otherwise be obtained. But ignoring knock-and-announce can realistically be expected to achieve absolutely nothing except the prevention of destruction of evidence and the avoidance of life-threatening resistance by occupants of the premises—dangers which, if there is even "reasonable suspicion" of their existence, *suspend the knock-and-announce requirement anyway*. Massive deterrence is hardly required.

It seems to us not true that without suppression there will be no deterrence of knock-and-announce violations at all. Even if this assertion were accurate, it would not necessarily justify suppression. Assuming that civil suit is not an effective deterrent, one can think of many forms of police misconduct that are similarly "undeterred." When, for example, a confessed suspect in the killing of a police officer, arrested (along with incriminating evidence) in a lawful warranted search, is subjected to physical abuse at the station house, would it seriously be suggested that the evidence must be excluded, since that is the only "effective deterrent"? And what, other than civil suit, is the "effective deterrent" of police violation of an already-confessed suspect's Sixth Amendment rights by denying him prompt access to counsel? Many would regard these violated rights as more significant than the right not to be intruded upon in one's nightclothes—and yet nothing but "ineffective" civil suit is available as a deterrent. And the police incentive for those violations is arguably greater than the incentive for disregarding the knock-and-announce rule.

We cannot assume that exclusion in this context is necessary deterrence simply because we found that it was necessary deterrence in different contexts long ago. Hudson complains that "it would be very hard to find a lawyer to take a case such as this," but Congress has authorized attorney's fees for civil-rights plaintiffs. This remedy was unavailable in the heydays of our exclusionary-rule jurisprudence. Hudson points out that few published decisions announce huge awards for knock-and-announce violations. Even if we thought that only large damages would deter police misconduct (and that police somehow are deterred by "damages" but indifferent to the prospect of large § 1988 attorney's fees), we do not know how many claims have been settled, or indeed how many violations have occurred that produced anything more than nominal injury. Lower courts are allowing colorable knock-and-announce suits to go forward, unimpeded by assertions of qualified immunity. As far as we know, civil liability is an effective deterrent here.

Another development over the past half-century that deters civil-rights violations is the increasing professionalism of police forces, including a new emphasis on internal police discipline. There have been "wide-ranging reforms in the education, training, and supervision of police officers." S. Walker, Taming the System: The Control of Discretion in Criminal Justice 1950–1990, p. 51 (1993). Failure to teach and enforce constitutional requirements exposes municipalities to financial liability. It is not credible to assert that internal discipline, which can limit successful careers, will not have a deterrent effect. There is also evidence that the increasing use of various forms of citizen review can enhance police accountability.

In sum, the social costs of applying the exclusionary rule to knock-and-announce violations are considerable; the incentive to such violations is minimal to begin with, and the extant deterrences against them are substantial—incomparably greater than the factors deterring warrantless entries when *Mapp* was decided. Resort to the massive remedy of suppressing evidence of guilt is unjustified.

For the foregoing reasons we affirm the judgment of the Michigan Court of Appeals.

It is so ordered.

JUSTICE KENNEDY, concurring in part and concurring in the judgment.

The continued operation of the exclusionary rule is not in doubt. Today's decision determines only that in the specific context of the knock-and-announce requirement, a violation is not sufficiently related to the later discovery of evidence to justify suppression.

JUSTICE BREYER, with whom JUSTICE STEVENS, JUSTICE SOUTER, and JUSTICE GINSBURG join, dissenting.

In *Wilson,* we traced the lineage of the knock-and-announce rule back to the 13th century and concluded that "there was 'little doubt that the Framers of the Fourth Amendment thought that the method of an officer's entry into a dwelling was among the factors to be considered in assessing the reasonableness of a search or seizure." An unreasonable search or seizure is, constitutionally speaking, an illegal search or seizure. The driving legal purpose underlying the exclusionary rule, namely, the deterrence of unlawful government behavior, argues strongly for suppression. Failure to apply the exclusionary rule would make the Fourth Amendment's promise a hollow one, reducing it to "a form of words," "of no value" to those whom it seeks to protect. What reason is there to believe that alternative remedies (such as private damages actions under 42 U.S.C. § 1983), which the Court found inadequate in *Mapp,* can adequately deter unconstitutional police behavior here? The need for deterrence—the critical factor driving this Court's Fourth Amendment cases for close to a century—argues with at least comparable strength for evidentiary exclusion here.

The Court has declined to apply the exclusionary rule only: (1) where there is a specific reason to believe that application of the rule would "not result in appreciable deterrence," or (2) where admissibility in proceedings other than criminal trials was at issue. Neither of these two exceptions applies here. The first does not apply because there is no reason to think that, in the case of knock-and-announce violations by the police, "the exclusion of evidence at trial would not sufficiently deter future errors," or "further the ends of the exclusionary rule in any appreciable way."

It is difficult for me to see how the presence of a warrant that does not authorize the entry in question has anything to do with the "inevitable discovery" exception or otherwise diminishes the need to enforce the knock-and-announce requirement through suppression. The knock-and-announce rule protects the occupants' privacy by assuring them that government agents will not enter their home without complying with those requirements (among others) that diminish the offensive nature of any such intrusion. The knock-and-announce requirement is no less a part of the "centuries-old principle" of special protection for the privacy of the home than the warrant requirement. The Court is therefore wrong to reduce the essence of its protection to "the right not to be intruded upon in one's night-clothes." Failure to comply with the knock-and-announce rule renders the related search unlawful. And where a search is unlawful, the law insists upon suppression of the evidence consequently discovered, even if that evidence or its possession has little or nothing to do with the reasons underlying the unconstitutionality of a search. Ordinarily a court will simply look to see if the unconstitutional search produced the evidence.

Food for Thought

In *State v. Cable,* 51 So.3d 434 (Fla. 2010), applying its state constitution, the Florida Supreme Court held that a violation of Florida's knock-and-announce statute vitiated the ensuing arrest and required suppression of the evidence obtained in connection with the arrest. The court concluded that, "even if probable cause exists for the arrest of a person, our statute is violated by an unannounced intrusion in the form of a breaking and entering any building, including a private home, except (1) where the person within already knows of the officer's authority and purpose; (2) where the officers are justified in the belief that the persons within are in imminent peril of bodily harm; (3) if the officer's peril would have been increased had he demanded entrance and stated the purpose, or (4) where those within made aware of the presence of someone outside are then engaged in activities which justify the officers in the belief that an escape or destruction of evidence is being attempted." The court reasoned as follows: "A citizen's obligation to respond to a request to allow a law enforcement officer into his or her home depends on the purpose of the law enforcement officer's request. While a citizen has every right to refuse entry to an officer who may be merely seeking information or conducting an investigation, the citizen has no right to refuse entry by an officer whose purpose in seeking entry is to execute an arrest warrant or search warrant. Before law enforcement officials may properly enter a private building to effect an arrest and 'use all necessary and reasonable force to enter any building or property,' § 901.19(1), Fla. Stat., they are required to announce their purpose." Is the Florida approach preferable?

Hypo 1: *The Delayed Search*

Pursuant to a warrant authorizing them to search for stolen and forged checks, the police search defendant's home. During the search, they find two locked safes capable of holding checks. Police seize the safes and transport them to the police station. A state court finds that it would have been permissible for the police to search the safes at the time of the original search, but that it was impermissible to seize them and search them later. Under *Hudson*, does the violation of defendant's possessory rights require exclusion of evidence found in the safes (methamphetamine)?

What arguments might you make on the defense's behalf? How might the prosecution respond to these arguments? *See State v. Powell*, 306 S.W.3d 761 (Tex. Crim. App. 2010).

Hypo 2: *More on Deterrence*

After some suspicious transactions, police investigate two fraudulent bank accounts opened in the name of "Ousmane Diallo" who used a passport from Guinea. However, they were unable to locate Diallo. When a man named Fode Fofana arrives at a U.S. airport under conditions that flag him as a "selectee" for additional screening, he is individually questioned and searched. During the search, a TSA agent finds various envelopes containing large amounts of cash, as well as two unsealed envelopes that "contain something hard and unbendable," but unidentifiable. The TSA agent opens the envelopes and finds three passports bearing Fofana's picture, but with different names. One of the passports contains the name "Ousmane Diallo." Because of the passport, later determined to be illegal, police link Fofana to the fraudulent bank accounts. Fofana moves to suppress the seized passports, as the fruit of an illegal search, as well as information regarding his identity, on the basis that TSA did not have the authority to open the envelopes. If the passports are excluded, must the court also exclude evidence regarding the link between Fofana and Diallo? Is sufficient deterrence obtained by the fact that the passports are excluded? *See United States v. Fofana*, 666 F.3d 985 (6th Cir. 2012).

Hypo 3: *The Exclusionary Rule and State Law*

While investigating a cocaine ring, a state warrant authorized the police to eavesdrop on digital pager communications. Consistently with Title III of the Omnibus Crime Control and Safe Streets Act of 1968, as amended by Title I of the Electronic Communications Privacy Act of 1986 (the "ECPA"), the warrant specifically required the police to capture, keep and store the communications on a police department computer "in a manner that will protect the records from editing and alteration." The warrant also authorized the monitoring of communications via a duplicate or "clone" paging device, which would display the same information as that shown on the device being monitored. When the police chose to monitor the clone pager, and failed to comply with a local law requiring that the information be stored on a police department computer, defendant moved to suppress the evidence. Assuming that the warrant was supported by probable cause, and was otherwise in order, should noncompliance with the ECPA's recording requirement trigger application of the exclusionary rule? See *United States v. Amanuel*, 615 F.3d 117 (2d Cir. 2010).

Hypo 4: *Arrest by an Officer in Excess of Jurisdiction.*

On Christmas Eve, a city officer observes an automobile traveling in excess of the speed limit on a road near the city limits. The officer mistakenly believes that the road is within the city limits. The officer begins pursuit with the intention of giving the driver a warning. However, the driver does not respond to the officer's blue lights, increases his speed, and runs a stop sign. When the officer finally catches up to the driver, he realizes that the driver has been driving under the influence of alcohol. If the officer does not have the authority to exercise police powers outside of the city limits, should the evidence of intoxication be suppressed? Should it matter that the officer acted in good faith? See *Delker v. State*, 50 So.3d 300 (Miss. 2010).

Hypo 5: *Jones and the Good Faith Exception*

As you may recall, in *United States v. Jones*, 565 U.S. 400 (2012), the Court held that the police violated the Fourth Amendment when they attached a GPS tracking device to a vehicle in order to track the vehicle's movements. The Court's prior decisions, particularly *United States v. Knotts*, 460 U.S. 276 (1983), had held that the police could track GPS devices without violating the Fourth Amendment. However, the facts were somewhat different in *Knotts*, because rather than attaching a GPS device to Knotts' car, the police inserted the GPS device in a bottle of chloroform before Knotts purchased it. Lower court decisions had construed *Knotts* as applying to situations when the police attach a GPS device to a suspect's vehicle. Should evidence obtained through direct attachment be admitted under the good faith exception? See *Kelly v. State*, 82 A.3d 205 (Md. 2013); *United States v. Aguiar*, 737 F.3d 251 (2nd Cir. 2013); *United States v. Smith*, 741 F.3d 1211 (11th Cir. 2013).

> ### Hypo 6: *Good Faith and Jardines*
>
> In *Florida v. Jardines*, 569 U.S. 1 (2013), the Court invalidated a canine sniff at an individual's residence as a violation of the Fourth Amendment. If lower court decisions had held that a dog sniff under similar circumstances was permissible, does the good faith exception apply? *See State v. Scull*, 843 N.W.2d 859 (Wis. App. 2014). *see also State v. Scull*, 361 Wis.2d 288, 862 N.W.2d 562 (2015); *United States v. Davis*, 760 F.3d 901 (8th Cir. 2014); *United States v. Gutierrez*, 760 F.3d 750 (7th Cir. 2014).

C. The Rule's Application in Other Contexts

Should the exclusionary rule apply in other contexts (*e.g.*, civil proceedings)? Consider the following case.

United States v. Janis

428 U.S. 433 (1976).

MR. JUSTICE BLACKMUN delivered the opinion of the Court.

In November 1968 the Los Angeles police obtained a warrant directing a search for bookmaking paraphernalia at two specified apartment locations in the city and, as well, on the respective persons of Morris Aaron Levine and respondent Max Janis. The warrant was issued by a judge of the Municipal Court of the Los Angeles Judicial District. It was based upon the affidavit of Officer Leonard Weissman. After the search, both the respondent and Levine were arrested and the police seized from respondent property consisting of $4,940 in cash and certain wagering records.

Officer Weissman telephoned an agent of the United States Internal Revenue Service and informed the agent that Janis had been arrested for bookmaking activity. With the assistance of Weissman, who was familiar with bookmakers' codes, the revenue agent analyzed the wagering records that had been seized and determined from them the gross volume of respondent's gambling activity for the five days immediately preceding the seizure. Weissman informed the agent that he had conducted a surveillance of respondent's activities that indicated that respondent had been engaged in bookmaking during the 77-day period from September 14 through November 30, 1968, the day of the arrest.

Respondent had not filed any federal wagering tax return pertaining to book-making activities for that 77-day period. Based exclusively upon its examination of the evidence so obtained by the Los Angeles police, the Internal Revenue Service made an assessment jointly against respondent and Levine for wagering taxes, under § 4401 of the Internal Revenue Code of 1954, in the amount of $89,026.09, plus interest. The assessment having been made, the Internal Revenue Service exercised its statutory authority, under 26 U.S.C. § 6331, to levy upon the $4,940 in cash in partial satisfaction of the assessment against respondent. Charges were filed in due course against respondent and Levine in Los Angeles Municipal Court for violation of the local gambling laws. The judge concluded that the evidence had been illegally obtained, and granted a motion to quash the warrant.

In June 1969 respondent filed a claim for refund of the $4,940. The claim was not honored, and respondent filed suit. The Government counterclaimed for the substantial unpaid balance of the assessment. In pretrial proceedings, it was agreed that the "sole basis of the computation of the civil tax assessment was the items obtained pursuant to the search warrant and the information furnished to (the revenue agent) by Officer Weissman with respect to the duration of (respondent's) alleged wagering activities." Respondent then moved to suppress the evidence seized, and all copies thereof in the possession of the Service, and to quash the assessment. The District Court granted the motion to suppress. Because of the obvious importance of the question, we granted certiorari.

In the complex and turbulent history of the rule, the Court never has applied it to exclude evidence from a civil proceeding, federal or state. In the present case we are asked to create judicially a deterrent sanction by holding that evidence obtained by a state criminal law enforcement officer in good-faith reliance on a warrant that later proved to be defective shall be inadmissible in a federal civil tax proceeding. Clearly, the enforcement of valid laws would be hampered by so extending the exclusionary rule, and concededly relevant and reliable evidence would be rendered unavailable.

In evaluating the need for a deterrent sanction, one must first identify those who are to be deterred. In this case it is the state officer who is the primary object of the sanction. Two factors suggest that a sanction in addition to those that presently exist is unnecessary. First, the local law enforcement official is already "punished" by the exclusion of the evidence in the state criminal trial. That, necessarily, is of substantial concern to him. Second, the evidence is also excludable in the federal criminal trial so that the entire criminal enforcement process, which is the concern and duty of these officers, is frustrated.

Jurists and scholars have recognized that the exclusionary rule imposes a substantial cost on the societal interest in law enforcement by its proscription of what concededly is relevant evidence. And alternatives that would be less costly to societal interests have been the subject of extensive discussion and exploration. If the exclusionary rule is the "strong medicine" that its proponents claim it to be, then its use in the situations in which it is now applied (resulting in frustration of the Los Angeles police officers' good-faith duties as enforcers of the criminal laws) must be assumed to be a substantial and efficient deterrent. Assuming this efficacy, the additional marginal deterrence provided by forbidding a different sovereign from using the evidence in a civil proceeding surely does not outweigh the cost to society of extending the rule to that situation. If, on the other hand, the exclusionary rule does not result in appreciable deterrence, then, clearly, its use in the instant situation is unwarranted.

In short, we conclude that exclusion from federal civil proceedings of evidence unlawfully seized by a state criminal enforcement officer has not been shown to have a sufficient likelihood of deterring the conduct of the state police so that it outweighs the societal costs imposed by the exclusion. This Court, therefore, is not justified in so extending the exclusionary rule. Imposition of the exclusionary rule in this case is unlikely to provide significant, much less substantial, additional deterrence. It falls outside the offending officer's zone of primary interest. The extension of the exclusionary rule would be an unjustifiably drastic action by the courts in the pursuit of what is an undesired and undesirable supervisory role over police officers.

In the situation before us, we do not find sufficient justification for the drastic measure of an exclusionary rule. There comes a point at which courts, consistent with their duty to administer the law, cannot continue to create barriers to law enforcement in the pursuit of a supervisory role that is properly the duty of the Executive and Legislative Branches. We therefore hold that the judicially created exclusionary rule should not be extended to forbid the use in the civil proceeding of one sovereign of evidence seized by a criminal law enforcement agent of another sovereign.

The judgment of the Court of Appeals is reversed, and the case is remanded for further proceedings consistent with this opinion.

It is so ordered.

MR. JUSTICE BRENNAN, with whom MR. JUSTICE MARSHALL concurs, dissenting.

The exclusionary rule is a necessary and inherent constitutional ingredient of the protections of the Fourth Amendment.

Mr. Justice Stewart, dissenting.

Federal officials responsible for the enforcement of the wagering tax provisions regularly cooperate with federal and local officials responsible for enforcing criminal laws restricting or forbidding wagering. Similarly, federal and local law enforcement personnel regularly provide federal tax officials with information, obtained in criminal investigations, indicating liability under the wagering tax. The pattern is one of mutual cooperation and coordination, with the federal wagering tax provisions buttressing state and federal criminal sanctions. If state police officials can effectively crack down on gambling law violators by the simple expedient of violating their constitutional rights and turning the illegally seized evidence over to Internal Revenue Service agents on the proverbial "silver platter," then the deterrent purpose of the exclusionary rule is wholly frustrated. "If, on the other hand, it is understood that the fruit of an unlawful search by state agents will be inadmissible in a federal trial, there can be no inducement to subterfuge and evasion with respect to federal-state cooperation in criminal investigation." *Elkins v. United States*, 364 U.S. 206, 222 (1960).

Points for Discussion

a. The Exclusionary Rule and Immigration Proceedings

Janis was followed by the Court's decision in *Immigration and Naturalization Service v. Lopez-Mendoza*, 468 U.S. 1032 (1984), in which the Court refused to apply the exclusionary rule in a deportation proceeding even though the officials who conducted an unlawful arrest were the same officials who brought a subsequent deportation proceeding (in other words, there was no "intrasovereign" violation). The Court justified its decision as follows:

> Several factors significantly reduce the deterrent value of the exclusionary rule in a civil deportation proceeding. First, deportation will still be possible when evidence not derived directly from the arrest is sufficient to support deportation. Since the person and identity of the respondent are not themselves suppressible, the INS must prove only alienage, and that will sometimes be possible using evidence gathered independently of, or sufficiently attenuated from, the original arrest. There is no provision which forbids drawing an adverse inference from the fact of standing mute. The second factor is a practical one. In the course of a year the average INS agent arrests almost 500 illegal aliens. Over 97.5% apparently agree to voluntary deportation without a formal hearing. When an occasional challenge is brought, the arresting officer is most unlikely to shape his conduct in anticipation of the exclusion of evidence at a formal deportation hearing. Third, and perhaps most important, the INS has its own comprehensive scheme for deterring Fourth Amendment violations by its officers. Evidence

seized through intentionally unlawful conduct is excluded by Department of Justice policy from the proceeding for which it was obtained. The INS also has in place a procedure for investigating and punishing immigration officers who commit Fourth Amendment violations. The INS's attention to Fourth Amendment interests reduces the likely deterrent value of the exclusionary rule. Deterrence must be measured at the margin. Finally, the deterrent value of the exclusionary rule in deportation proceedings is undermined by the availability of alternative remedies for institutional practices by the INS that might violate Fourth Amendment rights.

On the other side of the scale, the social costs of applying the exclusionary rule in deportation proceedings are unusual and significant. Applying the exclusionary rule in proceedings that are intended not to punish past transgressions but to prevent their continuance or renewal would require the courts to close their eyes to ongoing violations of the law. This Court has never before accepted costs of this character in applying the exclusionary rule. Sandoval is a person whose unregistered presence in this country, without more, constitutes a crime. His release within our borders would immediately subject him to criminal penalties. His release would clearly frustrate the express public policy against an alien's unregistered presence in this country. Even the objective of deterring Fourth Amendment violations should not require such a result. The constable's blunder may allow the criminal to go free, but we have never suggested that it allows the criminal to continue in the commission of an ongoing crime.

Other factors also weigh against applying the exclusionary rule in deportation proceedings. The INS currently operates a deliberately simple deportation hearing system, streamlined to permit the quick resolution of very large numbers of deportation actions, and it is against this backdrop that the costs of the exclusionary rule must be assessed. Finally, the INS advances the credible argument that applying the exclusionary rule to deportation proceedings might well result in the suppression of large amounts of information that had been obtained entirely lawfully. INS arrests occur in crowded and confused circumstances. In these circumstances we are persuaded that the *Janis* balance between costs and benefits comes out against applying the exclusionary rule in civil deportation hearings held by the INS.

Justice Brennan, dissenting, argued that "the Government has an obligation to obey the Fourth Amendment; that obligation is not lifted simply because the evidence was to be used in civil deportation proceedings." Justice White, also dissenting, contended that: "Because INS agents are law enforcement officials whose mission is analogous to that of police officers and because civil deportation proceedings are to INS agents what criminal trials are to police officers, the costs and benefits of applying the exclusionary rule in civil deportation proceedings do not differ from the costs and benefits of applying the rule in ordinary criminal proceedings." Justice Marshall also dissented: "There is no other way than exclusion to achieve 'the twin goals of enabling the judiciary to avoid the taint of partnership in official lawlessness and of assuring the people—all potential victims of unlawful government conduct—that the government would not profit from its lawless behavior.' "

b. More on the Exclusionary Rule and Deportation Proceedings

In *Lopez-Rodriguez v. Mukasey,* 536 F.3d 1012 (9th Cir. 2008), the court applied the exclusionary rule in a deportation proceeding on the basis that the Fourth Amendment violation was "egregious." In that case, officers entered the suspects' home without a warrant, consent or exigent circumstances.

c. The Exclusionary Rule in Grand Jury Proceedings

In *United States v. Calandra,* 414 U.S. 338 (1974), the Court refused to apply the exclusionary rule to a witness summoned to appear and testify before a grand jury who refused to answer questions on the ground that they were based on evidence obtained from an unlawful search and seizure. The Court justified its decision as follows: "This extension of the exclusionary rule would seriously impede the grand jury. Because the grand jury does not finally adjudicate guilt or innocence, it has traditionally been allowed to pursue its investigative and accusatorial functions unimpeded by the evidentiary and procedural restrictions applicable to a criminal trial. Any incremental deterrent effect which might be achieved by extending the rule to grand jury proceedings is uncertain at best. Such an extension would deter only police investigation consciously directed toward the discovery of evidence solely for use in a grand jury investigation. The incentive to disregard the requirement of the Fourth Amendment solely to obtain an indictment from a grand jury is substantially negated by the inadmissibility of the illegally seized evidence in a subsequent criminal prosecution of the search victim. A prosecutor would be unlikely to request an indictment where a conviction could not be obtained." Justice Brennan dissented: "The exclusionary rule is 'an essential part of both the Fourth and Fourteenth Amendments,' that 'gives to the individual no more than that which the Constitution guarantees him, to the police officer no less than that to which honest law enforcement is entitled, and, to the courts, that judicial integrity so necessary in the true administration of justice.' "

d. Armed Forces Enforcement of Civilian Law

In *United States v. Dreyer,* 767 F.3d 826 (9th Cir. 2014), a special agent in the Naval Criminal Investigative Service (NCIS), who was investigating the distribution of child pornography using special surveillance software, came across evidence of a civilian's downloading of child pornography onto his computer. After determining that the person involved was not in the military, the NCIS alerted civilian authorities who investigated and prosecuted the civilian. The Ninth Circuit held that The Posse Comitatus Act (PCA), 18 U.S.C. § 1385, "prohibits Army and Air Force military personnel from participating in civilian law enforcement activities." *United States v. Chon*, 210 F.3d 990, 993 (9th Cir. 2000). In addition, Congress has directed "the Secretary of Defense to prescribe such regulations as may be necessary" to prevent "direct participation by a member of the Army, Navy, Air Force, or Marine Corps" in civilian law enforcement activities unless otherwise authorized by law. Congress has authorized certain exceptions to § 375, such as permitting the military to make equipment and facilities available to civilian law enforcement and allowing the military to provide support in particular situations, such as during an emergency situation involving a weapon of mass destruction. However, the Court concluded that none of the exceptions were applicable. Finding a pattern of violations by the military, the Court applied the exclusionary rule to the case.

Food for Thought

In *Sanchez-Llamas v. Oregon*, 548 U.S. 331 (2006), the Court refused to apply the exclusionary rule to a violation of Article 36 of the Vienna Convention on Consular Relations (Vienna Convention or Convention). Article 36 provides that, when a national of one country is detained by authorities in another, the authorities must notify the consular officers of the detainee's home country if the detainee so requests. In addition, the authorities must inform the detainee of his right to request consular assistance. Sanchez-Llamas was detained for shooting a police officer, and given a *Miranda* warning, but not informed of his right to consular assistance. He sought to suppress his statements because of noncompliance with Article 36. Another foreign national raised similar claims as well. After noting that Article 36 does not provide for the remedy of suppression, the Court held that U.S. law does not require suppression: "It is beyond dispute that we do not hold a supervisory power over the courts of the several States. Where a treaty does not provide a particular remedy, either expressly or implicitly, it is not for the federal courts to impose one on the States through lawmaking of their own. Even if Sanchez-Llamas is correct that Article 36 implicitly requires a judicial remedy, the Convention equally states that Article 36 rights 'shall be exercised in conformity with the laws and regulations of the receiving State.' Art. 36(2), 21 U.S.T., at 101. Under our domestic law, the exclusionary rule is not a remedy we apply lightly. The violation of the right to consular notification, in contrast, is at best remotely connected to the gathering of evidence." Justice Breyer, joined by Justices Stevens and Souter, dissented: "*Sometimes* suppression could prove the only effective remedy. And, if that is so, then the Convention, which insists upon effective remedies, would require suppression in an appropriate case."

Hypo 1: *More on the Rule's Application to Civil Proceedings*

Does *Janis* suggest that the exclusionary rule should never be applied in administrative proceedings? Suppose that the *Janis* search had been conducted by IRS investigators rather than by the police. Would the Court's "cost-benefit" analysis require exclusion of the evidence when the IRS sought to use it? Suppose that IRS investigators enter Grace Harlow's home in hopes of finding evidence of illegal gambling. The investigators are acting without a warrant even though one is required. When Harlow confronts the investigators, they beat and restrain her. Ultimately, the investigators uncover evidence of illegal gambling and seek to use that evidence against Harlow in a civil tax proceeding. If you are hired to represent Harlow, how can you distinguish *Janis* and *Lopez-Mendoza* and argue that the exclusionary rule should be applied to Harlow's case? How might the IRS respond to those arguments? In light of *Lopez-Mendoza*, is the Court likely to apply the exclusionary rule in administrative proceedings? When will the "benefits" of the exclusionary rule outweigh the "costs" in a manner that justifies application of the exclusionary rule in an administrative proceeding?

Hypo 2: *The Exclusionary Rule and Cooperative Investigations*

Commonly, the police and the IRS work together on criminal investigations. Suppose that Janis can produce proof that the police and the IRS were working together in investigating him? Under such circumstances, should the Court apply the exclusionary rule? Would it matter whether the IRS was actually involved, or helped plan, the illegal search?

Hypo 3: *Evaluating Calandra*

Do you agree with *Calandra's* conclusion that a prosecutor would have no incentive to seek an indictment based on evidence that could not be admitted at trial? Suppose that the prosecutor believes that defendant is part of a conspiracy to commit bank robberies, and uses the illegal evidence to indict one of the conspirators. What advantage might the prosecutor gain from the simple fact of the indictment?

D. The Scope of the Exclusionary Rules

The exclusionary rule is subject to various rules and doctrines that expand or contract the scope of the rule.

1. Standing

Standing concepts limit the exclusionary rule's application. In the Fifth Amendment area, the Court treats the privilege against self-incrimination as "personal" and has held that it can only be asserted by the person whose rights have been violated. This limitation is seemingly implicit in the Fifth Amendment itself which states that "no person shall be compelled in any criminal case to be a witness against himself." U.S. Constitution, Amendment V. As the Court stated in *Hale v. Henkel*, 201 U.S. 43 (1906): "The right of a person under the 5th Amendment to refuse to incriminate himself is purely a personal privilege of the witness. It was never intended to permit him to plead the fact that some third person might be incriminated by his testimony, even though he were the agent of such person. A privilege so extensive might be used to put a stop to the examination of every witness who was called upon to testify before the grand jury with regard to the doings or business of his principal, whether such principal were an individual or a corporation."

Even though the Fourth Amendment is not phrased in such personal terms, the Court has also applied the standing requirement to Fourth Amendment violations. In *Alderman v. United States*, 394 U.S. 165 (1969), the Court stated: "Fourth Amendment rights are personal rights which, like some other constitutional rights, may not be vicariously asserted. If the police make an unwarranted search of a house and seize tangible property belonging to third parties, the homeowner may object to its use against him, not because he had any interest in the seized items as 'effects' protected by the Fourth Amendment, but because they were the fruits of an unauthorized search of his house, which is itself expressly protected by the Fourth Amendment."

At one point, the standing requirement was modified by an "automatic standing" rule articulated in *Jones v. United States*, 362 U.S. 257 (1960). Jones, who was prosecuted for the possession of narcotics, moved to suppress evidence obtained via a search warrant on the basis that the warrant had been issued without probable cause. The judge denied the motion for lack of standing, and the Court reversed: "Since narcotics charges may be established through proof solely of possession of narcotics, a defendant seeking to comply with the conventional standing requirement has been forced to allege facts the proof of which would tend, if indeed not be sufficient, to convict him. He has been faced, not only with the chance that the allegations made on the motion to suppress may be used against him at the trial, but also with the encouragement that he perjure himself if he seeks to establish 'standing' while maintaining a defense to the charge of possession. The possession on the basis of which petitioner is to be and was convicted suffices to give him standing under any fair and rational conception of the requirements of Rule 41(e)."

Rakas v. Illinois

439 U.S. 128 (1978).

MR. JUSTICE REHNQUIST delivered the opinion of the Court.

A police officer on a routine patrol received a radio call notifying him of a robbery of a clothing store and describing the getaway car. Shortly thereafter, the officer spotted an automobile which he thought might be the getaway car. After following the car for some time, he and several other officers stopped the vehicle. The occupants of the automobile, petitioners and two female companions, were ordered out of the car and two officers searched the interior of the vehicle. They discovered a box of rifle shells in the glove compartment, which had been locked, and a sawed-off rifle under the front passenger seat. After discovering the rifle and the shells, the officers placed petitioners under arrest.

Petitioners moved to suppress the rifle and shells on the ground that the search violated the Fourth and Fourteenth Amendments. They conceded that they did not own the automobile and were simply passengers; the owner of the car had been the driver of the vehicle at the time of the search. Nor did they assert that they owned the rifle or the shells seized. The prosecutor challenged petitioners' standing to object to the lawfulness of the search of the car. The trial court held that petitioners lacked standing and denied the motion to suppress the evidence. Petitioners were convicted and the conviction was affirmed.

Petitioners urge us to relax or broaden the rule of standing enunciated in *Jones v. United States*, 362 U.S. 257 (1960), so that any criminal defendant at whom a search was "directed" would have standing to contest the legality of that search and object to the admission of evidence obtained as a result of the search. Alternatively, petitioners argue that they have standing to object to the search under *Jones* because they were "legitimately on the premises" at the time of the search.

Jones focuses on whether the person seeking to challenge the legality of a search was himself the "victim" of the search or seizure. Adoption of the so-called "target" theory advanced by petitioners would in effect permit a defendant to assert that a violation of the Fourth Amendment rights of a third party entitled him to have evidence suppressed at his trial. We decline to extend the rule of standing. As we stated in *Alderman v. United States*, 394 U.S. 165, 174 (1969), "Fourth Amendment rights are personal rights which, like some other constitutional rights, may not be vicariously asserted." A person who is aggrieved by an illegal search and seizure only through the introduction of damaging evidence secured by a search of a third person's premises or property has not had any of his Fourth Amendment rights infringed. Since the exclusionary rule is an attempt to effectuate the guarantees of the Fourth Amendment, it is proper to permit only defendants whose Fourth Amendment rights have been violated to benefit from the rule's protections. There is no reason to think that a party whose rights have been infringed will not, if evidence is used against him, have ample motivation to move to suppress it. Even if such a person is not a defendant in the action, he may be able to recover damages for the violation of his Fourth Amendment rights, or seek redress under state law for invasion of privacy or trespass.

In support of their target theory, petitioners rely on the following quotation from *Jones*: "In order to qualify as a 'person aggrieved by an unlawful search and seizure' one must have been a victim of a search or seizure, one against whom the search was directed, as distinguished from one who claims prejudice only through the use of evidence gathered as a consequence of a search or seizure directed at someone else." This statement suggests that the language was meant merely as a parenthetical equivalent of the previous phrase "a victim of a search or seizure." To the extent that the language might be read more broadly, it is dictum which was impliedly repudiated in *Alderman* and which we now expressly reject. In *Alderman*, Mr. Justice Fortas argued that the Court should "include within the category of those who may object to the introduction of illegal evidence 'one against whom the search was directed.' " The Court rejected this theory holding that persons who were not parties to unlawfully overheard conversations or who did not own the premises on which such conversations took place did not have standing to contest the legality of the surveillance, regardless of whether or not they were the "targets" of the surveillance. Mr. Justice Harlan identified administrative problems posed by the target theory: "The target rule would entail very substantial administrative difficulties. In the majority of cases, the police plant a bug with the expectation that it may well produce leads to a large number of crimes. A lengthy hearing would then be necessary in order to determine whether the police knew of an accused's criminal activity at the time the bug was planted and whether the police decision to plant a bug was motivated by an effort to obtain information against the accused or some other individual. I do not believe that this administrative burden is justified in any substantial degree by the hypothesized marginal increase in Fourth Amendment protection." We cannot but give weight to practical difficulties such as those foreseen by Mr. Justice Harlan in the quoted language.

Conferring standing to raise vicarious Fourth Amendment claims would necessarily mean a more widespread invocation of the exclusionary rule during criminal trials. *Alderman* counseled against such an extension of the exclusionary rule: "We are not convinced that the additional benefits of extending the exclusionary rule to other defendants would justify further encroachment upon the public interest in prosecuting those accused of crime and having them acquitted or convicted on the basis of all the evidence which exposes the truth." Each time the exclusionary rule is applied it exacts a substantial social cost for the vindication of Fourth Amendment rights. Relevant and reliable evidence is kept from the trier of fact and the search for truth at trial is deflected. Since our cases generally have held that one whose Fourth Amendment rights are violated may successfully suppress evidence obtained in the course of an illegal search and seizure, misgivings as to the benefit of enlarging the class of persons who may invoke that rule are properly considered when deciding whether to expand standing to assert Fourth Amendment violations.

We can think of no decided cases that would have come out differently had we concluded, as we do now, that the type of standing requirement discussed in *Jones* and reaffirmed today is more properly subsumed under substantive Fourth Amendment doctrine. We think the better analysis forthrightly focuses on the extent of a particular defendant's rights under the Fourth Amendment, rather than on any theoretically separate, but invariably intertwined concept of standing.

The issue of standing involves two inquiries: first, whether the proponent of a particular legal right has alleged "injury in fact," and, second, whether the proponent is asserting his own legal rights and interests rather than basing his claim for relief upon the rights of third parties. The question is whether the challenged search or seizure violated the Fourth Amendment rights of a criminal defendant who seeks to exclude the evidence obtained during it. That inquiry in turn requires a determination of whether the disputed search and seizure has infringed an interest of the defendant which the Fourth Amendment was designed to protect. We are under no illusion that by dispensing with the rubric of standing used in *Jones* we have rendered any simpler the determination of whether the proponent of a motion to suppress is entitled to contest the legality of a search and seizure. But we think the decision of this issue will rest on sounder logical footing.

Petitioners, who were passengers occupying a car which they neither owned nor leased, seek to analogize their position to that of the defendant in *Jones*. In *Jones*, petitioner was present at the time of the search of an apartment which was owned by a friend. The friend had given Jones permission to use the apartment and a key to it, with which Jones had admitted himself on the day of the search. He had a suit and shirt at the apartment and had slept there "maybe a night," but his home was elsewhere. At the time of the search, Jones was the only occupant of the apartment because the lessee was away for a period of several days. Under these circumstances, this Court stated that while one wrongfully on the premises could not move to suppress evidence obtained as a result of searching them, "anyone legitimately on premises where a search occurs may challenge its legality." Petitioners argue that their occupancy of the automobile was comparable to that of Jones in the apartment and that they therefore have standing to contest the legality of the search—or as we rephrased the inquiry, that they, like Jones, had their Fourth Amendment rights violated by the search.

We do not question the conclusion in *Jones*. Nonetheless, we believe that the phrase "legitimately on premises" coined in *Jones* creates too broad a gauge for measurement of Fourth Amendment rights. Applied literally, this statement would permit a casual visitor who has never seen, or been permitted to visit, the basement of another's house to object to a search of the basement if the visitor happened to be in the kitchen of the house at the time of the search. Likewise, a casual visitor who walks into a house one minute before a search of the house commences and leaves one minute after the search ends would be able to contest the legality of the search. The first visitor would have absolutely no interest or legitimate expectation of privacy in the basement, the second would have none in the house, and it advances no purpose served by the Fourth Amendment to permit either of them to object to the lawfulness of the search.

We think that *Jones* stands for the unremarkable proposition that a person can have a legally sufficient interest in a place other than his own home so that the Fourth Amendment protects him from unreasonable governmental intrusion into that place. In defining the scope of that interest, arcane distinctions developed in property and tort law between guests, licensees, invitees, and the like, ought not to control. But the *Jones* statement that a person need only be "legitimately on premises" in order to challenge the validity of the search of a dwelling place cannot be taken in its full sweep beyond the facts of that case.

Katz held that capacity to claim the protection of the Fourth Amendment depends not upon a property right in the invaded place but upon whether the person who claims the protection of the Amendment has a legitimate expectation of privacy in the invaded place. *Jones* can best be explained by the fact that Jones had a legitimate expectation of privacy in the premises he was using and therefore could claim the protection of the Fourth Amendment with respect to a governmental invasion of those premises, even though his "interest" in those premises might not have been a recognized property interest at common law.[12]

In abandoning "legitimately on premises" for the doctrine that we announce today, we are rejecting blind adherence to a phrase which at most has superficial clarity and which conceals underneath that thin veneer all of the problems of line drawing which must be faced in any conscientious effort to apply the Fourth Amendment. We would not wish to be understood as saying that legitimate presence on the premises is irrelevant to one's expectation of privacy, but it cannot be deemed controlling.

Judged by this analysis, petitioners' claims must fail. They asserted neither a property nor a possessory interest in the automobile, nor an interest in the property seized. The fact that they were "legitimately on the premises" in the sense that they were in the car with the permission of its owner is not determinative of whether they had a legitimate expectation of privacy in the particular areas of the automobile searched. It is unnecessary to decide whether the same expectations of privacy are warranted in a car as in a dwelling place in analogous circumstances. Petitioners' claim is one which would fail even in an analogous situation in a dwelling place, since they made no showing that they had any legitimate expectation of privacy in the glove compartment or area under the seat of the car in which they were merely passengers. Like the trunk of an automobile, these are areas in which a passenger qua passenger would not normally have a legitimate expectation of privacy.

Jones and *Katz* involved significantly different factual circumstances. Jones not only had permission to use the apartment of his friend, but also had a key to the apartment with which he admitted himself on the day of the search and kept possessions in the apartment. Except with respect to his friend, Jones had complete dominion and control over the apartment and could exclude others

---

[12] A "legitimate" expectation of privacy by definition means more than a subjective expectation of not being discovered. A burglar plying his trade in a summer cabin may have a subjective expectation of privacy, but it is not one which the law recognizes as "legitimate." Legitimate expectations must have a source outside of the Fourth Amendment, either by reference to concepts of real or personal property law or to understandings that are recognized and permitted by society. Expectations of privacy need not be based on a common-law interest in real or personal property, or on the invasion of such an interest. But the Court has not altogether abandoned use of property concepts in determining the presence or absence of the privacy interests protected by that Amendment. In *Alderman*, the Court held that an individual's property interest in his own home was so great as to allow him to object to electronic surveillance of conversations emanating from his home, even though he himself was not a party to the conversations. On the other hand, even a property interest in premises may not be sufficient to establish a legitimate expectation of privacy with respect to particular items located on the premises or activity conducted thereon.

from it. Likewise in *Katz*, the defendant occupied the telephone booth, shut the door behind him to exclude all others and paid the toll, which "entitled him to assume that the words he uttered into the mouthpiece would not be broadcast to the world." Katz and Jones could legitimately expect privacy in the areas which were the subject of the search and seizure each sought to contest. No such showing was made by petitioners with respect to those portions of the automobile which were searched.[17]

The Illinois courts were correct in concluding that it was unnecessary to decide whether the search of the car might have violated the rights secured to someone else by the Fourth and Fourteenth Amendments to the United States Constitution. Since it did not violate any rights of these petitioners, their judgment of conviction is

Affirmed.

MR. JUSTICE POWELL, with whom THE CHIEF JUSTICE joins, concurring.

None of the passengers had control of the vehicle or the keys. It is unrealistic to suggest that these passengers had any reasonable expectation that the car in which they had been riding would not be searched after they were lawfully stopped and made to get out. The minimal privacy that existed simply is not comparable to that, for example, of an individual in his place of abode.

MR. JUSTICE WHITE, with whom MR. JUSTICE BRENNAN, MR. JUSTICE MARSHALL, and MR. JUSTICE STEVENS join, dissenting.

When a person is legitimately present in a private place, his right to privacy is protected from unreasonable governmental interference even if he does not own the premises. An expectation of privacy does not hinge on ownership. Surely a person riding in an automobile next to his friend the owner, or a child or wife with the father or spouse, must have some protection. If a nonowner may consent to a search merely because he is a joint user or occupant of a "premises," then that same nonowner must have a protected privacy interest.

The Court asserts that it is not limiting the bar against unreasonable searches to the protection of property rights, but in reality it is doing exactly that.[18] Petitioners

---

[17] Our dissenting Brethren criticize our "holding" that unless one has a common-law property interest in the premises searched, one cannot object to the search. To the contrary, we have taken pains to reaffirm the statements in *Jones* and *Katz* that "arcane distinctions developed in property law ought not to control."

[18] The Court's reliance on property law concepts is shown by its suggestion that visitors could "contest the lawfulness of the seizure of evidence or the search if their own property were seized during the search." What difference should that property interest make to constitutional protection against unreasonable searches, which is concerned with privacy? A passenger in a car expects to enjoy the privacy of the vehicle whether or not he happens to carry some item along for the ride. Even a person living in a barren room without possessions is entitled to expect that the police will not intrude without cause.

were in a private place with the permission of the owner. If that is not sufficient, what would be? It is hard to imagine anything short of a property interest that would satisfy the majority. Insofar as the Court's rationale is concerned, no passenger in an automobile, without an ownership or possessory interest and regardless of his relationship to the owner, may claim Fourth Amendment protection against illegal stops and searches of the automobile in which he is rightfully present. The Court approves the result in *Jones*, but it fails to give any explanation why the facts in *Jones* differ, in a fashion material to the Fourth Amendment, from the facts here.[15] More importantly, how is the Court able to avoid answering the question why presence in a private place with the owner's permission is insufficient?

As a control on governmental power, the Fourth Amendment assures that some expectations of privacy are justified and will be protected from official intrusion. If protected zones of privacy can only be purchased or obtained by possession of property, then much of our daily lives will be unshielded from unreasonable governmental prying, and the reach of the Fourth Amendment will have been narrowed to protect chiefly those with possessory interests in real or personal property. *Katz* firmly established that the Fourth Amendment was intended as more than simply a trespass law applicable to the government. Katz had no possessory interest in the public telephone booth, at least no more than petitioners had in their friend's car; Katz was simply legitimately present. And the decision in *Katz* was based not on property rights, but on the theory that it was essential to securing "conditions favorable to the pursuit of happiness" that the expectation of privacy in question be recognized. One could say that perhaps the Constitution provides some degree less protection for the personal freedom from unreasonable governmental intrusion when one does not have a possessory interest in the invaded private place. But that would only change the extent of the protection; it would not free police to do the unreasonable.

The Court's holding is contrary to the everyday expectations of privacy that we all share. If the owner of the car had not only invited petitioners to join her but had said to them, "I give you a temporary possessory interest in my vehicle so that you will share the right to privacy that I own," then apparently the majority would reverse. But people seldom say such things, though they may mean their invitation to encompass them if only they had thought of the problem. If the nonowner were the spouse or child of the owner, would the Court recognize a sufficient interest? If so, would distant relatives somehow have more of an expectation of privacy than close friends? What if the nonowner were driving with the

---

[15] Jones had permission to use the apartment, had slept in it one night, had a key, had left a suit and a shirt there, and was the only occupant at the time of the search. Petitioners here had permission to be in the car and were occupying it at the time of the search. Thus the only distinguishing fact is that Jones could exclude others from the apartment by using his friend's key. But petitioners and their friend the owner had excluded others by entering the automobile and shutting the doors.

owner's permission? *Katz* expressly recognized protection for such passengers. Why should Fourth Amendment rights be present when one pays a cabdriver for a ride but be absent when one is given a ride by a friend?

This decision invites police to engage in patently unreasonable searches every time an automobile contains more than one occupant. Should something be found, only the owner of the vehicle, or of the item, will have standing to seek suppression, and the evidence will presumably be usable against the other occupants. The danger of such bad faith is especially high in cases where the officers are only after the passengers.

Take Note

The concept of "automatic standing," first articulated in *Jones*, did not survive long after the *Rakas* decision. The Court laid the groundwork for the rule's demise in *Simmons v. United States*, 390 U.S. 377 (1968), a case in which petitioner was arrested for armed robbery based on an illegal search of a house. Petitioner testified that he thought he was the owner of the seized items. Using a self-incrimination analysis, the Court held that petitioner's testimony could not be used against him: "when a defendant testifies in support of a motion to suppress evidence on Fourth Amendment grounds, his testimony may not be admitted against him at trial on the issue of guilt unless he makes no objection." *But see United States v. Kahan*, 415 U.S. 239 (1974) (Court refused to apply *Simmons* to a prosecution for perjury: "*Simmons* barred the use of pretrial testimony at trial to prove its incriminating content. Here, by contrast, the incriminating component of respondent's pretrial statements derives not from their content, but from respondent's knowledge of their falsity."). The Court followed with its decision in *United States v. Salvucci*, 448 U.S. 83 (1980): "Defendants charged with crimes of possession may only claim the benefits of the exclusionary rule if their own Fourth Amendment rights have been violated. The automatic standing rule of *Jones* is therefore overruled. The 'dilemma' identified in *Jones*, that a defendant charged with a possessory offense might only be able to establish his standing to challenge a search and seizure by giving self-incriminating testimony admissible as evidence of his guilt, was eliminated by our decision in *Simmons*. *Simmons* grants a form of 'use immunity' to those defendants charged with nonpossessory crimes. We decline to use possession of a seized good as a substitute for a factual finding that the owner of the good had a legitimate expectation of privacy in the area searched." Justice Marshall dissented: "*Simmons* does not provide complete protection against the 'self-incrimination dilemma.' The use of the testimony for impeachment purposes would subject a defendant to precisely the same dilemma, unless he was prepared to relinquish his constitutional right to testify in his own defense, and would thereby create a strong deterrent to asserting Fourth Amendment claims. One of the purposes of *Jones* and *Simmons* was to remove such obstacles. Moreover, the opportunity for cross-examination at the suppression hearing may enable the prosecutor to elicit incriminating information beyond that offered on direct examination to establish the requisite Fourth Amendment interest. Even if such information could not be introduced at the subsequent trial, it might be helpful to the prosecution in developing its case or deciding its trial strategy. The furnishing of such a tactical advantage to the prosecution should not be the price of asserting a Fourth Amendment claim." The automatic standing rule is still applied by some state courts under their state constitutions. *See Commonwealth v. Enimpah*, 106 A.3d 695 (Penn. 2014).

Food for Thought

Does *Rakas* use any standard other than property principles to define the expectation of privacy test? If so, what are those principles? Does *Rakas* apply the "expectation of privacy" test in the same manner as *Katz*? If not, how do you explain the difference in application?

Hypo 1: *Denying Ownership*

The police wish to search a vehicle that is on a car transport carrier. They inquire of a man, standing near the vehicle, whether they may conduct the search. The man adamantly denies that he owns the vehicle. After the police conduct the search, and find contraband, and eventually link the man to the vehicle, he wants to challenge the search as a violation of the Fourth Amendment. Can the man establish standing to challenge the search after he originally denied ownership of the vehicle? *See United States v. Castellanos,* 716 F.3rd 828 (4th Cir. 2013). Likewise, does a passenger in an automobile have standing to challenge a search of his luggage that was left in the trunk of another person's automobile? Does it matter whether the luggage has tags identifying the owner? Does it matter whether, at the time of the search, the owner claimed ownership of the bag, and demanded that the police not search the bag? *See United States v. Iraheta*, 764 F.3d 455 (5th Cir. 2014).

Food for Thought

Consider Justice Fortas' opinion, concurring in part and dissenting in part, in *Alderman*: "In recognition of the principle that lawlessness on the part of the Government must be stoutly condemned, this Court has ruled that the Government may not profit from its fruits. For reasons which are related more to convenience and judicial prudence than to constitutional principles, courts of all states except California and of the federal system have allowed in evidence material obtained by police agents in direct and acknowledged violation of the Fourth Amendment. They have allowed this evidence except where a defendant who moves for suppression of the material can show that his personal right of privacy was violated by the unlawful search or seizure. If the exclusionary rule follows from the Fourth Amendment itself, there is no basis for confining its invocation to persons whose right of privacy has been violated by an illegal search. The Fourth Amendment is couched in terms of a guarantee that the Government will not engage in unreasonable searches and seizures. It is a general prohibition, a fundamental part of the constitutional compact, the observance of which is essential to the welfare of all persons. Accordingly, the necessary implication is that any defendant against whom illegally acquired evidence is offered, whether or not it was obtained in violation of his right to privacy, may have the evidence excluded. The Fourth Amendment is an assurance to all that the Government will exercise its formidable powers to arrest and to investigate only subject to the rule of law." Do you agree with Justice Fortas?

Hypo 2: *Rakas and Familial Relations*

In *Rakas*, Justice White asks whether the Court would have reached the opposite result (in other words, it would have found that "standing" existed), had the passengers been related to the driver. Suppose that you have been hired to represent the driver's teenage son. Following a search of the car, the police find illegal drugs (rather than a shotgun) under the seat. Would the son have standing to challenge the search if he had been a passenger in his father's car? In light of the *Rakas* decision, how would you argue the case on his behalf?

Hypo 3: *More on Passenger Standing*

In *Rakas*, the police also find shotgun shells in the glove compartment. Would a passenger have standing to challenge the search if the glove compartment was locked, and the passenger had possession of the key? Would it matter whether the owner/driver also had a key? If you are the prosecutor, how would you argue that the passenger does not have standing under these circumstances? How would you expect the defense to respond? Would your decision be affected by the fact that the passenger (who was not the owner of the car) was driving the car, and the owner was in the passenger seat? *See United States v. Almeida,* 748 F.3d 41 (1st Cir. 2014).

Hypo 4: *Challenging the Stop*

Would the result in *Rakas* have been different if, instead of challenging the search, the passengers had claimed that the police illegally stopped the car in which they were riding? How might Rakas have argued that he has standing to challenge the illegal stop? Would his standing to challenge the stop also give him standing to challenge the subsequent search?

Hypo 5: *Jones and Passenger Standing*

Now, recall the holding in *United States v. Jones* (discussed in chapter 4) which held that the police commit a trespass when they attach a GPS device to a vehicle in order to track it. Under *Jones*, we know that the owner of the vehicle has standing to challenge the attachment of the GPS system. What about a passenger in the vehicle? *See United States v. Davis, 750 F.3d 1186 (10th Cir. 2014).* Would a driver, who did not own the vehicle, but simply borrowed it, have standing to challenge the GPS? *See United States v. Gibson, 708 F.3d 1256 (11th Cir. 2013).*

Hypo 6: *Standing to Challenge Corporate Office Searches*

IRS agents obtain warrants authorizing a search of a corporation's headquarters and principal business offices for evidence of health care fraud and tax evasion. The search leads to an indictment, alleging a conspiracy with physicians, cardiac diagnostic providers, and others to bill for work that they did not actually perform. Subsequently, the corporation and its officers challenge the warrant on the basis that it fails the particularity requirement. Does the corporation have standing to challenge the warrant? Do corporate officers or part owners of the corporation also have standing to challenge the warrant? *See United States v. SDI Future Health, Inc., 553 F.3d 1246 (9th Cir. 2009).*

Hypo 7: *Standing in an Internet Age*

The police believe that defendant is transmitting child pornography via the internet. In an effort to catch defendant, the police obtain a warrant to search Google's computer records regarding defendant's internet search requests. When the Google search uncovers information that incriminates defendant, defendant moves to suppress on the basis that the Google search was a "fishing expedition" that was not justified based on probable cause. Does defendant have standing to challenge the Google search?

Hypo 8: *Fraudulent Access to Property*

Rigmaiden uses fake identities to rent an apartment, as well as to purchase a computer and aircard that he uses to perpetrate tax fraud. When the police track the aircard, the IP address for the computer, and search the apartment, Rigmaiden claims that the police violated his REOP. Can Rigmaiden have a REOP in property obtained through fake identities? *See United States v. Rigmaiden, 2013 WL 1932800 (Ariz.).*

Hypo 9: More on Standing

Suppose that a woman consents to a body cavity search that reveals the existence of illegal drugs. A reviewing court concludes that the consent was coerced for a variety of reasons: the police held the woman under difficult conditions for several hours; the police implied that they had obtained a warrant for the search when they had not; and the woman appeared groggy when she gave the consent. Suppose that, after the appellate court concludes that the evidence cannot be used against the woman, the prosecution tries to use it to prosecute her husband. Can the evidence be introduced against the husband? More to the point, can he object to the coercive tactics used against his wife, and use those tactics to obtain exclusion of the evidence against himself? Would it matter that the police conduct is regarded as so "egregious" as to violate substantive due process? *See United States v. Anderson*, 772 F.3d 969 (2d Cir. 2014).

Minnesota v. Olson

495 U.S. 91 (1990).

JUSTICE WHITE delivered the opinion of the Court.

On July 18, 1987, a lone gunman robbed an Amoco gasoline station in Minneapolis, Minnesota, and fatally shot the station manager. A police officer heard the police dispatcher report and suspected Joseph Ecker. The officer and his partner drove immediately to Ecker's home, arriving at about the same time that an Oldsmobile arrived. The driver of the Oldsmobile took evasive action, and the car spun out of control and came to a stop. Two men fled the car on foot. Ecker, who was later identified as the gunman, was captured shortly thereafter inside his home. The second man escaped. Inside the abandoned Oldsmobile, police found a sack of money and the murder weapon. They also found a title certificate with the name Rob Olson crossed out as a secured party, a letter addressed to a Roger R. Olson of 3151 Johnson Street, and a videotape rental receipt made out to Rob Olson and dated two days earlier. The police verified that a Robert Olson lived at 3151 Johnson Street.

The next morning, a woman identifying herself as Dianna Murphy called the police and said that a man by the name of Rob drove the car in which the gas station killer left the scene and that Rob was planning to leave town by bus. About noon, the same woman called again, gave her address and phone number, and said that a man named Rob had told a Maria and two other women, Louanne and Julie, that he was the driver in the Amoco robbery. The caller stated that Louanne was Julie's mother and that the two women lived at 2406 Fillmore Northeast. Police officers were sent to 2406 Fillmore to check out Louanne and Julie. When police arrived they determined that the dwelling was a duplex and that Louanne Bergstrom and her daughter Julie lived in the upper unit but were not home. Police spoke to Louanne's mother, Helen Niederhoffer, who lived in the lower unit. She confirmed that a Rob Olson had been staying upstairs but was not then in the unit. She promised to call the police when Olson returned. At 2 p.m., a "probable cause arrest bulletin," was issued for Olson's arrest. The police were instructed to stay away from the duplex.

At approximately 2:45 p.m., Niederhoffer called police and said Olson had returned. The detective-in-charge instructed police officers to go to the house and surround it. He then telephoned Julie from headquarters and told her Rob should come out of the house. The detective heard a male voice say, "tell them I left." Julie stated that Rob had left, whereupon at 3 p.m. the detective ordered the police to enter the house. Without seeking permission and with weapons drawn, the police entered the upper unit and found respondent hiding in a closet. Less than an hour after his arrest, respondent made an inculpatory statement at police headquarters.

The trial court denied respondent's motion to suppress his statement which was admitted into evidence and Olson was convicted of first-degree murder, three counts of armed robbery, and three counts of second-degree assault. The Minnesota Supreme Court reversed, holding that respondent had a sufficient interest in the Bergstrom home to challenge the legality of his warrantless arrest there, that the arrest was illegal because there were no exigent circumstances to justify a warrantless entry, and that respondent's statement was tainted by that illegality and should have been suppressed. We granted the State's petition for certiorari and now affirm.

It was held in *Payton v. New York*, 445 U.S. 573 (1980), that a suspect should not be arrested in his house without an arrest warrant, even though there is probable cause to arrest him. The purpose of the decision was not to protect the person of the suspect but to protect his home from entry in the absence of a magistrate's finding of probable cause. The State argues that Olson's relationship to the premises does not satisfy the 12 factors which in its view determine whether a dwelling is a "home." We need go no further than to conclude that Olson's status as an overnight guest is alone enough to show that he had an expectation of privacy in the home that society is prepared to recognize as reasonable.

The facts of this case are similar to those in *Jones v. United States*, 362 U.S. 257 (1960). In *Jones*, the defendant was arrested in a friend's apartment during the execution of a search warrant and sought to challenge the warrant as not supported by probable cause. "Jones testified that the apartment belonged to a friend, Evans, who had given him the use of it, and a key, with which Jones had admitted himself on the day of the arrest. Jones testified that he had a suit and shirt at the apartment, that his home was elsewhere, that he paid nothing for the use of the apartment, that Evans had let him use it 'as a friend,' that he had slept there 'maybe a night,' and that at the time of the search Evans had been away in Philadelphia for about five days."[6]

The Court ruled that Jones could challenge the search of the apartment because he was "legitimately on the premises." Although the "legitimately on the premises" standard was rejected in *Rakas* as too broad, *Rakas* explicitly reaffirmed the factual holding in *Jones*. *Rakas* thus recognized that, as an overnight guest, Jones was much more than just legitimately on the premises.

The State emphasizes that in this case Olson was never left alone in the duplex or given a key, whereas in Jones the owner of the apartment was away and Jones had a key with which he could come and go and admit and exclude others. We do not understand *Rakas* to hold that an overnight guest can never have a legitimate expectation of privacy except when his host is away and he has a key. To hold that an overnight guest has a legitimate expectation of privacy in his host's home merely recognizes the everyday expectations of privacy that we all share. Staying overnight in another's home is a longstanding social custom that serves functions recognized as valuable by society. Society recognizes that a houseguest has a legitimate expectation of privacy in his host's home.

From the overnight guest's perspective, he seeks shelter in another's home precisely because it provides him with privacy, a place where he and his possessions will not be disturbed by anyone but his host and those his host allows inside. We are at our most vulnerable when we are asleep because we cannot monitor our own safety or the security of our belongings. It is for this reason that, although we may spend all day in public places, when we cannot sleep in our own home we seek out another private place to sleep, whether it be a hotel room, or the home of a friend. Society expects at least as much privacy in these places as in a telephone booth—"a temporarily private place whose momentary occupants' expectations of freedom from intrusion are recognized as reasonable," *Katz*, 389 U.S., at 361 (Harlan, J., concurring).

That the guest has a host who has ultimate control of the house is not inconsistent with the guest having a legitimate expectation of privacy. The houseguest is there with the permission of his host, who is willing to share his house and his privacy with his guest. It is unlikely that the guest will be confined to a restricted area of the house; and when the host is away or asleep, the guest will have a measure of control over the premises. The host may admit or exclude from the

---

[6] Olson, who had been staying at Ecker's home for several days before the robbery, spent the night of the robbery on the floor of the Bergstroms' home, with their permission. He had a change of clothes with him at the duplex.

house as he prefers, but it is unlikely that he will admit someone who wants to see or meet with the guest over the objection of the guest. On the other hand, few houseguests will invite others to visit them while they are guests without consulting their hosts; but the latter, who have the authority to exclude despite the wishes of the guest, will often be accommodating. The point is that hosts will more likely than not respect the privacy interests of their guests, who are entitled to a legitimate expectation of privacy despite the fact that they have no legal interest in the premises and do not have the legal authority to determine who may or may not enter the household. If the untrammeled power to admit and exclude were essential to Fourth Amendment protection, an adult daughter temporarily living in the home of her parents would have no legitimate expectation of privacy because her right to admit or exclude would be subject to her parents' veto.

Because respondent's expectation of privacy in the Bergstrom home was rooted in "understandings that are recognized and permitted by society," it was legitimate, and respondent can claim the protection of the Fourth Amendment. We therefore affirm the judgment of the Minnesota Supreme Court.

It is so ordered.

Take Note

In *Minnesota v. Carter*, 525 U.S. 83 (1998), a police officer peered through a gap in a closed window blind into a ground floor apartment, and observed respondent bagging cocaine. The Court held that respondent lacked standing to challenge the officer's action because he was a temporary out-of-state visitor to the apartment: "If we regard the overnight guest in *Olson* as typifying those who may claim the protection of the Fourth Amendment in the home of another, and one merely 'legitimately on the premises' as typifying those who may not do so, the present case is obviously somewhere in between. The purely commercial nature of the transaction engaged in here, the relatively short period of time on the premises, and the lack of any previous connection between respondents and the householder, all lead us to conclude that respondents' situation is closer to that of one simply permitted on the premises. Any search which may have occurred did not violate their Fourth Amendment rights."

Points for Discussion

a. Controlled Substances in Another's Purse

In *Rawlings v. Kentucky*, 448 U.S. 98 (1980), petitioner was convicted of trafficking and possession of controlled substances based on evidence seized during the search of a purse. Petitioner, who was staying at a friend's home, carried drugs in a green bank bag. He asked a woman friend whether she would carry it for him and she said "yes." Shortly after she agreed to do so, the police arrived. In response to a police request, Cox poured the contents of her purse onto a coffee table, and told petitioner "to take what was his." Petitioner immediately claimed ownership of the controlled substances. The trial court admitted the drugs against him. The Court held that petitioner lacked standing to challenge the search: "At the time petitioner dumped thousands of dollars worth of illegal drugs into Cox's purse, he had known her for only a few days and had never sought or received access to her purse. Nor did petitioner have any right to exclude other persons from access to Cox's purse. Even assuming that petitioner's version of the bailment is correct and that Cox did consent to the transfer of possession, the precipitous nature of the transaction hardly supports a reasonable inference that petitioner took normal precautions to maintain his privacy. The record contains a frank admission by petitioner that he had no subjective expectation that Cox's purse would remain free from governmental intrusion. While petitioner's ownership of the drugs is undoubtedly one fact to be considered, *Rakas* emphatically rejected the notion that 'arcane' concepts of property law ought to control the ability to claim the protections of the Fourth Amendment. Petitioner had no legitimate expectation of privacy in Cox's purse." Justice Marshall dissented: "When the government seizes a person's property, it interferes with his constitutionally protected right to be secure in his effects. That interference gives him the right to challenge the reasonableness of the government's conduct, including the seizure. If the defendant's property was seized as the result of an unreasonable search, the seizure cannot be other than unreasonable. *Jones* and *Katz* expanded our view of the protections afforded by the Fourth Amendment by recognizing that privacy interests are protected even if they do not arise from property rights. But that recognition was never intended to exclude interests that had historically been sheltered by the Fourth Amendment from its protection."

b. A Search of a Union Office

In *Mancusi v. DeForte*, 392 U.S. 364 (1968), DeForte was convicted of conspiracy, coercion and extortion based on evidence seized from a union office where DeForte and several other union officials worked. The search was conducted without a warrant and over DeForte's objections. The Court concluded that DeForte had standing to object to the search even though the papers belonged to the union: "One has standing to object to a search of his office, as well as of his home. If DeForte had occupied a 'private' office in the union headquarters, and union records had been seized from a desk or a filing cabinet in that office, he would have had standing. In such a 'private' office, DeForte would have been entitled to expect that he would not be disturbed except by personal or business invitees, and that records would not be taken except with his permission or that of his union superiors. The situation was not fundamentally changed because DeForte shared an office with other union officers. DeForte still could reasonably have expected that only those persons and their personal or business guests would enter the office, and that records would not be touched except with their permission or that of union higher-ups. This expectation was defeated by the entrance of state officials, their conduct of a general search, and their removal of records which were in DeForte's custody. It is irrelevant that the Union or some of its officials might validly have consented to a search of the area where the records were kept, regardless of DeForte's wishes, for it is not claimed that any such consent was given." Justice Black dissented: "A corporate or union official suffers no personal injury when the business office he occupies as an agent of the corporation or union is invaded and when records he has prepared and safeguarded as an agent are seized. The organization has every right to challenge such intrusions if the seizure is illegal, the records can be suppressed in a prosecution against the organization, and if no prosecution is initiated, the organization can obtain return of all the documents by bringing a civil action. Such intrusions, however, involve absolutely no invasion of the 'personal privacy' or security of the agent or employee as an individual, and he accordingly has no right to seek suppression of records that the corporation or union itself has made no effort to regain."

Hypo 1: *The Protective Order*

Suppose that, rather than simply being an overnight guest, Olson had previously been involved in an intimate relationship with the woman who owned the house. However, after Olson became violent, she obtained a protective order prohibiting him from coming within 500 feet of her. The police receive a report, indicating that the woman has allowed Olson (the bank robber) into the house. Does Olson still have a REOP inside the house? *See United States v. Cortez-Dutreiville*, 743 F.3d 881 (3rd Cir. 2014).

Hypo 2: *Motel Rooms*

Police receive a tip regarding "suspicious activity" at a nearby motel and they respond. One officer stands behind a motel room (outside a frosted over bathroom window) while the other two officers approach the front door. When the two officers knock on the door, the third officer sees the bathroom light go on and a figure bending over. The third officer bursts through the window, believing that evidence is being flushed down the toilet. When the officers at the door hear the commotion, they burst through the door and observe two brothers in the room with counterfeit money, women, drugs, and guns. At trial, one woman testified that one brother paid for the rooms and told the other brother to "rent them for the group's use." Did the other brothers have a reasonable expectation of privacy in the motel room? *See United States v. Domenech*, 623 F.3d 325 (6th Cir. 2010).

Hypo 3: *Standing and GPS Tracking Systems*

Drug Enforcement Agency agents are alerted to a drug trafficking operation in Des Moines, Iowa. Using magnetic strips, they place a Global Positioning Satellite (GPS) tracking device on the bumper of a Ford truck while it is parked in a Walmart parking lot in Des Moines. The tracking device allows police to follow the truck back and forth to Denver. Investigators access the device to change the battery seven times during the course of the investigation, each time while the vehicle is parked in a public place. The device can relay the location of the vehicle only while the vehicle is outdoors, and investigators in Iowa work with police in Denver to monitor the truck while it is in Denver. In addition, they install stationary "pole cameras" in two locations in Des Moines. During the investigation, investigators observe Acosta operating and riding in some of the trucks used in the drug ring. He is seen at a house on Broadway Avenue that appears to be the transfer point for drug deliveries from Denver. The GPS device tracks the Ford on trips to Denver, and Acosta is observed following the Ford in another truck. However, the evidence shows that Acosta neither owns nor drives the Ford, but that he is only an occasional passenger therein. Does Acosta have standing to contest the installation and use of the GPS device? *See United States v. Marquez*, 605 F.3d 604 (8th Cir. 2010).

Hypo 4: *Cell Phone Monitoring*

In the prior problem, in addition to installing a GPS device on the truck, enforcement officers also arrange with an undercover agent to allow them to overhear the content of cell phone conversations between the criminals. Does a participant in those conversations (who did not know about the confederate or the consent) have standing to challenge the monitoring of the conversations? What about one of the criminals who participated in the endeavor, but not in the conversations? *See United States v. Marquez*, 605 F.3d 604 (8th Cir. 2010).

Hypo 5: *Standing and the Unclaimed Duffle Bag*

Drug enforcement authorities receive a tip suggesting that defendant, who is traveling by bus, is carrying illegal drugs on his person. When the bus stops at a rest area, an officer enters the bus, informs the passengers that he is conducting an investigation and states that he needs to verify their luggage by checking their claim tickets. The passengers claim their luggage, but one large duffel bag remains unclaimed. The detective then asks defendant if the bag belongs to him, and defendant replies, "No." A K-9 drug-detecting dog, transported to the scene, then alerts to the unclaimed duffel bag. Police search the bag and find heroin, as well as identification cards with defendant's name. Given that defendant denied that the duffle bag belonged to him, does he have standing to challenge a search of the bag? *See State v. Carvajal*, 202 N.J. 214, 996 A.2d 1029 (2010).

Hypo 6: *Standing and the Evicted Tenant*

Defendant's landlord sues to evict him for failure to pay rent. The court issues an eviction order requiring defendant to vacate the property within three days, and authorizing the constable to put the landlord in possession of the property. Unable to find defendant at home, officers attach a copy of the writ to defendant's door on two occasions over the next week. At that point, the constable decides to forcibly remove defendant and his possessions from the property. Before he does, he runs an identity check and learns that defendant has two felony convictions. When the police arrive, defendant is present, the police secure him in the hallway, and conduct a security sweep of the home. In plain view, they find marijuana. Given the eviction order, did defendant have standing to challenge the search of the house? *See United States v. Curlin*, 638 F.3d 562 (7th Cir. 2011).

Hypo 7: *Standing and the Use of an Alias*

Alejandro paid for two hotel rooms and directed Rogelio to rent them for the group's use. All of the participants were in one of the rooms when the police arrived. Does the fact that Alejandro used an agent (Rogelio) to rent the rooms deprive him of standing to challenge a search of the rooms? Does the fact that Rogelio registered for the rooms under an alias deprive him of standing to challenge the search? Would you reach the same result if a celebrity's agent registers him for a room under an alias in order to avoid paparazzi? *See United States v. Domenech*, 623 F.3d 325 (6th Cir. 2010).

Hypo 8: *The Escaping Thief*

An undercover store detective, who believes that defendant is engaged in shoplifting, tries to approach defendant. Defendant elbows the detective and a scuffle ensues. When the detective grabs hold of the back of defendant's jacket, defendant slips his arms out of the jacket and runs away. In the jacket, the detective finds stolen merchandise and a cell phone (which the police used to identify defendant). Does defendant have standing to challenge the search of his jacket and his cell phone given that he voluntarily left them behind? *See State v. Dailey*, 2010 WL 3836204 (Ohio App. 3 Dist. 2010).

Hypo 9: *Dogs in the Aunt's Backyard*

Betts kept dogs in his aunt's backyard. He used to live at the aunt's home, and she gave him permission to keep the dogs there after he moved to another address, and also authorized him to enter the premises in order to water and feed his dogs, which he did on a daily basis. The backyard was fenced on three sides with two-wire fencing, and the fourth side was enclosed by a neighbor's wood privacy fence. The dogs were kept approximately 70 yards from the road, behind the house, in a central part of the back yard. Some of the dogs were chained to the ground near dog-house structures, and others were in pens surrounded by chainlink. Does Betts have standing to challenge the fact that police made a warrantless entry into the backyard to inspect and seize the dogs? See *State v. Betts*, 397 S.W. 3d 198 (Tex. Crim. App. 2013).

United States v. Payner

447 U.S. 727 (1980).

Mr. Justice Powell delivered the opinion of the Court.

Respondent Payner was indicted on a charge of falsifying his 1972 federal income tax return in violation of 18 U.S.C. § 1001. The indictment alleged that respondent denied maintaining a foreign bank account at a time when he knew that he had such an account in the Bahama Islands. The Government's case rested on a loan guarantee agreement dated April 28, 1972, in which respondent pledged the funds in his account as security for a $100,000 loan.

The events are not in dispute. The Internal Revenue Service launched an investigation into the financial activities of American citizens in the Bahamas. The project, known as "Operation Trade Winds," was headquartered in Jacksonville, Fla. Suspicion focused on the Castle Bank in 1972, when investigators learned that a suspected narcotics trafficker had an account there. Special Agent Richard Jaffe of the Jacksonville office asked Norman Casper, a private investigator and occasional informant, to learn what he could about the Castle Bank and its depositors. Casper cultivated his friendship with Castle Bank vice president Michael Wolstencroft. Casper introduced Wolstencroft to Sybol Kennedy, a private investigator and former employee. When Casper discovered that the banker intended to spend a few days in Miami in January 1973, he devised a scheme to gain access to the bank records he knew Wolstencroft would be carrying in his briefcase. Agent Jaffe approved the basic outline of the plan.

Wolstencroft arrived in Miami on January 15 and went directly to Kennedy's apartment. At about 7:30 p.m., the two left for dinner at a Key Biscayne restaurant. Shortly thereafter, Casper entered the apartment using a key supplied by Kennedy. He removed the briefcase and delivered it to Jaffe. While the agent supervised the copying of approximately 400 documents taken from the briefcase, a "lookout" observed Kennedy and Wolstencroft at dinner. The observer notified Casper when the pair left the restaurant, and the briefcase was replaced. The documents photographed that evening included papers evidencing a close working relationship between the Castle Bank and the Bank of Perrine, Fla. Subpoenas issued to the Bank of Perrine ultimately uncovered the loan guarantee agreement at issue in this case.

The District Court found that the United States, acting through Jaffe, "knowingly and willfully participated in the unlawful seizure of Michael Wolstencroft's briefcase." According to that court, "the Government affirmatively counsels its agents that the Fourth Amendment standing limitation permits them to purposefully conduct an unconstitutional search and seizure of one individual in order to obtain evidence against third parties." The documents seized from Wolstencroft provided the leads that ultimately led to the discovery of the critical loan guarantee agreement. Although the search did not impinge upon the respondent's Fourth Amendment rights, the District Court believed that the Due Process Clause of the Fifth Amendment and the inherent supervisory power of the federal courts required it to exclude evidence tainted by the Government's "knowing and purposeful bad faith hostility to any person's fundamental constitutional rights." The Court of Appeals for the Sixth Circuit affirmed. We granted certiorari, and we now reverse.

Respondent lacks standing under the Fourth Amendment to suppress the documents illegally seized from Wolstencroft. The [lower courts] believed, however, that a federal court should use its supervisory power to suppress evidence tainted by gross illegalities that did not infringe the defendant's constitutional rights. We understand the commendable desire to deter deliberate intrusions into the privacy of persons who are unlikely to become defendants in a criminal prosecution. No court should condone the unconstitutional and possibly criminal behavior of those who planned and executed this "briefcase caper." But our cases do not command the exclusion of evidence in every case of illegality. The illegality must be weighed against the considerable harm that would flow from indiscriminate application of an exclusionary rule.

The exclusionary rule "has been restricted to those areas where its remedial objectives are most efficaciously served." The Court has acknowledged that the suppression of probative but tainted evidence exacts a costly toll upon the ability of courts to ascertain the truth in a criminal case. Our cases have consistently recognized that unbending application of the exclusionary sanction to enforce ideals of governmental rectitude would impede unacceptably the truth-finding functions of judge and jury. After all, it is the defendant, and not the constable, who stands trial.

The same societal interests are at risk when a criminal defendant invokes the supervisory power to suppress evidence seized in violation of a third party's constitutional rights. The supervisory power is applied with some caution even when the defendant asserts a violation of his own rights. In *United States v. Caceres*, 440 U.S. 741 (1979), we refused to exclude all evidence tainted by violations of an executive department's rules. And in *Elkins v. United States*, 364 U.S. 206 (1960), the Court called for a restrained application of the supervisory power. "Any apparent limitation upon the process of discovering truth in a federal trial ought to be imposed only upon the basis of considerations which outweigh the general need for untrammeled disclosure of competent and relevant evidence in a court of justice."

We conclude that the supervisory power does not authorize a federal court to suppress otherwise admissible evidence on the ground that it was seized unlawfully from a third party not before the court. Our Fourth Amendment decisions have established beyond any doubt that the interest in deterring illegal searches does not justify the exclusion of tainted evidence at the instance of a party who was not the victim of the challenged practices. The values assigned to the competing interests do not change because a court has elected to analyze the question under the supervisory power instead of the Fourth Amendment. In either case, the need to deter the underlying conduct and the detrimental impact of excluding the evidence remain precisely the same.

The District Court erred, therefore, when it concluded that "society's interest in deterring bad faith conduct by exclusion outweighs society's interest in furnishing the trier of fact with all relevant evidence." Were we to accept this use of the supervisory power, we would confer on the judiciary discretionary power to disregard the considered limitations of the law it is charged with enforcing. We hold that the supervisory power does not extend so far.

The judgment of the Court of Appeals is

Reversed.

MR. JUSTICE MARSHALL, with whom MR. JUSTICE BRENNAN and MR. JUSTICE BLACKMUN join, dissenting.

This Court has on several occasions exercised its supervisory powers over the federal judicial system in order to suppress evidence that the Government obtained through misconduct. The rationale for such suppression is twofold: to deter illegal conduct by Government officials, and to protect the integrity of the federal courts. The Court has stressed the need to use supervisory powers to prevent the federal courts from becoming accomplices to such misconduct.

The need to use the Court's supervisory powers to suppress evidence obtained through governmental misconduct was perhaps best expressed by Mr. Justice Brandeis in his famous dissenting opinion in *Olmstead v. United States*, 277 U.S. 438 (1928): "Decency, security and liberty alike demand that government officials shall be subjected to the same rules of conduct that are commands to the citizen. In a government of laws, existence of the government will be imperiled if it fails to observe the law scrupulously. If the Government becomes a lawbreaker, it breeds contempt for law; it invites every man to become a law unto himself; it invites anarchy. To declare that in the administration of the criminal law the end justifies the means—to declare that the Government may commit crimes in order to secure the conviction of a private criminal—would bring terrible retribution. Against that pernicious doctrine this Court should resolutely set its face." If the federal court permits the introduction of evidence, the intended product of deliberately illegal Government action, to be used to obtain a conviction, it places its imprimatur upon such lawlessness and thereby taints its own integrity.

The present case falls within that category. The District Court found a deliberate decision by Government agents to violate the constitutional rights of Wolstencroft for the explicit purpose of obtaining evidence against persons such as Payner. The actions of the Government agents—stealing the briefcase, opening it, and photographing all the documents inside—were patently in violation of the Fourth Amendment rights of Wolstencroft and plainly in violation of the criminal law. The Government knew exactly what information it wanted. Similarly, the Government knew that it wanted to prosecute persons such as Payner, and it made a conscious decision to forgo any opportunity to prosecute Wolstencroft in order to obtain illegally the evidence against Payner and others. Since the supervisory powers are exercised to protect the integrity of the court, rather than to vindicate the constitutional rights of the defendant, it is hard to see why the Court today bases its analysis entirely on Fourth Amendment standing rules. The federal judiciary should not be made accomplices to the crimes of Casper, Jaffe, and others.

2. "Fruit of the Poisonous Tree" Doctrine

When the exclusionary rule is applied, it prohibits the prosecution from using evidence directly obtained from a constitutional violation. Thus, if the police coerce a suspect into confessing, the exclusionary rule prohibits the use of that confession. The "derivative evidence rule," also known as the "Fruit of the Poisonous Tree" doctrine, prohibits the police from using other evidence "derived" (or indirectly obtained) from the direct evidence.

> If an illegal stop leads to a confession, the derivative evidence rule might prohibit the prosecution from using the confession as evidence. As the Court stated in *Nardone v. United States*, 308 U.S. 338 (1939), "the essence of a provision forbidding the acquisition of evidence in a certain way is that not merely evidence so acquired shall not be used before the Court but that it shall not be used at all."

Brown v. Illinois

422 U.S. 590 (1975).

MR. JUSTICE BLACKMUN delivered the opinion of the Court.

Petitioner Richard Brown was arrested for murder while attempting to enter his Chicago apartment. The arrest was illegal because the police lacked probable cause. The police then took petitioner to the police station. During the 20-minute drive Nolan again asked Brown, who then was sitting with him in the back seat of the car, whether his name was Richard Brown and whether he owned a 1966 Oldsmobile. Brown evaded these questions or answered them falsely. Upon arrival at the station house Brown was placed in the second-floor central interrogation room. The room was bare, except for a table and four chairs. He was left alone, without handcuffs, for some minutes while the officers obtained the file on the homicide. They returned with the file, sat down at the table, one across from Brown and the other to his left, and spread the file on the table in front of him.

The officers warned Brown of his rights under *Miranda*. They then informed him that they knew of an incident that had occurred in a poolroom when Brown, angry at having been cheated at dice, fired a shot from a revolver into the ceiling. Brown answered: "Oh, you know about that." Lenz informed him that a bullet had been obtained from the ceiling of the poolroom and had been taken to the crime laboratory to be compared with bullets taken from the victim's body. Brown responded: "Oh, you know that, too." At this point—it was about 8:45 p.m.—

Lenz asked Brown whether he wanted to talk about the homicide. Petitioner answered that he did. For the next 20 to 25 minutes Brown answered questions put to him by Nolan, as Lenz typed.

This questioning produced a two-page statement in which Brown acknowledged that he and a man named Jimmy Claggett visited Corpus on the evening of May 5; that the three for some time sat drinking and smoking marihuana; that Claggett ordered him at gunpoint to bind Corpus' hands and feet with cord from the headphone of a stereo set; and that Claggett, using a .38-caliber revolver sold to him by Brown, shot Corpus three times through a pillow. The statement was signed by Brown.

Later that night, after the police apprehended Claggett, Brown was again placed in the interrogation room. He was given coffee and was left alone, for the most part, until 2 a.m. when Assistant State's Attorney Crilly arrived. Crilly, too, informed Brown of his *Miranda* rights. After a half hour's conversation, a court reporter appeared. Once again the *Miranda* warnings were given: "I read him the card." Crilly told him that he "was sure he would be charged with murder." Brown gave a second statement, providing a factual account of the murder substantially in accord with his first statement, but containing factual inaccuracies with respect to his personal background. When the statement was completed, at about 3 a.m., Brown refused to sign it. An hour later he made a phone call to his mother. At 9:30 that morning, about 14 hours after his arrest, he was taken before a magistrate. At trial, the State introduced evidence of both statements, and the jury found petitioner guilty of murder. The conviction was affirmed on appeal.

In *Wong Sun v. United States*, 371 U.S. 471 (1963), the Court pronounced the principles to be applied when the issue is whether statements and other evidence obtained after an illegal arrest or search should be excluded. In that case, federal agents elicited an oral statement from defendant Toy after forcing entry at 6 a.m. into his laundry, at the back of which he had his living quarters. The agents followed Toy down the hall to the bedroom and placed him under arrest. There was no probable cause for the arrest. Toy's statement, which bore upon his participation in the sale of narcotics, led the agents to question another person, Johnny Yee, who actually possessed narcotics. Yee stated that heroin had been brought to him earlier by Toy and another Chinese known to him only as "Sea Dog." Under questioning, Toy said that "Sea Dog" was Wong Sun. Toy led agents to a multifamily dwelling where, he said, Wong Sun lived. Gaining admittance to the building through a bell and buzzer, the agents climbed the stairs and entered the apartment. One went into the back room and brought Wong Sun out in handcuffs. After arraignment, Wong Sun was released on his own recognizance. Several days later, he returned voluntarily to give an unsigned confession.

This Court ruled that Toy's declarations and the contraband taken from Yee were the fruits of the agents' illegal action and should not have been admitted as evidence against Toy. The statement did not result from "an intervening independent act of a free will," and was not "sufficiently an act of free will to purge the primary taint of the unlawful invasion." With respect to Wong Sun's confession, however, the Court held that in the light of his lawful arraignment and release on his own recognizance, and of his return voluntarily several days later to make the statement, the connection between his unlawful arrest and the statement "had become so attenuated as to dissipate the taint." The Court said: "We need not hold that all evidence is 'fruit of the poisonous tree' simply because it would not have come to light but for the illegal actions of the police. Rather, the more apt question is 'whether, granting establishment of the primary illegality, the evidence to which instant objection is made has been come at by exploitation of that illegality or instead by means sufficiently distinguishable to be purged of the primary taint.' Maguire, Evidence of Guilt, 221 (1959)."

The exclusionary rule thus was applied in *Wong Sun* primarily to protect Fourth Amendment rights. Protection of the Fifth Amendment right against self-incrimination was not the Court's paramount concern there. To the extent that the question whether Toy's statement was voluntary was considered, it was only to judge whether it "was sufficiently an act of free will to purge the primary taint of the unlawful invasion."

The Court in *Wong Sun*, as is customary, emphasized that application of the exclusionary rule on Toy's behalf protected Fourth Amendment guarantees in two respects: "in terms of deterring lawless conduct by federal officers," and by "closing the doors of the federal courts to any use of evidence unconstitutionally obtained."

The Illinois courts refrained from resolving the question whether Brown's statements were obtained by exploitation of the illegality of his arrest. They assumed that the *Miranda* warnings, by themselves, assured that the statements (verbal acts, as contrasted with physical evidence) were of sufficient free will as to purge the primary taint of the unlawful arrest.

This Court has described the *Miranda* warnings as a "prophylactic rule," and as a "procedural safeguard," employed to protect Fifth Amendment rights against "the compulsion inherent in custodial surroundings." The function of the warnings relates to the Fifth Amendment's guarantee against coerced self-incrimination, and the exclusion of a statement made in the absence of the warnings, serves to deter the taking of an incriminating statement without first informing the individual of his Fifth Amendment rights.

Although, almost 90 years ago, the Court observed that the Fifth Amendment is in "intimate relation" with the Fourth, the *Miranda* warnings thus far have not been regarded as a means either of remedying or deterring violations of Fourth Amendment rights. Frequently, rights under the two Amendments may appear to coalesce since "the 'unreasonable searches and seizures' condemned in the Fourth Amendment are almost always made for the purpose of compelling a man to give evidence against himself, which in criminal cases is condemned in the Fifth Amendment." The exclusionary rule, however, when utilized to effectuate the Fourth Amendment, serves interests and policies that are distinct from those it serves under the Fifth. It is directed at all unlawful searches and seizures, and not merely those that happen to produce incriminating material or testimony as fruits. In short, exclusion of a confession made without *Miranda* warnings might be regarded as necessary to effectuate the Fifth Amendment, but it would not be sufficient fully to protect the Fourth. *Miranda* warnings, and the exclusion of a confession made without them, do not alone sufficiently deter a Fourth Amendment violation.

Thus, even if the statements in this case were found to be voluntary under the Fifth Amendment, the Fourth Amendment issue remains. In order for the causal chain, between the illegal arrest and the statements made subsequent thereto, to be broken, *Wong Sun* requires not merely that the statement meet the Fifth Amendment standard of voluntariness but that it be "sufficiently an act of free will to purge the primary taint." *Wong Sun* thus mandates consideration of a statement's admissibility in light of the distinct policies and interests of the Fourth Amendment.

If *Miranda* warnings were held to attenuate the taint of an unconstitutional arrest, regardless of how wanton and purposeful the Fourth Amendment violation, the effect of the exclusionary rule would be substantially diluted. Arrests made without warrant or without probable cause, for questioning or "investigation," would be encouraged by the knowledge that evidence derived therefrom could well be made admissible at trial by the simple expedient of giving *Miranda* warnings. Any incentive to avoid Fourth Amendment violations would be eviscerated by making the warnings, in effect, a "cure-all," and the constitutional guarantee against unlawful searches and seizures could be said to be reduced to "a form of words."

It is possible, of course, that persons arrested illegally may decide to confess, as an act of free will unaffected by the initial illegality. But the *Miranda* warnings, alone and *per se*, cannot always make the act sufficiently a product of free will to break, for Fourth Amendment purposes, the causal connection between the illegality and the confession. They cannot assure that the Fourth Amendment violation has not been unduly exploited.

The question whether a confession is the product of a free will under *Wong Sun* must be answered on the facts of each case. No single fact is dispositive. The workings of the human mind are too complex, and the possibilities of misconduct too diverse, to permit protection of the Fourth Amendment to turn on such a talismanic test. The *Miranda* warnings are an important factor in determining whether the confession is obtained by exploitation of an illegal arrest. But they are not the only factor to be considered. The temporal proximity of the arrest and the confession, the presence of intervening circumstances, and, particularly, the purpose and flagrancy of the official misconduct are all relevant. The voluntariness of the statement is a threshold requirement. And the burden of showing admissibility rests on the prosecution.

The State failed to sustain the burden of showing that the evidence in question was admissible under *Wong Sun*. Brown's first statement was separated from his illegal arrest by less than two hours, and there was no intervening event of significance whatsoever. His situation is remarkably like that of James Wah Toy in *Wong Sun*. And the second statement was clearly the result and the fruit of the first.[12]

The illegality here, moreover, had a quality of purposefulness. The impropriety of the arrest was obvious; awareness of that fact was virtually conceded by the two detectives when they repeatedly acknowledged that the purpose of their action was "for investigation" or for "questioning." The detectives embarked upon this expedition for evidence in the hope that something might turn up. The manner in which Brown's arrest was affected gives the appearance of having been calculated to cause surprise, fright, and confusion.

We decide only that the Illinois courts were in error in assuming that the *Miranda* warnings, by themselves, under *Wong Sun* always purge the taint of an illegal arrest.

The judgment of the Supreme Court of Illinois is reversed and the case is remanded for further proceedings not inconsistent with this opinion.

It is so ordered.

MR. JUSTICE POWELL, with whom MR. JUSTICE REHNQUIST joins, concurring in part.

---

[12] The fact that Brown had made one statement, believed by him to be admissible, and his cooperation with the arresting and interrogating officers in the search for Claggett, with his anticipation of leniency, bolstered the pressures for him to give the second, or at least vitiated any incentive on his part to avoid self-incrimination.

The point at which the taint can be said to have dissipated should be related, in the absence of other controlling circumstances, to the nature of that taint. That police have not succeeded in coercing the accused's confession through willful or negligent misuse of the power of arrest does not remove the fact that they may have tried. The impermissibility of the attempt, and the extent to which such attempts can be deterred by the use of the exclusionary rule, are of primary relevance in determining whether exclusion is an appropriate remedy. The basic purpose of the rule is to remove possible motivations for illegal arrests. Given this purpose the notion of voluntariness has practical value in deciding whether the rule should apply to statements removed from the immediate circumstances of the illegal arrest. If an illegal arrest merely provides the occasion of initial contact between the police and the accused, and because of time or other intervening factors the accused's eventual statement is the product of his own reflection and free will, application of the exclusionary rule can serve little purpose: the police normally will not make an illegal arrest in the hope of eventually obtaining such a truly volunteered statement. In a similar manner, the role of the *Miranda* warnings in the *Wong Sun* inquiry is indirect. To the extent that they dissipate the psychological pressures of custodial interrogation, *Miranda* warnings serve to assure that the accused's decision to make a statement has been relatively unaffected by the preceding illegal arrest. Correspondingly, to the extent that the police perceive *Miranda* warnings to have this equalizing potential, their motivation to abuse the power of arrest is diminished. Bearing these considerations in mind, and recognizing that the deterrent value of the Fourth Amendment exclusionary rule is limited to certain kinds of police conduct, the following general categories can be identified.

Those most readily identifiable are on the extremes: the flagrantly abusive violation of Fourth Amendment rights, on the one hand, and "technical" Fourth Amendment violations, on the other. In my view, these extremes call for significantly different judicial responses. I would require the clearest indication of attenuation in cases in which official conduct was flagrantly abusive of Fourth Amendment rights. In such cases, I would consider the equalizing potential of *Miranda* warnings rarely sufficient to dissipate the taint. In such cases the deterrent value of the exclusionary rule is most likely to be effective, and the corresponding mandate to preserve judicial integrity, most clearly demands that the fruits of official misconduct be denied. I thus would require some demonstrably effective break in the chain of events leading from the illegal arrest to the statement, such as actual consultation with counsel or the accused's presentation before a magistrate for a determination of probable cause, before the taint can be deemed removed. At the opposite end of the spectrum lie "technical" violations of Fourth Amendment rights where, for example, officers in good faith arrest an individual in reliance on a warrant later invalidated or pursuant to a statute that subsequently is declared unconstitutional. I would not require more than proof that effective *Miranda* warnings were given and that the ensuing statement was voluntary in the Fifth Amendment sense. Absent aggravating circumstances, I would consider a statement given at the station house after one has been advised of *Miranda* rights to be sufficiently removed from the immediate circumstances of the illegal arrest to justify its admission at trial.

Points for Discussion

a. Illustrating the FOPT Doctrine

After *Brown*, the Court has decided several similar cases. In *Dunaway v. New York*, 442 U.S. 200 (1979), the Court held that the police violated petitioner's rights when they seized him and took him to the stationhouse for custodial questioning absent probable cause. Because of the illegal seizure, the Court refused to admit petitioner's incriminating statements at the stationhouse: "The situation in this case is virtually a replica of the situation in *Brown*. Petitioner was seized without probable cause in the hope that something might turn up, and confessed without any intervening event of significance." Chief Justice Rehnquist dissented: "The connection between petitioner's allegedly, unlawful detention and the incriminating statements and sketches is sufficiently attenuated to permit their use at trial. Where police have acted in good faith and not in a flagrant manner, I would require no more than that proper *Miranda* warnings be given and that the statement be voluntary within the meaning of the Fifth Amendment." *See also Taylor v. Alabama*, 457 U.S. 687 (1982) (Court suppressed confession when "petitioner was arrested without probable cause in the hope that something would turn up, and he confessed shortly thereafter without any meaningful intervening event" even though petitioner was given three *Miranda* warnings).

In *Rawlings v. Kentucky*, 448 U.S. 98 (1980), petitioner was convicted of trafficking in, and possession of, various controlled substances. The conviction was based, in part, on statements made by petitioner at the scene of the arrest. Even though the Court concluded that petitioner was illegally detained at the time he made the statements, the Court felt that the connection between the seizure and the statements was sufficiently attenuated: "Petitioner received *Miranda* warnings only moments before he made his incriminating statements. Petitioner and his companions were detained for a period of approximately 45 minutes. The three people sat quietly in the living room, or at least initially, moved freely about the first floor of the house. Petitioner's admissions were apparently spontaneous reactions to the discovery of his drugs in Cox's purse, and this factor weighs heavily in favor of a finding that petitioner acted 'of free will unaffected by the initial illegality.' The conduct of the police does not rise to the level of conscious or flagrant misconduct. Petitioner has not argued that his admission to ownership of the drugs was anything other than voluntary." Justice Marshall dissented: "Petitioner's admissions, far from being 'spontaneous,' were made in response to Vanessa Cox's demand that petitioner 'take what was his.' Her statement was the direct product of the illegal search of her purse. That search was made possible only because the police refused to let anyone in the house depart unless they 'consented' to a body search; that detention was illegal."

Take Note

The Court addressed an important "fruits" issue in *United States v. Patane,* 542 U.S. 630 (2004), in which a plurality of the Court held that police failure to give the *Miranda* warnings did not require suppression of the physical fruits of a defendant's unwarned statements. After officers arrested Patane, but before they gave him complete *Miranda* warnings, they asked him about the location of a gun. He told them the location and they seized it. The *Patane* plurality held that the statement was inadmissible, but that the gun was admissibile: "Introduction of the nontestimonial fruit of a voluntary statement, such as Patane's gun, does not implicate the Self-Incrimination Clause. The admission of such fruit presents no risk that a defendant's coerced statements will be used against him at a criminal trial and 'the exclusion of unwarned statements is a complete and sufficient remedy' for any perceived *Miranda* violation. There is simply no need to extend the prophylactic rule of *Miranda* to require the exclusion of physical evidence. Although the Court requires the exclusion of the physical fruit of actually coerced statements, it must be remembered that statements taken without sufficient *Miranda* warnings are presumed to have been coerced only for certain purposes and then only when necessary to protect the privilege against self-incrimination. We decline to extend that presumption further." Justices Kennedy, joined by Justice O'Connor, concurred, opining that "the important probative value of reliable physical evidence" made it "doubtful that exclusion of the gun can be justified by a deterrence rationale." The *Patane* dissenters argued that the admissible status of physical evidence "fruits" of *Miranda* violations would serve as an "invitation to law enforcement officers to flout *Miranda* when there may be physical evidence to be gained."

b. A Witness as a "Fruit" of an Illegal Search

In *United States v. Ceccolini,* 435 U.S. 268 (1978), while the police were investigating illegal gambling, Biro, a police officer entered respondent's place of business (a flower shop), went behind the customer counter and spent his break talking with his friend (Hennessey), an employee of the shop. During the conversation, he spotted an envelope with money lying on the cash register. Biro picked up the envelope, examined its contents, and discovered that it contained not only money but betting slips. He placed the envelope back on the register and, without telling his friend what he had seen, asked her who owned it. She replied that the envelope belonged to respondent, and that he had instructed her to give it to someone. Later, when respondent testified before a grand jury that he had never taken bets, Hennessey gave contrary testimony. The Court held that the friend's testimony was not subject to exclusion: "The evidence indicates overwhelmingly that the testimony given by the witness was an act of her own free will in no way coerced or even induced by official authority as a result of Biro's discovery of the policy slips. Nor were the slips themselves used in questioning Hennessey. Substantial periods of time elapsed between the time of the illegal search and the initial contact with the witness, on the one hand, and between the latter and the testimony at trial on the other. While the particular knowledge to which Hennessey testified at trial can be logically traced back to Biro's discovery of the policy slips both the identity of Hennessey and her relationship with the respondent were well known to those investigating the case. There is, in addition, not the slightest evidence to suggest that Biro entered the shop or picked up the envelope with the intent of finding tangible evidence bearing on an illicit gambling operation, much less any suggestion that he entered the shop and searched with the intent of finding a willing and knowledgeable witness to testify against respondent."

Likewise, in *Michigan v. Tucker*, 417 U.S. 433 (1974), a plurality of the Court held that the testimony of a witness could be used in the prosecution's case in chief, notwithstanding the fact that the identity of the witness was provided in a defendant's statement obtained by police in violation of *Miranda*. The Court reasoned that where the police committed the *Miranda* violation in good faith, "the deterrent effect" of reducing future *Miranda* violations would not be "significantly augmented" by excluding the testimony of "a third party who was subject to no custodial pressures." The *Tucker* defendant did not receive complete *Miranda* warnings, and therefore the statement he made after waiver, identifying the name of an alibi witness, was inadmissible at his trial. Although the witness's name and testimony were "fruits" of the *Miranda* violation, they were deemed admissible in *Tucker*.

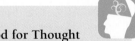

Food for Thought

What might the police have done differently in *Brown* that might have altered the result?

Utah v. Strieff

136 S.Ct. 2056 (2016).

JUSTICE THOMAS delivered the opinion of the Court.

The question in this case is whether the attenuation doctrine applies when an officer makes an unconstitutional investigatory stop; learns during that stop that the suspect is subject to a valid arrest warrant; and proceeds to arrest the suspect and seize incriminating evidence during a search incident to that arrest. We hold that the evidence the officer seized as part of the search incident to arrest is admissible because the officer's discovery of the arrest warrant attenuated the connection between the unlawful stop and the evidence seized incident to arrest.

In December 2006, someone called the South Salt Lake City police's drug-tip line to report "narcotics activity" at a particular residence. Narcotics detective Fackrell investigated the tip. Over the course of a week, Fackrell conducted intermittent surveillance of the home. He observed visitors who left a few minutes after arriving at the house. These visits were sufficiently frequent to raise his suspicion that the occupants were dealing drugs. One of those visitors was respondent Edward Strieff. Fackrell observed Strieff exit the house and walk toward a nearby convenience store. In the store's parking lot, Officer Fackrell detained Strieff, identified himself, and asked Strieff what he was doing at the residence. As part of the stop, Officer Fackrell requested Strieff's identification, and Strieff produced his Utah identification card. Officer Fackrell relayed Strieff's information to a police dispatcher, who reported that Strieff had an outstanding arrest warrant for a traffic violation. Officer Fackrell then arrested Strieff pursuant to that warrant. When Officer Fackrell searched Strieff incident to the arrest, he discovered a baggie of methamphetamine and drug paraphernalia.

The State charged Strieff with unlawful possession of methamphetamine and drug paraphernalia. Strieff moved to suppress the evidence, arguing that the evidence was inadmissible because it was derived from an unlawful investigatory stop. The prosecutor conceded that Officer Fackrell lacked reasonable suspicion for the stop but argued that the evidence should not be suppressed because a valid arrest warrant attenuated the connection between the unlawful stop and discovery of the contraband. The trial court admitted the evidence. The Utah Court of Appeals affirmed. The Utah Supreme Court reversed. We granted certiorari and reverse.

Because officers who violated the Fourth Amendment were traditionally considered trespassers, individuals subject to unconstitutional searches or seizures historically enforced their rights through tort suits or self-help. In the 20th century, the exclusionary rule—the rule that often requires trial courts to exclude unlawfully seized evidence in a criminal trial—became the principal judicial remedy to deter Fourth Amendment violations. See, *e.g., Mapp v. Ohio,* 367 U. S. 643 (1961). The exclusionary rule encompasses both the "primary evidence obtained as a direct result of an illegal search or seizure" and "evidence later discovered and found to be derivative of an illegality," the so-called "fruit of the poisonous tree." *Segura v. United States,* 468 U. S. 796 (1984). But the significant costs of this rule have led us to deem it "applicable only where its deterrence benefits outweigh its substantial social costs." *Hudson v. Michigan,* 547 U. S. 586 (2006). "Suppression of evidence has always been our last resort, not our first impulse." *Ibid.*

We have recognized several exceptions to the rule. Three of these exceptions involve the causal relationship between the unconstitutional act and the discovery of evidence. First, the independent source doctrine allows trial courts to admit evidence obtained in an unlawful search if officers independently acquired it from a separate, independent source. See *Murray v. United States,* 487 U. S. 533 (1988). Second, the inevitable discovery doctrine allows for the admission of evidence that would have been discovered even without the unconstitutional source. See

Nix v. Williams, 467 U. S. 431 (1984). Third is the attenuation doctrine: Evidence is admissible when the connection between unconstitutional police conduct and the evidence is remote or has been interrupted by some intervening circumstance, so that "the interest protected by the constitutional guarantee that has been violated would not be served by suppression of the evidence obtained." *Hudson, supra,* at 593.

Turning to the attenuation doctrine, we first address a threshold question: whether this doctrine applies at all to a case like this, where the intervening circumstance that the State relies on is the discovery of a valid, pre-existing, and untainted arrest warrant. The Utah Supreme Court declined to apply the attenuation doctrine because it read our precedents as applying the doctrine only "to circumstances involving an independent act of a defendant's 'free will' in confessing to a crime or consenting to a search." We disagree. The attenuation doctrine evaluates the causal link between the government's unlawful act and the discovery of evidence, which often has nothing to do with a defendant's actions. The logic of our prior attenuation cases is not limited to independent acts by the defendant.

It remains for us to address whether the discovery of a valid arrest warrant was a sufficient intervening event to break the causal chain between the unlawful stop and the discovery of drug-related evidence on Strieff's person. The three factors articulated in *Brown v. Illinois,* 422 U. S. 590 (1975), guide our analysis. First, we look to the "temporal proximity" between the unconstitutional conduct and the discovery of evidence to determine how closely the discovery of evidence followed the unconstitutional search. Second, we consider "the presence of intervening circumstances." Third, and "particularly" significant, we examine "the purpose and flagrancy of the official misconduct." In evaluating these factors, we assume that Officer Fackrell lacked reasonable suspicion to initially stop Strieff. Because we conclude that the warrant breaks the causal chain, we have no need to decide whether the warrant's existence alone would make the initial stop constitutional even if Officer Fackrell was unaware of its existence.

The first factor, temporal proximity between the initially unlawful stop and the search, favors suppressing the evidence. Our precedents have declined to find that this factor favors attenuation unless "substantial time" elapses between an unlawful act and when the evidence is obtained. Here, Officer Fackrell discovered drug contraband on Strieff's person only minutes after the illegal stop. As the Court explained in *Brown,* such a short time interval counsels in favor of suppression; there, we found that the confession should be suppressed, relying in part on the "less than two hours" that separated the unconstitutional arrest and the confession.

The second factor, the presence of intervening circumstances, strongly favors the State. In *Segura,* 468 U. S. 796, the Court addressed similar facts to those here and found sufficient intervening circumstances to allow the admission of evidence. There, agents had probable cause to believe that apartment occupants were dealing cocaine. They sought a warrant. In the meantime, they entered the apartment, arrested an occupant, and discovered evidence of drug activity during a limited search for security reasons. The next evening, the Magistrate Judge issued the search warrant. This Court deemed the evidence admissible notwithstanding the illegal search because the information supporting the warrant was "wholly unconnected with the arguably illegal entry and was known to the agents well before the initial entry." *Segura,* of course, applied the independent source doctrine because the unlawful entry "did not contribute in any way to discovery of the evidence seized under the warrant." But Segura suggested that the existence of a valid warrant favors finding that the connection between unlawful conduct and the discovery of evidence is "sufficiently attenuated to dissipate the taint."

In this case, the warrant was valid, it predated Officer Fackrell's investigation, and it was entirely unconnected with the stop. Once Officer Fackrell discovered the warrant, he had an obligation to arrest Strieff. "A warrant is a judicial mandate to an officer to conduct a search or make an arrest, and the officer has a sworn duty to carry out its provisions." *United States v. Leon,* 468 U. S. 897, 920 (1984). Officer Fackrell's arrest of Strieff thus was a ministerial act that was independently compelled by the pre-existing warrant. Once Officer Fackrell was authorized to arrest Strieff, it was undisputedly lawful to search Strieff as an incident of his arrest to protect Officer Fackrell's safety. See *Arizona v. Gant,* 556 U. S. 332 (2009).

Finally, the third factor, "the purpose and flagrancy of the official misconduct" also strongly favors the State. The exclusionary rule exists to deter police misconduct. *Davis v. United States,* 564 U. S. 229 (2011). The third factor of the attenuation doctrine reflects that rationale by favoring exclusion only when the police misconduct is most in need of deterrence—that is, when it is purposeful or flagrant.

Officer Fackrell was at most negligent. In stopping Strieff, Officer Fackrell made two good-faith mistakes. First, he had not observed what time Strieff entered the suspected drug house, so he did not know how long Strieff had been there. Fackrell thus lacked a sufficient basis to conclude that Strieff was a short-term visitor who may have been consummating a drug transaction. Second, because he lacked confirmation that Strieff was a short-term visitor, Fackrell should have asked Strieff whether he would speak with him, instead of demanding that Strieff do so. Officer Fackrell's stated purpose was to "find out what was going on in the house." Nothing prevented him from approaching Strieff simply to ask. But these errors in judgment hardly rise to a purposeful or flagrant violation of Strieff's Fourth Amendment rights.

While Officer Fackrell's decision to initiate the stop was mistaken, his conduct thereafter was lawful. The officer's decision to run the warrant check was a "negligibly burdensome precaution" for officer safety. *Rodriguez v. United States,* 575 U. S. ___, ___ (2015) (slip op., at 7). Officer Fackrell's actual search of Strieff was a lawful search incident to arrest. Moreover, there is no indication that this unlawful stop was part of any systemic or recurrent police misconduct. The evidence suggests that the stop was an isolated instance of negligence that occurred in connection with a bona fide investigation of a suspected drug house. Officer Fackrell saw Strieff leave a suspected drug house. His suspicion about the house was based on an anonymous tip and his personal observations.

Applying these factors, we hold that the evidence discovered on Strieff's person was admissible because the unlawful stop was sufficiently attenuated by the pre-existing arrest warrant. Although the illegal stop was close in time to Strieff's arrest, that consideration is outweighed by two factors supporting the State. The outstanding arrest warrant for Strieff's arrest is a critical intervening circumstance that is wholly independent of the illegal stop. The discovery of that warrant broke the causal chain between the unconstitutional stop and the discovery of evidence by compelling Officer Fackrell to arrest Strieff. It is especially significant that there is no evidence that Officer Fackrell's illegal stop reflected flagrantly unlawful police misconduct.

Strieff argues that the attenuation doctrine should not apply because the officer's stop was purposeful and flagrant. But Officer Fackrell sought information from Strieff to find out what was happening inside a house whose occupants were legitimately suspected of dealing drugs. This was not a suspicionless fishing expedition "in the hope that something would turn up." For the violation to be flagrant, more severe police misconduct is required than the mere absence of proper cause for the seizure. Second, Strieff argues that, because of the prevalence of outstanding arrest warrants in many jurisdictions, police will engage in dragnet searches if the exclusionary rule is not applied. We think that this outcome is unlikely. Such wanton conduct would expose police to civil liability. See 42 U. S. C. §1983; *Monell v. New York City Dept. of Social Servs.,* 436 U. S. 658 (1978). In any event, the *Brown* factors take account of the purpose and flagrancy of police misconduct. Were evidence of a dragnet search presented here, the application of the Brown factors could be different. But there is no evidence that the concerns that Strieff raises with the criminal justice system are present in South Salt Lake City, Utah.

We hold that the evidence Officer Fackrell seized as part of his search incident to arrest is admissible because his discovery of the arrest warrant attenuated the connection between the unlawful stop and the evidence seized from Strieff incident to arrest. The judgment of the Utah Supreme Court, accordingly, is reversed.

It is so ordered.

Justice Sotomayor, with whom Justice Ginsburg joins as to Parts I, II, and III, dissenting.

This case allows the police to stop you on the street, demand your identification, and check it for outstanding traffic warrants—even if you are doing nothing wrong. If the officer discovers a warrant for a fine you forgot to pay, courts will now excuse his illegal stop and will admit into evidence anything he happens to find by searching you after arresting you on the warrant. I dissent.

I

This stop was illegal. The Fourth Amendment protects people from "unreasonable searches and seizures." An officer breaches that protection when he detains a pedestrian to check his license without any evidence that the person is engaged in a crime. *Delaware v. Prouse,* 440 U. S. 648 (1979). The officer deepens the breach when he prolongs the detention just to fish further for evidence of wrongdoing. In his search for lawbreaking, the officer in this case himself broke the law.

II

It is tempting, where illegal conduct by an officer uncovers illegal conduct by a civilian, to forgive the officer. After all, his instincts, although unconstitutional, were correct. But two wrongs don't make a right. When "lawless police conduct" uncovers evidence of lawless civilian conduct, this Court has long required later criminal trials to exclude the illegally obtained evidence. *Mapp v. Ohio,* 367 U. S. 643 (1961). If an officer breaks into a home and finds a forged check lying around, that check may not be used to prosecute the homeowner for bank fraud. We would describe the check as "fruit of the poisonous tree." *Wong Sun v. United States,* 371 U. S. 471 (1963). Fruit that must be cast aside includes not only evidence directly found by an illegal search but also evidence "come at by exploitation of that illegality." *Ibid.*

The "exclusionary rule" removes an incentive for officers to search without proper justification. It also keeps courts from being "made party to lawless invasions of the constitutional rights of citizens by permitting unhindered governmental use of the fruits of such invasions." *Id.,* at 13. When courts admit only lawfully obtained evidence, they encourage "those who formulate law enforcement polices, and the officers who implement them, to incorporate Fourth Amendment ideals into their value system." *Stone v. Powell,* 428 U. S. 465 (1976). But when courts admit illegally obtained evidence as well, they reward "manifest neglect if not an open defiance of the prohibitions of the Constitution." *Weeks,* 232 U. S., at 394.

Applying the exclusionary rule, the officer found the drugs only after learning of Strieff's traffic violation; and he learned of Strieff's traffic violation only because he unlawfully stopped Strieff to check his driver's license. These factors confirm that the officer discovered Strieff's drugs by exploiting his own illegal conduct. The officer did not ask Strieff to volunteer his name only to find out, days later, that Strieff had a warrant against him. The officer illegally stopped Strieff and immediately ran a warrant check. The officer's sole reason for stopping Strieff, he acknowledged, was investigative—he wanted to discover whether drug activity was going on in the house Strieff had just exited. The warrant check was not an "intervening circumstance" separating the stop from the search for drugs. It was part and parcel of the officer's illegal "expedition for evidence in the hope that something might turn up." *Brown,* 422 U. S., at 605. Because the officer found Strieff's drugs by exploiting his own constitutional violation, the drugs should be excluded.

III

The majority misses the point when it calls the warrant check here a "negligibly burdensome precaution" taken for the officer's "safety." The officer stopped Strieff without suspecting him of committing any crime. By his own account, the officer did not fear Strieff. Moreover, the safety rationale is conspicuously absent here. A warrant check on a highway "ensures that vehicles on the road are operated safely and responsibly." We allow such checks during legal traffic stops because the legitimacy of a person's driver's license has a "close connection to roadway safety." A warrant check of a pedestrian on a sidewalk, "by contrast, is a measure aimed at 'detecting evidence of ordinary criminal wrongdoing.' " *Ibid.* (quoting *Indianapolis v. Edmond,* 531 U. S. 32 (2000)). Surely we would not allow officers to warrant-check random joggers, dog walkers, and lemonade vendors just to ensure they pose no threat to anyone else.

The officer's sole purpose was to fish for evidence. The majority casts his unconstitutional actions as "negligent" and therefore incapable of being deterred by the exclusionary rule. Even officers prone to negligence can learn from courts that exclude illegally obtained evidence. Indeed, they are perhaps the most in need of the education, whether by the judge's opinion, the prosecutor's future guidance, or an updated manual on criminal procedure. If the officers are in doubt about what the law requires, exclusion gives them an "incentive to err on the side of constitutional behavior." *United States v. Johnson,* 457 U. S. 537, 561 (1982).

Most striking about the Court's opinion is its insistence that the event here was "isolated," with "no indication that this unlawful stop was part of any systemic or recurrent police misconduct." Outstanding warrants are surprisingly common. The States and Federal Government maintain databases with over 7.8 million outstanding warrants, the vast majority for minor offenses. Most officers act in "good faith" and do not set out to break the law. That does not mean these stops are "isolated instances of negligence." The New York City Police Department long trained officers to "stop and question first, develop reasonable suspicion later."

IV

Unlawful "stops" have severe consequences. Although many Americans have been stopped for speeding or jaywalking, few may realize how degrading a stop can be when the officer is looking for more. This Court has allowed an officer to stop you for whatever reason he wants—so long as he can point to a pretextual justification after the fact. *Whren v. United States*, 517 U. S. 806 (1996). That justification must provide specific reasons why the officer suspected you were breaking the law, but it may factor in your ethnicity, where you live, what you were wearing, and how you behaved. The officer does not even need to know which law you might have broken so long as he can later point to any possible infraction—even one that is minor, unrelated, or ambiguous.

The indignity of the stop is not limited to an officer telling you that you look like a criminal. The officer may next ask for your "consent" to inspect your bag or purse without telling you that you can decline. Regardless of your answer, he may order you to stand "helpless, perhaps facing a wall with your hands raised." If the officer thinks you might be dangerous, he may then "frisk" you for weapons. The officer's control over you does not end with the stop. If the officer chooses, he may handcuff you and take you to jail for doing nothing more than speeding, jaywalking, or "driving your pickup truck with your 3-year-old son and 5-year-old daughter without your seatbelt fastened." *Atwater v. Lago Vista*, 532 U. S. 318 (2001). At the jail, he can fingerprint you, swab DNA from the inside of your mouth, and force you to "shower with a delousing agent" while you "lift your tongue, hold out your arms, turn around, and lift your genitals." *Florence v. Board of Chosen Freeholders of County of Burlington*, 566 U. S. ___, ___ ___ (2012). Even if you are innocent, you will now join the 65 million Americans with an arrest record and experience the "civil death" of discrimination by employers, landlords, and whoever else conducts a background check. Of course, if you fail to pay bail or appear for court, a judge will issue a warrant to render you "arrestable on sight" in the future.

This case involves a *suspicionless* stop, one in which the officer initiated this chain of events without justification. This case tells everyone, white and black, guilty and innocent, that an officer can verify your legal status at any time. We must not pretend that the countless people who are routinely targeted by police are "isolated." They are the ones who recognize that unlawful police stops corrode all our civil liberties and threaten all our lives. I dissent.

JUSTICE KAGAN, with whom JUSTICE GINSBURG joins, dissenting.

The question here is whether the prohibition on admitting evidence dissolves if the officer discovers, after making the stop but before finding the drugs, that the person has an outstanding arrest warrant. Because that added wrinkle makes no difference under the Constitution, I respectfully dissent.

The exclusionary rule serves a crucial function—to deter unconstitutional police conduct. By barring the use of illegally obtained evidence, courts reduce the temptation for police officers to skirt the Fourth Amendment's requirements. But suppression of evidence also "exacts a heavy toll": Its consequence in many cases is to release a criminal without just punishment. Our decisions have thus endeavored to strike a sound balance between those two competing considerations— rejecting the "reflexive" impulse to exclude evidence every time an officer runs afoul of the Fourth Amendment, but insisting on suppression when it will lead to "appreciable deterrence" of police misconduct.

This case requires the Court to determine whether excluding the fruits of Officer Douglas Fackrell's unjustified stop would significantly deter police from committing similar constitutional violations in the future. That inquiry turns on application of the "attenuation doctrine." Since *Brown v. Illinois,* 422 U. S. 590 (1975), three factors have guided that analysis. First, the closer the "temporal proximity" between the unlawful act and the discovery of evidence, the greater the deterrent value of suppression. Second, the more "purposeful" or "flagrant" the police illegality, the clearer the necessity, and better the chance, of preventing similar misbehavior. And third, the presence (or absence) of "intervening circumstances" makes a difference: The stronger the causal chain between the misconduct and the evidence, the more exclusion will curb future constitutional violations. Each of those considerations points toward suppression: Nothing in Fackrell's discovery of an outstanding warrant so attenuated the connection between his wrongful behavior and his detection of drugs as to diminish the exclusionary rule's deterrent benefits.

The temporal proximity factor "favors suppressing the evidence." After all, Fackrell's discovery of drugs came just minutes after the unconstitutional stop. Only the lapse of "substantial time" between the two could favor admission. The majority chalks up Fackrell's Fourth Amendment violation to a couple of innocent "mistakes." It is not disputed that Fackrell stopped Strieff without reasonable suspicion. The illegality here had a quality of purposefulness. The impropriety of the stop was obvious. Fackrell embarked upon this expedition for evidence in the hope that something might turn up." Finally, consider whether any intervening circumstance "broke the causal chain" between the stop and the evidence. Fackrell's discovery of an arrest warrant—the only event the majority thinks intervened—was an eminently foreseeable consequence of stopping Strieff. The department's standard detention procedures—stop, ask for identification, run a check—are partly designed to find outstanding warrants. Find them they will, given the staggering number of such warrants on the books.

The majority's misapplication of *Brown*'s three-part inquiry creates unfortunate incentives for the police—indeed, practically invites them to do what Fackrell did here. Consider an officer who wishes to stop someone for investigative reasons, but does not have reasonable suspicion. If the officer believes that any evidence he discovers will be inadmissible, he is likely to think the unlawful stop not worth making—precisely the deterrence the exclusionary rule is meant to achieve. So long as the target is one of the many millions of people in this country with an outstanding arrest warrant, anything the officer finds in a search is fair game for use in a criminal prosecution. From here on, he sees potential advantage in stopping individuals without reasonable suspicion—exactly the temptation the exclusionary rule is supposed to remove. Because the majority thus places Fourth Amendment protections at risk, I respectfully dissent.

Hypo 1: *Identification as the "Fruit" of an Unlawful Arrest*

A woman was accosted and robbed at gunpoint by a man in the women's restroom at the Washington Monument. Six days later, two other women were assaulted and robbed in the same restroom. All three women gave the same description of the robber: a young male, 15–18 years old, approximately five feet, eight inches tall, slender in build, with a very dark complexion and smooth skin. When an officer spied respondent (who matched the description) in the vicinity of the Washington Monument restrooms, the officer took him into custody and transported him to the station where he was photographed and released. The detention was arguably illegal because, although the officer had a "reasonable suspicion," he lacked probable cause. Afterwards, police showed the victim of the first robbery an array of eight photographs. Although she had failed to identify the robber after previously viewing more than 100 pictures, she immediately identified respondent as her assailant. Afterwards, respondent was taken into custody and forced to participate in a lineup where he was positively identified by two victims. At respondent's trial, should the court suppress the photographic identifications and the lineup identification because of the illegal seizure? How would you argue the case for defendant? How might the prosecution respond? *See United States v. Crews*, 445 U.S. 463 (1980).

Hypo 2: *More on Identifications as "Fruits"*

In the prior hypo, instead of offering the photographic and lineup identifications in court, suppose that the prosecution seeks to have the witnesses identify respondent in court on the basis of their independent recollections. Should the witnesses be allowed to do so despite the illegal seizure? How would you argue the case for the defendant? How might the prosecution respond? How should the court rule? *See United States v. Crews*, 445 U.S. 463 (1980).

Hypo 3: *Confession as the "Fruit" of a Payton Violation?*

The police had probable cause to arrest Harris, but they arrested him at his home without an arrest warrant in contravention of *Payton v. New York*. Harris was *Mirandized* and admitted to committing a murder. Harris was then taken to the stationhouse where he was given a second *Miranda* warning and made a written incriminating statement. After reading Harris his rights a third time, the police videotaped his confession. Should the confession be suppressed as the "fruit" of an illegal arrest? *See New York v. Harris*, 495 U.S. 14 (1990).

Hypo 4: *Illegal Search Followed by Consent*

Police conduct a warrantless and illegal entry into defendant's garage, and use a drug sniffing dog that confirms the existence of marijuana. The police then leave the premises. When defendant's wife returns home, they ask her for permission to search the house, and she consents. Aware that the dog has alerted to the garage, police go there first and find a large quantity of marijuana. Should the prior illegal search render the subsequent consent invalid? How would you argue the case for the defendant? How might the state respond? *State v. Guillen*, 223 Ariz. 314, 223 P.3d 658 (2010).

Nix v. Williams

467 U.S. 431 (1984).

CHIEF JUSTICE BURGER delivered the opinion of the Court.

In *Brewer v. Williams*, the Court reversed Williams' murder conviction because it was based on a confession obtained in violation of his Sixth Amendment right to counsel. The Court found that the confession was deliberately elicited by the "Christian burial speech" that a police officer gave to respondent on route from Davenport to Des Moines. At Williams' second trial, the prosecution did not offer Williams' statements into evidence, nor did it seek to show that Williams had directed the police to the child's body. However, evidence of the condition of her body as it was found, articles and photographs of her clothing, and the results of post mortem medical and chemical tests on the body were admitted. The trial court concluded that the State had proved by a preponderance of the evidence that, if the search had not been suspended and Williams had not led the police to the victim, her body would have been discovered "within a short time" in essentially the same condition as it was actually found. The trial court also ruled that if the police had not located the body, "the search would clearly have been taken up again where it left off, given the extreme circumstances of this case and the body would have been found in short order." In finding that the body would have been discovered in essentially the same condition as it was actually found, the court noted that freezing temperatures had prevailed and tissue deterioration would have been suspended. The challenged evidence was admitted and the jury again found Williams guilty of first-degree murder; he was sentenced to life in prison. After respondent's conviction was affirmed, he sought a writ of habeas corpus challenging his conviction. The court denied the writ. The Eighth Circuit Court of Appeals reversed finding that, whether or not the body would have been discovered, suppression was required because the police acted in bad faith. We granted certiorari and we reverse.

The "vast majority" of courts, both state and federal, recognize an inevitable discovery exception to the exclusionary rule. We are now urged to adopt and apply the so-called ultimate or inevitable discovery exception to the exclusionary rule.

Williams contends that evidence of the body's location and condition is "fruit of the poisonous tree," *i.e.*, the "fruit" or product of Detective Leaming's plea to help the child's parents give her "a Christian burial," which this Court had already held equated to interrogation. He contends that admitting the challenged evidence violated the Sixth Amendment whether it would have been inevitably discovered or not. Williams also contends that, if the inevitable discovery doctrine is constitutionally permissible, it must include a threshold showing of police good faith.

The doctrine requiring courts to suppress evidence as the tainted "fruit" of unlawful governmental conduct had its genesis in *Silverthorne Lumber Co. v. United States*, 251 U.S. 385 (1920); there, the Court held that the exclusionary rule applies not only to the illegally obtained evidence itself, but also to other incriminating evidence derived from the primary evidence. The holding was carefully limited, for the Court emphasized that such information does not automatically become "sacred and inaccessible." "If knowledge of such facts is gained from an independent source, they may be proved like any others."

The core rationale consistently advanced by this Court for extending the exclusionary rule to evidence that is the fruit of unlawful police conduct has been that this admittedly drastic and socially costly course is needed to deter police from violations of constitutional and statutory protections. This Court has accepted the argument that the way to ensure such protections is to exclude evidence seized as a result of such violations notwithstanding the high social cost of letting persons obviously guilty go unpunished for their crimes. On this rationale, the prosecution is not to be put in a better position than it would have been in if no illegality had transpired.

By contrast, the derivative evidence analysis ensures that the prosecution is not put in a worse position simply because of some earlier police error or misconduct. The independent source doctrine allows admission of evidence that has been discovered by means wholly independent of any constitutional violation. That doctrine, although closely related to the inevitable discovery doctrine, does not apply here; Williams' statements to Leaming indeed led police to the child's body. The independent source doctrine teaches us that the interest of society in deterring unlawful police conduct and the public interest in having juries receive all probative evidence of a crime are properly balanced by putting the police in the same, not a worse, position than they would have been in if no police error or misconduct had occurred. When the challenged evidence has an independent source, exclusion of such evidence would put the police in a worse position than they would have been in absent any error or violation. Thus, while the independent source exception would not justify admission of evidence in this case, its rationale is wholly consistent with and justifies our adoption of the ultimate or inevitable discovery exception to the exclusionary rule.

Cases implementing the exclusionary rule "begin with the premise that the challenged evidence is the product of illegal governmental activity." *United States v. Crews*, 445 U.S. 463 (1980). This does not end the inquiry. If the prosecution can establish by a preponderance of the evidence that the information ultimately or inevitably would have been discovered by lawful means—here the volunteers' search—then the deterrence rationale has so little basis that the evidence should be received.[5] Anything less would reject logic, experience, and common sense.

---

[5] Williams argues that the preponderance-of-the-evidence standard is inconsistent with *United States v. Wade*, 388 U.S. 218 (1967). In requiring clear and convincing evidence of an independent source for

The requirement that the prosecution must prove the absence of bad faith would place courts in the position of withholding from juries relevant and undoubted truth that would have been available to police absent any unlawful police activity. That view would put the police in a worse position than they would have been in if no unlawful conduct had transpired. Of equal importance, it wholly fails to take into account the enormous societal cost of excluding truth in the search for truth in the administration of justice. Nothing in this Court's prior holdings supports any such formalistic, pointless, and punitive approach.

The Court of Appeals concluded that if an absence-of-bad-faith requirement were not imposed, "the temptation to risk deliberate violations of the Sixth Amendment would be too great, and the deterrent effect of the Exclusionary Rule reduced too far." We reject that view. A police officer who is faced with the opportunity to obtain evidence illegally will rarely, if ever, be in a position to calculate whether the evidence sought would inevitably be discovered. On the other hand, when an officer is aware that the evidence will inevitably be discovered, there will be little to gain from taking any dubious "shortcuts" to obtain the evidence. Significant disincentives to obtaining evidence illegally—including the possibility of departmental discipline and civil liability—also lessen the likelihood that the ultimate or inevitable discovery exception will promote police misconduct. In these circumstances, the societal costs of the exclusionary rule far outweigh any possible benefits to deterrence that a good-faith requirement might produce.

Williams contends that because he did not waive his right to the assistance of counsel, the Court may not balance competing values in deciding whether the challenged evidence was properly admitted. He argues that the Sixth Amendment exclusionary rule is designed to protect the right to a fair trial and the integrity of the factfinding process. Williams contends that, when those interests are at stake, the societal costs of excluding evidence obtained from responses presumed involuntary are irrelevant in determining whether such evidence should be excluded. We disagree. Exclusion of physical evidence that would inevitably have been discovered adds nothing to either the integrity or fairness of a criminal trial. Here, Detective Leaming's conduct did nothing to impugn the reliability of the evidence in question—the body of the child and its condition as it was found, articles of clothing found on the body, and the autopsy. Suppression, in these circumstances, would do nothing whatever to promote the integrity of the trial process, but would inflict a wholly unacceptable burden on the administration of criminal justice.

---

an in-court identification, the Court gave weight to the effect an uncounseled pretrial identification has in "crystallizing the witnesses' identification of the defendant for future reference." The Court noted as well that possible unfairness at the lineup "may be the sole means of attack upon the unequivocal courtroom identification," and recognized the difficulty of determining whether an in-court identification was based on independent recollection unaided by the lineup identification. By contrast, inevitable discovery involves no speculative elements but focuses on demonstrated historical facts capable of ready verification or impeachment and does not require a departure from the usual burden of proof at suppression hearings.

Nor would suppression ensure fairness on the theory that it tends to safeguard the adversary system of justice. If the government can prove that the evidence would have been obtained inevitably and, therefore, would have been admitted regardless of any overreaching by the police, there is no rational basis to keep that evidence from the jury in order to ensure the fairness of the trial proceedings. The State has gained no advantage at trial and the defendant has suffered no prejudice. Indeed, suppression of the evidence would operate to undermine the adversary system by putting the State in a worse position than it would have occupied without any police misconduct.

More than a half century ago, Judge, later Justice, Cardozo made his seminal observation that under the exclusionary rule "the criminal is to go free because the constable has blundered." Prophetically, he went on to consider "how far-reaching in its effect upon society" the exclusionary rule would be when "the pettiest peace officer would have it in his power through overzeal or indiscretion to confer immunity upon an offender for crimes the most flagitious." Some day, Cardozo speculated, some court might press the exclusionary rule to the outer limits of its logic—or beyond—and suppress evidence relating to the "body of a murdered" victim because of the means by which it was found. When, as here, the evidence in question would inevitably have been discovered without reference to the police error or misconduct, there is no nexus sufficient to provide a taint and the evidence is admissible.

Three courts independently reviewing the evidence have found that the body of the child inevitably would have been found by the searchers. The prosecution offered the testimony of Agent Ruxlow of the Iowa Bureau of Criminal Investigation. Ruxlow had organized and directed some 200 volunteers who were searching for the child's body. The searchers were instructed "to check all the roads, the ditches, any culverts. If they came upon any abandoned farm buildings, they were instructed to go onto the property and search those abandoned farm buildings or any other places where a small child could be secreted." Ruxlow testified that he marked off highway maps of Poweshiek and Jasper Counties in grid fashion, divided the volunteers into teams of four to six persons, and assigned each team to search specific grid areas. Ruxlow also testified that, if the search had not been suspended because of Williams' promised cooperation, it would have continued into Polk County, using the same grid system. Although he had previously marked off into grids only the highway maps of Poweshiek and Jasper Counties, Ruxlow had obtained a map of Polk County, which he said he would have marked off in the same manner had it been necessary for the search to continue.

The search had commenced at approximately 10 a.m. and moved westward through Poweshiek County into Jasper County. At approximately 3 p.m., after Williams had volunteered to cooperate with the police, Detective Leaming, who was in the police car with Williams, sent word to Ruxlow and the other Special

Agent directing the search and the search was suspended at that time. The search was not resumed once it was learned that Williams had led the police to the body, which was found two and one-half miles from where the search had stopped in what would have been the easternmost grid to be searched in Polk County. There was testimony that it would have taken an additional three to five hours to discover the body if the search had continued; the body was found near a culvert, one of the kinds of places the teams had been specifically directed to search.

On this record it is clear that the search parties were approaching the actual location of the body, and we are satisfied that the volunteer search teams would have resumed the search had Williams not earlier led the police to the body and the body inevitably would have been found. The evidence asserted by Williams as newly discovered, *i.e.*, certain photographs of the body and deposition testimony of Agent Ruxlow made in connection with the federal habeas proceeding, does not demonstrate that the material facts were inadequately developed in the suppression hearing in state court or that Williams was denied a full, fair, and adequate opportunity to present all relevant facts at the suppression hearing.

The judgment of the Court of Appeals is reversed, and the case is remanded for further proceedings consistent with this opinion.

It is so ordered.

Justice Stevens, concurring in the judgment.

Williams I grew out of a line of cases in which this Court made it clear that the adversarial process protected by the Sixth Amendment may not be undermined by the strategems [sic] of the police. The now-familiar plaint that "'the criminal is to go free because the constable has blundered,'" is entirely beside the point. More pertinent is what the chief justice wrote for the Court on another occasion: "This is not a case where 'the constable blundered,' rather, it is one where the 'constable' planned an impermissible interference with the right to the assistance of counsel."

Admission of the victim's body, if it would have been discovered anyway, means that the trial was not the product of an inquisitorial process; that process was untainted by illegality. The good or bad faith of Detective Leaming is therefore simply irrelevant. If the trial process was not tainted as a result of his conduct, this defendant received the type of trial that the Sixth Amendment envisions. The prosecution cannot escape responsibility for a constitutional violation through speculation. The need to adduce proof sufficient to discharge its burden, and the difficulty in predicting whether such proof will be available or sufficient, means that the inevitable discovery rule does not permit state officials to avoid the uncertainty they would have faced but for the constitutional violation.

The majority refers to the "societal cost" of excluding probative evidence. The more relevant cost is that imposed on society by police officers who decide to take procedural shortcuts instead of complying with the law. What is the consequence of the shortcut that Detective Leaming took when he decided to question Williams in this case and not to wait an hour or so until he arrived in Des Moines? The answer is years and years of unnecessary but costly litigation. Thanks to Detective Leaming, the State of Iowa has expended vast sums of money and countless hours of professional labor in his defense. That expenditure surely provides an adequate deterrent to similar violations; the responsibility for that expenditure lies not with the Constitution, but rather with the constable. Accordingly, I concur in the Court's judgment.

JUSTICE BRENNAN, with whom JUSTICE MARSHALL joins, dissenting.

The "inevitable discovery" exception to the exclusionary rule is consistent with the requirements of the Constitution. I would require clear and convincing evidence before concluding that the government had met its burden of proof on this issue. Increasing the burden of proof serves to impress the fact finder with the importance of the decision and thereby reduces the risk that illegally obtained evidence will be admitted. I would remand this case for application of this heightened burden of proof by the lower courts in the first instance.

Point for Discussion

Independent Source

In *Segura v. United States*, 468 U.S. 796 (1984), the police had probable cause to search Segura's apartment. However, because it was evening, they decided to secure the apartment until a warrant could be obtained the next day. After entering, the police made a limited check to make sure that no one was present who might pose a threat to their safety or destroy evidence. During this search, the police found evidence of drug trafficking in plain view, but did not disturb it. Because of administrative delays, the warrant was not obtained until 5 p.m. the next day, and the apartment was not searched until 6 p.m. (approximately 19 hours after the initial entry). The search turned up the items discovered the night before, as well as cocaine, 18 rounds of ammunition, more than $50,000 cash, and records of narcotics transactions. Defendants were convicted of conspiring to distribute cocaine, and of distributing and possessing with intent to distribute cocaine based, in part, on the evidence seized. The Court concluded that the initial seizure of the apartment was "reasonable," and that there was an "independent source" for the evidence: "Whether the initial entry was illegal or not is irrelevant to the admissibility of the challenged evidence because there was an independent source for the warrant under which that evidence was seized. None of the information on which the warrant was secured was derived from or related in any way to the initial entry into petitioners' apartment; the information came from sources wholly unconnected with the entry and was known to the agents well before the initial entry. It is therefore beyond dispute that the information possessed by the agents before they entered the apartment constituted an independent source for the discovery and seizure of the evidence now challenged. The valid warrant search was a 'means sufficiently distinguishable' to purge the evidence of any 'taint' arising from the entry." The Court rejected the argument that suppression was appropriate because the evidence might have been destroyed had the officers not secured the apartment: "the essence of the dissent is that there is some 'constitutional right' to destroy evidence. This concept defies both logic and common sense." Justice Stevens, joined by three other justices, dissented, arguing that "the agents' access to the fruits of the authorized search was a product of illegal conduct. If Segura had not returned home at all that night, or during the next day, it is probable that the occupants of the apartment would have become concerned and might have destroyed the records of their illegal transactions, or removed some of the evidence. If so, then that evidence would not have been accessible to the agents when the warrant finally was executed. If the evidence would not have been available to the agents at the time they finally executed the warrant had they not illegally entered and impounded petitioners' apartment, then it cannot be said that the agents' access to the evidence was 'independent' of the prior illegality. If we are to give more than lipservice to protection of the core constitutional interests that were twice violated in this case, some effort must be made to isolate and then remove the advantages the Government derived from its illegal conduct."

In *State v. Winterstein*, 167 Wash.2d 620, 220 P.3d 1226 (2009), the State of Washington's Supreme Court held that the inevitable discovery doctrine is incompatible with Washington's Constitution: "Based on the intent of the framers of the Washington Constitution, we have held that the choice of their language 'mandates that the right of privacy shall not be diminished by the judicial gloss of a selectively applied exclusionary remedy.' Because the intent was to protect personal rights rather than curb government actions, 'whenever the right is unreasonably violated, the remedy must follow.' The constitutionally mandated exclusionary rule provides a remedy for individuals whose rights have been violated and protects the integrity of the judicial system by not tainting the proceedings with illegally obtained evidence. Because of textual differences, state action may be valid under the Fourth Amendment but violate article I, section 7." Is the Washington approach preferable?

Food for Thought

In *Nix*, the Court emphasized the fact that the weather was sub-freezing and that the victim's body was preserved by the cold against deterioration. Had the search taken place in mid-summer, should the Court have reached a different result? Would that fact have made the discovery less "inevitable?"

Hypo 1: *Proving Inevitable Discovery*

In a murder case like *Nix*, the prosecution is able to prove inevitability by pointing to the fact that a search was already underway, and demonstrating that this search was likely to have uncovered the body. But suppose that the search had not begun at the time of the so-called Christian Burial Speech. Would it still have been possible for the prosecution to show inevitability? If so, how?

Hypo 2: *Inevitable Discovery and the Kidnapped Girl*

A teenage girl disappears, and police believe that she has been kidnapped. Johnson becomes a suspect when the police search the girl's cell phone, and find sexually explicit messages from him. If the police decide to make an illegal warrantless search of Johnson's home, can they argue that any evidence that they found would have been "inevitably discovered" because of the cell phone messages? Would you apply the exception if Johnson made calls to the girl's cell phone just prior to her disappearance? What if GPS tracking data shows that Johnson's phone had traveled from New Mexico (where he lived) to California (where the girl lived), and back, just prior to the disappearance? What if a police investigator goes to Johnson's home, peers through the window, and sees Christy engaged in sex with an unidentified teenage girl? *See United States v. Christy*, 810 F. Supp. 2d 1219 (D. Mexico 2014).

Food for Thought

Suppose that a police officer randomly pulls a motorist over and illegally searches his car (without a warrant, probable cause, or any other basis for the search). The trial court suppresses the evidence as the fruit of an illegal search. Would it be possible for the prosecution to prove inevitable discovery? If so, how?

Hypo 3: *The Inventory Exception and Inevitable Discovery*

When Ruckes is stopped for speeding, police learn that his license has been suspended and place him under arrest. The officer searches the vehicle and finds that it contains cocaine and a firearm (prohibited because he is a convicted felon). Although the search is invalid under *Arizona v. Gant*, the state claims that the evidence should be admitted under the inevitable discovery doctrine. The state claims that Ruckes would not have been allowed to drive the car away (since his license had been suspended), could not have driven the car because he was subject to a custodial arrest, and there was no one else available to assume control of the car. Hence, the police were going to impound the vehicle, and would have subjected it to an inventory search that would have turned up the cocaine and the firearm. Should the inevitable discovery doctrine apply under such circumstances? *See United States v. Ruckes*, 586 F.3d 713 (9th Cir. 2009). Would it matter whether local procedures specifically permit impoundment of a vehicle whenever an individual is found to be driving without a valid license? *See United States v. Cartwright*, 630 F.3d 610 (2010).

Hypo 4: *Inevitable Discovery and Subpoenas*

The government, trying to prove health care fraud, obtains a doctor's medical records pursuant to a search of his medical offices. When the doctor moves to suppress the results of the search, the government claims that discovery of the records was "inevitable" because the government could have subpoenaed the records. How does the government go about proving that discovery of this information was "inevitable"? Would it matter whether the government had served subpoenas on this particular doctor in the past, or against other doctors? Would it matter whether the government had actually contemplated obtaining this particular information by subpoena? *See United States v. Lazar*, 604 F.3d 230 (6th Cir. 2010).

Hypo 5: *An Independent Source?*

Working with the police, Sutton (a police informer) makes a series of telephone calls and texts to Moody (a dealer) requesting methamphetamine, and she arranges to meet him to complete the transaction. Law enforcement officials stop Moody on his way to meet with Sutton. During the stop, the police examine Moody's cell phone records and note that he has made a number of phone calls to a person identified in the cell phone records only as "G." Moody was convicted of distribution of illegal narcotics. Following Moody's release from prison, he resumes selling methamphetamine. One of the people to whom he regularly sells methamphetamine is Donald Blair, who resells it to others. Eventually, Blair who is cooperating with the police, seeks to make a controlled purchase of methamphetamine from Moody. Law enforcement place audio/video recording devices in Blair's house, and Blair himself is outfitted with an audio/video recording device. While Moody is at Blair's apartment and under the surveillance of officers, Moody receives a call on his cell phone from a man later identified as Moody's methamphetamine source (a/k/a, "G"). Moody indicates during the phone conversation that he will leave Blair's apartment to meet his methamphetamine source to obtain additional supplies. Surveillance officers follow Moody to a nearby truck stop where they observe a blue vehicle pull up beside Moody's truck. A Hispanic male (later identified as Gonzalo Gutierrez or "G") leaves the blue vehicle and enters Moody's truck. He remains in Moody's truck for approximately two minutes and then returns to his vehicle and drives away. Officers follow both Moody and Gutierrez, and eventually stop Gutierrez for speeding. Gutierrez is arrested and his vehicle is impounded. During an inventory search of the vehicle, officers find $6,290 in cash and a cell phone. Some of the currency seized from Gutierrez's vehicle matches the currency Blair gave to Moody earlier that day. Suppose that the police officers' initial search and seizure of Moody's cell phone (in which they learned about "G") was illegal. Did the police develop an independent source for the information so that there is nothing prohibiting the admission of that evidence against either Moody or Gutierrez? *See United States v. Moody*, 664 F.3d 164 (7th Cir. 2011).

> ## Hypo 6: *Proving Inevitable Discovery*
>
> Suppose that the police have probable cause to obtain a search warrant for a home. They suspect that there is a marijuana growing operation inside the house because a bail bondsman informed police that he saw it. Instead of obtaining a warrant, the police go immediately to the house where they seek consent to search. Although the consent is given, a reviewing later finds that the consent is invalid. Is the evidence obtained as a result of the search admissible anyway under the inevitable discovery exception? Should it matter whether police have taken any steps towards obtaining a warrant? *See Rodriguez v. State*, 187 So.3d 841 (Fl. 2015).

Executive Summary

The Exclusionary Rule's Function. The exclusionary evidence rule precludes the state from using evidence seized in violation of a defendant's constitutional rights to convict the defendant of a crime. Although the rule is frequently applied to violations of Fourth Amendment rights, it can be invoked to exclude evidence obtained in violation of other constitutional rights as well. The exclusionary rule has been applied in federal cases since the United States Supreme Court's 1914 decision in *Weeks v. United States*, 232 U.S. 383 (1914). However, the Court did not mandate its application in state proceedings until 1961 in *Mapp v. Ohio*, 367 U.S. 643 (1961).

The Good Faith Exception to the Exclusionary Rule. Because of the perceived "costs" of the exclusionary rule, some police and law enforcement officials have pressed for limitations on the exclusionary rule. In *United States v. Leon*, 468 U.S. 897 (1984), the Court created the "good faith" exception to the exclusionary rule. In doing so, the Court emphasized that the exclusionary rule is not constitutionally mandated, but instead is a judicially created remedy that is designed to safeguard Fourth Amendment rights by deterring police misconduct. Emphasizing the "substantial social costs" that the rule imposes, including the fact some guilty defendants may go free or receive reduced sentences as a result of favorable plea bargains, the Court concluded that the costs are too high "when law enforcement officers have acted in objective good faith or their transgressions have been minor."

The *Leon* Balancing Test. In *Leon*, the Court established a balancing test to use in evaluating the propriety of applying the exclusionary rule in a given case. The Court balances the costs of exclusion (principally, the notion that an innocent individual might go free) against the benefits (deterrence of police misconduct). In *Leon*, because the police relied in good faith on a warrant issued by a neutral and detached magistrate, the Court concluded that the costs of exclusion outweighed the benefits because one cannot hope to deter police who are acting in good faith reliance on a magistrate's finding of probable cause.

Situations When the Good Faith Exception is Inapplicable. The Court has found that good faith does not exist when the magistrate or judge who issued a warrant was misled by information in an affidavit that the affiant knew was false or would have known was false except for his reckless disregard of the truth, when the issuing magistrate wholly abandoned his judicial role, when the warrant is based on an affidavit "so lacking in indicia of probable cause as to render official belief in its existence entirely unreasonable," or "when the warrant is so facially deficient—*i.e.*, in failing to particularize the place to be searched or the things to be seized—that the executing officers cannot reasonably presume it to be valid." In these circumstances, the executing officers may be subject to civil liability.

Major Themes

a. The Exclusionary Rule's Function - The exclusionary evidence rule precludes the state from using evidence seized in violation of a defendant's constitutional rights to convict the defendant of a crime. In general, the exclusionary rule is applied when the benefits of applying it (deterrence of police misconduct) outweigh the costs. As a result, the Court has refused to apply the rule in some situations in which the police act in good faith, as well as in various other situations.

b. Limitations and Expansions of the Exclusionary Rule - The courts have applied a variety of principles that limit application of the exclusionary rule, including the requirement of standing and the concept of harmless error. They have also applied the "fruit of the poisonous tree" doctrine that tends to expand the scope of the exclusionary rule.

Proceedings When the Exclusionary Rule Does Not Apply. The Court has refused to apply the exclusionary rule in a variety of contexts: in grand jury proceedings when witnesses are asked about evidence obtained from an unlawful search or seizure; in federal civil proceedings; when a warrant is invalid because of a "technical error" by the issuing judge; when the police made a warrantless search in good faith reliance on a local law authorizing warrantless searches; when the police relied in good faith on precedent that was later overruled; when a police officer made an arrest based on an outstanding arrest warrant, but the warrant was invalid due to a negligent bookkeeping error; and when police officers, executing a search warrant, violated the "knock and announce" requirement. Although *Leon's* logic suggest that the good faith exception should apply when an officer makes a warrantless search in "good faith," the Court has extended the good faith exception to some warrantless searches (*e.g.*, good faith reliance on an invalid statute authorizing warrantless searches). However, as a general rule, the exception does not apply to warrantless searches.

Standing, the Exclusionary Rule, and the Fifth Amendment. Standing concepts limit the exclusionary rule's application. In the Fifth Amendment area, the Court treats the privilege against self-incrimination as "personal" and has held that it can only be asserted by the person whose rights have been violated. Even though the Fourth Amendment is not phrased in such personal terms, the Court has also applied the standing requirement to Fourth Amendment violations. At one point, the standing requirement was modified by an "automatic standing" rule. Automatic Standing no longer exists.

Standing in the Fourth Amendment Context. In the Fourth Amendment context, an individual can establish standing by showing that he owns or possesses the place that was searched, or that the police violated his "reasonable expectation of privacy" (REOP). Although an overnight guest may have a REOP in the place where he is staying, those who visit a house for only a short period of time may not. An individual who puts contraband in a friend's purse may not have a REOP in the purse.

Fruit of the Poisonous Tree Doctrine. When the exclusionary rule is applied, it prohibits the prosecution from using evidence directly obtained from a constitutional violation. Thus, if the police coerce a suspect into confessing, the exclusionary rule prohibits the use of that confession. The "derivative evidence rule," also known as the "Fruit of the Poisonous Tree" doctrine, prohibits the police from using other evidence "derived" from the direct evidence. In some instances, it is possible to "purge the taint" of illegal conduct so that it will not be treated as "fruit of the poisonous tree. The administration of *Miranda* warnings can be a factor in purging the taint, but it is only a factor. Courts will examine a variety of factors in determining whether the taint of a confession has been purged, including "the temporal proximity of the arrest and the confession, the presence of intervening circumstances, and, particularly, the purpose and flagrancy of the official misconduct are all relevant. The voluntariness of the statement is a threshold requirement. And the burden of showing admissibility rests on the prosecution." The Court has held that police failure to give the

Test Your Knowledge

To assess your understanding of the material in this chapter, click here to take a quiz.

Miranda warnings does not require suppression of the physical fruits of a defendant's unwarned statements, and they have held that a witness located through an illegal search need not be suppressed. In addition, courts have refused to apply the exclusionary rule when the "fruits" would have inevitably been discovered, as well as when the police have an "independent source" for the evidence.

For More Information

• WAYNE R. LaFAVE, JEROLD H. ISRAEL, NANCY J. KING & ORIN S. KERR, CRIMINAL PROCEDURE (5th ed. 2009).

• RUSSELL L. WEAVER, JOHN M. BURKOFF, CATHERINE HANCOCK, JANET HOEFFEL, STEVE FRIEDLAND & STEPHEN SINGER, PRINCIPLES OF CRIMINAL PROCEDURE Ch. 8 (6th ed. 2018).

CHAPTER 9

Introduction to the Adversary System

Unlike criminal justice systems in many parts of the world, the American criminal justice system is an adversary system. A criminal defendant's guilt or innocence is determined as a result of the adversarial arguments and presentations of evidence by a prosecutor and defense counsel, overseen by a neutral and impartial judge.

While such a system has the immediate virtue of familiarity to most Americans, it is difficult if not impossible to argue that this method of adjudication is the *only* fair way to determine the guilt or innocence of criminal defendants. Indeed, some commentators argue that the American adversarial system, in practice if not in theory, is not truly fair at all. In the face of such criticisms, it is worthwhile to consider whether or not an adversary criminal adjudication model is and continues to be the most appropriate way to try criminal defendants in this country. And, even if we decide on balance that it is, what does that mean in terms of the appropriate roles of defense counsel and prosecutors?

A. Costs and Benefits

Richard Klein—The Role of Defense Counsel In Ensuring a Fair Justice System

36 The Champion 38, 38-39, 43-44 (June 2012).

Warrior for justice. Maybe this is overly romanticized, but it is how I see the role of the criminal defense attorney. The defense attorney is on the front lines doing, if not God's work, surely something quite close to it. And, as is true with anything that

Who's That?

Richard Klein is Bruce K. Gould Distinguished Professor of Law at Touro Law Center. He worked for ten years as a trial attorney with the Criminal Defense Division of the Legal Aid Society of New York, New York County.

important, the work is anything but easy. Obstacles, barriers, and road blocks are on the path.

Defense counsel may accurately be considered law enforcers. While representing a lone individual against all the power of the state, counsel must "police the police" to determine if there has been an unconstitutional search, a coerced confession, an unlawfully suggestive lineup, or the fabrication of testimony. Defense counsel must attempt to ensure that the prosecutor is adhering to the professional requirement not merely to convict, but to do justice and comply with his obligations to turn over exculpatory material to the defense. Perhaps most challenging of all is the need to remind the judge of the constitutional mandate as well as the professional obligation to protect the rights of the defendant rather than treat him as a docket number to be quickly processed and sent to jail.

Supreme Court decisions are replete with statements about how crucial it is to have a defense attorney represent the person who is accused of crime:

> Even the intelligent and educated layman has small and sometimes no skill in the science of law. If charged with crime, he is incapable, generally, of determining for himself whether the indictment is good or bad. He is unfamiliar with the rules of evidence. Left without the aid of counsel he may be put on trial without a proper charge, and convicted upon incompetent evidence, or evidence irrelevant to the issue or otherwise inadmissible. He lacks both the skill and knowledge adequately to prepare his defense, even though he have a perfect one. He requires the guiding hand of counsel at every step in the proceedings against him. Without it, though he be not guilty, he faces the danger of conviction because he does not know how to establish his innocence. If that be true of men of intelligence, how much more true is it of the ignorant and illiterate, or those of feeble intellect.

It is somewhat odd to be doing (almost) God's work, yet to have so few people acknowledge the vital import of the work. When we challenge the validity of the search of a home by the police, we are not just representing a single individual. When vigorous advocacy informs the police that they will not be able to "get away with" an illegal, unconstitutional search of a particular person's home, the benefits accrue to and protect us all. If we did not keep them honest, or as honest as we can keep them, there would be

Take Note

Don't miss the "religious" imagery here. Many lawyers, judges, and legal commentators believe that criminal defense counsel should be "zealots" for their clients. A "zealot" is, of course, a person who is fanatical and uncompromising in pursuit of his or her religious, political, or other ideals. Indeed, many argue that zealousness is an obligation that outweighs the importance of a criminal trial as a (supposed) search for truth. Are you troubled by a professional obligation of this sort?

nothing to deter the police from entering any of our homes at will. One can succeed, probably, in not committing a crime, but may not be as successful in not being charged with a crime.

It is appropriate to view the role of the criminal defense attorney as, in some ways, that of a constitutional lawyer. We attempt to protect clients from violations of their Fourth Amendment rights by unlawful searches and seizures, their Fifth Amendment rights by coerced confessions, their Sixth Amendment rights by a lawyer who is not totally effective in all respects, and their Eight Amendment right to not be subjected to a sentence that is grossly disproportionate to the crime committed. We attempt to compensate for the severe racial disparities of those arrested and prosecuted by combating the prosecutorial and judicial abuse of discretion against minorities and to secure the equal protection of the laws. And underlying it all is our commitment to due process and our sometimes desperate struggles to have criminal proceedings that are fundamentally fair.

These battles are against odds that certainly appear to be overwhelming at times. The discrepancy between the resources available to the prosecutor and those for counsel for the indigent is legendary. The prosecutor has not only the tools of an office that is better funded, but typically has police department investigators and laboratory technicians available as well. Eighty percent of prosecutions nationwide are against indigents who are represented by a public defender's office, a private not-for-profit corporation such as a legal aid society, or court-appointed private attorneys. Things are certainly

Food for Thought

A successful suppression motion typically results in the suppression of "truth," e.g. the defendant really *did* "possess" the suppressed drugs and she really was "guilty" of possession of narcotics; *or* the defendant really *did* kill his victim as his now-suppressed, un-*Mirandized*, inculpatory statement baldly conceded. Are the values of our adversary system sufficiently important to us that they outweigh the value of ascertaining the truth in criminal proceedings? What do you think?

not getting easier. The recession has hit the criminal defense bar with full force. As states find themselves with fewer available funds, indigent defense monies are hard hit. Fire departments, police, schools, parks and libraries all have their constituents who fight aggressively against cutbacks. There is virtually no constituency for the indigent defendant charged with crime—none, except the Sixth Amendment.

Watching an arraignment in many of the large urban areas throughout the country can be an embarrassment for anyone concerned with a fair justice system. It can be assembly line justice at its worst. Human being after human being parades in front of the judge. Often, the only information brought before the court is what is in the police report. The prosecutor informs the judge of the accusation, and the judge assumes guilt. The defense counsel often has little or no information to add; there is no presumption of innocence. It is hard for anyone involved in this process to maintain their dignity. What is the proper response for the defender who is most concerned with a fair justice system? Defense counsel should strive to ensure that there is an awareness that these courts need to be concerned with preserving the due process protections of the Constitution.

The title of this article assumes that there is a fair justice system in America, but it is hard to claim that justice is fair for many of our clients. The lack of adequate funding for indigent defense services is sorely lacking and, therefore, many defenders have such extensive caseloads as to bring into doubt whether the mandate of *Gideon* has been met. No defender can provide effective assistance to his clients if he simply has too many of them.

Our work is so extraordinarily crucial. We struggle against all odds to bring truth to "Equal Justice Under the Law," when we see the reality of the treatment of the minorities and the poor by the criminal justice system. We fight for "Liberty and Justice for All," when we know that some of our clients have no liberty and are incarcerated in overcrowded jails simply because they have no funds for bail

Food for Thought

Do you agree? Does our criminal justice system operate in such a way that unfairness is intrinsic for many defendants? Can you imagine a criminal justice system (in the American context) that works differently . . . and works fairly, to boot?

and, therefore, cannot afford liberty. The Sixth Amendment right to counsel does not serve merely to supplement other constitutional rights. It is the basic right that serves to enable an individual to exercise his other constitutional rights. Counsel is there to ensure that the procedural protections, which exist on paper, are actually applied. This is no easy task. The best of us, the most passionate of us, the most committed of us, go beyond just perceiving the job as one that "the adversary system and our constitution requires to be done;" we add, "by me."

W. William Hodes—Seeking the Truth Versus Telling the Truth At the Boundaries of the Law: Misdirection, Lying, and "Lying With An Explanation"

44 S. Tex. L. Rev. 53, 57-62 (2002).

One of the most brutal clashes between competing values is that between "truth" and "justice," with implications for the very nature of the legal system itself. Finding the truth and then resolving disputes on the basis of that truth ranks very highly in our value system. But so does achieving justice, even though justice as Peter defines it, it will often be purchased at Paul's expense, and even though some of the truth is frequently obscured or even sacrificed along the way. And, of course, the elusive and essentially fatuous concept of "the whole truth" is always lost in the fog of adversarial combat.

Who's That?

W. William Hodes is Professor of Law Emeritus at the Indiana University Robert H. McKinney School of Law, and is currently engaged in solo law practice at The William Hodes Law Firm in Florida.

The tension between truth on the one hand, and justice on the other-the latter often equated in our culture simply with winning-has long engaged both the legal profession and the public. This clash of values arises most dramatically in the context of high profile criminal trials, which correspondingly receive the most media attention and public debate.

The public is offended enough when a criminal defense is based on suppression of evidence or some other legal or "technical" defense. But that pales in comparison to the outrage expressed when it appears that the defense lawyers knew the truth of a client's factual guilt, but nonetheless attempted to achieve an acquittal on the merits. This is often seen as a form of "lying," and it must be conceded that the lawyer's plan in such a case is to induce the jury to come to a conclusion that the lawyer knows is factually wrong, namely that someone other than the accused physically did the deeds in question.

Defense lawyers, on the other hand, and allies in the bar generally, are typically angered by such attacks, and point to a lawyer's obligation-rooted in both professional ethics and in the Sixth Amendment to the United States Constitution-to use all legal means to mount a defense, whether or not the client is known to be factually guilty. More important, for present purposes, they reject any claim that they have "lied," if no false evidence has been introduced, and if they have engaged only in argumentation, pointing out inconsistencies and trying to punch logical holes in the government's case, and suggesting alternative "narratives" that the jury is free to accept or reject.

Take Note

Hodes clearly strikes a more "moderate" tone than Professor Klein in the preceding article excerpt, but note that he still contends that the present balance between zealous representation and concern for the truth has been struck correctly.

This quarrel can be seen as no more than a variant on the distinction between active and passive behavior, but I prefer the shorthand implicit in the title of this essay-that while lawyers must tell the truth, they are not required to seek the truth or to aid in the search. Instead, they are often required by their roles to work to obscure inconvenient truths and to prevent the truth from coming out.

Moreover, although I have my moments of queasiness, like everyone else, and although I struggle along with everyone else to locate the exact boundary line between truth and justice, I am convinced that the law of lawyering has drawn this particular line roughly where it ought to be drawn.

Deborah L. Rhode—The Future of the Legal Profession: Institutionalizing Ethics

44 Case W. Res. L.Rev. 665, 667-73 (1994).

Who's That?

Deborah L. Rhode is the Ernest W. McFarland Professor of Law, the Director of the Center on the Legal Profession, and the Director of the Program in Law and Social Entrepreneurship at Stanford University.

The central norm of contemporary American legal practice is one of neutral partisanship; the attorney's role is to advance client interests "zealously within the bounds of the law" regardless of the attorney's own assessment of their underlying merits. Although lawyers have certain obligations as officers of the court, these are quite limited and largely track the prohibitions on criminal and fraudulent conduct that govern all participants in the legal process.

This neutral partisanship model rests on two assumptions. The first is that an adversarial clash between two zealous advocates is the best way to discover truth and to promote accurate legal decision making. A second assumption is that partisan advocacy provides the most effective protection for individual rights. [The] first assumption, that an adversarial clash yields accurate outcomes, is not self-evident. As many commentators have observed, this is not how most countries adjudicate disputes, how most professionals investigate facts, or even how most lawyers conduct inquiries outside the courtroom.

In an adversarial model, the merits prevail only if the contest is a balanced one-that is, if each side has roughly equal access to relevant legal information, resources, and capabilities. Yet how often a fully balanced contest occurs in practice is open to doubt. American lawyers practice in a social order that tolerates vast disparities in wealth, makes most litigation enormously expensive, and allocates civil legal assistance almost entirely through market mechanisms. Under these circumstances, one would expect that the "haves" generally come out ahead.

Among defenders of current partisan norms, the conventional "solution" to the problem of unequal advocacy "is not to impose on counsel the burden of representing interests other than those of his client, but rather to take appropriate steps to ensure that all interests are effectively represented." Exactly what those steps might be have never been satisfactorily elaborated. Inequalities in access have been seriously confronted only at a rhetorical level.

The unqualified pursuit of client interests carries obvious costs: It obstructs the decision-making process, imposes unnecessary delays and expense, and deters meritorious claims. In response to such criticisms, proponents of neutral partisanship typically invoke a second line of defense. Whatever its effectiveness or efficiency in promoting truth, this partisan framework is an indispensable safeguard of individual rights. On this view, respect for clients' autonomy implies respect for their pursuit of legal claims and demands largely undivided loyalty from their legal advisors. By absolving attorneys from accountability for clients' acts, the traditional advocacy role encourages representation of those most vulnerable to public prejudice and state oppression. The promise of non-judgmental advocacy may also encourage legal consultation by those most in need of ethical counseling. Any alternative system, it is argued, would threaten "rule by an oligarchy of lawyers." To demand that attorneys judge, rather than simply defend, their clients would be "equivalent to saying that saints must have a monopoly of lawsuits" and that the lawyers should have a monopoly of deciding who qualifies for sainthood.

From an ethical standpoint, this justification for neutral partisanship presents two central difficulties. First, it conflates legal and moral entitlements; it assumes that society wishes to permit whatever lawmakers do not prohibit. Yet some conduct that is clearly antithetical to broader public interests may nonetheless remain legal—either because prohibitions appear too difficult or costly to enforce, or because decision makers are too uninformed,

Food for Thought

Professor Rhode takes issue with other commentators' "neutral partisanship model" of criminal defense counsel's role, noting, *inter alia*, the costs of what she deems to be *excessively* partisan practices. Perhaps her strongest criticism is that such a model "fail[s] to explain why the rights of clients should trump those of all other parties whose interests are inadequately represented." What is your position on this question? Should criminal defense counsel consider interests other than his or her client's? Whose? The victim's? The victim's family's? The community's? Which community? Would you prefer a justice system where defense counsel is obliged to determine the client's guilt and, in essence, disclose it to the court? Doesn't such a system at least have the virtue of better producing the truth? Or does it? Is there any actor in such a (hypothesized) system who will make the effort to insure that the defendant is being treated fairly? Is that important? More or as important as discovering the truth? At the very minimum, you should see how hard these policy choices are to make.

overworked, or pressured by special interests. Although lawyers may have no special moral expertise, they at least have a more disinterested perspective than clients on the ethical dimensions of certain practices. Attorneys can accept moral responsibility without necessarily imposing it. Unless the lawyer is the last in town, his or her refusal of the neutral partisan role may simply impose on clients the psychological and financial cost of finding alternative counsel.

A second problem with rights-based justifications for partisanship is that they fail to explain why the rights of clients should trump those of all other parties whose interests are inadequately represented.

Much of the appeal of rights-based justifications for partisanship draws on the lawyer's role in criminal defense proceedings. Yet such proceedings are distinctive in their potential for governmental oppression and in their impact on individual life, liberty, and reputation. For the same reasons that our constitutional traditions impose special protections for criminal cases, most commentators suggest that the justifications for neutral partisanship are strongest in that context.

Hypo: *Role of Judge*

Should judges have a greater role in the trial process in order to insure fairness and increase the odds of discovering the truth? What do you think? Would our system benefit from more intervention and tighter control by the trial judge? Less strategic posturing by counsel? Such dramatic changes in our system—even if we agree that they are desirable—may not be possible in a practical sense given defendants' constitutional rights in our system, e.g. the Sixth Amendment right to effective assistance of counsel. Would you be willing to trade away (the current scope of) some of these rights for a more efficient and less adversarial criminal justice system?

Daniel Markovits—Adversary Advocacy and the Authority of Adjudication

75 Fordham L. Rev. 1367, 1367-1369, 1370, 1391-1393, 1395 (2006).

Should lawyers detach their professional activities from their personal factual, legal, and moral views and promote even clients' causes that they would oppose as citizens and reject as judges or jurors, or should lawyers

Who's That?

Daniel Markovits is Guido Calabresi Professor of Law at Yale Law School.

constrain the professional services that they provide to suit their personal views? Should lawyers serve particular clients as partisans, or should they serve justice writ large?

The lore of the bar-think of Lord Brougham's remark that a lawyer should serve his client "by all expedient means" and "reckless of the consequences," and even though he should "involve his country in confusion for his client's protection"—tends towards the first alternative in each pair. Moreover, the positive law governing lawyers also elaborates a partisan conception of lawyers' professional role. Broad and organic principles of lawyer loyalty and client control require lawyers zealously to pursue ends that their clients have wide discretion in setting. In addition, a broad and organic principle of professional detachment, although usually understood as an effort to shield lawyers from legal or even moral responsibility for their clients' concerns, also acts as a sword to forbid lawyers from imposing their personal doubts about the merits of claims that clients nevertheless wish to pursue. To be sure, these duties are ringed round by constraints on any number of forms of partisan excess-including, for example, rules that forbid lying to tribunals or assisting fraud, and bringing frivolous or malicious claims. And lawyers are permitted, and indeed in some measure encouraged, to counsel clients on the broader legal and moral implications of the positions that the clients take. But the constraints that the positive law places on adversary excess are technical and mechanical and therefore only constrain, and cannot possibly eliminate, the organic duties towards partisanship. The lawyer's counseling role must give way to the duties of lawyer loyalty and client control when confronted with recalcitrant clients. The genetic structure of the positive law of lawyering tends towards partisanship.

Moreover, the adversary system defense, which has traditionally dominated theoretical work in legal ethics, roughly supports this account of the lawyer's professional role. It proposes that lawyers' partisanship plays an essential part in an impartially justified moral division of labor-that competition among partisan advocates concerned exclusively (or at least primarily) for their clients produces, on balance, the best justice for all.

But this argument has repeatedly been shown to be not just mistaken but simply implausible. To begin with, its factual predicates do not generally obtain. Even in an ideal legal system, in which the underlying substantive laws are just and access to legal services is fairly distributed, it remains uncertain how much partisanship in fact best serves the law's underlying purposes. Certainly, a lawyer whose aggressive manipulations were on the verge of successfully subverting these purposes would better serve justice by stepping back in ways that neither the bar's self-conception nor its current rules contemplate. And the adversary system defense stands on shakier ground still in nonideal legal systems (and therefore in every actual legal system), in which substantive laws are not perfectly just and legal services are not perfectly fairly distributed. When adversary lawyers are more available to some persons than to others, for example, it becomes quite incredible that lawyers' adversary loyalty will best serve justice for all, even only on balance.

Moreover, the adversary system defense's theoretical predicates also stand on shaky ground. The aggregative conception of fairness on which the adversary system defense relies faces challenges from competitor conceptions, associated with rights-based moral theories, that apply the demands of fairness separately to every relation between persons. These theories suggest that a lawyer's preference for her client that violates a third-party's rights cannot, as the adversary system defense would have it, be simply offset by benefits that arise elsewhere in the adversary administration of justice. And accordingly, notwithstanding the commonplaces of legal ethics, the partisan conception of lawyering remains in need of a defense.

I argue that partisan client-centered rather than impartial justice-centered lawyers are necessary for the legitimacy of adjudication (and indeed for the broader practices of applying general laws to particular cases). The adversariness of lawyers is necessary for sustaining all the transformations that the legal process engenders-from the shallowest to the deepest. Even the most superficial transformations, associated with the mere translation of claims from ordinary into legal language, will be stable only if clients place a high degree of trust in lawyer-translators. Specifically, clients must trust first in lawyers' capacity to understand their claims and, second, in lawyers' commitments to fidelity in translation (even when fidelity requires lawyers to ignore their own assessments of the clients' claims). Only loyally partisan lawyers can earn and sustain such trust, because only loyal partisans have the empathy necessary for understanding their clients and the open-mindedness necessary to avoid judging them. If lawyers retreat from adversary ideals of lawyer loyalty and client control, their efforts at translation will no longer be trusted by clients but will instead be experienced as foreign and hostile, so that they disrupt rather than enhance the clients' engagements with the legal process. Insofar as lawyers reject adversary advocacy in favor of a more positively capable conception of their professional roles, lawyers' professional behavior "grows introverted, preoccupied with its own norms and activities," so that the "institution of the legal profession develops a carapace, impermeable to external information, prescription, or influence." And when this happens, lawyers' efforts at translation inevitably fail, and "the problems the legal profession handles are the problems defined by the institution, not the society; the solutions it generates are solutions for the institution, not the society." Rather than serving as intermediaries whose interpretive efforts connect clients to the legal process, non-adversary lawyers confront clients as an unmediated part of the process; and rather than bringing clients into the legal process in ways that support its practical legitimacy, non-adversary lawyers alienate clients in ways that undermine the legal process's legitimacy.

Moreover, lawyers' ability to dampen disputes by encouraging clients to abandon or modify their most unreasonable positions also depends on their commitment to adversary advocacy. This is, to begin with, a matter of psychology and even of emotion. Disputants' most unreasonable positions often reflect frustration and anger rather than considered judgments, so that they are open to being talked down and may even seek it out. But only a sympathetic and nonjudgmental counsel will inspire the trust needed to cool passions in this way. In addition, the adversary lawyer's unique capacity to deflate her clients' most extreme claims has an ethical component. Both ethical theory and empirical research suggest that disputants have a natural ethical inclination in favor of resolving disputes through reasonable reciprocal concessions. But most clients, being inexperienced in the disputes in which they are engaged, will be uncertain which concessions are in fact reasonable. Lawyers have experience and expertise that clients do not and can therefore help to resolve this uncertainty. But lawyers will be trusted to do so only when clients are confident that their deflationary advice serves the clients' interests alone, rather than the interests of the legal system or the other disputants-only, that is, when lawyers accept the adversary obligations associated with lawyer loyalty and client control. In these ways, adversary advocates support both the psychological and ethical mechanisms through which engagements with the legal process persuade disputants voluntarily to abandon their most aggressive and unreasonable demands. And adversary advocates therefore transform disputants' attitudes in legitimacy-enhancing ways, whereas lawyers who abandon their adversary obligations and judge their clients rather than serving them have an opposite, de-legitimating effect.

Finally, lawyers' adversary commitments are especially important for transforming clients' claims from brute demands into assertions of right whose implicitly defeasible character makes the deepest contribution to the legitimacy of the legal process. Once again, "a high degree of trust and confidence are usually necessary if lawyers are to 'sell' the new definition of the situation" that the conversion of brute demands into claims of right involves, and lawyers' adversary commitments justify their clients' trust. Accordingly, the lawyers who help disputants to transform their brute demands into assertions of right must leave no available right unasserted. (Unasserted rights cannot be addressed in adjudication and therefore threaten to undermine legitimacy by coming between disputants and the resolutions to disputes that the legal process proposes.) And lawyers can do this only if they function as adversary advocates, amplifying and refining all their clients' claims rather than evaluating and choosing among them. Lawyers who abandon their adversary role in favor of personal assessments of their clients' claims quite literally prejudge these claims. And when this happens, the legitimacy of the legal process becomes dependent on the legitimacy of the lawyers' judgments. But these judgments, being creatures of the lawyers' individual minds, are virtually impossible to legitimate, and certainly cannot be legitimated by reference to the transformative powers of a legal process that has not yet begun. Lawyers who abandon their adversary role to pursue the law's underlying purposes merely shift the burden of legitimation forward to their own assessments of these purposes, which necessarily address their clients' demands in an untransformed, and hence intractable, state.

The law integrates through the transformative powers of the legal process, which operates through the efforts of the lawyers who administer the legal process and invite disputants to engage it. And lawyers can successfully invite litigants to engage the legal process (and open themselves up to the transformations that the process engenders) only if they themselves resist judging their clients—only, that is, if they serve their clients loyally. Partisan advocacy is therefore revealed to lie at the very center of the law's claim to legitimacy—as a retail analog to the democratic virtues that are so notoriously celebrated throughout the civilized world.

Food for Thought

Does it make sense to you that clients are more likely to listen to and respect the tactical judgment of those attorneys they truly trust? In any event, do you believe that the virtue of client trust in his or her legal representative is outweighed by the downside of permitting and legitimizing adversariness that so often is viewed as (and may really be) excessive?

Monroe H. Freedman & Abbe Smith—Misunderstanding Lawyers' Ethics (Book Review of Daniel Markovits, A Modern Legal Ethics: Adversary Ethics in a Democratic Age (2008))

108 Mich. L. Rev. 925, 925-26, 927. 929, 931-34, 935-36, 937-38 (2010).

Markovits is concerned with how a lawyer's professional life can be ethically satisfying. He contends that lawyers' lives are not "well-lived," because they feel guilty. The source of that guilt, according to Markovits, is that lawyers are compelled to lie and cheat, routinely and viciously.

Markovits begins his analysis with the adversary system, which combines partisan representation with impartial adjudication. He notes that the law-

Who's That?

Monroe Freedman is the late Professor of Law and former Dean at the Maurice A. Deane School of Law at Hofstra University. Abbe Smith is Professor of Law, Director of the Criminal Defense & Prisoner Advocacy Clinic, and Co-Director of the E. Barrett Prettyman Fellowship, at Georgetown University Law Center. Professor Smith began her legal career at the Defender Association of Philadelphia, where she was an Assistant Defender, a member of the Special Defense Unit, and a Senior Trial Attorney.

yer's role in an adversary system is client-centered—lawyers are required to be loyal to the clients they serve. That loyalty obliges the lawyer to accept what the client wishes to achieve in the representation and to use lawful and ethical means for achieving client interests, in particular by maintaining the client's position against any present or potential adversary.

This simplified, formalistic description of the lawyer's role is fine as far as it goes. From there, however, Markovits relies on erroneous and unsupported assumptions regarding the nature of law practice and the mental and emotional state of lawyers. The nature of the lawyers' role, he asserts, requires that they violate what everyone, including lawyers themselves, consider moral conduct. His chief evidence of immorality, however, is a peculiar definition of lying and cheating. Because of this lying and cheating, and the guilt suffered as a result, it is not possible for a lawyer to have self-respect.

Markovits contends further that the "adversary system excuse"—that is, the lawyer's critical role in an adversary system—cannot salve this inevitable and pervasive sense of guilt. He says that focusing on the lawyer's adversarial role may excuse such conduct, but it does not deny its "viciousness." Thus, lawyers remain in a state of moral self-hatred.

As Professor Geoffrey Hazard notes, Markovits purveys the idea that the practice of law, "as defined by its function, its traditions, and its ethical norms is ethically suspect, perhaps evil." We agree with Hazard that this view is not just incorrect, but "demoralizing," especially to law students.

It is not clear where Markovits got the notion that practicing lawyers spend their lives agonizing over (or denying) their viciousness. Certainly, that is not our experience. For us and for the countless others we have known, the practice of law has been an exhilarating, gratifying, and essentially moral profession of serving others and of maintaining the ideals of our constitutional democracy.

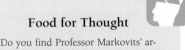

Food for Thought

Do you find Professor Markovits' arguments (as described by Professors Freedman and Smith, at least) "demoralizing," as they suggest? Do you think that you would feel "guilty" and unhappy in defending a guilty defendant in this fashion? And if so, is that important, i.e. should defense counsel's feelings dictate the nature of an accused person's representation? What do you think?

We know of no study that documents widespread lawyer unhappiness due to the ethics of law practice. On the other hand, we are well aware of unhappiness—even some agonizing—among associates at large law firms. But the agonizing we have observed and read about has been over the unreasonable demands on their time, which has significantly interfered with family life.

We should note that in our own practice, we have often argued for a result that we would not have adopted as a judge. This is partly the result of our choice of practice area and clients and partly the result of sound tactics.

But even if we do not "privately believe" in a particular case theory or argument, few judges expect advocates to be stating a personal view of the facts or law. They understand that we are engaged in advocacy. Both lawyer and judge understand that the lawyer is saying, in effect, "Your Honor, this is the way you can render an objectively sound and reasonable judgment that favors my client." That is a service to the court (which is free to adopt the argument or not) as well as to the client. To call this kind of advocacy a lie, much less vicious, is, again, silly.

Half a century ago, legal philosopher Lon Fuller analogized a lawyer's argument in court to a baseball catcher "riding with the pitch" and "pulling" a pitch into the strike zone. As is true of Markovits's fancied lying and cheating by lawyers, it is fatuous to think of catchers as lying and cheating when they pull pitches, or base runners as being dishonest when they "steal" bases, or pitchers as deceitful when they throw a change-up. These are all tactics that are analogous to lawyers' conduct that is "permitted by the law and the Disciplinary Rules" and that are expected, accepted, and respected by those engaged in the particular undertaking.

Clearly, therefore, the context of one's actions is critical. Inevitably, Markovits identifies the source of what he sees as lawyers' pervasive immorality in role differentiation, specifically in the lawyers' role in our adversary system. As he explains, adversary lawyers "commonly do, and indeed are often required to do, things in their professional capacities, which, if done by ordinary people in ordinary circumstances, would be straightforwardly immoral." Thus, Markovits repeatedly criticizes what has come to be called "the adversary system excuse."

We count ourselves among the defenders of the adversary system—what Markovits correctly calls the "traditionalists." We believe that lawyers' ethics are rooted in the Bill of Rights and in the autonomy and dignity of the individual, and reflecting the traditional client-centered view of the lawyer's role in an adversary system. The adversary system has been constitutionalized in this country by a panoply of fundamental rights that were incorporated into the First, Fourth, Fifth, Sixth, Seventh, and Fourteenth Amendments to the Constitution, and that have been elaborated upon by the Supreme Court throughout history. Those constitutional values express the deeply moral ideals of individual dignity and autonomy, and serve to safeguard individual liberties against oppressive government power.

In addition, the adversary system is the most effective means of determining the truth, particularly in cases in which facts are in dispute. It has historically been an effective method for peacefully resolving disputes, including those coming from serious political and racial discord. Further, the adversary system reflects a belief in democratic decision making through the jury system, and in the importance of giving individuals control over their cases, which gives them a greater sense of having been treated fairly and helps to legitimize the system generally. We want to state clearly that there are compelling reasons for a principled person to choose to be a lawyer and to carry out her professional responsibilities with a sense of moral conviction and personal gratification.

Food for Thought

What about Professors Freedman's and Smith's argument that the adversary system is the best way to determine the truth? Do you agree with that? Is that what defense counsel wants to accomplish? *Really?*

There is an additional aspect of the lawyer's relationship to her client that bears heavily on her moral responsibilities and which is ignored by Markovits and other scholars who criticize client-centered lawyering.

When a lawyer chooses to represent a client, she necessarily becomes the client's fiduciary. Thus, the lawyer assumes the responsibility to make the client's cause her own and to carry out the client's lawful objectives by all lawful and ethical means that are reasonably available. In this way, the lawyer honors the client's status as a free person in a free society, respects the client's dignity as an individual, and assists the client in exercising his or her autonomy. Of course, a lawyer may simply decline a particular representation, and the lawyer's power to do that is quite broad.

What this means is that the lawyer will have made a promise—expressly or impliedly given her word upon which the client can be expected to rely—that she will use all lawful and ethical means that are reasonably available to advance the client's lawful interests in all aspects of the representation. Promises, of course, are generally recognized as among the heaviest of moral obligations.

Although other critics think the "adversary excuse" is most justified in a criminal context, Markovits barely discusses criminal defense, explaining that "the distinctiveness of the criminal context should not be overstated."

Restraint in lawyering seems to be what Markovits is after; restraint and a kind of purity. Lawyers should be more dignified, they shouldn't be so aggressive, and they should be absolutely convinced of the righteousness of their cause. Yet, in our experience, the very people who claim to disdain zealous lawyering seek exactly that when they or a loved one needs a lawyer.

Markovits's "positive conclusion" for the profession is not that lawyers are heroic defenders of individual liberties who serve the essential function in a constitutional democracy of maintaining individual dignity and autonomy. His final judgment is that his argument "has the form of tragedy, and that lawyers are tragic villains."

We disagree. Although the practice of law has its share of tragedy—whether due to random misfortune or pervasive injustice—it is ultimately uplifting and gratifying. We know we are not alone in this conviction. This is not the time to discourage lawyers and prospective lawyers from the zealous, client-centered practice of law. On the contrary, there has never been a greater need for lawyers willing to champion individual liberties and human rights.

Exercise: *Observe Criminal Proceedings*

Spend at least half a day observing a criminal trial or hearings at your local courthouse. Write a paper briefly reporting the nature of your observations and addressing all of the following questions where they are applicable: Were defense counsel and the prosecutor contentious in their advocacy? Should they have been more zealous or adversarial in their advocacy? In what ways did the outcome of the proceedings you observed turn on the adversarial manner of presentation of arguments and/or evidence? What difference do you think it would have made if the proceedings had taken place in a less adversarial fashion?

B. Defense Counsel's Role

Accepting the present reality, i.e. that criminal trials take place in an adversary setting, what does adversariness mean *in practice* for defense counsel? Is it possible to be an able and effective defense attorney and to be a "good person" at the same time? Is it possible to stay emotionally healthy?

Robert P. Mosteller—Why Defense Attorneys Cannot, But Do, Care About Innocence

50 Santa Clara L. Rev. 1, 3-4, 40-41, 58-59, 60-62 (2010).

Defense counsel focus on what is useful to the conduct of their representation that relates to innocence—its proof. When such proof is available, they develop it and present it. Assuredly, when innocence is not present, they defend anyway, but their reaction is connected to the irrelevance of guilt to the duty to represent the client and does not dictate the irrelevance of innocence.

Belief in innocence without proof is a different matter. Unlike prosecutors, defense attorneys lack the power to dismiss a case because they believe the defendant is, or may be, innocent. In the courtroom, their belief is treated as inadmissible, and therefore it is functionally irrelevant. In contrast to guilt, where defense attorneys may have unique personal knowledge because the client unequivocally

Who's That?

Robert Mosteller is the J. Dickson Phillips Distinguished Professor of Law at the University of North Carolina. He worked for seven years with the Washington, D.C. Public Defender Service where he was Director of Training and Chief of the Trial Division.

admitted guilt to them, a client's impassioned protestation of innocence hardly constitutes knowledge of innocence. Usually, the evidence defense attorneys possess that is not also available to the prosecution merely supports the likelihood of innocence, but does not prove it.

My experience is that defense attorneys do care about innocence when they see it or they think they see it. However, defenders who search among their clients for those who are innocent are inviting personal and professional destruction. A defender's belief in her client's innocence must be backed by evidence; otherwise, it largely only torments the defender and interferes with the performance of the attorney's professional duty to all of her other clients. Furthermore, because this can become disabling, it can harm even a client the defender believes to be innocent.

In the end, I conclude that the concern for innocence will likely continue to be handled individually by attorneys responding to the torment by giving special attention to those clients, and attempting to limit the damage that special attention may cause to others who they represent.

In meeting hundreds of clients and examining their cases, attentive defense attorneys build a knowledge base, which enables most to analyze criminal cases with skill and judgment. One also develops a cynical side and sees the world as a hard place. Optimists—those who believe in the possibility of human perfection and consider most of their clients innocent or perfectible—do not survive long. Although I rationally understood that I could not actually know which clients were the innocent ones, I now recognize that I had a false sense of confidence that I would have a relatively accurate inclination of innocence, which I suspect many defenders share. My suspicion is that this false confidence arose from a self-protective instinct designed to lower the pressure of the work, which was much easier if the system's expectation that all clients were guilty was true.

I do not assume that many of my clients were innocent, but what I have come to appreciate more over time is that I could not tell the innocent from the large percentage that were guilty. This point may be criticized because I have no proof that I had any other innocent client beyond those who were discovered. I do not know.

Global View

A number of countries around the world have begun a transition to a more adversarial criminal justice system, including adopting the concept of appointed public defenders for indigent clients. But the U.S. public defender system hasn't always been a successful transplant in other countries. Consider the example of Chile. See John D. King, *The Public Defender as International Transplant*, 38 U. Pa. J. Int'l L. 831 (2017).

In assessing the possible impact that a focus on guilt and innocence might have on defenders, some typology of the motivations of defenders is helpful. I suggest there are four major categories: (1) The Tester of Factual or Legal Guilt, (2) The Rights Protector, (3) The Protector of and Aid to the Downtrodden, and (4) The Competitor.

The first category—The Tester of Factual or Legal Guilt—is the one most directly involved in this article. The motivation of these lawyers roughly centers on the arguments that determining facts is often difficult, leading to inherent uncertainty as to factual guilt, and thus, despite the good faith efforts of prosecutors, conviction of the innocent remains a reality. As a result, defense lawyers are needed to protect the factually innocent. Even if we know what happened, many cases turn on issues of human motivation and responsibility, which may remain uncertain or which may properly be viewed from different perspectives. Thus, lawyers also play this role, even when the issue is legal guilt rather than factual innocence. Finally, in death penalty cases, defense attorneys are critical to reaching an appropriate judgment as to punishment.

The second category—The Rights Protector—houses arguments flowing from the command of the Sixth Amendment under our adversarial system for equal justice and the contention that in protecting those least loved, defenders support the foundation of the liberties of all. The third category—The Protector of the Downtrodden—contains elements of social work and political cause. Most of those charged with crimes come from impoverished backgrounds and present a host of social maladies. Somewhere in the mix of motivations to enter defender work is likely at least the potential for empathy for defendants who typically come from impoverished backgrounds and may be members of racial minority groups. Few defenders are likely drawn to the work to perform a social work function, but in reality, much of a defender's work has this function. For those who endure, success in the social work function often becomes a fulfilling element of the job. The fourth category—The Competitor—captures the personal ego satisfaction that sustains litigators. It is the selfish joy of winning. For defenders, this joy may be more infrequent because the prosecution typically has the stronger case, but the victories are more enjoyable when they come to an underdog.

At PDS [the Washington, D.C. Public Defender Service], as I assume with public defenders generally, we had no clearly articulated justifications for our work either at an office-wide level or individually. I saw and felt elements of all four of the motivational categories described above. The most common articulation was the systemic justification set out in the second category— "The Protector of Rights." We certainly believed that a major consequence and purpose of our work was to keep the criminal justice process honest, which should help those who are innocent, but our focus was on the immediate goal of maintaining a fair process. We were, in this way, lawyers working for a cause. Thus, working for a larger cause is somewhere in their motivation, but for most defenders, that is not what sustains them on a day-to-day basis.

Food for Thought

What do you think about Professor Mosteller's description of the types of PD motivations? Overly simplistic? Or . . . right on? If you are considering criminal defense practice after law school, which of these might apply to you? And given the fact that many, many civil practice clients are every bit as unpleasant, culpable, and discomfiting, do you think that criminal defense practice is really a more emotionally demanding setting in which to practice law?

In her insightful article, Repression and Denial in Criminal Lawyering, 9 Buff. Crim. L. Rev. 339, 359 (2006), Professor Susan Bandes examines the emotional and psychological impact upon defenders of representing largely, but not universally, guilty individuals, many of whom have caused pain to others and face the prospect of harsh punishment themselves. On the support side of the ledger, Bandes, drawing from numerous personal accounts of defenders, notes the central focus and sustaining motivation is the client: "One common thread among those who maintain a commitment to defense work is the importance of the connection to one's client, and the importance of keeping his needs concrete and immediate."

As Professor Bandes describes, the lawyers at the Public Defender Service most centrally represented people in need—we had clients and saw ourselves as their vigorous and loyal lawyers. Representing clients is the obvious centerpiece of what public defenders do. Lawyers, no doubt, go into defender work because they are drawn to a general cause, but the sense of mission at PDS was not felt immediately as being to a cause—the cause of justice—but to individual clients. We defended the guilty and innocent alike, but we tried to win cases and more particularly to do our best for our clients, whom we saw principally as clients and individuals rather than consciously recognizing them as either guilty or innocent clients.

Hypo: *Defending Bad Guys*

How do you feel about representing criminal defendants who you believe (or know) have committed serious or, often, heinous offenses? Could you do it? Should you do it? How do you feel about others doing it? Do you respect the people who have the fortitude to engage in such a practice, or do you look down upon them? Are you comfortable with criminal defense counsel's coping mechanism of "not knowing" whether his or her client is guilty? Maybe this is the moment to reflect on these issues and decide whether you screwed up and should have gone into the family dry-cleaning business instead of coming to law school.

Abbe Smith—*Defending Those People*
10 Ohio St. J. Crim. L. 277, 283-285, 287-288, 290-291, 298, 300, 301 (2012).

I am drawn to people in trouble. Maybe this is because I had a little sister who was often in trouble. My sister had "problems" as a young child. Once, in kindergarten, she was finger-painting. When it was time to clean up and move to the next activity, the teacher said, "Okay, class. Time to put everything away." My sister ignored her. The teacher approached my sister and, calling her by name, directed her to put the paints away. My sister kept painting. When the teacher repeated her request, my sister picked up her paint-covered hands and wiped them on the teacher's dress.

Who's That?

Abbe Smith is Professor of Law, Director of the Criminal Defense & Prisoner Advocacy Clinic, and Co-Director of the E. Barrett Prettyman Fellowship, at Georgetown University Law Center. Professor Smith began her legal career at the Defender Association of Philadelphia, where she was an Assistant Defender, a member of the Special Defense Unit, and a Senior Trial Attorney.

I grew up intervening on my sister's behalf, fighting her battles-at home, school, and in the neighborhood. Sometimes I literally fought for her. There was a red-haired boy named Alan who, in second grade, called my sister a name. I gave him a bloody lip, which got me sent to the principal's office. This was my first and only visit to the principal. It was worth it.

I don't think I've punched anyone since. I tend to fight my battles in court.

From that point on, it wasn't a great leap to others in trouble. I mean "trouble" broadly, not just the kind my sister got in, or the kind that lands people in the criminal justice system. I feel a natural sympathy for people in difficulty or distress. It doesn't matter who they are. The fact that they are in trouble is what makes me want to defend them.

This is ironic since patience is generally not my strong suit-I can be brusque and dismissive. I am not known for my attention span-I tend to lose interest quickly (except when it's me who's talking, then I'm riveted). I have many more flaws: I can be a smart aleck, sarcasm is second nature, I don't suffer fools gladly. If I am any guide, you don't need to be the nicest person on earth to want to help people in trouble.

I am probably nicer to people in trouble than I am to ordinary people-even more so if I don't know them. No one should take from this kindness to strangers any great meaning, biblical or otherwise. I might be nicer to strangers only in comparison to people I know. I laugh when a friend or family member takes a pratfall. I can barely stop laughing long enough to help them up.

I seem to broadcast a certain receptiveness to trouble. I am regularly accosted and confided in by people with problems: on the street, in the subway, and at the grocery store. This is multiplied many times in the courthouse. It never fails: the anxious person with a summons, subpoena, or son in jail manages to find me. I don't know why this is.

Ordinarily, I am not terribly interested in "needy" people. I don't have the stamina to weed through layers of need. But with people in criminal trouble there is a built-in narrative that draws me in-something happened and something else will happen to resolve it one way or another. It doesn't need to be a serious or high profile crime for there to be a good story: A gripping tale of comedy, tragedy, theater.

Most of those accused and convicted of crime are poor. Disproportionate numbers are nonwhite. There are now more black people currently under the control of the criminal justice system than were enslaved in 1850. I suppose this is why "nobody really cares" about the quality of criminal justice in the United States, or the fact that we currently lock up more people than any other nation on earth in the "history of the free world." Who gives a damn about a bunch of poor, black people in prison?

I do. And so does every public defender in America-or at least they should.

I often tell students I became a criminal lawyer because I read the book To Kill a Mockingbird (and saw the movie version) too many times as an impressionable child. For me, there is no more compelling figure than Atticus Finch, the archetypal criminal lawyer defending a wrongly accused poor black man. That Gregory Peck played Finch in the movie only contributes to his iconic stature.

Criminal defenders are, by and large, poverty lawyers. You can't spend any amount of time in criminal court and not see that it is a poor people's court. You can't step foot in a jail or prison and not notice they are full of poor people.

But I confess that I am also drawn to any underdog-the little guy, not the big one; David, not Goliath; the Cubs, not the Yankees. I often tell students that growing up a Chicago Cubs fan probably helped pave my life path. Moreover, some criminal justice underdogs were once top dogs. That's the terrifying thing about a criminal prosecution-the once mighty can suddenly be brought low. Although I have represented very few non-indigent clients, the fear, anxiety, and vulnerability that accompany a criminal accusation transcend class.

There's also something fun about fighting for the underdog in criminal court: the stakes are high, the battle hard-fought, the outcome uncertain. The lines are also refreshingly clear. Defenders fight for underdogs against the enormous power of the State. It's the Good Fight.

What's more, we have to be that much better-tougher, smarter, more creative, more resourceful-in order to level the playing field. As one writer puts it: "It's always a stacked deck for the state and often the defense attorney's very best work is simply not good enough to overcome the power and the might." This can be frightening, but it is also exciting. Sometimes you can literally beat the government. There's nothing more thrilling than this, nothing more intoxicating. The wins help keep you going.

But the thing about siding with the underdog is you don't always win-in fact mostly you don't-and it can be devastating when the government puts a human being under your care in a steel cage or kills them. Each defender has to figure out a reason to continue the fight. The opportunity to challenge authority on behalf of another-in fact, the duty to do so-is oddly satisfying and somehow freeing. It doesn't feel that way when I have to confront authority on my own behalf. Then I fold like a cheap tent. But for a client, I am easily indignant and outraged. I tone it down because those feelings are not necessarily the most effective advocacy. But I am happy to go toe-to-toe with prosecutors, police officers, probation officers, and parole officers for a client if I have to-likewise with judges: I am willing to court contempt if need be.

For all of these reasons-the fact that I'm drawn to people in trouble, under-dogs, and the guilty, and I enjoy challenging authority-I am what might be called a natural defender. But that doesn't mean there's nothing hard about it. There is plenty that's hard about it. The hardest part is the randomness of justice and the pervasiveness of injustice. Too much depends on the luck of the draw: which lawyer, prosecutor, judge, or jury you happen to get. And too much depends on the resources of the accused.

In her classic article on criminal defense, Barbara Babcock concludes that the real question is not "How can you defend the guilty?" but "Why don't you defend the guilty?" She means two things by this. First, that lawyers who are supposed to be defending the accused often fail to do so because of crushing caseloads and lack of resources. Second, that there should be more lawyers doing criminal defense. Babcock believes that the criminal justice system and the legal profession would be better off if more lawyers did criminal work.

Food for Thought

Does this article excerpt make you think that criminal defense attorneys—and maybe prosecutors, too—are drawn to the different sides of criminal justice practice in some part for psychological, character-ological, and/or emotional reasons? Is that a surprise to you? And if there is some truth to this notion, what accounts for lawyers who move from defense to prosecutorial practice, and vice versa? Schizophrenic?

All of this is true. But I would add one more thing: There is nothing more stimulating, fun, challenging, and rewarding than representing people accused or convicted of crime.

William H. Simon—The Ethics of Criminal Defense

91 Mich. L. Rev. 1703, 1707-08 (June 1993).

Libertarians claim that aggressive advocacy is distinctively appropriate to the criminal sphere because it serves to check oppression by the "state." Such arguments invoke the image of the "isolated," "lone," "friendless," or "naked" individual faced with the "enormous power and resources of the

Who's That?

William H. Simon is Arthur Levitt Professor of Law at Columbia Law School.

state." Aggressive defense is supposed to level the playing field and turn the trial into a "contest of equals," or at least express the system's commitment to treat all citizens with respect.

Aggressive defense is also supposed to protect against the abuse of state power. The danger of abuse is most commonly attributed to the inherently corrupting nature of state power and the consequent aggression and rapacity of state officials. The aggressive defense lawyer inhibits such abuse by increasing the difficulty of conviction. In David Luban's rhetoric:

> We want to handicap the state in its power even legitimately to punish us, for we believe as a matter of political theory and historical experience that if the state is not handicapped or restrained ex ante, our political and civil liberties are jeopardized. Power-holders are inevitably tempted to abuse the criminal justice system to persecute political opponents, and overzealous police will trample civil liberties in the name of crime prevention and order.

This type of rhetoric has been exempt from critical reflection for so long that even a small amount should raise doubts. In the first place, the image of the lonely individual facing Leviathan is misleading. Let us grant the lonely part even though some defendants have lots of friends. But, what about the state? Libertarian rhetoric tends to suggest that the individual defendant takes on the entire state. But, of course, the state has other concerns besides this defendant. From the state's point of view, the defendant may be part of an enormous class of criminal defendants and suspects with which it can hardly begin to cope.

It is more plausible to portray the typical defendant as facing a small number of harassed, overworked bureaucrats. Of course, state agencies can focus their resources on particular defendants and, when they do so, their power can be formidable. But the state cannot possibly focus its power this way on all defendants or even most of them. Yet, aggressive defense treats all defendants as if they faced the full concentrated power of the state.

Second, victims do not appear in the libertarian picture. The "victims' rights" movement has worked for the past two decades to replace in the popular consciousness the defense lawyer's image of the criminal trial as a state-versus-defendant contest with that of a victim-versus-defendant contest. The

Food for Thought

Professor Simon attacks the underpinnings of some of the justifications for zealous representation by criminal defense counsel put forward by previous commentators, such as Professor Smith. In your opinion, does he succeed in his arguments? He contends, for example, that "[t]he problem with aggressive defense is that it impedes the state's ability to convict the guilty without affording any significant protection to the innocent." Such an argument, of course, raises a host of questions addressed in previous article excerpts in this Chapter. Should defense counsel ever assist the State (in any fashion, however indirect) in proving guilt? Is aggressive defense necessarily bad for the community? Does it make it more difficult to achieve justice? Are accused persons who are actually guilty *not* entitled to such protections? Only the innocent, as Professor Simon implies? What do you think?

movement is often naive, even blind, about the efficacy of criminal punishment in deterring future wrongs or aiding victims, but its imagery seems as plausible as that of the defense lawyer.

A frequent concomitant of the idea that aggressive defense checks the rapacity of the state is the idea that it expresses respect for the "dignity of the individual." The idea that helping the accused escape substantively appropriate punishment through aggressive defense serves individual dignity is hard to square with the legitimacy of punishment after conviction. A viable ideal of dignity has to make room for respect for the rights of others and, at least in our system, for acceptance of punishment when the individual violates such rights.

Hypo: *Withholding Evidence*

Two part-time public defenders, brothers George and Walter Stenhach, were appointed to represent Richard Buchanan who was charged in Potter County, Pennsylvania, with murder. In discussing the events surrounding the alleged homicide with George Stenhach, Buchanan revealed the locations of some pieces of physical evidence. An investigator for the brothers went to one of the locations and discovered a broken rifle stock which had apparently been used in the homicide. The investigator retrieved and turned the stock over to the Stenhach brothers who withheld it from the prosecution on the theory that "they were obligated to retain the rifle stock to protect their client." During Buchanan's murder trial, the prosecution learned of the existence of the rifle stock and the trial judge subsequently ordered the Stenhach brothers to produce it, which they did. After Buchanan was convicted of murder, the Stenhach brothers were themselves charged with various criminal offenses relating to obstruction of justice.

Do you think that the Stenhach brothers were guilty of criminal activity on these facts or were they, instead, simply acting zealously and professionally in the best interests of their client? Does it make any difference in your analysis that the prosecutor never asked the Stenhach brothers, formally or informally, to produce any relevant evidence that they may have had in their possession? Would it make any difference in your analysis if the evidence that the Stenhach brothers withheld was testimonial rather than physical, e.g. Buchanan's confidential statements to them confessing to the crime? See *Commonwealth v. Stenhach*, 356 Pa.Super. 5, 514 A.2d 114 (1986).

C. The Prosecutor's Role

Prosecutors, like defense counsel, often struggle with the appropriate contours of their role in the American adversarial criminal justice system. If "justice" requires that criminal defense counsel defend their clients' zealously, does the same hold true for prosecutors? Do—should—prosecutors have professional duties that differ from those assigned to defense counsel? And how do we—should we—regulate prosecutors' exercise of those duties?

David Luban—The Conscience of a Prosecutor

45 Val. U. L. Rev. 1, 15-18, 20-22, 31 (2010).

Prosecutors are not supposed to win at all costs. In a time-honored formula, their job is to seek justice, not victory. This is a mantra that appears in all the crucial ethics documents. It appears in a comment to the current ABA Model Rules of Professional Conduct: "A prosecutor has the responsibility of a minister of justice and not simply that of an advocate." It appears in the Model Rules' predecessor, the ABA Code of Professional Responsibility: "The responsibility of a public prosecutor differs from that of the usual advocate; his duty is to seek justice, not merely to convict." The same language appears in the ABA's Standards for the Prosecution Function.

> **Who's That?**
>
> David Luban is University Professor and Professor of Law and Philosophy at Georgetown University.

The ancestor of all these pronouncements is the Supreme Court's dictum in a 1935 case, *Berger v. United States*:

> The United States Attorney is the representative not of an ordinary party to a controversy, but of a sovereignty whose obligation to govern impartially is as compelling as its obligation to govern at all; and whose interest, therefore, in a criminal prosecution is not that it shall win a case, but that justice shall be done. As such, he is in a peculiar and very definite sense the servant of the law, the twofold aim of which is that guilt shall not escape or innocence suffer.

This is a very different way to think about a lawyer's role in the adversary system than we are used to in other contexts. It is especially different from the criminal defense attorney's role, which most lawyers and scholars agree requires maximum zeal on the client's behalf. Now in one way, this stark difference between the prosecutor's mission and the mission assigned to other advocates in the adversary system is obvious: the criminal justice system would be a travesty if a prosecutor, holding years of someone's life in her hands, cared about nothing but notching another victory.

But I do want to point out that the *Berger* dictum, with its "seek justice not victory" formula, runs entirely against the grain of popular anti-crime sentiment as well as the way people commonly think about the adversary system. In popular sentiment, criminals are by definition bad guys, prosecutors who lock them up are, for that reason, good guys, and defense lawyers live under a perpetual cloud of suspicion, reflected in endless griping about clever lawyers who get crooks off on technicalities. Criminal defenders constantly face the question "[h]ow can you represent people like that?"-or the more sophisticated law student's version, "I understand why the system needs defense lawyers, but personally I could never do that kind of work." As for our conventional understanding of the adversary system, it envisions complete symmetry of obligation between the two sides: they are both supposed to fight as hard as they can to win.

The "seek justice not victory" formula, coupled with the view that criminal defense requires the maximum level of zealous advocacy, presents an entirely upside down model. Now, we have asymmetrical obligations: the defender is supposed to seek victory, not justice, while the prosecutor is constrained to seek justice, not victory. Prosecutors, it seems, are simply not supposed to fight to win the way defenders are.

Food for Thought

What do you think about Professor Luban's point that this ethical obligation for prosecutors is at odds with the popular, anti-crime perception? Does this/should this make a difference? Should prosecutors be "freed" to be zealous, too? Or is this all a theoretical debate in the sense that many (most?) prosecutors are zealots now anyway, ethics rules notwithstanding?

Admittedly, there is a delphic quality to the "seek justice not victory" formula. Justice is a grandiose and vague word. Oliver Wendell Holmes famously said "I hate justice, which means that I know if a man begins to talk about that, for one reason or another he is shirking thinking in legal terms." The formal ethics rules-as opposed to aspirational standards like the ABA's Standards for the Prosecution Function-take a pretty minimalist view of the prosecutor's obligations. Prosecutors should not proceed without probable cause, they should make a reasonable effort to ensure that the accused has been informed of his rights, they should not try to get an unrepresented person to waive rights, and they should do timely *Brady* disclosures. They should not subpoena defense lawyers unless they have to. And they should refrain from inflammatory public comments about their cases-a rule all too often honored in the breach. In most jurisdictions, that is the extent of their ethical obligations. These rules leave loads of leeway for prosecutors to seek victory regardless of justice, without facing even a whiff of professional discipline.

Fred Zacharias, in a leading scholarly article on the "seek justice not victory" formula, thinks that the justice prosecutors seek "has two fairly limited prongs: (1) prosecutors should not prosecute unless they have a good faith belief that the defendant is guilty; and, (2) prosecutors must ensure that the basic elements of the adversary system exist at trial." The formal ethics rules do not go even that far.

And yet I have spoken with a lot of prosecutors who take "seek justice not victory" seriously, even if they are not 100% confident they know exactly what it requires. At the very least, as Zacharias's first point indicates, they know you should not try to keep people behind bars if you think they didn't do it.

In 2008, the ABA House of Delegates agreed. The ABA added two Model Rules to deal with prosecutors' obligations when new evidence suggests that they obtained wrongful convictions. One requires a prosecutor who learns of "new, credible and material evidence creating a reasonable likelihood that a convicted defendant did not commit an offense of which the defendant was convicted," to disclose the evidence to the proper authorities as well as the defendant and to initiate an investigation. If the evidence is clear and convincing, the prosecutor must "seek to remedy the conviction." Two prominent scholars have argued that these rules do not go far enough because evidence that a convicted person is probably innocent should impel a conscientious prosecutor to try to remedy the injustice, even if the evidence is not clear and convincing.

An important point is lurking in the background here. One reason some lawyers feel uncomfortable with the adage "seek justice not victory" is that there is no consensus about what justice is, and we have every reason to doubt there ever will be. Philosophers who spend their lives thinking about the theory of justice don't agree about whose theory is right. But you do not need a philosophical theory of justice to recognize gross injustice when you see it. Our sense of injustice is more basic, less controversial, and less dependent on philosophical arguments than propositions about justice. "Avoid injustice" might be a more useful imperative than "seek justice," even if it is less catchy and less inspirational. It is probably what prosecutors actually do when they take "seek justice not victory" seriously.

Scholars have advanced two theories for why the prosecutor's job is to seek justice not victory. One points to the power differential between the state and the accused individual. The state has tremendous resources: police to investigate cases, crime labs to examine evidence, and—of course—the charging power to flip witnesses and induce plea bargains. The accused typically has an overworked defender with little or no capacity to investigate; in many cases, the accused is in jail. Even the names attached to criminal cases show the power imbalance: State v. Defendant, People v. Defendant, United States v. Defendant. Because of the power imbalance, it is essential that prosecutors not take victory as their sole goal. Call this the power theory.

The other theory focuses not on the power imbalance between the government and the accused, but on the special duty of the executive to govern justly and impartially. That is the theory in the *Berger* case, which I quoted earlier: the prosecutor "is the representative not of an ordinary party to a controversy, but of a sovereignty whose obligation to govern impartially is as compelling as its obligation to govern at all." Call this the sovereignty theory.

In my view, neither theory tells the whole story. The sovereignty theory does not explain why prosecutors, seeking victory in an adversary contest where the defense is doing the same, are not governing impartially. Why isn't procedural justice within in the adversary system all the justice prosecutors need to seek? Surely part of the explanation is the power imbalance: giving the state most of the cards in a purely competitive contest, where the only goal is victory, means that it will win even when the defense would prevail in a more even context. So the sovereignty theory needs the power theory to back it up—otherwise, it does not adequately explain why prosecutors should seek justice not victory.

Conversely, the power theory does not explain what is wrong with a pro-government power imbalance, which, after all, many people think is the best way to fight crime. The answer must be that we want more from government than fighting crime: we want government to bend over backwards to achieve fairness and avoid collateral damage to the innocent in the war against crime. In other words, the power theory needs the sovereignty theory to back it up.

In short, each theory needs the other. But even combining them leaves out something essential: the stakes are so much higher in criminal law than anywhere else. We have one of the world's harshest criminal justice systems, with lengthy sentences, draconian conditions of confinement, little if any interest in rehabilitation, loss of rights to convicted felons even after they serve their time, and stigma that follows convicts forever, blighting their chances to make a fresh start. As everyone knows or should know, the United States currently has more people locked up than any nation in history, both per capita and in absolute numbers.

But the United States also has a constitution built on principles of limited government and individual rights. It is an interesting puzzle how the same country that traditionally fears government abuse and rallies around the libertarian slogan "don't tread on me!" can at the same time be so addicted to harsh punishment-but this is not the occasion to address the puzzle.

Instead, I want to emphasize that the protection of individual rights from government abuse is a key part of our political tradition, and the harshness of our punishments makes the protection of rights in the criminal process a matter of life and death. That is why the power imbalance in the criminal justice system and the government's commitment to impartiality are so important. "Seek justice not victory" weaves together all three concerns. Prosecutors should not exploit the power imbalance, and they should care immensely about the rights of the accused, including the substantive right to stay out of jail when you are innocent, because of the enormously high stakes in these cases. Every good prosecutor understands that she holds years of a person's life in her hands.

Obviously, prosecutors are not responsible for mass incarceration-they deal with criminal cases retail, not wholesale, and legislatures' addiction to ratcheting up punishments is not the prosecutor's fault. But the prosecutor is the gatekeeper of the system, the one who decides which cases go from the paddy wagon to the courtroom. The prosecutor's conscience is the invisible guardian of our rights, just as the defense lawyer is the visible guardian.

Conscience is not the special property of moralists and saints. It is not the property of humanitarians with refined sensibilities-prosecuting felonies is not the career choice of delicate people. If you are lucky, you may never encounter a conscience case, although I suspect that prosecutors encounter them more often than they recognize. The test of character is whether, when you do, you can be stubborn enough and creative enough to rise to the occasion.

Hypo: *Voir Dire*

When a prosecutor is engaging in the *voir dire* process, should he or she seek to seat jurors who appear to favor the government's case (as the defense will be doing in reverse), or does the duty to "do justice" mean, at least as a matter of theory, that prosecutors should seek to seat only neutral and seemingly unbiased jurors?

Bruce Green & Ellen Yaroshefsky—Prosecutorial Accountability 2.0

92 Notre Dame L. Rev. 51, 114-16 (2016)

Who's That?

Bruce Green is the Louis Stein Chair at Fordham Law School, where he directs the Louis Stein Center for Law and Ethics. Ellen Yaroshefsky is Howard Lichtenstein Distinguished Professor of Legal Ethics and Executive Director of the Monroe H. Freedman Institute for the Study of Legal Ethics at Hofstra Law School.

Attention to prosecutorial misconduct has grown in the Internet era. Traditionally, prosecutorial misconduct was viewed as episodic, where the perception was that only a few "rogue prosecutors" engaged in such conduct. Historically, there was limited examination of the issue beyond some defense organizations and a few judges, and regulation of prosecutorial conduct, either by courts or disciplinary authorities, was scant. Discipline within prosecutors' offices was considered ineffective. It was difficult to obtain information about prosecutorial misconduct in cases and, to the extent the issues were exposed, discussions reached a limited audience.

This has changed significantly in the Internet era. The rhetorical shift has moved toward the perception that prosecutorial misconduct is recurring and systemic. Moreover, there has been a regulatory shift toward examining prosecutorial conduct more broadly. Judges more readily express skepticism about prosecutorial compliance with law and ethics rules, and legislative reform has targeted prosecutorial conduct, most notably in areas regarding compliance with discovery in criminal cases. Even disciplinary authorities have stepped up action against errant prosecutors.

The reasons for the shift in attention to prosecutorial misconduct are multiple and interrelated. We have highlighted five necessary social conditions, beginning with the obvious one--the recurrence of prosecutorial misconduct.

Second, failings of the criminal justice system are front and center in the American discourse. Over-criminalization, mass incarceration, racial disparity in policing, and a myriad of other criminal justice concerns are the fodder of daily news stories. Many of these implicate prosecutors' work, especially their exercise of discretion in investigation, charging, plea bargaining, and sentencing. Concern about prosecutorial conduct is no longer limited to intentional lawbreaking.

Third, hundreds of DNA exonerations and the work of innocence projects exposing the causes of wrongful convictions have prompted public and professional discourse about the prosecutorial responsibility to avert wrongful convictions. Years of litigation, scientific research, and policy work exposed cases where prosecutors relied upon faulty eyewitness identification, false confessions, bad science, and police misconduct in obtaining criminal convictions of innocent people. Many of those cases also involved intentional and negligent failure to disclose evidence favorable to the defense.

Fourth, academic scholarship, particularly in the social sciences, has demonstrated deficiencies in the

Barry Scheck and Peter Neufeld, who met as public defenders at the Bronx Legal Aid Society, started the Innocence Project in 1992 as a legal clinic at Benjamin N. Cardozo School of Law. The idea was simple: If DNA technology could prove people guilty of crimes, it could also prove that people who had been wrongfully convicted were innocent. Since 1992, Innocence Project efforts have resulted in 350 DNA exonerations of convicted prisoners. See https://25years.innocenceproject.org/.

criminal justice process that prosecutors can ameliorate, and deficiencies in prosecutors' decisionmaking. The scholarship has contributed to the expansion of concern from deliberate prosecutorial wrongdoing to a concept of misconduct that encompasses both negligent wrongdoing and failures to take reasonable measures to ensure the fairness and reliability of the criminal process.

Fifth, as a consequence of and contributor to increased public attention to prosecutorial misconduct, reform organizations slowly built momentum toward discovery reform and other reform directed at prosecutors' conduct.

However, it is unlikely that any of these conditions, individually or collectively, would have resulted in the rhetorical and regulatory shift we describe but for a change in the medium by which prosecutors' conduct is catalogued and debated and made a subject of reform. Information technology has served as a catalyst for change. The Internet has expanded public exposure to wrongful conviction cases, the fault lines in the criminal justice system, the misconduct of prosecutors, and work of reform organizations. Blogs, listservs, Twitter, evolving sites, and new applications contribute to a flurry and exchange of information that was impossible in the pre-Internet days.

There has been a shifting discourse about prosecutorial misconduct, its causes, and potential remedies. Attention to the issue has not waned in the past decade. If anything, public attention is relatively constant and sustained by Internet exposure of new cases, issues, proposed reforms, and new programs. Slowly, but in significant measure, courts, legislatures, and disciplinary authorities have responded to the call for enhanced accountability measures. One cannot predict the future, but the inevitable increase in the sources, availability, and dissemination of information suggests that at the very least, information technology will continue to fuel a movement toward expanded judicial, legislative, and disciplinary regulation of prosecutors and attention to systemic changes in the role of prosecutors in our criminal justice system.

Hypo: *Prosecutors' Duty to Rape Victims and Their Families*

American Bar Association (ABA) Standards for Criminal Justice, Prosecution Function Standard 3-3.4(i) (4th ed. 2015) provides, *inter alia*, that "consistent with any specific laws or rules governing victims, the prosecutor should provide victims of serious crimes, or their representatives, an opportunity to consult with and to provide information to the prosecutor, prior to making significant decisions such as whether or not to prosecute, to pursue a disposition by plea, or to dismiss charges."

Since the victim of an alleged criminal offense is not the prosecutor's "client," do you think it appropriate in the following situations for a prosecutor to either consider the victim's (or the victim's representatives') input or to require the victim's (or representatives') approval before taking the action proposed:

Go Online

You can take a look at all of the current ABA Standards for Criminal Justice: Prosecution and Defense Function, 4th ed. (2015) at https://www.americanbar.org/groups/criminal_justice/standards/ProsecutionFunctionFourthEdition-TableofContents.

(1) A rape victim does not want her attacker to be prosecuted because she fears the humiliation and embarrassment of having to recount the circumstances of the rape on the witness stand;

(2) A rape victim does not want her attacker to be prosecuted because she fears that he or friends of his will harm her or her family;

(3) The family of a murdered victim wants the prosecutor to seek the death penalty in a homicide prosecution;

(4) The family of a murdered victim wants the prosecutor not to seek the death penalty in a homicide prosecution;

(5) An armed robbery victim does not want the prosecution to offer the defendant a proposed plea bargain which would not include incarceration. (Should it make a difference in this situation how strong the prosecution thinks its case is?)

In addition to ethical constraints and quandaries, prosecutors must operate in a setting where they often do not control their own investigative resources. In considering the following excerpt discussing this issue in the federal setting, consider the ways in which this dynamic might influence prosecutorial decision-making.

Daniel Richman—Prosecutors and Their Agents, Agents and Their Prosecutors

103 Colum. L. Rev. 749, 756-763, 786-790 (2003).

Although all federal prosecutors are housed within the Justice Department (either in the litigating divisions of "Main Justice" or in United States Attorneys' Offices), not all federal investigative agencies are. The Secret Service (which handles financial and computer crimes in addition to its protective duties) and the Customs Service, previously in the Treasury Department, are now both in the Department of Homeland Security, as is the enforcement arm of the Immigration and Naturalization Service, hitherto in the Justice Department. The criminal agents in the Internal Revenue Service report to the Secretary of the Treasury. Postal Inspectors-whose jurisdiction over mail fraud sweeps in a broad array of criminal activity, and who gained a new visibility in the anthrax investigation-are part of the U.S. Postal Service. And criminal investigations are also conducted by personnel within various regulatory agencies, including the Securities and Exchange Commission and the Environmental Protection Agency, and such executive departments as Agriculture, Labor, and Interior. Even within the Justice Department, special agents in the FBI, DEA, and (since the 2002 Homeland Security legislation) the renamed "Bureau of Alcohol, Tobacco, Firearms and Explosives" report not to prosecutors, but to other agency officials, with only the Attorney General and Deputy Attorney General exercising (or at least possessing) hierarchical authority over them. One often hears rookie prosecutors refer to 'my agents." Most soon learn to drop the possessive.

Who's That?

Daniel Richman is Paul J. Kellner Professor of Law at Columbia Law School. He is a former Chief Appellate Attorney and Assistant United States Attorney in the Southern District of New York.

If neither a line prosecutor nor her chief can dictate how an agency should deploy its resources or run an investigation, and agency officials cannot control the adjudicative process, how are the terms of this coordinate relationship set? Part of the answer lies in the macro policymaking that comprises an administration's criminal justice agenda. Congressional agendas may have similar effects as well. Policy formation and decisions about implementation (assuming for the moment that the two are analytically distinct) will also occur at the subcabinet level, within the Justice Department or at the upper reaches of enforcement agency hierarchies. Even specific cases, because of their importance and national ramifications, may be coordinated and controlled at the highest levels of the executive branch.

My focus here is on micro policymaking-the interaction between prosecutors and agents in the run-of-the-mill cases that have not been selected out for special attention by Washington. These cases are generally handled by prosecutors in the ninety-four U.S. Attorney's Offices, and by field agents scattered across the country (but concentrated in the bigger cities). In the absence of a clear bureaucratic command, how are they able to achieve a modus vivendi? What are the structures that drive agencies and prosecutors to negotiate the terms of their interaction and that set those terms?

At its heart, the relationship between federal prosecutors and federal enforcement agents is a bilateral monopoly. Prosecutors are the exclusive gatekeepers over federal court, but they need agents to gather evidence. Agencies control investigative resources, but they are not free to retain separate counsel. If agents want criminal charges to be pursued against the target of an investigation, they will have to convince a prosecutor to take the case. To focus on these truisms, however, is to ignore the interactions that determine how enforcement discretion is exercised on the ground.

Let us refine the prosecutorial side of the equation. Federal prosecutors would have monopoly power only if they were able to act through some central "purchasing" agent. And they aren't. Traditions of local independence, advantages of local knowledge, and the limited resources they have because of Congress's affinity for decentralized power are all barriers to the entry of litigating units from Main Justice into a district without cooperation from the U.S. Attorney. Those units remain at least potential entrants, however, offering a limited counterweight to the U.S. Attorney's Office's control over its district's criminal docket.

One U.S. Attorney's Office can face competition from another. Where a metropolitan area is divided among two or more federal districts (as when a large city lies near a district's border), flexible federal venue rules will allow an aggressive investigative agency to play one U.S. Attorney's Office off against another, steering its "best" cases to the district that has given the agency the best service by taking less alluring cases or offering the "best" (i.e., the most accommodating) legal support for investigations.

The possibility that another federal prosecutorial office can take cases from its jurisdiction may not be of great concern to a U.S. Attorney's Office. Disputes may occur when two offices simultaneously reach for a high-profile case holding the promise of institutional and personal glory, but ordinarily the universe of potential federal cases is large enough (and low profile enough) to allow any number of offices to pursue territorially overlapping matters with little friction. The important point for our purposes, however, is that the overlap of prosecutorial authority inevitably reduces the ability of each office to control investigative agencies' access to federal court, and consequentially reduces the extent to which an office can leverage its gatekeeping power into control of those agencies' agendas.

The overlap between state and federal criminal law also offers agencies some choice, at least in theory. Although the federal system is generally thought to offer significant procedural and resource advantages over state criminal processes, the difference will not always be significant, or, if significant, may still be outweighed by the desire to circumvent federal prosecutorial gatekeeping. A U.S. Attorney will not mourn whenever federal agencies take cases to the local D.A.'s office and will often want cases falling below some threshold level to go there. Yet an agency's interaction with local authorities will limit the U.S. Attorney's control, and even knowledge, of agency activity.

Finally, the size and organization of a single U.S. Attorney's Office can limit its power if agents can play one assistant or unit off against another. If agents can "shop" cases around until they find a sympathetic assistant, gatekeeping standards can fall victim to a "race to the bottom," in which those individual prosecutors with the lowest standards (or, from another perspective, the greatest zeal) will be the ones to whom agents most prefer to take cases. Since there are limits to how many cases even the most acquiescent assistant can take, office standards are unlikely to fall all the way to his level. But the risk is that agents will reserve for him the cases over which they want to exercise the most control-which may be precisely those cases most in need of prosecutorial oversight. If, because of their significance, these cases are among the most personally rewarding for prosecutors to work on, other assistants will be tempted to lower their standards as well. Offices can, and do, counter this problem by establishing some centralized screening mechanism. But circumvention may still be possible, as sometimes occurs when an assistant pursues a "related" matter.

Whatever their legal and institutional obligations to work together, prosecutors and agents are sometimes pushed apart by their membership in distinct, even antagonistic, professional cultures.

The basics are well known. Although the FBI has a long tradition of lawyer-agents, most agencies do not. And even the FBI has changed a lot since the Hoover years. As a general rule, then, most agents have not been exposed to the acculturation process at law school, which not only tends to be process oriented when it addresses criminal enforcement issues, but also exalts a norm of moral neutrality that can (but need not) lead prosecutors to distance themselves from the enforcement projects of the agents they deal with. Law school is only the beginning of the story, though. Far more influential are the differences in the career paths of agents and prosecutors and the aftermarkets they face. There are many career, or at least long-serving, prosecutors. But a great many view the job as a way station, a means of acquiring human capital (litigation experience, familiarity with local legal practices and personalities) that will facilitate their representation of private clients thereafter. Even those prosecutors who plan to stay with the government will often orient themselves toward their professional counterparts through participation in local bar activities and the like. In contrast, agents stay a long time. A 1994 RAND report found that "overall attrition in the FBI is low," and that, while some agents resign in their first five years, "most agents either retire at the earliest opportunity [age 50] or remain in the bureau until mandatory retirement [age 57].'"

Agents and prosecutors also have different geographical orientations. AUSAs wishing to move may try to transfer to another U.S. Attorney's Office. They may even be asked by Washington to take on jobs in another city. But the typical AUSA stays in one city and builds her professional reputation there. Life is very different for agents. According to the RAND report, upon graduation from the FBI Academy, an FBI agent starts with a three-to-five-year assignment to a field office that cannot be near her home. After that, she typically will be sent to another field office— "often one of the 'top 12' offices that are larger, have broader operational requirements, and are sometimes difficult to staff-or to headquarters in Washington D.C." Reassignments are "based on the needs of the FBI and whether agents choose to compete for management positions in other locations."

These cultural differences can drive a powerful wedge between agents and prosecutors. Agents or even agencies seeking to justify their refusal to share information about sources and methods with prosecutors will assert a fear that such data will be misused once the prosecutors enter private practice. This tendency toward non-disclosure is bolstered by concerns that prosecutors have far less "on the line" when it comes to investigative security. An agent's promise to

Practice Pointer

This article excerpt should give you some very interesting insights into the relationship between federal prosecutors and their offices, and federal investigators and their investigative agencies. All of these individuals, offices, and agencies in the federal criminal justice system are, of course, on the "same side." But this realistic—and pragmatic—look at the difference between prosecutorial and investigative mindsets and cultures can help you appreciate the fact that lawyers (defense counsel, too) need to consider not simply prosecutorial concerns, but law enforcement perspectives and priorities as well. They can be—and often are—different.

an informant is bonded by his and his agency's professional reputation. The prosecutor who will soon move into another world is not so bound. Agents may worry that prosecutors looking for lucrative private practice berths will be too quick to compromise cases with, or extend professional courtesies to, prospective professional allies, or, alternatively, too quick to tax agency resources by taking cases to trial unnecessarily in order to gain marketable litigation experience. Agents may also see prosecutors as all too ready to credit defense allegations of agent misconduct. Part of the problem may be sheer resentment on the part of agents at the rewards that private practice will bring prosecutors, and perhaps some disdain for the unworldliness of young prosecutors' law school experience. Prosecutors, for their part, may tend to identify with professional adversaries and see their job as reining in "cowboy" line agents who pay little heed to the niceties of due process.

Executive Summary

Adversary System. The American criminal justice system is an adversary system where a criminal defendant's guilt or innocence is determined as a result of the adversarial arguments and presentations of evidence by a prosecutor and defense counsel, overseen by a neutral and impartial judge.

Defense Counsels' Dilemma. Criminal defense counsel need to represent their clients effectively, whether or not they know that they are or may be guilty. Nonetheless, representing guilty clients as if they are innocent often can be troubling for defense counsel (and their families) personally, emotionally, and sometimes professionally.

Prosecutors' Dilemma. Prosecutors are supposed to fight crime and convict the guilty. However, they are also supposed to "seek justice, not victory," and this obligation counsels prosecutors not to try to win at all costs, a stricture that can be difficult for prosecutors to follow personally, emotionally, and professionally.

Major Themes

a. Defense Counsel as Zealots—Many criminal defense counsel believe that they must or should represent their clients "zealously." But sometimes zealous representation of criminal defendants raises concerns about real or apparent conflicts with defense counsel's simultaneous role as an officer of the court.

b. Prosecutor's Clients—Prosecutors are said to be "ministers of justice," whose clients are *all* of the people in their jurisdiction, not the victims of a crime. But sometimes it can be difficult for prosecutors to resist the urge to act in just as adversarial a fashion as criminal defense counsel, considering primarily the victims' interests, whether or not securing a conviction actually reflects the overall community's interests.

c. Due Process vs. Truth—The American criminal justice system sometimes values adherence to proper procedures, e.g. avoiding police misconduct, over finding the truth, e.g. determining whether the defendant is actually innocent or guilty. This important and overriding systemic respect for fair and lawful methods of proceeding creates a persistent tension in the criminal justice system, however, and it sometimes results in public misunderstanding of—and displeasure with—events that may take place in a criminal prosecution, e.g. the suppression of otherwise inculpatory evidence.

Test Your Knowledge

To assess your understanding of the material in this chapter, click here to take a quiz.

CHAPTER 10

Initial Appearance and Pretrial Release

A. Initial Appearance

Following an arrest and administrative "booking" procedures, the accused must be brought before a judge or other judicial officer (such as a magistrate) for a proceeding usually called a "first appearance" "initial appearance," "presentment," or "preliminary arraignment." There are three main determinations that are normally accomplished at the initial appearance: a determination of probable cause, a determination regarding bond, and appointment of counsel if necessary.

Federal Rule of Criminal Procedure 5(d) is typical of most rules setting the procedures for the initial appearance in court. Under Rule 5(d), the judge must inform the accused of the following:

1. The charges;

2. The right to remain silent;

3. The right to request or retain an attorney;

4. The fact that any statements that he/she makes may be used against him/her;

5. The circumstances under which the accused may secure pretrial release;

6. The right to a preliminary hearing;

7. A reasonable time to consult with an attorney; and

8. The setting or denying bail.

In some jurisdictions, including in the federal courts, at the initial appearance an accused is charged by the prosecuting authority by way of a complaint or similar document.

Take Note

In many jurisdictions, however, there may be no charging document that is issued by the prosecuting authority at the time of the initial appearance. Instead, he court makes determinations regarding probable cause and bond based on sworn information from the police.

Whether there is a charging document from the prosecution or simply an accusation from the police (commonly referred to as a "police charge"), the court must make the defendant aware of the accusation(s) against him.

Most jurisdictions require that the accused be brought before the nearest available judicial officer without unnecessary delay. Many jurisdictions have a provision like Fed. R. Crim. P. 5, which permits the judicial officer to conduct the initial appearance by video teleconference, with the defendant's consent. Under Fed. R. Crim. P. 5, the judge also has flexibility as to the district in which the initial appearance may be held. In *United States v. Alvarez-Sanchez*, 511 U.S. 350 (1994), the Supreme Court held that the period of delay in federal courts usually is measured from the time the accused is arrested on federal charges. An unreasonable delay between arrest and the initial appearance may violate due process. In evaluating an allegation of unreasonable delay, courts analyze the amount of time that has passed as well as how and why the delay occurred.

When there is a charging document from the prosecutor, and the charging document is an indictment, or when an indictment is not necessary, then the defendant normally enters a plea to the charges, usually "Not Guilty" at this early stage of the case. If a defendant chooses to stand mute, the court, by rule or its inherent authority, enters a not guilty plea on the defendant's behalf.

Take Note

Confessions that are obtained during periods of unnecessary delay prior to the initial appearance may be inadmissible. For example, under 18 U.S.C. § 3501, delay is one of several statutory factors considered in deciding whether a confession was given voluntarily during the period of unreasonable delay. *See McNabb v. United States*, 318 U.S. 332 (1943); *Mallory v. United States*, 354 U.S. 449 (1957).

Point for Discussion

Assignment of Counsel

In *Rothgery v. Gillespie County, Texas*, 554 U.S. 191 (2008), the Court made clear that the defendant's Sixth Amendment right to counsel attaches at the initial appearance, regardless of whether there is a formal charging document. *See also* Fed. R. Crim. P. 44. In many jurisdictions, this means that while counsel may be "appointed,"

Food for Thought

What problems do you see if there is no counsel present at the initial appearance? What role should a lawyer play at the initial appearance? What problems might be created by the fact that a single lawyer stands in for all defendants? What should the remedy be for the lack of counsel at the first appearance?

specific counsel may not actually be assigned at the initial appearance, thereby creating the possibility that defendant will not have an assigned attorney for an extended period of time. In such situations, there is usually one attorney from the local public defenders' office who will stand in and represent all indigent defendants at first appearances. In more urban or larger jurisdictions, this may mean twenty or more defendants at once. However, sometimes there is no counsel present at the first appearance.

Gerstein v. Pugh

420 U.S. 103 (1975).

MR. JUSTICE POWELL delivered the opinion of the Court.

Hear It

You can hear the oral argument in *Gerstein* at: http://www.oyez.org/cas es/1970-1979/1973/1973_73_477.

In March 1971 respondents Pugh and Henderson were arrested in Dade County, Fla. Each was charged with several offenses under a prosecutor's information. Pugh was denied bail because one of the charges against him carried a potential life sentence, and Henderson remained in custody because he was unable to post a $4,500 bond.

In Florida, indictments are required only for prosecution of capital offenses. Prosecutors may charge all other crimes by information, without a prior preliminary hearing and without obtaining leave of court. The Florida courts have held that the filing of an information foreclosed the suspect's right to a preliminary hearing. They have also held that habeas corpus could not be used, except perhaps in exceptional circumstances, to test the probable cause for detention under an information. The only possible methods for obtaining a judicial determination of probable cause were a special statute allowing a preliminary hearing after 30 days and arraignment, which the District Court found was often delayed a month or more after arrest. As a result, a person charged by information could be detained for a substantial period solely on the decision of a prosecutor.

Take Note

The defendants were arrested without a warrant. Had they been arrested on a warrant, the Court in *Gerstein* stated that an arrest warrant previously issued by a magistrate would satisfy the probable cause determination for the imposition of bail, temporarily detaining a defendant.

This case presents two issues: whether a person arrested and held for trial on an information is entitled to a judicial determination of probable cause for detention, and if so, whether the adversary hearing ordered by the District Court and approved by the Court of Appeals is required by the Constitution.

To implement the Fourth Amendment's protection against unfounded invasions of liberty and privacy, the Court has required that the existence of probable cause be decided by a neutral and detached magistrate whenever possible. The classic statement of this principle appears in *Johnson v. United States*, 333 U.S. 10, 13–14 (1948):

> The point of the Fourth Amendment, which often is not grasped by zealous officers, is not that it denies law enforcement the support of the usual inferences which reasonable men draw from evidence. Its protection consists in requiring that those inferences be drawn by a neutral and detached magistrate instead of being judged by the officer engaged in the often competitive enterprise of ferreting out crime.

Maximum protection of individual rights could be assured by requiring a magistrate's review of the factual justification prior to any arrest, but such a requirement would constitute an intolerable handicap for legitimate law enforcement. Thus, while the Court has expressed a preference for the use of arrest warrants when feasible it has never invalidated an arrest supported by probable cause solely because the officers failed to secure a warrant.

Under this practical compromise, a policeman's on-the-scene assessment of probable cause provides legal justification for arresting a person suspected of crime, and for a brief period of detention to take the administrative steps incident to arrest. Once the suspect is in custody, however, the reasons that justify dispensing with the magistrate's neutral judgment evaporate. There no longer is any danger that the suspect will escape or commit further crimes while the police submit their evidence to a magistrate. And, while the State's reasons for taking summary action subside, the suspect's need for a neutral determination of probable cause increases significantly. The consequences of prolonged detention may be more serious than the interference occasioned by arrest. Pretrial confinement may imperil the suspect's job, interrupt his source of income, and impair his family relationships. Even pretrial release may be accompanied by burdensome conditions that effect a significant restraint of liberty. When the stakes are this high, the detached judgment of a neutral magistrate is essential if the Fourth Amendment is to furnish meaningful protection from unfounded interference with liberty. Accordingly, we hold that the Fourth Amendment requires a judicial determination of probable cause as a prerequisite to extended restraint of liberty following arrest.

Both the District Court and the Court of Appeals held that the determination of probable cause must be accompanied by the full panoply of adversary safeguards—counsel, confrontation, cross-examination, and compulsory process for witnesses. A full preliminary hearing of this sort is modeled after the procedure used in many States to determine whether the evidence justifies going to trial under an information or presenting the case to a grand jury.

These adversary safeguards are not essential for the probable cause determination required by the Fourth Amendment. The sole issue is whether there is probable cause for detaining the arrested person pending further proceedings. This issue can be determined reliably without an adversary hearing. The standard is the same as that for arrest. That standard—probable cause to believe the suspect has committed a crime—traditionally has been decided by a magistrate in a nonadversary proceeding on hearsay and written testimony, and the Court has approved these informal modes of proof.

The use of an informal procedure is justified not only by the lesser consequences of a probable cause determination but also by the nature of the determination itself. It does not require the fine resolution of conflicting evidence that a reasonable-doubt or even a preponderance standard demands, and credibility determinations are seldom crucial in deciding whether the evidence supports a reasonable belief in guilt. This is not to say that confrontation and cross-examination might not enhance the reliability of probable cause determinations in some cases. In most cases, however, their value would be too slight to justify holding, as a matter of constitutional principle, that these formalities and safeguards designed for trial must also be employed in making the Fourth Amendment determination of probable cause.

Because of its limited function and its nonadversary character, the probable cause determination is not a "critical stage" in the prosecution that would require appointed counsel. The Court has identified as "critical stages" those pretrial procedures that would impair defense on the merits if the accused is required to proceed without counsel. *Coleman v. Alabama*, 399 U.S. 1 (1970); *United States v. Wade*, 388 U.S. 218, 226–227 (1967). The Fourth Amendment probable cause determination is addressed only to pretrial custody. To be sure, pretrial custody may affect to some extent the defendant's ability to assist in preparation of his defense, but this does not present the high probability of substantial harm identified as controlling in *Wade* and *Coleman*.

Food for Thought

Is the Court right? Why is this not a "critical stage"? Why aren't some adversarial safeguards necessary at this point, now that the defendant is in court? Is there something between what the District Court required and what the Court here suggests, which is reliance on an *ex parte* determination of probable cause by a judicial officer without the opportunity for a lawyer representing the defense to point out any problems or defects?

Although we conclude that the Constitution does not require an adversary determination of probable cause, we recognize that state systems of criminal procedure vary widely. There is no single preferred pretrial procedure, and the nature of the probable cause determination usually will be shaped to accord with a State's pretrial procedure viewed as a whole. Whatever procedure a State may adopt, it must provide a fair and reliable determination of probable cause as a condition for any significant pretrial restraint of liberty,[26] and this determination must be made by a judicial officer either before or promptly after arrest.

We agree with the Court of Appeals that the Fourth Amendment requires a timely judicial determination of probable cause as a prerequisite to detention, and we accordingly affirm that much of the judgment. As we do not agree that the Fourth Amendment requires the adversary hearing outlined in the District Court's decree, we reverse in part and remand to the Court of Appeals for further proceedings consistent with this opinion.

It is so ordered.

> **Make the Connection**
>
> This case was brought as a civil rights action pursuant to U.S.C. §1983, as was *Rothgery*. However, the Supreme Court suggests in *Gerstein* that the case could have been brought as a pretrial petition for a writ of habeas corpus challenging the pretrial detention as unlawful under the Fourth Amendment. Lawyers and judges usually think of habeas corpus petitions as solely designed to address post-conviction constitutional issues (see Chapter 23), but that is not the case.

Points for Discussion

a. The *Gerstein* Proceeding

At a *Gerstein* hearing, hearsay and written testimony are permitted, as long as the statements have been sworn to under oath. While the *Gerstein* determination is not an adversarial proceeding and the accused has no right to be present, to have counsel, or to question witnesses, in practice it often occurs at the initial appearance with the accused and counsel present, and counsel may be allowed to point out defects in the government's presentation.

> Because of the similarity between the timing of the initial appearance and the timing of the *Gerstein* determination following a warrantless arrest, a judge may conduct both proceedings at the time of the initial appearance.

---

[26] Because the probable cause determination is not a constitutional prerequisite to the charging decision, it is required only for those suspects who suffer restraints on liberty other than the condition that they appear for trial. There are many kinds of pretrial release and many degrees of conditional liberty. We cannot define specifically those that would require a prior probable cause determination, but the key factor is significant restraint on liberty.

b. A Finding of No Probable Cause

When a court determines that there is no probable cause, the defendant must be released from custody on that charge. A finding of no probable cause does not foreclose a later prosecution.

Make the Connection

What happens if the defendant is arrested under a warrant and the affidavit does not establish probable cause, or if the judicial officer at first appearance finds probable cause but is wrong? Does the defendant have a constitutional remedy? *Gerstein* does not answer these questions but does the Fourth Amendment require a remedy?

c. The Forty-Eight Hour Rule

In *County of Riverside v. McLaughlin*, 500 U.S. 44 (1991), the Court held that absent "emergency or other extraordinary circumstances" the judicial determination of probable cause must occur "soon as is reasonably feasible, but in no event later than 48 hours after arrest."

Hypo: *Did the Police Comply with Riverside?*

The police arrest Frank Johnson for murder on a Saturday at 11:00 a.m. as he is fleeing the scene of a homicide. The police hold Frank for interrogation until Monday morning while they complete their investigation. In this jurisdiction, the court holds first appearances at 10:00 a.m. and at 3:00 p.m. every day Monday through Friday, but only at 5:00 pm on Saturdays, Sundays and holidays. Monday morning the police take Frank to court for the 10:00 a.m. initial appearance session. Did the police comply with *Riverside*? *See Lopez v. City of Chicago*, 464 F. 3d 711 (7th Cir. 2006).

B. Pretrial Release

A defendant's pretrial release from custody typically is in exchange for a pledge of something of value designed to insure he will appear in court and will comply with the court's orders in a pending criminal case. Bail provides the Anglo-American criminal justice system's solution to the problem of how to handle an accused, who is presumed innocent, during the time period between arrest and trial. Conceptually, bail accommodates the defendant's interest in pretrial liberty (consistent with the presumption of innocence) and society's interest in assuring that the accused is present for trial so that the case can be properly adjudicated. In each case, a must judge decide whether to grant pretrial release, and if so, what monetary amount and/or conditions of release are needed to assure the defendant's presence. There are a variety of release conditions that a court may impose.

Points for Discussion

a. Recognizance Bond

Release on recognizance is a long-standing practice, and for good reason. If the defendant is likely return to court, even without the imposition of conditions, the bond requirement may not be needed, and may impose a substantial and unnecessary hardship upon a defendant of limited resources. Perhaps for this reason, the law acknowledges the power of the courts to release a defendant on recognizance,

Under a recognizance bond, commonly called "personal recognizance" ("PR" for short) or "release on recognizance" ("ROR"), the court allows the defendant to be at liberty in return for a written promise to return and to comply with the orders of the court throughout the case.

and indeed entitles a defendant to ROR unless the court finds that something more is required to insure the defendant's appearance in court. In other words, under the law (though perhaps not in practice), release on recognizance should be the norm or "default" position.

b. Unsecured Bond

An unsecured bond is a pledge by the defendant to be liable for a specified sum if the defendant should breach a material condition of release. The unsecured bond is advantageous over the release on personal recognizance when defendant is a person of means. The bond gives the defendant a financial stake in obeying the orders of the court and thus helps insure the defendant's appearance.

c. Release on Nonfinancial Conditions

The court has the power and flexibility to place nonfinancial conditions on the defendant as long as they are limited to conditions designed to insure the presence of the accused at future court proceedings. Courts must impose the least onerous conditions that will insure defendant's presence in court. Such conditions may include, but are not limited to, placing defendant in the custody of a person or agency, placing restrictions upon travel, association or place of abode, drug testing or treatment, enrollment in school or pursuit of employment, electronic monitoring, or requiring confinement at home, a jail, a halfway house or other facility during specified hours.

d. Cash Bond

A defendant may be released from custody by depositing cash (or its equivalent) in the amount of the bail with the court. The money is deposited by the clerk in an escrow account and is returned, usually minus an administrative fee, at the conclusion of the proceedings—assuming that the accused has appeared as directed. A major advantage of the cash bond is that it gives defendant an immediate stake in appearing for court proceedings. In the event of non-appearance, defendant faces an immediate financial loss, rather than some sort of distant civil liability, as would be true under an unsecured bond. Moreover, if defendant does appear in court as ordered, the money may be recovered rather than be retained by the bondsman who may have done little to advance the justice system's interests. A cash bond may also be available for forfeiture or for application to indebtedness upon judgment in the case.

Food for Thought

Compare the differences between cash and the surety bonds. Is there any advantage of one over the other for criminal justice purposes? Why might judges prefer surety bonds? Is there a rational basis for that preference?

e. Personal Surety Bond

The defendant may also be able to obtain release by pledging his real property (or arranging for his/her friends do so). If defendant fails to appear in court, the property is forfeited. On the other hand, if the defendant appears as directed, the property or any lien on the real estate is released at the conclusion of the proceedings.

f. Surety Bond

The court may require defendant to post a bond underwritten by one or more sureties. This is the classic bail bond situation. The defendant or his or her family or friends pay a fee, typically 10%, to a bondsman, and the bondsman posts the entire amount of the bond with the court. The bondsman keeps the 10% as a fee at the conclusion of the case. If defendant fails to appear in court, the bondsman is on the hook for the bond amount and therefore has an incentive to find

Take Note

While bail bondsmen may have made sense in earlier times, the need for bondsmen is obsolete with the advent of modern policing and computer systems: (1) once the bondsman is paid his fee, the bond no longer provides the defendant with an incentive to appear; (2) in actual practice, bondsmen do very little because a defendant who fails to appear is usually returned to court by law enforcement; (3) even if a bondsman does attempt to return defendant to court, it is questionable whether public safety is advanced by "Dog the Bounty Hunter" going out into the community armed with a gun to protect his own money. Isn't this better handled by trained law enforcement?

the defendant and get him to court, much in the vein of the Old West bounty hunters.

1. Release Determinations

Stack v. Boyle

342 U.S. 1 (1951).

MR. CHIEF JUSTICE VINSON delivered the opinion of the Court.

Indictments have been returned in the Southern District of California charging the twelve petitioners with conspiring to violate the Smith Act, 18 U.S.C. (Supp. IV) §§ 371, 2385. Upon their arrest, bail was fixed for each petitioner in the widely varying amounts of $2,500, $7,500, $75,000 and $100,000. On motion of petitioner Schneiderman following arrest in the Southern District of New York, his bail was reduced to $50,000 before his removal to California. On motion of the Government to increase bail in the case of other petitioners, bail was fixed in the District Court for the Southern District of California in the uniform amount of $50,000 for each petitioner.

Petitioners moved to reduce bail on the ground that bail as fixed was excessive under the Eighth Amendment.[1] In support of their motion, petitioners submitted statements as to their financial resources, family relationships, health, prior criminal records, and other information. The only evidence offered by the Government was a certified record showing that four persons previously convicted under the Smith Act in the Southern District of New York had forfeited bail. No evidence was produced relating those four persons to the petitioners in this case. At a hearing on the motion, petitioners were examined by the District Judge and cross-examined by an attorney for the Government. Petitioners' factual statements stand uncontroverted.

After their motion to reduce bail was denied, petitioners filed applications for habeas corpus in the same District Court. Upon consideration of the record on the motion to reduce bail, the writs were denied. The Court of Appeals for the Ninth Circuit affirmed.

From the passage of the Judiciary Act of 1789 to the present Federal Rules of Criminal Procedure, Rule 46 (a)(1), federal law has unequivocally provided that a person arrested for a non-capital offense *shall* be admitted to bail. This traditional

---

[1] Excessive bail shall not be required, nor excessive fines imposed, nor cruel and unusual punishments inflicted." U.S. Const., Amend. VIII.

right to freedom before conviction permits the unhampered preparation of a defense, and serves to prevent the infliction of punishment prior to conviction. *See Hudson v. Parker,* 156 U.S. 277, 285 (1895). Unless this right to bail before trial is preserved, the presumption of innocence, secured only after centuries of struggle, would lose its meaning.

The right to release before trial is conditioned upon the accused's giving adequate assurance that he will stand trial and submit to sentence if found guilty. *Ex parte Milburn,* 9 Pet. 704, 710 (1835). Like the ancient practice of securing the oaths of responsible persons to stand as sureties for the accused, the modern practice of requiring a bail bond or the deposit of a sum of money subject to forfeiture serves as additional assurance of the presence of an accused. Bail set at a figure higher than an amount reasonably calculated to fulfill this purpose is "excessive" under the Eighth Amendment.

Since the function of bail is limited, the fixing of bail for any individual defendant must be based upon standards relevant to the purpose of assuring the presence of that defendant. The traditional standards as expressed in the Federal Rules of Criminal Procedure are to be applied in each case to each defendant. In this case petitioners are charged with offenses under the Smith Act and, if found guilty, their convictions are subject to review with the scrupulous care demanded by our Constitution. Upon final judgment of conviction, petitioners face imprisonment of not more than five years and a fine of not more than $10,000. It is not denied that bail for each petitioner has been fixed in a sum much higher than that usually imposed for offenses with like penalties and yet there has been no factual showing to justify such action in this case. The Government asks the courts to depart from the norm by assuming, without the introduction of evidence, that each petitioner is a pawn in a conspiracy and will, in obedience to a superior, flee the jurisdiction. To infer from the fact of indictment alone a need for bail in an unusually high amount is an arbitrary act. Such conduct would inject into our own system of government the very principles of totalitarianism which Congress was seeking to guard against in passing the statute under which petitioners have been indicted.

If bail in an amount greater than that usually fixed for serious charges of crimes is required in the case of any of the petitioners, that is a matter to which evidence should be directed in a hearing so that the constitutional rights of each petitioner may be preserved. In the absence of such a showing, we are of the opinion that the fixing of bail before trial in these cases cannot be squared with the statutory and constitutional standards for admission to bail.

The Court concludes that bail has not been fixed by proper methods in this case and that petitioners' remedy is by motion to reduce bail, with right of appeal to the Court of Appeals. Accordingly, the judgment of the Court of Appeals is vacated and the case is remanded to the District Court with directions to vacate its order denying petitioners' applications for writs of habeas corpus and to dismiss the applications without prejudice. Petitioners may move for reduction of bail in the criminal proceeding so that a hearing may be held for the purpose of fixing reasonable bail for each petitioner.

By MR. JUSTICE JACKSON, whom MR. JUSTICE FRANKFURTER joins dissenting.

The principles governing allowance of bail have been misunderstood or too casually applied in these cases and they should be returned to the Circuit Justice or the District Courts for reconsideration in the light of standards which it is our function to determine.

The practice of admission to bail, as it has evolved in Anglo-American law, is not a device for keeping persons in jail upon mere accusation until it is found convenient to give them a trial. On the contrary, the spirit of the procedure is to enable them to stay out of jail until a trial has found them guilty.

Without this conditional privilege, even those wrongly accused are punished by a period of imprisonment while awaiting trial and are handicapped in consulting counsel, search-ing for evidence and witnesses, and preparing a defense. To open a way of escape from this handicap and possible injustice, Congress commands allowance of bail for one under charge of any offense not punishable by death, Fed. Rules Crim. Proc., 46 (a)(1) providing: "A person arrested for an offense not punishable by death shall be admitted to bail" before conviction.

Food for Thought

The view of bail articulated in this opinion is not reflective of what the vast majority of judges actually do when setting bond. For example, when a judge sets a million dollar bond for an indigent defendant in a murder or rape case, does the judge expect defendant to post the bond, giving him an adequate incentive to return to court, or does he expect that the accused will stay in jail?

Admission to bail always involves a risk that the accused will take flight. That is a calculated risk which the law takes as the price of our system of justice. We know that Congress anticipated that bail would enable some escapes, because it provided a procedure for dealing with them. Fed. Rules Crim. Proc., 46 (f).

In allowance of bail, the duty of the judge is to reduce the risk by fixing an amount reasonably calculated to hold the accused available for trial and its consequence. Fed. Rules Crim. Proc., 46 (c). But the judge is not free to make the sky the limit, because the Eighth Amendment to the Constitution says: "Excessive bail shall not be required."

Congress has reduced this generality in providing more precise standards, stating that "the amount thereof shall be such as in the judgment of the commissioner or court or judge or justice will insure the presence of the defendant, having regard to the nature and circumstances of the offense charged, the weight of the evidence against him, the financial ability of the defendant to give bail and the character of the defendant." Fed. Rules Crim. Proc., 46 (c).

It is complained that the District Court fixed a uniform blanket bail chiefly by consideration of the nature of the accusation and did not take into account the difference in circumstances between different defendants. If this occurred, it is a clear violation of Rule 46 (c). Each defendant stands before the bar of justice as an individual. Even on a conspiracy charge defendants do not lose their separateness or identity. While it might be possible that these defendants are identical in financial ability, character and relation to the charge—elements Congress has directed to be regarded in fixing bail—I think it violates the law of probabilities. Each accused is entitled to any benefits due to his good record, and misdeeds or a bad record should prejudice only those who are guilty of them. The question when application for bail is made relates to each one's trustworthiness to appear for trial and what security will supply reasonable assurance of his appearance.

But the protest charges, and the defect in the proceedings below appears to be, that, provoked by the flight of certain Communists after conviction, the Government demands and public opinion supports a use of the bail power to keep Communist defendants in jail before conviction. Thus, the amount is said to have been fixed not as a reasonable assurance of their presence at the trial, but also as an assurance they would remain in jail. There seems reason to believe that this may have been the spirit to which the courts below have yielded, and it is contrary to the whole policy and philosophy of bail. This is not to say that every defendant is entitled to such bail as he can provide, but he is entitled to an opportunity to make it in a reasonable amount. I think the whole matter should be reconsidered by the appropriate judges in the traditional spirit of bail procedure.

Go Online

To learn more about the relationship between high money bonds and poverty, race and pretrial detention, see: http://www.bjs.gov/content/pub/pdf/prfdsc.pdf; http://www.pretrial.org; http://www.npr.org/2010/01/21/122725771/Bail-Burden-Keeps-U-S-Jails-Stuffed-With-Inmates.

Hypo 1: *Proper Bond?*

Joe is charged with theft in a jurisdiction where he has lived all of his life. He lives with his wife and children, and he has a steady job at a local manufacturing plant but no savings. The court sets a bond of $10,000 cash or surety. Is the bond amount proper? What if instead, Joe was arrested and charged with armed robbery after being identified by two witnesses and bond is set at $50,000? In each case, what are the best defense and prosecution arguments?

Hypo 2: *Escalating Priors*

Steve is charged with possession of cocaine. Steve recently moved to the jurisdiction from out of state to live with his girlfriend. Steve has no prior convictions and no assets. The court sets a bond of $5,000 cash or surety. What are the arguments for and against this bond? Does it change the analysis if Steve has two prior misdemeanor convictions, one for criminal trespass and one for simple assault? What if, instead of those two convictions, Steve has two prior felony convictions that significantly enhance the potential sentence he could receive upon conviction for possession of cocaine? In the last two situations what additional information might you want regarding the prior cases?

Hypo 3: *The Question of Assets*

Barbara is an executive at a large national bank. She is charged with defrauding the bank and its customers out of millions of dollars. She is single, has no family, but owns a multi-million dollar downtown condo, a brand new Lexus, and has other assets in the form of stocks, bonds, and cash totaling $2.5 million. What arguments for bail will the defense and prosecution make?

Hypo 4: *The Addict Mother*

Thirty-six year-old Susan is charged with burglary. She is a heroin addict, and has a record of seven prior convictions, five for theft and two for possession of narcotics. She works part-time and lives with her three children and her husband who is a high school math teacher. The court is contemplating setting a $15,000 cash or surety bond, which she does not have the financial ability to make. What position(s) will the defense advance on Susan's behalf? How should the prosecution respond?

Hypo 5: *Same Crime, Same Bond*

Two men rob a local convenience store. The owner gives a very detailed description of the two men that a police detective recognizes as David and John. David is single, unemployed, and mostly lives with his parents but stays "off and on" with his girlfriend. John is married with one infant child and has a steady job at McDonalds. The detective has both men brought in for questioning. David immediately asserts his right to remain silent and is booked for robbery and taken to court that day for his initial appearance. Bond is set at $25,000 which must be provided by a commercial surety. John waives his rights and eventually confesses that he and David robbed the store together. As a result of the interrogation, John isn't brought to court for his initial appearance until the next day. The prosecutor informs the magistrate about David's bond, and the magistrate immediately sets John's bond at the same amount. What statutory and/or constitutional arguments can John's attorney make to challenge the bail? How might the prosecution respond?

Hypo 6: *The Buyer and the Seller*

Michael is twenty-three years old and shares an apartment with three other men in their 20's and one of their girlfriends. All of them have no steady employment but work at odd jobs. Based on tips, the police set up an observation post at a street corner near the apartment that is known for narcotics activity. The police see Michael walk up to a man later identified as Patrick standing near the corner, and hand Patrick money. Patrick then signals to another man who retrieves a small, ziplock plastic bag containing an off-white rock-like substance from a bush. The man hands the bag to Michael and leaves. The police radio a description of Michael to other officers who stop and arrest Michael around the corner on his way back to the apartment. A search of Michael yields the plastic bag along with a small pipe. The substance tests positive for cocaine. The police also arrest Patrick at the corner but the other man gets away. A search of Patrick yields about $700 in cash. In the bush, police locate a large plastic bag containing twenty-five small ziplock bags each containing crack cocaine.

The magistrate sets Michael's bond at $2500 cash or surety. Patrick's bond is set at $50,000 cash or surety. Do these bonds make sense? What arguments can be made for and against these bonds?

Hypo 7: *Funds Used to Hire Lawyer*

Susan is a twenty-two year-old single mother of three children who is charged with theft. She has one prior conviction for possession of marijuana. Susan has a full-time waitressing job and over the years has managed to put about $1000 of her tips into a savings account. Susan's best friend looks everywhere for an attorney to take Susan's case and finally one agrees to take it for $750. The attorney shows up for the initial appearance, but when the judge learns about Susan's employment and savings account the judge sets bond at $2500 cash or surety. What arguments might her attorney make on a motion to reconsider the bond? What if no attorney will agree to take the case for less than $2500 so Susan is instead represented by a public defender?

Hypo 8: *Wealthy Parents*

Frank is a twenty-one year-old full-time college student. Pursuant to a valid search warrant, the police search his dorm room and find fifty individually packaged ziplock bags each containing twenty-five dollars' worth of marijuana. Frank is arrested and charged with possession with intent to distribute marijuana. Frank has no car or other large assets (just a two-year-old computer, clothes and other small, personal belongings). His mother is a cardiologist and his father is a successful business executive and they are quite wealthy with combined yearly earnings around $1 million. They own a large suburban home (mortgage has been paid off) and a Lexus and an Audi. They are paying Frank's way through college including his $40,000 per year tuition and expenses through their savings and income. As soon as Frank is arrested he contacts his parents and they retain the best lawyer in town for $25,000. The judge sets Frank's bond at $100,000. What are the arguments in favor and against this amount?

2. The Bail Reform Act

Most states rely upon statutes to define the circumstances under which an accused may obtain pretrial release. The Bail Reform Act of 1984 (18 U.S.C. §§ 3141–3150) governs release determinations in federal courts, and may serve as a reference. For minor misdemeanors, many jurisdictions provide a uniform schedule of bail, though even then defendants may alternatively avail themselves of the regular bail provisions.

An initial determination is made by the court about whether the accused is a flight or safety risk. If not a flight or safety risk, § 3142(b) mandates a recognizance bond or an unsecured appearance bond. If the court believes that the accused presents either risk, the court is to inquire whether the risk can be minimized by measures short of pretrial detention, *i.e.*, by imposing conditions under § 3142(c), after considering the § 3142(g) factors. If the risk can be minimized, the court tailors conditions to address the risk posed. Under particular circumstances, including a serious risk that the defendant will not appear, the defendant may be subject to pretrial detention without the possibility of release, § 3142(e)–(g).

Regardless of the type of release, it is always subject to the condition that the person not commit another crime. § 3142(b). When a defendant commits a crime while released, an independent, mandatory, consecutive, additional sentence (up to ten years for felonies and one year for misdemeanors) is imposed after conviction. § 3147. In addition, the sentencing judge may increase the sentence for crimes committed while on pretrial release. *United States Sentencing Commission, Federal Sentencing Guidelines Manual*, §§ 2J1.7, 4A1.3. However, a separate prosecution for contempt for violation of the release order raises complicated double jeopardy issues.

Section 3142(c)(2) prohibits the imposition of financial conditions that are so burdensome that the defendant is effectively subject to preventive detention. Does that mean that a court cannot set a bail that the defendant cannot meet immediately? Although the United States Supreme Court has never firmly resolved the issue, one Circuit held in *United States v. Mantecon-Zayas*, 949 F.2d 548 (1st Cir. 1991) that a court can impose a financial condition exceeding a defendant's means as long as the amount of bail is reasonably necessary to assure the defendant's presence at trial.

3. Pretrial Detention

The Bail Reform Act of 1984 not only governs pretrial release decisions but, for the first time in our nation's history, explicitly authorized the government to hold a defendant charged with an ordinary criminal offense in jail pending trial without any means for release—so called "preventive detention." Title 18 U.S.C. § 3142 authorizes a judicial officer to order the detention of a defendant pending trial if the prosecution demonstrates by clear and convincing evidence that no release conditions will reasonably assure the safety of the community or assure the defendant's appearance at future court proceedings. It was only a matter of time before the United States Supreme Court reviewed the constitutionality of this novel and controversial statute.

United States v. Salerno

481 U.S. 739 (1987).

CHIEF JUSTICE REHNQUIST delivered the opinion of the Court.

Hear It

You can hear the oral argument in *Salerno* at: http://www.oyez.org/cas es/1980-1989/1986/1986_86_87.

The Bail Reform Act of 1984 (Act) allows a federal court to detain an arrestee pending trial if the Government demonstrates by clear and convincing evidence after an adversary hearing that no release conditions "will reasonably assure the safety of any other person and the community." The United States Court of Appeals for the Second Circuit struck down this provision of the Act as facially unconstitutional, because, in that court's words, this type of pretrial detention violates "substantive due process."

Responding to "the alarming problem of crimes committed by persons on release," Congress formulated the Bail Reform Act of 1984, 18 U.S.C. § 3141 et seq. (1982 ed., Supp. III), as the solution to a bail crisis in the federal courts. The Act represents the National Legislature's considered response to numerous perceived deficiencies in the federal bail process. By providing for sweeping changes in both the way federal courts consider bail applications and the circumstances under which bail is granted, Congress hoped to "give the courts adequate authority to make release decisions that give appropriate recognition to the danger a person may pose to others if released."

To this end, § 3141(a) of the Act requires a judicial officer to determine whether an arrestee shall be detained. Section 3142(e) provides that "if, after a hearing pursuant to the provisions of subsection (f), the judicial officer finds that no condition or combination of conditions will reasonably assure the appearance of the person as required and the safety of any other person and the community, he shall order the detention of the person prior to trial." Section 3142(f) provides the arrestee with a number of procedural safeguards. He may request the presence of counsel at the detention hearing, he may testify and present witnesses in his behalf, as well as proffer evidence, and he may cross-examine other witnesses appearing at the hearing. If the judicial officer finds that no conditions of pretrial release can reasonably assure the safety of other persons and the community, he must state his findings of fact in writing, § 3142(i), and support his conclusion with "clear and convincing evidence," § 3142(f).

The judicial officer is not given unbridled discretion in making the detention determination. Congress has specified the considerations relevant to that decision. These factors include the nature and seriousness of the charges, the substantiality of the Government's evidence against the arrestee, the arrestee's background and characteristics, and the nature and seriousness of the danger posed by the suspect's release. § 3142(g). Should a judicial officer order detention, the detainee is entitled to expedited appellate review of the detention order. §§ 3145(b), (c).

Respondents Anthony Salerno and Vincent Cafaro were arrested on March 21, 1986, after being charged in a 29-count indictment alleging various Racketeer Influenced and Corrupt Organizations Act (RICO) violations, mail and wire fraud offenses, extortion, and various criminal gambling violations. The RICO counts alleged 35 acts of racketeering activity, including fraud, extortion, gambling, and conspiracy to commit murder. At respondents' arraignment, the Government moved to have Salerno and Cafaro detained pursuant to § 3142(e), on the ground that no condition of release would assure the safety of the community or any person. The District Court held a hearing at which the Government made a detailed proffer of evidence. The Government's case showed that Salerno was the "boss" of the Genovese crime family of La Cosa Nostra and that Cafaro was a "captain" in the Genovese family. According to the Government's proffer, based in large part on conversations intercepted by a court-ordered wiretap, respondents had participated in wide-ranging conspiracies to aid their illegitimate enterprises through violent means. The Government also offered the testimony of two of its trial witnesses, who would assert that Salerno personally participated in two murder conspiracies. Salerno opposed the motion for detention, challenging the credibility of the Government's witnesses. He offered the testimony of several character witnesses as well as a letter from his doctor stating that he was suffering from a serious medical condition. Cafaro presented no evidence at the hearing, but instead characterized the wiretap conversations as merely "tough talk."

A facial challenge to a legislative Act is, of course, the most difficult challenge to mount successfully, since the challenger must establish that no set of circumstances exists under which the Act would be valid. The fact that the Bail Reform Act might operate unconstitutionally under some conceivable set of circumstances is insufficient to render it wholly invalid, since we have not recognized an "overbreadth" doctrine outside the limited context of the First Amendment. *Schall v. Martin*, 467 U.S. 253 (1984). We think respondents have failed to shoulder their heavy burden to demonstrate that the Act is "facially" unconstitutional.

Respondents present two grounds for invalidating the Bail Reform Act's provisions permitting pretrial detention on the basis of future dangerousness. First, they rely upon the Court of Appeals' conclusion that the Act exceeds the limitations placed upon the Federal Government by the Due Process Clause of the Fifth Amendment. Second, they contend that the Act contravenes the Eighth Amendment's proscription against excessive bail. We treat these contentions in turn.

The Due Process Clause of the Fifth Amendment provides that "No person shall . . . be deprived of life, liberty, or property, without due process of law." This Court has held that the Due Process Clause protects individuals against two types of government action. So-called "substantive due process" prevents the government from engaging in conduct that "shocks the conscience," *Rochin v. California*, 342 U.S. 165 (1952), or interferes with rights "implicit in the concept of ordered liberty," *Palko v. Connecticut*, 302 U.S. 319 (1937). When government action depriving a person of life, liberty, or property survives substantive due process scrutiny, it must still be implemented in a fair manner. *Mathews v. Eldridge*, 424 U.S. 319 (1976). This requirement has traditionally been referred to as "procedural" due process.

Respondents first argue that the Act violates substantive due process because the pretrial detention it authorizes constitutes impermissible punishment before trial. *See Bell v. Wolfish*, 441 U.S. 520 (1979). The Government, however, has

Take Note

These particular defendants—dangerous and notorious mafia crime bosses—presented the Court with the best scenario for preventive detention. Indeed, by the time the case reached the Supreme Court, the Court did not have to decide the case: Salerno had been convicted and sentenced and Cafaro had been released at the government's request because he had agreed to be a government informant (apparently making him no longer dangerous in the government's eyes). The issue of preventive detention was therefore moot for both defendants. Yet the Court decided the issue anyway because it presented such a compelling case for preventive detention.

never argued that pretrial detention could be upheld if it were "punishment." The Court of Appeals assumed that pretrial detention under the Bail Reform Act is regulatory, not penal, and we agree that it is.

As an initial matter, the mere fact that a person is detained does not inexorably lead to the conclusion that the government has imposed punishment. To determine whether a restriction on liberty constitutes impermissible punishment or permissible regulation, we look to legislative intent. Unless Congress expressly intended to impose punitive restrictions, the punitive/regulatory distinction turns on "whether an alternative purpose to which the restriction may rationally be connected is assignable for it, and whether it appears excessive in relation to the alternative purpose assigned to it." *Schall v. Martin*, 467 U.S. at 269.

We conclude that the detention imposed by the Act falls on the regulatory side of the dichotomy. The legislative history of the Bail Reform Act clearly indicates that Congress did not formulate the pretrial detention provisions as punishment for dangerous individuals. Congress instead perceived pretrial detention as a potential solution to a pressing societal problem. There is no doubt that preventing danger to the community is a legitimate regulatory goal.

Nor are the incidents of pretrial detention excessive in relation to the regulatory goal Congress sought to achieve. The Bail Reform Act carefully limits the circumstances under which detention may be sought to the most serious of crimes. *See* 18 U.S.C. § 3142(f). The arrestee is entitled to a prompt detention hearing, and the maximum length of pretrial detention is limited by the stringent time limitations of the Speedy Trial Act. *See* 18 U.S.C. § 3161 *et seq.* Moreover, as in *Schall v. Martin*, the conditions of confinement envisioned by the Act "appear to reflect the regulatory purposes relied upon by the" Government. As in *Schall*, the statute requires that detainees be housed in a "facility separate, to the extent practicable, from persons awaiting or serving sentences or being held in custody pending appeal." 18 U.S.C. § 3142(i)(2). We conclude, therefore, that the pretrial detention contemplated by the Bail Reform Act is regulatory in nature, and does not constitute punishment before trial in violation of the Due Process Clause.

The Court of Appeals nevertheless concluded that "the Due Process Clause prohibits pretrial detention on the ground of danger to the community as a regulatory measure, without regard to the duration of the detention." Respondents characterize the Due Process Clause as erecting an impenetrable "wall" in this area that "no governmental interest—rational, important, compelling or otherwise—may surmount."

We do not think the Clause lays down any such categorical imperative. We have repeatedly held that the Government's regulatory interest in community safety can, in appropriate circumstances, outweigh an individual's liberty interest. For example, in times of war or insurrection, when society's interest is at its peak, the Government may detain individuals whom the Government believes to be dangerous. *See Ludecke v. Watkins,* 335 U.S. 160 (1948); *Moyer v. Peabody,* 212 U.S. 78 (1909). Even outside the exigencies of war, we have found that sufficiently compelling governmental interests can justify detention of dangerous persons. Thus, we have found no absolute constitutional barrier to detention of potentially dangerous resident aliens pending deportation proceedings. *Carlson v. Landon,* 342 U.S. 524 (1952); *Wong Wing v. United States,* 163 U.S. 228 (1896). We have also held that the government may detain mentally unstable individuals who present a danger to the public, *Addington v. Texas,* 441 U.S. 418 (1979), and dangerous defendants who become incompetent to stand trial, *Jackson v. Indiana,* 406 U.S. 715 (1972); *Greenwood v. United States,* 350 U.S. 366 (1956). We have approved of post arrest regulatory detention of juveniles when they present a continuing danger to the community. *Schall v. Martin, supra.* Even competent adults may face substantial liberty restrictions as a result of the operation of our criminal justice system. If the police suspect an individual of a crime, they may arrest and hold him until a neutral magistrate determines whether probable cause exists. *Gerstein v. Pugh,* 420 U.S. 103 (1975). Finally, respondents concede and the Court of Appeals noted that an arrestee may be incarcerated until trial if he presents a risk of flight, *see Bell v. Wolfish,* 441 U.S., at 534, or a danger to witnesses.

Respondents characterize all of these cases as exceptions to the "general rule" of substantive due process that the government may not detain a person prior to a judgment of guilt in a criminal trial. Such a "general rule" may freely be conceded, but these cases show a sufficient number of exceptions to the rule that the congressional action challenged here can hardly be characterized as totally novel. Given the well-established authority of the government, in special circumstances, to restrain individuals' liberty prior to or even without criminal trial and conviction, we think that the present statute providing for pretrial detention on the basis of dangerousness must be evaluated in precisely the same manner that we evaluated the laws in the cases discussed above.

The government's interest in preventing crime by arrestees is both legitimate and compelling. In *Schall* we recognized the strength of the State's interest in preventing juvenile crime. This general concern with crime prevention is no less compelling when the suspects are adults. Indeed, "the harm suffered by the victim of a crime is not dependent upon the age of the perpetrator." *Schall v. Martin.* The Bail Reform Act of 1984 responds to an even more particularized governmental interest than the interest we sustained in *Schall.* The statute we upheld in

Schall permitted pretrial detention of any juvenile arrested on any charge after a showing that the individual might commit some undefined further crimes. The Bail Reform Act, in contrast, narrowly focuses on a particularly acute problem in which the Government interests are overwhelming. The Act operates only on individuals who have been arrested for a specific category of extremely serious offenses. 18 U.S.C. § 3142(f). Congress specifically found that these individuals are far more likely to be responsible for dangerous acts in the community after arrest. Nor is the Act by any means a scattershot attempt to incapacitate those who are merely suspected of these serious crimes. The Government must first of all demonstrate probable cause to believe that the charged crime has been committed by the arrestee, but that is not enough. In a full-blown adversary hearing, the Government must convince a neutral decisionmaker by clear and convincing evidence that no conditions of release can reasonably assure the safety of the community or any person. 18 U.S.C. § 3142(f). While the Government's general interest in preventing crime is compelling, even this interest is heightened when the Government musters convincing proof that the arrestee, already indicted or held to answer for a serious crime, presents a demonstrable danger to the community. Under these narrow circumstances, society's interest in crime prevention is at its greatest.

On the other side of the scale is the individual's strong interest in liberty. We do not minimize the importance and fundamental nature of this right. But, as our cases hold, this right may, in circumstances where the government's interest is sufficiently weighty, be subordinated to the greater needs of society. Congress' careful delineation of the circumstances under which detention will be permitted satisfies this standard. When the Government proves by clear and convincing evidence that an arrestee presents an identified and articulable threat to an individual or the community, consistent with the Due Process Clause, a court may disable the arrestee from executing that threat. Under these circumstances, we cannot categorically state that pretrial detention "offends some principle of justice so rooted in the traditions and conscience of our people as to be ranked as fundamental." *Snyder v. Massachusetts*, 291 U.S. 97 (1934).

Finally, we may dispose briefly of respondents' facial challenge to the procedures of the Bail Reform Act. To sustain them against such a challenge, we need only find them "adequate to authorize the pretrial detention of at least some persons charged with crimes," *Schall, supra*, at 264, whether or not they might be insufficient in some particular circumstances. We think they pass that test. As we stated in *Schall*, "there is nothing inherently unattainable about a prediction of future criminal conduct." 467 U.S., at 278.

Under the Bail Reform Act, the procedures by which a judicial officer evaluates the likelihood of future dangerousness are specifically designed to further the accuracy of that determination. Detainees have a right to counsel at the detention hearing. 18 U.S.C. § 3142(f). They may testify in their own behalf, present information by proffer or otherwise, and cross-examine witnesses who appear at the hearing. The judicial officer charged with the responsibility of determining the appropriateness of detention is guided by statutorily enumerated factors, which include the nature and the circumstances of the charges, the weight of the evidence, the history and characteristics of the putative offender, and the danger to the community. § 3142(g). The Government must prove its case by clear and convincing evidence. § 3142(f). Finally, the judicial officer must include written findings of fact and a written statement of reasons for a decision to detain. § 3142(i). The Act's review provisions provide for immediate appellate review of the detention decision. Given the legitimate and compelling regulatory purpose of the Act and the procedural protections it offers, we conclude that the Act is not facially invalid under the Due Process Clause of the Fifth Amendment.

Respondents also contend that the Bail Reform Act violates the Excessive Bail Clause of the Eighth Amendment. We think that the Act survives a challenge founded upon the Eighth Amendment. The Eighth Amendment addresses pretrial release by providing merely that "excessive bail shall not be required." This Clause, of course, says nothing about whether bail shall be available at all. Respondents nevertheless contend that this Clause grants them a right to bail calculated solely upon considerations of flight. They rely on *Stack v. Boyle*, 342 U.S. 1 (1951), in which the Court stated that "bail set at a figure higher than an amount reasonably calculated [to ensure the defendant's presence at trial] is 'excessive' under the Eighth Amendment." In respondents' view, since the Bail Reform Act allows a court essentially to set bail at an infinite amount for reasons not related to the risk of flight, it violates the Excessive Bail Clause. Respondents concede that the right to bail they have discovered in the Eighth Amendment is not absolute. A court may, for example, refuse bail in capital cases. And, as the Court of Appeals noted and respondents admit, a court may refuse bail when the defendant presents a threat to the judicial process by intimidating witnesses. Respondents characterize these exceptions as consistent with what they claim to be the sole purpose of bail—to ensure the integrity of the judicial process.

While we agree that a primary function of bail is to safeguard the courts' role in adjudicating the guilt or innocence of defendants, we reject the proposition that the Eighth Amendment categorically prohibits the government from pursuing other admittedly compelling interests through regulation of pretrial release. The above-quoted dictum in *Stack v. Boyle* is far too slender a reed on which to rest this argument. The Court in *Stack* had no occasion to consider whether the Excessive Bail Clause requires courts to admit all defendants to bail, because the statute before the Court in that case in fact allowed the defendants to be bailed. Thus, the Court had to determine only whether bail, admittedly available in that case, was excessive if set at a sum greater than that necessary to ensure the arrestees' presence at trial.

The holding of *Stack* is illuminated by the Court's holding just four months later in *Carlson v. Landon*, 342 U.S. 524, 545–46 (1952):

> The bail clause was lifted with slight changes from the English Bill of Rights Act. In England that clause has never been thought to accord a right to bail in all cases, but merely to provide that bail shall not be excessive in those cases where it is proper to grant bail. When this clause was carried over into our Bill of Rights, nothing was said that indicated any different concept. The Eighth Amendment has not prevented Congress from defining the classes of cases in which bail shall be allowed in this country. Thus, in criminal cases bail is not compulsory where the punishment may be death. Indeed, the very language of the Amendment fails to say all arrests must be bailable.

Carlson v. Landon was a civil case, and we need not decide today whether the Excessive Bail Clause speaks at all to Congress' power to define the classes of criminal arrestees who shall be admitted to bail. For even if we were to conclude that the Eighth Amendment imposes some substantive limitations on the National Legislature's powers in this area, we would still hold that the Bail Reform Act is valid. Nothing in the text of the Bail Clause limits permissible Government considerations solely to questions of flight. The only arguable substantive limitation of the Bail Clause is that the Government's proposed conditions of release or detention not be "excessive" in light of the perceived evil. Of course, to determine whether the Government's response is excessive, we must compare that response against the interest the Government seeks to protect by means of that response. Thus, when the Government has admitted that its only interest is in preventing flight, bail must be set by a court at a sum designed to ensure that goal, and no more. *Stack v. Boyle, supra.* We believe that when Congress has mandated detention on the basis of a compelling interest other than prevention of flight, as it has here, the Eighth Amendment does not require release on bail.

In our society liberty is the norm, and detention prior to trial or without trial is the carefully limited exception. We hold that the provisions for pretrial detention in the Bail Reform Act of 1984 fall within that carefully limited exception. The Act authorizes detention prior to trial of arrestees charged with serious felonies who are found after an adversary hearing to pose a threat to the safety of individuals or to the community which no condition of release can dispel. The numerous procedural safeguards detailed above must attend this adversary hearing. We are unwilling to say that this congressional determination, based as it is upon that primary concern of every government—a concern for the safety and indeed the lives of its citizens—on its face violates either the Due Process Clause of the Fifth Amendment or the Excessive Bail Clause of the Eighth Amendment.

The judgment of the Court of Appeals is therefore *reversed*.

Justice Marshall, with whom Justice Brennan joins, dissenting.

This case brings before the Court a statute in which Congress declares that a person innocent of any crime may be jailed indefinitely, pending the trial of allegations which are legally presumed to be untrue, if the Government shows to the satisfaction of a judge that the accused is likely to commit crimes, unrelated to the pending charges, at any time in the future. Such statutes, consistent with the usages of tyranny and the excesses of what bitter experience teaches us to call the police state, have long been thought incompatible with the fundamental human rights protected by our Constitution. Today this Court holds otherwise. Its decision disregards basic principles of justice established centuries ago and enshrined beyond the reach of governmental interference in the Bill of Rights.

The majority approaches respondents' challenge to the Act by dividing the discussion into two sections, one concerned with the substantive guarantees implicit in the Due Process Clause, and the other concerned with the protection afforded by the Excessive Bail Clause of the Eighth Amendment. This is a sterile formalism, which divides a unitary argument into two independent parts and then professes to demonstrate that the parts are individually inadequate.

On the due process side appears an argument concerning the distinction between regulatory and punitive legislation. The majority concludes that the Act is a regulatory rather than a punitive measure. The major premise is that "unless Congress expressly intended to impose punitive restrictions, the punitive/regulatory distinction turns on 'whether an alternative purpose to which the restriction may rationally be connected is assignable for it, and whether it appears excessive in relation to the alternative purpose assigned to it.' " The majority finds that "Congress did not formulate the pretrial detention provisions as punishment for dangerous individuals," but instead was pursuing the "legitimate regulatory goal" of "preventing danger to the community." Concluding that pretrial detention is not an excessive solution to the problem of preventing danger to the community, the majority thus finds that no substantive element of the guarantee of due process invalidates the statute. This argument does not demonstrate the conclusion it purports to justify. Let us apply the majority's reasoning to a similar, hypothetical case. After investigation, Congress determines (not unrealistically) that a large proportion of violent crime is perpetrated by persons who are unemployed. It also determines, equally reasonably, that much violent crime is committed at night. From amongst the panoply of "potential solutions," Congress chooses a statute which permits, after judicial proceedings, the imposition of a dusk-to-dawn curfew on anyone who is unemployed. Since this is not a measure enacted for the purpose of punishing the unemployed, and since the majority finds that preventing danger to the community is a legitimate regulatory goal, the curfew statute would, according to the majority's analysis, be a mere "regulatory" detention statute, entirely compatible with the substantive components of the Due Process Clause.

The absurdity of this conclusion arises, of course, from the majority's cramped concept of substantive due process. The majority proceeds as though the only substantive right protected by the Due Process Clause is a right to be free from punishment before conviction. The majority's technique for infringing this right is simple: merely redefine any measure which is claimed to be punishment as "regulation," and, magically, the Constitution no longer prohibits its imposition. Because the Due Process Clause protects other substantive rights which are infringed by this legislation, the majority's argument is merely an exercise in obfuscation.

The Eighth Amendment, as the majority notes, states that "excessive bail shall not be required." The majority then declares that: "this Clause, of course, says nothing about whether bail shall be available at all." If excessive bail is imposed the defendant stays in jail. The same result is achieved if bail is denied altogether. Whether the magistrate sets bail at $1 billion or refuses to set bail at all, the consequences are indistinguishable. It would be mere sophistry to suggest that the Eighth Amendment protects against the former decision, and not the latter. But perhaps, the majority says, this manifest absurdity can be avoided. Perhaps the Bail Clause is addressed only to the Judiciary. "We need not decide today," the majority says, "whether the Excessive Bail Clause speaks at all to Congress' power to define the classes of criminal arrestees who shall be admitted to bail." This question was decided long ago. Federal and state statutes which purport to accomplish what the Eighth Amendment forbids, such as imposing cruel and unusual punishments, may not stand. *See, e. g., Trop v. Dulles,* 356 U.S. 86 (1958). The text of the Amendment, which provides simply that "excessive bail shall not be required, nor excessive fines imposed, nor cruel and unusual punishments inflicted," provides absolutely no support for the majority's speculation that both courts and Congress are forbidden to inflict cruel and unusual punishments, while only the courts are forbidden to require excessive bail.

The majority's attempts to deny the relevance of the Bail Clause to this case are unavailing, but the majority is nonetheless correct that the prohibition of excessive bail means that in order "to determine whether the Government's response is excessive, we must compare that response against the interest the Government seeks to protect by means of that response." The majority concedes that "when the Government has admitted that its only interest is in preventing flight, bail must be set by a court at a sum designed to ensure that goal, and no more." But, the majority says, "when Congress has mandated detention on the basis of a compelling interest other than prevention of flight, as it has here, the Eighth Amendment does not require release on bail." This conclusion follows only if the "compelling" interest upon which Congress acted is an interest which the Constitution permits Congress to further through the denial of bail. The majority does not ask, as a result of its disingenuous division of the analysis, if there are any substantive limits contained in both the Eighth Amendment and the Due Process Clause which render this system of preventive detention unconstitutional. The majority does not ask because the answer is apparent and, to the majority, inconvenient.

The essence of this case may be found, ironically enough, in a provision of the Act to which the majority does not refer. Title 18 U.S.C. § 3142(j) provides that "nothing in this section shall be construed as modifying or limiting the presumption of innocence." But the very pith and purpose of this statute is an abhorrent limitation of the presumption of innocence. The majority's untenable conclusion that the present Act is constitutional arises from a specious denial of the role of the Bail Clause and the Due Process Clause in protecting the invaluable guarantee afforded by the presumption of innocence.

"The principle that there is a presumption of innocence in favor of the accused is the undoubted law, axiomatic and elementary, and its enforcement lies at the foundation of the administration of our criminal law." *Coffin v. United States*, 156 U.S. 432, 453 (1895). Our society's belief, reinforced over the centuries, that all are innocent until the state has proved them to be guilty, like the companion principle that guilt must be proved beyond a reasonable doubt, is "implicit in the concept of ordered liberty," *Palko v. Connecticut*, 302 U.S. 319 (1937), and is established beyond legislative contravention in the Due Process Clause. *See In re Winship*, 397 U.S. 358 (1970).

The statute now before us declares that persons who have been indicted may be detained if a judicial officer finds clear and convincing evidence that they pose a danger to individuals or to the community. The statute does not authorize the Government to imprison anyone it has evidence is dangerous; indictment is necessary. But let us suppose that a defendant is indicted and the Government shows by clear and convincing evidence that he is dangerous and should be detained pending a trial, at which trial the defendant is acquitted. May the Government continue to hold the defendant in detention based upon its showing that he is dangerous? The answer cannot be yes, for that would allow the Government to imprison someone for uncommitted crimes based upon "proof" not beyond a reasonable doubt. The result must therefore be that once the indictment has failed, detention cannot continue. But our fundamental principles of justice declare that the defendant is as innocent on the day before his trial as he is on the morning after his acquittal. Under this statute an untried indictment somehow acts to permit a detention, based on other charges, which after an acquittal would be unconstitutional. The conclusion is inescapable that the indictment has been turned into evidence, if not that the defendant is guilty of the crime charged, then that left to his own devices he will soon be guilty of something else. "If it suffices to accuse, what will become of the innocent?" *Coffin v. United States, supra*, at 455.

To be sure, an indictment is not without legal consequences. It establishes that there is probable cause to believe that an offense was committed, and that the defendant committed it. Upon probable cause a warrant for the defendant's arrest may issue; a period of administrative detention may occur before the evidence of probable cause is presented to a neutral magistrate. *See Gerstein v. Pugh*, 420 U.S. 103 (1975). Once a defendant has been committed for trial he may be detained in custody if the magistrate finds that no conditions of release will prevent him from becoming a fugitive. But in this connection the charging instrument is evidence of nothing more than the fact that there will be a trial, and "release before trial is conditioned upon the accused's giving adequate assurance that he will stand trial and submit to sentence if found guilty. Like the ancient practice of securing the oaths of responsible persons to stand as sureties for the accused, the modern practice of requiring a bail bond or the deposit of a sum of money subject to forfeiture serves as additional assurance of the presence of an accused." *Stack v. Boyle*, 342 U.S. 1, 4–5 (1951).

The finding of probable cause conveys power to try, and the power to try imports of necessity the power to assure that the processes of justice will not be evaded or obstructed. "Pretrial detention to prevent future crimes against society at large, however, is not justified by any concern for holding a trial on the charges for which a defendant has been arrested." *Salerno*, 794 F.2d 64, 73 (2d Cir. 1986). The detention purportedly authorized by this statute bears no relation to the Government's power to try charges supported by a finding of probable cause, and thus the interests it serves are outside the scope of interests which may be considered in weighing the excessiveness of bail under the Eighth Amendment.

It is not a novel proposition that the Bail Clause plays a vital role in protecting the presumption of innocence. Reviewing the application for bail pending appeal by members of the American Communist Party convicted under the Smith Act, 18 U.S.C. § 2385, Justice Jackson wrote:

Grave public danger is said to result from what the defendants may be expected to do, in addition to what they have done since their conviction. If I assume that defendants are disposed to commit every opportune disloyal act helpful to Communist countries, it is still difficult to reconcile with traditional American law the jailing of persons by the courts because of anticipated but as yet uncommitted crimes. Imprisonment to protect society from predicted but unconsummated offenses is unprecedented in this country and fraught with danger of excesses and injustice.

Williamson v. United States, 95 L. Ed. 1379, 1382 (1950) (opinion in chambers).

As Chief Justice Vinson wrote for the Court in *Stack v. Boyle*: "Unless the right to bail before trial is preserved, the presumption of innocence, secured only after centuries of struggle, would lose its meaning."

There is a connection between the peculiar facts of this case and the evident constitutional defects in the statute which the Court upholds today. Respondent Cafaro was originally incarcerated for an indeterminate period at the request of the Government, which believed (or professed to believe) that his release imminently threatened the safety of the community. That threat apparently vanished, from the Government's point of view, when Cafaro agreed to act as a covert agent of the Government. There could be no more eloquent demonstration of the coercive power of authority to imprison upon prediction, or of the dangers which the almost inevitable abuses pose to the cherished liberties of a free society.

"It is a fair summary of history to say that the safeguards of liberty have frequently been forged in controversies involving not very nice people." *United States v. Rabinowitz*, 339 U.S. 56, 69 (1950) (Frankfurter, J., dissenting). Honoring the presumption of innocence is often difficult; sometimes we must pay substantial social costs as a result of our commitment to the values we espouse. But at the end of the day the presumption of innocence protects the innocent; the shortcuts we take with those whom we believe to be guilty injure only those wrongfully accused and, ultimately, ourselves.

Throughout the world today there are men, women, and children interned indefinitely, awaiting trials which may never come or which may be a mockery of the word, because their governments believe them to be "dangerous." Our Constitution, whose construction began two centuries ago, can shelter us forever from the evils of such unchecked power. Over 200 years it has slowly, through our efforts, grown more durable, more expansive, and more just. But it cannot protect us if we lack the courage, and the self-restraint, to protect ourselves. Today a majority of the Court applies itself to an ominous exercise in demolition. Theirs is truly a decision which will go forth without authority, and come back without respect. I dissent.

JUSTICE STEVENS, dissenting.

There may be times when the Government's interest in protecting the safety of the community will justify the brief detention of a person who has not committed any crime. It is indeed difficult to accept the proposition that the Government is without power to detain a person when it is a virtual certainty that he or she would otherwise kill a group of innocent people in the immediate future. Nonetheless, I firmly agree with Justice Marshall that the provision of the Bail Reform Act

Food for Thought

Who has the better argument, the majority or the dissent? What reasoning is most persuasive and why? In terms of the kinds of cases to which they apply, are the preventive detention provisions of the Bail Reform Act of 1984 as limited as the majority asserts? What happens when these provisions are replicated on the State level?

allowing pretrial detention on the basis of future dangerousness is unconstitutional. Whatever the answers are to the questions I have mentioned, it is clear to me that a pending indictment may not be given any weight in evaluating an individual's risk to the community or the need for immediate detention. If the evidence of imminent danger is strong enough to warrant emergency detention, it should support that preventive measure regardless of whether the person has been charged, convicted, or acquitted of some other offense. Justice Marshall has demonstrated that the fact of indictment cannot, consistent with the presumption of innocence and the Eighth Amendment's Excessive Bail Clause, be used to create a special class, the members of which are, alone, eligible for detention because of future dangerousness. I respectfully dissent.

Points for Discussion

a. High Money Bonds Versus Preventive Detention

After *Salerno*, many States have adopted similar preventive detention statutes. Nevertheless, in most States, the use of these statutes is relatively limited, and there continue to be many defendants held in jail pretrial on money bonds that they are financially unable to satisfy. Why do you think this is? In this respect, are there actually any advantages to the defendant to the use of the preventive detention scheme in the Bail Reform Act of 1984? If so, what are they?

b. Crimes of Violence

Under § 3142(f)(1)(A), the United States Attorney can seek preventive detention in any case that "involves a crime of violence." Is the crime of being a felon in possession of a firearm "a crime of violence" eligible for preventive detention? What are the arguments in favor of and against this interpretation? Compare *United States v. Ingle*, 454 F.3d 1082 (10th Cir. 2006) with *United States v. Dillard*, 214 F. 3d 88 (2d Cir. 2000).

Hypo 1: *A Case for Preventive Detention?*

Defendant is charged with drug trafficking and illegal possession of firearms. A firearm was present in defendant's residence when police executed a search warrant and the firearm was in close proximity to drugs that defendant was alleged to have distributed. Seven years ago, defendant was sentenced to ten years' probation for theft, burglary, and burglary of auto; that probation was successfully completed. He also had convictions for obstructing an officer, trafficking in marijuana and marijuana paraphernalia, public intoxication, and failure to return rental property, for which prison sentences were imposed. All of the convictions occurred at least five years ago. Defendant has family ties in the area, including his responsibility to care for his minor child. Under the preventive detention provision of the Bail Reform Act, what arguments will the prosecution make in favor of pretrial detention? What arguments will the defense make in opposition?

Hypo 2: *Another Case for Preventive Detention?*

Defendant has no prior criminal record, but was recently arrested for drug trafficking. He is 27 years old, has lived his entire life in Pennsylvania, and has a history of steady employment. He has worked in his father's construction business since graduating from high school nine years ago. He has also worked as a personal fitness trainer for the past 2 years. He has close ties to his family. Until last year, he lived with his parents. His younger sister stated that since his arrest, she has maintained his apartment and would offer to help her brother post a bond and supervise her brother if he is released. She indicated that her parents are also willing to provide support. She also found someone willing to employ defendant should he be released. Finally, the DEA agents who arrested defendant said that upon his arrest, he expressed concern about his parents' reaction to his arrest because his brother had been murdered in a drug-related incident last year. Defendant's only assets are $400 in a checking account and a Pontiac valued at approximately $200. Defendant was apprehended during a government sting operation. A confidential informant, who cooperated with the government in hope of obtaining more lenient treatment, called defendant and asked him to meet him at a hotel. The informant then produced a kilo of cocaine to sell to defendant. When he indicated that he had no money, the informant gave him the kilo on consignment. Under the Bail Reform Act, what are the prosecutor's best arguments in favor of preventive detention? What are the defense arguments in opposition?

Executive Summary

No Unnecessary Delay Between Arrest and Appearance. An accused must be taken before a judge without unnecessary delay following arrest.

Notice and Advice at First Appearance. The judge must advise the accused about the charges and several constitutional rights.

***Gerstein* Probable Cause Finding.** Under *Gerstein*, a judge must make a determination of probable cause prior to setting or denying bail pending trial.

No Probable Cause Finding Not Bar Further Proceedings. Whether a court finds probable cause at first appearance has no effect on whether the proceedings against the defendant go forward.

No Excessive Bail. The Eighth Amendment prohibits excessive bail. Bail becomes excessive when it is set higher than reasonably necessary to assure a defendant's appearance at trial.

Major Themes

a. Lack of Counsel—The right to counsel attaches at an accused person's initial appearance in court but an accused may nonetheless not actually have counsel in court representing his interests during proceedings where a judge or magistrate makes important decisions regarding probable cause to detain the accused pretrial and what bond to set.

b. Bail—While *Stack v. Boyle* holds that bail is set for purposes of conditions of release in order to guarantee return to court, state judges and magistrates nonetheless set bail in amounts that accused persons cannot make.

c. Preventive Detention—*Salerno*'s facts and holding would have indicated a much more limited use of preventive detention, holding defendant in jail pretrial, in opposition to the current practice in many states of allowing preventive detention for many different felonies and for persons with no prior record of violence or dangerousness.

Preventive Detention by Statute. By federal statute and some state statutes, a defendant can be preventatively detained prior to trial if the prosecution makes a showing that the defendant presents a danger to the community.

Preventive Detention Constitutional. Preventive detention was held constitutional by the Supreme Court in *United States v. Salerno*, 481 U.S. 739 (1987).

Test Your Knowledge

To assess your understanding of the material in this chapter, click here to take a quiz.

For More Information

• MARK E. CAMMACK & NORMAN M. GARLAND, ADVANCED CRIMINAL PROCEDURE (2006).

• WAYNE R. LAFAVE, JEROLD H. ISRAEL, NANCY J. KING & ORIN S. KERR, CRIMINAL PROCEDURE (5th ed. 2009).

• JEROLD H. ISRAEL & WAYNE R. LAFAVE, CRIMINAL PROCEDURE: CONSTITUTIONAL LIMITATIONS (8th ed. 2006).

• RUSSELL L. WEAVER, JOHN M. BURKOFF, CATHERINE HANCOCK, JANET HOEFFEL, STEVE FRIEDLAND & STEPHEN SINGER, PRINCIPLES OF CRIMINAL PROCEDURE Ch. 9 (6th ed. 2018).

CHAPTER 11

Prosecutorial Discretion

A. Introduction

A major feature of prosecutorial power is the exercise of discretion regarding whether to bring charges against a suspect, and, if charges are initiated, what to charge. This aspect of prosecutorial power is a very significant but often over-looked component of the prosecutor's broad array of powers. Prosecutors have considerable leeway in making strategic decisions, a power that can be controversial in high-profile cases, such as those involving the shooting deaths by Officer Darryl Wilson and neighborhood watchman George Zimmerman. In those cases, the prosecutor applied its discretion differently to Wilson, who shot teenager Michael Brown, and Zimmerman, who shot teenager Trayvon Martin.

Of course, the greater the prosecutorial discretion, the greater the potential for abuse. Recurring questions arise about how much power prosecutors ought to be able to wield and what checks can and should exist on that power. High profile cases often raise issues relating to prosecutorial discretion, including the nature and scope of charges that are appropriately filed.

Points for Discussion

a. Zimmerman & Martin

A controversial case that raised prosecutorial discretion issues was *Florida v. Zimmerman*, a case involving the shooting of unarmed teenager Trayvon Martin on February 26, 2012, by neighborhood watchman volunteer, George Zimmerman, in Sanford, Florida. After a trial of a little more than a month starting on June 13, 2013, the jury acquitted Zimmerman, who raised a claim of self-defense. A preliminary issue involved the process by which charges should have been initiated—through a grand jury derived from the public or an information filed by the prosecutor? The Governor of Florida appointed a special prosecutor who decided to charge Zimmerman with second-degree murder instead of seeking an indictment from a Grand Jury. The charging process, like many other aspects of the case, was controversial. There were those who thought the case should have gone to the grand jury. Others thought the defendant was over-charged based on the facts. The media provided numerous reports and experts, flooding the Internet and airwaves with commentary. After the case was tried and Zimmerman was acquitted, the prosecutor's discretion in charging obscured by the decision.

b. *United States v. John Edwards*

John Edwards, a former senator from North Carolina and presidential candidate, was indicted by a Grand Jury in 2011 for violating federal campaign finance laws. The violations primarily stemmed from the cover-up of a sexual affair that Mr. Edwards had during his presidential campaign, which began in December of 2006. After a lengthy pre-trial run-up involving motions and discovery, he was tried in federal court in Greensboro, NC, in the late spring of 2012. In May of 2012, the jury acquitted him of one charge and hung on five other counts, leading to a mistrial. The government decided not to retry him on the remaining counts.

Food for Thought

The *Edwards* case raises several questions about prosecutorial discretion. Is the government using its resources wisely if it goes forward with a relatively weak case? Should such cases be reviewed to ensure that a reasonably objective prosecutor would proceed based on the evidence? Should there be different prosecutorial discretion standards in high-profile cases, especially costly ones? Should the government bring cases that they hope to win but are based on novel or questionable grounds?

c. Wilson & Brown

On August 9, 2014, a confrontation between Officer Darryl Wilson and teenager Michael Brown left Brown dead. The prosecutor, Robert P. McCulloch, of St. Louis County, resisted the appointment of a special prosecutor and gave the case to the Grand Jury to see if there was probable cause to believe Wilson had committed a crime. The officer essentially alleged self-defense, and witnesses before the Grand Jury gave conflicting stories. In the end, the Grand Jury refused to return a true bill. One of the controversial issues focused on prosecutorial discretion. Usually, a prosecutor seeks indictment for a specific crime, and offers a minimal number of witnesses in a largely one-sided affair, especially given the defense does not have an attorney in the Grand Jury room and cannot cross-examine any witnesses. In this case, the prosecutor offered all of the evidence and witnesses it found to the Grand Jury so that the jury would be free to draw its own conclusions about what happened. By not returning a true bill, the Grand Jury (or at least four of the jurors (only 9 of the 12 were needed to vote for probable cause under Missouri law)) found no probable cause to believe a crime had been committed by the officer. While the prosecutor could offer additional evidence or seek an alternative route, Mr. McCulloch made it apparent he would decline to prosecute in light of the Grand Jury's decision.

d. *United States v. Blankenship*

It is not unusual to see periodically a coal mine disaster where workers get trapped and killed far below ground. What is unusual is to see the management of the company held criminally responsible. In 2010, there was an explosion in the Upper Big Branch mine in West Virginia. Methane gas surged through two miles of tunnels, killing 29 miners. The explosion was allegedly caused by unlawful conditions, including high levels of coal dust in the mine. In late 2014, the then CEO of Massey Energy, one of the largest coal companies in the United States and the company that owned the mine, Mr. Donald L. Blankenship, was indicted on criminal charges related to that event. The Grand Jury found probable cause to believe that Mr. Blankenship engaged in conspiracy, fraud, and numerous safety violations and returned a true bill in the form of the indictment. Federal prosecutors in Charleston, West Virginia, then moved forward on the charges. Trip Gabriel, *West Virginia Coal Country Sees New Era as Donald Blankenship Is Indicted*, N.Y. Times (Nov. 30, 2014). For a copy of the indictment, see: http://www.nytimes.com/2014/12/01/us/west-virginia-coal-country-sees-new-era-as-a-mine-boss-is-indicted.html.

Hypo: *Charging Choices*

Three men, Al, age 46, Peter, age 19, and James, age 16, decide to rob a local convenience store around 9 a.m. one November morning in southern Georgia. Al tells the others how easy it will be and how they will never put anyone in danger, especially because they will not have any weapons. After robbing the proprietor of the convenience store of $2,000, the men decide to rob the jewelry store down the street, where they net $5,000. They are efficient and do not threaten the sole employee in the store. They all get into Al's car and he drives them to Atlanta, where, after getting gas, they rob another jewelry store at Al's urging. When the proprietor of this jewelry store starts to reach into a drawer, Al, takes out of his pocket a starter's pistol that looks like a real gun but fires blanks, points it at the proprietor, and says, "Do not move!" The proprietor quickly closes the drawer, which has a loaded gun in it. As the men are driving away, they are caught by the police. After a quick pat-down at the scene, Peter is found to have two marijuana joints in his pants pocket. A) With what crimes would you charge them if you were the prosecutor assigned to the case and why? B) Should a prosecutor's personal views about marijuana matter if given discretion on how to charge the possession of the substance? Explain. C) What should be the proper penalty for each participant? D) What, if any, plea bargains would you accept? Explain.

* * *

These questions pose dilemmas for prosecutors that are within the purview of the prosecutorial discretion subject area. From whether to charge, to how to charge and how to dispose of cases, prosecutors have considerable leeway in making strategic decisions. Of course, the greater this prosecutorial power is, the greater the possibility of abuse.

B. Overview of Prosecutorial Discretion

Prosecutors have broad discretion about when and whether to investigate and prosecute cases. Broad discretion is required as a matter of separation of powers because prosecutors act as part of the Executive Branch. Courts also have noted repeatedly that the decision to prosecute is particularly ill-suited to judicial review. Among the discretionary factors involved in the decisions on whether and how to charge cases that are not easily reviewable are the strength of the case, the prosecution's general deterrence value, the State's enforcement priorities, and the case's relationship to the State's overall enforcement plans. As Congress and state legislatures have criminalized more and more behavior and provided duplicative ways in which to charge an individual, the prosecutor has arguably become the most powerful figure in the criminal justice system, inviting both vigorous critique and defense of the prosecutor's role. While discretion can be dangerous in how it is deployed, so is rigidity, prohibiting individualized treatment that might be based on common sense.

Why is prosecutorial discretion so important? While it can be attributed to the fact that specific circumstances often dictates what is fair in criminal cases, it also could be due in part to scarcity of resources. A commentator recently reflected on the difficulty caused by policies that affect prosecutorial discretion through the way limited resources in the criminal

Food for Thought

You are the new state budget chief. You have an unexpected budget surplus of $1 million. You must allocate it to the following three areas: hiring additional police officers; hiring more prosecutors; hiring additional prison guards. How do you allocate the funds? What are your rationales for doing so?

justice system are allocated. "Procedural justice is undermined because over-policing increases the number of cases in lower criminal courts, overwhelming prosecutors, defenders, and judges." K. Babe Howell, *Prosecutorial Discretion and the Duty to Seek Justice in an Overburdened System*, 27 Geo. J. L. Ethics 285 (2014).

Some approach prosecutorial discretion as a necessity, both in terms of pragmatism and jurisprudence. Then-Professor, now U.S. Third Circuit Court of Appeals Judge Stephanos Bibas, in his article, *The Need for Prosecutorial Discretion*, 19 Temp. Pol. & Civ. Rts. L. Rev. 369 (2009-2010), argues that U.S. criminal court dockets are so congested that prosecutors have no choice but to "plea bargain away most of their cases." He argues that the problem is caused by the fact that legislatures often "pass overbroad and overlapping criminal statutes instead of drawing them so narrowly that some scoundrels might escape." The breadth of these laws necessarily leaves prosecutors with broad discretion which they exercise in different ways. For example, prosecutors might choose not to prosecute more minor offenses (e.g., jaywalking or speeders who are only slightly above the speed limit) in favor of prosecuting more serious offenses (e.g., murder). However, in some instances, prosecutors will charge defendants for more minor offenses if an effort to encourages potential witnesses to turn state's evidence. However, prosecutorial discretion is hardly limited to the question of whether or not to charge a defendant with a crime. If a defendant is convicted, the prosecutor has discretion regarding whether to recommend a high sentence, a low sentence, or even probation.

Bibas believes that prosecutorial discretion is not simply a function of scarce resources. He notes that, in some European countries (e.g., Germany) " "prosecutors are supposed to charge and prosecute all defendants for whom they have enough evidence of guilt." *Id*. He notes that some U.S. jurisdictions take a similar approach. However, he also argues that "justice" requires the exercise of discretion so that prosecutors can make "fine-grained moral evaluations and distinctions." Judges and juries should make more of these judgment calls than they do now, but prosecutors also deserve large roles. He notes that, even though some jurisdictions ban "weapons" from school grounds, it would make no sense to prosecute a grandmother who sends a birthday cake, and a knife to cut it, to school with her granddaughter.

However, the fact that prosecutors have broad discretion creates the potential for abuse. Under constitutionally imposed rules, prosecutors are required to disclose exculpatory evidence to defendants. *See Editorial—Justice and Prosecutorial Misconduct?, N.Y. Times* (Dec. 28, 2011). However, there is evidence suggesting that prosecutors do not always turn over exculpatory evidence, and that they rarely suffer consequences for their failure to do so. As the Court recognized in *Berger v. United States*, 295 U.S. 78 (1935), a "prosecutor is the representative not of an ordinary party to a controversy but a sovereignty whose obligation to govern impartially is as compelling as its obligation to govern at all; and whose interest, therefore, in a criminal prosecution is not that it shall win a case, but that justice shall be done." The ultimate objective is that "guilt shall not escape or innocence suffer." However, while a prosecutor may "strike hard blows, he is not at liberty to strike foul ones. It is as much his duty to refrain from improper methods calculated to produce a wrongful conviction as it is to use every legitimate means to bring about a just one." Moreover, prosecutors have a "nullification power" that they can use to nullify a "law by not bringing charges when they should, or by bringing different charges than they should," as well as by deciding the venue where a case will be litigated.

Prosecutorial discretion is not always cabined by decisions on whether to charge at all or what charges to bring, but rather by how to conduct the prosecution. Sometimes, prosecutors do things that jump the line of acceptability. This was the case in *United States v. Bowen,* 799 F3d. 336 (5th Cir. 2015), which married prosecutorial ethics, discretion and the use of the Internet. In *Bowen,* police officers were convicted of felonies relating to the killing of several unarmed men after Hurricane Katrina in New Orleans and then orchestrating a cover-up. The primary issue in the government's appeal, though, was whether anonymous online posting by government prosecutors would, when discovered, warrant a new trial. In Bowen, the majority of a split three-judge panel wrote:

> In the anarchy following Hurricane Katrina, a group of heavily armed New Orleans police officers were dispatched to the Danziger Bridge in response to an emergency call reporting shots being fired at police. There, amid chaos, they shot and killed two unarmed men, one of them developmentally disabled, and wounded four other unarmed civilians. The police then allegedly orchestrated a cover-up to deny what happened. Some of those involved were tried by the state, but a mistrial was ordered. The federal government took over the prosecution and has also bungled it. Five former officers have been convicted of serious crimes and received lengthy sentences. Yet they appear in this court as Appellees, and the federal government as the Appellant, because the district court granted a new trial.

> The reasons for granting a new trial are novel and extraordinary. No less than three high-ranking federal prosecutors are known to have been posting online, anonymous comments to newspaper articles about the case throughout its duration. The government makes no attempt to justify the prosecutors' ethical lapses, which the court described as having created an "online 21st century carnival atmosphere." Not only that, but the government inadequately investigated and substantially delayed the ferreting out of information about its in-house contributors to the anonymous postings. The district court also found that cooperating defendants called to testify by the government lied, an FBI agent overstepped, defense witnesses were intimidated from testifying, and inexplicably gross sentencing disparities resulted from the government's plea bargains and charging practices.

Like the district court, we are well aware of our duty normally to affirm convictions that are tainted only by harmless error. In this extraordinary case, however, harmless error cannot even be evaluated because the full consequences of the federal prosecutors' misconduct remain uncertain after less-than-definitive DOJ internal investigations. The trial, in any event, was permeated by the cumulative effect of the additional irregularities found by the district court. We conclude that the grant of a new trial was not an abuse of the district court's discretion.

Factually, the order relies on a number of events. Foremost are the online comments of Perricone and Dobinski, which in tandem tended to create an "On-Line 21st Century 'Carnival Atmosphere'," as graphically depicted in the district court's quotation of all of the comments posted by these two. *September Order,* 969 F. Supp. 2d at 588–603. Second is Jan Mann's testimony, which includes the implications that Letten was aware of her online posting activity in March 2012.

In its footnote 127, the district court identified some of the outstanding issues:

> As HenryL.Mencken_1951, Perricone made two very correct statements: "There are NO secrets in New Orleans," and "Perhaps the truth will surface. God knows, we need more truth in this city." Yet the Court, even with the capable assistance of Mr. Horn and Ms. Alexander, remains unaware of: the identity of the source of the "leak" of the Lohman plea, in possible violation of Rule 6(e); the earlier user IDs of Perricone and Jan Mann, and how many other user IDs might be involved; the identities of ten of the eleven user IDs that were the subject of the DOJ administrative subpoena; the information which could have been obtained from a forensic recovery of computer data for years 2010 and 2011 (prior to December 19, 2011) by the DOJ; whether USA Letten agrees with his former First Assistant that she disclosed her online posting activity in March 2012, and whether that information was conveyed to others in DOJ over six months prior to its public disclosure in early November 2012; whether Karla Dobinski's posting was known to others at DOJ; whether "123ac" is an AUSA; whether other government agency employees posted comments on this case, as did government agency employee "A" and whether any of the three defense witnesses who refused to testify at trial will ever be charged with the crimes for which they were threatened prior to this trial. These are but a few of the outstanding issues which would be the subject of an evidentiary hearing. It is anticipated that surely others would surface upon learning further information at such a hearing.

What the government nowhere confronts is the incomplete, dilatory, and evasive nature of its efforts to respond to the district court's inquiries about the full extent of online activity by government employees and the source of the Lohman plea leak. The district court was stymied and frustrated for more than twelve months (June 2012–July 2013) by the government's tactics, while private sources like a local magazine and an individual under federal investigation repeatedly leapfrogged government admissions of official misbehavior.

Ignoring the procedural deficiencies of its misconduct investigation, the government's defense against a new trial consists of two essential premises: first, only a finding of specific prejudice to the verdict will suffice to support a new trial; and second, prejudice was not shown on the record developed in the district court. We disagree that specific prejudice is a necessary prerequisite to a new trial in this *sui generis* case. But even if required, prejudice here was shown both from this pattern of misconduct and evasion and from other abusive prosecutorial actions.

The "unprecedented" *Harbin* case, 250 F.3d at 539, is instructive. In *Harbin*, the court allowed the prosecutor to "save" until mid-trial a peremptory juror challenge, which he exercised to replace one juror with an alternate. The replacement juror was not shown to have been biased, nor could any impact on the verdict be proven. Nevertheless, the Seventh Circuit held that the error was precisely the type that "defies harmless error analysis." *Id.* at 545. The defendants had been denied a comparable right to excise a juror during trial not only because they had previously used all of their peremptory challenges, but also because they were not even informed of the possibility of delayed exercise. *Harbin* held that this error affected the fundamental fairness of the trial and demanded a new trial without harmless error proof, because the imbalance in peremptory challenges "gave the prosecutor unilateral discretionary control over the composition of the jury mid-trial." And it was "simply impossible as a practical matter to assess the impact on the jury of such an error."

So too here, the breadth of the government's misconduct and continued obfuscation, as the district court found, makes this the "unusual case" contemplated by *Brecht*. The online commenting alone, which breached all standards of prosecutorial ethics, gave the government a surreptitious advantage in influencing public opinion, the venire panel, and the trial itself.

The fact that there is no proof that members of the venire panel or actual jurors read or were influenced by the online comments exacerbates rather than alleviates prejudice here. Anonymous postings prevent uncovering the extent of improper influence, adding injury to the insult of the biased, inflammatory, and improper communications themselves. Had the comments in this case been delivered by the prosecutors without the shield of anonymity, the extent of the harm would have been quantifiable, but their actions eliminated the measurement of harm. Moreover, the government overlooks that potential harm extends not just to jurors but others involved in the case.

The government also argues that official and professional discipline were adequate to rebuke Perricone, Jan Mann, and Dobinski and should have sufficed in lieu of a new trial. Like the district court, we disagree. To begin with, whether those who committed misconduct were disciplined simply does not bear on whether the defendants received a fair trial. It is clear from Perricone, Mann, and Dobinski's testimony that none of them is particularly remorseful about the misconduct, and they claimed to believe their individual First Amendment rights were separable from their positions of public trust. Perricone and Jan Mann both resigned from office with benefits as far as the record shows, although they were referred for professional discipline to the State Bar of Louisiana. Dobinski remains in federal employment with only a bare reproof for her online commenting. Their misdeeds are compounded by the government's insouciant investigation, which leaves open only three inferences concerning this prosecutorial breakdown: the government is not serious about controlling extracurricular, employment- related online commenting by its officials; the government feared what it might uncover by a thorough and timely investigation; or the government's investigation was incompetent. Exerting professional discipline on three individual government lawyers does nothing to solve the systemic problem, and it is not a sufficient answer to the miscarriage of justice in this case.

Edward C. Prado, Circuit Judge, dissenting:

I agree with the majority that the actions of the government attorneys in this case demean the integrity of the judiciary and merit the most severe sanctions. But we "cannot permit" these considerations "to alter our analysis, for we are not at liberty to ignore the mandate" of the Federal Rules of Criminal Procedure "in order to obtain 'optimal' . . . results," *Carlisle v. United States*, 517 U.S. 416, 430 (1996). Because the majority opinion relies on extraordinary facts to skirt ordinary procedure, I respectfully dissent. Before this Court is an appeal of a new-trial order granted under Rule 33(b)(1) of the Federal Rules of Criminal Procedure. Rule 33 contemplates two kinds of motions for new trial: one "grounded on newly discovered evidence," and one "grounded on any reason other than newly discovered evidence." Fed. R. Crim. P. 33(b). The former "must be filed within 3 years after the verdict or finding of guilty," whereas the latter "must be filed within 14 days after the verdict or finding of guilty." *Id.*

Therefore, in the present case, the district court had authority to consider—and we have authority to review—*only* a motion for a new trial based on newly discovered evidence. Neither the district court nor the majority opinion has applied the appropriate standard: "In order to warrant a new trial on the basis of newly discovered evidence, [the defendant] must demonstrate that (1) the evidence is newly discovered and was unknown to the defendant at the time of trial; (2) failure to detect the evidence was not due to a lack of diligence by the defendant; (3) the evidence is not merely cumulative or impeaching; (4) the evidence is material; and (5) *the evidence introduced at a new trial would probably produce an acquittal.* Unless all factors are met, the motion should be denied."

In sum, I would conclude that the district court abused its discretion in granting a new trial. The district court erred in not applying our established Rule 33(b)(1) standard, and the defendants have not carried their heavy burden to prove that "the evidence introduced at a new trial would probably produce an acquittal," Bowler, 252 F.3d at 747. In holding otherwise, the majority opinion puts us at odds with binding Fifth Circuit precedent as well as authority from our sister circuits.

C. The Decision to Investigate or Charge

1. Discretionary Authority

Prosecutors have broad discretion—rather than an obligation or a duty—about when and whether to investigate and/or to prosecute. Arguably, broad discretion is required as a matter of separation of powers because prosecutors act as part of the Executive Branch. Courts also have noted repeatedly that the decision to prosecute is particularly ill-suited to judicial review. Among the discretionary factors that are not easily reviewable are the strength of the case, the prosecution's general deterrence value, the Government's enforcement priorities, and the case's relationship to the Government's overall enforcement plans. With numerous criminal statutes providing different levels of punishment, should prosecutors have the power to select which statutes to enforce?

United States v. Batchelder

442 U.S. 114 (1979).

MR. JUSTICE MARSHALL delivered the opinion of the Court.

At issue in this case are two overlapping provisions of the Omnibus Crime Control and Safe Streets Act of 1968 (Omnibus Act). Both prohibit convicted felons from receiving firearms, but each authorizes different maximum penalties. We must determine whether a defendant convicted of the offense carrying the greater penalty may be sentenced only under the more lenient provision when his conduct violates both statutes.

Who's That?

Thurgood Marshall was an associate justice on the United States Supreme Court for 24 years, from 1967–1991. The first African-American justice, he was well-known before his appointment to the high court, having won many arguments before the same court, including *Brown v. Board of Education* in his role as chief counsel and executive director for the NAACP Legal Defense Fund. He also was the Solicitor General, appointed by President Lyndon Johnson.

Respondent, a previously convicted felon, was found guilty of receiving a firearm that had traveled in interstate commerce, in violation of 18 U.S.C. § 922(h). The District Court sentenced him under 18 U.S.C. § 924(a) to five years' imprisonment, the maximum term authorized for violation of § 922(h).

The Court of Appeals affirmed the conviction but, by a divided vote, remanded for resentencing. The majority recognized that respondent had been indicted and convicted under § 922(h) and that § 924(a) permits five years' imprisonment for such violations. However, noting that the substantive elements of § 922(h) and 18 U.S.C.App. § 1202(a) are identical as applied to a convicted felon who unlawfully receives a firearm, the court interpreted the Omnibus Act to allow no more than the 2-year maximum sentence provided by § 1202(a).

This Court has previously noted the partial redundancy of §§ 922(h) and 1202(a), both as to the conduct they proscribe and the individuals they reach. However, we find nothing in the language, structure, or legislative history of the Omnibus Act to suggest that because of this overlap, a defendant convicted under § 992(h) may be imprisoned for no more than the maximum term specified in § 1202(a). As we read the Act, each substantive statute, in conjunction with its own sentencing provision, operates independently of the other.

In construing § 1202(a) to override the penalties authorized by § 924(a), the Court of Appeals relied, we believe erroneously, on three principles of statutory interpretation. First, the court invoked the well-established doctrine that ambiguities in criminal statutes must be resolved in favor of lenity. Although this principle of construction applies to sentencing as well as substantive provisions, in the instant case there is no ambiguity to resolve. Respondent unquestionably violated § 922(h), and § 924(a) unquestionably permits five years' imprisonment for such a violation. That § 1202(a) provides different penalties for essentially the same conduct is no justification for taking liberties with unequivocal statutory language. Where, as here, "Congress has conveyed its purpose clearly, we decline to manufacture ambiguity where none exists."

Nor can § 1202(a) be interpreted as implicitly repealing § 924(a) whenever a defendant's conduct might violate both Titles. In this case, however, the penalty provisions are fully capable of coexisting because they apply to convictions under different statutes. Finally, the maxim that statutes should be construed to avoid constitutional questions offers no assistance here.

We find no constitutional infirmities. It is a fundamental tenet of due process that "[n]o one may be required at peril of life, liberty or property to speculate as to the meaning of penal statutes." A criminal statute is therefore invalid if it "fails to give a person of ordinary intelligence fair notice that his contemplated conduct is forbidden." So too, vague sentencing provisions may pose constitutional questions if they do not state with sufficient clarity the consequences of violating a given criminal statute.

The provisions in issue here, however, unambiguously specify the activity proscribed and the penalties available upon conviction. That this particular conduct may violate both Titles does not detract from the notice afforded by each.

This Court has long recognized that when an act violates more than one criminal statute, the Government may prosecute under either so long as it does not discriminate against any class of defendants.

The provisions at issue plainly demarcate the range of penalties that prosecutors and judges may seek and impose. In light of that specificity, the power that Congress has delegated to those officials is no broader than the authority they routinely exercise in enforcing the criminal laws. Having informed the courts, prosecutors, and defendants of the permissible punishment alternatives available under each Title, Congress has fulfilled its duty.

Accordingly, the judgment of the Court of Appeals is reversed.

Immigration. Prosecutorial discretion arises in many places and contexts. This year, the immigration context took on a higher profile, particularly given the posture of President Trump concerning deportation. In immigration cases, prosecutorial discretion involves the power to choose whether to seek deportation of a per-

Food for Thought

A prosecutor in a large urban city decides that controversial stop-and-frisk policies do not justify pressing criminal charges against individuals, given the sweeping number of arrests and trespass charges. The prosecutor wishes to provide diversion, meaning non-prosecution of charges, for all persons who have no prior serious criminal offenses on their criminal records. A) Would this be an appropriate policy? Is there an alternative policy that you might impose if you were the prosecutor? B) What articulable criteria would you use for your decision-making process? (Examples of such criteria are provided in Part E. infra.)

son under the circumstances. One particular immigration issue involves the scope of prosecutorial power to denaturalize persons who lied to immigration officials in the process of becoming a citizen, and prosecute that person for violating a federal law that subjects a person to prison if the person "knowingly procures or attempts to procure, contrary to any law, the naturalization of any person." The question in the case of Divna Maslenjak, *Maslenjak v. United States,* heard on oral argument before the United States Supreme Court on April 26, 2017, is whether a naturalized person can be stripped of citizenship based on an immaterial lie. The justices were not sure a clear line could be drawn between materiality and immateriality. As Justice Anthony Kennedy stated at the oral argument, "You can have a statement that everyone thinks is immaterial, it's subjectively immaterial, but it might have a causal connection at the end of the day."

2. Criteria for the Exercise of Discretion

While not formally binding on a prosecutor's decision whether or who to investigate, or whether, who, and/or what to charge, the American Bar Association has adopted standards intended to assist prosecutors in the principled exercise of their investigatory and charging discretion. Consider two examples of policy questions that arise regarding discretion. First, are the age and medical status of suspects relevant criteria in determining whether and how to prosecute? How, if at all, should these factors be weighed? Second, should the criteria for the prosecutor's exercise of discretion be disclosed to the defense or the public or should it be hidden?

In *Inmates of Attica Correctional Facility v. Rockefeller*, 477 F.2d 375 (2d Cir. 1973), the court held that the federal judiciary, even at the behest of crime victims, lack the authority to compel federal and state officials to investigate and prosecute persons who have violated criminal statutes. Because prosecutors possess discretion (rather than an obligation or duty) to investigate and prosecute, they are not legally bound to do either. From the perspective of the separation of powers, the Judicial Branch should not be interfering with the executive prerogatives of prosecutors who are part of the Executive Branch. As the court points out, we do not want courts to become "superprosecutors", without anyone to check the exercise (and abuse) of such authority.

Hypo 1: *Homicide Charge*

If you are a prosecutor faced with the following factual scenarios, would you charge the potential accused with homicide? If you don't feel that you can fairly make such a decision based on these limited facts, what further facts would you ask the police to obtain for you? What significance would you attach to these further facts, i.e., would they make you more or less likely to charge? Suppose that Terry, a Hispanic-American, is a neighborhood watch coordinator for his gated community. Terry sees a person in his neighborhood that he does not recognize, Alan, a young African American. Terry calls the local police to report suspicious behavior, saying that the person is walking leisurely in the neighborhood and cutting in-between houses, but not engaging in any criminal behavior. After the phone call ends, there is a violent confrontation between the two individuals. During the incident, Terry shoots Alan in the chest area once, killing him. Terry claimed self-defense. Assume the law states in pertinent part: "A person is justified in using force, except deadly force, against another when and to the extent that the person reasonably believes that such conduct is necessary to defend himself or herself or another against the other's imminent use of unlawful force. However, a person is justified in the use of deadly force and does not have a duty to retreat if: (1) He or she reasonably believes that such force is necessary to prevent imminent death or great bodily harm to himself or herself or another or to prevent the imminent commission of a forcible felony; or (2) Under those circumstances permitted pursuant to defense of one's home." If you decide to charge, would you seek a Grand Jury indictment or charge the case yourself by information (if you were not required by law to seek an indictment for the crimes charged)?

Hypo 2: *More Decisions*

What decisions would you make as a prosecutor in each of the following scenarios—and why?

A. A medical associate of the late Dr. Jack Kevorkian, who believed strongly in euthanasia, has flown to your jurisdiction and, at the request of his spouse, obtained drugs with which her 72-year-old husband, who had terminal cancer, killed himself. Your jurisdiction's Crimes Code contains a section which provides that "a person who intentionally aids or solicits another to commit suicide is guilty of a felony punishable by up to 10 years in prison if the person's conduct causes such suicide or an attempted suicide." Do you charge Dr. Kevorkian and/or the deceased's spouse?

B. The day after a defendant is arrested for the sexual abuse of a 10-year-old boy, the boy's distraught mother shoots and kills the defendant at his arraignment. She tells you that she bought the gun that morning in order to shoot and kill the deceased. (The state's Crimes Code provides that: an intentional, premeditated killing is first-degree murder; an otherwise malicious killing is second-degree murder; and a provoked killing is voluntary manslaughter, although the provocation must be "sudden." With what, if anything, do you charge the mother?

C. A woman who had been physically and emotionally abused by her husband for a period of three years killed him by pouring gasoline on him and lighting it while he had passed out on his bed in an alcoholic stupor. The last time he was abused her had been three days earlier. Your jurisdiction's Crimes Code does not expressly recognize a "battered spouse" defense. Your jurisdiction's self-defense provisions require that a defendant establish, *inter alia,* that he or she used defensive deadly force in response to the "imminent" use of deadly force against him or her. Do you charge her with murder?

D. A college student, Anthony, spied on his new roommate, making a secret tape of the student while that student was with another student on a date in their dormitory room. The student who spied put the tape up on his Facebook page. When the roommate found out, an altercation ensued. Assume that Anthony is charged with battery and invasion of privacy. Also assume that Anthony's immigration status would be adversely affected by a plea of guilty to a felony or misdemeanor charge. What criteria would you use for determining whether and with what to charge Anthony? Would you take his immigration status into account?

D. Prosecutorial Discretion in Plea Bargaining

Prosecutorial discretion frequently comes into play in plea bargaining—when prosecutors and attorneys for the accused—or the accused directly, if she is unrepresented—attempt to reach an alternate disposition to a trial. It is the functional equivalent of settlement negotiations in civil cases.

The bargaining generally involves the degree or a specific type of crime and potential outcomes (jail? probation? diversion?), and it is no surprise to those who participate in the criminal justice system that most criminal cases do not go to trial and instead utilize plea bargaining agreements between prosecutors and defendants. It might be surprising to realize, however, the extent to which cases end up with plea-bargained dispositions. For example, in 2011, fewer than 1 in 40 criminal cases went to trial. See http://www.nytimes.com/2011/09/26/us/tough-sentences-help-prosecutors-push-for-plea-bargains.html?pagewanted=all.

According to one commentator: "Beginning in the 1960s, and escalating thereafter, Congress and most state legislatures, largely in response to public pressure, decreed that those convicted of crimes would serve ever-longer prison sentences. In the federal system, for example, this trend took the form of mandatory minimum sentences, sentencing guidelines, and the abolition of parole. Faced with the knowledge that their clients, if convicted after trial, would be sentenced to very long periods of incarceration, prudent defense counsel increasingly sought to negotiate plea bargains that would allow their clients to obtain lower sentences by pleading guilty to lesser counts or narrower charges, or in exchange for other sentencing concessions. The direct result was to increase greatly the percentage of criminal cases resolved by guilty pleas; such pleas now account for ninety-seven percent of all federal criminal convictions and ninety-four percent of all state criminal convictions." Jed. S. Rakoff, Frye *and* Lafler: *Bearers of Mixed Messages*, 122 Yale L.J. Online 25 (2012).

There is a risk, that arises from plea bargaining, that an innocent defendant will plead guilty to a crime that he did not commit. *See* Gary Fields & John Emshwiller, Federal Guilty Pleas Soar as Bargains Trump Trials, Wall St. Journal, U.S. News Section. A.1 (Sept. 23, 2012). Defendants sometimes plead guilty (even when innocent) because they fear that, if they do not, they may be convicted and spend years or decades in prison. By pleading guilty, defendants sometimes receive lesser sentences. Prosecutors can exacerbate these fears by overcharging defendants. Indeed, in 2011, guilty pleas were entered in 97% of all federal cases, an increase of 84% from 1990. *Id.* At the same time, because of a crackdown on various crimes, the number of prosecutions dramatically increased two-fold. *Id.* Sometimes, defendants pleaded guilty without attempting to discover whether the prosecution has exculpatory evidence. *Id.* As a result, some have begun to question whether plea bargains should be allowed or should be more carefully scrutinized. *Id.* As a result, some believe that defendants who plea bargain should receive the types of protection that they would have received had they gone to trial.

Point for Discussion

Effective Assistance of Counsel

In 2012, the Supreme Court dealt with two cases that involved plea bargaining. These cases intersect with other areas of criminal procedure, but have some relevance in the plea bargaining context. In particular, the cases show that in the plea bargaining arena, defendants have constitutional rights in that process. Moreover, even if prosecutors exercised their discretion properly, the Sixth Amendment right to counsel still limits what bargaining will suffice for a permissible outcome.

In the first case, Missouri v. Frye, 566 U.S. 133 (2012), the Supreme Court considered whether the Sixth Amendment right to the effective assistance of counsel extended to the consideration and negotiation of plea agreements. The Court held that it did. Because 95% of cases result in plea bargains, the Court held that it was improper to think that the trial process alone would protect criminal defendants against errors occurring in the pre-trial phase. As Justice Kennedy noted, plea bargaining, "is not some adjunct to the criminal justice system, it is the criminal justice system."

In *Lafler v. Cooper,* 566 U.S. 156 (2012), the Supreme Court considered a habeas corpus claim concerning an alleged violation of the Six Amendment right to the effective assistance of counsel, specifically whether a state court's application of the right to effective assistance was contrary to the standard set forth in *Strickland v. Washington,* 466 U.S. 668 (1984). In the trial court, the defendant Cooper had rejected two plea offers and chose to go to trial. The majority in this 5-4 decision found that the state appellate court applied a standard contrary to Strickland and vacated the decision below, remanding for further proceedings. The Court concluded that when a defendant claims that ineffective assistance of counsel led to the improper rejection of a plea offer, defendant has the burden of showing by a reasonable probability that the prejudice resulting from a more severe conviction and sentence after standing trial would not have occurred but for the ineffective assistance.

Ineffective assistance is an extremely important aspect of the process. When he was Attorney General of the United States, John Ashcroft issued a memo limiting the authority of prosecutors to enter into plea bargains. See David Rosenzweig, *L.A. Attorneys Divided on Ashcroft Directive: Some Defense Lawyers Fear That Placing Restrictions on Prosecutors Who are Seeking Plea Bargains Will Strain the System,* L.A. Times p. B2 (October 17, 2003). Some commentators suggested that the entire criminal justice system might collapse if the new memo limited and constrained plea bargaining. *Id.* In Los Angeles, at the time, some 97.2% of all cases are settled through plea bargaining (the rate is 96% nationally). *Id.* As a result, if only a fraction of defendants who currently plead guilty were to choose trials because prosecutors had become uncompromising, the courts would be inundated in no time, said defense lawyers." *Id.*

The Ashcroft policy change altered a policy previously issued by former Attorney General Janet Reno in 1993 which "allowed prosecutors engaged in plea negotiations to make individualized assessments of the circumstances and seriousness of a crime and whether the sentence would be appropriate." *Id.* However, the Reno memo left intact "a requirement that prosecutors proceed on the most serious 'readily provable' charges and not arrive at a plea agreement 'that fails to reflect the seriousness of the defendant's conduct.' " *Id.* So, the Ashcroft memo seemed designed to limit prosecutorial discretion.

E. Pretrial Diversion for Defendants

In addition to a significant measure of discretion with respect to who and when to investigate and who, what, and whether to charge, prosecutors in many jurisdictions also possess substantial authority to divert accused persons into whatever pretrial intervention (PTI) programs that may have been established in their jurisdiction. In effect, prosecutors have essentially the same unfettered discretion with respect to a diversion decision as they possess in deciding who to investigate or to charge. The prosecutor is presumed to have considered all relevant factors in making his or her decision. In *State v. Rosario,* 237 N.J.Super. 63, 566 A.2d 1173 (App. Div. 1989) (distinguished by *State v. Green,* 413 N.J. Super. 556, 997 A.2d 242 (2010)), the court upheld the discretion of a prosecutor to refuse to consent to the defendant's participation in a diversion program. In Rosario's situation, evidence that his residence was used as a source of narcotics trafficking, even though he was not charged with trafficking, justified the prosecutor's refusal to consent to Rosario's diversion. "Abandonment of the prosecution would be more harmful to society than admission into the diversion program would be beneficial to defendant."

Food for Thought

What would happen if a prosecutor's office prohibited plea bargaining and allowed only straight pleas of guilty, dismissal, or diversion? For example, consider the statement by the District Attorney of the Bronx, New York, Robert T. Johnson, made on November 24, 1992: Last week, I directed my staff not to plea bargain any case which had been indicted by a grand jury. Of course, defendants were free to plead to the crimes as charged in the indictment, or to attempt to negotiate a plea before an indictment resulted. This direction was met by protests from some that the system would collapse. In my view, this objection demonstrates the need for the system to take stock of itself and answer this question: is it actually accomplishing what it was designed to accomplish. For if the system really will collapse unless we plea bargain, then there must be something terribly wrong with the system. It means that those charged with crime have a stranglehold on the rest of us; it means that society has ceded control to those it has accused of violating its laws; and it means that our system is running us, instead of the other way around.

Typically, the successful completion by an accused of the conditions set upon entry into the PTI program results in the dismissal of the pending charges that led to the PTI diversion. Concomitantly, failure to meet those PTI requirements results in the prosecutorial office taking the charges to trial. The National District Attorneys Association (NDAA) has created a set of model standards for the prosecutorial exercise of discretion relating to PTI referrals, standards which have not been expressly adopted in any jurisdiction, but which will illustrate the sorts of concerns and criteria prosecutors should have and use in deciding how to exercise this discretion.

National District Attorneys Association—National Prosecution Standards

STANDARDS 4-3.1 through 4-3.8 (3d ed. 2009).

Diversion

4-3.1 Prosecutorial Responsibility: The decision to divert cases from the criminal justice system should be the responsibility of the prosecutor. The prosecutor should, within the exercise of his or her discretion, determine whether diversion of an offender to a treatment alternative best serves the interests of justice.

4-3.2 Diversion Alternatives: A prosecutor should be aware and informed of the scope and availability of all alternative diversion programs. The prosecutor's office should take steps to help ensure that all diversion programs are credible and effective.***

4-3.4 Information Gathering: The prosecutor should have all relevant investigative information, personal data, case records, and criminal history information necessary to render sound and reasonable decisions on diversion of individuals from the criminal justice system. The chief prosecutor should take steps to ensure the enactment of appropriate legislation and court rules to enable the prosecutor to obtain such information from appropriate agencies.

4-3.5 Factors to Consider: The prosecutor may divert individuals from the criminal justice system when he or she considers it to be in the interest of justice and beneficial to both the community and the individual. Factors which may be considered in this decision include:

a. The nature and severity of the offense;

b. Any special characteristics or difficulties of the offender;

c. Whether the defendant is a first-time offender;

d. The likelihood that the defendant will cooperate with and benefit from the diversion program;

e. Whether an available program is appropriate to the needs of the offender;

f. The impact of diversion upon the community;

g. Recommendations of the relevant law enforcement agency;

h. The likelihood that the defendant will recidivate;

i. The extent to which diversion will enable the defendant to maintain employment or remain in school.

j. The opinion of the victim;

k. Provisions for restitution;

l. The impact of the crime on the victim; and

m. Diversion decisions with respect to similarly situated defendants.

4-3.6 Diversion Procedures: The process of diverting a defendant should include the following procedures:

a. A signed agreement or court record specifying all requirements of the accused;

b. A signed waiver of speedy trial requirements, where applicable;

c. The right of the prosecutor, for a designated time period, to proceed with the criminal case when, in the prosecutor's judgment, such action would be in the interest of justice;

d. Appropriate mechanisms to safeguard the prosecution of the case, such as admissions of guilt, stipulations of facts, and depositions of witnesses.

Commentary

An alternative available to prosecutors in the processing of a criminal complaint is that of diversion - the channeling of criminal defendants and even potential defendants, into programs that may not result in a criminal conviction. The purposes of diversion programs include:

1. Unburdening court dockets and conserving judicial resources for more serious cases;

2. Reducing the incidence of offender recidivism by providing community-based rehabilitation that would be more effective and less costly than the alternatives available in continued criminal prosecution.

Food for Thought

What is your opinion of the appropriateness of the factors set forth to guide the prosecutor's discretion in NDAA Standard 4-3? Are all of these factors appropriate for a prosecutor's consideration given the fact that there is unlikely to be any judicial review of this decision? Is it appropriate for a prosecutor, for example, to take account of the political impact of a decision to divert an accused into an otherwise available PTI program: Is the "political reaction" of individuals in the community (including, perhaps, whether or not to vote for the prosecutor in the next election) different from the "community reaction" which Standard 4-3 provides should be appropriate for the prosecutor to consider? In your opinion, are there any other factors not set forth in Standard 4-3 that should be considered by a prosecutor in making these decisions? What are they?

Determination of the appropriateness of diversion in a specified case will involve a subjective determination that, after consideration of all circumstances, the offender and the community will both benefit more by diversion than by prosecution.

Equally important as protecting the rights of the individual is the necessity to protect the interests of society. It must be remembered that the individual involved in the diversion process is accused of having committed a criminal act and is avoiding prosecution only because an alternative procedure is thought to be more appropriate and more beneficial.

For the rules, go to: http://www.ndaa.org/pdf/NDAA%20NPS%203rd%20 Ed.%20w%20Revised%20Commentary.pdf.

Hypo: *The Ray Rice Case*

Ray Rice, a running back with the National Football League (NFL) Baltimore Ravens, was videotaped on Valentine's Day weekend, 2014, punching and knocking out his then-fiancée, Janay—and now wife—in an elevator of an Atlantic City Hotel and Casino. Rice was indicted for aggravated assault on March 27, 2014, and then accepted into a diversion program on May 23, 2014. For a timeline, see: http://sports.yahoo.com/blogs/nfl-shutdown-corner/a-timeline-of-the-ray-rice-nfl-saga-this-week-024851003.html.

For the elevator video, *see* http://www.tmz.com/videos/0_ekaflcqq/.

For Judge Jones' arbitration decision of Rice's appeal of his NFL suspension, go to: https://s3.amazonaws.com/s3.documentcloud.org/documents/1372767/judge-ruling-ray-rice-decision.pdf. Based on the NDAA standards above, was the granting of diversion appropriate? What would you have done?

F. Selective Prosecution

As a result of the wide discretion prosecutors have in prosecuting criminal cases, potential exists for abuse of that discretion. Misuse of that discretion especially presents itself when a prosecutor, with the requisite amount of probable cause, purposefully chooses to pursue a case because of the defendant's race, religion, or some other arbitrary classification.

Wayte v. United States

470 U.S. 598 (1985).

JUSTICE POWELL delivered the opinion of the Court.

The question presented is whether a passive enforcement policy under which the Government prosecutes only those who report themselves as having violated the law, or who are reported by others, violates the First and Fifth Amendments.

On July 2, 1980, pursuant to his authority under § 3 of the Military Selective Service Act, the President issued Presidential Proclamation No. 4771. This Proclamation directed male citizens and certain male residents born during 1960 to register with the Selective Service System during the week of July 21, 1980. Petitioner fell within that class but did not register. Instead, he wrote several letters to Government officials, including the President, stating that he had not registered and did not intend to do so.

Petitioner's letters were added to a Selective Service file of young men who advised that they had failed to register or who were reported by others as having failed to register. For reasons we discuss, Selective Service adopted a policy of passive enforcement under which it would investigate and prosecute only the cases of nonregistration contained in this file. In furtherance of this policy, Selective Service sent a letter on June 17, 1981, to each reported violator who had not registered and for whom it had an address. The letter explained the duty to register, and warned that a violation could result in criminal prosecution and specified penalties.

On July 20, 1981, Selective Service transmitted to the Department of Justice, for investigation and potential prosecution, the names of petitioner and 133 other young men identified under its passive enforcement system—all of whom had not registered in response to the Service's June letter. At two later dates, it referred the names of 152 more young men similarly identified. After screening out the names of those who appeared not to be in the class required to register, the Department of Justice referred the remaining names to the Federal Bureau of Investigation for additional inquiry and to the United States Attorneys for the districts in which the nonregistrants resided. Petitioner's name was one of those referred.

Pursuant to Department of Justice policy, those referred were not immediately prosecuted. Instead, the appropriate United States Attorney was required to notify identified nonregistrants by registered mail that, unless they registered within a specified time, prosecution would be considered. In addition, an FBI agent was usually sent to interview the nonregistrant before prosecution was instituted. This effort to persuade nonregistrants to change their minds became known as the "beg" policy. Under it, young men who registered late were not prosecuted, while those who never registered were investigated further by the Government. Pursuant to the "beg" policy, the United States Attorney for the Central District of California sent petitioner a letter on October 15, 1981, urging him to register or face possible prosecution. Again petitioner failed to respond.

On December 9, 1981, the Department of Justice instructed all United States Attorneys not to begin seeking indictments against nonregistrants until further notice. On January 7, 1982, the President announced a grace period to afford nonregistrants a further opportunity to register without penalty. This grace period extended until February 28, 1982. Petitioner still did not register.

Over the next few months, the Department decided to begin prosecuting those young men who, despite the grace period and "beg" policy, continued to refuse to register. It recognized that under the passive enforcement system those prosecuted were "liable to be vocal proponents of nonregistration" or persons "with religious or moral objections." It also recognized that prosecutions would "undoubtedly result in allegations that the case was brought in retribution for the nonregistrant's exercise of his first amendment rights." The Department was advised, however, that Selective Service could not develop a more "active" enforcement system for quite some time. Because of this, the Department decided to begin seeking indictments under the passive system without further delay. On May 21, 1982, United States Attorneys were notified to begin prosecution of nonregistrants. On June 28, 1982, FBI agents interviewed petitioner, and he continued to refuse to register. Accordingly, on July 22, 1982, an indictment was returned against him for knowingly and willfully failing to register with the Selective Service.

Petitioner moved to dismiss the indictment on the ground of selective prosecution. He contended that he and the other indicted nonregistrants were "vocal" opponents of the registration program who had been impermissibly targeted (out of an estimated 674,000 nonregistrants) for prosecution on the basis of their exercise of First Amendment rights.

[The federal district court found that the government had engaged in impermissible selective prosecution; the Ninth Circuit Court of Appeals reversed.]

In our criminal justice system, the Government retains "broad discretion" as to whom to prosecute. "So long as the prosecutor has probable cause to believe that the accused committed an offense defined by statute, the decision whether or not to prosecute, and what charge to file or bring before a grand jury, generally rests entirely in his discretion." This broad discretion rests largely on the recognition that the decision to prosecute is particularly ill-suited to judicial review. Such factors as the strength of the case, the prosecution's general deterrence value, the Government's enforcement priorities, and the case's relationship to the Government's overall enforcement plan are not readily susceptible to the kind of analysis the courts are competent to undertake. Judicial supervision in this area, moreover, entails systemic costs of particular concern. Examining the basis of a prosecution delays the criminal proceeding, threatens to chill law enforcement by subjecting the prosecutor's motives and decision-making to outside inquiry, and may undermine prosecutorial effectiveness by revealing the Government's enforcement policy. All these are substantial concerns that make the courts properly hesitant to examine the decision whether to prosecute.

As we have noted in a slightly different context, however, although prosecutorial discretion is broad, it is not "'unfettered.' Selectivity in the enforcement of criminal laws is subject to constitutional constraints." In particular, the decision to prosecute may not be "deliberately based upon an unjustifiable standard such as race, religion, or other arbitrary classification," including the exercise of protected statutory and constitutional rights.

It is appropriate to judge selective prosecution claims according to ordinary equal protection standards. Under our prior cases, these standards require petitioner to show both that the passive enforcement system had a discriminatory effect and that it was motivated by a discriminatory purpose. All petitioner has shown here is that those eventually prosecuted, along with many not prosecuted, reported themselves as having violated the law. He has not shown that the enforcement policy selected nonregistrants for prosecution on the basis of their speech. Indeed, he could not have done so given the way the "beg" policy was carried out. The Government did not prosecute those who reported themselves but later registered. Nor did it prosecute those who protested registration but did not report themselves or were not reported by others. In fact, the Government did not even investigate those who wrote letters to Selective Service criticizing registration unless their letters stated affirmatively that they had refused to comply with the law. The Government, on the other hand, did prosecute people who reported themselves or were reported by others but who did not publicly protest. These facts demonstrate that the Government treated all reported nonregistrants similarly. It did not subject vocal nonregistrants to any special burden. Indeed, those prosecuted in effect selected themselves for prosecution by refusing to register after being reported and warned by the Government.

Even if the passive policy had a discriminatory effect, petitioner has not shown that the Government intended such a result. The evidence he presented demonstrated only that the Government was aware that the passive enforcement policy would result in prosecution of vocal objectors and that they would probably make selective prosecution claims. As we have noted, however: "'Discriminatory purpose' implies more than intent as awareness of consequences. It implies that the decisionmaker selected or reaffirmed a particular course of action at least in part 'because of,' not merely 'in spite of,' its adverse effects upon an identifiable group." In the present case, petitioner has not shown that the Government prosecuted him *because of* his protest activities. Absent such a showing, his claim of selective prosecution fails.

We conclude that the Government's passive enforcement system together with its "beg" policy violated neither the First nor Fifth Amendment. Accordingly, we affirm the judgment of the Court of Appeals.

It is so ordered.

Justice Marshall, with whom Justice Brennan joins, dissenting.

The Court correctly points out that Wayte's selective prosecution claims must be judged according to ordinary equal protection standards. Wayte presents an equal protection challenge to the "passive" enforcement system, under which Selective Service refers to the Justice Department for further investigation and possible prosecution *only* the "names of young men who fall into two categories: (1) those who wrote to Selective Service and said that they refused to register and (2) those whose neighbors and others reported them as persons who refused to register." Wayte argues that the scheme purposefully singled out these individuals as a result of their exercise of First Amendment rights. The claim here is not that the Justice Department discriminated among *known* violators of the draft registration law either in its administration of the "beg" policy, which gave such individuals the option of registering to avoid prosecution, or in prosecuting only some reported nonregistrants. Instead, the claim is that the system by which the Department defined the class of possible prosecutees—the "passive" enforcement system—was designed to discriminate against those who had exercised their First Amendment rights. Such governmental action cannot stand if undertaken with discriminatory intent. As this Court has clearly stated, "for an agent of the State to pursue a course of action whose objective is to penalize a person's reliance on his legal rights is 'patently unconstitutional.'" If the Government intentionally discriminated in defining the pool of potential prosecutees, it cannot immunize itself from liability merely by showing that it used permissible methods in choosing whom to prosecute from this previously tainted pool.

Take Note

Sometimes, politics is alleged to be the real reason for a prosecution. For example, Professor Alan Dershowitz of Harvard Law School claimed that the felony prosecution of conservative filmmaker and author Dinesh D'Souza is an improper use of prosecutorial discretion. Jacob Gershman, "Dershowitz Says D'Souza Case 'Smacks of Selective Prosecution,'" Wall St. Journal Law Blog (Jan. 31, 2014).

United States v. Armstrong

517 U.S. 456 (1996).

CHIEF JUSTICE REHNQUIST delivered the opinion of the Court.

In this case, we consider the showing necessary for a defendant to be entitled to discovery on a claim that the prosecuting attorney singled him out for prosecution on the basis of his race. We conclude that respondents failed to satisfy the threshold showing: They failed to show that the Government declined to prosecute similarly situated suspects of other races.

Practice Pointer

When a trial court denies a defense motion to compel discovery, the standard applied by many appellate courts is abuse of discretion, *see, e.g., United States v. Hirsch*, 360 F.3d 860 (8th Cir. 2004), while a few courts apply a de novo standard of review, *see, e.g., United States v. James*, 257 F.3d 1173 (10th Cir. 2001).

In April 1992, respondents were indicted in the United States District Court for the Central District of California on charges of conspiring to possess with intent to distribute more than 50 grams of cocaine base (crack) and conspiring to distribute the same, in violation of 21 U.S.C. §§ 841 and 846, and federal firearms offenses. For three months prior to the indictment, agents had infiltrated a suspected crack distribution ring by using three confidential informants. On seven separate occasions during this period, the informants had bought a total of 124.3 grams of crack from respondents and witnessed respondents carrying firearms during the sales. The agents searched the hotel room in which the sales were transacted, arrested respondents Armstrong and Hampton in the room, and found more crack and a loaded gun. The agents later arrested the other respondents as part of the ring.

Respondents filed a motion for discovery to support their selective prosecution claim. The motion was opposed by the Government, but granted by the District Court. The Supreme Court considered whether this discovery request was warranted.

A selective-prosecution claim is not a defense on the merits to the criminal charge itself, but an independent assertion that the prosecutor has brought the charge for reasons forbidden by the Constitution. Our cases delineating the necessary elements to prove a claim of selective prosecution have taken great pains to explain that the standard is a demanding one. These cases afford a "background presumption" that the showing necessary to obtain discovery should itself be a significant barrier to the litigation of insubstantial claims.

A selective-prosecution claim asks a court to exercise judicial power over a "special province" of the Executive. The Attorney General and United States Attorneys retain "'broad discretions' 'to enforce the Nation's criminal laws.' They have this latitude because they are designated by statute as the President's delegates to help him discharge his constitutional responsibility to 'take Care that the Laws be faithfully executed.'" In the ordinary case, "so long as the prosecutor has probable cause to believe that the accused committed an offense defined by statute, the decision whether or not to prosecute, and what charge to file or bring before a grand jury, generally rests entirely in his discretion."

Of course, a prosecutor's discretion is "subject to constitutional constraints." One of these constraints, imposed by the equal protection component of the Due Process Clause of the Fifth Amendment, is that the decision whether to prosecute may not be based on "an unjustifiable standard such as race, religion, or other arbitrary classification." A defendant may demonstrate that the administration of a criminal law is "directed so exclusively against a particular class of persons . . . with a mind so unequal and oppressive" that the system of prosecution amounts to "a practical denial" of equal protection of the law.

In order to dispel the presumption that a prosecutor has not violated equal protection, a criminal defendant must present "clear evidence to the contrary." The high standard stems from a concern not to unnecessarily impair the performance of a core executive constitutional function. "Examining the basis of a prosecution delays the criminal proceeding, threatens to chill law enforcement by subjecting the prosecutor's motives and decisionmaking to outside inquiry, and may undermine prosecutorial effectiveness by revealing the Government's enforcement policy."

The requirements for a selective-prosecution claim draw on "ordinary equal protection standards." The claimant must demonstrate that the federal prosecutorial policy "had a discriminatory effect and that it was motivated by a discriminatory purpose." To establish a discriminatory effect in a race case, the claimant must show that similarly situated individuals of a different race were not prosecuted.

We turn to the showing necessary to obtain discovery in support of such a claim. If discovery is ordered, the Government must assemble from its own files documents which might corroborate or refute the defendant's claim. Discovery thus imposes many of the costs present when the Government must respond to a prima facie case of selective prosecution. It will divert prosecutors' resources and may disclose the Government's prosecutorial strategy. The justifications for a rigorous standard for the elements of a selective-prosecution claim thus require a correspondingly rigorous standard for discovery in aid of such a claim.

The Courts of Appeals "require some evidence tending to show the existence of the essential elements of the defense," discriminatory effect and discriminatory intent.

In this case we consider what evidence constitutes "some evidence tending to show the existence" of the discriminatory effect element. The Court of Appeals held that a defendant may establish a colorable basis for discriminatory effect without evidence that the Government has failed to prosecute others who are similarly situated to the defendant. We think it was mistaken in this view. The vast majority of the Courts of Appeals require the defendant to produce some evidence that similarly situated defendants of other races could have been prosecuted, but were not, and this requirement is consistent with our equal protection case law. As the three-judge panel explained, "'selective prosecution' implies that a selection has taken place."

We think the required threshold—a credible showing of different treatment of similarly situated persons—adequately balances the Government's interest in vigorous prosecution and the defendant's interest in avoiding selective prosecution.

In the case before us, respondents' "study" did not constitute "some evidence tending to show the existence of the essential elements of" a selective-prosecution claim. The study failed to identify individuals who were not black, could have been prosecuted for the offenses for which respondents were charged, but were not so prosecuted. This omission was not remedied by respondents' evidence in opposition to the Government's motion for reconsideration. The newspaper article which discussed the discriminatory effect of federal drug sentencing laws, was not relevant to an allegation of discrimination in decision prosecuted. This omission was not evidence in opposition to the reconsideration. The newspaper article, discriminatory effect of federal drug sentencing laws, was not relevant to an allegation of discrimination in decisions to prosecute. Respondents' affidavits, which recounted one attorney's conversation with a drug treatment center employee and the experience of another attorney defending drug prosecutions in state court, recounted hearsay and reported personal conclusions based on anecdotal evidence. The judgment of the Court of Appeals is therefore reversed, and the case is remanded for proceedings consistent with this opinion.

It is so ordered.

JUSTICE STEVENS, dissenting.

The Court correctly concludes that in this case the facts presented to the District Court in support of respondents' claim that they had been singled out for prosecution because of their race were not sufficient to prove that defense. Like Chief Judge Wallace of the Court of Appeals, I am persuaded that the District Judge did not abuse her discretion when she concluded that the factual showing was sufficiently disturbing to require some response from the United States Attorney's Office. Perhaps the discovery order was broader than necessary, but I cannot agree with the Court's apparent conclusion that no inquiry was permissible.

The District Judge's order should be evaluated in light of three circumstances that underscore the need for judicial vigilance over certain types of drug prosecutions. First, the Anti-Drug Abuse Act of 1986 and subsequent legislation established a regime of extremely high penalties for the possession and distribution of so-called "crack" cocaine. Those provisions treat one gram of crack as the equivalent of 100 grams of powder cocaine. The distribution of 50 grams of crack is thus punishable by the same mandatory minimum sentence of 10 years in prison that applies to the distribution of 5,000 grams of powder cocaine.

Second, the disparity between the treatment of crack cocaine and powder cocaine is matched by the disparity between the severity of the punishment imposed by federal law and that imposed by state law for the same conduct. Finally, it is undisputed that the brunt of the elevated federal penalties falls heavily on blacks. While 65% of the persons who have used crack are white, in 1993 they represented only 4% of the federal offenders convicted of trafficking in crack. Eighty-eight percent of such defendants were black.

The extraordinary severity of the imposed penalties and the troubling racial patterns of enforcement give rise to a special concern about the fairness of charging practices for crack offenses. Evidence tending to prove that black defendants charged with distribution of crack in the Central District of California are prosecuted in federal court, whereas members of other races charged with similar offenses are prosecuted in state court, warrants close scrutiny by the federal judges in that District. In my view, the District Judge, who has sat on both the federal and the state benches in Los Angeles, acted well within her discretion to call for the development of facts that would demonstrate what standards, if any, governed the choice of forum where similarly situated offenders are prosecuted.

In this case, the evidence was sufficiently disturbing to persuade the District Judge to order discovery that might help explain the conspicuous racial pattern of cases before her Court I cannot accept the majority's conclusion that the District Judge either exceeded her power or abused her discretion when she did so. I therefore respectfully dissent.

United States v. Bass

536 U.S. 862 (2002).

PER CURIAM.

A federal grand jury sitting in the Eastern District of Michigan returned a second superseding indictment charging respondent with, *inter alia*, the intentional firearm killings of two individuals. The United States filed a notice of intent to seek the death penalty. Respondent, who is black, alleged that the Government had determined to seek the death penalty against him because of his race. He moved to dismiss the death penalty notice and, in the alternative, for discovery of information relating to the Government's capital charging practices. The District Court granted the motion for discovery, and after the Government informed the court that it would not comply with the discovery order, the court dismissed the death penalty notice. A divided panel of the United States Court of Appeals for the Sixth Circuit affirmed the District Court's discovery order. We grant the petition for a writ of certiorari and now summarily reverse.

In *United States v. Armstrong*, we held that a defendant who seeks discovery on a claim of selective prosecution must show some evidence of both discriminatory effect and discriminatory intent. We need go no further in the present case than consideration of the evidence supporting discriminatory effect. As to that, *Armstrong* says that the defendant must make a "credible showing" that "similarly situated individuals of a different race were not prosecuted." The Sixth Circuit concluded that respondent had made such a showing based on nationwide statistics demonstrating that "[t]he United States charges blacks with a death-eligible offense more than twice as often as it charges whites" and that the United States enters into plea bargains more frequently with whites than it does with blacks. Even assuming that the *Armstrong* requirement can be satisfied by a nationwide showing (as opposed to a showing regarding the

Food for Thought

Neither *Armstrong* nor *Bass* specified how the showing of "some evidence" of discriminatory effect could be satisfied, *e.g.*, by affidavit, by other admissible documentation, or by specific allegations. In *McNeil v. State*, 112 Md.App. 434, 685 A.2d 839 (1996), the court suggested that presentation of verifiable facts in some form would be sufficient as long as it went beyond a mere general allegation of prosecutorial misconduct. Thus, even if a defense motion to dismiss for selective prosecution were not supported by an affidavit, it would nevertheless suffice if it was verifiable by review of the court file. In *United States v. Alameh*, 341 F.3d 167 (2d Cir. 2003), statistical evidence and affidavits showed increased prosecutions of people with Arab names after September 11, 2001, but the court held that was insufficient to support discovery because most of the investigation had occurred prior to that date.

record of the decisionmakers in respondent's case), raw statistics regarding overall charges say nothing about charges brought against *similarly situated defendants*. And the statistics regarding plea bargains are even less relevant, since respondent *was* offered a plea bargain but declined it. Under *Armstrong*, because respondent failed to submit relevant evidence that similarly situated persons were treated differently, he was not entitled to discovery.

The Sixth Circuit's decision is contrary to *Armstrong* and threatens the "performance of a core executive constitutional function." For that reason, we reverse.

Hypo 1: *Latin Kings*

"King Paradise," a/k/a George Boyd, has retained you to represent him following his federal indictment for racketeering and murder. You have filed motions to dismiss his indictment due to selective prosecution and to gain access to information about governmental charging policies. The indictment charges George and all of the "Kings" who are officers and have prior criminal histories (*e.g.*, King Guy, King Bullet, King Humpty, King Biz); they are also the older male members of the local chapter of the Almighty Latin King Nation. Among the other members of the local chapter who were not indicted are its only three women members, who were officers and associates (commonly referred to as, you guessed it, "Queens") of the Latin Kings. In the Latin Kings organization, because women are prohibited from holding positions of authority, the highest office open to women is "Secretary," who is responsible for keeping records of all Latin King meetings. Your initial interview with George indicates that some of the unindicted male members and all of the female members will testify for the Government. Evaluate whether the court will deny your motions.

Hypo 2: *Selective Prosecution*

Following discovery of a large and violent crack cocaine conspiracy, the United States Attorney indicted 25 persons, all of whom are African-American. Of the 55 unindicted persons who were involved in the conspiracy, 50 are African-American and five are white. Twenty-five African-Americans were granted immunity from prosecution as were three whites. Defendant Sterling moved to dismiss the indictment, claiming that he had been selected for prosecution because of his race. He argued that the five unindicted white persons were similarly situated to him and that more than 90% of those indicted in the metro area since 1992 for crack cocaine trafficking are African-Americans. An officer in the local police department testified that he did not choose individuals to violate the law. "They choose to violate the law themselves. And when they violate the law, if we can prove it, we prosecute them, regardless of their race, sex, where they were born, or their family identity." He also testified about the reason that each white conspirator identified in Sterling's motion had not been indicted. One had agreed to work undercover, another was a target but the evidence against him was still insufficient, and the third had proven himself to be truthful and cooperative with the investigation.

The trial court concluded that Sterling had made a nonfrivolous showing in raising a claim of selective prosecution and ordered the prosecution to respond to Sterling's formal requests for discovery into its criteria for selecting whom to prosecute. The court also found that Sterling and the unindicted white conspirators were "similarly situated" for a selective prosecution claim and that Sterling's statistical data made a nonfrivolous showing of discriminatory intent. Do you agree?

G. Vindictive Prosecution

The line between selective and vindictive prosecution is not always clear. The Court in the next case, *United States v. Brown*, 862 F.Supp.2d 1276 (N.D. Ala. 2012), took pains to describe each.

United States v. Brown

862 F.Supp.2d 1276 (N.D. Ala. 2012).

Memorandum Opinion and Order

Vindictive prosecution is distinguishable from selective prosecution in that vindictive prosecution arises when the severity of the charges against a defendant is increased after the defendant exercises a constitutional right after criminal charges have begun, while selective prosecution occurs when a person is prosecuted based on an immutable personal characteristic, such as race or religion, or in response to some constitutionally-protected act that a person has done prior to the criminal charge being brought against him. The court will set out the standard for each theory in turn.

1. Selective Prosecution

Claims of selective prosecution have been recognized by the Supreme Court for well over a century. In *Yick Wo v. Hopkins*, 118 U.S. 356 (1886), two Chinese subjects raised challenges under the Fourteenth Amendment's Equal Protection Clause to their incarceration for violating a San Francisco ordinance requiring operators of laundries in wooden buildings to obtain a permit from the city. About 200 Chinese owners of wooden laundries had been denied permits, whereas 80 non-Chinese owners had been granted permits to carry on their businesses under similar conditions. The Supreme Court reversed the convictions, declaring:

Though the law itself be fair on its face and impartial in appearance, yet, if it is applied and administered by public authority with an evil eye and an unequal hand, so as practically to make unjust and illegal discriminations between persons in similar circumstances, material to their rights, the denial of equal justice is within the prohibition of the Constitution. In other words, a decision to prosecute that is "deliberately based upon an unjustifiable standard such as race, religion, or other arbitrary classification" is a denial of equal protection. *Oyler v. Boles*, 368 U.S. 448, 456 (1962). The ban on discriminatory prosecution is not limited to the states but also applies to the federal government under the Fifth Amendment's Due Process Clause. As noted by the Magistrate Judge, in *Wayte*, the Supreme Court set out the constitutional constraints on prosecutorial discretion as follows:

Although prosecutorial discretion is broad, it is not " 'unfettered.' Selectivity in the enforcement of criminal laws is subject to constitutional constraints." In particular, the decision to prosecute may not be " 'deliberately based upon an unjustifiable standard such as race, religion, or other arbitrary classification,'" including the exercise of protected statutory and constitutional rights. *Wayte v. United States*, 470 U.S. 598, 608. *Wayte* instructs that selective prosecution cases are to be "judged according to ordinary equal protection standards." Unless the equal protection claim is based on an overtly discriminatory classification, "these standards require petitioner to show both that the passive enforcement system had a discriminatory effect and that it was motivated by a discriminatory purpose."

2. Vindictive Prosecution

"As long as the prosecutor has probable cause to believe the accused has committed a crime, the courts have no authority to interfere with a prosecutor's decision to prosecute." *United States v. Barner*, 441 F. 3d 1310, 1315 (11th Cir. 2006). The prosecutor will violate due process, however, if he obtains new charges out of vindictiveness, *i.e.*, a "desire to punish a person for exercising his statutory or constitutional rights." *Id.*; *see also United States v. Goodwin*, 457 U.S. 368 (1982).

There are two ways to prove a prosecutorial vindictiveness claim: (1) by showing that a presumption of vindictiveness arises from the government's conduct; or (2) by showing actual vindictiveness. *See, e.g.*, *United States v. Saltzman*, 537 F.3d 353, 359 (5th Cir. 2008).

Brown's claim of vindictive prosecution is based on his allegation that he was prosecuted when others who are similarly situated were not because, before the charge he seeks to have dismissed was brought: (1) Brown was the victim of an assault by a BOP guard for which the guard had entered a guilty plea; (2) Brown had filed a civil suit in relation to that assault; (3) prison personnel were aware of those facts; and (4) Brown wrote an "inordinate number" of grievances against prison staff. However, even assuming that Brown has asserted a claim of presumptive or actual vindictiveness, he has failed to show the existence of either.

"A prosecutor's decision to seek heightened charges after a defendant successfully appeals his conviction for the same conduct is presumed to be vindictive." *Barner,* 441 F. 3d at 1315-16 There is, however, no automatic presumption of vindictiveness when a prosecutor decides to increase charges after a defendant exercises a legal right in the pretrial context. *Barner*, 441 F. 3d at 1316; *Goodwin*, 457 U.S. at 381. Although the Eleventh Circuit has not definitively determined whether the presumption of vindictiveness can ever arise in the pretrial—much less precharge—context, that court did note that such a presumption could arise in the pretrial context only if the facts of the case "form a realistic likelihood of vindictiveness." *Barner*, 441 F.3d at 1318. For such a presumption to arise, the defendant must first show that his exercise of pretrial rights was followed by charges of increased severity. If this threshold showing is made, the defendant then must identify other factors to raise a realistic likelihood of vindictiveness.

To establish actual vindictiveness, a defendant must prove that: (1) the prosecutor wanted to punish the defendant for exercising his rights (animus); and (2) the prosecutor's animus caused the prosecutor to bring charges of increased severity (causation). *See Barner,* 441 F. 3d at 1322. A showing of actual vindictiveness is "exceedingly difficult to make." Moreover, it would be unduly burdensome on any person challenging a prosecution as vindictive to limit the motive which must be shown to the subjective motive of the actual prosecutor, or even to the United States Attorneys office. *Simms v. United States*, 41 A.3d 482 (D.C. Court of Appeals, 2012) (To impose a "'personal stake' requirement unduly constricts the inquiry of prosecutorial vindictiveness, which is not limited to the motives of an individual prosecutor and may focus on the motivations of the government as an institution.").

Not surprisingly, *Brown* has not established actual vindictiveness. Crucially, Brown has not alleged a set of circumstances showing that "a reasonable likelihood of vindictiveness exists." *Goodwin*, 457 U.S. at 373. All Brown has done is shown that he was assaulted by a guard, the guard was prosecuted and plead guilty, Brown filed a civil suit related to the assault, and Brown was indicted for assaulting a guard by throwing feces and urine in the guard's face although other inmates who had engaged in similar assaults were not indicted. Thus, the Government was not required to come up with a reasonable explanation for the difference in Brown's treatment. *See Simms*, 41 A.3d 482. Government's obligation to answer or explain allegations of prosecutorial vindictiveness does not arise unless "the accumulation of circumstances of record, without more, give rise to a realistic likelihood of prosecutorial vindictiveness."

Points for Discussion

a. Causing a Retrial

"Should there be a presumption of vindictiveness when a prosecutor increases criminal charges after a defendant exercises a constitutional right that causes a retrial after conviction? Suppose the following situation occurred: "Goodwin was charged with several misdemeanor and petty offenses, including assault on a United States Park Policeman. He initiated plea negotiations with the prosecutor, but later advised the prosecutor that he did not wish to plead guilty and desired a trial by jury in the District Court. The case was transferred from the United States Magistrate to the District Court and responsibility for the prosecution was assumed by an Assistant United States Attorney. About six weeks later, after reviewing the case, the prosecutor obtained a four-count indictment charging respondent with one felony count of forcibly assaulting a federal officer and three related counts arising from the same incident. A jury convicted respondent on the felony count and on one misdemeanor count." Should a presumption of vindictiveness have attached to this case? *See United States v. Goodwin*, 457 U.S. 368 (1982).

b. Different Prosecutors

Should a presumption of vindictiveness arise if the defendant can prove that separate prosecutors filed the related indictments? Can a persuasive argument be made that the vindictiveness is institutional rather than personal? See *Thigpen v. Roberts*, 468 U.S. 27, 31–32 (1984), where the Court noted that the addition of another prosecutor changed "little," but then stated:

> It might be argued that if two different prosecutors are involved, a presumption of vindictiveness, which arises in part from assumptions about the individual's personal stake in the proceedings, is inappropriate. On

the other hand, to the extent the presumption reflects "institutional pressure that might subconsciously motivate a vindictive prosecutorial response to a defendant's exercise of his right to obtain a retrial of a decided question," it does not hinge on the continued involvement of a particular individual. A district attorney burdened with the retrial of an already-convicted defendant might be no less vindictive because he did not bring the initial prosecution. Indeed, *Blackledge* referred frequently to actions by "the State," rather than "the prosecutor."

We need not determine the correct rule when two independent prosecutors are involved, however.

c. Mistrial

Should a presumption of vindictiveness exist when the prosecutor brings additional charges after a mistrial but before a retrial? *See, e.g., United States v. Poole*, 407 F.3d 767 (6th Cir. 2005) (no presumption of vindictiveness for adding charges following a mistrial due to a hung jury).

Hypo: *Vindictive Extra Count*

Three defendants were indicted for narcotics and firearms offenses. At their initial appearance, two of the defendants requested that they be released on bail pending trial, but the government was strongly opposed. Apparently, the third defendant had turned state's evidence and had been threatened. The government responded by placing her in the federal witness protection program and urged that the other two defendants not be released on bail. Based on testimony by the Assistant United States Attorney regarding the threats, the magistrate judge denied bail and remanded the two defendants to federal custody. The jailed defendants appealed that decision to the district judge who released them on bond. Two days later, the Assistant United States Attorney sought and obtained a superseding indictment charging defendants with an additional conspiracy count. Should the conspiracy charge be dismissed as vindictive?

---

d. Malicious Prosecution

Usually, a prosecutor has immunity from exercising prosecutorial discretion. Sometimes, however, it seems there might be an alternative path to a lawsuit. After Freddy Gray died while being transported by the police in Baltimore in April of 2015, District Attorney Marilyn Mosby filed charges against six police officers. Three of the cases resulted in acquittal and three were dismissed. Five of the six police officers filed suit in federal court for malicious prosecution, among other grounds. In January 2017, a federal district court judge refused to dismiss the case against Mosby at this juncture because her office asserted it did its own investigative work and therefore functioned as an investigator in part, and not as a prosecutor. See, e.g., Justin Fenton, "Judge Orders Discovery and Depositions to Move Forward in Mosby Malicious Prosecution Lawsuit," Baltimore Sun, Maryland News (Feb. 3, 2017). Available at: http://www.baltimoresun.com/news/maryland/crime/bs-md-ci-mosby-lawsuit-discovery-20170203-story.htm

Executive Summary

Prosecutorial Discretion is Designed to Promote Fairness. Discretion is built into the system in the investigative and prosecution phases to allow the system to be flexible enough to mold itself around the facts of individual cases. This flexibility promotes fairness.

Prosecutors Have Broad Discretion. Prosecutors have discretion over when and how to investigate a potential case and how to charge it.

Use of Grand Juries. While some jurisdictions require grand juries to proceed in a case, such as a capital murder action, prosecutors can use the grand jury to determine whether charges are appropriate.

Discretion Has Limits. Prosecutors can't use their discretion in violation of the law, particularly the Constitution.

Major Themes

a. Discretion is Widespread—Prosecutorial discretion exists in many aspects of the criminal justice system, from investigating leads, to plea bargaining, to calling witnesses, to sentencing allocution.

b. Discretion Can be Controversial—Prosecutorial discretion, particularly whether and how to charge cases, can be controversial, indicating a need to limit and guide discretion, when appropriate.

c. Selective and Vindictive Prosecution— Certain types of misuse of discretion are not permitted, such as selective and vindictive prosecution.

Test Your Knowledge

To assess your understanding of the material in this chapter, click here to take a quiz.

No Selective Prosecution. Prosecutors cannot prosecute defendants based on immutable characteristics, such as race or national origin, in violation of equal protection principles.

No Vindictive Prosecution.   Prosecutors cannot penalize defendants for exercising their constitutional or statutory rights after proceedings have commenced by subsequently increasing charges.

For More Information

• D. Lieb, Note, *Vindicating Vindictiveness: Prosecutorial Discretion and Plea Bargaining, Past and Future*, 123 YALE L. J. 1014 (2014).

http://www.yalelawjournal.org/note/vindicating-vindictiveness-prosecutorial-discretion-and-plea-bargaining-past-and-future

• Tracy Vedder, Conviction tossed for man who claimed 'vindictive prosecution', komonews.com, (Nov. 21, 2012)

http://www.komonews.com/news/local/Man-who-accused-city-of-vindictive-prosecution-has-conviction-tossed-180450601.html

• RUSSELL L. WEAVER, JOHN M. BURKOFF, CATHERINE HANCOCK & STEVEN I. FRIEDLAND, PRINCIPLES OF CRIMINAL PROCEDURE, Ch. 10 (6th ed. 2018).

CHAPTER 12

Case Screening: Preliminary Hearings & Grand Juries

A. Introduction

There are three basic processes by which a case is screened for a determination whether it will proceed to a formal prosecution. First, a prosecutor has discretion to decide not to file a formal charge, as discussed in Chapter 11. The two other processes are the subjects of this chapter: preliminary hearings and grand juries. Both preliminary hearings and grand jury review test the government's case for the quantum of proof required to proceed to trial, although each requires only proof of probable cause (as opposed to proof beyond a reasonable doubt) that a crime has been committed and that a particular defendant committed the crime.

Take Note

Preliminary hearings and grand juries differ, in important respects. For example: preliminary hearings are public, while grand jury proceedings are secret. Preliminary hearings are adversary proceedings in which the defense can challenge the prosecution's case, while grand juries normally hear only the prosecution's case and prospective defendants and defense counsel are excluded from the grand jury proceedings. Judges preside over preliminary hearings, while grand jury proceedings are run by the prosecution and occur with little judicial participation. Finally, judges determine the sufficiency of the evidence in preliminary hearings, while grand jurors (citizens of the local community) make this determination in grand jury proceedings.

B. Preliminary Hearings

In most jurisdictions, the accused may request that, within a short period after the initial appearance, the judge conduct an adversarial hearing to determine whether there is probable cause to believe that a crime was committed and that the defendant committed it. Recall that the *Gerstein* determination of probable cause discussed in Chapter 10, *supra*, may be *ex parte*, without any input from the defendant. Federal Rule of Criminal Procedure 5.1, which is typical, specifies that a defendant who requests one should have a preliminary hearing within 10 days, if he or she is incarcerated, and within 20 days, if he or she is not. Without a finding of probable cause, the accused must be released from custody or from any bail obligation.

In Coleman v. Alabama, 399 U.S. 1 (1970), the Supreme Court concluded that when a state grants the accused a preliminary hearing, the Sixth Amendment right to counsel applies to that hearing. Counsel is necessary, the Court said, to try to rebut the showing of probable cause, discover the prosecution's case, build a record for later impeachment, preserve the testimony of witnesses who are unavailable for trial, and make effective arguments on matters like the necessity for bail.

Points for Discussion

a. Screening

Whether or not the preliminary hearing serves a screening function for the prosecution depends on the circumstances. Some prosecutors' offices may spend substantial resources before the first appearance, or before a formal charge is filed, screening the case for merit and not bringing charges in cases that are weak. As a result, the screening for meritorious prosecutions has often already been done before the preliminary hearing. In addition, in federal court, and in state cases involving a grand jury prior to bringing of formal charging through an indictment, if the indictment is returned before the preliminary hearing, then the accused is usually not entitled to a preliminary hearing. The grand jury will have already determined that there is probable cause to go forward. For example, 18 U.S.C. § 3060(e) provides that no preliminary hearing is required for an arrested person if at any time subsequent to the initial appearance of that person and prior to the date fixed for the preliminary examination, an indictment is returned.

If a prosecutor's office does not do significant screening in advance of the preliminary hearing and does not proceed through an indictment before the preliminary hearing, then the hearing may indeed serve a screening function. With the opportunity to hear from a witness in the case (typically a police officer), it may become apparent that the charge lacks probable cause or that the prosecution's case is weak and not worth pursuing. Normally, a finding of no probable cause at a preliminary hearing does not preclude future prosecution of the case, especially if further investigation unearths additional evidence.

b. Pretrial Discovery

In practice, the preliminary hearing may provide defense counsel with a valuable discovery technique. Presentation of the prosecution's case necessarily provides the defense with some discovery. Defense counsel may obtain even more discovery by cross-examining the prosecution's witnesses at the hearing and by subpoenaing other potential witnesses to testify as defense witnesses at the hearing.

c. Future Impeachment

Extensive cross-examination of prosecution witnesses at the preliminary hearing stage may be of value to the defense even though there is little likelihood of successfully challenging the prosecution's showing of probable cause and little to be gained by way of

Practice Pointer

The importance to the defense of the limited discovery accessible through the preliminary hearing depends in large part on the availability of alternative discovery procedures. For example, if prior statements of prospective witnesses and the arresting officer's report are readily accessible, the hearing's discovery potential may be relatively unimportant. On the other hand, if state law and practice, like federal court practice, provide for little pretrial discovery, the preliminary hearing may serve as an important discovery device. Similarly, if discovery does not occur until after the critical time for plea negotiations, the preliminary hearing may serve as the main discovery device for the large percentage of cases resolved by guilty pleas.

Practice Pointer

Of course, cross-examination designed to lay the foundation for future impeachment carries dangers for the defense. By focusing on potential weaknesses in a witness's testimony, a witness may be rehabilitated for trial and state that at the preliminary hearing she was confused but now is clear and certain . Cross-examination may also harden a witness's position, making the witness less able to retreat to a more friendly position. Finally, if the witness becomes unavailable at trial, the earlier testimony can be used, and the perpetuated testimony may be more damaging than that which would have existed without the cross-examination.

discovery. The skilled interrogation of witnesses can be a vital impeachment tool for use in cross-examination later at trial. Witnesses are more likely to make damaging admissions or contradictory statements at the preliminary hearing because they are less thoroughly briefed for that proceeding than they are for trial. In addition, the more some witnesses say before trial, the more likely that there will be some inconsistency between their trial testimony and their previous statements.

d. Perpetuation of Testimony

The admission of the preliminary hearing testimony of a prosecution witness who is unavailable for trial must be reconciled with the defendant's constitutional right of confrontation. Preliminary hearing testimony may be admissible as substantive evidence at trial if: 1) it was given under oath; 2) the declarant is unavailable to testify at trial; and 3) a reasonable opportunity, whether exercised or not, for cross-examination on substantially the same issues was afforded the opposing party at the preliminary hearing. *See Crawford v. Washington*, 541 U.S. 36 (2004), and its progeny.

e. Pretrial Release

Where bail is set at the initial appearance on the basis of sketchy facts, the preliminary hearing provides the judge with the first extensive adversary examination of the facts of the individual case. The testimony may persuade the court to reduce or increase bail, or impose other terms or conditions of pretrial release. The hearing also insures that a person who has been unjustifiably accused will be promptly released from custody or from any bail obligations.

Take Note

Given all of the possible strategies for a defense attorney at a preliminary hearing, the motives and extent of cross-examination of a witness at a preliminary hearing may be different from the motives and extent of cross-examination of that same witness at a future trial. If so, then it may violate the Confrontation Clause to allow the preliminary hearing testimony of that witness to come in as evidence at trial in lieu of live testimony and cross-examination at trial.

f. Plea Bargaining

A preliminary hearing may be an "educational experience" for the defendant who is not persuaded by defense counsel's opinion that the prosecution has such a strong case that a negotiated plea is in the defendant's best interest. Conversely, the proof at the hearing may be insufficient on the charged offenses, and require reduction of excessive charges. It thereby may serve as a check against the prosecutorial practice of "overcharging" (by the number of charges and/or the severity of charges) in anticipation of plea negotiations. However, this latter function is mitigated by the fact that a finding of no probable cause at the preliminary hearing does not necessarily preclude the later filing of the charge.

Practice Pointer

There is typically no reason a defendant would waive a preliminary hearing as it is an important avenue of discovery. However, on occasion a prosecutor may offer more robust "open file" discovery in return for the defendant's waiver of the preliminary hearing. In those cases, a defendant receives the benefit of better discovery and may want to consider waiving the hearing.

g. Motion to Dismiss

At the close of the prosecution's case at a preliminary hearing, whenever possible, defense counsel should move to dismiss the charges, based upon the failure of the proof to establish: 1) That an offense was committed; 2) That the accused is the one who committed it; and/or 3) That proper venue is locking (usually, the place where the offense took place), for jurisdictional purposes. Sometimes, if the judge denies defense counsel's motion for a dismissal based upon the above grounds, as will usually be the case, the defense will move the court to reduce the original charge to a lesser offense, e.g., from a felony to a misdemeanor, have the accused plead guilty to the reduced charge, and thereby dispose of the case. If the accused is permitted to enter a guilty plea to an amended charge that is a lesser-included offense of the original charge, double jeopardy will prevent the prosecution from reinstituting the original charge against the accused.

Hypo 1: *Present the Alibi?*

The F.B.I. arrests Jack Penny for federal bank robbery on October 21 at approximately 11:00 a.m. Mr. Penny contacts you to represent him on the charge. Mr. Penny is detained pretrial. From the documents you have been able to obtain, it appears that someone robbed the employees of a federally insured bank in a small town located about seventy-five miles from the city where your client resides. From the photographs taken by the bank camera, the F.B.I. located Mr. Penny and arrested him. In addition, several employees of the bank identified him in a line-up held on October 23 at the local Federal Building. Mr. Penny has told you that, during the late morning of October 21, he was visiting his hometown methadone center receiving his weekly dosage. You are able to corroborate this information with the receptionist on duty at that time. At the preliminary hearing, the Assistant United States Attorney presented the evidence described in the first paragraph. In addition, bank employees identified Mr. Penny as he sat next to you at counsel table in the small courtroom where the United States Magistrate Judge was conducting the proceedings. You dutifully conduct your cross-examination of the prosecution witnesses, but you are unable to make much progress in challenging their identification. At the conclusion of the government's case, you move to dismiss the charges because there was inadequate proof of probable cause, but you are unsuccessful. Now you must decide whether to present the receptionist or even your client. What should you do?

Hypo 2: *Present the Driver?*

Four men are driving around in a car at 2:00 a.m. The police conduct a traffic stop and discover a gun under the driver's seat, also accessible to the back seat passenger, Ronald Martin. Ronald Martin is charged with unlawful possession of a firearm. You are appointed to represent Mr. Martin, who is not incarcerated; he is out on personal recognizance. He tells you that when the officer approached the driver of the car that he asked the driver if he had any guns or drugs and the driver offered that he had a gun and turned over to the officer both the gun and the registration papers for the gun. You speak to the driver and he confirms this and agrees to testify if necessary. At the preliminary hearing, the prosecution puts on a police officer who testifies to the simple fact of the gun being found near Mr. Martin, likely enough for probable cause. Should you call the driver to testify? Why or why not?

Hypo 3: *Call the Eyewitness?*

You are assigned to be the prosecutor for the preliminary hearing on a robbery charge. You have a police officer available to testify to the facts of the robbery, and that there was an eyewitness identification of the defendant as the robber. Should you also call the eyewitness to the robbery? Why or why not?

Hypo 4: *A Domestic Violence Victim*

You are a prosecutor assigned to prosecute domestic violence cases. You have a preliminary hearing in a case where a man beat his girlfriend of five years, who is also the mother of two of their children. This is not the first time this defendant has been arrested for beating this same victim. He has yet to be convicted for any of the assaults on her. You have the police officer who arrested the defendant and can testify to what the victim told him about the beating. Should you also call the victim to testify? Why or why not?

C. Grand Juries

The grand jury is an ancient common law entity that originated as a body of local citizens who helped look into possible crimes in the community. This investigative function of a grand jury has been characterized as a sword to root out crime. However, by the time of the American Revolution, the colonists, and ultimately the founding fathers, rejected the grand jury as a sword because the British authorities had engaged in malicious prosecutions, particularly on charges of sedition and libel against the King. Hence, the founding fathers viewed the grand jury's function as a shield to protect citizens against unfounded prosecutions. As you read through this Chapter, you will see that the two functions of the grand jury ebb and flow with the times. The dual functions of the grand jury are considered separately in this Chapter.

In the federal system, the view that the grand jury acts as a "shield" or "screen" against improper prosecutions is embodied in U.S. Constitution, Amendment V which provides: "No person shall be held to answer for a capital, or otherwise infamous crime, unless on a presentment or indictment of a Grand Jury." The grand jury requirement has not been "incorporated" and made applicable to the States through the Due Process Clause of the Fourteenth Amendment. *See* Hurtado v. California, 110 U.S. 516 (1884). As a result, States have their own statutory or constitutional provisions regarding grand juries. In general, there are two methods by which the prosecution can formally charge a defendant with a crime: (1) by grand jury indictment; or (2) by information. An information is a charge drawn up by the prosecutor and not submitted to a grand jury, and it may or may not be screened by a judicial officer at a preliminary hearing.

Many states have either eliminated grand juries, allowing prosecution by information, or permit the prosecutor to choose between grand jury indictment and information. Other states require indictment by a grand jury for only certain offenses (usually serious felonies) and permit prosecution by information for less serious charges. Also, the states that use grand juries may have rules comparable to the federal rules, permitting defendants to waive the right to indictment and proceed by information.

Points for Discussion

a. Selection of the Grand Jury

Grand juries in individual jurisdictions differ greatly in their composition and selection processes. At common law, the grand jury was comprised of twenty-three persons, at least twelve of whom had to agree in order to hand down an indictment for a criminal offense. Today, federal grand juries consist of between sixteen and twenty-three jurors, twelve of whom must agree to indict the defendant for any charge. Other jurisdictions utilize much smaller grand juries, although all jurisdictions require that an indictment be based on the concurrence of at least a majority of the grand jurors empanelled to review the charges.

The process of selecting grand jurors begins with the court's summoning of a number of persons qualified to serve as grand jurors. The qualifications for grand jury service are set out in the jurisdiction's statutes and normally include requirements (usually similar to or identical to the requirements for regular jury service) that the prospective grand juror be: (1) a citizen of the jurisdiction; (2) reside in the jurisdiction; (3) be over eighteen years of age; and (4) be a person of honesty, intelligence, and good demeanor. Purging the grand jury is the process of narrowing the number of qualified grand jurors to the number of jurors who will actually serve. The process eliminates otherwise qualified grand jurors who have legitimate excuses for not serving, such as health problems, family obligations and the like.

Although the States are not required to utilize grand juries, if they choose to do so, the Equal Protection Clause of the U.S. Constitution requires that no State may deliberately and systematically exclude individuals because of race, class, gender, or national origin. *Taylor v. Louisiana*, 419 U.S. 522 (1975). The basic elements of an equal protection challenge to the grand jury are the same as required for challenges to the trial jury. Constitutional infirmities in the composition of a grand jury may invalidate a conviction even though the trial jury was legally constituted and guilt was established beyond a reasonable doubt. *Vasquez v. Hillery*, 474 U.S. 254 (1986).

Take Note

Defense counsel does not participate in the selection of the grand jury. Thus any deficiencies in the composition of the grand jury must be raised when the defendant is brought to trial (objections cannot be raised for the first time on appeal). A timely and well-founded pretrial objection allows the trial court to void the indictment and send the prosecutor back to a lawfully constituted grand jury. Challenges to the composition of the grand jury are made by a motion to dismiss or quash the indictment returned by the grand jury. Generally, the courts have recognized only two proper grounds for objecting to the composition of the grand jury: (1) one or more of the grand jurors failed to meet the statutory qualifications for service; or (2) the process for selecting grand jurors violated constitutional standards, *i.e.*, usually discrimination based on suspect classifications such as race and gender.

Hypo 1: *Project Exile*

The police observed defendant Jones, an African-American, drive in the wrong direction on a one-way street. The officer stops defendant's vehicle and determines that defendant's driver's license is suspended. During a search of the vehicle subsequent to the stop, the police officer discovers marijuana, a nine-millimeter pistol, and drug paraphernalia. However, a program designated "Project Exile" results in the transfer of Jones' case to a federal grand jury which issues a four-count indictment against Jones. The federal indictment covers precisely the same conduct originally prosecuted in the state proceedings. Project Exile is jointly undertaken by the prosecutor for the City of Richmond, Virginia and the United States Attorney for the Eastern District of Virginia. Although Richmond possesses only three percent of the State's population, it accounts for twenty-seven percent of the State's homicides. The stated goal of Project Exile is to reduce violent crime by federally prosecuting firearm-related crimes whenever possible. The parties are unable to obtain precise empirical data concerning the race of Project Exile defendants or the racial composition of the relevant grand jury pools. However, the parties agree to these general facts: The vast majority, and perhaps as many as ninety percent of the defendants prosecuted under Project Exile are African-American. The jury pool for the Circuit Court for the City of Richmond is approximately seventy-five percent African-American. The jury pool for the Richmond Division of the Eastern District of Virginia is drawn from a broader geographic area. In contrast to the state jury pool, it is only about ten percent African-American. At a local Bench-Bar Conference discussing the issue, an Assistant United States Attorney stated that one goal of Project Exile is to avoid "Richmond juries." As defense counsel for Mr. Jones, what arguments would you make in a motion to quash the indictment issued by the federal grand jury? As the prosecutor, how would you respond to the motion to quash?

Hypo 2: *Foreperson Selection*

Assume a system where grand jurors are selected at random and the supervising judge chooses the foreperson for the grand jury. The judge chooses the foreperson from the venire (the entire pool) and not from those who were already selected to serve. Assume that for the past twenty years, no black person has ever been chosen to be foreperson even though the pool is 20% black. What arguments will you make to dismiss the indictment? What are the likely responses by the prosecution? *See* Campbell v. Louisiana, 523 U.S. 392 (1998).

b. Scope of Grand Jury Investigation

Once the grand jury is selected and empanelled, the judge will charge the grand jury. This charge may range from the judge's statements about the general state of the Union, to suggestions about particular matters that will come before the grand jury. All judges, however, will caution the grand jury to maintain the secrecy of its proceedings. Once the judge has charged the grand jury, the prosecutor leads the jury in its investigation of alleged criminal offenses. Unlike preliminary hearings, the judge does not preside over grand jury proceedings.

Take Note

The grand jury's refusal to return a true bill does not preclude the prosecutor from resubmitting the evidence to another grand jury. Double Jeopardy does not protect the accused from undergoing successive grand jury investigations.

The prosecutor chooses what cases to present to a grand jury and what witnesses to call before the grand jury for each case. After the presentation of witnesses and evidence in a case, the prosecutor instructs the grand jury on the elements of the offenses and the grand jury decides whether to return an indictment, a written accusation of crime prepared by the prosecutor. If the grand jury agrees that the evidence established probable cause for a charge, it will return a "true bill" of indictment upon which the accused will face trial. If the grand jury concludes that the evidence does not establish probable cause, it will return "no true bill."

Very rarely, a grand jury may go beyond the prosecutor's direction and investigate additional crimes, but this is unusual. The grand jury typically follows the prosecutor's lead. Because the prosecution typically presents only its own witnesses and its own side of the case, the grand jury virtually always returns an indictment.

i. Rare Decision Not to Indict

On August 9, 2014, Michael Brown, an unarmed black teenager, was shot and killed by Darren Wilson, a white police officer, in Ferguson, Missouri. The incident set off waves of protests around the country. Some witnesses claimed Michael Brown was shot when he was doing nothing and his arms were up in the air while police witnesses said Brown was shot after struggling for Darren Wilson's gun. The St. Louis County Prosecutor decided to convene a grand jury to decide whether to indict the officer for the killing. The typical grand jury hears testimony on a case in a single day, of only a few prosecution witnesses, usually police officers, not defense witnesses or the defendant, and is instructed on potential charges by the prosecutor. In the *Brown* case, the grand jury listened to evidence for 25 days, with over 60 witnesses, mainly defense, including four hours of testimony by the defendant, and the Prosecutor did not suggest any charges. On November 24, 2014, the Prosecutor announced that the grand jury had decided not to indict. Given that the grand jury's purpose is to screen cases for probable cause and not to decide guilt, was the Prosecutor's use of the grand jury proper?

See It

Shortly after the grand jury in Ferguson, Missouri decided not to indict, on December 3, 2014, a grand jury in Staten Island decided not to indict a white police officer who killed Eric Garner, an unarmed black man, by using an unauthorized chokehold causing him to suffocate to death. Whereas there was debate over what had occurred in Ferguson, here, the entire incident was captured on video: http://www.theguardian.com/us-news/video/2014/dec/04/i-cant-breathe-eric-garner-chokehold-death-video.

c. Grand Jury Secrecy

Unlike most stages of a criminal prosecution, grand jury proceedings are conducted in secret. The Supreme Court has explained that the secrecy requirement is designed to serve five important objectives: (1) to prevent the escape of those whose indictment may be contemplated; (2) to insure the utmost freedom to the grand jury in its deliberations, and to prevent persons subject to indictment or their friends from importuning the grand jurors; (3) to prevent subornation of perjury or tampering with the witnesses who may testify before the grand jury and later appear at the trial of those indicted by it; (4) to encourage free and untrammeled disclosures by persons who have information with respect to the commission of crimes; (5) to protect the innocent accused who is exonerated from disclosure of the fact that he has been under investigation, and from the expense

Grand jury secrecy requirements vary among jurisdictions, but generally the prosecutor and the grand jurors are prohibited from disclosing grand jury testimony except when authorized by court order. Most jurisdictions do not impose an obligation of secrecy upon grand jury witnesses, and the Supreme Court has held that a State may not prohibit grand jury witnesses from disclosing their own testimony after the term of the grand jury has ended. *Butterworth v. Smith*, 494 U.S. 624 (1990).

of standing trial where there was no probability of guilt. *United States v. Procter & Gamble Co.*, 356 U.S. 677, 681 n.6 (1958). Whether, and to what extent, these stated reasons are the current and actual motivations for maintaining grand jury secrecy is open to question.

Federal Rule of Criminal Procedure 6(e)(3)(D) follows the Patriot Act, § 203, to allow disclosure of Grand Jury information that "involves foreign intelligence or counterintelligence" to intelligence, defense, national security, or immigration officials.

1. The Grand Jury as a Shield

In the federal system, the constitutional requirement for grand jury indictment has continuing vitality. When a properly constituted grand jury returns an indictment, courts will not review the adequacy of evidence presented to a grand jury. In *Wood v. Georgia*, 370 U.S. 375, 390 (1962), the Court described the grand jury as "a primary security to the innocent against hasty, malicious and oppressive persecution; it serves the invaluable function in our society of standing between the accuser and the accused, whether the latter be an individual, minority group, or other, to determine whether a charge is founded upon reason or was dictated by an intimidating power or by malice and personal ill will." However, the view of the *Wood* Court has given way over the years as issues of crime control and punishment have loomed large since the 1980's War on Crime. The shield function has eroded in rhetoric and the sword function has become primary again. The majority view is that the shielding function of the grand jury, while attractive rhetoric, is illusory in practice. Statistics show that grand juries rarely refuse to indict, an understandable result in light of the fact that grand jury proceedings are not adversarial. Without a defense counsel to challenge the government's evidence or to present exculpatory evidence, it is rather like a football game where only one team is on the field.

See It

The prosecutor who conducted the grand jury proceedings in the high profile shooting death of Michael Brown in Ferguson took the unusual step of releasing volumes of transcripts to the public after the grand jury controversially decided not to indict. You can see and read them at: http://www.nytimes.com/interactive/2014/11/25/us/evidence-released-in-michael-brown-case.html.

United States v. Williams

504 U.S. 36 (1992).

JUSTICE SCALIA delivered the opinion of the Court.

The question presented in this case is whether a district court may dismiss an otherwise valid indictment because the Government failed to disclose to the grand jury "substantial exculpatory evidence", in its possession.

Hear It

You can hear the oral argument in *Williams* at: http://www.oyez.org/cases/1990-1999/1991/1991_90_1972.

On May 4, 1988, respondent John H. Williams, Jr., a Tulsa, Oklahoma, investor, was indicted by a federal grand jury on seven counts of "knowingly making a false statement or report for the purpose of influencing the action of a federally insured financial institution," in violation of 18 U.S.C. § 1014 (1988 ed., Supp. 11). According to the indictment, between September 1984 and November 1985 Williams supplied four Oklahoma banks with "materially false" statements that variously overstated the value of his current assets and interest income in order to influence the banks' actions on his loan requests.

Shortly after arraignment, the District Court granted Williams' motion for disclosure of all exculpatory portions of the grand jury transcripts. Upon reviewing this material, Williams demanded that the District Court dismiss the indictment, alleging that the Government had failed to fulfill its obligation to present "substantial exculpatory evidence" to the grand jury. His contention was that evidence which the Government had chosen not to present to the grand jury—in particular, Williams' general ledgers and tax returns, and Williams' testimony in his contemporaneous Chapter 11 bankruptcy proceeding—disclosed that, for tax purposes and otherwise, he had regularly accounted for the "notes receivable" (and the interest on them) in a manner consistent with the Balance Sheet and the Income Statement. This, he contended, belied an intent to mislead the banks, and thus directly negated an essential element of the charged offense.

The District Court found, after a hearing, that the withheld evidence was "relevant to an essential element of the crime charged," created " 'a reasonable doubt about respondent's guilt,' " and thus "rendered the grand jury's decision to indict gravely suspect." The Court of Appeals affirmed the District Court's order. Under these circumstances, the Tenth Circuit concluded, it was not an abuse of discretion for the District Court to require the Government to begin anew before the grand jury. We granted certiorari.

Bank of Nova Scotia v. United States, 487 U.S. 250 (1988), makes clear that the supervisory power can be used to dismiss an indictment because of misconduct before the grand jury, at least where that misconduct amounts to a violation of one of those "few, clear rules which were carefully drafted and approved by this Court and by Congress to ensure the integrity of the grand jury's functions." We did not hold in *Bank of Nova Scotia*, however, that the courts' supervisory power could be used, not merely as a means of enforcing or vindicating legally compelled standards of prosecutorial conduct before the grand jury, but as a means of prescribing those standards of prosecutorial conduct in the first instance—just as it may be used as a means of establishing standards of prosecutorial conduct before the courts themselves. It is this latter exercise that respondent demands. Because the grand jury is an institution separate from the courts, over whose functioning the courts do not preside, we think it clear that, as a general matter at least, no such "supervisory" judicial authority exists, and that the disclosure rule applied here exceeded the Tenth Circuit's authority.

"Rooted in long centuries of Anglo-American history," the grand jury is mentioned in the Bill of Rights, but not in the body of the Constitution. It has not been textually assigned, therefore, to any of the branches described in the first three Articles. In fact the whole theory of its function is that it belongs to no branch of the institutional government, serving as a kind of buffer or referee between the Government and the people. Although the grand jury normally operates, of course, in the courthouse and under judicial auspices, its institutional relationship with the judicial branch has traditionally been, so to speak, at arm's length. Judges' direct involvement in the functioning of the grand jury has generally been confined to the constitutive one of calling the grand jurors together and administering their oaths of office.

We have insisted that the grand jury remain "free to pursue its investigations unhindered by external influence or supervision so long as it does not trench upon the legitimate rights of any witness called before it." Recognizing this tradition of independence, we have said that the Fifth Amendment's "constitutional guarantee presupposes an investigative body 'acting independently of either prosecuting attorney or judge'."

Given the grand jury's operational separateness from its constituting court, it should come as no surprise that we have been reluctant to invoke the judicial supervisory power as a basis for prescribing modes of grand jury procedure. Over the years, we have received many requests to exercise supervision over the grand jury's evidence-taking process, but we have refused them all, including some more appealing than the one presented today.

Any power federal courts may have to fashion, on their own initiative, rules of grand jury procedure is a very limited one, not remotely comparable to the power they maintain over their own proceedings. It certainly would not permit judicial reshaping of the grand jury institution, substantially altering the traditional relationships between the prosecutor, the constituting court, and the grand jury itself.

Requiring the prosecutor to present exculpatory as well as inculpatory evidence would alter the grand jury's historical role, transforming it from an accusatory to an adjudicatory body. Imposing upon the prosecutor a legal obligation to present exculpatory evidence in his possession would be incompatible with this system. If a "balanced" assessment of the entire matter is the objective, surely the first thing to be done—rather than requiring the prosecutor to say what he knows in defense of the target of the investigation—is to entitle the target to tender his own defense. To require the former while denying (as we do) the latter would be quite absurd. It would also be quite pointless, since it would merely invite the target to circumnavigate the system by delivering his exculpatory evidence to the prosecutor, whereupon it would have to be passed on to the grand jury—unless the prosecutor is willing to take the chance that a court will not deem the evidence important enough to qualify for mandatory disclosure.

Respondent insists that courts must require the modern prosecutor to alert the grand jury to the nature and extent of the available exculpatory evidence, because otherwise the grand jury "merely functions as an arm of the prosecution." We reject the attempt to convert a nonexistent duty of the grand jury itself into an obligation of the prosecutor. The authority of the prosecutor to seek an indictment has long been understood to be "coterminous with the authority of the grand jury to entertain the prosecutor's charges." If the grand jury has no obligation to consider all "substantial exculpatory" evidence, we do not understand how the prosecutor can be said to have a binding obligation to present it.

There is yet another respect in which respondent's proposal not only fails to comport with, but positively contradicts, the "common law" of the Fifth Amendment grand jury. Motions to quash indictments based upon the sufficiency of the evidence relied upon by the grand jury were unheard of at common law in England. And the traditional American practice was described by Justice Nelson as follows: "No case has been cited, nor have we been able to find any, furnishing an authority for looking into and revising the judgment of the grand jury upon the evidence, for the purpose of determining whether or not the finding was founded upon sufficient proof, or whether there was a deficiency in respect to any part of the complaint." It would make little sense, we think, to abstain from reviewing the evidentiary support for the grand jury's judgment while scrutinizing the sufficiency of the prosecutor's presentation. A complaint about the quality or adequacy of the evidence can always be recast as a complaint that the prosecutor's presentation was "incomplete" or "misleading." Our words in *Costello* bear repeating: Review of facially valid indictments on such grounds "would run counter to the whole history of the grand jury institution, and neither justice nor the concept of a fair trial requires it."

Respondent argues that a rule requiring the prosecutor to disclose exculpatory evidence to the grand jury would, by removing from the docket unjustified prosecutions, save valuable judicial time. That depends, we suppose, upon what the ratio would turn out to be between unjustified prosecutions eliminated and grand jury indictments challenged—for the latter as well as the former consume "valuable judicial time." We need not pursue the matter; if there is an advantage to the proposal, Congress is free to prescribe it. For the reasons set forth above, we conclude that courts have no authority to prescribe such a duty pursuant to their inherent supervisory authority over their own proceedings. The judgment of the Court of Appeals is accordingly reversed and the cause remanded for further proceedings consistent with this opinion.

JUSTICE STEVENS, with whom JUSTICE BLACKMUN and JUSTICE O'CONNOR join, and with whom JUSTICE THOMAS joins as to Parts II and III, dissenting.

I agree with the Government that the prosecutor is not required to place all exculpatory evidence before the grand jury. A grand jury proceeding is an ex parte investigatory proceeding to determine whether there is probable cause to believe a violation of the criminal laws has occurred, not a trial. Requiring the prosecutor to ferret out and present all evidence that could be used at trial to create a reasonable doubt as to the defendant's guilt would be inconsistent with the purpose of the grand jury proceeding and would place significant burdens on the investigation. But that does not mean that the prosecutor may mislead the grand jury into believing that there is probable cause to indict by withholding clear evidence to the contrary. I thus agree with the Department of Justice that "when a prosecutor conducting a grand jury inquiry is personally aware of substantial evidence which directly negates the guilt of a subject of the investigation, the prosecutor must present or otherwise disclose such evidence to the grand jury before seeking an indictment against

Make the Connection

In Constitutional Law class, you likely learned the importance of originalism to justices like Justice Scalia as a method for interpreting the Constitution. In history classes, you might have learned that the Founding Fathers were deeply skeptical of prosecutions by the Crown for crimes like seditious libel. There is little doubt that the founders believed the grand jury was a shield and not a sword, preventing abuses of wrongful and unjust charging. It is not at all clear that originalism dictates that the founders would have agreed that substantial exculpatory information in the hands of the prosecution should not have to be presented to a grand jury.

such a person." U.S. Dept. of Justice, United States Attorneys' Manual, Title 9, ch. 11, & 9–11.233, 88 (1988).

Although I question whether the evidence withheld in this case directly negates respondent's guilt, I need not resolve my doubts because the Solicitor General did not ask the Court to review the nature of the evidence withheld. Instead, he asked us to decide the legal question whether an indictment may be dismissed because the prosecutor failed to present exculpatory evidence. Unlike the Court and the Solicitor General, I believe the answer to that question is yes, if the withheld evidence would plainly preclude a finding of probable cause. I therefore cannot endorse the Court's opinion.

Points for Discussion

a. Admissibility of "Inadmissible Evidence"

The Court set the stage for *Williams* in two prior cases. In Costello v. United States, 350 U.S. 359 (1956), the Court held that hearsay was admissible in a grand jury proceeding. The holding rested on the assumption that the "accused will get his fair, judicial, hearing at his trial." But if the grand jury is to protect the innocent against oppression and unjust prosecution, should a defendant be compelled to go to trial to prove the insufficiency of the charge? The Second Circuit described the effect of an investigation as follows:" A wrongful indictment is no laughing matter; often it works a grievous irreparable injury to the person indicted. The stigma cannot be easily erased. In the public mind, the blot on a man's escutcheon, resulting from such a public accusation of wrongdoing, is seldom wiped out by a subsequent judgment of not guilty. Frequently, the public remembers the accusation, and still suspects guilt, even after an acquittal. *In re Fried*, 161 F.2d 453 (2d Cir.1947) (concurring opinion).

In the second case, United States v. Calandra, 414 U.S. 338, 349 (1974), the Supreme Court indicated that the *Costello* rationale also barred a challenge to an indictment issued on the basis of unconstitutionally obtained evidence. In *Calandra* the district court held that the defendant "need not answer any of the grand jury's questions based on" evidence obtained from an unconstitutional search. The Supreme Court reversed stating:" It is evident that this extension of the exclusionary rule would seriously impede the grand jury. Because the grand jury does not finally adjudicate guilt or innocence, it has traditionally been allowed to pursue its investigative and accusatorial functions unimpeded by the evidentiary and procedural restrictions applicable to a criminal trial. Permitting witnesses to invoke the exclusionary rule before a grand jury would precipitate adjudication of issues hitherto reserved for the trial on the merits and would delay and disrupt grand jury proceedings."

b. What is Exculpatory?

Despite the *Williams* decision, most state courts that have confronted the issue have imposed a duty on prosecutors to disclose exculpatory evidence to the grand jury in the unique cases where the prosecutor has evidence in her file. *See, e.g.,* State v. Hogan, 144 N.J. 216, 676 A.2d 533 (1996). In order to reduce the circumstances in which a prosecutor's duty will arise, most courts rejecting the *Williams* approach have also ignored an alternative rule that imposed a requirement on prosecutors to disclose evidence that "reasonably tends to negate the guilt of the accused." Instead, most state courts have imposed a limited duty on the prosecutor to inform the grand jury of evidence which directly negates the guilt of the accused and is clearly exculpatory.

Food for Thought

In the following situations, would the prosecutor have an obligation to disclose that: 1. The accused did not have a motive to commit the crime? 2. The State's witnesses have criminal records? 3. The testimony of an eyewitness is potentially biased? 4. The testimony of an eyewitness is contradicted by other witnesses? 5. The accused denied involvement in the crime? 6. A reliable alibi witness is available to testify? 7. Reliable exculpatory physical evidence is available? 8. The prosecution's main witness has recanted her testimony? 9. The target of the grand jury's investigation was insane at the time of the offense?

c. Duty to Present Possible Defenses?

In a later opinion arising from the same facts, the appellate court in *State v. Hogan*, 336 N.J.Super. 319, 764 A.2d 1012, 1025 (2001) opined:

> In our view, a prosecutor's obligation to instruct the grand jury on possible defenses is a corollary to his responsibility to present exculpatory evidence. The extent of the prosecutor's duty must be defined with reference to the role of the grand jury—to protect the innocent, and bring to trial those who may be guilty. Viewed from this perspective, the question of whether a particular defense need be charged depends upon its potential for eliminating a needless or unfounded prosecution. The appropriate distinction for this purpose is between exculpatory and mitigating defenses. An exculpatory defense is one that would, if believed, result in a finding of no criminal liability, *i.e.*, a complete exoneration. The rule accords with common sense and promotes the ability of a grand jury to filter out cases that should never be tried. We adopt that rule to the extent that it defines the existence of the prosecutor's duty.
>
> We now focus upon the scope of the prosecutor's duty. The first question is when such a duty arises. We do not believe that the prosecutor has the obligation on his own meticulously to sift through the entire

record of investigative files to see if some combination of facts and inferences might rationally sustain a defense or justification. The rule should be that it is only when the facts known to the prosecutor clearly indicate or clearly establish the appropriateness of an instruction that the duty of the prosecution arises.

d. Non-Constitutional Errors Cured by Conviction at Trial

In United States v. Mechanik, 475 U.S. 66 (1986), the grand jury process violated Fed. R. Crim P. 6(d) by allowing two witnesses to be present in the grand jury room at the same time. The issue was raised after the defendant was convicted at a jury trial. The Court held that "the petit jury's subsequent guilty verdict means not only that there was probable cause to believe that the defendants were guilty as charged, but

Food for Thought

Faced with the option of proceeding by information or seeking a grand jury indictment, would any prosecutor pay attention to the "shielding" function of a grand jury? Consider the following situation: in the course of an alleged robbery of an inner-city grocery store, the grocer shot and killed the fleeing robber, a member of a racial minority. Local merchant groups are insisting that no charges be brought, while various civil rights groups are demanding prosecution of the grocer. You are the prosecutor, an elected official. How will you proceed? If you opt to submit the matter to a grand jury, will you allow the local merchants association and/or the civil rights groups to address the grand jury? How would you respond to the grand jury's request that you furnish them with statistical evidence of inter-racial violence in the city?

also that they are in fact guilty as charged beyond a reasonable doubt. Measured by the petit jury's verdict, then, any error in the grand jury proceeding connected with the charging decision was harmless beyond a reasonable doubt." *Id.* at 70. Errors of constitutional dimension can be challenged, however. *See, e.g., Campbell v. Louisiana*, 523 U.S. 392 (1998) (equal protection claim), *supra*.

e. Dismissal of Grand Jury

May the court dismiss the grand jury? Refuse to extend its term? Refuse to issue or enforce subpoenas requested by the grand jury? Some jurisdictions permit the judge to dismiss the grand jury at any time; other jurisdictions prohibit dismissal because of fears that a judge will thwart a legitimate investigation, particularly an investigation into government corruption. Refusal to extend the grand jury term or to enforce its subpoenas are less blatant forms of controlling a runaway grand jury.

During the early stages of the Watergate investigation, Federal District Judge Sirica was hailed as a hero for extending the grand jury's term until it could pierce the suspected cover-up.

2. The Grand Jury as a Sword

In practice, the grand jury's potential to "shield" innocent citizens is often subordinate to its functioning as a "sword" to root out crime through use of its investigative authority. Rather than viewing grand jury indictment as an unnecessary burden, many prosecutors favor use of grand jury proceedings in hopes of uncovering additional evidence. They seek to use the grand jury's broad subpoena powers over witnesses and documents.

A witness who is not a target of the grand jury investigation and who is subpoenaed to appear before the grand jury has no general right to remain silent or to refuse to cooperate. Nor is a subpoena to appear before a grand jury a "seizure" of the person under the Fourth Amendment. United States v. Dionisio, 410 U.S. 1 (1973). In the absence of a constitutional provision such as the Fifth Amendment privilege against self-incrimination or a common law communication privilege, the witness "must tell what he knows" or risk being punished for contempt. Branzburg v. Hayes, 408 U.S. 665 (1972). The contempt sanction makes the grand jury subpoena particularly useful in obtaining statements from persons who will not voluntarily furnish information to the police. Failure to comply with a grand jury subpoena may constitute contempt, but in the federal system it may also subject the party to prosecution for violating 18 U.S.C. § 1503, which prohibits "corruptly influencing, obstructing, or impeding, or endeavoring to influence, obstruct, or impede, the due administration of justice." *See* United States v. Erickson, 561 F. 3d 1150 (10th Cir. 2009). Even when an individual invokes the privilege against self-incrimination, the prosecutor may, if authorized by law, grant the witness immunity and thus force an answer to its question.

a. Fifth Amendment Rights Applicable to Testimony

Any witness appearing before a grand jury to testify may assert the Fifth Amendment privilege against self-incrimination. Whether and under what circumstances the courts will uphold a witness's assertion of the privilege, and decline to compel the witness to testify under the threat of contempt and possible incarceration has been the subject of considerable dispute and litigation.

Hoffman v. United States

341 U.S. 479 (1951).

MR. JUSTICE CLARK delivered the opinion of the Court.

Petitioner has been convicted of criminal contempt for refusing to obey a federal court order requiring him to answer certain questions asked in a grand jury investigation. He raises here important issues as to the application of the privilege against self-incrimination under the Fifth Amendment, claimed to justify his refusal.

A special federal grand jury was convened at Philadelphia on September 14, 1950.

The pertinent interrogation, in which [Hoffman] refused to answer, follows:

"Q. What do you do now, Mr. Hoffman?

"A. I refuse to answer.

"Q. Have you been in the same undertaking since the first of the year?

"A. I don't understand the question.

"Q. Have you been doing the same thing you are doing now since the first of the year?

"A. I refuse to answer.

"Q. Do you know Mr. William Weisberg?

"A. I do.

"Q. How long have you known him?

"A. Practically twenty years, I guess.

"Q. When did you last see him?

"A. I refuse to answer.

"Q. Have you seen him this week?

"A. I refuse to answer.

"Q. Do you know that a subpoena has been issued for Mr. Weisberg?

"A. I heard about it in Court.

"Q. Have you talked with him on the telephone this week?

"A. I refuse to answer.

"Q. Do you know where Mr. William Weisberg is now?

"A. I refuse to answer."

It was stipulated that petitioner declined to answer on the ground that his answers might tend to incriminate him of a federal offense.

Petitioner's claim of privilege was challenged by the Government in the Federal District Court for the Eastern District of Pennsylvania, which found no real and substantial danger of incrimination to petitioner and ordered him to return to the grand jury and answer. Petitioner stated in open court that he would not obey the order, and on October 5 was adjudged in criminal contempt and sentenced to five months imprisonment.

This is another of five proceedings before this Court during the present Term in each of which the privilege against self-incrimination has been asserted in the course of federal grand-jury investigations.

A number of similar cases have been considered recently by the lower courts. The increase in such litigation emphasizes the continuing necessity that prosecutors and courts alike be "alert to repress" any abuses of the investigatory power invoked, bearing in mind that while grand juries "may proceed, either upon their own knowl-

edge or upon the examination of witnesses, to inquire whether a crime cognizable by the court has been committed," *Hale v. Henkel*, 201 U.S. 43, 65 (1906), yet "the most valuable function of the grand jury has been not only to examine into the commission of crimes, but to stand between the prosecutor and the accused," *id.* at 59. Enforcement officials taking the initiative in grand-jury proceedings and courts charged with their superintendence should be sensitive to the considerations making for wise exercise of such investigatory power, not only where constitutional issues may be involved but also where the noncoercive assistance of other federal agencies may render it unnecessary to invoke the compulsive process of the grand jury.

The Fifth Amendment declares in part that "No person shall be compelled in any criminal case to be a witness against himself." This guarantee against testimonial compulsion, like other provisions of the Bill of Rights, "was added to the original Constitution in the conviction that too high a price may be paid even for the unhampered enforcement of the criminal law and that, in its attainment, other social objects of a free society should not be sacrificed." *Feldman v. United States*,

322 U.S. 487, 489 (1944). This provision of the Amendment must be accorded liberal construction in favor of the right it was intended to secure.

The privilege afforded not only extends to answers that would in themselves support a conviction under a federal criminal statute but likewise embraces those which would furnish a link in the chain of evidence needed to prosecute the claimant for a federal crime. But this protection must be confined to instances where the witness has reasonable cause to apprehend danger from a direct answer. The witness is not exonerated from answering merely because he declares that in so doing he would incriminate himself—his say-so does not of itself establish the hazard of incrimination. It is for the court to say whether his silence is justified, and to require him to answer if "it clearly appears to the court that he is mistaken." *Temple v. Commonwealth*, 75 Va. 892, 899 (1881). However, if the witness, upon interposing his claim, were required to prove the hazard in the sense in which a claim is usually required to be established in court, he would be compelled to surrender the very protection which the privilege is designed to guarantee. To sustain the privilege, it need only be evident from the implications of the question, in the setting in which it is asked, that a responsive answer to the question or an explanation of why it cannot be answered might be dangerous because injurious disclosure could result. The trial judge in appraising the claim "must be governed as much by his personal perception of the peculiarities of the case as by the facts actually in evidence." *See* Taft, J., in *Ex parte Irvine*, 74 F. 954, 960 (C.C.S.D. Ohio 1896).

The judge who ruled on the privilege had himself impaneled the special grand jury to investigate "rackets" in the district. He had explained to the jury that "the Attorney General's office has come into this district to conduct an investigation that will run the gamut of all crimes covered by federal statute." "If rackets infest or encrust our system of government," he instructed, "just as any blight attacks any other growth, it withers and dies. . . ." Subpoenas had issued for some twenty witnesses, but only eleven had been served; as the prosecutor put it, he was "having trouble finding some big shots." Several of those who did appear and were called into the grand-jury room before petitioner had refused to answer questions until ordered to do so by the court. The prosecutor had requested bench warrants for eight of the nine who had not appeared the first day of the session, one of whom was William Weisberg. Petitioner had admitted having known Weisberg for about twenty years. In addition, counsel for petitioner had advised the court that "It has been broadly published that petitioner has a police record."

The court should have considered, in connection with the business questions, that the chief occupation of some persons involves evasion of federal criminal laws, and that truthful answers by petitioner to these questions might have disclosed that he was engaged in such proscribed activity.

Also, the court should have recognized, in considering the Weisberg questions, that one person with a police record summoned to testify before a grand jury investigating the rackets might be hiding or helping to hide another person of questionable repute sought as a witness. To be sure, the Government may inquire of witnesses before the grand jury as to the whereabouts of unlocated witnesses; ordinarily the answers to such questions are harmless if not fruitless. But of the seven questions relating to Weisberg (of which three were answered), three were designed to draw information as to petitioner's contacts and connection with the fugitive witness; and the final question, perhaps an afterthought of the prosecutor, inquired of Weisberg's whereabouts at the time. All of them could easily have required answers that would forge links in a chain of facts imperiling petitioner with conviction of a federal crime. The three questions, if answered affirmatively, would establish contacts between petitioner and Weisberg during the crucial period when the latter was eluding the grand jury; and in the context of these inquiries the last question might well have called for disclosure that Weisberg was hiding away on petitioner's premises or with his assistance. Petitioner could reasonably have sensed the peril of prosecution for federal offenses ranging from obstruction to conspiracy.

In this setting it was not "perfectly clear, from a careful consideration of all the circumstances in the case, that the witness is mistaken, and that the answers cannot possibly have such tendency" to incriminate. *Temple v. Commonwealth*, 75 Va. 892, 898 (1881).

"The immediate and potential evils of compulsory self-disclosure transcend any difficulties that the exercise of the privilege may impose on society in the detection and prosecution of crime." *United States v. White*, 322 U.S. 694, 698 (1944). Pertinent here is the observation of Mr. Justice Brandeis for this Court in *McCarthy v. Arndstein*, 266 U.S. 34, 42 (1924): "If Congress should hereafter conclude that a full disclosure by the witnesses is of greater importance than the possibility of punishing them for some crime in the past, it can, as in other cases, confer the power of unrestricted examination by providing complete immunity."

Take Note

If a witness has a valid Fifth Amendment privilege, the prosecutor can still obtain the witness's testimony by giving the witness immunity from prosecution. *See* Part 2.c. ("The Use of 'Compelled' Disclosures in Subsequent Proceedings") *infra.*

Reversed.

Points for Discussion

a. A Fifth Amendment Privilege for Claimed Innocence?

In Ohio v. Reiner, 532 U.S. 17, 21 (2001), the Supreme Court stated that, "We have never held that the privilege is unavailable to those who claim innocence. To the contrary, we have emphasized that one of the Fifth Amendment's 'basic functions is to protect innocent men "who otherwise might be ensnared by ambiguous circumstances."'"

b. *Miranda* Warnings?

There is no requirement that a grand jury witness who might have a Fifth Amendment privilege be given *Miranda* warnings. United States v. Mandujano, 425 U.S. 564 (1976). As a matter of practice, however, good prosecutors typically warn such a witness that the witness need not answer any questions if the questions may incriminate the witness and that the witness is entitled to a lawyer.

c. Warnings to Targets?

In *United States v. Washington*, 431 U.S. 181, 188 (1977), the Court held that a witness need not be warned that he is a target of the grand jury investigation:

> After being sworn, respondent was explicitly advised that he had a right to remain silent and that any statements he did make could be used to convict him of crime. It is inconceivable that such a warning would fail to alert him to his right to refuse to answer any questions which might incriminate him. Even in the presumed psychologically coercive atmosphere of police custodial interrogation, Miranda does not require that any additional warnings be given simply because the suspect is a potential defendant; indeed, such suspects are potential defendants more often than not. Respondent points out that unlike one subject to custodial interrogation, whose arrest should inform him only too clearly that he is a potential criminal defendant, a grand jury witness may well be unaware that he is targeted for possible prosecution. While this may be so, it is an overdrawn generalization. In any case, events here prior to questioning by the prosecutor clearly put respondent on notice that he was a suspect in the motorcycle theft.

d. Sixth Amendment Right to Counsel

The Supreme Court has indicated, though never explicitly held, that a witness before a grand jury has no Sixth Amendment right to be represented by counsel. *See* Anonymous v. Baker, 360 U.S. 287 (1959). While that means that an indigent person has no right to counsel at the State's expense, citizens can choose to employ counsel at their own expense. Whatever the status of a Sixth Amendment or Due Process right to counsel at grand jury proceedings, consultation between a witness and counsel may be necessary in order that the witness may determine whether to invoke the Fifth Amendment privilege against self-incrimination in response to a particular question. In such situations, the witness has a right to consult with an attorney outside the grand jury room.

e. Witness Protection Against Perjury

In *United States v. Sarihifard*, 155 F. 3d 301 (4th Cir. 1998), the Court recognized the possibility of perjury entrapment when a witness is called more than once before the grand jury and held that a witness called multiple times is entitled to review their prior transcripts. The Supreme Court also held in Rehberg v. Paulk, 566 U.S. 356 (2012), that, as a state actor, a grand jury witness is entitled to absolute immunity from a § 1983 civil suit brought by the grand jury target claiming that the witness conspired to present false testimony before the grand jury.

Take Note

This right to consult with, but not have counsel present, often leads to almost farcical scenes where the grand jurors pose a question to a witness who then asks to be excused so that he may consult with his attorney in the hallway. The witness will repeat the question to the attorney who will advise whether the question calls for self-incrimination. The witness will return to the grand jury room, inform the grand jury of whether or not he will answer the question, and then may repeat the scenario after each question is posed. Some courts permit the witness to consult with counsel after each question, *see, e.g., United States v. George*, 444 F.2d 310 (6th Cir.1971), while other courts deem this to be obstructionist and limit the witness to consulting with counsel on only three or four questions, *see, e.g., In re Tierney*, 465 F.2d 806 (5th Cir.1972). Some states explicitly permit counsel to be in the grand jury room when the witness is a target or has a Fifth Amendment privilege. *See, e.g.*, La C.Cr.P. Art. 433A(2) (2013).

b. Fifth Amendment and Compliance With Subpoena Duces Tecum

The grand jury may issue a subpoena duces tecum, which is a command to a person to produce writings or objects described in the subpoena. A subpoena issued by a grand jury is presumed reasonable and the burden is on the recipient to prove that requiring compliance would be unreasonable. United States v. R. Enterprises, Inc., 498 U.S. 292 (1991). The only constitutional limitations on subpoenas duces tecum or other grand jury investigative powers are the constitutional rights of individual witnesses, particularly the Fifth Amendment right against self-incrimination. This area of law is very complex.

With respect to subpoenas duces tecum for written materials, the Fifth Amendment applies to the person producing the materials subpoenaed when three conditions are met: (1) the government seeks to "compel" compliance with its demand that the person produce documents or tangible items; (2) the compelled material is "testimonial" in nature; and (3) the material "incriminates" the person required to produce it. The requirements that the material be both "compelled" and "testimonial" in nature has led the Court to distinguish between the *creation* of and *production* of the document. When the government seeks documents previously created by the defendant, the act of creation is deemed to have been voluntary, not compelled. The act of producing the voluntarily created documents, however, may be deemed "testimonial" *only* if the act establishes incriminating aspects *unrelated* to the contents of the document. For example, the act of production may establish the existence of the documents; the defendant's control over the documents; or may constitute authentication of the documents, *i.e.*, that the documents are those described by the subpoena. In such cases, the Fifth Amendment privilege may apply to the production of the documents even if the documents were voluntarily created. *See* Fisher v. United States, 425 U.S. 391 (1976).

Doe v. United States

487 U.S. 201 (1988).

JUSTICE BLACKMUN delivered the opinion of the Court.

This case presents the question whether a court order compelling a target of a grand jury investigation to authorize foreign banks to disclose records of his accounts, without identifying those documents or acknowledging their existence, violates the target's Fifth Amendment privilege against self-incrimination.

Hear It

You can hear the oral argument in *Doe* at: http://www.oyez.org/cases/1980-1989/1987/1987_86_1753.

Appearing before the grand jury pursuant to subpoena directing him to produce records of transactions in accounts at three named banks in the Cayman Islands and Bermuda, petitioner produced some records and testified that no additional records were within his possession. When questioned about the existence of additional records, he invoked the Fifth Amendment privilege against self-incrimination. Grand jury subpoenas then were issued to United States branches of each of the banks, but the banks refused to comply because their governments' laws prohibited disclosure of account records without the customer's consent. The prosecution then filed a motion with the district court requesting that petitioner be ordered to sign forms stating that he was "directing any bank at which I may have a bank account of any kind or at which a corporation has a bank account of any kind upon which I am authorized to draw" to deliver records of those accounts to the grand jury. The form specifically noted that petitioner's directive was being made pursuant to court order, and that the directive was intended to provide compliance with the bank secrecy laws of the Cayman Islands and Bermuda. Petitioner refused to sign the consent directive on self-incrimination grounds, and after being held in contempt, sought appellate review. The Court of Appeals affirmed.

Petitioner's sole claim is that his execution of the consent forms directing the banks to release records as to which the banks believe he has the right of withdrawal has independent testimonial significance that will incriminate him, and that the Fifth Amendment prohibits governmental compulsion of that act. The question is whether the act of executing the form is a "testimonial communication." The parties disagree about both the meaning of "testimonial" and whether the consent directive fits the proposed definitions.

Petitioner contends that a compelled statement is testimonial if the Government could use the content of the speech or writing, as opposed to its physical characteristics, to further a criminal investigation of the witness. The second half of petitioner's "testimonial" test is that the statement must be incriminating, which is, of course, already a separate requirement for invoking the privilege. Thus, Doe contends, in essence, that every written and oral statement significant for its content is necessarily testimonial for purposes of the Fifth Amendment. Under this view, the consent directive is testimonial because it is a declarative statement of consent made by Doe to the foreign banks, a statement that the Government will use to persuade the banks to produce potentially incriminating account records that would otherwise be unavailable to the grand jury.

While the Court in *Fisher v. United States*, 425 U.S. 391 (1976) and *United States v. Doe*, 465 U.S. 605 (1984) did not purport to announce a universal test for determining the scope of the privilege, it also did not purport to establish a more narrow boundary applicable to acts alone. To the contrary, the Court applied basic Fifth Amendment principles. An examination of the Court's application of these principles in other cases indicates the Court's recognition that, in order to be testimonial, an accused's communication must itself, explicitly or implicitly, relate a factual assertion or disclose information. Only then is a person compelled to be a "witness" against himself.

This understanding is perhaps most clearly revealed in those cases in which the Court has held that certain acts, though incriminating, are not within the privilege. Thus, a suspect may be compelled to furnish a blood sample, to provide a handwriting exemplar or a voice exemplar, to stand in a lineup, and to wear particular clothing. These decisions are grounded on the proposition that "the privilege protects an accused only from being compelled to testify against himself, or otherwise provide the State with evidence of a testimonial or communicative nature." *Schmerber v. California*, 384 U.S. 757, 761 (1966). It is the "extortion of information from the accused," the attempt to force him "to disclose the contents of his own mind," that implicates the Self-Incrimination Clause. "Unless some attempt is made to secure a communication—written, oral or otherwise—upon which reliance is to be placed as involving the accused's consciousness of the facts and the operations of his mind in expressing it, the demand made upon him is not a testimonial one."

It is consistent with the history of and the policies underlying the Self-Incrimination Clause to hold that the privilege may be asserted only to resist compelled explicit or implicit disclosures of incriminating information. Historically, the privilege was intended to prevent the use of legal compulsion to extract from the accused a sworn communication of facts which would incriminate him. Such was the process of the ecclesiastical courts and the Star Chamber—the inquisitorial method of putting the accused upon his oath and compelling him to answer questions designed to uncover uncharged offenses, without evidence from another source. The major thrust of the policies undergirding the privilege is to prevent such compulsion. The Court in *Murphy v. Waterfront Comm'n of New York Harbor*, 378 U.S. 52, 55 (1964) explained that the privilege is founded on:

> [1] our unwillingness to subject those suspected of crime to the cruel trilemma of self-accusation, perjury or contempt; [2] our preference for an accusatorial rather than an inquisitorial system of criminal justice; [3] our fear that self-incriminating statements will be elicited by inhumane treatment and abuses; [4] our sense of fair play which dictates "a fair state-individual balance by requiring the government to leave the individual alone until good cause is shown for disturbing him and by requiring the government in its contest with the individual to shoulder the entire load,"; [5] our respect for the inviolability of the human personality and of the right of each individual "to a private enclave where he may lead a private life,"; [6] our distrust of self-deprecatory statements; and [7] our realization that the privilege, while sometimes "a shelter to the guilty," is often "a protection to the innocent."

These policies are served when the privilege is asserted to spare the accused from having to reveal, directly or indirectly, his knowledge of facts relating him to the offense or from having to share his thoughts and beliefs with the Government.

We are not persuaded by petitioner's arguments that our articulation of the privilege fundamentally alters the power of the Government to compel an accused to assist in his prosecution. There are very few instances in which a verbal statement, either oral or written, will not convey information or assert facts. The vast majority of verbal statements thus will be testimonial and, to that extent, will fall within the privilege. Furthermore, there are many restrictions on the Government's prosecutorial practices in addition to the Self-Incrimination Clause. Indeed, there are other protections against governmental efforts to compel an unwilling suspect to cooperate in an investigation, including efforts to obtain information from him. We are confident that these provisions, together with the Self-Incrimination Clause, will continue to prevent abusive investigative techniques.

We turn to consider whether Doe's execution of the consent directive at issue here would have testimonial significance. We agree that it would not, because neither the form, nor its execution, communicates any factual assertions, implicit or explicit, or conveys any information to the Government.

The consent directive itself is not "testimonial." It is carefully drafted not to make reference to a specific account, but only to speak in the hypothetical. Thus, the form does not acknowledge that an account in a foreign financial institution is in existence or that it is controlled by petitioner. Nor does the form indicate whether documents or any other information relating to petitioner are present at the foreign bank, assuming that such an account does exist. The form does not even identify the relevant bank. Although the executed form allows the Government access to a potential source of evidence, the directive does not point the Government toward hidden accounts or otherwise provide information that will assist the prosecution in uncovering evidence. The Government must locate that evidence "by the independent labor of its officers." As in *Fisher*, the Government is not relying upon the "truthtelling" of Doe's directive to show the existence of, or his control over, foreign bank account records.

Given the consent directive's phraseology, petitioner's compelled act of executing the form has no testimonial significance either. By signing the form, Doe makes no statement, explicit or implicit, regarding the existence of a foreign bank account or his control over any such account. Nor would his execution of the form admit the authenticity of any records produced by the bank. Not only does the directive express no view on the issue, but because petitioner did not prepare the document, any statement by Doe to the effect that it is authentic would not establish that the records are genuine. Authentication evidence would have to be provided by bank officials.

We read the directive as equivalent to a statement by Doe that, although he expresses no opinion about the existence of, or his control over, any such account, he is authorizing the bank to disclose information relating to accounts over which, in the bank's opinion, Doe can exercise the right of withdrawal. When forwarded to the bank along with a subpoena, the executed directive, if effective under local law, will simply make it possible for the recipient bank to comply with the Government's request to produce such records. If the Government obtains bank records after Doe signs the directive, the only factual statement made by anyone will be the bank's implicit declaration, by its act of production in response to the subpoena, that it believes the accounts to be petitioners'. *Cf. Fisher.* The fact that the bank's customer has directed the disclosure of his records "would say nothing about the correctness of the bank's representations." Indeed, the Second and Eleventh Circuits have concluded that consent directives virtually identical to the one here are inadmissible as an admission by the signator of either control or existence.

JUSTICE STEVENS, dissenting.

A defendant can be compelled to produce material evidence that is incriminating. Fingerprints, blood samples, voice exemplars, handwriting specimens or other items of physical evidence may be extracted from a defendant against his will. But can he be compelled to use his mind to assist the prosecution in convicting him of a crime? I think not. He may in some cases be forced to surrender a key to a strong box containing incriminating documents, but I do not believe he can be compelled to reveal the combination to his wall safe—by word or deed.

The document the Government seeks to extract from John Doe purports to order third parties to take action that will lead to the discovery of incriminating evidence. The directive itself may not betray any knowledge petitioner may have about the circumstances of the offenses being investigated by the Grand Jury, but it nevertheless purports to evidence a reasoned decision by Doe to authorize action by others. The forced execution of this document differs from the forced production of physical evidence just as human beings differ from other animals.

If John Doe can be compelled to use his mind to assist the Government in developing its case, I think he will be forced "to be a witness against himself." The fundamental purpose of the Fifth Amendment was to mark the line between the kind of inquisition conducted by the Star Chamber and what we proudly describe as our accusatorial system of justice. It reflects "our respect for the inviolability of the human personality." In my opinion that protection gives John Doe the right to refuse to sign the directive authorizing access to the records of any bank account that he may control. Accordingly, I respectfully dissent.

Food for Thought

What is the basis for Justice Stevens' distinction between what he concedes is permissible—forcing the defendant "to surrender a key to a strong box containing incriminating documents"—and what he considers impermissible—compelling the defendant "to reveal the combination to his wall safe by word or deed?" Does it matter if the combination to the safe has been memorized (and must be disclosed by the defendant's verbal statement) or if the combination was written on a piece of paper that the defendant is ordered to physically surrender to the government? Is there a meaningful distinction between a physical act (deemed non-testimonial) and a mental process (deemed testimonial)?

Food for Thought

The Fifth Amendment privilege only protects testimonial evidence from a witness. A blood test is not testimonial because it is not a communication from the witness's mind but rather a naturally occurring element in the body. *Schmerber v. California*, 384 U.S. 757 (1966). What about the following:

1. A compelled voice exemplar from a witness, where the witness was told to read a portion of a transcript of an intercepted conversation into a recording device. The grand jury scrutinized the exemplars in an attempt to identify the voices in the intercepted conversation. *See United States v. Dionisio*, 410 U.S. 1 (1973);

2. A videotape of a compelled sobriety test where the witness exhibited slurred speech, the witness could not walk in a straight line, the witness was asked the date of his sixth birthday and could not remember, or the witness could not touch his nose with his index finger.

See Pennsylvania v. Muniz, 496 U.S. 582 (1990).

Hypo: *Computers and Incrimination*

How would the Supreme Court deal with the following court orders to a defendant? 1) Tell us what is on the computer disk you prepared on September 1; 2) Surrender the disk to the U.S. Attorney; or 3) Surrender the password and code used to encrypt the disk.

Points for Discussion

a. What is the Corporate Custodian of Records to Do?

Collective entities such as corporations, partnerships, and labor unions have no Fifth Amendment privilege against self-incrimination. In *Braswell v. United States*, 487 U.S. 99 (1988), the Supreme Court held that the custodian of records of a collective entity cannot resist a subpoena for entity records by claiming the privilege against self-incrimination on behalf of the corporation. The corporate custodian has no privilege as to the corporate records, even though the act of production may be personally incriminating. Because the Court had used a fiction, *i.e.*, the corporate employee acts only as an agent when asked to produce corporate documents in response to a subpoena, the Court addressed the issue of personal incrimination for the custodian. To insure that the compelled act does not violate the custodian's personal Fifth Amendment privilege, the Court stated that the government cannot disclose to the jury who produced the documents. If the jury is not told that the custodian produced the records, the act of production by the custodian merely implies possession and authentication by the corporation but not by the custodian. Therefore, production of the corporate documents is not incriminating to the custodian.

b. Use of "Compelled" Disclosures in Subsequent Proceedings

If the court upholds a witness's assertion of the Fifth Amendment privilege, or if the prosecutor (or other authority seeking evidence such as Congress) agrees that the witness has a valid Fifth Amendment privilege, it is not the end of the matter. The prosecutor (or Congress or other lawful authority) may still seek to compel disclosure by granting the witness immunity from prosecution. The theory here is that the Fifth Amendment only protects a person from being compelled to be a witness against himself at a criminal proceeding. If the "witness" cannot be prosecuted because she has been granted immunity, then anything that they are compelled to disclose cannot violate the Fifth Amendment privilege because it cannot be used in a subsequent prosecution. Therefore, while the witness has been "compelled" to disclose, she has not been compelled to be a "witness" at a criminal proceeding because there will not be a subsequent criminal prosecution due to the grant of immunity.

Historically, two types of immunity have developed. Originally, what has come to be known as transactional immunity was thought to be necessary in order to overcome a valid assertion of Fifth Amendment privilege. Under transactional immunity, the witness is given complete immunity from criminal prosecution for any offenses committed in connection with the criminal incident(s) for which the immunity has been granted. In other words, the witness simply cannot be prosecuted for anything in connection with the incident(s). For almost 200 years, transactional immunity was the sole type of immunity. It was during the Watergate era, however, that attorneys at the Department of Justice came up with the concept of use immunity.

FYI

Ironically, the person under whose watch use immunity arose was President Richard Nixon's Attorney General John Mitchell, who was subsequently jailed for his role in the Watergate scandals.

Under use immunity, anything that the witness is compelled to say or disclose cannot be "used" against them at a subsequent criminal proceeding. However, a subsequent criminal proceeding is not completely barred (as under transactional immunity). Instead, the witness may still in fact later be prosecuted for offenses committed in connection with the criminal incident(s) about which they were compelled to testify, as long as the compelled disclosures are not used, and the prosecution is based entirely on other evidence completely separate and apart from any compelled disclosures. *See* Kastigar v. United States, 406 U.S. 441 (1972). Since *Kastigar*, this form of immunity has come to be known as "use and derivative use immunity" because *Kastigar* requires not only that no compelled disclosures be directly used at a subsequent criminal prosecution, but also that no compelled disclosures be indirectly used as leads or otherwise to obtain other evidence. In other words, all of the evidence used

Practice Pointer

For a defense lawyer representing an individual with a potential privilege, it is important to raise the privilege regardless of whether the judge upholds the privilege. This is because if the judge denies the privilege and the defendant has to testify, that testimony is compelled and cannot be used against him in a future proceeding.

at a subsequent criminal prosecution must be completely independent of any compelled disclosures. A pretrial hearing, sometimes referred to as a *"Kastigar"* hearing, may be necessary in order to determine compliance.

United States v. Hubbell

530 U.S. 27 (2000).

JUSTICE STEVENS delivered the opinion of the Court.

The two questions presented concern the scope of a witness' protection against compelled self-incrimination: (1) whether the Fifth Amendment privilege protects a witness from being

Hear It

You can hear the oral argument in *Hubbell* at: http://www.oyez.org/cases/1990-1999/1999/1999_99_166.

compelled to disclose the existence of incriminating documents that the Government is unable to describe with reasonable particularity; and (2) if the witness produces such documents pursuant to a grant of immunity, whether 18 U.S.C. § 6002 prevents the Government from using them to prepare criminal charges against him.

This proceeding arises out of the second prosecution of respondent, Webster Hubbell, commenced by the Independent Counsel appointed in August 1994 to investigate possible violations of federal law relating to the Whitewater Development Corporation. The first prosecution was

The Whitewater investigation is famous for ultimately leading to the exposure of President Bill Clinton's affair with Monica Lewinsky and subsequent impeachment proceedings.

terminated pursuant to a plea bargain. In December 1994, respondent pleaded guilty to charges of mail fraud and tax evasion arising out of his billing practices as a member of an Arkansas law firm from 1989 to 1992, and was sentenced to 21 months in prison. In the plea agreement, respondent promised to provide the Independent Counsel with "full, complete, accurate, and truthful information" about matters relating to the Whitewater investigation.

The second prosecution resulted from the Independent Counsel's attempt to determine whether respondent had violated that promise. In October 1996, while respondent was incarcerated, the Independent Counsel served him with a subpoena duces tecum calling for the production of 11 categories of documents before a grand jury sitting in Little Rock, Arkansas. On November 19, he appeared before the grand jury and invoked his Fifth Amendment privilege against self-incrimination. In response to questioning by the prosecutor, respondent refused "to state whether there are documents within my possession, custody, or control responsive to the Subpoena." Thereafter, the prosecutor produced an order, which had previously been obtained from the District Court pursuant to 18 U.S.C. § 6003(a), directing him to respond to the subpoena and granting him immunity "to the extent allowed by law." Respondent then produced 13,120 pages of documents and records and responded to a series of questions that established that those were all of the documents in his custody or control that were responsive to the commands in the subpoena, with the exception of a few documents he claimed were shielded by the attorney-client and attorney work-product privileges.

The contents of the documents produced by respondent provided the Independent Counsel with the information that led to this second prosecution. On April 30, 1998, a grand jury in the District of Columbia returned a 10-count indictment charging respondent with various tax-related crimes and mail and wire fraud. The District Court dismissed the indictment relying, in part, on the ground that the Independent Counsel's use of the subpoenaed documents violated § 6002 because all of the evidence he would offer against respondent at trial derived either directly or indirectly from the testimonial aspects of respondent's immunized act of producing those documents. Noting that the Independent Counsel had admitted that he was not investigating tax-related issues when he issued the subpoena, and that he had "learned about the unreported income and other crimes from studying the records' contents, 'the District Court characterized the subpoena as the quintessential fishing expedition.'"

The Court of Appeals vacated the judgment and remanded for further proceedings. The majority concluded that the District Court had incorrectly relied on the fact that the Independent Counsel did not have prior knowledge of the contents of the subpoenaed documents. The question the District Court should have addressed was the extent of the Government's independent knowledge of the documents' existence and authenticity, and of respondent's possession or control of them. It explained:

> On remand, the district court should hold a hearing in which it seeks to establish the extent and detail of the Government's knowledge of Hubbell's financial affairs (or of the paperwork documenting it) on the day the subpoena issued. It is only then that the court will be in a position to assess the testimonial value of Hubbell's response to the subpoena. Should the Independent Counsel prove capable of demonstrating with reasonable particularity a prior awareness that the exhaustive litany of documents sought in the subpoena existed and were in Hubbell's possession, then the wide distance evidently traveled from the subpoena to the substantive allegations contained in the indictment would be based upon legitimate intermediate steps. To the extent that the information conveyed through Hubbell's compelled act of production provides the necessary linkage, however, the indictment deriving therefrom is tainted.

In the opinion of the dissenting judge, the majority failed to give full effect to the distinction between the contents of the documents and the limited testimonial significance of the act of producing them. In his view, as long as the prosecutor could make use of information contained in the documents or derived therefrom without any reference to the fact that respondent had produced them in response to a subpoena, there would be no improper use of the testimonial aspect of the immunized act of production. In other words, the constitutional privilege and the statute conferring use immunity would only shield the witness from the use of any information resulting from his subpoena response "beyond what the prosecutor would receive if the documents appeared in the grand jury room or in his office unsolicited and unmarked, like manna from heaven."

On remand, the Independent Counsel acknowledged that he could not satisfy the "reasonable particularity" standard prescribed by the Court of Appeals and entered into a conditional plea agreement with respondent. In essence, the agreement provides for the dismissal of the charges unless this Court's disposition of the case makes it reasonably likely that respondent's "act of production immunity" would not pose a significant bar to his prosecution. The case is not moot, however, because the agreement also provides for the entry of a guilty plea and a sentence that will not include incarceration if we should reverse and issue an opinion that is sufficiently favorable to the Government to satisfy that condition. Despite that agreement, we granted the Independent Counsel's petition for a writ of certiorari in order to determine the precise scope of a grant of immunity with respect to the production of documents in response to a subpoena. We now affirm.

It is useful to preface our analysis of the constitutional issue with a restatement of certain propositions that are not in dispute. The term "privilege against self-incrimination" is not an entirely accurate description of a person's constitutional protection against being "compelled in any criminal case to be a witness against himself."

The word "witness" in the constitutional text limits the relevant category of compelled incriminating communications to those that are "testimonial" in character. As Justice Holmes observed, there is a significant difference between the use of compulsion to extort communications from a defendant and compelling a person to engage in conduct that may be incriminating. Thus, even though the act may provide incriminating evidence, a criminal suspect may be compelled to put on a shirt, to provide a blood sample or handwriting exemplar, or to make a recording of his voice. The act of exhibiting such physical characteristics is not the same as a sworn communication by a witness that relates either express or implied assertions of fact or belief.

More relevant to this case is the settled proposition that a person may be required to produce specific documents even though they contain incriminating assertions of fact or belief because the creation of those documents was not "compelled" within the meaning of the privilege. It is clear, therefore, that respondent Hubbell could not avoid compliance with the subpoena served on him merely because the demanded documents contained incriminating evidence, whether written by others or voluntarily prepared by himself.

On the other hand, we have also made it clear that the act of producing documents in response to a subpoena may have a compelled testimonial aspect. We have held that "the act of production" itself may implicitly communicate "statements of fact." By "producing documents in compliance with a subpoena, the witness would admit that the papers existed, were in his possession or control, and were authentic." Moreover, as was true in this case, when the custodian of documents responds to a subpoena, he may be compelled to take the witness stand and answer questions designed to determine whether he has produced everything demanded by the subpoena. The answers to those questions, as well as the act of production itself, may certainly communicate information about the existence, custody, and authenticity of the documents. Whether the constitutional privilege protects the answers to such questions, or protects the act of production itself, is a question that is distinct from the question whether the unprotected contents of the documents themselves are incriminating.

Finally, the phrase "in any criminal case" in the text of the Fifth Amendment might have been read to limit its coverage to compelled testimony that is used against the defendant in the trial itself. It has, however, long been settled that its protection encompasses compelled statements that lead to the discovery of incriminating evidence even though the statements themselves are not incriminating and are not introduced into evidence. Thus, a half-century ago we held that a trial judge had erroneously rejected a defendant's claim of privilege on the ground that his answer to the pending question would not itself constitute evidence of the charged offense. As we explained: "The privilege afforded not only extends to answers that would in themselves support a conviction under a federal criminal statute but likewise embraces those which would furnish a link in the chain of evidence needed to prosecute the claimant for a federal crime." *Hoffman v. United States*, 341 U.S. 479, 486 (1951). Compelled testimony that communicates information that may "lead to incriminating evidence" is privileged even if the information itself is not inculpatory. *Doe v. United States*, 487 U.S. 201, 208 n.6 (1988). It is the Fifth Amendment's protection against the prosecutor's use of incriminating information derived directly or indirectly from the compelled testimony of the respondent that is of primary relevance in this case.

Acting pursuant to 18 U.S.C. § 6002, the District Court entered an order compelling respondent to produce "any and all documents" described in the grand jury subpoena and granting him "immunity to the extent allowed by law." In *Kastigar v. United States*, 406 U.S. 441 (1972), we upheld the constitutionality of § 6002 because the scope of the "use and derivative-use" immunity that it provides is coextensive with the scope of the constitutional privilege against self-incrimination.

The "compelled testimony" in this case is not to be found in the contents of the documents produced in response to the subpoena. It is, rather, the testimony inherent in the act of producing those documents. The disagreement between the parties focuses entirely on the significance of that testimonial aspect.

The Government correctly emphasizes that the testimonial aspect of a response to a subpoena duces tecum does nothing more than establish the existence, authenticity, and custody of items that are produced. We assume that the Government is entirely correct in its submission that it would not have to advert to respondent's act of production in order to prove the existence, authenticity, or custody of any documents that it might offer in evidence at a criminal trial; indeed, the Government disclaims any need to introduce any of the documents produced by respondent into evidence in order to prove the charges against him. It follows, according to the Government, that it has no intention of making improper "use" of respondent's compelled testimony.

The question, however, is not whether the response to the subpoena may be introduced into evidence at his criminal trial. That would surely be a prohibited "use" of the immunized act of production. But the fact that the Government intends no such use of the act of production leaves open the separate question whether it has already made "derivative use" of the testimonial aspect of that act in obtaining the indictment against respondent and in preparing its case for trial. It clearly has.

It is apparent from the text of the subpoena itself that the prosecutor needed respondent's assistance both to identify potential sources of information and to produce those sources. Given the breadth of the description of the 11 categories of documents called for by the subpoena, the collection and production of the materials demanded was tantamount to answering a series of interrogatories asking a witness to disclose the existence and location of particular documents fitting certain broad descriptions. The assembly of literally hundreds of pages of material in response to a request for "any and all documents reflecting, referring, or relating to any direct or indirect sources of money or other things of value received by or provided to" an individual or members of his family during a 3-year period, is the functional equivalent of the preparation of an answer to either a detailed written interrogatory or a series of oral questions at a discovery deposition. Entirely apart from the contents of the 13,120 pages of materials that respondent produced in this case, it is undeniable that providing a catalog of existing documents fitting within any of the 11 broadly worded subpoena categories could provide a prosecutor with a "lead to incriminating evidence," or "a link in the chain of evidence needed to prosecute."

Indeed, the record makes it clear that that is what happened in this case. The documents were produced before a grand jury sitting in the Eastern District of Arkansas in aid of the Independent Counsel's attempt to determine whether respondent had violated a commitment in his first plea agreement. The use of those sources of information eventually led to the return of an indictment by a grand jury sitting in the District of Columbia for offenses that apparently are unrelated to that plea agreement. What the District Court characterized as a "fishing expedition" did produce a fish, but not the one that the Independent Counsel expected to hook. It is abundantly clear that the testimonial aspect of respondent's act of producing subpoenaed documents was the first step in a chain of evidence that led to this prosecution. The documents did not magically appear in the prosecutor's office like "manna from heaven." They arrived there only after respondent asserted his constitutional privilege, received a grant of immunity, and—under compulsion of the District Court's order—took the mental and physical steps necessary to provide the prosecutor with an accurate inventory of the many sources of potentially incriminating evidence sought by the subpoena. It was only through respondent's truthful reply to the subpoena that the Government received the incriminating documents of which it made "substantial use in the investigation that led to the indictment."

For these reasons, we cannot accept the Government's submission that respondent's immunity did not preclude its derivative use of the produced documents because its "possession of the documents was the fruit only of a simple physical act—the act of producing the documents." It was necessary for respondent to make extensive use of "the contents of his own mind" in identifying the hundreds of documents responsive to the requests in the subpoena. The assembly of those documents was like telling an inquisitor the combination to a wall safe, not like being forced to surrender the key to a strongbox. The Government's anemic view of respondent's act of production as a mere physical act that is principally non-testimonial in character and can be entirely divorced from its "implicit" testimonial aspect so as to constitute a "legitimate, wholly independent source" (as required by *Kastigar*) for the documents produced simply fails to account for these realities.

We have no doubt that the constitutional privilege against self-incrimination protects the target of a grand jury investigation from being compelled to answer questions designed to elicit information about the existence of sources of potentially incriminating evidence. That constitutional privilege has the same application to the testimonial aspect of a response to a subpoena seeking discovery of those sources. Before the District Court, the Government arguably conceded that respondent's act of production in this case had a testimonial aspect that entitled him to respond to the subpoena by asserting his privilege against self-incrimination. On appeal and again before this Court, the Government has argued that the communicative aspect of respondent's act of producing ordinary business records is insufficiently "testimonial" to support a claim of privilege because the existence and possession of such records by any businessman is a "foregone conclusion" under our decision in *Fisher v. United States*, 425 U.S. 391 (1976). This argument misreads *Fisher* and ignores our subsequent decision in *United States v. Doe*, 465 U.S. 605 (1984).

Whatever the scope of this "foregone conclusion" rationale, the facts of this case plainly fall outside of it. While in *Fisher* the Government already knew that the documents were in the attorneys' possession and could independently confirm their existence and authenticity through the accountants who created them, here the Government has not shown that it had any prior knowledge of either the existence or the whereabouts of the 13,120 pages of documents produced by respondent. The Government cannot cure this deficiency through the overbroad argument that a businessman such as respondent will always possess general business and tax records that fall within the broad categories described in this subpoena. The Doe subpoenas also sought several broad categories of general business records, yet we upheld the finding that the act of producing those records would involve testimonial self-incrimination.

Given our conclusion that respondent's act of production had a testimonial aspect, at least with respect to the existence and location of the documents sought by the Government's subpoena, respondent could not be compelled to produce those documents without first receiving a grant of immunity under § 6003. As we construed § 6002 in *Kastigar*, such immunity is co-extensive with the constitutional privilege. *Kastigar* requires that respondent's motion to dismiss the indictment on immunity grounds be granted unless the Government proves that the evidence it used in obtaining the indictment and proposed to use at trial was derived from legitimate sources "wholly independent" of the testimonial aspect of respondent's immunized conduct in assembling and producing the documents described in the subpoena. The Government does not claim that it could make such a showing. Rather, it contends that its prosecution of respondent must be considered proper unless someone—presumably respondent—shows that "there is some substantial relation between the compelled testimonial communications implicit in the act of production (as opposed to the act of production standing alone) and some aspect of the information used in the investigation or the evidence presented at trial." We could not accept this submission without repudiating the basis for our conclusion in *Kastigar* that the statutory guarantee of use and derivative-use immunity is as broad as the constitutional privilege itself. This we are not prepared to do.

Accordingly, the indictment against respondent must be dismissed. The judgment of the Court of Appeals is affirmed. It is so ordered.

Points for Discussion

a. Foregone Conclusion

What is the nature of the foregone conclusion discussion in *Hubbell*? In *Fisher v. United States*, 425 U.S. 391 (1976), and other cases, the Court had discussed this concept: "It is doubtful that implicitly admitting the existence and possession of the papers rises to the level of testimony within the protection of the Fifth Amendment. The papers belong to the accountant, were prepared by him, and are the kind usually prepared by an accountant working on the tax returns of his client. Surely the Government is in no way relying on the 'truthtelling' of the taxpayer to prove the existence of or his access to the documents. The existence and location of the papers are a foregone conclusion and the taxpayer adds little or nothing to the sum total of the Government's information by conceding that he in fact has the papers. Under these circumstances by enforcement of the summons "no constitutional rights are touched. The question is not of testimony but of surrender." Besides noting that the papers were of the kind usually prepared by an accountant, the Court never explained why the existence and location of the accountant's work papers were a foregone conclusion. *Doe* also tied authenticity to the foregone conclusion. Authenticity concerns whether a document is genuine, rather than a forgery or fabrication. The act of production confirms that the person responding to the subpoena believes the documents are those described in the subpoena.

b. Prosecution's Burden

The Ninth Circuit, in *In re Grand Jury Subpoena, Dated April 18, 2003*, 383 F. 3d 905 (9th Cir. 2004), held that the trial court erred in concluding that the prosecution had proved that the existence, possession, and authenticity of the documents sought was a foregone conclusion and in refusing to examine the documents in camera to determine whether the act of producing them would be incriminating:

> The government was not required to have actual knowledge of the existence and location of each and every responsive document; the government was required, however, to establish the existence of the documents sought and Doe's possession of them with "reasonable particularity" before the existence and possession of the documents could be considered a foregone conclusion and production therefore would not be testimonial. Although the government possessed extensive knowledge about Doe's price-fixing activities as a result of interviews with cooperating witnesses and Doe's own incriminating statements made to federal agents on April 26, 2003, it is the government's knowledge of the existence and possession of the actual documents, not the information contained therein, that is central to the foregone conclusion inquiry. The breadth of the subpoena in this case far exceeded the government's knowledge about the actual documents that Doe created or possessed during his former employment and that he retained after he terminated his employment. The government probably could identify with sufficient particularity the existence of e-mails between Doe and some of his competitors, e-mails between Doe and his superiors regarding pricing, phone records corroborating that Doe spoke to his competitors, and records establishing meetings with certain competitors because Doe made substantial admissions to investigators during his living room interview regarding these documents. The government, however, failed to draft the subpoena narrowly to identify the documents that it could establish with reasonable particularity. Thus, on the record before us, the subpoena's breadth far exceeded the reasonably particular knowledge that the government actually possessed when it served the subpoena on Doe.

> The authenticity prong of the foregone conclusion doctrine requires the government to establish that it can independently verify that the compelled documents "are in fact what they purport to be." Independent verification not only requires the government to show that the documents sought to be compelled would be admissible independent of the witness' production of them, but also inquires into whether the government is compelling the witness to use his discretion in selecting and assembling the responsive documents, and thereby tacitly providing identifying information that is necessary to the government's authentication of the subpoenaed documents.

Although the government could probably authenticate the writing on Doe's handwritten documents through handwriting analysis, it made little effort to demonstrate how anyone beside Doe could sift through his handwritten notes, personal appointment books, and diaries to produce what Doe's attorney estimates may be 4,500 documents. Such a response by Doe would provide the government with the identifying information that it would need to authenticate these documents. Doe's notes to himself would be difficult, if not impossible, to authenticate by anyone besides Doe. In this case, the government has failed to demonstrate that it can authenticate the documents so broadly described in the subpoena without the identifying information that Doe would provide by using his knowledge and judgment to sift through, select, assemble, and produce the documents.

c. Oliver North Prosecution

For another good illustration of the *Kastigar* problem regarding whether, after disclosures made pursuant to a grant of immunity, a subsequent criminal prosecution may go forward, see *United States v. North*, 910 F.2d 843 (D.C. Cir. 1990). In that case, Oliver North was prosecuted for violating the Boland Amendments, which barred the United States government from providing resources to rebels (so called "Contras") battling the Nicaraguan government. Congress conducted hearings to investigate whether President Reagan's administration was violating these provisions. Retired Colonel Oliver North, then a member of the National Security Administration staff, was subpoenaed to testify. He asserted his Fifth Amendment privilege. Congress decided that getting to the truth of whether the Reagan administration was violating the law was more important than criminal prosecution and decided to grant North immunity (use and derivative use) in order to compel his testimony. North provided extensive testimony on how the administration had violated the law by funneling money from secret sales of weapons to Iran to the Contras in Nicaragua. Special Prosecutor Lawrence Walsh subsequently prosecuted North for his lead role in violating the Boland Amendments. North was convicted but his conviction was subsequently overturned by the D.C. Circuit principally because in the appellate court's view, the prosecution had failed to satisfy the dictates of *Kastigar* by demonstrating that every piece of its evidence was obtained wholly independent of North's testimony. While in the North case the D.C. Circuit wrote about the prosecution's "heavy burden" under *Kastigar*, to show an independent source for each piece of evidence, it is worth noting that the decision came in a divided 2–1 opinion in which the two judges in the majority were both Reagan appointees. North was a high official in the Reagan administration and, according to news accounts, other, even higher administration officials, such as Secretary of Defense Caspar Weinberger may have been implicated. The degree of protection afforded by *Kastigar* to the run of the mill defendant is questionable.

Executive Summary

Screening a Case. There are three basic ways in which a case may be "screened" to determine whether it will proceed: (1) by the prosecution within the prosecutor's office; (2) through a preliminary hearing; (3) through a grand jury.

Preliminary Hearing. A preliminary hearing is an adversary proceeding that occurs in open court, is presided over by a judge, and the accused has the right to counsel, to cross examine witnesses presented by the prosecution, and to present evidence.

No Probable Cause Not a Barrier to Prosecution. A finding of no probable cause by the judge at a preliminary hearing does not necessarily preclude the prosecution from prosecuting the charge.

Effect of Indictment. The return of an indictment establishes probable cause and may eliminate the accused's right to a preliminary hearing.

Major Themes

a. Discretion—The main source for screening whether a case will go forward is the vast discretion of the prosecutor whether to charge. The preliminary hearing rarely leads to a dismissal of the charges, and the grand jury rarely refuses to return an indictment.

b. Sword—While the grand jury was born of the founders' interest in having it serve as a shield to governmental over-reaching in charging, it rarely if ever serves that purpose now. It is a sword in the prosecution's possession used to investigate and bring charges in serious or high profile cases.

c. Immunity—In high profile or complex investigations, in order to gain important information through testimony in the grand jury, the prosecution has complete discretion to offer a witness who may incriminate himself transactional or use immunity.

Unbiased Grand Juror Selection. Grand jurors must be selected without systematic exclusion of individuals based on race, gender, or national origin.

Rules on Disclosure of Grand Jury Testimony. The prosecutor and grand jurors are generally prohibited from disclosing grand jury testimony to others, but witnesses are not prohibited from disclosing their own testimony.

No Court Review of Grand Jury Findings. Courts will not review the adequacy of evidence presented to a grand jury.

Evidence Submitted to Grand Jury. Hearsay and evidence obtained in violation of the Fourth Amendment is admissible in grand jury proceedings, and prosecutors have no constitutional duty to present exculpatory evidence to a grand jury.

Fifth Amendment Privilege. In response to a grand jury subpoena to testify or subpoena duces tecum, a person may claim that testifying or compliance with the subpoena would violate the Fifth Amendment right against self-incrimination.

Immunity. A prosecutor may grant a witness "use" immunity in order to overcome a witness's assertion of a Fifth Amendment privilege and compel the witness to testify or comply with a subpoena duces tecum.

Overcoming Fifth Amendment Privilege. In order to overcome an assertion of a Fifth Amendment privilege with respect to a subpoena duces tecum, a prosecutor must show that at the time the subpoena issued, the government knew that the material sought existed, knew who had the material, and knew that the material sought was that described by the subpoena.

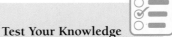

Test Your Knowledge

To assess your understanding of the material in this chapter, click here to take a quiz.

For More Information

• MARK E. CAMMACK & NORMAN M. GARLAND, ADVANCED CRIMINAL PROCEDURE (2006).

• WAYNE R. LaFAVE, JEROLD H. ISRAEL, NANCY J. KING & ORIN S. KERR, CRIMINAL PROCEDURE (5th ed. 2009).

• JEROLD H. ISRAEL & WAYNE R. LaFAVE, CRIMINAL PROCEDURE: CONSTITUTIONAL LIMITATIONS (8th ed. 2006).

• RUSSELL L. WEAVER, JOHN M. BURKOFF, CATHERINE HANCOCK, JANET HOEFFEL, STEVE FRIEDLAND & STEPHEN SINGER, PRINCIPLES OF CRIMINAL PROCEDURE Ch. 11 (6th ed. 2018).

CHAPTER 13

Discovery and Disclosure

Discovery in criminal cases is conceptually similar to discovery in civil cases: it is the process of exchanging information between the parties, which in a criminal case are the prosecution and the defense. This exchange of information is to be contrasted with other avenues for gathering information, such as factual investigation. In practice, however, criminal and civil discovery are very different. While discovery in civil cases is broad and evenly pursued, in criminal cases, the prosecution holds the vast majority of the information. The reason for this is in part structural—the prosecution gathers information from the police, who report to the scene of the crime and investigate immediately; the defense is not able to begin investigating the crime until the defendant obtains counsel (who has access to an investigator), and that may not occur until weeks or months after the crime. In addition, law enforcement possesses formal statutory authority to investigate criminal activity and the defense does not. The other reason for the uneven balance is the availability of resources. The prosecution has a plethora of government agents at its disposal for investigation, forensic examination and other expertise. The typical criminal defense attorney is a public defender, who is often underpaid, overworked and underresourced. Therefore, discovery disputes are most often about the defendant trying to obtain information from the prosecution, and most litigation in the discovery area involves allegations that the prosecution failed to disclose certain information.

There are two sources for the right to discovery: constitutional and

Practice Pointer

It is crucial that defense counsel be aware of how discovery obligations are triggered in the particular jurisdiction. In the federal court and in many state jurisdictions, the requirement to disclose information is triggered simply by a request for the information by the opposing party, usually in writing and pursuant to a statute that sets forth what must be disclosed. Further, some jurisdictions require a party to assert that it has engaged in diligent efforts to obtain the discovery by request or other means before the party can file a motion regarding discovery from the opposing party. On the other hand, some state jurisdictions provide that a party's obligation to provide discovery pursuant to statute is only triggered by filing a formal motion for discovery with the court.

statutory. The United States Constitution sets a floor, giving minimal rights of discovery to a criminal defendant through the Due Process Clause of the Fifth Amendment. *See Armstrong v. Manzo*, 380 U.S. 545 (1965). Every jurisdiction also has a statute governing criminal discovery that sets forth more information that must be given to the other party. Most meaningful discovery will come from the statutory obligations as opposed to the Constitutional obligations.

It is here, when we discuss discovery obligations, that the arraignment becomes important. An arraignment is the court proceeding whereby the accused is given formal notice of the charges through the court reading the indictment or information. The accused will then enter a plea. This is not to be confused with the first appearance, where formal charges are often not yet filed. The defendant's right to statutory discovery is usually not triggered until arraignment and an entry of a plea of not guilty.

There are two basic discovery issues under the United States Constitution. One involves the defendant's due process right to notice of the charges, and the other involves the defendant's due process right to discover exculpatory evidence.

A. Notice and Motion for Bill of Particulars

After the defendant is arraigned on the charges in open court, he or she may seek additional information about those charges by filing a motion for a bill of particulars. This motion is limited to clarifying the charging document, whether indictment or information, so that the defendant has adequate notice of the charges. *See Armstrong v. Manzo*, 380 U.S. 545 (1965) (defendant's right to notice of charges is basic to due process). For example, defendant may request the date, time and place of the alleged incident or incidents, the nature of the alleged acts which comprise the elements of the charged crime, or which subsection of a multi-sectioned criminal statute forms the basis of the charge. "The decisive consideration in each case is whether the matter claimed to be left out of the indictment has resulted in depriving the accused of a substantial right and subjects him to danger of being tried upon a charge for which he has not been indicted." *Ward v. Commonwealth*, 205 Va. 564, 138 S.E.2d 293 (1964).

Practice Pointer

Given the limited information provided by a bill of particulars, such motions are rarely filed in routine criminal cases where that information is usually clear. It is more likely that a defense attorney may seek a bill of particulars in a case where the charges are either very serious, such as in a capital case, or very complex, such as in conspiracy or RICO prosecutions, and clarification of basic information about the charges is needed.

B. Discovery of Exculpatory Evidence

By far, the largest area of contention and confusion between prosecutors and defense attorneys is the requirement set forth in *Brady v. Maryland*, 373 U.S. 83 (1963), and its progeny. Loosely stated, these cases hold that the prosecution has an obligation under the Due Process Clause to disclose exculpatory information. However, the parameters of this obligation are contested. The issue often arises when a defendant learns of withheld information after conviction.

Brady v. Maryland

373 U.S. 83 (1963).

Opinion of the Court by Mr. Justice Douglas.

Petitioner and a companion, Boblit, were found guilty of murder in the first degree and were sentenced to death. At his trial Brady took the stand and admitted his participation in the crime, but he claimed that Boblit did the actual killing. In his summation to the jury, Brady's counsel conceded that Brady was guilty of murder in the first degree, asking only that the jury return that verdict "without capital punishment." Prior to the trial petitioner's counsel had requested the prosecution to allow him to examine Boblit's extrajudicial statements. Several of those statements were shown to him; but one dated July 9, 1958, in which Boblit admitted the actual homicide, was withheld by the prosecution and did not come to petitioner's notice until after he had been tried, convicted, and sentenced, and after his conviction had been affirmed.

Take Note

The undisclosed statement did not exculpate Brady of the crime of first-degree murder—he was an accomplice to the felony and so was liable for felony-murder even if Boblit did the killing. The statement was only potentially relevant to whether he received a life sentence or capital punishment.

We agree with the Maryland Court of Appeals that suppression of this confession was a violation of the Due Process Clause of the Fourteenth Amendment. This ruling is an extension of *Mooney v. Holohan,* 294 U.S. 103, 112 (1935), where the Court ruled on what nondisclosure by a prosecutor violates due process:

> It is a requirement that cannot be deemed to be satisfied by mere notice and hearing if a State has contrived a conviction through the pretense of a trial which in truth is but used as a means of depriving a defendant of liberty through a deliberate deception of court and jury by

the presentation of testimony known to be perjured. Such a contrivance by a State to procure the conviction and imprisonment of a defendant is as inconsistent with the rudimentary demands of justice as is the obtaining of a like result by intimidation.

In *Pyle v. Kansas,* 317 U.S. 213, 215–216 (1942), we phrased the rule in broader terms:

> Petitioner's papers are inexpertly drawn, but they do set forth allegations that his imprisonment resulted from perjured testimony, knowingly used by the State authorities to obtain his conviction, and from the deliberate suppression by those same authorities of evidence favorable to him. These allegations sufficiently charge a deprivation of rights guaranteed by the Federal Constitution, and, if proven, would entitle petitioner to release from his present custody.

The Third Circuit has construed that statement in *Pyle* v. *Kansas* to mean that the "suppression of evidence favorable" to the accused was itself sufficient to amount to a denial of due process. In *Napue v. Illinois,* 360 U.S. 264, 269 (1959), we extended the test formulated in *Mooney* v. *Holohan* when we said: "The same result obtains when the State, although not soliciting false evidence, allows it to go uncorrected when it appears."

We now hold that the suppression by the prosecution of evidence favorable to an accused upon request violates due process where the evidence is material either to guilt or to punishment, irrespective of the good faith or bad faith of the prosecution.

The principle of *Mooney* v. *Holohan* is not punishment of society for misdeeds of a prosecutor but avoidance of an unfair trial to the accused. Society wins not only when the guilty are convicted but when criminal trials are fair; our system of the administration of justice suffers when any accused is treated unfairly. An inscription on the walls of the Department of Justice states the proposition candidly for the federal domain: "The United States wins its point whenever justice is done its citizens in the courts." A prosecution that withholds evidence on demand of an accused which, if made available, would tend to exculpate him or reduce the penalty helps shape a trial that bears heavily on the defendant. That casts the prosecutor in the role of an architect of a proceeding that does not comport with standards of justice, even though, as in the present case, his action is not "the result of guile."

Affirmed.

United States v. Bagley

473 U.S. 667 (1985).

JUSTICE BLACKMUN announced the judgment of the Court and delivered an opinion of the Court except as to Part III.

Hear It

You can hear the oral argument in *Bagley* at: http://www.oyez.org/cases/1980-1989/1984/1984_84_48.

In *Brady v. Maryland*, 373 U.S. 83 (1963), this Court held that "the suppression by the prosecution of evidence favorable to an accused upon request violates due process where the evidence is material either to guilt or punishment." The issue in the present case concerns the standard of materiality to be applied in determining whether a conviction should be reversed because the prosecutor failed to disclose requested evidence that could have been used to impeach Government witnesses.

In October 1977, respondent Hughes Anderson Bagley was indicted in the Western District of Washington on 15 charges of violating federal narcotics and firearms statutes. On November 18, 24 days before trial, respondent filed a discovery motion. The sixth paragraph of that motion requested:

> "The names and addresses of witnesses that the government intends to call at trial. Also the prior criminal records of witnesses, and any deals, promises or inducements made to witnesses in exchange for their testimony."

The Government's two principal witnesses at the trial were James F. O'Connor and Donald E. Mitchell. O'Connor and Mitchell were state law-enforcement officers employed by the Milwaukee Railroad as private security guards. Between April and June 1977, they assisted the federal Bureau of Alcohol, Tobacco and Firearms (ATF) in conducting an undercover investigation of respondent.

The Government's response to the discovery motion did not disclose that any "deals, promises or inducements" had been made to O'Connor or Mitchell. In apparent reply to a request in the motion's ninth paragraph for "copies of all Jencks Act material," the Government produced a series of affidavits that O'Connor and Mitchell had signed between April 12 and May 4, 1977, while the undercover investigation was in progress. These affidavits recounted in detail the undercover dealings that O'Connor and Mitchell were having at the time with respondent. Each affidavit concluded with the statement, "I made this statement freely and voluntarily without any threats or rewards, or promises of reward having been made to me in return for it."

Respondent waived his right to a jury trial and was tried before the court in December 1977. At the trial, O'Connor and Mitchell testified about both the firearms and the narcotics charges. On December 23, the court found respondent guilty on the narcotics charges, but not guilty on the firearms charges. [In a subsequent habeas corpus action, the district court found that the prosecution had failed to disclose the existence of agreements with O'Connor and Mitchell to pay them for their testimony if it proved to be useful. These agreements would have provided impeachment material when O'Connor and Mitchell testified.]

The District Court found beyond a reasonable doubt, however, that had the existence of the agreements been disclosed to it during trial, the disclosure would have had no effect upon its finding that the Government had proved beyond a reasonable doubt that respondent was guilty of the offenses for which he had been convicted. The District Court reasoned: Almost all of the testimony of both witnesses was devoted to the firearms charges in the indictment. Respondent, however, was acquitted on those charges. The testimony of O'Connor and Mitchell concerning the narcotics charges was relatively very brief. On cross-examination, respondent's counsel did not seek to discredit their testimony as to the facts of distribution but rather sought to show that the controlled substances in question came from supplies that had been prescribed for respondent's personal use. The answers of O'Connor and Mitchell to this line of cross-examination tended to be favorable to respondent. Thus, the claimed impeachment evidence would not have been helpful to respondent and would not have affected the outcome of the trial. Accordingly, the District Court denied respondent's motion to vacate his sentence.

The holding in *Brady v. Maryland* requires disclosure only of evidence that is both favorable to the accused and "material either to guilt or to punishment." The *Brady* rule is based on the requirement of due process. Its purpose is not to displace the adversary system as the primary means by which truth is uncovered, but to ensure that a miscarriage of justice does not occur. Thus, the prosecutor is not required to deliver his entire file to defense counsel, but only to disclose evidence favorable to the accused that, if suppressed, would deprive the defendant of a fair trial. In *Brady* and *United States v. Agurs*, 427 U.S. 97 (1976), the prosecutor failed to disclose exculpatory evidence. In the present case, the prosecutor failed to disclose evidence that the defense might have used to impeach the Government's witnesses by showing bias or interest. Impeachment evidence, however, as well as exculpatory evidence, falls within the *Brady* rule. Such evidence is "evidence favorable to an accused," so that, if disclosed and used effectively, it may make the difference between conviction and acquittal.

The constitutional error, if any, in this case was the Government's failure to assist the defense by disclosing information that might have been helpful in conducting the cross-examination. As discussed above, such suppression of evidence amounts to a constitutional violation only if it deprives the defendant of a fair trial. Consistent with "our overriding concern with the justice of the finding of guilt," a constitutional error occurs, and the conviction must be reversed, only if the evidence is material in the sense that its suppression undermines confidence in the outcome of the trial.

It remains to determine the standard of materiality applicable to the non-disclosed evidence at issue. Our starting point is the framework for evaluating the materiality of *Brady* evidence established in *United States v. Agurs. Agurs* distinguished three situations involving the discovery, after trial, of information favorable to the accused that had been known to the prosecution but unknown to the defense. The first situation was the prosecutor's knowing use of perjured testimony or, equivalently, the prosecutor's knowing failure to disclose that testimony used to convict the defendant was false. The Court noted the well-established rule that "a conviction obtained by the knowing use of perjured testimony is fundamentally unfair, and must be set aside if there is any reasonable likelihood that the false testimony could have affected the judgment of the jury." Although this rule is stated in terms that treat the knowing use of perjured testimony as error subject to harmless-error review, it may as easily be stated as a materiality standard under which the fact that testimony is perjured is considered material unless failure to disclose it would be harmless beyond a reasonable doubt. *Agurs* justified this standard of materiality on the ground that the knowing use of perjured testimony involves prosecutorial misconduct and, more importantly, involves "a corruption of the truth-seeking function of the trial process."

At the other extreme is the situation in *Agurs* itself, where the defendant does not make a *Brady* request and the prosecutor fails to disclose evidence favorable to the accused. The Court rejected a harmless-error rule in that situation, because under that rule every nondisclosure is treated as error, thus imposing on the prosecutor a constitutional duty to deliver his entire file to defense counsel. At the same time, the Court rejected a standard that would require the defendant to demonstrate that the evidence if disclosed probably would have resulted in acquittal. The Court reasoned: "If the standard applied to the usual motion for a new trial based on newly discovered evidence were the same when the evidence was in the State's possession as when it was found in a neutral source, there would be no special significance to the prosecutor's obligation to serve the cause of justice." The standard of materiality applicable in the absence of a specific Brady request is therefore stricter than the harmless-error standard but more lenient to the defense than the newly-discovered-evidence standard.

The third situation identified by *Agurs* is where the defense makes a specific request and the prosecutor fails to disclose responsive evidence. The Court did not define the standard of materiality applicable in this situation, but suggested that the standard might be more lenient to the defense than in the situation in which the defense makes no request or only a general request. The Court also noted: "When the prosecutor receives a specific and relevant request, the failure to make any response is seldom, if ever, excusable."

The Court has relied on and reformulated the *Agurs* standard for the materiality of undisclosed evidence in two subsequent cases arising outside the *Brady* context. In neither case did the Court's discussion of the *Agurs* standard distinguish among the three situations described in *Agurs*. In *Strickland v. Washington*, 466 U.S. 668 (1984), the Court held that a new trial must be granted when evidence is not introduced because of the incompetence of counsel only if "there is a reasonable probability that, but for counsel's unprofessional errors, the result of the proceeding would have been different." The *Strickland* Court defined a "reasonable probability" as "a probability sufficient to undermine confidence in the outcome."

We find the *Strickland* formulation of the *Agurs* test for materiality sufficiently flexible to cover the "no request," "general request," and "specific request" cases of prosecutorial failure to disclose evidence favorable to the accused: The evidence is material only if there is a reasonable probability that, had the evidence been disclosed to the defense, the result of the proceeding would have been different. A "reasonable probability" is a probability sufficient to undermine confidence in the outcome.

The Government suggests that a materiality standard more favorable to the defendant reasonably might be adopted in specific request cases. The Government notes that an incomplete response to a specific request not only deprives the defense of certain evidence, but also has the effect of representing to the defense that the evidence does not exist. In reliance on this misleading representation, the defense might abandon lines of independent investigation, defenses, or trial strategies that it otherwise would have pursued.

We agree that the prosecutor's failure to respond fully to a *Brady* request may impair the adversary process in this manner. And the more specifically the defense requests certain evidence, thus putting the prosecutor on notice of its value, the more reasonable it is for the defense to assume from the nondisclosure that the evidence does not exist, and to make pretrial and trial decisions on the basis of this assumption. This possibility of impairment does not necessitate a different standard of materiality, however, for under the *Strickland* formulation the reviewing court may consider directly any adverse effect that the prosecutor's failure to respond might have had on the preparation or presentation of the defendant's case. The reviewing court should assess the possibility that such effect might have occurred in light of the totality of the circumstances and with an awareness of the difficulty of reconstructing in a post-trial proceeding the course that the defense and the trial would have taken had the defense not been misled by the prosecutor's incomplete response.

In the present case, we think that there is a significant likelihood that the prosecutor's response to respondent's discovery motion misleadingly induced defense counsel to believe that O'Connor and Mitchell could not be impeached on the basis of bias or interest arising from inducements offered by the Government. Defense counsel asked the prosecutor to disclose any inducements that had been made to witnesses, and the prosecutor failed to disclose that the possibility of a reward had been held out to O'Connor and Mitchell if the information they supplied led to "the accomplishment of the objective sought to be obtained to the satisfaction of the Government." This possibility of a reward gave O'Connor and Mitchell a direct, personal stake in respondent's conviction. The fact that the stake was not guaranteed through a promise or binding contract, but was expressly contingent on the Government's satisfaction with the end result, served only to strengthen any incentive to testify falsely in order to secure a conviction.

The District Court, nonetheless, found beyond a reasonable doubt that, had the information that the Government held out the possibility of reward to its witnesses been disclosed, the result of the criminal prosecution would not have been different. If this finding were sustained by the Court of Appeals, the information would be immaterial even under the standard of materiality applicable to the prosecutor's knowing use of perjured testimony. Although the express holding of the Court of Appeals was that the nondisclosure in this case required automatic reversal, the Court of Appeals "disagreed" with the District Court's finding of harmless error. In particular, the Court of Appeals disagreed with the factual premise on which this finding expressly was based. The District Court reasoned that O'Connor's and Mitchell's testimony was exculpatory on the narcotics charges. The Court of Appeals, however, concluded, after reviewing the record, that O'Connor's and Mitchell's testimony was in fact inculpatory on those charges. Accordingly, we reverse the judgment of the Court of Appeals and remand the case to that court for a determination whether there is a reasonable probability that, had the inducement offered by the Government to O'Connor and Mitchell been disclosed to the defense, the result of the trial would have been different.

JUSTICE WHITE, with whom THE CHIEF JUSTICE and JUSTICE REHNQUIST join, concurring in part and concurring in the judgment.

I agree with the Court that respondent is not entitled to have his conviction overturned unless he can show that the evidence withheld by the Government was "material." I also agree with Justice Blackmun that for purposes of this inquiry, "evidence is material only if there is a reasonable probability that, had the evidence been disclosed to the defense, the result of the proceeding would have been different." As the Justice correctly observes, this standard is "sufficiently flexible" to cover all instances of prosecutorial failure to disclose evidence favorable to the accused. Given the flexibility of the standard and the inherently factbound nature of the cases to which it will be applied, I see no reason to attempt to elaborate on the relevance to the inquiry of the specificity of the defense's request for disclosure, either generally or with respect to this case. I would hold simply that the proper standard is one of reasonable probability and that the Court of Appeals' failure to apply this standard necessitates reversal. I therefore concur in the judgment.

JUSTICE MARSHALL, with whom JUSTICE BRENNAN joins, dissenting.

When the Government withholds from a defendant evidence that might impeach the prosecution's only witnesses, that failure to disclose cannot be deemed harmless error. I would affirm the judgment of the Court of Appeals and would not remand for further proceedings.

Once the prosecutor suspects that certain information might have favorable implications for the defense, either because it is potentially exculpatory or relevant to credibility, I see no reason why he should not be required to disclose it. After all, favorable evidence indisputably enhances the truth-seeking process at trial. And it is the job of the defense, not the prosecution, to decide whether and in what way to use arguably favorable evidence. In addition, to require disclosure of all evidence that might reasonably be considered favorable to the defendant would have the precautionary effect of assuring that no information of potential consequence is mistakenly overlooked. A clear rule of this kind, coupled with a presumption in favor of disclosure, also would facilitate the prosecutor's admittedly difficult task by removing a substantial amount of unguided discretion.

The Court, however, offers a complex alternative. It defines the right not by reference to the possible usefulness of the particular evidence in preparing and presenting the case, but retrospectively, by reference to the likely effect the evidence will have on the outcome of the trial.

The result is to veer sharply away from the basic notion that the fairness of a trial increases with the amount of existing favorable evidence to which the defendant has access, and to disavow the ideal of full disclosure.

I simply cannot agree with the Court that the due process right to favorable evidence recognized in Brady was intended to become entangled in prosecutorial determinations of the likelihood that particular information would affect the outcome of trial. In so saying, I recognize that a failure to divulge favorable information should not result in reversal in all cases. The benefits of disclosure may at times be tempered by the state's legitimate desire to avoid retrial when error has been harmless. However, in making the determination of harmlessness, I would apply our normal constitutional error test and reverse unless it is clear beyond a reasonable doubt that the withheld evidence would not have affected the outcome of the trial.

Food for Thought

How does a trial prosecutor employ such a retrospective standard before the trial has even occurred? For years, defense attorneys have maintained that *Bagley's* materiality standard is strictly for appellate courts to apply in determining whether a *Brady* violation warranting reversal has occurred, and that at the trial level the question is simply whether the information is favorable to the defense. In other words, materiality cannot be known in advance before all of the evidence is in, but only on a review of the complete record on appeal. As one appellate court explained, at the trial level "no one has the gift of prophecy. To argue that the [trial] court [or prosecutor] can apply a material-to-outcome test before trial is to argue a contradiction." *Lewis v. United States*, 408 A.2d 303, 307 (D.C. 1979). *See* Discussion Point f below for some views of current Supreme Court Justices on the issue.

JUSTICE STEVENS, dissenting.

Two situations in which the rule applies are those demonstrating the prosecution's knowing use of perjured testimony, exemplified by *Mooney v. Holohan*, and the prosecution's suppression of favorable evidence specifically requested by the defendant, exemplified by *Brady* itself. In both situations, the prosecution's deliberate nondisclosure constitutes constitutional error—the conviction must be set aside if the suppressed or perjured evidence was "material" and there was "any reasonable likelihood" that it "could have affected" the outcome of the trial. The combination of willful prosecutorial suppression of evidence and, "more importantly," the potential "corruption of the truth-seeking function of the trial process" requires that result. Suppression in response to a request is far more serious than mere nondisclosure of evidence in which the defense has expressed no particular interest. A reviewing court should attach great significance to silence in the face of a specific request, when responsive evidence is later shown to have been in the Government's possession. Such silence actively misleads in the same way as would an affirmative representation that exculpatory evidence does not exist when, in fact, it does (i.e., perjury)—indeed, the two situations are aptly described as "sides of a single coin."

Turner v. United States

137 S.Ct. 1885 (2017).

JUSTICE BREYER delivered the opinion of the Court.

In *Brady v. Maryland*, 373 U.S. 83 (1963), this Court held that the government violates the Constitution's Due Process Clause "if it withholds evidence that is favorable to the defense and material to the defendant's guilt or punishment." *Smith v. Cain*, 565 U.S. 73, 75 (2012). In 1985 the seven petitioners in these cases were tried together in the Superior Court for the District of Columbia for the kidnaping, armed robbery, and murder of Catherine Fuller. Long after petitioners' convictions became final, it emerged that the Government possessed certain evidence that it failed to disclose to the defense. The question is whether that evidence was "material" under Brady. The D.C. Superior Court, after a 16–day hearing, determined that the withheld evidence was not material. The D.C. Court of Appeals reviewed the record, reached the same conclusion, and affirmed. We reach the same conclusion.

Food for Thought

Assume you are Bagley's defense attorney on remand to the Court of Appeals. Assume that O'Connor and Mitchell were the only prosecution witnesses linking Bagley to the narcotics. Articulate your argument to the Court that there is a reasonable probability that the outcome of the trial would have been different if you had known of the impeaching evidence. What difficulties are there in making this argument? Now articulate your argument under the dissent's desired harmless error standard—that the prosecution cannot prove beyond a reasonable doubt that the outcome would not have been different with the impeaching evidence. Which standard makes more sense and why? What values does each standard serve?

Before *Bagley*, in *Giglio v. United States*, 405 U.S. 150 (1972), the Supreme Court made clear that *Brady* applies not only to evidence that affirmatively helps show that the defendant is innocent of the crime but also to evidence which merely weakens or undermines the strength of the prosecution's case, such as impeachment evidence. In *Giglio*, the impeachment evidence at issue was a deal between the prosecution and its main witness—that the witness would receive favorable treatment on other charges in return for his testimony. The Court in *Bagley* then held that all impeachment evidence was subject to disclosure, not just deals with prosecution witnesses.

In these fact-intensive cases, we set out here only a basic description of the record facts along with our reasons for reaching our conclusion. We refer those who wish more detail to the opinions of the lower courts.

The Trial. On March 22, 1985, a grand jury indicted the seven petitioners— Timothy Catlett, Russell Overton, Levy Rouse, Kelvin Smith, Charles Turner, Christopher Turner, and Clifton Yarborough—and several others for the kidnaping, robbery, and murder of Catherine Fuller. The evidence showed that on October 1, 1984, at around 4:30 p.m., Catherine Fuller left her home to go shopping. At around 6 p.m., William Freeman, a street vendor, found Fuller's body inside an alley garage between Eighth and Ninth Street N. E., just a few blocks from Fuller's home. Fuller had been robbed, severely beaten, and sodomized with an object that caused extensive internal injuries. The Government advanced the theory at trial that Fuller had been attacked in the alley by a large group of individuals, including petitioners; codefendants Steve Webb, Alfonso Harris, and Felicia Ruffin; as well as by Calvin Alston and Harry Bennett. The Government's evidentiary centerpiece consisted of testimony by Alston and Bennett, who confessed to participating in the offense and who cooperated with the Government in return for leniency. Although the testimony of Alston and Bennett diverged on minor details, it was consistent in stating that, and describing how, Fuller was attacked by a sizable group of individuals, including petitioners and themselves.

Alston testified that at about 4:10 p.m. on the day of the murder, he arrived in a park located on H Street. He found a group of people gathered there. It included petitioners Levy Rouse, Russell Overton, Christopher Turner, Charles Turner, Kelvin Smith, Clifton Yarborough, and Timothy Catlett, as well as several codefendants and others. Those in the group were talking and singing while Catlett was banging out a beat. Alston suggested "getting paid" by robbing someone. Catlett, Overton, Rouse, Smith, Charles Turner, Christopher Turner, Yarborough, and several others agreed. Alston pointed at Catherine Fuller, who was walking on the other side of H Street near the corner of H and Eighth Streets. Those in the group were "game for getting paid." Alston, Rouse, Yarborough, and Charles Turner crossed H Street moving toward Eighth Street and followed Fuller down Eighth Street. The rest of the group crossed H Street and moved toward Ninth Street. When Alston's group approached Fuller, Charles Turner shoved her into an alley that runs between Eighth and Ninth Streets. Charles Turner, Rouse, and Alston began punching Fuller. They were soon joined by Christopher Turner, Smith, and others. All of them continued to hit and kick Fuller until she fell to the ground. Rouse and Charles Turner then carried Fuller to the center of the alley and dropped her in front of a garage located at the point where the alley joins another, perpendicular alley that runs toward I Street. Someone dragged Fuller into the garage. Alston, Rouse, Charles Turner, Overton, Yarborough, and Catlett followed. Others stood outside. Members of the group tore Fuller's clothes off and struggled over her change purse. Overton and Charles Turner then held Fuller's legs, and Alston, Catlett, Harris, and Yarborough stood around her while Rouse sodomized her with a foot-long pipe. Shortly after, the group dispersed and left the alley.

Harry Bennett's testimony was similar. Bennett also described a group attack. He had gone to the H Street park, where he saw Rouse, Overton, Christopher Turner, Smith, Catlett, and others gathered. Alston was talking to the group about "getting paid" and said "let's go get that lady." At that point Alston, Rouse, Overton, and Webb crossed H Street and approached Fuller, while Catlett, Christopher Turner, Charles Turner, and Harris followed in a separate group. Bennett added that he himself went to the corner of Eighth and H Streets to watch for police. He then went into the alley and joined the group in kicking and beating Fuller. He testified that at least 12 people were there, with some beating Fuller and others watching or picking up her jewelry. Overton then dragged Fuller into the garage, and Bennett, Rouse, Christopher Turner, Charles Turner, Catlett, Smith, Harris, and Webb followed, as did some "girls." Alston and Steve Webb held Fuller's legs, and Rouse sodomized her with a pole. The group then dispersed from the garage and alley.

The Government presented several other witnesses who corroborated aspects of Alston's and Bennett's testimony, including the fact that Fuller was attacked by a group. Melvin Montgomery testified that he was in the H Street park on the afternoon of the murder. He saw Overton, Catlett, Rouse, Charles Turner, and others gathered there. The group was being noisy and singing a song about needing money. Somebody then said they were "going to get that one," and Montgomery saw that Overton was pointing to a woman standing on the corner of Eighth Street. Overton, Catlett, Rouse, Charles Turner, and others crossed H Street. Some headed toward Eighth Street while others went toward Ninth Street. Montgomery did not follow them. Maurice Thomas, then 14 years old, testified that he witnessed the attack itself. Thomas lived in the neighborhood and knew many of the defendants. As he was walking home, he glanced down the Eighth Street alley and saw a group surrounding Fuller. Thomas saw Catlett pat Fuller down and then hit her. He then saw everyone in the group join in hitting her. Thomas said he knew Catlett, Yarborough, Rouse, Charles Turner, Christopher Turner, and Smith and recognized them in the group. Thomas heard Fuller calling for help. He ran home where he found his aunt, who told him not to tell anyone what he saw. Later that day, Thomas saw Catlett at a corner store, and heard Catlett say to someone that they "had to kill her" because "she spotted someone he was with." On the afternoon of the murder, Carrie Eleby and Linda Jacobs were looking for petitioner Smith, who was Eleby's boyfriend, near the corner of H and Eighth Streets. They heard screams coming from where a "gang of boys" was beating somebody near the garage in the alley. Eleby and Jacobs approached the group. Eleby recognized

Christopher Turner, Smith, Catlett, Rouse, Overton, Alston, and Webb kicking Fuller while Yarborough stood nearby. Both Eleby and Jacobs testified that they saw Rouse sodomize Fuller with a pole. Eleby added that Overton held Fuller's legs. Finally, the Government played a videotape of a recorded statement that Yarborough, one of the petitioners, had given to detectives approximately two months after the murder. Names were redacted. The video shows Yarborough describing in detail how he was part of a large group that forced Fuller into the alley, jointly robbed and assaulted her, and dragged her into the garage.

None of the defendants testified, nor did any of them try to rebut the prosecution witnesses' claim that Fuller was killed in a group attack. Rather, each petitioner pursued what was essentially a "not me, maybe them" defense, namely, that he was not part of the group that attacked Fuller. Each tried to establish this defense by impeaching witnesses who had placed that particular petitioner at the scene. Some provided evidence that Eleby and Jacobs had used PCP the day of Fuller's murder. Some tried to establish alibis for the time of Fuller's death. The jury convicted all seven petitioners, along with codefendant Steve Webb (who subsequently died).

The jury acquitted codefendants Alfonso Harris and Felicia Ruffin. On appeal, the D.C. Court of Appeals affirmed petitioners' convictions, though it remanded for resentencing. The trial court resentenced petitioners to the same amount of prison time.

The Brady *Claims.* In 2010, petitioners pursued postconviction proceedings to vacate their convictions or be granted a new trial. After petitioners' convictions became final, it emerged that the Government possessed certain evidence that it had withheld from the defense at the time of trial. Petitioners discovered other withheld evidence in their review of the trial prosecutor's case file, which the Government turned over to petitioners in the course of the postconviction proceedings. Petitioners contended that the withheld evidence was both favorable and material, entitling them to relief under *Brady.* The D.C. Superior Court rejected those claims, finding that "none of the undisclosed information was material." The D.C. Court of Appeals affirmed.

At issue in those proceedings were the following seven specific pieces of evidence: 1. *The identity of James McMillan.* Freeman, the vendor who discovered Fuller's body in the alley garage, testified at trial that, while he was waiting for police to arrive, he saw two men run into the alley and stop near the garage for about five minutes before running away when an officer approached. One of the men had a bulge under his coat. Early in the trial, codefendant Harris' counsel had requested the identity of the two men to confirm that her client was not one of them. But the Government refused to disclose the men's identity. In their postconviction review of the prosecutor's files, petitioners learned that

Freeman had identified the two men he saw in the alley as James McMillan and Gerald Merkerson. McMillan lived in a house which opens in the back onto a connecting alley. In the weeks following Fuller's murder, but before petitioners' trial, McMillan was arrested for beating and robbing two women in the neighborhood. Neither attack included a sexual assault. Separately, petitioners learned that seven years after petitioners' trial, McMillan had robbed, sodomized, and murdered a young woman in an alley. 2. *The interview with Willie Luchie.* The prosecutor's notes also recorded an undisclosed interview with Willie Luchie, who told the prosecutor that he and three others walked through the alley on their way to an H Street liquor store between 5:30 and 5:45 p.m. on the evening of the murder. As the group walked by the garage, Luchie "heard several groans" and "remembers the doors to the garage being closed." Another person in the group recalled "hearing some moans," while the other two persons did not recall hearing anything unusual. The group continued walking without looking into the garage or otherwise investigating the source of the sounds. They did not see McMillan or any other person in the alley when they passed through. 3. *The interviews with Ammie Davis.* Undisclosed notes written by a police officer and the prosecutor refer to two interviews with Ammie Davis, who had been arrested for disorderly conduct a few weeks after Fuller's murder. Davis initially told a police investigator that she had seen another individual, James Blue, beat Fuller to death in the alley. Shortly thereafter, she said she only saw Blue grab Fuller and push her into the alley. Davis also said that a girlfriend, whom she did not name, accompanied her. She promised to call the investigator with more details, but she did not do so. About 9 months later (after petitioners were indicted but 11 weeks before trial), a prosecutor learned of the investigator's notes and interviewed Davis. The prosecutor's notes state that Davis did not provide any more details, except to say that the girlfriend who accompanied her was nicknamed "Shorty." About two months later, shortly before petitioners' trial, Blue murdered Davis in an unrelated drug dispute. During the postconviction evidentiary hearing, the prosecutor who interviewed Davis testified that he did not disclose Davis' statement because she acted "playful" and "not serious" during the interview and he found her to be "totally incredible." Additionally, the prosecutor stated that he knew Davis had previously falsely accused Blue of a different murder, and on another occasion had falsely accused a different individual of a different murder. 4. *Impeachment of Kaye Porter and Carrie Eleby.* Kaye Porter accompanied Eleby during an initial interview with homicide detectives. Porter agreed with Eleby that she had also heard Alston state that he was involved in robbing Fuller. An undisclosed prosecutorial note states that in a later interview with detectives, Porter stated that she did not actually recall hearing Alston's statement and just went along with what Eleby said. The note also states that Eleby likewise admitted that she had lied about Porter being present during Alston's statement and had asked Porter to support her. 5. *Impeachment of Carrie Eleby.* A prosecutor's undisclosed note revealed that Eleby said she had been high on PCP during a January 9, 1985, meeting with investigators. 6. *Impeachment of Linda Jacobs.* An undisclosed note of an interview with Linda Jacobs said that the detective had "questioned her hard," and that she had "vacillated" about what she saw. The prosecutor recalled that the detective "kept raising his voice" and was "smacking his hand on the desk" during the interview. 7. *Impeachment of Maurice Thomas.* An undisclosed note of an interview with Maurice Thomas' aunt stated that she "does not recall Maurice ever telling her anything such as this."

The Government does not contest petitioners' claim that the withheld evidence was "favorable to the accused, either because it is exculpatory, or because it is impeaching." *Strickler v. Greene,* 527 U.S. 263, 281 (1999). Neither does the Government contest petitioners' claim that it "suppressed" the evidence, "either willfully or inadvertently." It does concede that the *Brady* rule's "overriding concern is with the justice of the finding of guilt," *United States v. Bagley,* 473 U.S. 667, 678 (1985), and that the Government's "interest in a criminal prosecution is not that it shall win a case, but that justice shall be done," *Kyles v. Whitley,* 514 U.S. 419, 439 (1995). Consistent with these principles, the Government assured the Court that subsequent to petitioners' trial, it has adopted a "generous policy of discovery" in criminal cases under which it discloses any "information that a defendant might wish to use." "This is as it should be."

Petitioners and the Government do contest the materiality of the undisclosed *Brady* information. "Evidence is 'material' within the meaning of *Brady* when there is a reasonable probability that, had the evidence been disclosed, the result of the proceeding would have been different." *Cone v. Bell,* 556 U.S. 449, 469 (2009). "A 'reasonable probability' of a different result" is one in which the suppressed evidence "undermines confidence in the outcome of the trial." *Kyles, supra,* at 434. In other words, petitioners are entitled to a new trial only if they "establish the prejudice necessary to satisfy the 'materiality' inquiry." *Strickler, supra,* at 282.

The issue before us is legally simple but factually complex. We must examine the trial record, "evaluate" the withheld evidence "in the context of the entire record," and determine in light of that examination whether "there is a reasonable probability that, had the evidence been disclosed, the result of the proceeding would have been different." We agree with the lower courts that there was no such reasonable probability.

Petitioners' main argument is that, had they known about McMillan's identity and Luchie's statement, they could have challenged the Government's basic theory that Fuller was killed in a group attack. Petitioners contend that they could have raised an alternative theory, namely, that a single perpetrator (or two at most) had attacked Fuller. According to petitioners, the groans that Luchie and his companion heard when they walked through the alley between 5:30 and 5:45 p.m.

suggest that the attack was taking place inside the garage at that moment. The fact that the garage was small and that Luchie's group saw no one in the alley could bolster a "single attacker" theory. Freeman's recollection that one garage door was open when he found Fuller's body at around 6 p.m., combined with Luchie's recollection that both doors were shut around 5:30 or 5:45 p.m., could suggest that one or two perpetrators were in the garage when Luchie walked by but left before Freeman arrived. McMillan's identity as one of the men Freeman saw enter the alley after Freeman discovered Fuller's body would have revealed McMillan's criminal convictions in the months before petitioners' trial. Petitioners argue that together, this evidence would have permitted the defense to knit together a theory that the group attack did not occur at all—and that it was actually McMillan, alone or with an accomplice, who murdered Fuller. They add that they could have used the investigators' failure to follow up on Ammie Davis' claim about James Blue, and the various pieces of withheld impeachment evidence, to suggest that an incomplete investigation had ended up accusing the wrong persons.

Considering the withheld evidence "in the context of the entire record," we conclude that it is too little, too weak, or too distant from the main evidentiary points to meet *Brady*'s standards. McMillan's guilt (or that of any other single, or near single, perpetrator) is inconsistent with petitioners' guilt only if there was no group attack. But a group attack was the very cornerstone of the Government's case. The witnesses may have differed on minor details, but virtually every witness agreed as to a main theme: that Fuller was killed by a large group of perpetrators. The evidence was such that, even though petitioners knew that Freeman saw two men enter the alley after he discovered Fuller's body, that one appeared to have a bulky object hidden under his coat, and that both ran when the police arrived, none of the petitioners attempted to mount a defense that implicated those men as alternative perpetrators acting alone.

Is it reasonably probable that adding McMillan's identity, and Luchie's ambiguous statement that he heard groans but saw no one, could have led to a different result at trial? It is not. The problem for petitioners is that their current alternative theory would have had to persuade the jury that both Alston and Bennett falsely confessed to being active participants in a group attack that never occurred; that Yarborough falsely implicated himself in that group attack and, through coordinated effort or coincidence, gave a highly similar account of how it occurred; that Thomas, a disinterested witness who recognized petitioners when he happened upon the attack and heard Catlett refer to it later that night, wholly fabricated his story; that both Eleby and Jacobs likewise testified to witnessing a group attack that did not occur; and that Montgomery in fact did not see petitioners and others, as a group, identify Fuller as a target and leave the park to rob her.

With respect to the undisclosed impeachment evidence, it was largely cumulative of impeachment evidence petitioners already had used at trial. For example, the jury heard multiple times about Eleby's frequent PCP use, including Eleby's own testimony that she and Jacobs had smoked PCP shortly before they witnessed Fuller's attack. It would not have surprised the jury to learn that Eleby used PCP on yet another occasion. Porter was a minor witness who was also impeached at trial with evidence about changes in her testimony over time, leaving little added significance to the note that she changed her mind about having agreed with Eleby's claims. The jury was also well aware of Jacobs' vacillation, as she was impeached on the stand with her shifting stories about what she witnessed. Knowledge that a detective raised his voice during an interview with her would have added little more. Nor do we see how the note about the statement by Thomas' aunt could have mattered much, given the facts that neither side chose to call the aunt as a witness and that the jury already knew, from Thomas' testimony, that his aunt had told him not to tell anyone what he saw. As for James Blue, petitioners argue that the investigators' delay in following up on Ammie Davis' statement could have led the jury to doubt the thoroughness of the investigation. But this likelihood is seriously undercut by notes about Davis' demeanor and lack of detail, and by her prior false accusations that Blue committed a different murder and that yet another person committed yet a different murder.

We do not suggest that impeachment evidence is immaterial with respect to a witness who has already been impeached with other evidence. We conclude only that in the context of this trial, with respect to these witnesses, the cumulative effect of the withheld evidence is insufficient to "undermine confidence" in the jury's verdict. On the basis of our review, we agree with the lower courts that there is not a "reasonable probability" that the withheld evidence would have changed the outcome of petitioners' trial. The judgment of the D.C. Court of Appeals, accordingly, is affirmed.

It is so ordered.

Justice GORSUCH took no part in the consideration or decision of these cases.

Justice Kagan, with whom Justice Ginsburg joins, dissenting.

Consider two criminal cases. In the first, the government accuses ten defendants of acting together to commit a vicious murder and robbery. At trial, each defendant accepts that the attack occurred almost exactly as the government describes—contending only that *he* wasn't part of the rampaging group. The defendants thus undermine each other's arguments at every turn. In the second case, the government makes the same arguments. But this time, all of the accused adopt a common defense, built around an alternative account of the crime. Armed with new evidence that someone else perpetrated the murder, the defendants vig-orously dispute the government's gang-attack narrative and challenge the credibil-ity of its investigation. The question this case presents is whether such a unified defense, relying on evidence unavailable in the first scenario, had a "reasonable probability" (less than a preponderance) of shifting even one juror's vote. *Cone v. Bell*, 556 U.S. 449 (2009).

The Government knew about but withheld the evidence of an alternative perpetrator—and so prevented the defendants from coming together to press that theory of the case. If the Government's non-disclosure was material, this Court's decision in *Brady* demands a new trial. The Court today holds it was not material: In light of the evidence, the majority argues, the transformed defense stood little chance of persuading a juror to vote to acquit. That conclusion is not indefensible: The Government put on quite a few witnesses who said that the defendants com-mitted the crime. But the majority gets the answer wrong. With the undisclosed evidence, the whole tenor of the trial would have changed. Rather than relying on a "not me, maybe them" defense, defendants would have relentlessly impeached the Government's (thoroughly impeachable) witnesses and offered the jurors a way to view the crime in a different light. That could well have flipped one or more jurors—which is all *Brady* requires.

The majority and I share some common ground. We agree on the exculpa-tory or impeaching evidence suppressed in this case. We also agree that such evidence ought to be disclosed to defendants as a matter of course. Constitutional requirements aside, turning over exculpatory materials is a core responsibility of all prosecutors—whose professional interest and obligation is not to win cases but to ensure justice is done. Finally, we agree on the legal standard by which to assess the materiality of undisclosed evidence for purposes of applying the constitutional rule: Courts are to ask whether there is a "reasonable probability" that disclosure of the evidence would have led to a different outcome—*i.e.,* an acquittal or hung jury rather than a conviction. I part ways with the majority in applying that standard to the evidence withheld in this case. That evidence falls into three basic categories. Taken together, the materials would have recast the trial significantly—so as to "undermine confidence" in the guilty verdicts reached in their absence. *Kyles*, 514 U.S., at 434.

First, the Government suppressed information identifying a possible alterna-tive perpetrator. Defendants knew that, shortly before the police arrived, wit-nesses had observed two men acting suspiciously near the alleyway garage where Catherine Fuller's body was found. They did not know—because the Govern-ment never told them—that a witness had identified one of those men as James McMillan. With that information, defendants would have discovered that in the weeks following Fuller's murder, McMillan assaulted and robbed two other women of comparable age in the same neighborhood. Using *that* information, defendants would have united around a common defense. They would have pointed their fingers at McMillan (rather than at each other), arguing that he committed Fuller's murder as part of a string of similar crimes.

Second, the Government suppressed witness statements suggesting that one or two perpetrators—not a large group—carried out the attack. Those statements were given by two individuals who walked past the garage around the time of Fuller's death. They told the police that they heard groans coming from inside the garage; and one remarked that the garage's doors were closed. Introducing that evidence would have sown doubt about the Government's group-attack narrative, because that many people couldn't have fit inside the small garage. The questions thus raised would have further supported the defendants' theory that McMillan (and perhaps an accomplice) had committed the murder.

Third and finally, the Government suppressed a raft of evidence discrediting its investigation and impeaching its witnesses. Undisclosed files, for example, showed that the police took more than nine months to look into a witness's claim that a man named James Blue had murdered Fuller. Evidence of that kind of negligence could easily have led jurors to wonder about the competence of the police work done in the case. Other withheld documents revealed that one of the Government's main witnesses was high on PCP when she met with investigators to identify participants in the crime—and that she also encouraged a friend to lie to the police to support her story. Using that sort of information, defendants could have undercut the Government's witnesses—even while presenting their own account of the murder.

The majority argues that "none of the accused attempted to mount an alternative-perpetrator defense" and that such a defense would have challenged "the very cornerstone of the Government's case." That proves my point. The defendants didn't offer an alternative-perpetrator defense because the Government prevented them from learning what made it credible: that one of the men seen near the garage had a record of assaulting and robbing middle-aged women, and that witnesses would back up the theory that only one or two individuals had committed the murder. Moreover, that defense had game-changing potential exactly *because* it challenged the cornerstone of the Government's case. Without the withheld evidence, defendants had little choice but to accept the Government's framing of the crime as a group attack—and argue only that *he* wasn't there. That meant the defendants often worked at cross-purposes. Each defendant not identified by a Government witness sought to bolster that witness's credibility, no matter the harm to his co-defendants. Credible alternative-perpetrator evidence would have allowed the defendants to escape this cycle of mutually assured destruction. By enabling the defendants to jointly attack the Government's "cornerstone" theory, the withheld evidence would have reframed the case presented to the jury.

The majority claims, an alternative-perpetrator defense would have had no realistic chance of changing the outcome because the Government had ample evidence of a group attack, including five witnesses who testified that they had participated in it or seen it happen. But the Government's case wasn't nearly the slam-dunk the majority suggests. No physical evidence tied any of the defendants to the crime—a highly surprising fact if, as the Government claimed, more than ten people carried out a spur-of-the-moment, rampage-like attack in a confined space. The Government's five eyewitnesses had some serious credibility deficits. Two had been charged as defendants, and agreed to testify only in exchange for favorable plea deals. Two admitted they were high on PCP at the time. (one was also high when she later met with police to identify the culprits.) One was an eighth-grader whose own aunt contradicted parts of his trial testimony. Even in the absence of an alternative account of the crime, the jury took more than a week—and many dozens of votes—to reach its final verdict. Had defendants offered a unified counter-narrative, based on the withheld evidence, one or more jurors could well have concluded that the Government had not proved its case beyond a reasonable doubt.

Again, the issue here concerns the difference between two criminal cases. The Government got the case it most wanted—the one in which the defendants, each in an effort to save himself, formed something of a circular firing squad. The Government avoided the case it most feared—the one in which the defendants acted jointly to show that a man known to assault women like Fuller committed her murder. The difference between the two cases lay in the Government's files—evidence of obvious relevance that prosecutors nonetheless chose to suppress. I think it could have mattered to the trial's outcome. For that reason, I respectfully dissent.

Points for Discussion

a. Prosecutorial Duty to Seek Evidence from Prosecution Team

In *Kyles v. Whitley*, 514 U.S. 419 (1995), the Court clarified that the duty to turn over to the defense exculpatory evidence encompasses a duty to actively seek out any such evidence from the extended members of the prosecution "team," *i.e.,* "others acting on the government's behalf in the case, including the police." In *Kyles*, the prosecution failed to learn of exculpatory evidence in the hands of the police who were involved in the investigation of the case. While the state argued that the prosecution should not be held responsible for exculpatory evidence the police did not disclose to it, the Court responded, "any argument for excusing a prosecutor from disclosing what he does not happen to know about boils down to a plea to substitute the police for the prosecutor, and even for the courts themselves, as the final arbiters of the government's obligation to ensure fair trials."

b. Disclosure of Confidential Information

The defendant's right to *Brady* evidence generally overcomes statutory rules of privilege or confidentiality. *See Davis v. Alaska*, 415 U.S. 308 (1974) (withholding of presumptively confidential juvenile criminal record violated defendant's Confrontation Clause right to impeach the witness with the record); *Pennsylvania v. Ritchie*, 480 U.S. 39 (1987) (holding that, while a criminal defendant charged with child abuse cannot conduct an unsupervised search of child welfare agency confidential files to find exculpatory evidence, the defendant could request specific information, and the trial court could decide the exculpatory value of the evidence in chambers); *Roviaro v. United States*, 353 U.S. 53 (1957) (establishing an exception to the general rule against disclosure of an informant's identity, holding that "where the disclosure of an informer's identity is relevant and helpful to the defense of an accused, or is essential to a fair determination of a cause, the privilege of nondisclosure must give way.")

c. Disclosure of Inadmissible Evidence

In *Wood v. Bartholmew*, 526 U.S. 1 (1995), the Court held that the failure to disclose a polygraph test showing that a prosecution witness had lied did not have to be disclosed under *Brady* because the polygraph test results would be inadmissible at trial. Since *Wood*, lower courts have divided over whether it means all inadmissible evidence is automatically excluded from *Brady*. In *Commonwealth v. Willis*, 46 A.3d 648 (Pa. 2012), the Pennsylvania Supreme Court summarized the nature of the division among the lower courts as divided into three camps. Some hold inadmissible evidence is immaterial as a matter of law. *See Hoke v. Netherland*, 92 F.3d 1350 (4th Cir. 1996); *State v. Pena*, 353 S.W.3d 797 (Tex. Crim. App. 2011). Others hold that evidence that is inadmissible at trial may be material under *Brady* if it would lead to admissible evidence. *See, e.g., United States v. Gil*, 297 F.3d 93 (2d Cir. 2002); *United States v. Sudikoff*, 36 F. Supp. 2d 1196 (C.D. Cal. 1999). Still a third group treat the admissibility of derivative evidence as simply one factor to consider in the totality of the circumstances regarding whether the disclosure would have "put the whole case in such a different light as to undermine confidence in the verdict." *See, e.g., Unites States v. Sipe*, 388 F.3d 471 (5th Cir. 2004). In *Willis*, a plurality of the Pennsylvania Supreme Court placed itself in this third camp.

d. The *Bagley* Materiality Standard

In *Smith v. Cain*, 565 U.S. 73 (2012), a prosecutor withheld a police report that undermined its case. The police report had prior inconsistent statements of the sole eyewitness indicating he could not identify anyone from the killing. Although the Court's opinion in *Smith* is rather short and unexceptional, the oral argument was extremely illuminating on the contested issue of whether the materiality standard from *Bagley* should be applied in a trial or pretrial setting. In other words, if pretrial or at trial the prosecution has exculpatory evidence or information, can the prosecution nonetheless not disclose the evidence or information, taking the position that the evidence or information is not "material" under *Bagley*— that is, there is no reasonable probability that disclosure will alter the result of the proceeding?

The Supreme Court has never had to decide this issue in a written opinion, as it only ever reviews the error on appeal. In oral argument in *Smith v. Cain*, however, members of the Court expressed their strong belief that the standard for disclosure at trial is not the standard for discerning error on appeal. The Justices were incredulous that the prosecutor's office made the argument that, although the undisclosed information was exculpatory in that it was helpful to the defense, it did not need to be disclosed because it was not "material" under *Bagley*. An excerpt from the oral argument demonstrates the Justices' view:

> JUSTICE SOTOMAYOR: Tell me why [the witness's statements] didn't on their face constitute Brady materials that needed to be turned over. What's the legal principle that doesn't make them Brady?
>
> [PROSECUTOR]: Because if they had been presented—if those statements had been presented to defense—or presented to a jury, the—the outcome would have remained the same. The jury—
>
> JUSTICE GINSBURG: How do you know? How do you know? How can you possibly know? The jury is supposed to decide on the credibility of this witness.
>
> JUSTICE KENNEDY: And with all respect I think you misspoke when you—you were asked what is—the test for when Brady material must be turned over. And you said whether or not there's a reasonable probability—reasonable likelihood—pardon me—a reasonable probability that the result would have been different. That's the test for when there has been a Brady violation. You don't determine your Brady obligation by the test for the Brady violation. You're transposing two very different things. And so, that's incorrect.
>
> JUSTICE KAGAN: Did your office ever consider just confessing error in this case? You've had a bunch of time to think about it. You know? We took cert a while ago. I'm just wondering whether you've ever considered confessing error.
>
> [PROSECUTOR]: Your Honor, we believe that we have an argument that these statements are not material.
>
> JUSTICE SCALIA: I—may I suggest that—

[PROSECUTOR]: Yes.

JUSTICE SCALIA:—you stop fighting as to whether it should be turned over? Of course, it should have been turned over. . . . Why don't you give that up?

Hear It

To listen to the oral argument in Smith, go to: http://www.oyez.org/cas es/2010-2019/2011/2011_10_8145.

e. Remedying *Brady* Violations

Just nine months before *Smith v. Cain*, the Court considered another case of withheld exculpatory evidence out of the same prosecutor's office—Orleans Parish District Attorney. In *Connick v. Thompson*, 563 U.S. 51 (2011), John Thompson sued Orleans Parish District Attorney Harry Connick, Sr. and his office alleging that their deliberate indifference to *Brady* violations and failure to train caused the *Brady* violation in his case which led to his spending 14 years on death row in solitary confinement. The jury had awarded John Thompson $14 million in damages. A deeply divided Supreme Court reversed. Justice Thomas wrote for the majority that, because Thompson did not allege a pattern of violations (although there had been four reversals of convictions from that office on *Brady* violations), and his theory of recovery was based on the egregiousness of one violation, the single incident by a rogue prosecutor was not the result of a failure to train. Justice Thomas indicated that prosecutors are given tools in law school and beyond to ensure they can follow the dictates of *Brady*. The four-member dissent disagreed that this was a one-violation case, cataloguing the many *Brady* violations in the case, and arguing that Connick's office demonstrated a deliberate indifference to *Brady* violations and training. Harry Connick testified that he had "stopped reading law books and looking at opinions" after being elected District Attorney in 1974 and that there was a need for *Brady* training in the office. Not only did the dissent find any training absent and the understanding of *Brady* in the office deficient, it found that there is no requirement in law school or for the Bar exam that future lawyers learn *Brady*.

f. *Brady* and Guilty Pleas

In *United States v. Ruiz*, 536 U.S. 622 (2002), the Supreme Court held that prosecutors are not required to disclose impeachment information relating to informants or other witnesses before entering into a binding plea agreement with a criminal defendant. Although constitutional fair trial guarantees provide that defendants have the right to receive exculpatory impeachment material for trial, Justice Breyer stated that a defendant who pleads guilty foregoes a fair trial and various other constitutional guarantees. *See* Chapter 16, Guilty Pleas, *infra*.

g. Post-Conviction Discovery of Exculpatory Evidence

There is a division of opinion regarding whether prosecutors must turn over exculpatory evidence that comes to light post-conviction. While the American Bar Association amended Model Rule 3.8 to require the disclosure of such evidence, some courts disagree. See *Commission for Lawyer Discipline v. Hanna*, 513 S.W.3d 175 (Tex. App. 2016).

Food for Thought

Which of the following pieces of information must be disclosed by the prosecution? A) The main homicide detective in a murder case was accused in another murder case of fabricating a police report. That accusation is being investigated by the police department's internal investigation unit; B) In a murder prosecution, a prosecution witness with an unrelated pending charge asks the prosecutor whether she can help him get out of that charge. The prosecutor responds that she can make no promises; C) A police report indicating that an eyewitness to the murder initially tells the police she cannot identify the killer. (Subsequently, she identifies the defendant and says she was just too scared the first time they asked.); D) Information that the police first pursued another suspect in the murder, but which investigation was dropped when that suspect's alibi was confirmed. Prosecutors are obligated to turn over favorable evidence in a timely manner. In deciding what is timely, consider the prosecutions' reasons for wanting to turn over the evidence later and the defense attorney's reasons for needing the evidence earlier to make effective use of it. Go back through the examples in the following Hypo, assuming it is favorable, consider whether it would be "timely" to turn over that information just before trial.

Hypo: *Police Activity Sheet*

James Lambert was convicted and sentenced to death for the murder of two patrons during a robbery of Prince's Lounge. One of the main prosecution witnesses was Bernard Jackson, who admitted being involved in the robbery and who named Lambert and Bruce Reese as his accomplices. The state failed to disclose a "police activity sheet" which noted that a photo display containing a photo of a man named Lawrence

Woodlock was shown to two witnesses to the Prince's Lounge robbery but no identification was made. The sheet also noted that Woodlock was named as a co-defendant by Bernard Jackson. The defense argues that the sheet is exculpatory because it suggested that someone other than him or in addition to him committed the crime, and also it could have been used to further impeach Jackson who named Woodlock as an accomplice before he named Lambert. The state argues that the activity sheet contains nothing more than an "ambiguously worded notation" because Jackson at the time was under investigation for at least 13 armed robberies of bars and that he was more likely naming Woodlock as a codefendant in one of those other robberies, considering the police never pursued Woodlock for this charge. What do you think? *See Wetzel v. Lambert, 565 U.S. 520 (2012).*

C. Preservation of Evidence

Under normal circumstances, the duty to disclose evidence encompasses the duty to preserve evidence once it comes within the custody and control of the government. The question that arises, however, is what should be the consequences of the government's failure to meet this responsibility of preservation.

Arizona v. Youngblood

488 U.S. 51 (1988).

CHIEF JUSTICE REHNQUIST delivered the opinion of the Court.

Respondent Larry Youngblood was convicted by a Pima County, Arizona, jury of child molestation, sexual assault, and kidnaping. The Arizona Court of Appeals reversed his conviction on the ground that the State had failed to preserve semen samples from the victim's body and clothing. We granted certiorari to consider the extent to which the Due Process Clause of the Fourteenth Amendment requires the State to preserve evidentiary material that might be useful to a criminal defendant.

On October 29, 1983, David L., a 10-year-old boy, attended a church service with his mother. After he left the service at about 9:30 p.m., the boy went to a

Hear It

You can hear the oral argument in *Youngblood* at: http://www.oyez.org/cases/1980-1989/1988/1988_86_1904.

carnival behind the church, where he was abducted by a middle-aged man of medium height and weight. The assailant drove the boy to a secluded area near a ravine and molested him. He then took the boy to an unidentified, sparsely furnished house where he sodomized the boy four times. Afterwards, the assailant tied the boy up while he went outside to start his car. Once the assailant started the car, albeit with some difficulty, he returned to the house and again sodomized the boy. The assailant then sent the boy to the bathroom to wash up before he returned him to the carnival. He threatened to kill the boy if he told anyone about the attack. The entire ordeal lasted about 1½ hours.

After the boy made his way home, his mother took him to Kino Hospital. At the hospital, a physician treated the boy for rectal injuries. The physician also used a "sexual assault kit" to collect evidence of the attack. The Tucson Police Department provided such kits to all hospitals in Pima County for use in sexual assault cases. Under standard procedure, the victim of a sexual assault was taken to a hospital, where a physician used the kit to collect evidence. The kit included paper to collect saliva samples, a tube for obtaining a blood sample, microscopic slides for making smears, a set of Q-Tip-like swabs, and a medical examination report. Here, the physician used the swab to collect samples from the boy's rectum and mouth. He then made a microscopic slide of the samples. The doctor also obtained samples of the boy's saliva, blood, and hair. The physician did not examine the samples at any time. The police placed the kit in a secure refrigerator at the police station. At the hospital, the police also collected the boy's underwear and T-shirt. This clothing was not refrigerated or frozen.

Nine days after the attack, on November 7, 1983, the police asked the boy to pick out his assailant from a photographic lineup. The boy identified respondent as the assailant. Respondent was not located by the police until four weeks later; he was arrested on December 9, 1983.

On November 8, 1983, Edward Heller, a police criminologist, examined the sexual assault kit. He testified that he followed standard department procedure, which was to examine the slides and determine whether sexual contact had occurred. After he determined that such contact had occurred, the criminologist did not perform any other tests, although he placed the assault kit back in the refrigerator. He testified that tests to identify blood group substances were not routinely conducted during the initial examination of an assault kit and in only about half of all cases in any event. He did not test the clothing at this time.

Respondent was indicted on charges of child molestation, sexual assault, and kidnaping. The State moved to compel respondent to provide blood and saliva samples for comparison with the material gathered through the use of the sexual assault kit, but the trial court denied the motion on the ground that the State had not obtained a sufficiently large semen sample to make a valid comparison. The prosecutor then asked the State's criminologist to perform an ABO blood group test on the rectal swab sample in an attempt to ascertain the blood type of the boy's assailant. This test failed to detect any blood group substances in the sample.

In January 1985, the police criminologist examined the boy's clothing for the first time. He found one semen stain on the boy's underwear and another on the rear of his T-shirt. The criminologist tried to obtain blood group substances from both stains using the ABO technique, but was unsuccessful. He also performed a P–30 protein molecule test on the stains, which indicated that only a small quantity of semen was present on the clothing; it was inconclusive as to the assailant's identity. The Tucson Police Department had just begun using this test, which was then used in slightly more than half of the crime laboratories in the country.

Respondent's principal defense at trial was that the boy had erred in identifying him as the perpetrator of the crime. In this connection, both a criminologist for the State and an expert witness for respondent testified as to what might have been shown by tests performed on the samples shortly after they were gathered, or by later tests performed on the samples from the boy's clothing had the clothing been properly refrigerated. The court instructed the jury that if they found the State had destroyed or lost evidence, they might "infer that the true fact is against the State's interest."

The jury found respondent guilty as charged, but the Arizona Court of Appeals reversed the judgment of conviction. It stated that " 'when identity is an issue at trial and the police permit the destruction of evidence that could eliminate the defendant as the perpetrator, such loss is material to the defense and is a denial of due process.' " The Court of Appeals concluded on the basis of the expert testimony at trial that timely performance of tests with properly preserved semen samples could have produced results that might have completely exonerated respondent. The Court of Appeals reached this conclusion even though it did "not imply any bad faith on the part of the State." The Supreme Court of Arizona denied the State's petition for review, and we granted certiorari. We now reverse.

Our most recent decision in this area of the law, *California v. Trombetta*, 467 U.S. 479 (1984), arose out of a drunk-driving prosecution in which the State had introduced test results indicating the concentration of alcohol in the blood of two motorists. The defendants sought to suppress the test results on the ground that the State had failed to preserve the breath samples used in the test. We rejected this argument for several reasons: first, "the officers here were acting in 'good faith and in accord with their normal practice,' second, in the light of the procedures actually used the chances that preserved samples would have exculpated the defendants were slim, and, third, even if the samples might have shown inaccuracy in the tests, the defendants had 'alternative means of demonstrating their innocence.' " In the present case, the likelihood that the preserved materials would have enabled the defendant to exonerate himself appears to be greater than it was in *Trombetta*, but here, unlike in *Trombetta*, the State did not attempt to make any use of the materials in its own case in chief.

Our decisions in related areas have stressed the importance for constitutional purposes of good or bad faith on the part of the Government when the claim is based on loss of evidence attributable to the Government. In *United States v. Marion*, 404 U.S. 307 (1971), we said that "no actual prejudice to the conduct of the defense is alleged or proved, and there is no showing that the Government intentionally delayed to gain some tactical advantage over appellees or to harass them." Similarly, in *United States v. Valenzuela-Bernal*, [458 U.S. 858 (1982)] we considered whether the Government's deportation of two witnesses who were illegal aliens violated due process. We held that the prompt deportation of the witnesses was justified "upon the Executive's good-faith determination that they possess no evidence favorable to the defendant in a criminal prosecution."

The Due Process Clause of the Fourteenth Amendment, as interpreted in *Brady*, makes the good or bad faith of the State irrelevant when the State fails to disclose to the defendant material exculpatory evidence. But we think the Due Process Clause requires a different result when we deal with the failure of the State to preserve evidentiary material of which no more can be said than that it could have been subjected to tests, the results of which might have exonerated the defendant. Part of the reason for the difference in treatment is found in the observation made by the Court in *Trombetta*, that "whenever potentially exculpatory evidence is permanently lost, courts face the treacherous task of divining the import of materials whose contents are unknown and, very often, disputed." Part of it stems from our unwillingness to read the "fundamental fairness" requirement of the Due Process Clause, as imposing on the police an undifferentiated and absolute duty to retain and to preserve all material that might be of conceivable evidentiary significance in a particular prosecution. We think that requiring a defendant to show bad faith on the part of the police both limits the extent of the police's obligation to preserve evidence to reasonable bounds and confines it to that class of cases where the interests of justice most clearly require it, *i.e.*, those cases in which the police themselves by their conduct indicate that the evidence could form a basis for exonerating the defendant. We therefore hold that unless a criminal defendant can show bad faith on the part of the police, failure to preserve potentially useful evidence does not constitute a denial of due process of law.

In this case, the police collected the rectal swab and clothing on the night of the crime; respondent was not taken into custody until six weeks later. The failure of the police to refrigerate the clothing and to perform tests on the semen samples can at worst be described as negligent. None of this information was concealed from respondent at trial, and the evidence—such as it was—was made available to respondent's expert who declined to perform any tests on the samples. The

Arizona Court of Appeals noted that there was no suggestion of bad faith on the part of the police. It follows, therefore, that there was no violation of the Due Process Clause.

The Arizona Court of Appeals also referred somewhat obliquely to the State's "inability to quantitatively test" certain semen samples with the newer P–30 test. If the court meant by this statement that the Due Process Clause is violated when the police fail to use a particular investigatory tool, we strongly disagree. The situation here is no different than a prosecution for drunken driving that rests on police observation alone; the defendant is free to argue to the finder of fact that a breathalyzer test might have been exculpatory, but the police do not have a constitutional duty to perform any particular tests.

The judgment of the Arizona Court of Appeals is reversed, and the case is remanded for further proceedings not inconsistent with this opinion.

Reversed.

Justice Stevens, concurring in the judgment.

Three factors are of critical importance. First, at the time the police failed to refrigerate the victim's clothing, and thus negligently lost potentially valuable evidence, they had at least as great an interest in preserving the evidence as did the person later accused of the crime. Indeed, at that time it was more likely that the evidence would have been useful to the police—who were still conducting an investigation—and to the prosecutor—who would later bear the burden of establishing guilt beyond a reasonable doubt—than to the defendant. Even without a prophylactic sanction such as dismissal of the indictment, the State has a strong incentive to preserve the evidence.

Second, although it is not possible to know whether the lost evidence would have revealed any relevant information, it is unlikely that the defendant was prejudiced by the State's omission. In examining witnesses and in her summation, defense counsel impressed upon the jury the fact that the State failed to preserve the evidence and that the State could have conducted tests that might well have exonerated the defendant. The trial judge instructed the jury: "If you find that the State has allowed to be destroyed or lost any evidence whose content or quality are in issue, you may infer that the true fact is against the State's interest." As a result, the uncertainty as to what the evidence might have proved was turned to the defendant's advantage.

Third, the fact that no juror chose to draw the permissive inference that proper preservation of the evidence would have demonstrated that the defendant was not the assailant suggests that the lost evidence was "immaterial." "The proper standard of materiality must reflect our overriding concern with the justice of the finding of guilt," and a State's failure to turn over (or preserve) potentially exculpatory evidence therefore "must be evaluated in the context of the entire record." *United States v. Agurs*, 427 U.S. 97, 112 (1976). In declining defense counsel's and the court's invitations to draw the permissive inference, the jurors in effect indicated that, in their view, the other evidence at trial was so overwhelming that it was highly improbable that the lost evidence was exculpatory. In this case, the jury has already performed this calculus based on its understanding of the evidence introduced at trial. Presumably, in a case involving a closer question as to guilt or innocence, the jurors would have been more ready to infer that the lost evidence was exculpatory.

With these factors in mind, I concur in the Court's judgment. I do not, however, join the Court's opinion because it announces a proposition of law that is much broader than necessary to decide this case. It states that "unless a criminal defendant can show bad faith on the part of the police, failure to preserve potentially useful evidence does not constitute a denial of due process of law." In my opinion, there may well be cases in which the defendant is unable to prove that the State acted in bad faith but in which the loss or destruction of evidence is nonetheless so critical to the defense as to make a criminal trial fundamentally unfair. This, however, is not such a case. Accordingly, I concur in the judgment.

JUSTICE BLACKMUN, with whom JUSTICE BRENNAN and JUSTICE MARSHALL join, dissenting.

The Constitution requires that criminal defendants be provided with a fair trial, not merely a "good faith" try at a fair trial. Respondent here, by what may have been nothing more than police ineptitude, was denied the opportunity to present a full defense. That ineptitude deprived respondent of his guaranteed right to due process of law. In reversing, this Court, in my view, misreads the import of its prior cases and unduly restricts the protections of the Due Process Clause. An understanding of due process demonstrates that the evidence which was allowed to deteriorate was "constitutionally material," and that its absence significantly prejudiced respondent. I dissent.

The majority has identified clearly one type of violation, for police action affirmatively aimed at cheating the process undoubtedly violates the Constitution. But to suggest that this is the only way in which the Due Process Clause can be violated cannot be correct. Regardless of intent or lack thereof, police action that results in a defendant's receiving an unfair trial constitutes a deprivation of due process. The Court in *Brady* ruled that "the suppression by the prosecution of evidence favorable to an accused upon request violates due process where the evidence is material either to guilt or to punishment, irrespective of the good faith or bad faith of the prosecution." The *Brady* Court went on to explain that the principle underlying earlier cases, *e.g., Mooney v. Holohan,* 294 U.S. 103 (1935) (violation of due process when prosecutor presented perjured testimony), is "not punishment of society for misdeeds of a prosecutor but avoidance of an unfair trial to the accused." The failure to turn over material evidence "casts the prosecutor in the role of an architect of a proceeding that does not comport with standards of justice, even though, as in the present case, his action is not 'the result of guile.' "

In *Trombetta,* the Court also relied on *United States v. Agurs,* which required a prosecutor to turn over to the defense evidence that was "clearly supportive of a claim of innocence" even without a defense request. The Court noted that the prosecutor's duty was not one of constitutional dimension unless the evidence was such that its "omission deprived the defendant of a fair trial," and explained:

> Nor do we believe the constitutional obligation is measured by the moral culpability, or the willfulness, of the prosecutor. If evidence highly probative of innocence is in his file, he should be presumed to recognize its significance even if he has actually overlooked it. If the suppression of evidence results in constitutional error, it is because of the character of the evidence, not the character of the prosecutor.

Agurs thus made plain that the prosecutor's state of mind is *not* determinative. Rather, the proper standard must focus on the materiality of the evidence, and that standard "must reflect our overriding concern with the justice of the finding of guilt."

Brady and *Agurs* could not be more clear in their holdings that a prosecutor's bad faith in interfering with a defendant's access to material evidence is *not* an essential part of a due process violation. Nor did *Trombetta* create such a requirement. *Trombetta* demonstrates that the absence of bad faith does not end the analysis. The determination in *Trombetta* that the prosecution acted in good faith and according to normal practice merely prefaced the primary inquiry, which centers on the "constitutional materiality" of the evidence itself. There is nothing in *Trombetta* that intimates that good faith alone should be the measure.

The cases in this area clearly establish that police actions taken in bad faith are not the only species of police conduct that can result in a violation of due process. As *Agurs* points out, it makes no sense to overturn a conviction because a malicious prosecutor withholds information that he mistakenly believes to be material, but which actually would have been of no help to the defense. In the same way, it makes no sense to ignore the fact that a defendant has been denied a fair trial because the State allowed evidence that was material to the defense to deteriorate beyond the point of usefulness, simply because the police were inept rather than malicious.

I also doubt that the "bad faith" standard creates the bright-line rule sought by the majority. Apart from the inherent difficulty a defendant would have in obtaining evidence to show a lack of good faith, the line between "good faith" and "bad faith" is anything but bright, and the majority's formulation may well create more questions than it answers. What constitutes bad faith for these purposes? Does a defendant have to show actual malice, or would recklessness, or the deliberate failure to establish standards for maintaining and preserving evidence, be sufficient? Does "good faith police work" require a certain minimum of diligence, or will a lazy officer, who does not walk the few extra steps to the evidence refrigerator, be considered to be acting in good faith? While the majority leaves

Food for Thought

Why should the good faith or the bad faith of the police matter when the issue is loss of evidence that could have proven innocence? In 2000, Youngblood's attorneys requested testing of the degraded semen sample through the technology of DNA testing. The testing excluded Youngblood and he was exonerated. Does that information influence your view of what the standard should be for loss of evidence today, at least in particular kinds of cases where DNA testing is possible?

these questions for another day, its quick embrace of a "bad faith" standard has not brightened the line; it only has moved the line so as to provide fewer protections for criminal defendants.

Point for Discussion

Distinguishing *Youngblood*

At least one state has distinguished the situation in *Youngblood*, where the results of the testing are not known, from the situation where it is known it would have been favorable to the defense. In *Galbraith v. Commonwealth*, 18 Va. App. 734, 446 S.E.2d 633 (1994), the court stated that, "If it is clear that, had the evidence been properly preserved, it would have formed a basis for exonerating the defendant, then absent a showing to the contrary we must assume that the police were not acting in good faith."

Hypo 1: *Discovery of File of Exoneree*

Kurt Cross is prosecuted for aggravated rape and convicted. Years later, Cross is exonerated through DNA testing. The result of the DNA test is run through the CODIS database (storing DNA profiles of convicted felons) and there is a "match" with the DNA profile of Gregory Forman. The prosecution now charges Forman with the aggravated rape. Forman's lawyer requests under *Brady* the prosecution's file from Cross's previous prosecution. After a diligent search and investigation, the prosecution cannot find the Cross file at all. What result under *Youngblood*?

> ## Hypo 2: *Lost Gun and Bullet*
>
> In a murder investigation, a bullet is recovered from the decedent's body. The police execute a search warrant on suspect Frank Girard's house. A gun is located in a dresser drawer and taken to the crime laboratory. The lab finds a "match" between the bullet and the gun. An officer transporting the gun and bullet back to the courthouse is in an accident while crossing a bridge. The accident is not the officer's fault, but nonetheless, it causes the evidence he is carrying to fall to the river below never to be seen or found again. At trial, the state introduces the ballistics report about the match over the defendant's objection. What are the defendant's options in terms of requests made to the court? If the ballistics report comes in and the defendant is convicted, what result on appeal?

D. Discovery Under Rules and Statutes

Most jurisdictions provide statutory discovery that is more extensive than what the Constitution requires, but less than what is granted in civil cases. For example, very few jurisdictions provide for depositions of witnesses. While states vary, most state discovery rules are variations on Federal Rule of Criminal Procedure 16. The rules and statutes provide for discovery in a number of generalized areas as follows: defendant's own statements to law enforcement, whether written, oral or recorded; defendant's own criminal records; documents and tangible evidence, such as weapons, clothing, drugs, photographs and the like, intended for use at trial; scientific evidence and reports intended for use at trial. Some subsidiary rules also include: other crimes evidence (Fed. R. Evid. 404(b)); co-defendants' statements; co-conspirators' statements.

Federal and most State discovery rules do not require prosecutors to disclose witness statements or even the identity of its witnesses, the general rationale being the importance of witness safety. The defense is often not specifically entitled to police reports either, although redacted reports are typically turned over as the most efficient way for busy prosecutors to comply with their discovery obligations.

Food for Thought

Why are there such strict limits on disclosure by the prosecution? Why is the presumption exclusion from discovery and not open file discovery, where the prosecution must disclose information unless the prosecution can give valid reasons why that material should not be turned over? What are the benefits of open file discovery?

Generally, the prosecution cannot seek reciprocal discovery from the defendant until the defendant has sought discovery first through a request or motion. Disclosure under discovery rules is considered an ongoing obligation as parties learn about and gather new evidence and information. Discretion is normally left to the court to on how and whether to sanction a party for noncompliance with discovery rules. Noncompliance does not always result in exclusion of the evidence.

Points for Discussion

a. The Jencks Act

In the federal system, the *Jencks* rule strikes an accommodation between protecting witnesses from possible pretrial harassment and providing the defense with an opportunity to impeach witnesses who have made statements inconsistent with their trial testimony. In *Jencks v. United States*, 353 U.S. 657 (1957), the Court exercised its supervisory power over federal courts to require disclosure of prior statements by witnesses *after* they testify. Congress then enacted the Jencks Act, 18 U.S.C. § 3500, and the essence of the Jencks Act is now contained in Rule 26.2 of the Federal Rules of Criminal Procedure. The Jencks Act and Rule 26.2 require both parties—the prosecution and the defense—to provide to the opposition prior statements by its own witnesses.

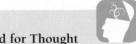

Food for Thought

Suppose the government introduces in evidence the out-of-court statements of the defendant's unindicted co-conspirator, who has fled the country and cannot be called to the witness stand. Could you invoke the Jencks Act to obtain any prior statements by the co-conspirator? Federal Rule of Evidence 806 equates hearsay with live testimony to the extent that if an out-of-court statement is admitted, the opposing party may impeach the statement with "any evidence which would be admissible for those purposes if the declarant had testified as a witness." In light of Rule 806, can you invoke the Jencks Act to obtain other statements made by the co-conspirator after he "testifies" via hearsay?

In order to qualify as "Jencks" and trigger disclosure, the statement must: (1) be that of a witness called by the party possessing the statement; (2) have been contemporaneously recorded (whether by means of writing, audio, or video); and (3) relate to the subject matter of the witness' testimony.

b. Jencks and Non-Testifying Witnesses

The Second and Fourth Circuits have held that the underlying "witness safety" purposes of the Jencks Act require that non-testifying declarants be treated like testifying government witnesses, thus their statements are shielded from pretrial discovery. *In re United States*, 834 F.2d 283 (2d Cir.1987); *United States v. Roberts*, 811 F.2d 257 (4th Cir.1987) (en banc). Does this inconsistent judicial interpretation of the Jencks Act allow the government to employ a "Heads I win. Tails you lose" approach, *i.e.* when defendants seek pretrial discovery, courts shield hearsay from disclosure by ruling that hearsay declarants are "witnesses" under the Jencks Act, but when defendants seek discovery at trial, courts deny disclosure on grounds that declarants are not witnesses within the meaning of the Jencks Act?

Hypo: *Videotape Request*

Your client was caught in a major DEA "sting" operation focusing on the manufacture and sale of PCP. Your client allegedly delivered certain controlled chemicals often used in the manufacture of PCP, and was paid for these chemicals with a large quantity of PCP. The exchange was made with Melvin Jones, an undercover agent of the Drug Enforcement Agency. You interviewed Mr. Jones who related that your client was merely one of many persons who had purchased drugs and chemicals during the two-month sting.

Your client denies dealing with Mr. Jones, and you question whether Mr. Jones can remember the details of this one alleged "drug-deal" during a lengthy sting operation involving many people. You also are aware that the DEA often uses a hidden video camera to record its sting operations. You would like to discover if there is any record of the alleged exchange between your client and Mr. Jones. On what grounds can you request disclosure of any existing videotape?

In addition to, or in place of the videotape, can you request disclosure of: the identity of any other DEA agents or law enforcement officials who were present and observed the alleged exchange? any summary or memorandum of the exchange prepared by law enforcement officials? che identity of other defendants who had dealings with the DEA sting operation within a one-week period of your client's alleged exchange? the status of charges against other defendants prosecuted because of the sting operation? any plea bargains struck between the prosecution and these other defendants?

E. Discovery by the Prosecution

Many jurisdictions give the prosecution an unconditional right to be notified prior to trial that the defendant intends to raise the defense of insanity and to present expert testimony to support this claim. Such provisions allow the prosecution the time to prepare its own expert witnesses to rebut the claim of insanity. Federal Rule 12.1 embodies the approach utilized by a majority of states. Federal Rules of Criminal Procedure 12.2, 12.3 and 12.4 also mandate, respectively, the disclosure of defendant's intent to raise the defense of alibi, an actual or believed exercise of public authority on behalf of a law enforcement or federal intelligence agency, or the names of corporate parties with an interest in the case.

Williams v. Florida

399 U.S. 78 (1970).

JUSTICE WHITE delivered the opinion of the Court.

Hear It

You can hear the oral argument in *Williams* at: http://www.oyez.org/cases/1960-1969/1969/1969_927. (Note that a separate issue argued in this case, the constitutionality of a jury of less that twelve, is covered in Chapter 17.)

Prior to his trial for robbery in the State of Florida, petitioner filed a "Motion for a Protective Order," seeking to be excused from the requirements of Rule 1.200 of the Florida Rules of Criminal Procedure, 33 F.S.A. That rule requires a defendant, on written demand of the prosecuting attorney, to give notice in advance of trial if the defendant intends to claim an alibi, and to furnish the prosecuting attorney with information as to the place where he claims to have been and with the names and addresses of the alibi witnesses he intends to use. In his motion petitioner openly declared his intent to claim an alibi, but objected to the further disclosure requirements on the ground that the rule "compels the Defendant in a criminal case to be a witness against himself" in violation of his Fifth and Fourteenth Amendment rights. The motion was denied.

Florida's notice-of-alibi rule is in essence a requirement that a defendant submit to a limited form of pretrial discovery by the State whenever he intends to rely at trial on the defense of alibi. In exchange for the defendant's disclosure of the witnesses he proposes to use to establish that defense, the State in turn is required to notify the defendant of any witnesses it proposes to offer in rebuttal to that defense. Both sides are under a continuing duty promptly to disclose the names and addresses of additional witnesses bearing on the alibi as they become available. The threatened sanction for failure to comply is the exclusion at trial of the defendant's alibi evidence—except for his own testimony—or, in the case of the State, the exclusion of the State's evidence offered in rebuttal of the alibi.

In this case, following the denial of his Motion for a Protective Order, petitioner complied with the alibi rule and gave the State the name and address of one Mary Scotty. Mrs. Scotty was summoned to the office of the State Attorney on the morning of the trial, where she gave pretrial testimony. At the trial itself, Mrs. Scotty, petitioner, and petitioner's wife all testified that the three of them had been in Mrs. Scotty's apartment during the time of the robbery. On two occasions during cross-examination of Mrs. Scotty, the prosecuting attorney confronted her with her earlier deposition in which she had given dates and times that in some respects did not correspond with the dates and times given at trial. Mrs. Scotty adhered to her trial story, insisting that she had been mistaken in her earlier testimony. The State also offered in rebuttal the testimony of one of the officers investigating the robbery who claimed that Mrs. Scotty had asked him for directions on the afternoon in question during the time when she claimed to have been in her apartment with petitioner and his wife.

We need not linger over the suggestion that the discovery permitted the State against petitioner in this case deprived him of "due process" or a "fair trial." Florida law provides for liberal discovery by the defendant against the State, and the notice-of-alibi rule is itself carefully hedged with reciprocal duties requiring state disclosure to the defendant. Given the ease with which an alibi can be fabricated, the State's interest in protecting itself against an eleventh-hour defense is both obvious and legitimate. Reflecting this interest, notice-of-alibi provisions, dating at least from 1927, are now in existence in a substantial number of States. The adversary system of trial is hardly an end in itself; it is not yet a poker game in which players enjoy an absolute right always to conceal their cards until played. We find ample room in that system, at least as far as "due process" is concerned, for the instant Florida rule, which is designed to enhance the search for truth in the criminal trial by insuring both the defendant and the State ample opportunity to investigate certain facts crucial to the determination of guilt or innocence.

Petitioner's major contention is that he was "compelled to be a witness against himself" contrary to the commands of the Fifth and Fourteenth Amendments because the notice-of-alibi rule required him to give the State the name and address of Mrs. Scotty in advance of trial and thus to furnish the State with information useful in convicting him. No pretrial statement of petitioner was introduced at trial; but armed with Mrs. Scotty's name and address and the knowledge that she was to be petitioner's alibi witness, the State was able to take her deposition in advance of trial and to find rebuttal testimony. Also, requiring him to reveal the elements of his defense is claimed to have interfered with his right to wait until after the State had presented its case to decide how to defend against it. We conclude, however, as has apparently every other court that has considered the issue, that the privilege against self-incrimination is not violated by a requirement that the defendant give notice of an alibi defense and disclose his alibi witnesses.

The defendant in a criminal trial is frequently forced to testify himself and to call other witnesses in an effort to reduce the risk of conviction. When he presents his witnesses, he must reveal their identity and submit them to cross-examination which in itself may prove incriminating or which may furnish the State with leads to incriminating rebuttal evidence. That the defendant faces such a dilemma demanding a choice between complete silence and presenting a defense has never been thought an invasion of the privilege against compelled self-incrimination. The pressures generated by the State's evidence may be severe but they do not vitiate the defendant's choice to present an alibi defense and witnesses to prove it, even though the attempted defense ends in catastrophe for the defendant. However "testimonial" or "incriminating" the alibi defense proves to be, it cannot be considered "compelled" within the meaning of the Fifth and Fourteenth Amendments.

Very similar constraints operate on the defendant when the State requires pretrial notice of alibi and the naming of alibi witnesses. Nothing in such a rule requires the defendant to rely on an alibi or prevents him from abandoning the defense; these matters are left to his unfettered choice. That choice must be made, but the pressures that bear on his pretrial decision are of the same nature as those that would induce him to call alibi witnesses at the trial: the force of historical fact beyond both his and the State's control and the strength of the State's case built on these facts. Response to that kind of pressure by offering evidence or testimony is not compelled self-incrimination transgressing the Fifth and Fourteenth Amendments.

In the case before us, the notice-of-alibi rule by itself in no way affected petitioner's crucial decision to call alibi witnesses or added to the legitimate pressures leading to that course of action. At most, the rule only compelled petitioner to accelerate the timing of his disclosure, forcing him to divulge at an earlier date information that the petitioner from the beginning planned to divulge at trial. Nothing in the Fifth Amendment privilege entitles a defendant as a matter of constitutional right to await the end of the State's case before announcing the nature of his defense, any more than it entitles him to await the jury's verdict on the State's case-in-chief before deciding whether or not to take the stand himself.

Petitioner concedes that absent the notice-of-alibi rule the Constitution would raise no bar to the court's granting the State a continuance at trial on the ground of surprise as soon as the alibi witness is called. Nor would there be self-incrimination problems if, during that continuance, the State was permitted to do precisely what it did here prior to trial: take the deposition of the witness and find rebuttal evidence. But if so utilizing a continuance is permissible under the Fifth and Fourteenth Amendments, then surely the same result may be accomplished through pretrial discovery, as it was here, avoiding the necessity of a disrupted trial. We decline to hold that the privilege against compulsory self-incrimination guarantees the defendant the right to surprise the State with an alibi defense.

JUSTICE BLACK, with whom JUSTICE DOUGLAS joins, concurring in part and dissenting in part.

The Court today holds that a State can require a defendant in a criminal case to disclose in advance of trial the nature of his alibi defense and give the names and addresses of witnesses he will call to support that defense. This requirement, the majority says, does

> **Food for Thought**
>
> A defendant's filing of a Notice of Alibi does not bind him to that defense. If the defendant does not pursue the alibi at trial, the prosecution cannot use the Notice and subsequent withdrawal against him. Why do you think that is?

not violate the Fifth Amendment prohibition against compelling a criminal defendant to be a witness against himself. Although this case itself involves only a notice-of-alibi provision, it is clear that the decision means that a State can require a defendant to disclose in advance of trial any and all information he might possibly use to defend himself at trial. This decision, in my view, is a radical and dangerous departure from the historical and constitutionally guaranteed right of a defendant in a criminal case to remain completely silent, requiring the State to prove its case without any assistance of any kind from the defendant himself.

> **Food for Thought**
>
> Other than notices of an insanity or alibi defense, many states condition the prosecution's right to discovery upon whether the defense has been granted discovery. The defense may then be required to provide the prosecutor with an opportunity to inspect or copy any physical evidence or reports of any scientific expert or test that the defense intends to use at trial. Why is it that the prosecution's right to reciprocal discovery would be dependent on its compliance with its own discovery obligation first? Why isn't it simply a two-way street?

F. Regulation of Discovery

The criminal defendant's right to pretrial discovery may come in conflict with the privacy rights of victims or other third parties. All jurisdictions empower the court to issue protective orders or limit the scope and terms of discovery, subject of course to constitutional limitations. If either party fails to comply with the court's discovery orders the court generally has a number of options for dealing with the violation.

Possible sanctions authorized in various states include: instruct the jury to assume the accuracy of certain facts that might have been established through the non-disclosed material;

Ethical Issue

Regardless of whether the identity of the opposing party's witness is learned through discovery or through investigation, a witness does not "belong" to either side and cannot be instructed not to speak with the opposing party. The American Bar Association, Model Rules of Professional Conduct, 3.4(a) provides: "A lawyer shall not unlawfully obstruct another party's access to evidence or unlawfully alter, destroy or conceal a document or other material having potential evidentiary value. A lawyer shall not counsel or assist another to do such act."

hold the offending party in contempt of court; declare a mistrial; or, in the case of a violation by the government, dismiss the prosecution. The least drastic and preferred remedy for violations of discovery orders is to order immediate disclosure and offer a continuance for the party to examine the material.

Point for Discussion

Preclusion Sanction

In *Taylor v. Illinois*, 484 U.S. 400 (1988), a trial court became frustrated with what it found were repeated and blatant discovery violations by the defense attorney such that when the defense attorney called a witness to testify whose identity had not been disclosed to the prosecution despite repeated requests, the trial court refused to allow the witness to testify. The Supreme Court held that the extreme sanction of precluding the witness's testimony did not violate the defendant's Sixth Amendment right to present witnesses on his behalf under the Compulsory Process Clause. In dissent, Justices Brennan, Marshall and Blackmun argued that it would have been fairer and more effective to directly sanction the offending attorney: "Deities may be able to visit the sins of the father on the son, but I cannot agree that courts should be permitted to visit the sins of the lawyer on the innocent client."

Executive Summary

Bill of Particulars. The defendant may move for a bill of particulars if the charging instrument does not give sufficient notice of the charges.

Prosecutor's Duty to Disclose Exculpatory Information. A prosecutor must disclose to the defendant exculpatory and impeachment information before trial.

Statutory Discovery by Defendant. Statutory and procedural rules provide for the defendant to request information from the prosecution about defendants' statements to law enforcement, and documents and tangible objects, reports of scientific tests.

Reciprocal Discovery by Prosecution. If a defendant requests and obtains information from the prosecution, the prosecution may obtain disclosure of documents and tangible objects as well as reports of scientific evidence in the possession of the defense and intended for use at trial.

Alibi Demand. Most jurisdictions permit the prosecution pretrial discovery about a defendant's alibi or a defendant's mental condition.

Sanctions for Discovery Violations. A court has the discretion to refuse to allow a party to introduce evidence at trial that was not produced pursuant to pretrial discovery rules.

Major Themes

a. Duty to Disclose—If the prosecution withholds information that is favorable to the defense and material to the defendant's guilt or punishment, the conviction violates due process and must be reversed.

b. Materiality—Favorable information is "material" if it had a reasonable probability of changing the outcome of the trial or sentence.

c. Pre-Trial Disclosure—While Supreme Court case law indicates in dicta that the standard for whether the prosecutor must disclose favorable information before trial is the same as the standard for reversal on appeal (*i.e.*, whether there was a reasonable probability the withheld evidence would have made a difference in the outcome), the ethical rules, common sense, and five Justices of the Court in a recent oral argument, all indicate that the prosecutor's duty at trial is simply to disclose favorable information, without reference to outcome or prejudice.

d. Team—The prosecutor's duty to disclose favorable evidence at trial includes evidence in the hands of any member of the prosecution team, including the police.

e. Guilty Plea—The prosecution does not have to disclose impeachment information prior to a guilty plea, but the Court has not yet ruled on whether it has to disclose non-impeachment exculpatory information for a valid guilty plea.

Test Your Knowledge

To assess your understanding of the material in this chapter, click here to take a quiz.

For More Information

• MARK E. CAMMACK & NORMAN M. GARLAND, ADVANCED CRIMINAL PROCEDURE (2006).

• WAYNE R. LAFAVE, JEROLD H. ISRAEL, NANCY J. KING & ORIN S. KERR, CRIMINAL PROCEDURE (5th ed. 2009).

• JEROLD H. ISRAEL & WAYNE R. LAFAVE, CRIMINAL PROCEDURE: CONSTITUTIONAL LIMITATIONS (8th ed. 2006).

• RUSSELL L. WEAVER, JOHN M. BURKOFF, CATHERINE HANCOCK, JANET HOEFFEL, STEVE FRIEDLAND & STEPHEN SINGER, PRINCIPLES OF CRIMINAL PROCEDURE Ch. 12 (6th ed. 2018).

CHAPTER 14

Joinder and Severance

A. Introduction

Joinder and severance of defendants or offenses revolve around the prosecution's charging instruments, such as the indictment or information. The primary issue is whether principles of fairness require that offenses or defendants should be joined or severed from the same charging instruments and cases. Most state criminal procedure rules as well as the Federal Rules of Criminal Procedure allow a prosecutor to combine offenses or defendants simply by charging multiple offenses and defendants in the same indictment or information.[1] In addition, if offenses or parties are charged separately but initially *could* have been joined together in a single indictment or information, the criminal rules give a trial judge the discretion to do so, with or without a motion. This delayed joinder is called consolidation of the charges.

Food for Thought

Joinder is really a marriage of claims or defendants, combining for better or worse for a trip through the criminal system. Severance is really a divorce, separating cases and claims for good.

The importance of joinder and severance cannot be overstated. It is a key decision often lying with the prosecutor's discretion. As one commentator has noted:

> The way in which the prosecutor chooses to combine offenses or defendants in a single indictment is perhaps second in importance only to his decision to prosecute.

Go Online

To best understand joinder and severance, it is useful to become acquainted with charging instruments. The main charging instruments are informations, pieces of paper filed by the prosecutor, and indictments, returned by grand juries. For the Federal Rule of Criminal Procedure on charging instruments, see Fed. R. Crim. P. 7: http://www.law.cornell.edu/rules/frcrmp/rule_7. For an actual indictment, go to: https://www.justice.gov/sites/default/files/usao-edpa/legacy/2014/10/22/liciardello_indictment.pdf

---

[1] When charging multiple offenses in a single charging document, each crime must be alleged in a separate count. A prosecutor must be careful to avoid charging separate crimes in a single count because to do so will cause the count to be duplicitous.

Whether a defendant is tried *en masse* with many other participants in an alleged crime, or in a separate trial of his own, will often be decisive of the outcome. Equally decisive may be the number of offenses which are cumulated against a single defendant, particularly if they are unconnected. 8 Moore's Federal Practice 8-3 (Cipes ed. 1993).

Joint trials have an important role in the criminal justice system by promoting efficiency and serving the interests of justice, *i.e.*, avoiding the shame and unfairness of inconsistent verdicts. They also save state funds, reduce inconvenience to witnesses and law enforcement authorities, and reduce delays in bringing defendants to trial.

Joint trials also offer strategic opportunities. Prosecutors might have the chance to paint a more complete picture of events with all or many of the defendants associated with a single case. Prosecutors also have greater opportunities to contrast stories and arguments of individual defendants and even to pit them against each other. On the other hand, defendants can be obscured sometimes when multiple parties are in the same courtroom and juries can compare the relative blameworthiness of behavior.

Once multiple offenses or defendants are joined, either by charging document or by court order, the defense or prosecution may ask the court to sever one or more of them. A motion for severance may be based on misjoinder of either offenses or defendants, sometimes based on the idea that the joinder rules have not been followed. In federal courts, even if joinder is otherwise proper, a pretrial motion to sever under Fed. R. Crim. P. 14 may assert prejudicial joinder. Rule 14 leaves the determination of risk of prejudice, and any remedy that may be necessary, to the sound discretion of the trial, court. If prejudice develops at trial after a motion to sever has been overruled, the defendant should renew the motion and move for a mistrial.

Go Online

Some famous joint trials included Lewis Powell and David Herold (co-conspirators in the killing of Abraham Lincoln); Sacco and Vanzetti; and Leopold and Loeb. http://law2. umkc.edu/faculty/projects/ftrials/ SaccoV/SaccoV.htm; http://law2. umkc.edu/faculty/projects/ftrials/ lincolnconspiracy/lincolnaccount. html; http://www.crimelibrary.com/ notorious_murders/famous/loeb/ index_1.html.

Make the Connection

In addition to joinder and severance issues, the exercise of prosecutorial discretion to join or not join offenses or defendants may have constitutional consequences. These consequences relate primarily to Fifth Amendment Double Jeopardy and collateral estoppel issues, discussed in Chapter 21, as well as Sixth Amendment Confrontation Clause matters, discussed in Chapter 18.

B. Joinder and Severance of Offenses

The joinder and severance of offenses can have a significant impact on how cases are approached and tried. Public policy, especially fairness and efficiency concerns, underlies joinder and severance analysis. How people are tried matters, and fairness of process is of the utmost importance.

When a defendant is charged with multiple offenses, procedural rules usually govern the joinder and severance of the offenses and whether there will be a single trial or several trials. In general, the rules give the prosecution the discretion to charge in a single prosecution all of the offenses that a defendant allegedly committed in a closely connected series of events within the same time sequence. Conversely, the rules permit the defendant to seek a severance of offenses that have been joined. Rules like Fed. R. Crim. P. 8(a) are typical, allowing, but not requiring, joinder of offenses. It states that two or more offenses may be charged together against a defendant if they are based upon: 1) the same act or transaction (*e.g.,* a rape and assault); or 2) a series of acts or transactions constituting a common scheme (*e.g.,* armed robbery, auto theft, possession of weapon); or 3) the offenses being of similar character (*e.g.,* bank robberies in same neighborhood two months apart).

Take Note

The "same or same series of acts or transactions" requirement comes up often in this and other procedural areas. This is the type of language referred to as "boiler plate," meaning often used language in a particular area. In this instance, though, it is a very significant part of the rules and really concerns the nexus of the conduct in question.

Because the rule is permissive rather than mandatory, a defendant has no right to have all alleged offenses tried together. However, a defendant's motion to consolidate charges under Fed. R. Crim. P. 13 may succeed *if* the charges could have been brought together under Rule 8(a). Rule 13 states in part: "The court may order two or more indictments or informations or both to be tried together if the offenses, and the defendants if there is more than one, could have been joined in a single indictment or information."

Joinder is usually upheld when the crimes are closely related in character, circumstances, and time. One example of a common scheme or plan is when the offenses show a near identical *modus operandi* and the offenses occur within such a close proximity of time and location to each other that there can be little doubt that the offenses were committed by the same person. A second type of case occurs when the crimes are somewhat similar in nature but are closely related in an overall scheme.

The efficiency realized from joining "same act" offenses or "same series" offenses may vanish when the only basis for the joinder is the similarity of charged offenses which were committed in different places, at different times, or in different ways. When evidence of one offense is not admissible at the trial of another offense, joinder is inefficient, and separate trials are preferable. Case law suggests, however, that if evidence of each crime is simple and distinct, though not admissible in separate trials, joinder may be proper if the trial judge properly instructs the jury about the dangers of cumulating evidence. If evidence of one crime *is* admissible at the trial of the other, the court may not find the joinder of offenses prejudicial and determine that separate trials of the similar offenses are unnecessary.

Arguably, any joinder of offenses is prejudicial to some extent, but where joinder is otherwise proper under the rules of procedure, the defendant must prove prejudice to justify and obtain a severance. There are several general discretionary considerations which may persuade a court to grant severance. First, the jury may consider the defendant a "bad person" or infer a criminal propensity by the defendant simply because he is charged with so many offenses. Second, proof of one charge may "spill over" and assist in a conviction on another charge. Unless there is a high probability of an

Practice Pointer

Note that the prosecutor or defendant should *move* to join or sever. It is not up to the judge to try the cases for the parties. Generally, motions will be filed in writing and then sometimes argued, as compared to a simple objection, which is often only oral and about the admissibility of evidence. Sometimes motions and objections are inappropriately mixed, so that a party objects to the joinder of parties or offenses, instead of moving to have joinder or severance.

acquittal on one count, courts will usually deny a severance on this ground. *See, e.g., United States v. Moyer*, 313 F.3d 1082 (8th Cir. 2002) (joinder of crimes not prejudicial solely because evidence of some crimes is stronger than evidence of other crimes). Third, the defendant may wish to testify about one offense, but not about another offense. *See, e.g., United States v. Saadey*, 393 F.3d 669 (6th Cir. 2005) (defendant failed to show trial court how testifying about one charge would violate his Fifth Amendment privilege against self-incrimination on another charge when he had asserted that the charges were unrelated). The defendant must convince the trial court that he has important testimony to give concerning one count, but that there is a strong need to assert the Fifth Amendment Privilege Against Self-Incrimination and refrain from testifying on the other count. Finally, the defendant may wish to assert antagonistic defenses to the joinable charges. For example, if he is charged with two assaults, he may want to claim an alibi as to one assault and insanity as to the other. Because one of the defenses is likely to diminish the credibility of the other, prejudice may be asserted in support of a motion for a severance.

The motion for severance of offenses in the case that follows illustrates that the test for joinder of offenses is about a fair trial as much as it is about the same, similar or connected transaction test of Fed. R. Cr. P. 8(a).

United States v. Angell

2017 WL 1364893 (D. Utah, Apr. 12, 2017).

DISTRICT JUDGE CLARK WADDOUPS

Before the court is Defendant Misty Angell's Motion for Separate Trial, in which Defendant argues that the counts against her were improperly joined in the indictment or, alternatively, that the two counts should be severed to avoid prejudice to her defense. After careful consideration, the court now DENIES Defendant's motion.

Defendant was charged by a two-count indictment on January 11, 2017. The indictment accuses her of mail theft and simple possession of methamphetamine. The government alleges [that] approximately five grams of methamphetamine were found in Defendant's possession during prebooking for her arrest for mail theft. That arrest occurred seven days after Defendant was observed stealing mail from mailboxes in Magna, Utah. And Defendant was not employed at the time of the charged conduct. The government further represented to the court during the status conference on the day Defendant filed the motion to severe that the arresting officer would testify regarding both counts. Defendant has not at this time presented a contrary factual account.

Federal Rule of Criminal Procedure 8(a) permits joinder of multiple charges against a defendant in the same indictment. Such joinder is proper "if the offenses charged are of the same or similar character, or are based on the same transaction, or are connected with or constitute parts of a common scheme or plan." Fed. R. Crim. P. 8(a).

First, joinder is proper here because the facts as alleged demonstrate that the charges are based on the same act or transaction and are connected as a part of a common plan. Defendant argues for misjoinder, claiming that the charged conduct in this case is not "connected in any way." Her argument focuses on the dissimilarity between drug possession and theft and the lack of overlapping evidence between the two counts. But the charged offenses were separated by a mere seven days—a substantially shorter period than in the case Defendant relies upon to argue that time between criminal acts can justify misjoinder, *see United States v. Chavis*, 296 F.3d 450, 458 (6th Cir. 2002) (joinder improper when gun purchased two years prior to possession of cocaine and there was no evidence or allegation that the two offenses connected), and a shorter time than in many cases in which courts have held joinder was proper, *see, e.g., United States v. Bagby*, 696 F.3d 1074, 1086 (10th Cir. 2012) (plain error not to sever counts of drug possession and ammunition possession when the ammunition and drugs were found three months apart in different locations); *United States v. Holland*, 10 F.3d 696, 697, 699 (10th Cir. 1993) (affirming joinder when gun and drug possession were separated by three months). And while theft and drug use are not the same conduct, there is a logical inference that Defendant committed the theft to facilitate drug use, especially because Defendant had no income.

Second, Defendant will not be so prejudiced as to require severance. Severance is necessary when a defendant's "right to a fair trial is threatened or actually deprived." *United States v. Johnson*, 130 F.3d 1420, 1427 (10th Cir. 1997). That is, severance is appropriate when there is a serious risk that joinder would "compromise a specific trial right" of the defendant or "prevent the jury from making a reliable judgment about guilt or innocence." *Zafiro v. United States*, 506 U.S. 534, 539 (1993); *Valentine*, 706 F.2d at 290. But defendants are not prejudiced simply because severance would have given them a better chance of acquittal. And where the jury can be instructed to consider the charges separately, courts have presumed their ability to do so and have thus denied severance.

There is not such a risk of prejudice to Defendant that severance is necessary. Defendant first argues that failure to sever would require a later trial date in violation of her rights under the Speedy Trial Act. Her motion to sever, however, tolls the Speedy Trial Act, and the currently scheduled trial date is within the Speedy Trial period. She then claims that introduction of evidence of the drugs in support of Count Two of the indictment "would severely impact Ms. Angell's ability to receive a fair trial on Count One." While evidence of one count may in theory influence juror thinking on the other count, that does not rise to the level of prejudice where the court can, and will in this case, issue a limiting instruction to the jury. In sum, severance is not necessary to avoid prejudice to the defense in this case.

Defendant's Motion for Separate Trial is hereby DENIED. The two counts will be tried together according to the schedule set out in the final pretrial order.

Hypo 1: *Permissible Joinder?*

In the following situations, determine whether joinder is permissible under the applicable criminal procedure rule (meaning federal, the state where you attend law school or the state where you intend to practice). If joinder is permissible, determine whether the joinder under that rule is nonetheless prejudicial: A) Tom Slime was charged in a single indictment with the rape of one of his daughters, allegedly occurring in 2009, and a separate rape of his stepdaughter in 2006; B) Dick was charged with robbing Smith's Drug Store on July 1, 2014, with assaulting Jim Johnson on February 3, 2005, and with being a career criminal (two or more prior felony convictions); C) Harry was charged with sixteen robberies over a 28-month period. The robberies were committed in the same manner and at about the same time of day by a man wearing similar clothing.

Hypo 2: *Severance*

In the early hours of June 19, Tom allegedly entered a convenience store, brandished a 12-inch knife, and demanded that the clerk hand over all the money in the store's two cash registers. Two weeks later, in the early morning of July 3, Tom allegedly returned to the store, demanded that another clerk hand over money from the same registers, and threatened the clerk with the jagged edge of a broken bottle. After the robberies, each clerk gave slightly different descriptions of the robber. Later, both clerks picked Tom out of a photographic display. A) As defense counsel for Tom, describe the arguments you would make in a motion to the court for a severance of the two robbery counts based upon prejudicial joinder. B) If you were the prosecutor in the case, how would you respond to Tom's motion? C) As the trial judge, how would you rule on Tom's motion for a severance of the robbery charges?

C. Joinder and Severance of Defendants

1. Joinder of Defendants Under the Rules

Criminal procedure rules address joinder and severance procedures in situations when multiple defendants are jointly alleged to have committed one or more crimes. The policy behind this type of rule is to improve judicial economy, since one trial is faster and less expensive than two. The joinder of defendants is permissive, and severance is discretionary with the court. When multiple defendants are jointly charged, a severance may be available based upon specific allegations of prejudice. A more general request for severance may be grounded on the proposition that the defendants should not have been joined in the first place. This is similar to the problem that arises when there is misjoinder of unrelated offenses.

Take Note

While the rules might overlap, it is important to distinguish the joinder of defendants from the joinder of claims, particularly regarding the policy concerns and practical impact underlying each type of rule.

In most jurisdictions, joinder of defendants is permitted when the defendants allegedly participated either in the same act or transaction or in the same series of acts or transactions. Unlike the rules on joinder of offenses, before defendants can be joined, they must have committed offenses which are part of the same series of acts rather than being of a similar character. Joinder of defendants looks to the factual connecting link. Where the link is part of some larger plan, or there is some commonality of proof, joinder is permitted. Even when the connecting link is absent, and joinder is not permitted under the rules, misjoinder is subject to harmless error analysis. *United States v. Lane*, 474 U.S. 438 (1986). Most procedural rules also provide that defendants may be charged in one or more counts together or separately, but each defendant does not have to be charged in each count. *See, e.g.,* Fed. R. Crim. P. 8(b) in the statutory supplement.

Assuming that joinder is proper under the applicable rules, severance of defendants may be based upon specific allegations of prejudice that may result from a joint trial. The prejudicial aspects of a joint trial are commonly considered as 1) the "spill over" effect of one defendant's heinous conduct affecting the jury's view of the other co-defendants; and 2) the dangers of any one attorney not having total control over the defense. While the prosecution is unified, the defense is fragmented because each defendant has an attorney and each attorney's view of the case may differ. Specific grounds for severance of defendants for factual prejudice relate to: (1) the weight or type of proof as to one defendant; (2) antagonistic defenses or positions; (3) the desire to call the codefendant as a witness; and (4) the confession of a codefendant.

When there is a great disparity in the weight or type of the evidence against the defendants, with the evidence against one or more defendants far more damaging than the evidence against the moving defendant, severance may be appropriate. Otherwise, the guilt of others may "rub off" on the moving defendant. For example, a defendant being tried for a single offense may seek a severance from being jointly tried with a defendant who is charged with both the same offense as the other defendant and with being a recidivist.

If antagonistic defenses are alleged as the basis for a motion for separate trials, the moving defendant must show that the antagonism with a codefendant will mislead or confuse the jury, thereby rendering his defense ineffective. In *Zafiro v. United States*, 506 U.S. 534 (1993), the Court rejected a bright line test that severance is required whenever defendants have mutually antagonistic defenses. The four *Zafiro* defendants did not articulate any specific instances of prejudice but merely argued that the "very nature of their defenses, without more, prejudiced them." Writing for the Court, Justice O'Connor responded that "it is well settled that defendants are not entitled to a severance merely because they may have a better chance of acquittal in separate trials." Instead, a court:

> should grant a severance only if there is a serious risk that a joint trial would compromise a specific right of one of the defendants, or prevent the jury from making a reliable judgment about guilt or innocence. Such a risk might occur when evidence that the jury should not consider against a defendant and that would not be admissible if a defendant were tried alone is admitted against a codefendant. For example, evidence of a codefendant's wrongdoing in some circumstances erroneously could lead a jury to conclude that a defendant was guilty. When many defendants are tried together in a complex case and they have markedly different degrees of culpability, this risk of prejudice is heightened. Evidence that is probative of a defendant's guilt but technically admissible only against a codefendant also might present a risk of prejudice. Conversely, a defendant might suffer prejudice if essential exculpatory evidence that would be available to a defendant tried alone were unavailable in a joint trial.

Who's That?

To find out about Justice Sandra Day O'Connor, see: http://www.biography.com/people/sandra-day-oconnor-9426834.

Even if there is some risk of prejudice, it may be curable with proper instructions. Justice O'Connor noted that the trial court in that case instructed the jury to give separate consideration to each defendant, and that each defendant was entitled to have his or her case judged only on the basis of the evidence applicable to him/her. Thus, the instructions "sufficed to cure any possibility of prejudice."

The problem of calling a codefendant as a witness may conflict with the codefendant's privilege against self-incrimination. If the cases are severed, and the codefendant's trial is held first, the self-incrimination problem might be eliminated by virtue of a conviction or acquittal. Courts faced with severance motions based on the prospect of calling a codefendant often require specific statements of 1) a bona fide need for the codefendant's testimony, 2) the substance of the codefendant's testimony, 3) the exculpatory nature and effect of the codefendant's testimony, and 4) the likelihood that the codefendant will in fact testify at a separate trial. For example, in *United States v. Hall*, 473 F.3d 1295 (10th Cir. 2007), the court upheld the denial of a severance because the exculpatory value of the codefendant's testimony was minimal.

Point for Discussion

Sufficient Prejudice

Consider whether sufficient prejudice is present in a trial of two defendants when: 1) One defendant testifies and the other does not; 2) Evidence is introduced that is competent as to one defendant but incompetent as to another; 3) One defendant claims merely to have been present at the crime scene and the other claims entrapment; 4) The chances for acquittal for one defendant are better if there are separate trials; 5) The expense or strain of a joint trial is harmful to the defendant.

Food for Thought

What effect should a court give to each of the following when ruling on a motion to sever based upon the ground of calling a codefendant? 1) The sufficiency of a showing that the codefendant would testify at a severed trial. 2) The degree to which the exculpatory testimony would be cumulative. 3) Judicial economy. 4) The likelihood that the testimony would be substantially impeached.

Hypo 1: *Permissible But Prejudicial?*

In the following situations, determine whether the joinder of defendants is permissible under the applicable criminal procedure rules, and if so, determine whether the joinder, though permissible, is nonetheless prejudicial.

A. In two counts of a ten-count indictment, the prosecutor has charged Joan and Buffy with illegally trafficking in controlled substances. In the remaining counts, Joan alone is charged with trafficking in controlled substances on eight other occasions.

B. The prosecution charges Jill, Sally, and others with trafficking illegally in controlled substances. Jill's defense is that she merely aided and abetted the other defendants; Sally's defense is entrapment.

C. Alice and Deborah face multiple criminal tax charges arising from their business ventures. Alice is willing to give exculpatory evidence for Deborah, but without a severance of her case from Deborah's, she will invoke her privilege against self-incrimination.

Hypo 2: *Arguing a Motion*

Charles asked his friend Phil if he knew where Charles could purchase some cocaine. Phil checked with his friend Harry, who in turn found Dave, who said that he would sell a kilogram of cocaine to Charles for $25,000. Late one night, the four men met in a parking lot of a shopping mall to consummate the transaction. Charles gave Dave the cash for the drugs, thinking that Dave had already given the drugs to Phil. When Dave and Harry quickly drove off in Dave's car, Charles asked Phil for the drugs. Phil replied that he did not have them and thought that Dave had given them to Charles when Charles paid the money to Dave. Phil and Charles jumped into Phil's pickup truck and started chasing Dave and Harry. During the chase, both cars collided with another vehicle, killing the two occupants. No cocaine was found in Dave's car. Immediately after he was arrested, Charles gave the police a statement in which he described the drug sale gone bad, and implicated Dave as the culprit. The prosecutor charged Charles and Dave each with two counts of wanton murder, and also charged Dave with trafficking in a controlled substance and theft by deception. The prosecutor allowed Phil and Harry to plead guilty to minor offenses in return for their testimony at Charles' and Dave's trial.

The law provides that wanton murder occurs when a defendant operates a motor vehicle under circumstances manifesting extreme indifference to human life and kills another person. Trafficking in cocaine occurs when a defendant sells, transfers or possesses with intent to sell cocaine. One way in which theft by deception may occur is when a defendant creates a false impression as to his intention and obtains the property of another with intent to deceive that person of the property. Nothing in the statutes or their legislative histories indicates that cumulative punishments for trafficking and theft by deception are permitted.

A. As defense counsel for Charles, describe the nature of the arguments you would make in a motion to the court for a severance of his wanton murder charge from Dave's charges.

B. If you are the prosecutor in the case, how would you respond to Charles' motion?

C. As the trial judge, how would you rule on Charles' motion for a severance of his case from Dave's?

D. As the trial judge, how would you rule on Dave's motion: 1) To compel the prosecution to elect between prosecuting him for trafficking or for theft by deception because they are the same offense; and 2) To exclude his name or any reference to his participation from Charles' statement when it is introduced during the prosecution's case-in-chief?

2. Impact of Severance

Severance of defendants also involves calculating the relative interests of the government and the defense. The authors of an empirical study involving the impact of severance in a case reached these conclusions based on the following study:

> In addition to offering empirical findings, we have argued that courts currently miscalculate the defense and governmental interests when deciding whether to sever. In particular, we claim that judges undervalue the defendants' interests, in part because they may assume that defendants are trying to gain some tactical or unfair advantage from separate trials. This fear seems exaggerated; we could not identify any illegitimate reason why a defendant would seek severance. At the same time, the fear of increased trials in a world of more generous severance also seems overdone. More severance would undoubtedly lead to some

increase in the number of proceedings, but given the predictive effect of the first trial outcome on the rest of the cases, it is questionable whether all, or even most, subsequent trials would find their way to the courtroom. Andrew D. Leipold and Hossein A. Abbasi, The Impact of Joinder and Severance on Federal Cases: An Empirical Study, 59 Vand. L. Rev. 349 (2006).

Executive Summary

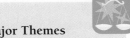

Rationale. Joinder and severance issues involve issues of fairness and efficiency.

Basic Definitions. Joinder involves combining offenses or defendants in the same proceeding; severance involves separating them into separate proceedings. Joinder and severance can apply to both offenses and defendants.

Strategies and Tactics. As a general rule, prosecutors prefer to join defendants for the resulting efficacy, completeness of the narrative, and potential impact on the jury. Defendants generally prefer to be tried separately to avoid guilt by association. The same positioning of defendants is not so clear for offenses, where joinder of offenses might depend on the circumstances. Often, defendants prefer to have charges consolidated in order to give the prosecution only "one bite at the apple." There is a lower standard for motions made pretrial as compared to motions made during trial.

Major Themes

a. Start with the Pleadings—Joinder of offenses and defendants commences with the pleadings but often continues as an issue up to and through the trial. Joinder of offenses and defendants depends on the circumstances of the case and will be impermissible if prejudice will result.

b. "Same Transaction or Series of Transactions"—Joinder of offenses often is based on the same transactions or series of transactions (or the offenses are of a similar character).

c. Delays—Delayed joinder is also permitted, and is called consolidation.

d. Severance Considerations and Context—Severance of defendants or offenses often depends on the evidence, whether disparity or quantity differentials will cause prejudice for one or more defendants. It also depends on process, whether the defenses offered by a defendant are sufficiently antagonistic to warrant separation of defendants or offenses.

Test Your Knowledge

To assess your understanding of the material in this chapter, click here to take a quiz.

For More Information

For a recent opinion on joinder and severance, see *Microsoft Corp. v. Surf cast, Inc.*, Case IPR 2014-00271 (Patent Trial and Appeal Board).

RUSSELL L. WEAVER, JOHN M. BURKOFF, CATHERINE HANCOCK & STEVEN I. FRIEDLAND, PRINCIPLES OF CRIMINAL PROCEDURE Ch. 13 (6th ed. 2018).

Article: http://www.natlawreview.com/article/microsoft-corporation-v-surfcast-inc-decision-denying-institution-and-motion-joinder.

Opinion: http://ptabtrialblog.com/wp-content/uploads/2014/06/IPR2014-00271-Decision-Denying-Institution-and-Motion-for-Joinder-20140613.pdf.

CHAPTER 15

Pre-Charge Delay and Speedy Trial

A. Delay in Bringing the Charge

To establish a federal due process violation based on pre-charge delay, a defendant must show that: 1) the delay resulted in actual prejudice to the ability of the defense to present its case; and 2) the prosecution's conduct was intentional and motivated by an intent to harass the defendant or to gain a tactical advantage over the defendant. In each case, the reasons for the delay and the prospective impact on a trial are relevant. The burden of proving prosecutorial intent and of establishing actual prejudice is a heavy one.

> **Take Note**
>
> Defendants have two constitutional rights related to issues of delay. First, the Due Process Clauses of the Fifth and Fourteenth Amendments offer some protection to an accused for delay between commission of the crime and arrest, indictment, or information, whichever comes first. Second, the Sixth Amendment protects a defendant from undue delay in bringing the case to trial after charging. The Sixth Amendment states, in relevant part, "In all criminal prosecutions, the accused shall enjoy the right to a speedy . . . trial." This Chapter covers pre-charge delay, delay implicating the Sixth Amendment speedy trial right, and delay implicating the statutory rights created by the federal Speedy Trial Act.

United States v. Lovasco

431 U.S. 783 (1977).

Mr. Justice Marshall delivered the opinion of the Court.

On March 6, 1975, respondent was indicted for possessing eight firearms stolen from the United States mails, and for dealing in firearms without a license. The offenses were alleged

> **Hear It**
>
> You can hear the oral argument in *Lovasco* at: http://www.oyez.org/cases/1970-1979/1976/1976_75_1844.

to have occurred between July 25 and August 31, 1973, more than 18 months before the indictment was filed. Respondent moved to dismiss the indictment due to the delay.

The District Court conducted a hearing at which respondent sought to prove that the delay was unnecessary and that it had prejudiced his defense. Respondent presented a Postal Inspector's report on his investigation that was prepared one month after the crimes were committed, and a stipulation concerning the post-report progress of the probe. The report stated, in brief, that within the first month of the investigation respondent had admitted to Government agents that he had possessed and then sold five of the stolen guns, and that the agents had developed strong evidence linking respondent to the remaining three weapons. The report also stated, however, that the agents had been unable to confirm or refute respondent's claim that he had found the guns in his car after visiting his son, a mail handler, at work. The stipulation the Assistant United States Attorney entered indicated that little additional information concerning the crimes was uncovered in the 17 months following the preparation of the Inspector's report.

To establish prejudice, respondent testified that he had lost the testimony of two material witnesses due to the delay. The first witness, Tom Stewart, died more than a year after the alleged crimes occurred. Respondent claimed that Stewart had been his source for two or three of the guns. The second witness, respondent's brother, died in April 1974, eight months after the crimes were completed. Respondent testified that his brother was present when respondent called Stewart to secure the guns, and witnessed all of respondent's sales. Respondent did not state how the witnesses would have aided the defense had they been willing to testify.

The Government made no systematic effort to explain its long delay. The Assistant United States Attorney did expressly disagree with defense counsel's suggestion that the investigation had ended after the Postal Inspector's report was prepared. The prosecutor also stated that it was the Government's theory that respondent's son, who had access to the mail at the railroad terminal from which the guns were "possibly stolen," was responsible for the thefts. Finally, the prosecutor elicited somewhat cryptic testimony from the Postal Inspector indicating that the case "as to these particular weapons involves other individuals"; that information had been presented to a grand jury "in regard to this case other than on the day of the indictment itself"; and that he had spoken to the prosecutors about the case on four or five occasions.

Following the hearing, the District Court filed a brief opinion and order. The court found that by October 2, 1973, the date of the Postal Inspector's report, "the Government had all the information relating to defendant's alleged commission of the offenses charged against him," and that the 17-month delay before the case was presented to the grand jury "had not been explained or justified" and was "unnecessary and unreasonable." The court also found that "as a result of the delay defendant has been prejudiced by reason of the death of Tom Stewart, a material witness on his behalf." Accordingly, the court dismissed the indictment. The Eighth Circuit Court of Appeals affirmed. We granted certiorari and reverse.

In *United States v. Marion*, 404 U.S. 307 (1971), this Court considered the significance, for constitutional purposes, of a lengthy preindictment delay. We held that as far as the Speedy Trial Clause of the Sixth Amendment is concerned, such delay is wholly irrelevant, since our analysis of the language, history, and purposes of the Clause persuaded us that only "a formal indictment or information or else the actual restraints imposed by arrest and holding to answer a criminal charge engage the particular protections" of that provision. We went on to note that statutes of limitations, which provide predictable, legislatively enacted limits on prosecutorial delay, provide "the primary guarantee, against bringing overly stale criminal charges." But we did acknowledge that the "statute of limitations does not fully define defendants' rights with respect to the events occurring prior to indictment," and that the Due Process Clause has a limited role to play in protecting against oppressive delay.

Marion makes clear that proof of prejudice is generally a necessary but not sufficient element of a due process claim, and that the due process inquiry must consider the reasons for the delay as well as the prejudice to the accused. It requires no extended argument to establish that prosecutors do not deviate from "fundamental conceptions of justice" when they defer seeking indictments until they have probable cause to believe an accused is guilty; indeed it is unprofessional conduct for a prosecutor to recommend an indictment on less than probable cause. It should be equally obvious that prosecutors are under no duty to file charges as soon as probable cause exists but before they are satisfied they will be able to establish the suspect's guilt beyond a reasonable doubt. To impose such a duty "would have a deleterious effect both upon the rights of the accused and upon the ability of society to protect itself." From the perspective of potential defendants, requiring prosecutions to commence when probable cause is established is undesirable because it would increase the likelihood of unwarranted charges being filed, and would add to the time during which defendants stand accused but untried. From the perspective of law enforcement officials, a requirement of immediate prosecution upon probable cause is equally unacceptable because it could make obtaining proof of guilt beyond a reasonable doubt impossible by causing potentially fruitful sources of information to evaporate before they are fully exploited. From the standpoint of the courts, such a requirement is unwise because it would cause scarce resources to be consumed on cases that prove to be insubstantial, or that involve only some of the responsible parties or some of the criminal acts. Thus, no one's interests would be well served by compelling prosecutors to initiate prosecutions as soon as they are legally entitled to do so.

It might be argued that once the Government has assembled sufficient evidence to prove guilt beyond a reasonable doubt, it should be constitutionally required to file charges promptly, even if its investigation of the entire criminal transaction is not complete. Adopting such a rule, however, would have many of the same consequences as adopting a rule requiring immediate prosecution upon probable cause.

First, compelling a prosecutor to file public charges as soon as the requisite proof has been developed against one participant on one charge would cause numerous problems in those cases in which a criminal transaction involves more than one person or more than one illegal act. In some instances, an immediate arrest or indictment would impair the prosecutor's ability to continue his investigation, thereby preventing society from bringing lawbreakers to justice. In other cases, the prosecutor would be able to obtain additional indictments despite an early prosecution, but the necessary result would be multiple trials involving a single set of facts. Such trials place needless burdens on defendants, law enforcement officials, and courts.

Second, insisting on immediate prosecution once sufficient evidence is developed to obtain a conviction would pressure prosecutors into resolving doubtful cases in favor of early and possibly unwarranted prosecutions. The determination of when the evidence available to the prosecution is sufficient to obtain a conviction is seldom clear-cut, and reasonable persons often will reach conflicting conclusions. In the instant case, since respondent admitted possessing at least five of the firearms, the primary factual issue in dispute was whether respondent knew the guns were stolen as required by 18 U.S.C. § 1708. Not surprisingly, the Postal Inspector's report contained no direct evidence on this issue. The decision whether to prosecute, therefore, required a necessarily subjective evaluation of the strength of the circumstantial evidence available and the credibility of respondent's denial. Even if a prosecutor concluded that the case was weak and further investigation appropriate, he would have no assurance that a reviewing court would agree. To avoid the risk that a subsequent indictment would be dismissed for preindictment delay, the prosecutor might feel constrained to file premature charges, with all the disadvantages that would entail.

Finally, requiring the Government to make charging decisions immediately upon assembling evidence sufficient to establish guilt would preclude the Government from giving full consideration to the desirability of not prosecuting in particular cases. The decision to file criminal charges, with the awesome consequences it entails, requires consideration of a wide range of factors in addition to the strength of the Government's case, in order to determine whether prosecution would be in the public interest. Prosecutors often need more information than proof of a suspect's guilt, therefore, before deciding whether to seek an indictment. Again the instant case provides a useful illustration. Although proof of the identity of the mail thieves was not necessary to convict respondent of the possessory crimes with which he was charged, it might have been crucial in assessing respondent's culpability, as distinguished from his legal guilt. If further investigation were to show that respondent had no role in or advance knowledge of the theft and simply agreed, out of paternal loyalty, to help his son dispose of the guns once respondent discovered his son had stolen them, the United States Attorney might have decided not to prosecute, especially since respondent was over 60 years old and had no prior criminal record. Requiring prosecution once the evidence of guilt is clear could prevent a prosecutor from awaiting the information necessary for such a decision.

We would be reluctant to adopt a rule which would have these consequences absent a clear constitutional command to do so. We can find no such command in the Due Process Clause of the Fifth Amendment. Investigative delay is fundamentally unlike delay undertaken by the Government solely "to gain tactical advantage over the accused," *United States v. Marion*, 404 U.S., at 324, precisely because investigative delay is not so one-sided.[17] Rather than deviating from elementary standards of "fair play and decency," a prosecutor abides by them if he refuses to seek indictments until he is completely satisfied that he should prosecute and will be able promptly to establish guilt beyond a reasonable doubt. Penalizing prosecutors who defer action for these reasons would subordinate the goal of "orderly expedition" to that of "mere speed." This the Due Process Clause does not require. We therefore hold that to prosecute a defendant following investigative delay does not deprive him of due process, even if his defense might have been somewhat prejudiced by the lapse of time.

In *Marion* we conceded that we could not determine in the abstract the circumstances in which preaccusation delay would require dismissing prosecutions. More than five years later, that statement remains true. Indeed, in the intervening years so few defendants have established that

Food for Thought

When and how did Justice Marshall decide that due process gives him leeway rather than restricts his ability to decide pre-charge delay cases?

---

[17] In *Marion* we noted with approval that the Government conceded that a "tactical" delay would violate the Due Process Clause. The Government renews that concession here by stating: "A due process violation might also be made out upon a showing of prosecutorial delay incurred in reckless disregard of circumstances, known to the prosecution, suggesting that there existed an appreciable risk that delay would impair the ability to mount an effective defense." However, there is no evidence of recklessness here.

they were prejudiced by delay that neither this Court nor any lower court has had a sustained opportunity to consider the constitutional significance of various reasons for delay. We therefore leave to the lower courts, in the first instance, the task of applying the settled principles of due process that we have discussed to the particular circumstances of individual cases. We simply hold that in this case the lower courts erred in dismissing the indictment.

Reversed.

Points for Discussion

a. Prosecutorial Intent

Suppose a defendant is able to show prejudice from the delay between the crime and the arrest, how can the defendant prove an improper prosecutorial motive? Occasionally, courts decide that proof of prejudice to the defense is sufficient to afford the defendant a dismissal of the charge, without a showing of improper prosecutorial motive. *See, e.g.,* Howell v. Barker, 904 F.2d 889 (4th Cir. 1990); State v. Cyr, 588 A.2d 753 (Me. 1991).

Food for Thought

The Court observed the impossibility of deciding in the abstract when due process relief is required, and it left to the lower courts the task of applying "settled principles of due process" to the particular circumstances of individual cases. How settled could those principles have been if the courts were lacking in the experience of deciding the significance of various reasons for delay?

b. Statutes of Limitations

Besides constitutional restrictions on charging defendants, there may be statutes of limitations for charging defendants with felonies or misdemeanors. What is the purpose of such statutes? In *United States v. Marion,* 404 U.S. 307 (1971), the Court stated: "The purpose of a statute of limitations is to limit exposure to prosecution to a fixed period of time and to protect individuals from having to defend themselves against charges when the basic facts may have become obscured by the passage of time. Such a time limit may also have the salutary effect of encouraging law enforcement officials promptly to

Take Note

When a defendant alleges, without substantiation, prejudice from witnesses' faded memories, the defendant's inability to locate witnesses, the loss of evidence, or the refusal of witnesses to testify, courts generally refuse to find substantial prejudice to the defendant's ability to present a defense at trial. *See, e.g.,* United States v. Gilbert, 266 F.3d 1180 (9th Cir.2001) (no showing of how testimony of "lost" witnesses would have assisted defendant).

investigate suspected criminal activity." Many states have no time limit within which felony charges must be brought. The limitations period for many federal felonies is five years. *See* 18 U.S.C. § 3282. By contrast, misdemeanor charges typically must be commenced within a time certain, *e.g.,* one year, from the last act constituting the offense.

Hypo: *A Case for Unconstitutional Pre-Indictment Delay?*

In 1990, Sue acquired a building in Metro that she converted into a country-western nightclub known as Sue's. The nightclub opened in early 1991, but was damaged severely by a fire two months later. Sue was on the premises at the time the fire broke out and the evidence clearly indicates that the fire was arson. Sue was alone at the time and claims that the fire was started by a masked man who accosted her at the nightclub, stole all the money, tied her to a chair, and started the fire. Sue escaped after she began to smell smoke, and went to a nearby convenience store for help. Store clerks later stated that Sue appeared to have been beaten and her hands were tied with wire. The police took a number of pictures of Sue's face showing cuts and bruises. Local police and fire departments and Sue's insurance carrier conducted extensive investigations to determine the origin and cause of the fire. The investigations were completed in April 1991. While insurance investigators were suspicious of Sue's story, they paid her insurance claim during the summer of 1991

During May 1996, the local grand jury indicted Sue and an associate on charges of arson. Between April 1991 and May 1996 there were no new developments in the case—no new evidence was found, no new studies were conducted, and no new witnesses or statements about the fire were made available to authorities. However, in the intervening five years, the police lost the photos of Sue's injuries and one of the two store clerks moved and could not be found. Prior to trial, Sue moved to dismiss the indictment on the ground that the pre-charge delay and the State's loss of potentially exculpatory evidence had prejudiced her case. The court reserved judgment on the motion until after trial. During the trial, the State entered evidence showing that Sue was heavily in debt, that she set the fire to her business intentionally in order to collect insurance proceeds, and that she inflicted her own injuries to support her story that a robber set the fire. Sue testified and also put on a store clerk who testified about her injuries and her tied hands. The jury found Sue guilty of arson.

> The trial judge then granted Sue's pretrial motion to dismiss the indictment on the ground of prejudicial pre-indictment delay. Do you agree with the decision? If the standard for appellate review is whether the trial judge's factual and legal findings were clearly erroneous, will the prosecutor be successful on appeal of the trial judge's grant of the dismissal?

B. Delay in Bringing Defendant to Trial

An accused's right to a speedy trial is guaranteed by the Sixth Amendment. Because a defendant has no duty to bring himself to trial, the duty of executing the right is the responsibility of the prosecution. The right is intended to spare the accused those penalties and disabilities that spring from delays in the criminal process, as well as to provide protection for society's interest in effective prosecution. *Dickey v. Florida*, 398 U.S. 30 (1970). The constitutional right to a speedy trial protects the accused from arrest through trial but does not apply to sentencing, i.e., once a defendant has been found guilty at trial or has pleaded guilty to criminal charges. *Betterman v. Montana*, 136 S.Ct. 1609 (2016). The speedy trial right helps to implement the presumption of innocence and hence loses force upon conviction. In the seminal case of *Barker v. Wingo*, the Court set out the balancing inquiry for deciding whether the right has been violated.

Barker v. Wingo

407 U.S. 514 (1972).

MR. JUSTICE POWELL delivered the opinion of the Court.

The right to a speedy trial is generically different from any of the other rights enshrined in the Constitution for the protection of the accused. In addition to the general concern that

Hear It

You can hear the oral argument in *Barker v. Wingo* at: http://www.oyez.org/cases/1970-1979/1971/1971_71_5255.

all accused persons be treated according to decent and fair procedures, there is a societal interest in providing a speedy trial which exists separate from, and at times in opposition to, the interests of the accused. The inability of courts to provide a prompt trial has contributed to a large backlog of cases in urban courts which, among other things, enables defendants to negotiate more effectively for pleas of guilty to lesser offenses and otherwise manipulate the system. In addition, persons released on bond for lengthy periods awaiting trial have an opportunity to commit other crimes. It must be of little comfort to the residents of Christian County, Kentucky, to know that Barker was at large on bail for over four years while accused of a vicious and brutal murder of which he was ultimately convicted. Moreover, the longer an accused is free awaiting trial, the more tempting becomes his opportunity to jump bail and escape. Finally, delay between arrest and punishment may have a detrimental effect on rehabilitation.

If an accused cannot make bail, he is generally confined, as was Barker for 10 months, in a local jail. This contributes to the overcrowding and generally deplorable state of those institutions. Lengthy exposure to these conditions "has a destructive effect on human character and makes the rehabilitation of the individual offender much more difficult." At times the result may even be violent rioting. Finally, lengthy pretrial detention is costly. The cost of maintaining a prisoner in jail varies from $3 to $9 per day, and this amounts to millions across the Nation. In addition, society loses wages which might have been earned, and it must often support families of incarcerated breadwinners.

Take Note

While the right to a speedy trial applies equally to defendants who are detained as to those who are out on bond, most appellate courts do not take seriously a speedy trial claim unless the defendant is or was incarcerated. Courts assume (usually correctly) that if the defendant is at liberty, the defense is either primarily or equally responsible for the delay or at least has acquiesced in the delay.

A second difference between the right to speedy trial and the accused's other constitutional rights is that deprivation of the right may work to the accused's advantage. Delay is not an uncommon defense tactic. As the time between the commission of the crime and trial lengthens, witnesses may become unavailable or their memories may fade. If the witnesses support the prosecution, its case will be weakened, sometimes seriously so. And it is the prosecution which carries the burden of proof. Thus, unlike the right to counsel or the right to be free from compelled self-incrimination, deprivation of the right to speedy trial does not *per se* prejudice the accused's ability to defend himself.

Finally, and perhaps most importantly, the right to speedy trial is a more vague concept than other procedural rights. It is, for example, impossible to determine with precision when the right has been denied. We cannot definitely say how long is too long in a system where justice is supposed to be swift but deliberate. As a consequence, there is no fixed point in the criminal process when the State can put the defendant to the choice of either exercising or waiving the right to a speedy trial. If, for example, the State moves for a 60-day continuance, granting that continuance is not a violation of the right to speedy trial unless the circumstances of the case are such that further delay would endanger the values the right protects. It is impossible to do more than generalize about when those circumstances exist. There is nothing comparable to the point in the process when a defendant exercises or waives his right to counsel or his right to a jury trial.

The amorphous quality of the right also leads to the unsatisfactorily severe remedy of dismissal of the indictment when the right has been deprived. This is indeed a serious consequence because it means that a defendant who may be guilty of a serious crime will go free, without having been tried. Such a remedy is more serious than an exclusionary rule or a reversal for a new trial, but it is the only possible remedy.

Perhaps because the speedy trial right is so slippery, two rigid approaches are urged upon us as ways of eliminating some of the uncertainty which courts experience in protecting the right. The first suggestion is that we hold that the Constitution requires a criminal defendant to be offered a trial within a specified time period. The result of such a ruling would have the virtue of clarifying when the right is infringed and of simplifying courts' application of it. Recognizing this, some legislatures have enacted laws, and some courts have adopted procedural rules which more narrowly define the right. The United States Court of Appeals for the Second Circuit has promulgated rules for the district courts in that Circuit establishing that the government must be ready for trial within six months of the date of arrest, except in unusual circumstances, or the charge will be dismissed. This type of rule is also recommended by the American Bar Association.

But such a result would require this Court to engage in legislative or rulemaking activity, rather than in the adjudicative process to which we should confine our efforts. We do not establish procedural rules for the States, except when mandated by the Constitution. We find no constitutional basis for holding that the speedy trial right can be quantified into a specified number of days or months. The States, of course, are free to prescribe a reasonable period consistent with constitutional standards, but our approach must be less precise.

The second suggested alternative would restrict consideration of the right to those cases in which the accused has demanded a speedy trial. Most States have recognized what is loosely referred to as the "demand rule," although eight States reject it. It is not clear precisely what is meant by that term. Although every federal court of appeals that has considered the question has endorsed some kind of demand rule, some have regarded the rule within the concept of waiver, whereas others have viewed it as a factor to be weighed in assessing whether there has been a deprivation of the speedy trial right. We shall refer to the former approach as the demand-waiver doctrine. The demand-waiver doctrine provides that a defendant waives any consideration of his right to speedy trial for any period prior to which he has not demanded a trial. Under this rigid approach, a prior demand is a necessary condition to the consideration of the speedy trial right.

Such an approach, by presuming waiver of a fundamental right from inaction, is inconsistent with this Court's pronouncements on waiver of constitutional rights. The Court has defined waiver as "an intentional relinquishment or abandonment of a known right or privilege." *Johnson v. Zerbst*, 304 U.S. 458, 464 (1938). Courts should "indulge every reasonable presumption against waiver," *Aetna Ins. Co. v. Kennedy*, 301 U.S. 389, 393 (1937), and they should "not presume acquiescence in the loss of fundamental rights," *Ohio Bell Tel. Co. v. Public Utilities Comm'n*, 301 U.S. 292, 307 (1937). In *Carnley v. Cochran*, 369 U.S. 506 (1962), we held: "Presuming waiver from a silent record is impermissible. The record must show, or there must be an allegation and evidence which show, that an accused was offered counsel but intelligently and understandably rejected the offer. Anything less is not waiver." The Court has ruled similarly with respect to waiver of other rights designed to protect the accused. *See, e.g., Miranda v. Arizona*, 384 U.S. 436 (1966); *Boykin v. Alabama*, 395 U.S. 238 (1969).

In excepting the right to speedy trial from the rule of waiver we have applied to other fundamental rights, courts that have applied the demand-waiver rule have relied on the assumption that delay usually works for the benefit of the accused and on the absence of any readily ascertainable time in the criminal process for a defendant to be given the choice of exercising or waiving his right. But it is not necessarily true that delay benefits the defendant. There are cases in which delay harms the defendant's ability to defend himself. Moreover, a defendant confined to jail prior to trial is obviously disadvantaged by delay as is a defendant released on bail but unable to lead a normal life because of community suspicion and his own anxiety.

The nature of the speedy trial right does make it impossible to pinpoint a precise time in the process when the right must be asserted or waived, but that fact does not argue for placing the burden of protecting the right solely on defendants. A defendant has no duty to bring himself to trial; the State has that duty as well as the duty of insuring that the trial is consistent with due process. Moreover, for the reasons earlier expressed, society has a particular interest in bringing swift prosecutions, and society's representatives are the ones who should protect that interest.

It is also noteworthy that such a rigid view of the demand-waiver rule places defense counsel in an awkward position. Unless he demands a trial early and often, he is in danger of frustrating his client's right. If counsel is willing to tolerate some delay because he finds it reasonable and helpful in preparing his own case, he may be unable to obtain a speedy trial for his client at the end of that time. Since under the demand-waiver rule no time runs until the demand is made, the government will have whatever time is otherwise reasonable to bring the defendant to trial after a demand has been made. Thus, if the first demand is made three months after arrest in a jurisdiction which prescribes a six-month rule, the prosecution will have a total of nine months—which may be wholly unreasonable under the circumstances. The result in practice is likely to be either an automatic, *pro forma* demand made immediately after appointment of counsel or delays which, but for the demand-waiver rule, would not be tolerated. Such a result is not consistent with the interests of defendants, society, or the Constitution.

We reject, therefore, the rule that a defendant who fails to demand a speedy trial forever waives his right. This does not mean, however, that the defendant has no responsibility to assert his right. We think the better rule is that the defendant's assertion of or failure to assert his right to a speedy trial is one of the factors to be considered in an inquiry into the deprivation of the right. Such a formulation avoids the rigidities of the demand-waiver rule and the resulting possible unfairness in its application. It allows the trial court to exercise a judicial discretion based on the circumstances, including due consideration of any applicable formal procedural rule. It would permit, for example, a court to attach a different weight to a situation in which the defendant knowingly fails to object from a situation in which his attorney acquiesces in long delay without adequately informing his client, or from a situation in which no counsel is appointed. It would also allow a court to weigh the frequency and force of the objections as opposed to attaching significant weight to a purely *pro forma* objection.

The rule we announce today, which comports with constitutional principles, places the primary burden on the courts and the prosecutors to assure that cases are brought to trial. If delay is attributable to the defendant, then his waiver may be given effect under standard waiver doctrine, the demand rule aside.

We, therefore, reject both of the inflexible approaches—the fixed-time period because it goes further than the Constitution requires; the demand-waiver rule because it is insensitive to a right which we have deemed fundamental. The approach we accept is a balancing test, in which the conduct of both the prosecution and the defendant are weighed.[29]

---

[29] Nothing we have said should be interpreted as disapproving a presumptive rule adopted by a court in the exercise of its supervisory powers which establishes a fixed time period within which cases must normally be brought.

A balancing test necessarily compels courts to approach speedy trial cases on an *ad hoc* basis. We can do little more than identify some of the factors which courts should assess in determining whether a particular defendant has been deprived of his right. Though some might express them in different ways, we identify four such factors: Length of delay, the reason for the delay, the defendant's assertion of his right, and prejudice to the defendant.

The length of the delay is to some extent a triggering mechanism. Until there is some delay which is presumptively prejudicial, there is no necessity for inquiry into the other factors that go into the balance. Nevertheless, because of the imprecision of the right to speedy trial, the length of delay that will provoke such an inquiry is necessarily dependent upon the peculiar circumstances of the case.[31] To take but one example, the delay that can be tolerated for an ordinary street crime is considerably less than for a serious, complex conspiracy charge.

Closely related to length of delay is the reason the government assigns to justify the delay. Here, too, different weights should be assigned to different reasons. A deliberate attempt to delay the trial in order to hamper the defense should be weighted heavily against the government. A more neutral reason such as negligence or overcrowded courts should be weighted less heavily but nevertheless should be considered since the ultimate responsibility for such circumstances must rest with the government rather than with the defendant. Finally, a valid reason, such as a missing witness, should serve to justify appropriate delay.

We have already discussed the third factor, the defendant's responsibility to assert his right. Whether and how a defendant asserts his right is closely related to the other factors we have mentioned. The strength of his efforts will be affected by the length of the delay, to some extent by the reason for the delay, and most particularly by the personal prejudice, which is not always readily identifiable, that he experiences. The more serious the deprivation, the more likely a defendant is to complain. The defendant's assertion of his speedy trial right, then, is entitled to strong evidentiary weight in determining whether the defendant is being deprived of the right. We emphasize that failure to assert the right will make it difficult for a defendant to prove that he was denied a speedy trial.

A fourth factor is prejudice to the defendant. Prejudice, of course, should be assessed in the light of the interests of defendants which the speedy trial right was designed to protect. This Court has identified three such interests: (i) to prevent oppressive pretrial incarceration; (ii) to minimize anxiety and concern of the accused; and (iii) to limit the possibility that the defense will be impaired. Of these, the most serious is the last, because the inability of a defendant adequately

---

[31] For example, the First Circuit thought a delay of nine months overly long, absent a good reason, in a case that depended on eyewitness testimony. *United States v. Butler*, 426 F.2d 1275, 1277 (1970).

to prepare his case skews the fairness of the entire system. If witnesses die or disappear during a delay, the prejudice is obvious. There is also prejudice if defense witnesses are unable to recall accurately events of the distant past. Loss of memory, however, is not always reflected in the record because what has been forgotten can rarely be shown.

We have discussed previously the societal disadvantages of lengthy pretrial incarceration, but obviously the disadvantages for the accused who cannot obtain his release are even more serious. The time spent in jail awaiting trial has a detrimental impact on the individual. It often means loss of a job; it disrupts family life; and it enforces idleness. Most jails offer little or no recreational or rehabilitative programs. The time spent in jail is simply dead time. Moreover, if a defendant is locked up, he is hindered in his ability to gather evidence, contact witnesses, or otherwise prepare his defense.[35] Imposing those consequences on anyone who has not yet been convicted is serious. It is especially unfortunate to impose them on those persons who are ultimately found to be innocent. Finally, even if an accused is not incarcerated prior to trial, he is still disadvantaged by restraints on his liberty and by living under a cloud of anxiety, suspicion, and often hostility.

Food for Thought

Why must prejudice be a factor? Do you agree that the anxiety and "lack of repose" from pending charges for the non-incarcerated defendant is not that serious compared to other constitutional violations? And should the fact that a defendant is incarcerated pretrial for months without good reason for the delay become a constitutional violation without regard to prejudice? As a practical matter, courts only become interested in the delay if there is prejudice to presenting a defense. Of course, that is the hardest showing for a defendant—how does he prove he would have found a helpful witness or evidence when there now appears to be no helpful witness or evidence?

We regard none of the four factors identified above as either a necessary or sufficient condition to the finding of a deprivation of the right of speedy trial. Rather, they are related factors and must be considered together with such other circumstances as may be relevant. In sum, these factors have no talismanic qualities; courts must still engage in a difficult and sensitive balancing process. But, because we are dealing with a fundamental right of the accused, this process must be carried out with full recognition that the accused's interest in a speedy trial is specifically affirmed in the Constitution.

---

[35] There is statistical evidence that persons who are detained between arrest and trial are more likely to receive prison sentences than those who obtain pretrial release, although other factors bear upon this correlation. *See* Wald, *Pretrial Detention and Ultimate Freedom: A Statistical Study*, 39 N.Y.U.L. REV. 631 (1964).

Points for Discussion

a. CIA Interrogation

In *United States v. Ghailani,* 733 F.3d 29 (2nd Cir. 2013), the Second Circuit held that a five-year delay due to the detention and interrogation of the defendant by the CIA did not count against the government under the Sixth Amendment's Speedy Trial Clause. The Court reasoned that the government does not have to choose between national security and criminal prosecution.

The right to a speedy trial attaches from the earlier of the date of the indictment or information, or the date of the arrest, *i.e.,* when the person becomes "accused." Similarly, the right to a speedy trial attaches when a detainer is lodged against an accused in custody on other charges. Once the right to a speedy trial attaches, it continues until the charges are dismissed.

b. Reasons for the Delay

Courts weigh delays intended to gain a trial advantage more heavily against the prosecution than unintentional delays resulting from institutional dysfunction. Neutral reasons such as negligence and overcrowded calendars weigh less heavily, but are still considered because responsibility for such conditions rests with the prosecution. Delays attributable to court appointed defense counsel are not to be counted against the State. *Vermont v. Brillon,* 556 U.S. 945 (2009).

Take Note

In *United States v. MacDonald,* 456 U.S. 1 (1982), the Court held that the time period between dismissal of charges and reinstatement of those charges is a part of the pre-charge period to which the Sixth Amendment right to a speedy trial is inapplicable. *MacDonald* was deemed controlling in *United States v. Loud Hawk,* 474 U.S. 302 (1986), where the Court held that the time during which the prosecution appealed a dismissal, while the defendants were not incarcerated and not subject to bail, did not count in the Sixth Amendment speedy trial analysis. The Court stated that an interlocutory appeal is "ordinarily a valid reason that justifies the delay."

c. Delay Caused By Lack of Funding for Defense

In *Boyer v. Louisiana,* 133 S.Ct. 1702 (2013), the Supreme Court split 5–4 in favor of dismissing the case. The issue the Court would have taken up was "whether a state's failure to fund counsel for an indigent defendant for five years, particularly where failure was the direct result of the prosecution's choice to seek the death penalty, should be weighed against the state for speedy trial purposes." The Louisiana

Take Note

In the following Sixth Amendment speedy trial case, notice the extent to which the Court has altered *Barker's* balancing test.

courts had answered no, that funding was a circumstance out of the prosecution's control. For the four dissenters, Justice Sotomayor wrote that the reasoning of *Barker* "requires that a delay caused by a State's failure to provide funding for an indigent's defense must count against the State, and not the accused. We held there that even a more 'neutral reason' for a delay such as 'overcrowded courts' should be weighed against the State, because 'the ultimate responsibility for such circumstances' lies squarely with the state system as a whole."

d. Role of Speedy Trial Demand

A defendant's failure to demand a speedy trial undercuts the defendant's constitutional argument. By contrast, a vigorous and timely assertion of the right provides strong evidence that the defendant is interested in a speedy disposition. A court will not treat a claim seriously that a trial started too late unless the defendant continuously has sought a speedy trial. *See, e.g., United States v. Vachon,* 869 F.2d 653 (1st Cir.1989) (defendant did not assert right until two days before trial after thirteen-month delay).

e. Harsh Remedy

Barker expressly stated that dismissal with prejudice is the only possible remedy for a violation of the Sixth Amendment speedy trial right. Trial courts therefore cannot devise less extreme remedies such as a sentence reduction. *Strunk v. United States,* 412 U.S. 434 (1973). The re-prosecution prohibition undoubtedly results in courts finding fewer constitutional violations because of the extreme nature of the remedy. An alternative disposition is to find a violation of the relevant speedy trial statute (*e.g.,* 18 U.S.C. § 3161 *et seq.*) or the relevant docket control rule (*e.g.,* Fed.R.Crim.P. 48(b)), both of which may prescribe dismissal without prejudice as an available method of enforcement. Still another remedy is to provide a writ of mandamus to compel a trial court to set a trial date for the defendant's case.

> **Food for Thought**
>
> If a defendant is denied a speedy trial but is found not guilty, does the defendant have any remedy? If so, what? If not, should there be one?

Doggett v. United States

505 U.S. 647 (1992).

JUSTICE SOUTER delivered the opinion of the Court.

In this case we consider whether the delay of 8½ years between petitioner's indictment and arrest violated his Sixth Amendment right to a speedy trial. We hold that it did.

On February 22, 1980, petitioner Marc Doggett was indicted for conspiring with several others to import and distribute cocaine. Douglas Driver, the Drug Enforcement Administration's principal agent investigating the conspiracy, told the United States Marshal's Service that the DEA would

Hear It

You can hear the oral argument in *Doggett* at: http://www.oyez.org/cases/1990-1999/1991/1991_90_857.

oversee the apprehension of Doggett and his confederates. On March 18, 1980, two police officers set out under Driver's orders to arrest Doggett at his parents' house in Raleigh, North Carolina, only to find that he was not there. His mother told the officers that he had left for Colombia four days earlier.

To catch Doggett on his return to the United States, Driver sent word of his outstanding arrest warrant to all United States Customs stations and to a number of law enforcement organizations. He also placed Doggett's name in the Treasury Enforcement Communication System (TECS), a computer network that helps Customs agents screen people entering the country, and in the National Crime Information Center computer system, which serves similar ends. The TECS entry expired that September, however, and Doggett's name vanished from the system.

In September 1981, Driver found out that Doggett was under arrest on drug charges in Panama and, thinking that a formal extradition request would be futile, simply asked Panama to "expel" Doggett to the United States. Although the Panamanian authorities promised to comply when their own proceedings had run their course, they freed Doggett the following July and let him go to Colombia, where he stayed with an aunt for several months. On September 25, 1982, he passed unhindered through Customs in New York City and settled down in Virginia. Since his return to the United States, he has married, earned a college degree, found a steady job as a computer operations manager, lived openly under his own name, and stayed within the law.

Doggett's travels abroad had not wholly escaped the Government's notice, however. In 1982, the American Embassy in Panama told the State Department of his departure to Colombia, but that information, for whatever reason, eluded the DEA, and Agent Driver assumed for several years that his quarry was still serving time in a Panamanian prison. Driver never asked DEA officials in Panama to check into Doggett's status, and only after his own fortuitous assignment to that country in 1985 did he discover Doggett's departure for Colombia. Driver then simply assumed Doggett had settled there, and he made no effort to find out for sure or to track Doggett down, either abroad or in the United States. Thus Doggett remained lost to the American criminal justice system until September 1988, when the Marshal's Service ran a simple credit check on several thousand people subject to outstanding arrest warrants and, within minutes, found out where Doggett lived and worked. On September 5, 1988, nearly 6 years after his return to the United States and 8½ years after his indictment, Doggett was arrested.

He naturally moved to dismiss the indictment, arguing that the Government's failure to prosecute him earlier violated his Sixth Amendment right to a speedy trial. The Federal Magistrate hearing his motion applied the criteria for assessing speedy trial claims set out in *Barker v. Wingo*, 407 U.S. 514 (1972): "length of delay, the reason for the delay, the defendant's assertion of his right, and prejudice to the defendant." The Magistrate found that the delay between Doggett's indictment and arrest was long enough to be "presumptively prejudicial," that the delay "clearly was attributable to the negligence of the government," and that Doggett could not be faulted for any delay in asserting his right to a speedy trial, there being no evidence that he had known of the charges against him until his arrest. The Magistrate also found, however, that Doggett had made no affirmative showing that the delay had impaired his ability to mount a successful defense or had otherwise prejudiced him. In his recommendation to the District Court, the Magistrate contended that this failure to demonstrate particular prejudice sufficed to defeat Doggett's speedy trial claim. The District Court took the recommendation and denied Doggett's motion.

The Sixth Amendment guarantees that, "in all criminal prosecutions, the accused shall enjoy the right to a speedy trial." On its face, the Speedy Trial Clause is written with such breadth that, taken literally, it would forbid the government to delay the trial of an "accused" for any reason at all. Our cases have qualified the literal sweep of the provision by specifically recognizing the relevance of four separate enquiries: whether delay before trial was uncommonly long, whether the government or the criminal defendant is more to blame for that delay, whether, in due course, the defendant asserted his right to a speedy trial, and whether he suffered prejudice as the delay's result.

The first of these is actually a double enquiry. Simply to trigger a speedy trial analysis, an accused must allege that the interval between accusation and trial has crossed the threshold dividing ordinary from "presumptively prejudicial" delay, since, by definition, he cannot complain that the government has denied him a "speedy" trial if it has, in fact, prosecuted his case with customary promptness. If the accused makes this showing, the court must then consider, as one factor among several, the extent to which the delay stretches beyond the bare minimum needed to trigger judicial examination of the claim. This latter enquiry is significant to the speedy trial analysis because, as we discuss below, the presumption that pretrial delay has prejudiced the accused intensifies over time. In this case, the extraordinary 8½ year lag between Doggett's indictment and arrest clearly suffices to trigger the speedy trial enquiry;[1] its further significance within that enquiry will be dealt with later.

As for *Barker's* second criterion, the Government claims to have sought Doggett with diligence. The findings of the courts below are to the contrary, and we review trial court determinations of negligence with considerable deference. The Government gives us nothing to gainsay the findings that have come to us, and we see nothing fatal to them in the record. For six years, the Government's investigators made no serious effort to test their progressively more questionable assumption that Doggett was living abroad, and they could have found him within minutes. While the Government's lethargy may have reflected no more than Doggett's relative unimportance in the world of drug trafficking, it was still findable negligence, and the finding stands.

The Government goes against the record again in suggesting that Doggett knew of his indictment years before he was arrested. Were this true, *Barker's* third factor, concerning invocation of the right to a speedy trial, would be weighed heavily against him. But the Government is trying to revisit the facts. At the hearing on Doggett's speedy trial motion, it introduced no evidence challenging the testimony of Doggett's wife, who said that she did not know of the charges until his arrest, and of his mother, who claimed not to have told him or anyone else that the police had come looking for him.

The Government is left, then, with its principal contention: that Doggett fails to make out a successful speedy trial claim because he has not shown precisely how he was prejudiced by the delay between his indictment and trial.

We have observed in prior cases that unreasonable delay between formal accusation and trial threatens to produce more than one sort of harm, including "oppressive pretrial incarceration," "anxiety and concern of the accused," and "the possibility that the accused's defense will be impaired" by dimming memories and loss of exculpatory evidence. Of these forms of prejudice, "the most serious is the last, because the inability of a defendant adequately to prepare his case skews the fairness of the entire system." Doggett claims this kind of prejudice, and there is probably no other kind that he can claim, since he was subjected neither to pretrial detention nor, he has successfully contended, to awareness of unresolved charges against him.

---

[1] Depending on the nature of the charges, the lower courts have generally found postaccusation delay "presumptively prejudicial" at least as it approaches one year. We note that, as the term is used in this threshold context, "presumptive prejudice" does not necessarily indicate a statistical probability of prejudice; it simply marks the point at which courts deem the delay unreasonable enough to trigger the *Barker* enquiry.

The Government answers Doggett's claim by citing language in three cases for the proposition that the Speedy Trial Clause does not significantly protect a criminal defendant's interest in fair adjudication. The Government asks us, in effect, to read part of *Barker* right out of the law, and that we will not do. In context, the cited passages support nothing beyond the principle, which we have independently based on textual and historical grounds, that the Sixth Amendment right of the accused to a speedy trial has no application beyond the confines of a formal criminal prosecution. Once triggered by arrest, indictment, or other official accusation, the speedy trial enquiry must weigh the effect of delay on the accused's defense just as it has to weigh any other form of prejudice that *Barker* recognized.

As an alternative to limiting *Barker*, the Government claims Doggett has failed to make any affirmative showing that the delay weakened his ability to raise specific defenses, elicit specific testimony, or produce specific items of evidence. Though Doggett did indeed come up short in this respect, the Government's argument takes it only so far: consideration of prejudice is not limited to the specifically demonstrable, and, as it concedes, affirmative proof of particularized prejudice is not essential to every speedy trial claim. *Barker* explicitly recognized that impairment of one's defense is the most difficult form of speedy trial prejudice to prove because time's erosion of exculpatory evidence and testimony "can rarely be shown." And though time can tilt the case against either side, one cannot generally be sure which of them it has prejudiced more severely. Thus, we generally have to recognize that excessive delay presumptively compromises the reliability of a trial in ways that neither party can prove or, for that matter, identify. While such presumptive prejudice cannot alone carry a Sixth Amendment claim without regard to the other *Barker* criteria, it is part of the mix of relevant facts, and its importance increases with the length of delay.

This brings us to an enquiry into the role that presumptive prejudice should play in the disposition of Doggett's speedy trial claim. We begin with hypothetical and somewhat easier cases and work our way to this one. Our speedy trial standards recognize that pretrial delay is often both inevitable and wholly justifiable. The government may need time to collect witnesses against the accused, oppose his pretrial motions, or, if he goes into hiding, track him down. We attach great weight to such considerations when balancing them against the costs of going forward with a trial whose probative accuracy the passage of time has begun by degrees to throw into question. In this case, if the Government had pursued Doggett with reasonable diligence from his indictment to his arrest, his speedy trial claim would fail. Indeed, that conclusion would generally follow as a matter of course however great the delay, so long as Doggett could not show specific prejudice to his defense.

The Government concedes that Doggett would prevail if he could show that the Government had intentionally held back in its prosecution of him to gain some impermissible advantage at trial. That we cannot doubt. *Barker* stressed that official bad faith in causing delay will be weighed heavily against the government, and a bad-faith delay the length of this negligent one would present an overwhelming case for dismissal. Between diligent prosecution and bad-faith delay, official negligence in bringing an accused to trial occupies the middle ground. While not compelling relief in every case where bad-faith delay would make relief virtually automatic, neither is negligence automatically tolerable simply because the accused cannot demonstrate exactly how it has prejudiced him. It was on this point that the Court of Appeals erred, and on the facts before us, it was reversible error.

Barker made it clear that "different weights are to be assigned to different reasons" for delay. Although negligence is to be weighed more lightly than a deliberate intent to harm the accused's defense, it still falls on the wrong side of the divide between acceptable and unacceptable reasons for delaying a criminal prosecution once it has begun. Such is the nature of the prejudice presumed that the weight we assign to official negligence compounds over time as the presumption of evidentiary prejudice grows. Thus, our toleration of negligence varies inversely with its protractedness, and its consequent threat to the fairness of the accused's trial. Condoning prolonged and unjustifiable delays in prosecution would both penalize many defendants for the state's fault and simply encourage the government to gamble with the interests of criminal suspects assigned a low prosecutorial priority. The Government can hardly complain too loudly, for persistent neglect in concluding a criminal prosecution indicates an uncommonly feeble interest in bringing an accused to justice; the more weight the Government attaches to securing a conviction, the harder it will try to get it.

To be sure, to warrant granting relief, negligence unaccompanied by particularized trial prejudice must have lasted longer than negligence demonstrably causing such prejudice. But the Government's egregious persistence in failing to prosecute Doggett is clearly sufficient. The lag between Doggett's indictment and arrest was 8½ years, and he would have faced trial 6 years earlier than he did but for the Government's inexcusable oversights. The portion of the delay attributable to the Government's negligence far exceeds the threshold needed to state a speedy trial claim; indeed, we have called shorter delays "extraordinary." When the Government's negligence thus causes delay six times as long as that generally sufficient to trigger judicial review, and when the presumption of prejudice, albeit unspecified, is neither extenuated, as by the defendant's acquiescence, nor persuasively rebutted, the defendant is entitled to relief.

We reverse the judgment of the Court of Appeals and remand the case for proceedings consistent with this opinion.

JUSTICE O'CONNOR, dissenting.

I believe the Court of Appeals properly balanced the considerations set forth in *Barker v. Wingo*. Although the delay between indictment and trial was lengthy, petitioner did not suffer any anxiety or restriction on his liberty. The only harm to petitioner from the lapse of time was potential prejudice to his ability to defend his case. We have not allowed such speculative harm to tip the scales. Instead, we have required a showing of actual prejudice to the defense before weighing it in the balance. As we stated in *United States v. Loud Hawk*, 474 U.S. 302, 315 (1986), the "possibility of prejudice is not sufficient to support respondents' position that their speedy trial rights were violated. In this case, delay is a two-edged sword. It is the Government that bears the burden of proving its case beyond a reasonable doubt. The passage of time may make it difficult or impossible for the Government to carry this burden." The Court of Appeals followed this holding, and I believe we should as well. For this reason, I respectfully dissent.

JUSTICE THOMAS, with whom THE CHIEF JUSTICE and JUSTICE SCALIA join, dissenting.

Just as "bad facts make bad law," so too odd facts make odd law. Doggett's 8½-year odyssey from youthful drug dealing in the tobacco country of North Carolina, through stints in a Panamanian jail and in Colombia, to life as a computer operations manager, homeowner, and registered voter in suburban Virginia, is extraordinary. But even more extraordinary is the Court's conclusion that the Government denied Doggett his Sixth Amendment right to a speedy trial despite the fact that he has suffered none of the harms that the right was designed to prevent. I respectfully dissent.

In my view, the choice presented is not a hard one. *Barker's* suggestion that preventing prejudice to the defense is a fundamental and independent objective of the Clause is plainly dictum. Never, until today, have we confronted a case where a defendant subjected to a lengthy delay after indictment nonetheless failed to suffer any substantial impairment of his liberty. *Barker* simply did not contemplate such an unusual situation. Moreover, to the extent that the *Barker* dictum purports to elevate considerations of prejudice to the defense to fundamental and independent status under the Clause, it cannot be deemed to have survived our subsequent decisions.

Therefore, I see no basis for the Court's conclusion that Doggett is entitled to relief under the Speedy Trial Clause simply because the Government was negligent in prosecuting him and because the resulting delay may have prejudiced his defense.

It remains to be considered whether Doggett is entitled to relief under the Speedy Trial Clause because of the disruption of his life years after the criminal events at issue. In other words, does the Clause protect a right to repose, free from secret or unknown indictments? In my view, it does not.

There is no basis for concluding that the disruption of an accused's life years after the commission of his alleged crime is an evil independently protected by the Speedy Trial Clause. Such disruption occurs regardless of whether the individual is under indictment during the period of delay. Thus, had Doggett been indicted shortly before his 1988 arrest rather than shortly after his 1980 crime, his repose would have been equally shattered—but he would not have even a colorable speedy-trial claim. To recognize a constitutional right to repose is to recognize a right to be tried speedily after the offense. That would, of course, convert the Speedy Trial Clause into a constitutional statute of limitations—a result with no basis in the text or history of the Clause or in our precedents.

Food for Thought

Both *Barker* and *Doggett*, like most (if not all) speedy trial cases, come to the Court on appeal after conviction. Is there anything a defendant who is being denied a speedy trial can do pretrial? What?

Today's opinion, I fear, will transform the courts of the land into boards of law-enforcement supervision. For the Court compels dismissal of the charges against Doggett not because he was harmed in any way by the delay between his indictment and arrest, but simply because the Government's efforts to catch him are found wanting. Our Constitution neither contemplates nor tolerates such a role. I respectfully dissent.

Points for Discussion

Food for Thought

Does *Doggett* offer insight into the interrelationships among the *Barker* factors? For example, if the reason for the delay is the reasonable diligence of the government, a defendant's speedy trial claim probably will fail unless there is a showing of specific prejudice. Conversely, if the reason for the delay is the prosecution's attempt to gain some impermissible tactical advantage, a rebuttal presumption of prejudice exists. As a prosecutor, how would you rebut the presumption of prejudice? If the reason for the delay is the prosecution's negligence, is some showing of prejudice by the defendant necessary or is a presumption of prejudice created? What is the distinction between governmental negligence and bad faith?

a. Shorter Delays in "Uncomplicated Cases"

In weighing the four *Barker* factors, a court may well find a shorter delay less tolerable in a minor, less complicated, case. In *State v. Cahill*, 61 A.2d 1278 (N.J. 2013), for example, the New Jersey Supreme Court held that a 16-month delay in a DWI case violated the defendant's right to a speedy trial. The defendant's failure to assert the right was outweighed by the state's complete failure to justify the long delay in a straightforward, uncomplicated quasi-criminal matter.

b. Lack of Speedy Trial Demand by Counsel

In the absence of a demand by defense counsel, does the demand "require-ment" result in the defendant paying for the omission of counsel? Is a successful claim of ineffective assistance of counsel necessary to relieve the defendant of the failure to make a demand for a speedy trial? Should the defendant's failure to request a speedy trial be treated differently when the defendant is representing herself?

c. Mistrials

States are divided over whether the speedy trial clock continues to tick or whether it restarts after the declaration of a mistrial. What are the arguments in favor of restarting the clock? Against? If the clock keeps running, how should the mistrial factor into the speedy trial analysis? *See, e.g., Goncalves v. State*, 404 S.W.3d 180 (Ky. 2013).

Food for Thought

In *Reed v. Farley*, 512 U.S. 339 (1994), the Court, citing *Barker*, asserted: "A showing of prejudice is required to establish a violation of the Sixth Amendment Speedy Trial Clause, and that necessary ingredient is entirely missing here." Does *Reed* further modify or rebalance the statements in *Doggett* about the interrelationship of the *Barker* factors?

Hypo: Speedy Trial and Retrials

A man is convicted of sexually assaulting his young daughter, but the conviction is overturned because of a confrontation clause violation. Regarding his retrial, the man contended that he had an independent and absolute right to a speedy trial, which he contended precluded continuances or exceptions. The prosecution claimed that a delay was justified by the primary witness's refusal to cooperate, as well as by the fact that she had married, changed her name, and had moved, making it difficult to locate her. The prosecution located her in California, and moved for a continuance, claiming that they had exercised due diligence in trying to locate her. Would it violate the right to a speedy trial to grant the continuance under these circumstances? *See Mosley v. People,* 393 P.3d 480 (Colo. 2017).

Hypo 1: *Locating the Defendant*

In early 2006, Bob and John arranged to purchase cocaine from Sam. Sam, acting as a "middleman," set up a meeting with Bob, John and a cocaine supplier, who in fact was an undercover federal agent working with the Metro Police. The meeting took place on March 30, 2006, at which time Bob and John were arrested by the federal agent on suspicion of state law drug violations. Because of the amount of drugs involved, the Metro Police requested federal prosecution. John was soon released from custody.

A federal indictment was returned on May 8, 2006. John, however, was not arrested until October 16, 2007. Metro Police Officer Bill Green later testified that during the time between John's indictment and arrest, he spent several nights looking for John, including driving by and watching John's house, which Green said looked vacant. At one point, Green knocked on John's door, but John's wife said he was at work. Green left a message with John's wife, but did not mention that John was under federal indictment. In June, 2006, Green suspended efforts to locate John, apparently under the impression that United States Marshals would take over the case. In October, 2007, however, Green happened to drive by John's house, saw that the lights were on, and knocked on the door. John answered, and was arrested.

John moves to dismiss the indictment because of unconstitutional delay. The United States, of course, opposes the motion. What are the merits of the motion to dismiss? Would you grant it?

Hypo 2: *Clerical Error*

Willie was indicted on April 23, 2006, for polluting streams near his home. After indictment, the state moves for three continuances of six months each to allow the prosecutor additional time to prepare her case. In addition, the trial judge's clerk forgot to redocket the case for trial for one year. During this time of two and a half years, public opinion had become less tolerant of water pollution. In October 2008, Willie was found guilty by a jury and sentenced to ten years. Willie's counsel objected to the proceedings before and during trial, but the trial judge denied his motions to dismiss. Willie wants you to help him file an appeal. What speedy trial arguments will you make on Willie's behalf? Are they likely to be successful?

C. Statutory Prompt Disposition Provisions

In addition to the constitutional speedy trial standard, many state legislatures and the Congress have enacted speedy trial legislation that establishes specific time limits for completing stages of a criminal prosecution. For example, the federal Speedy Trial Act (18 U.S.C. § 3161 *et seq.*) requires that an arrested defendant be formally charged within thirty days after the arrest and that the defendant's trial begin within seventy days after the formal charge was filed. In addition, the trial cannot begin earlier than thirty days from the date the defendant first appeared before the court unless the defendant consents in writing to an earlier trial. Unlike the constitutional standard that makes the passage of time a "triggering mechanism," the statute makes the passage of time dispositive of whether there is a violation. Many speedy trial statutes, like the federal Act, do not require a defendant to show either a demand for a speedy trial or that the effect of the delay was prejudicial.

Certain types of pretrial delays are automatically excluded from the computation of legislative time limits, *e.g.,* periods of delay like the absence or unavailability of the defendant or an essential witness (as long as it is not the result of a lack of due diligence), delays resulting from the joinder of a codefendant, and delays resulting from "other proceedings" involving the defendant. In *Henderson v. United States*, 476 U.S. 321 (1986), the Court held that Congress intended the "other proceedings" provision to require exclusion of all delays attributable to pendency of pretrial motions regardless of whether the delays are reasonably necessary. 18 U.S.C. § 3161(h)(1)(D) covers the delay from the filing of any pretrial motion through the hearing or other disposition of the motion. The running of the 70-day period from indictment to trial stops upon the filing of the pretrial motion, regardless of whether it actually causes a delay in starting the trial. *See United States v. Tinklenberg*, 563 U.S. 647 (2011). However, time granted by the trial court to *prepare* pretrial motions is not necessarily automatically excludable. *See Bloate v. United States*, 559 U.S. 196 (2010).

To give trial judges some flexibility, continuances may be granted when the "ends of justice" outweigh the interest of the public and the defendant in a speedy trial. By contrast, a court cannot grant a continuance for delays caused by general congestion of the court calendar, or by the prosecution's failure to prepare diligently or obtain available witnesses.

To compute whether there has been a statutory violation, the court calculates the gross elapsed days and subtracts the number of days attributable to excludable time, leaving the net elapsed days. If the Act's time limits are not met, the charges against a defendant must be dismissed. The key determination for the trial judge is whether the dismissal must be with or without prejudice ("with prejudice" means the prosecution cannot re-bring the charges later). As stated in 18 U.S.C. §§ 3162(a)(1)–(2), the judge should consider three factors in exercising discretion to dismiss charges with or without prejudice: 1) the seriousness of the offense; 2) the circumstances leading to dismissal; and 3) the effect of reprosecution on the administration of justice and the speedy trial legislation. In *United States v. Taylor*, 487 U.S. 326 (1988), the Court held that it is an abuse of discretion for the trial judge to fail to consider each statutory factor and explain other factors relied upon in deciding whether to dismiss charges.

Points for Discussion

a. Waiver of Speedy Trial

Is a defendant permitted to waive the requirements of the Speedy Trial Act? For example, can a defendant execute a written waiver of speedy trial rights based on an "ends of justice" continuance under § 3161(h)(8)? In *Zedner v. United States*, 547 U.S. 489 (2006), the Supreme Court stated that, under § 3162(a)(2), a waiver of the right to dismissal for a past statutory violation occurs when a defendant fails to file a motion for dismissal before trial or before entering a guilty plea. However, that provision does not indicate that Congress intended to permit prospective waivers, *i.e.*, a defendant cannot opt out of the Act's requirements prior to a violation. The Act was intended to serve public interests that would be subverted by an interpretation that allowed prospective waivers.

Food for Thought

The Speedy Trial Act (STA) requires that an information or indictment be filed within thirty days after arrest or service of a summons on the defendant. Does the thirty-day period begin to run when a defendant is arrested and released without being charged and then is indicted after the thirty-day period has run? *See United States v. Gaskin,* 364 F. 3d 438 (2d Cir. 2004).

Food for Thought

The STA requires that the trial begin within seventy days of the filing of an information or indictment, or of the date the defendant appears before an officer of the court in which the charge is pending, whichever is later.

b. Superseding Indictment

Does the filing of a superseding indictment for offenses charged affect the seventy-day period? *See United States v. Apperson,* 441 F. 3d 1162 (10th Cir. 2006).

c. Pretrial Period

What trial event constitutes the end of the pretrial period? *See United States v. Rodriguez,* 63 F. 3d 1159 (1st Cir. 1995).

Food for Thought

After the Speedy Trial Act's time limit has passed, the trial court grants a detained defendant's motion to dismiss. As the defendant is about to be released, the government refiles a new indictment. Can the government keep the defendant in custody? *Compare United States v. Tirasso,* 532 F.2d 1298 (9th Cir. 1976), *with United States v. Worthy,* 699 F.3d 661 (1st Cir. 2012).

Hypo: A State Statutory Problem

The state of Pennsylvania failed to prosecute the defendant for kidnapping and rape within the one-year statutory period. The preliminary hearing judge failed to forward the case to the court's central docketing system; the state failed to follow up and track the case itself; and the defendant did not mention the issue until he moved for a speedy trial dismissal just after the one-year period. Should the case be dismissed on speedy trial grounds? *See Commonwealth v. Bradford,* 46 A.3d 693 (Pa. 2012).

Executive Summary

Pre-Charge Delay. Due process may protect an accused from delay between the crime and the earlier of an arrest, indictment or information.

Speedy Trial Right. The Sixth Amendment speedy trial right protects a defendant from delay from the earlier of arrest or formal charge to trial.

When Violated. A balancing of the length of the delay, reasons for the delay, assertion of the speedy trial right, and any prejudice from the delay determines whether there is a violation of the constitutional right to a speedy trial under the Sixth Amendment.

Speedy Trial Statutes. Most jurisdictions, including the federal law, have speedy trial statutes that measure a violation exclusively by the lapse of a specific length of time, after subtracting time attributable to specific types of excludable delay.

Major Themes

a. Defense Burden—While there is a due process right against undue pretrial delay, it is almost impossible for a defendant to meet the burden of proving that the prosecutor's delay in charging was in bad faith and resulted in actual prejudice to the defendant's ability to present a case.

b. Prejudice—While there are four *Barker v. Wingo* factors for courts to consider, by far the most important to most courts is the ability of the defendant to show prejudice from the delay. Without prejudice, courts are reluctant to grant the extreme remedy for a speedy trial delay, which is dismissal. *Doggett* gave defendants the benefit of a presumption of prejudice if the delay has reached one year.

Test Your Knowledge

To assess your understanding of the material in this chapter, click here to take a quiz.

For More Information

• MARK E. CAMMACK & NORMAN M. GARLAND, ADVANCED CRIMINAL PROCEDURE (2006).

• WAYNE R. LAFAVE, JEROLD H. ISRAEL, NANCY J. KING & ORIN S. KERR, CRIMINAL PROCEDURE (5th ed. 2009).

• JEROLD H. ISRAEL & WAYNE R. LAFAVE, CRIMINAL PROCEDURE: CONSTITUTIONAL LIMITATIONS (8th ed. 2006).

• RUSSELL L. WEAVER, JOHN M. BURKOFF, CATHERINE HANCOCK, JANET HOEFFEL, STEVE FRIEDLAND & STEPHEN SINGER, PRINCIPLES OF CRIMINAL PROCEDURE Ch. 14 (6th ed. 2018).

CHAPTER 16

Guilty Pleas

A. Introduction

After an indictment or criminal information has been filed, the defendant is typically arraigned on that charging document and is asked to enter a plea in open court. At that time, the defendant may plead guilty, not guilty, or, in many jurisdictions—if permitted by the court in the interests of justice—enter a plea of *nolo contendere*, *i.e.* indicating that he or she is simply not contesting the charges. *See, e.g.,* Fed.R.Crim.P. 11(b). Generally a "nolo plea" (as they are commonly called) is identical to a guilty plea except that a nolo plea cannot be used as an admission of guilt against the defendant in a subsequent civil proceeding. In addition, in most jurisdictions, instead of pleading guilty or not guilty (or entering a nolo plea), the defendant can invoke a psychological condition by pleading "not guilty by reason of insanity" or, in some jurisdictions, "guilty but mentally ill."

In many states, a defendant may enter a conditional guilty plea, reserving the right to appeal specified pretrial motions without having to proceed to a complete trial in order to preserve the issues for appeal. *See, e.g.,* Fed.R.Crim.P. 11(a)(2). Conditional pleas generally require that the court and the prosecutor approve the conditional guilty plea, and any defendant who prevails on appeal may later withdraw the conditional plea.

According to the Bureau of Justice Statistics of the U.S. Department of Justice (BJS), of the estimated 1,132,290 felons convicted in state courts in 2006, the vast majority (94%) of those sentenced for a felony pleaded guilty. The remaining 6% were found guilty either by a jury (4%) or by a judge in a bench trial (2%). BJS, Felony Sentences in State Court, 2006, http://www.bjs.gov/content/pub/pdf/fssc 06st.pdf (last visited 12/14/14). Moreover, "the predominance of guilty pleas is not new in the criminal justice system. A study in Connecticut covering 75 years (1880 to 1954) concludes that between 1880 and 1910 10% of all convictions were obtained by trial." U.S. Department of Justice, Report to the Nation on Crime and Justice 83 (2d ed. 1988).

B. Policy Concerns

Most cases in which criminal charges are filed never go to trial and are resolved by a guilty plea. In deciding to plead guilty, defendant gives up his right to a trial, and (of course) the possibility of an acquittal. By contrast, the prosecution usually agrees to a lower sentence for defendant, and sometimes agrees to convict defendant of only less serious charges. On balance, those who agree to plead guilty serve shorter sentences than those who do not. *See* Robert E. Scott William J. Stuntz, Plea Bargaining as Contract, 101 Yale L.J. 1909–10 (1992).

Who's That?

Robert Scott is a Professor of Law at Columbia Law School. You can read about him at http://www.law.columbia.edu/fac/Robert_Scott. William Stuntz was a Professor of Law at Harvard Law School until he passed away in 2011. You can read about him at http://www.nytimes.com/2011/03/21/us/21stuntz.html.

Of course, the plea bargaining process produces unique results. While many perceive the criminal justice process as involving elaborate trials—in which there is a clash of lawyers through argument, the production of witnesses, and the production of physical evidence—plea bargains essentially involve little more than agreements between the prosecution and the defense. The vast majority of cases are resolved through this bargaining/contract process. These "bargains" have enormous real world consequences that place individuals in prison, sometimes for long prison terms. They are entered into because the prosecution seeks to avoid the risk and expense of a trial, with the possibility of an acquittal, and the defendant receives a guarantee of a lower sentence. Moreover, since plea bargains are so much more efficient than trials, prosecutors can handle far more cases through plea bargaining than they could handle if all cases had to be tried.

The plea bargaining process has been subject to numerous criticisms. Unlike defendants who go to trial, and whose cases are subject to elaborate investigation and fact-finding processes, defendants who enter into plea bargains are subjected to only limited investigation and fact-finding. Fearing more severe punishments, poor defendants often agree to plead guilty and forego the right to a trial. As a result, they may never find out about exculpatory evidence that may exist in the prosecutor's file. Because of the limited nature of the process, judges often do not have sufficient information to decide whether to accept or reject a plea deal. Although most "legal scholars oppose plea bargaining," most "participants generally approve of it." *Id.*

The absence of complete information complicates the plea bargaining process. Since most criminal defendants assert their innocence, prosecutors may have difficulty distinguishing between guilty defendants and innocent defendants. Moreover, truly innocent defendants may encounter difficulty signaling their innocence to prosecutors. As a result, prosecutors may not be able to accurately calculate the possibility that a given defendant will be convicted at trial. By contrast, defendants have reasons to be risk adverse and plead guilty despite their innocence. Thus, there is no assurance that the plea bargaining process will produce satisfactory or desirable results. These factors can distort the process:

Food for Thought

What do you think? Is plea bargaining a positive good for the criminal justice system, a necessary evil, or a feature that needs to be eliminated, whether due to the unequal bargaining power between the parties or the risk of innocent persons pleading guilty?

> By failing to enforce prosecutors' sentencing promises, the law encourages courts to raise sentences in precisely those cases where the defendant is most likely to be innocent. By under protecting against defense attorney error, the law increases the chances of risk averse innocent defendants accepting deals that treat them as certain convictions. And by permitting prosecutorial manipulation of broad mandatory sentencing statutes, the doctrine reduces prosecutors' incentives to separate innocent from guilty defendants at the charging stage. All these effects are unnecessary. By following appropriate contract models, one can devise different rules that reduce the harm to innocent defendants and meanwhile reduce transaction costs and inefficiency for everyone else.

Id.

Points for Discussion

a. Bargain as Contract

Courts have generally applied the law of contracts to plea agreements. *See, e.g., United States v. Vaval*, 404 F. 3d 144 (2d Cir. 2005). As such, one or both parties may breach the agreement, although determining the existence of a breach tends to be very fact-specific. Some courts have held that due process requires that any ambiguity in the terms of an agreement should be construed against the prosecution, consistent with the defendant's reasonable understanding of the agreement. *See, e.g., United States v. Guzman*, 318 F. 3d 1191 (10th Cir. 2003) (court construes any ambiguities against government as drafter of the agreement); *United States v. Bownes*, 405 F. 3d 634 (7th Cir. 2005) (although plea agreements are generally analyzed under contract law, analogy to contract law is not complete because guilty plea involves waiver of fundamental constitutional rights).

Several Supreme Court cases have analyzed plea bargains as contracts. In *Ricketts v. Adamson*, 483 U.S. 1 (1987), Ricketts was charged with first-degree murder. Ricketts and the prosecutor reached an agreement whereby Ricketts agreed that, in return for a guilty plea to the lesser charge of second-degree murder, he would testify against two other individuals allegedly involved in the murder. He agreed to do so "in any Court, State or Federal, when requested by proper authorities against any and all parties involved in the murder." Further, "should the defendant refuse to testify or should he at any time testify untruthfully then this entire agreement is null and void and the original charge will be automatically reinstated." The state trial court accepted the plea agreement and found Ricketts guilty of second-degree murder. Ricketts then testified as obligated under the agreement, and both other individuals were convicted of first-degree murder. Ricketts was sentenced, but then the convictions of the two other individuals were reversed by an appellate court and a new trial was ordered. The State again sought Ricketts' testimony but he refused, claiming he had fulfilled his side of the bargain and his obligation was met. The State disagreed and called him to testify but he refused, claiming a Fifth Amendment privilege. The State then reinstituted the first-degree murder charge against Ricketts and he claimed a retrial violated double jeopardy. A majority of the Supreme Court rejected this claim and held that the defendant had violated the agreement, which thereby removed the double jeopardy bar to prosecution of Ricketts on the first-degree murder charge.

Whereas *Ricketts* is a case where the defendant breached the contract, *Santobello v. New York*, 404 U.S. 257 (1971), is one where the prosecution failed to uphold its end of the bargain. The State charged Santobello with two felony counts. After negotiations, the prosecution agreed to permit petitioner to plead guilty to a lesser-included offense that would carry a maximum prison sentence of one year. The prosecutor agreed to make no recommendation as to the actual sentence within the one-year maximum. At sentencing, another prosecutor had replaced the prosecutor who negotiated the plea. The new prosecutor recommended the maximum one-year sentence, denied knowledge of any agreement, and the court sentenced Santobello to one year. The Supreme Court held that "the interests of justice and appropriate recognition of the duties of the prosecution in relation to promises made in the negotiation of pleas of guilty will be best served" by recognizing the breach of agreement and remanding the case for an appropriate solution. In so holding the Court underscored the legitimate value of plea bargains:

> This record represents another example of an unfortunate lapse in orderly prosecutorial procedures, in part, no doubt, because of the enormous increase in the workload of the often understaffed prosecutor's offices. The heavy workload may well explain these episodes, but it does not excuse them. The disposition of criminal charges by agreement between the prosecutor and the accused, sometimes loosely called "plea

bargaining," is an essential component of the administration of justice. Properly administered, it is to be encouraged. If every criminal charge were subjected to a full-scale trial, the States and the Federal Government would need to multiply by many times the number of judges and court facilities.

Disposition of charges after plea discussions is not only an essential part of the process but a highly desirable part for many reasons. It leads to prompt and largely final disposition of most criminal cases; it avoids much of the corrosive impact of enforced idleness during pre-trial confinement for those who are denied release pending trial; it protects the public from those accused persons who are prone to continue criminal conduct even while on pretrial release; and, by shortening the time between charge and disposition, it enhances whatever may be the rehabilitative prospects of the guilty when they are ultimately imprisoned.

b. Remedy for Breach?

If a defendant is able to prove that the prosecution has breached a plea agreement, what is the appropriate remedy for the defendant? Withdrawal of the plea? Specific performance of the agreement? Alteration of the sentence? In *Santobello*, the issue of the appropriate remedy was left to the discretion of the trial court. Should the defendant who seeks specific performance be required to prove prejudice? *See, e.g., United States v. Manzo*, 675 F. 3d 1204 (9th Cir. 2012) (court orders specific performance of plea agreement where government promised a certain base offense level under the Sentencing Guidelines and reneged by going along with the presentence report which grouped the offenses together and came up with a higher base level).

Food for Thought

Defendant Carlton Legall executed a plea agreement with the government in which both sides agreed to take no appeal if Legall's sentence for the offense of conspiracy to import a controlled substance fell within a range of 120 to 135 months imprisonment. The district court sentenced Legall to 135 months and he appealed, claiming that the federal sentencing guidelines permit an appeal when the sentence is in violation of a statutory provision as this one was since the trial judge imposed this sentence without a proper specification of reasons. The government agrees that an appeal would normally be appropriate in these circumstances except that Legall waived his right to appeal from a sentence in this range in his plea agreement. Who do you think is right? Why? Should it matter that the 135-month sentence may be illegal under the applicable sentencing guidelines? *United States v. Yemitan*, 70 F. 3d 746 (2d Cir. 1995).

---

c. Sentencing Recommendations

In a federal plea agreement between a defendant and the government under Fed.R.Crim.P. 11(c)(1)(B), the prosecutor may be responsible for making a nonbinding sentencing recommendation to the court. In *United States v. Benchimol*, 471 U.S. 453 (1985), the Court held that the prosecutor does not have to "enthusiastically" defend its sentencing recommendation. Is a promise by the government to recommend a sentence at the low end of the sentencing guideline range breached when the government recommendation is in the presentence report but it does not affirmatively advocate that sentence to the trial court? Yes, said the appellate court in *United States v. Barnes*, 278 F. 3d 644 (6th Cir. 2002). On the other hand, when the government keeps its promise about not making a sentencing recommendation, courts usually do not preclude additional comments as long as a specific sentence is not being recommended. *See, e.g., Colvin v. Taylor*, 324 F. 3d 583 (8th Cir.2003) (no breach when prosecutor rebutted factual assertions that supported defendant's request); *United States v. Gerace*, 997 F.2d 1293 (9th Cir.1993) (no breach when prosecutor was silent at sentencing but opposed leniency at later probation revocation hearing).

d. Binding on Non-Party Authorities?

Assuming that a plea agreement exists between a defendant and the prosecution, who is bound by that agreement? In *Santobello*, the successor of the prosecutor who made a promise to the defendant was bound by that promise. Generally, a plea agreement in a state prosecution is not binding on prosecutors in other jurisdictions or on officials in other parts of the same jurisdiction if they are not parties to the agreement. *See, e.g., Montoya v. Johnson*, 226 F. 3d 399 (5th Cir. 2000) (binding on federal officials).

e. Fleeing Defendant

After entry of a negotiated guilty plea but prior to sentencing, a defendant flees by failing to appear for sentencing. He is later caught and brought back to court. Under the circumstances, may the government renege on its obligations under the agreement if there is no express provision regarding flight? If the government does renege, can defendant back out of the agreement and insist on a trial? *See United States v. Hallahan*, 744 F.3d 497 (7th Cir. 2014).

* * *

Some argue that the plea bargaining process is unfair to minority groups, especially when they are confronted by police who sometimes arrest and charge minorities based on "suspicious" activity rather than based on probable cause. See Chester Mirsky, *Plea Reform is No Bargain*, Newsday p.70 (City edition, March 4, 1994). The vast majority of these cases are resolved through plea bargains. When these defendants do plead guilty, judges are inclined to accept the pleas for a variety of reasons. Sadly, some courts may not rigorously examine the evidence to make sure that defendants are actually guilty. Rather, they may assume guilt based on a defendant's race or socioeconomic status.

Food for Thought

In one jurisdiction, local rules require that a plea bargain involve conviction for the most serious charge in an indictment, thereby eliminating the possibility for defendants to receive a lesser sentence based on a reduced charge. Is such an approach desirable? Might such an approach help ensure that drug dealers and violent individuals receive more severe sentences? Might such rule discourage defendants from engaging in plea bargaining because they will receive less benefit? If so, what is the potential impact on the criminal justice system? Might cases languish longer? Might defendants remain in jail longer? Might the prosecution's evidence disappear or go stale as time passes? Can such a policy be manipulated to continue "business as usual?"

C. The Legal Requirements of a Valid Guilty Plea

In order for a guilty plea to be constitutionally valid, three requirements must be satisfied. The plea must have been made "knowingly" and "voluntarily," and there must be a "factual basis" for the plea. *See Boykin v. Alabama*, 395 U.S. 238 (1969). To ensure that a valid guilty plea satisfies these basic constitutional requirements, most states follow procedures similar to those set out in Federal Rule of Criminal Procedure 11. These procedures are usually satisfied by a "colloquy" (a conversation) in open court between the trial judge, the defendant and the prosecution.

Boykin v. Alabama

395 U.S. 238 (1969).

MR. JUSTICE DOUGLAS delivered the opinion of the Court.

In the spring of 1966, within the period of a fortnight, a series of armed robberies occurred in Mobile, Alabama. The victims, in each case,

Hear It

You can hear the oral argument in *Boykin* at: http://www.oyez.org/cases/1960-1969/1968/1968_642.

were local shopkeepers open at night who were forced by a gunman to hand over money. While robbing one grocery store, the assailant fired his gun once, sending a bullet through a door into the ceiling. A few days earlier in a drugstore, the robber had allowed his gun to discharge in such a way that the bullet, on ricochet from the floor, struck a customer in the leg. Shortly thereafter, a local grand jury returned five indictments against petitioner, a 27-year-old Negro, for common law robbery—an offense punishable in Alabama by death.

Before the matter came to trial, the court determined that petitioner was indigent and appointed counsel to represent him. Three days later, at his arraignment, petitioner pleaded guilty to all five indictments. So far as the record shows, the judge asked no questions of petitioner concerning his plea, and petitioner did not address the court.

Trial strategy may of course make a plea of guilty seem the desirable course. But the record is wholly silent on that point and throws no light on it.

Alabama provides that when a defendant pleads guilty, "the court must cause the punishment to be determined by a jury" (except where it is required to be fixed by the court) and may "cause witnesses to be examined, to ascertain the character of the offense." In the present case a trial of that dimension was held, the prosecution presenting its case largely through eyewitness testimony. Although counsel for petitioner engaged in cursory cross-examination, petitioner neither testified himself nor presented testimony concerning his character and background. There was nothing to indicate that he had a prior criminal record.

In instructing the jury, the judge stressed that petitioner had pleaded guilty in five cases of robbery, defined as "the felonious taking of money from another against his will by violence or by putting him in fear carrying from ten years minimum in the penitentiary to the supreme penalty of death by electrocution." The jury, upon deliberation, found petitioner guilty and sentenced him severally to die on each of the five indictments. The Alabama Supreme Court affirmed.

It was error, plain on the face of the record, for the trial judge to accept petitioner's guilty plea without an affirmative showing that it was intelligent and voluntary.

A plea of guilty is more than a confession which admits that the accused did various acts; it is itself a conviction; nothing remains but to give judgment and determine punishment. Admissibility of a confession must be based on a "reliable determination on the voluntariness issue which satisfies the constitutional rights of the defendant." The requirement that the prosecution spread on the record the prerequisites of a valid waiver is no constitutional innovation. In *Carnley v. Cochran*, 369 U.S. 506, we dealt with a problem of waiver of the right to counsel, a Sixth Amendment right. We held: "Presuming waiver from a silent record is impermissible. The record must show, or there must be an allegation and evidence which show, that an accused was offered counsel but intelligently and understandingly rejected the offer. Anything less is not waiver."

We think that the same standard must be applied to determining whether a guilty plea is voluntarily made. For, as we have said, a plea of guilty is more than an admission of conduct; it is a conviction. Ignorance, incomprehension, coercion, terror, inducements, subtle or blatant threats might be a perfect cover-up of unconstitutionality. The question of an effective waiver of a federal constitutional right in a proceeding is of course governed by federal standards.

Several federal constitutional rights are involved in a waiver that takes place when a plea of guilty is entered in a state criminal trial. First, is the privilege against compulsory self-incrimination guaranteed by the Fifth Amendment and applicable to the States by reason of the Fourteenth. Second, is the right to trial by jury. Third, is the right to confront one's accusers. We cannot presume a waiver of these three important federal rights from a silent record.

What is at stake for an accused facing death or imprisonment demands the utmost solicitude of which courts are capable in canvassing the matter with the accused to make sure he has a full understanding of what the plea connotes and of its consequence. When the judge discharges that function, he leaves a record adequate for any review that may be later sought and forestalls the spin-off of collateral proceedings that seek to probe murky memories.

Reversed.

Points for Discussion

a. Rule 11 and *Boykin*

The Court regards the Fed.R.Crim.P. 11(b)(1)(C)–(E) list of rights as merely a codification of *Boykin*'s requirements regarding the waiver of constitutional rights. *Libretti v. United States*, 516 U.S. 29 (1995). The reading of these rights and their knowing and voluntary waiver is often called the *Boykin* inquiry. Among the rights the trial judge will confirm that the defendant is knowingly and voluntarily waiving are the right to a judge or jury trial where the prosecution would be required to prove every element of every offense beyond a reasonable doubt, the right to have counsel cross-examine the prosecution's witnesses, the right to call witnesses in his defense, and the right to appeal errors in the trial if there is a conviction.

b. No Constitutional Right to a Deal

A defendant has no constitutional right to plea bargain with the prosecutor. *Weatherford v. Bursey*, 429 U.S. 545 (1977). Indeed, prosecutors have discretion to plea bargain with some defendants but not with others. Similarly, prosecutors have discretion to offer "package deals" (often referred to as "wired" deals) to all defendants or no deal at all. *See United States v. Crain,* 33 F. 3d 480 (5th Cir. 1994). Prosecutors nevertheless cannot base the decision to plea bargain upon unjustifiable standards such as race, religion or other arbitrary classification. *Bordenkircher v. Hayes,* 434 U.S. 357 (1978). *See* Chapter 11 on Prosecutorial Discretion.

c. What is "Knowing"?

The trial judge has an obligation to determine that the defendant understands what he is doing when he decides to plead guilty. In *Godinez v. Moran,* 509 U.S. 389, 396–402 (1993), the Court held that the competency standard for pleading guilty is no higher than the competency standard for standing trial:

> A criminal defendant may not be tried unless he is competent and he may not plead guilty unless he does so "competently and intelligently." In *Dusky v. United States,* 362 U.S. 402 (1960), we held that the standard for competence to stand trial is whether the defendant has "sufficient present ability to consult with his lawyer with a reasonable degree of rational understanding" and has "a rational as well as factual understanding of the proceedings against him." While we have described the standard for competence to stand trial, we have never expressly articulated a standard for competence to plead guilty. Even assuming that there is some meaningful distinction between the capacity for "reasoned choice" and a "rational understanding" of the proceedings, we reject the notion that competence to plead guilty must be measured by a standard that is higher than (or even different from) the *Dusky* standard.

> We begin with the guilty plea. A defendant who stands trial is likely to be presented with choices that entail relinquishment of the same rights that are relinquished by a defendant who pleads guilty: He will ordinarily have to decide whether to waive his "privilege against compulsory self-incrimination" by taking the witness stand; if the option is available, he may have to decide whether to waive his "right to trial by jury"; and, in consultation with counsel, he may have to decide whether to waive his "right to confront his accusers" by declining to cross-examine witnesses for the prosecution. A defendant who pleads not guilty faces still other strategic choices: In consultation with his attorney, he may be called upon to decide, among other things, whether (and how) to put on a defense and whether to raise one or more affirmative defenses. In sum, all criminal defendants—not merely those who plead guilty—may be required to make important decisions once criminal proceedings have been initiated. And while the decision to plead guilty is undeniably a profound one, it is no more complicated than the sum total of decisions that a defendant may be called upon to make during the course of a trial. (The decision to plead guilty is also made over a shorter period of time, without the distraction and burden of a trial.) This being so, we can conceive of no basis for demanding a higher level of competence for those

defendants who choose to plead guilty. If the *Dusky* standard is adequate for defendants who plead not guilty, it is necessarily adequate for those who plead guilty.

Requiring that a criminal defendant be competent has a modest aim: It seeks to ensure that he has the capacity to understand the proceedings and to assist counsel. While psychiatrists and scholars may find it useful to classify the various kinds and degrees of competence, and while States are free to adopt competency standards that are more elaborate than the *Dusky* formulation, the Due Process Clause does not impose these additional requirements.

d. Voluntariness and Knowledge of Elements

Can a guilty plea be voluntary if the defendant is unaware of the essential elements of the offense to which he is pleading? In *Henderson v. Morgan*, 426 U.S. 637, 644–46 (1976), the Court held that a plea was involuntary when neither defense counsel nor the trial court explained that intent was an element of second-degree murder:

> We assume, as petitioner argues, that the prosecutor had overwhelming evidence of guilt available. We also accept petitioner's characterization of the competence of respondent's counsel and of the wisdom of their advice to plead guilty to a charge of second-degree murder. Nevertheless, such a plea cannot support a judgment of guilt unless it was voluntary in a constitutional sense. And clearly the plea could not be voluntary in the sense that it constituted an intelligent admission that he committed the offense unless the defendant received "real notice of the true nature of the charge against him, the first and most universally recognized requirement of due process." *Smith v. O'Grady*, 312 U.S. 329, 334.
>
> There is nothing in this record that can serve as a substitute for either a finding after trial, or a voluntary admission, that respondent had the requisite intent. Defense counsel did not purport to stipulate to that fact; they did not explain to him that his plea would be an admission of that fact; and he made no factual statement or admission necessarily implying that he had such intent. In these circumstances it is impossible to conclude that his plea to the unexplained charge of second-degree murder was voluntary.

Should the trial judge be able to rely on defense counsel disclosing the important elements of the offense to the defendant? In *Bradshaw v. Stumpf*, 545 U.S. 175 (2005), the Court held that "where a defendant is represented by competent counsel, the court usually may rely on that counsel's assurance that the defendant has been properly informed of the nature and elements of the charge to which he is pleading guilty."

e. Factual Basis for the Plea

In *McCarthy v. United States*, 394 U.S. 459 (1969), the Court noted that the requirement of agreeing to a factual basis protects a defendant from pleading voluntarily without realizing that her conduct is not actually within the charge. In court, after the judge makes the proper *Boykin* inquiries to ensure that the defendant is entering the plea knowingly and voluntarily, the judge turns to the prosecutor to provide the factual basis for the plea. The prosecutor reads a short statement of facts, which may be a police report, of what would have been proven had the case gone to trial, and then the judge asks the defendant if the facts are true. The defendant may disagree with some of the stated facts, but the plea will be valid as long as the facts necessary to constitute the elements of the charge are agreed upon.

f. *Alford* Plea

A court may, in its discretion, accept a plea when there is a factual basis for the charges even though the defendant asserts his innocence. In *North Carolina v. Alford*, 400 U.S. 25 (1970), Alford was indicted for first-degree murder, a capital offense. His appointed counsel questioned witnesses who Alford said would substantiate his claim of innocence. The witnesses, however, did not support Alford's story but gave statements that strongly indicated his guilt. Faced with strong evidence of guilt and no substantial evidentiary support for the claim of innocence, Alford's attorney recommended that he plead guilty, but left the ultimate decision to Alford himself. The prosecutor agreed to accept a plea of guilty to a charge of second-degree murder, and Alford pleaded guilty to the reduced charge. The Supreme Court approved this plea:

> State and lower federal courts are divided upon whether a guilty plea can be accepted when it is accompanied by protestations of innocence and hence contains only a waiver of trial but no admission of guilt. Some courts, giving expression to the principle that "our law only authorizes a conviction where guilt is shown," require that trial judges reject such pleas. But others have concluded that they should not "force any defense on a defendant in a criminal case," particularly when advancement of the defense might "end in disaster." Since "guilt, or the degree of guilt, is at times uncertain and elusive," "an accused, though believing in or entertaining doubts respecting his innocence, might reasonably conclude a jury would be convinced of his guilt and that he would fare better in the sentence by pleading guilty." As one state court observed nearly a century ago, "reasons other than the fact that he is guilty may induce a defendant to so plead, and he must be permitted to judge for himself in this respect."

We cannot perceive any material difference between a plea that refuses to admit commission of the criminal act and a plea containing a protestation of innocence when, as in the instant case, a defendant intelligently concludes that his interests require entry of a guilty plea and the record before the judge contains strong evidence of actual guilt. Here the State had a strong case of first-degree murder against Alford. Whether he realized or disbelieved his guilt, he insisted on his plea because in his view he had absolutely nothing to gain by a trial and much to gain by pleading. Because of the overwhelming evidence against him, a trial was precisely what neither Alford nor his attorney desired. Confronted with the choice between a trial for first-degree murder, on the one hand, and a plea of guilty to second-degree murder, on the other, Alford quite reasonably chose the latter and thereby limited the maximum penalty to a 30-year term. When his plea is viewed in light of the evidence against him, which substantially negated his claim of innocence and which further provided a means by which the judge could test whether the plea was being intelligently entered, its validity cannot be seriously questioned. In view of the strong factual basis for the plea demonstrated by the State and Alford's clearly expressed desire to enter it despite his professed belief in his innocence, we hold that the trial judge did not commit constitutional error in accepting it.

Food for Thought

Alford pleas are atypical. Why do you think that is? How do you think the judge, who will sentence the defendant, views an *Alford* plea? Is it appropriate for the judge to take into account a defendant's lack of admission of guilt as a reason to increase sentence? *See* Chapter 20, Sentencing, *infra.*

400 U.S. at 33–38. Whether a prosecutor agrees to an *Alford* plea and whether the trial court accepts one is discretionary.

g. The Judge's Role

Fed.R.Crim.P. 11(c)(1) prohibits the judge from participating in plea negotiations. In federal court, therefore, the plea negotiation takes place solely between the prosecution and the defendant. While the judge may decide whether to accept a plea negotiated between the prosecution and the defense, the judge cannot participate in the process. *See, e.g., United States v. Hemphill*, 748 F.3d 666 (5th Cir. 2014) (holding trial court's comments about strength of prosecution's evidence and reference to fate befallen similarly situated defendants constituted improper participation in plea negotiations).

Food for Thought

Federal courts have interpreted Rule 11's prohibition on judicial involvement in plea negotiations to include a prohibition on letting the parties know what sentence the court will impose under a particular plea. This would seem to deprive of all meaning the constitutional requirements that a plea reflect the accused's "knowing and intelligent waiver of constitutional rights." What could be more important to the accused than knowing what sentence will be imposed upon pleading guilty? And as far as contract law goes, isn't this a bit like negotiating over a purchase without knowing either the price or the value of the thing being purchased?

Professor Albert Alschuler made the following argument on the trial judge's role:

Apologists for plea bargaining often contend that, when a plea agreement satisfies the parties, no one else can have legitimate reason for complaint. A bargain that a defendant, advised by able counsel, finds advantageous cannot properly be criticized on the ground that it is unfair to him, and if occasional cases of incompetence or corruption are set aside, the prosecutor's acquiescence in the bargain insures that it is fair to the state as well. A jurisprudential assessment of this argument would require consideration of the concept of voluntariness, of the goals of criminal proceedings, of the mechanisms by which those goals can best be achieved, and, perhaps, of the reasons for prohibiting a variety of consensual arrangements in other contexts. It is sufficient for present purposes to note that one who accepts this central argument for plea bargaining cannot consistently oppose judicial participation in the process, for judicial bargaining apparently meets with the approval of most defense attorneys and a great many prosecutors. At the very least, if the consent of the parties is regarded as determinative, a trial judge should be permitted to negotiate with a defense attorney when both the prosecutor and the defendant acquiesce in this procedure. If the opponents of judicial bargaining are unwilling to create this exception to the prohibition that they propose, some of them must apparently reconsider the significance that the consent of the parties should have in criminal proceedings.

Albert Alschuler, *The Trial Judge's Role in Plea Bargaining, Part I*, 76 Colum. L. Rev. 1059, 1152 (1976). Do you agree or disagree with this excerpt? Why or why not? Do you think that there is something "unseemly" or otherwise inappropriate about judges being involved in plea bargaining? If so, is that a commentary upon the judicial role or on plea bargaining itself?

FYI

In State courts, the source of most of the nation's criminal justice action, where dockets have large backlogs and resources are vastly less than in the federal system, there are generally no impediments to active judicial participation in plea negotiations, and most plea bargains involve a guaranteed sentence agreed upon by all participants, including the judge.

h. Collateral Consequences

Fed.R.Crim.P. 11(b)(1) lists some consequences of a guilty plea, *e.g.,* mandatory minimum penalty & maximum possible penalty. A defendant need not be advised of every collateral consequence of a guilty plea (*e.g.,* loss of government benefits, voting rights, housing, professional licensing), but the Supreme Court held in *Padilla v. Kentucky,* 559 U.S. 356 (2010), that ineffective assistance of counsel occurs when a defendant's lawyer does not advise a client of deportation risks, including a requirement of at least advising in general terms if the exact immigration consequences are unclear.

What about mandatory sex offender registration obligations? Must a guilty plea advisory warn defendants of this consequence? Courts have split on the issue. *See, e.g., People v. Fonville*, 804 N.W.2d 878 (Mich. App. 2011) (warning required because sex offender registration is like deportation as a serious and intimately-connected consequence of conviction); *People v. Gravino*, 928 N.E.2d 1048 (N.Y. 2010) (pre-*Padilla* case holding that because registration is a "collateral" and not "direct" consequence, warning not required).

i. Presumption of Validity

Constitutionally, when a prior conviction based upon a guilty plea is used to enhance the defendant's sentence for the current offense, in the absence of a transcript of the prior guilty plea proceeding, the burden is on the defendant to show a *Boykin* violation. The *Boykin* "presumption of invalidity" is trumped by the presumption of regularity attaching to final judgments. *Parke v. Raley*, 506 U.S. 20 (1992).

j. Contract Null if Court Rejects Plea

In *United States v. Hyde*, 520 U.S. 670 (1997), the Court observed that the Federal Rules: "explicitly envision a situation in which the defendant performs his side of the bargain (the guilty plea) before the Government is required to perform its side (here, the motion to dismiss four counts). If the court accepts the agreement and thus the Government's promised performance, then the contemplated agreement is complete and the defendant gets the benefit of his bargain. But if the court rejects the Government's promised performance, then the agreement is terminated and the defendant has the right to back out of his promised performance (the guilty plea), just as a binding contractual duty may be extinguished by the nonoccurrence of a condition subsequent.

k. Use of Statements Made in Plea Negotiations

Notwithstanding Fed.R.Crim.P. 11(f)'s general prohibition on the admissibility of plea-statements, the Court in *United States v. Mezzanatto*, 513 U.S. 196 (1995), held that a defendant could agree prior to plea discussions that any statement he made during those discussions could be used to impeach any contradictory statement he might make if the case is tried. The Court found that waiver is not inconsistent with the rule's goal of encouraging voluntary settlement, because it "makes no sense to conclude that mutual settlement will be encouraged by precluding negotiation over an issue that may be particularly important to one of the parties to the transaction."

l. Involuntariness as Basis for Negating Plea

One of the few grounds upon which a guilty plea may be set aside is if a court determines that it was involuntary. In *Brady v. United States*, 397 U.S. 742 (1970), the Court held that the defendant must prove that the fear of the possible consequences of not pleading guilty destroyed the ability to balance the risks and benefits of going to trial. The Court found that Brady's plea was voluntary even though it was motivated by his desire to avoid the death penalty.

Hypo: *Withdrawal of Plea?*

Jonathan Pollard, an Intelligence Research Specialist with the United States Navy, admitted spying for the Israeli government. Ultimately, he pleaded guilty to one count of conspiracy to deliver national defense information to a foreign government. Anne Pollard, Jonathan Pollard's wife, was also implicated in this spy affair. Despite the fact that Anne Pollard had a debilitating gastrointestinal disorder prior to her arrest and, seriously ill, lost forty pounds over a period of three months while confined in the District of Columbia jail after her arrest, the government refused to offer her a plea agreement unless Jonathan Pollard also pleaded guilty. Such plea arrangements are commonly called "wired pleas," *i.e.*, each plea is inextricably linked to the other; if one defendant fails to abide by his or her plea agreement terms, both plea deals fail. After Anne Pollard served three years in prison and was paroled and moved to Israel, Jonathan Pollard sought to withdraw his plea arguing that the government overreached by using unconstitutional pressure (his concern about his wife's health) to force him to plead guilty, in effect, coercing an involuntary plea. Do you think this is a good argument? Why or why not? Does it (should it) make any difference in your analysis that Pollard did not contest his actual guilt?

United States v. Ruiz

536 U.S. 622 (2002).

JUSTICE BREYER delivered the opinion of the Court.

In this case we primarily consider whether the Fifth and Sixth Amendments require federal prosecutors, before entering into a binding plea agreement with a criminal defendant,

Hear It

You can hear the oral argument in *Ruiz* at: http://www.oyez.org/cases/2000-2009/2001/2001_01_595.

to disclose "impeachment information relating to any informants or other witnesses." We hold that the Constitution does not require that disclosure.

After immigration agents found 30 kilograms of marijuana in Angela Ruiz's luggage, federal prosecutors offered her what is known in the Southern District of California as a "fast track" plea bargain. That bargain—standard in that district—asks a defendant to waive indictment, trial, and an appeal. In return, the Government agrees to recommend to the sentencing judge a two-level departure downward from the otherwise applicable United States Sentencing Guidelines sentence. In Ruiz's case, a two-level departure downward would have shortened the ordinary Guidelines-specified 18-to-24-month sentencing range by 6 months, to 12-to-18 months.

The prosecutors' proposed plea agreement contains a set of detailed terms. Among other things, it specifies that "any known information establishing the factual innocence of the defendant" "has been turned over to the defendant," and it acknowledges the Government's "continuing duty to provide such information." At the same time it requires that the defendant "waive the right" to receive "impeachment information relating to any informants or other witnesses" as well as the right to receive information supporting any affirmative defense the defendant raises if the case goes to trial. Because Ruiz would not agree to this last-mentioned waiver, the prosecutors withdrew their bargaining offer. The Government then indicted Ruiz for unlawful drug possession. Despite the absence of any agreement, Ruiz ultimately pleaded guilty.

At sentencing, Ruiz asked the judge to grant her the same two-level downward departure that the Government would have recommended had she accepted the "fast track" agreement. The Government opposed her request, and the District Court denied it, imposing a standard Guideline sentence instead.

The Ninth Circuit vacated the District Court's sentencing determination. The Ninth Circuit pointed out that the Constitution requires prosecutors to make certain impeachment information available to a defendant before trial. It decided that this obligation entitles defendants to receive that same information before they enter into a plea agreement. The Ninth Circuit also decided that the Constitution prohibits defendants from waiving their right to that information. And it held that the prosecutors' standard "fast track" plea agreement was unlawful because it insisted upon that waiver. We granted the Government's petition for certiorari.

The constitutional question concerns a federal criminal defendant's waiver of the right to receive exculpatory impeachment material from prosecutors—a right that the Constitution provides as part of its basic "fair trial" guarantee. *See* U.S. Const., Amdts. 5, 6. *See also Brady v. Maryland,* 373 U.S. 83 (1963) (Due process requires prosecutors to "avoid an unfair trial" by making available "upon request" evidence "favorable to an accused where the evidence is material either to guilt or to punishment"); *Giglio v. United States,* 405 U.S. 150, 154 (1972) (exculpatory evidence includes "evidence affecting" witness "credibility," where the witness' "reliability" is likely "determinative of guilt or innocence").

When a defendant pleads guilty he or she, of course, forgoes not only a fair trial, but also other accompanying constitutional guarantees. *Boykin v. Alabama,* 395 U.S. 238, 243 (1969) (pleading guilty implicates the Fifth Amendment privilege against self-incrimination, the Sixth Amendment right to confront one's accusers, and the Sixth Amendment right to trial by jury). Given the seriousness of the matter, the Constitution insists, among other things, that the defendant enter a guilty plea that is "voluntary" and that the defendant must make related waivers "knowingly, intelligently, and with sufficient awareness of the relevant circumstances and likely consequences."

We must decide whether the Constitution requires that preguilty plea disclosure of impeachment information. We conclude that it does not.

Due process considerations, the very considerations that led this Court to find trial-related rights to exculpatory and impeachment information in *Brady* and *Giglio*, argue against the existence of the "right" that the Ninth Circuit found here. This Court has said that due process considerations include not only (1) the nature of the private interest at stake, but also (2) the value of the additional safeguard, and (3) the adverse impact of the requirement upon the Government's interests.

Food for Thought

The Court here seems unable to see why an innocent person would plead guilty. Can you? Is the Court's discounting of this possibility warranted?

Ake v. Oklahoma, 470 U.S. 68 (1985). Here, as we have just pointed out, the added value of the Ninth Circuit's "right" to a defendant is often limited, for it depends upon the defendant's independent awareness of the details of the Government's case. And in any case, as the proposed plea agreement at issue here specifies, the Government will provide "any information establishing the factual innocence of the defendant" regardless. That fact, along with other guilty-plea safeguards, diminishes the force of Ruiz's concern that, in the absence of impeachment information, innocent individuals, accused of crimes, will plead guilty.

At the same time, a constitutional obligation to provide impeachment information during plea bargaining, prior to entry of a guilty plea, could seriously interfere with the Government's interest in securing those guilty pleas that are factually justified, desired by defendants, and help to secure the efficient administration of justice. The Ninth Circuit's rule risks premature disclosure of Government witness information, which, the Government tells us, could "disrupt ongoing investigations" and expose prospective witnesses to serious harm. And the careful tailoring that characterizes most legal Government witness disclosure requirements suggests recognition by both Congress and the Federal Rules Committees that such concerns are valid. *See, e.g.,* 18 U.S.C. § 3432 (witness list disclosure required in capital cases three days before trial with exceptions); § 3500 (Government witness statements ordinarily subject to discovery only after testimony given); Fed. Rule Crim. Proc. 16(a)(2) (embodies limitations of 18 U.S.C. § 3500).

FYI

Ruiz is a federal case. To the extent there is any legitimacy to the Court's assumptions in *Ruiz* about the lack of costs to innocent defendants and the high costs to the government, those assumptions are not as warranted in state criminal cases. While in the vast majority of federal cases, involving drug, gun and white-collar offenses, the witnesses are government agents or are known to the defendant, state criminal prosecutions rely far more heavily on civilian witnesses.

Consequently, the Ninth Circuit's requirement could force the Government to abandon its "general practice" of not "disclosing to a defendant pleading guilty information that would reveal the identities of cooperating informants, undercover investigators, or other prospective witnesses." It could require the Government to devote substantially more resources to trial preparation prior to plea bargaining, thereby depriving the plea-bargaining process of its main resource-saving advantages. Or it could lead the Government instead to abandon its heavy reliance upon plea bargaining in a vast number—90% or more—of federal criminal cases. We cannot say that the Constitution's due process requirement demands so radical a change in the criminal justice process in order to achieve so comparatively small a constitutional benefit.

These considerations, taken together, lead us to conclude that the Constitution does not require the Government to disclose material impeachment evidence prior to entering a plea agreement with a criminal defendant.

In addition, we note that the "fast track" plea agreement requires a defendant to waive her right to receive information the Government has regarding any "affirmative defense" she raises at trial. We do not believe the Constitution here requires provision of this information to the defendant prior to plea bargaining—for most (though not all) of the reasons previously stated. That is to say, in the context of this agreement, the need for this information is more closely related to the *fairness* of a trial than to the *voluntariness* of the plea; the value in terms of the defendant's added awareness of relevant circumstances is ordinarily limited; yet the added burden imposed upon the Government by requiring its provision well in advance of trial (often before trial preparation begins) can be serious, thereby significantly interfering with the administration of the plea bargaining process.

For these reasons the decision of the Court of Appeals for the Ninth Circuit is reversed.

Points for Discussion

a. Non-Impeachment Evidence

The facts of *Ruiz* do not reach the issue of a guilty plea where a defendant agrees to forego discovery of withholding non-impeachment exculpatory evidence, such as evidence indicating someone else may have committed the crime. Should such an agreement be treated differently? What about evidence that would undermine the identification of an eyewitness? Is that covered by *Ruiz*? Is that impeachment evidence? *Compare Matthew v. Johnson*, 201 F.3d 353 (5th Cir. 2000) (holding defendants cannot challenge guilty pleas on basis on undisclosed *Brady* information) *with State v. Heubler*, 275 P.3d 91 (Nev. 2012) (holding defendants can challenge guilty pleas on basis of withheld non-impeachment or affirmatively exculpatory evidence).

b. Interests of Justice Involved

Are there valid interests to be protected by requiring prosecutors to disclose all exculpatory evidence before a guilty plea, or, similarly, behind not allowing defendants to waive the right to this disclosure?

c. Pre-plea Request

Does *Ruiz* apply when a defendant already had made a pre-plea discovery request for any potentially *exculpatory* evidence in the state's control? Should the court require the prosecutor to provide the defendant with the evidence before accepting the plea? *See, e.g., State v. Harris*, 266 Wis.2d 200, 667 N.W.2d 813 (App. 2003) (defendant allowed to withdraw guilty plea when prosecutor failed to disclose exculpatory information prior to entry of plea).

D. Plea Negotiation Roles

Some have argued that, during the plea bargaining process, prosecutors must play multiple roles: 1) "administrator" in the sense of disposing of cases in the "fastest, most efficient manner"; 2) "advocate" in the sense of trying "to maximize both the number of convictions and the severity of the sentences that are imposed after conviction"; "judge" in the sense that the prosecutor may be trying to do the 'right thing' for the defendant in view of the defendant's social circumstances or in view of the peculiar circumstances of his crime—with the qualification, of course, that the 'right thing' will not be done unless the defendant pleads guilty; "legislator" because he "may grant concessions because the law is "too harsh," not only for this defendant but for all defendants." *See* Albert W. Alschuler, *The Prosecutor's Role in Plea Bargaining*, 36 U. CHI. L.REV. 52–53 (1968).

Point for Discussion

ABA Standards

The relevant portions of the ABA Prosecution Function Standards warn prosecutors against misleading criminal defendants in plea discussions. However, law enforcement personnel are entitled under existing Fifth, Sixth and Fourteenth Amendment law to "mislead" accused defendants who have properly received Miranda warnings, *e.g.*, about inculpatory statements supposedly made by co-defendants or the existence of fingerprints supposedly left at the scene of the crime. Do the ethics rules conflict with prevailing constitutional law? If so, which body of law or rules should a prosecutor follow?

Some argue that there is a widespread perception that criminal attorneys are romantic figures who serve as "an antidote to the fear, ignorance, and bewilderment of the impoverished and uneducated defendant, not only in the courtroom but throughout the criminal process." See Albert W. Alschuler, The Defense Attorney's Role in Plea Bargaining, 84 Yale L.J. 1179, 1181–82 (1975). The hope is that "a guilty plea is truthful, based on consent, and entered with an awareness of the consequences and of the defendant's rights."

Alschuler argues that the economics of criminal defense work tend to undercut this romantic image. Some lawyers are able to develop "a reputation as an outstanding trial lawyer" that allows them to attract wealthy clients who can pay higher fees. Many other criminal defense attorneys handle "a large volume of cases for less-than-spectacular fees," and that is usually accomplished by having lots of clients agree to plea bargains. Indeed, lawyers never make much money on cases that they try. As one prominent attorney said, "A guilty plea is a quick buck." *Id.*

As another attorney noted "Half of the regular defense bar are guys who plead out constantly." As another lawyer said "Of the lawyers who sometimes appear in criminal cases here, there are no more than five whom I would hire. There may be 30 others who do a more-or-less conscientious job. And there are probably 50 or 55 cop-out lawyers." Another believed that the number of lawyers "who hustle business, never see their clients, and plead all of them guilty." Nevertheless, "at least half of all defense attorneys never take a case intending to prepare for trial." *Id.*

As a result, although plea bargaining seems to occur in "an atmosphere of informed choice," the participating parties (private defense attorneys, public defenders, and appointed attorneys) "are all subject to bureaucratic pressures and conflicts of interest that seem unavoidable in any regime grounded on the guilty plea." *Id.*

Alschuler goes on to argue that, unless it is possible to remedy these defects in the plea bargaining process, "we must either endure these abuses or else restructure our criminal justice system to eliminate the overwhelming importance of the defendant's choice of plea, a choice that is usually bent to the purposes of defense attorneys and other participants in the criminal justice system rather than to the interests of the defendant or society." *Id.* He concludes:

> The problem of providing adequate resources for criminal courts, for prosecutor and defender offices, and for other criminal justice agencies is undeniably difficult. Nevertheless, even the poorest and most primitive societies manage to guarantee a right to trial, and it is hard to believe that our nation cannot find the resources to guarantee this right as well. Rather than rationalize the familiar, the cheap, and the easy, it may be time to reassert the judgment of the framers of the Sixth Amendment: the cost of jury trials is worth paying.

Id.

Food for Thought

Professor Alschuler describes the problems defense attorneys bring to the plea bargaining system. What are the pressures and problems prosecutors (the executive branch), judges, and legislators bring to this system? Consider the pressures on judges to move overcrowded dockets and obtain resources to run the court. Judges know well that setting high bail amounts that result in incarceration of a defendant pretrial force quicker guilty pleas, and that guilty pleas allow an imposition of fines and fees that are relied upon to finance the court system. Legislators pass draconian sentencing schemes, and prosecutors can leverage those schemes to force defendants to plead guilty regardless of a meritorious defense or actual innocence.

Exercise: *Plea Bargaining*

Your class should be split evenly between those assigned the role of prosecutors and those assigned to be defense counsel. Both groups should consider the following factual scenario:

Peter Lane is observed by police in an area known for drug dealing. They see Peter talking to known addicts, and at one point they see him reach into his front right pocket and pull something out and give it to someone. The officers cannot see what Peter has pulled out and this is not a two-way exchange of items. An officer approaches Peter and puts him against the wall for a frisk. Upon feeling a plastic baggie in Peter's front right pocket, which in the officer's experience feels like it contains rocks consistent with cocaine, the officer pulls the baggie out of Peter's pocket. The officer finds that it contains six rocks of cocaine. Police arrest Peter.

The prosecutor assigned to the charging division charged Peter with possession with intent to distribute cocaine. Possession with intent to distribute cocaine carries a maximum term of imprisonment of 10 years and a mandatory minimum of one year. Simple possession of cocaine carries a maximum term of imprisonment of five years and no mandatory minimum.

Peter has one prior arrest for possession of cocaine where the case was dismissed and one prior conviction for simple assault.

At a time to be set by your professor, selected prosecutors and defense counsel should simulate a meeting between the two sides (a meeting requested by defense counsel) to discuss whether there might be a plea deal. Both sides should come to class having prepared a "pre-negotiation memorandum," referring to, *inter alia*: A) the considerations (policy, political, ethical, moral, penological, community, etc.) relevant to this charging decision (from the defendant's side and from the State's side respectively); B) what additional information, if any, about Peter Lane should be acquired by defense counsel or the District Attorney's Office to better determine an appropriate plea; C) strengths and weaknesses in the State's case; D) specific recommendations for the deal, and arguments in support thereof.

Two student observers should monitor each of the plea negotiation sessions. The observers should draft a memorandum analyzing what

> they observed, *e.g.*, how did the negotiation proceed?; was a fair resolution reached?; how could each of the sides have better maximized their respective positions?

E. Withdrawing a Guilty Plea

It is not uncommon for a defendant who has previously tendered a guilty plea to subsequently seek to withdraw that plea, whether it is days, months, or even years later. Aside from the broken plea agreement cases, there are innumerable reasons why a defendant might later seek to withdraw his or her guilty plea. Such reasons range from mere second thoughts about the strategic thinking (defendant's and/or defense counsel's) that resulted in a guilty plea, to dissatisfaction with or surprise at the severity of the sentence received, to the emergence of new evidence or new witnesses (or the disappearance of evidence or witnesses). However, once properly tendered, a defendant does not generally have the right to withdraw a guilty plea. Nonetheless, prior to the imposition of sentence, most courts can and do permit withdrawal if the defendant presents "any fair and just" reason to do so. After the imposition of sentence, withdrawal is rarely permitted absent a finding of manifest injustice or a miscarriage of justice. *See* Fed.R.Crim.P. 11(d)(2).

In *United States v. Hyde*, 520 U.S. 670 (1997), the Court reversed a case in which the trial court permitted the defendant to withdraw a guilty plea after acceptance of a plea but before sentencing, without offering any justification. The Court observed:

> After the defendant has sworn in open court that he actually committed the crimes, after he has stated that he is pleading guilty because he is guilty, after the court has found a factual basis for the plea, and after the court has explicitly announced that it accepts the plea, the Court of Appeals would allow the defendant to withdraw his guilty plea simply on a lark. The Advisory Committee, in adding the "fair and just reason" standard to Rule 32(e) in 1983, explained why this cannot be so: "Given the great care with which pleas are taken under revised Rule 11, there is no reason to view pleas so taken as merely 'tentative,' subject to withdrawal before sentence whenever the government cannot establish prejudice. Were withdrawal automatic in every case where the defendant decided to alter his tactics and present his theory of the case to the jury, the guilty plea would become a mere gesture, a temporary and meaningless formality reversible at the defendant's whim. In fact, however, a guilty plea is no such trifle, but a "grave and solemn act," which is "accepted only with care and discernment." We think the Court of Appeals' holding would

degrade the otherwise serious act of pleading guilty into something akin to a move in a game of chess.

In addition, if the reason a defendant pleaded guilty was that he or she relied on the incompetent legal or tactical advice of defense counsel, where he or she can demonstrate that "there is a reasonable probability that, but for counsel's errors, defendant would not have pleaded guilty and would have insisted on going to trial," the guilty plea may be withdrawn based upon ineffective assistance of counsel. *Hill v. Lockhart,* 474 U.S. 52, 59 (1985).

Executive Summary

Types of Pleas. In many jurisdictions, a defendant may enter either a plea of not guilty, nolo contendere, guilty, guilty but mentally ill, not guilty by reason of insanity, an *Alford* plea, or a conditional guilty plea.

Knowing and Voluntary Plea. A judge must address a defendant personally in open court to determine if a plea is voluntary and if the defendant understands the rights being waived by entering the plea.

Factual Basis Required. There must be a factual basis for the plea stated on the record.

Major Themes

a. Vast Majority—The role of prosecutors and defense attorneys in criminal cases is largely one of negotiating pleas; the vast majority of charged defendants plead guilty on lesser charges as opposed to risk more severe sentences by proceeding to trial.

b. Contracts—Promises or agreements that form the basis of a plea generally must be fulfilled as under the law of contracts. Both sides of the agreement must fulfill their promises.

Competency to Plead Guilty. To enter a guilty plea a defendant must be competent which is determined by the same standards as competency to stand trial.

Withdrawing a Guilty Plea. Procedural rules may allow to defendant to withdraw a guilty plea under specified circumstances, though it is much easier to withdraw a guilty plea prior to sentencing than after a sentence has been imposed.

Non-Disclosure of Impeachment Evidence. Prosecutors may withhold impeachment evidence regarding prosecution witnesses prior to entry of a guilty plea.

Test Your Knowledge

To assess your understanding of the material in this chapter, click here to take a quiz.

For More Information

• WAYNE R. LAFAVE, JEROLD H. ISRAEL, NANCY J. KING & ORIN S. KERR, CRIMINAL PROCEDURE (5th ed. 2009).

• JEROLD H. ISRAEL & WAYNE R. LAFAVE, CRIMINAL PROCEDURE: CONSTITUTIONAL LIMITATIONS (8th ed. 2006).

• RUSSELL L. WEAVER, JOHN M. BURKOFF, CATHERINE HANCOCK, JANET HOEFFEL, STEVE FRIEDLAND & STEPHEN SINGER, PRINCIPLES OF CRIMINAL PROCEDURE CH. 15 (6th ed. 2018).

CHAPTER 17

Jury Trials

A. Right to Jury Trial

The Sixth Amendment provides in pertinent part that "in all criminal prosecutions an accused shall enjoy the right to a speedy and public trial, by an impartial jury of the State and district wherein the crime shall have been committed." Further, Article III of the Constitution states that "the trial of all crimes . . . shall be by jury; and such trial shall be held in the state where the said crimes shall have been committed." In *Duncan v. Louisiana*, 391 U.S. 145 (1968), the Supreme Court held that the right to trial by jury is a fundamental right that is applicable to the states through the Due Process Clause of the Fourteenth Amendment.

In *Duncan*, defendant was convicted of simple battery, a misdemeanor under Louisiana law, a crime punishable by a maximum of two years' imprisonment and a $300 fine. Appellant sought trial by jury, but the trial judge denied the request because the state constitution granted jury trials only when capital punishment or imprisonment at hard labor may be imposed. Appellant was convicted and sentenced to serve 60 days in the parish prison and was required to pay a fine of $150. Justice White upheld the defendant's right to a jury trial, with the following broad reasoning:

> The guarantees of jury trial in the Federal and State Constitutions reflect a profound judgment about the way in which law should be enforced and justice administered. A right to jury trial is granted to criminal defendants in order to prevent oppression by the Government. Those who wrote our constitutions knew from history and experience that it was necessary to protect against unfounded criminal charges brought to eliminate enemies and against judges too responsive to the voice of higher authority. The framers of the constitutions strove to create an independent judiciary but insisted upon further protection against arbitrary action. Providing an accused with the right to be tried by a jury of his peers gave him an inestimable safeguard against the corrupt or overzealous prosecutor and against the compliant, biased, or eccentric judge. If the defendant preferred the common-sense judgment of a jury to the more tutored but perhaps less sympathetic reaction of the single judge, he was to have it. Beyond this, the jury trial provisions in the Federal and

State Constitutions reflect a fundamental decision about the exercise of official power—a reluctance to entrust plenary powers over the life and liberty of the citizen to one judge or to a group of judges. Fear of unchecked power, so typical of State and Federal Governments in other respects, found expression in the criminal law in this insistence upon community participation in the determination of guilt or innocence. The deep commitment of the Nation to the right of jury trial in serious criminal cases as a defense against arbitrary law enforcement qualifies for protection under the Due Process Clause of the Fourteenth Amendment, and must therefore be respected by the States.

Food for Thought

You learned in Chapter 16 that approximately 95% of defendants charged with crimes plead guilty rather than risk trial. Does this mean that the judgment of guilt or innocence is largely entrusted to the unchecked decisions of a prosecutor? Does the right to a jury trial have meaning in this context?

In determining whether the length of the authorized prison term or the seriousness of other punishment is enough in itself to require a jury trial, we refer to objective criteria, chiefly the existing laws and practices in the Nation. In the federal system, petty offenses are defined as those punishable by no more than six months in prison and a $500 fine. In 49 of the 50 States, crimes subject to trial without a jury (which occasionally include simple battery) are punishable by no more than one year in jail. We need not, however, settle in this case the exact location of the line between petty offenses and serious crimes. It is sufficient for our purposes to hold that a crime punishable by two years in prison is, based on past and contemporary standards in this country, a serious crime and not a petty offense. Consequently, appellant was entitled to a jury trial and it was error to deny it.

Blanton v. City of North Las Vegas

489 U.S. 538 (1989).

JUSTICE MARSHALL delivered the opinion of the Court.

The issue in this case is whether there is a constitutional right to a trial by jury for persons charged under Nevada law with driving under the influence of alcohol (DUI). Nev.Rev. Stat. § 484.379(1) (1987). We hold that there is not.

Hear It

You can listen to the oral argument in *Blanton* at: http://www.oyez.org/cases/1980-1989/1988/1988_87_1437.

DUI is punishable by a minimum term of two days' imprisonment and a maximum term of six months' imprisonment. Alternatively, a trial court may order defendant "to perform 48 hours of work for the community while dressed in distinctive garb which identifies him" as a DUI offender. Defendant also must pay a fine ranging from $200 to $1,000. In addition, defendant automatically loses his driver's license for 90 days, and he must attend, at his own expense, an alcohol abuse education course. Repeat DUI offenders are subject to increased penalties.

Petitioners Melvin R. Blanton and Mark D. Fraley were charged with DUI in separate incidents. Neither petitioner had a prior DUI conviction. The North Las Vegas, Nevada, Municipal Court denied their respective pretrial demands for a jury trial. On appeal, the Eighth Judicial District Court denied Blanton's request for a jury trial but, a month later, granted Fraley's. Blanton then appealed to the Supreme Court of Nevada, as did respondent city of North Las Vegas with respect to Fraley. After consolidating the two cases along with several others raising the same issue, the Supreme Court concluded, *inter alia*, that the Federal Constitution does not guarantee a right to a jury trial for a DUI offense because the maximum term of incarceration is only six months and the maximum possible fine is $1,000. We granted *certiorari* to consider whether petitioners were entitled to a jury trial, and now affirm.

It has long been settled that "there is a category of petty crimes or offenses which is not subject to the Sixth Amendment jury trial provision." *Duncan v. Louisiana*, 391 U.S. 145, 159 (1968). In determining whether a particular offense should be categorized as "petty," our early decisions focused on the nature of the offense and on whether it was triable by a jury at common law. In recent years, however, we have sought more "objective indications of the seriousness with which society regards the offense." *Frank v. United States*, 395 U.S. 147, 148 (1969). "We have found the most relevant such criteria in the severity of the maximum authorized penalty." *Baldwin v. New York*, 399 U.S. 66, 68 (1970) (plurality opinion). In fixing the maximum penalty for a crime, a legislature "includes within the definition of the crime itself a judgment about the seriousness of the offense."

In using the word "penalty," we do not refer solely to the maximum prison term authorized for a particular offense. A legislature's view of the seriousness of an offense also is reflected in the other penalties that it attaches to the offense. We thus examine "whether the length of the authorized prison term or the seriousness of other punishment is enough in itself to require a jury trial." *Duncan*, 391 U.S., at 161. Primary emphasis, however, must be placed on the maximum authorized period of incarceration. Penalties such as probation or a fine may engender "a significant infringement of personal freedom," but they cannot approximate in severity the loss of liberty that a prison term entails. Indeed, because incarceration is an "intrinsically different" form of punishment, it is the most powerful indication whether an offense is "serious."

Following this approach, our decision in *Baldwin* established that a defendant is entitled to a jury trial whenever the offense for which he is charged carries a maximum authorized prison term of greater than six months. The possibility of a sentence exceeding six months, we determined, is "sufficiently severe by itself" to require the opportunity for a jury trial. As for a prison term of six months or less, we recognized that it will seldom be viewed by the defendant as "trivial or 'petty.'" But we found that the disadvantages of such a sentence, "onerous though they may be, may be outweighed by the benefits that result from speedy and inexpensive nonjury adjudications."

Although we did not hold in *Baldwin* that an offense carrying a maximum prison term of six months or less automatically qualifies as a "petty" offense, and decline to do so today, we do find it appropriate to presume for purposes of the Sixth Amendment that society views such an offense as "petty." A defendant is entitled to a jury trial in such circumstances only if he can demonstrate that any additional statutory penalties, viewed in conjunction with the maximum authorized period of incarceration, are so severe that they clearly reflect a legislative determination that the offense in question is a "serious" one.

Applying these principles here, it is apparent that petitioners are not entitled to a jury trial. The maximum authorized prison sentence for first-time DUI offenders does not exceed six months. A presumption therefore exists that the Nevada Legislature views DUI as a "petty" offense for purposes of the Sixth Amendment. Considering the additional statutory penalties as well, we do not believe that the Nevada Legislature has clearly indicated that DUI is a "serious" offense.

In the first place, it is immaterial that a first-time DUI offender may face a minimum term of imprisonment. In settling on six months' imprisonment as the constitutional demarcation point, we have assumed that a defendant convicted of the offense in question would receive the maximum authorized prison sentence. It is not constitutionally determinative, therefore, that a particular defendant may be required to serve some amount of jail time less than six months. Likewise, it is of little moment that a defendant may receive the maximum prison term because of the prohibitions on plea bargaining and probation. As for the 90-day license suspension, it, too, will be irrelevant if it runs concurrently with the prison sentence, which we assume for present purposes to be the maximum of six months.[9]

---

[9] It is unclear whether the license suspension and prison sentence in fact run concurrently. Furthermore, the requirement that an offender attend an alcohol abuse education course can only be described as *de minimis*.

We are also unpersuaded by the fact that, instead of a prison sentence, a DUI offender may be ordered to perform 48 hours of community service dressed in clothing identifying him as a DUI offender. Even assuming the outfit is the source of some embarrassment during the 48-hour period, such a penalty will be less embarrassing and less onerous than six months in jail. As for the possible $1,000 fine, it is well below the $5,000 level set by Congress in its most recent definition of a "petty" offense, and petitioners do not suggest that this congressional figure is out of step with state practice for offenses carrying prison sentences of six months or less. Finally, we ascribe little significance to the fact that a DUI offender faces increased penalties for repeat offenses. Recidivist penalties of the magnitude imposed for DUI are commonplace and, in any event, petitioners do not face such penalties here.

Viewed together, the statutory penalties are not so severe that DUI must be deemed a "serious" offense for purposes of the Sixth Amendment. It was not error, therefore, to deny petitioners jury trials. Accordingly, the judgment of the Supreme Court of Nevada is

Affirmed.

Food for Thought

Do you agree with the Court that the combination of sanctions described in the first paragraph of the decision is not sufficiently "serious"? Does the Court give guidelines for what is "serious" enough to require a jury trial besides the maximum jail time?

Points for Discussion

a. Six Months or Less

In *United States v. Nachtigal*, 507 U.S. 1 (1993), the Court relied on *Blanton* in holding that a DUI charge with a maximum penalty of six months' imprisonment, a $5,000 fine, a five-year term of probation, and other penalties was not constitutionally serious. The Court reiterated *Blanton's* presumption that offenses for which the maximum authorized period of incarceration is six months or less are presumptively "petty." That legislative judgment, plus the possibility of a probationary sentence or a $5,000 fine, was not sufficiently severe to overcome the presumption. Compare *Richter v. Fairbanks*, 903 F.2d 1202 (8th Cir. 1990), where the court found that a possible 15-year driver's license revocation for a third DUI offense justified a jury trial even though the maximum authorized sentence was six months.

b. Aggregate Terms

In *Lewis v. United States*, 518 U.S. 322 (1996), the Supreme Court held that the scope of the federal jury trial right does not change when a defendant faces a potential aggregate prison term in excess of six months because multiple petty offenses are charged. "By setting the maximum authorized prison term at six months, the legislature categorized the offense as petty. The fact that Lewis was charged with two counts of a petty offense does not revise the legislative judgment as to the gravity of the particular offense, nor does it transform the petty offense into a serious one."

c. Contempt Proceedings

Contempt proceedings are at least quasi-criminal in nature, and a jury must be afforded before a sentence of confinement for more than six months may be imposed for a post-verdict finding of contempt. In *Codispoti v. Pennsylvania*, 418 U.S. 506 (1974), the Court held that a contemnor has a right to a jury trial if the aggregate sentences imposed on multiple contempt convictions was more than six months even though each count was only punishable up to six months. The *Lewis* Court distinguished *Codispoti* because the legislature usually has not set a specific penalty for criminal contempt. Instead, "courts use the severity of the penalty actually imposed as the measure of the character of the particular offense."

d. Jury Trials and Fines

Is a jury trial constitutionally required when the authorized statutory punishment is six months or less, but the penalty includes a fine? Does *Blanton* suggest that the magnitude of a fine may take the case out of the "petty offense" category? Many courts apply the federal statutory standard of a fine of $5,000 or less as the petty offense upper limit. A jury trial is required when a court imposes serious fines for criminal contempt. In *International Union, United Mine Workers of Am. v. Bagwell*, 512 U.S. 821 (1994), the Court held that contempt fines of $52 million for violation of a labor injunction were criminal and were subject to the jury trial right. However, the Court reiterated the long-accepted idea that direct contempt in the presence of the court is subject to immediate summary adjudication without jury trial.

e. Juvenile Court

Juvenile court proceedings against a youthful offender are not considered to be criminal in nature, and there is no right to a jury trial in such proceedings. *McKeiver v. Pennsylvania*, 403 U.S. 528 (1971).

f. Bench Trials

Virtually all jurisdictions allow the constitutional right to a jury trial to be waived by the defendant in favor of a bench trial in most circumstances, although a defendant does not have a constitutional right to a bench trial. *Patton v. United States*, 281 U.S. 276 (1930). Consequently statutory rules like Fed. R. Crim.

Pro. 23, which require a prosecutor's consent to a bench trial, are constitutional. In *Singer v. United States,* 380 U.S. 24 (1965), the Court left open the possibility that the right to waive could belong to the defendant alone: "We need not determine in this case whether there might be some circumstances where a defendant's reasons for wanting to be tried by a judge alone are so compelling that the Government's insistence on trial by jury would result in the denial to a defendant of an impartial trial."

g. Sentencing Enhancements and Jury Trials

In *Apprendi v. New Jersey,* 530 U.S. 466 (2000), the Court struck down a sentencing law enabling a judge to lengthen a jury-imposed sentence by two years if the judge determined it to be a hate crime. The Court held that, other than the fact of a prior conviction, any fact increasing the penalty beyond the prescribed statutory maximum, whether the statute calls it an element or a sentencing factor, must be submitted to a jury, and proved beyond a reasonable doubt. *See* Chapter 20, Sentencing, *infra.*

Food for Thought

A determination that the waiver is made voluntarily and with a full understanding of its consequences must precede the acceptance of a waiver by the court. *See Singer v. United States, supra.* Assuming that the prosecutor and the court are willing to concur in any decision by the defendant to waive a jury trial, what strategic considerations may affect a defendant's decision to waive a jury trial?

B. Jury Size and Unanimity

Williams v. Florida

399 U.S. 78 (1970).

MR. JUSTICE WHITE delivered the opinion of the Court.

[Williams's motion to impanel a 12-person jury, rather than the six-person jury provided by Florida law in noncapital cases, was denied. Thereafter he was convicted of robbery and sentenced to life imprisonment.]

Hear It

You can listen to the oral argument in *Williams* at: http://www.oyez.org/cases/1960-1969/1969/1969_927.

In *Duncan v. Louisiana,* 391 U.S. 145 (1968), we held that the Fourteenth Amendment guarantees a right to trial by jury in all criminal cases that—were they in a federal court—would come within the Sixth Amendment's guarantee. Petitioner's trial for robbery on July 3, 1968, clearly falls within the scope of that holding. The question is whether the constitutional guarantee of a trial by "jury" necessarily requires trial by exactly 12 persons, rather than some lesser number—in this case six. We hold that the 12-man panel is not a necessary ingredient of "trial by jury," and that respondent's refusal to impanel more than the six members provided for by Florida law did not violate petitioner's Sixth Amendment rights as applied to the States through the Fourteenth.

We had occasion in *Duncan v. Louisiana* to review the history of the development of trial by jury in criminal cases. That history revealed a long tradition attaching great importance to the concept of relying on a body of one's peers to determine guilt or innocence as a safeguard against arbitrary law enforcement. That same history affords little insight into the considerations that gradually led the size of that body to be generally fixed at 12. Some have suggested that the number 12 was fixed upon simply because that was the number of the presentment jury from the hundred, from which the petit jury developed. Other, less circular but more fanciful reasons for the number 12 have been given, "but they were all brought forward after the number was fixed," and rest on little more than mystical or superstitious insights into the significance of "12." Lord Coke's explanation that the "number of twelve is much respected in holy writ, as 12 apostles, 12 stones, 12 tribes, etc.," is typical. In short, while sometime in the 14th century the size of the jury at common law came to be fixed generally at 12, that particular feature of the jury system appears to have been a historical accident, unrelated to the great purposes which gave rise to the jury in the first place. The question is whether this accidental feature of the jury has been immutably codified into our Constitution.

The relevant inquiry must be the function that the particular feature performs and its relation to the purposes of the jury trial. Measured by this standard, the 12-man requirement cannot be regarded as an indispensable component of the Sixth Amendment. The purpose of the jury trial, as we noted in *Duncan*, is to prevent oppression by the Government. Given this purpose, the essential feature of a jury obviously

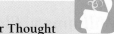

Food for Thought

Is the mode of analysis used by Justice White here, which is also used in the next case on unanimity, *Apodaca v. Oregon*, consistent with the Court's current emphasis on applying text and history? Does this affect the outcome in these cases?

lies in the interposition between the accused and his accuser of the commonsense judgment of a group of laymen, and in the community participation and shared responsibility that results from that group's determination of guilt or innocence. The performance of this role is not a function of the particular number of the body that makes up the jury. To be sure, the number should probably be large enough to promote group deliberation, free from outside attempts at intimidation, and to provide a fair possibility for obtaining a representative cross-section of the community. But we find little reason to think that these goals are in any meaningful sense less likely to be achieved when the jury numbers six, than when it numbers 12—particularly if the requirement of unanimity is retained. Certainly the reliability of the jury as a factfinder hardly seems likely to be a function of its size.

It might be suggested that the 12-man jury gives a defendant a greater advantage since he has more "chances" of finding a juror who will insist on acquittal and thus prevent conviction. But the advantage might just as easily belong to the State, which also needs only one juror out of twelve insisting on guilt to prevent acquittal. What few experiments have occurred—usually in the civil area—indicate that there is no discernible difference between the results reached by the two different-sized juries. In short, neither currently available evidence nor theory suggests that the 12-man jury is necessarily more advantageous to the defendant than a jury composed of fewer members.

Similarly, while in theory the number of viewpoints represented on a randomly selected jury ought to increase as the size of the jury increases, in practice the difference between the 12-man and the six-man jury in terms of the cross-section of the community represented seems likely to be negligible. Even the 12-man jury cannot insure representation of every distinct voice in the community, particularly given the use of the peremptory challenge.

> **FYI**
>
> Despite the *Williams* holding—that the federal constitution does not require that a jury be composed of twelve members—many state constitutions require a twelve-person jury for all felony prosecutions and a six-person jury for misdemeanor prosecutions.

Point for Discussion

Six-Person Jury

In *Ballew v. Georgia*, 435 U.S. 223 (1978), the Court used empirical data to establish a constitutional minimum of six-person juries and to reject a jury of only five persons as violative of the Sixth and Fourteenth Amendments:

> Recent empirical data suggest that progressively smaller juries are less likely to foster effective group deliberation. At some point, this decline leads to inaccurate fact-finding and incorrect application of the common sense of the community to the facts. Generally, a positive correlation exists between group size and the quality of both group per-

formance and group productivity. A variety of explanations have been offered for this conclusion. Several are particularly applicable in the jury setting. The smaller the group, the less likely are members to make critical contributions necessary for the solution of a given problem. Because most juries are not permitted to take notes, memory is important for accurate jury deliberations. As juries decrease in size, they are less likely to have members who remember each of the important pieces of evidence or argument. Furthermore, the smaller the group, the less likely it is to overcome the biases of its members to obtain an accurate result. The data now raise doubts about the accuracy of the results achieved by smaller and smaller panels. The data suggest that the verdicts of jury deliberation in criminal cases will vary as juries become smaller, and that the variance amounts to an imbalance to the detriment of one side, the defense. What has just been said about the presence of minority viewpoint as juries decrease in size foretells problems not only for jury decisionmaking, but also for the representation of minority groups in the community. We do not pretend to discern a clear line between six members and five. But the assembled data raise substantial doubt about the reliability and appropriate representation of panels smaller than six. Because of the fundamental importance of the jury trial to the American system of criminal justice, any further reduction that promotes inaccurate and possibly biased decisionmaking, that causes untoward differences in verdicts, and that prevents juries from truly representing their communities, attains constitutional significance.

Apodaca v. Oregon

406 U.S. 404 (1972).

MR. JUSTICE WHITE announced the judgment of the Court in an opinion in which THE CHIEF JUSTICE, MR. JUSTICE BLACKMUN, and MR. JUSTICE REHNQUIST joined.

Hear It

You can listen to the oral argument in *Apodaca* at: https://www.oyez.org/cases/1971/69-5046.

[Three men were convicted in separate trials by Oregon juries which returned less than unanimous (11–1 and 10–2) verdicts.]

In *Williams v. Florida*, 399 U.S. 78 (1970), we had occasion to consider a related issue: whether the Sixth Amendment's right to trial by jury requires that all juries consist of 12 men. After considering the history of the 12-man requirement and the functions it performs in contemporary society, we concluded that it was not of constitutional stature. We reach the same conclusion today with regard to the requirement of unanimity.

As in *Williams*, we must accordingly consider what is meant by the concept "jury" and determine whether a feature commonly associated with it is constitutionally required. And, as in *Williams*, our inability to divine "the intent of the Framers" when they eliminated references to the "accustomed requisites" requires that in determining what is meant by a jury we must turn to other than purely historical considerations.

Our inquiry must focus upon the function served by the jury in contemporary society. As we said in *Duncan*, the purpose of trial by jury is to prevent oppression by the Government by providing a "safeguard against the corrupt or overzealous prosecutor and against the compliant, biased, or eccentric judge." "Given this purpose, the essential feature of a jury obviously lies in the interposition between the accused and his accuser of the commonsense judgment of a group of laymen." A requirement of unanimity, however, does not materially contribute to the exercise of this commonsense judgment. As we said in *Williams*, a jury will come to such a judgment as long as it consists of a group of laymen representative of a cross section of the community who have the duty and the opportunity to deliberate, free from outside attempts at intimidation, on the question of a defendant's guilt. In terms of this function we perceive no difference between juries required to act unanimously and those permitted to convict or acquit by votes of 10 to two or 11 to one. Requiring unanimity would obviously produce hung juries in some situations where nonunanimous juries will convict or acquit. But in either case, the interest of the defendant in having the judgment of his peers interposed between himself and the officers of the State who prosecute and judge him is equally well served.

Petitioners argue that unanimity serves other purposes constitutionally essential to the continued operation of the jury system. Their principal contention is that a Sixth Amendment 'jury trial' made mandatory on the States by virtue of the Due Process Clause of the Fourteenth Amendment, should be held to require a unanimous jury verdict in order to give substance to the reasonable-doubt standard otherwise mandated by the Due Process Clause. We are quite sure, however, that the Sixth Amendment itself has never been held to require proof beyond a reasonable doubt in criminal cases. The reasonable-doubt standard developed separately from both the jury trial and the unanimous verdict. As the Court noted in *In re Winship*, 397 U.S. 358, the rule requiring proof of crime beyond a reasonable doubt did not crystallize in this country until after the Constitution was adopted. In that case, which held such a burden of proof to be constitutionally required, the Court purported to draw no support from the Sixth Amendment.

Petitioners also cite quite accurately a long line of decisions of this Court upholding the principle that the Fourteenth Amendment requires jury panels to reflect a cross section of the community. They contend that unanimity is a necessary precondition for effective application of the cross-section requirement, because a rule permitting less than unanimous verdicts will make it possible for convictions to occur without the acquiescence of minority elements within the community.

There are two flaws in this argument. One is petitioners' assumption that every distinct voice in the community has a right to be represented on every jury and a right to prevent conviction of a defendant in any case. All that the Constitution forbids is systematic exclusion of identifiable segments of the community from jury panels. We also cannot accept petitioners' second assumption—that minority groups, even when they are represented on a jury, will not adequately represent the viewpoint of those groups simply because they may be outvoted in the final result. They will be present during all deliberations, and their views will be heard. We cannot assume that the majority of the jury will refuse to weigh the evidence and reach a decision upon rational grounds, just as it must now do in order to obtain unanimous verdicts, or that a majority will deprive a man of his liberty on the basis of prejudice when a minority is presenting a reasonable argument in favor of acquittal. We simply find no proof for the notion that a majority will disregard its instructions and cast its votes for guilt or innocence based on prejudice rather than the evidence.

MR. JUSTICE POWELL, concurring in the judgment.

I concur in the plurality opinion insofar as it concludes that a defendant in a state court may constitutionally be convicted by less than a unanimous verdict, but I am not in accord with a major premise upon which that judgment is based. Its premise is that the concept of jury trial, as applicable to the States under the Fourteenth Amendment, must be identical in every detail to the concept required in federal courts by the Sixth Amendment. I do not think that all of the elements of jury trial within the meaning of the Sixth Amendment are necessarily embodied in or incorporated into the Due Process Clause of the Fourteenth Amendment.

In an unbroken line of cases reaching back into the late 1800's, the Justices of this Court have recognized, virtually without dissent, that unanimity is one of the indispensable features of federal jury trial. In these cases, the Court has presumed that unanimous verdicts are essential in federal jury trials, not because unanimity is necessarily fundamental to the function performed by the jury, but because that result is mandated by history. The reasoning that runs throughout this Court's Sixth Amendment precedents is that, in amending the Constitution to guarantee the right to jury trial, the framers desired to preserve the jury safeguard as it was known to them at common law. At the time the Bill of Rights was adopted, unanimity had long been established as one of the attributes of a jury conviction at common law. It therefore seems to me, in accord both with history and precedent, that the Sixth Amendment requires a unanimous jury verdict to convict in a federal criminal trial.

But it is the Fourteenth Amendment, rather than the Sixth, that imposes upon the States the requirement that they provide jury trials to those accused of serious crimes. This Court has said that due process does not require that the States apply the federal jury-trial right with all its gloss. In *Maxwell v. Dow*, 176 U.S. 581, 605 (1900), Mr. Justice Peckham, speaking for eight of the nine members of the Court, so stated:

> When providing in their constitution and legislation for the manner in which civil or criminal actions shall be tried, it is in entire conformity with the character of the Federal Government that (the States) should have the right to decide for themselves what shall be the form and character of the procedure in such trials, whether there shall be a jury of twelve or a lesser number, and whether the verdict must be unanimous or not.

Again, in *Jordan v. Massachusetts*, 225 U.S. 167, 176 (1912), the Court concluded that 'in criminal cases due process of law is not denied by a state law which dispenses with the necessity of a jury of twelve, or unanimity in the verdict.'

It is true that the *Maxwell* and *Jordan* Courts went further and concluded that the States might dispense with jury trial altogether. That conclusion, grounded on a more limited view of due process than has been accepted by this Court in recent years, was rejected by the Court in *Duncan v. Louisiana*, 391 U.S. 145 (1968). But I find nothing in the constitutional principle upon which *Duncan* is based, or in other precedents, that requires repudiation of the views expressed in *Maxwell* and *Jordan* with respect to the size of a jury and the unanimity of its verdict. Mr. Justice Fortas, concurring in *Duncan*, commented on the distinction between the requirements of the Sixth Amendment and those of the Due Process Clause and suggested the appropriate framework for analysis of the issue in this case.

> 'I see no reason whatever to assume that our decision today should require us to impose federal requirements such as unanimous verdicts or a jury of 12 upon the States. We may well conclude that these and other features of federal jury practice are by no means fundamental—that they are not essential to due process of law and that they are not obligatory on the States.'

Duncan v. Louisiana, 391 U.S. at 213.

The importance that our system attaches to trial by jury derives from the special confidence we repose in a 'body of one's peers to determine guilt or innocence as a safeguard against arbitrary law enforcement.' *Williams v. Florida*, 399 U.S. 78, 87 (1970). It is this safeguarding function, preferring the commonsense judgment of a jury as a bulwark 'against the corrupt or overzealous prosecutor and against the complaint, biased, or eccentric judge,' that lies at the core of our dedication to the principles of jury determination of guilt or innocence. This is the fundamental of jury trial that brings it within the mandate of due process. It seems to me that this fundamental is adequately preserved by the jury-verdict provision of the Oregon Constitution. There is no reason to believe, on the basis of experience in Oregon or elsewhere, that a unanimous decision of 12 jurors is more likely to serve the high purpose of jury trial, or is entitled to greater respect in the community, than the same decision joined in by 10 members of a jury of 12.

JUSTICE STEWART, with whom JUSTICE BRENNAN and JUSTICE MARSHALL join, dissenting.

In *Duncan v. Louisiana*, the Court squarely held that the Sixth Amendment right to trial by jury in a federal criminal case is made wholly applicable to state criminal trials by the Fourteenth Amendment. Unless *Duncan* is to be overruled, therefore, the only relevant question here is whether the Sixth Amendment's guarantee of trial by jury embraces a guarantee that the verdict of the jury must be unanimous. The answer to that question is clearly 'yes,' as my Brother Powell has cogently demonstrated in that part of his concurring opinion that reviews almost a century of Sixth Amendment adjudication.

Until today, it has been universally understood that a unanimous verdict is an essential element of a Sixth Amendment jury trial. I would follow these settled Sixth Amendment precedents and reverse the judgment before us.

> **Food for Thought**
>
> Based on what you have read so far, can you predict how the Court ruled when the issue of unanimity for juries of six came before the Court? (Hint: look at *Ballew v. Georgia* in "Point for Discussion" *supra* and do the math!). *See Burch v. Louisiana*, 441 U.S. 130 (1979).

JUSTICE DOUGLAS, with whom JUSTICE BRENNAN and JUSTICE MARSHALL join, dissenting.

It is said, however, that the Sixth Amendment, as applied to the States by reason of the Fourteenth, does not mean what it does in federal proceedings, that it has a 'due process' gloss on it, and that that gloss gives the States power to experiment with the explicit or implied guarantees in the Bill of Rights. Do today's decisions mean that States may apply a 'watered down' version of the Just Compensation Clause? Or are today's decisions limited to a paring down of civil rights protected by the Bill of Rights and up until now as fully applicable to the States as to the Federal Government?

These civil rights—whether they concern speech, searches and seizures, self-incrimination, criminal prosecutions, bail, or cruel and unusual punishments extend, of course, to everyone, but in cold reality touch mostly the lower castes in our society. I refer to the blacks, the Chicanos, the one-mule farmers, the agricultural workers, the off-beat students, the victims of the ghetto. Are we giving the States the power to experiment in diluting their civil rights? It has long been thought that the 'thou shalt nots' in the Constitution and Bill of Rights protect everyone against governmental intrusion or overreaching. The idea has been obnoxious that there are some who can be relegated to second-class citizenship. But if we construe the Bill of Rights and the Fourteenth Amendment to permit States to 'experiment' with the basic rights of people, we open a veritable Pandora's box. Hate and prejudice are versatile forces that can degrade the constitutional scheme.

Take Note

No other Justice agreed with Powell's theory of "partial incorporation" whereby the Sixth Amendment jury trial guarantee requires unanimity in federal cases but does not when applied to the States through the Fourteenth Amendment's Due Process Clause. Yet, because of the 4-4 split among the other justices, that became the law. Thus, in perhaps the truest case of judicial irony, a legal theory that lost 8-1 in the Supreme Court is the law of the land!

Points for Discussion

a. Less than Unanimous

Currently, only Louisiana and Oregon allow juries to convict on less than unanimous votes in felony cases. In *Johnson v. Louisiana*, 406 U.S. 356 (1972), the Court upheld a conviction based upon a 9–3 vote. In dissent, Justice Blackmun wondered where the mathematical niceties would end, claiming that under the Court's reasoning, a vote of 8–4 or 7–5 was permissible.

b. Federal Rule on Unanimity

In federal cases, unanimous jury verdicts are required by the Federal Rules unless the parties stipulate otherwise. *See* Fed. R. Crim. P. 31.

c. Uncertain Verdicts

In *Schad v. Arizona*, 501 U.S. 624 (1991), defendant was convicted of first-degree murder and sentenced to death. First-degree murder included both premeditated and felony-murder theories, and the prosecution offered proof on both. With a general verdict, it was uncertain whether the jury had been unanimous about premeditated murder. A plurality of the Court said that the issue "is one of the permissible limits in defining criminal conduct, not one of jury unanimity," and held that Schad's due process rights had not been violated when the trial court grouped felony murder and premeditated murder as alternative ways of committing the single crime of first-degree murder.

Compare *Richardson v. United States*, 526 U.S. 813 (1999), in which a federal statute prohibits engaging in a continuing criminal enterprise, which is defined as a violation of the drug statutes where the "violation is part of a continuing series of violations." 21 U.S.C § 848. The Court had to decide whether the phrase "series of violations" refers to one element—a "series"—or whether it creates several elements, or violations, each of which requires unanimity. If the Court concluded that the former approach applied, the jury would simply have to find that the defendant engaged in a series of violations, without regard to whether there was jury unanimity about which violations constituted the series. The Court opted for the latter formulation, and held that a jury must agree unanimously not only that a defendant committed a "continuing series of violations" but also which specific violations made up that "continuing series of violations."

d. Deadlocked Jury

In some instances the jury will report that it is "hung" and is unable to reach a unanimous verdict. If this situation continues the judge may declare a mistrial. A mistrial because of a hung jury usually does not bar a retrial of the defendant. *See* Chapter 21, Double Jeopardy, *infra*.

When a jury reports that it is unable to reach a verdict, but the trial court believes that further deliberations may be useful, the court may give the jury what is commonly called an anti-deadlock instruction. Such an instruction is normally given only once, as more than one such instruction can be considered coercive. Judges often give what is known as an "Allen charge," named after the decision in *Allen v. United States*, 164 U.S. 492 (1896). In *Allen*, the Court repeated the approved instruction as follows:

> Although the verdict must be the verdict of each individual juror, and not a mere acquiescence in the conclusion of his fellows, yet they should examine the question submitted with candor, and with a proper regard and deference to the opinions of each other; that it was their duty to decide the case if they could conscientiously do so; that they should listen, with a disposition to be convinced, to each other's arguments; that, if much the larger number were for conviction, a dissenting juror should consider whether his doubt was a reasonable one which made no impression upon the minds of so many men, equally honest,

equally intelligent with himself. If, on the other hand, the majority were for acquittal, the minority ought to ask themselves whether they might not reasonably doubt the correctness of a judgment which was not concurred in by the majority.

164 U.S. at 501.

Some judges opt for a less "coercive" charge. *See also Lowenfield v. Phelps*, 484 U.S. 231 (1988) (a supplemental instruction, which does not speak specifically to minority jurors but does serve the purpose of avoiding a retrial, is permissible after consideration of the context and circumstances in which it is given). While an anti-deadlock instruction may usually be read only once, a judge may send a jury back to continue deliberations without instruction multiple times. There is considerable debate about how often a judge can do this without being coercive. When a jury has been kept together until it appears that there is no probability of agreement upon a verdict, the court may discharge the jury without a verdict.

e. Inconsistent Verdicts

Because of the possibility of trial on multiple charges, the jury may convict on one or more counts and acquit on others. Inconsistency in the verdict is typically not grounds for a retrial. For example, a jury might decide to convict a defendant of a homicide charge, when the homicide was accomplished with a firearm, and acquit of the charge of illegal possession of a firearm, even if obviously proven. Some states may place some limits on inconsistent verdicts, but they are rare and specialized.

C. Selecting Prospective Jurors

In most states, the master list for prospective jurors is drawn from voter registration lists for the county or a list of persons over the age of eighteen holding valid drivers' licenses issued in the county or a compilation from both sources. A computer periodically may generate a randomized jury list of prospective jurors. A court that conducts felony trials will summon as many potential jurors for jury service as deemed necessary for the impaneling of juries for the number of trials requiring juries. The total number of people drawn for jury service on any given day may be called alternatively, the "jury pool" or the "jury venire." Of that group, the group called up to a courtroom for jury selection is called either the "jury panel" or the "jury venire," depending on the usage of the terms in that courthouse. The people actually selected to serve on a jury comprise the "petit jury."

Each person drawn for jury service may be served with a summons directing him or her to report at a specified time and place and to be available for jury service for a period of time. Often, the summons is accompanied by a jury qualification form that must be completed and returned. The form may seek information about the person's address, date of birth, level of education, employer, and members of the immediate family. The form also may seek information about whether the person has ever sued or been sued, as well as information which could statutorily disqualify the person from serving as a juror, *e.g.*, citizenship, inability to speak and understand English, physical or mental disabilities which may prevent effective jury service, a current indictment or a past felony conviction against the prospective juror, or recent jury service. Unless the court determines in a particular case that the information contained on the form must be kept confidential, or its use restricted in the interest of justice, the information is generally made available to the parties or their attorneys.

1. The Fair Cross-Section Requirement

The Sixth Amendment grants to criminal defendants the right to a "jury of the State and district wherein the crime shall have been committed." From this language has evolved the concept that the petit jury in a criminal case must be selected from a fair cross-section of the community where the crime occurred. Note that this requirement applies only to the jury panel from which the petit jury is selected. The jury that actually decides the case does not have to reflect a cross-section of the community. *Holland v. Illinois*, 493 U.S. 474 (1990). As discussed, *infra*, the Equal Protection Clause of the Fourteenth Amendment dictates restrictions on the composition of the petit jury.

The purposes of the cross-section requirement are: (1) avoiding "the possibility that the composition of juries would be arbitrarily skewed in such a way as to deny criminal defendants the benefit of the common-sense judgment of the community;" (2) avoiding an "appearance of unfairness;" and (3) ensuring against deprivation of "often historically disadvantaged groups of their right as citizens to serve on juries in criminal cases." *Lockhart v. McCree*, 476 U.S. 162 (1986). Most of the early fair cross-section cases concerned the systematic exclusion of racial or ethnic groups from the jury panel. Later cases recognized violations of the fair cross-section requirement on the basis of gender. In *Taylor v. Louisiana*, 419 U.S. 522 (1975), the Supreme Court held that a male defendant had standing to challenge the constitutionality of a state law excluding women from jury service unless they had filed a written declaration. The Court also found that a petit jury must be selected from a representative cross-section of the community because it is a fundamental aspect of the jury trial guarantee in the Sixth Amendment. A cross-section of the community is composed of "large, distinctive groups" which play "major roles in the community."

Duren v. Missouri

439 U.S. 357 (1979).

Mr. Justice White delivered the opinion of the Court.

In *Taylor v. Louisiana*, 419 U.S. 522 (1975), this Court held that systematic exclusion of women during the jury-selection process, resulting in jury

Hear It

You can listen to the oral argument in *Duren* at: http://www.oyez.org/cases/1970-1979/1978/1978_77_6067.

pools not "reasonably representative" of the community, denies a criminal defendant his right, under the Sixth and Fourteenth Amendments, to a petit jury selected from a fair cross section of the community. Under the system invalidated in *Taylor*, a woman could not serve on a jury unless she filed a written declaration of her willingness to do so. As a result, although 53% of the persons eligible for jury service were women, less than 1% of the 1,800 persons whose names were drawn from the jury wheel during the year in which appellant Taylor's jury was chosen were female.

At the time of our decision in *Taylor* no other State provided that women could not serve on a jury unless they volunteered to serve. However, five States, including Missouri, provided an automatic exemption from jury service for any women requesting not to serve. Subsequent to *Taylor*, three of these States eliminated this exemption. Only Missouri and Tennessee continue to exempt women from jury service upon request. Today we hold that such systematic exclusion of women that results in jury venires averaging less than 15% female violates the Constitution's fair-cross-section requirement.

Petitioner Duren was indicted in 1975 in the Circuit Court of Jackson County, Mo., for first-degree murder and first-degree robbery. In a pretrial motion to quash his petit jury panel and again in a post-conviction motion for a new trial, he contended that his right to trial by a jury chosen from a fair cross section of his community was denied by provisions of Missouri law granting women who so request an automatic exemption from jury service. Both motions were denied.

The jury-selection process in Jackson County begins with the annual mailing of a questionnaire to persons randomly selected from the Jackson County voter registration list. Approximately 70,000 questionnaires were mailed in 1975. The questionnaire contains a list of occupations and other categories which are the basis under Missouri law for either disqualification[9] or exemption[10] from jury

---

[9] Felons, illiterates, attorneys, judges, members of the Armed Forces, and certain others are ineligible for jury service.

[10] In addition to women, the following are exempted from jury service upon request: persons over age 65, medical doctors, clergy, teachers, persons who performed jury service within the preceding year, "any person whose absence from his regular place of employment would, in the judgment of the court, tend materially and adversely to affect the public safety, health, welfare or interest," and "any person upon whom service as a juror would in the judgment of the court impose an undue hardship."

service. Included on the questionnaire is a paragraph prominently addressed "TO WOMEN" that states in part: "Any woman who elects not to serve will fill out this paragraph and mail this questionnaire to the jury commissioner at once."

The names of those sent questionnaires are placed in the master jury wheel for Jackson County, except for those returning the questionnaire who indicate disqualification or claim an applicable exemption. Summonses are mailed on a weekly basis to prospective jurors randomly drawn from the jury wheel. The summons, like the questionnaire, contains special directions to men over 65 and to women, this time advising them to return the summons by mail if they desire not to serve. The practice is that even those women who do not return the summons are treated as having claimed exemption if they fail to appear for jury service on the appointed day. Other persons seeking to claim an exemption at this stage must make written or personal application to the court.

Petitioner established that according to the 1970 census, 54% of the adult inhabitants of Jackson County were women. He also showed that for the periods June–October 1975 and January–March 1976, 11,197 persons were summoned and that 2,992 of these or 26.7%, were women. Of those summoned, 741 women and 4,378 men appeared for service. Thus, 14.5% (741 of 5,119) of the persons on the post summons weekly venires during the period in which petitioner's jury was chosen were female. In March 1976, when petitioner's trial began, 15.5% of those on the weekly venires were women (110 of 707). Petitioner's jury was selected from a 53-person panel on which there were 5 women; all 12 jurors chosen were men. None of the foregoing statistical evidence was disputed. The Missouri Supreme Court affirmed.

In certain crucial respects the Missouri Supreme Court misconceived the nature of the fair-cross-section inquiry set forth in *Taylor*. In holding that "petit juries must be drawn from a source fairly representative of the community," we explained that: "jury wheels, pools of names, panels, or venires from which juries are drawn must not systematically exclude distinctive groups in the community and thereby fail to be reasonably representative thereof."

In order to establish a prima facie violation of the fair-cross-section requirement, defendant must show (1) that the group alleged to be excluded is a "distinctive" group in the community; (2) that the representation of this group in venires from which juries are selected is not fair and reasonable in relation to the number of such persons in the community; and (3) that this underrepresentation is due to systematic exclusion of the group in the jury-selection process.

With respect to the first part of the prima facie test, Taylor without doubt established that women "are sufficiently numerous and distinct from men" so that "if they are systematically eliminated from jury panels, the Sixth Amendment's fair-cross-section requirement cannot be satisfied."

The second prong of the prima facie case was established by petitioner's statistical presentation. Initially, defendant must demonstrate the percentage of the community made up of the group alleged to be underrepresented, for this is the conceptual benchmark for the Sixth Amendment fair-cross-section requirement. In *Taylor*, the State stipulated that 53% of the population eligible for jury service was female, while petitioner Duren has relied upon a census measurement of the actual percentage of women in the community (54%). In the trial court, the State of Missouri never challenged these data. Although the Missouri Supreme Court speculated that changing population patterns between 1970 and 1976 and unequal voter registration by men and women rendered the census figures a questionable frame of reference, there is no evidence whatsoever to suggest that the 1970 census data significantly distorted the percentage of women in Jackson County at the time of trial. Petitioner's presentation was clearly adequate prima facie evidence of population characteristics for the purpose of making a fair-cross-section violation.

Given petitioner's proof that in the relevant community slightly over half of the adults are women, we disagree with the conclusion of the court below that jury venires containing approximately 15% women are "reasonably representative" of this community. If the percentage of women appearing on jury pools in Jackson County had precisely mirrored the percentage of women in the population, more than one of every two prospective jurors would have been female. In fact, less than one of every six prospective jurors was female; 85% of the average jury was male. Such a gross discrepancy between the percentage of women in jury venires and the percentage of women in the community requires the conclusion that women were not fairly represented in the source from which petit juries were drawn in Jackson County.

Finally, in order to establish a prima facie case, it was necessary for petitioner to show that the underrepresentation of women, generally and on his venire, was due to their systematic exclusion in the jury-selection process. Petitioner's proof met this requirement. His undisputed demonstration that a large discrepancy occurred not just occasionally but in every weekly venire for a period of nearly a year manifestly indicates that the cause of the underrepresentation was systematic—that is, inherent in the particular jury-selection process utilized.

Duren's statistics and other evidence also established when in the selection process the systematic exclusion took place. There was no indication that underrepresentation of women occurred at the first stage of the selection process—the questionnaire canvass of persons randomly selected from the relevant voter registration list. The first sign of a systematic discrepancy is at the next stage—the construction of the jury wheel from which persons are randomly summoned for service. Less than 30% of those summoned were female, demonstrating that a substantially larger number of women answering the questionnaire claimed either ineligibility or exemption from jury service. Moreover, at the summons stage women were not only given another opportunity to claim exemption, but also were presumed to have claimed exemption when they did not respond to the summons. Thus, the percentage of women at the final, venire, stage (14.5%) was much lower than the percentage of women who were summoned for service (26.7%).

The resulting disproportionate and consistent exclusion of women from the jury wheel and at the venire stage was quite obviously due to the system by which juries were selected. Petitioner demonstrated that the underrepresentation of women in the final pool of prospective jurors was due to the operation of Missouri's exemption criteria—whether the automatic exemption for women or other statutory exemptions—as implemented in Jackson County. Women were therefore systematically underrepresented within the meaning of *Taylor*.

Once defendant has made a prima facie showing of an infringement of his constitutional right to a jury drawn from a fair cross section of the community, the State bears the burden of justifying this infringement by showing attainment of a fair cross section to be incompatible with a significant state interest. Assuming, arguendo, that the exemptions mentioned by the court below would justify failure to achieve a fair community cross section on jury venires, the State must demonstrate that these exemptions caused the underrepresentation. The record contains no such proof, and mere suggestions or assertions to that effect are insufficient.

The other possible cause of the disproportionate exclusion of women on Jackson County jury venires is, of course, the automatic exemption for women. Neither the Missouri Supreme Court nor respondent has offered any substantial justification for this exemption. In response to questioning at oral argument, counsel for respondent ventured that the only state interest advanced by the exemption is safeguarding the important role played by women in home and family life. But exempting all women because of the preclusive domestic responsibilities of some women is insufficient justification for their disproportionate exclusion on jury venires. What we stated in *Taylor* with respect to the system there challenged under which women could "opt in" for jury service is equally applicable to Missouri's "opt out" exemption:

> It is untenable to suggest these days that it would be a special hardship for each and every woman to perform jury service or that society

cannot spare any women from their present duties. This may be the case with many, and it may be burdensome to sort out those who should be exempted from those who should serve. But that task is performed in the case of men and the administrative convenience in dealing with women as a class is insufficient justification for diluting the quality of community judgment represented by the jury in criminal trials. If it was ever the case that women were unqualified to sit on juries or were so situated that none of them should be required to perform jury service, that time has long since passed.

We recognize that a State may have an important interest in assuring that those members of the family responsible for the care of children are available to do so. An exemption appropriately tailored to this interest would survive a fair-cross-section challenge. However, the constitutional guarantee to a jury drawn from a fair cross section of the community requires that States exercise proper caution in exempting broad categories of persons from jury service. Although most occupational and other reasonable exemptions may

Justice Rehnquist alone dissented in both *Taylor* and *Duren*, lamenting in his dissent in *Duren*, "Eventually, the Court will insist that women be treated identically to men for purposes of jury selection."

inevitably involve some degree of overinclusiveness or underinclusiveness, any category expressly limited to a group in the community of sufficient magnitude and distinctiveness so as to be within the fair-cross-section requirement—such as women—runs the danger of resulting in underrepresentation sufficient to constitute a prima facie violation of that constitutional requirement. We repeat the observation made in *Taylor* that it is unlikely that reasonable exemptions, such as those based on special hardship, incapacity, or community needs, "would pose substantial threats that the remaining pool of jurors would not be representative of the community."

Points for Discussion

a. Who is "Distinctive"?

A jury panel from which a cognizable class of citizens has been systematically excluded is not a representative jury. Thus far, the Court has not extended the category of those classes of citizens who are "distinctive" beyond the constitutionally "suspect classes" (*e.g.*, racial minorities and women). *See Castaneda v. Partida*, 430 U.S. 482 (1977) (racial minorities is such a class). Young adults and college students are not a distinctive group. Likewise, the exclusion of young people that results from the intermittent recompiling of the jury lists has been justified in the interest of judicial economy. *See Hamling v. United States*, 418 U.S. 87 (1974).

b. Felons as a Distinctive Group

If convicted felons are excluded from jury service, how might you make an argument that they represent a "distinctive" class under *Taylor*?

2. Jury Selection Process

In the typical large urban courthouse, a large pool of 300 to 500 people is called on any given day for potential jury service. When a judge informs the clerk that a jury is needed, the clerk randomly calls out the numbers of forty to seventy jurors to go to that courtroom to participate in the *voir dire*, or jury selection, process. As their names are called, the jurors are tentatively seated in the jury box to be examined under oath concerning their qualifications. If jurors are excused from service following their examination, the judge's clerk draws additional names until they are replaced.

Because of its central role in the selection of a fair and impartial jury, the *voir dire* examination is one of the most important parts of the trial. Its importance is augmented by the fact that it is the first opportunity afforded to counsel to address the jury in connection with the case. Impressions that the jurors have about the case and about counsel at the conclusion of the examination may last throughout the entire trial.

There are two kinds of challenges to jurors. The first is known as a "challenge for cause." A challenge for cause can be made, and will be sustained by the judge, whenever it appears that a juror will not be able to be fair and impartial in a case. That may happen by the juror's own admission or through questioning that makes the bias known. Examples of categories of inquiries plumbed for challenges for cause are: prior knowledge about the parties, judge, witnesses, or the crime; attitudes or prejudices that will likely have a bearing on the case; prior experience as a crime victim, a law enforcement officer, or as a juror; inability to follow the presumption of innocence or other rules of law. The number of jurors who may be struck by challenges for cause is unlimited.

If there are reasonable grounds to believe that a juror cannot render a fair and impartial verdict, the juror shall be excused for cause. However, disqualification is not required merely because a juror does not understand or immediately accept every legal concept presented during *voir dire*. The test is not whether a juror agrees with the law when it is presented; it is whether, after having heard all of the evidence, the prospective juror can adjust his views to the requirements of the law and render a fair and impartial verdict. Even if the parties fail to make a challenge for cause, the court has an affirmative duty to explore undisclosed information of which it is aware affecting the qualification of an individual juror.

The other kind of challenge to jurors is the peremptory challenge. While peremptory challenges are not constitutionally required, the peremptory challenge is so historically ingrained that every jurisdiction provides parties with a set number of peremptory challenges. The parties can exercise their peremptory challenges without giving any reason whatsoever (with the limited exception described in Part 3, *infra*). If multiple defendants are being tried, each defendant gets his own set number of peremptories, and the prosecution, in turn, gets its allotted number for each defendant added together.

Practice Pointer

The purposes of *voir dire* examination are to determine any possible basis for challenging jurors for cause, to develop background information that can be considered so that peremptory challenges can be exercised intelligently, to learn about jurors' backgrounds and receptiveness to particular arguments, and to educate jurors about the law and factors at issue in the case.

The court may exercise considerable discretion in deciding whether to excuse an individual juror for cause. Usually, to show prejudice from any abuse of discretion in denying a for cause challenge, the party challenging the juror must first use all peremptory challenges. *Ross v. Oklahoma*, 487 U.S. 81 (1988).

In federal court, the judge typically asks the questions and conducts the *voir dire*, and the lawyers have a very limited role. In most state courts, the judges permit far more involvement by the lawyers. Even if the court conducts the examination, the parties are often entitled to submit supplemental inquiries. Moreover, the initial responses of individual jurors to questions may require further inquiry. There are also some questions, such as those covering sensitive matters, which are best conducted through a private examination of individual jurors, either at the bench or in the judge's chambers. As another example, the ABA Standards Relating to Fair Trial and Free Press, §§ 3, 4, recommends the separate examination of jurors concerning pretrial publicity in order to avoid the incidental exposure of other members of the panel to affirmative responses.

Point for Discussion

Purpose of Peremptories

Why do you think parties get peremptory challenges?

3. Constitutional Limits on Peremptory Challenges

Traditionally, a party could exercise peremptory challenges without offering any justification or explanation. The issue eventually arose, however, regarding the constitutionality of striking potential jurors based on race. In *Swain v. Alabama*, 380 U.S. 202 (1965), the Court held that the defendant's showing that no African American had served on a petit jury for a number of years did not give rise to an inference of systematic discrimination on the part of the State through its use of peremptory challenges. However, in the watershed case of *Batson v. Kentucky*, 476 U.S. 79 (1986), the Court rejected that conclusion. In *Batson*, the Supreme Court described the basic principles that apply to challenges against the exercise of peremptory challenges based on race:

Food for Thought

Voir dire can be an art form. Uncovering true bias will never happen by asking questions like, "Are you racist?" Subtle background questions can be asked to get at this information, and lawyers will often use one person's answers to a question to educate others. For example, if you are a prosecutor in a domestic violence case, and one of the potential jurors being questioned has worked in a battered women's shelter, you know it is likely the defense will strike that juror. Nonetheless, you might ask that juror questions to educate the other jurors. Formulate a series of questions for the following purposes: 1) To uncover bias against African Americans; 2) To discover if jurors will hold a defendant's right not to testify against him (asked by a defense attorney); 3) To discover jurors attitudes toward the believability of a government witness who took a deal (asked by a prosecutor).

A defendant may establish a prima facie case of purposeful discrimination in selection of the petit jury solely on evidence concerning the prosecutor's exercise of peremptory challenges at the defendant's trial. To establish such a case, the defendant first must show that he is a member of a cognizable racial group, and that the prosecutor has exercised peremptory challenges to remove from the venire members of the defendant's race. Second, the defendant is entitled to rely on the fact, as to which there can be no dispute, that peremptory challenges constitute a jury selection practice that permits "those to discriminate who are of a mind to discriminate." Finally, defendant must show that these facts and any other relevant circumstances raise an inference that the prosecutor used that practice to exclude veniremen from the petit jury on account of their race. This combination of factors in the empanelling of the petit jury, as in the selection of the venire, raises the necessary inference of purposeful discrimination.

In deciding whether defendant has made the requisite showing, the trial court should consider all relevant circumstances. For example, a "pattern" of strikes against black jurors included in the particular venire might give rise to an inference of discrimination. Similarly, the prosecutor's questions and statements during *voir dire* examination and in exercising his challenges may support or refute an inference of discriminatory purpose. These examples are merely illustrative. We have confidence that trial judges, experienced in supervising *voir dire*, will be able to decide if the circumstances concerning the prosecutor's use of peremptory challenges creates a prima facie case of discrimination against black jurors.

Once the defendant makes a prima facie showing, the burden shifts to the State to come forward with a neutral explanation for challenging black jurors. Though this requirement imposes a limitation in some cases on the full peremptory character of the historic challenge, we emphasize that the prosecutor's explanation need not rise to the level justifying exercise of a challenge for cause. But the prosecutor may not rebut the defendant's prima facie case of discrimination by stating merely that he challenged jurors of the defendant's race on the assumption—or his intuitive judgment—that they would be partial to the defendant because of their shared race. The core guarantee of equal protection, ensuring citizens that their State will not discriminate on account of race, would be meaningless were we to approve the exclusion of jurors on the basis of such assumptions, which arise solely from the jurors' race. Nor may the prosecutor rebut the defendant's case merely by denying that he had a discriminatory motive or "affirming his good faith in making individual selections." If these general assertions were accepted as rebutting a defendant's prima facie case, the Equal Protection Clause "would be but a vain and illusory requirement." The prosecutor therefore must articulate a neutral explanation related to the particular case to be tried. The trial court then will have the duty to determine if the defendant has established purposeful discrimination.

After *Batson*, several cases significantly broadened its scope. First, in *Powers v. Ohio*, 499 U.S. 400 (1991), a white defendant alleged that the prosecutor used peremptory challenges to exclude African-American jurors based on their race. Using third-party standing principles, the Court held that the white defendant had standing to assert an equal protection claim on behalf of the excluded African-American jurors. Second, the Court held that a criminal defendant also cannot engage in purposeful discrimination in the exercise of peremptory challenges. *Georgia v. McCollum*, 505 U.S. 42 (1992). The Court relied on *Powers* to find that the prosecution had third-party standing to assert the equal protection rights of excluded jurors. "As the representative of all its citizens, the State is the logical and proper party to assert the invasion of the constitutional rights of the excluded jurors in a criminal trial." Third, the Court emphasized that *Batson* applied to both race and gender. In *Hernandez v. New York*, 500 U.S. 352 (1991), the Court found that Hispanics have a right to be free from discrimination in jury selection. Then, in *J.E.B. v. Alabama ex rel. T.B.*, 511 U.S. 127 (1994), the Court held that the Equal Protection Clause forbids the exercise of a peremptory challenge based upon the gender of a prospective juror.

A generation after *Batson*, the Court continued to offer guidance to lower courts for applying the steps of the constitutional analysis.

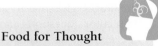

Food for Thought

While clearly illegal under *Batson*, is there any legitimacy to a decision to strike a juror based on his or her race? Assume the parties receive very little printed information about the jurors and the judge conducts a fairly limited *voir dire* to determine only strikes for cause. If you represent an African-American man accused of a crime against a white person, would you consider striking white jurors? Is there a legitimate purpose?

Miller-El v. Dretke

545 U.S. 231 (2005).

JUSTICE SOUTER delivered the opinion of the Court.

The numbers describing the prosecution's use of peremptories [in defendant's capital murder trial] are remarkable. Out of 20 black members of the 108-person venire panel for

Hear It

You can listen to the oral argument in *Miller-El* at: http://www.oyez.org/cases/2000-2009/2004/2004_03_9659.

Miller-El's trial, only 1 served. Although 9 were excused for cause or by agreement, 10 were peremptorily struck by the prosecution.

More powerful than these bare statistics, however, are side-by-side comparisons of some black venire panelists who were struck and white panelists allowed to serve. If a prosecutor's proffered reason for striking a black panelist applies just as well to an otherwise-similar nonblack who is permitted to serve, that is evidence tending to prove purposeful discrimination to be considered at *Batson*'s third step.

The prosecution used its second peremptory strike to exclude Billy Jean Fields, a black man who expressed unwavering support for the death penalty. On the questionnaire filled out by all panel members before individual examination on the stand, Fields said that he believed in capital punishment, and during questioning he disclosed his belief that the State acts on God's behalf when it imposes the death penalty. "Therefore, if the State exacts death, then that's what it should be." He testified that he had no religious or philosophical reservations about the death penalty and that the death penalty deterred crime. He twice averred, without apparent hesitation, that he could sit on Miller-El's jury and make a decision to impose this penalty.

Although at one point in the questioning, Fields indicated that the possibility of rehabilitation might be relevant to the likelihood that a defendant would commit future acts of violence, he responded to ensuing questions by saying that although he believed anyone could be rehabilitated, this belief would not stand in the way of a decision to impose the death penalty.

Fields was struck peremptorily by the prosecution, with prosecutor James Nelson offering a race-neutral reason:

> We have concern with reference to some of his statements as to the death penalty in that he said that he could only give death if he thought a person could not be rehabilitated and he later made the comment that any person could be rehabilitated if they find God or are introduced to God and the fact that we have a concern that his religious feelings may affect his jury service in this case.

Thus, Nelson simply mischaracterized Fields's testimony. He represented that Fields said he would not vote for death if rehabilitation was possible, whereas Fields unequivocally stated that he could impose the death penalty regardless of the possibility of rehabilitation. Perhaps Nelson misunderstood, but unless he had an ulterior reason for keeping Fields off the jury we think he would have proceeded differently. In light of Fields's outspoken support for the death penalty, we expect the prosecutor would have cleared up any misunderstanding by asking further questions before getting to the point of exercising a strike.

If, indeed, Fields's thoughts on rehabilitation did make the prosecutor uneasy, he should have worried about a number of white panel members he accepted with no evident reservations. Sandra Hearn said that she believed in the death penalty "if a criminal cannot be rehabilitated and continues to commit the same type of crime." Hearn went so far as to express doubt that at the penalty phase of a capital case she could conclude that a convicted murderer "would probably commit some criminal acts of violence in the future." "People change," she said, making it hard to assess the risk of someone's future dangerousness. "The evidence would have to be awful strong." But the prosecution did not respond to Hearn the way it did to Fields, and without delving into her views about rehabilitation with any further question, it raised no objection to her serving on the jury. White panelist Mary Witt said she would take the possibility of rehabilitation into account in deciding at the penalty phase of the trial about a defendant's probability of future dangerousness, but the prosecutors asked her no further question about her views on reformation, and they accepted her as a juror. Latino venireman Fernando Gutierrez, who served on the jury, said that he would consider the death penalty for someone who could not be rehabilitated, but the prosecutors did not question him further about this view. In sum, non-black jurors whose remarks on rehabilitation could well have signaled a limit on their willingness to impose a death sentence were not questioned further and drew no objection, but the prosecution expressed apprehension about a black juror's belief in the possibility of reformation even though he repeatedly stated his approval of the death penalty and testified that he could impose it according to state legal standards even when the alternative sentence of life imprisonment would give a defendant (like everyone else in the world) the opportunity to reform.

In sum, when we look for nonblack jurors similarly situated to Fields, we find strong similarities as well as some differences. But the differences seem far from significant, particularly when we read Fields's *voir dire* testimony in its entirety. Upon that reading, Fields should have been an ideal juror in the eyes of a prosecutor seeking a death sentence, and the prosecutors' explanations for the strike cannot reasonably be accepted.

The prosecution's proffered reasons for striking Joe Warren, another black venireman, are comparably unlikely. Warren gave this answer when he was asked what the death penalty accomplished: "I don't know. It's really hard to say because I know sometimes you feel that it might help to deter crime and then you feel that the person is not really suffering. You're taking the suffering away from him. So it's like I said, sometimes you have mixed feelings about whether or not this is punishment or, you know, you're relieving personal punishment."

The prosecution said nothing about these remarks when it struck Warren from the panel, but prosecutor Paul Macaluso referred to this answer as the first of his reasons when he testified at the later *Batson* hearing: "I thought [Warren's statements on *voir dire*] were inconsistent responses. At one point he says, you know, on a case-by-case basis and at another point he said, well, I think—I got the impression, at least, that he suggested that the death penalty was an easy way out, that they should be made to suffer more."

On the face of it, the explanation is reasonable from the State's point of view, but its plausibility is severely undercut by the prosecution's failure to object to other panel members who expressed views much like Warren's. Sandra Jenkins, whom the State accepted (but who was then struck by the defense) testified that she thought "a harsher treatment is life imprisonment with no parole." Leta Girard, accepted by the State (but also struck by the defense) gave her opinion that "living sometimes is a worse—is worse to me than dying would be." The fact that Macaluso's reason also applied to these other panel members, most of them white, none of them struck, is evidence of pretext.

The suggestion of pretext is not, moreover, mitigated much by Macaluso's explanation that Warren was struck when the State had 10 peremptory challenges left and could afford to be liberal in using them. If that were the explanation for striking Warren and later accepting panel members who thought death would be too easy, the prosecutors should have struck Sandra Jenkins, whom they examined and accepted before Warren. Indeed, the disparate treatment is the more remarkable for the fact that the prosecutors repeatedly questioned Warren on his capacity and willingness to impose a sentence of death and elicited statements of his ability to do so if the evidence supported that result and the answer to each special question was yes, whereas the record before us discloses no attempt to determine whether Jenkins would be able to vote for death in spite of her view that it was easy on the convict. Yet the prosecutors accepted the white panel member Jenkins and struck the black venireman Warren.

When illegitimate grounds like race are in issue, a prosecutor simply has got to state his reasons as best he can and stand or fall on the plausibility of the reasons he gives. A *Batson* challenge does not call for a mere exercise in thinking up any rational basis. If the stated reason does not hold up, its pretextual significance does not fade because a trial judge, or an appeals court, can imagine a reason that might not have been shown up as false.

The whole of the *voir dire* testimony subject to consideration casts the prosecution's reasons for striking Warren in an implausible light. Comparing his strike with the treatment of panel members who expressed similar views supports a conclusion that race was significant in determining who was challenged and who was not. We do not decide whether there were white jurors who expressed ambivalence just as much as these black members of the venire panel. There is no need to go into these instances, for the prosecutors' treatment of Fields and Warren supports stronger arguments that *Batson* was violated.

The case for discrimination goes beyond these comparisons to include broader patterns of practice during the jury selection. The prosecution's shuffling of the venire panel, its enquiry into views on the death penalty, its questioning about minimum acceptable sentences: all indicate decisions probably based on race. Finally, the appearance of discrimination is confirmed by widely known evidence of the general policy of the Dallas County District Attorney's Office to exclude black venire members from juries at the time Miller-El's jury was selected.

The first clue to the prosecutors' intentions, distinct from the peremptory challenges themselves, is their resort during *voir dire* to a procedure known in Texas as the jury shuffle. In the State's criminal practice, either side may literally reshuffle the cards bearing panel members' names, thus rearranging the order in which members of a venire panel are seated and reached for questioning. Once the order is established, the panel members seated at the back are likely to escape *voir dire* altogether, for those not questioned by the end of the week are dismissed.

In this case, the prosecution and then the defense shuffled the cards at the beginning of the first week of *voir dire*; the record does not reflect the changes in order. At the beginning of the second week, when a number of black members were seated at the front of the panel, the prosecution shuffled. At the beginning of the third week, the first four panel members were black. The prosecution shuffled, and these black panel members ended up at the back. Then the defense shuffled, and the black panel members again appeared at the front. The prosecution requested another shuffle, but the trial court refused. Finally, the defense shuffled at the beginning of the fourth and fifth weeks of *voir dire*; the record does not reflect the panel's racial composition before or after those shuffles.

The State notes in its brief that there might be racially neutral reasons for shuffling the jury, and we suppose there might be. But no racially neutral reason has ever been offered in this case, and nothing stops the suspicion of discriminatory intent from rising to an inference.

The next body of evidence that the State was trying to avoid black jurors is the contrasting *voir dire* questions posed respectively to black and nonblack panel members, on two different subjects. First, there were the prosecutors' statements preceding questions about a potential juror's thoughts on capital punishment. Some of these prefatory statements were cast in general terms, but some followed the so-called graphic script, describing the method of execution in rhetorical and clinical detail. It is intended, Miller-El contends, to prompt some expression of hesitation to consider the death penalty and thus to elicit plausibly neutral grounds for a peremptory strike of a potential juror subjected to it, if not a strike for cause. If the graphic script is given to a higher proportion of blacks than whites, this is evidence that prosecutors more often wanted blacks off the jury, absent some neutral and extenuating explanation.

Of the 10 nonblacks whose questionnaires expressed ambivalence or opposition, only 30% received the graphic treatment. But of the seven blacks who expressed ambivalence or opposition, 86% heard the graphic script. The reasonable inference is that race was the major consideration when the prosecution chose to follow the graphic script.

The same is true for another kind of disparate questioning, which might fairly be called trickery. The prosecutors asked members of the panel how low a sentence they would consider imposing for murder. Most potential jurors were first told that Texas law provided for a minimum term of five years, but some members of the panel were not, and if a panel member then insisted on a minimum above five years, the prosecutor would suppress his normal preference for tough jurors and claim cause to strike.

It is entirely true that prosecutors struck a number of nonblack members of the panel (as well as black members) for cause or by agreement before they reached the point in the standard *voir dire* sequence to question about minimum punishment. But this is no answer; 8 of the 11 nonblack individuals who voiced opposition or ambivalence were asked about the acceptable minimum only after being told what state law required. Hence, only 27% of nonblacks questioned on the subject who expressed these views were subjected to the trick question, as against 100% of black members. Once again, the implication of race in the prosecutors' choice of questioning cannot be explained away.

In the course of drawing a jury to try a black defendant, 10 of the 11 qualified black venire panel members were peremptorily struck. At least two of them, Fields and Warren, were ostensibly acceptable to prosecutors seeking a death verdict, and Fields was ideal. The prosecutors' chosen race-neutral reasons for the strikes do not hold up and are so far at odds with the evidence that pretext is the fair conclusion, indicating the very discrimination the explanations were meant to deny.

The strikes that drew these incredible explanations occurred in a selection process replete with evidence that the prosecutors were selecting and rejecting potential jurors because of race. At least two of the jury shuffles conducted by the State make no sense except as efforts to delay consideration of black jury panelists to the end of the week, when they might not even be reached. The State has in fact never offered any other explanation. Nor has the State denied that disparate lines of questioning were pursued: 53% of black panelists but only 3% of nonblacks were questioned with a graphic script meant to induce qualms about applying the death penalty (and thus explain a strike), and 100% of blacks but only 27% of nonblacks were subjected to a trick question about the minimum acceptable penalty for murder, meant to induce a disqualifying answer. The State's attempts to explain the prosecutors' questioning of particular witnesses on nonracial grounds fit the evidence less well than the racially discriminatory hypothesis.

If anything more is needed for an undeniable explanation of what was going on, history supplies it. The prosecutors took their cues from a 20-year old manual of tips on jury selection, as shown by their notes of the race of each potential juror. By the time a jury was chosen, the State had peremptorily challenged 12% of qualified nonblack panel members, but eliminated 91% of the black ones.

It blinks reality to deny that the State struck Fields and Warren, included in that 91%, because they were black. The strikes correlate with no fact as well as they correlate with race, and they occurred during a selection infected by shuffling and disparate questioning that race explains better than any race-neutral reason advanced by the State. The State's pretextual positions confirm Miller-El's claim, and the prosecutors' own notes proclaim that the Sparling Manual's emphasis on race was on their minds when they considered every potential juror.

The state court's conclusion that the prosecutors' strikes of Fields and Warren were not racially determined is shown up as wrong to a clear and convincing degree; the state court's conclusion was unreasonable as well as erroneous. The judgment of the Court of Appeals is reversed, and the case is remanded for entry of judgment for petitioner together with orders of appropriate relief.

It is so ordered.

JUSTICE BREYER, concurring.

In *Batson v. Kentucky*, 476 U.S. 79 (1986), the Court adopted a burden-shifting rule designed to ferret out the unconstitutional use of race in jury selection. In his separate opinion, Justice Thurgood Marshall predicted that the Court's rule would not achieve its goal. The only way to "end the racial discrimination that peremptories inject into the jury-selection process," he concluded, was to "eliminate peremptory challenges entirely." Today's case reinforces Justice Marshall's concerns.

This case illustrates the practical problems of proof that Justice Marshall described. Miller-El marshaled extensive evidence of racial bias. Despite the strength of his claim, Miller-El's challenge has resulted in 17 years of largely unsuccessful and protracted litigation—including 8 different judicial proceedings and 8 different judicial opinions, and involving 23 judges, of whom 6 found the *Batson* standard violated and 16 the contrary.

The complexity of this process reflects the difficulty of finding a legal test that will objectively measure the inherently subjective reasons that underlie use of a peremptory challenge. *Batson* seeks to square this circle by (1) requiring defendants to establish a prima facie case of discrimination, (2) asking prosecutors then to offer a race-neutral explanation for their use of the peremptory, and then (3) requiring defendants to prove that the neutral reason offered is pretextual. But *Batson* embodies defects intrinsic to the task.

At *Batson*'s first step, litigants remain free to misuse peremptory challenges as long as the strikes fall below the prima facie threshold level. At *Batson*'s second step, prosecutors need only tender a neutral reason, not a "persuasive, or even plausible" one. *Purkett v. Elem*, 514 U.S. 765 (1995) (per curiam). Most importantly, at step three, *Batson* asks judges to engage in the awkward, sometime hopeless, task of second-guessing a prosecutor's instinctive judgment—the underlying basis for which may be invisible even to the prosecutor exercising the challenge.

Given the inevitably clumsy fit between any objectively measurable standard and the subjective decisionmaking at issue, I am not surprised to find studies and anecdotal reports suggesting that, despite *Batson*, the discriminatory use of peremptory challenges remains a problem.

Practical problems of proof to the side, peremptory challenges seem increasingly anomalous in our judicial system.

The use of race-and gender-based stereotypes in the jury-selection process seems better organized and more systematized than ever before. *See, e.g.,* Post, A Loaded Box of Stereotypes: Despite "Batson," Race, Gender Play Big Roles in Jury Selection., Nat. L. J., Apr. 25, 2005, pp. 1, 18 (discussing common reliance on race and gender in jury selection). For example, one jury-selection guide counsels attorneys to perform a "demographic analysis" that assigns numerical points to characteristics such as age, occupation, and marital status—in addition to race as well as gender. *See* V. Starr & A. McCormick, Jury Selection 193–200 (3d ed. 2001). Thus, in a hypothetical dispute between a white landlord and an African-American tenant, the authors suggest awarding two points to an African-American venire member while subtracting one point from her white counterpart. *Id.,* at 197–199.

These examples reflect a professional effort to fulfill the lawyer's obligation to help his or her client. Nevertheless, the outcome in terms of jury selection is the same as it would be were the motive less benign. And as long as that is so, the law's anti-discrimination command and a peremptory jury-selection system that permits or encourages the use of stereotypes work at cross-purposes.

I recognize that peremptory challenges have a long historical pedigree. They may help to reassure a party of the fairness of the jury. But long ago, Blackstone recognized the peremptory challenge as an "arbitrary and capricious species of a challenge." 4 W. Blackstone, Commentaries on the Laws of England 346 (1769). If used to express stereotypical judgments about race, gender, religion,

Food for Thought

Is the elimination of peremptory challenges raised by Justice Breyer's concurrence the best solution to discrimination problems in jury selection? Other members of the judiciary have endorsed the elimination of peremptory challenges. *See, e.g., Commonwealth v. Maldonado,* 439 Mass. 460, 788 N.E.2d 968 (2003); *People v. Brown,* 97 N.Y.2d 500, 743 N.Y.S.2d 374, 769 N.E.2d 1266 (2002). What arguments can you make for and against the elimination of peremptory strikes?

or national origin, peremptory challenges betray the jury's democratic origins and undermine its representative function. *See* 1 A. de Tocqueville, Democracy in America 287 (H. Reeve transl. 1900) ("The institution of the jury raises the people to the bench of judicial authority and invests them with the direction of society"). In light of the considerations I have mentioned, I believe it necessary to reconsider *Batson*'s test and the peremptory challenge system as a whole. With that qualification, I join the Court's opinion.

[The dissenting opinion of Justice Thomas, which questions whether Miller-El established racial discrimination, is omitted.]

Points for Discussion

a. Explaining *Miller-El*

After *Miller-El*, it seems clear that not all members of a racial group must be excluded from a jury in order for *Batson* to apply. How would you describe to a colleague the basis of the Court's holding? Which step(s) of the three-step *Batson* analysis is (are) addressed by Justice Souter?

b. The "Neutral" Explanation

Batson does not require the neutral explanation for peremptorily striking a potential juror to be derived from *voir dire*, nor does the neutral explanation have to rise to a level sufficient to satisfy a strike for cause. A prosecutor may use her own personal knowledge concerning a juror and information supplied from outside sources. The test is not whether the information is true or false; it is whether she has a good-faith belief in the information and whether she can articulate the reason to the trial court in a race-neutral or gender-neutral way that does not violate the defendant's constitutional rights. The trial court then decides whether the prosecutor has acted with a prohibited intent.

c. A *McCullom* Challenge

In *Gilchrist v. Maryland*, 667 A.2d 876 (Md.1995), before the jury box was full, each side exercised one peremptory challenge. After twelve jurors were seated, defense counsel then continue to exercise peremptory challenges as each new prospective juror was seated. All of the peremptory challenges had been used by the defense against white prospective jurors. After the seventh prospective juror was peremptorily challenged by defense counsel, the prosecutor objected, arguing that the defense was attempting to remove all white prospective jurors from the jury in violation of *Batson*. The following colloquy occurred out of the hearing of the jury. As you read the transcript, consider whether there was a *McCollum* violation? Did the prosecutor establish a prima facie case? Did the trial judge find a prima facie case? Were the explanations given by defense counsel racially neutral?

> THE COURT: Which juror are you questioning or do you want to go through a reason for each one of them?

> ASSISTANT STATE'S ATTORNEY: For each one.

> THE COURT: All right. That's seven jurors you've struck. They were all white. Let's go through them one by one and give me the reasons you struck them.

Two of the jurors were challenged by the defendant because they were crime victims, and the other juror was challenged because the defendant was uncomfortable with the way the juror stared at him. The court found that these were acceptable explanations. The conversation moved on to the other strikes.

> DEFENSE COUNSEL: Judge, I personally, by looking at her—I see jurors in the box and I look at the way they relate to each other.

> THE COURT: Well, how did she look?

> DEFENSE COUNSEL: She reminded me of my Catholic School teacher that I didn't particularly like. Her look at the other people who were in the jury box.

> DEFENSE COUNSEL: Judge, The next juror was young. I didn't think particularly he would be a strong juror for my case by looking at him.

> THE COURT: And why was that?

> DEFENSE COUNSEL: Because I look at the way he fits into the persons that are on the panel. And what I'm trying to accomplish from the look of him, from the way he sat—

> THE COURT: Well, how did he look from the way he was sitting that made you feel he was not good, other than the fact he was white and young?

> DEFENSE COUNSEL: Well, he—number one, most of the jurors would look at my client and look over at the table. He was just like sitting there not relating to anything in the room.

> THE COURT: Because he wasn't relating to your client?

> DEFENSE COUNSEL: Not relating to anything or anyone in the room. Frankly, I don't think he even wanted to be here.

> THE COURT: For the next juror?

DEFENSE COUNSEL: Why? He was—I don't have anything written on here.

THE COURT: Let the record reflect he was a young white male in a navy blazer and khaki slacks.

DEFENSE COUNSEL: I believe he was—I remember him, Judge, and . . . we say he was unacceptable.

THE COURT: And why was that?

DEFENSE COUNSEL: His clothing, his manner.

THE COURT: What was wrong with his clothing and his manner?

DEFENSE COUNSEL: Well, his manner and his clothing suggest to me that he wouldn't be able to relate to my client because in this particular case there are—there is the police officer's word against my client's word. My client may very well testify. And because of those things—

THE COURT: Well, how does his clothing have anything to do with it? I don't make the connection.

DEFENSE COUNSEL: The clothing, Judge, means when you go to Brooks Brothers and buy a suit, and maybe not the suit—

THE COURT: The people who go to Brooks Brothers are more likely to believe police than defendants; is that what you're saying?

DEFENSE COUNSEL: Not necessarily so. But given the little information I have about them, I must make judgments about these individuals.

THE COURT: Well, what—well, all right. That's right. So what information did you have that required you to strike him?

DEFENSE COUNSEL: He's a student. We don't know what he's studying—

THE COURT: Well, we could have asked him.

DEFENSE COUNSEL: Well, some courts don't let you bring them up and ask them.

THE COURT: But you didn't ask.

DEFENSE COUNSEL: He seems rather studious.

THE COURT: Well, so what if he's studious? He's 21 years old.

DEFENSE COUNSEL: Right. He has 16 years of education.

THE COURT: Right.

DEFENSE COUNSEL: That means he's done his college.

THE COURT: Right.

DEFENSE COUNSEL: Those are my reasons.

THE COURT: When you say that someone comes in a navy blazer and khaki slacks, and because he's a student and because of his address that's a reason for striking him—

DEFENSE COUNSEL: I said I don't know anything about his address because I don't know the address. But, Judge, that could have been a black man. Are we saying that black men don't wear blazers and khaki pants?

d. A *Batson* Challenge

In *Gibson v. State*, 117 S.W.3d 567 (Tex.Ct.App.2003), the defense made a *Batson* challenge. As you read the following colloquy, ask yourself: is it different in any respects from the previous colloquy? Did the judge make the right decision on the challenge? Are you satisfied with the "race neutral" reasons given in both this and the previous case?

THE COURT: Now, you have a *Batson* challenge, [Defense Counsel]. Would you tell me the jurors that you challenge or believe the State struck for racial reasons? I'd like the number only, please, and I will take judicial notice that the Defendant is—the Defendant's race.

DEFENSE COUNSEL: Your Honor, that would go to Juror Number 6 and 11.

THE COURT: Thank you, sir. Will the State give me a race neutral reason why you struck Juror Number 6?

PROSECUTOR: Judge, I struck [Juror 6] among other reason because he's a substance abuse counselor.

THE COURT: Okay.

PROSECUTOR: And he told us as much during *voir dire*.

PROSECUTOR: Judge, I struck Juror 11 because she had spoken up and said that she would require more than one witness to testify.

THE COURT: All right.

DEFENSE COUNSEL: Your Honor, in response to that, [Juror 7] stated the same thing, that he would need more evidence than one witness though he was not struck by the State.

THE COURT: All right. Can you answer that, please?

PROSECUTOR: I can, Judge. He qualified his answer—And we can go back to the record. But he qualified his record at one point and said, but if there is more evidence I would be okay. And, in fact, there is more evidence in this case. I can't state strongly enough, Judge—I don't want to—We want to give Mr. Gibson a fair trial and if there's anything here that's not fair—

THE COURT: Well, that's what I'm trying to find out. You struck Number 11 for the reason you stated and did not strike Number 7 for the reason you stated; is that correct?

PROSECUTOR: That is correct with the caveat I just added.

THE COURT: Okay, I'm going to deny the *Batson* challenge. He's given race neutral reasons. Yes, sir.

DEFENSE COUNSEL: Just as a request to clarify your ruling. Their reason for striking [Juror 11], that he needed more evidence and the similar and same reason [Juror 7] was not struck, is that—has he given a sufficient race neutral reason to strike [Juror 11]?

THE COURT: In my judgment he has. They're pre-emptory [sic] challenges and he's given a race neutral reason.

e. The Logic of *Batson*

Batson demands that litigants be color-blind. However, they do not always act in a color-blind manner, and will often use race as a proxy for beliefs and biases, the same as they use a person's occupation or how they dress. When a defense attorney assumes that white jurors will be less sympathetic to his African-American client than African-American jurors, is that racism or common sense? Given the ease with which litigants can give "race neutral" reasons for strikes, what value does *Batson* serve? Would you keep it?

f. Deficient Performance

A state petitioner on habeas made a claim of ineffective assistance of counsel because his trial counsel chose to strike all women jurors on the belief women would be biased against the defendant in a sexual assault case. The federal court held that violating *Batson* is always deficient performance by counsel (even when allegedly violated for the benefit of the defendant) and normally

FYI

Sometimes a *Batson* violation is easy to spot. In *Foster v. Chatman*, 136 S.Ct. 1737 (2016), the Court found such a clear violation in a 30-year-old death penalty case. Not only did the state exercise its peremptory strikes against all four prospective black jurors qualified to serve, but the Court found the prosecutor's strikes of two black jurors were motivated by discriminatory intent, given shifting explanations, misrepresentations of the record and a prosecutor file focused on the race of the potential jurors, including placement of the letter "B" next to black jurors' names and a statement next to one that "if it comes down to having to pick one of the black jurors this one might be okay."

would be prejudicial *per se*, as *Batson* violations are always structural error. *See Winston v. Boatwright*, 649 F. 3d 618 (7th Cir. 2011) (upholding conviction, however, as it was not clearly established at the time that the state court should not have used harmless error analysis.)

Hypo 1: *Gender Plus*

Defense counsel raised a *Batson* objection after the prosecutor used all peremptory strikes to remove men from the jury pool. The trial court then asked the prosecutor to explain the challenges. The prosecutor candidly admitted that he considered gender, but claimed that other factors such as age, education and employment motivated the strikes as well. The trial court announced that the fact that the four strikes were all males did not establish a prima facie case of discrimination, and the court accepted the prosecutor's explanation that he had used "other rationales" in making his strikes. On appeal, as an appellate judge, how would you rule? Did defense counsel establish a prima facie case? If so, did the explanations offered by the prosecutor show what factors related to each juror and how these factors made him believe that each of these jurors should not be on the jury? *See State v. Jagodinsky*, 209 Wis.2d 577, 563 N.W.2d 188 (App.1997).

Hypo 2: *Racial Strikes and the KKK*

On April 13, the Ku Klux Klan held a rally on the steps of the local courthouse. Although the rally itself occurred without incidents leading to arrests, a member of the Klan, Karl Kody, a 25-year-old unemployed Caucasian, was arrested for wanton endangerment as he left the gathering when he swung his uniform at a crowd of people who were protesting the Klan's presence. At his jury trial, Karl's attorney, Kalvin Cline, used all three of the defense's available peremptory challenges to remove African-Americans from the jury. After the defense used its peremptory challenges, no African-American jurors remained on the jury. Articulate the real reason Cline struck those jurors. How might Cline distinguish his strikes of African-Americans from the *Batson* rationale? Would he succeed?

Hypo 3: *Batson Violation?*

In a capital murder case involving a black defendant, the prosecution used the vast majority of its early peremptory challenges against black jurors. It accepted two black jurors, but only after defense counsel's repeated objections and after it was running out of peremptory strikes. In addition, in its earlier strikes, the prosecution did not strike a white juror who was essentially similar to two of the black jurors who were struck. Did the prosecutor act unconstitutionally based on race? *See Chamberlin v. Fisher*, 855 F.3d 657 (5th Cir. 2017).

Hypo 4: *Striking Females in Stalker Cases*

A woman is charged with "stalking" a man that she met online. During jury selection, the prosecution struck only females from the jury. When the defense challenged the strikes, the prosecution offered gender-neutral reasons for the strikes, including age, health and apparent disinterest in the legal process. Did the strikes involve improper gender discrimination? *See People v. Beauvais*, 393 P.3d 509 (Colo. 2017).

D. The No Impreachment Rule

Peña-Rodriguez v. Colorado

137 S.Ct. 855 (2017).

JUSTICE KENNEDY delivered the opinion of the Court.

The jury is a central foundation of our justice system and our democracy as a necessary check on governmental power. The jury, over the centuries, has been an inspired, trusted, and effective instrument for resolving factual disputes and determining ultimate questions of guilt or innocence in criminal cases. Its judgments find acceptance in the community, an acceptance essential to respect for the rule of law. The jury is a tangible implementation of the principle that the law comes from the people.

In the era of our Nation's founding, the right to a jury trial already had existed and evolved for centuries, through and alongside the common law. The jury was considered a fundamental safeguard of individual liberty. *See* THE FEDERALIST No. 83, p. 451 (B. Warner ed. 1818) (A. Hamilton). The right to a jury trial in criminal cases was part of the Constitution as first drawn, and it was restated in the Sixth Amendment. Art. III, § 2, cl. 3; Amdt. 6. By operation of the Fourteenth Amendment, it is applicable to the States. *Duncan v. Louisiana*, 391 U.S. 145 (1968).

Like all human institutions, the jury system has its flaws, yet experience shows that fair and impartial verdicts can be reached if the jury follows the court's instructions and undertakes deliberations that are honest, candid, robust, and based on common sense. A general rule has evolved to give substantial protection to verdict finality and to assure jurors that, once their verdict has been entered, it will not later be called into question based on the comments or conclusions they expressed during deliberations. This principle, centuries old, is referred to as the no-impeachment rule. The instant case presents the question whether there is an exception to the no-impeachment rule when, after the jury is discharged, a juror comes forward with compelling evidence that another juror made clear and explicit statements indicating that racial animus was a significant motivating factor in his or her vote to convict.

In 2007, in the bathroom of a Colorado horse-racing facility, a man sexually assaulted two teenage sisters. The girls told their father and identified the man as an employee of the racetrack. The police located and arrested petitioner. Each girl separately identified petitioner as the man who had assaulted her. The State charged petitioner with harassment, unlawful sexual contact, and attempted sexual assault on a child. Before the jury was empanelled, members of the venire were repeatedly asked whether they believed that they could be fair and impartial in the case. None of the empanelled jurors expressed any reservations based on racial or any other bias. And none asked to speak with the trial judge. After a 3–day trial, the jury found petitioner guilty of unlawful sexual contact and harassment, but it failed to reach a verdict on the attempted sexual assault charge. When the jury was discharged, the court gave them this instruction, as mandated by Colorado law: "The question may arise whether you may now discuss this case with the lawyers, defendant, or other persons. For your guidance the court instructs you that whether you talk to anyone is entirely your own decision. If any person persists in discussing the case over your objection, or becomes critical of your service either before or after any discussion has begun, please report it to me."

Following the discharge of the jury, petitioner's counsel entered the jury room to discuss the trial with the jurors. Two jurors remained to speak with counsel in private. They stated that, during deliberations, another juror had expressed anti-Hispanic bias toward petitioner and petitioner's alibi witness. Petitioner's counsel reported this to the court and, with the court's supervision, obtained sworn affidavits from the two jurors. The affidavits described a number of biased statements made by another juror, identified as Juror H.C. According to the two jurors, H.C. told the other jurors that he "believed the defendant was guilty because, in H.C.'s experience as an ex-law enforcement officer, Mexican men had a bravado that caused them to believe they could do whatever they wanted with women." The jurors reported that H.C. stated his belief that Mexican men are physically controlling of women because of their sense of entitlement, and further stated, "I think he did it because he's Mexican and Mexican men take whatever they want." According to the jurors, H.C. further explained that, in his experience, "nine times out of ten Mexican men were guilty of being aggressive toward women and young girls." Finally, the jurors recounted that Juror H.C. said that he did not find petitioner's alibi witness credible because, among other things, the witness was "an illegal." (In fact, the witness was a legal resident of the United States.)

After reviewing the affidavits, the trial court acknowledged H.C.'s apparent bias. But the court denied petitioner's motion for a new trial, noting that "the actual deliberations that occur among the jurors are protected from inquiry under Colorado Rule of Evidence 606(b)." Like its federal counterpart, Colorado's Rule 606(b) generally prohibits a juror from testifying as to any statement made during deliberations in a proceeding inquiring into the validity of the verdict. See Fed. Rule Evid. 606(b). The Colorado Rule reads as follows:"(b) Inquiry into validity of verdict or indictment. Upon an inquiry into the validity of a verdict or indictment, a juror may not testify as to any matter or statement occurring during the course of the jury's deliberations or to the effect of anything upon his or any other juror's mind or emotions as influencing him to assent to or dissent from the verdict or indictment or concerning his mental processes in connection therewith. But a juror may testify about (1) whether extraneous prejudicial information was improperly brought to the jurors' attention, (2) whether any outside influence was improperly brought to bear upon any juror, or (3) whether there was a mistake in entering the verdict onto the verdict form. A juror's affidavit or evidence of any statement by the juror may not be received on a matter about which the juror would be precluded from testifying." Colo. Rule Evid. 606(b) (2016)." The verdict deemed final, petitioner was sentenced to two years' probation and was required to register as a sex offender. A divided panel of the Colorado Court of Appeals affirmed petitioner's conviction. The Colorado Supreme Court affirmed by a vote of 4 to 3. The prevailing opinion relied on two decisions of this Court rejecting constitutional challenges to the federal no-impeachment rule as applied to evidence of juror misconduct or bias. See *Tanner v. United States,* 483 U.S. 107 (1987). This Court granted certiorari to decide whether there is a constitutional exception to the no-impeachment rule for instances of racial bias.

At common law jurors were forbidden to impeach their verdict, either by affidavit or live testimony. This rule originated in *Vaise v. Delaval,* 1 T.R. 11, 99 Eng. Rep. 944 (K.B. 1785). There, Lord Mansfield excluded juror testimony that the jury had decided the case through a game of chance. The Mansfield rule, as it came to be known, prohibited jurors, after the verdict was entered, from testifying either about their subjective mental processes or about objective events that occurred during deliberations.

American courts adopted the Mansfield rule as a matter of common law, though not in every detail. Some jurisdictions adopted a different, more flexible version of the no-impeachment bar known as the "Iowa rule." Under that rule, jurors were prevented only from testifying about their own subjective beliefs, thoughts, or motives during deliberations. Jurors, however, could testify about objective facts and events occurring during deliberations, in part because other jurors could corroborate that testimony. An alternative approach, referred to as the federal approach, stayed closer to the original Mansfield rule. Under this version, the no-impeachment bar permitted an exception only for testimony about events extraneous to the deliberative process, such as reliance on outside evidence—newspapers, dictionaries, and the like—or personal investigation of the facts.

This Court's early decisions did not establish a clear preference for a particular version of the no-impeachment rule. In *United States v. Reid*, 12 How. 361, 13 L.Ed. 1023 (1852), the Court appeared open to the admission of juror testimony that the jurors had consulted newspapers during deliberations, but in the end it barred the evidence because the newspapers "had not the slightest influence" on the verdict. *Reid* warned that juror testimony "ought always to be received with great caution." Yet it added an important admonition: "cases might arise in which it would be impossible to refuse" juror testimony "without violating the plainest principles of justice." In a following case the Court required the admission of juror affidavits stating that the jury consulted information that was not in evidence, including a prejudicial newspaper article. *Mattox v. United States,* 146 U.S. 140 (1892). The Court suggested that the admission of juror testimony might be governed by a more flexible rule, one permitting jury testimony even where it did not involve consultation of prejudicial extraneous information.Later, however, the Court rejected the more lenient Iowa rule. In *McDonald v. Pless,* 238 U.S. 264 (1915), the Court affirmed the exclusion of juror testimony about objective events in the jury room. There, the jury allegedly had calculated a damages award by averaging the numerical submissions of each member. As the Court explained, admitting that evidence would have "dangerous consequences": "no verdict would be safe" and the practice would "open the door to the most pernicious arts and tampering with jurors." Yet the Court reiterated its admonition from *Reid,* cautioning that the no-impeachment rule might recognize exceptions "in the gravest and most important cases" where exclusion of juror affidavits might well violate "the plainest principles of justice."

The common-law development of the no-impeachment rule reached a milestone in 1975, when Congress adopted the Federal Rules of Evidence, including

Rule 606(b). Congress, like the *McDonald* Court, rejected the Iowa rule. Instead it endorsed a broad no-impeachment rule, with only limited exceptions. The Advisory Committee drafted a rule reflecting the Iowa approach, prohibiting admission of juror testimony only as it related to jurors' mental processes in reaching a verdict. The Department of Justice, however, expressed concern. The Advisory Committee then drafted the more stringent version now in effect, prohibiting all juror testimony, with exceptions only where the jury had considered prejudicial extraneous evidence or was subject to other outside influence. Rules of Evidence for United States Courts and Magistrates, 56 F.R.D. 183 (1972). The Court adopted this second version and transmitted it to Congress. The House favored the Iowa approach, but the Senate expressed concern that it did not sufficiently address the public policy interest in the finality of verdicts. Siding with the Senate, the Conference Committee adopted, Congress enacted, and the President signed the Court's proposed rule. The substance of the Rule has not changed since 1975, except for a 2006 modification.

The current version of Rule 606(b) states as follows: "(1) *Prohibited Testimony or Other Evidence*. During an inquiry into the validity of a verdict or indictment, a juror may not testify about any statement made or incident that occurred during the jury's deliberations; the effect of anything on that juror's or another juror's vote; or any juror's mental processes concerning the verdict or indictment. The court may not receive a juror's affidavit or evidence of a juror's statement on these matters. (2) *Exceptions*. A juror may testify about whether: (A) extraneous prejudicial information was improperly brought to the jury's attention; (B) an outside influence was improperly brought to bear on any juror; or (C) a mistake was made in entering the verdict on the verdict form." This version of the no-impeachment rule has substantial merit. It promotes full and vigorous discussion by providing jurors with considerable assurance that after being discharged they will not be summoned to recount their deliberations, and they will not otherwise be harassed or annoyed by litigants seeking to challenge the verdict. The rule gives stability and finality to verdicts.

Some version of the no-impeachment rule is followed in every State and the District of Columbia. Variations make classification imprecise, but, as a general matter, 42 jurisdictions follow the Federal Rule, while 9 follow the Iowa Rule. Within both classifications there is a diversity of approaches. Nine jurisdictions that follow the Federal Rule have codified exceptions other than those listed in Federal Rule 606(b). At least 16 jurisdictions, 11 of which follow the Federal Rule, have recognized an exception to the no-impeachment bar under the circumstances the Court faces here: juror testimony that racial bias played a part in deliberations. Only one State other than Colorado has addressed this issue and declined to recognize an exception for racial bias. See *Commonwealth v. Steele*, 961 A.2d 786 (2008).

The federal courts are governed by Federal Rule 606(b). Various Courts of Appeals have had occasion to consider a racial bias exception and have reached different conclusions. Three have held or suggested there is a constitutional exception for evidence of racial bias. One court of appeals has declined to find an exception, reasoning that other safeguards inherent in the trial process suffice to protect defendants' constitutional interests. Another has suggested in the habeas context that an exception for racial bias was not clearly established but indicating in dicta that no such exception exists. One Court of Appeals has held that evidence of racial bias is excluded by Rule 606(b), without addressing whether the Constitution may at times demand an exception. In addressing the scope of the common-law no-impeachment rule before Rule 606(b)'s adoption, the *Reid* and *McDonald* Courts noted the possibility of an exception to the rule in the "gravest and most important cases." *Reid,* 12 How., at 366; *McDonald,* 238 U.S., at 269. Yet since the enactment of Rule 606(b), the Court has addressed the precise question whether the Constitution mandates an exception to it in just two instances.

In its first case, *Tanner,* 483 U.S. 107, the Court rejected a Sixth Amendment exception for evidence that some jurors were under the influence of drugs and alcohol during the trial. Central to the Court's reasoning were the "long-recognized and very substantial concerns" supporting "the protection of jury deliberations from intrusive inquiry." *Tanner* echoed *McDonald*'s concern that, if attorneys could use juror testimony to attack verdicts, jurors would be "harassed and beset by the defeated party," thus destroying "all frankness and freedom of discussion and conference." The Court was concerned, moreover, that attempts to impeach a verdict would "disrupt the finality of the process" and undermine both "jurors' willingness to return an unpopular verdict" and "the community's trust in a system that relies on the decisions of laypeople." *Tanner* outlined existing, significant safeguards for the defendant's right to an impartial and competent jury beyond post-trial juror testimony. *Voir dire* provides an opportunity for the court and counsel to examine members of the venire for impartiality. As a trial proceeds, the court, counsel, and court personnel have some opportunity to learn of any juror misconduct. Before the verdict, jurors themselves can report misconduct to the court. These procedures do not undermine the stability of a verdict once rendered. Even after the trial, evidence of misconduct other than juror testimony can be used to attempt to impeach the verdict. Balancing these interests and safeguards against the defendant's Sixth Amendment interest in that case, the Court affirmed the exclusion of affidavits pertaining to the jury's inebriated state.

The second case was *Warger.* The Court again rejected the argument that the jury trial right required an exception to the no-impeachment rule. *Warger* involved a civil case where, after the verdict was entered, the losing party sought to proffer evidence that the jury forewoman had failed to disclose prodefendant bias during *voir dire.* As in *Tanner,* the Court put substantial reliance on existing safeguards for a fair trial. The Court stated: "Even if jurors lie in *voir dire* in a way that conceals bias, juror impartiality is adequately assured by the parties' ability to bring to the court's attention any evidence of bias before the verdict is rendered, and to employ nonjuror evidence even after the verdict is rendered." In *Warger,* the Court did reiterate that the no-impeachment rule may admit exceptions. As in *Reid* and *McDonald,* the Court warned of "juror bias so extreme that, almost by definition, the jury trial right has been abridged." "If and when such a case arises," the Court indicated it would "consider whether the usual safeguards are or are not sufficient to protect the integrity of the process." The recognition in *Warger* that there may be extreme cases where the jury trial right requires an exception to the no-impeachment rule must be interpreted in context as a guarded, cautious statement. This caution is warranted to avoid formulating an exception that might undermine the jury dynamics and finality interests the no-impeachment rule seeks to protect. Today, the Court must decide whether the Constitution requires an exception to the no-impeachment rule when a juror's statements indicate that racial animus was a significant motivating factor in his or her finding of guilt.

It must become the heritage of our Nation to rise above racial classifications that are so inconsistent with our commitment to the equal dignity of all persons. This imperative to purge racial prejudice from the administration of justice was given new force and direction by the ratification of the Civil War Amendments. "The central purpose of the Fourteenth Amendment was to eliminate racial discrimination emanating from official sources in the States." *McLaughlin v. Florida,* 379 U.S. 184, 192 (1964). In the years before and after the ratification of the Fourteenth Amendment, racial discrimination in the jury system posed a particular threat both to the promise of the Amendment and to the integrity of the jury trial. "Almost immediately after the Civil War, the South began a practice that would continue for many decades: All-white juries punished black defendants particularly harshly, while simultaneously refusing to punish violence by whites, including Ku Klux Klan members, against blacks and Republicans." In the years 1865 and 1866, all-white juries in Texas decided a total of 500 prosecutions of white defendants charged with killing African–Americans. All 500 were acquitted. The stark and unapologetic nature of race-motivated outcomes challenged the American belief that "the jury was a bulwark of liberty," and prompted Congress to pass legislation to integrate the jury system and to bar persons from eligibility for jury service if they had conspired to deny the civil rights of African–Americans. Members of Congress stressed that the legislation was necessary to preserve the right to a fair trial and to guarantee the equal protection of the laws.

The duty to confront racial animus in the justice system is not the legislature's alone. Time and again, this Court has been called upon to enforce the Constitution's guarantee against state-sponsored racial discrimination in the jury system.

Beginning in 1880, the Court interpreted the Fourteenth Amendment to prohibit the exclusion of jurors on the basis of race. *Strauder v. West Virginia,* 100 U.S. 303 (1880). The Court has repeatedly struck down laws and practices that systematically exclude racial minorities from juries. To guard against discrimination in jury selection, the Court has ruled that no litigant may exclude a prospective juror on the basis of race. *Batson v. Kentucky,* 476 U.S. 79 (1986). In an effort to ensure that individuals who sit on juries are free of racial bias, the Court has held that the Constitution at times demands that defendants be permitted to ask questions about racial bias during *voir dire.* The unmistakable principle underlying these precedents is that discrimination on the basis of race, "odious in all aspects, is especially pernicious in the administration of justice." *Rose v. Mitchell,* 443 U.S. 545, 555 (1979). The jury is to be "a criminal defendant's fundamental 'protection of life and liberty against race or color prejudice.'" *McCleskey v. Kemp,* 481 U.S. 279, 310 (1987). Permitting racial prejudice in the jury system damages "both the fact and the perception" of the jury's role as "a vital check against the wrongful exercise of power by the State." *Powers v. Ohio,* 499 U.S. 400, 411 (1991).

This case lies at the intersection of the Court's decisions endorsing the no-impeachment rule and its decisions seeking to eliminate racial bias in the jury system. The two lines of precedent, however, need not conflict. Racial bias of the kind alleged in this case differs in critical ways from the compromise verdict in *McDonald,* the drug and alcohol abuse in *Tanner,* or the pro-defendant bias in *Warger.* The behavior in those cases is troubling and unacceptable, but each involved anomalous behavior from a single jury—or juror—gone off course. Jurors are presumed to follow their oath, and neither history nor common experience show that the jury system is rife with mischief of these or similar kinds. To attempt to rid the jury of every irregularity of this sort would be to expose it to unrelenting scrutiny. "It is not at all clear that the jury system could survive such efforts to perfect it."

The same cannot be said about racial bias, a familiar and recurring evil that, if left unaddressed, would risk systemic injury to the administration of justice. Racial bias implicates unique historical, constitutional, and institutional concerns. An effort to address the most grave and serious statements of racial bias is not an effort to perfect the jury but to ensure that our legal system remains capable of coming ever closer to the promise of equal treatment under the law that is so central to a functioning democracy.

Racial bias is distinct in a pragmatic sense. In past cases this Court has relied on other safeguards to protect the right to an impartial jury. Some of those safeguards can disclose racial bias. *Voir dire,* observation of juror demeanor and conduct during trial, juror reports before the verdict, and nonjuror evidence after trial are important mechanisms for discovering bias. Yet their operation may be compromised, or they may prove insufficient. This Court has noted the dilemma faced by trial court judges and counsel in deciding whether to explore potential racial bias at *voir dire*. Generic questions about juror impartiality may not expose specific attitudes or biases that can poison jury deliberations. Yet more pointed questions "could well exacerbate whatever prejudice might exist without substantially aiding in exposing it."

The stigma that attends racial bias may make it difficult for a juror to report inappropriate statements during the course of juror deliberations. It is one thing to accuse a fellow juror of having a personal experience that improperly influences her consideration of the case. It is quite another to call her a bigot. The recognition that certain of the *Tanner* safeguards may be less effective in rooting out racial bias than other kinds of bias is not dispositive. All forms of improper bias pose challenges to the trial process. But there is a sound basis to treat racial bias with added precaution. A constitutional rule that racial bias in the justice system must be addressed—including after the verdict has been entered—is necessary to prevent a systemic loss of confidence in jury verdicts, a confidence that is a central premise of the Sixth Amendment trial right.

The Court now holds that where a juror makes a clear statement that indicates he or she relied on racial stereotypes or animus to convict a criminal defendant, the Sixth Amendment requires that the no-impeachment rule give way in order to permit the trial court to consider the evidence of the juror's statement and any resulting denial of the jury trial guarantee. Not every offhand comment indicating racial bias or hostility will justify setting aside the no-impeachment bar to allow further judicial inquiry. For the inquiry to proceed, there must be a showing that one or more jurors made statements exhibiting overt racial bias that cast serious doubt on the fairness and impartiality of the jury's deliberations and resulting verdict. To qualify, the statement must tend to show that racial animus was a significant motivating factor in the juror's vote to convict. Whether that threshold showing has been satisfied is a matter committed to the substantial discretion of the trial court in light of all the circumstances, including the content and timing of the alleged statements and the reliability of the proffered evidence.

The practical mechanics of acquiring and presenting such evidence will no doubt be shaped and guided by state rules of professional ethics and local court rules, both of which often limit counsel's post-trial contact with jurors. These limits seek to provide jurors some protection when they return to their daily affairs after the verdict has been entered. But while a juror can always tell counsel they do not wish to discuss the case, jurors in some instances may come forward of their own accord. That is what happened here. In this case the alleged statements by a juror were egregious and unmistakable in their reliance on racial bias. Not only did juror H.C. deploy a dangerous racial stereotype to conclude petitioner was guilty and his alibi witness should not be believed, but he encouraged other jurors to join him in convicting on that basis.

Petitioner's counsel did not seek out the two jurors' allegations of racial bias. Pursuant to Colorado's mandatory jury instruction, the trial court had set limits on juror contact and encouraged jurors to inform the court if anyone harassed them about their role in the case. Similar limits on juror contact can be found in other jurisdictions that recognize a racial-bias exception. With the understanding that they were under no obligation to speak out, the jurors approached petitioner's counsel, within a short time after the verdict, to relay their concerns about H.C.'s statements. Pursuant to local court rules, petitioner's counsel then sought and received permission from the court to contact the two jurors and obtain affidavits limited to recounting the exact statements made by H.C. that exhibited racial bias. While the trial court concluded that Colorado's Rule 606(b) did not permit it even to consider the resulting affidavits, the Court's holding today removes that bar. When jurors disclose an instance of racial bias as serious as the one involved in this case, the law must not wholly disregard its occurrence.

The Court relies on the experiences of the 17 jurisdictions that have recognized a racial-bias exception to the no-impeachment rule—some for over half a century—with no signs of an increase in juror harassment or a loss of juror willingness to engage in searching and candid deliberations. The experience of these jurisdictions, and the experience of the courts going forward, will inform the proper exercise of trial judge discretion in these and related matters. This case does not ask, and the Court need not address, what procedures a trial court must follow when confronted with a motion for a new trial based on juror testimony of racial bias. The Court also does not decide the appropriate standard for determining when evidence of racial bias is sufficient to require that the verdict be set aside and a new trial be granted.

There are standard and existing processes designed to prevent racial bias in jury deliberations. The advantages of *voir dire* have already been noted. Other safeguards deserve mention. Trial courts, often at the outset of the case and again in their final jury instructions, explain the jurors' duty to review the evidence and reach a verdict in a fair and impartial way, free from bias of any kind. Some instructions are framed by trial judges based on their own learning and experience. Model jury instructions likely take into account these continuing developments and are common across jurisdictions. Instructions may emphasize the group dynamic of deliberations by urging jurors to share their questions and conclusions with their colleagues. Probing and thoughtful deliberation improves the likelihood that jurors can confront the flawed nature of reasoning that is prompted or influenced by improper biases, whether racial or otherwise. These dynamics help ensure that the exception is limited to rare cases.

The Nation must continue to make strides to overcome race-based discrimination. The progress that has already been made underlies the Court's insistence that blatant racial prejudice is antithetical to the functioning of the jury system and must be confronted in egregious cases like this one despite the general bar of the no-impeachment rule. It is the mark of a maturing legal system that it seeks to understand and to implement the lessons of history. The Court now seeks to strengthen the broader principle that society can and must move forward by achieving the thoughtful, rational dialogue at the foundation of both the jury system and the free society that sustains our Constitution.

The judgment of the Supreme Court of Colorado is reversed, and the case is remanded for further proceedings not inconsistent with this opinion.

It is so ordered.

JUSTICE THOMAS, dissenting.

The Court's holding cannot be squared with the original understanding of the Sixth or Fourteenth Amendments. The common-law right to a jury trial did not guarantee a defendant the right to impeach a jury verdict with juror testimony about juror misconduct, including "a principal species of juror misbehaviour"— "notorious partiality." 3 Blackstone 388. Although partiality was a ground for setting aside a jury verdict, the English common-law rule did not allow jurors to supply evidence of that misconduct. *Rex v. Almon,* 5 Burr. 2687, 98 Eng. Rep. 411 (K.B.).[4]

At the time of the founding, the States took mixed approaches to this issue. Many States followed Lord Mansfield's no-impeachment rule and refused to receive juror affidavits. By the time the Fourteenth Amendment was ratified, Lord Mansfield's no-impeachment rule had become firmly entrenched in American law. The vast majority of States adopted the no-impeachment rule as a matter of common law. Our common-law history does not establish that—in either 1791 (when the Sixth Amendment was ratified) or 1868 (when the Fourteenth Amendment was ratified)—a defendant had the right to impeach a verdict with juror testimony of juror misconduct. In fact, such evidence was prohibited. Perhaps good reasons exist to curtail or abandon the no-impeachment rule. Some States have

---

[4] Prior to 1770, juror affidavits were sometimes received to impeach a verdict on the ground of juror misbehavior, although only "with great caution." *McDonald v. Pless,* 238 U.S. 264, 268 (1915). But "previous to our Revolution, and at least as early as 1770, the doctrine in England was distinctly the other way, and has so stood ever since." 3 T. WATERMAN, A TREATISE ON THE PRINCIPLES OF LAW AND EQUITY WHICH GOVERN COURTS IN THE GRANTING OF NEW TRIALS IN CASES CIVIL AND CRIMINAL 1429 (1855).

done so and others have not. Ultimately, that question should be left to the political process. The Court today ends the political process and imposes a uniform, national rule. The Constitution does not require such a rule. Neither should we. I respectfully dissent.

JUSTICE ALITO, with whom THE CHIEF JUSTICE and JUSTICE THOMAS join, dissenting.

For centuries, it has been the judgment of experienced judges, trial attorneys, scholars, and lawmakers that allowing jurors to testify after a trial about what took place in the jury room would undermine the system of trial by jury that is integral to our legal system. Juries occupy a unique place in our justice system. When jurors retire to deliberate, they enter a space that is not regulated. Jurors are ordinary people. They are expected to speak, debate, argue, and make decisions the way ordinary people do in their daily lives. Our Constitution places great value on this way of thinking, speaking, and deciding. The jury trial right protects parties in court cases from being judged by a special class of trained professionals who do not speak the language of ordinary people and may not understand or appreciate the way ordinary people live their lives. To protect that right, the door to the jury room has been locked, and the confidentiality of jury deliberations has been closely guarded.

Today, with the admirable intention of providing justice for one criminal defendant, the Court not only pries open the door; it rules that respecting the privacy of the jury room, as our legal system has done for centuries, violates the Constitution. This is a startling development, and it is doubtful that there are principled grounds for preventing the expansion of today's holding. The Court justifies its decision on the ground that the nature of the confidential communication at issue—a clear expression of what the Court terms racial bias—is uniquely harmful to our criminal justice system. The Court is surely correct that even a tincture of racial bias can inflict great damage on that system, which is dependent on the public's trust. But until today, the argument that the Court now finds convincing has not been thought to be sufficient to overcome confidentiality rules like the one at issue here.

The firm no-impeachment approach taken in *McDonald* came to be known as "the federal rule." This approach categorically bars testimony about jury deliberations, except where it is offered to demonstrate that the jury was subjected to an extraneous influence (for example, an attempt to bribe a juror). Some jurisdictions, notably Iowa, adopted a more permissive rule. Under the Iowa rule, jurors were generally permitted to testify about any subject except their "subjective intentions and thought processes in reaching a verdict." Accordingly, the Iowa rule allowed jurors to "testify as to events or conditions which might have improperly influenced the verdict, even if these took place during deliberations within the jury room."

Debate between proponents of the federal rule and the Iowa rule emerged during the framing and adoption of Federal Rule of Evidence 606(b). In the end the strict federal approach was retained. The process that culminated in the adoption of Federal Rule of Evidence 606(b) was the epitome of reasoned democratic rulemaking. The matter went to Congress, which "specifically understood, considered, and rejected a version of the rule that would have allowed jurors to testify on juror conduct during deliberations." *Tanner*, 483 U.S., at 125. Colorado considered this same question, made the same judgment as the federal process, and adopted a very similar rule. In doing so, it joined the overwhelming majority of States. In the great majority of jurisdictions, strong no-impeachment rules continue to be "viewed as both promoting the finality of verdicts and insulating the jury from outside influences."

Recognizing the importance of Rule 606(b), this Court has twice rebuffed efforts to create a Sixth Amendment exception—first in *Tanner* and then in *Warger*. *Warger* explained that "even if jurors lie in *voir dire* in a way that conceals bias, juror impartiality is adequately assured by" two of the other *Tanner* safeguards: pre-verdict reports by the jurors and non-juror evidence. Today, the Court creates a constitutional exception to no-impeachment rules. The Court attempts to distinguish *Tanner* and *Warger*, but its efforts fail. *Tanner* and *Warger* rested on two basic propositions. First, no-impeachment rules advance crucial interests. Second, the right to trial by an impartial jury is adequately protected by mechanisms other than the use of juror testimony regarding jury deliberations. *Tanner* identified four "aspects of the trial process" that protect a defendant's Sixth Amendment rights: (1) *voir dire* ; (2) observation by the court, counsel, and court personnel; (3) pre-verdict reports by the jurors; and (4) non-juror evidence. Although the Court insists that that these mechanisms "may be compromised" in cases involving allegations of racial bias, it addresses only two of them and fails to make a sustained argument about either.

The Court contends that the effectiveness of *voir dire* is questionable in cases involving racial bias because pointed questioning about racial attitudes may highlight racial issues and thereby exacerbate prejudice. The suggestion that *voir dire* is ineffective in unearthing bias runs counter to decisions of this Court holding that *voir dire* on the subject of race is constitutionally required in some cases, mandated as a matter of federal supervisory authority in others, and typically advisable in any case if a defendant requests it. If *voir dire* were not useful in identifying racial prejudice, those decisions would be pointless. Even the majority recognizes the "advantages of careful *voir dire*" as a "process designed to prevent racial bias in jury deliberations." And reported decisions substantiate that *voir dire* can be effective in this regard. Thus, while *voir dire* is not a magic cure, there are good reasons to think that it is a valuable tool. In any event, the critical point for present purposes is that the effectiveness of *voir dire* is a debatable empirical proposition. Its assessment should be addressed in the process of developing federal and state evidence rules. Federal and state rulemakers can try a variety of approaches, and they can make changes in response to the insights provided by experience and research. The approach taken by today's majority—imposing a federal constitutional rule on the entire country—prevents experimentation and makes change exceedingly hard.

The majority argues that "racial bias may make it difficult for a juror to report inappropriate statements during the course of juror deliberations" because it is difficult to "call another juror a bigot." Jurors *do* report biased comments made by fellow jurors prior to the beginning of deliberations. Even if there is something to the distinction that the Court makes between pre- and post-verdict reporting, it is debatable whether the difference is significant enough to merit different treatment. Post-verdict reporting is both more disruptive and may be the result of extraneous influences. A juror who is initially in the minority but is ultimately persuaded by other jurors may have second thoughts after the verdict and may be angry with others on the panel who pressed for unanimity. If a verdict is unpopular with a particular juror's family, friends, employer, co-workers, or neighbors, the juror may regret his or her vote and may feel pressured to rectify what the jury has done.

The thrust of the opinion is that the Constitution is less tolerant of racial bias than other forms of juror misconduct, but it is hard to square this argument with the nature of the Sixth Amendment right. What the Sixth Amendment protects is the right to an "impartial jury." Nothing in the text or history of the Amendment or in the inherent nature of the jury trial right suggests that the extent of the protection provided by the Amendment depends on the nature of a jury's partiality or bias. It is true that "racial bias implicates unique historical, constitutional, and institutional concerns." But it is hard to see what that has to do with the scope of an *individual criminal defendant's* Sixth Amendment right to be judged impartially. Imagine two cellmates serving lengthy prison terms. Both were convicted for homicides committed in unrelated barroom fights. At the trial of the first prisoner, a juror expressed animosity toward the defendant because of his race. At the trial of the second prisoner, a juror expressed animosity toward the defendant because he was wearing the jersey of a hated football team. In both cases, jurors come forward after the trial and reveal what the biased juror said in the jury room. The Court would say to the first prisoner: "You are entitled to introduce the jurors' testimony, because racial bias is damaging to our society." To the second, the Court would say: "Even if you did not have an impartial jury, you must stay in prison because sports rivalries are not a major societal issue." This disparate treatment is unsupportable under the Sixth Amendment. Statements or conduct showing partiality should be treated the same way.

Recasting this as an equal protection case would not provide a ground for limiting the holding to cases involving racial bias. At a minimum, cases involving bias based on any suspect classification—such as national origin or religion— would merit equal treatment. So would bias based on sex, or the exercise of the First Amendment right to freedom of expression or association. Indeed, convicting a defendant on the basis of any irrational classification would violate the Equal Protection Clause.

The Court says that only "clear" expressions of bias must be admitted, but judging whether a statement is sufficiently "clear" will often not be easy. Suppose that the allegedly biased juror in this case never made reference to Peña–Rodriguez's race or national origin but said that he had a lot of experience with "this macho type" and knew that men of this kind felt that they could get their way with women. Suppose that other jurors testified that they were certain that "this macho type" was meant to refer to Mexican or Hispanic men. Under today's decision it will be difficult for judges to discern the dividing line between those that are "clearly" based on racial or ethnic bias and those that are at least somewhat ambiguous.

Today's decision—especially if it is expanded in ways that seem likely—will invite the harms that no-impeachment rules were designed to prevent. As the Court explained in *Tanner,* "post verdict scrutiny of juror conduct" will inhibit "full and frank discussion in the jury room." Today's ruling will also prompt losing parties and their friends, supporters, and attorneys to contact and seek to question jurors, and this pestering may erode citizens' willingness to serve on juries. Where post-verdict approaches are permitted or occur, there is almost certain to be an increase in harassment, arm-twisting, and outright coercion. The majority's approach will also undermine the finality of verdicts. Accusations of juror bias—which may be "raised for the first time days, weeks, or months after the verdict"—can "seriously disrupt the finality of the process." *Tanner, supra,* at 120. The Court's only response is that some jurisdictions already make an exception for racial bias, and the Court detects no signs of "a loss of juror willingness to engage in searching and candid deliberations."

The Court's decision is well-intentioned. It seeks to remedy a flaw in the jury trial system, but it is questionable whether our system of trial by jury can endure this attempt to perfect it.

Hypo: *The Juror's Blog*

During a criminal trial of a man charged with fraud, a blog was found to contain numerous negative comments about the defendant. When it became clear that a juror had posted a comment on the blog, the court made inquiry and determined that the individual was a juror who had been removed from the jury. Later, a second juror posted anonymous comments that referred to the removed juror and comments that she had made during the trial: "Mama June, and those who were there know what I'm talking about, she was spouting about the 'shots in the dark' blog since day one. It's why she conveniently got 'sick' and didn't finish her service. Several other jurors told her to stfu and got annoyed. 'Idiot' doesn't describe the half of it." Does the fact that one juror appeared to be talking about the blog to other jurors during the trial justify holding a hearing regarding to determine what happened? *See United States v. Zimny*, 846 F.3d 458 (1st Cir. 2017).

Executive Summary

Right to a Jury Trial. A defendant has a Sixth Amendment right to a jury trial when the authorized maximum punishment for a charge exceeds six months.

Less Than Six Months But "Serious." For offenses with shorter authorized sentences, no jury trial right exists unless the other statutory penalties, such as fines, are so severe as to render the offense "serious."

Jury of Twelve Not Required. A jury of twelve persons is not constitutionally mandated in State court proceedings and juries may be composed of as few as six persons, but a jury of six must be unanimous.

Unanimity Not Required. While unanimity is not constitution-

Major Themes

a. Limited Right—While the Court has recognized the great importance of a trial by jury to the founders, it has nonetheless chipped away at the edges of the right using a historical analysis (not agreed upon by all members of the Court), resulting in conclusions that the right never applied to all offenses, and never required unanimity nor a jury of twelve persons.

b. Jury Selection—Jury selection procedures are governed by several constitutional rights, from a fairly limited right to a jury chosen from a fair-cross section of the community, to the right to an impartial jury, allowing the court to remove jurors for cause who could not be fair, and the right of jurors to equal protection of the laws, such that neither the prosecution nor the defense can strike jurors based on race or gender.

ally required in State court proceedings, all but two States and the federal courts require unanimous jury verdicts.

Fair Cross-Section Requirement. Prospective jurors must be selected from a fair cross-section of the population of the place where the crime was committed. Exclusion of large distinctive groups from jury service, such as women or on the basis of race, violates the constitution.

Challenges for Cause. Prospective trial jurors may be questioned during *voir dire* to determine whether they can be excluded from the jury for cause because they cannot be fair and impartial.

Peremptory Challenges. Peremptory challenges to jurors may be based on any reason or no reason at all except that neither party can exercise peremptory challenges to exclude jurors based on race or gender.

Test Your Knowledge

To assess your understanding of the material in this chapter, click here to take a quiz.

For More Information

• WAYNE R. LAFAVE, JEROLD H. ISRAEL, NANCY J. KING & ORIN S. KERR, CRIMINAL PROCEDURE (5th ed. 2009).

• JEROLD H. ISRAEL & WAYNE R. LAFAVE, CRIMINAL PROCEDURE: CONSTITUTIONAL LIMITATIONS (8th ed. 2006).

• RUSSELL L. WEAVER, JOHN M. BURKOFF, CATHERINE HANCOCK, JANET HOEFFEL, STEVE FRIEDLAND & STEPHEN SINGER, PRINCIPLES OF CRIMINAL PROCEDURE Ch. 16 (6th ed. 2018).

CHAPTER 18

The Confrontation Clause

A. Introduction

The Sixth Amendment provides that: "In all criminal prosecutions, the accused shall enjoy the right . . . to be confronted with the witnesses against him." The Confrontation Clause protects criminal defendants by affording them the opportunity to confront the witnesses against them at trial. What "confronting witnesses" means, however, is far from clear. Instead, the phrase long has depended on judicial interpretation, especially by the Supreme Court. The Clause protects the accused in federal court cases directly through the Sixth Amendment, and in state court cases through the Fourteenth Amendment's Due Process Clause.

Over the past several decades, two distinct threads of Confrontation Clause analysis have developed. One thread involves the potential exclusion of hearsay statements offered by the prosecution against defendants in criminal cases. Another thread involves issues of whether defendants in sexual assault cases have the right to be face-to-face observation with child witnesses.

What's That?

Hearsay is an out-of-court statement offered to prove the truth of the matter asserted. Fed. R. Evid. 801. Under the rules of evidence, hearsay is generally excluded. Fed. R. Evid. 802. Even so, there are a litany of exceptions to the hearsay rule. See Fed. R. Evid. 803 and 804. Hearsay statements raise both evidentiary issues and Confrontation Clause questions. This chapter is concerned only with the Confrontation Clause.

The hearsay statement thread of Confrontation Clause analysis was well-established until it was wrested from its moorings in *Crawford v. Washington*, 541 U.S. 36 (2004) and became the subject of renewed interest and volatility. In *Crawford*, Justice Scalia altered the entire foundation of when and how the Clause applied. *Crawford* divided the constitutional firmament for hearsay statements into two categories: testimonial hearsay and everything else. The Confrontation Clause now focused only on testimonial statements, not the remainder.

Crawford's new structure emphasized the defendant's ability to examine a declarant about his hearsay statements. If the statement is regarded as testimonial, then defendant must have an opportunity to examine the declarant about the statement; it is not necessary that the accused in fact examine the declarant. If the declarant is available at trial, the declarant generally must be called as a witness. If the declarant is not available, no matter how firmly rooted or reliable the testimonial statements are, the statements only will be admissible if the defendant had a prior opportunity to cross-examine the now unavailable declarant. Otherwise the statements are excluded from evidence under the Confrontation Clause.

Take Note

The pre-*Crawford* Confrontation Clause approach applied to all hearsay and was grounded on the reliability of the statement. As the Court found in the seminal case of *Ohio v. Roberts*, 448 U.S. 56 (1980), if the hearsay was located within a "firmly rooted" exception or had "particularized guarantees of trustworthiness," it was considered to have presumptive reliability. The reliability analysis of *Roberts* no longer governs, replaced instead by the testimonial hearsay inquiry of *Crawford*. In effect, instead of changing the oil in a car, *Crawford* seemingly traded in the entire vehicle for replacement.

Crawford's meaning has developed as a result of a case-by-case analysis in hundreds of subsequent state and federal actions, including several Supreme Court cases. For example, after *Crawford*, Justice Scalia recognized a significant exclusion under the Confrontation Clause for statements made for the primary purpose of responding to an on-going emergency, as compared to statements relating to eliciting the facts of a past crime. *Davis v. Washington*, 547 U.S. 813 (2006).

What's That?

Since the lynchpin of the *Crawford* analysis is whether a statement is considered to be testimonial, the definition of this term is critical. What is included in the testimonial statements category, though, has not been starkly illuminated by the Court, but rather revolves around context. Justice Scalia in *Crawford* indicated that affidavits, statements produced by custodial police interrogation, depositions, courtroom testimony, and "statements that were made under circumstances which would lead an objective witness reasonably to believe that the statement would be available for use at a later trial" are included. These statements thus could be formal, as evidenced by affidavits, or informal, such as those made during on-the-street police questioning.

Even if statements are deemed to be testimonial and the Confrontation Clause applies, the accused still can waive his or her rights. The waiver can be express or implied. One notable type of implied waiver involves forfeiture by wrongdoing, when an accused who intentionally acts to prevent a declarant from testifying cannot use the Confrontation Clause as a shield.

The second thread of Confrontation Clause analysis applies to sexual assault cases involving children. This thread usually concerns the circumstances surrounding how victimized children are required to testify at a trial, if at all. A significant question revolves around the meaning of "face-to-face" confrontation.

> **Food for Thought**
>
> The fact that a hearsay statement survives Confrontation Clause analysis does not guarantee that it will be admissibile at trial. Under the rules of evidence, hearsay analysis, and other potential exclusions, could render the evidence inadmissible.

B. Modern Hearsay Thread Confrontation Clause Analysis

Modern "hearsay" Confrontation Clause analysis revolves around *Crawford v. Washington*, 541 U.S. 36 (2004), which follows. The case raises constitutional interpretation issues, using the text and framers' intent.

Crawford v. Washington

541 U.S. 36 (2004).

JUSTICE SCALIA delivered the opinion of the Court.

> **Who's That?**
>
> Justice Scalia was appointed to the Supreme Court as an Associate Justice by President Ronald Reagan in 1986 and served until his death in 2016. With nine children, he was a former professor at the University of Virginia Law School and judge on the D.C. Circuit Court of Appeals. His interest in the Confrontation Clause is apparent, if only from the number and importance of his Confrontation opinions. Often labeled a textualist, who tries to divine meaning from the text of statutes and the Constitution, he is known for asking many questions during oral arguments and sometimes writing sharp-tongued dissents.

On August 5, 1999, Kenneth Lee was stabbed at his apartment. Police arrested petitioner later that night. After giving petitioner and his wife *Miranda* warnings, detectives interrogated each of them twice. Petitioner eventually confessed that he and Sylvia had gone in search of Lee because he was upset over an earlier incident in which Lee had tried to rape her. The two had found Lee at his apartment, and a fight ensued in which Lee was stabbed in the torso and petitioner's hand was cut. Petitioner claimed that he saw something in Lee's hand, possibly a weapon, right before he stabbed him. Sylvia generally corroborated petitioner's story about the events leading up to the fight, but her account of the fight itself was arguably different—particularly with respect to whether Lee had drawn a weapon before petitioner assaulted him. She denied seeing anything in Lee's hands.

The State charged petitioner with assault and attempted murder. At trial, he claimed self-defense. Sylvia did not testify because of the state marital privilege, which generally bars a spouse from testifying without the other spouse's consent. In Washington, this privilege does not extend to

Hear It

Listen to the oral argument of *Crawford* at: http://www.oyez.org/cases/2000-2009/2003/2003_02_9410.

a spouse's out-of-court statements admissible under a hearsay exception, so the State sought to introduce Sylvia's tape-recorded statements to the police as evidence that the stabbing was not in self-defense. Noting that Sylvia had admitted she led petitioner to Lee's apartment and thus had facilitated the assault, the State invoked the hearsay exception for statements against penal interest.

Petitioner countered that, state law notwithstanding, admitting the evidence would violate his federal constitutional right to be "confronted with the witnesses against him." Amdt. 6. According to our description of that right in *Ohio v. Roberts, 448 U.S. 56 (1980)*, it does not bar admission of an unavailable witness's statement against a criminal defendant if the statement bears "adequate 'indicia of reliability.' " To meet that test, evidence must either fall within a "firmly rooted hearsay exception" or bear "particularized guarantees of trustworthiness." The trial court admitted the statement, offering several reasons why it was trustworthy. The Washington Court of Appeals reversed concluding that, although Sylvia's statement did not fall under a firmly rooted hearsay exception, it bore guarantees of trustworthiness. We granted certiorari to determine whether the State's use of Sylvia's statement violated the Confrontation Clause.

The Sixth Amendment's Confrontation Clause provides that, "in all criminal prosecutions, the accused shall enjoy the right . . . to be confronted with the witnesses against him." We have held that this bedrock procedural guarantee applies to both federal and state prosecutions. *Roberts* says that an unavailable witness's out-of-court statement may be admitted so long as it has "adequate indicia of reliability"—*i.e.,* falls within a "firmly rooted hearsay exception" or bears "particularized guarantees of trustworthiness." Petitioner argues that this test strays from the original meaning of the Confrontation Clause.

The Constitution's text does not alone resolve this case. One could plausibly read "witnesses against" a defendant to mean those who actually testify at trial, those whose statements are offered at trial, or something in-between. We must therefore turn to the historical background of the Clause to understand its meaning.

English common law tradition is one of live testimony in court subject to adversarial testing. See 3 W. Blackstone, Commentaries on the Laws of England 373–374 (1768). Many declarations of rights adopted around the time of the Revolution guaranteed a right of confrontation. See Virginia Declaration of Rights § 8 (1776). The proposed Federal Constitution, however, did not. When there was an outcry against this omission, the First Congress responded by including the Confrontation Clause in the proposal that became the Sixth Amendment. Early state decisions shed light upon the original understanding of the common-law right. *State v. Webb,* 2 N.C. 103 (1794) (per curium), held: "It is a rule of the common law, founded on natural justice, that no man shall be prejudiced by evidence which he had not the liberty to cross examine."

This history supports two inferences about the meaning of the Sixth Amendment. First, the principal evil at which the Confrontation Clause was directed was the civil-law mode of criminal procedure, and particularly its use of *ex parte* examinations as evidence against the accused. It was these practices that the Crown deployed in notorious treason cases and that the founding-era rhetoric decried. The Sixth Amendment must be interpreted with this focus in mind.

We reject the view that the Confrontation Clause applies of its own force only to in-court testimony, and that its application to out-of-court statements introduced at trial depends upon "the law of Evidence for the time being." Leaving the regulation of out-of-court statements to the law of evidence would render the Confrontation Clause powerless to prevent even the most flagrant inquisitorial practices. This focus also suggests that not all hearsay implicates the Sixth Amendment's core concerns. An off-hand, overheard remark might be unreliable evidence and thus a good candidate for exclusion under hearsay rules, but it bears little resemblance to the civil-law abuses the Confrontation Clause targeted. On the other hand, *ex parte* examinations might sometimes be admissible under modern hearsay rules, but the Framers certainly would not have condoned them.

The text of the Confrontation Clause reflects this focus. It applies to "witnesses" against the accused—in other words, those who "bear testimony." "Testimony," in turn, is typically "a solemn declaration or affirmation made for the purpose of establishing or proving some fact." An accuser who makes a formal statement to government officers bears testimony in a sense that a person who makes a casual remark to an acquaintance does not.

Various formulations of this core class of "testimonial" statements exist: "*ex parte* in-court testimony or its functional equivalent—that is, material such as affidavits, custodial examinations, prior testimony that the defendant was unable to cross-examine, or similar pretrial statements that declarants would reasonably expect to be used prosecutorially," "extrajudicial statements contained in formalized testimonial materials, such as affidavits, depositions, prior testimony, or confessions," *White v. Illinois,* 502 U.S. 346 (1992) (Thomas, J., joined by Scalia, J., concurring in part and concurring in judgment); "statements that were made under circumstances which would lead an objective witness reasonably to believe that the statement would be available for use at a later trial."

Statements taken by police officers in the course of interrogations are also testimonial under even a narrow standard. That interrogators are police officers rather than magistrates does not change the picture. Even if the Sixth Amendment is not solely concerned with testimonial hearsay, that is its primary object, and interrogations by law enforcement officers fall squarely within that class.

The historical record also supports a second proposition: that the Framers would not have allowed admission of testimonial statements of a witness who did not appear at trial unless he was unavailable to testify, and the defendant had had a prior opportunity for cross-examination. The text of the Sixth Amendment does not suggest any open-ended exceptions from the confrontation requirement to be developed by the courts. Rather, the "right to be confronted with the witnesses against him" is most naturally read as a reference to the right of confrontation at common law, admitting only those exceptions established at the time of the founding. As the English authorities reveal, the common law in 1791 conditioned admissibility of an absent witness's examination on unavailability and a prior opportunity to cross-examine. The Sixth Amendment therefore incorporates those limitations.

We do not read the historical sources to say that a prior opportunity to cross-examine was merely a sufficient, rather than a necessary, condition for admissibility of testimonial statements. They suggest that this requirement was dispositive, and not merely one of several ways to establish reliability. Our case law has been largely consistent with these two principles. In *Mattox v. United States,* 156 U.S. 237 (1895), we relied on the fact that the defendant had had, at the first trial, an adequate opportunity to confront the witness. Even our recent cases, in their outcomes, hew closely to the traditional line. *Ohio v. Roberts,* 448 U.S., at 67–70, admitted testimony from a preliminary hearing at which the defendant had examined the witness. *Lilly v. Virginia,* excluded testimonial statements that the defendant had had no opportunity to test by cross-examination. *Bourjaily v. United States,* 483 U.S. 171 (1987), admitted statements made unwittingly to an FBI informant after applying a more general test that did *not* make prior cross-examination an indispensable requirement.

Our cases have thus remained faithful to the Framers' understanding: Testimonial statements of witnesses absent from trial have been admitted only where the declarant is unavailable, and only where the defendant has had a prior opportunity to cross-examine. When the declarant appears for cross-examination at trial, the Confrontation Clause places no constraints at all on the use of his prior testimonial statements. See *Tennessee v. Street,* 471 U.S. 409 (1985).

Although the results of our decisions have generally been faithful to the original meaning of the Confrontation Clause, the same cannot be said of our rationales. *Roberts* conditions the admissibility of all hearsay evidence on whether it falls under a "firmly rooted hearsay exception" or bears "particularized guarantees of trustworthiness." This test departs from the historical principles identified above in two respects. It applies the same mode of analysis whether or not the hearsay consists of *ex parte* testimony. This often results in close constitutional scrutiny in cases that are far removed from the core concerns of the Clause. At the same time, however, the test is too narrow: It admits statements that *do* consist of *ex parte* testimony upon a mere finding of reliability. This malleable standard often fails to protect against paradigmatic confrontation violations.

Where testimonial statements are involved, we do not think the Framers meant to leave the Sixth Amendment's protection to the vagaries of the rules of evidence, much less to amorphous notions of "reliability." Admitting statements deemed reliable by a judge is fundamentally at odds with the right of confrontation. Dispensing with confrontation because testimony is obviously reliable is akin to dispensing with jury trial because a defendant is obviously guilty. This is not what the Sixth Amendment prescribes. The legacy of *Roberts* in other courts vindicates the Framers' wisdom in rejecting a general reliability exception. The framework is so unpredictable that it fails to provide meaningful protection from even core confrontation violations. Reliability is an amorphous, if not entirely subjective, concept. Whether a statement is deemed reliable depends heavily on which factors the judge considers and how much weight he accords each of them. Some courts wind up attaching the same significance to opposite facts.

The unpardonable vice of the *Roberts* test, however, is not its unpredictability, but its demonstrated capacity to admit core testimonial statements that the Confrontation Clause plainly meant to exclude. One recent study found that, after *Lilly,* appellate courts admitted accomplice statements to the authorities in 25 out of 70 cases—more than one-third of the time. Courts have invoked *Roberts* to admit other sorts of plainly testimonial statements despite the absence of any opportunity to cross-examine.

To add insult to injury, some of the courts that admit untested testimonial statements find reliability in the very factors that *make* the statements testimonial. One court relied on the fact that the witness's statement was made to police while in custody on pending charges—the theory being that this made the statement more clearly against penal interest and thus more reliable. That inculpating statements are given in a testimonial setting is not an antidote to the confrontation problem, but rather the trigger that makes the Clause's demands most urgent.

Roberts' failings were on full display in the proceedings below. Sylvia Crawford made her statement while in police custody, herself a potential suspect in the case. Indeed, she had been told that whether she would be released "depended on how the investigation continues." In response to often leading questions from police detectives, she implicated her husband in Lee's stabbing and at least arguably undermined his self-defense claim. Despite all this, the trial court admitted her statement, listing several reasons why it was reliable. In its opinion reversing, the Court of Appeals listed several *other* reasons why the statement was *not* reliable. Finally, the State Supreme Court relied exclusively on the interlocking character of the statement and disregarded every other factor the lower courts had considered. The case is thus a self-contained demonstration of *Roberts'* unpredictable and inconsistent application. Each of the courts also made assumptions that cross-examination might well have undermined.

To reverse the Washington Supreme Court's decision after conducting our own reliability analysis would perpetuate what the Sixth Amendment condemns. The Constitution prescribes a procedure for determining the reliability of testimony in criminal trials, and we lack authority to replace it with one of our own devising. The Framers knew that judges, like other government officers, could not always be trusted to safeguard the rights of the people.

Where nontestimonial hearsay is at issue, it is wholly consistent with the Framers' design to afford the States flexibility in their development of hearsay law—as does *Roberts,* and as would an approach that exempted such statements from Confrontation Clause scrutiny altogether. Where testimonial evidence is at issue, the Sixth Amendment demands what the common law required: unavailability and a prior opportunity for cross-examination. We leave for another day any effort to spell out a comprehensive definition of "testimonial." Whatever else the term covers, it applies at a minimum to prior testimony at a preliminary hearing, before a grand jury, or at a former trial; and to police interrogations.

In this case, the State admitted Sylvia's testimonial statement against petitioner, despite the fact that he had no opportunity to cross-examine her. That alone is sufficient to make out a violation of the Sixth Amendment. *Roberts* notwithstanding, we decline to mine the record in search of indicia of reliability. Where testimonial statements are at issue, the only indicium of reliability sufficient to satisfy constitutional demands is the one the Constitution actually prescribes: confrontation.

The judgment of the Washington Supreme Court is reversed, and the case is remanded for further proceedings not inconsistent with this opinion.

It is so ordered.

CHIEF JUSTICE REHNQUIST, with whom JUSTICE O'CONNOR joins, concurring in the judgment.

I dissent from the Court's decision to overrule *Roberts*. The Court's distinction between testimonial and nontestimonial statements is no better rooted in history than our current doctrine. Testimonial statements such as accusatory statements to police officers likely would have been disapproved of in the 18th century, not necessarily because they resembled *ex parte* affidavits or depositions as the Court reasons, but more likely than not because they were not made under oath. See *King v. Woodcock,* 1 Leach 500, 503, 168 Eng. Rep. 352, 353 (1789). Without an oath, one usually did not get to the second step of whether confrontation was required.

While I agree that the Framers were mainly concerned about sworn affidavits and depositions, it does not follow that they were similarly concerned about the Court's broader category of testimonial statements. Unsworn testimonial statements were treated no differently at common law than were nontestimonial statements, and it seems to me any classification of statements as testimonial beyond that of sworn affidavits and depositions will be somewhat arbitrary, merely a proxy for what the Framers might have intended had such evidence been liberally admitted as substantive evidence like it is today. I therefore see no reason why the distinction the Court draws is preferable to our precedent. Exceptions to confrontation have always been derived from the experience that some out-of-court statements are just as reliable as cross-examined in-court testimony due to the circumstances under which they were made.

"In a given instance cross-examination may be superfluous; it may be sufficiently clear that the statement offered is free enough from the risk of inaccuracy and untrustworthiness, so that the test of cross-examination would be a work of supererogation." 5 Wigmore § 1420, at 251. In choosing the path it does, the Court of course overrules *Roberts,* a case decided nearly a quarter of a century ago. The Court grandly declares that "we leave for another day any effort to spell out a comprehensive definition of 'testimonial,' "But the thousands of federal prosecutors and the tens of thousands of state prosecutors need answers as to what beyond the specific kinds of "testimony" the Court lists is covered by the new rule. They need them now,

Who's That?

Chief Justice Rehnquist, considered a conservative justice, was originally appointed to the Supreme Court as an Associate Justice by President Richard Nixon in 1971. He was elevated to Chief Justice in 1986 by President Ronald Reagan, where he remained until his death in 2005. Justice Rehnquist presided over many important cases, including *Bush v. Gore*, and the impeachment trial of President Bill Clinton. He oversaw a very different Supreme Court than his predecessor, Chief Justice Burger, or successor, Chief Justice Roberts. Biographical information about Chief Justice Rehnquist can be found at the following link: http://www.biography.com/people/william-rehnquist-9454479#death-and-legacy.

not months or years from now. Rules of criminal evidence are applied every day in courts throughout the country, and parties should not be left in the dark in this manner.

The result the Court reaches follows inexorably from *Roberts* and its progeny without any need for overruling that line of cases. In *Idaho v. Wright*, 497 U.S. 805 (1990), we held that an out-of-court statement was not admissible simply because the truthfulness of that statement was corroborated by other evidence at trial. A citation to *Wright,* would suffice. This would be a far preferable course for the Court to take here.

Point for Discussion

Expecting to Bear Witness

Other federal courts subsequently articulated their understanding of testimonial statements. The Court observed in *United States v. Dargan*, 738 F.3d 643 (4th Cir. 2013):

> As *Crawford* and later Supreme Court cases make clear, a statement must be 'testimonial' to be excludable under the Confrontation Clause. The primary determinant of a statement's testimonial quality is "whether a reasonable person in the declarant's position would have expected his statements to be used at trial—that is, whether the declarant would have expected or intended to 'bear witness' against another in a later proceeding." *Crawford,* 541 U.S. at 52. This definition flows from the Court's recognition that "the principal evil at which the Confrontation Clause was directed was the civil-law mode of criminal procedure, and particularly its use of ex parte examinations as evidence against the accused."

Hypo 1: *Does Crawford Apply to Pretrial Suppression Hearings?*

Jones was stopped by the police for erratic driving. In the audiotape of the initial conversation between Officer Pelts and Jones after the stop, Pelts could be heard stating, "I saw you cross over the center line twice, in violation of the law. That is why I stopped you." Jones was arrested for DUI and the possession of guns. In a subsequent suppression hearing, the audiotape was offered by the prosecution because Officer Pelts had since passed away. Jones claimed the tape violated his Confrontation Clause rights. What should be the ruling of the court and why? *State v. Zamzow,* 374 Wis.2d 220 (2017)

Hypo 2: *Testimonial Statements*

Please consider whether the following statements are "testimonial" and therefore within the scope of the Confrontation Clause:

A) An eighty-year-old woman is battered and injured in her apartment by a younger woman who asks for money and ransacks the apartment. The assailant left the scene, and the police were called. After the police arrive, the police officer talks with the bruised woman and calls emergency medical services to help treat her and prepare for transport to the hospital. During the conversation, the woman provides a description of her assailant. Missing additional forensic evidence, such as fingerprints, hairs, or fibers, the victim's statements are important to the prosecution's case. At the defendant's trial for battery with a deadly weapon and robbery, the victim is unavailable to testify. Are the victim's statements to the police testimonial?

B) Defendants Donnie and Charlie are selling drugs at a local schoolyard. When a police officer stops Charlie and questions him, Charlie responds with ane alibi he and Donnie were using about working for a charity, seeking donations. After more questioning, Charlie inadvertently admits to committing the crime. He then confesses. Were Charlie's statements testimonial? Explain.

C) Jones is prosecuted for selling large quantities of counterfeit goods. At trial, the prosecution calls Detective Peabody, who testifies that the accused was not at first a suspect but became one after interviewing Jones' former roommate, Manfred. Manfred had been hit by a car and was in a coma at the time of trial. Did Detective Peabody's testimony violate defendant's rights? Could the appellate court consider whether defendant's rights were violated if the defense attorney did not object or in any other way preserve the question for appeal?

D) In a sexual assault action, the prosecution offers a psychiatric social worker to testify about what various complainants had told her concerning assaults against them. Most of the people who were the sources of the information testified. Some of the sources did not testify. The evidence presented by the social worker about the assaults was not duplicated by other sources or physical evidence. Was the testimony permissible under the Confrontation Clause? What if some statements were made for the purposes of medical treatment? Would these statements still be regarded as testimonial?

E) A victim of an armed robbery spoke to the police shortly after the crime and identified defendant, who was in custody, as the perpetrator. The victim was bleeding profusely and did not have time to reflect on or think about the statement concerning the events surrounding the attack. At the time of the declarant's statement, defendant had been arrested. At trial, the declarant was unavailable to testify. If a judge decides that these statements meet the excited utterance requirements under Federal Rule of Evidence 803(2), should the statement be admitted on behalf of the prosecution?

F) On March 4th, a bank was robbed in downtown Greensboro. The suspect was George Peabody, a student, who claimed at trial that he was in class at the date and time of the robbery. The prosecutor offered the statement of defendant's teacher who told a detective, before trial, that she had checked the class rolls for that date and that defendant was not in at class at that day and time. The defense attorney objected, claiming that the detective's testimony violated the Confrontation Clause. Was the testimony about the teacher's search of the class rolls testimonial? Why or why not?

Hypo 3: *Availability to Testify*

How should the following situations be handled under the Confrontation Clause: A) Suzie had been married to Decker for 10 years when she was asked by the police about the whereabouts and conduct of her husband on a certain date. After Suzie spoke voluntarily with the police, her husband was charged with two counts of burglary. At trial, the prosecution called Suzie to the witness stand, but she invoked the spousal testimony privilege and refused to testify. The prosecution wants to read her statement to the jury over the defense objection. Should the trial court admit the testimony? B) At trial, the witness was called to the stand in an armed robbery case to establish the existence of other prior robberies with the same *modus operandi*. The witness, a co-defendant, raised the Fifth Amendment and refused to answer any questions. The prosecutor was allowed to read the witness' prior statement made to the police during interrogation. Was the prosecutor's conduct permissible?

Hypo 4: *Opportunity to Examine*

Arthur Smitts is charged with grand theft auto. Before trial, the prosecution takes a discovery deposition of a witness who does not testify at trial. Defendant was permitted to attend the deposition by stipulation of both parties. Would Smitts have a viable Confrontation Clause claim if he did not attend the deposition and never cross-examined the witness? Explain.

C. Distinguishing Testimonial Statements From Statements Made for the Primary Purpose of Resolving an On-Going Emergency

The Court was confronted by how to categorize statements made by persons for the purpose of resolving on-going emergency situations, such as statements made during 911 calls. Should these statements be considered "testimonial," and therefore subject to the Confrontation Clause? In particular, after the following decision, could 911 calls include both testimonial and non-testimonial statements?

Hammon v. Indiana; Davis v. Washington

547 U.S. 813 (2006).

JUSTICE SCALIA delivered the opinion of the Court.

These cases require us to determine when statements made to law enforcement personnel during a 911 call or at a crime scene are "testimonial" and thus subject to the requirements of the Sixth Amendment's Confrontation Clause.

Hear It

You can hear the oral argument in *Hammon* at: http://www.oyez.org/cases/2000-2009/2005/2005_05_570.

The relevant statements in *Davis v. Washington*, No. 05–5224, were made to a 911 emergency operator on February 1, 2001. In the ensuing conversation, the operator ascertained that the 911 caller McCottry was involved in a domestic disturbance with her former boyfriend Adrian Davis, the petitioner in this case:

"911 Operator: Hello.

"Complainant: Hello.

"911 Operator: What's going on?

"Complainant: He's here jumpin' on me again.

"911 Operator: Listen to me carefully. Do you know his last name?

"Complainant: It's Davis.

"911 Operator: Davis? Okay, what's his first name?

"Complainant: Adrian

"Complainant: Martell. He's runnin' now."

McCottry described the context of the assault, after which the operator told her that the police were on their way. The police arrived within four minutes of the 911 call and observed McCottry's shaken state, the "fresh injuries on her forearm and her face," and her "frantic efforts to gather her belongings and her children so that they could leave the residence."

The State charged Davis with felony violation of a domestic no-contact order. "The State's only witnesses were the two police officers who responded to the 911 call. Both officers testified that McCottry exhibited injuries that appeared to be recent, but neither officer could testify as to the cause of the injuries." McCottry presumably could have testified as to whether Davis was her assailant, but she did not appear. Over Davis's objection, based on the Confrontation Clause of the Sixth Amendment, the trial court admitted the recording of her exchange with the 911 operator, and the jury convicted him. The Washington Court of Appeals and Supreme Court of Washington affirmed. We granted certiorari.

In *Hammon v. Indiana*, police responded late on the night of February 26, 2003, to a "reported domestic disturbance" at the home of Hershel and Amy Hammon. They found Amy alone on the front porch, appearing "somewhat frightened," but she told them that "nothing was the matter." She gave them permission to enter the house, where an officer saw "a gas heating unit in the corner of the living room" that had "flames coming out of the partial glass front. Hershel, meanwhile, was in the kitchen. He told the police "that he and his wife had 'been in an argument' but 'everything was fine now' and the argument 'never became physical.' " By this point Amy had come back inside. After hearing Amy's account, the officer "had her fill out and sign a battery affidavit." Amy handwrote the following: "Broke our Furnace & shoved me down on the floor into the broken glass. Hit me in the chest and threw me down. Broke our lamps & phone. Tore up my van where I couldn't leave the house. Attacked my daughter."

The State charged Hershel with domestic battery and with violating his probation. Amy was subpoenaed, but she did not appear at his subsequent bench trial.

The State called the officer who had questioned Amy, and asked him to recount what Amy told him and to authenticate the affidavit. Hershel's counsel repeatedly objected to the admission of this evidence. Nonetheless, the trial court admitted the affidavit as a "present sense impression," and Amy's statements as "excited utterances" that "are expressly permitted in these kinds of cases even if the declarant is not available to testify." The officer thus testified that Amy: "informed me that she and Hershel had been in an argument. That he became irrate [sic] over the fact of their daughter going to a boyfriend's house. The argument became physical after being verbal. She informed me Mr. Hammon had pushed her onto the ground, had shoved her head into the broken glass of the heater and that he had punched her in the chest twice I believe."

The trial judge found Hershel guilty on both charges, and the Indiana Court of Appeals affirmed in relevant part. The Indiana Supreme Court also affirmed, concluding that Amy's statement was admissible for state-law purposes as an excited utterance, that "a 'testimonial' statement is one given or taken in significant part for purposes of preserving it for potential future use in legal proceedings," where "the motivations of the questioner and declarant are the central concerns," and that Amy's oral statement was not "testimonial" under these standards. It also concluded that, although the affidavit was testimonial and thus wrongly admitted, it was harmless beyond a reasonable doubt, largely because the trial was to the bench. We granted certiorari.

The Confrontation Clause of the Sixth Amendment provides: "In all criminal prosecutions, the accused shall enjoy the right to be confronted with the witnesses against him." In 2004, we held that this provision bars "admission of testimonial statements of a witness who did not appear at trial unless he was unavailable to testify, and the defendant had had a prior opportunity for cross-examination." A critical portion of this holding, and the portion central to resolution of the cases before us, is the phrase "testimonial statements." Only statements of this sort cause the declarant to be a "witness" within the meaning of the Confrontation Clause. It is the testimonial character of the statement that separates it from other hearsay that, while subject to traditional limitations upon hearsay evidence, is not subject to the Confrontation Clause.

Our opinion in *Crawford* set forth "various formulations" of the core class of "testimonial" statements, but found it unnecessary to endorse any of them, because "some statements qualify under any definition." Among those, we said, were "statements taken by police officers in the course of interrogations. Questioning that generated the deponent's statement in *Crawford*—which was made and recorded while she was in police custody, after having been given *Miranda* warnings as a possible suspect herself—"qualifies under any conceivable definition" of an "interrogation." We therefore did not define that term, except to say that "we use it in its colloquial, rather than any technical legal, sense," and that "one can imagine various definitions, and we need not select among them in this case."

It suffices to decide the present cases to hold as follows: Statements are nontestimonial when made in the course of police interrogation under circumstances objectively indicating that the primary purpose of the interrogation is to enable police assistance to meet an ongoing emergency. They are testimonial when the circumstances objectively indicate that there is no such ongoing emergency, and that the primary purpose of the interrogation is to establish or prove past events potentially relevant to later criminal prosecution.

We must decide, therefore, whether the Confrontation Clause applies only to testimonial hearsay; and, if so, whether the recording of a 911 call qualifies as an interrogation by law enforcement officers. The answer to the first question was suggested in *Crawford*: "The text of the Confrontation Clause reflects this focus on testimonial hearsay. It applies to 'witnesses' against the accused—in other words, those who 'bear testimony.' 1 N. Webster, An American Dictionary of the English Language (1828). 'Testimony,' in turn, is typically 'a solemn declaration or affirmation made for the purpose of establishing or proving some fact.' An accuser who makes a formal statement to government officers bears testimony in a sense that a person who makes a casual remark to an acquaintance does not." A limitation so clearly reflected in the text of the constitutional provision must fairly be said to mark out not merely its "core," but its perimeter.

We are not aware of any early American case invoking the Confrontation Clause or the common-law right to confrontation that did not clearly involve testimony as thus defined. Even our later cases, conforming to the reasoning of *Roberts*, never in practice dispensed with the Confrontation Clause requirements of unavailability and prior cross-examination in cases that involved testimonial hearsay, *Crawford*, 541 U.S., at 57–59, with one arguable exception, (discussing *White v. Illinois*, 502 U.S. 346). Where our cases did dispense with those requirements—even under the *Roberts* approach—the statements at issue were clearly nontestimonial. See, e.g., *Bourjaily v. United States*, 483 U.S. 171, 181 (1987) (statements made unwittingly to a Government informant).

The question before us in *Davis* is whether, objectively considered, the interrogation that took place in the course of the 911 call produced testimonial statements. When we said in *Crawford* that "interrogations by law enforcement officers fall squarely

> **Food for Thought**
>
> Does *White v. Illinois* undermine the Court's review of precedent?

within the class" of testimonial hearsay, we had immediately in mind (for that was the case before us) interrogations solely directed at establishing the facts of a past crime, in order to identify (or provide evidence to convict) the perpetrator. The product of such interrogation, whether reduced to a writing signed by the declarant or embedded in the memory (and perhaps notes) of the interrogating officer, is testimonial. A 911 call, on the other hand, and at least the initial interrogation conducted in connection with a 911 call, is ordinarily not designed primarily to "establish or prove" some past fact, but to describe current circumstances requiring police assistance.

The difference between the interrogation in *Davis* and the one in *Crawford* is apparent on the face of things. In *Davis*, McCottry was speaking about events *as they were actually happening,* rather than "describing past events," *Lilly v. Virginia,* 527 U.S. 116 (1999) (plurality opinion). Sylvia Crawford's interrogation, on the other hand, took place hours after the events she described had occurred. Moreover, any reasonable listener would recognize that McCottry (unlike Sylvia Crawford) was facing an ongoing emergency. Although one *might* call 911 to provide a narrative report of a crime absent any imminent danger, McCottry's call was plainly a call for help against bona fide physical threat. Third, the nature of what was asked and answered in *Davis,* again viewed objectively, was such that the elicited statements were necessary to be able to *resolve* the present emergency, rather than simply to learn (as in *Crawford*) what had happened in the past. That is true even of the operator's effort to establish the identity of the assailant, so that the dispatched officers might know whether they would be encountering a violent felon. Finally, the difference in the level of formality between the two interviews is striking. Crawford was responding calmly, at the station house, to a series of questions, with the officer-interrogator taping and making notes of her answers; McCottry's frantic answers were provided over the phone, in an environment that was not tranquil, or even (as far as any reasonable 911 operator could make out) safe.

We conclude that the circumstances of McCottry's interrogation objectively indicate its primary purpose was to enable police assistance to meet an ongoing emergency. She simply was not acting as a *witness;* she was not *testifying.* What she said was not "a weaker substitute for live testimony" at trial, *United States v. Inadi,* 475 U.S. 387, 394 (1986), like Lord Cobham's statements in *Raleigh's Case,* 2 How. St. Tr. 1 (1603), or Jane Dingler's *ex parte* statements against her husband in *King v. Dingler,* 2 Leach 561, 168 Eng. Rep. 383 (1791), or Sylvia Crawford's statement in *Crawford.* In each of those cases, the *ex parte* actors and the evidentiary products of the *ex parte* communication aligned perfectly with their courtroom analogues. McCottry's emergency statement does not. No "witness" goes into court to proclaim an emergency and seek help.

Davis seeks to cast McCottry in the unlikely role of a witness by pointing to English cases. None of them involves statements made during an ongoing emergency. In *King v. Brasier,* 1 Leach 199, 168 Eng. Rep. 202 (1779), for example, a young rape victim, "immediately on her coming home, told all the circumstances of the injury" to her mother. The case would be helpful to Davis if the relevant statement had been the girl's screams for aid as she was being chased by her assailant. But by the time the victim got home, her story was an account of past events.

This is not to say that a conversation which begins as an interrogation to determine the need for emergency assistance cannot "evolve into testimonial statements," once that purpose has been achieved. In this case, after the operator gained the information needed to address the exigency of the moment, the emergency appears to have ended (when Davis drove away from the premises). The operator then told McCottry to be quiet, and proceeded to pose a battery of questions. It could readily be maintained that, from that point on, McCottry's statements were testimonial, not unlike the "structured police questioning" that occurred in *Crawford.* This presents no great problem. Through *in limine* procedure, they should redact or exclude the portions of any statement that have become testimonial, as they do, for example, with unduly prejudicial portions of otherwise admissible evidence. Davis's jury did not hear the *complete* 911 call, although it may well have heard some testimonial portions. We were asked to classify only McCottry's early statements identifying Davis as her assailant, and we agree that they were not testimonial. That court also concluded that, even if later parts of the call were testimonial, their admission was harmless beyond a reasonable doubt. Davis does not challenge that holding, and we assume it to be correct.

Determining the testimonial or nontestimonial character of the statements that were the product of the interrogation in *Hammon* is a much easier task, since they were not much different from the statements we found to be testimonial in *Crawford.* It is entirely clear from the circumstances that the interrogation was part of an investigation into possibly criminal past conduct—as, indeed, the testifying officer expressly acknowledged. There was no emergency in progress; the interrogating officer testified that he had heard no arguments or crashing and saw no one throw or break anything. When the officer questioned Amy for the second time, and elicited the challenged statements, he was not seeking to determine (as in Davis) "what is happening," but rather "what happened." Objectively viewed, the primary, if not indeed the sole, purpose of the interrogation was to investigate a possible crime—which is, of course, precisely what the officer should have done.

It is true that the *Crawford* interrogation was more formal. But Amy's interrogation was formal enough that Amy's interrogation was conducted in a separate room, away from her husband (who tried to intervene), with the officer receiving her replies for use in his "investigation." What we called the "striking resemblance" of the *Crawford* statement to civil-law *ex parte* examinations is shared by Amy's statement here. Both declarants were actively separated from the defendant—officers forcibly prevented Hershel from participating in the interrogation. Both statements deliberately recounted, in response to police questioning, how potentially criminal past events began and progressed. Both took place sometime after the events described were over.

Respondents in both cases contend that the nature of the offenses charged in these two cases—domestic violence—requires greater flexibility in the use of testimonial evidence. This particular type of crime s notoriously susceptible to intimidation or coercion of the victim to ensure that she does not testify at trial. When this occurs, the Confrontation Clause gives the criminal a windfall. We may not, however, vitiate constitutional guarantees when they have the effect of allowing the guilty to go free. But when defendants seek to undermine the judicial process by procuring or coercing silence from witnesses and victims, the Sixth Amendment does not require courts to acquiesce. We reiterate what we said in *Crawford:* that "the rule of forfeiture by wrongdoing extinguishes confrontation claims on essentially equitable grounds." That is, one who obtains the absence of a witness by wrongdoing forfeits the constitutional right to confrontation.

We have determined that, absent a finding of forfeiture by wrongdoing, the Sixth Amendment operates to exclude Amy Hammon's affidavit. The Indiana courts may (if they are asked) determine on remand whether such a claim of forfeiture is properly raised and, if so, whether it is meritorious.

We affirm the judgment of the Supreme Court of Washington. We reverse the judgment of the Supreme Court of Indiana, and remand the case to that court for proceedings not inconsistent with this opinion.

It is so ordered.

JUSTICE THOMAS, concurring in the judgment in part and dissenting in part.

In *Crawford v. Washington,* 541 U.S. 36 (2004), we abandoned the general reliability inquiry we had long employed to judge the admissibility of hearsay evidence under the Confrontation Clause, describing that inquiry as "*inherently, and therefore permanently,* unpredictable." Today, a mere two years after the Court decided *Crawford,* it adopts an equally unpredictable test, under which district courts are charged with divining the "primary purpose" of police interrogations. Besides being difficult for courts to apply, this test characterizes as "testimonial," and therefore inadmissible, evidence that bears little resemblance to what we have recognized as the evidence targeted by the Confrontation Clause. Because neither of the cases before the Court today would implicate the Confrontation Clause under an appropriately targeted standard, I concur only in the judgment in *Davis v. Washington,* and dissent from the Court's resolution of *Hammon v. Indiana.*

Neither the 911 call at issue in *Davis* nor the police questioning at issue in *Hammon* is testimonial under the appropriate framework. Neither the call nor the questioning is itself a formalized dialogue. Nor do any circumstances surrounding the taking of the statements render those statements sufficiently formal to resemble the Marian examinations; the statements were neither *Mirandized* nor custodial, nor accompanied by any similar indicia of formality. Finally, there is no suggestion that the prosecution attempted to offer the women's hearsay evidence at trial in order to evade confrontation. Accordingly, the statements at issue in both cases are nontestimonial and admissible under the Confrontation Clause.

Because the standard adopted by the Court today is neither workable nor a targeted attempt to reach the abuses forbidden by the Clause, I concur in the judgment in *Davis* and respectfully dissent from the Court's resolution of *Hammon*.

Hypo 1: *Primary Purpose of Interrogation*

How does the Confrontation Clause apply to the following two situations: A) A victim of domestic violence places a 911 call to the police for help. The first part of the call involves the imminent safety of the caller. When it is established that the perpetrator rode away on a bicycle, the rest of the call concerns the identity of the perpetrator and the relevant circumstances. A timely objection has been lodged. You are the judge. Would you admit testimony regarding the 911 call? B) The county coroner conducts an autopsy on a 72-year-old male. After the autopsy, the coroner concludes that the decedent died from strangulation. The prosecution offers a forensic pathologist to testify about the autopsy report in a subsequent murder case. Is the report testimonial? Is the primary purpose of the report to create evidence for trial? If not, what is the primary purpose?

Hypo 2: *Judicial Error*

How would the Confrontation Clause apply to the following two situations: A) Defendant is on trial for eluding a police officer after being pulled over for a traffic violation and then driving off, creating a wild and dangerous chase through a highly populated area. The declarant, while being questioned by the police after the defendant was been arrested, informed the police that she loaned defendant her car. Declarant also provides considerable information about the defendant's state of mind.

The Court admitted the declarant's statement over objection, saying it was part of "an on-going emergency" and that it met the excited utterance foundation and was important to the prosecution's case, establishing how defendant obtained the car and the motive for driving off. If you are an appellate court judge considering whether the admission of the declarant's statements was harmless error, how would you rule on the issue? B) A police officer at a valid traffic stop discovers a baggie containing a white substance in plain view. Based on what he sees, the officer arrests defendant for the possession of cocaine. At trial for possession with intent to distribute cocaine, a report by a non-testifying chemist is offered in evidence without objection during the testimony of the arresting officer. On appeal, petitioner claims that it was unconstitutional and plain error to admit the evidence. How should the appellate court rule on the claim of error?

Michigan v. Bryant

562 U.S. 344 (2011).

JUSTICE SOTOMAYOR delivered the opinion of the Court.

At respondent Richard Bryant's trial, the court admitted statements that the victim, Anthony Covington, made to police officers who discovered him mortally wounded in a gas station parking lot. A jury convicted Bryant of second-degree murder. On appeal, the Supreme Court of Michigan held that the Sixth Amendment's Confrontation Clause rendered Covington's statements inadmissible testimonial

Who's That?

Sonia Sotomayor was appointed as an Associate Justice to the Supreme Court by President Obama in 2009, replacing David Souter. She first served as a federal district court judge, appointed by President George H.W. Bush. A graduate of Princeton University and Yale Law School, she was an assistant district attorney and international commercial litigator while in practice.

hearsay, and the court reversed Bryant's conviction. We granted the State's petition for a writ of certiorari. We hold that the circumstances of the interaction between Covington and the police objectively indicate that the "primary purpose of the interrogation" was "to enable police assistance to meet an ongoing emergency." *Davis, 547 U.S., at 822.* Therefore, Covington's identification and description of the shooter and the location of the shooting were not testimonial statements, and their admission at Bryant's trial did not violate the Confrontation Clause. We vacate the judgment of the Supreme Court of Michigan and remand.

This case requires further explanation of the "ongoing emergency" circumstance addressed in *Davis*. Because *Davis* and *Hammon* arose in the domestic violence context, that was the situation "we had immediately in mind." We now face a new context: a nondomestic dispute, involving a victim found in a public location, suffering from a fatal gunshot wound, and a perpetrator whose location was unknown at the time the police located the victim.

To determine whether the "primary purpose" of an interrogation is "to enable police assistance to meet an ongoing emergency," which would render the resulting statements non-testimonial, we objectively evaluate the circumstances in which the encounter occurs and the statements and actions of the parties. An objective analysis of the circumstances of an encounter and the statements and actions of the parties to it provides the most accurate assessment of the "primary purpose of the interrogation." The circumstances in which an encounter occurs— *e.g.,* at or near the scene of the crime versus at a police station, during an ongoing emergency or afterwards—are clearly matters of objective fact. The statements and actions of the parties must also be objectively evaluated. That is, the relevant inquiry is not the subjective or actual purpose of the individuals involved in a particular encounter, but rather the purpose that reasonable participants would have had, as ascertained from the individuals' statements and actions and the circumstances in which the encounter occurred.

Whether an ongoing emergency exists is simply one factor—albeit an important factor—that informs the ultimate inquiry regarding the "primary purpose" of an interrogation. Another factor the Michigan Supreme Court did not sufficiently account for is the importance of *informality* in an encounter between a victim and police. Formality is not the sole touchstone of our primary purpose inquiry because, although formality suggests the absence of an emergency and therefore an increased likelihood that the purpose of the interrogation is to "establish or prove past events potentially relevant to later criminal prosecution," informality does not necessarily indicate the presence of an emergency or the lack of testimonial intent. As we explain below, the questioning in this case occurred in an exposed, public area, prior to the arrival of emergency medical services, and in a disorganized fashion. All of those facts make this case distinguishable from the formal station-house interrogation in *Crawford*.

In addition to the circumstances in which an encounter occurs, the statements and actions of both the declarant and interrogators provide objective evidence of the primary purpose of the interrogation. *Davis* requires a combined inquiry that accounts for both the declarant and the interrogator. In many instances, the primary purpose of the interrogation will be most accurately ascertained by looking to the contents of both the questions and the answers. To give an extreme example, if the police say to a victim, "Tell us who did this to you so that we can arrest and prosecute them," the victim's response that "Rick did it," appears purely accusatory because by virtue of the phrasing of the question, the victim necessarily has prosecution in mind when she answers.

The combined approach also ameliorates problems that could arise from looking solely to one participant. Predominant among these is the problem of mixed motives on the part of both interrogators and declarants. Police officers in our society function as both first responders and criminal investigators. Their dual responsibilities may mean that they act with different motives simultaneously or in quick succession. See *New York v. Quarles*, 467 U.S. 649, 656 (1984).

As the context of this case brings into sharp relief, the existence and duration of an emergency depend on the type and scope of danger posed to the victim, the police, and the public. We first examine the circumstances in which the interrogation occurred. The parties disagree over whether there was an emergency when the police arrived at the gas station. The record reveals little about the motive for the shooting. What Covington did tell the officers was that he fled Bryant's back porch, indicating that he perceived an ongoing threat. The police did not know, and Covington did not tell them, whether the threat was limited to him. The potential scope of the dispute and therefore the emergency in this case thus stretches more broadly than those at issue in *Davis* and *Hammon* and encompasses a threat potentially to the police and the public.

This is also the first of our post-*Crawford* Confrontation Clause cases to involve a gun. The physical separation that was sufficient to end the emergency in *Hammon* was not necessarily sufficient to end the threat in this case; Covington was shot through the back door of Bryant's house. Bryant's argument that there was no ongoing emergency because "no shots were being fired," surely construes ongoing emergency too narrowly. At bottom, there was an ongoing emergency here where an armed shooter, whose motive for and location after the shooting were unknown, had mortally wounded Covington within a few blocks and a few minutes of the location where the police found Covington.

For their part, the police responded to a call that a man had been shot. They did not know why, where, or when the shooting had occurred. Nor did they know the location of the shooter or anything else about the circumstances in which the crime occurred. The questions they asked—"what happened, who shot him, and where the shooting occurred,"—were the exact type of questions necessary to allow the police to "assess the situation, the threat to their own safety, and possible danger to the potential victim" and to the public, *Davis*, 547 U.S., at 832, including to allow them to ascertain "whether they would be encountering a violent felon," *Davis* at 827. In other words, they solicited the information necessary to enable them "to meet an ongoing emergency exception."

Nothing in Covington's responses indicated to the police that, contrary to their expectation upon responding to a call reporting a shooting, there was no emergency or that a prior emergency had ended. Covington did indicate that he had been shot at another location about 25 minutes earlier, but he did not know the location of the shooter at the time the police arrived and he gave no indication that the shooter, having shot at him twice, would be satisfied that Covington was only wounded. In fact, Covington did not indicate any possible motive for the shooting, and thereby gave no reason to think that the shooter would not shoot again if he arrived on the scene. As in *Davis,* "initial inquiries" may "*often* produce nontestimonial statements. The initial inquiries in this case resulted in the type of nontestimonial statements we contemplated in *Davis.*

Finally, we consider the informality of the situation and the interrogation. This situation is more similar, though not identical, to the informal, harried 911 call in *Davis* than to the structured, station-house interview in *Crawford.* As the officers' trial testimony reflects, the situation was fluid and somewhat confused: the officers arrived at different times; apparently each, upon arrival, asked Covington "what happened?"; and, contrary to the dissent's portrayal, they did not conduct a structured interrogation. The informality suggests that the interrogators' primary purpose was simply to address what they perceived to be an ongoing emergency, and the circumstances lacked any formality that would have alerted Covington to or focused him on the possible future prosecutorial use of his statements.

Because the circumstances of the encounter as well as the statements and actions of Covington and the police objectively indicate that the "primary purpose of the interrogation" was "to enable police assistance to meet an ongoing emergency," Covington's identification and description of the shooter and the location of the shooting were not testimonial hearsay. The Confrontation Clause did not bar their admission at Bryant's trial.

For the foregoing reasons, we hold that Covington's statements were not testimonial and that their admission at Bryant's trial did not violate the Confrontation Clause. We leave for the Michigan courts to decide on remand whether the statements' admission was otherwise permitted by state hearsay rules. The judgment of the Supreme Court of Michigan is vacated, and the case is remanded for further proceedings not inconsistent with this opinion.

Food for Thought

Is *Michigan v. Bryant* consistent with *Hammon* and *Davis*? Apply *Bryant* to the hypos after *Hammon* and *Davis* to see if it invariably leads to the same results.

It is so ordered.

JUSTICE KAGAN took no part in the consideration or decision of this case.

JUSTICE THOMAS, concurring in the judgment.

I agree that the admission of Covington's out-of-court statements did not violate the Confrontation Clause, but I reach this conclusion because Covington's questioning by police lacked sufficient formality and solemnity for his statements to be considered "testimonial." See *Crawford v. Washington, 541 U.S. 3 (2004)*.

In determining whether Covington's statements to police implicate the Confrontation Clause, the Court evaluates the "primary purpose" of the interrogation. The majority's analysis which relies on what the police knew when they arrived at the scene, the specific questions they asked, the particular information Covington conveyed, the weapon involved, and Covington's medical condition illustrates the uncertainty that this test creates for law enforcement and the lower courts. I have criticized the primary-purpose test as "an exercise in fiction" that is "disconnected from history" and "yields no predictable results."

Rather than attempting to reconstruct the "primary purpose" of the participants, I would consider the extent to which the interrogation resembles those historical practices that the Confrontation Clause addressed. This interrogation bears little if any resemblance to the historical practices that the Confrontation Clause aimed to eliminate. Covington thus did not "bear testimony" against Bryant, and the introduction of his statements at trial did not implicate the Confrontation Clause. I concur in the judgment.

JUSTICE SCALIA, dissenting.

Today's tale—a story of five officers conducting successive examinations of a dying man with the primary purpose, not of obtaining and preserving his testimony regarding his killer, but of protecting him, them, and others from a murderer somewhere on the loose—is so transparently false that professing to believe it demeans this institution. But reaching a patently incorrect conclusion on the facts is a relatively benign judicial mischief; it affects, after all, only the case at hand. In its vain attempt to make the incredible plausible, today's opinion distorts our Confrontation Clause jurisprudence and leaves it in a shambles. Instead of clarifying the law, the Court makes itself the obfuscator of last resort. Because I continue to adhere to the Confrontation Clause that the People adopted, as described in *Crawford*, I dissent.

A declarant-focused inquiry is the only inquiry that would work in every fact pattern implicating the Confrontation Clause. An inquiry into an officer's purposes would make no sense when a declarant blurts out "Rick shot me" as soon as the officer arrives on the scene. I see no reason to adopt a different test—one that accounts for an officer's intent—when the officer asks "what happened" before the declarant makes his accusation. (This does not mean the interrogator is irrelevant.

The identity of an interrogator, and the content and tenor of his questions, can bear upon whether a declarant intends to make a solemn statement, and envisions its use at a criminal trial. But none of this means that the interrogator's purpose matters.)

Looking to the declarant's purpose (as we should), this is an absurdly easy case. Roughly 25 minutes after Anthony Covington had been shot, Detroit police responded to a 911 call reporting that a gunshot victim had appeared at a neighborhood gas station. They quickly arrived at the scene, and in less than 10 minutes five different Detroit police officers questioned Covington about the shooting. Each asked him a similar battery of questions: "what happened" and when, "who shot the victim," and "where" did the shooting take place. After Covington would answer, they would ask follow-up questions, such as "how tall is" the shooter. The battery relented when the paramedics arrived and began tending to Covington's wounds.

From Covington's perspective, his statements had little value except to ensure the arrest and eventual prosecution of Richard Bryant. He knew the "threatening situation" had ended six blocks away and 25 minutes earlier when he fled from Bryant's back porch. Bryant had not confronted him face-to-face before he was mortally wounded, instead shooting him through a door. Even if Bryant had pursued him (unlikely), and after seeing that Covington had ended up at the gas station was unable to confront him there before the police arrived (doubly unlikely), it was entirely beyond imagination that Bryant would again open fire while Covington was surrounded by five armed police officers. And Covington knew the shooting was the work of a drug dealer, not a spree killer who might randomly threaten others.

The Court's distorted view creates an expansive exception to the Confrontation Clause for violent crimes. Because Bryant posed a continuing threat to public safety in the Court's imagination, the emergency persisted for confrontation purposes at least until the police learned his "motive for and location after the shooting." It may have persisted in this case until the police "secured the scene of the shooting" two-and-a-half hours later. In *Crawford v. Washington*, this Court

Food for Thought

A commentator has suggested that Justice Sotomayor might have been reinstating the *Ohio v. Roberts* reliability analysis when she said, "Implicit in *Davis* is the idea that because the prospect of fabrication in statements given for the primary purpose of resolving that emergency is presumably significantly diminished, the Confrontation Clause does not require such examinations to be subject to the crucible of cross-examination." The commentator noted, "This logic of focusing on whether there is an ongoing emergency such as to render a statement non-testimonial is not unlike that justifying the excited utterance exception in hearsay law." I. Bennett Capers, "Reading *Michigan v. Bryant*, "Reading" Justice Sotomayor," 123 Yale L. Forum 427 (2014).

noted that, in the law we inherited from England, there was a well-established exception to the confrontation requirement: The cloak protecting the accused against admission of out-of-court testimonial statements was removed for dying declarations. This historic exception, we recalled in *Giles v. California*, 554 U.S. 353 (2008), applied to statements made by a person about to die and aware that death was imminent. Were the issue properly tendered here, I would take up the question whether the exception for dying declarations survives our recent Confrontation Clause decisions.

Hypo: *Shotgun*

The defendant was tried for the unlawful possession of a shotgun. At trial, an investigating police officer testified that she was at the scene after a 911 call and the victim returned to the scene and told the officer that the accused had possessed the gun and pointed it at her, identifying the accused in the process. A timely objection was made to the investigator's testimony. The judge permitted a brief *voir dire* of the witness to determine whether the victim's statements were testimonial. You are asked to conduct the *voir dire*, meaning a brief cross-examination of the witness, in this case outside the hearing of the jury. What questions would you ask about the location of the defendant when the victim's statements were made? What other questions might you ask about the incident in question?

An important and evolving focus of courts in the aftermath of *Crawford* has been the development of the "primary purpose" test in determining whether evidence is testimonial. If the primary purpose of the evidence is to create an out-of-court substitute for trial testimony, it will fall within the ambit of the Confrontation Clause. On the other hand, if the evidence is intended to help resolve an on-going emergency or for some other purpose, it is not testimonial. *Ohio v. Clark* provides a good summary of the winding road leading to the current stasis of the rule.

Ohio v. Clark

135 S.Ct. 2173 (2015)

JUSTICE ALITO delivered the opinion of the Court.

Darius Clark, who went by the nickname "Dee," lived in Cleveland, Ohio, with his girlfriend, T.T., and her two children: L.P., a 3-year-old boy, and A.T., an

18-month-old girl. Clark was also T.T.'s pimp, and he would regularly send her on trips to Washington, D. C., to work as a prostitute. In March 2010, T.T. went on one such trip, and she left the children in Clark's care. The next day, Clark took L.P. to preschool. In the lunchroom, one of L.P.'s teachers, Ramona Whitley, observed that L.P.'s left eye appeared bloodshot. She asked him "what happened," and he initially said nothing. Eventually, however, he told the teacher that he "fell." When they moved into the brighter lights of a classroom, Whitley noticed "red marks, like whips of some sort," on L.P.'s face. She notified the lead teacher, Debra Jones, who asked L.P., "Who did this? What happened to you?" According to Jones, L.P. "seemed kind of bewildered" and "said something like, Dee, Dee." Jones asked L.P. whether Dee is "big or little," to which L.P. responded that "Dee is big." Jones then brought L.P. to her supervisor, who lifted the boy's shirt, revealing more injuries. Whitley called a child abuse hotline to alert authorities about the suspected abuse. When Clark later arrived at the school, he denied responsibility for the injuries and quickly left with L.P. The next day, a social worker found the children at Clark's mother's house and took them to a hospital, where a physician discovered additional injuries suggesting child abuse. L.P. had a black eye, belt marks on his back and stomach, and bruises all over his body. A.T. had two black eyes, a swollen hand, and a large burn on her cheek, and two pigtails had been ripped out at the roots of her hair.

Clark moved to exclude testimony about L.P.'s out-of-court statements under the Confrontation Clause. The trial court denied the motion, ruling that L.P.'s responses were not testimonial statements covered by the Sixth Amendment. The jury found Clark guilty on all counts except for one assault count related to A.T., and it sentenced him to 28 years' imprisonment. Clark appealed his conviction, and a state appellate court reversed on the ground that the introduction of L.P.'s out-of-court statements violated the Confrontation Clause. The Supreme Court of Ohio affirmed. We granted certiorari and reverse.

The Sixth Amendment's Confrontation Clause, which is binding on the States through the Fourteenth Amendment, provides: "In all criminal prosecutions, the accused shall enjoy the right . . . to be confronted with the witnesses against him." In *Ohio v. Roberts*, 448 U. S. 56, 66 (1980), we interpreted the Clause to permit the admission of out-of-court statements by an unavailable witness, so long as the statements bore "adequate 'indicia of reliability.' " Such indicia are present, we held, if "the evidence falls within a firmly rooted hearsay exception" or bears "particularized guarantees of trustworthiness."

Our more recent cases have labored to flesh out what it means for a statement to be "testimonial." In *Davis v. Washington and Hammon v. Indiana*, 547 U. S. 813 (2006), which we decided together, we dealt with statements given to law enforcement officers by the victims of domestic abuse. The victim in *Davis* made statements to a 911 emergency operator during and shortly after her boyfriend's violent attack. In *Hammon*, the victim, after being isolated from her abusive husband, made statements to police that were memorialized in a "battery affidavit." We held that the statements in *Hammon* were testimonial, while the statements in *Davis* were not. Announcing what has come to be known as the "primary purpose" test, we explained: "Statements are nontestimonial when made in the course of police interrogation under circumstances objectively indicating that the primary purpose of the interrogation is to enable police assistance to meet an ongoing emergency. They are testimonial when the circumstances objectively indicate that there is no such ongoing emergency, and that the primary purpose of the interrogation is to establish or prove past events potentially relevant to later criminal prosecution."

In *Michigan v. Bryant*, 562 U. S. 344 (2011), we further expounded on the primary purpose test. The inquiry, we emphasized, must consider "all of the relevant circumstances." The existence *vel non* of an ongoing emergency is not the touchstone of the testimonial inquiry." Instead, "whether an ongoing emergency exists is simply one factor that informs the ultimate inquiry regarding the 'primary purpose' of an interrogation." One additional factor is "the informality of the situation and the interrogation." A "formal station-house interrogation," like the questioning in *Crawford*, is more likely to provoke testimonial statements, while less formal questioning is less likely to reflect a primary purpose aimed at obtaining testimonial evidence against the accused. In determining whether a statement is testimonial, "standard rules of hearsay, designed to identify some statements as reliable, will be relevant." In the end, the question is whether, in light of all the circumstances, viewed objectively, the "primary purpose" of the conversation was to "create an out-of-court substitute for trial testimony."

In this case, we consider statements made to preschool teachers, not the police. We are therefore presented with the question we have repeatedly reserved: whether statements to persons other than law enforcement officers are subject to the Confrontation Clause. Because at least some statements to individuals who are not law enforcement officers could conceivably raise confrontation concerns, we decline to adopt a categorical rule excluding them from the Sixth Amendment's reach. Nevertheless, such statements are much less likely to be testimonial than statements to law enforcement officers. Considering all the relevant circumstances here, L.P.'s statements clearly were not made with the primary purpose of creating evidence for Clark's prosecution. Thus, their introduction at trial did not violate the Confrontation Clause.

We reverse the judgment of the Supreme Court of Ohio and remand the case for further proceedings not inconsistent with this opinion.

It is so ordered.

Point for Discussion

Ohio v. Clark's **Progeny.**

After *Ohio v. Clark*, lower courts were left with the task of determining whether hearsay evidence was testimonial because the primary purpose of the evidence was to create an out-of-court substitute for trial testimony – or whether the primary purpose was for some other purpose such as addressing an on-going emergency. In *Oregon v. Rafeh*, 361 Ore. 423 (2017), the Oregon Supreme Court considered whether a document was testimonial and subject to Confrontation Clause scrutiny. The Court found that the document, a certification of notice given, was not testimonial:

> In 2012, the Driver and Motor Vehicle Services Division (DMV) of the Department of Transportation suspended defendant's driver's license for three years for refusing to submit voluntarily to a blood alcohol test. Approximately two and one-half years later, defendant was stopped while driving without a license, and the state charged her with driving while suspended (DWS). See ORS 811.182 (defining that crime). The question that this case presents is whether the federal Confrontation Clause prohibits the admission, in defendant's DWS trial, of an earlier certification that defendant had been given notice that the state intended to suspend her driver's license. The trial court admitted the certification over defendant's objection, and the jury found her guilty of DWS. The Court of Appeals summarily affirmed the resulting judgment. Having allowed defendant's petition for review, we now affirm the Court of Appeals decision and the trial court's judgment.
>
> The question in *Bryant* and in *Crawford* was whether police officers were seeking to create "an out-of-court substitute" for testimony in a criminal trial. To accept defendant's expansive interpretation of the Confrontation Clause, not only would we have to overlook the context in which the statements on which he relies were made, but we also would have to ignore the Court's holding in *Clark* that only out-of-court statements made or elicited primarily for use in a criminal proceeding are testimonial. Following *Clark* and *Copeland*, we conclude that the certification in the Implied Consent Combined Report was not made for "the primary purpose of assisting in defendant's prosecution." Rather, as explained above, the primary purpose of the certification is administrative. It confirmed that defendant had received sufficient notice for DMV to proceed with an administrative license suspension hearing. The decision whether to suspend defendant's license was undertaken to ensure the safety of the other drivers on the state's roads, much in the same way that the child's statement in *Clark* identifying who had harmed him was elicited to protect the child from further harm. Indeed, the challenged certification—that defendant had been given a copy of the report as

written notice—would have no relevance to a prosecution for DUII. And, as explained above, the prospect that the certification might become relevant in some future prosecution for DWS turns on far too many contingencies to say that the certification's primary purpose was for use in a criminal proceeding.

A similar issue arose in *United States v. Fryberg*, 854 F. 3rd 1126 (9th Cir. 2017), which involved a completed service of return of notice of a hearing on the restraining order. In that case before a tribal court, a key question was whether the defendant had received notice of a hearing on a restraining order. The government offered in evidence a document, the completed return of service showing notice, and not witness testimony. The question on appeal was whether that service of return was testimonial within the Confrontation Clause. The Court ruled that "the admission of the return of service did not violate either the rule against hearsay or the Confrontation Clause of the Sixth Amendment, and we affirm Defendant's conviction." A predicate question involved whether the return of service complied with the hearsay limits imposed by the Federal Rules of Evidence. The Court held that it did. The Court found that the officer was "under a legal duty to report when he completed the return of service," and that the service was a ministerial part of the officer's duties, making the service document a public record under Fed. R. Evid. 803(8)(A)(ii). The Court's reasoning in its Confrontation Clause analysis was more nuanced. It stated:

> A business or public record is not 'testimonial' due to 'the mere possibility' that it could be used in a later criminal prosecution." *United State v. Morales*, 720 F.3d 1194, 1200 (9th Cir. 2013). The inquiry is whether the primary purpose of the record is "for use as evidence at a future criminal trial." Here, the primary purpose of the return of service was to inform the tribal court that Defendant had been served with notice of the hearing on the protection order, which enabled the hearing to proceed. Perhaps it was foreseeable to Officer Echevarria that the return of service might later be used in a criminal trial to establish the fact that Defendant had been served with notice, but that fact does not necessarily render the return of service It is generally true that one who violates a domestic violence protection order is subject to criminal penalties. See, e.g., Wash. Rev. Code § 26.50.110 (2016). Had the Government not produced a copy of the return of service but, instead, attempted to introduce a 2015 affidavit signed by Officer Echevarria stating that he had served Defendant with notice in 2002, this case would be closer to *Bustamante*. As it is, however, the Government introduced the return of service itself, a contemporaneous document owing its existence primarily to the tribal court's administrative needs. We hold that the admission of the return of service did not violate Defendant's rights under the Confrontation Clause.

D. Expert Reports and Confrontation

It is common for the prosecution to use experts and their reports in criminal cases. Experts testify about the *modus operandi* of criminal operations, and test for contraband substances in laboratories across the country. Prior to *Crawford*, the experts could submit their test results as part of reliable reports under the heasay exception recognized in state and federal courts alike, the public records exception. *See, e.g.*, Fed. R. Evid. 803(8).

Melendez-Diaz v. Massachusetts

557 U.S. 305 (2009).

JUSTICE SCALIA delivered the opinion of the Court, joined by JUSTICE STEVENS, JUSTICE SOUTER, JUSTICE THOMAS, and JUSTICE GINSBURG.

The Massachusetts courts in this case admitted into evidence affidavits reporting the results of forensic analysis which showed that material seized by the police and connected to the defendant was cocaine. The question presented is whether those affidavits are "testimonial," rendering the affiants "witnesses" subject to the defendant's right of confrontation under the Sixth Amendment.

In 2001, Boston police officers arrested several men in a drug sting, one of whom was petitioner Luis Melendez-Diaz. The officers placed all three men in a police cruiser. During the short drive to the police station, the officers observed their passengers fidgeting and making furtive movements in the back of the car. After depositing the men at the station, they searched the police cruiser and found a plastic bag containing 19 smaller plastic bags hidden in the partition between the front and back seats. They submitted the seized evidence to a state laboratory required by law to conduct chemical analysis upon police request. Melendez-Diaz was charged with distributing cocaine and with trafficking in cocaine in an amount between 14 and 28 grams. At trial, the prosecution placed into evidence the bags seized from Wright and from the police cruiser. It also submitted three "certificates of analysis" showing the results of the forensic analysis performed on the seized substances. The certificates reported the weight of the seized bags and stated that the bags "have been examined with the following results: The substance was found to contain: Cocaine." The certificates were sworn to before a notary public by analysts at the State Laboratory Institute of the Massachusetts Department of Public Health, as required under Massachusetts law. Petitioner objected to the admission of the certificates, asserting that our Confrontation Clause decision required the analysts to testify in person. The objection was overruled, and the certificates were admitted pursuant to state law as "prima facie evidence of the composition, quality, and the net weight of the narcotic analyzed." The jury found Melendez-Diaz guilty. He appealed, contending, among other things, that admission of the certificates violated his Sixth Amendment right to be confronted with the witnesses against him. We granted certiorari.

The Sixth Amendment to the United States Constitution, made applicable to the States via the Fourteenth Amendment, provides that "in all criminal prosecutions, the accused shall enjoy the right ... to be confronted with the witnesses against him." In *Crawford,* after reviewing the Clause's historical underpinnings, we held that it guarantees a defendant's right to confront those "who 'bear testimony' " against him. A witness's testimony against a defendant is thus inadmissible unless the witness appears at trial or, if the witness is unavailable, the defendant had a prior opportunity for cross-examination.

Our opinion described the class of testimonial statements covered by the Confrontation Clause as follows:

> "Various formulations of this core class of testimonial statements exist: *ex parte* in-court testimony or its functional equivalent-that is, material such as affidavits, custodial examinations, prior testimony that the defendant was unable to cross-examine, or similar pretrial statements that declarants would reasonably expect to be used prosecutorially; extrajudicial statements ... contained in formalized testimonial materials, such as affidavits, depositions, prior testimony, or confessions; statements that were made under circumstances which would lead an objective witness reasonably to believe that the statement would be available for use at a later trial."

There is little doubt that the documents at issue in this case fall within the "core class of testimonial statements" thus described. The documents, while denominated by Massachusetts law "certificates," are quite plainly affidavits: "declarations of facts written down and sworn to by the declarant before an officer authorized to administer oaths." Black's Law Dictionary 62 (8th ed.2004). They are incontrovertibly a "solemn declaration or affirmation made for the purpose of establishing or proving some fact." *Crawford, supra,* at 51. The fact in question is that the substance found in the possession of Melendez-Diaz and his codefendants was, as the prosecution claimed, cocaine-the precise testimony the analysts would be expected to provide if called at trial. The "certificates" are functionally identical to live, in-court testimony, doing "precisely what a witness does on direct examination." *Davis v. Washington,* 547 U.S. 813, 830 (2006).

Here, not only were the affidavits "made under circumstances which would lead an objective witness reasonably to believe that the statement would be available for use at a later trial," but under Massachusetts law the *sole purpose* of the affidavits was to provide "prima facie evidence of the composition, quality, and the net weight" of the analyzed substance, Mass. Gen. Laws, ch. 111, § 13. We can safely assume that the analysts were aware of the affidavits' evidentiary purpose, since that purpose-as stated in the relevant state-law provision-was reprinted on the affidavits themselves. In short, under our decision in *Crawford* the analysts' affidavits were testimonial statements, and the analysts were "witnesses" for purposes of the Sixth Amendment. Absent a showing that the analysts were unavailable to testify at trial *and* that petitioner had a prior opportunity to cross-examine them, petitioner was entitled to "be confronted with" the analysts at trial.

The vast majority of the state-court cases the dissent cites in support of its claim that established precedent is being swept away come not from the last 90 years, but from the last 30, and not surprisingly nearly all of them rely on our decision in *Ohio v. Roberts,* 448 U.S. 56 (1980), or its since-rejected theory that unconfronted testimony was admissible as long as it bore indicia of reliability, As for the cases cited by the dissent, five of them postdated and expressly relied on *Roberts.* This much is entirely clear: In faithfully applying *Crawford* to the facts of this case, we are not overruling 90 years of settled jurisprudence. It is the dissent that seeks to overturn precedent by resurrecting *Roberts* a mere five years after it was rejected in *Crawford.*

The dissent contends that a "conventional witness recalls events observed in the past, while an analyst's report contains near-contemporaneous observations of the test." It is doubtful that the analyst's reports in this case could be characterized as reporting "near-contemporaneous observations"; the affidavits were completed almost a week after the tests were performed. (the tests were performed on November 28, 2001, and the affidavits sworn on December 4, 2001). Regardless, the dissent misunderstands the role that "near-contemporaneity" has played in our case law. The dissent notes that that factor was given "substantial weight" in *Davis,* but in fact that decision *disproves* the dissent's position. There the Court considered the admissibility of statements made to police officers responding to a report of a domestic disturbance. By the time officers arrived the assault had ended, but the victim's statements-written and oral-were sufficiently close in time to the alleged assault that the trial court admitted her affidavit as a "present sense impression." *Davis, 547 U.S., at 820.* Though the witness's statements in *Davis* were "near-contemporaneous" to the events she reported, we nevertheless held that they could *not* be admitted absent an opportunity to confront the witness. A second reason the dissent contends that the analysts are not "conventional witnesses" (and thus not subject to confrontation) is that they "observed neither the crime nor any human action related to it." The dissent provides no authority for this particular limitation of the type of witnesses subject to confrontation. The dissent's novel exception from coverage of the Confrontation Clause would exempt all expert witnesses-a hardly "unconventional" class of witnesses. Respondent and the dissent may be right that there are other ways-and in some cases better ways-to challenge or verify the results of a forensic test. But the Constitution guarantees one way: confrontation. We do not have license to suspend the Confrontation Clause when a preferable trial strategy is available.

Nor is it evident that what respondent calls "neutral scientific testing" is as neutral or as reliable as respondent suggests. Forensic evidence is not uniquely immune from the risk of manipulation. A forensic analyst responding to a request from a law enforcement official may feel pressure-or have an incentive-to alter the evidence in a manner favorable to the prosecution.

Confrontation is one means of assuring accurate forensic analysis. While it is true, as the dissent notes, that an honest analyst will not alter his testimony when forced to confront the defendant, the same cannot be said of the fraudulent analyst. This case is illustrative. The affidavits submitted by the analysts contained only the bare-bones statement that "the substance was found to contain: Cocaine." At the time of trial, petitioner did not know what tests the analysts performed, whether those tests were routine, and whether interpreting their results required the exercise of judgment or the use of skills that the analysts may not have possessed. The same is true of many of the other types of forensic evidence commonly used in criminal prosecutions. "There is wide variability across forensic science disciplines with regard to techniques, methodologies, reliability, types and numbers of potential errors, research, general acceptability, and published material." National Academy Report S-5.

Respondent argues that the analysts' affidavits are admissible without confrontation because they are "akin to the types of official and business records admissible at common law." But the affidavits do not qualify as traditional official or business records, and even if they did, their authors would be subject to confrontation nonetheless. Documents kept in the regular course of business may ordinarily be admitted at trial despite their hearsay status. See Fed. Rule Evid. 803(6). But that is not the case if the regularly conducted business activity is the production of evidence for use at trial. Our decision in *Palmer v. Hoffman,* 318 U.S. 109 (1943), made that distinction clear. There we held that an accident report provided by an employee of a railroad company did not qualify as a business record because, although kept in the regular course of the railroad's operations, it was "calculated for use essentially in the court, not in the business." The analysts' certificates-like police reports generated by law enforcement officials-do not qualify as business or public records for precisely the same reason. See Rule 803(8) (defining public records as "excluding, however, in criminal cases matters observed by police officers and other law enforcement personnel").

Respondent asserts that we should find no Confrontation Clause violation in this case because petitioner had the ability to subpoena the analysts. But that power-whether pursuant to state law or the Compulsory Process Clause-is no substitute for the right of confrontation. Unlike the Confrontation Clause, those provisions are of no use to the defendant when the witness is unavailable or simply refuses to appear. More fundamentally, the Confrontation Clause imposes a burden on the prosecution to present its witnesses, not on the defendant to bring those adverse witnesses into court. Finally, respondent asks us to relax the requirements of the Confrontation Clause to accommodate the "necessities of trial and the adversary process." It is not clear

Food for Thought

Suppose five analysts all do pieces of DNA testing. Do all of the analysts have to testify? Does it matter if an analyst does only a small part of the testing in a laboratory, but it is a very important link in the chain? What if the work the analyst does in the testing process involves the use of judgment or discretion? Must the analyst testify?

whence we would derive the authority to do so. Perhaps the best indication that the sky will not fall after today's decision is that it has not done so already. Many States have already adopted the constitutional rule we announce today, and there is no evidence that the criminal justice system has ground to a halt in the States that, one way or another, empower a defendant to insist upon the analyst's appearance at trial. Indeed, in Massachusetts itself, a defendant may subpoena the analyst to appear at trial, and yet there is no indication that obstructionist defendants are abusing the privilege.

This case involves little more than the application of our holding in *Crawford*. The Sixth Amendment does not permit the prosecution to prove its case via *ex parte* out-of-court affidavits, and the admission of such evidence against Melendez-Diaz was error. We therefore reverse the judgment of the Appeals Court of Massachusetts and remand the case for further proceedings not inconsistent with this opinion.

It is so ordered.

JUSTICE THOMAS, concurring.

I write separately to note that I continue to adhere to my position that "the Confrontation Clause is implicated by extrajudicial statements only insofar as they are contained in formalized testimonial materials, such as affidavits, depositions, prior testimony, or confessions." *White v. Illinois,* 502 U.S. 346, 365, (1992). I join the Court's opinion because the documents at issue in this case "are quite plainly affidavits." As such, they "fall within the core class of testimonial statements" governed by the Confrontation Clause.

JUSTICE KENNEDY, with whom THE CHIEF JUSTICE, JUSTICE BREYER, and JUSTICE ALITO join, dissenting.

The Court sweeps away an accepted rule governing the admission of scientific evidence. Until today, scientific analysis could be introduced into evidence without testimony from the "analyst" who produced it. This rule has been established for at least 90 years. It extends across at least 35 States and six Federal Courts of Appeals. Yet the Court undoes it based on two recent opinions that say nothing about forensic analysts: *Crawford* and *Davis.*

It is remarkable that the Court so confidently disregards a century of jurisprudence. We learn that we have misinterpreted the Confrontation Clause-hardly an arcane or seldom-used provision of the Constitution-for the first 218 years of its existence. The immediate systemic concern is that the Court makes no attempt to acknowledge the real differences between laboratory analysts who perform scientific tests and other, more conventional witnesses-"witnesses" being the word the Framers used in the Confrontation Clause.

Because *Crawford* and *Davis* concerned typical witnesses, the Court should have done the sensible thing and limited its holding to witnesses as so defined. Indeed, as Justice THOMAS warned in *Davis,* the Court's approach has become "disconnected from history and unnecessary to prevent abuse." The Court's reliance on the word "testimonial" is of little help for that word does not appear in the text of the Clause.

The Court dictates to the States, as a matter of constitutional law, an as-yet-undefined set of rules governing what kinds of evidence may be admitted without in-court testimony. Indeed, under today's opinion the States bear an even more onerous burden than they did before *Crawford.*

The Court's opinion suggests this will be a body of formalistic and wooden rules, divorced from precedent, common sense, and the underlying purpose of the Clause. The Court says that, before the results of a scientific test may be introduced into evidence, the defendant has the right to confront the "analyst." There is no accepted definition of analyst, and there is no established precedent to define that term. Outside this narrow category, the range of other scientific tests that may be affected by the Court's new confrontation right is staggering.

Food for Thought

Suppose the Court agreed with Justice Ginsburg 9-0. Would that change the importance and impact of the case? Has the Confrontation Clause analysis been obscured by disagreements between the justices regarding the shape of the doctrine?

For the sake of negligible benefits, the Court threatens to disrupt forensic investigations across the country and to put prosecutions nationwide at risk of dismissal based on erratic, all-too-frequent instances when a particular laboratory technician, now invested by the Court's new constitutional designation as the analyst, simply does not or cannot appear. The Court's holding is a windfall to defendants, one that is unjustified by any demonstrated deficiency in trials, any well-understood historical requirement, or any established constitutional precedent. I respectfully dissent.

Points for Discussion

a. *Melendez-Diaz* on Remand

On remand, the prosecutor argued that the defense had failed to make the identity of the substance a live issue in the case and therefore the admission of the drug certificates were harmless beyond a reasonable doubt. The Court disagreed, finding there was harm and that "the defense was hardly in a position to argue that the substances were not cocaine. See *Commonwealth v. Melendez-Diaz,* 921 N.E.2d 108 (Mass. App. Ct. 2010) *on remand from sub nom. Massachusetts v. Melendez-Diaz,* 557 U.S. 305 (2009).

b. DWI Testing

Bullcoming v. New Mexico

564 U.S. 647 (2011).

Petitioner Donald Bullcoming was arrested on charges of driving while intoxicated (DWI). Principal evidence against Bullcoming was a forensic laboratory report certifying that Bullcoming's blood-alcohol concentration was well above the threshold for aggravated DWI. At trial, the prosecution did not call as a witness the analyst who signed the certification. Instead, the State called another analyst who was familiar with the laboratory's testing procedures, but had neither participated in nor observed the test on Bullcoming's blood sample. The Court concluded that the Confrontation Clause was violated: "We hold that surrogate testimony of that order does not meet the constitutional requirement. The accused's right is to be confronted with the analyst who made the certification, unless that analyst is unavailable at trial, and the accused had an opportunity, pretrial, to cross-examine that particular scientist."

Hypo 1: *Who Must Testify*

A forensic chemist testified about mass spectrometer testing of controlled substances. The test examines the color produced by controlled substances and creates a graph that can then be analyzed by an expert chemist. In this case, the chemist who testified was not the chemist who did the analysis of the drugs in question. While the testifying chemist did not give her own opinion about the analysis, she did summarize and explain the analysis performed by her colleague who wrote the report. The colleague who wrote the report was unavailable for trial. The testifying chemist also described how peer review checks expert opinions and that the test yields inferences about the type as well as weight of the illegal drug. Is this testimony permitted? Why or why not? Suppose that Dr. Melinda Kite did the testing of narcotics in the testing laboratory, while Dr. Shamus Treadstone did the recording and analysis. Lab assistant Horris Houston was in charge of the entry of data, finalizing all reports. In the case of the lab report on Sample 26X4T, which was the main evidence in the case of the government prosecution of one Miles Austin, all of the above individuals participated in the drug sample concerning Austin's case. Who must the prosecution call to the witness stand to satisfy *Melendez-Diaz*? Why?

Hypo 2: "Who Done It"?

The police find a body in a remote wilderness in Montana. They do all kinds of testing in a nearby laboratory, including regarding blood, hair, and bite marks. After five analysts participate in the testing, a report is drawn up. All five analysts write their name on the report as "contributors." Twenty years later, after the DNA from the samples is entered into a nation-wide registry, a hit occurs, and defendant is accused of murder. At trial, can the government offer the twenty-year-old report without any of the five analysts who helped to prepare it? Explain. whether the government acted constitutionally?

Hypo 3: *Breathalyzer Calibration Records*

Should a court treat breathalyzer calibration records as testimonial? Assume that these calibration records occur regularly as a part of police department policy and as required by applicable regulations and statutes. Are these records investigative, or do they simply reflect the level of operability of the breathalyzers? Are they reflective of objective facts or have sufficient human input to categorize them as investigatory? *See People v. Pealer,_20 N.Y.App. 447 (2013).*

Hypo 4: *Field Test Tales*

A police officer, Sgt. Smith, testified at defendant's criminal trial for possession of marijuana and other contraband. The officer stated that she field-tested the substance in accordance with her training, and the test was positive for the controlled substance in question. Defendant objected, claiming that *Melendez-Diaz v. Massachusetts*, 557 U.S. 305 (2009), required the person who trained the Sgt. Smith to testify as well. Is defendant correct? *See Newman v. United States*, 49 A.3d 321 (D.C. 2012).

E. The Basis of Expert Testimony

Another corollary issue that arose regarding *Crawford's* meaning related to the applicability of the Confrontation Clause to the bases of expert testimony. Experts regularly rely on inadmissible evidence, including hearsay. Is this practice consistent with *Crawford*? Would the bases of expert testimony depend on whether the reliance was brought to the jury's attention? Whether the hearsay was being offered for the truth of the matter asserted? Or simply whether the hearsay was considered testimonial? The next case, *Williams v. Illinois*, attempted to answer these questions, but with a fractured court, perhaps illustrating that the Confrontation Clause analysis remains in a state of flux.

What's That?

As you might recall from your Evidence Law course, expert testimony is admissible if it meets certain prerequisites, showing that the expert is qualified and demonstrating that the theory upon which the expert is testifying is reliable. See Fed. R. Evid. 702. The basis for the expert's opinion might not necessarily be admissible in evidence. Instead, it simply must be "reasonably relied on" by an expert in the particular field. Sometimes the bases for the expert's opinions can be offered to show how the expert reached her conclusions even if the evidence is otherwise inadmissible. See Fed. R. Evid. 703. The next case, *Williams v. Illinois*, concerns these bases and how they are treated for Confrontation Clause purposes.

Williams v. Illinois

567 U.S. 50 (2012).

JUSTICE ALITO announced the judgment of the Court and delivered an opinion, in which THE CHIEF JUSTICE, JUSTICE KENNEDY, and JUSTICE BREYER join.

In this case, we decide whether *Crawford v. Washington*, 541 U.S. 36 (2004), precludes an expert witness from testifying in a manner that has long been allowed under the law of evidence. Specifically, does *Crawford* bar an expert from expressing an opinion based on facts about a case that have been made known to the expert but about which the expert is not competent to testify? We also decide whether *Crawford* substantially impedes the ability of prosecutors to introduce DNA evidence and thus may effectively relegate the prosecution in some cases to reliance on older, less reliable forms of proof.

In petitioner's bench trial for rape, the prosecution called an expert who testified that a DNA profile produced by an outside laboratory, Cellmark, matched a profile produced by the state police lab using a sample of petitioner's blood. On direct examination, the expert testified that Cellmark was an accredited laboratory and that Cellmark provided the police with a DNA profile. The expert also explained the notations on documents admitted as business records, stating that, according to the records, vaginal swabs taken from the victim were sent to and received back from Cellmark. The expert made no other statement that was offered for the purpose of identifying the sample of biological material used in deriving the profile or for the purpose of establishing how Cellmark handled or tested the sample. Nor did the expert vouch for the accuracy of the profile that Cellmark produced.

We conclude that this form of expert testimony does not violate the Confrontation Clause because that provision has no application to out-of-court statements that are not offered to prove the truth of the matter asserted. When an expert testifies for the prosecution in a criminal case, the defendant has the opportunity to cross-examine the expert about any statements that are offered for their truth. Out-of-court statements that are related by the expert solely for the purpose of explaining the assumptions on which that opinion rests are not offered for their truth and thus fall outside the scope of the Confrontation Clause. Applying this rule to the present case, we conclude that the expert's testimony did not violate the Sixth Amendment.

As a second, independent basis for our decision, we conclude that even if the report produced by Cellmark had been admitted into evidence, there would have been no Confrontation Clause violation. The Cellmark report is very different from the sort of extrajudicial statements, such as affidavits, depositions, prior testimony, and confessions that the Confrontation Clause was originally understood to reach. The report was produced before any suspect was identified. The report was sought not for the purpose of obtaining evidence to be used against petitioner, who was not even under suspicion at the time, but for the purpose of finding a rapist who was on the loose. The profile that Cellmark provided was not inherently inculpatory. On the contrary, a DNA profile is evidence that tends to exculpate all but one of the more than 7 billion people in the world today.

In this case, a young woman, L.J., had been raped in Chicago, Illinois, in 2000. Various DNA testing occurred, and a perpetrator was identified and prosecuted. At a later bench trial, various experts testified about their DNA analysis. A forensic specialist, Sandra Lambatos, also testified. Lambatos testified that she had compared samples tested by others, a practice she said was "commonly accepted" when it came to "one DNA expert relying on records from another DNA expert." One of the samples was prepared by Cellmark Diagnostics Laboratory, an "accredited crime lab." Lambatos then testified that as a result of the comparison, the defendant could not be excluded as a perpetrator. The trial court found petitioner guilty of the charges against him. The state appeals court and Illinois Supreme Court affirmed the decision.

The Confrontation Clause of the Sixth Amendment provides that, "in all criminal prosecutions, the accused shall enjoy the right . . . to be confronted with the witnesses against him." Our decision in *Crawford* has resulted in a steady stream of new cases in this Court. Two of these decisions involved scientific reports. In *Melendez-Diaz*, the defendant was arrested and charged with distributing and trafficking in cocaine. The trial court admitted into evidence three "certificates of analysis" from the state forensic laboratory stating that the bags contained cocaine. The Court held that the admission of these certificates, which were executed under oath before a notary, violated the Sixth Amendment. They were "quite plainly affidavits" used to prove the truth of the matter they asserted. In *Bullcoming*, we held that another scientific report could not be used as substantive evidence against the defendant unless the analyst who prepared and certified the report was subject to confrontation. The Court declined to accept a surrogate expert's testimony, despite the fact that the testifying analyst was a "knowledgeable representative of the laboratory" who could "explain the lab's processes and the details of the report." The Court stated simply: "The accused's right is to be confronted with the analyst who made the certification." In concurrence, Justice Sotomayor highlighted the importance of the fact that the forensic report had been admitted into evidence for the purpose of proving the truth of the matter it asserted. "We would face a different question," she observed, "if asked to determine the constitutionality of allowing an expert witness to discuss others' testimonial statements if the testimonial statements were not themselves admitted as evidence." We now confront that question.

It has long been accepted that an expert witness may voice an opinion based on facts concerning the events at issue in a particular case even if the expert lacks firsthand knowledge of those facts. At common law, courts developed two ways to deal with this situation. An expert could rely on facts that had already been established in the record. Because it was not always possible to proceed in this manner, and because record evidence was often disputed, courts developed the alternative practice of allowing an expert to testify in the form of a "hypothetical question." Under this approach, the expert would be asked to assume the truth of certain factual predicates, and was then asked to offer an opinion based on those assumptions. There is a long tradition of the use of hypothetical questions in American courts. Modern rules of evidence continue to permit experts to express opinions based on facts about which they lack personal knowledge, but these rules dispense with the need for hypothetical questions. Under both the Illinois and the Federal Rules of Evidence, an expert may base an opinion on facts that are "made known to the expert at or before the hearing," but such reliance does not constitute admissible evidence of this underlying information. Fed. R. Evid. 703.

Crawford, while departing from prior Confrontation Clause precedent in other respects, took pains to reaffirm the proposition that the Confrontation Clause "does not bar the use of testimonial statements for purposes other than establishing the truth of the matter asserted." 541 U.S. at 59-60, n. 9 (citing *Tennessee v. Street*, 471 U.S. 409).

The principal argument advanced to show a Confrontation Clause violation concerns the phrase that Lambatos used when she referred to the DNA profile that the ISP lab received from Cellmark. In the view of the dissent, the following is the critical portion of Lambatos' testimony, with the particular words that the dissent finds objectionable italicized:

"Q. Was there a computer match generated of the male DNA profile *found in semen from the vaginal swabs of L.J.* to a male DNA profile that had been identified as having originated from Sandy Williams?

"A. Yes, there was."

According to the dissent, the phrase violated petitioner's confrontation right because Lambatos lacked personal knowledge that the profile produced by Cellmark was based on the vaginal swabs taken from the victim, L.J. As the dissent acknowledges, there would have been "nothing wrong with Lambatos's testifying that two DNA profiles—the one shown in the Cellmark report and the one derived from Williams's blood—matched each other; that was a straightforward application of Lambatos's expertise." Thus, if Lambatos' testimony had been slightly modified as follows, the dissent would see no problem.

"Q Was there a computer match generated of the male DNA profile produced by Cellmark found in semen from the vaginal swabs of L.J. to a male DNA profile that had been identified as having originated from Sandy Williams?

"A. Yes, there was."

The defect in this argument is that under Illinois law (like federal law) it is clear that the putatively offending phrase in Lambatos' testimony was not admissible for the purpose of proving the truth of the matter asserted—*i.e.*, that the matching DNA profile was "found in semen from the vaginal swabs." There is no reason to think that the trier of fact took Lambatos' answer as substantive evidence to establish where the DNA profiles came from.

The dissent's argument would have force if petitioner had elected to have a jury trial. In that event, there would have been a danger of the jury's taking Lambatos' testimony as proof that the Cellmark profile was derived from the sample obtained from the victim's vaginal swabs. Absent an evaluation of the risk of juror confusion and careful jury instructions, the testimony could not have gone to the jury. This case, however, involves *a bench trial* and we must assume that the trial judge understood that the portion of Lambatos' testimony to which the dissent objects was not admissible to prove the truth of the matter asserted. The dissent, on the other hand, reaches the truly remarkable conclusion that the wording of Lambatos' testimony confused the trial judge. This argument reflects a profound lack of respect for the acumen of the trial judge. We conclude that petitioner's Sixth Amendment confrontation right was not violated.

Even if the Cellmark report had been introduced for its truth, we would nevertheless conclude that there was no Confrontation Clause violation. The abuses that the Court has identified as prompting the adoption of the Confrontation Clause shared the following two characteristics: (a) they involved out-of-court statements having the primary purpose of accusing a targeted individual of engaging in criminal conduct and (b) they involved formalized statements such as affidavits, depositions, prior testimony, or confessions. The Cellmark report is very different. It plainly was not prepared for the primary purpose of accusing a targeted individual. In identifying the primary purpose of an out-of-court statement, we apply an objective test. We look for the primary purpose that a reasonable person would have ascribed to the statement, taking into account all of the surrounding circumstances.

Here, the primary purpose of the Cellmark report, viewed objectively, was not to accuse petitioner or to create evidence for use at trial. When the ISP lab sent the sample to Cellmark, its primary purpose was to catch a dangerous rapist who was still at large, not to obtain evidence for use against petitioner, who was neither in custody nor under suspicion at that time. Similarly, no one at Cellmark could have possibly known that the profile that it produced would turn out to inculpate petitioner— or for that matter, anyone else whose DNA profile was in a law enforcement database. Under these circumstances, there was no "prospect of fabrication" and

Food for Thought

Why isn't face-to-face confrontation indispensible? Are the justices "watering down" the right by saying that it is just a "preference"? Explain.

no incentive to produce anything other than a scientifically sound and reliable profile. It is also significant that in many labs, numerous technicians work on each DNA profile. ("Approximately 10 Cellmark analysts were involved in the laboratory work in this case"). When the work of a lab is divided up in such a way, it is likely that the sole purpose of each technician is simply to perform his or her task in accordance with accepted procedures.

For the two independent reasons explained above, we conclude that there was no Confrontation Clause violation in this case. Accordingly, the judgment of the Supreme Court of Illinois is

Affirmed.

JUSTICE THOMAS, concurring in the judgment.

I agree with the plurality that the disclosure of Cellmark's out-of-court statements through the expert testimony of Sandra Lambatos did not violate the Confrontation Clause. I reach this conclusion, however, solely because Cellmark's statements lacked the requisite "formality and solemnity" to be considered "'testimonial'" for purposes of the Confrontation Clause. See *Michigan v. Bryant,* 131 S.Ct. 1143 (2011) (Thomas, J., concurring in judgment).

JUSTICE KAGAN, with whom JUSTICE SCALIA, JUSTICE GINSBURG, and JUSTICE SOTOMAYOR join, dissenting.

Some years ago, the State of California prosecuted a man named John Kocak for rape. At a preliminary hearing, the State presented testimony from an analyst at the Cellmark Diagnostics Laboratory—the same facility used to generate DNA evidence in this case. The analyst had extracted DNA from a bloody sweatshirt found at the crime scene and then compared it to two control samples—one from Kocak and one from the victim. The analyst's report identified a single match: As she explained on direct examination, the DNA found on the sweatshirt belonged to Kocak. But after undergoing cross-examination, the analyst realized she had made a mortifying error. She took the stand again, but this time to admit that the report listed the victim's control sample as coming from Kocak, and Kocak's as coming from the victim. So the DNA on the sweatshirt matched not Kocak, but the victim herself. In trying Kocak, the State would have to look elsewhere for its evidence.

Our Constitution contains a mechanism for catching such errors—the Sixth Amendment's Confrontation Clause. That Clause, and the Court's recent cases interpreting it, require that testimony against a criminal defendant be subject to cross-examination. That command applies with full force to forensic evidence of the kind involved in both the Kocak case and this one. In two decisions issued in the last three years, this Court held that if a prosecutor wants to introduce the results of forensic testing into evidence, he must afford the defendant an opportunity to cross-examine an analyst responsible for the test.

Under our Confrontation Clause precedents, this is an open-and-shut case. The State of Illinois prosecuted Sandy Williams for rape based in part on a DNA profile created in Cellmark's laboratory. Yet the State did not give Williams a chance to question the analyst who produced that evidence. Instead, the prosecution introduced the results of Cellmark's testing through an expert witness who had no idea how they were generated. That approach—no less (perhaps more) than the confrontation-free methods of presenting forensic evidence we have formerly banned—deprived Williams of his Sixth Amendment right to "confront . . . the witnesses against him."

The Court today disagrees, though it cannot settle on a reason why. Justice Alito, joined by three other Justices, advances two theories—that the expert's summary of the Cellmark report was not offered for its truth, and that the report is not the kind of statement triggering the Confrontation Clause's protection. In the pages that follow, I call Justice Alito's opinion "the plurality," But in all except its disposition, his opinion is a dissent: Five Justices specifically reject every aspect of its reasoning and every paragraph of its explication. Justice Thomas, for his part, contends that the Cellmark report is non-testimonial on a different rationale. No other Justice joins his opinion or subscribes to the test he offers.

That creates five votes to approve admission of the Cellmark report, but not a single good explanation. The plurality's first rationale endorses a prosecutorial dodge; its second relies on distinguishing indistinguishable forensic reports. Justice Thomas's concurrence, though positing an altogether different approach, suffers in the end from similar flaws. I would choose another path—to adhere to the simple rule established in our decisions, for the good reasons we have previously given. Because defendants like Williams have a constitutional right to confront the witnesses against them, I dissent from the Court's fractured decision.

The report at issue here shows a DNA profile produced by an analyst at Cellmark's laboratory, allegedly from a vaginal swab taken from a young woman, L.J., after she was raped. That report is identical to the one in *Bullcoming* (and *Melendez-Diaz*) in "all material respects." (Once again, the report was made to establish "'some fact' in a criminal proceeding"—here, the identity of L.J.'s attacker. Once again, it details the results of forensic testing on evidence gathered by the police. Viewed side-by-side with the *Bullcoming* report, the Cellmark analysis has a comparable title; similarly describes the relevant samples, test methodology, and results; and likewise includes the signatures of laboratory officials. Under this Court's prior analysis, the substance of the report could come into evidence only if Williams had a chance to cross-examine the responsible analyst.

But that is not what happened. Instead, the prosecutor used Sandra Lamba-tos—a state-employed scientist who had not participated in the testing—as the conduit for this piece of evidence. Lambatos came to the stand after two other state analysts testified about forensic tests they had performed. One recounted how she had developed a DNA profile of Sandy Williams from a blood sample drawn after his arrest. Another told how he had confirmed the presence of (unidentified) semen on the vaginal swabs taken from L.J. All this was by the book: Williams had an opportunity to cross-examine both witnesses about the tests they had run. But of course, the State still needed to supply the missing link—it had to show that DNA found in the semen on L.J.'s vaginal swabs matched Williams's DNA. To fill that gap, the prosecutor could have called the analyst from Cellmark to testify about the DNA profile she had produced from the swabs. But instead, the State called Lambatos as an expert witness and had her testify that the semen on those swabs contained Sandy Williams's DNA:

"Q. Was there a computer match generated of the male DNA profile found in semen from the vaginal swabs of L.J. to a male DNA profile that had been identi-fied as having originated from Sandy Williams?

"A. Yes, there was.

"Q. Did you compare the semen from the vaginal swabs of L.J. to the male DNA profile from the blood of Sandy Williams?

"A. Yes, I did. "Q. Is the semen identified in the vaginal swabs of L.J. consis-tent with having originated from Sandy Williams?

"A. Yes."

And so it was Lambatos, rather than any Cellmark employee, who informed the trier of fact that the testing of L.J.'s vaginal swabs had produced a male DNA profile implicating Williams.

Have we not already decided this case? Lambatos's testimony is functionally identical to the "surrogate testimony" that New Mexico proffered in *Bullcoming*, which did nothing to cure the problem identified in *Melendez-Diaz* (which, for its part, straightforwardly applied our decision in *Crawford*). Like the surrogate witness in *Bullcoming*, Lambatos "could not convey what the actual analyst knew or observed about the events, i.e., the particular test and testing process he employed." *Bullcoming*, 131 S. Ct. at 2715.

Under our case law, that is sufficient to resolve this case. "When the State elected to introduce" the substance of Cellmark's report into evidence, the analyst who generated that report "became a witness" whom Williams "had the right to confront." *Bullcoming*, 131 S. Ct. at 2716 n. 7. As we stated just last year, "Our precedents cannot sensibly be read any other way." *Id.*

Point for Discussion

Expert Testimony After *Williams*

What does *Williams* mean for expert testimony? There are at least a dozen cases pending before the Court seeking clarification of *Williams*, a case that exemplifies the difficulties of creating coherence from a multiplicity of doctrinal rationales. The splintered Court, with a 4-1-4 plurality, left many questions about the admissibility of experts testifying to statements by non-testifying persons and left lower courts grasping for a predictable pronouncement to follow. While there is a rule courts follow for plurality decisions—e.g., "when a fragmented Court decides a case and no single rationale explaining the result enjoys the assent of five Justices, the holding of the Court may be viewed as the position taken by those members who concurred in the judgments on the narrowest grounds." *Marks v. United States*, 430 U.S. 188, 193 (1977)—no such clear lowest common denominator is apparent in *Williams*. What statements are admissible, and under what rationale, is still open to debate.

Hypo: *Drugged Victim*

In a true story, two ladies in their mid-70s were convicted of murdering two elderly men six years apart to collect life insurance proceeds. The women lived in Los Angeles and were listed as beneficiaries on several life insurance policies taken out on the men. The women ran the men over with their cars and collected more than half a million dollars. At trial, the prosecution alleged that at least one of the men was drugged beforehand. A laboratory director testified for the prosecution that blood analysis reports showed that one of the men had a drug in his blood that caused drowsiness. The director did not perform the tests in the reports. Did the laboratory director's testimony violate the accused's Confrontation Clause rights? Explain.

F. Other Confrontation Issues

1. Forfeiture of Confrontation Clause Rights by Wrongdoing

In *Giles v. California*, 554 U.S. 353 (2008), the Supreme Court held that right to Confrontation could be forfeited by wrongdoing. Giles was convicted of murder after the trial court permitted prosecutors to introduce hearsay statements made by the victim to a police officer who was responding to a domestic violence alert. At issue before the Supreme Court was whether the un-confronted testimony of the victim was properly admitted, or whether the forfeiture exception applied only when there was an intentional act to prevent the witness from testifying or simply an intentional criminal act that does not permit the witness to testify. The Supreme Court, led again by Justice Scalia, adopted the former approach because it was established at the founding of the Amendment that there must be conduct designed to prevent subsequent testimony. As applied to Giles, the intentionality of the criminal act does not suffice to show there was a design to prevent testimony at a subsequent time. Because the intent of the defendant was not considered in determining whether there was such a design, whether intent existed was a matter to be considered by the court below on remand. As noted in the casebook and last year's supplement, the seminal Confrontation Clause case of *Crawford v. Washington*, 541 U.S. 36 (2004), continues to produce a plethora of cases attempting to cabin and explain the scope the Clause.

The Louisiana Supreme Court has held that witness intimidation creates "unavailability" under the "forfeiture by wrongdoing" doctrine of the Confrontation Clause, even if it is not violent. In *State v. Aguilar*, 2015 BL 303182 (La. 2015), the Court concluded that domestic violence victims were unavailable after the defendant violated a protective order barring contact with the victims and the victims subsequently recanted their original testimony. The Court stated:

The district court erred in denying the State's motion to introduce the victims' statements at trial pursuant to La. Code Evid. art. 804B(7), forfeiture by wrongdoing. The State established by a preponderance of the evidence that the victims (the defendant's girlfriend and their daughter) recanted their testimony and ultimately became uncooperative with the prosecution of the case after the defendant repeatedly violated the protective order forbidding the defendant from contact with the victims. The lower courts both found the victims were unavailable as witnesses within the meaning of La. Code Evid. art. 804A. Thus, to introduce the victims' out of court statements, the State was required to show that the defendant engaged or acquiesced in wrongdoing that was intended to, and did, procure the unavailability of the declarants as witnesses. La. Code Evid. art. 804B(7); *Giles v. California*, 554 U.S. 353 (2008).

Contrary to the court of appeal's reasoning, there is no requirement in the code article that the defendant must engage in violence or employ threats of physical violence to cause fear in the victim in order to procure the witness's unavailability. The link between the defendant's actions and the victim's unavailability may be established when "a defendant puts forward to a witness the idea to avoid testifying, either by threats, coercion, persuasion, or pressure " *Commonwealth v. Edwards*, 444 Mass. 526, 541, 830 N.E.2d 158 (2005). Here, the defendant, in violation of the protective order, repeatedly suggested and encouraged the victims to recant their statements to the police and to avoid testifying against him at trial, thereby applying pressure on the witnesses through persistent contact. Because the witnesses' unavailability is a logical outgrowth of the defendant's actions in this domestic violence case, the forfeiture by wrongdoing doctrine is properly applied. For these reasons, the trial court's ruling is reversed, and the matter is remanded to that court for further proceedings.

Hypos: *The Intimidator & The Killer*

A) A man, known in the neighborhood as "the intimidator," was charged with brutally beating up another man who lived in the same neighborhood. Frank was an eyewitness who was interviewed by the prosecution in a discovery deposition, which the defendant was not permitted to attend, and was subpoenaed to testify at trial. Frank was visited by several aides of the accused who, in a not-so-subtle fashion, indicated he should be careful about what he said. When Frank showed up at trial, claiming that he could no longer speak, the prosecution offered the discovery deposition instead. How should the judge rule if the defense objects to the deposition?

B) Jones was prosecuted for murder of his ex-girlfriend. His ex had texted others on several occasions about how scared she was of Jones, and had reported his threats to the police. On one occasion, the police visited her home and took down a statement. The prosecution wants to offer the various prior statements of the victim at Jones' trial. The defense objects. What ruling and why?

---

2. Impeachment Evidence

To what extent is impeachment evidence protected by the Confrontation Clause? In *Davis v. Alaska*, 415 U.S. 308 (1974), the Supreme Court held that a criminal defendant has the right to cross-examine prosecution witnesses about their convictions, including sometimes their juvenile adjudications, particularly to show bias if on probation. Chief Justice Burger observed that subject to "the broad discretion of a trial judge to preclude repetitive and unduly harassing interrogation, the cross-examiner has traditionally been allowed to impeach, *i. e.,* discredit, the witness." He added:

> Cross-examination is the principal means by which the believability of a witness and the truth of his testimony are tested.

A more particular attack on the witness' credibility is effected by means of cross-examination directed toward revealing possible biases, prejudices, or ulterior motives of the witness as they may relate directly to issues or personalities in the case at hand.

> We cannot speculate as to whether the jury, as sole judge of the credibility of a witness, would have accepted this line of reasoning had counsel been permitted to fully present it. But we do conclude that the jurors were entitled to have the benefit of the defense theory before them so that they could make an informed judgment as to the weight to place on Green's testimony which provided "a crucial link in the proof of petitioner's act." *Douglas* v. *Alabama,* 380 U. S., at 419. The accuracy and truthfulness of Green's testimony were key elements in the State's case against petitioner. The claim of bias which the defense sought to develop was admissible to afford a basis for an inference of undue pressure because of Green's vulnerable status as a probationer, as well as of Green's possible concern that he might be a suspect in the investigation.

Subsequently, the Court reaffirmed the protection for cross-examination to uncover bias in *Olden v. Kentucky,* 488 U.S. 227 (1988). In *Olden,* a defendant accused of sexual assault attempted to cross-examine the complaining witness by impeaching the witness' credibility attempting to reveal that the witness might have had a motive to lie about the assault to protect an on-going extra-marital affair. The defense was not permitted to do so and on appeal in the state court, the appeal was denied based on harmless error. The Court, in a *per curiam* opinion, concluded that such a denial violated defendant's Confrontation Clause rights and was not harmless error under the *Chapman v. California,* 386 U.S. 18 (1967). The Court noted that "the correct inquiry is whether, assuming that the damaging potential of the cross-examination were fully realized, a reviewing court might nonetheless say that the error was harmless beyond a reasonable doubt." *Delaware v. VanArsdall,* 475 U.S. 673, 679 (1986). The Court explained that exclusion of the impeachment evidence was not harmless:

> In the instant case, petitioner has consistently asserted that he and Matthews engaged in consensual sexual acts and that complaining witness Matthews—out of fear of jeopardizing her relationship with Russell—lied when she told Russell she had been raped and has continued to lie since. It is plain to us that "a reasonable jury might have received a significantly different impression of the witness' credibility had defense counsel been permitted to pursue his proposed line of cross-examination." *Delaware v. Van Arsdall, supra,* at 680. Here, Matthews' testimony was central, indeed crucial, to the prosecution's case. Her story, which was directly contradicted by that of petitioner and Harris, was corroborated only by the largely derivative testimony of Russell, whose

impartiality would also have been somewhat impugned by revelation of his relationship with Matthews. Finally, the State's case against petitioner was far from overwhelming. In sum, considering the relevant *Van Arsdall* factors within the context of this case, we find it impossible to conclude "beyond a reasonable doubt" that the restriction on petitioner's right to confrontation was harmless.

Hypo: *Corruption Evidence*

Defendant Jones was charged in a drive-by shooting murder case. Jones offered extrinsic bias and corruption evidence about a testifying police detective. In particular, the defense wanted to show that the officer was the subject of an on-going investigation about coaching witnesses in another case. If you are the judge, would you allow this evidence? *Compare Longus v. United States*, 52 A.3d 836 (D.C. 2012), where the Court found that a trial court's "refusal to allow questioning about facts indicative of a witness's bias from which the jury could reasonably draw adverse inferences of reliability is an error of constitutional dimension." Moreover, evidence from which the jury can infer bias may be presented not only through cross-examination, but also by the introduction of extrinsic evidence. *See In re C.B.N.*, 499 A.2d 1215, 1218 (D.C. 1985)

---

3. Interpreter Statements

The circuits are split over whether statements by non-testifying interpreters violate the Confrontation Clause. In the Fourth and Ninth Circuits, courts view interpreters as language conduits, meaning agents of the speaker, and these statements are not considered testimonial. *See United States v. Shibin*, 722 F.3d 233 (4th Cir. 2013); and *United States v. Romo-Chavez*, 681 F.3d 955, 961 (9th Cir. 2013) (stating that a translator was serving as a "mere conduit" for the statements of the defendant.)

In *Shibin*, the defendant, a Somali, was tried for his involvement in the piracy of a ship off of the Somali coast. The defendant negotiated a ransom from the owners of the ship. After his involvement in another ship hijacking, Shibin was captured and brought to Virginia to stand trial. Shibin was convicted and appealed. He raised the Confrontation Clause as it related to the interpreter used for one of his witnesses as the basis for one of the grounds of alleged error. The Court rejected Shibin's claims: "Here, the statements were introduced as prior inconsistent statements. The interpreter was nothing more than a language conduit. He interpreted the statements of Salad Ali [the defendant's witness] and FBI Agent Coughlin, both of whom were subject to cross-examination." The Eleventh Circuit disagreed with the *Shibin* approach. In *United States v. Charles*, 722 F.3d 1319 (11th Cir. 2013), in an opinion issued shortly after the Fourth Circuit's opinion, the Court found that statements by interpreters were indeed testimonial and subject to the Confrontation Clause. The Court also found, though, that the trial court's failure to allow confrontation based on the facts of the case was not plain error.

a. Forfeiture of Confrontation Clause Rights By Wrongdoing

As noted in the casebook and last year's supplement, the seminal Confrontation Clause case of *Crawford v. Washington*, continues to produce a plethora of cases attempting to cabin and explain the scope the Clause. The Louisiana Supreme Court has held that witness intimidation creates "unavailability" under the "forfeiture by wrongdoing" doctrine of the Confrontation Clause, even if it is not violent. *In State v. Aguilar*, 2015 BL 303182 (La. 2015), the Court concluded that domestic violence victims were unavailable after the defendant violated a protective order barring contact with the victims and the victims subsequently recanted their original testimony. The Court stated:

> The district court erred in denying the State's motion to introduce the victims' statements at trial pursuant to La. Code Evid. art. 804B(7), forfeiture by wrongdoing. The State established by a preponderance of the evidence that the victims (the defendant's girlfriend and their daughter) recanted their testimony and ultimately became uncooperative with the prosecution of the case after the defendant repeatedly violated the protective order forbidding the defendant from contact with the victims. The lower courts both found the victims were unavailable as witnesses within the meaning of La. Code Evid. art. 804A. Thus, to introduce the victims' out of court statements, the State was required to show that the defendant engaged or acquiesced in wrongdoing that was intended to, and did, procure the unavailability of the declarants as witnesses. La. Code Evid. art. 804B(7); *Giles v. California*, 554 U.S. 353 (2008).

> Contrary to the court of appeal's reasoning, there is no requirement in the code article that the defendant must engage in violence or employ threats of physical violence to cause fear in the victim in order to procure the witness's unavailability. The link between the defendant's actions and the victim's unavailability may be established when "a defendant puts forward to a witness the idea to avoid testifying, either by threats, coercion, persuasion, or pressure " *Commonwealth v. Edwards*, 444 Mass. 526, 830 N.E.2d 158 (2005). Here, the defendant, in violation of the protective order, repeatedly suggested and encouraged the victims

to recant their statements to the police and to avoid testifying against him at trial, thereby applying pressure on the witnesses through persistent contact. Because the witnesses' unavailability is a logical outgrowth of the defendant's actions in this domestic violence case, the forfeiture by wrongdoing doctrine is properly applied. For these reasons, the trial court's ruling is reversed, and the matter is remanded to that court for further proceedings.

4. Harmless Error

When is a violation of the Confrontation Clause harmless error? In *Johnson v. Lamas*, 850 F.3d 119 (3rd Cir. 2017), the Court observed, "to be entitled to habeas relief, a habeas petitioner must establish that the trial error "had a substantial and injurious effect or influence in determining the jury's verdict." *Brecht v. Abrahamson*, 507 U.S. 619, 637 (1993). Under this test, we may grant relief only if we have a "grave doubt" as to whether the error at trial had a substantial and injurious effect or influence. *Davis v. Ayala*, 135 S.Ct. 2187, 2198 (2015). In other words, "there must be more than a 'reasonable probability' that the error was harmful." *Id.* The Court provided a list of factors that assisted in its analysis.

> Several factors guide our review of Confrontation Clause errors, including "the importance of the witness' testimony in the prosecution's case, whether the testimony was cumulative, the presence or absence of evidence corroborating or contradicting the testimony of the witness on material points, the extent of cross-examination otherwise permitted, and, of course, the overall strength of the prosecution's case. U.S. Const. Amend. 6.

G. Confrontation in Sexual Assault Cases

A special Confrontation Clause issue arises in sexual assault cases—what are the requirements for confrontation in testimony by a complaining witness? Is the Clause only satisfied by face-to-face confrontation or are alternatives permitted? In *Maryland v. Craig*, 497 U.S. 839 (1990), the Court held that a child witness in a child abuse case can testify outside the defendant's physical presence, through a closed circuit television. Justice O'Connor, for the Court, stated:

> We have never held, however, that the Confrontation Clause guarantees criminal defendants the *absolute* right to a face-to-face meeting with witnesses against them at trial. Indeed, in *Coy v. Iowa*, we expressly "left for another day the question whether any exceptions exist" to the "irreducible literal meaning of the Clause: 'a right to *meet face to face* all those who appear and give evidence *at trial*.' " In sum, our precedents establish that "the Confrontation Clause reflects a *preference* for face-to-face con-

frontation at trial," a preference that "must occasionally give way to considerations of public policy and the necessities of the case." Thus, though we reaffirm the importance of face-to-face confrontation with witnesses appearing at trial, we cannot say that such confrontation is an indispensable element of the Sixth Amendment's guarantee of the right to confront one's accusers. Accordingly, we hold that, if the State makes an adequate showing of necessity, the state interest in protecting child witnesses from the trauma of testifying in a child abuse case is sufficiently important to justify the use of a special procedure that permits a child witness in such cases to testify at trial against a defendant in the absence of face-to-face confrontation with the defendant.

Hypo: *Remote Testimony*

Suppose a sexual abuse trial is scheduled to occur and the complaining witness is: (a) eight years old and her mother does not want her to testify in front of the defendant; (b) 10 years old and nervous about testifying; (c) 12 years old and on a long-planned vacation with her family. Would any of these situations violate the Confrontation Clause? Would a remote studio location without face-to-face confrontation for the testimony suffice in any of these three situations? Why or why not?

Executive Summary

The Confrontation Clause applies to both state and federal governments and has two strands—putative hearsay and face-to-face positioning. The more volatile and dynamic analysis concerns hearsay. After *Crawford v. Washington*, the Clause only applies to testimonial statements, for which the Court did not provide a comprehensive definition. These statements include affidavits, *ex parte* statements, and any statements that are made to prove a fact that previously happened likely will fall within the embrace of the Clause, regardless of their reliability. Reliability

Major Themes

a. Testimonial—Hearsay must be testimonial for the Confrontation right to apply.

b. Opportunity—An accused must have the opportunity to cross-examine a declarant whose statement is testimonial, or a witness when the declarant is unavailable.

was the lynchpin under the prior seminal case, *Ohio v. Roberts*, but was abandoned in *Crawford*.

The Initial Issue is Whether the Statement is Testimonial. The hearsay strand applies only to testimonial statements. If such a statement is offered by the prosecution, the accused must first have had the opportunity to examine the subsequently unavailable declarant before the statement is potentially admitted.

Testimonial Statements Can Still Satisfy Confrontation Requirements. If a statement is testimonial, the accused must have been afforded the opportunity to examine the declarant. If the declarant testifies, that satisfies the Sixth Amendment. If the declarant is unavailable, the accused must have been afforded the opportunity to examine the witness.

Opportunity Does Not Require Examination. The accused can waive the opportunity to examine the witness—all that is required is an opportunity. Of course, it is generally beneficial to cross-examine the opponent's witnesses.

The Clause Does Not Apply to All Statements. The Clause does not apply to statements offered by the defense, including statements not offered for their truth, or statements made for the primary purpose of resolving an on-going emergency.

Admissibility Ultimately Depends on Evidence Rules As Well. Even if a statement survives the Confrontation Clause analysis, evidentiary and other rules apply and could preclude admissibility.

Exceptions. The Confrontation Clause has several exceptions and the rights it affords can be waived by the accused, either expressly or implicitly. These exceptions include forfeiture by wrongdoing, which occurs when an accused intentionally renders a witness unavailable for testifying.

For More Information

• "Confrontation Clause: Continuing Uncertainty For Expert Testimony Following Williams v. Illinois," Federal Evidence Review (6/17/2013), http://federalevidence.com/blog/2013/june/confrontation-clause-continuing-uncertainty-expert-testimony-following-williams-v-ill.

• J. Smith, "Understanding the New Confrontation Clause Analysis: *Crawford, Davis, Melendez-Diaz*," Administration of Justice Bulletin, UNC School of Government (2010) http://sogpubs.unc.edu/electronicversions/pdfs/aojb1002.pdf.

RUSSELL L. WEAVER, JOHN M. BURKOFF, CATHERINE HANCOCK & STEVEN I. FRIEDLAND, PRINCIPLES OF CRIMINAL PROCEDURE Ch. 17 (6th ed. 2018).

Test Your Knowledge

To assess your understanding of the material in this chapter, click here to take a quiz.

CHAPTER 19

Freedom of the Press and Fair Trials

Guarantees of expressive freedom and a fair trial are fundamental values in American society, but these guarantees do not always coexist harmoniously. Indeed, freedom of the press may both promote and undermine the criminal justice process. An unfettered right to free expression promotes self-government by exposing judicial or prosecutorial corruption or incompetence, and it can be a catalyst for reform by heightening the public's political awareness and understanding of the criminal process. Thus, the media's presence and influence avoid proceedings akin to the star chamber and practices inimical to fundamental fairness. But, while the press can serve many useful functions, its presence has the potential to disrupt and undermine the fairness of the trial process. Consider the following case.

A. Failing to Control the Press

Sheppard v. Maxwell

384 U.S. 333 (1966).

MR. JUSTICE CLARK delivered the opinion of the Court.

Marilyn Sheppard, petitioner's pregnant wife, was bludgeoned to death in the upstairs bedroom of their lakeshore home in Bay Village, Ohio, a suburb of Cleveland. On the day of the tragedy, July 4, 1954, Sheppard pieced together for several local officials the following story: after dinner Sheppard became drowsy and dozed off on a couch. The next thing he remembered was hearing his wife cry out in the early morning hours. He hurried upstairs and in the dim light from the hall saw a "form" standing next to his wife's bed. As he struggled with the "form" he was struck on the back of the neck and rendered unconscious.

From the outset officials focused suspicion on Sheppard. After a search of the house and premises on the morning of the tragedy, Dr. Gerber, the Coroner, is reported to have told his men, "Well, it is evident the doctor did this, so let's go get the confession out of him." On July 20th, the press opened fire with a front-page charge that somebody is "getting away with murder." The newspapers emphasized evidence that tended to incriminate Sheppard and pointed out discrepancies in his statements to authorities. At the same time, Sheppard made many public statements to the press and wrote feature articles asserting his innocence.

The case came to trial two weeks before the November general election at which the chief prosecutor was a candidate for common pleas judge and the trial judge, Judge Blythin, was a candidate to succeed himself. Twenty-five days before the case was set, 75 veniremen were called as prospective jurors. All three Cleveland newspapers published the names and addresses of the veniremen. As a consequence, anonymous letters and telephone calls, as well as calls from friends, regarding the impending prosecution were received by all of the prospective jurors.

The courtroom in which the trial was held measured 26 by 48 feet. A long temporary table was set up inside the bar, in back of the single counsel table. It ran the width of the courtroom, parallel to the bar railing, with one end less than three feet from the jury box. Approximately 20 representatives of newspapers and wire services were assigned seats at this table by the court. Behind the bar railing there were four rows of benches. These seats were likewise assigned by the court for the entire trial. The first row was occupied by representatives of television and radio stations, and the second and third rows by reporters from out-of-town newspapers and magazines. One side of the last row, which accommodated 14 people, was assigned to Sheppard's family and the other to Marilyn's. The public was permitted to fill vacancies in this row on special passes only. Representatives of the news media also used all the rooms on the courtroom floor, including the room where cases were ordinarily called and assigned for trial. Private telephone lines and telegraphic equipment were installed in these rooms so that reports from the trial could be speeded to the papers. Station WSRS was permitted to set up broadcasting facilities on the third floor of the courthouse next door to the jury room, where the jury rested during recesses in the trial and deliberated. Newscasts were made from this room throughout the trial, and while the jury reached its verdict.

On the sidewalk and steps in front of the courthouse, television and newsreel cameras were occasionally used to take motion pictures of the participants in the trial, including the jury and the judge. Indeed, one television broadcast carried a staged interview of the judge as he entered the courthouse. In the corridors outside the courtroom there was a host of photographers and television personnel with flash cameras, portable lights and motion picture cameras. This group photographed the prospective jurors during selection of the jury. After the trial opened, the witnesses, counsel, and jurors were photographed and televised whenever they entered or left the courtroom. Sheppard was brought to the courtroom about

10 minutes before each session began; he was surrounded by reporters and extensively photographed for the newspapers and television. A rule of court prohibited picture-taking in the courtroom during the actual sessions of the court, but no restraints were put on photographers during recesses, which were taken once each morning and afternoon, with a longer period for lunch.

All of these arrangements with the news media and their massive coverage of the trial continued during the entire nine weeks of the trial. The courtroom remained crowded to capacity with representatives of news media. Their movement in and out of the courtroom often caused so much confusion that, despite the loud-speaker system installed in the courtroom, it was difficult for the witnesses and counsel to be heard. Furthermore, the reporters clustered within the bar of the small courtroom made confidential talk among Sheppard and his counsel almost impossible during the proceedings. They frequently had to leave the courtroom to obtain privacy. And many times when counsel wished to raise a point with the judge out of the hearing of the jury it was necessary to move to the judge's chambers. Even then, news media representatives so packed the judge's anteroom that counsel could hardly return from the chambers to the courtroom. The reporters vied with each other to find out what counsel and the judge had discussed, and often these matters later appeared in newspapers accessible to the jury.

The jurors themselves were constantly exposed to the news media. Every juror, except one, testified at *voir dire* to reading about the case in the Cleveland papers or to having heard broadcasts about it. Seven of the 12 jurors who rendered the verdict had one or more Cleveland papers delivered in their home; the remaining jurors were not interrogated on the point. Nor were there questions as to radios or television sets in the jurors' homes, but we must assume that most of them owned such conveniences. As the selection of the jury progressed, individual pictures of prospective members appeared daily. During the trial, pictures of the jury appeared over 40 times in the Cleveland papers alone. The court permitted photographers to take pictures of the jury in the box, and individual pictures of the members in the jury room. One newspaper ran pictures of the jurors at the Sheppard home when they went there to view the scene of the murder. Another paper featured the home life of an alternate juror. The day before the verdict was rendered—while the jurors were at lunch and sequestered by two bailiffs—the jury was separated into two groups to pose for photographs which appeared in the newspapers.

While we cannot say that Sheppard was denied due process by the judge's refusal to take precautions against the influence of pretrial publicity alone, the court's later rulings must be considered against the setting in which the trial was held. In light of this background, we believe that the arrangements made by the judge with the news media caused Sheppard to be deprived of that "judicial serenity and calm to which he was entitled." Bedlam reigned at the courthouse during the trial and newsmen took over practically the entire courtroom, hounding most of the participants in the trial, especially Sheppard. At a temporary table within a few feet of the jury box and counsel table sat some 20 reporters staring at Sheppard and taking notes. The erection of a press table for reporters inside the bar is unprecedented. The bar of the court is reserved for counsel, providing them a safe place in which to keep papers and exhibits, and to confer privately with client and co-counsel. It is designed to protect the witness and the jury from any distractions, intrusions or influences, and to permit bench discussions of the judge's rulings away from the hearing of the public and the jury. Having assigned almost all of the available seats in the courtroom to the news media the judge lost his ability to supervise that environment.

The carnival atmosphere at trial could easily have been avoided since the courtroom and courthouse premises are subject to the control of the court. The presence of the press at judicial proceedings must be limited when it is apparent that the accused might otherwise be prejudiced or disadvantaged. Bearing in mind the massive pretrial publicity, the judge should have adopted stricter rules governing the use of the courtroom by newsmen, as Sheppard's counsel requested. The number of reporters in the courtroom itself could have been limited at the first sign that their presence would disrupt the trial. They certainly should not have been placed inside the bar. Furthermore, the judge should have more closely regulated the conduct of newsmen in the courtroom. For instance, the judge belatedly asked them not to handle and photograph trial exhibits lying on the counsel table during recesses.

Secondly, the court should have insulated the witnesses. All of the newspapers and radio stations apparently interviewed prospective witnesses at will, and in many instances disclosed their testimony. A typical example was the publication of numerous statements by Susan Hayes, before her appearance in court, regarding her love affair with Sheppard. Although the witnesses were barred from the courtroom during the trial the full verbatim testimony was available to them in the press. This completely nullified the judge's imposition of the rule.

Thirdly, the court should have made some effort to control the release of leads, information, and gossip to the press by police officers, witnesses, and the counsel for both sides. The trial court might well have proscribed extrajudicial statements by any lawyer, party, witness, or court official which divulged prejudicial matters, such as the refusal of Sheppard to submit to interrogation or take any lie detector tests; any statement made by Sheppard to officials; the identity of prospective witnesses or their probable testimony; any belief in guilt or innocence; or like statements concerning the merits of the case. Being advised of the great public interest in the case, the mass coverage of the press, and the potential prejudicial impact of publicity, the court could also have requested the appropriate city and county officials to promulgate a regulation with respect to dissemination of information about the case by their employees. In addition, reporters who wrote or broadcast prejudicial stories, could have been warned as to the impropriety of publishing material not introduced in the proceedings.

From the cases coming here we note that unfair and prejudicial news comment on pending trials has become increasingly prevalent. Due process requires that the accused receive a trial by an impartial jury free from outside influences. Given the pervasiveness of modern communications and the difficulty of effacing prejudicial publicity from the minds of the jurors, trial courts must take strong measures to ensure that the balance is never weighed against the accused. And appellate tribunals have the duty to make an independent evaluation of the circumstances. Of course, there is nothing that proscribes the press from reporting events that transpire in the courtroom. But where there is a reasonable likelihood that prejudicial news prior to trial will prevent a fair trial, the judge should continue the case until the threat abates, or transfer it to another county not so permeated with publicity. In addition, sequestration of the jury was something the judge should have raised *sua sponte* with counsel. If publicity during the proceedings threatens the fairness of the trial, a new trial should be ordered. But we must remember that reversals are but palliatives; the cure lies in those remedial measures that prevent the prejudice at its inception. The courts must take such steps by rule and regulation that will protect their processes from prejudicial outside interferences. Neither prosecutors, counsel for defense, the accused, witnesses, court staff nor enforcement officers coming under the jurisdiction of the court should be permitted to frustrate its function. Collaboration between counsel and the press as to information affecting the fairness of a criminal trial is not only subject to regulation, but is highly censurable and worthy of disciplinary measures.

Since the state trial judge did not fulfill his duty to protect Sheppard from the inherently prejudicial publicity which saturated the community and to control disruptive influences in the courtroom, we must reverse the denial of the habeas petition. The case is remanded to the District Court with instructions to issue the writ and order that Sheppard be released from custody unless the State puts him to its charges again within a reasonable time.

It is so ordered.

B. Pretrial Publicity and Defendant's Right to a Fair Trial

In order to preserve a defendant's right to a fair trial, there are several steps that a judge might take to limit the impact of media publicity.

1. Change of Venue

While a defendant has a right to a state criminal trial in the county of the crime, the defendant may desire a trial in another county and may file a motion for a change of venue. The right to request a change of venue belongs to either the defendant or the prosecution. Since venue is largely a creature of statute, statutory procedures should be followed before relief may be granted. On the other hand, a change of venue is a federally protected right which may require the court to overlook statutory procedures in some instances. *Groppi v. Wisconsin*, 400 U.S. 505 (1971). Statutes may permit each party only one application for a change of venue. The application for a change of venue must be timely made or it may be waived.

When potential jurors have read or heard prejudicial publicity, a trial judge should inquire into the nature and extent of the exposure. To prove juror partiality, a defendant must show that the publicity either actually prejudiced a juror or so pervaded the proceedings that it raised a presumption of inherent prejudice. Recall *Sheppard v. Maxwell*, in which the Court noted that "where there is a reasonable likelihood that prejudicial news prior to trial will prevent a fair trial, the judge should continue the case until the threat abates, or transfer it to another county not so permeated with publicity." During trial, a judge also has broad discretion to sequester the jury and caution the jurors to avoid media accounts of the proceedings.

After an application has been made, the court must determine whether the application establishes a *prima facie* case for granting a change of venue. If it does not, the application may be denied. If a *prima facie* showing has been made, the opposing party must then controvert the allegations or the change of venue must be granted. In making its determination the trial court has wide discretion which will not be disturbed if it is supported by sufficient evidence. In many instances the trial judge will defer a decision about the motion until *voir dire* has indicated whether there is a valid prospect of a fair trial for the defendant. Once in a while, however, circumstances suggest the need to grant the change of venue without the necessity of weighing the nature and extent of awareness about the defendant and the charge.

United States v. Lindh

212 F. Supp. 2d 541 (E.D. Va. 2002).

ELLIS, DISTRICT JUDGE.

John Phillip Walker Lindh ("Lindh") is an American citizen who, according to the Indictment filed against him, joined certain foreign terrorist organizations in Afghanistan and served these organizations there in combat against Northern

Alliance and American forces until his capture in November 2001. Lindh sought dismissal of certain counts of the Indictment on a variety of grounds, including lawful combatant immunity and selective prosecution. Lindh also sought dismissal, or alternatively, transfer of venue, arguing that he could not receive a fair trial in this district owing to pre-trial publicity. All motions were denied following extensive briefing and oral argument.

Lindh requests dismissal on the ground that the media attention surrounding this case has been so prejudicial as to deprive him of his Sixth Amendment right to a fair trial. He alternatively requests a transfer of venue to the Northern District of California, the district in which he spent his childhood and where he claims the pre-trial publicity has not been as prejudicial. Lindh also claims that the Northern District of California is more convenient for the parties and witnesses, pursuant to Rule 21(b), Fed.R.Crim.P.

The principles that govern resolution of this motion are clear and well settled. The Sixth Amendment guarantees that in all criminal prosecutions, the defendant shall enjoy the right to trial "by an impartial jury." In certain extraordinary, circumstances, this fundamental right to trial "by an impartial jury" may be compromised by the presence of pervasive and inflammatory pre-trial publicity. To warrant a dismissal of an indictment on this ground, a defendant must establish that he cannot obtain a fair trial anywhere in the country owing to prejudicial pre-trial publicity. See *United States v. Abbott Laboratories*, 505 F.2d 565, 571 (4th Cir.1974). In other words, dismissal is appropriate only where a defendant establishes that prejudicial pre-trial publicity is "so widespread and pervasive that a change of venue would be ineffective to assure a defendant a fair trial." *Id*. In this regard, it is important to note that "sheer volume of publicity alone does not deny a defendant a fair trial." *United States v. Bakker*, 925 F.2d 728, 732 (4th Cir.1991).

Dismissal of an indictment as a remedy for prejudicial pre-trial publicity is severe and rarely warranted, as it is unlikely that fair and impartial jurors cannot be found in any district. The less severe remedy of transfer is also unwarranted unless a defendant can show that the pre-trial publicity in the district "is so inherently prejudicial that trial proceedings must be presumed to be tainted." *Bakker*, 925 F.2d at 732. Moreover, transfers of venue based on pre-trial publicity are not often granted, as "the effects of pre-trial publicity on the pool from which jurors are drawn is generally determined by a careful and searching *voir dire* examination." *United States v. McVeigh*, 918 F.Supp. 1467 (W.D.Okla.1996). Indeed, "only where *voir dire* reveals that an impartial jury cannot be impaneled would a change of venue be justified." *Bakker*, 925 F.2d at 732. In this regard, "it is not required that jurors be totally ignorant of the facts and issues involved." *Id*. at 734. Rather, "it is sufficient if the juror can lay aside his impression or opinion and render a verdict based on the evidence presented in court." *Id*.

All prospective jurors in this case, as in all cases, will be questioned carefully as to what they have seen or read or heard about the case and whether they have formed any opinions or impressions. No juror will be qualified to serve unless the Court is satisfied that the juror (i) is able to put aside any previously formed opinions or impressions, (ii) is prepared to pay careful and close attention to the evidence as it is presented in the case and finally (iii) is able to render a fair and impartial verdict based solely on the evidence adduced at trial and the Court's instructions of law.

Just as the sheer volume of pre-trial publicity in this case does not compel dismissal or transfer, neither does the nature of that publicity. The bulk of the pre-trial publicity relating to this case is factual, rather than inflammatory, and hence less likely to poison the venire pool. No doubt the publicity also includes some expressions of opinions on newspaper editorial pages or the Internet that were specifically designed to inflame or persuade readers. Yet, on the whole, the record does not warrant a conclusion that prejudicial pre-trial publicity has been so "inherently prejudicial that trial proceedings must be presumed to be tainted" or that Lindh cannot receive a fair trial. And, in any event, the proof of this pudding will be the *voir dire* results; only those prospective jurors found to be capable of fair and impartial jury service after careful *voir dire* will be declared eligible to serve as jurors. Past experience provides reasonable assurance that more than a sufficient number of qualified, impartial jurors will be identified as a result of the *voir dire* in this case.

Nor are Lindh's expert reports—one prepared by Neil Vidmar and the other by Steven Penrod—to the contrary; neither persuasively supports dismissal of the Indictment or transfer to another district. Vidmar developed a survey interview questionnaire to assess the impact of pre-trial publicity in this case. He later supervised the Evans McDonough Company in conducting random telephone interviews of 400 individuals in this district and, for comparison purposes, 200 individuals in Chicago, Minneapolis, San Francisco and Seattle.[8] Penrod, on the other hand, conducted a content analysis of the pre-trial newspaper coverage concerning Lindh and other issues, as reported in the two major newspapers circulated in Alexandria (the Washington Post and the Washington Times) and,

---

[8] Among the questions asked of the respondents were (i) what information they know about Lindh; (ii) whether they have a strongly favorable, somewhat favorable, somewhat unfavorable or strongly unfavorable opinion of Lindh; (iii) whether they view Lindh as a terrorist, a traitor, a confused young man or a person on a religious journey; (iv) whether they believe Lindh was involved in the death of CIA agent Spann; (v) whether they believe there is a connection between Lindh and the September 11, 2001 terrorist attacks; (vi) whether they knew someone who was killed or injured in the September 11, 2001 terrorist attacks; (vii) whether they believe Lindh is guilty, probably guilty, probably not guilty or definitely not guilty of the charges against him; (viii) whether they would consider a not guilty verdict very acceptable, acceptable, not acceptable or very unacceptable; (ix) what punishment they believe Lindh should receive if found guilty of the charges against him; and (x) whether they could be fair and impartial if seated as a juror at Lindh's trial.

for comparison purposes, the two major newspapers circulated in Minneapolis (the Minneapolis Star Tribune and the St. Paul Pioneer Press).[9]

Despite Lindh's arguments to the contrary, the Vidmar report actually supports the conclusion that Lindh is just as likely to receive a fair trial in this district as he is elsewhere in the country. Indeed, Vidmar concludes that "the stated attitudes of jury eligible respondents in Virginia toward Mr. Lindh between April 29 and May 2 did not differ from stated attitudes in the rest of the country." Moreover, according to the Vidmar data, approximately three quarters (74%) of the Northern Virginia residents who were polled indicated that they could be fair and impartial if seated as a juror at Lindh's trial. Significantly, this percentage exceeds the corresponding percentage reported by Vidmar for California (68.6%), the jurisdiction to which Lindh seeks a transfer. And, contrary to Lindh's assertions, the fact that a number of the individuals polled in both Virginia and elsewhere knew someone injured or killed in the September 11, 2001 terrorist attacks does not warrant dismissal of the Indictment or a change of venue. Rather, such personal connections to the terrorist attacks are matters adequately addressed and dealt with during the *voir dire* process.

The Penrod report also does not support dismissal or transfer of the case. Indeed, on more than half the subjects covered by the survey, the Minneapolis newspapers were either harsher in their assessment of Lindh or expressed "unfavorable" opinions to the same extent as did the Alexandria newspapers. Additionally, on those subjects where the Alexandria newspapers were found to be less favorable toward Lindh than the Minneapolis newspapers, the percentages were often so close as to be statistically insignificant. Finally, it is worth noting that Lindh is not entitled to a "favorable" jury, as Penrod appears to suggest; nor is he entitled to a jury that has not been privy to any media reports regarding the instant prosecution, favorable or unfavorable. Rather, what the Sixth Amendment guarantees Lindh, and all criminal defendants, is a fair and impartial jury. Nothing in the studies and data Lindh submitted supports a conclusion that Lindh cannot receive a fair and impartial jury trial in this district.

Lindh's motion to transfer the case to the Northern District of California for purposes of convenience, pursuant to Rule 21(b) is equally unpersuasive. Indeed, contrary to Lindh's contentions, there are multiple reasons for concluding that transfer from this district is inappropriate, including the following: (i) the trial will proceed more expeditiously in this district; (ii) this district is equipped and prepared to cope with the significant security concerns associated with this

---

[9] Specifically, the newspaper articles were coded as either favorable or unfavorable toward Lindh on a number of issues, including (i) the personal characteristics of Lindh; (ii) Lindh's connections to the Taliban, al Qaeda and bin Laden; (iii) Lindh's connection to the QIJ prison uprising resulting in the death of CIA agent Spann; (iv) the regional economic and emotional impact of the September 11, 2001 attack on the Pentagon; and (v) the instant charges against Lindh.

case; (iii) the prosecution team is comprised largely of attorneys from this district; (iv) the relevant documents are located in this district; (v) the defendant is present in this district, subject to security measures already in place; and (vi) a number of potential witnesses are located in or near this district. Moreover, the fact that four of Lindh's attorneys reside in California rather than in this district is an inconvenience of his own choosing. No claim is made, or can be made, that competent and experienced counsel cannot be found in this district. Of course, Lindh has a Sixth Amendment right to select competent and experienced counsel from another district, which he has done, but he is not entitled to rely on the exercise of that right to effect a change of venue.

In conclusion, it is clear that neither a dismissal of the Indictment nor a transfer of venue is warranted in this case. Lindh has failed to meet his burden of establishing that the pre-trial publicity generated in this case, by both the government and the defense, "has been so inflammatory and prejudicial that a fair trial is absolutely precluded and the indictment should be dismissed without an initial attempt to see if an impartial jury can be impaneled." *Abbott*, 505 F.2d at 571. He has also failed to establish that a transfer of venue based on pre-trial publicity is appropriate, as the publicity involved here is not "so inherently prejudicial that trial proceedings in this district must be presumed to be tainted." *Bakker*, 925 F.2d at 732.[15] Nor is a transfer of venue for purposes of convenience warranted under Rule 21(b), Fed.R.Crim.P. Rather, the appropriate course of action in the circumstances is to continue the proceedings in this district and to conduct a thorough *voir dire* of all potential jurors to ensure the selection of a fair and impartial jury that is able to set aside any pre-conceived notions regarding this case and render an impartial verdict based solely on the evidence presented in the case and the Court's instructions of law.

Points for Discussion

a. Factors Supporting a Change of Venue

Other factors may support a motion for a change of venue:

1) The peculiar influence which a trial participant may have in the community may also preclude a fair trial, even if a jury with no actual knowledge of the case could be empanelled;

---

[15] This case is easily distinguishable from *United States v. McVeigh*, 918 F. Supp. 1467 (W.D. Okla.1996), where a transfer of venue was ultimately granted based on the impact of defendant's conduct—the bombing of the Murrah Federal Office Building in Oklahoma City. This unique and extraordinary local impact led the district judge to conclude that "there is so great a prejudice against these two defendants in the State of Oklahoma that they cannot obtain a fair and impartial trial at any place [in] that state." In *McVeigh*, the very courthouse where the case would have been tried suffered collateral damage from the bombing. None of the features that motivated transfer in *McVeigh* is present to the same degree in the instant case.

2) A state of lawlessness which threatens to erupt into mob violence or which might influence the conduct of the trial may also form the basis for a change of venue;

3) The need to transfer the defendant to another place for safekeeping pending trial may require a change of venue. Ultimately, the question remains whether an impartial jury might be had in the community, and neither pretrial publicity nor hostility on the part of some members of the community requires a change of venue if a fair and impartial jury may be empanelled and a fair trial held.

b. Choosing an Alternate Venue

Statutes differ regarding where a case should be sent if the court grants a motion for a change of venue. For example, if a state court determines that a case should be removed due to emergency conditions, it may transfer the case to any other county within the state in which a fair trial may be held. Or, a statute may provide that, if a court decides to grant a change of venue, it must transfer the case to an adjoining county if a fair trial can be held there. If the court finds that a fair trial cannot be had in any adjoining county, the case may then be transferred to the most convenient county in which a fair trial may be had. In your state, where is a judge allowed to transfer a case after granting a change of venue? With cable television and the Internet, is there a strong likelihood that no place exists within a state where a defendant can receive a fair trial? The court to which a case is removed has the same jurisdiction to dispose of the case as the original court that ordered the transfer. If the indictment is dismissed,

While a change of venue is frequently thought of as a matter relating to a fair trial, a somewhat different procedure may exist that allows the transfer of venue to another county for purposes of a plea. The purpose of this latter transfer provision is to permit a defendant to plead guilty in one place based on charges pending in another place. Fed.R.Crim.P. 20 and many corresponding state rules allow a defendant physically located in one place to plead guilty to charges pending in another place. While the federal rule deals with avoiding transportation problems, there is an added benefit in that a defendant can dispose of multiple cases in a single court. For example, defendants are sometimes charged with multiple crimes, such as bad checks, that occur in several adjacent counties. By appropriate plea negotiations with the various prosecutors involved, the defendant may get a "package deal" on all of his pending charges. In this fashion a single judge may take the plea and impose sentence in consideration of all the charges. Attorneys who have clients with multi-county charges should consider suggesting to the District Attorney that the transfer provision be utilized to consolidate and dispose of the charges. The transfer provisions only apply when there is going to be a guilty plea. If the defendant changes his mind and pleads not guilty, the proceedings are transferred back to the county where the prosecution was initially commenced. Where transfer has to be terminated, any statement that the defendant may have made expressing his desire to plead guilty cannot be used against him.

the grand jury in the county to which the case has been transferred may thereafter be able to prosecute the action as if the offense had been committed in that county originally. The original court making the transfer has no further jurisdiction to prosecute the action as long as the transfer is in effect.

Hypo 1: *The Drug Conspiracy*

Three defendants, all from New York City, are charged in a drug conspiracy in a rural area. One defendant previously was convicted of an informer's girlfriend's death in Vermont state court. Pretrial publicity included local newspaper and television coverage of (1) the defendants' drug arrests, (2) the defendant's prior murder conviction, and (3) the effects of the victim's death on the community. Defendants contended that common knowledge of these events within the venue prevents a fair trial. During *voir dire*, the court excuses any jurors who either (1) knew of defendant's guilty verdict in the earlier trial for murder, or (2) had formed an opinion about the case that prevented their impartial deliberation. The court does not excuse jurors reporting exposure to pre-trial publicity who stated that they could try the case fairly. Defendants further argue that as three black men from New York City, they cannot obtain an impartial jury from a largely white population in a rural area. The court inquires whether any of the remaining panel members have beliefs about drugs, firearms, defendants' race, or the fact that defendants hailed from New York City, that would prevent their impartial deliberation; no juror so indicated. As a judge, how would you exercise your discretion in this case if the defendants seek a change of venue?

Hypo 2: *Extensive Pre-Trial Publicity*

Defendants claimed extensive pretrial publicity. Defendants submitted scores of national and local newspaper and magazine reports about drug-related issues. They also presented radio and television news transcripts describing the growing problem of drug availability for young children. Only about one-third of the articles mentioned the defendants, and those articles were primarily factual in nature, only once referring to confessions given by the defendants. As a judge, how would you exercise your discretion in this case if defendants seek a change of venue?

Hypo 3: *Pre-Trial Polling*

At the time of his arraignment, defendant moved for a change of venue. The public opinion survey/poll which was filed with the motion indicated that in 100 calls, 98 persons had read or heard about the crime. Eighty-nine of the 100 polled were aware of defendant's name; 73 knew that he had been in prison previously; and 60 were aware of that charge. Ninety-three persons had heard both radio and television stories, some up to at least 100 such reports. Eighty-five considered defendant guilty, while 15 did not respond or stated they did not know. Sixty-five thought he would receive a fair trial in the county. Defendant renewed his motion during the course of *voir dire* as prospective jurors gave repeated voice to the community's sentiment that was widespread against him. All potential jurors, save one, had knowledge of the case. Of the 153 or more jurors that were *voir dired* individually, 112 were excused because they had preconceived opinions about defendant's guilt, could not presume him innocent, or admitted to knowledge of his prior manslaughter conviction. Of 38 jurors who were accepted by the court to comprise the pool from which the trial jury would be selected, 19 had an initial opinion that he was guilty. As a judge, how would you exercise your discretion in this case if defendants seek a change of venue?

2. Due Process and Pretrial Publicity

Despite concerns about pretrial publicity and juror impartiality, jurors need not be completely ignorant of the facts and issues. A trial judge must assess the jurors' opinions to determine whether the jurors can impartially decide the case. In *Irvin v. Dowd*, 366 U.S. 717 (1961), petitioner was convicted of murder following a trial that was "extensively covered" by the news media and aroused "great excitement and indignation." The press reported defendant's prior convictions, his confession to 24 burglaries and six murders including the one for which he was tried, and his unaccepted offer to plead guilty in order to avoid the death sentence. The trial court granted a change of venue to an adjoining county. The court refused an additional request for change of venue on the basis that Indiana law provided for only a single change of venue. The Court reversed:

> Here the "pattern of deep and bitter prejudice" shown to be present throughout the community was clearly reflected in the sum total of the *voir dire* examination of a majority of the jurors finally placed in the jury box. Eight out of the 12 thought petitioner was guilty. With such an opinion permeating their minds, it would be difficult to say that each

could exclude this preconception of guilt from his deliberations. The influence that lurks in an opinion once formed is so persistent that it unconsciously fights detachment from the mental processes of the average man. Where one's life is at stake—and accounting for the frailties of human nature—we can only say that in the light of the circumstances here the finding of impartiality does not meet constitutional standards. Two-thirds of the jurors had an opinion that petitioner was guilty and were familiar with the material facts and circumstances involved, including the fact that other murders were attributed to him, some going so far as to say that it would take evidence to overcome their belief. One said that he "could not give the defendant the benefit of the doubt that he is innocent." Another stated that he had a "somewhat" certain fixed opinion as to petitioner's guilt. No doubt each juror was sincere when he said that he would be fair and impartial to petitioner, but psychological impact requiring such a declaration before one's fellows is often its father. Where so many, so many times, admitted prejudice, such a statement of impartiality can be given little weight. As one of the jurors put it, "You can't forget what you hear and see." With his life at stake, it is not requiring too much that petitioner be tried in an atmosphere undisturbed by so huge a wave of public passion and by a jury other than one in which two-thirds of the members admit, before hearing any testimony, to possessing a belief in his guilt.

Irvin was followed by a couple of other major decisions. In *Murphy v. Florida*, 421 U.S. 794 (1975), the Court upheld petitioner's conviction for breaking and entering a home, while armed, with intent to commit robbery and of assault with intent to commit robbery. In that case, there was extensive press coverage because petitioner had been involved in the theft of the Star of India sapphire from a museum in New York. His flamboyant lifestyle made him a continuing subject of press interest, and the press referred to him as "Murph the Surf." Relying on *Irvin, Rideau v. Louisiana*, 373 U.S. 723 (1963), and *Estes v. Texas*, 381 U.S. 532 (1965), as well as on *Sheppard*, the Court concluded that the *voir dire* showed that the jurors did not have undue hostility towards petitioner, the situation in the community was not regarded as "inflammatory," and the Court was unable to conclude that Murphy did not receive a fair trial. *Patton v. Yount*, 467 U.S. 1025 (1984), was a murder case in which there had been publicity regarding Yount's prior conviction for murder, his confession, and his prior plea of temporary insanity, information not admitted into evidence at trial. The Court refused to overturn the conviction even though *voir dire* showed that all but 2 of 163 veniremen questioned about the case had heard of it, and that, 126, or 77%, admitted they would carry an opinion into the jury box. 8 of the 14 jurors and alternates actually seated admitted that at some time they had formed an opinion as to Yount's guilt. The Court focused on the fact that a year and a half had elapsed between the reversal and the start of the second trial. During this period, the two local newspapers published an average of less than one article per month about the case. Many of these articles were extremely brief announcements of the trial dates and scheduling such as are common in rural newspapers. During the *voir dire* the newspapers published articles on an almost daily basis, but these too were purely factual articles generally discussing not the crime or prior prosecution, but the prolonged process of jury selection. In short, the record of publicity in the months preceding, and at the time of, the second trial does not reveal the "barrage of inflammatory publicity immediately prior to trial," amounting to a "huge wave of public passion," that the Court found in *Irvin*.

Skilling v. United States

561 U.S. 358 (2010).

JUSTICE GINSBURG delivered the opinion of the Court.

In 2001, Enron Corporation, then the seventh highest-revenue-grossing company in America, crashed into bankruptcy. We consider in this opinion whether pretrial publicity and community prejudice presented Skilling from obtaining a fair trial. Skilling, we hold, did not establish that a presumption of juror prejudice arose or that actual bias infected the jury that tried him.

Founded in 1985, Enron Corporation grew from its headquarters in Houston, Texas, into one of the world's leading energy companies. Skilling launched his career there in 1990 when Kenneth Lay, the company's founder, hired him to head an Enron subsidiary. Skilling steadily rose through the corporation's ranks, serving as president and chief operating officer, and then, beginning in February 2001, as chief executive officer. Six months later, on August 14, 2001, Skilling resigned from Enron.

Less than four months after Skilling's departure, Enron spiraled into bankruptcy. The company's stock, which had traded at $90 per share in August 2000, plummeted to pennies per share in late 2001. Attempting to comprehend what caused the corporation's collapse, the U.S. Department of Justice formed an Enron Task Force, comprising prosecutors and FBI agents from around the Nation. The Government's investigation uncovered an elaborate conspiracy to prop up Enron's short run stock prices by overstating the company's financial well-being. In the years following Enron's bankruptcy, the Government prosecuted dozens of Enron employees who participated in the scheme. In time, the Government worked its way up the corporation's chain of command: On July 7, 2004, a grand jury indicted Skilling, Lay, and Richard Cause, Enron's former chief accounting officer for securities and wire fraud, and insider trading.

In November 2004, Skilling moved to transfer the trial to another venue; he contended that hostility toward him in Houston, coupled with extensive pretrial publicity, had poisoned potential jurors. Skilling, aided by media experts, submitted hundreds of news reports detailing Enron's downfall; he also presented affidavits from the experts he engaged portraying community attitudes in Houston in comparison to other potential venues. The U.S. District Court for the Southern District of Texas denied the venue-transfer motion. Despite "isolated incidents of intemperate commentary," the court observed, media coverage "had mostly been objective and unemotional," and the facts of the case were "neither heinous nor sensational." Moreover, "courts had commonly" favored "effective *voir dire* to ferret out any juror bias." Pretrial publicity about the case, the court concluded, did not warrant a presumption that Skilling would be unable to obtain a fair trial in Houston.

In the months leading up to the trial, the District Court solicited from the parties questions the court might use to screen prospective jurors. Unable to agree on a questionnaire's format and content, Skilling and the Government submitted dueling documents. On venire members' sources of Enron-related news, for example, the Government proposed that they tick boxes from a checklist of generic labels such as "television," "newspaper," and "radio"; Skilling proposed more probing questions asking venire members to list the specific names of their media sources and to report on "what stood out in their minds" of "all the things they had seen, heard or read about Enron."

The District Court rejected the Government's sparer inquiries in favor of Skilling's submission. Skilling's questions "were more helpful," the court said, "because they were generally open-ended and would allow the potential jurors to give us more meaningful information." The court converted Skilling's submission, with slight modifications, into a 77-question, 14-page document that asked prospective jurors about, *inter alia,* their sources of news and exposure to Enron-related publicity, beliefs concerning Enron and what caused its collapse, opinions regarding the defendants and their possible guilt or innocence, and relationships to the company and to anyone affected by its demise.[4]

---

[4] Questions included the following: "What are your opinions about the compensation that executives of large corporations receive?"; "Have you, any family members, or friends ever worked for or applied for work with," "done business with," or "owned stock in Enron Corporation or any Enron subsidiaries and partnership?"; "Do you know anyone who has been negatively affected or hurt in any way by what happened at Enron?"; "Do you have an opinion about the cause of the collapse of Enron? If YES, what is your opinion? On what do you base your opinion?"; "Have you heard or read about any of the Enron cases? If YES, please tell us the name of all sources from which you have heard or read about the Enron cases."; "Have you read any books or seen any movies about Enron? If YES, please describe."; "Are you angry about what happened with Enron? If YES, please explain."; "Do you have an opinion about Jeffrey Skilling? If YES, what is your opinion? On what do you base your opinion?"; "Based on anything you have heard, read, or been told, do you have any opinion about the guilt or innocence of Jeffrey Skilling? If YES, please explain."; "Would any opinion you may have formed regarding Enron or

In November 2005, the District Court mailed the questionnaire to 400 prospective jurors and received responses from nearly all the addressees. The court granted hardship exemptions to approximately 90 individuals, and the parties, with the court's approval, further winnowed the pool by excusing another 119 for cause, hardship, or physical disability. The parties agreed to exclude, in particular, "each and every" prospective juror who said that a preexisting opinion about Enron or the defendants would prevent her from impartially considering the evidence at trial. Denying Skilling's request for attorney-led *voir dire*, the court promised to give counsel an opportunity to ask follow-up questions, and it agreed that venire members should be examined individually about pretrial publicity.

After questioning the venire as a group, the District Court brought prospective jurors one by one to the bench for individual examination. Although the questions varied, the process generally tracked the following format: The court asked about exposure to Enron-related news and the content of any stories that stood out in the prospective juror's mind. Next, the court homed in on questionnaire answers that raised a red flag signaling possible bias. The court then permitted each side to pose follow-up questions. Finally, after the venire member stepped away, the court entertained and ruled on challenges for cause. In all, the court granted one of the Government's for-cause challenges and denied four; it granted three of the defendants' challenges and denied six. The parties agreed to excuse three additional jurors for cause and one for hardship.

Following a 4-month trial and nearly five days of deliberation, the jury found Skilling guilty of 19 counts, including the honest-services-fraud conspiracy charge, and not guilty of 9 insider-trading counts. The District Court sentenced Skilling to 292 months' imprisonment, 3 years' supervised release, and $45 million in restitution.

On appeal, Skilling raised a host of challenges to his convictions, including the fair-trial arguments he presses here. The Fifth Circuit initially determined that the volume and negative tone of media coverage generated by Enron's collapse created a presumption of juror prejudice.

Pointing to "the community passion aroused by Enron's collapse and the vitriolic media treatment" aimed at him, Skilling argues that his trial "never should have proceeded in Houston." Even if it had been possible to select impartial jurors in Houston, "the truncated *voir dire* did almost nothing to weed out prejudices," he contends, so "far from rebutting the presumption of prejudice, the record below affirmatively confirmed it." Skilling's fair-trial claim thus raises two distinct questions. First, did the District Court err by failing to move the trial to a differ-

---

any of the defendants prevent you from impartially considering the evidence presented during the trial of Jeffrey Skilling? If YES or UNSURE, please explain."; "Is there anything else you feel is important for the court to know about you?"

ent venue based on a presumption of prejudice? Second, did actual prejudice contaminate Skilling's jury?

The Sixth Amendment secures to criminal defendants the right to trial by an impartial jury. By constitutional design, that trial occurs "in the State where the Crimes have been committed." Art. III, § 2, cl. 3. "The theory of our trial system is that the conclusions to be reached in a case will be induced only by evidence and argument in open court, and not by any outside influence, whether of private talk or public print." *Patterson v. Colorado ex rel. Attorney General of Colo.*, 205 U.S. 454, 462 (1907). When does the publicity attending conduct charged as criminal dim prospects that the trier can judge a case, as due process requires, impartially, unswayed by outside influence? Because most cases of consequence garner at least some pretrial publicity, courts have considered this question in diverse settings. We begin our discussion by addressing the presumption of prejudice from which the Fifth Circuit's analysis in Skilling's case proceeded. The foundation precedent is *Rideau v. Louisiana*, 373 U.S. 723 (1963).

Wilbert Rideau robbed a bank in a small Louisiana town, kidnapped three bank employees, and killed one of them. Police interrogated Rideau in jail without counsel present and obtained his confession. Without informing Rideau, no less seeking his consent, the police filmed the interrogation. On three separate occasions shortly before the trial, a local television station broadcast the film to audiences ranging from 24,000 to 53,000 individuals. Rideau moved for a change of venue, arguing that he could not receive a fair trial in the parish where the crime occurred, which had a population of approximately 150,000 people. The trial court denied the motion, and a jury eventually convicted Rideau. The Supreme Court of Louisiana upheld the conviction. We reversed. "What the people in the community saw on their television sets," we observed, "was Rideau, in jail, flanked by the sheriff and two state troopers, admitting in detail the commission of the robbery, kidnapping, and murder." "To the tens of thousands of people who saw and heard it," we explained, the interrogation "in a very real sense *was* Rideau's trial-at which he pleaded guilty." We therefore "did not hesitate to hold, without pausing to examine a particularized transcript of the *voir dire*," that "the kangaroo court proceedings" trailing the televised confession violated due process.

We followed *Rideau's* lead in two later cases in which media coverage manifestly tainted a criminal prosecution. In *Estes v. Texas*, 381 U.S. 532, 538 (1965), extensive publicity before trial swelled into excessive exposure during preliminary court proceedings as reporters and television crews overran the courtroom and "bombarded the community with the sights and sounds of" the pretrial hearing. The media's overzealous reporting efforts, we observed, "led to considerable disruption" and denied the "judicial serenity and calm to which Billie Sol Estes was entitled."

Similarly, in *Sheppard v. Maxwell,* 384 U.S. 333 (1966), news reporters extensively covered the story of Sam Sheppard, who was accused of bludgeoning his pregnant wife to death. "Bedlam reigned at the courthouse during the trial and newsmen took over practically the entire courtroom," thrusting jurors "into the role of celebrities." Pretrial media coverage, which we characterized as "months of virulent publicity about Sheppard and the murder," did not alone deny due process, we noted. But Sheppard's case involved more than heated reporting pretrial: We upset the murder conviction because a "carnival atmosphere" pervaded the trial.

In each of these cases, we overturned a "conviction obtained in a trial atmosphere that was utterly corrupted by press coverage"; our decisions, however, "cannot be made to stand for the proposition that juror exposure to news accounts of the crime alone presumptively deprives the defendant of due process." *Murphy v. Florida,* 421 U.S. 794, 798–799 (1975). See also, *e.g., Patton v. Yount,* 467 U.S. 1025 (1984). Prominence does not necessarily produce prejudice, and juror *impartiality,* we have reiterated, does not require *ignorance.*

Relying on *Rideau, Estes,* and *Sheppard,* Skilling asserts that we need not pause to examine the screening questionnaires or the *voir dire* before declaring his jury's verdict void. We are not persuaded. Important differences separate Skilling's prosecution from those in which we have presumed juror prejudice.

First, we have emphasized in prior decisions the size and characteristics of the community in which the crime occurred. In *Rideau,* for example, we noted that the murder was committed in a parish of only 150,000 residents. Houston, in contrast, is the fourth most populous city in the Nation: At the time of Skilling's trial, more than 4.5 million individuals eligible for jury duty resided in the Houston area. Given this large, diverse pool of potential jurors, the suggestion that 12 impartial individuals could not be empanelled is hard to sustain.[15] See *Mu'Min v. Virginia,* 500 U.S. 415, 429 (1991); *Gentile v. State Bar of Nev.,* 501 U.S. 1030, 1044 (1991) (plurality opinion).

Second, although news stories about Skilling were not kind, they contained no confession or other blatantly prejudicial information of the type readers or viewers could not reasonably be expected to shut from sight. Rideau's dramatically staged admission of guilt, for instance, was likely imprinted indelibly in the mind of anyone who watched it. Pretrial publicity about Skilling was less memorable

---

[15] According to a survey commissioned by Skilling in conjunction with his first motion for a venue change, only 12.3% of Houstonians named him when asked to list Enron executives they believed guilty of crimes. In response to the follow-up question "what words come to mind when you hear the name Jeff Skilling?", two-thirds of respondents failed to say a single negative word: 43% either had never heard of Skilling or stated that nothing came to mind when they heard his name, and another 23% knew Skilling's name was associated with Enron but reported no opinion about him.

and prejudicial. No evidence of the smoking-gun variety invited prejudgment of his culpability.

Third, unlike cases in which trial swiftly followed a widely reported crime, over four years elapsed between Enron's bankruptcy and Skilling's trial. Although reporters covered Enron-related news throughout this period, the decibel level of media attention diminished somewhat in the years following Enron's collapse.

Finally, and of prime significance, Skilling's jury acquitted him of nine insider-trading counts. Similarly, earlier instituted Enron-related prosecutions yielded no overwhelming victory for the Government. In *Rideau, Estes,* and *Sheppard,* in marked contrast, the jury's verdict did not undermine in any way the supposition of juror bias. It would be odd for an appellate court to presume prejudice in a case in which jurors' actions run counter to that presumption.

Skilling's trial, in short, shares little in common with those in which we approved a presumption of juror prejudice. The Fifth Circuit reached the opposite conclusion based primarily on the magnitude and negative tone of media attention directed at Enron. But "pretrial publicity—even pervasive, adverse publicity—does not inevitably lead to an unfair trial." *Nebraska Press Assn. v. Stuart,* 427 U.S. 539, 554 (1976). In this case, news stories about Enron did not present the kind of vivid, unforgettable information we have recognized as particularly likely to produce prejudice, and Houston's size and diversity diluted the media's impact.[17]

Nor did Enron's "sheer number of victims," trigger a presumption of prejudice. Although the widespread community impact necessitated careful identification and inspection of prospective jurors' connections to Enron, the extensive screening questionnaire and follow-up *voir dire* were well suited to that task. And hindsight shows the efficacy of these devices; jurors' links to Enron were either nonexistent or attenuated.

Finally, although a codefendant's "well-publicized decision to plead guilty" shortly before trial created a danger of juror prejudice, the District Court took appropriate steps to reduce that risk. The court delayed the proceedings by two weeks, lessening the immediacy of that development. And during *voir dire,* the court asked about prospective jurors' exposure to recent publicity, including news regarding the codefendant. Only two venire members recalled the plea; neither mentioned the codefendant by name, and neither ultimately served on Skilling's jury. Although publicity about a codefendant's guilty plea calls for inquiry to guard against actual prejudice, it does not ordinarily—and, we are satisfied, it did not here—warrant an automatic presumption of prejudice.

---

[17] Data submitted by Skilling in support of his first motion for a venue transfer suggested that a slim percentage of Enron-related stories specifically named him[.]

Persuaded that no presumption arose, we conclude that the District Court, in declining to order a venue change, did not exceed constitutional limitations.

We next consider whether actual prejudice infected Skilling's jury. *Voir dire,* Skilling asserts, did not adequately detect and defuse juror bias. "The record affirmatively confirms" prejudice, he maintains, because several seated jurors "prejudged his guilt." We disagree with Skilling's characterization of the *voir dire* and the jurors selected through it.

No hard-and-fast formula dictates the necessary depth or breadth of *voir dire.* Jury selection, we have repeatedly emphasized, is "particularly within the province of the trial judge." *Ristaino v. Ross,* 424 U.S. 589, 594–595 (1976). Appellate courts making after-the-fact assessments of the media's impact on jurors should be mindful that their judgments lack the on-the-spot comprehension of the situation possessed by trial judges.

Reviewing courts are properly resistant to second-guessing the trial judge's estimation of a juror's impartiality, for that judge's appraisal is ordinarily influenced by a host of factors impossible to capture fully in the record—among them, the prospective juror's inflection, sincerity, demeanor, candor, body language, and apprehension of duty. In contrast to the cold transcript received by the appellate court, the in-the-moment *voir dire* affords the trial court a more intimate and immediate basis for assessing a venire member's fitness for jury service. We consider the adequacy of jury selection in Skilling's case, therefore, attentive to the respect due to district-court determinations of juror impartiality and of the measures necessary to ensure that impartiality.

Skilling deems the *voir dire* insufficient because, he argues, jury selection lasted "just five hours," "most of the court's questions were conclusory, high-level, and failed adequately to probe jurors' true feelings," and the court "consistently took prospective jurors at their word once they claimed they could be fair, no matter what other indications of bias were present." Our review of the record, however, yields a different appraisal.

The District Court initially screened venire members by eliciting their responses to a comprehensive questionnaire drafted in large part by Skilling. That survey helped to identify prospective jurors excusable for cause and served as a springboard for further questions put to remaining members of the array. *Voir dire* thus was, in the court's words, the "culmination of a lengthy process." In other Enron-related prosecutions, District Courts, after inspecting venire members' responses to questionnaires, completed the jury-selection process within one day.

The District Court conducted *voir dire,* moreover, aware of the greater-than-normal need, due to pretrial publicity, to ensure against jury bias. At Skilling's urging, the court examined each prospective juror individually, thus preventing the spread of any prejudicial information to other venire members. To encourage candor, the court repeatedly admonished that there were "no right and wrong answers to the questions." The court denied Skilling's request for attorney-led *voir dire* because, in its experience, potential jurors were "more forthcoming" when the court, rather than counsel, asked the question. The parties, however, were accorded an opportunity to ask follow-up questions of every prospective juror brought to the bench for colloquy. Skilling's counsel declined to ask anything of more than half of the venire members questioned individually, including eight eventually selected for the jury, because, he explained, "the Court and other counsel have covered" everything he wanted to know.

Inspection of the questionnaires and *voir dire* of the individuals who actually served as jurors satisfies us that, notwithstanding the flaws Skilling lists, the selection process successfully secured jurors who were largely untouched by Enron's collapse. Eleven of the seated jurors and alternates reported no connection at all to Enron, while all other jurors reported at most an insubstantial link. As for pretrial publicity, jurors and alternates specifically stated that they had paid scant attention to Enron-related news. The remaining two jurors indicated that nothing in the news influenced their opinions about Skilling.

The questionnaires confirmed that, whatever community prejudice existed in Houston generally, Skilling's jurors were not under its sway. Although many expressed sympathy for victims of Enron's bankruptcy and speculated that greed contributed to the corporation's collapse, these sentiments did not translate into animus toward Skilling. When asked whether they "had an opinion about Jeffrey Skilling," none of the seated jurors and alternates checked the "yes" box. And in response to the question whether "any opinion they may have formed regarding Enron or Skilling would prevent" their impartial consideration of the evidence at trial, every juror—despite options to mark "yes" or "unsure"—instead checked "no."

The District Court, Skilling asserts, should not have "accepted at face value jurors' promises of fairness." In *Irvin v. Dowd*, 366 U.S. at 727–728, Skilling points out, we found actual prejudice despite jurors' assurances that they could be impartial. We disagree. The facts of *Irvin* are worlds apart from those presented here. Leslie Irvin stood accused of a brutal murder and robbery spree in a small rural community. In the months before Irvin's trial, "a barrage" of publicity was "unleashed against him," including reports of his confessions to the slayings and robberies. "Newspapers in which these stories appeared were delivered regularly to 95% of the dwellings in" the county where the trial occurred, which had a population of only 30,000; "radio and TV stations, which likewise blanketed that county, also carried extensive newscasts covering the same incidents." In this case, news stories about Enron contained nothing resembling the horrifying information rife in reports about Irvin's rampage of robberies and murders. Of key importance, Houston shares little in common with the rural community in which Irvin's trial proceeded, and circulation figures for Houston media sources were far lower than the 95% saturation level recorded in *Irvin*. Skilling's seated jurors, moreover, exhibited nothing like the display of bias shown in *Irvin*. In light of these large differences, the District Court had far less reason than did the trial court in *Irvin* to discredit jurors' promises of fairness.

The District Court, moreover, did not simply take venire members who proclaimed their impartiality at their word. As noted, all of Skilling's jurors had already affirmed on their questionnaires that they would have no trouble basing a verdict only on the evidence at trial. Nevertheless, the court followed up with each individually to uncover concealed bias. This face-to-face opportunity to gauge demeanor and credibility, coupled with information from the questionnaires regarding jurors' backgrounds, opinions, and sources of news, gave the court a sturdy foundation to assess fitness for jury service. The jury's not-guilty verdict on nine insider-trading counts after nearly five days of deliberation, meanwhile, suggests the court's assessments were accurate. Skilling, we conclude, failed to show that his *voir dire* fell short of constitutional requirements.

In sum, Skilling failed to establish that a presumption of prejudice arose or that actual bias infected the jury that tried him. Jurors, the trial court correctly comprehended, need not enter the box with empty heads in order to determine the facts impartially. "It is sufficient if the jurors can lay aside their impressions or opinions and render a verdict based on the evidence presented in court." Taking account of the full record, rather than incomplete exchanges selectively culled from it, we find no cause to upset the lower courts' judgment that Skilling's jury met that measure. We therefore affirm the Fifth Circuit's ruling that Skilling received a fair trial.

For the foregoing reasons, we affirm the Fifth Circuit's ruling on Skilling's fair-trial argument.

It is so ordered.

Justice Sotomayor, with whom Justice Stevens and Justice Breyer join, concurring in part and dissenting in part.

I dissent from the Court's conclusion that Jeffrey Skilling received a fair trial before an impartial jury. The more intense the public's antipathy toward a defendant, the more careful a court must be to prevent that sentiment from tainting the jury. In this case, passions ran extremely high. The sudden collapse of Enron directly affected thousands of people in the Houston area and shocked the entire community. As Enron's one-time CEO, Skilling was at the center of the storm. Even if these extraordinary circumstances did not constitutionally compel a change of venue, they required the District Court to conduct a thorough *voir dire* in which prospective jurors' attitudes about the case were closely scrutinized. The District Court's inquiry lacked the necessary thoroughness and left serious doubts about whether the jury empanelled to decide Skilling's case was capable of rendering an impartial decision based solely on the evidence presented in the courtroom.

Local media coverage of the story saturated the community. The *Houston Chronicle*—the area's leading newspaper—assigned as many as 12 reporters to work on the Enron story full time. The paper mentioned Enron in more than 4,000 articles during the 3-year period following the company's bankruptcy filing. Hundreds of articles discussed Skilling by name. Many stories conveyed and amplified the community's outrage at the top executives perceived to be responsible for the company's bankruptcy. There were also articles expressing sympathy toward and solidarity with the company's many victims. Skilling's media expert counted nearly a hundred victim-related stories in the Chronicle which poignantly described the gut-wrenching experiences of former employees who lost vast sums of money, faced eviction from their homes, could not afford Christmas gifts for their children, and felt "scared," "hurt," "humiliated," "helpless," and "betrayed." More than one-third of the prospective jurors (approximately 99 of 283, by my count) indicated that they or persons they knew had lost money or jobs as a result of the Enron bankruptcy. Two-thirds of the jurors (about 188 of 283) expressed views about Enron or the defendants that suggested a potential predisposition to convict.

As the tide of public enmity rises, so too does the danger that the prejudices of the community will infiltrate the jury. In selecting a jury, a trial court must take measures adapted to the intensity, pervasiveness, and character of the pretrial publicity and community animus. Reviewing courts, meanwhile, must assess whether the trial court's procedures sufficed under the circumstances to keep the jury free from disqualifying bias.

I agree that the prospect of seating an unbiased jury in Houston was not so remote as to compel the conclusion that the District Court acted unconstitutionally in denying Skilling's motion to change venue. However, the devastating impact of Enron's collapse and the relentless media coverage demanded exceptional care on the part of the District Court to ensure the seating of an impartial jury. While the procedures employed by the District Court might have been adequate in the typical high-profile case, they did not suffice in the extraordinary circumstances of this case to safeguard Skilling's constitutional right to a fair trial before an impartial jury. Any doubt that the prevailing mindset in the Houston community remained overwhelmingly negative was dispelled by prospective jurors' responses to the written questionnaires. More than one-third of the prospective jurors either knew victims of Enron's collapse or were victims themselves, and two-thirds gave responses suggesting an ant defendant bias. In many instances their contempt for Skilling was palpable. Only a small fraction of the prospective jurors raised no red flags in their responses. And this was *before* Causey's guilty plea and the flurry of news reports that accompanied the approach of trial. Given the extent of the antipathy evident both in the community at large and in the responses to the written questionnaire, it was critical for the District Court to take "strong measures" to ensure the selection of "an impartial jury free from outside influences." *Sheppard,* 384 U.S. at 362. The District Court's 5-hour *voir dire* was manifestly insufficient to identify and remove biased jurors. The court asked very few prospective jurors any questions directed to their knowledge of or feelings about that event.

The court also rarely asked prospective jurors to describe personal interactions they may have had about the case, or to consider whether they might have difficulty avoiding discussion of the case with family, friends, or colleagues during the course of the lengthy trial. The tidbits of information that trickled out on these subjects provided cause for concern. In response to general media-related questions, several prospective jurors volunteered that they had spoken with others about the case. The court, however, did not seek elaboration about the substance of these interactions. Surely many prospective jurors had similar conversations, particularly once they learned upon receiving the written questionnaire that they might end up on Skilling's jury.

Prospective jurors' personal interactions, moreover, may well have left them with the sense that the community was counting on a conviction. On the few occasions when prospective jurors were asked whether they would feel pressure from the public to convict, they acknowledged that it might be difficult to return home after delivering a not-guilty verdict. Most prospective jurors were asked just a few yes/no questions about their general exposure to media coverage and a handful of additional questions concerning any responses to the written questionnaire that suggested bias. The court rarely sought to draw them out with open-ended questions about their impressions of Enron or Skilling and showed limited patience for counsel's follow-up efforts.

The District Court failed to make a sufficiently critical assessment of prospective jurors' assurances of impartiality. The District Court essentially took jurors at their word when they promised to be fair. Worse still, the District Court on a number of occasions accepted declarations of impartiality that were equivocal on their face. The majority takes solace in the fact that most of the persons actually seated as jurors and alternates "specifically stated that they had paid scant attention to Enron-related news." In context, however, these general declarations reveal little about the seated jurors' actual knowledge or views. Jurors who did not "get into details" of Enron's complicated accounting schemes, nevertheless knew the outline of the oft-repeated story, including that Skilling and Lay had been cast as the leading villains.

When the District Court asked the prospective jurors as a group whether they had any reservations about their ability to presume innocence and put the Government to its proof, only two answered in the affirmative, and both were excused for cause. The District Court's individual questioning exposed disqualifying prejudices among numerous additional prospective jurors who had earlier expressed no concerns about their impartiality. It thus strikes me as highly likely that at least some of the seated jurors, despite stating that they could be fair, harbored similar biases that a more probing inquiry would likely have exposed. The majority suggests that the jury's decision to acquit Skilling on nine relatively minor insider trading charges confirms its impartiality. Jurors who act in good faith and sincerely believe in their own fairness may nevertheless harbor disqualifying prejudices.

Points for Discussion

a. More on *Irwin v. Dowd*

Consider the following language from *Irwin v. Dowd, supra*:

Although this Court has said that the Fourteenth Amendment does not demand the use of jury trials in a State's criminal procedure, every State has constitutionally provided trial by jury. In essence, the right to jury trial guarantees to the criminally accused a fair trial by a panel of impartial, "indifferent" jurors. The failure to accord an accused a fair hearing violates even the minimal standards of due process. In the ultimate analysis, only the jury can strip a man of his liberty or his life. In the language of Lord Coke, a juror must be as "indifferent as he stands unsworn." His verdict must be based upon the evidence developed at the trial. This is true, regardless of the heinousness of the crime charged, the apparent guilt of the offender or the station in life which he occupies. "The theory of the law is that a juror who has formed an opinion cannot be impartial." *Reynolds v. United States*, 98 U.S. 145, 155.

It is not required, however, that the jurors be totally ignorant of the facts and issues involved. In these days of swift, widespread and diverse methods of communication, an important case can be expected to arouse the interest of the public in the vicinity, and scarcely any of those best qualified to serve as jurors will not have formed some impression or opinion as to the merits of the case. This is particularly true in criminal cases. To hold that the mere existence of any preconceived notion as to the guilt or innocence of an accused, without more, is sufficient to rebut the presumption of a prospective juror's impartiality would be to establish an impossible standard. It is sufficient if the juror can lay aside his impression or opinion and render a verdict based on the evidence presented in court.

b. The Judicial Duty

When pretrial publicity threatens to prejudice a trial, the trial judge has a duty to ensure that prospective jurors have not formed preconceptions of the defendant's guilt. In *Mu'Min v. Virginia*, 500 U.S. 415 (1991), 8 of the 12 persons sworn as jurors answered on *voir dire* that they had read or heard something about the case. The defendant argued that his Sixth Amendment right to an impartial jury and his right to due process under the Fourteenth Amendment were violated because the trial judge refused to question further prospective jurors about the specific content of the news reports to which they had been exposed. Citing *Patton v. Yount* and *Irwin v. Dowd*, the Court found that it was sufficient for a trial judge to ask a panel of prospective jurors collectively and in groups of four whether they had formed opinions based on publicity.

Hypo 1: *Seating an Unbiased Jury*

How is it possible to get an unbiased jury in a case that generates extensive national publicity? Numerous examples abound of cases in which there has been excessive press coverage. Examples include the Rodney King case in which news organizations played videos of the beating over and over to a national and international audience, and the O.J. Simpson case received obsessive national attention. Does the fact that both trials resulted in not guilty verdicts (at least, the first Rodney King verdict was "not guilty") suggest that jurors can retain their independence despite extensive press coverage? Do those verdicts suggest that the press may have less impact than we suspect?

Hypo 2: *Docudrama and Change of Venue*

In one month, the National Broadcasting Company (NBC) plans to air a "docudrama" entitled "The Billionaire Boys Club." The docudrama portrays Joe Bobson planning and committing a murder, and suggests a possible motive for the murder. In addition, the docudrama show Bobson's involvement with a social group referred to as the "Billionaire Boys Club," and portrays "Bobson's personality, activities, and business affairs in ways that further connect him to this murder." Bobson has already been convicted of murdering one person, and is about to stand trial for the murder depicted in the docudrama. Bobson believes that the film will severely prejudice his right to a fair trial in the second case. In addition, since Bobson's conviction in the first case is on appeal, Bobson worries that the airing of the docudrama will prejudice his right to a fair trial in that case should it be retried. Suppose that you are Bobson's attorney in the criminal trial. What steps might you to take to ensure Bobson's right to a fair trial?

Hypo 3: *The Obligation to Voir Dire*

Defendants were charged with engaging in a pattern of racketeering activity involving participation in the "Chicago Outfit"—the long-running lineal descendant of Al Capone's gang—and engaging in extortion, obstruction of justice, and other crimes. In order to protect the jury, the judge granted jury members anonymity. The notoriety of the Outfit guaranteed extensive press coverage, resulting in such tidbits as an interview with the government's mob expert, name-calling by a victim's brother, a story that Marcello had been "humiliated" by his mistress's testimony, and an opinion piece saying that the jurors would be "basically stupid" if they didn't convict the defendants. The judge told the jurors not to pay attention to the media and not to do research on their own. As a result, the judge refused to *voir dire* the jury each time a new article was published. In the absence of evidence that jurors have disobeyed his orders, is a judge required to *voir dire* the jury after every inflammatory article is published? *See United States v. Schiro*, 679 F. 3d 521 (7th Cir. 2012).

C. Gagging the Press

Nebraska Press Association v. Stuart

427 U.S. 539 (1976).

MR. CHIEF JUSTICE BURGER delivered the opinion of the Court.

The respondent judge entered an order restraining the petitioners from publishing or broadcasting accounts of confessions or admission made by the accused or facts "strongly implicative" of the accused in a widely reported murder of six persons. We granted certiorari to decide whether the entry of such an order on the showing made before the state court violated the constitutional guarantee of freedom of the press.

On the evening of October 18, 1975, local police found the six members of the Henry Kellie family murdered in their home in Sutherland, Neb., a town of about 850 people. Police released the description of a suspect, Erwin Charles Simants, to the reporters who had hastened to the scene of the crime. Simants was arrested and arraigned in Lincoln County Court the following morning, ending a tense night for this small rural community.

The crime immediately attracted widespread news coverage, by local, regional, and national newspapers, radio and television stations. Three days after the crime, the County Attorney and Simants' attorney joined in asking the County Court to enter a restrictive order relating to "matters that may or may not be publicly reported or disclosed to the public," because of the "mass coverage by news media" and the "reasonable likelihood of prejudicial news which would make difficult, if not impossible, the impaneling of an impartial jury and tend to prevent a fair trial." The County Court heard oral argument but took no evidence; no attorney for members of the press appeared at this stage. The County Court granted the prosecutor's motion for a restrictive order and entered it the next day, October 22. The order prohibited everyone in attendance from "releasing or authorizing the release for public dissemination in any form or manner whatsoever any testimony given or evidence adduced"; the order also required members of the press to observe the Nebraska Bar-Press Guidelines.

Simants' preliminary hearing was held the same day, open to the public but subject to the order. The County Court bound over the defendant for trial to the State District Court. The charges, as amended to reflect the autopsy findings, were that Simants had committed the murders in the course of a sexual assault.

Petitioners—several press and broadcast associations, publishers, and individual reporters—moved on October 23 for leave to intervene in the District Court, asking that the restrictive order imposed by the County Court be vacated. The District Court conducted a hearing, at which the County Judge testified and newspaper articles about the *Simants* case were admitted in evidence. The District Judge granted petitioners' motion to intervene and, on October 27, entered his own restrictive order. The judge found "because of the nature of the crimes charged in the complaint that there is a clear and present danger that pre-trial publicity could impinge upon the defendant's right to a fair trial." The order applied only until the jury was impaneled, and specifically prohibited petitioners from reporting five subjects: (1) the existence or contents of a confession Simants had made to law enforcement officers, which had been introduced in open court at arraignment; (2) the fact or nature of statements Simants had made to other persons; (3) the contents of a note he had written the night of the crime;

(4) certain aspects of the medical testimony at the preliminary hearing; and (5) the identity of the victims of the alleged sexual assault and the nature of the assault. It also prohibited reporting the exact nature of the restrictive order itself. Like the County Court's order, this order incorporated the Nebraska Bar-Press Guidelines. Finally, the order set out a plan for attendance, seating, and court-house traffic control during the trial.

The thread running through earlier cases is that prior restraints on speech and publication are the most serious and the least tolerable infringement on First Amendment rights. A criminal penalty or a judgment in a defamation case is subject to the whole panoply of protections afforded by deferring the impact of the judgment until all avenues of appellate review have been exhausted. Only after judgment has become final, correct or otherwise, does the law's sanction become fully operative.

A prior restraint, by contrast and by definition, has an immediate and irreversible sanction. If it can be said that a threat of criminal or civil sanctions after publication "chills" speech, prior restraint "freezes" it at least for the time. The damage can be particularly great when the prior restraint falls upon the communication of news and commentary on current events. Truthful reports of public judicial proceedings have been afforded special protection against subsequent punishment.

We turn now to the record in this case to determine whether, as Learned Hand put it, "the gravity of the 'evil,' discounted by its improbability, justifies such invasion of free speech as is necessary to avoid the danger." To do so, we must examine the evidence before the trial judge when the order was entered to determine (a) the nature and extent of pretrial news coverage; (b) whether other measures would be likely to mitigate the effects of unrestrained pretrial publicity; and (c) how effectively a restraining order would operate to prevent the threatened danger. The precise terms of the restraining order are also important. We must then consider whether the record supports the entry of a prior restraint on publication, one of the most extraordinary remedies known to our jurisprudence.

Our review of the pretrial record persuades us that the trial judge was justified in concluding that there would be intense and pervasive pretrial publicity concerning this case. He could also reasonably conclude, based on common man experience, that publicity might impair the defendant's right to a fair trial. He did not purport to say more, for he found only "a clear and present danger that pre-trial publicity *could* impinge upon the defendant's right to a fair trial." (Emphasis added.) His conclusion as to the impact of such publicity on prospective jurors was of necessity speculative, dealing as he was with factors unknown and unknowable.

We find little in the record that goes to another aspect of our task, determining whether measures short of an order retraining all publication would have insured the defendant a fair trial. Although the entry of the order might be read as a judicial determination that other measures would not suffice, the trial court made no express findings to that effect; the Nebraska Supreme Court referred to the issue only by implication.

Most of the alternatives to prior restraint of publication in these circumstances were discussed with obvious approval in *Sheppard v. Maxwell*: (a) change of trial venue to a place less exposed to the intense publicity that seemed imminent in Lincoln County; (b) postponement of the trial to allow public attention to subside; (c) searching questioning of prospective jurors, as Mr. Chief Justice Marshall used in the Aaron Burr Case, to screen out those with fixed opinions as to guilt or innocence; (d) the use of emphatic and clear instructions on the sworn duty of each juror to decide the issues only on evidence presented in open court. Sequestration of jurors is, of course, always available. Although that measure insulates jurors only after they are sworn, it also enhances the likelihood of dissipating the impact of pretrial publicity and emphasizes the elements of the jurors' oaths.

We must also assess the probable efficacy of prior restraint on publication as a workable method of protecting Simants' right to a fair trial, and we cannot ignore the reality of the problems of managing and enforcing pretrial restraining orders. The territorial jurisdiction of the issuing court is limited by concepts of sovereignty. The need for *in personam* jurisdiction also presents an obstacle to a restraining order that applies to publication at large as distinguished from restraining publication within a given jurisdiction.

The events disclosed by the record took place in a community of 850 people. It is reasonable to assume that, without any news accounts being printed or broadcast, rumors would travel swiftly by word of mouth. One can only speculate on the accuracy of such reports, given the generative propensities of rumors; they could well be more damaging than reasonably accurate news accounts. But plainly a whole community cannot be restrained from discussing a subject intimately affecting life within it.

Given these practical problems, it is far from clear that prior restraint on publication would have protected Simants' rights.

MR. JUSTICE BRENNAN, with whom MR. JUSTICE STEWART and MR. JUSTICE MARSHALL join, concurring in the judgment.

The right to a fair trial by a jury of one's peers is unquestionably one of the most precious and sacred safeguards enshrined in the Bill of Rights. I would hold, however, that resort to prior restraints on the freedom of the press is a constitutionally impermissible method for enforcing that right; judges have at their disposal a broad spectrum of devices for ensuring that fundamental fairness is accorded the accused without necessitating so drastic an incursion on the equally fundamental and salutary constitutional mandate that discussion of public affairs in a free society cannot depend on the preliminary grace of judicial censors.

Points for Discussion

a. The Heavy Presumption Against Gag Orders

Restraining the press from reporting on judicial proceedings is a method for protecting the defendant's right to a fair trial. However, gag orders implicate First Amendment interests. As a preemptive restriction upon expression, such methods trigger the "heavy presumption" that exists against the constitutionality of "any system of prior restraint." *New York Times Co. v. United States*, 403 U.S. 713, 714 (1971) (per curiam). They also impose upon government "a heavy burden of justification." Given the constitutional interest that is present, when the goal is ensuring a fair trial, compelling regulatory interests are identifiable at least in the abstract. The Court has established standards allowing gag orders, but not when the risks to a fair trial are merely speculative but only when those risks are demonstrable. Even then, prior restraint is permissible, they can be imposed only after methods less burdensome to First Amendment interests have been found inapt.

b. Juror Sequestration

Critics of prior restraint analysis fault the Court for exalting form over substantive values and risks. *See, e.g.*, James Calvin Jeffries, Jr., *Rethinking Prior Restraint*, 92 Yale L.J. 409 (1983). Insofar as the doctrinal deck is stacked in favor of First Amendment interests, concern with the deficiencies of less restrictive alternatives predictably magnifies. Questions have been raised with respect to whether sequestration, especially in lengthy trials, breeds a state of mind that is inimical to fairness. *See, e.g.*, Bernard P. Bell, *Closure of Pretrial Suppression Hearings: Resolving the Free Trial/Free Press Conflict*, 51 Fordham L. Rev. 1297, 1315 (1983) (noting costs and burdens of sequestration and potential for causing "juror resentment"). Even if the formalities of prior restraint were subtracted from the analysis, it is reasonable to assume that review still would be probing.

> **Food for Thought**
>
> In a number of other countries (England and Canada), the courts restrict press coverage of pending criminal matters through the contempt power. *See* Geoffrey Robertson & Andrew G.L. Nicol, Media Law: The Rights of Journalists and Broadcasters 161–85 (3d ed. 1992); *see also* David A. Anderson, *Democracy and the Demystification of Courts: An Essay*, Rev. Litig. 627, 639 (1995). Should U.S. courts be equally free to restrict such coverage?

Because profound interests of self-governance vie against fair trial concerns, as they do when access is at issue, logic ordains that review be no less searching than when closure is at stake.

Hypo: *More on Gag Orders*

Defendants are being prosecuted for corruption in a case involving allegations that some defendants had bribed elected legislative representatives. The case generated very substantial media coverage, including a live blog and Twitter feed. Prosecutors had significant interactions with the press during the pretrial phase of the proceeding: a prosecutor held a press conference to announce the indictment; a prosecutor tipped the press off to the fact that defendant was going to be arrested at his home; and a prosecutor issued press releases when two of the defendants pled guilty. Attorneys for some defendants were particularly vocal during the first trial, and would talk to the press as they left the courthouse on a daily basis. During these news conferences, the attorneys would comment on the credibility of the witnesses, discuss trial strategy, and speculate as to the cooperating witnesses' motives in testifying. Updates concerning the trial were posted by the media on an almost minute-by-minute basis. One particular revelation at the first trial garnered national media attention (allegedly racist comments made by some elected officials about African-American voters). At the first trial, the trial court tried to minimize jurors' exposure to the media by designating an area outside the courthouse for the media, and by instructing jurors to enter and exit the courthouse from the other side of the building. The court also set up an over-flow room where journalists could watch the court proceedings via closed-circuit video; no televised images of the trial aired publicly. Once the jury panel was selected, the court issued preliminary jury instructions ordering jurors scrupulously to avoid media coverage of the trial. In the six months between the first trial and the retrial, the case remained a prominent feature of Alabama politics. A state senator cited his participation in the case in his primary campaign to unseat an incumbent member of the United States House of Representatives, and sent out anti-gambling campaign literature. For the retrial, *voir dire* focused extensively on potential jurors' knowledge of the first trial, but the jury was sequestered and jurors were instructed not to view media coverage about the trial. Shortly before the retrial, the government has moved for a gag order which would provide that "apart from court hearings or filings, no participating attorney or any member of their trial team shall make any extrajudicial comments about questions, or commentary." Thus, the attorneys could not inform the press that a specific witness would be testifying the next day or direct the press to examine a recent filing. If you are the judge, should you grant the gag order? *See United States v. McGregor*, 838 F.Supp.2d 1256 (M.D. Ala. March 14, 2012).

D. Press Access to Judicial Proceedings

Even though the courts cannot prohibit the press from reporting on a trial, must the courts give the press access to the proceeding? Trials themselves historically have been open to the press and public, and the Court has established a presumption in favor of access. *Globe Newspaper Co. v. Superior Court*, 457 U.S. 596, 607 (1982). Tradition, however, has not always cut in favor of open preliminary proceedings. In *Gannett, Inc. v. DePasquale*, 443 U.S. 368, 394 (1979), the Court upheld a trial judge's order closing a suppression hearing at the defendant's request. The outcome in *Gannett* reflected an understanding that the Sixth Amendment guarantee of a public trial accrued not to the press or public but to the defendants. The decision's bottom line was that the Sixth Amendment established no constitutional right for the press or public to attend a criminal trial. The determination rested on the premise that "that the public interest is fully protected by the participants in the litigation."

One year after *Gannett*, a defendant's motion to close a trial was defeated by First Amendment concerns. In *Richmond Newspapers, Inc. v. Virginia*, 448 U.S. 555 (1980), opinions by eight justices endorsed the notion of an access right for the press and public even over the defendant's objections. Chief Justice Burger, stressing the presumptive openness of criminal trials, observed that the right to attend such proceedings "is implicit in guarantees of the First Amendment; without the freedom to attend such trials, which people have exercised for centuries, important aspects of freedom of speech and of the press could be eviscerated." Consistent with established First Amendment doctrine, access to trials was configured coextensively for the press and public.

Globe Newspaper Co. v. Superior Court

457 U.S. 596 (1982).

JUSTICE BRENNAN delivered the opinion of the Court.

Section 16A of Chapter 278 of the Massachusetts General Laws, as construed by the Massachusetts Supreme Judicial Court, requires trial judges, at trials for specific sexual offenses involving a victim under the age of 18, to exclude the press and general public from the courtroom during the testimony of that victim. The question presented is whether the statute thus construed violates the First Amendment as applied to the States through the Fourteenth Amendment.

The Court's recent decision in *Richmond Newspapers* firmly established for the first time that the press and general public have a constitutional right of access to criminal trials. Of course, this right of access to criminal trials is not explicitly mentioned in terms in the First Amendment. But we have long eschewed any "narrow, literal conception" of the Amendment's terms, for the Framers were concerned with broad principles, and wrote against a background of shared values and practices. The First Amendment is thus broad enough to encompass those rights that, while not unambiguously enumerated in the very terms of the Amendment, are nonetheless necessary to the enjoyment of other First Amendment rights. Thus to the extent that the First Amendment embraces a right of access to criminal trials, it is to ensure that this constitutionally protected "discussion of governmental affairs" is an informed one.

Two features of the criminal justice system, emphasized in the various opinions in *Richmond Newspapers*, serve to explain why a right of access to criminal trials in particular is properly afforded protection by the First Amendment. First, the criminal trial historically has been open to the press and general public. "At the time when our organic laws were adopted, criminal trials both here and in England had long been presumptively open." Since that time, the presumption of openness has remained secure. Indeed, at the time of this Court's decision in *In re Oliver*, the presumption was so solidly grounded that the Court was "unable to find a single instance of a criminal trial conducted in camera in any federal, state, or municipal court during the history of this country." This uniform rule of openness has been viewed as significant in constitutional terms not only "because the Constitution carries the gloss of history," but also because "a tradition of accessibility implies the favorable judgment of experience."

Second, the right of access to criminal trials plays a particularly significant role in the functioning of the judicial process and the government as a whole. Public scrutiny of a criminal trial enhances the quality and safeguards the integrity of the fact-finding process, with benefits to both the defendant and to society as a whole. Moreover, public access to the criminal trial fosters an appearance of fairness, thereby heightening public respect for the judicial process. And in the broadest terms, public access to criminal trials permits the public to participate in and serve as a check upon the judicial process—an essential component in our structure of self-government. In sum, the institutional value of the open criminal trial is recognized in both logic and experience.

Although the right of access to criminal trials is of constitutional stature, it is not absolute. But the circumstances under which the press and public can be barred from a criminal trial are limited; the State's justification in denying access must be a weighty one. Where, as in the present case, the State attempts to deny the right of access in order to inhibit the disclosure of sensitive information, it must be shown that the denial is necessitated by a compelling governmental interest, and is narrowly tailored to serve that interest.

The state interests asserted to support § 16A, though articulated in various ways, are reducible to two: the protection of minor victims of sex crimes from further trauma and embarrassment; and the encouragement of such victims to come forward and testify in a truthful and credible manner. We consider these interests in turn.

We agree with appellee that the first interest—safeguarding the physical and psychological well-being of a minor—is a compelling one. But as compelling as that interest is, it does not justify a *mandatory* closure rule, for it is clear that the circumstances of the particular case may affect the significance of the interest. A trial court can determine on a case-by-case basis whether closure is necessary to protect the welfare of a minor victim. Among the factors to be weighed are the minor victim's age, psychological maturity and understanding, the nature of the crime, the desires of the victim, and the interests of parents and relatives. Section 16A, in contrast, requires closure even if the victim does not seek the exclusion of the press and general public and would not suffer injury by their presence.

Nor can § 16A be justified on the basis of the Commonwealth's second asserted interest—the encouragement of minor victims of sex crimes to come forward and provide accurate testimony. The Commonwealth has offered no empirical support for the claim that the rule of automatic closure contained in § 16A bars the press and general public from the courtroom during the testimony of minor sex victims, the press is not denied access to the transcript, court personnel, or another possible source that could provide an account of the minor victim's testimony. Thus § 16A cannot prevent the press from publicizing the substance of a minor victim's testimony, as well as his or her identity. If the commonwealth's interest in encouraging minor victim's to come forward depends on keeping such matters secret, § 16A hardly advances that interest in an effective manner. And even if § 16A effectively advanced the State's interest, it is doubtful that the interest would be sufficient to overcome the constitutional attack, for that same interest could be relied on to support an array of mandatory closure rules designed to encourage victims to come forward: Surely it cannot be suggested that minor victims of sex crimes are the *only* crime victims who, because of publicity attendant to criminal trials, are reluctant to come forward and testify. The State's argument based on this interest therefore proves too much, and runs contrary to the very foundation of the right of access recognized in *Richmond Newspapers*: namely, "that a presumption of openness inheres in the very nature of a criminal trial under our system of justice." (plurality opinion).

For the foregoing reasons, we hold that § 16A, as construed by the Massachusetts Supreme Judicial Court, violates the First Amendment to the Constitution. Accordingly, the judgment of the Massachusetts Supreme Judicial Court is *Reversed.*

CHIEF JUSTICE BURGER, with whom JUSTICE REHNQUIST joins, dissenting.

Historically our society has gone to great lengths to protect minors *charged* with crime, particularly by prohibiting the release of the names of offenders, barring the press and public from juvenile proceedings, and sealing the records of those proceedings. Yet today the Court holds unconstitutional a state statute designed to protect not the *accused*, but the minor *victims* of sex crimes. In doing so, it advances a disturbing paradox. Although states are permitted, for example, to mandate the closure of all proceedings in order to protect a 17-year-old charged with rape, they are not permitted to require the closing of part of criminal proceedings in order to protect an innocent child who has been raped or otherwise sexually abused.

The Court has tried to make its holding a narrow one by not disturbing the authority of state legislatures to enact more narrowly drawn statutes giving trial judges the discretion to exclude the public and the press from the courtroom during the minor victim's testimony.

I also do not read the Court's opinion as foreclosing a state statute which mandates closure except in cases where the victim agrees to testify in open court. But the Court's decision is nevertheless a gross invasion of state authority and a state's duty to protect its citizens—in this case minor victims of crime. I cannot agree with the Court's expansive interpretation of our decision in *Richmond Newspapers, Inc. v. Virginia*, or its cavalier rejection of the serious interests supporting Massachusetts' mandatory closure rule. Accordingly, I dissent.

Press-Enterprise Co. v. Superior Court

478 U.S. 1 (1986).

CHIEF JUSTICE BURGER delivered the opinion of the Court.

The right to an open public trial is a shared right of the accused and the public, the common concern being the assurance of fairness. Only recently, in *Waller v. Georgia*, for example, we considered whether the defendant's Sixth Amendment right to an open trial prevented the closure of a suppression hearing over the defendant's objection. We noted that the First Amendment right of access would in most instances attach to such proceedings and that "the explicit Sixth Amendment right of the accused is no less protective of a public trial than the implicit First Amendment right of the press and public." When the defendant objects to the closure of a suppression hearing, therefore, the hearing must be open unless the party seeking to close the hearing advances an overriding interest that is likely to be prejudiced.

Here, unlike *Waller*, the right asserted is not the defendant's Sixth Amendment right to a public trial since the defendant requested a *closed* preliminary hearing. Instead, the right asserted here is that of the public under the First Amendment. The California Supreme Court concluded that the First Amendment was not implicated because the proceeding was not a criminal trial, but a preliminary hearing. However, the First Amendment question cannot be resolved solely on the label we give the event, *i.e.*, "trial" or otherwise, particularly where the preliminary hearing functions much like a full-scale trial.

In California, to bring a felon to trial, the prosecutor has a choice of securing a grand jury indictment or a finding of probable cause following a preliminary hearing. Even when the accused has been indicted by a grand jury, however, he has an absolute right to an elaborate preliminary hearing before a neutral magistrate. The accused has the right to personally appear at the hearing, to be represented by counsel, to cross-examine hostile witnesses, to present exculpatory evidence, and to exclude illegally obtained evidence. If the magistrate determines that probable cause exists, the accused is bound over for trial; such a finding leads to a guilty plea in the majority of cases.

It is true that unlike a criminal trial, the California preliminary hearing cannot result in the conviction of the accused and the adjudication is before a magistrate or other judicial officer without a jury. But these features, standing alone, do not make public access any less essential to the proper functioning of the proceedings in the overall criminal justice process. Because of its extensive scope, the preliminary hearing is often the final and most important step in the criminal proceeding.

As the California Supreme Court has stated the preliminary hearing in many cases provides "the sole occasion for public observation of the criminal justice system."

Similarly, the absence of a jury, long recognized as "an inestimable safeguard against the corrupt or overzealous prosecutor and against the complaint, biased, or eccentric judge," makes the importance of public access to a preliminary hearing even more significant. "People in an open society do not demand infallibility from their institutions, but it is difficult for them to accept what they are prohibited from observing."

Denying the transcript of a 41-day preliminary hearing would frustrate what we have characterized as the "community therapeutic value" of openness. Criminal acts, especially certain violent crimes, provoke public concern, outrage, and hostility. "When the public is aware that the law is being enforced and the criminal justice system is functioning, an outlet is provided for these understandable reactions and emotions." In sum:

> The value of openness lies in the fact that people not actually attending trials can have confidence that standards of fairness are being observed; the sure knowledge that anyone is free to attend gives assurance that established procedures are being followed and that deviations will become known. Openness thus enhances both the basic fairness of the criminal trial and the appearance of fairness so essential to public confidence in the system. *Press-Enterprise I, supra*, at 508 (emphasis in original).

We therefore conclude that the qualified First Amendment right of access to criminal proceedings applies to preliminary hearings as they are conducted in California.

Points for Discussion

a. Press Privilege?

Modern First Amendment doctrine has trumpeted the theme that the press and media have no special status or priority in accessing proceedings or information. This premise is consistent with determinations that the press has no special privilege, rooted in the First Amendment, against having to disclose sources when asked to identify them in grand jury proceedings. The Court,

Consistent with its refusal to protect functions that arguably advance the aims of press freedom in the grand jury context, the Court has resisted arguments for recognizing media access rights in various criminal justice venues and processes. Although acknowledging that freedom of the press is crucial to informed self-government, it has brooked no distinction between press and public when access to facilities or proceedings is at stake. Questions of access have arisen most notably in the context of prisons, pretrial proceedings and trials. The common constitutional denominator in each of those settings is a refusal to set separate standards for the press and public.

in *Branzburg v. Hayes*, 408 U.S. 665, 688 (1972) (plurality opinion), not only stressed that the grand jury has the "right to everyman's evidence" but repudiated the notion that the media's role as the public's proxy would be undermined if confidentiality of sources was not protected. Although the newsgathering function may be perceived as essential to effective functioning of the press, insofar as it facilitates enhanced public knowledge and understanding, the Court has been loath to develop penumbras of press freedom that might be the equivalent of what freedom of association is to freedom of speech.

b. More on Public Access to Preliminary Hearings

Nevertheless, *Press-Enterprise* emphasized the tradition of open preliminary hearings and their similarity to trials in the state. The relevance of First Amendment priorities thus was referenced not to national norms, as was the case with trials, but to state customs. At least when the nature and traditions of a preliminary hearing are congruent with a trial, it is predictable that First Amendment values will be a dominant factor. Justice Stevens criticized the ruling as inconsistent with *Gannett's* determination that the press and public have no First Amendment right to attend pretrial proceedings. Closure of pretrial hearings under *Press-Enterprise* is justifiable only if "specific findings are made that there is a substantial probability that the defendant's right to a fair trial will be prejudiced by publicity that closure would prevent, and reasonable alternatives to closure cannot adequately protect the defendant's free trial rights." Even if those standards were satisfied and proceedings were closed, First Amendment interests would not vanish. As the *Gannett* Court itself indicated, the judge must provide a transcript of the proceeding when the risk of prejudice abates. *Gannett Co., Inc. v. DePasquale*, 443 U.S. 368, 393 (1979).

c. Public Access to *Voir Dire*

Once trumpeted, the values supporting open trials invariably exerted pressure against the logic of *Gannett* in the pretrial context. Several decisions over the course of the 1980s significantly broadened the scope of access in pretrial proceedings. In *Press-Enterprise Co. v. Superior Court (I)*, the Court extended the First Amendment zone of interest to include *voir dire*. *Press-Enterprise Co. v. Superior Court*, 464 U.S. 501, 505–10 (1984). Finding that jury selection in criminal trials was presumptively

Take Note

In *Presley v. Georgia*, 558 U.S. 209 (2010), the Court held that trial courts must consider alternatives to closing courtrooms during *voir dire*, even if no one identifies the nature of such alternatives, because the "public has a right to be present whether or not any party has asserted the right" and "trial courts are obligated to take every reasonable measure to accommodate public attendance at criminal trials."

open, the Court stressed the public interest in openness referenced in *Globe Newspaper* and *Richmond Newspapers*. Consistent with those decisions, it also noted that the presumption against closure could be overcome only by a higher interest and narrowly tailored method.

Hypo 1: *Closing Voir Dire*

Defendant was charged with "disorderly and disruptive conduct" when he yelled at General David Petraeus "You are trying to set a trap for us to bomb the helpless people of Iran. Aren't 750,000 deaths enough for your blood thirst?" during a Senate Foreign Relations Committee hearing. During *voir dire*, the judge asked everyone to leave the courtroom: "I'm going to ask everybody in the courtroom, just for *voir dire*, to please leave the courtroom, because I'm going to have to fill up the chairs in the back, okay. Is that okay with everybody? Not okay?" The trial judge then directed his attention to one spectator and said, "Okay. Ma'am, do you understand why you have to leave?" That unidentified spectator answered, "Yes. Thank you." The judge then explained to another spectator why he wanted to close the courtroom during *voir dire:* "Well ma'am, it's kind of hard for you to stay while we do this because I don't want to get confused as to who you are and who the jurors are. But after *voir dire* is over, you all—when the trial starts, you all are welcome to come in. Okay? It's an open court, okay. All right." Should *voir dire* have remained open to the press and the public? *See Barrows v. United States*, 15 A.3d 673 (D.C. App. 2011).

Hypo 2: *Frisk and State Employee Identification*

Prison inmate Conrad Lilly was charged with two counts of assault on a public servant. He moved to transfer his trial proceedings from the chapel courthouse at the prison to the public county courthouse. The trial judge denied the motion and Lilly pled guilty in a proceeding in the chapel. For an observer of the proceedings to get to the chapel, he or she must pass through a front gate, where one is frisked, then through two razor wire fences and three locked metal doors. A person can only gain entry with a valid state employee ID or with approval from the warden on duty. No unaccompanied minors or persons who have been released from confinement within the past two years may enter. In Lilly's case, no one was actually excluded from the proceedings. Was Lilly denied his Sixth Amendment right to a public trial? *See Lilly v. State*, 365 S.W.3d 321 (Tex. Crim. App. 2012).

Hypo 3: *Closing the Trial*

In a drug trial, suppose that a police officer who served in an undercover capacity will give testimony against the defendant. The prosecution, concerned about the safety of the witness given threats against his life, wants to close the trial. Is closure permissible during the witness' testimony? Is the trial court required to consider alternatives to closure? If so, what might they be? *See Moss v. Colvin*, 845 F.3d 516 (2nd Cir. 2017).

E. Broadcasting Legal Proceedings

Cameras in the courtroom have become a staple in state courts, but except for some experimentation in the civil context, have been disallowed at the federal level. The Judicial Conference, after overseeing an experiment with cameras in six federal districts and two courts of appeals, voted to maintain a policy against their presence. The Conference's report is set forth in M. Johnson, Federal Judicial Center, *Electronic Media Coverage of Federal Civil Proceedings, An Evaluation of the Pilot Program in Six District Courts and Two Courts of Appeals* (1994). There, a plurality of the Court concluded that televised proceedings entail "such a probability that prejudice will result that it is deemed inherently lacking in due process." *Estes v. Texas*, 381 U.S. 532, 542 (1965). In a concurring opinion of significant durability, Justice Harlan stressed the need for adaptability in the event future circumstances warranted it. As he put it

The right of access to trials and pretrial hearings does not incorporate any freedom for the media to use a particular technology to cover such proceedings. To the contrary, even as cameras and other electronic instrumentalities have become increasingly common in state courts, the judiciary still exercises considerable control over the extent (if any) to which they may be used.

Permitting television in the courtroom undeniably has mischievous potentialities for intruding upon the detached atmosphere which should always surround the judicial process. Forbidding this innovation, however, would doubtless impinge upon one of the valued attributes of our federalism by preventing the States from pursuing a novel course of procedural experimentation. My conclusion is that there is no constitutional requirement that television be allowed in the courtroom, and, at least as to a notorious criminal trial such as this one, the considerations against allowing television in the courtroom so far outweigh the countervailing factors advanced in its support as to require a holding that what was done in this case infringed the fundamental right to a fair trial assured by the Due Process Clause of the Fourteenth Amendment. Some preliminary observations are in order: All would agree, I am sure, that at its worst, television is capable of distorting the trial process so as to deprive it of fundamental fairness. Cables, kleig lights, interviews with the principal participants, commentary on their performances, "commercials" at frequent intervals, special wearing apparel and makeup for the trial participants—certainly such things would not conduce to the sound administration of justice by any acceptable standard.

Take Note

As technology reinvented the electronic instrumentalities of trial coverage, so that intrusiveness and distraction were diminished, case law veered in the direction of Justice Harlan's concurring opinion. Responding to liberalized provisions for electronic coverage of judicial proceedings, the Court in *Chandler v. Florida* repudiated the notion that cameras in the courtroom *per se* offended due process.

Chandler v. Florida

449 U.S. 560 (1981).

CHIEF JUSTICE BURGER delivered the opinion of the Court.

The question is whether, consistent with constitutional guarantees, a state may provide for radio, television, and still photographic coverage of a criminal trial for public broadcast, notwithstanding the objection of the accused.

The Florida Supreme Court concluded "that on balance there was more to be gained than lost by permitting electronic media coverage of judicial proceedings subject to standards for such coverage." The Florida court was of the view that because of the significant effect of the courts on the day-to-day lives of the citizenry, it was essential that the people have confidence in the process. It felt that broadcast coverage of trials would contribute to wider public acceptance and understanding of decisions. Consequently, after revising the 1977 guidelines to reflect its evaluation of the pilot program, the Florida Supreme Court promulgated a revised Canon 3A(7). The Canon provides:

"Subject at all times to the authority of the presiding judge to (I) control the conduct of proceedings before the court, (ii) ensure decorum and prevent distractions, and (iii) ensure the fair administration of justice in the pending cause, electronic media and still photography coverage of public judicial proceedings in the appellate and trial courts of this state shall be allowed in accordance with standards of conduct and technology promulgated by the Supreme Court of Florida."

The implementing guidelines specify in detail the kind of electronic equipment to be used and the manner of its use. For example, no more than one television camera and only one camera technician are allowed. Existing recording systems used by court reporters are used by broadcasters for audio pickup. Where more than one broadcast news organization seeks to cover a trial, the media must pool coverage. No artificial lighting is allowed. The equipment is positioned in a fixed location, and it may not be moved during trial. Videotaping equipment must be remote from the courtroom. Film, videotape, and lenses may not be changed while the court is in session. No audio recording of conferences between lawyers, between parties and counsel, or at the bench is permitted. The judge has sole and plenary discretion to exclude coverage of certain witnesses, and the jury may not be filmed. The judge has discretionary power to forbid coverage whenever satisfied that coverage may have a deleterious effect on the paramount right of the defendant to a fair trial. The Florida Supreme Court has the right to revise these rules as experience dictates, or indeed to bar all broadcast coverage or photography in courtrooms.

Appellants rely chiefly on *Estes v. Texas*, and Chief Justice Warren's separate concurring opinion in that case. They argue that the televising of criminal trials is inherently a denial of due process, and they read *Estes* as announcing a *per se* constitutional rule to that effect.

Chief Justice Warren's concurring opinion, in which he was joined by Justices Douglas and Goldberg, indeed provides some support for the appellants' position:

> "While I join the Court's opinion and agree that the televising of criminal trials is inherently a denial of due process, I desire to express additional views on why this is so. In doing this, I wish to emphasize that our condemnation of televised criminal trials is not based on generalities or abstract fears. The record in this case presents a vivid illustration of the inherent prejudice of televised criminal trials and supports our conclusion that this is the appropriate time to make a definitive appraisal of television in the courtroom."

If appellants' reading of *Estes* were correct, we would be obliged to apply that holding and reverse the judgment under review.

Justice Harlan's concurring opinion, upon which analysis of the constitutional holding of *Estes* turns, must be read as defining the scope of that holding; we conclude that *Estes* is not to be read as announcing a constitutional rule barring still photographic, radio, and television coverage in all cases and under all circumstances. It does not stand as an absolute ban on state experimentation with an evolving technology, which, in terms of modes of mass communication, was in its relative infancy in 1964, and is, even now, in a state of continuing change.

Since we are satisfied that *Estes* did not announce a constitutional rule that all photographic or broadcast coverage of criminal trials is inherently a denial of due process, we turn to consideration, as a matter of first impression, of the appellants' suggestion that we now promulgate such a *per se* rule.

Not unimportant to the position asserted by Florida and other states is the change in television technology since 1962, when Estes was tried. It is urged, and some empirical data are presented, that many of the negative factors found in *Estes*—cumbersome equipment, cables, distracting lighting, numerous camera technicians—are less substantial factors today than they were at that time.

It is also significant that safeguards have been built into the experimental programs in state courts, and into the Florida program, to avoid some of the most egregious problems envisioned by the six opinions in the *Estes* case. Florida admonishes its courts to take special pains to protect certain witnesses—for example, children, victims of sex crimes, some informants, and even the very timid witness or party—from the glare of publicity and the tensions of being "on camera."

Inherent in electronic coverage of a trial is a risk that the very awareness by the accused of the coverage and the contemplated broadcast may adversely affect the conduct of the participants and the fairness of the trial, yet leave no evidence of how the conduct or the trial's fairness was affected. Given this danger, it is significant that Florida requires that objections of the accused to coverage be heard and considered on the record by the trial court. In addition to providing a record for appellate review, a pretrial hearing enables a defendant to advance the basis of his objection to broadcast coverage and allows the trial court to define the steps necessary to minimize or eliminate the risks of prejudice to the accused. Experiments such as the one presented here may well increase the number of appeals by adding a new basis for claims to reverse, but this is a risk Florida has chosen to take after preliminary experimentation. Here, the record does not indicate that appellants requested an evidentiary hearing to show adverse impact or injury. Nor does the record reveal anything more than generalized allegations of prejudice.

To say that the appellants have not demonstrated that broadcast coverage is inherently a denial of due process is not to say that the appellants were in fact accorded all of the protections of due process in their trial. As noted earlier, a defendant has the right on review to show that the media's coverage of his case—printed or broadcast—compromised the ability of the jury to judge him fairly. Alternatively, a defendant might show that broadcast coverage of his particular case had an adverse impact on the trial participants sufficient to constitute a denial of due process. Neither showing was made in this case.

To demonstrate prejudice in a specific case a defendant must show something more than juror awareness that the trial is such as to attract the attention of broadcasters. No doubt the very presence of a camera in the courtroom made the jurors aware that the trial was thought to be of sufficient interest to the public to warrant coverage. Jurors, forbidden to watch all broadcasts, would have had no way of knowing that only fleeting seconds of the proceeding would be reproduced. But the appellants have not attempted to show with any specificity that the presence of cameras impaired the ability of the jurors to decide the case on only the evidence before them or that their trial was affected adversely by the impact on any of the participants of the presence of cameras and the prospect of broadcast.

Although not essential to our holding, we note that at *voir dire*, the jurors were asked if the presence of the camera would in any way compromise their ability to consider the case. Each answered that the camera would not prevent him or her from considering the case solely on the merits. The trial court instructed the jurors not to watch television accounts of the trial, and the appellants do not contend that any juror violated this instruction. The appellants have offered no evidence that any participant in this case was affected by the presence of cameras. In short, there is no showing that the trial was compromised by television coverage, as was the case in *Estes*.

Point for Discussion

Cameras in Federal Court Proceedings

Despite upholding broadcast and photographic coverage of criminal proceedings in a state court, Federal Rule of Criminal Procedure 53 states that such activity "shall not be permitted" in federal courtrooms. In *United States v. Moussaoui*, 205 F.R.D. 183 (E.D.Va. 2002), Court TV unsuccessfully sought to intervene in order to record and telecast the pretrial and trial proceedings:

Since *Chandler*, and notwithstanding federal repudiation of cameras following an experimentation period from 1991–94, electronic coverage has become common in state proceedings. At least 47 states allow cameras in their courtrooms.

The words "shall not be permitted" make clear that this rule is mandatory, leaving the Court with no discretion to ignore the categorical ban. Nor can Rule 53 be rewritten or finessed through technical hairsplitting.

Advances in broadcast technology have created new threats to the integrity of the fact finding process. The traditional public spectator or media representative who attends a federal criminal trial leaves the courtroom with his or her memory of the proceedings and any notes he or she may have taken. These spectators do not leave with a permanent photograph. However, once a witness' testimony has been televised, the witness' face has not just been publicly observed, it has also become eligible for preservation by VCR or DVD recording, digitizing by the new generation of cameras or permanent placement on Internet web sites and chat rooms. Today, it is not so much the small, discrete cameras or microphones in the courtroom that are likely to intimidate witnesses, rather, it is the witness' knowledge that his or her face or voice may be forever publicly known and available to anyone in the world.

As the United States argues, this intimidation could lead foreign prosecution witnesses, outside the jurisdiction of the Court, to refuse to testify or withhold their full testimony out of reasonable fears for their personal safety. It could similarly lead witnesses favorable to the defense to refrain from coming forward for fear of being ostracized. The permanent preservation of images of law enforcement witnesses could also jeopardize their future careers or personal safety. How could an agent whose face was known throughout the world ever be able to work undercover or interview witnesses on the street effectively?

Knowledge that the proceedings were being broadcast may also intimidate jurors. Excluding cameras and other recording devices from the courtroom will help preserve the anonymity of the jurors who are selected to serve and minimize the potential for a "popular verdict."

Executive Summary

Conflicting Values. Guarantees of expressive freedom and a fair trial are fundamental values in American society, but these guarantees do not always coexist harmoniously. Indeed, freedom of the press may both promote and undermine the criminal justice process. An unfettered right to free expression promotes self-government by exposing judicial or prosecutorial corruption or incompetence, and can be a catalyst for reform by heightening the public's political awareness and understanding of the criminal process. But, while the press can serve many useful functions, its presence has the potential to disrupt and undermine the fairness of the trial process.

Remedies for Prejudicial Publicity. "Where there is a reasonable likelihood that prejudicial news prior to trial will prevent a fair trial, the judge should continue the case until the threat abates, or transfer it to another county not so permeated with publicity." During trial, a judge also has broad discretion to sequester the jury, to caution jurors to avoid media accounts of the proceedings, and to provide clear instructions to jurors to decide the issues only on evidence presented in open court. Publicity alone does not deny a defendant a fair trial. The less severe remedy of transfer is also unwarranted unless a defendant can show that the pre-trial publicity in the district is so inherently prejudicial that trial proceedings must be presumed to be tainted. Gag orders are also disfavored.

Voir Dire. No juror will be disqualified from service unless the Court is satisfied that the juror (i) is unable to put aside any previously formed opinions or impressions, (ii) is not prepared to pay careful and close attention to the evidence as it is presented in the case and finally (iii) is unable to render a fair and impartial verdict based solely on the evidence adduced at trial and the Court's instructions of law.

Press Access to Judicial Proceedings. Trials historically have been open to the press and public, and the Court has established presumptions in favor of openness and access. Although the right of access to criminal trials is of constitutional stature, it is not absolute, but can only be impinged when there is a compelling governmental interest that is narrowly tailored to serve that interest. The right of access to trials and pretrial hearings does not incorporate any freedom for the media

Major Themes

a. Conflicting Values—Guarantees of expressive freedom and a fair trial are fundamental values in American society, but these guarantees do not always coexist harmoniously. Freedom of the press may both promote and undermine the criminal justice process. Substantial and prejudicial publicity can undermine a defendant's right to a fair trial.

b. Remedies for Prejudicial Publicity—Trial courts have a variety of remedies available to them to preserve the right to a fair trial against prejudicial publicity. The judge can continue the case until the threat abates, grant a change of venue to a different location, *voir dire* the jury, sequester the jury, and caution jurors to avoid media accounts of the proceedings. As a general rule, courts may not impose gag orders on the media. However, the right to access is not absolute and can be overridden by a compelling governmental interest, but the restriction must be narrowly tailored to serve that interest.

c. Press Coverage of Criminal Proceedings—However, the right of access to trials and pretrial hearings does not include the right to use any particular technology to cover such proceedings. To the contrary, even as cameras and other electronic instrumentalities have become increasingly common in state courts, the judiciary still exercises considerable control over the extent (if any) to which they may be used.

Test Your Knowledge

To assess your understanding of the material in this chapter, click here to take a quiz.

to use a particular technology to cover such proceedings. To the contrary, even as cameras and other electronic instrumentalities have become increasingly common in state courts, the judiciary still exercises considerable control over the extent (if any) to which they may be used.

For More Information

• MARK E. CAMMACK & NORMAN M. GARLAND, ADVANCED CRIMINAL PROCEDURE (2006).

• WAYNE R. LAFAVE, JEROLD H. ISRAEL, NANCY J. KING & ORIN S. KERR, CRIMINAL PROCEDURE (5th ed. 2009).

• JEROLD H. ISRAEL & WAYNE R. LAFAVE, CRIMINAL PROCEDURE: CONSTITUTIONAL LIMITATIONS (8th ed. 2006).

• RUSSELL L. WEAVER, JOHN M. BURKOFF, CATHERINE HANCOCK, JANET HOEFFEL, STEVE FRIEDLAND & STEPHEN SINGER, PRINCIPLES OF CRIMINAL PROCEDURE CH. 18 (6th ed. 2018).

CHAPTER 20

Sentencing

A. Sentencing Procedures

Formal sentencing consists of pronouncing sentence in accordance with the previous plea or adjudication of guilt.[1] If the defendant has been convicted, the case should proceed to sentencing without unreasonable delay. However, it is customary to postpone sentencing for a short period of time to enable the court to obtain a presentence report. Typically, the presentence report is prepared by the probation office or other court officer. It usually includes an analysis of the defendant's background, such as prior arrests and convictions, mental health issues, school and employment history, family history, and it also may include a victim impact statement under appropriate circumstances. If the defendant wishes to dispute any portion of the contents of the report, the court must afford a fair opportunity and a reasonable period of time to challenge it. However, the court normally need not disclose the sources of confidential information contained in the report.

Normally, the judge who presided at the trial conducts the sentencing. Unlike the evidentiary restrictions at trial, the judge can take into account a vast array of information in making the sentencing decision, including proffers by counsel, hearsay, prior bad acts of the defendant not admissible at trial, expressions of remorse and the like. The judge should consider the presentence report, sentencing alternatives if any, evidence concerning the nature and characteristics of the criminal conduct, and whether to run any multiple sentences on different counts concurrently (at the same time) or consecutively (when the second or subsequent sentence does not start until the first sentence is completed). In addition, the judge may weigh untruthfulness by the defendant or weigh a defendant's cooperation

Food for Thought

Why at sentencing can the judge consider inadmissible evidence, such as hearsay and arrests or other bad acts that did not result in a conviction? What are the arguments in favor of allowing this and what are the arguments against this?

---

[1] This chapter addresses only non-capital sentencing and sentencing procedures. Capital sentencing procedures are highly specialized and have special constitutional requirements and limitations.

with law enforcement in favor of the defendant. The judge "must be permitted to consider any and all information that reasonably might bear on the proper sentence for the particular defendant, given the crime committed." *Wasman v. United States*, 468 U.S. 559 (1984).

At the sentencing hearing, defendant must be given the right of allocution, which is the right to speak to the judge to identify any reason why the sentence should not be pronounced or why a particular sentence is appropriate. *See* Fed. R. Crim. P. 32(i)(4)(A)(ii). It thus affords regularity to the proceedings and reduces the likelihood of a subsequent attack on the judgment. Additionally, the judge must advise the defendant of his right to appeal his conviction.

In terms of the sentence, a judge may impose, the maximum punishment (term of imprisonment and/or fine), and any mandatory minimum punishment, is usually contained in the statutory definition of the offense. Although the statute usually defines the range of defendant's "exposure," most statutes articulate a sentencing range that gives judges discretion to impose a penalty within that range. When there is no mandatory minimum term of imprisonment, the judge can consider alternatives to imprisonment. There are a variety of such alternatives.

Hypo: *Always the Same Sentence*

A New Jersey judge remarked in a status conference in a case where a defendant charged with first-degree murder rejected a plea of 45 years that he "always" dishes out 60-year terms in first-degree murder cases and that he could "check his record" on that. A defendant previously convicted of first-degree murder by a jury and sentenced by this judge to 60 years learned of this and now appeals his sentence. Note that the judge did weigh aggravating and mitigating circumstances as required by the statute before declaring the sentence to be 60 years. Is this a problem? See State v. McFarlane, 134 A.3d 956 (N.J. 2016).

Points for Discussion

a. Fines

The punishment for a violation of the law may include a fine in addition to, or in some cases instead of, imprisonment. A court's authority to impose fines for violations of criminal statutes is set forth in the statutes themselves. The procedure for the collection of fines is governed largely by statute. Due to certain constitutional limitations, an indigent person may not usually be imprisoned for failure to pay the fine or costs. *See Bearden v. Georgia*, 461 U.S. 660 (1983). When the defendant seeks to appeal a fine, the trial judge may grant a stay of the payment and require bail.

b. Restitution

By statute, a person can be ordered to make restitution of property or its value to the victim in cases involving the taking of, injury to, or destruction of property. An order of restitution may defer payment until the person is released from custody. However, the decision by a trial judge not to use this remedy does not deprive the victim of a civil action for the damage sustained.

c. Forfeiture or Confiscation of Property

A person convicted of certain types of crimes, such as possession of controlled substances, intoxicating liquors, eavesdropping devices, deadly weapons, gambling devices, and obscene matter, can be ordered to forfeit that property if it was used in the commission of the offense. Forfeitures, as payments in kind, are "fines" if they constitute punishment for an offense. *Austin v. United States,* 509 U.S. 602 (1993). Thus, the forfeiture of vehicles and property used to facilitate commission of drug trafficking is allowed, because it serves as a punishment under the Eighth Amendment's Excessive Fines Clause.

Generally, under the Due Process Clause, the Government must provide notice and a meaningful opportunity to be heard before seizing real property subject to civil forfeiture. *United States v. James Daniel Good Real Property,* 510 U.S. 43 (1993). The Due Process Clause does not preclude forfeiture of property used for unlawful purposes by a defendant but which belongs to another person. *Bennis v. Michigan,* 516 U.S. 442 (1996).

d. Probation and Conditional Discharge

Probation is granted when the sentencing court suspends the execution or imposition of a sentence of imprisonment conditionally and releases the defendant under the supervision of a probation officer. Statutes may provide that probation is prohibited after convictions for certain offenses, such as crimes of violence, sex offenses, and the like, or for offenders who have one or more prior felony convictions. Otherwise, many states require that a defendant be considered for probation and conditional discharge unless the court finds that imprisonment is necessary to protect the public. When a defendant is sentenced to a period of incarceration followed by probation (as opposed to parole), the sentence is referred to as a "split sentence"—because part of the sentence is suspended and the sentence is "split" between time in prison and a period of probation).

Conditions of probation are usually stated in writing and furnished to the defendant. All defendants are required to refrain from committing another offense. They may also be subject to other conditions such as drug testing and treatment, restitution, counseling or any other condition that the court deems reasonably necessary to enable defendant to lead a law-abiding life. In addition to reasonable conditions, a court may require a defendant to submit to a period of imprisonment, such as weekends in the local jail. The court, the probation officer, or the prosecution may initiate proceedings to determine whether to revoke the probation because of a violation of its conditions.

Food for Thought

Many State and local court systems get a substantial portion of their funding from fines and fees collected from convicted defendants. Fines and fees are difficult, if not impossible, to collect from someone sentenced to prison. Think about how this affects the choice of sentencing alternatives, particularly probation. Also, consider how this relates to Chapter 17's discussion of the jury trial guarantee and the Supreme Court's holding that that right does not apply to so called "petty" offenses.

e. Home Incarceration

Many states permit defendants convicted of minor offenses to serve all or part of a definite term of imprisonment through "home incarceration." The sentencing judge may have discretion to order home incarceration as a form of "split sentence" under which defendant serves part of the sentence at home and part of it in the local jail. As with probation and conditional discharge, a defendant under home incarceration must sign an agreement that lists all of the conditions of confinement.

f. Continuous Confinement for a Definite Term or Indeterminate Term

An indeterminate sentence is set within statutory limits, with the parole board having responsibility for deciding precisely when the defendant is eligible for early release. Many states use indeterminate sentences. A determinate sentence (also known as "flat time") is for a fixed period without the possibility of early release, but supervision often accompanies that release.

B. Proportionality of Punishment

The Eighth Amendment prohibits cruel and unusual punishments, which includes punishments that are deemed to be "excessive." In a series of Supreme

Court cases, described in *Ewing v. California*, the Court greatly restricted the judiciary's ability to find punishments excessive once set by legislatures.

Ewing v. California

538 U.S. 11 (2003).

JUSTICE O'CONNOR announced the judgment of the Court and delivered an opinion in which THE CHIEF JUSTICE and JUSTICE KENNEDY join.

> **Hear It**
>
> You can listen to the oral argument in *Ewing* at: http://www.oyez.org/cases/2000-2009/2002/2002_01_6978.

In this case, we decide whether the Eighth Amendment prohibits the State of California from sentencing a repeat felon to a prison term of 25 years to life under the State's "Three Strikes and You're Out" law.

According to the law, if the defendant has one prior "serious" or "violent" felony conviction, he must be sentenced to "twice the term otherwise provided as punishment for the current felony conviction." If the defendant has two or more prior "serious" or "violent" felony convictions, he must receive "an indeterminate term of life imprisonment." Defendants sentenced to life under the three strikes law become eligible for parole on a date calculated by reference to a "minimum term," which is the greater of (a) three times the term otherwise provided for the current conviction, (b) 25 years, or (c) the term determined by the court pursuant to § 1170 for the underlying conviction, including any enhancements.

On parole from a 9-year prison term, petitioner Gary Ewing walked into the pro shop of the El Segundo Golf Course in Los Angeles County on March 12, 2000. He walked out with three golf clubs, priced at $399 apiece, concealed in his pants leg. A shop employee, whose suspicions were aroused when he observed Ewing limp out of the pro shop, telephoned the police. The police apprehended Ewing in the parking lot.

Ewing is no stranger to the criminal justice system. In 1984, at the age of 22, he pleaded guilty to theft. Only 10 months later, Ewing stole the golf clubs at issue in this case. He was charged with, and ultimately convicted of, one count of felony grand theft of personal property in excess of $400. As required by the three strikes law, the prosecutor formally alleged, and the trial court found, that Ewing had been convicted previously of four serious or violent felonies for the three burglaries and the robbery in the Long Beach apartment complex. The trial judge determined that the grand theft should remain a felony. The court also ruled that the four prior strikes for the three burglaries and the robbery in Long Beach should stand. As a newly convicted felon with two or more "serious" or "violent" felony convictions in his past, Ewing was sentenced under the three strikes law to 25 years to life. The California Court of Appeal affirmed. Relying on our decision in *Rummel v. Estelle*, 445 U.S. 263 (1980), the court rejected Ewing's claim that his sentence was grossly disproportionate under the Eighth Amendment. Enhanced sentences under recidivist statutes like the three strikes law, the court reasoned, serve the "legitimate goal" of deterring and incapacitating repeat offenders. The Supreme Court of California denied Ewing's petition for review, and we granted certiorari. We now affirm.

The Eighth Amendment, which forbids cruel and unusual punishments, contains a "narrow proportionality principle" that "applies to noncapital sentences." We have most recently addressed the proportionality principle as applied to terms of years in a series of cases beginning with *Rummel v. Estelle*. In *Rummel*, we held that it did not violate the Eighth Amendment for a State to sentence a three-time offender to life in prison with the possibility of parole. Like Ewing, Rummel was sentenced to a lengthy prison term under a recidivism statute. Rummel's two prior offenses were a 1964 felony for "fraudulent use of a credit card to obtain $80 worth of goods or services," and a 1969 felony conviction for "passing a forged check in the amount of $28.36." His triggering offense was a conviction for felony theft—"obtaining $120.75 by false pretenses."

Three years after *Rummel*, in *Solem v. Helm*, 463 U.S. 277, 279 (1983), we held that the Eighth Amendment prohibited "a life sentence without possibility of parole for a seventh nonviolent felony." The triggering offense in *Solem* was "uttering a 'no account' check for $100." We specifically stated that the Eighth Amendment's ban on cruel and unusual punishments "prohibits sentences that are disproportionate to the crime committed," and that the "constitutional principle of proportionality has been recognized explicitly in this Court for almost a century." The *Solem* Court explained that three factors may be relevant to a determination of whether a sentence is so disproportionate that it violates the Eighth Amendment: "(i) the gravity of the offense and the harshness of the penalty; (ii) the sentences imposed on other criminals in the same jurisdiction; and (iii) the sentences imposed for commission of the same crime in other jurisdictions." Applying these factors in *Solem*, we struck down the defendant's sentence of life without parole. We specifically noted the contrast between that sentence and the sentence in *Rummel*, pursuant to which the defendant was eligible for parole. Indeed, we explicitly declined to overrule *Rummel*: "Our conclusion today is not inconsistent with *Rummel v. Estelle*."

Eight years after *Solem*, we grappled with the proportionality issue again in *Harmelin v. Michigan*, 501 U.S. 957 (1991). Harmelin was not a recidivism case, but rather involved a first-time offender convicted of possessing 672 grams of cocaine. He was sentenced to life in prison without possibility of parole. A majority of the Court rejected Harmelin's claim that his sentence was so grossly disproportionate that it violated the Eighth Amendment. The Court, however, could not agree on why his proportionality argument failed. Justice Scalia, joined by The Chief Justice, wrote that the proportionality principle was "an aspect of our death penalty jurisprudence, rather than a generalizable aspect of Eighth Amendment law." He would thus have declined to apply gross disproportionality principles except in reviewing capital sentences. Justice Kennedy, joined by two other Members of the Court, concurred in part and concurred in the judgment. Justice Kennedy specifically recognized that "the Eighth Amendment proportionality principle also applies to noncapital sentences." He then identified four principles of proportionality review—"the primacy of the legislature, the variety of legitimate penological schemes, the nature of our federal system, and the requirement that proportionality review be guided by objective factors"—that "inform the final one: The Eighth Amendment does not require strict proportionality between crime and sentence. Rather, it forbids only extreme sentences that are 'grossly disproportionate' to the crime." Justice Kennedy's concurrence also stated that *Solem* "did not mandate" comparative analysis "within and between jurisdictions."

The proportionality principles in our cases distilled in Justice Kennedy's concurrence guide our application of the Eighth Amendment in the new context that we are called upon to consider. Throughout the States, legislatures enacting three strikes laws made a deliberate policy choice that individuals who have repeatedly engaged in serious or violent criminal behavior, and whose conduct has not been deterred by more conventional approaches to punishment, must be isolated from society in order to protect the public safety. Though three strikes laws may be relatively new, our tradition of deferring to state legislatures in making and implementing such important policy decisions is longstanding. Our traditional deference to legislative policy choices finds a corollary in the principle that the Constitution "does not mandate adoption of any one penological theory." A sentence can have a variety of justifications, such as incapacitation, deterrence, retribution, or rehabilitation. Some or all of these justifications may play a role in a State's sentencing scheme. Selecting the sentencing rationales is generally a policy choice to be made by state legislatures, not federal courts.

When the California Legislature enacted the three strikes law, it made a judgment that protecting the public safety requires incapacitating criminals who have already been convicted of at least one serious or violent crime. California's justification is no pretext. Recidivism is a serious public safety concern in California and throughout the Nation. According to a recent report, approximately 67 percent of former inmates released from state prisons were charged with at least one "serious" new crime within three years of their release. The State's interest in deterring crime also lends some support to the three strikes law. We have long viewed both incapacitation and deterrence as rationales for recidivism statutes: "A recidivist statute's primary goals are to deter repeat offenders and, at some point in the life of one who repeatedly commits criminal offenses serious enough to be punished as felonies, to segregate that person from the rest of society for an extended period of time." *Rummel.* Four years after the passage of California's three strikes law, the recidivism rate of parolees returned to prison for the commission of a new crime dropped by nearly 25 percent.

Against this backdrop, we consider Ewing's claim that his three strikes sentence of 25 years to life is unconstitutionally disproportionate to his offense of "shoplifting three golf clubs." We first address the gravity of the offense compared to the harshness of the penalty. Ewing incorrectly frames the issue. The gravity of his offense was not merely "shoplifting three golf clubs." Rather, Ewing was convicted of felony grand theft for stealing nearly $1,200 worth of merchandise after previously having been convicted of at least two "violent" or "serious" felonies. Even standing alone, Ewing's theft should not be taken lightly. His crime was certainly not "one of the most passive felonies a person could commit." To the contrary, the Supreme Court of California has noted the "seriousness" of grand theft in the context of proportionality review. In weighing the gravity of Ewing's offense, we must place on the scales not only his current felony, but also his long history of felony recidivism. Any other approach would fail to accord proper deference to the policy judgments that find expression in the legislature's choice of sanctions. In imposing a three strikes sentence, the State's interest is not merely punishing the offense of conviction, or the "triggering" offense: "It is in dealing in a harsher manner with those who by repeated criminal acts have shown that they are simply incapable of conforming to the norms of society as established by its criminal law." To give full effect to the State's choice of this legitimate penological goal, our proportionality review of Ewing's sentence must take that goal into account.

Ewing's sentence is justified by the State's public-safety interest in incapacitating and deterring recidivist felons, and amply supported by his own long, serious criminal record. Ewing has been convicted of numerous misdemeanor and felony offenses, served nine separate terms of incarceration, and committed most of his crimes while on probation or parole. His prior "strikes" were serious felonies including robbery and three residential burglaries. To be sure, Ewing's sentence is a long one. But it reflects a rational legislative judgment, entitled to deference, that offenders who have committed serious or violent felonies and who continue to commit felonies must be incapacitated. The State of California "was entitled to place upon Ewing the onus of one who is simply unable to bring his conduct within the social norms prescribed by the criminal law of the State." Ewing's is not "the rare case in which a threshold comparison of the crime committed and the sentence imposed leads to an inference of gross disproportionality."

We hold that Ewing's sentence of 25 years to life in prison, imposed for the offense of felony grand theft under the three strikes law, is not grossly disproportionate and therefore does not violate the Eighth Amendment's prohibition on cruel and unusual punishments. The judgment of the California Court of Appeal is affirmed.

Food for Thought

What values are espoused by Justice O'Connor in her opinion?

JUSTICE BREYER, with whom JUSTICE STEVENS, JUSTICE SOUTER, and JUSTICE GINSBURG join, dissenting.

The constitutional question is whether the "three strikes" sentence imposed by California upon repeat-offender Gary Ewing is "grossly disproportionate" to his crime. The sentence amounts to a real prison term of at least 25 years. The sentence-triggering criminal conduct consists of the theft of three golf clubs priced at a total of $1,197. The offender has a criminal history that includes four felony convictions arising out of three separate burglaries (one armed). In *Solem v. Helm*, the Court found grossly disproportionate a somewhat longer sentence imposed on a recidivist offender for triggering criminal conduct that was somewhat less severe. In my view, the differences are not determinative, and the Court should reach the same ultimate conclusion here.

The plurality applies Justice Kennedy's analytical framework in *Harmelin*. To implement this approach, courts faced with a "gross disproportionality" claim must first make "a threshold comparison of the crime committed and the sentence imposed." If a claim crosses that threshold—itself a rare occurrence—then the court should compare the sentence at issue to other sentences "imposed on other criminals" in the same, or in other, jurisdictions. The comparative analysis will "validate" or invalidate "an initial judgment that a sentence is grossly disproportionate to a crime." I recognize the warnings implicit in the Court's frequent repetition of words such as "rare." Nonetheless I believe that the case before us is a "rare" case—one in which a court can say with reasonable confidence that the punishment is "grossly disproportionate" to the crime.

Ewing's claim crosses the gross disproportionality "threshold." First, precedent makes clear that Ewing's sentence raises a serious disproportionality question. Ewing is a recidivist. Hence the two cases most directly in point are those in which the Court considered the constitutionality of recidivist sentencing: *Rummel* and *Solem*. Ewing's claim falls between these two cases. It is stronger than the claim presented in *Rummel*, where the Court upheld a recidivist's sentence as constitutional. It is weaker than the claim presented in *Solem*, where the Court struck down a recidivist sentence as unconstitutional.

Three kinds of sentence-related characteristics define the relevant comparative spectrum: (a) the length of the prison term in real time, i.e., the time that the offender is likely actually to spend in prison; (b) the sentence-triggering criminal conduct, i.e., the offender's actual behavior or other offense-related circumstances; and (c) the offender's criminal history. The length of the real prison term—the factor that explains the *Solem/Rummel* difference in outcome—places Ewing closer to *Solem* than to *Rummel*, though the greater value of the golf clubs that Ewing stole moves Ewing's case back slightly in *Rummel*'s direction. Overall, the comparison places Ewing's sentence well within the twilight zone between *Solem* and *Rummel*—a zone where the argument for unconstitutionality is substantial, where the cases themselves cannot determine the constitutional outcome. Second, Ewing's sentence on its face imposes one of the most severe punishments available upon a recidivist who subsequently engaged in one of the less serious forms of criminal conduct. I do not deny the seriousness of shoplifting, which costs retailers in the range of $30 billion annually. This case, of course, involves shoplifting engaged in by a recidivist. One might argue that any crime committed by a recidivist is a serious crime potentially warranting a 25-year sentence. But this Court rejected that view in *Solem*, and in *Harmelin*, with the recognition that "no penalty is *per se* constitutional." Third, some objective evidence suggests that many experienced judges would consider Ewing's sentence disproportionately harsh. The United States Sentencing Commission (having based the federal Sentencing Guidelines primarily upon its review of how judges had actually sentenced offenders) does not include shoplifting (or similar theft-related offenses) among the crimes that might trigger especially long sentences for recidivists.

A comparison of Ewing's sentence with other sentences requires answers to two questions. First, how would other jurisdictions (or California at other times, i.e., without the three strikes penalty) punish the same offense conduct? Second, upon what other conduct would other jurisdictions (or California) impose the same prison term? Moreover, since hypothetical punishment is beside the point, the relevant prison time, for comparative purposes, is real prison time, i.e., the time that an offender must actually serve. As to California itself, we know the following: First, between the end of World War II and 1994 (when California enacted the three strikes law), no one like Ewing could have served more than 10 years in prison. We know that for certain because the maximum sentence for Ewing's crime of conviction, grand theft, was for most of that period 10 years. We also know that the time that any offender actually served was likely far less than 10 years. This is because statistical data shows that the median time actually served for grand theft (other than auto theft) was about two years, and 90 percent of all those convicted of that crime served less than three or four years.

Second, statistics suggest that recidivists of all sorts convicted during that same time period in California served a small fraction of Ewing's real-time sentence. On average, recidivists served three to four additional (recidivist-related) years in prison, with 90 percent serving less than an additional real seven to eight years. Third, we know that California has reserved, and still reserves, Ewing-type prison time, i.e., at least 25 real years in prison, for criminals convicted of crimes far worse than was Ewing's. Statistics for the years 1945 to 1981, for example, indicate that typical (nonrecidivist) male first-degree murderers served between 10 and 15 real years in prison, with 90 percent of all such murderers serving less than 20 real years. Moreover, California, which has moved toward a real-time sentencing system (where the statutory punishment approximates the time served), still punishes far less harshly those who have engaged in far more serious conduct.

As to other jurisdictions, the United States, bound by the federal Sentencing Guidelines, would impose upon a recidivist, such as Ewing, a sentence that, in any ordinary case, would not exceed 18 months in prison. With three exceptions, we do not have before us information about actual time served by Ewing-type offenders in other States. We do know, that the law would make it legally impossible for a Ewing-type offender to serve more than 10 years in prison in 33 jurisdictions, as well as the federal courts, more than 15 years in 4 other States, and more than 20 years in 4 additional States. In nine other States, the law might make it legally possible to impose a sentence of 25 years or more—though that fact by itself, of course, does not mean that judges have actually done so.

Food for Thought

As compared to Justice O'Connor, what values are espoused in the dissent?

Points for Discussion

a. *Ewing's* Value Judgments

Does the O'Connor threesome or the dissent have the better argument under precedent? As a matter of policy? If you feel Ewing's punishment was wrong, what exactly was wrong with it?

b. Proportionality and Forfeiture

Proportionality limitations may apply to forfeitures as well. In *United States v. Bajakajian*, 524 U.S. 321 (1998), the defendant was arrested while trying to take $357,144 on a flight to Cyprus, because he had failed to report that he possessed or had control of more than $10,000. After a bench trial on a criminal forfeiture charge, the trial court found the entire amount subject to forfeiture. The court, however, ordered only $15,000 forfeited, reasoning that forfeiture of more than that amount would be "grossly disproportional" to Bajakajian's culpability and thus unconstitutional under the Excessive Fines Clause. The court expressly found that all of the money came from a lawful source and was to be used for a lawful purpose. The Court agreed that the forfeiture of currency permissible under the statute constituted punishment because the forfeiture only became possible upon conviction of willfully violating the reporting statute. After concluding that the forfeiture qualified as a "fine," and therefore "punishment," the Court turned to the question of excessiveness. Bajakajian's crime was "solely a reporting offense," and the harm Bajakajian's caused was "minimal" in the sense that the government would be deprived only of information that the $357,144 left the country. Thus, the gravity of the crime compared to the amount in forfeiture sought would be "grossly disproportional" if the entire amount were forfeited.

c. Enhanced Sentences for Recidivists

Recidivist offender statutes like the one applied in *Ewing* are used by many states. A defendant is entitled to notice of being charged as a recidivist before the trial of the underlying substantive offense. A separate indictment meets this requirement just as does a separate count in the indictment charging the substantive offense to which it refers. It is common practice for the indictment to specify the nature, time and place of the prior conviction.

d. Maximum Sentences for Juveniles

Under the Eighth Amendment's Cruel and Unusual Punishment Clause, a juvenile cannot be sentenced to life without parole for non-homicide crimes. *Graham v. Florida*, 560 U.S. 48 (2010). The Eighth Amendment also forbids a sentencing scheme that *mandates* life without parole for any juvenile offender, regardless of the crime. *Miller v. Alabama*, 567 U.S. 460 (2012). In *Montgomery v. Louisiana*, 136 S.Ct. 718 (2016), the United States Court held *Miller* was to be retroactively applied, potentially sending hundreds of inmates in several states back to court for resentencing.

C. The Right to a Jury Trial Meets Sentencing

1. *Apprendi's* Sea Change

Throughout most of the history of the United States, legislatures gave trial judges considerable and broad discretion to sentence an individual convicted of a crime within a wide range of punishment. In addition, judges

Assuming a defendant is properly charged as a recidivist, trial initially takes place on the underlying felony. During this initial trial, no mention is made of the prior convictions, except for impeachment. The determination of whether the defendant is a recidivist must occur in a separate proceeding from the trial on the underlying felony. This penalty phase usually is conducted with the same jury. The evidence at the hearing is very narrow. The only function of the jury is to hear proof of prior convictions and to determine if a defendant's record of recidivism warrants punishment. Accordingly, the courts have denied defendant an opportunity to introduce evidence of mitigation. During the hearing, the prosecution must prove every element of the recidivist charge beyond a reasonable doubt. A defendant charged with being a recidivist may plead guilty to the charge.

had broad authority to impose probation and suspend imprisonment when they thought it was warranted.

In the late 1970s and 1980s, during the War on Crime and the War on Drugs, legislatures began to adopt a new tough-on-crime attitude, and began to establish mandatory minimum terms of incarceration for certain kinds of crimes, eliminating judicial discretion to impose probation in those cases. Close on the heels of mandatory minimums, legislatures began to pass sentencing "enhancements", which allowed a judge to increase a penalty by a certain amount upon a finding, for example, that defendant used a firearm during the crime, that the crime was perpetrated on an elderly or very young victim, or the crime was perpetrated on a victim because of his or her race or ethnicity. As judicial discretion was narrowed and the plethora of sentencing enhancements grew, litigants seized upon the right to a trial by jury to attack the constitutionality of the enhancements. In *Apprendi*, the Court accepted the challenge.

Apprendi v. New Jersey

530 U.S. 466 (2000).

JUSTICE STEVENS delivered the opinion of the Court.

A New Jersey hate crime statute provided for an "extended term" of imprisonment if the trial judge found, by a preponderance of the evidence, that "the defendant in committing the

Hear It

You can listen to the oral argument in *Apprendi* at: http://www.oyez.org/cases/1990-1999/1999/1999_99_478.

crime acted with a purpose to intimidate an individual or group of individuals because of race, color, gender, handicap, religion, sexual orientation or ethnicity." The extended term authorized by the hate crime law is imprisonment for "between 10 and 20 years." After his indictment, Apprendi agreed to plead guilty to possession of a firearm for an unlawful purpose, punishable by five to ten years. The plea agreement allowed the prosecution to request that the sentence be enhanced due to a biased purpose. After an adversarial hearing, the trial court concluded that the crime was motivated by racial bias.

The question is whether the Due Process Clause of the Fourteenth Amendment requires that a factual determination authorizing an increase in the maximum prison sentence for an offense from 10 to 20 years be made by a jury on the basis of proof beyond a reasonable doubt. At stake in this case are constitutional protections of surpassing importance: the proscription of any deprivation of liberty without "due process of law," Amdt. 14, and the guarantee that "in all criminal prosecutions, the accused shall enjoy the right to a speedy and public trial, by an impartial jury," Amdt. 6.

Any possible distinction between an "element" of a felony offense and a "sentencing factor" was unknown to the practice of criminal indictment, trial by jury, and judgment by court as it existed during the years surrounding our Nation's founding. As a general rule, criminal proceedings were submitted to a jury after being initiated by an indictment containing "all the facts and circumstances which constitute the offence, stated with such certainty and precision, that the defendant may be enabled to determine the species of offence they constitute, in order that he may prepare his defence accordingly *and that there may be no doubt as to the judgment which should be given*, if the defendant be convicted." J. ARCHBOLD, PLEADING AND EVIDENCE IN CRIMINAL CASES 44 (15th ed. 1862). The defendant's ability to predict with certainty the judgment from the face of the felony indictment flowed from the invariable linkage of punishment with crime.

Just as the circumstances of the crime and the intent of the defendant at the time of commission were often essential elements to be alleged in the indictment, so too were the circumstances mandating a particular punishment. "Where a statute annexes a higher degree of punishment to a common-law felony, if committed under particular circumstances, an indictment for the offence, in order to bring the defendant within that higher degree of punishment, must expressly charge it to have been committed under those circumstances, and must state the circumstances with certainty and precision. 2 M. HALE, PLEAS OF THE CROWN." ARCHBOLD, PLEADING AND EVIDENCE IN CRIMINAL CASES, at 51. If, then, "upon an indictment under the statute, the prosecutor prove the felony to have been committed, but fail in proving it to have been committed under the circumstances specified in the statute, the defendant shall be convicted of the common-law felony only." *Id.*, at 188.

We should be clear that nothing in this history suggests that it is impermissible for judges to exercise discretion—taking into consideration various factors relating both to offense and offender—in imposing a judgment within the range prescribed by statute. We have often noted that judges in this country have long exercised discretion of this nature in imposing sentence within statutory limits in the individual case. As in *Williams v. New York*, our periodic recognition of judges' broad discretion in sentencing—since the 19th-century shift in this country from statutes providing fixed-term sentences to those providing judges discretion within a permissible range, has been regularly accompanied by the qualification that that discretion was bound by the range of sentencing options prescribed by the legislature.

We do not suggest that trial practices cannot change in the course of centuries and still remain true to the principles that emerged from the Framers' fears "that the jury right could be lost not only by gross denial, but by erosion." But practice must at least adhere to the basic principles undergirding the requirements of trying to a jury all facts necessary to constitute a statutory offense, and proving those facts beyond reasonable doubt.

In *McMillan v. Pennsylvania*, 477 U.S. 79 (1986), this Court, for the first time, coined the term "sentencing factor" to refer to a fact that was not found by a jury but that could affect the sentence imposed by the judge. We concluded that the Pennsylvania statute did not run afoul of our previous admonitions against relieving the State of its burden of proving guilt. We did not, however, there budge from the position that (1) constitutional limits exist to States' authority to define away facts necessary to constitute a criminal offense, *id.*, at 85–88, and (2) that a state scheme that keeps from the jury facts that "expose defendants to greater or additional punishment," may raise serious constitutional concern.

Almendarez-Torres v. United States, 523 U.S. 224 (1998), represents at best an exceptional departure from the historic practice that we have described. Because Almendarez-Torres had admitted the three earlier convictions for aggravated felonies—all of which had been entered pursuant to proceedings with substantial procedural safeguards of their own—no question concerning the right to a jury trial or the standard of proof that would apply to a contested issue of fact was before the Court. Although our conclusion in that case was based in part on our application of the criteria we had invoked in *McMillan*, the specific question decided concerned the sufficiency of the indictment. More important, our conclusion in *Almendarez-Torres* turned heavily upon the fact that the additional sentence to which the defendant was subject was "the prior commission of a serious crime." Both the certainty that procedural safeguards attached to any "fact" of prior conviction, and the reality that Almendarez-Torres did not challenge the accuracy of that "fact" in his case, mitigated the due process and Sixth Amendment concerns otherwise implicated in allowing a judge to determine a "fact" increasing punishment beyond the maximum of the statutory range.

This explanation of *Almendarez-Torres* was articulated in an important case decided between *Almendarez-Torres* and *Apprendi*: *Jones v. United States*, 526 U.S. 226 (1999).

Even though it is arguable that *Almendarez-Torres* was incorrectly decided, and that a logical application of our reasoning today should apply if the recidivist issue were contested, Apprendi does not contest the decision's validity and we need not revisit it for purposes of our decision today to treat the case as a narrow exception to the general rule we recalled at the outset. Given its unique facts, it surely does not warrant rejection of the otherwise uniform course of decision during the entire history of our jurisprudence.

In sum, our reexamination of our cases in this area, and of the history upon which they rely, confirms the opinion that we expressed in *Jones v. United States*, 526 U.S. 227 (1999). Other than the fact of a prior conviction, any fact that increases the penalty for a crime beyond the prescribed statutory maximum must be submitted

Take Note

Despite the plethora of progeny spawned by *Apprendi* and the expansion of its application to a host of different areas, the Court has never revisited *Almendarez-Torres*.

to a jury, and proved beyond a reasonable doubt. With that exception, we endorse the statement of the rule set forth in the concurring opinions in that case: "It is unconstitutional for a legislature to remove from the jury the assessment of facts that increase the prescribed range of penalties to which a criminal defendant is exposed. It is equally clear that such facts must be established by proof beyond a reasonable doubt."

JUSTICE O'CONNOR, with whom THE CHIEF JUSTICE, JUSTICE KENNEDY, and JUSTICE BREYER join, dissenting.

The Court today casts aside our traditional cautious approach and instead embraces a universal and seemingly bright-line rule limiting the power of Congress and state legislatures to define criminal offenses and the sentences that follow from convictions thereunder. The Court marshals virtually no authority to support its extraordinary rule. Indeed, it is remarkable that the Court cannot identify a single instance, in the over 200 years since the ratification of the Bill of Rights, that our Court has applied, as a constitutional requirement, the rule it announces today.

New Jersey could cure its sentencing scheme, and achieve virtually the same results, by drafting its weapons possession statute in the following manner: First, New Jersey could prescribe, in the weapons possession statute itself, a range of 5 to 20 years' imprisonment for one who commits that criminal offense. Second, New Jersey could provide that only those defendants convicted under the statute who are found by a judge, by a preponderance of the evidence, to have acted with a purpose to intimidate an individual on the basis of race may receive a sentence greater than 10 years' imprisonment.

Under another reading of the Court's decision, it may mean only that the Constitution requires that a fact be submitted to a jury and proved beyond a reasonable doubt if it, as a formal matter, increases the range of punishment beyond that which could legally be imposed absent that fact. A State could, however, remove from the jury (and subject to a standard of proof below "beyond a reasonable doubt") the assessment of those facts that, as a formal matter, decrease the range of punishment below that which could legally be imposed absent that fact. Thus, consistent with our decision in *Patterson v. New York*, 432 U.S. 197 (1977), New Jersey could cure its sentencing scheme, and achieve virtually the same results, by drafting its weapons possession statute in the following manner: First, New Jersey could prescribe, in the weapons possession statute itself, a range of 5 to 20 years' imprisonment for one who commits that criminal offense. Second, New Jersey could provide that a defendant convicted under the statute whom a judge finds, by a preponderance of the evidence, not to have acted with a purpose to intimidate an individual on the basis of race may receive a sentence no greater than 10 years' imprisonment.

If either of the above readings is all that the Court's decision means, "the Court's principle amounts to nothing more than chastising the New Jersey Legislature for failing to use the approved phrasing in expressing its intent as to how unlawful weapons possession should be punished." If New Jersey can, consistent with the Constitution, make precisely the same differences in punishment turn on precisely the same facts, and can remove the assessment of those facts from the jury and subject them to a standard of proof below "beyond a reasonable doubt," it is impossible to say that the Fifth, Sixth, and Fourteenth Amendments require the Court's rule. For the same reason, the "structural democratic constraints" that might discourage a legislature from enacting either of the above hypothetical statutes would be no more significant than those that would discourage the enactment of New Jersey's present sentence-enhancement statute. In all three cases, the legislature is able to calibrate punishment perfectly, and subject to a maximum penalty only those defendants whose cases satisfy the sentence-enhancement criterion.

Take Note

Apprendi was the product of a hotly contested debate within the Court drawn out over a number of years and encompassing at least three cases from *Almendarez-Torres* to *Jones v. United States*, and culminating in *Apprendi*. *Almendarez-Torres*, held that sentences could be enhanced with prior convictions when there had *not* been a jury determination of guilt, was a 5-4 decision in which Justice Scalia authored a vigorous dissent, joined by the three more liberal members of the Court (Justices Ginsberg, Souter, Stevens). Justice Thomas, who is usually aligned with Justice Scalia, curiously joined the majority to provide the critical fifth vote. However, Justice Scalia eventually convinced Justice Thomas to take his view. Justice Thomas' switch between *Almendarez-Torres* and *Apprendi* (using remarkably frank language: "one of the chief errors of *Almendarez-Torres*—an error to which I succumbed") led to the opposite result in *Apprendi*, also a sharply divided 5-4 opinion.

One important purpose of the Sixth Amendment's jury trial guarantee is to protect the criminal defendant against potentially arbitrary judges. It effectuates this promise by preserving, as a constitutional matter, certain fundamental decisions for a jury of one's peers, as opposed to a judge. Clearly, the concerns animating the Sixth Amendment's jury trial guarantee, if they were to extend to the sentencing context at all, would apply with greater strength to a discretionary-sentencing scheme than to determinate sentencing. In the former scheme, the potential for mischief by an arbitrary judge is much greater, given that the judge's decision of where to set the defendant's sentence within the prescribed statutory range is left almost entirely to discretion. In contrast, under a determinate-sentencing system, the discretion the judge wields within the statutory range is tightly constrained. Accordingly, our approval of discretionary-sentencing schemes, in which a defendant is not entitled to have a jury make factual findings relevant to sentencing despite the effect those findings have on the severity of the defendant's sentence, demonstrates that the defendant should have no right to demand that a jury make the equivalent factual determinations under a determinate-sentencing scheme.

> **FYI**
>
> Justice Breyer, dissenting here, became the leading dissenter in *Apprendi*'s progeny (until he finally gave up in 2013 in *Alleyne*, *infra*). As the first Chairman of the Committee that created the Federal Sentencing Guidelines, of which he was very proprietary, he was able to see that *Apprendi* contained the seeds of the Guidelines' destruction. *See Booker*, *infra*.

The Court appears to hold today, that a defendant is entitled to have a jury decide, by proof beyond a reasonable doubt, every fact relevant to the determination of sentence under a determinate-sentencing scheme. If this is an accurate description of the constitutional principle underlying the Court's opinion, its decision will have the effect of invalidating significant sentencing reform accomplished at the federal and state levels over the past three decades.

Points for Discussion

a. Aggravators and the Death Penalty

In *Ring v. Arizona*, 536 U.S. 584 (2002), the Court concluded that it was a violation of *Apprendi* for a sentencing judge sitting without a jury to find an aggravating circumstance necessary for imposition of the death penalty. When the judge made that finding, the defendant was exposed to a penalty greater than that authorized by the jury's verdict alone, in violation of *Apprendi*.

b. Mandatory Minimums

Soon after *Apprendi* was decided, scores of challengers attempted to take advantage of what Justice O'Connor had termed a "watershed change in constitutional law." While *Apprendi* made clear that a jury was required for a finding of facts which increased the statutory *maximum* sentence, it did not resolve whether a jury finding was also required for facts which increased the statutory *minimum* for a sentence. In 2002, the Court decided that *Apprendi* did not apply to mandatory minimum sentences. *Harris v. United States*, 536 U.S. 545 (2002). However, in 2013, showing the issues surrounding *Apprendi* are still alive and well, the Court overruled *Harris*. In *Alleyne v. United States*, 570 U.S. 99 (2013), the Court, in a 5–4 decision, held that any fact that increases the mandatory minimum sentence for a crime is an "element" of the crime that must be submitted to a jury, and not a so-called "sentencing factor" that a judge alone can decide. Therefore, when a finding that a defendant had brandished, as opposed to merely carried, a firearm in connection with crime of violence would elevate a mandatory minimum term for the offense from five to seven years, it was therefore an "element" of a separate, aggravated offense that had to found by jury. According to Justice Thomas for the majority:

> The essential Sixth Amendment inquiry is whether a fact is an element of the crime. When a finding of fact alters the legally prescribed punishment so as to aggravate it, the fact necessarily forms a constituent part of a new offense and must be submitted to the jury. It is no answer to say that the defendant could have received the same sentence with or without that fact. It is obvious, for example, that a defendant could not be convicted and sentenced for assault, if the jury only finds the facts for larceny, even if the punishments prescribed for each crime are identical. One reason is that each crime has different elements and a defendant can be convicted only if the jury has found each element of the crime of conviction.

Justice Thomas was careful to add that nothing in the opinion was meant to circumscribe a judge's traditional discretion to take into account any facts and circumstances she found relevant to the offender or offense that affected her decision as to the appropriate sentence within the statutory range.

c. Harmless Error

Apprendi violations are subject to constitutional harmless error analysis. *See Chapman v. California*, 386 U.S. 18 (1967). As with the failure to submit elements of a crime to the jury, the failure to submit a sentencing factor to the jury is not a "structural" error. *Washington v. Recuenco*, 548 U.S. 212 (2006).

d. Findings for Consecutive Sentencing

In *Oregon v. Ice*, 555 U.S. 160 (2009), the Court found it did not violate the Sixth Amendment (or *Apprendi*) for a judge to make factual findings for his decision to impose consecutive sentences as opposed to concurrent sentences.

e. Imposition of Fine

In *Southern Union Co. v. United States*, 567 U.S. 343 (2012), the Supreme Court held that the principles of *Apprendi* extend to the imposition of criminal fines, which are also a form of punishment. Where the jury made a finding of guilt only on the charged offense—that Southern Union violated the Resource Conservation and Recovery Act of 1976 "on or about September 19, 2002 to October 19, 2004"—the trial court could not impose a fine for every day in that period because the jury never specifically found more than one day's violation.

2. *Blakely* and *Booker*

The next step in *Apprendi* litigation was an attack on sentencing guidelines. Sentencing guidelines came about because members of the criminal justice community and the public became dissatisfied with the wide disparity in sentencing practices among judges, amounting to different sentences for similarly situated individuals. In response to this disparity and in league with the tough-on-crime attitude, the Federal Sentencing Guidelines were developed. The Guidelines were widely regarded as resulting in harsher penalties than were meted out under the previous sentencing scheme that gave judges wide latitude. The mandatory nature of the Guidelines also had the effect of cramping judges' ability to deal with inequities that were built into the system. Perhaps the most notorious of these inequities was the imposition of far more severe penalties on those who possessed or distributed crack cocaine, which was a largely African-American population, than those who possessed or distributed powder cocaine, which was a whiter and wealthier population. Judges could take fewer individualities of the defendant into account and virtually the only way for a defendant to get out from under severe Guidelines sentences was to cooperate with the prosecution, pursuant to Section 5K of the Sentencing Guidelines (lending the name "5K letters" to the prosecutor's letter to a judge detailing the cooperation). In *Blakely v. Washington*, 542 U.S. 296 (2004), the Court struck down as unconstitutional Washington State's determinate sentencing scheme as a violation of the right to a trial by jury. That decision is explained in *Booker*, below, and set the stage for the upset of the Federal Sentencing Guidelines in *Booker*.

United States v. Booker

543 U.S. 220 (2005).

Justice Stevens delivered the opinion of the Court in part [in which Justice Scalia, Justice Souter, Justice Thomas, and Justice Ginsburg join].

Hear It

You can listen to the oral argument in *Booker* at: http://www.oyez.org/cases/2000-2009/2004/2004_04_104/.

The question is whether an application of the Federal Sentencing Guidelines violated the Sixth Amendment. In each case, the courts below held that binding rules set forth in the Guidelines limited the severity of the sentence that the judge could lawfully impose on the defendant based on the facts found by the jury at his trial. In both cases the courts rejected, on the basis of our decision in *Blakely v. Washington*, 542 U.S. 296 (2004), the Government's recommended application of the Sentencing Guidelines because the proposed sentences were based on additional facts that the sentencing judge found by a preponderance of the evidence. We hold that both courts correctly concluded that the Sixth Amendment as construed in *Blakely* does apply to the Sentencing Guidelines. In a separate opinion authored by Justice Breyer, the Court concludes that in light of this holding, two provisions of the Sentencing Reform Act of 1984 (SRA) that have the effect of making the Guidelines mandatory must be invalidated in order to allow the statute to operate in a manner consistent with congressional intent.

Respondent Booker was charged with possession with intent to distribute at least 50 grams of cocaine base (crack). Having heard evidence that he had 92.5 grams in his duffel bag, the jury found him guilty of violating 21 U.S.C. § 841(a)(1). That statute prescribes a minimum sentence of 10 years in prison and a maximum sentence of life for that offense. § 841(b)(1)(A)(iii). Based upon Booker's criminal history and the quantity of drugs found by the jury, the Sentencing Guidelines required the District Court Judge to select a "base" sentence of not less than 210 nor more than 262 months in prison. *See* United States Sentencing Commission, Guidelines Manual §§ 2D1.1(c)(4), 4A1.1 (Nov. 2003) (USSG). The judge held a post-trial sentencing proceeding and concluded by a preponderance of the evidence that Booker had possessed an additional 566 grams of crack and that he was guilty of obstructing justice. Those findings mandated that the judge select a sentence between 360 months and life imprisonment; the judge imposed a sentence at the low end of the range. Thus, instead of the sentence of 21 years and 10 months that the judge could have imposed on the basis of the facts proved to the jury beyond a reasonable doubt, Booker received a 30-year sentence.

Over the dissent of Judge Easterbrook, the Court of Appeals for the Seventh Circuit held that this application of the Sentencing Guidelines conflicted with our holding in *Apprendi v. New Jersey*, 530 U.S. 466 (2000), that "other than the fact of a prior conviction, any fact that increases the penalty for a crime beyond the prescribed statutory maximum must be submitted to a jury, and proved beyond a reasonable doubt." The majority relied on our holding in *Blakely v. Washington* that "the 'statutory maximum' for *Apprendi* purposes is the maximum sentence a judge may impose solely on the basis of the facts reflected in the jury verdict or admitted by the defendant." The court held that the sentence violated the Sixth Amendment, and remanded with instructions to the District Court either to sentence respondent within the sentencing range supported by the jury's findings or to hold a separate sentencing hearing before a jury. It has been settled throughout our history that the Constitution protects every criminal defendant "against conviction except upon proof beyond a reasonable doubt of every fact necessary to constitute the crime with which he is charged." *In re Winship*, 397 U.S. 358, 364, (1970). It is equally clear that the "Constitution gives a criminal defendant the right to demand that a jury find him guilty of all the elements of the crime with which he is charged." *United States v. Gaudin*, 515 U.S. 506, 511, (1995). These basic precepts, firmly rooted in the common law, have provided the basis for recent decisions interpreting modern criminal statutes and sentencing procedures.

In *Blakely v. Washington*, 542 U.S. 296 (2004), we dealt with a determinate sentencing scheme similar to the Federal Sentencing Guidelines. There the defendant pleaded guilty to kidnaping, a class B felony punishable by a term of not more than 10 years. Other provisions of Washington law, comparable to the Federal Sentencing Guidelines, mandated a "standard" sentence of 49-to-53 months, unless the judge found aggravating facts justifying an exceptional sentence. Although the prosecutor recommended a sentence in the standard range, the judge found that the defendant had acted with "deliberate cruelty" and sentenced him to 90 months.

The application of Washington's sentencing scheme violated the defendant's right to have the jury find the existence of "any particular fact" that the law makes essential to his punishment. That right is implicated whenever a judge seeks to impose a sentence that is not solely based on "facts reflected in the jury verdict or admitted by the defendant." We rejected the State's argument that the jury verdict was sufficient to authorize a sentence within the general 10-year sentence for Class B felonies, noting that under Washington law, the judge was required to find additional facts in order to impose the greater 90-month sentence. Our precedents, we explained, make clear "that the 'statutory maximum' for *Apprendi* purposes is the maximum sentence a judge may impose solely on the basis of the facts reflected in the jury verdict or admitted by the defendant." The determination that the defendant acted with deliberate cruelty, like the determination in *Apprendi* that the defendant acted with racial malice, increased the sentence that the defendant could have otherwise received. Since this fact was found by a judge using a preponderance of the evidence standard, the sentence violated Blakely's Sixth Amendment rights.

As the dissenting opinions in *Blakely* recognized, there is no distinction of constitutional significance between the Federal Sentencing Guidelines and the Washington procedures at issue in that case. This conclusion rests on the premise, common to both systems, that the relevant sentencing rules are mandatory and impose binding requirements on all sentencing judges.

If the Guidelines as currently written could be read as merely advisory provisions that recommended, rather than required, the selection of particular sentences in response to differing sets of facts, their use would not implicate the Sixth Amendment. We have never doubted the authority of a judge to exercise broad discretion in imposing a sentence within a statutory range. Indeed, everyone agrees that the constitutional issues presented by these cases would have been avoided entirely if Congress had omitted from the SRA the provisions that make the Guidelines binding on district judges; it is that circumstance that makes the Court's answer to the second question presented possible. For when a trial judge exercises his discretion to select a specific sentence within a defined range, the defendant has no right to a jury determination of the facts that the judge deems relevant.

The Guidelines as written are not advisory; they are mandatory and binding on all judges. While subsection (a) of § 3553 of the sentencing statute lists the Sentencing Guidelines as one factor to be considered in imposing a sentence, subsection (b) directs that the court "shall impose a sentence of the kind, and within the range" established by the Guidelines, subject to departures in specific, limited cases. Because they are binding on judges, we have consistently held that the Guidelines have the force and effect of laws.

The Guidelines permit departures from the prescribed sentencing range in cases in which the judge "finds that there exists an aggravating or mitigating circumstance of a kind, or to a degree, not adequately taken into consideration by the Sentencing Commission in formulating the guidelines that should result in a sentence different from that described." 18 U.S.C.A. § 3553(b)(1) (Supp.2004). At first glance, one might believe that the ability of a district judge to depart from the Guidelines means that she is bound only by the statutory maximum. Were this the case, there would be no *Apprendi* problem. Importantly, however, departures are not available in every case, and in fact are unavailable in most. In most cases, as a matter of law, the Commission will have adequately taken all relevant factors into account, and no departure will be legally permissible.

Booker's case illustrates the mandatory nature of the Guidelines. The jury convicted him of possessing at least 50 grams of crack in violation of 21 U.S.C. § 841(b)(1)(A)(iii) based on evidence that he had 92.5 grams of crack in his duffel bag. Under these facts, the Guidelines specified an offense level of 32, which, given the defendant's criminal history category, authorized a sentence of 210-to-262 months. *See* USSG § 2D1.1(c)(4). Booker's is a run-of-the-mill drug case, and does not present any factors that were inadequately considered by the Commission. The sentencing judge would therefore have been reversed had he not imposed a sentence within the level 32 Guidelines range. Booker's actual sentence was 360 months, almost 10 years longer than the Guidelines range supported by the jury verdict alone. To reach this sentence, the judge found facts beyond those found by the jury: namely, that Booker possessed 566 grams of crack in addition to the 92.5 grams in his duffel bag. The jury never heard any evidence of the additional drug quantity, and the judge found it true by a preponderance of the evidence. Just as in *Blakely*, "the jury's verdict alone does not authorize the sentence. The judge acquires that authority only upon finding some additional fact." There is no relevant distinction between the sentence imposed pursuant to the Washington statutes in *Blakely* and the sentences imposed pursuant to the Federal Sentencing Guidelines in these cases.

The Government advances three arguments in support of its submission that we should not apply our reasoning in *Blakely* to the Federal Sentencing Guidelines. It contends that *Blakely* is distinguishable because the Guidelines were promulgated by a commission rather than the Legislature; that principles of *stare decisis* require us to follow four earlier decisions that are arguably inconsistent with *Blakely*; and that the application of *Blakely* to the Guidelines would conflict with separation of powers principles reflected in *Mistretta v. United States*, 488 U.S. 361 (1989). These arguments are unpersuasive.

All of the foregoing support our conclusion that our holding in *Blakely* applies to the Sentencing Guidelines. We recognize that in some cases jury fact-finding may impair the most expedient and efficient sentencing of defendants. But the interest in fairness and reliability protected by the right to a jury trial—a common-law right that defendants enjoyed for centuries and that is now enshrined in the Sixth Amendment—has always outweighed the interest in concluding trials swiftly.

Accordingly, we reaffirm our holding in *Apprendi*: Any fact (other than a prior conviction) which is necessary to support a sentence exceeding the maximum authorized by the facts established by a plea of guilty or a jury verdict must be admitted by the defendant or proved to a jury beyond a reasonable doubt.

JUSTICE BREYER delivered the opinion of the Court in part [in which THE CHIEF JUSTICE, JUSTICE O'CONNOR, JUSTICE KENNEDY, and JUSTICE GINSBURG join].

We answer the question of remedy by finding the provision of the federal sentencing statute that makes the Guidelines mandatory incompatible with today's constitutional holding. This provision must be severed and excised, as must one other statutory section which depends upon the Guidelines' mandatory nature. So modified, the federal sentencing statute makes the Guidelines effectively advisory. It requires a sentencing court to consider Guidelines ranges, but it permits the court to tailor the sentence in light of other statutory concerns as well.

We answer the remedial question by looking to legislative intent. We seek to determine what "Congress would have intended" in light of the Court's constitutional holding. In this instance, we must determine which of the two following remedial approaches is the more compatible with the legislature's intent as embodied in the 1984 Sentencing Act. One approach, that of Justice Stevens' dissent, would retain the Sentencing Act (and the Guidelines) as written, but would engraft onto the existing system today's Sixth Amendment "jury trial" requirement. The addition would change the Guidelines by preventing the sentencing court from increasing a sentence on the basis of a fact that the jury did not find (or that the offender did not admit). The other approach, which we now adopt, would (through severance and excision of two provisions) make the Guidelines system advisory while maintaining a strong connection between the sentence imposed and the offender's real conduct—a connection important to the increased uniformity of sentencing that Congress intended its Guidelines system to achieve.

Both approaches would significantly alter the system that Congress designed. But today's constitutional holding means that it is no longer possible to maintain the judicial fact-finding that Congress thought would underpin the mandatory Guidelines system that it sought to create and that Congress wrote into the Act in 18 U.S.C.A. §§ 3553(a) and 3661 (main ed. and Supp.2004). Hence we must decide whether we would deviate less radically from Congress' intended system (1) by superimposing the constitutional requirement announced today or (2) through elimination of some provisions of the statute.

Several considerations convince us that, were the Court's constitutional requirement added onto the Sentencing Act as currently written, the requirement would so transform the scheme that Congress created that Congress likely would not have intended the Act as so modified to stand. First, the statute's text states that "the court" when sentencing will consider "the nature and circumstances of the offense and the history and characteristics of the defendant." 18 U.S.C.A. § 3553(a)(1). In context, the words "the court" mean "the judge without the jury," not "the judge working together with the jury."

Second, Congress' basic statutory goal—a system that diminishes sentencing disparity—depends for its success upon judicial efforts to determine, and to base punishment upon, the real conduct that underlies the crime of conviction. That determination is particularly important where an act that meets the statutory definition can be committed in a host of different ways. Judges have long looked to real conduct when sentencing. Federal judges have long relied upon a presentence report, prepared by a probation officer, for information (often unavailable until after the trial) relevant to the manner in which the convicted offender committed the crime of conviction.

To engraft the Court's constitutional requirement onto the sentencing statutes would destroy the system. It would prevent a judge from relying upon a presentence report for factual information, relevant to sentencing, uncovered after the trial. In doing so, it would, even compared to pre-Guidelines sentencing, weaken the tie between a sentence and an offender's real conduct. It would thereby undermine the sentencing statute's basic aim of ensuring similar sentences for those who have committed similar crimes in similar ways.

Several examples help illustrate the point. Imagine Smith and Jones, each of whom violates the Hobbs Act in very different ways. *See* 18 U.S.C. § 1951(a) (forbidding "obstructing, delaying, or affecting commerce or the movement of any article or commodity in commerce, extortion"). Smith threatens to injure a co-worker unless the co-worker advances him a few dollars from the interstate company's till; Jones, after similarly threatening the co-worker, causes far more harm by seeking far more money, by making certain that the co-worker's family is aware of the threat, by arranging for deliveries of dead animals to the co-worker's home to show he is serious, and so forth. The offenders' behavior is very different; the known harmful consequences of their actions are different; their punishments both before, and after, the Guidelines would have been different. But, under the dissenters' approach, unless prosecutors decide to charge more than the elements of the crime, the judge would have to impose similar punishments. Now imagine two former felons, Johnson and Jackson, each of whom engages in identical criminal behavior: threatening a bank teller with a gun, securing $50,000, and injuring an innocent bystander while fleeing the bank. Suppose prosecutors charge Johnson with one crime (say, illegal gun possession), and Jackson with another (say, bank robbery.) Before the Guidelines, a single judge faced with such similar real conduct would have been able (within statutory limits) to impose similar sentences upon the two similar offenders despite the different charges brought against them. The Guidelines themselves would ordinarily have required judges to sentence the two offenders similarly. But under the dissenters' system, in these circumstances the offenders likely would receive different punishments.

Third, the sentencing statutes, read to include the Court's Sixth Amendment requirement, would create a system far more complex than Congress could have intended. How would courts and counsel work with an indictment and a jury trial that involved not just whether a defendant robbed a bank but also how? Would the indictment have to allege, in addition to the elements of robbery, whether the defendant possessed a firearm, whether he brandished or discharged it, whether he threatened death, whether he caused bodily injury, whether any such injury was ordinary, serious, permanent or life threatening, whether he abducted or physically restrained anyone, whether any victim was unusually vulnerable, how much money was taken, and whether he was an organizer, leader, manager, or supervisor in a robbery gang? *See* USSG §§ 2B3.1, 3B1.1. If so, how could a defendant mount a defense against some or all such specific claims should he also try simultaneously to maintain that the Government's evidence failed to place him at the scene of the crime?

Plea bargaining would not significantly diminish the consequences of the Court's constitutional holding for the operation of the Guidelines. Rather, plea bargaining would make matters worse. Congress enacted the sentencing statutes in major part to achieve greater uniformity in sentencing, *i.e.*, to increase the likelihood that offenders who engage in similar real conduct would receive similar sentences. The statutes reasonably assume that their efforts to move the trial-based sentencing process in the direction of greater sentencing uniformity would have a similar positive impact upon plea-bargained sentences, for plea bargaining takes place in the shadow of (*i.e.*, with an eye towards the hypothetical result of) a potential trial. That, too, is why Congress, understanding the realities of plea bargaining, authorized the Commission to promulgate policy statements that would assist sentencing judges in determining whether to reject a plea agreement after reading about the defendant's real conduct in a presentence report (and giving the offender an opportunity to challenge the report). This system has not worked perfectly; judges have often simply accepted an agreed-upon account of the conduct at issue. But compared to pre-existing law, the statutes try to move the system in the right direction, *i.e.*, toward greater sentencing uniformity.

The Court's constitutional jury trial requirement, however, if patched onto the present Sentencing Act, would move the system backwards in respect both to tried and to plea-bargained cases. In respect to tried cases, it would effectively deprive the judge of the ability to use post-verdict-acquired real-conduct information; it would prohibit the judge from basing a sentence upon any conduct other than the conduct the prosecutor chose to charge; and it would put a defendant to a set of difficult strategic choices as to which prosecutorial claims he would contest. The sentence that would emerge in a case tried under such a system would likely reflect real conduct less completely, less accurately, and less often than did a pre-Guidelines, as well as a Guidelines, trial.

Because plea bargaining inevitably reflects estimates of what would happen at trial, plea bargaining too under such a system would move in the wrong direction. That is to say, in a sentencing system modified by the Court's constitutional requirement, plea bargaining would likely lead to sentences that gave greater weight, not to real conduct, but rather to the skill of counsel, the policies of the prosecutor, the caseload, and other factors that vary from place to place, defendant to defendant, and crime to crime. Compared to pre-Guidelines plea bargaining, plea bargaining of this kind would necessarily move federal sentencing in the direction of diminished, not increased, uniformity in sentencing. It would tend to defeat, not to further, Congress' basic statutory goal.

Such a system would have particularly troubling consequences with respect to prosecutorial power. Until now, sentencing factors have come before the judge in the presentence report. But in a sentencing system with the Court's constitutional requirement engrafted onto it, any factor that a prosecutor chose not to charge at the plea negotiation would be placed beyond the reach of the judge entirely. Prosecutors would thus exercise a power the Sentencing Act vested in judges: the power to decide, based on relevant information about the offense and the offender, which defendants merit heavier punishment.

For all these reasons, Congress, had it been faced with the constitutional jury trial requirement, likely would not have passed the same Sentencing Act. It likely would have found the requirement incompatible with the Act as written. Hence the Act cannot remain valid in its entirety. Severance and excision are necessary.

We now turn to the question of which portions of the sentencing statute we must sever and excise as inconsistent with the Court's constitutional requirement. Although we believe that Congress would have preferred the total invalidation of the statute to the dissenters' remedial approach, we nevertheless do not believe that the entire statute must be invalidated. Most of the statute is perfectly valid. We must sever and excise two specific statutory provisions: the provision that requires sentencing courts to impose a sentence within the applicable Guidelines range (in the absence of circumstances that justify a departure), *see* 18 U.S.C. § 3553(b)(1), and the provision that sets forth standards of review on appeal, including *de novo* review of departures from the applicable Guidelines range, *see* § 3742(e). With these two sections excised (and statutory cross-references to the two sections consequently invalidated), the remainder of the Act satisfies the Court's constitutional requirements. As the Court today recognizes in its first opinion in these cases, the existence of § 3553(b)(1) is a necessary condition of the constitutional violation.

Without the "mandatory" provision, the Act nonetheless requires judges to take account of the Guidelines together with other sentencing goals. The Act still requires judges to consider the Guidelines "sentencing range established for an offense committed by the applicable category of defendant," the pertinent Sentencing Commission policy statements, the need to avoid unwarranted sentencing disparities, and the need to provide restitution to victims. And the Act nonetheless requires judges to impose sentences that reflect the seriousness of the offense, promote respect for the law, provide just punishment, afford adequate deterrence, protect the public, and effectively provide the defendant with needed educational or vocational training and medical care.

Despite the absence of § 3553(b)(1), the Act continues to provide for appeals from sentencing decisions (irrespective of whether the trial judge sentences within or outside the Guidelines range in the exercise of his discretionary power under § 3553(a)). We concede that the excision of § 3553(b)(1) requires the excision of a different, appeals-related section, namely § 3742(e), which sets forth standards of review on appeal. That section contains critical cross-references to the (now-excised) § 3553(b)(1) and consequently must be severed and excised for similar reasons.

Excision of § 3742(e), however, does not pose a critical problem for the handling of appeals. That is because a statute that does not explicitly set forth a standard of review may nonetheless do so implicitly. We infer appropriate review standards from related statutory language, the structure of the statute, and the "sound administration of justice." And in this instance those factors, in addition to the past two decades of appellate practice in cases involving departures, imply a practical standard of review already familiar to appellate courts: review for "unreasonableness." 18 U.S.C. § 3742(e)(3). Ours, of course, is not the last word: The ball now lies in Congress' court. The National Legislature is equipped to devise and install, long-term, the sentencing system, compatible with the Constitution, that Congress judges best for the federal system of justice.

In respondent Booker's case, the District Court applied the Guidelines as written and imposed a sentence higher than the maximum authorized solely by the jury's verdict. The Court of Appeals held *Blakely* applicable to the Guidelines, concluded that Booker's sentence violated the Sixth Amendment, vacated the judgment of the District Court, and remanded for resentencing. We affirm the judgment of the Court of Appeals and remand the case. On remand, the District Court should impose a sentence in accordance with today's opinions, and, if the sentence comes before the Court of Appeals for review, the Court of Appeals should apply the review standards set forth in this opinion.

[Justice STEVENS also dissented in part, arguing that the prosecution should be permitted to empanel juries to find "sentencing facts" that would increase a sentence above the maximum term of a presumptive range. Justice SCALIA's dissenting opinion criticized the severance remedy, preferring a reasonableness standard.]

Points for Discussion

a. Appellate Advice for Prospective Trial Court Sentencing

For future cases, the circuits attempted to prescribe a sentencing method, after the mandatory nature of the Guidelines was determined unconstitutional:

At this point, we can identify several essential aspects of *Booker* that concern the selection of sentences. First, the Guidelines are no longer mandatory. Second, the sentencing judge must consider the Guidelines and all of the other factors listed in section 3553(a). Third, consideration of the Guidelines will normally require determination of the applicable Guidelines range, or at least identification of the arguably applicable ranges, and consideration of applicable policy statements. Fourth, the sentencing judge should decide, after considering the Guidelines and all the other factors set forth in section 3553(a), whether (i) to impose the sentence that would have been imposed under the Guidelines, i.e., a sentence within the applicable Guidelines range or within permissible departure authority, or (ii) to impose a non-Guidelines sentence. Fifth, the sentencing judge is entitled to find all the facts appropriate for determining either a Guidelines sentence or a non-Guidelines sentence.

United States v. Crosby, 397 F. 3d 103 (2d Cir. 2005).

b. What is a "Reasonable" Sentence?

Justice Breyer's opinion (in part) in *Apprendi* held that the remedy for the constitutional violation was to make the Guidelines advisory and to replace *de novo* appellate review of sentences with a reasonableness standard of review. In *United States v. Fleming*, 397 F. 3d 95, 100 (2d Cir. 2005), the Second Circuit described how an appellate court would assess the reasonableness of a federal sentence:

> The appellate function in this context should exhibit restraint, not micromanagement. In addition to their familiarity with the record, including the presence report, district judges have discussed sentencing with a probation officer and gained an impression of a defendant from the entirety of the proceedings, including the defendant's opportunity for sentencing allocution. The appellate court proceeds only with the record. Although the brevity or length of a sentence can exceed the bounds of "reasonableness," we anticipate encountering such circumstances infrequently.

Food for Thought

Given the predilection of many federal judges to adhere to the Guidelines, as well as the reluctance of other circuits to adhere to the principle of restraint espoused in the Second Circuit's decision in *Fleming* in reviewing sentences that depart from the Guidelines, Justice Breyer's fears that *Apprendi* meant the demise of the Sentencing Guidelines are not fully warranted.

In the pending case, the District Court sentenced a defendant who had served three sentences of imprisonment and was appearing for his third violation of a term of supervised release. Judge Gershon considered the current violations "massive." She noted that the Defendant had been given the benefit of a substantial departure for his cooperation in connection with his sentence on the prisoner assault charge. *See* U.S.S.G.

§ 7B1.4, comment. (n.4) ("Where the original sentence was the result of a downward departure (*e.g.,* as a reward for substantial assistance), an upward departure may be warranted."). She identified as the "primary purpose" of her sentence "the necessity for both punishment for Fleming's behavior and deterrence." The District Court's explanation was sufficient to facilitate appellate review. Under all the circumstances, we cannot say that the two-year sentence was unreasonable.

Executive Summary

Sentencing Alternatives. A variety of sentencing alternatives to incarceration are available for courts.

Proportionality Challenge. A criminal sentence may be challenged as grossly disproportionate under the Eighth Amendment.

Sentence Enhancements. Enhanced sentences for defendants with prior felony convictions may lead to a life sentence.

Due Process. Sentencing procedures must satisfy due process regarding judicial consideration of all information relating to the defendant.

Jury Requirements. Any factual information, other than a prior conviction where there was a right to a jury trial, that increases the maximum penalty for a crime must be charged in the charging instrument, submitted to a jury, and proved beyond a reasonable doubt.

Major Themes

a. Judicial Discretion—Unlike pretrial and trial procedures, sentencing procedures are bound by few rules as long as the sentencing judge stays within the sentencing range set by the legislature. A judge can take into account and consider relevant to punishment almost any information, whether admissible or proven.

b. Constitutional Limits—The constitutional limits on a judge's sentencing discretion are the Eighth Amendment's prohibition on excessive punishment, which is practically no limit at all as it sets an extremely high bar for a showing of disproportionate punishment, and the right to a jury trial for the finding of facts that would increase a defendant's maximum sentencing exposure, which, unlike the Eighth Amendment, has led to substantial changes in sentencing procedures.

Test Your Knowledge

To assess your understanding of the material in this chapter, click here to take a quiz.

For More Information

• DEBORAH YOUNG, PETER HOFFMAN, SIGMUND POPKO & THOMAS HUTCHINSON, FEDERAL SENTENCING LAW & PRACTICE (2014 ed.).

• Douglas A. Berman, SENTENCING LAW AND POLICY, sentencing.typepad. com.

• WAYNE R. LAFAVE, JEROLD H. ISRAEL, NANCY J. KING & ORIN S. KERR, CRIMINAL PROCEDURE (5th ed. 2009).

• JEROLD H. ISRAEL & WAYNE R. LAFAVE, CRIMINAL PROCEDURE: CONSTITUTIONAL LIMITATIONS (8th ed. 2006).

• RUSSELL L. WEAVER, JOHN M. BURKOFF, CATHERINE HANCOCK, JANET HOEFFEL, STEVE FRIEDLAND & STEPHEN SINGER, PRINCIPLES OF CRIMINAL PROCEDURE CH. 19 (6th ed. 2018).

CHAPTER 21

Double Jeopardy

No person shall "be subject for the same offense to be twice put in jeopardy of life or limb."—The Fifth Amendment Double Jeopardy Clause

"At its core, the Double Jeopardy Clause reflects the wisdom of the founding generation that one's acquittal or conviction should satisfy the law,"—Justice Sonia Sotomayor, *Blueford v. Arkansas*, 566 U.S. 599, 609 (2012) (dissenting opinion)

A. Introduction

Double jeopardy doctrine is layered, complex, and nuanced, contrary to its compact reference in the Constitution. The initial determination that must be made is whether double jeopardy analysis is triggered by a particular charge or proceeding, especially a second or succeeding one. The clause applies only in a criminal case. It does not prevent criminal and civil punishment for the same offense—just no multiple criminal punishments. What constitutes a civil or criminal penalty is sometimes fuzzy, and the interpretation of legislative intent generally controls.

The Clause offers three primary protections: (1) against a second prosecution for the same offense following an acquittal; (2) against a second prosecution for the same offense after a conviction; and (3) against multiple punishments for the same offense.

A defendant has both federal and state constitutional protections against being placed in jeopardy twice for the same offense. While the Fifth Amendment double jeopardy protection applies only to the federal government directly, it also applies to the states through the Fourteenth Amendment. *Benton v. Maryland*, 395 U.S. 784 (1969).

Make the Connection

Kansas v. Hendricks, 521 U.S. 346 (1997) involved the involuntary civil commitment of sex offenders following the completion of a criminal sentence. Justice Thomas distinguished what constituted civil from criminal actions, mostly deferring to the treatment accorded the action by the legislature that created it. Find it at the Oyez Project: http://www.oyez.org/cases/1990-1999/1996/1996_95_1649.

Because the debates of the constitutional framers offer little guidance regarding the intended scope of double jeopardy protection, the courts have interpreted the Double Jeopardy Clause in light of their understanding of its underlying purposes. The essence of the prohibition against double jeopardy is not that a defendant may incur a greater risk of being found guilty in a second trial than in a first trial, or that a second trial may be conducted prejudicially, but rather that the defendant cannot be forced to face the risk of conviction for an offense regarding which defendant already has been placed on trial and in jeopardy.

Double jeopardy notions also are predicated on the principle that the United States has two sovereigns or governments. Thus, the state government can prosecute the same conduct that has been prosecuted in federal court, *Bartkus v. Illinois*, 359 U.S. 121 (1959), and, vice versa, the federal government can prosecute the same conduct that has been prosecuted in state court, *Abbate v. United States*, 359 U.S. 187 (1959), pursuant to federalism principles. These types of successive prosecutions generally do not violate double jeopardy principles.

A successful claim involving double jeopardy will bar a succeeding trial on an indictment or information or any punitive government act considered criminal in nature based on the first trial. The objection to the succeeding government action may be raised by a motion to dismiss at any time before trial. Although a failure to raise the objection before the second adjudication may operate as a waiver, it can be raised for the first time in a reviewing court if the double jeopardy issue can be decided as a matter of law on the facts established by the record. *Menna v. New York*, 423 U.S. 61 (1975).

One of the requirements for the attachment of jeopardy is that the court hearing the case must have proper jurisdiction. When the court exceeds its jurisdiction, a conviction is void, and there is no bar to a new trial.

"Wild Bill" Hickok and Double Jeopardy?

What does James Butler "Wild Bill" Hickok have to do with double jeopardy analysis? On August 2, 1876, Jack McCall murdered the 39-year-old Hickok by shooting him from behind as a result of a perceived slight. The shooting occurred in the town of Deadwood, South Dakota, where McCall was subsequently held for trial by local townspeople in an impromptu setting and acquitted. Shortly thereafter, McCall left for the Wyoming territory, where he was captured and returned to Yankton, in the South Dakota Territory. There, he was again tried for the murder. The South Dakota court found that there was no violation of double jeopardy as a result of the second trial because Deadwood, where the first trial occurred, was technically in what was then known as Indian territory, while the South Dakota trial was in U.S. territory. At the second trial, McCall was convicted and later executed. Go online: "This Day In History," The History Channel, http://www.history.com/this-day-in-history/wild-bill-hickok-is-murdered. Absent a facial jurisdictional defect, the original adjudication is presumed to have been within the court's jurisdiction. Likewise, a prior conviction or acquittal procured by the defendant to defraud the government of an opportunity to attain the proper sentence does not bar a new prosecution.

Take Note

The doctrine of dual sovereignty does not prohibit multiple prosecutions for the same offense by courts of different sovereigns. *See, e.g., Heath v. Alabama,* 474 U.S. 82 (1985) (successive prosecutions by different states permissible); *Bartkus v. People of State of Illinois,* 359 U.S. 121 (1959) (successive state and federal trials for same offense permissible). On the other hand, the dual sovereignty theory does not apply to state and municipal prosecutions for the same act because the state and the municipality are regarded as the same sovereign, regardless of how the state chooses to classify its governmental subunits: the subunits derive their power to exist from the sovereign. *See, e.g., Waller v. Florida,* 397 U.S. 387 (1970) (successive prosecutions for same offense based upon violations of state statute and local ordinance prohibited by double jeopardy).

B. Does Jeopardy Attach?

The initial question to ask in analyzing double jeopardy questions is whether jeopardy has attached. If jeopardy has attached in the original proceeding, it leads to the second major question of whether the government is precluded from retrying or recharging the defendant. This does not mean that a jury trial must be completed in the first proceeding or that evidence was offered or argument given by counsel; it does not even require a balancing of factors. Rather, there are judicially-created standards as to when jeopardy attaches and when a retrial is permitted. The standard for jeopardy attaching is singular and falls along a bright line. Courts generally find that if the jury has been empanelled and sworn, jeopardy has attached. The standard for the second question, whether a retrial is permitted, is a more nuanced matter.

Double jeopardy bars a second prosecution only if the prerequisite jeopardy attached in the original proceeding. The analysis of when jeopardy attaches (and if it does, when a bar from further charges or retrial occurs) can be straight forward. In a jury trial, jeopardy generally attaches when the jury is sworn. *Crist v. Bretz,* 437 U.S. 28 (1978). But what if there is no jury? If a case is tried before a judge, after waiver of a jury, jeopardy attaches when the first witness is sworn. Jeopardy also attaches when the trial court accepts a guilty plea. Conversely, withdrawal of a guilty plea is a waiver of the double jeopardy protection against trial on the charge in the indictment or information. If a case is dismissed or terminated prior to the attachment of jeopardy, jeopardy has not attached, and the defendant may have to respond to the same criminal charges in subsequent proceedings.

Martinez v. Illinois

134 S.Ct. 2070 (2014).

PER CURIAM.

The State of Illinois indicted Marti-nez in August 2006 on charges of aggra-vated battery and mob action against Avery Binion and Demarco Scott. But Martinez's trial date did not arrive for nearly four years. The story picks up for present purposes on July 20, 2009, when the State moved to continue an August 3 trial date because it had not located the complaining witnesses, Binion and Scott. The State subpoe-naed both men four days later, and the

It's Latin to Me

What is "*per curiam*?" This means, in Latin, "by the court." A *per curiam* decision is issued by the court in-stead of specific judges. *Per curiam* decisions have been criticized as for-saking the tradition of individual ac-countability of judges, who usually sign the written opinions.

court rescheduled Martinez's trial to September 28. But the State sought another continuance, shortly before that date, because it still had not found Binion and Scott. The court rescheduled the trial to November 9, and the State reissued sub-poenas. Still, the witnesses could not be located. On the morning of May 17, [the reset trial date], Binion and Scott were again nowhere to be found. At 8:30, when the trial was set to begin, the State asked for a brief continuance. The court offered to delay swearing the jurors until a complete jury had been empanelled and told the State that it could at that point either have the jury sworn or move to dismiss its case. When Binion and Scott still had not shown up after the jury was chosen, the court offered to call the other cases on its docket so as to delay swearing the jury a bit longer. But when all these delays had run out, Binion and Scott were still nowhere in sight. The State filed a written motion for a continuance, arguing that it was "unable to proceed" without Binion and Scott. The court denied that motion:

> "The case before the Court began on July 7, 2006. In two months we will then be embarking upon half a decade of pending a Class 3 felony. Avery Binion, Jr., and Demarco Scott are well known in Elgin, both are convicted felons. One would believe that the Elgin Police Department would know their whereabouts. They were ordered to be in court today. The Court will issue body writs for both of these gentlemen.

> "In addition, the State's list of witnesses indicates twelve witnesses. Excluding Mr. Scott and Mr. Binion, that's ten witnesses. The Court would anticipate it would take every bit of today and most of tomorrow to get through ten witnesses. By then the People may have had a chance to execute the arrest warrant body writs for these two gentlemen. The Court will deny the motion for continuance. I will swear the jury in 15, 20 minutes. Perhaps you might want to send the police out to find these two gentlemen."

After a brief recess, the court offered to delay the start of the trial for several more hours if the continuance would "be of any help" to the State. But when the State made clear that Binion and Scott's "whereabouts" remained "unknown," the court concluded that the delay "would be a further waste of time."

The following colloquy ensued:

"THE COURT: It's a quarter to eleven and Binion and Scott have not appeared on their own will, so I'm going to bring the jury in now then to swear them.

"The Prosecutor: Okay. Your Honor, may I approach briefly?

"THE COURT: Yes.

"The Prosecutor: Your Honor, just so your Honor is aware, I know that it's the process to bring them in and swear them in; however, the State will not be participating in the trial. I wanted to let you know that.

"THE COURT: Very well. We'll see how that works."

The jury was then sworn. After instructing the jury, the court directed the State to proceed with its opening statement. The prosecutor demurred: "Your Honor, respectfully, the State is not participating in this case." After the defense waived its opening statement, the court directed the State to call its first witness. Again, the prosecutor demurred: "Respectfully, your Honor, the State is not participating in this matter." The defense then moved for a judgment of acquittal. The Court replied, "The Court will grant the motion for a directed finding and dismiss the charges."

The State appealed, arguing that the trial court should have granted a continuance. Martinez responded that the State's appeal was improper because he had been acquitted. The Illinois Appellate Court sided with the State, holding that jeopardy had never attached and that the trial court had erred in failing to grant a continuance. The Illinois Supreme Court granted review on the jeopardy issue and affirmed. It began by recognizing that "generally, in cases of a jury trial, jeopardy attaches when a jury is empanelled and sworn, as that is the point when the defendant is 'put to trial before the trier of the facts.'" But it reasoned that under this Court's precedents, " 'rigid, mechanical' rules" should not govern the inquiry into whether jeopardy has attached. Rather, it opined, the relevant question is whether a defendant was "subjected to the hazards of trial and possible conviction." Here, the court concluded, Martinez "was never at risk of conviction"—and jeopardy therefore did not attach—because "the State indicated it would not participate prior to the jury being sworn Because Martinez was not placed in jeopardy," the court held, the trial court's entry of directed verdicts of not guilty did not constitute true acquittals. Indeed, the court remarked, the trial court repeatedly referred to its action as a "dismissal" rather than an acquittal.

This case presents two issues. First, did jeopardy attach to Martinez? Second, if so, did the proceeding end in such a manner that the Double Jeopardy Clause bars his retrial? Our precedents clearly dictate an affirmative answer to each question.

There are few if any rules of criminal procedure clearer than the rule that "jeopardy attaches when the jury is empanelled and sworn." *Crist*, 437 U.S., at 35; see also *United States v. Martin Linen Supply Co.*, 430 U.S. 564, 569 (1977). Our clearest exposition of this rule came in *Crist*. As *Crist* explains, "the precise point at which jeopardy attaches in a jury trial might have been open to argument before this Court's decision in *Downum v. United States*, 372 U.S. 734 (1963)," but *Downum* put any such argument to rest: Its holding "necessarily pinpointed the stage in a jury trial when jeopardy attaches, and it has since been understood as explicit authority for the proposition that jeopardy attaches when the jury is empanelled and sworn." The Illinois Supreme Court misread our precedents in suggesting that the swearing of the jury is anything other than a bright line at which jeopardy attaches.

The Illinois Supreme Court's error was consequential, for it introduced confusion into what we have consistently treated as a bright-line rule: A jury trial begins, and jeopardy attaches, when the jury is sworn. We have never suggested the exception perceived by the Illinois Supreme Court—that jeopardy may not have attached where, under the circumstances of a particular case, the defendant was not genuinely at risk of conviction. Martinez was subjected to jeopardy because the jury in his case was sworn.

The remaining question is whether the jeopardy ended in such a manner that the defendant may not be retried. Here, there is no doubt that Martinez's jeopardy ended in a manner that bars his retrial: The trial court acquitted him of the charged offenses. "Perhaps the most fundamental rule in the history of double jeopardy jurisprudence has been that 'a verdict of acquittal could not be reviewed without putting a defendant twice in jeopardy, and thereby violating the Constitution.' " *Martin Linen,* 97 S.Ct. 1349.

"Our cases have defined an acquittal to encompass any ruling that the prosecution's proof is insufficient to establish criminal liability for an offense." *Evans v. Michigan*, 133 S.Ct. 1069, 1074. The trial court clearly made such a ruling here. After the State declined to present evidence against Martinez, his counsel moved for "directed findings of not guilty to both counts," and the court "granted the motion for a directed finding." That is a textbook acquittal: a finding that the State's evidence cannot support a conviction.

The Illinois Supreme Court thought otherwise. The court went on to "note that, in directing findings of not guilty," the trial court "referred to its action as a 'dismissal' rather than an acquittal." Under our precedents, however, that is immaterial. Here, as in *Evans* and *Martin Linen*, the trial court's action was an acquittal because the court "acted on its view that the prosecution had failed to prove its case." *Evans,* 133 S.Ct., at 1078; Because Martinez was acquitted, the State cannot retry him.

The functional rule adopted by the Illinois Supreme Court is not necessary to avoid unfairness to prosecutors or to the public. The Court repeatedly delayed that act to give the State additional time to find its witnesses. It had previously granted the State a number of continuances for the same purpose. Critically, the court told the State on the day of trial that it could "move to dismiss its case" before the jury was sworn. Had the State accepted that invitation, the Double Jeopardy Clause would not have barred it from recharging Martinez. Instead, the State participated in the selection of jurors and did not ask for dismissal before the jury was sworn. Here, the State knew, or should have known, that an acquittal forever bars the retrial of the defendant when it occurs after jeopardy has attached. The Illinois Supreme Court's holding is understandable, given the significant consequence of the State's mistake, but it runs directly counter to our precedents and to the protection conferred by the Double Jeopardy Clause.

Go Online

For the full case: https://a.next.west law.com/Link/Document/FullText?f indType=Y&serNum=1975129745 &pubNum=708&originationConte xt=document&transitionType=Docu mentItem&contextData=(sc.Search).

The judgment of the Supreme Court of Illinois is reversed, and the case is remanded for further proceedings not inconsistent with this opinion.

It is so ordered.

Hypo: *Does Jeopardy Attach?*

In the following situations, does double jeopardy apply?

1) Jonas is prosecuted for drug possession in his car. After obtaining a conviction, the prosecution sought forfeiture of the car under a civil forfeiture statute. *See Porter v. Coughlin,* 421 F.3d 141, 146 (2d Cir. 2005);

2) Felix is charged with failing to report transporting over $10,000 into the United States and making false statements to U.S. officials about the same. Felix is prosecuted for these acts under separate statutory provisions and given cumulative punishments. *See United States v. Woodward*, 469 U.S. 105 (1985) (*per curiam*); 3) Alberto is given consecutive sentences for possession with intent to distribute heroin and contempt of court, after committing a drug offense while on pre-trial release and after the court commanded the defendant to not commit any unlawful act. *See United States v. Henry*, 519 F.3d 68 (1st Cir. 2008).

While jurisdictions have allowed separate prosecutions for the same conduct in federal and state courts under the rationale that the federal and state governments are dual sovereigns, the doctrine is not beyond reproach. In the following case, the court found that a double jeopardy violation occurred when the state initiated prosecution for conduct the defendant had been prosecuted for and convicted of by the federal government.

State v. Robertson

2017 UT 27 (2017)

CHIEF JUSTICE DURRANT, opinion of the Court:

Defendant D. Chris Robertson was prosecuted and convicted by the federal government for possession of child pornography. The State of Utah subsequently charged him with twenty counts of sexual exploitation of a minor based on the same conduct. Robertson argues that Utah Code section 76-1-404 prohibits this subsequent state prosecution. That statute provides that—if a defendant's conduct establishes the commission of one or more offenses within the concurrent jurisdiction of this state and of another jurisdiction, federal or state, the prosecution in the other jurisdiction is a bar to a subsequent prosecution in this state if the former prosecution resulted in an acquittal, conviction, or termination of prosecution .and the subsequent prosecution is for the same offense or offenses.

Under our previous interpretation of section 404, this statute would present no barrier to the current prosecution. In *State v. Franklin*, we concluded that section 404 incorporated the—dual sovereignty doctrine, a principle of double jeopardy law that permits subsequent prosecutions by different sovereigns, even for the—same offense. The court of appeals affirmed Robertson's convictions in accordance with this precedent.

Today, we reassess that earlier interpretation and conclude that it was wrongly decided. Taking into account *stare decisis* considerations, we overrule *Franklin* as to that issue and hold that the legislature's use of the phrase—same offense in section 404 is an express rejection of the dual sovereignty doctrine. Properly interpreted, section 404 requires courts to employ only the *Blockburger-Sosa* test for determining whether two offenses are the—same offense. Under this test, two offenses are not the same if each requires proof of an element that the other does not.

After articulating the correct interpretation of the statute, we apply it to this case. Because the charged offenses in his federal and state prosecutions are the—same offense under the *Blockburger-Sosa* test, and because the record shows that the state prosecution is based on the same conduct that was at issue in the initial federal prosecution, we conclude that section 404, properly interpreted, prohibits the State from prosecuting Robertson. We therefore reverse the decision of the court of appeals.

[Defendant was found to have possessed child pornography and subsequently prosecuted and convicted in federal court. He was then charged in state court based on the same conduct.]

We hold that—Same Offense in Section 76-1-404 Incorporates the *Blockburger-Sosa* Test but Rejects the Dual Sovereignty Doctrine, Overruling in Part *State v. Franklin* Having clarified the precedential value of *State v. Franklin*, we now discuss whether our decision therein that Utah Code section 76-1-404 incorporated the dual sovereignty doctrine should be overruled. We do not overrule a prior interpretation of a statute lightly, out of respect for the *stare decisis* principles of—predictability and fairness. But even though overruling a prior interpretation of a statute is an—unusual step,—the doctrine of stare decisis is neither mechanical nor rigid as it relates to courts of last resort. As we discuss below, we believe that the portion of *Franklin* interpreting the—same offense language of section 404 to incorporate the dual sovereignty doctrine should be overruled. We hold today that—same offense, as used in section 404, should be interpreted as incorporating only the *Blockburger-Sosa* test and that section 404 is an express rejection of the dual sovereignty doctrine.

We Are Persuaded that *Franklin's* Interpretation of Section 76-1-404 Should Be Overruled. We consider at least three factors when deciding whether to overrule a prior interpretation of a statute:—the plausibility of the existing interpretation given the statute, the degree to which that interpretation has worked itself into the state of the law, and the strength of the arguments for changing that interpretation. We discuss each factor below and conclude that they weigh in favor of overruling *State v. Franklin*.

Prior to deciding whether section 76-1-404 prohibits the State's prosecution of Robertson, we must first address the State's argument that our decision to overrule *Franklin* should be applied prospectively only. We conclude that section 404 is a substantive statute that creates an affirmative defense to avoid the dual sovereignty exception to double jeopardy118 and that the new interpretation of it announced in this case applies retroactively to cases on direct and collateral review. We then apply our interpretation of section 404 to the facts of this case. We hold that the federal and state offenses are the same under *Blockburger-Sosa* and that the record shows that federal prosecution encompassed all of the conduct for which Robertson was subsequently prosecuted by the State.

Section 76-1-404 Is a Substantive Statute that Creates an Affirmative Defense to Avoid the Dual Sovereignty Exception to Double Jeopardy, and We Apply It Retroactively to Cases on Direct and Collateral Review. The Record Shows that the State Premised Its Prosecution of Robertson on Conduct that Constitutes the "Same Offense" for Which He Was Prosecuted Federally As discussed, Utah Code section 76-1-404 prohibits the State from prosecuting a defendant if the defendant has already been prosecuted in another jurisdiction provided two conditions are satisfied. First, the former prosecution must result in an acquittal, conviction, or termination of prosecution. The parties agree that Robertson's federal prosecution satisfies this requirement. The second condition requires that—the subsequent prosecution be for the same offense or offenses, as we have described above. It is on this condition that the parties disagree—whether the Utah prosecution can be said to be for the—same offense as the federal prosecution.

As we have explained, determining whether a prior foreign prosecution qualifies as the—same offense under section 404 requires a two-part analysis: whether the offenses for which an individual was prosecuted are the same under *Blockburger-Sosa* and, if they are, whether the conduct establishing the offenses is also the same. In this case, there is no dispute that the two relevant statutes are the—same offense under a *Blockburger-Sosa* analysis.

We do not reach the question whether there may be some exception to the general rule we adopt today. *See, e.g., Luurtsema,* 12 A.3d at 832 (adopting a—general presumption in favor of full retroactivity for judicial decisions that narrow the scope of liability of a criminal statute, but denying retroactive application of a new rule of substantive criminal law where such a denial did not constitute a—gross miscarriage of justice). Robertson was charged in both federal and state court with possession of child pornography. The federal child pornography statute, 18 U.S.C. section 2252A(a)(5)(B) (2008), criminalizes the—knowing possession of—any material that contains an image of child pornography that has been transported using any means or facility of interstate or foreign commerce. The equivalent Utah statute, section 76-5a-3 (2004), makes it a crime to—knowingly possess. child pornography. The definition of—child pornography is the same under both statutes. And though the federal offense requires proof of an element that the Utah statute does not—interstate commerce—the Utah statute does not require proof of an element that the federal statute does not. Thus, the Utah crime is a lesser-included offense of the federal offense, rendering it the—same offense under a *Blockburger-Sosa* analysis.

Our conclusion in *State v. Franklin* that Utah Code section 76-1-404's use of—same offense incorporated the dual sovereignty doctrine is overruled. The language of the statute unmistakably operates as a legislative rejection of the dual sovereignty doctrine. We accordingly clarify today that section 404's use of—same offense encompasses only the *Blockburger-Sosa* test. Thus, section 404 prohibits Utah prosecutions following prosecutions in other jurisdictions so long as the offenses are the same under *Blockburger-Sosa* and the conduct at issue in the previous prosecution encompasses the same conduct at issue in the Utah prosecution, as informed by the relevant units of prosecution and evidence. The interpretation of section 404 that we announce today applies retroactively and, applying this interpretation to Robertson's case, we hold that section 404 prohibited the State from prosecuting him after the federal prosecution. We therefore reverse the court of appeals' decision.

C. Double Jeopardy and Multiple Offenses

1. Generally

When the prosecution charges a defendant with multiple offenses, a double jeopardy issue might arise in determining whether the two charges are considered to be the "same offense." Thus, double jeopardy might arise not only in the traditional scenario involving successive prosecutions for related acts, but also in a single prosecution involving multiple offenses and punishments.

A constitutional violation does not occur if the legislature intended to impose cumulative punishments for a single act that constitutes more than one crime. In *Missouri v. Hunter*, 459 U.S. 359 (1983), the Supreme Court held that "where a legislature specifically authorizes cumulative punishment under two statutes, the prosecutor may seek and the trial court or jury may impose cumulative punishment under such statutes in a single trial." *Hunter* held that to show legislative intent, the statutes defining the two offenses must require: 1) a "clearly expressed legislative intent" that supports the imposition of cumulative punishments; or 2) proof of different elements.

Either the legislative history of the statute or the language or organization of a statute may reveal the legislative intent. "If the offenses are set forth in different statutes or in distinct sections of a statute, and each provision or section unambiguously sets forth punishment for its violation, then courts generally infer that Congress intended to authorize multiple punishments." *United States v. Gugino*, 860 F.2d 546, 549 (2d Cir. 1988).

In *Brown v. Ohio*, 432 U.S. 161 (1977), the Court suggested that the legislature may divide a continuous course of conduct into separate offenses, even for conduct which occurs within a very short period of time. *See, e.g., Hennemeyer v. Commonwealth*, 580 S.W.2d 211 (Ky. 1979), when the court held that six gunshots fired at police during a chase resulted in six different counts of wanton endangerment.

When the legislative intent to impose multiple charges or punishments is ambiguous, the Supreme Court test from *Blockburger v. United States*, 284 U.S. 299 (1932), governs whether multiple offenses and punishments in a single or successive prosecutions are constitutionally permissible. *Blockburger* held that two offenses do not constitute the same offense when *each* offense requires proof of elements that the other offense does not. The test may be satisfied despite substantial overlap in the evidence used to prove the offenses. In *United States v. Felix*, 503 U.S. 378 (1992), the Supreme Court held that an attempt to commit a substantive offense and a conspiracy to commit that offense are not the same offense for double jeopardy purposes even if they are based upon the same underlying facts. A conspiracy is distinct from the substantive offense that is the object of the conspiracy because the former requires proof of an agreement while the latter requires proof of an overt act.[1]

On the other hand, two offenses *do* constitute the same offense when only *one* of the offenses requires proof that the other offense does not. A lesser included offense is the same as the greater offense because by definition the greater offense includes all the elements of the lesser. Thus, multiple punishments following a single prosecution for both offenses are barred, in the absence of a clearly expressed legislative intent to the contrary.

---

[1] When a single act affects multiple victims, different offenses are committed. If one person is killed and another is wounded by the same bullet, multiple criminal offenses have been committed. *See, e.g., Smith v. Commonwealth*, 734 S.W.2d 437 (Ky. 1987).

Points for Discussion

a. Applying *Blockburger*

Applying the *Blockburger* test, the Court unanimously held that a charge of conspiracy to distribute controlled substances in violation of 21 U.S.C. § 846 is a lesser included offense of conducting a continuing criminal enterprise "in concert" with others in violation of 21 U.S.C. § 848 when the "in concert" element of the latter offense is based upon the same agreement as the conspiracy offense. *Rutledge v. United States*, 517 U.S. 292 (1996). Therefore, convictions of both charges in one trial violate double jeopardy, even when the trial court imposes concurrent life sentences. The Court remanded the case to the trial court to determine which conviction must be vacated.

b. The *Jeffers* Case

In *Jeffers v. United States*, 432 U.S. 137 (1977), a plurality of the Court found:

If the defendant expressly asks for separate trials on the greater and the lesser offenses, or, in connection with his opposition to trial together, fails to raise the issue that one offense might be a lesser included offense of the other, an exception to the same offense rule emerges. Although a defendant is normally entitled to have charges on a greater and a lesser offense resolved in one proceeding, there is no violation of the Double Jeopardy Clause when he elects to have the two offenses tried separately and persuades the trial court to honor his election.

Hypo: *Multiple and Same Offenses*

In each of the following examples, identify whether the multiple offenses charged in one indictment, and arising from the same transaction, constitute the "same offense" under the Hunter or the Blockburger/ Dixon cases. In essence, could each listed offense have been committed, regardless of whether the other listed offense was committed? Use the applicable criminal law of your jurisdiction. The prosecutor charged: 1) Basil with rape and kidnapping arising from the same event; 2) Betty with wanton murder and driving while under the influence of controlled substances, based on the same course of conduct; 3) Larry with theft by deception and forgery. He entered into a CD burner rental agreement. The CD burner was valued at approximately $150. Larry forged the name of "Earl Wheeler," his cousin, on the rental agreement. After the CD burner in question was not returned pursuant to the rental agreement, theft by deception and forgery charges were brought against Larry; 4) Otis with DUI and attempted murder. Barney was on bike patrol in front of the Mayberry Hotel at 3 a.m., when he heard tires squealing. He rode to the back of the parking lot where he saw Otis driving a white F-10 truck with its headlights off. Otis was speeding up to the back of a van several times as the van was leaving the parking lot. Otis then turned the F-10 truck in the direction of Barney, who told him twice to stop. As Barney pedaled his bike away from the truck, the truck hit the bike's back tire, spinning the bike around as Barney jumped off and hit the ground.

In another part of the Double Jeopardy universe lies *United States v. Faulkner*, 793 F.3d 752 (7th Cir. 2015). In *Faulkner*, the defendant pled guilty to certain charges under a 2011 indictment and received an enhanced sentence based on conduct used to bring another indictment in 2013. The Court found that the new indictment did not constitute multiple punishments, either on the facts or as a matter of law, and thus did not violate Double Jeopardy precepts. The court relied on *Witte v. United States*, 515 U.S. 389 (1995): "The Supreme Court has held that the "use of evidence of related criminal conduct to enhance a defendant's sentence for a separate crime within the authorized statutory limits does not constitute punishment for that conduct within the meaning of the Double Jeopardy Clause." *Witte*, 515 U.S. at 399. Thus, for purposes of the Double Jeopardy Clause, any use the judge made of evidence of Faulkner's involvement with controlled substances, gangs, and violence did not constitute "punishment" for that conduct, and thus a later conviction on the basis of that conduct does not violate the Clause."

2. Collateral Estoppel and the Relitigation of Facts

As previously discussed, when there is a single criminal transaction or activity, it may be divided into multiple statutory crimes. If the prosecution chooses to divide the offenses into separate prosecutions or to bring the charges successively rather than simultaneously, an acquittal on one offense may preclude a trial on the other offense under the doctrine of collateral estoppel, also known as issue preclusion. This doctrine provides that determination of a factual issue in a defendant's favor at one proceeding may estop the prosecution from disputing the fact in another proceeding against the same defendant. Thus, when different offenses are charged and double jeopardy would normally not bar a second prosecution, collateral estoppel may, in effect, bar the second trial when a fact previously found in the defendant's favor is necessary to the second conviction.

For collateral estoppel to apply, the defendant must be contesting relitigation of an issue of ultimate fact previously determined in that defendant's favor by a valid and final judgment. First, the second prosecution must involve the same parties as the first trial. A defendant cannot estop the prosecution from relitigating a fact found against the prosecution in a proceeding against a different defendant. In *Standefer v. United States,* 447 U.S. 10 (1980), a unanimous Court held that one defendant's acquittal on a bribery charge did not preclude a later prosecution of another defendant for aiding and abetting the same bribery. Second, the fact finder must have "actually and certainly" determined the issue of fact in the earlier proceeding. For example, in *Schiro v. Farley,* 510 U.S. 222 (1994), a homicide case, the jury was given ten possible verdicts and returned a verdict on only one of the verdict sheets, convicting the defendant for rape felony murder. Defendant claimed that the state was collaterally estopped from showing

Take Note

Collateral estoppel and res judicata are cousins—doctrines that prevent retrials. They have different focuses, however, on what is precluded from retrial, and differ in their elements. Collateral estoppel is about retrying facts while res judicata is about retrying legal claims. Collateral estoppel prevents the relitigation of an ultimate fact that has been necessarily and actually litigated, with a resolution, generally against the same party. Res judicata prevents a party from splitting and retrying claims subject to a final judgment on the merits in successive actions. Both doctrines also apply in the civil domain and are often taught in a Civil Procedure course.

intentional killing (one of the other verdict sheet possibilities) as an aggravated factor supporting a death sentence. The Court held that "failure to return a verdict does not have collateral estoppel effect unless the record establishes that the issue was actually and necessarily decided in the defendant's favor."

The most difficult problem in applying collateral estoppel is ascertaining what facts were established in the earlier case. Because juries render general rather than special verdicts in most criminal cases, a determination of which facts support the verdict requires careful analysis of the trial record. Only those fact determinations essential to the first decision are conclusive in later proceedings.

Not only must a court be able to determine that the fact issue was litigated in defendant's first trial, but also the nature of the reason for acquitting defendant in the earlier trial determines whether collateral estoppel applies in the current case. For example, assume that Donna Defendant is charged with assaults against two victims at the same time and place, but the offenses are not joined. If Donna is acquitted at the first trial for assaulting Victim #1 because there is doubt as to whether she was present at the time of the assaults, her acquittal acts as a collateral estoppel defense to the second assault charge. On the other hand, if the acquittal at the first trial resulted from doubt about whether Donna actually assaulted Victim #1, the prosecutor can still try to prove that Donna assaulted Victim #2.

Bravo-Fernandez v. United States

137 S.Ct. 352 (2016).

JUSTICE GINSBURG delivered the opinion of the Court.

This case concerns the issue-preclusion component of the Double Jeopardy Clause. In criminal prosecutions, as in civil litigation, the issue-preclusion principle means that "when an issue of ultimate fact has once been determined by a valid and final judgment, that issue cannot again be litigated between the same parties in any future lawsuit." *Ashe v. Swenson,* 397 U.S. 436, 443 (1970). Does issue preclusion apply when a jury returns inconsistent verdicts, convicting on one count and acquitting on another count, where both counts turn on the very same issue of ultimate fact? In such a case, this Court has held, both verdicts stand. The Government is barred by the Double Jeopardy Clause from challenging the acquittal, see *Green v. United States,* 355 U.S. 184, 188 (1957), but because the verdicts are rationally irreconcilable, the acquittal gains no preclusive effect, *United States v. Powell,* 469 U.S. 57, 68 (1984). Does issue preclusion attend a jury's acquittal verdict if the same jury in the same proceeding fails to reach a verdict on a different count turning on the same critical issue? This Court has answered yes, in those circumstances, the acquittal has preclusive force. *Yeager v. United States,* 557 U.S. 110, 121 (2009). As "there is no way to decipher what a hung count represents," we reasoned, a jury's failure to decide "has no place in the issue-preclusion analysis." *Ibid.*

In the case before us, the jury returned irreconcilably inconsistent verdicts of conviction and acquittal. Without more, *Powell* would control. There could be no retrial of charges that yielded acquittals but, in view of the inconsistent verdicts, the acquittals would have no issue-preclusive effect on charges that yielded convictions. In this case, however, unlike *Powell,* the guilty verdicts were vacated on appeal because of error in the judge's instructions unrelated to the verdicts' inconsistency. Petitioners urge that, just as a jury's failure to decide has no place in issue-preclusion analysis, so vacated guilty verdicts should not figure in that analysis.

We hold otherwise. One cannot know from the jury's report why it returned no verdict. "A host of reasons" could account for a jury's failure to decide—"sharp disagreement, confusion about the issues, exhaustion after a long trial, to name but a few." *Yeager,* 557 U.S., at 121. But actual inconsistency in a jury's verdicts is a reality; vacatur of a conviction for unrelated legal error does not reconcile the jury's inconsistent returns. We therefore bracket this case with *Powell,* not *Yeager,* and affirm the judgment of the Court of Appeals, which held that issue preclusion does not apply when verdict inconsistency renders unanswerable "what the jury necessarily decided."

The doctrine of claim preclusion instructs that a final judgment on the merits "forecloses successive litigation of the very same claim." *New Hampshire v. Maine*, 532 U.S. 742, 748 (2001); see Restatement (Second) of Judgments § 19, p. 161 (1980). So instructing, the doctrine serves to "avoid multiple suits on identical entitlements or obligations between the same parties." 18 C. Wright, A. Miller, & E. Cooper, Federal Practice and Procedure § 4402, p. 9 (2d ed. 2002). Long operative in civil litigation, claim preclusion is also essential to the Constitution's prohibition against successive criminal prosecutions. No person, the Double Jeopardy Clause states, shall be "subject for the same offense to be twice put in jeopardy of life or limb." Amdt. 5. The Clause "protects against a second prosecution for the same offense after conviction"; as well, "it protects against a second prosecution for the same offense after acquittal." *North Carolina v. Pearce*, 395 U.S. 711, 717 (1969). "A verdict of acquittal in our justice system is final," the last word on a criminal charge, and therefore operates as "a bar to a subsequent prosecution for the same offense." *Green v. United States*, 355 U.S. 184, 188 (1957).

The allied doctrine of issue preclusion ordinarily bars relitigation of an issue of fact or law raised and necessarily resolved by a prior judgment. It applies in both civil and criminal proceedings, with an important distinction. In civil litigation, where issue preclusion and its ramifications first developed, the availability of appellate review is a key factor. In significant part, preclusion doctrine is premised on "an underlying confidence that the result achieved in the initial litigation was substantially correct." *Standefer v. United States*, 447 U.S. 10, 23 (1980). "In the absence of appellate review," we have observed, "such confidence is often unwarranted." *Standefer*, 447 U.S., at 23.

In civil suits, inability to obtain review is exceptional; it occurs typically when the controversy has become moot. In criminal cases, however, only one side (the defendant) has recourse to an appeal from an adverse judgment on the merits. The Government "cannot secure appellate review" of an acquittal, even one "based upon an egregiously erroneous foundation," *Arizona v. Washington*, 434 U.S. 497, 503 (1978). Juries enjoy an " unreviewable power to return a verdict of not guilty for impermissible reasons," for "the Government is precluded from appealing or otherwise upsetting such an acquittal by the Constitution's Double Jeopardy Clause." *United States v. Powell*, 469 U.S. 57, 63 (1984). The absence of appellate review of acquittals, we have cautioned, calls for guarded application of preclusion doctrine in criminal cases. See *Standefer*, 447 U.S., at 22–23. Particularly where it appears that a jury's verdict is the result of compromise, compassion, lenity, or misunderstanding of the governing law, the Government's inability to gain review "strongly militates against giving an acquittal issue preclusive effect." *Id.*, at 23.

This case requires us to determine whether an appellate court's vacatur of a conviction alters issue-preclusion analysis under the Double Jeopardy Clause.

Three prior decisions guide our disposition. This Court first interpreted the Double Jeopardy Clause to incorporate the principle of issue preclusion in *Ashe v. Swenson*, 397 U.S. 436 (1970). *Ashe* involved a robbery of six poker players by a group of masked men. Ashe was charged with robbing one of the players, but a jury acquitted him "due to insufficient evidence." The State then tried Ashe again, this time for robbing another of the poker players. Aided by "substantially stronger" testimony from "witnesses who were for the most part the same," the State secured a conviction. We held that the second prosecution violated the Double Jeopardy Clause. Because the sole issue in dispute in the first trial was whether Ashe had been one of the robbers, the jury's acquittal verdict precluded the State from trying to convince a different jury of that very same fact in a second trial. *Ashe* explained that issue preclusion in criminal cases must be applied with "realism and rationality." To identify what a jury in a previous trial necessarily decided, we instructed, a court must "examine the record of a prior proceeding, taking into account the pleadings, evidence, charge, and other relevant matter." This inquiry "must be set in a practical frame and viewed with an eye to all the circumstances of the proceedings." We have also made clear that "the burden is on the defendant to demonstrate that the issue whose relitigation he seeks to foreclose was actually decided" by a prior jury's verdict of acquittal. *Schiro v. Farley*, 510 U.S. 222, 233 (1994).

In *United States v. Powell*, 469 U.S. 57, we held that a defendant cannot meet this burden when the same jury returns irreconcilably inconsistent verdicts on the question she seeks to shield from reconsideration. *Powell's* starting point was our holding in *Dunn v. United States*, 284 U.S. 390 (1932), that a criminal defendant may not attack a jury's finding of guilt on one count as inconsistent with the jury's verdict of acquittal on another count. The Court's opinion in *Dunn* stated no exceptions to this rule, and after *Dunn* the Court had several times "alluded to the rule as an established principle." Nevertheless, several Courts of Appeals had "recognized exceptions to the rule," and Powell sought an exception for the verdicts of guilt she faced. At trial, a jury had acquitted Powell of various substantive drug charges but convicted her of using a telephone in "causing and facilitating" those same offenses. She appealed, arguing that "the verdicts were inconsistent, and that she therefore was entitled to reversal of the telephone facilitation convictions." Issue preclusion, she maintained, barred "acceptance of the guilty verdicts" on the auxiliary offenses because the same jury had acquitted her of the predicate felonies. Rejecting Powell's argument, we noted that issue preclusion is "predicated on the assumption that the jury acted rationally." When a jury returns irreconcilably inconsistent verdicts, we said, one can glean no more than that "either in the acquittal or the conviction the jury did not speak their real conclusions." Although it is impossible to discern which verdict the jurors arrived at rationally, we observed, "that does not show that they were not convinced of the defendant's guilt." In the event of inconsistent verdicts, we pointed out, it is just as likely that "the jury, convinced of guilt, properly reached its conclusion on one count, and then through mistake, compromise, or lenity, arrived at an inconsistent conclusion on the related offense." Because a court would be at a loss to know which verdict the jury "really meant," we reasoned, principles of issue preclusion are not useful, for they are "predicated on the assumption that the jury acted rationally and found certain facts in reaching its verdict." Holding that the acquittals had no preclusive effect on the counts of conviction, we reaffirmed *Dunn's* rule, under which both Powell's convictions and her acquittals, albeit inconsistent, remained undisturbed.

Finally, in *Yeager v. United States*, 557 U.S. 110 (2009), we clarified that *Powell's* holding on inconsistent verdicts does not extend to an apparent inconsistency between a jury's verdict of acquittal on one count and its inability to reach a verdict on another count. Yeager was tried on charges of fraud and insider trading. The jury acquitted him of the fraud offenses, which the Court of Appeals concluded must have reflected a finding that he "did not have any insider information that contradicted what was presented to the public." Yet the jury failed to reach a verdict on the insider-trading charges, as to which "the possession of insider information was likewise a critical issue of ultimate fact." Arguing that the jury had therefore acted inconsistently, the Government sought to retry Yeager on the hung counts. We ruled that retrial was barred by the Double Jeopardy Clause.

A jury "speaks only through its verdict," we noted. Any number of reasons— including confusion about the issues and sheer exhaustion, we observed—could cause a jury to hang. Accordingly, only "a jury's decisions, not its failures to decide," identify "what a jury necessarily determined at trial." Because a hung count reveals nothing more than a jury's failure to reach a decision, we further reasoned, it supplies no evidence of the jury's irrationality. Hung counts, we therefore held, "have no place in the issue-preclusion analysis": When a jury acquits on one count while failing to reach a verdict on another count concerning the same issue of ultimate fact, the acquittal, and only the acquittal, counts for preclusion purposes. Given the preclusive effect of the acquittal, the Court concluded, Yeager could not be retried on the hung count.

With our controlling precedent in view, we turn to the inconsistent verdicts rendered in this case. The prosecution stemmed from an alleged bribe paid by petitioner Juan Bravo–Fernandez (Bravo), an entrepreneur, to petitioner Hector Martínez–Maldonado (Martínez), then a senator serving the Commonwealth of Puerto Rico. The alleged bribe took the form of an all-expenses-paid trip to Las Vegas, including a $1,000 seat at a professional boxing match featuring a popular Puerto Rican contender. According to the Government, Bravo intended the bribe to secure Martínez' help in shepherding legislation through the Puerto Rico Senate that, if enacted, would "provide substantial financial benefits" to Bravo's enterprise. In the leadup to the Las Vegas trip, Martínez submitted the legislation for the Senate's consideration and issued a committee report supporting it; within a week of returning from Las Vegas, Martínez issued another favorable report and voted to enact the legislation.

Based on these events, a federal grand jury in Puerto Rico indicted petitioners for, *inter alia,* federal-program bribery, in violation of 18 U.S.C. § 666; conspiracy to violate § 666, in violation of § 371; and traveling in interstate commerce to further violations of § 666, in violation of the Travel Act, § 1952(a)(3)(A). Following a three-week trial, a jury convicted Bravo and Martínez of the standalone § 666 bribery offense, but acquitted them of the related conspiracy and Travel Act charges. Each received a sentence of 48 months in prison. The Court of Appeals for the First Circuit vacated the § 666 convictions for instructional error. In the First Circuit's view, the jury had been erroneously charged on what constitutes criminal conduct under that statute. The charge permitted the jury to find Bravo and Martínez "guilty of offering and receiving a gratuity," but, the appeals court held, § 666 proscribes only *quid pro quo* bribes, and not gratuities. True, the court acknowledged, the jury was instructed on both theories of bribery, and the evidence at trial sufficed to support a guilty verdict on either theory. But the Court of Appeals could not say with confidence that the erroneous charge was harmless, so it vacated the § 666 convictions and remanded for further proceedings.

On remand, relying on the issue-preclusion component of the Double Jeopardy Clause, Bravo and Martínez moved for judgments of acquittal on the standalone § 666 charges. They could not be retried on the bribery offense, they insisted, because the jury necessarily determined that they were not guilty of violating § 666 when it acquitted them of conspiring to violate § 666 and traveling in interstate commerce to further violations of § 666. That was so, petitioners maintained, because the only contested issue at trial was whether Bravo had offered, and Martínez had accepted, a bribe within the meaning of § 666.. The District Court denied the motions. If the sole issue disputed at trial was whether Bravo and Martínez had violated § 666, the court explained, then "the jury had acted irrationally." Because the same jury had simultaneously *convicted* Bravo and Martínez on the standalone § 666 charges, "the verdict simply was inconsistent." The First Circuit affirmed, agreeing that the jury's inconsistent returns were fatal to petitioners' issue-preclusion plea. The jury received the same bribery instructions for each count involving § 666, the court noted, so the § 666–based verdicts—convicting on the standalone bribery charges but acquitting on the related Travel Act and conspiracy counts—could not be reconciled. We granted certiorari to resolve a conflict among courts on this question: Does the issue-preclusion component of the Double Jeopardy Clause bar the Government from retrying defendants, like Bravo and Martínez, after a jury has returned irreconcilably inconsistent verdicts of conviction and acquittal, and the convictions are later vacated for legal error unrelated to the inconsistency? Holding that the Double Jeopardy Clause does not bar retrial in these circumstances, we affirm the First Circuit's judgment.

When a conviction is overturned on appeal, "the general rule is that the Double Jeopardy Clause does not bar reprosecution." *Justices of Boston Municipal Court v. Lydon*, 466 U.S. 294, 308 (1984). The ordinary consequence of vacatur, if the Government so elects, is a new trial shorn of the error that infected the first trial. This "continuing jeopardy" rule neither gives effect to the vacated judgment nor offends double jeopardy principles. Rather, it reflects the reality that the "criminal proceedings against an accused have not run their full course." *Ibid.* And by permitting a new trial post vacatur, the continuing-jeopardy rule serves both society's and criminal defendants' interests in the fair administration of justice. "It would be a high price indeed for society to pay," we have recognized, "were every accused granted immunity from punishment because of any defect sufficient to constitute reversible error in the proceedings leading to conviction." *United States v. Tateo*, 377 U.S. 463, 466 (1964). The rights of criminal defendants would suffer too, for "it is at least doubtful that appellate courts would be as zealous as they now are in protecting against the effects of improprieties at the trial or pretrial stage if they knew that reversal of a conviction would put the accused irrevocably beyond the reach of further prosecution." *Ibid.*

Bravo and Martínez ask us to deviate from the general rule that, post vacatur of a conviction, a new trial is in order. When a conviction is vacated on appeal, they maintain, an acquittal verdict simultaneously returned should preclude the Government from retrying the defendant on the vacated count. Our precedent, harmonious with issue-preclusion doctrine, opposes the foreclosure petitioners seek.

Bravo and Martínez bear the burden of demonstrating that the jury necessarily resolved in their favor the question whether they violated § 666. *Schiro*, 510 U.S., at 233. But, as we have explained, a defendant cannot meet that burden where the trial yielded incompatible jury verdicts on the issue the defendant seeks to insulate from relitigation. Here, the jury convicted Bravo and Martínez of violating § 666 but acquitted them of conspiring, and traveling with the intent, to violate § 666. The convictions and acquittals are irreconcilable because other elements of the Travel Act and conspiracy counts were not disputed. It is unknowable "which of the inconsistent verdicts—the acquittals or the convictions—'the jury really meant.'" In view of the Government's inability to obtain review of the acquittals, *Powell*, 469 U.S., at 68 the inconsistent jury findings weigh heavily against according those acquittals issue-preclusive effect. See *Standefer*, 447 U.S., at 23.

That petitioners' bribery convictions were later vacated for trial error does not alter our analysis. The critical inquiry is whether the jury actually decided that Bravo and Martínez did not violate § 666. *Ashe* counsels us to approach that task with "realism and rationality," in particular, to examine the trial record "with an eye to all the circumstances of the proceedings." As the Court of Appeals explained, "the fact that the jury convicted Bravo and Martínez of violating § 666 would seem to be of quite obvious relevance" to this practical inquiry, "even though the convictions were later vacated." Because issue preclusion "depends on the jury's assessment of the facts in light of the charges as presented at trial," a conviction overturned on appeal is "appropriately considered in our assessment of an acquittal verdict's preclusive effect." *United States v. Citron,* 853 F.2d 1055, 1061 (C.A.2 1988). Indeed, the jurors in this case might not have acquitted on the Travel Act and conspiracy counts absent their belief that the § 666 bribery convictions would stand.

Bravo and Martínez could not be retried on the bribery counts, of course, if the Court of Appeals had vacated their § 666 convictions because there was insufficient evidence to support those convictions. For double jeopardy purposes, a court's evaluation of the evidence as insufficient to convict is equivalent to an acquittal and therefore bars a second prosecution for the same offense. See *Burks v. United States,* 437 U.S. 1, 10 (1978). But this is scarcely a case in which the prosecution "failed to muster" sufficient evidence in the first proceeding. *Burks,* 437 U.S., at 11. Quite the opposite. The evidence presented at petitioners' trial supported a guilty verdict on the gratuity theory *as well as* the *quid pro quo* theory. Vacatur was compelled for the sole reason that the First Circuit found the jury charge erroneous to the extent that it encompassed gratuities. Therefore, the general rule of "allowing a new trial to rectify trial error" applied. *Burks,* 437 U.S., at 14. Nor, as the Government acknowledges, would retrial be tolerable if the trial error could resolve the apparent inconsistency in the jury's verdicts. But the instructional error here cannot account for the jury's contradictory determinations because the error applied equally to every § 666–related count.

As in *Powell,* "the problem is that the same jury reached inconsistent results." The convictions' later invalidation on an unrelated ground does not erase or reconcile that inconsistency: It does not bear on "the factual determinations actually and necessarily made by the jury," nor does it "serve to turn the jury's otherwise inconsistent and irrational verdict into a consistent and rational verdict." *People v. Wilson,* 496 Mich. 91, 125, 852 N.W.2d 134, 151 (2014) (Markman, J., dissenting). Bravo and Martínez, therefore, cannot establish the factual predicate necessary to preclude the Government from retrying them on the standalone § 666 charges—namely, that the jury in the first proceeding actually decided that they did not violate the federal bribery statute.

To support their argument for issue preclusion, Bravo and Martínez highlight our decision in *Yeager.* In *Yeager,* we recognized that hung counts "have never been accorded respect as a matter of law or history." That is also true of vacated convictions, they urge, so vacated convictions, like hung counts, should be excluded from the *Ashe* inquiry into what the jury necessarily determined. Asserting that we have "never held an invalid conviction relevant to or evidence of anything," Bravo and Martínez argue that taking account of a vacated conviction in our issue-preclusion analysis would impermissibly give effect to "a legal nullity."

This argument misapprehends the *Ashe* inquiry. It is undisputed that petitioners' convictions are invalid judgments that may not be used to establish their guilt. The question is whether issue preclusion stops the Government from prosecuting them anew. On that question, Bravo and Martínez bear the burden of showing that the issue whether they violated § 666 has been "determined by a valid and final judgment of acquittal." *Yeager,* 557 U.S., at 119. To judge whether they carried that burden, a court must realistically examine the record to identify the ground for the § 666–based *acquittals. Ashe,* 397 U.S., at 444. A conviction that contradicts those acquittals is plainly relevant to that determination, no less so simply because it is later overturned on appeal for unrelated legal error: The split verdict—finding § 666 violated on the standalone counts, but not violated on the related Travel Act and conspiracy counts—tells us that, on one count or the other, "the jury did not follow the court's instructions," whether because of "mistake, compromise, or lenity." *Powell,* 469 U.S., at 65. Petitioners' acquittals therefore do not support the application of issue preclusion here.

Relying on *Yeager,* Bravo and Martínez contend that their vacated convictions should be ignored because, as with hung counts, "there is no way to decipher" what they represent. The § 666 convictions are meaningless, they maintain, because the jury was allowed to convict on the basis of conduct not criminal in the First Circuit—payment of a gratuity. This argument trips on *Yeager's* reasoning. *Yeager* did not rest on a court's inability to detect the basis for a jury's decision. Rather, this Court reasoned that, when a jury hangs, there is *no decision,* hence no evidence of irrationality. A verdict of guilt, by contrast, *is* a jury decision, even if subsequently vacated on appeal. It therefore can evince irrationality. That is the case here. Petitioners do not dispute that the Government's evidence at trial supported a guilty verdict on the *quid pro quo* theory, or that the gratuity instruction held erroneous by the Court of Appeals applied to every § 666–based offense. Because no rational jury could have reached conflicting verdicts on those counts, petitioners' § 666 convictions "reveal the jury's inconsistency—which is the relevant issue here—even if they do not reveal which theory of liability jurors relied upon in reaching those inconsistent verdicts." In other words, because we do not know what the jury would have concluded had there been no instructional error, a new trial on the counts of conviction is in order. Bravo and Martínez have succeeded on appeal to that extent, but they are entitled to no more. The split verdict does not impede the Government from renewing the prosecution.

The Double Jeopardy Clause forever bars the Government from again prosecuting Bravo and Martínez on the § 666–based conspiracy and Travel Act offenses; "the acquittals themselves remain inviolate." Bravo and Martínez have also gained "the benefit of their appellate victory," a second trial on the standalone bribery charges, in which the Government may not invoke a gratuity theory. But issue preclusion is not a doctrine they can commandeer when inconsistent verdicts shroud in mystery what the jury necessarily decided.

For the reasons stated, the judgment of the Court of Appeals for the First Circuit is

Affirmed.

JUSTICE THOMAS, concurring.

As originally understood, the Double Jeopardy Clause does not have an issue-preclusion prong. "The English common-law pleas of *auterfoits acquit* and *auterfoits convict,* on which the Clause was based, barred only repeated 'prosecution for the same identical act *and* crime.' " "In *Ashe* the Court departed from the original meaning of the Double Jeopardy Clause, holding that it precludes successive prosecutions on distinct crimes when facts essential to conviction of the second crime have necessarily been resolved in the defendant's favor by a verdict of acquittal of the first crime." *Yeager, supra,* at 128 (Scalia, J., dissenting). "*Ashe* held only that the Clause sometimes bars successive prosecution of facts found during 'a prior proceeding.' " *Yeager,* however, "barred retrial on hung counts after what was not a prior proceeding but simply an earlier stage of the same proceeding." In an appropriate case, we should reconsider the holdings of *Ashe* and *Yeager.* Because the Court today properly declines to extend those cases, and indeed reaches the correct result under the Clause's original meaning, I join its opinion.

Evidence of a crime for which the defendant was acquitted sometimes may be introduced at a later trial involving the same circumstances. In *Dowling v. United States,* 493 U.S. 342 (1990), while prosecuting a defendant for bank robbery, the Court held that the prosecution may introduce relevant other acts of evidence of a burglary for which the defendant had been acquitted. The Court reasoned that the evidence was admissible at the robbery trial because the acquittal did not prove that the defendant was innocent but only that there was a reasonable doubt about the defendant's guilt. The difference in burdens of proof was the key distinction for the Court: in the first trial, the government failed to show beyond a reasonable doubt that Dowling had committed the act; to introduce evidence of the same act in another trial, the government need show only that a jury could reasonably conclude that the defendant committed the first act.

3. Mistrial of Offenses and the "Continuation" of Jeopardy

What does it mean when a jury does not reach a verdict on a particular charge? Does that count as an acquittal or instead something else that would permit a retrial? The 9th Circuit Court of Appeals took up this question in *Lemke v. Ryan*, 719 F.3d 1093 (9th Cir. 2013).

Lemke v. Ryan

719 F.3d 1093 (9th Cir. 2013).

Mr. Justice Burns delivered the opinion of the Court.

Petitioner Robert D. Lemke appeals the district court's denial of his petition for a writ of habeas corpus brought under 28 U.S.C. § 2254. Lemke contends that subjecting him to retrial for felony murder violated the Double Jeopardy Clause because a jury earlier had impliedly acquitted him of the robbery underlying the felony murder charge. We conclude that the Arizona Court of Appeals' holding that double jeopardy did not bar Lemke's retrial was not "contrary to, or an unreasonable application of, clearly established Federal law, as determined by the Supreme Court of the United States." 28 U.S.C. § 2254(d)(1). Accordingly, we affirm.

In August 2002, Charles Chance was robbed and shot once in the chest. He died at the scene. Petitioner was indicted in Arizona state court on three counts stemming from that incident: (1) felony murder predicated on armed robbery; (2) armed robbery; and (3) conspiracy to commit armed robbery. At trial, the court instructed the jury that the armed robbery charge in Count II included the lesser offense of theft and, similarly, that the charge of conspiracy to commit armed robbery in Count III included the lesser charge of conspiracy to commit theft. In accordance with Arizona law, the trial court also provided a *LeBlanc* instruction, which allowed the jurors to consider a lesser included offense if, after reasonable effort, they could not agree on the greater charged offense. The jury was not instructed on any lesser included offense for Count I, felony murder. After seven days of deliberation, the jury returned guilty verdicts on the lesser included offenses of theft and conspiracy to commit theft. The jury left blank the verdict forms for armed robbery and conspiracy to commit armed robbery. As to felony murder predicated on armed robbery, the jury reported that it could not reach a verdict. The court declared a mistrial on the felony murder count and sentenced Lemke to a total of twenty-seven years' imprisonment for the theft and conspiracy convictions.

The State then sought retrial on the felony murder count. Lemke moved for dismissal, arguing that double jeopardy barred his retrial for felony murder predicated on armed robbery. The trial court denied Lemke's motion, the Arizona Court of Appeals rejected Lemke's double jeopardy claim in a reasoned decision, and the Arizona Supreme Court denied review. Thereafter, Lemke pleaded guilty to felony murder in exchange for a concurrent life sentence with the possibility of parole after 25 years.

The Double Jeopardy Clause provides that no person shall "be subject for the same offence to be twice put in jeopardy of life or limb." U.S. Const. Amend. V. The claim preclusion aspect of the Double Jeopardy Clause bars successive prosecutions for charges that are, for double jeopardy purposes, the same offense. *United States v. Dixon*, 509 U.S. 688 (1993). The issue preclusion, or collateral estoppel, aspect of double jeopardy "precludes the Government from relitigating any issue that was necessarily decided by a jury's acquittal in a prior trial." *Yeager v. United States*, 557 U.S. 110 (2009).

The Arizona Court of Appeals held that neither aspect of double jeopardy barred Lemke's retrial for felony murder. We now consider whether that conclusion constituted an unreasonable application of clearly established Supreme Court precedent, and we hold that it did not.

The Supreme Court has held that the Double Jeopardy Clause "protects against successive prosecutions for the same offense after acquittal or conviction." *Monge v. California*, 524 U.S. 721 (1998). Under this formulation and others put forth by the Supreme Court, the prosecution of Lemke for armed robbery felony murder after his implied acquittal of armed robbery was indeed prosecution for the "same offense." Supreme Court precedent, however, does not clearly establish that, under the circumstances of his case, the continued prosecution was "successive" and therefore prohibited.

Two charges constitute the "same offense" for double jeopardy purposes unless "each provision requires proof of a fact which the other does not." *Blockburger v. United States*, 284 U.S. 299 (1932). The State admits, and the Arizona Court of Appeals held, that armed robbery and felony murder predicated on armed robbery are the "same offense" under the *Blockburger* test because the felony murder includes all of the elements of armed robbery. *See, e.g., Harris v. Oklahoma*, 433 U.S. 682 (1977) (holding that, for double jeopardy purposes, robbery with a firearm is the same offense as felony murder predicated on armed robbery). The Arizona Court of Appeals also assumed that, by convicting Lemke of theft and remaining silent as to the charge of armed robbery, the jury impliedly acquitted Lemke of armed robbery. The Arizona Court of Appeals was thus confronted with a situation in which the jury had convicted the defendant of theft, impliedly acquitted him of armed robbery, and deadlocked on felony murder, and all three of those charges constituted the "same offense" for double jeopardy purposes. Lemke argues that, once the Arizona Court of Appeals reached this point in its analysis, *Blockburger* compelled the court to hold that double jeopardy barred his retrial for felony murder. His argument is attractively simple. Under *Blockburger,* the offenses for which he was convicted (theft) and impliedly acquitted (armed robbery) are the "same offense" as felony murder. Accordingly, the State could not place him twice in jeopardy for the "same offense" by retrying him on the felony murder charge.

The Arizona Court of Appeals, however, did not follow the straightforward approach that Lemke advocates. Citing *Richardson v. United States,* 468 U.S. 317, the court noted that the protections afforded by the Double Jeopardy Clause apply only after original jeopardy has terminated, and jeopardy "continues" on counts for which the jury has failed to reach a verdict. The Arizona Court of Appeals therefore held that, although jeopardy had terminated as to the armed robbery count of the indictment, it had never terminated as to the felony murder count. Thus, retrial for felony murder would not expose Lemke to a *successive* prosecution or place him "*twice* in jeopardy."

Case law from our sister circuits that conflicts with *Wilson* also buttresses our conclusion that Lemke's double jeopardy claim is not founded on clearly established Supreme Court law. *See Carey v. Musladin,* 549 U.S. 70 (2006). Several decisions from other circuits suggest that double jeopardy does not necessarily bar retrial on a hung count after jeopardy has terminated on a lesser included or greater inclusive offense charged in the same indictment. *See, e.g., United States v. Jackson,* 658 F.3d 145, 151 (2d Cir. 2011) (finding no double jeopardy violation where defendant had been convicted of lesser included offense and retried on deadlocked greater offense, but suggesting that collateral estoppel might have barred retrial had defendant been acquitted, rather than convicted, of lesser offense); *Delgado v. Fla. Dep't of Corrections,* 659 F.3d 1311, 1330 (11th Cir. 2011) (noting that jeopardy can continue on one charge even after it terminates on a lesser or greater offense charged in the same indictment); *United States v. Howe,* 538 F.3d 820, 827 (8th Cir. 2008) (holding that, when a jury acquits a defendant of a greater offense and deadlocks as to a lesser offense, "jeopardy continues as to the lesser offense, notwithstanding the defendant's acquittal on the greater offense"), *abrogated on other grounds by Yeager v. United States,* 557 U.S. 110 (2009). These cases cast doubt on the proposition that Supreme Court precedent clearly establishes that double jeopardy bars retrial on a deadlocked count once jeopardy has terminated on another count in the indictment that constitutes the "same offense."

We conclude, therefore, that Lemke has failed to meet the requirement of 28 U.S.C. § 2254(d)(1) that the decision of the Arizona Court of Appeals rejecting double jeopardy claim preclusion "was contrary to, or involved an unreasonable application of, clearly established Federal law, as determined by the Supreme Court of the United States."

We also conclude that the Arizona Court of Appeals did not unreasonably apply clearly established federal law in holding that collateral estoppel did not bar Lemke's retrial for felony murder. Collateral estoppel would apply if Lemke's retrial for felony murder would involve "relitigating any issue that was necessarily decided by a jury's acquittal in a prior trial." *Yeager*, 557 U.S. at 119. In deciding whether an issue was "necessarily decided" by the jury, the court must "examine the record of a prior proceeding, taking into account the pleadings, evidence, charge, and other relevant matter, and conclude whether a rational jury could have grounded its verdict upon an issue other than that which the defendant seeks to foreclose from consideration." *Ashe v. Swenson*, 397 U.S. 436 (1970).

The Arizona Court of Appeals reasonably concluded that Petitioner could not carry his burden of demonstrating that the jury "necessarily decided" that he had not committed armed robbery. The court noted that "the *LeBlanc* instruction prevents us from knowing whether the jury unanimously acquitted defendant of armed robbery or simply could not agree." Although the jury's silence on armed robbery constituted an implied acquittal of that charge for the purposes of the claim preclusion aspect of double jeopardy, it does not have an issue preclusive effect unless the record indicates that the jury necessarily decided the issue in Lemke's favor. Here, the record did not establish that the jury had necessarily decided that Lemke did not commit armed robbery.

The judgment of the district court is *AFFIRMED*.

MR. JUSTICE BURNS concurring in part and dissenting in part.

I agree that the decision of the Arizona Court of Appeals rejecting Lemke's double jeopardy claim was not contrary to, or an unreasonable application of, clearly established Federal law. I don't agree, though, that Lemke still had a double jeopardy claim left after he pled guilty to felony murder. Lemke signed a plea agreement in which he bargained away his right to pursue "any and all motions, defenses, objections or requests which he had made or raised, or could assert hereafter, to the court's entry of judgment against him." But after he got what he bargained for—namely, a favorable sentence—he reneged on his promise to drop his defenses and appeals. We shouldn't let him get away with such perfidy.

D. Termination of the Case by Dismissal, Mistrial or Acquittal

Take Note

Once jeopardy has attached, the way in which a trial ends is critical to double jeopardy application. Whether the cessation of a trial is a dismissal or acquittal is important to resolving whether the government can appeal the adverse termination of the case, and whether the defendant can be reprosecuted. For example, if a case is terminated by mistrial, manifest necessity for the mistrial declaration is crucial for the prosecution to retry a defendant who objected to a mistrial. The assumption underlying the mistrial was that the reason for terminating the first trial was not a fatal defect to a second trial.

All jurisdictions provide statutory authority for the government to appeal from an adverse termination. *See, e.g.,* 18 U.S.C. § 3731. In the absence of a double jeopardy prohibition, the government can appeal under statutory authority and, if successful, can reprosecute the defendant.

1. Termination of a Trial Because of Judicial Error

Can a premature ending to a trial due to a judicial error, namely an erroneous directed verdict of acquittal by a trial judge, be appealed and retried? The Supreme Court confronted this question in *Evans v. Michigan,* below.

Evans v. Michigan

568 U.S. 313 (2013).

JUSTICE SOTOMAYOR delivered the opinion of the Court.

When the State of Michigan rested its case at petitioner Lamar Evans' arson trial, the court entered a directed verdict of acquittal, based upon its view that the State had not provided sufficient evidence of a particular element of the offense. It turns out that the unproven "element" was not actually a required element at all. We must decide whether an erroneous acquittal such as this nevertheless constitutes an acquittal for double jeopardy purposes, which would mean that Evans could not be retried. This Court has previously held that a judicial acquittal premised upon a "misconstruction" of a criminal statute is an "acquittal on the merits that bars retrial." *Arizona v. Rumsey,* 467 U.S. 203 (1984). Seeing no meaningful constitutional distinction between a trial court's "misconstruction" of a statute and its erroneous addition of a statutory element, we hold that a midtrial acquittal in these circumstances is an acquittal for double jeopardy purposes as well.

The State charged Evans with burning "other real property," a violation of Mich. Comp. Laws § 750.73 (1981). The State's evidence suggested that Evans had burned down an unoccupied house. At the close of the State's case, however, Evans moved for a directed verdict of acquittal. He pointed the court to the applicable Michigan Criminal Jury Instructions, which listed as the "Fourth" element of the offense "that the building was not a dwelling house." The commentary to the Instructions emphasized, "an essential element is that the structure burned is *not* a dwelling house." Evans argued that Mich. Comp. Laws § 750.72 criminalizes common-law arson, which requires that the structure burned be a dwelling, while the provision under which he was charged, § 750.73, covers all other real property. Persuaded, the trial court granted the motion. The court explained that the "testimony of the homeowner was this was a dwelling house," so the non-dwelling requirement of Section 750.73 was not met.

On the State's appeal, the Michigan Court of Appeals reversed and remanded. Evans had conceded, and the court held, that under controlling precedent, burning "other real property" is a lesser included offense under Michigan law, and disproving the greater offense is not required. The court thus explained it was "undisputed that the trial court misperceived the elements of the offense with which Evans was charged and erred by directing a verdict." But the court rejected Evans' argument that the Double Jeopardy Clause barred retrial.

In answering this question, we do not write on a clean slate. Quite the opposite. It has been half a century since we first recognized that the Double Jeopardy Clause bars retrial following a court-decreed acquittal, even if the acquittal is "based upon an egregiously erroneous foundation." Fong Foo v. United States, 369 U.S. 141 (*per curiam*). A mistaken acquittal is an acquittal nonetheless, and we have long held that "a verdict of acquittal could not be reviewed, on error or otherwise, without putting a defendant twice in jeopardy, and thereby violating the Constitution." United States v. Ball, 163 U.S. 662, 671 (1896).

Our cases have defined an acquittal to encompass any ruling that the prosecution's proof is insufficient to establish criminal liability for an offense. *See ibid.*, Burks v. United States, 437 U.S. 1 (1978); United States v. Martin Linen Supply Co., 430 U.S. 564 (1977). Thus an "acquittal" includes "a ruling by the court that the evidence is insufficient to convict," a "factual finding that necessarily establishes the criminal defendant's lack of criminal culpability," and any other "ruling which relates to the ultimate question of guilt or innocence." *Scott*, 437 U.S. at 91, 98. These sorts of substantive rulings stand apart from procedural rulings that may also terminate a case midtrial, which we generally refer to as dismissals or mistrials. Procedural dismissals include rulings on questions that "are unrelated to factual guilt or innocence," but "which serve other purposes," including "a legal judgment that a defendant, although criminally culpable, may not be punished" because of some problem like an error with the indictment.

The court below saw things differently. It identified a "constitutionally meaningful difference" between this case and our previous decisions. Those cases, the court found, "involved evidentiary errors regarding the proof needed to establish a factual element of the crimes at issue," but still ultimately involved "a resolution regarding the sufficiency of the factual elements of the charged offense." When a court mistakenly "identifies an extraneous element and dismisses the case solely on that basis," however, it has "not resolved or even addressed any factual element necessary to establish" the offense. As a result, the court below reasoned, the case terminates "based on an error of law unrelated to the defendant's guilt or innocence on the elements of the charged offense," and thus falls outside the definition of an acquittal.

We fail to perceive the difference. This case, like our previous ones, involves an antecedent legal error that led to an acquittal because the State failed to prove some fact it was not actually required to prove. We hold that Evans' trial ended in an acquittal when the trial court ruled the State had failed to produce sufficient evidence of his guilt. The Double Jeopardy Clause thus bars retrial for his offense and should have barred the State's appeal. The judgment of the Supreme Court of Michigan is

Reversed.

JUSTICE ALITO, dissenting.

The Court holds that the Double Jeopardy Clause bars petitioner's retrial for arson because his attorney managed to convince a judge to terminate petitioner's first trial prior to verdict on the specious ground that the offense with which he was charged contains an imaginary "element" that the prosecution could not prove. The Court's decision makes no sense. It is not consistent with the original meaning of the Double Jeopardy Clause; it does not serve the purposes of the prohibition against double jeopardy; and contrary to the Court's reasoning, the trial judge's ruling was not an "acquittal," which our cases have "consistently" defined as a decision that "actually represents a resolution, correct or not, of some or all of the factual *elements of the offense charged.*" *E.g., Smith v. Massachusetts,* 543 U.S. 462 *(quoting*

Food for Thought

Wrong! What if the attorney was correct in *Evans* about the extra element, but the Court mistakenly thought the element had been met by the state and proceeded with a resulting conviction. Would a retrial be a violation of double jeopardy?

United States v. Martin Linen Supply Co., 430 U.S. 564 (1977)). For no good reason, the Court deprives the State of Michigan of its right to have one fair opportunity to convict petitioner, and I therefore respectfully dissent.

2. Midtrial Dismissal of Charges

If a case or charge is dismissed before the conclusion of proceedings, even during a trial, whether a retrial of a case can occur is dependent on differing considerations. Who sought the dismissal, the prosecution or defense? Was the dismissal based on guilt or innocence or some other ground? Can the government appeal at all? Does it matter how the trial judge characterized her dismissal of the case or charge? These and other questions are considered in the following case.

United States v. Scott

437 U.S. 82 (1978).

MR. JUSTICE REHNQUIST delivered the opinion of the Court.

On March 5, 1975, respondent, a member of the police force in Muskegon, Mich., was charged in a three-count indictment with distribution of narcotics. Both before his trial in the United States District Court for the Western District of Michigan, and twice during the trial, respondent moved to dismiss the two counts of the indictment which concerned transactions that took place during the preceding September, on the ground that his defense had been prejudiced by pre-indictment delay. At the close of the evidence, the court granted respondent's motion. Although the court did not explain its reasons for dismissing the second count, it explicitly concluded that respondent had "presented sufficient proof of prejudice with respect to Count I."

The Government sought to appeal the dismissals of the first two counts to the United States Court of Appeals for the Sixth Circuit. That court, relying on our opinion in *United States v. Jenkins*, 420 U.S. 358 (1975), concluded that any further prosecution of respondent was barred by the Double Jeopardy Clause of the Fifth Amendment, and therefore dismissed the appeal. The Government sought review in this Court only with regard to the dismissal of the first count. We granted certiorari to give further consideration to the applicability of the Double Jeopardy Clause to Government appeals from orders granting defense motions to terminate a trial before verdict. We now reverse.

The problem presented by this case could not have arisen during the first century of this Court's existence. The Court has long taken the view that the United States has no right of appeal in a criminal case, absent explicit statutory authority. Such authority was not provided until the enactment of the Criminal Appeals Act, Act of Mar. 2, 1907, which permitted the United States to seek a writ of error in this Court from any decision dismissing an indictment on the basis of "the invalidity, or construction of the statute upon which the indictment is founded." In 1971, Congress adopted the current language of the Act, permitting Government appeals from any decision dismissing an indictment, "except that no appeal shall lie where the Double Jeopardy Clause of the United States Constitution prohibits further prosecution." 18 U.S.C. § 3731.

These, at least, are two venerable principles of double jeopardy jurisprudence. The successful appeal of a judgment of conviction, on any ground other than the insufficiency of the evidence to support the verdict, *Burks v. United States*, 437 U.S. 1, poses no bar to further prosecution on the same charge. A judgment of acquittal, whether based on a jury verdict of not guilty or on a ruling by the court that the evidence is insufficient to convict, may not be appealed and terminates the prosecution when a second trial would be necessitated by a reversal.

Although the primary purpose of the Double Jeopardy Clause was to protect the integrity of a final judgment, this Court has also developed a body of law guarding the separate but related interest of a defendant in avoiding multiple prosecutions even where no final determination of guilt or innocence has been made. Such interests may be involved in two different situations: the first, in which the trial judge declares a mistrial; the second, in which the trial judge terminates the proceedings favorably to the defendant on a basis not related to factual guilt or innocence.

Our opinion in *Burks* necessarily holds that there has been a "failure of proof," requiring an acquittal when the Government does not submit sufficient evidence to rebut a defendant's essentially factual defense of insanity, though it may otherwise be entitled to have its case submitted to the jury. The defense of insanity, like the defense of entrapment, arises from "the notion that Congress could not have intended criminal punishment for a defendant who has committed all the elements of a proscribed offense," *United States v. Russell*, 411 U.S. 423 (1973), where other facts established to the satisfaction of the trier of fact provide a legally adequate justification for otherwise criminal acts. Such a factual finding does "necessarily establish the criminal defendant's lack of criminal culpability," (Brennan, J., dissenting), under the existing law; the fact that "the acquittal may result from erroneous evidentiary rulings or erroneous interpretations of governing legal principles," affects the accuracy of that determination, but it does not alter its essential character. By contrast, the dismissal of an indictment for pre-indictment delay represents a legal judgment that a defendant, although criminally culpable, may not be punished because of a supposed constitutional violation.

In the present case, defendant successfully avoided such a submission of the first count of the indictment by persuading the trial court to dismiss it on a basis which did not depend on guilt or innocence. He was thus neither acquitted nor convicted, because he himself successfully undertook to persuade the trial court not to submit the issue of guilt or innocence to the jury which had been empanelled to try him.

Defendant has not been "deprived" of his valued right to go to the first jury; only the public has been deprived of its valued right to "one complete opportunity to convict those who have violated its laws." *Arizona v. Washington*. No interest protected by the Double Jeopardy Clause is invaded when the Government is allowed to appeal and seek reversal of such a midtrial termination of the proceedings in a manner favorable to the defendant.[2]

We, of course, do not suggest that a midtrial dismissal of a prosecution, in response to a defense motion on grounds unrelated to guilt or innocence, is necessarily improper. Such rulings may be necessary to terminate proceedings marred by fundamental error. But where a defendant prevails on such a motion, he takes the risk that an appellate court will reverse the trial court.

It is obvious from what we have said that we believe we pressed too far in *Jenkins*, the concept of the "defendant's valued right to have his trial completed by a particular tribunal." We now conclude that where the defendant himself seeks to have the trial terminated without any submission to either judge or jury as to his guilt or innocence, an appeal by the Government from his successful effort to do so is not barred by 18 U.S.C. § 3731.

MR. JUSTICE BRENNAN, with whom MR. JUSTICE WHITE, MR. JUSTICE MARSHALL, and MR. JUSTICE STEVENS join, dissenting.

While the Double Jeopardy Clause often has the effect of protecting the accused's interest in the finality of particular favorable determinations, this is not its objective. For the Clause

Food for Thought

In the three years between the *Jenkins* and *Scott* cases, the Court's philosophy about Double Jeopardy changed—from shielding a defendant from the burden of multiple prosecutions (*i.e.*, running the gauntlet twice), to preserving determinations only of innocence via an acquittal, but allowing retrials following dismissals or mistrials.

---

[2] We should point out that it is entirely possible for a trial court to reconcile the public interest in the Government's right to appeal from an erroneous conclusion of law, with the defendant's interest in avoiding a second prosecution. In *Wilson*, the court permitted the case to go to the jury, which returned a verdict of guilty, but it subsequently dismissed the indictment for preindictment delay on the basis of evidence adduced at trial.

often permits Government appeals from final judgments favorable to the accused. The purpose of the Clause, which the Court today fails sufficiently to appreciate, is to protect the accused against the agony and risks attendant upon undergoing more than one criminal trial for any single offense. Society's "willingness to limit the Government to a single criminal proceeding to vindicate its very vital interest in enforcement of criminal laws" bespeaks society's recognition of the gross unfairness of requiring the accused to undergo the strain and agony of more than one trial for any single offense. The policies of the Double Jeopardy Clause mandate that the Government be afforded but one complete opportunity to convict an accused and that when the first proceeding terminates in a final judgment favorable to the defendant any retrial be barred. The rule as to acquittals can only be understood as simply an application of this larger principle.

Food for Thought

As *Scott* states, an acquittal occurs when the judge's ruling represents a "resolution in the defendant's favor, correct or not, of some or all of the factual elements of the offense charged." In *Sanabria v. United States*, 437 U.S. 54 (1978), decided the same day as *Scott*, the Court held that when a defendant is acquitted at trial, he cannot be retried for the same charge, even if the legal rulings underlying the acquittal were erroneous. By contrast, the Court has held that the government may appeal the grant of *pretrial* motions to dismiss. *Serfass v. United States*, 420 U.S. 377 (1975). Even though a successful government appeal can lead to a new prosecution, the Double Jeopardy doctrine does not bar the appeal because jeopardy had not attached at the time the trial court dismissed the charges. The policy supporting this disposition is that the defendant is not running the gauntlet more than once, i.e., a reprosecution does not provide a second chance for the prosecution because it has not yet had a first chance.

Hypo: *Appealing the Acquittal*

Defendants are charged with conspiracy and concealing material facts in a federal court case. Suppose, after trial has commenced, and during the prosecution's case, the district court judge concludes that the prosecutor's conduct is improper and that the prosecution's witnesses lack credibility. The judge then orders the jury to acquit the defendant, which it does, and a judgment of acquittal is promptly entered. The district court judge, however, does not have the power to direct the jury to render an acquittal. If the prosecutor appeals the acquittal, and wins, can the accused be retried? *See Fong Foo v. United States*, 369 U.S. 141 (1962).

3. Mistrials and Hung Juries

If a jury announces through a foreperson in a report on its status during deliberations that it is unanimously against the capital and first-degree murder charges, but deadlocked on the manslaughter charge, and the judge subsequently declares a mistrial, can the state retry the defendant on all three charges? In *Blueford v. Arkansas*, the Supreme Court said that a retrial on all charges was permitted. Chief Justice Roberts found that the jury's deliberations were not final and that because there was manifest necessity for a mistrial, a retrial was permitted.

Blueford v. Arkansas

566 U.S. 599 (2012).

CHIEF JUSTICE ROBERTS delivered the opinion of the Court.

The Double Jeopardy Clause protects against being tried twice for the same offense. The Clause does not, however, bar a second trial if the first ended in a mistrial. Before the jury concluded deliberations in this case, it reported that it was unanimous against guilt on charges of capital murder and

Hear It

You can hear the oral argument in *Blueford* at: http://www.oyez.org/cases/2010-2019/2011/2011_10_1320.

first-degree murder, was deadlocked on manslaughter, and had not voted on negligent homicide. The court told the jury to continue to deliberate. The jury did so but still could not reach a verdict, and the court declared a mistrial. All agree that the defendant may be retried on charges of manslaughter and negligent homicide. The question is whether he may also be retried on charges of capital and first-degree murder.

One-year-old Matthew McFadden, Jr., suffered a severe head injury on November 28, 2007, while home with his mother's boyfriend, Alex Blueford. Despite treatment at a hospital, McFadden died a few days later. The State of Arkansas charged Blueford with capital murder, but waived the death penalty. The State's theory at trial was that Blueford had injured McFadden intentionally, causing the boy's death "under circumstances manifesting extreme indifference to the value of human life." Ark. Code Ann. §5–10–101(a)(9)(A) (Supp. 2011). The defense, in contrast, portrayed the death as the result of Blueford accidentally knocking McFadden onto the ground. The trial court instructed the jury that the charge of capital murder included three lesser offenses: first-degree murder, manslaughter, and negligent homicide.

Blueford's primary submission is that he cannot be retried for capital and first-degree murder because the jury actually acquitted him of those offenses, claiming it was an acquittal in substance, if not form. Here, according to Blueford, the foreperson's announcement of the jury's unanimous votes on capital and first-degree murder represented just that: a resolution of some or all of the elements of those offenses in Blueford's favor. We disagree. The foreperson's report was not a final resolution of anything. The jurors in fact went back to the jury room to deliberate further, even after the foreperson had delivered her report. When they emerged a half hour later, the foreperson stated only that they were unable to reach a verdict.

Blueford also contends that there was no necessity for a mistrial on capital and first-degree murder, given the foreperson's report that the jury had voted unanimously against guilt on those charges. According to Blueford, the court at that time should have taken "some action," whether through partial verdict forms or other means, to allow the jury to give effect to those votes, and then considered a mistrial only as to the remaining charges. We reject that suggestion. We have never required a trial court, before declaring a mistrial because of a hung jury, to consider any particular means of breaking the impasse—let alone to consider giving the jury new options for a verdict. See *Renico v. Lett,* 559 U. S. 766, (2010). As permitted under Arkansas law, the jury's options in this case were limited to two: either convict on one of the offenses, or acquit on all. The instructions explained those options in plain terms, and the verdict forms likewise contemplated no other outcome. There were separate forms to convict on each of the possible offenses, but there was only one form to acquit, and it was to acquit on all of them. When the foreperson disclosed the jury's votes on capital and first-degree murder, the trial court did not abuse its discretion by refusing to add another option—that of acquitting on some offenses but not others. That, however, is precisely the relief Blueford seeks—relief the Double Jeopardy Clause does not afford him.

The jury in this case did not convict Blueford of any offense, but it did not acquit him of any either. When the jury was unable to return a verdict, the trial court properly declared a mistrial and discharged the jury. As a consequence, the Double Jeopardy Clause does not stand in the way of a second trial on the same offenses.

The judgment of the Supreme Court of Arkansas is

Affirmed.

E. Termination of the Case by Conviction

The general rule is that when a defendant appeals or collaterally attacks a conviction successfully, double jeopardy does not preclude a re-prosecution.

When a defendant chooses to appeal from a conviction, he seeks to nullify the conviction. If successful, the courts treat the conviction as a nullity, meaning no trial ever occurred. Thus, the slate is wiped clean, the defendant never ran the gauntlet, and he can be tried "again." The following case provides some insight into this general rule.

Lockhart v. Nelson

488 U.S. 33 (1988).

CHIEF JUSTICE REHNQUIST delivered the opinion of the Court.

In this case a reviewing court set aside a defendant's conviction of enhanced sentence because certain evidence was erroneously admitted against him, and further held that the Double Jeopardy Clause forbade the State to retry him as a habitual offender because the remaining evidence adduced at trial was legally insufficient to support a conviction. Nothing in the record suggests any misconduct in the prosecutor's submission of the evidence. We conclude that in cases such as this, where the evidence offered by the State and admitted by the trial court—whether erroneously or not—would have been sufficient to sustain a guilty verdict, the Double Jeopardy Clause does not preclude retrial.

Respondent Johnny Lee Nelson pleaded guilty in Arkansas state court to burglary, a class B felony, and misdemeanor theft. He was sentenced under Arkansas' habitual criminal statute, which provides that a defendant who is convicted of a class B felony and "who has previously been convicted of or found guilty of four [4] or more felonies," may be sentenced to an enhanced term of imprisonment of between 20 and 40 years. To have a convicted defendant's sentence enhanced under the statute, the State must prove beyond a reasonable doubt, at a separate sentencing hearing, that the defendant has the requisite number of prior felony convictions.

At respondent's sentencing hearing, the State introduced, without objection from the defense, certified copies of four prior felony convictions. The case was submitted to the jury, which found that the State had met its burden of proving four prior convictions and imposed an enhanced sentence. The State courts upheld the enhanced sentence on both direct and collateral review, despite respondent's protestations that one of the convictions relied upon by the State had been pardoned.

After finding that one conviction had been pardoned upon a writ of habeas corpus, the State desired to resentence the defendant as a habitual offender based on a different conviction. The District Court decided that the Double Jeopardy

Clause prevented the State from attempting to resentence respondent as a habitual offender on the burglary charge. The Court of Appeals for the Eighth Circuit affirmed. The Court of Appeals reasoned that the pardoned conviction was not admissible under state law, and that "without it, the state has failed to provide sufficient evidence" to sustain the enhanced sentence. We granted certiorari to review this interpretation of the Double Jeopardy Clause.

It has long been settled that the Double Jeopardy Clause's general prohibition against successive prosecutions does not prevent the government from retrying a defendant who succeeds in getting his first conviction set aside, through direct appeal or collateral attack, because of some error in the proceedings leading to conviction. *United States v. Ball,* 163 U.S. 662 (1896); *United States v. Tateo,* 377 U.S. 463 (1964). This rule is necessary in order to ensure the "sound administration of justice":

> Corresponding to the right of an accused to be given a fair trial is the societal interest in punishing one whose guilt is clear after he has obtained such a trial. It would be a high price indeed for society to pay were every accused granted immunity from punishment because of any defect sufficient to constitute reversible error in the proceedings leading to conviction.

Permitting retrial after a conviction has been set aside also serves the interests of defendants, for "it is at least doubtful that appellate courts would be as zealous as they now are in protecting against the effects of improprieties at the trial or pretrial stage if they knew that reversal of a conviction would put the accused irrevocably beyond the reach of further prosecution." *Ibid.*

In *Burks v. United States,* 437 U.S. 1 (1978), we recognized an exception to the general rule—when a defendant's conviction is reversed by an appellate court on the sole ground that the evidence was insufficient to sustain the jury's verdict, the Double Jeopardy Clause bars a retrial on the same charge.

Burks was based on the view that an appellate court's reversal for insufficiency of the evidence is in effect a determination that the government's case against the defendant was so lacking that the trial court should have entered a judgment of acquittal, rather than submitting the case to the jury. *Burks* was careful to point out that a reversal based solely on evidentiary insufficiency has fundamentally different implications, for double jeopardy purposes, than a reversal based on such ordinary "trial errors" as the "incorrect receipt or rejection of evidence." While the former is in effect a finding "that the government has failed to prove its case" against the defendant, the latter "implies nothing with respect to the guilt or innocence of the defendant," but is simply "a determination that he has been convicted through a judicial *process* which is defective in some fundamental respect."

It appears to us to be beyond dispute that this case is a situation described in *Burks* as reversal for "trial error"—the trial court erred in admitting a particular piece of evidence, and without it there was insufficient evidence to support a judgment of conviction. But clearly with that evidence, there was enough to support the sentence: the court and jury had before them certified copies of four prior felony convictions, and that is sufficient to support a verdict of enhancement under the statute. The fact that one of the convictions had been later pardoned by the Governor vitiated its legal effect, but it did not deprive the certified copy of that conviction of its probative value under the statute. It is quite clear from our opinion in *Burks* that a reviewing court must consider all of the evidence admitted by the trial court in deciding whether retrial is permissible under the Double Jeopardy Clause—indeed, that was the *ratio decidendi* of *Burks*, and the overwhelming majority of appellate courts considering the question have agreed.

What's That?

What is a felony? While the term lies comfortably within the popular culture, its legal definition does not. A felony generally refers to a serious crime for which the potential incarceration is more than one year. The key is not what the accused actually receives as a sentence, but what the accused could receive. Thus, a charge of aggravated battery, with a sentence of two years, would still be a felony even if the accused were released on probation after a conviction. Note that lesser offenses, for which incarceration could occur up to one year, are called misdemeanors.

Permitting retrial in this instance is not the sort of governmental oppression at which the Double Jeopardy Clause is aimed; rather, it serves the interest of the defendant by affording him an opportunity to "obtain a fair readjudication of his guilt free from error." Had the defendant offered evidence at the sentencing hearing to prove that the conviction had become a nullity by reason of the pardon, the trial judge would presumably have allowed the prosecutor an opportunity to offer evidence of another prior conviction to support the habitual offender charge. Our holding today thus merely recreates the situation that would have been obtained if the trial court had excluded the evidence of the conviction because of the showing of a pardon.

The judgment of the Court of Appeals is accordingly *reversed*.

JUSTICE MARSHALL, with whom JUSTICE BRENNAN and JUSTICE BLACKMUN join, dissenting.

It seems to me that the Court's analysis of this issue should begin with the recognition that, in deciding when the double jeopardy bar should apply, we are balancing two weighty interests: the defendant's interest in repose and society's interest in the orderly administration of justice. *See, e.g., United States v. Tateo*. At first blush, it would seem that the defendant's interest is every bit as great in this situation as in the *Burks* situation. Society's interest, however, would appear to turn on a number of variables. The chief one is the likelihood that retrying the defendant will lead to conviction. In appraising this likelihood, one might inquire into whether prosecutors tend in close cases to hold back probative evidence of a defendant's guilt; if they do not, there would be scant societal interest in permitting retrial given that the State's remaining evidence is, by definition, insufficient. Alternatively, one might inquire as to why the evidence at issue was deemed inadmissible. Where evidence was stricken for reasons having to do with its unreliability, it would seem curious to include it

Practice Pointer

Should the defense attorney appeal issues of trial error as well as issues relating to evidentiary insufficiency? In practice, a convicted defendant will seek reversal for any reason regardless of the Double Jeopardy consequences. After *Burks* and *Nelson*, the risk in offering judges multiple grounds for reversal may lead judges to reverse for trial error because of the possibility of a new trial. Of course, there may not be another trial. Instead, a prosecutor may be willing to plea bargain because the witnesses' memories are faded, public sentiment about the type of offense has changed, or simply for judicial economy purposes.

in the sufficiency calculus. Inadmissible hearsay evidence, for example, or evidence deemed defective or nonprobative as a matter of law thus might not be included. By contrast, evidence stricken in compliance with evidentiary rules grounded in other public policies—the policy of encouraging subsequent remedial measures embodied in Federal Rule of Evidence 407, for example, or the policy of deterring unconstitutional searches and seizures embodied in the exclusionary rule—might more justifiably be included in a double jeopardy sufficiency analysis.

Point for Discussion

a. The Thirteenth-Juror Reversal.

Unlike *Burks*, the Court in *Tibbs v. Florida*, 457 U.S. 31 (1982), held that when an appellate court reverses a conviction because the verdict is against the weight of the evidence, there can be a retrial because such a reversal assumes that there was

Food for Thought

Suppose that a state has two degrees of murder and the jury is instructed on both degrees. The jury convicts on the less serious murder charge, which is reversed on appeal for trial error. At a retrial, what can be the maximum charge against the defendant? In *Morris v. Mathews*, 475 U.S. 237 (1986), the Court held that if the trial court erred and did retry and convict the defendant on the more serious charge at a second trial, the appellate court can reduce the charge from a jeopardy-barred offense of the more serious charge to the permissible, less serious charge. By contrast, if the second trial for the jeopardy-barred offense, *e.g.*, murder, results in a conviction for the less serious charge which was not jeopardy-barred, *e.g.*, voluntary manslaughter, a retrial must occur because of the possible prejudicial effect on the jury of prosecuting the accused on a higher charge. *Price v. Georgia*, 398 U.S. 323 (1970).

sufficient evidence at the first trial. The appellate judge simply disagreed with the way in which the jury decided the case.

F. Retrials and Increased Penalties

If there is a retrial and the prosecution seeks and the judge provides increased penalties, does this violate double jeopardy principles? This issue, overlapping with vindictive prosecution, was resolutely answered in *North Carolina v. Pearce*, 395 U.S. 711, 722 (1969), where Justice Stewart, for the Court, held:

Neither the double jeopardy provision nor the Equal Protection Clause imposes an absolute bar to a more severe sentence upon reconviction. A trial judge is not constitutionally precluded, in other words, from imposing a new sentence, whether greater or less than the original sentence, in the light of events subsequent to the first trial that may have thrown new light upon the defendant's "life, health, habits, conduct, and mental and moral propensities." *Williams v. New York*, 337 U.S. 241. Such information may come to the judge's attention from evidence adduced at the second trial itself, from a new presentence investigation, from the defendant's prison record, or possibly from other sources. The freedom of a sentencing judge to consider the defendant's conduct subsequent to the first conviction in imposing a new sentence is no more than consonant with the principle, fully approved in *Williams*, that a State may adopt the "prevalent modern philosophy of penology that the punishment should fit the offender and not merely the crime."

The Court recognized that this principle has limits, particularly in the form of the Due Process Clause of the Fourteenth Amendment. Justice Stewart observed: "It can hardly be doubted that it would be a flagrant violation of the Fourteenth Amendment for a state trial court to follow an announced practice of imposing a heavier sentence upon every reconvicted defendant for the explicit purpose of punishing the defendant for his having succeeded in getting his original conviction set aside. Where, as in each of the cases before us, the original conviction has been set aside because of a constitutional error, the imposition of such a punishment, "penalizing those who choose to exercise" constitutional rights, "would be patently unconstitutional." *United States v. Jackson*, 390 U.S. 570, 581. The very threat inherent in the existence of such a punitive policy would, with respect to those still in prison, serve to "chill the exercise of basic constitutional rights." But even if the first conviction has been set aside for non-constitutional error, the imposition of a penalty upon the defendant for having successfully pursued a statutory right of appeal or collateral remedy would be no less a violation of due process of law. A court is "without right to put a price on an appeal. A defendant's exercise of a right of appeal must be free and unfettered. It is unfair to use the great power given to the court to determine sentence to place a defendant in the dilemma of making an unfree choice."

Due process of law, then, requires that vindictiveness against a defendant for having successfully attacked his first conviction must play no part in the sentence he receives after a new trial. Since the fear of such vindictiveness may unconstitutionally deter a defendant's exercise of the right to appeal or collaterally attack his first conviction, due process also requires that a defendant be freed of apprehension of such a retaliatory motivation on the part of the sentencing judge.

In order to assure the absence of such a motivation, we have concluded that whenever a judge imposes a more severe sentence upon a defendant after a new trial, the reasons for his doing so must affirmatively appear. Those reasons must be based upon objective information concerning identifiable conduct on the part of the defendant occurring after the time of the original sentencing proceeding. And the factual data upon which the increased sentence is based must be made part of the record, so that the constitutional legitimacy of the increased sentence may be fully reviewed on appeal.

Points for Discussion

a. Sentencing Considerations.

A court sentencing a defendant after retrial can consider any event committed before the original sentencing, such as a conviction. *Texas v. McCullough*, 475 U.S. 134 (1986); *Wasman v. United States*, 468 U.S. 559 (1984). When a jury imposes the second sentence, the jury's independence minimizes the possibility that prosecutorial vindictiveness will influence the sentence. *Chaffin v. Stynchcombe*, 412 U.S. 17 (1973). Where the court imposes sentence, the Double Jeopardy Clause applies, because the judge could retaliate against the defendant for taking an appeal by imposing a higher sentence on retrial. However, the presumption of vindictiveness does not apply when the initial sentence was based on a guilty plea and the higher sentence follows from a trial on the merits. *Alabama v. Smith*, 490 U.S. 794 (1989).

The availability of an appeal by the defendant does not prohibit a higher punishment on a trial *de novo* on the same charge. *Colten v. Kentucky*, 407 U.S. 104 (1972). However, a higher offense cannot be charged in the *de novo* appeal. *Thigpen v. Roberts*, 468 U.S. 27 (1984); *Blackledge v. Perry*, 417 U.S. 21 (1974). The prosecution may also appeal a sentence imposed by the judge without violation of double jeopardy. *Pennsylvania v. Goldhammer*, 474 U.S. 28 (1985); *United States v. DiFrancesco*, 449 U.S. 117 (1980).

b. Double Jeopardy and Sentencing Considerations.

The double jeopardy prohibition of multiple prosecutions for the same offense limits a court's ability to impose or alter sentences. *See Ex parte Lange*, 85 U.S. (18 Wall.) 163, 21 L.Ed. 872 (1873) (defendant cannot be subjected to another sentence after suffering fully one punishment for the offense). A sentence imposed at a proceeding sufficiently similar to a trial may be sufficiently final to invoke the protection of the Double Jeopardy Clause. For example, if a life sentence is imposed in a bifurcated sentencing proceeding for a capital offense that resembles a trial on guilt or innocence, the Double Jeopardy Clause prohibits the imposition of the death penalty following a successful appeal and retrial. *Bullington v. Missouri*, 451 U.S. 430 (1981). When a jury's verdict in a capital sentencing proceeding is merely advisory, a court may impose the death penalty despite the jury's verdict of life imprisonment. *Spaziano v. Florida*, 468 U.S. 447 (1984).

Food for Thought

Can a court increase the sentence when an appellate court rules that the first sentence was invalid, unlawful or erroneous? *See, e.g., Jones v. Thomas*, 491 U.S. 376 (1989). Can a trial judge increase a valid sentence after the defendant begins to serve the sentence? *Compare United States v. Arrellano-Rios*, 799 F.2d 520 (9th Cir.1986) with *United States v. Lopez*, 706 F.2d 108 (2d Cir.1983).

Does *Bullington* extend to enhancement/recidivist proceedings on the theory that because such proceedings resemble trials, a decision not to enhance acts as an acquittal on the factual findings necessary to enhance? No, said the Court in *Monge v. California*, 524 U.S. 721 (1998). *Bullington* is limited to capital cases due to its unique character, such that it produces a "heightened interest in accuracy."

In *Schiro v. Farley*, 510 U.S. 222 (1994), the trial court found defendant guilty of murder while committing rape but made no finding on a count of intentional murder. It then imposed the death penalty after finding a statutory aggravating circumstance of intentionally killing while committing rape. The Court rejected the defendant's claim that the jury's failure to convict him on the intentional murder count operated as an acquittal of intentional murder and that double jeopardy prohibited the use of the intentional murder aggravating circumstance for sentencing purposes. The Court distinguished *Bullington* by noting that the case referred only to second capital sentencing proceedings.

Executive Summary

The Double Jeopardy Clause protects criminal defendants from having to "run the gauntlet" of criminal proceedings or charges multiple times. Its purpose is to shield defendants against the potential oppression of successive prosecutions and to promote the finality of judgments. This protection extends not only to successive prosecutions but also to convictions on multiple offenses considered to be the same offense. Double jeopardy analysis usually commences with the question of whether jeopardy attaches. In the trial setting, jeopardy attaches when a jury is empanelled and sworn. If jeopardy attaches, the next question is whether a retrial of a defendant is permitted. This question is not a mere formality but is nuanced and complex. Retrials of prosecutions are authorized by statute today but are limited by double jeopardy principles. The issue of the permissibility of a retrial arises in

Major Themes

a. Attachment—What does it mean for jeopardy to "attach?" The line between jeopardy attaching and not is an important one, generally limiting the prosecution to a "use it or lose it" situation.

b. Posture of Case—The applicability of Double Jeopardy depends on the posture of the case - for example, was the initial case a dismissal, mistrial, completed trial with acquittal or conviction, or a charging of multiple offenses arising out of the same conduct?

c. Retrials—Even if jeopardy applies, retrials are sometimes permitted. The question of whether a retrial is permitted, and whether a higher sentence can be imposed on remand than in the first sentence, depends on the circumstances and the applicable rules.

different contexts, such as whether there has been an acquittal, mistrial, dismissal, or conviction. If there has been an acquittal, no retrial is generally permitted. If there has been a conviction that has been set aside, the initial conviction is generally considered a nullity, and a retrial is permitted. Mistrials usually can be retried if there was manifest necessity for the mistrial. If there has been a dismissal prior to a final judgment, a retrial is often permitted, unless the basis for the dismissal was insufficiency of the evidence. If the dismissal was grounds other than insufficiency of the evidence, such as prejudice or a judicial error, a fair conclusion of the proceedings through a retrial is generally considered to be appropriate.

Test Your Knowledge

To assess your understanding of the material in this chapter, click here to take a quiz.

For More Information

- RUSSELL L. WEAVER, JOHN M. BURKOFF, CATHERINE HANCOCK, JANET HOEFFEL, STEVE FRIEDLAND & STEPHEN SINGER, PRINCIPLES OF CRIMINAL PROCEDURE CH. 21 (6th ed. 2018).

CHAPTER 22

Post-Trial Motions and Direct Appeals

There are significant differences between the trial and appellate stages of a criminal proceeding. The purpose of the trial stage from the State's point of view is to convert a criminal defendant from a person presumed innocent to one found guilty beyond a reasonable doubt. By contrast, it is ordinarily the defendant, rather than the State, who initiates the appellate process, seeking not to fend off the efforts of the State's prosecutor but rather to overturn a finding of guilt made by a judge or a jury below.

Ross v. Moffitt, 417 U.S. 600, 610 (1974).

Take Note

Following conviction, the defendant has several avenues of relief available and has access to a number of forums where he can obtain review of his conviction. Motions to set aside the verdict and motions for a new trial are addressed to the trial court. Direct appeal lies to the state appellate courts, while habeas corpus petitions can be filed in both state and federal court. This chapter addresses the forms of judicial review in the order in which they normally arise, and highlights substantive differences between the forms of judicial review, as well as distinct procedural requirements relating to time and form. Post-conviction remedies are addressed in the next Chapter.

A. Review by the Trial Court

1. Trial *De Novo*

In most appeals, a higher court is asked to scrutinize the trial record for errors that would require reversal of the conviction. In some states, however, misdemeanor charges are tried in lower courts, such as police courts or magistrate courts, from which no record or transcript of the proceedings is available for review by a higher court. These lower courts are sometimes referred to as courts-not-of-record and usually operate without a jury and without all of the procedural safeguards provided in the trial of felony cases. A defendant convicted in such a lower court is often granted an absolute right to a trial *de novo* in a superior court, sometimes called a court-of-record. Although occasionally referred to as an appeal, the granting of a trial *de novo* is normally automatic upon the defendant's request. Thus no error need be alleged as to the first trial, and a defendant who exercises his right to a trial *de novo* is not entitled to judicial review of the sufficiency of the evidence presented to the lower court. *Justices of Boston Municipal Court v. Lydon*, 466 U.S. 294 (1984).

Food for Thought

Why might some jurisdictions choose to have such a system? What are the benefits? What are the costs? Do the benefits outweigh the costs?

The right to a trial *de novo* generally exists even when the defendant pled guilty in the lower court. Neither the defendant's plea nor the lower court's judgment is admissible evidence at the trial *de novo*, but the defendant's prior testimony is admissible at the trial in the higher court. Due Process prohibits prosecutorial vindictiveness in increasing the charges at the trial *de novo*. *Blackledge v. Perry*, 417 U.S. 21 (1974); *Thigpen v. Roberts*, 468 U.S. 27 (1984). However, the punishment imposed at the trial *de novo* may be harsher than that imposed by the lower court. *Colten v. Kentucky*, 407 U.S. 104 (1972).

2. Motions for New Trial and to Set Aside the Verdict

Prior to appeal to an appellate court, the defense may ask the trial court to set aside the guilty verdict and/ or for a new trial. The procedures for such motions are very specific to individual jurisdictions and are governed by statute. A motion to set aside the verdict can be made after a guilty verdict is returned, and the motion can be based

In some jurisdictions, a motion to set aside the verdict is referred to as a "judgment NOV" or "judgment notwithstanding the verdict." It also may simply be a "motion for a new trial," depending upon the grounds.

on: (1) the insufficiency or weight of the evidence; (2) error committed during trial; or (3) newly discovered evidence. Motions to set aside the verdict because of insufficiency of the evidence or error occurring at trial require the trial judge to review the case, the evidence submitted, and any errors in dealing with the introduction of evidence.

Defendants making motions to set aside the verdict and for a new trial because of newly discovered evidence have a high burden. The courts generally require that defense counsel prove: (1) the evidence was discovered after the trial concluded; (2) the evidence could not, by the exercise of diligence, have been discovered before the trial terminated; (3) the evidence is material and likely to produce a different verdict at the new trial; and (4) the evidence is not merely cumulative, corroborative, or collateral.

Hypo 1: *New Evidence of Self-Defense*

A defendant charged with murder testified that the deceased said, "I will kill you," and reached into his right pocket. The defendant maintained that he acted in self-defense because he knew the deceased often carried a razor and a pistol, and the defendant thought the deceased was reaching for a weapon. While the jury was deliberating, a spectator approached defense counsel and related that he had seen a knife in the deceased's hand. Following conviction, defense moves for a new trial based on this newly discovered evidence. What result? *See Connell v. Commonwealth*, 144 Va. 553, 131 S.E. 196 (1926).

Hypo 2: *Sister's Withheld Testimony*

The government charged defendant with knowingly purchasing a fully automatic M–16 rifle at a gun show and later selling it to a pawn shop. Defendant claimed that Rogers, his sister's boyfriend, was the one who purchased the M–16, and that the next time that he saw the rifle was when his sister asked him to pawn it on Rogers's behalf. Defendant did not dispute that he possessed and eventually transferred the firearm described in the indictment. Instead, he argued that he was unaware at the time that the internal mechanism of the M–16 had been altered to convert it to a fully automatic weapon. At trial, the central issue was whether defendant knew that the M–16 was a fully automatic weapon when he sold it to the pawn shop. The jury found the government's evidence convincing and convicted defendant. Three weeks later, defendant's sister informed defense counsel that the M–16 belonged to Rogers, and that she had asked defendant to pawn it on Rogers's behalf. She further stated that neither she nor defendant knew that the M–16 had been converted into a machine gun. At the time of her brother's trial, she told defendant that she would not testify truthfully on his behalf because she was involved in an intimate relationship with Rogers and did not want to place her boyfriend in jeopardy. As defense counsel, how would you argue a motion for a new trial based on the information supplied by defendant's sister? As the prosecutor, on what grounds would you oppose the motion?

B. Direct Appeal in the State Courts

1. The Right to Appeal

There was no right to appeal in criminal cases at common law, and England did not permit appeals from a criminal conviction until 1907. Appeals as of right in federal courts were nonexistent for the first century of our nation, and appellate review of any sort was rarely allowed. The States did not generally recognize an appeal as of right until 1889.

The United States Supreme Court has noted, at least in dicta, that "a review by an appellate court of the final judgment in a criminal case, however grave the offense of which the accused is convicted, was not at common law and is not now a necessary element of due process." *McKane v. Durston*, 153 U.S. 684 (1894). Justice Scalia cited *McKane* for the proposition that "there is no constitutional right to appeal," and "a State could, as far as the federal Constitution is concerned, subject its trial-court determinations to no review whatever." *Martinez v. Court of Appeal*, 528 U.S. 152 (2000). However, by statute or State constitution, a right of appeal is now universal for all significant convictions.

The distinction between a right of appeal and discretionary review by an appellate court is important because the United States Supreme Court has held that in felony cases, counsel must be provided to indigent persons exercising their state-given right to appeal. *Douglas v. California*, 372 U.S. 353 (1963). However, counsel need not be provided to indigent defendants seeking discretionary review. *Ross v. Moffitt*, 417 U.S. 600 (1974). The right to counsel on appeal stems from the due process and equal protection clauses of the Fourteenth Amendment, not from the Sixth Amendment. Thus, although the Sixth Amendment guarantees the defendant's right to self-representation at trial, there is no such right at the appellate stage. *Martinez v. Court of Appeal*, 528 U.S. 152 (2000).

Food for Thought

Given that a right of appeal is not constitutionally mandated, why do the States and the federal government nonetheless provide for at least one appeal as of right? What are the values or goals involved? Does the benefit only inure to the criminal defendant or is there also some benefit to the State or the criminal justice system generally?

Most jurisdictions have created a two-tiered appellate structure in which the convicted defendant has a right of appeal to an intermediate appellate court; a further appeal to a higher court, usually the State Supreme Court, may be discretionary.

The appellate process begins with defendant's filing of a notice or petition of appeal. Such notice informs the parties, the trial judge and the appellate court that the case is being appealed. All jurisdictions require that the notice of appeal be filed within a specified period of time. For example, in the federal system the notice of appeal must be filed within ten days of the date of judgment.

At the time the notice of appeal is filed, or at a subsequent specified date, the parties must designate portions of the trial record that will be sent to the appellate court. The appellate court bases its review of the case on the trial record which commonly includes: (1) jury instructions given or refused by the trial judge; (2) exhibits offered in evidence; (3) any orders entered by the trial court; (4) any opinion or memorandum decision rendered by the trial judge; (5) any pretrial discovery material requested; and (6) the entire trial transcript or just portions in which the judge ruled upon objections to the introduction of evidence.

Counsel also must alert the appellate court to the basis of appeal by filing a statement of issues that the appellate court is asked to resolve. These issues will be expanded upon in counsels' written briefs that summarize the factual background of the case and set forth relevant legal arguments. The appellate court, usually in its discretion, may hear oral arguments on the issues raised.

2. Standards of Review

The thorniest legal issue on appeal is what standard of review the appellate court must apply. As an initial matter, the standard of review will depend in part on whether defense counsel preserved the issue for appeal by making a contemporaneous objection. The contemporaneous objection requirement is designed to afford opposing counsel an opportunity to respond to the objection, to allow the trial court to rule in the first instance as to the propriety of the objection, and to preclude defense counsel from "sandbagging" the trial court by not calling possible errors to its attention.

Many appellate courts also require opposing counsel to state the basis for opposing the objection, and require the trial judge to "state on the record" the grounds on which his ruling is

Practice Pointer

Criminal defense attorneys need to be aware of the importance of preserving issues for appeal because an unpreserved issue will face a much higher standard of review on appeal. To preserve an issue, a defense attorney must make a contemporaneous objection to a ruling of the court and articulate the reasons for the objection. It is critical that a defense attorney's reasons include those that are federally-based (*i.e.*, constitutional claims) along with those that are state-based. Preserved federal issues are the only ones that may be reviewed on habeas corpus, discussed in the next Chapter.

based. In *United States v. Williams*, 951 F.2d 1287 (D.C. Cir. 1991), the court explained the purpose of the federal version of the rule:

> Rule 12(e) of the Federal Rules of Criminal Procedure commands the court to "state its essential findings on the record." The rule serves several functions. Findings on the record inform the parties and other interested persons of the grounds of the ruling, add discipline to the process of judicial decision-making and enable appellate courts properly to perform their reviewing function. If the district court not only fails to make "essential findings on the record," but also expresses nothing in the way of legal reasoning, if it simply announces a result, it may frustrate these objectives. We say "may" because there are cases in which the facts are so certain, and the legal consequences so apparent, that little guesswork is needed to determine the grounds for the ruling.

Williams was a case where guesswork was needed, however. The court had to balance a countervailing appellate rule that allowed a reviewing court to sustain the trial court's ruling "if there is any reasonable view of the evidence that will support it." Because the appellate court had nothing on the record to suggest a factual or legal basis for the ruling, however, the *Williams* court remanded the case for the factual findings required by Rule 12(e).

a. Harmless Error Review and Structural Error

Trial errors can be of constitutional dimension—a violation of a constitutional right of the defendant, such as the Sixth Amendment right to confront witnesses—or non-constitutional, such as an error excluding a piece of evidence contrary to state evidence rules. A trial error that is not of constitutional dimension is harmless when it plainly appears from the facts and circumstances of the case that the error did not affect the verdict. Reversal is required for a non-constitutional error only if it "had substantial and injurious effect or influence in determining the jury's verdict." *United States v. Lane*, 474 U.S. 438 (1986).

Application of the harmless error doctrine to constitutional error depends upon the nature of the error, *i.e.,* whether the error is a "structural error" or not. Structural errors "are so intrinsically harmful as to require automatic reversal (*i.e.,* "affect substantial rights") without regard to their effect on the outcome." *Neder v. United States*, 527 U.S. 1 (1999). They are the type of errors whose effect is impossible to measure. The Supreme Court has recognized a limited number of structural errors requiring automatic reversal. They include: (1) unlawful exclusion of members of the defendant's race from a grand jury, *Vasquez v. Hillery*, 474 U.S. 254 (1986), (2) exclusion of a juror reluctant to impose the death penalty (but not opposed under all circumstances), *Gray v. Mississippi*, 481 U.S. 648 (1987), (3) absolute denial of the right to a public trial, *Waller v. Georgia*, 467 U.S. 39 (1984), (4) denial of the right of self-representation, *McKaskle v. Wiggins*, 465 U.S. 168

(1984), (5) a trial presided over by a biased judge, *Tumey v. Ohio*, 273 U.S. 510 (1927), (6) absolute denial of the right to counsel, *Gideon v. Wainwright*, 372 U.S. 335 (1963), and (7) a constitutionally inadequate jury instruction on reasonable doubt, *Sullivan v. Louisiana*, 508 U.S. 275 (1993).

Constitutional errors that are not structural are treated differently depending on whether they are raised on direct appeal or collateral review. On collateral review (*e.g.*, habeas corpus petitions), trial errors require reversal of the conviction only if the defendant proves "actual prejudice," *i.e.*, the error had a "substantial and injurious effect or influence in determining the jury's verdict." *Brecht v. Abrahamson*, 507 U.S. 619 (1993). On direct review, however, *Chapman v. California* held that trial errors require reversal of the conviction unless the reviewing court finds such errors to be harmless "beyond a reasonable doubt."

Food for Thought

Can you see why the errors listed as "structural" cannot be subject to harmless error analysis? Do the structural errors requiring automatic reversal reflect more serious errors than the constitutional errors that are subject to harmless error analysis (*i.e.*, right of confrontation, right to effective assistance of counsel, right to be present at all critical stages of the trial).

Chapman v. California

386 U.S. 18 (1967).

JUSTICE BLACK delivered the opinion of the Court.

Petitioners, Ruth Elizabeth Chapman and Thomas LeRoy Teale, were convicted in a California state court upon a charge that they robbed, kidnaped, and murdered a bartender. She was sentenced to life imprisonment and he to death. At the time of the trial, Art I, § 13, of the State's Constitution provided that 'in any criminal case, whether the defendant testifies or not, his failure to explain or to deny by his testimony any evidence or facts in the case against him may be commented upon by the court and by counsel, and may be considered by the court or the jury.' Both petitioners in this case chose not to testify at their trial, and the State's attorney prosecuting them took full advantage of his right under the State Constitution to comment upon their failure to testify, filling his argument to the jury from beginning to end with numerous references to their silence and inferences of their guilt resulting therefrom. The trial court

Hear It

You can listen to the oral argument in *Chapman* at: http://www.oyez.org/cases/1960-1969/1966/1966_95.

also charged the jury that it could draw adverse inferences from petitioners' failure to testify. Shortly after the trial, but before petitioners' cases had been considered on appeal by the California Supreme Court, this Court decided *Griffin v. State of California*, 380 U.S. 609, in which we held California's constitutional provision and practice invalid on the ground that they put a penalty on the exercise of a person's right not to be compelled to be a witness against himself, guaranteed by the Fifth Amendment to the United States Constitution and made applicable to California and the other States by the Fourteenth Amendment. On appeal, the State Supreme Court, admitting that petitioners had been denied a federal constitutional right by the comments on their silence, nevertheless affirmed, applying the State Constitution's harmless-error provision, which forbids reversal unless 'the court shall be of the opinion that the error complained of has resulted in a miscarriage of justice.'

We are urged to hold that all federal constitutional errors, regardless of the facts and circumstances, must always be deemed harmful. Such a holding would require an automatic reversal of their convictions. We decline to adopt any such rule. All 50 States have harmless-error statutes or rules, and the United States long ago through its Congress established for its courts the rule that judgments shall not be reversed for 'errors or defects which do not affect the substantial rights of the parties.' None of these rules on its face distinguishes between federal constitutional errors and errors of state law or federal statutes and rules. All of these rules, state or federal, serve a very useful purpose insofar as they block setting aside convictions for small errors or defects that have little, if any, likelihood of having changed the result of the trial. We conclude that there may be some constitutional errors which in the setting of a particular case are so unimportant and insignificant that they may, consistent with the Federal Constitution, be deemed harmless, not requiring the automatic reversal of the conviction.

In fashioning a harmless-constitutional-error rule, we must recognize that harmless-error rules can work very unfair and mischievous results when, for example, highly important and persuasive evidence, or argument, though legally forbidden, finds its way into a trial in which the question of guilt or innocence is a close one. What harmless-error rules all aim at is a rule that will save the good in harmless-error practices while avoiding the bad, so far as possible.

The federal rule emphasizes 'substantial rights' as do most others. The California constitutional rule emphasizes 'a miscarriage of justice,' but the California courts have neutralized this to some extent by emphasis, and perhaps overemphasis, upon the court's view of 'overwhelming evidence.' We prefer the approach of this Court in deciding what was harmless error in our recent case of *Fahy v. State of Connecticut*, 375 U.S. 85. There we said: 'The question is whether there is a reasonable possibility that the evidence complained of might have contributed to the conviction.' Although our prior cases have indicated that there are some constitutional rights so basic to a fair trial that their infraction can never be treated as harmless error, this statement in *Fahy* itself belies any belief that all trial errors which violate the Constitution automatically call for reversal. At the same time, like the federal harmless-error statute, it emphasizes an intention not to treat as harmless those constitutional errors that 'affect substantial rights' of a party. An error in admitting plainly relevant evidence which possibly influenced the jury adversely to a litigant cannot, under *Fahy*, be conceived of as harmless. Certainly error, constitutional error, in illegally admitting highly prejudicial evidence or comments, casts on someone other than the person prejudiced by it a burden to show that it was harmless. It is for that reason that the original common-law harmless-error rule put the burden on the beneficiary of the error either to prove that there was no injury or to suffer a reversal of his erroneously obtained judgment. There is little, if any, difference between our statement in *Fahy v. State of Connecticut* about 'whether there is a reasonable possibility that the evidence complained of might have contributed to the conviction' and requiring the beneficiary of a constitutional error to prove beyond a reasonable doubt that the error complained of did not contribute to the verdict obtained. We do no more than adhere to the meaning of our *Fahy* case when we hold, as we now do, that before a federal constitutional error can be held harmless, the court must be able to declare a belief that it was harmless beyond a reasonable doubt. While appellate courts do not ordinarily have the original task of applying such a test, it is a familiar standard to all courts, and its adoption will provide a more workable standard, although achieving the same result as that aimed at in our *Fahy* case.

Applying the foregoing standard, we have no doubt that the error in these cases was not harmless to petitioners. To reach this conclusion one need only glance at the prosecutorial comments compiled from the record by petitioners' counsel and (with minor omissions) set forth in the Appendix. The California Supreme Court fairly summarized the extent of these comments as follows:

> Such comments went to the motives for the procurement and handling of guns purchased by Mrs. Chapman, funds or the lack thereof in Mr. Teale's possession immediately prior to the killing, the amount of intoxicating liquors consumed by defendants at the Spot Club and other taverns, the circumstances of the shooting in the automobile and the removal of the victim's body therefrom, who fired the fatal shots, why defendants used a false registration at a motel shortly after the killing, the meaning of a letter written by Mrs. Chapman several days after the killing, why Teale had a loaded weapon in his possession when apprehended, the meaning of statements made by Teale after his apprehension, why certain clothing and articles of personal property were shipped by defendants to Missouri, what clothing Mrs. Chapman wore at the time of the killing, conflicting statements as to Mrs. Chapman's whereabouts immediately preceding the killing and, generally, the overall commission of the crime.

Thus, the state prosecutor's argument and the trial judge's instruction to the jury continuously and repeatedly impressed the jury that from the failure of petitioners to testify, to all intents and purposes, the inferences from the facts in evidence had to be drawn in favor of the State—in short, that by their silence petitioners had served as irrefutable witnesses against themselves. Though the case in which this occurred presented a reasonably strong 'circumstantial web of evidence' against petitioners, it was also a case in which, absent the constitutionally forbidden comments, honest, fair-minded jurors might very well have brought in not-guilty verdicts. Under these circumstances, it is impossible for us to say that the State has demonstrated, beyond a reasonable doubt, that the prosecutor's comments and the trial judge's instruction did not contribute to petitioners' convictions. Such a machine-gun repetition of a denial of constitutional rights, designed and calculated to make petitioners' version of the evidence worthless, can no more be considered harmless than the introduction against a defendant of a coerced confession. Petitioners are entitled to a trial free from the pressure of unconstitutional inferences.

Reversed and remanded.

Points for Discussion

a. Applying Harmless Error Anticipatorily at Trial?

In *Hackney v. Commonwealth*, 28 Va.App. 288, 504 S.E.2d 385 (1998), defendant was charged with grand larceny and possession of a firearm by a convicted felon. In light of well-settled precedent that justice requires separate trials "where evidence of one crime is not admissible in the trial of the others," the defendant filed a motion to sever the charge of possession of a firearm by a convicted felon from the larceny charge. The trial judge and defense counsel had the following discussion:

> **Food for Thought**
>
> Once an appellate court finds there is constitutional error, *Chapman* states that the prosecution must bear the burden of proving the error was harmless. Why is that so? Since the defendant was convicted and no longer presumed innocent, should the defendant bear the burden on all issues on appeal, including showing prejudice? What are the values *Chapman* is espousing by placing the burden on the prosecution?

THE COURT: The Commonwealth is going to ask the question, "Have you ever been convicted of a felony or a misdemeanor involving lying, cheating and stealing?" They're going to ask that question at some point during the trial as well.

DEFENSE COUNSEL: If he takes the stand.

THE COURT: If he takes the stand.

DEFENSE COUNSEL: If he takes the stand.

THE COURT: And the Court certainly can't rule that out. Previous cases recognized that if the defendant testifies, prior convictions are admissible for impeachment purposes, thus rendering harmless any error in denying a motion to sever the charges. I think the Court would have to overrule Counsel's motion here.

During its case-in-chief, the prosecution introduced prior convictions for three grand larceny and burglary offenses committed by defendant in order to prove a required element of the firearm charge, namely, that defendant was a convicted felon. Defendant testified in his defense to the larceny and firearm charges. On cross-examination, the prosecution elicited for impeachment purposes, testimony from the defendant that he had been previously convicted of three felonies. The jury found defendant guilty of grand larceny and possession of a firearm by a convicted felon.

A panel of the appellate court held that in light of the defendant's decision to testify, the trial court's refusal to sever the charges was harmless error. Upon a rehearing en banc, the full court reversed the panel's decision:

> We hold that, as a matter of policy, we will not condone a trial court's clear error in refusing to sever the possession of a firearm by a felony charge predicated on the assumption that an accused will testify and render the error harmless. The harmless error doctrine is applicable only upon appellate review or in the trial court upon consideration of a motion to set aside a verdict. When applicable, the harmless error doctrine enables an appellate court or a trial court when considering a motion to set aside a verdict to ignore the effect of an erroneous ruling when an error clearly has had no impact upon the verdict or sentence in a case. The harmless error doctrine should not be used prospectively by a trial court as a basis to disregard an established rule of law.

The Court held that the trial court's refusal to sever was not harmless beyond a reasonable doubt.

b. Correct Burden Allocation

In *Gamache v. California*, 562 U.S. 1083 (2010), the Court denied certiorari, but four Justices expressed concern about the denial because, contrary to *Chapman*, the California Supreme Court stated that the *defendant* had "to demonstrate prejudice under the usual standard for ordinary trial error." Justice Sotomayor objected, stating: "It is not clear what the court intended in allocating the burden to the defendant to demonstrate prejudice, but if it meant to convey that the defendant bore the burden of persuasion, that would contravene

Chapman. The allocation of the burden of proving harmlessness can be outcome determinative in some cases. With all that is at stake in capital cases, in future cases the California courts should take care to ensure that their burden allocation conforms to the commands of *Chapman*."

Hypo : *Harmless Error and Jury Instructions*

Defendant, who was charged with robbery, was positively identified by two victims (a cashier at a storage facility and a cashier at a convenience store). In addition, a security camera recorded his face and voice during one of the encounters. During his jury instructions, the judge failed to inform the jury of the elements or facts that must be shown in order to prove the crime of robbery (taking another's property, from his possession, in his presence, against his will, through force or fear). The judge did inform the jurors of the required mental state and the need to find that defendant used a weapon in the crime. Can this error be regarded as harmless? *See People v. Merritt*, 2 Cal.5th 819, 392 P.3d 421 (Cal. 2017).

---

b. Plain Error Review

When a defendant fails to object to an error at trial, whether one of constitutional or non-constitutional dimension, but later calls the error to the attention of the appellate court, the standard of review is for plain error, which is a much higher standard of review than harmless error. An appellate court may review the record for plain error and may reverse the conviction to attain the ends of justice.

United States v. Olano

507 U.S. 725 (1993).

JUSTICE O'CONNOR delivered the opinion of the Court.

Hear It

You can listen to the oral argument in *Olano* at: http://www.oyez.org/cases/1990-1999/1992/1992_91_1306.

The question is whether the presence of alternate jurors during jury deliberations was a "plain error" that the Court of Appeals was authorized to correct under Federal Rule of Criminal Procedure 52(b).

Each of the respondents, Guy W. Olano, Jr., and Raymond M. Gray, served on the board of directors of a savings and loan association. In 1986, the two were indicted in the Western District of Washington on multiple federal charges for their participation in an elaborate loan "kickback" scheme. Their joint jury trial with five other codefendants commenced in March 1987. All of the parties agreed that 14 jurors would be selected to hear the case, and that the 2 alternates would be identified before deliberations began. The matter arose again the next day, in an ambiguous exchange between Gray's counsel and the District Court:

> THE COURT: Have you given any more thought as to whether you want the alternates to go in and not participate, or do you want them out?
>
> MR. ROBISON counsel for Gray: We would ask they not.

One day later, on May 28, the last day of trial, the District Court for a third time asked the defendants whether they wanted the alternate jurors to retire into the jury room. Counsel for defendant Davy Hilling gave an unequivocal, affirmative answer.

> THE COURT: Well, Counsel, I received your alternates. Do I understand that the defendants now—it's hard to keep up with you, Counsel. It's sort of a day by day—but that's all right. You do all agree that all fourteen deliberate?
>
> Okay. Do you want me to instruct the two alternates not to participate in deliberation?
>
> MR. KELLOGG counsel for Hilling: That's what I was on my feet to say. It's my understanding that the conversation was the two alternates go back there instructed that they are not to take part in any fashion in the deliberations.

The District Court concluded that Hilling's counsel was speaking for the other defendants as well as his own client. None of the other counsel intervened during the colloquy between the District Court and Hilling's counsel on May 28, nor did anyone object later the same day when the court instructed the jurors that the two alternates would be permitted to attend but not participate in deliberations.

Both respondents were convicted on a number of charges. They appealed to the United States Court of Appeals for the Ninth Circuit. The Court of Appeals reversed certain counts for insufficient evidence and then considered whether the presence of alternate jurors during jury deliberations violated Federal Rule of Criminal Procedure 24(c): An alternate juror who does not replace a regular juror shall be discharged after the jury retires to consider its verdict.

Because respondents had not objected to the alternates' presence, the court applied a "plain error" standard under Rule 52(b). The court found that Rule 24(c) was violated in the instant case, because "the district court did not obtain individual waivers from each defendant personally, either orally or in writing." It then held that the presence of alternates in violation of Rule 24(c) was "inherently prejudicial" and reversible per se:

> We cannot fairly ascertain whether in a given case the alternate jurors followed the district court's prohibition on participation. However, even if they heeded the letter of the court's instructions and remained orally mute throughout, it is entirely possible that their attitudes, conveyed by facial expressions, gestures or the like, may have had some effect upon the decision of one or more jurors.

Finally, in a footnote, the court decided that "because the violation is inherently prejudicial and because it infringes upon a substantial right of the defendants, it falls within the plain error doctrine." We granted certiorari to clarify the standard for "plain error" review by the courts of appeals under Rule 52(b).

"No procedural principle is more familiar to this Court than that a constitutional right," or a right of any other sort, "may be forfeited in criminal as well as civil cases by the failure to make timely assertion of the right before a tribunal having jurisdiction to determine it." *Yakus v. United States*, 321 U.S. 414, 444 (1944). Federal Rule of Criminal Procedure 52(b) provides a court of appeals a limited power to correct errors that were forfeited because not timely raised in district court.

Although "a rigid and undeviating judicially declared practice under which courts of review would invariably and under all circumstances decline to consider all questions which had not previously been specifically urged would be out of harmony with the rules of fundamental justice," there must be an "error" that is "plain" and that "affects substantial rights." Moreover, Rule 52(b) leaves the decision to correct the forfeited error within the sound discretion of the court of appeals, and the court should not exercise that discretion unless the error "seriously affects the fairness, integrity or public reputation of judicial proceedings." *United States v. Young*, 470 U.S. 1, 15 (1985).

Rule 52(b) defines a single category of forfeited-but-reversible error. Although it is possible to read the Rule in the disjunctive, as creating two separate categories—"plain errors" and "defects affecting substantial rights"—that reading is surely wrong. As we explained in *Young*, the phrase "error or defect" is more simply read as "error." The forfeited error "may be noticed" only if it is "plain" and "affects substantial rights." More precisely, a court of appeals may correct the error (either vacating for a new trial, or reversing outright) only if it meets these criteria.

The first limitation on appellate authority under Rule 52(b) is that there indeed be an "error." Deviation from a legal rule is "error" unless the rule has been waived. For example, a defendant who knowingly and voluntarily pleads guilty in conformity with the requirements of Rule 11 cannot have his conviction vacated by court of appeals on the grounds that he ought to have had a trial. Because the right to trial is waivable, and because the defendant who enters a valid guilty plea waives that right, his conviction without a trial is not "error."

Waiver is different from forfeiture. Whereas forfeiture is the failure to make the timely assertion of a right, waiver is the "intentional relinquishment or abandonment of a known right." Whether a particular right is waivable; whether the defendant must participate personally in the waiver; whether certain procedures are required for waiver; and whether the defendant's choice must be particularly informed or voluntary, all depend on the right at stake. Mere forfeiture, as opposed to waiver, does not extinguish an "error" under Rule 52(b). If a legal rule was violated during the district court proceedings, and if the defendant did not waive the rule, then there has been an "error" within the meaning of Rule 52(b) despite the absence of a timely objection.

The second limitation on appellate authority under Rule 52(b) is that the error be "plain." "Plain" is synonymous with "clear" or, equivalently, "obvious." We need not consider the special case where the error was unclear at the time of trial but becomes clear on appeal because the applicable law has been clarified. At a minimum, court of appeals cannot correct an error pursuant to Rule 52(b) unless the error is clear under current law.

The third and final limitation on appellate authority under Rule 52(b) is that the plain error "affect substantial rights." This is the same language employed in Rule 52(a), and in most cases it means that the error must have been prejudicial: It must have affected the outcome of the district court proceedings. When the defendant has made a timely objection to an error and Rule 52(a) applies, a court of appeals normally engages in a specific analysis of the district court record—a

In *Henderson v. United States*, 568 U.S. 266 (2013), the Court held that an error is "plain" for "plain error" review, as long as the law was settled at the time of appellate review. The Court reasoned that adopting the "time of review" standard as opposed to the "time of error" standard puts appellants on equal footing and allows the appellate court to apply present law.

so-called "harmless error" inquiry—to determine whether the error was prejudicial. Rule 52(b) normally requires the same kind of inquiry, with one important difference: It is the defendant rather than the Government who bears the burden of persuasion with respect to prejudice. In most cases, a court of appeals cannot

correct the forfeited error unless the defendant shows that the error was prejudicial. This burden shifting is dictated by a subtle but important difference in
language between the two parts of Rule 52: While Rule 52(a) precludes error correction only if the error "does not affect substantial rights," Rule 52(b) authorizes
no remedy unless the error does "affect substantial rights."

Rule 52(b) is permissive, not mandatory. If the forfeited error is "plain" and
"affects substantial rights," the court of appeals has authority to order correction,
but is not required to do so. The language of the Rule ("may be noticed"), the
nature of forfeiture, and the established appellate practice that Congress intended
to continue all point to this conclusion. "In criminal cases, where the life, or as in
this case the liberty, of the defendant is at stake, the courts of the United States, in
the exercise of a sound discretion, may notice forfeited error."

The Court of Appeals should correct a plain forfeited error affecting substantial rights if the error "seriously affects the fairness, integrity or public reputation
of judicial proceedings." As we explained, the "standard laid down in *United States
v. Atkinson* was codified in Federal Rule of Criminal Procedure 52(b)," and we
repeatedly have quoted the *Atkinson* language in describing plain-error review. An
error may "seriously affect the fairness, integrity or public reputation of judicial
proceedings" independent of the defendant's innocence. Conversely, a plain error
affecting substantial rights does not, without more, satisfy the *Atkinson* standard,
for otherwise the discretion afforded by Rule 52(b) would be illusory.

With these basic principles in mind, we turn to the instant case. The Government essentially concedes that the "error" was "plain." We therefore focus our
attention on whether the error "affected substantial rights" within the meaning of
Rule 52(b), and conclude that it did not. The presence of alternate jurors during
jury deliberations is not the kind of error that "affects substantial rights" independent of its prejudicial impact. Nor have respondents made a specific showing of
prejudice.

Respondents have made no specific showing that the alternate jurors
in this case either participated in the
jury's deliberations or "chilled" deliberation by the regular jurors. Nor will
we presume prejudice for purposes
of the Rule 52(b) analysis here. The
Court of Appeals was incorrect in finding the error "inherently prejudicial."
Until the close of trial, the 2 alternate
jurors were indistinguishable from the

Take Note

As reiterated by the Court in
United States v. Marcus, 560 U.S. 258
(2010), plain error analysis requires
a "reasonable probability that the error affected the outcome of the trial,"
not just "any possibility no matter
how likely."

12 regular jurors. Along with the regular jurors, they commenced their office with an oath, received the normal initial admonishment, heard the same evidence and arguments, and were not identified as alternates until after the District Court gave a final set of instructions. In those instructions, the District Court specifically enjoined the jurors that "according to the law, the alternates must not participate in the deliberations," and reiterated, "we are going to ask that you not participate." The Court of Appeals should not have supposed that this injunction was contravened. "It is the almost invariable assumption of the law that jurors follow their instructions." "We presume that jurors, conscious of the gravity of their task, attend closely the particular language of the trial court's instructions in a criminal case and strive to understand, make sense of, and follow the instructions given them." Nor do we think that the mere presence of alternate jurors entailed a sufficient risk of "chill" to justify a presumption of prejudice on that score.

In sum, respondents have not met their burden of showing prejudice under Rule 52(b). Because the conceded error in this case did not "affect substantial rights," the Court of Appeals had no authority to correct it. The judgment of the Court of Appeals is reversed, and the case is remanded for further proceedings consistent with this opinion.

c. Review for Sufficiency of the Evidence

The one claim that a defendant can make without concern about preserving the issue at trial is that the jury or judge convicted him based upon insufficient evidence. In *In re Winship,* 397 U.S. 358 (1970), the Court held that the requirement that the prosecution prove every element of the charged offense beyond a reasonable doubt is essential to Fourteenth Amendment due process. In *Jackson v. Virginia,* 443 U.S. 307 (1979), the Court discussed how that requirement should be viewed on appeal:

Take Note

The "*any* rational trier of fact" standard makes appeals on the basis of insufficiency of the evidence very difficult to sustain: in essence, the prosecution must have neglected to produce *any* credible evidence in support of an element of the offense. If this were the case, a defense attorney should win a motion for a directed verdict or a motion to set aside the verdict, as described above in Part A.2.

After *Winship* the critical inquiry on review of the sufficiency of the evidence to support a criminal conviction must be not simply to determine whether the jury was properly instructed, but to determine whether the record evidence could reasonably support a finding of guilt beyond a reasonable doubt. But this inquiry does not require a court to "ask itself whether it believes that the evidence at the trial established guilt beyond a reasonable doubt." Instead, the relevant question is whether, after viewing the evidence in the light most favorable to the prosecution, *any* rational trier of fact could have found the essential elements of the crime beyond a reasonable doubt. This familiar standard gives full play to the responsibility of the trier of fact fairly to resolve conflicts in the testimony, to weigh the evidence, and to draw reasonable inferences from the basic facts to ultimate facts. Once a defendant has been found guilty of the crime charged, the fact finder's role as weigher of the evidence is preserved through a legal conclusion that upon judicial review *all of the evidence* is to be considered in the light most favorable to the prosecution. The criterion thus impinges upon "jury" discretion only to the extent necessary to guarantee the fundamental protection of due process of law.

3. Waiver of the Right to Appeal

As with all rights, a defendant can waive his right to appeal. For example, defendants can waive their right to appeal as part of a plea bargain. In *United States v. Wenger*, 58 F.3d 280 (7th Cir. 1995), the defendant waived his right to appeal his sentence in return for a plea and then in fact appealed, claiming that the trial judge did not make a specific inquiry as to whether he knowingly and voluntarily waived that right. The Seventh Circuit stated:

> Defendant has appealed, despite his promise not to do so. Waivers of appeal are enforceable. Defendant asks us to establish a procedural citadel around the right of appeal, so that waiver will be accepted only following elaborate warnings after the fashion of those used for the most vital constitutional rights. *See Johnson v. Zerbst*, 304 U.S. 458, 464 (1938) (sixth amendment right to counsel); Fed.R.Crim.P. 11(c). But other rights may be surrendered without warnings of any kind and with considerably less formality. E.g., *Schneckloth v. Bustamonte*, 412 U.S. 218 (1973) (fourth amendment right to privacy); *United States v. Mezzanatto*, 513 U.S. 196 (1995) (right to exclude from evidence proffer made as part of plea negotiations). The right to appeal is in the latter category—not simply because it depends on a statute rather than the Constitution but because it has long been seen as the kind of right that depends on assertion. A litigant who does not take a timely appeal has forfeited any entitlement to appellate review. Our legal system makes no appeal the default position. A defendant who finds this agreeable need do nothing. All the waiver in a plea agreement does is to make that outcome a part of the parties' bargain, so that a defendant inclined against appeal or willing to forgo it—perhaps to put an unpleasant episode behind him more quickly—may obtain a concession from the prosecutor. In this case the prosecutor agreed to support a downward departure for acceptance of responsibility, a boon that usually would be unavailable to a defendant arrested (as defendant was) for an intervening offense.

Empty promises are worthless promises; if defendants could retract their waivers (the practical effect, if the procedural hurdles to an effective waiver were set too high) then they could not obtain concessions by promising not to appeal. Although any given defendant would like to obtain the concession and exercise the right as well, prosecutors cannot be fooled in the long run. Right holders are better off if they can choose between exercising the right and exchanging that right for something they value more highly. Defendant exchanged the right to appeal for prosecutorial concessions; he cannot have his cake and eat it too.

In *United States v. Han*, 181 F. Supp. 2d 1039 (N.D. Cal. 2002), the court held that a waiver of the right to appeal a sentence that is made as part of a plea agreement is a waiver of an unknown error, that is, one which has yet to occur. In light of the requirement that a waiver must be knowing and voluntary, a sentence limited only by the statutory maximum and constitutional constraints does not allow the defendant a fair opportunity to contemplate the *actual*, not theoretical, range of sentence that may be imposed. Accordingly, "a plea agreement containing a waiver of judicial review, should, at the very least, set forth a maximum sentence which the defendant would accept based upon certain assumptions as they relate to sentencing factors, including criminal history." The court offered the following as "standard language of a waiver of appeal" that could be used in plea agreements:

> In exchange for the government's concessions in this plea agreement, defendant waives, to the full extent of the law, any right to appeal or collaterally attack the conviction and sentence, including any restitution order, unless the Court imposes a sentence in excess of ___ months. If the custodial sentence exceeds ___ months, the defendant may appeal, but the government will be free to support on appeal the sentence actually imposed.

A defendant may also forfeit his appeal as a sanction for escaping from the penal institution holding him. *Molinaro v. New Jersey*, 396 U.S. 365 (1970). However, the Court held that a fugitive defendant does not forfeit his right to appeal if he absconds while his case is pending in trial court but is recaptured before sentencing and appeal. *Ortega-Rodriguez v. United States*, 507 U.S. 234 (1993).

Ethical Issue

Your client was sentenced to death, but now tells you that he wants to be executed and orders you not to appeal his sentence. The defendant's mother intervenes and asks you to file a petition as defendant's "next friend" asking the appellate court to re-examine the legal and factual issues. Should the court honor the defendant's waiver? Should you enter into this new role? Is there something different about allowing a defendant to give up on appeals in a capital case as opposed to a non-capital case? Does the judge have an extra responsibility? *See, e.g., State v. Robbins*, 5 S.W.3d 51 (Ark. 1999).

4. Ethics and the Frivolous Appeal

In *Smith v. Robbins*, 528 U.S. 259 (2000), Justice Souter observed that "No one has a right to a wholly frivolous appeal, against which the judicial system's first line of defense is its lawyers. Being officers of the court, members of the bar are bound 'not to clog the courts with frivolous motions or appeals.'" 528 U.S. at 294 (Souter, J., dissenting).

In *Anders v. California*, 386 U.S. 738 (1967), the Court suggested that when an attorney appointed to represent an indigent defendant on direct appeal finds the case wholly frivolous, he should: (1) advise the court and request permission to withdraw; (2) submit a brief referring to anything in the record that might arguably support the appeal; (3) furnish a copy of the brief to the defendant in time to allow him to raise any points that he chooses; and (4) request the court to conduct a full examination and decide whether the case is wholly frivolous.

California replaced an *Anders* brief with a *Wende* brief that provides that "counsel, upon concluding that an appeal would be frivolous, files a brief with the appellate court that summarizes the procedural and factual history of the case, with citation of the record. He also attests that he has reviewed the record, explained his evaluation of the case to his client, provided the client with a copy of the brief, and informed the client of his right to file a *pro se* supplemental brief. He further requests that the court independently examine the record for arguable issues."

Take Note

An *Anders* brief creates tension between counsel's ethical duty as an officer of the court (which requires him not to present frivolous arguments) and counsel's duty to further his client's interests (which might not permit counsel to characterize his client's claims as frivolous). One former public defender bemoaned the fact that a client's desire to pursue a frivolous appeal requires defense counsel "to do something that the Code of Professional Responsibility describes as unethical; the only choice is as to which canon he or she prefers to violate." Pengilly, "Never Cry *Anders*: The Ethical Dilemma of Counsel Appointed to Pursue a Frivolous Criminal Appeal," 9 Crim. Justice J. 45, 64 (1986).

Food for Thought

What does it mean for an appellate attorney to decide that an appeal would be "frivolous"? Is there really such a thing as an error-free trial? Is an appeal frivolous if there are errors but they are minor and a reversal is highly unlikely?

The majority in *Smith v. Robbins, supra* approved the California approach: "The procedure we sketched in *Anders v. California*, is a prophylactic one; the States are free to adopt different procedures, so long as those procedures adequately safeguard a defendant's right to appellate counsel" and the State provides a review process that "reasonably ensures that an indigent's appeal will be resolved in a way that is related to the merit of that appeal." In dissent Justice Souter maintained:

> The rub is that although counsel may properly refuse to brief a frivolous issue and a court may just as properly deny leave to take a frivolous appeal, there needs to be some reasonable assurance that the lawyer has not relaxed his partisan instinct prior to refusing, in which case the court's review could never compensate for the lawyer's failure of advocacy. A simple statement by counsel that an appeal has no merit, coupled with an appellate court's endorsement of counsel's conclusion, gives no affirmative indication that anyone has sought out the appellant's best arguments or championed his cause to the degree contemplated by the adversary system.

Make the Connection

A defendant who fails to obtain a reversal on direct appeal may make collateral attacks on the conviction, such as a petition for a writ of habeas corpus discussed in the next chapter.

It is owing to the importance of assuring that an adversarial, not an inquisitorial system is at work that I disagree with the Court's statement today that our cases approve of any state procedure that "reasonably ensures that an indigent's appeal will be resolved in a way that is related to the merit of that appeal." A purely inquisitorial system could satisfy that criterion, and so could one that appoints counsel only if the appellate court deems it useful. But we have rejected the former and have explicitly held the latter unconstitutional.

528 U.S. at 294, 296 (Souter, J., dissenting).

5. Appeals of Last Resort

As a supplement to judicial review, all jurisdictions grant a convicted defendant an opportunity to appeal to executive authority for a pardon or grant of clemency. For example, Article 2, Section 2, Clause 1 of the U. S. Constitution gives the President "Power to grant Reprieves and Pardons for Offences against the United States, except in Cases of Impeachment."

President Gerald Ford gave former President Richard Nixon a "full pardon" for his role in the Watergate scandal. The President also has the power to "forgive the convicted person in part or entirely, to reduce a penalty in terms of a specified number of years, or to alter it with conditions which are in themselves constitutionally unobjectionable." *Schick v. Reed*, 419 U.S. 256 (1974).

Executive Summary

Trials *De Novo*. Some misdemeanor courts allow a defendant to try a case in front of a magistrate and then, if he loses, have a trial *de novo* in a superior court.

Post-Trial Motions. Defendants making motions to set aside the verdict and for a new trial because of newly discovered evidence have a high burden.

One Appeal as of Right. Most jurisdictions provide for one appeal of a criminal conviction as a matter of right.

Discretionary Appeals. A subsequent appeal may be heard only when the court exercises its discretion to accept the case.

Standards of Review. The standard of review on appeal depends both upon the kind of error alleged—whether constitutional or not—and whether it was preserved at trial.

Major Themes

a. Structural or Reversible Error— Automatic reversal is required in the rare case of a "structural error," a handful of scenarios where the effect of a trial error of constitutional dimension is impossible to measure. If not structural, a trial error of constitutional dimension is reversible unless the prosecution can prove the error was harmless beyond a reasonable doubt.

b. Plain Error— If the defendant failed to preserve an error for appeal, the standard of review is for "plain error," and the defendant bears the burden of proving a reasonable probability that the error affected the outcome.

c. Insufficient Evidence— A reversal for insufficiency of the evidence must meet a high burden—viewing the facts in the light most favorable to the prosecution, the appellate court must find that no reasonable juror could have found the defendant guilty beyond a reasonable doubt.

Waiver of Right to Appeal. A defendant can waive his right to appeal.

Test Your Knowledge

To assess your understanding of the material in this chapter, click here to take a quiz.

For More Information

- MAYER BROWN LLP, FEDERAL APPELLATE PRACTICE (2d ed. 2013).

- JAMES WILLIAM MOORE et al., MOORE'S FEDERAL PRACTICE (3d ed. 1977-date).

- CHARLES WRIGHT & ARTHUR MILLER, FEDERAL PRACTICE AND PROCEDURE (Rev. ed. 1971-date).

- MARK E. CAMMACK & NORMAN M. GARLAND, ADVANCED CRIMINAL PROCEDURE (2006).

- WAYNE R. LAFAVE, JEROLD H. ISRAEL, NANCY J. KING & ORIN S. KERR, CRIMINAL PROCEDURE (5th ed. 2009).

- JEROLD H. ISRAEL & WAYNE R. LAFAVE, CRIMINAL PROCEDURE: CONSTITUTIONAL LIMITATIONS (8th ed. 2006).

- RUSSELL L. WEAVER, JOHN M. BURKOFF, CATHERINE HANCOCK, JANET HOEFFEL, STEVE FRIEDLAND & STEPHEN SINGER, PRINCIPLES OF CRIMINAL PROCEDURE Ch. 21 (6th ed. 2018).

CHAPTER 23

Collateral Remedies

A. Introduction

A defendant who fails on direct appeal may file a collateral attack on the conviction, the most common form being a *habeas corpus* petition.

Petitioning for a writ of habeas corpus is a collateral attack: it is not a continuation of the criminal process but a civil suit brought to challenge the legality of the restraint under which a person is held. The petitioner in this civil suit, having lost the presumption of innocence upon conviction, has the burden to prove that his confinement is illegal. The respondent in a habeas action is the prisoner's custodian—the warden or other prison official. Habeas corpus has been called "the most celebrated writ in the English law," and the Supreme Court paid homage to this "Great Writ of Liberty" in *Fay v. Noia*, 372 U.S. 391 (1963):

It's Latin to Me

Habeas corpus is a Latin term meaning "you have the body."

Most states have habeas corpus-like proceedings that closely follow federal habeas corpus discussed in the remainder of this chapter. Failure to prevail in state habeas proceedings will not bar a subsequent federal habeas action.

We do well to bear in mind the extraordinary prestige of the Great Writ in Anglo-American jurisprudence. Received into our own law in the colonial period, given explicit recognition in the Federal Constitution, Art. I, section 9, cl. 2, incorporated in the first grant of federal court jurisdiction, habeas corpus was early confirmed by Chief Justice Marshall to be a "great constitutional privilege." Although in form the Great Writ is simply a mode of procedure, its history is inextricably intertwined with the growth of fundamental rights of personal liberty. For its function has been to provide a prompt and efficacious remedy for whatever society deems to be intolerable restraints. Its root principle is that in a civilized society, government must always be accountable to the judiciary for a man's imprisonment: if the imprisonment cannot be shown to conform with fundamental requirements of law, the individual is entitled to his immediate release. Thus, there is nothing novel in the fact that today habeas corpus in the federal courts provides a mode for the redress of denials of due process of law. Vindication of due process is precisely its historic office.

However grand the rhetoric in *Fay v. Noia*, the reality is that merely filing a habeas corpus petition does not insure that a federal court will review the merits of the petitioner's claim. As this Chapter will explain, the Court—beginning in the 1970s—and Congress in 1996 greatly narrowed the ability to achieve post-conviction relief for unlawful confinement.

1. Factual Basis for Claim

In *Williams v. Taylor*, the Court discusses one of the procedural hurdles to getting a hearing on a federal habeas petition: the requirement that petitioner must have developed the factual basis of his claim in state proceedings.

Williams v. Taylor

529 U.S. 420 (2000).

JUSTICE KENNEDY delivered the opinion of the Court.

Petitioner Michael Wayne Williams received a capital sentence for the murders of Morris Keller, Jr., and Keller's wife, Mary Elizabeth. Petitioner later sought a writ of habeas corpus in federal court. Accompany-

> **Hear It**
>
> You can listen to the oral argument in *Williams v. Taylor* at: http://www.oyez.org/cases/1990-1999/1999/1999_99_6615.

ing his petition was a request for an evidentiary hearing on constitutional claims which, he alleged, he had been unable to develop in state-court proceedings. The question is whether 28 U.S.C. § 2254(e)(2) bars the evidentiary hearing petitioner seeks. If petitioner "has failed to develop the factual basis of his claims in State court proceedings," his case is subject to § 2254(e)(2), and he may not receive a hearing because he concedes his inability to satisfy the statute's further stringent conditions for excusing the deficiency.

Petitioner filed a habeas petition in the United States District Court for the Eastern District of Virginia on November 20, 1996. The petition raised three claims relevant to questions now before us. First, petitioner claimed the prosecution had violated *Brady v. Maryland*, 373 U.S. 83 (1963), in failing to disclose a report of a confidential pre-trial psychiatric examination of prosecution witness Cruse. Second, petitioner alleged his trial was rendered unfair by the seating of a juror who at *voir dire* had not revealed possible sources of bias. Finally, petitioner alleged one of the prosecutors committed misconduct in failing to reveal his knowledge of the juror's possible bias. [The district court dismissed the petition, deciding that petitioner could not satisfy § 2254(e)(2)'s requirements.] The Court of Appeals concluded petitioner could not satisfy the statute's conditions for excusing his failure to develop the facts and held him barred from receiving an evidentiary hearing.

On October 18, 1999, petitioner filed an application for stay of execution and a petition for a writ of certiorari. On October 28, we stayed petitioner's execution and granted certiorari to decide whether § 2254(e)(2) precludes him from receiving an evidentiary hearing on his claims. We now affirm in part and reverse in part. Section 2254(e)(2), the provision which controls whether petitioner may receive an evidentiary hearing in federal district court on the claims that were not developed in the Virginia courts, becomes the central point of our analysis. It provides as follows:

> "If the applicant has failed to develop the factual basis of a claim in State court proceedings, the court shall not hold an evidentiary hearing on the claim unless the applicant shows that—
>
> "(A) the claim relies on—
>
> "(i) a new rule of constitutional law, made retroactive to cases on collateral review by the Supreme Court, that was previously unavailable; or
>
> "(ii) a factual predicate that could not have been previously discovered through the exercise of due diligence; and
>
> "(B) the facts underlying the claim would be sufficient to establish by clear and convincing evidence that but for constitutional error, no reasonable fact finder would have found the applicant guilty of the underlying offense."

By the terms of its opening clause the statute applies only to prisoners who have "failed to develop the factual basis of a claim in State court proceedings." If the prisoner has failed to develop the facts, an evidentiary hearing cannot be granted unless the prisoner's case meets the other conditions of § 2254(e)(2). Here, petitioner concedes his case does not comply with § 2254(e)(2)(B), so he may receive an evidentiary hearing only if his claims fall outside the opening clause.

We start with the language of the statute. Section 2254(e)(2) begins with a conditional clause, "if the applicant has failed to develop the factual basis of a claim in State court proceedings," which directs attention to the prisoner's efforts in state court. We ask first whether the factual basis was indeed developed in state court, a question susceptible, in the normal course, of a simple yes or no answer. Here the answer is no.

The Commonwealth would have the analysis begin and end there. Under its no-fault reading of the statute, if there is no factual development in the state court, the federal habeas court may not inquire into the reasons for the default when determining whether the opening clause of § 2254(e)(2) applies. We do not agree with the Commonwealth's interpretation of the word "failed."

We do not deny "fail" is sometimes used in a neutral way, not importing fault or want of diligence. So the phrase "We fail to understand his argument" can mean simply "We cannot understand his argument." This is not the sense in which the word "failed" is used here, however.

We give the words of a statute their "ordinary, contemporary, common meaning," absent an indication Congress intended them to bear some different import. In its customary and preferred sense, "fail" connotes some omission, fault, or negligence on the part of the person who has failed to do something. To say a person has failed in a duty implies he did not take the necessary steps to fulfill it. He is, as a consequence, at fault and bears responsibility for the failure. In this sense, a person is not at fault when his diligent efforts to perform an act are thwarted, for example, by the conduct of another or by happenstance. Fault lies, in those circumstances, either with the person who interfered with the accomplishment of the act or with no one at all. We conclude Congress used the word "failed" in the sense just described. Had Congress intended a no-fault standard, it would have had no difficulty in making its intent plain. It would have had to do no more than use, in lieu of the phrase "has failed to," the phrase "did not."

Under the opening clause of § 2254(e)(2), a failure to develop the factual basis of a claim is not established unless there is lack of diligence, or some greater fault, attributable to the prisoner or the prisoner's counsel. Now we apply the statutory test. If there has been no lack of diligence at the relevant stages in the state proceedings, the prisoner has not "failed to develop" the facts under § 2254(e)(2)'s opening clause, and he will be excused from showing compliance with the balance of the subsection's requirements. We find lack of diligence as to one of the three claims but not as to the other two.

Petitioner did not exercise the diligence required to preserve the claim that nondisclosure of Cruse's psychiatric report was in contravention of *Brady v.*

Maryland. The report concluded Cruse "had little recollection of the murders of the Kellers, other than vague memories, as he was intoxicated with alcohol and marijuana at the time." The report had been prepared in September 1993, before petitioner was tried; yet it was not mentioned by petitioner until he filed his federal habeas petition and attached a copy of the report. Petitioner explained that an investigator for his federal habeas counsel discovered the report in Cruse's court file but state habeas counsel had not seen it when he had reviewed the same file. State habeas counsel averred as follows:

Food for Thought

Is it right that a defendant's claim should stand or fall based on the diligence of his or her counsel? What if the attorney was known for laziness or inept work, or was a public defender with a burdensome caseload?

"Prior to filing petitioner's habeas corpus petition with the Virginia Supreme Court, I reviewed the Cumberland County court files of petitioner and of his co-defendant, Jeffrey Cruse. I have reviewed the attached psychiatric evaluation of Jeffrey Cruse. I have no recollection of seeing this report in Mr. Cruse's court file when I examined the file. Given the contents of the report, I am confident that I would remember it."

The trial court was not satisfied with this explanation for the late discovery. Nor are we. We conclude petitioner has met the burden of showing he was diligent in efforts to develop the facts supporting his juror bias and prosecutorial misconduct claims in collateral proceedings before the Virginia Supreme Court. Petitioner's claims are based on two of the questions posed to the jurors by the trial judge at *voir dire.* First, the judge asked prospective jurors, "Are any of you related to the following people who may be called as witnesses?" Then he read the jurors a list of names, one of which was "Deputy Sheriff Claude Meinhard." Bonnie Stinnett, who would later become the jury foreperson, had divorced Meinhard in 1979, after a 17-year marriage with four children. Stinnett remained silent, indicating the answer was "no." Meinhard, as the officer who investigated the crime scene and interrogated Cruse, would later become the prosecution's lead-off witness at trial.

After reading the names of the attorneys involved in the case, including one of the prosecutors, Robert Woodson, Jr., the judge asked, "Have you or any member of your immediate family ever been represented by any of the aforementioned attorneys?" Stinnett again said nothing, despite the fact Woodson had represented her during her divorce from Meinhard. In an affidavit she provided in the federal habeas proceedings, Stinnett claimed "she did not respond to the judge's first question because she did not consider herself 'related' to Claude Meinhard in 1994 at *voir dire.* Once our marriage ended in 1979, I was no longer related to him." As for Woodson's earlier representation of her, Stinnett explained as follows: "When Claude and I divorced in 1979, the divorce was uncontested and Mr. Woodson drew up the papers so that the divorce could be completed. Since neither Claude nor I was contesting anything, I didn't think Mr. Woodson 'represented' either one of us."

Woodson provided an affidavit in which he admitted "he was aware that Juror Bonnie Stinnett was the ex-wife of then Deputy Sheriff Claude Meinhard and he was aware that they had been divorced for some time." Woodson stated, however, "to his mind, people who are related only by marriage are no longer 'related' once the marriage ends in divorce."

Ethical Issue

Even if the prosecutor had a semantic point, should he have raised the marriage and divorce himself? Why or why not?

Woodson also "had no recollection of having been involved as a private attorney in the divorce proceedings between Claude Meinhard and Bonnie Stinnett." He explained that "whatever his involvement was in the 1979 divorce, by the time of trial in 1994 he had completely forgotten about it."

In ordering an evidentiary hearing on the juror bias and prosecutorial misconduct claims, the District Court concluded the factual basis of the claims was not reasonably available to petitioner's counsel during state habeas proceedings. The Court of Appeals held state habeas counsel was not diligent because petitioner's investigator on federal habeas discovered the relationships upon interviewing two jurors who referred in passing to Stinnett as "Bonnie Meinhard." The investigator later confirmed Stinnett's prior marriage to Meinhard by checking Cumberland County's public records. ("The documents supporting petitioner's Sixth Amendment claims have been a matter of public record since Stinnett's divorce became final in 1979. Indeed, because petitioner's federal habeas counsel located those documents, there is little reason to think that his state habeas counsel could not have done so as well"). We should be surprised, to say the least, if a district court familiar with the standards of trial practice were to hold that in all cases diligent counsel must check public records containing personal information pertaining to each and every juror. Because of Stinnett and Woodson's silence, there was no basis for an investigation into Stinnett's marriage history. Section 2254(e)(2) does not apply to petitioner's related claims of juror bias and prosecutorial misconduct.

The decision of the Court of Appeals is affirmed in part and reversed in part. The case is remanded for further proceedings consistent with this opinion.

Points for Discussion

a. Hearing, Bail, and Appeal

If a federal district court grants a hearing on a habeas petition, both the petitioner and the government must be given the opportunity to present evidence. Upon denial of the petition, the petitioner will be remanded to custody. If the court grants the petition, the petitioner shall be discharged from custody, but the court may suspend execution of its order to allow the government to appeal or to institute a new trial within a specified period of time. The court also has authority to admit the petitioner to bail, pending the government's appeal or initiation of a new trial. When deciding whether to grant release pending appeal to a state prisoner who has won habeas relief a federal court may consider: (1) the risk that the prisoner may flee; (2) the danger the prisoner may pose to the public; (3) the state's interest in continuing custody and rehabilitation; and (4) the prisoner's interest in release pending appeal. *Hilton v. Braunskill*, 481 U.S. 770 (1987).

b. Access to Habeas

The writ of habeas corpus may be suspended under the circumstances described in Art. I, § 2, cl. 2 of the Constitution: "The Privilege of the Writ of Habeas Corpus shall not be suspended unless when in Cases of Rebellion or Invasion the public Safety may require it."

In *Boumediene v. Bush*, 553 U.S. 723 (2008), the Court held that, in the case of enemy combatants held at Guantanamo Bay, Cuba, Congress had violated the Suspension Clause by improperly denying access to habeas corpus relief.

c. No Statutory Right to Competency in Habeas Proceeding

In *Ryan v. Gonzales*, 568 U.S. 57 (2013), the Court held that the federal habeas statute did not create a right of competency simply because it gave the defendant a right to counsel. Whereas the two rights are connected at the trial level, in that an incompetent defendant cannot effectively aid in the defense of his case by counsel at trial, at the habeas level, a competent defendant is not necessary to aid counsel because the review is a backward-looking, records-based process.

2. AEDPA Time Limits

At common law any person illegally detained could use the writ of habeas corpus to make repeated efforts to gain his freedom. "*Res judicata* did not attach to a court's denial of habeas relief. Instead a renewed application could be made to every other judge or court in the realm, and each court or judge was bound to consider the question of the prisoner's right to a discharge independently, and not to be influenced by the previous decisions refusing discharge." *McCleskey v. Zant*,

499 U.S. 467 (1991). The common law courts tolerated multiple petitions and petitions filed years after the initial trial because the writ of habeas corpus originally applied only to prisoners confined under federal authority and not under state authority, and review was limited primarily to testing the jurisdiction of the sentencing court. The scope of the writ later expanded beyond its original narrow purview to encompass review of constitutional error that had occurred in both state and federal proceedings leading to conviction. *See* Section C of this Chapter. The expanded coverage of the writ led the Supreme Court to formulate the doctrines of exhaustion and procedural default as means of limiting abusive and repetitive habeas petitions. In 1996, Congress passed The Antiterrorism and Effective Death Penalty Act (AEDPA), and it incorporated and expanded upon these doctrines. The current statutory provisions of the writ are found in 28 U.S.C.A. §§ 2241–2266.

Prior to enactment of AEDPA there was no time limitation on the filing of a writ of habeas corpus. Some courts applied the doctrine of laches on a case-by-case basis, *see e.g., Walker v. Mitchell*, 224 Va. 568, 299 S.E.2d 698 (1983) (six-and-a-half-year delay in filing a habeas corpus petition), but it did not operate as an effective statute of limitations due to the requirement that the government prove actual prejudice from the delay, *see id.* ("prejudice cannot be presumed solely from the passage of time").

What's That?

The "doctrine of laches" is based on the maxim that "equity aids the vigilant and not those who slumber on their rights." *Black's Law Dictionary*. When applied, a party's legal claim will not be enforced or allowed if delay in asserting the right or claim prejudiced the adverse party.

In order to promote speedy punishment and the finality of criminal justice proceedings, AEDPA created a rigid one-year limitation for filing a petition for habeas corpus relief. The limitation period begins to run on the latest date of the following: 1) when the judgment of conviction becomes final; 2) when a state action impeding making a motion was removed; 3) when a right asserted was initially recognized by the Supreme Court and made retroactive; or 4) when the facts supporting the claim presented could have been discovered through due diligence. *See* 28 U.S.C. § 2244(d)(1).

Because AEDPA limited the time for seeking habeas relief, case law has focused on the limitations period. For example, in *Johnson v. United States*, 544 U.S. 295 (2005), the Court held that the limitations period began to run when the petitioner received notice of the order vacating the state conviction that was used to enhance the federal sentence, provided that petitioner showed due diligence in seeking to vacate the state conviction. An application for state collateral review tolls the one-year limitations period during the interval between a lower state court's decision on collateral review and the filing of a notice of appeal to a higher state court. *Carey v. Saffold*, 536 U.S. 214 (2002). Judicial review of a state court judgment that is not part of a direct review, such as when a state prisoner requests that the trial court use its discretion to reduce his sentence, tolls the federal habeas statute of limitations. *Wall v. Kholi*, 562 U.S. 545 (2011). As for the third exception to the time limit for filing, the Court has held that any claim is time-barred if more than twelve months pass before the rule is held to be retroactive. *Dodd v. United States*, 545 U.S. 353 (2005).

If the habeas petition is filed in due time, a state prisoner seeking habeas review in a federal court must meet four requirements: (1) custody; (2) a violation of federal law; (3) exhaustion of other remedies; and (4) the absence of procedural default.

B. Custody

A person is in custody when he is presently serving a sentence for the conviction challenged by the writ, or when he has been released from confinement subject to the control of the parole board, probation officer, or a court that imposed a suspended sentence. In the latter case, a writ of habeas corpus is available if the conditions of release "significantly restrain" the petitioner's liberty. *Jones v. Cunningham*, 371 U.S. 236 (1963); *Hensley v. Municipal Court*, 411 U.S. 345 (1973). A prisoner serving consecutive sentences is "in custody" for purposes of challenging any of the sentences. *Peyton v. Rowe*, 391 U.S. 54 (1968). The writ may not be used to attack a conviction that imposed a fine or collateral civil disability and did not result in incarceration. Nor may the petitioner attack a sentence that has been fully served unless the prisoner is serving another sentence that was enhanced by the challenged sentence.

Garlotte v. Fordice

515 U.S. 39 (1995).

JUSTICE GINSBURG delivered the opinion of the Court.

To petition a federal court for habeas corpus relief from a state court conviction, the applicant must be "in custody in violation of the Constitution or laws or treaties of the United

Hear It

You can listen to the oral argument in *Garlotte* at: http://www.oyez.org/cases/1990-1999/1994/1994_94_6790.

States." In *Peyton v. Rowe*, 391 U.S. 54 (1968), we held that the governing federal prescription permits prisoners incarcerated under consecutive state court sentences to apply for federal habeas relief from sentences they had not yet begun to serve. We said in *Peyton* that, for purposes of habeas relief, consecutive sentences should be treated as a continuous series; a prisoner is "in custody in violation of the Constitution," we explained, "if any consecutive sentence the prisoner is scheduled to serve was imposed as the result of a deprivation of constitutional rights."

The case before us is appropriately described as *Peyton's* complement, or *Peyton* in reverse. Like the habeas petitioners in *Peyton*, petitioner Harvey Garlotte is incarcerated under consecutive sentences. Unlike the *Peyton* petitioners, Garlotte does not challenge a conviction underlying a sentence yet to be served. Instead, Garlotte seeks to attack a conviction underlying the sentence that ran first in a consecutive series, a sentence already served, but one that nonetheless persists to postpone Garlotte's eligibility for parole. Following *Peyton*, we do not desegregate Garlotte's sentences, but comprehend them as composing a continuous stream. We therefore hold that Garlotte remains "in custody" under all of his sentences until all are served, and now may attack the conviction underlying the sentence scheduled to run first in the series.

On September 16, 1985, at a plea hearing held in a Mississippi trial court, Harvey Garlotte entered simultaneous guilty pleas to one count of possession with intent to distribute marijuana and two counts of murder. Pursuant to a plea agreement, the State recommended that Garlotte be sentenced to a prison term of three years on the marijuana count, to run consecutively with two concurrent life sentences on the murder counts. The court imposed the sentences in this order: the three-year sentence first, then, consecutively, the concurrent life sentences.

Garlotte wrote to the trial court seven months after the September 16, 1985 hearing, asking for permission to withdraw his guilty plea on the marijuana count. The court's reply notified Garlotte of the Mississippi statute under which he could pursue post-conviction collateral relief. Garlotte unsuccessfully moved for such relief. Nearly two years after the denial of Garlotte's motion, the Mississippi Supreme Court rejected his appeal. On January 18, 1989, the Mississippi Supreme Court denied further post-conviction motions filed by Garlotte. By this time, Garlotte had completed the period of incarceration set for the marijuana offense, and had commenced serving the life sentences.

On October 6, 1989, Garlotte filed a habeas corpus petition in the United States District Court for the Southern District of Mississippi, naming as respondent Kirk Fordice, the Governor of Mississippi. Adopting the recommendation of a federal magistrate judge, the District Court denied Garlotte's petition on the merits. Before the United States Court of Appeals for the Fifth Circuit, the State argued for the first time that the District Court lacked jurisdiction over Garlotte's petition. The State asserted that Garlotte, prior to the District Court filing, had already served out the prison time imposed for the marijuana conviction; therefore, the State maintained, Garlotte was no longer "in custody" under that conviction within the meaning of the federal habeas statute. Garlotte countered that he remained "in custody" until all sentences were served, emphasizing that the marijuana conviction continued to postpone the date on which he would be eligible for parole. Adopting the State's position, the Fifth Circuit dismissed Garlotte's habeas petition for want of jurisdiction.

The Courts of Appeals have divided over the question whether a person incarcerated under consecutive sentences remains "in custody" under a sentence that (1) has been completed in terms of prison time served, but (2) continues to postpone the prisoner's date of potential release. We granted certiorari to resolve this conflict, and now reverse.

Had the Mississippi trial court ordered that Garlotte's life sentences run before his marijuana sentence—an option about which the prosecutor expressed indifference—*Peyton* unquestionably would have instructed the District Court to entertain Garlotte's present habeas petition. Because the marijuana term came first, and Garlotte filed his habeas petition after prison time had run on the marijuana sentence, Mississippi urges that *Maleng v. Cook*, 490 U.S. 488 (1989) (per curiam), rather than *Peyton*, controls.

The question presented in *Maleng* was "whether a habeas petitioner remains 'in custody' under a conviction after the sentence imposed for it has fully expired, merely because of the possibility that the prior conviction will be used to enhance the sentences imposed for any subsequent crimes of which he is convicted." We held that the potential use of a conviction to enhance a sentence for subsequent offenses did not suffice to render a person "in custody" within the meaning of the habeas statute.

Maleng recognized that we had "very liberally construed the 'in custody' requirement for purposes of federal habeas," but stressed that the Court had "never extended it to the situation where a habeas petitioner suffers no present restraint from a conviction." "Almost all States have habitual offender statutes, and many States provide for specific enhancement of subsequent sentences on the basis of prior convictions,"; hence, the construction of "in custody" urged by the habeas petitioner in *Maleng* would have left nearly all convictions perpetually open to collateral attack. The *Maleng* petitioner's interpretation, we therefore commented, "would read the 'in custody' requirement out of the statute."

Unlike the habeas petitioner in *Maleng*, Garlotte is serving consecutive sentences. In *Peyton*, we held that "a prisoner serving consecutive sentences is 'in custody' under any one of them" for purposes of the habeas statute. Having construed the statutory term "in custody" to require that consecutive sentences be viewed in the aggregate, we will not now adopt a different construction simply because the sentence imposed under the challenged conviction lies in the past rather than in the future.

Mississippi urges, as a prime reason for its construction of the 'in custody' requirement, that allowing a habeas attack on a sentence nominally completed would "encourage and reward delay in the assertion of habeas challenges." Mississippi argues that Garlotte's reading of the words "in custody" would undermine the expeditious adjudication rationale of *Peyton*.

Our holding today is unlikely to encourage delay. A prisoner naturally prefers release sooner to release later. Further, because the habeas petitioner generally bears the burden of proof, delay is apt to disadvantage the petitioner more than the State. Nothing in this record suggests that Garlotte has been dilatory in challenging his marijuana conviction. Finally, under Habeas Corpus Rule 9(a), a district court may dismiss a habeas petition if the State "has been prejudiced in its ability to respond to the petition by inexcusable delay in its filing."

> ### Take Note
>
> As a remedy of last resort, a convicted person no longer subject to confinement may seek a common law writ of *coram nobis* to challenge his prior conviction. *See United States v. Morgan*, 346 U.S. 502 (1954) (all federal courts may in exceptional cases grant relief in the nature of *coram nobis* to a person who is not in custody, under the "all-writs provision," 28 U.S.C. § 1651(a)). For example, in *Korematsu v. United States*, 323 U.S. 214 (1944), the Supreme Court upheld the conviction of an American citizen of Japanese ancestry for being in a location designated as off limits to all persons of Japanese ancestry. Forty years later, in *Korematsu v. United States*, 584 F. Supp. 1406 (N.D.Cal.1984), a federal district court granted a writ of *coram nobis* and vacated the conviction on grounds that the government had mislead the courts as to the military necessity of wartime relocation and internment of civilians in 1944.

> ### It's Latin to Me
>
> *Coram nobis* is Latin for "in our presence; before us." A writ of *coram nobis* is directed at the trial court alleged to have made an error of fact or law.

Under *Peyton*, we view consecutive sentences in the aggregate, not as discrete segments. Invalidation of Garlotte's marijuana conviction would advance the date of his eligibility for release from present incarceration. Garlotte's challenge, which will shorten his term of incarceration if he proves unconstitutionality, implicates the core purpose of habe-as review. We therefore hold that Garlotte was "in custody" under his marijuana conviction when he filed his federal habeas petition. Accordingly, the judgment of the Court of Appeals for the Fifth Circuit is reversed, and the case is remanded for proceedings consistent with this opinion.

JUSTICE THOMAS, with whom THE CHIEF JUSTICE joins, dissenting.

In my view, *Peyton* ought to be construed as limited to situations in which a habeas petitioner challenges a yet unexpired sentence. This would satisfy *Peyton's* policy concerns by permitting challenges to unserved sentences at an earlier time. More importantly, this interpretation would also make sense of *Maleng v. Cook's* proper insistence that the habeas statute does not permit prisoners to challenge expired convictions. The majority, however, relies upon broad language in one opinion to ignore language in another. Given the statute's text and the oddity of asserting that Garlotte is still serving time under the expired marijuana convic-tion, I would read *Peyton* narrowly. I dissent.

C. Violations of Federal Law

Only federal issues are cognizable in federal habeas proceedings; state consti-tutional or statutory violations are not. *See Rivera v. Illinois*, 556 U.S. 148 (2009) ("A mere error of state law is not a denial of due process. The Due Process Clause, our decisions instruct, safeguards not the meticulous observance of state proce-dural prescriptions, but 'fundamental elements of fairness in a criminal trial.'"). The most common habeas corpus claims are federal constitutional claims involv-ing ineffective assistance of counsel, illegal confessions obtained by the police, improper judicial or prosecutorial conduct, and insufficient evidence. In most cases errors concerning the admissibility of evidence or instructions to the jury do not amount to constitutional violations. The writ of habeas corpus focuses on the legality of the prisoner's detention under the Due Process Clause of the Fourteenth Amendment, rather than his ultimate guilt or innocence.

Although 28 U.S.C. § 2254 speaks of a "violation of the Constitution or laws or treaties of the United States," almost all federal habeas petitions allege a violation of the Constitution. A conviction obtained in violation of a federal statute does not warrant habeas review unless the statutory violation qualifies as a "fundamental defect which inherently results in a complete miscarriage of justice, or an omission inconsistent with the rudimentary demands of fair procedure." *Reed v. Farley*, 512 U.S. 339 (1994). Most statutory violations simply do not rise to that high standard to invoke habeas jurisdiction.

The breadth of coverage of federal habeas review of state court convictions increased dramatically throughout history and through the Warren Court of the 1960s:

> The writ of habeas corpus known to the Framers was quite different from that which exists today. The first Congress made the writ of habeas corpus available only to prisoners confined under the authority of the United States, not under state authority. It was not until 1867 that Congress made the writ generally available in "all cases where any person may be restrained of his or her liberty in violation of the constitution, or of any treaty or law of the United States." And it was not until well into this century that this Court interpreted that provision to allow a final judgment of conviction in a state court to be collaterally attacked on habeas.

Felker v. Turpin, 518 U.S. 651 (1996).

In *Stone v. Powell*, the Court limited the judicial availability of federal habeas relief in Fourth Amendment cases, its first step to rein in federal judges reared on the Warren Court's "judicial activism" and distrust of state courts.

FYI

The Warren Court's willingness to increase the scope of federal habeas review of state court convictions was partially premised on a belief that the state courts could not be trusted to protect the constitutional rights of criminal defendants. In the landmark case of *Gideon v. Wainwright*, 372 U.S. 335, 351 (1963), Justice Harlan expressed dissatisfaction with many state courts' discharge of their "front-line responsibility for the enforcement of constitutional rights." The Burger and Rehnquist Courts, however, embraced the concept of a "new federalism" and resurrected faith in the state courts as protectors of individual freedom. "The battle over habeas is driven, in the main, not by relatively sterile concerns for federalism and congested federal dockets, but by an ideological resistance to the Warren Court's innovative interpretations of substantive federal rights." Larry Yackle, *The Habeas Hagioscope*, 66 S. Cal. L. Rev. 2331 (1993).

Stone v. Powell

428 U.S. 465 (1976).

JUSTICE POWELL delivered the opinion of the Court.

Hear It

You can listen to the oral argument in *Stone v. Powell* at: http:// www.oyez.org/cases/1970-1979/ 1975/1975_74_1055.

[Respondent Powell was arrested for violating a vagrancy ordinance, but was later charged with murder and convicted on the basis of evidence seized during a search pursuant to the vagrancy arrest. Powell asserted that the vagrancy ordinance was unconstitutional and the subsequent arrest and search were illegal.]

Respondent alleges violations of Fourth Amendment rights guaranteed them through the Fourteenth Amendment. The question is whether state prisoners who have been afforded the opportunity for full and fair consideration of their reliance upon the exclusionary rule with respect to seized evidence by the state courts at trial and on direct review may invoke their claim again on federal habeas corpus review. The answer is to be found by weighing the utility of the exclusionary rule against the costs of extending it to collateral review of Fourth Amendment claims.

The costs of applying the exclusionary rule even at trial and on direct review are well known: the focus of the trial, and the attention of the participants therein, are diverted from the ultimate question of guilt or innocence that should be the central concern in a criminal proceeding. Moreover, the physical evidence sought to be excluded is typically reliable and often the most probative information bearing on the guilt or innocence of the defendant.

Application of the rule thus deflects the truth finding process and often frees the guilty. The disparity in particular cases between the error committed by the police officer and the windfall afforded a guilty defendant by application of the rule is contrary to the idea of proportionality that is essential to the concept of justice. Thus, although the rule is thought to deter unlawful police activity in part through the nurturing of respect for Fourth Amendment values, if applied indiscriminately it may well have the opposite effect of generating disrespect for the law and administration of justice. These long-recognized costs of the rule persist when a criminal conviction is sought to be overturned on collateral review on the ground that a search-and-seizure claim was erroneously rejected by two or more tiers of state courts.

Make the Connection

This weighing of costs and benefits should sound familiar to students of the Fourth Amendment. The Court has used the same cost/benefit analysis to restrict application of the exclusionary rule to violations of the Fourth Amendment, including exclusion of evidence at trial.

Evidence obtained by police officers in violation of the Fourth Amendment is excluded at trial in the hope that the frequency of future violations will decrease. Despite the absence of supportive empirical evidence, we have assumed that the immediate effect of exclusion will be to discourage law enforcement officials from violating the Fourth Amendment by removing the incentive to disregard it. More importantly, over the long term, this demonstration that our society attaches serious consequences to violation of constitutional rights is thought to encourage those who formulate law enforcement policies, and the officers who implement them, to incorporate Fourth Amendment ideals into their value system.

We adhere to the view that these considerations support the implementation of the exclusionary rule at trial and its enforcement on direct appeal of state-court convictions. But the additional contribution, if any, of the consideration of search-and-seizure claims of state prisoners on collateral review is small in relation to the costs. To be sure, each case in which such claim is considered may add marginally to an awareness of the values protected by the Fourth Amendment. There is no reason to believe, however, that the overall educative effect of the exclusionary rule would be appreciably diminished if search-and-seizure claims could not be raised in federal habeas corpus review of state convictions. Nor is there reason to assume that any specific disincentive already created by the risk of exclusion of evidence at trial or the reversal of convictions on direct review would be enhanced if there were the further risk that a conviction obtained in state court and affirmed on direct review might be overturned in collateral proceedings often occurring years after the incarceration of the defendant. The view that the deterrence of Fourth Amendment violations would be furthered rests on the dubious assump-

tion that law enforcement authorities would fear that federal habeas review might reveal flaws in a search or seizure that went undetected at trial and on appeal. Even if one rationally could assume that some additional incremental deterrent effect would be presented in isolated cases, the resulting advance of the legitimate goal of furthering Fourth Amendment rights would be outweighed by the acknowledged costs to other values vital to a rational system of criminal justice.

Food for Thought

Even if review of a Fourth Amendment violation on collateral review would not have significant deterrent effects, is there any other value favoring a review of a claimed Fourth Amendment violation?

In sum, we conclude that where the State has provided an opportunity for full and fair litigation of a Fourth Amendment claim, a state prisoner may not be granted federal habeas corpus relief on the ground that evidence obtained in an unconstitutional search or seizure was introduced at his trial. In this context the contribution of the exclusionary rule, if any, to the effectuation of the Fourth Amendment is minimal, and the substantial societal costs of application of the rule persist with special force.

Mr. Justice Brennan, with whom Mr. Justice Marshall concurs, dissenting.

It is simply inconceivable that a constitutional deprivation suddenly vanishes after the appellate process has been exhausted. Federal habeas corpus review of Fourth Amendment claims of state prisoners was merely one manifestation of the principle that "conventional notions of finality in criminal litigation cannot be permitted to defeat the manifest federal policy that federal constitutional rights of personal liberty shall not be denied without the fullest opportunity for plenary federal judicial review." *Fay v. Noia*, 372 U.S. 391, 424 (1963). This Court's precedents have been "premised in large part on a recognition that the availability of collateral remedies is necessary to insure the integrity of proceedings at and before trial where constitutional rights are at stake. Our decisions leave no doubt that the federal habeas remedy extends to state prisoners alleging that unconstitutionally obtained evidence was admitted against them at trial."

Food for Thought

Should every convicted defendant have at least one opportunity to litigate federal constitutional claims in federal court? In theory, a defendant convicted in state court could petition the Supreme Court for certiorari to review the conviction—without having to show that the state denied him a full and fair hearing on the constitutional claim. In practice, the Supreme Court is unlikely to grant certiorari. Should federal habeas be used to allow the lower federal courts to conduct the type of review that the Supreme Court is unable to provide because of its heavy caseload? On the other hand, if it is a perversion of federalist principles to have federal district courts essentially serve as appellate courts for the states who have "fully and fairly litigated" the federal issue, why shouldn't *Stone* apply to all claims of violation of federal law? What role does factual innocence play in defining habeas jurisdiction? *See* Section F of this Chapter.

The only result of today's holding will be that denials by the state courts of claims by state prisoners of violations of their Fourth Amendment rights will go unreviewed by a federal tribunal. I fear that the same treatment ultimately will be accorded state prisoners' claims of violations of other constitutional rights; thus the potential ramifications of this case for federal habeas jurisdiction generally are ominous. The Court, no longer content just to restrict forthrightly the constitutional rights of the citizenry, has embarked on a campaign to water down even such constitutional rights as it purports to acknowledge by the device of foreclosing resort to the federal habeas remedy for their redress.

Points for Discussion

a. *Miranda* Claims

In *Withrow v. Williams,* 507 U.S. 680 (1993), the Court declined an opportunity to apply *Stone v. Powell* to *Miranda v. Arizona,* 384 U.S. 436 (1966), despite the fact that *Miranda's* exclusionary rule, like that of the Fourth Amendment rule, is designed to deter police violations and is arguably unrelated to accurate fact-finding. Nevertheless, the *Withrow* Court found that a federal court can hear a petition concerning a *Miranda* violation. In rejecting an extension of *Stone v. Powell,* the Court stated that "prophylactic though it may be," *Miranda* safeguards the constitutional right against self-incrimination, a fundamental right that is not "necessarily divorced from the correct ascertainment of guilt." Justice Souter also noted that eliminating *Miranda* habeas claims simply would result in the substitution of due process voluntariness claims in their place. *See Miller v. Fenton,* 474 U.S. 104 (1985) ("the voluntariness of a confession is a legal question requiring independent federal determination upon a federal writ of habeas corpus").

Take Note

Although the Court's opinion in *Stone v. Powell* led to speculation that defendants might be denied habeas corpus review of other constitutional claims, this did not happen. The Supreme Court did not extend its limiting principle to constitutional violations impacting the guilt determination. For example, in *Jackson v. Virginia,* 443 U.S. 307 (1979), the Court held that a claim that a prisoner was convicted on insufficient evidence is cognizable on federal habeas corpus review as a violation of due process. Unlike the Fourth Amendment, which operates to exclude evidence that would have aided in the truth-finding function, whether the prosecution's evidence met the reasonable doubt standard of proof related to the accuracy of fact-finding. *Jackson's* holding, however, limited habeas relief to a showing that no rational trier of fact, viewing the evidence in the light most favorable to the prosecution, "could have found the essential elements of the crime beyond a reasonable doubt."

b. Grand Jury Discrimination

In *Rose v. Mitchell,* 443 U.S. 545 (1979), the Court held that a claim of racial discrimination in the selection of a state grand jury is cognizable on federal habeas corpus, even though the claimed error did not affect the determination of guilt and had been heard by the state court. The Court distinguished *Stone* on three grounds. First, the Court was unwilling to assume that state judges could fairly consider claims of grand jury discrimination, since those claims required the state courts to review their own procedures rather than those of the police. Second, the right to an indictment by a grand jury free from discrimination in its selection process is a personal constitutional right rather than a judicially created remedy. Third, state courts could be expected to respond to a determination that their grand jury selection procedures failed to meet constitutional requirements, *i.e.*, deterrence is effective.

Hypo: *Using Kimmelman*

Your client was convicted in State court based largely on evidence obtained from a warrantless search of his residence. Following direct appeal in the State courts, your client fired his trial counsel and retained you. Your review of the trial transcript convinces you that the State court incorrectly applied Fourth Amendment precedent and that the federal courts would not uphold the warrantless search. Is there any way that you can obtain federal review of the search without running afoul of *Stone v. Powell*? Consider whether the rationale of *Stone* be reconciled with the rationale of *Kimmelman v. Morrison*, 477 U.S. 365 (1986): "The constitutional rights of criminal defendants are granted to the innocent and the guilty alike. Consequently, we decline to hold either that the guarantee of effective assistance of counsel belongs solely to the innocent or that it attaches only to matters affecting the determination of actual guilt." In *Kimmelman v. Morrison* the Court ruled that *Stone v. Powell* did not preclude Sixth Amendment ineffective assistance of counsel claims based on defense counsel's failure to move to suppress illegally seized evidence. The Court emphasized that, unlike the Fourth Amendment exclusionary rule, Sixth Amendment rights are fundamental trial rights, going to the fairness of the judicial process. Although the Fourth Amendment claim was one element of proof of the Sixth Amendment claim, "the two claims have separate identities and reflect different constitutional values." Moreover, "in general, no comparable, meaningful opportunity exists for the full and fair litigation of a habeas petitioner's ineffective assistance claims at trial and on direct review." Is it possible for you use *Kimmelman* to create "backdoor" access to federal review of Fourth Amendment issues by combining the Fourth Amendment claim with a Sixth Amendment claim that trial counsel was ineffective in raising the Fourth Amendment claim?

c. *Stone v. Powell* and AEPDA

To what extent has *Stone v. Powell* been extended by AEDPA's provision that habeas relief will not be granted with respect to any claim that was adjudicated on the merits in state court unless the state adjudication "resulted in a decision that was contrary to, or involved an unreasonable application of, clearly established Federal law, as determined by the Supreme Court of the United States"? Is there a distinction between the "contrary to" category and the "unreasonable application" category? Consider the following case.

Williams v. Taylor

529 U.S. 362 (2000).

JUSTICE STEVENS announced the judgment of the Court and delivered the opinion of the Court with respect to Parts, I, III, and IV, and an opinion with respect to Parts II and V. Justice SOUTER, Justice GINSBURG, and Justice BREYER join this opinion in its entirety. Justice O'CONNOR and Justice KENNEDY join Parts I, III, and IV of this opinion.

Hear It

You can listen to the oral argument in *(Terry) Williams* at: http://www.oyez.org/cases/1990-1999/1999/1999_98_8384.

The questions presented are whether Terry Williams' constitutional right to the effective assistance of counsel as defined in *Strickland v. Washington*, 466 U.S. 668 (1984), was violated, and whether the judgment of the Virginia Supreme Court refusing to set aside his death sentence "was contrary to, or involved an unreasonable application of, clearly established Federal law, as determined by the Supreme Court of the United States," within the meaning of 28 U.S.C. § 2254(d)(1) (1994 ed., Supp. III). We answer both questions affirmatively.

In September 1986, Williams was convicted of robbery and capital murder. The jury found a probability of future dangerousness and unanimously fixed Williams' punishment at death. The trial judge concluded that such punishment was "proper" and "just" and imposed the death sentence. The Virginia Supreme Court affirmed the conviction and sentence.

In 1988 Williams filed for state collateral relief in the Danville Circuit Court. Judge Ingram (the same judge who presided over Williams' trial and sentencing) held an evidentiary hearing on Williams' claim that trial counsel had been ineffective. Based on the evidence adduced after two days of hearings, Judge Ingram found that Williams' conviction was valid, but that his trial attorneys had been ineffective during sentencing. Among the evidence reviewed that had not been presented at trial were documents prepared in connection with Williams' commitment when he was 11 years old that dramatically described mistreatment, abuse, and neglect during his early childhood, as well as testimony that he was "borderline mentally retarded," had suffered repeated head injuries, and might have mental impairments organic in origin. The habeas hearing also revealed that the same experts who had testified on the State's behalf at trial believed that Williams, if kept in a "structured environment," would not pose a future danger to society.

Judge Ingram found that counsel's failure to discover and present this and other significant mitigating evidence was "below the range expected of reasonable, professional competent assistance of counsel." Counsel's performance thus "did not measure up to the standard required under the holding of *Strickland v. Washington*, 466 U.S. 668 (1984), and if it had, there is a reasonable probability that the result of the sentencing phase would have been different." Judge Ingram therefore recommended that Williams be granted a rehearing on the sentencing phase of his trial.

The Virginia Supreme Court did not accept that recommendation. Although it assumed, without deciding, that trial counsel had been ineffective, it disagreed with the trial judge's conclusion that Williams had suffered sufficient prejudice to warrant relief. Treating the prejudice inquiry as a mixed question of law and fact, the Virginia Supreme Court accepted the factual determination that available evidence in mitigation had not been presented at the trial, but held that the trial judge had misapplied the law in two respects. First, relying on our decision in *Lockhart v. Fretwell*, 506 U.S. 364 (1993), the court held that it was wrong for the trial judge to rely "on mere outcome determination" when assessing prejudice. Second, it construed the trial judge's opinion as having "adopted a per se approach" that would establish prejudice whenever any mitigating evidence was omitted. The court then reviewed the prosecution evidence supporting the "future dangerousness" aggravating circumstance, reciting Williams' criminal history, including the several most recent offenses to which he had confessed. In comparison, it found that the excluded mitigating evidence—which it characterized as merely indicating "that numerous people, mostly relatives, thought that defendant was nonviolent and could cope very well in a structured environment,"—"barely would have altered the profile of this defendant that was presented to the jury." On this basis, the court concluded that there was no reasonable possibility that the omitted evidence would have affected the jury's sentencing recommendation, and that Williams had failed to demonstrate that his sentencing proceeding was fundamentally unfair.

Having exhausted his state remedies, Williams sought a federal writ of habeas corpus pursuant to 28 U.S.C. § 2254. After reviewing the state habeas hearing transcript and the state courts' findings of fact and conclusions of law, the federal trial judge agreed with the Virginia trial judge: The death sentence was constitutionally infirm. After noting that the Virginia Supreme Court had not addressed the question whether trial counsel's performance at the sentencing hearing fell below the range of competence demanded of lawyers in criminal cases, the District judge began by addressing that issue in detail. He identified five categories of mitigating evidence that counsel had failed to introduce, and he rejected the argument that counsel's failure to conduct an adequate investigation had been a strategic decision to rely almost entirely on the fact that Williams had voluntarily confessed.

According to Williams' trial counsel's testimony before the state habeas court, counsel did not fail to seek Williams' juvenile and social services records because he thought they would be counterproductive, but because counsel erroneously believed that "state law didn't permit it." Counsel also acknowledged in the course of the hearings that information about Williams' childhood would have been important in mitigation. And counsel's failure to contact a potentially persuasive character witness was likewise not a conscious strategic choice, but simply a failure to return that witness' phone call offering his service. Finally, even if counsel neglected to conduct such an investigation at the time as part of a tactical decision, the District Judge found, tactics as a matter of reasonable performance could not justify the omissions.

Turning to the prejudice issue, the judge determined that there was "a reasonable probability that, but for counsel's unprofessional errors, the result of the proceeding would have been different." He found that the Virginia Supreme Court had erroneously assumed that *Lockhart* had modified the *Strickland* standard for determining prejudice, and that it had made an important error of fact in discussing its finding of no prejudice. Having introduced his analysis of Williams' claim with the standard of review applicable on habeas appeals provided by 28 U.S.C. § 2254(d), the judge concluded that those errors established that the Virginia Supreme Court's decision "was contrary to, or involved an unreasonable application of, clearly established Federal law" within the meaning of § 2254(d)(1).

The Federal Court of Appeals reversed. It construed § 2254(d)(1) as prohibiting the grant of habeas corpus relief unless the state court "decided the question by interpreting or applying the relevant precedent in a manner that reasonable jurists would all agree is unreasonable." Applying that standard, it could not say that the Virginia Supreme Court's decision on the prejudice issue was an unreasonable application of the tests developed in either *Strickland* or *Lockhart*. It explained that the evidence that Williams presented a future danger to society was "simply overwhelming," it endorsed the Virginia Supreme Court's interpretation of *Lockhart*, and it characterized the state court's understanding of the facts in this case as "reasonable." We granted certiorari, and now reverse.

Over the years, the federal habeas corpus statute has been repeatedly amended, but the scope of that jurisdictional grant remains the same. It is, of course, well settled that the fact that constitutional error occurred in the proceedings that led to a state-court conviction may not alone be sufficient reason for concluding that a prisoner is entitled to the remedy of habeas. *See, e.g., Stone v. Powell.* On the other hand, errors that undermine confidence in the fundamental fairness of the state adjudication certainly justify the issuance of the federal writ. The deprivation of the right to the effective assistance of counsel recognized in *Strickland* is such an error.

The warden here contends that federal habeas corpus relief is prohibited by the amendment to 28 U.S.C. § 2254, enacted as a part of the Antiterrorism and Effective Death Penalty Act of 1996 (AEDPA). The relevant portion of that amendment provides:

> "(d) An application for a writ of habeas corpus on behalf of a person in custody pursuant to the judgment of a State court shall not be granted with respect to any claim that was adjudicated on the merits in State court proceedings unless the adjudication of the claim—

> "(1) resulted in a decision that was contrary to, or involved an unreasonable application of, clearly established Federal law, as determined by the Supreme Court of the United States."

The message that Congress intended to convey by using the phrases, "contrary to" and "unreasonable application of" is not entirely clear. The prevailing view in the Circuits is that the former phrase requires de novo review of 'pure' questions of law and the latter requires some sort of "reasonability" review of so-called mixed questions of law and fact.

We are not persuaded that the phrases define two mutually exclusive categories of questions. Most constitutional questions that arise in habeas corpus proceedings—and therefore most "decisions" to be made—require the federal judge to apply a rule of law to a set of facts, some of which may be disputed and some undisputed. For example, an erroneous conclusion that particular circumstances established the voluntariness of a confession, or that there exists a conflict of interest when one attorney represents multiple defendants, may well be described either as "contrary to" or as an "unreasonable application of" the governing rule of law. AEDPA plainly sought to ensure a level of "deference to the determinations of state courts," provided those determinations did not conflict with federal law or apply federal law in an unreasonable way. Congress wished to curb delays, to prevent "retrials" on federal habeas, and to give effect to state convictions to the extent possible under law. When federal courts are able to fulfill these goals within the bounds of the law, AEDPA instructs them to do so.

In sum, the statute directs federal courts to attend to every state-court judgment with utmost care, but it does not require them to defer to the opinion of every reasonable state-court judge on the content of federal law. If, after carefully weighing all the reasons for accepting a state court's judgment, a federal court is convinced that a prisoner's custody—or, as in this case, his sentence of death—violates the Constitution, that independent judgment should prevail. Otherwise the federal "law as determined by the Supreme Court of the United States" might be applied by the federal courts one way in Virginia and another way in California. In light of the well-recognized interest in ensuring that federal courts interpret federal law in a uniform way, we are convinced that Congress did not intend the statute to produce such a result.

In this case, Williams contends that he was denied his constitutionally guaranteed right to the effective assistance of counsel when his trial lawyers failed to investigate and to present substantial mitigating evidence to the sentencing jury. The threshold question under AEDPA is whether Williams seeks to apply a rule of law that was clearly established at the time his state-court conviction became final. That question is easily answered because the merits of his claim are squarely governed by our holding in *Strickland v. Washington*.

It is past question that the rule set forth in *Strickland* qualifies as "clearly established Federal law, as determined by the Supreme Court of the United States." That the *Strickland* test "of necessity requires a case-by-case examination of the evidence," obviates neither the clarity of the rule nor the extent to which the rule must be seen as "established" by this Court. This Court's precedent "dictated" that the Virginia Supreme Court apply the *Strickland* test at the time that court entertained Williams' ineffective-assistance claim. And it can hardly be said that recognizing the right to effective counsel "breaks new ground or imposes a new obligation on the States." Williams is therefore entitled to relief if the Virginia Supreme Court's decision rejecting his ineffective-assistance claim was either "contrary to, or involved an unreasonable application of," that established law. It was both.

The Virginia Supreme Court erred in holding that our decision in *Lockhart v. Fretwell*, modified or in some way supplanted the rule set down in *Strickland*. The trial judge analyzed the ineffective-assistance claim under the correct standard; the Virginia Supreme Court did not. We are also persuaded, unlike the Virginia Supreme Court, that counsel's unprofessional service prejudiced Williams within the meaning of *Strickland*.

In our judgment, the state trial judge was correct both in his recognition of the established legal standard for determining counsel's effectiveness, and in his conclusion that the entire post conviction record, viewed as a whole and cumulative of mitigation evidence presented originally, raised "a reasonable probability that the result of the sentencing proceeding would have been different" if competent counsel had presented and explained the significance of all the available evidence. It follows that the Virginia Supreme Court rendered a "decision that was contrary to, or involved an unreasonable application of, clearly established Federal law."

Accordingly, the judgment of the Court of Appeals is reversed, and the case is remanded for further proceedings consistent with this opinion.

Justice O'CONNOR delivered the opinion of the Court with respect to Part II, concurred in part, and concurred in the judgment. Justice KENNEDY joins this opinion in its entirety. THE CHIEF JUSTICE and Justice THOMAS join this opinion with respect to Part II. Justice SCALIA joins this opinion with respect to Part II.

Food for Thought

Are you persuaded? Having covered ineffective assistance of counsel in Chapter 3, *supra*, has the Supreme Court made it at all clear what sort of deficient performance and prejudice will result in a Sixth Amendment violation? Is it really "clearly established law"? And was the lower court's decision really "contrary to" *Strickland*? How much do you think the outcome in this case has to do with the fact that the deficient performance was in the penalty phase of a capital proceeding, as opposed to a less serious case?

Before 1996, this Court held that a federal court entertaining a state prisoner's application for habeas relief must exercise its independent judgment when deciding both questions of constitutional law and mixed constitutional questions (*i.e.*, application of constitutional law to fact). In other words, a federal habeas court owed no deference to a state court's resolution of such questions of law or mixed questions. If today's case were governed by the federal habeas statute prior to Congress' enactment of AEDPA in 1996, I would agree with Justice Stevens that Williams' petition for habeas relief must be granted if we, in our independent judgment, were to conclude that his Sixth Amendment right to effective assistance of counsel was violated.

II

Section 2254(d)(1) defines two categories of cases in which a state prisoner may obtain federal habeas relief with respect to a claim adjudicated on the merits in state court. Under the statute, a federal court may grant a writ of habeas corpus if the relevant state-court decision was either (1) "contrary to clearly established Federal law, as determined by the Supreme Court of the United States," or (2) "involved an unreasonable application of clearly established Federal law, as determined by the Supreme Court of the United States."

The Court of Appeals for the Fourth Circuit properly accorded both the "contrary to" and "unreasonable application" clauses independent meaning. With respect to the first of the two statutory clauses, the Fourth Circuit held in *Green* that a state-court decision can be "contrary to" this Court's clearly established precedent in two ways. First, a state-court decision is contrary to this Court's precedent if the state court arrives at a conclusion opposite to that reached by this Court on a question of law. Second, a state-court decision is also contrary to this Court's precedent if the state court confronts facts that are materially indistinguishable from a relevant Supreme Court precedent and arrives at a result opposite to ours.

The word "contrary" is commonly understood to mean "diametrically different," "opposite in character or nature," or "mutually opposed." The text of § 2254(d)(1) therefore suggests that the state court's decision must be substantially different from the relevant precedent of this Court. The Fourth Circuit's interpretation of the "contrary to" clause accurately reflects this textual meaning. A state-court decision will certainly be contrary to our clearly established precedent if the state court applies a rule that contradicts the governing law set forth in our cases. Take, for example, our decision in *Strickland v. Washington*. If a state court were to reject a prisoner's claim of ineffective assistance of counsel on the grounds that the prisoner had not established by a preponderance of the evidence that the result of his criminal proceeding would have been different, that decision would be "diametrically different," "opposite in character or nature," and "mutually opposed" to our clearly established precedent because we held in *Strickland* that the prisoner need only demonstrate a "reasonable probability that the result of the proceeding would have been different." A state-court decision will also be contrary to this Court's clearly established precedent if the state court confronts a set of facts that are materially indistinguishable from a decision of this Court and nevertheless arrives at a result different from our precedent. In either of these two scenarios, a federal court will be unconstrained by § 2254(d)(1) because the state-court decision falls within that provision's "contrary to" clause.

On the other hand, a run-of-the-mill state-court decision applying the correct legal rule from our cases to the facts of a prisoner's case would not fit comfortably within § 2254(d)(1)'s "contrary to" clause. Assume, for example, that a state-court decision on a prisoner's ineffective-assistance claim correctly identifies *Strickland* as the controlling legal authority and, applying that framework, rejects the prisoner's claim. Quite clearly, the state-court decision would be in accord with our decision in *Strickland* as to the legal prerequisites for establishing an ineffective-assistance claim, even assuming the federal court considering the prisoner's habeas application might reach a different result applying the *Strickland* framework itself. It is difficult to describe such a run-of-the-mill state-court decision as "diametrically different" from, "opposite in character or nature" from, or "mutually opposed" to *Strickland*, our clearly established precedent. Although the state-court decision may be contrary to the federal court's conception of how *Strickland* ought to be applied in that particular case, the decision is not "mutually opposed" to *Strickland* itself.

The Fourth Circuit's interpretation of the "unreasonable application" clause of § 2254(d)(1) is generally correct. A state-court decision can involve an "unreasonable application" of this Court's clearly established precedent in two ways. First, a state-court decision involves an unreasonable application of this Court's precedent if the state court identifies this Court's cases but unreasonably applies it to the facts of the particular state prisoner's case. Second, a state-court decision also involves an unreasonable application of this Court's precedent if the state court either unreasonably extends a legal principle from our precedent to a new context where it should not apply or unreasonably refuses to extend that principle to a new context where it should apply.

There remains the task of defining what exactly qualifies as an "unreasonable application" of law under § 2254(d)(1). Stated simply, a federal habeas court making the "unreasonable application" inquiry should ask whether the state court's application of clearly established federal law was objectively unreasonable. The federal habeas court should not transform the inquiry into a subjective one by resting its determination instead on the simple fact that at least one of the Nation's jurists has applied the relevant federal law in the same manner the state court did in the habeas petitioner's case.

Under § 2254(d)(1)'s "unreasonable application" clause, then, a federal habeas court may not issue the writ simply because that court concludes in its independent judgment that the relevant state-court decision applied clearly established federal law erroneously or incorrectly. Rather, that application must also be unreasonable.

In sum, § 2254(d)(1) places a new constraint on the power of a federal habeas court to grant a state prisoner's application for a writ of habeas corpus with respect to claims adjudicated on the merits in state court. Under § 2254(d)(1), the writ may issue only if one of the following two conditions is satisfied—the state-court adjudication resulted in a decision that (1) "was contrary to clearly established Federal law, as determined by the Supreme Court of the United States," or (2) "involved an unreasonable application of clearly established Federal law, as determined by the Supreme Court of the United States." Under the "contrary to" clause, a federal habeas court may grant the writ if the state court arrives at a conclusion opposite to that reached by this Court on a question of law or if the state court decides a case differently than this Court has on a set of materially indistinguishable facts. Under the "unreasonable application" clause, a federal habeas court may grant the writ if the state court identifies the correct governing legal principle from this Court's decisions but unreasonably applies that principle to the facts of the prisoner's case.

III

Although I disagree with Justice Stevens concerning the standard we must apply under § 2254(d)(1) in evaluating Williams' claims on habeas, I agree with the Court that the Virginia Supreme Court's adjudication of Williams' claim of ineffective assistance of counsel resulted in a decision that was

> **Food for Thought**
>
> As a matter of statutory interpretation of the phrases "contrary to" and "unreasonable application of," which group of Justices has it right? Did you count the votes? Part II that you just read is the controlling interpretation.

both contrary to and involved an unreasonable application of this Court's clearly established precedent. Specifically, I believe that the Court's discussion in Parts III and IV is correct and that it demonstrates the reasons that the Virginia Supreme Court's decision in Williams' case, even under the interpretation of § 2254(d)(1) I have set forth above, was both contrary to and involved an unreasonable application of our precedent.

> Justice Kennedy was the only Justice in the majority of all the 2007 habeas corpus cases decided by a vote of 5–4 under AEDPA.

Accordingly, although I disagree with the interpretation of § 2254(d)(1) set forth in Part II of Justice Stevens' opinion, I join Parts I, III, and IV of the Court's opinion and concur in the judgment of reversal.

Points for Discussion

> In *Carey v. Musladin*, 549 U.S. 70 (2006), the victim's family members sat in the audience during the trial wearing buttons displaying the victim's image. The defendant argued it denied him a fair trial. Contrary to the conclusion of the Ninth Circuit, the Court held that there was no "clearly established" federal law on the effect on a defendant's fair-trial rights of such spectator conduct. While the Court had held that there was inherent prejudice in certain government-sponsored conduct (*e.g.*, requiring the defendant to wear prison clothing, *see Estelle v. Williams*, 425 U.S. 501 (1976)), the Court had never addressed a claim that private-actor courtroom conduct was so inherently prejudicial that it deprived a defendant of a fair trial.

a. No Mitigating Evidence

In *Schriro v. Landrigan,* 550 U.S. 465 (2007), the Court upheld the denial of an evidentiary hearing in a case where the defendant refused to permit his counsel to present mitigating evidence on the penalty phase of a capital case. Under § 2254's deferential standards, the federal district court did not abuse its discretion in denying the petition for habeas relief, because regardless of what information defense counsel might have produced, the defendant would not have permitted him to present it.

Ethical Issue

A capital defense attorney's decision not to present mitigating evidence at the penalty phase of a capital case will likely help to secure a death verdict for her client. Should the decision be left up to the client? Why or why not?

b. Death Penalty *Voir Dire*

In *Uttecht v. Brown,* 551 U.S. 1 (2007), the Supreme Court emphasized again the AEDPA's "independent, high standard" before a habeas corpus writ can issue to set aside a state court ruling. At trial, defense counsel did not object to the removal for cause of a juror whose *voir dire* responses raised a question about his ability to consider the death penalty but which were not necessarily conclusive grounds for cause. The Court held that a reviewing court should consider the entire *voir dire* in the defendant's case as well as the questioning of the particular juror. Where "there is lengthy questioning of a prospective juror, and the trial court has supervised a diligent and thoughtful *voir dire*, the trial court has broad discretion." Here, the trial court's decision "was not contrary to, or an unreasonable application of, clearly established federal law" under 28 U.S.C. § 2254(d).

Take Note

The Court held in *Abdul-Kabir v. Quarterman,* 550 U.S. 233 (2007), and *Brewer v. Quarterman,* 550 U.S. 286 (2007), that the state courts' decisions in those cases were "contrary to" and "involved an unreasonable application of, clearly established Federal law, as determined by the Supreme Court of the United States." In both cases, the trial court's jury instructions prevented the jury from giving meaningful consideration and effect to relevant mitigating evidence during the capital trial's penalty phase, contrary to clear precedent in *Penry v. Lynaugh,* 492 U.S. 302 (1989).

c. Supreme Court Precedents

"Clearly established federal law, as determined by the Supreme Court" means law established in the Supreme Court's precedents and not in the federal circuit's precedents. *See Parker v. Matthews,* 567 U.S. 37 (2012) (per curiam) (reversing Sixth Circuit's use of a multi-step analysis for prosecutorial misconduct rather than the Supreme Court's more general standard). In addition, a Supreme Court case that was decided after the state court's findings does not qualify as "clearly established" for purposes of deference to the state court's findings. *See Greene v. Fisher*, 565 U.S. 34 (2011).

d. State Court Record Controls

When a federal court concludes that a state court's judgment is contrary to established federal law, or involves an unreasonable application of federal law, under 28 U.S.C. § 2254(d), it must be based on the record that was before the state court that decided the claim. *See Cullen v. Pinholster*, 563 U.S. 170 (2011).

When a state court denies post-conviction relief, but does not state its reasons, the denial nevertheless qualifies as an "adjudication on the merits" under § 2254(d), and therefore deserves deference. *See Harrington v. Richter*, 562 U.S. 86 (2011). The Supreme Court has taken to using *per curiam* opinions in unargued cases to reverse and chastise lower courts for their failure to sufficiently defer to state courts under AEDPA. For example, in *Parker v. Matthews*, 567 U.S.37 (2012) (per curiam), the Court reversed a lower court's findings of insufficiency of the evidence and prosecutorial misconduct, and opined as follows: "In this habeas case, the [federal circuit court] set aside two 29-year-old murder convictions based on the flimsiest of rationales. The court's decision is a textbook example of what the Antiterrorism and Effective Death Penalty Act of 1996 (AEDPA) proscribes: 'using federal habeas corpus review as a vehicle to second-guess the reasonable decisions of state courts.' " *See also Coleman v. Johnson*, 566 U.S. 650 (2012) (per curiam reversal of lower court's finding of insufficiency of the evidence).

D. Exhaustion of Remedies

Before a federal court will review a constitutional claim in a habeas corpus proceeding that seeks review of a state conviction, the claim first must be fairly presented to the state court system by properly pursuing a claim throughout the entire state appellate process. 28 U.S.C. § 2254(b)(1)(A). Exhaustion of remedies includes the presentation of claims to the state supreme court even though its review is discretionary, *O'Sullivan v. Boerckel*, 526 U.S. 838 (1999), and even though that court does not address her claim in a written opinion, *e.g.*, the court denies discretionary review, *Dye v. Hofbauer*, 546 U.S. 1 (2005). In order to have fairly presented the claim, a petitioner must have presented a substantially equivalent claim to the state courts as it presented to the federal courts. The state court need not actually address the claim in a written opinion to satisfy this requirement.

The exhaustion requirement does not preclude habeas review; it merely delays such review. In *Rose v. Lundy*, 455 U.S. 509 (1982), the Court held that, when faced with a petition that combines unexhausted and exhausted claims, a federal district court must either dismiss the petition without prejudice to allow the petitioner to return to the state court to exhaust the remaining claims and then return to

Take Note

This strict exhaustion requirement exists because of federalism concerns. It is contrary to federalism considerations to allow a state prisoner to bypass the state courts and initiate the first review of his conviction in the federal courts.

present all of the claims together in a single petition, or must allow the petitioner to drop the unexhausted claims. Because of the strict one-year time limitation for filing, a federal district court has discretion to stay a "mixed" petition while unexhausted claims are presented to a state court, and to return to federal court for review of the perfected petition without being time barred. *Rhines v. Weber*, 544 U.S. 269 (2005).

If the petitioner fails to exhaust his state remedies, the federal court may dismiss the petition until such time as the petitioner has exhausted available state remedies. The only exceptions to the exhaustion of remedies doctrine are when there is an absence of available state remedies or special circumstances render such remedies ineffective to protect the rights of the petitioner. Because the exhaustion of state remedies doctrine is based on comity and is not a jurisdictional requirement, the government may waive the requirement. 28 U.S.C. § 2254(b)(1), (3).

Points for Discussion

a. Denial on the Merits

In light of the stringent requirements for exhaustion of remedies, why would any federal district court apply AEDPA's provision that the "application for a writ of habeas corpus may be denied on the merits, notwithstanding the failure of the applicant to exhaust the remedies available in the courts of the State"? The Supreme Court advised that the district court "should determine whether the interests of comity and federalism will be better served by addressing the merits forthwith or by requiring a series of additional state and district court proceedings before reviewing the merits of the petitioner's claim." *Granberry v. Greer*, 481 U.S. 129 (1987).

b. Equitable Principles

In addition to interests of comity and federalism, federal habeas corpus has traditionally been governed by equitable principles. Consider the situation in *Whittlesey v. Circuit Court*, 897 F.2d 143 (4th Cir. 1990). Whittlesey was convicted and sentenced by a Maryland State court in 1978. In 1980 he escaped from prison, committed other crimes in Florida and began serving a 136-year sentence in the Florida State Prison. In 1986, he filed a petition for post-conviction relief in Maryland state court. The state court dismissed Whittlesey's petition without prejudice because his presence could not be secured for a post-conviction hearing. (Whittlesey sought unsuccessfully to invoke the Interstate Agreement on Detainers as a means of transfer to Maryland for a hearing). In 1987, Whittlesey filed a federal petition for habeas corpus, raising the same issues he had raised in his state petitions. The federal district court dismissed the petition without prejudice on the ground that Whittlesey had not exhausted his state post-conviction remedies.

On appeal to the circuit court, Whittlesey argued:

(1) that he had complied with § 2254(b)'s exhaustion requirement. By its own terms § 2254(b) requires only that an applicant for habeas relief have exhausted the state court remedies available to him, and that since Whittlesey is unable to return for the hearing there are no remedies available.

(2) that his petition falls within the futility exception of § 2254(b), which provides that a habeas writ may be granted despite a failure to exhaust state court remedies if "there is either an absence of available State corrective process or the existence of circumstances rendering such process ineffective to protect the rights of the prisoner." Whittlesey emphasized that since he is serving a 136-year sentence in Florida, it would be futile for him to wait until he has been released from prison in Florida to pursue his Maryland post-conviction remedy.

A majority of the Fourth Circuit panel held that Whittlesey had not exhausted his remedies because, "the doors of the Maryland state courts stand open for him to present his complaints; that he is unable to enter through those doors until completion of his Florida sentence is the price he must pay for having escaped from the Maryland prison and committed offenses in Florida. It is his own criminal misconduct which has denied Maryland courts the opportunity to hold a hearing, develop a record, and thereby address his claims on the merits. We will not command the district court to review his habeas petition when his own unlawful acts have prevented the state courts from reviewing his claims."

The dissent, however, maintained that "this is one of those hard cases that invites the making of bad law—specifically here, bad exhaustion law. A prisoner who escapes from incarceration in state A only to be incarcerated for conviction of another crime in state B while still a fugitive from state A makes an instinctively unattractive petitioner for federal habeas relief from the original incarceration." The fact of the escape, however, has no more legal relevance to the availability of a federal habeas forum than do any other of the usual run of unsavory events and prior conduct that exist in the backgrounds of many federal habeas petitioners. "The obvious question is: 'What else could the petitioner do?' And the answer, 'Nothing,' as obviously satisfies the ultimate concerns of comity underlying the exhaustion requirement. Whittlesey could spend the rest of his life in a Florida prison without the opportunity to litigate his constitutional claims. That is not right. Whittlesey has exhausted the state remedies that are available to him at the present time. He has the right to a federal habeas forum to present his constitutional claims."

E. Abuse of the Writ and Procedural Default

1. Successive Petitions as an Abuse of the Writ

AEPDA establishes procedures for the disposition of second or successive petitions. A second or successive petition must pass through a "gatekeeping" system which requires that petitioner seek an authorization order from a three-judge panel in the appropriate court of appeals before a district court may hear the petition. 28 U.S.C. § 2244(b)(3). In order to obtain an authorization order, a petitioner must make a prima facie showing that (1) the claim was not presented in a previous federal habeas petition, (2) this new claim relies on a new rule of constitutional law that was previously unavailable, or its factual basis "could not have been discovered previously through the exercise of due diligence," and (3) the facts underlying the claim, if proven and viewed in light of the whole evidence, show by clear and convincing evidence that, but for the constitutional error, no reasonable juror would have found the petitioner guilty of the offense. The panel's certification decision is not appealable and is not subject to rehearing.

Slack v. McDaniel

529 U.S. 473 (2000).

JUSTICE KENNEDY delivered the opinion of the Court.

Petitioner Antonio Slack was convicted of second-degree murder in Nevada state court in 1990. His direct appeal was unsuccessful. On November 27, 1991, Slack filed a petition for writ

Hear It

You can listen to the oral argument in *Slack* at: http://www.oyez.org/cases/1990-1999/1999/1999_98_6322.

of habeas corpus in federal court under 28 U.S.C. § 2254. Early in the federal proceeding, Slack decided to litigate claims he had not yet presented to the Nevada courts. He could not raise the claims in federal court because, under the exhaustion of remedies rule, a federal court was required to dismiss a petition presenting claims not yet litigated in state court. Accordingly, Slack filed a motion seeking to hold his federal petition in abeyance while he returned to state court to exhaust the new claims. Without objection by the State, the District Court ordered the habeas petition dismissed "without prejudice." The order, dated February 19, 1992, further stated, "Petitioner is granted leave to file an application to renew upon exhaustion of all State remedies." After an unsuccessful round of state postconviction proceedings, Slack filed a new federal habeas petition on May 30, 1995. The District Court later appointed counsel, directing him to file an amended petition or a notice of intention to proceed with the current petition. On December 24, 1997, counsel filed an amended petition presenting 14 claims for relief. The State moved to dismiss the petition because it was a mixed petition, that is to say a petition raising some claims which had been presented to the state courts and some which had not. As its second ground, the State cited *Farmer v. McDaniel*, 98 F. 3d 1548 (C.A.9 1996), and contended that claims Slack had not raised in his 1991 federal habeas petition must be dismissed as an abuse of the writ.

The District Court granted the State's motion. First, the court relied on *Farmer* to hold that Slack's 1995 petition was "a second or successive petition," even though his 1991 petition had been dismissed without prejudice for a failure to exhaust state remedies. The court then invoked the abuse of the writ doctrine to dismiss with prejudice the claims Slack had not raised in the 1991 petition. This left Slack with four claims, each having been raised in the 1991 petition; but one of these, the court concluded, had not yet been presented to the state courts. The court therefore dismissed Slack's remaining claims because they were in a mixed petition. Here, Slack seeks to challenge the dismissal of claims as abusive; he does not contend that all claims presented in the amended petition were exhausted. The District Court dismissed claims Slack failed to raise in his 1991 petition based on its conclusion that Slack's 1995 petition was a second or successive habeas petition. This conclusion was wrong. A habeas petition filed in the district court after an initial habeas petition was unadjudicated on its merits and dismissed for failure to exhaust state remedies is not a second or successive petition.

The phrase "second or successive petition" is a term of art given substance in our prior habeas corpus cases. The Court's decision in *Rose v. Lundy*, 455 U.S., at 510, instructs us in reaching our understanding of the term. *Rose* held that a federal district court must dismiss habeas corpus petitions containing both exhausted and unexhausted claims. The opinion, however, contemplated that the prisoner could return to federal court after the requisite exhaustion. It was only if a prisoner declined to return to state court and decided to proceed with his exhausted claims in federal court that the possibility arose that a subsequent petition would be considered second or successive and subject to dismissal as an abuse of the writ. A petition filed after a mixed petition has been dismissed under *Rose* before the district court adjudicated any claims is to be treated as "any other first petition" and is not a second or successive petition.

The State complains that this rule is unfair. The filing of a mixed petition in federal court requires it to appear and to plead failure to exhaust. The petition is then dismissed without prejudice, allowing the prisoner to make a return trip through the state courts to exhaust new claims. The State expresses concern that, upon exhaustion, the prisoner would return to federal court but again file a mixed petition, causing the process to repeat itself. In this manner, the State contends, a vexatious litigant could inject undue delay into the collateral review process. To the extent the tactic would become a problem, however, it can be countered without upsetting the established meaning of a second or successive petition.

First, the State remains free to impose proper procedural bars to restrict repeated returns to state court for postconviction proceedings. Second, provisions of AEDPA may bear upon the question in cases to which the Act applies. AEDPA itself demonstrates that Congress may address matters relating to exhaustion and mixed petitions through means other than rules governing "second or successive" petitions. E.g., 28 U.S.C. § 2254(b)(2). Third, the Rules of Civil Procedure, applicable as a general matter to habeas cases, vest the federal courts with due flexibility to prevent vexatious litigation. We reject the State's argument that refusing to give a new meaning to the established term "second or successive" opens the door to the abuses described.

It is so ordered.

Points for Discussion

a. Goal of Religitation

In *Felker v. Turpin*, 518 U.S. 651 (1996), the Supreme Court upheld the limits on second or successive petitions as "a modified *res judicata* rule, a restraint on what is called in habeas corpus practice 'abuse of the writ.'"

However, in *Calderon v. United States District Court*, 163 F. 3d 530 (9th Cir., en banc, 1998), the Ninth Circuit stated:

> We reject the panel majority's use of *res judicata* because it contravenes the longstanding rule that *res judicata* has no application in habeas corpus. The entire point

It's Latin to Me

Non constat
jus civile
a posteriori

In Latin, *res judicata* means "a thing adjudged." The doctrine of *res judicata* generally bars relitigation of claims between parties that were already decided on final judgment.

of a habeas petition that challenges a state conviction is to relitigate issues that were raised in the state case and resolved against the petitioner. Obviously, then, *res judicata*, in the traditional sense of that doctrine cannot apply in habeas corpus; otherwise, nearly every habeas petition would be barred by the original trial.

Federal courts have created a doctrine known as "abuse of the writ" that serves as a substitute for *res judicata* by limiting the availability of successive habeas petitions when a prior one has been denied. The reason why successive petitions are often deemed abusive is that the first petition provided an adequate opportunity for the petitioner to raise all of his claims, and the petitioner simply chose not to take advantage of that opportunity. Abuse of the writ evolved as a judicially created equitable doctrine, but it is now codified by the AEDPA.

We also reject the State's argument that the traditional rule against applying *res judicata* in habeas cases has somehow been abrogated by the AEDPA. Even after the AEDPA, federal habeas relief exists in order to relitigate claims that were previously decided in state court, so it is quite fanciful to suggest that the AEDPA *sub silento* introduced *res judicata* into habeas law. Further, the AEDPA includes specific provisions to govern successive habeas petitions, and *res judicata* would render those provisions largely superfluous. We conclude that even after the AEDPA, the rule is as it has always been: *Res judicata* does not apply to habeas cases.

Food for Thought

The doctrines of exhaustion and abuse of the writ are defenses invoked by the State to bar defendants who file multiple habeas petitions. May a prosecutor take a pro-active stance to bar possible habeas petitions? For example, if State law does not provide for a life-without-parole sentence, may the prosecutor plea bargain for the defendant's waiver of the right to file a habeas petition challenging a life sentence? Is such a waiver accomplished by the following plea agreement: "Defendant agrees that he will never apply, orally or in writing for parole, commutation of sentence, reprieve, or any other form of relief from life imprisonment. He understands this means he will be sentenced to serve the remainder of his natural life in the penitentiary. In consideration of the State waiving the death penalty, defendant also hereby gives up his right to ask for the Superior Court Sentence Review panel to review any sentence imposed upon him. He hereby states that the sentence of life imprisonment for his participation in the criminal acts is not excessive."

In *Allen v. Thomas*, 161 F. 3d 667 (11th Cir. 1998), The Eleventh Circuit noted the absence of any published decisions addressing plea-bargained waivers of the right to seek federal habeas review. The court held that if such a waiver is constitutionally permissible, it did not occur in this case because the defendant did not make a knowing and intelligent waiver of the right to seek federal habeas review. The catch-all phrase—"or any other form of relief from life imprisonment"—is far too general to constitute a valid waiver of a specific right. *Id. See also United States v. Goodman*, 165 F. 3d 169 (2d Cir. 1999).

b. "Second or Successive" Application

Any claim presented in a second or successive application must be dismissed if that issue was previously presented. Claims presented in the second or successive application that were not previously presented also must be dismissed, subject to two statutory exceptions under § 2244(b)(2)(A)–(B). The filing of such permitted claims in a second or successive application must be authorized by the Court of Appeals under § 2244(b)(3)(A).

In addition to *Slack v. McDaniel*, several other Court decisions have attempted to define the scope of the phrase "second or successive" application. For example, *Panetti v. Quarterman*, 551 U.S. 930 (2007) created an exception for a second application raising a claim that would have been unripe had the petitioner presented it in his first application. In *Magwood v. Patterson*, 561 U.S. 320 (2010), the Court addressed the issue of "whether an application is 'second or successive' if it challenges a new judgment." In *Burton v. Stewart*, 549 U.S. 147 (2007), the Court held that because both of the petitioner's habeas petitions had challenged the same judgment, the second petition was statutorily precluded. However, *Burton* acknowledged that the result might have been different if a new judgment had intervened between the habeas petitions. In *Magwood*, there was such an intervening judgment. Thus, Magwood's second petition was his first application to challenge the intervening judgment when the trial court had conducted a full resentencing.

2. Procedural Default

In *Justus v. Murray*, 897 F.2d 709 (4th Cir.1990), the court distinguished between procedural default and exhaustion as follows: "The doctrine of exhaustion and the procedural default rule are two different things. Exhaustion generally requires that before a federal court will review a constitutional claim in habeas, the claim must first be fairly presented to the state court system. The procedural default rule requires that if a state court rejects a habeas petitioner's federal constitutional challenge on the adequate and independent state ground that the claim is defaulted under a state procedural rule, a federal habeas court is ordinarily precluded from reviewing that claim unless the petitioner can show cause for the default and prejudice resulting from it."

The consequence of procedural default is that the petitioner may be barred from judicial review of the forfeited claims in both state and federal courts. The most common form of procedural default is the defendant's failure to present a federal constitutional claim to the trial court and thus preserve the issue for appellate review. Unlike *Stone v. Powell* which bars federal habeas relief only when Fourth Amendment issues are given a full and fair hearing in the state courts, if there is a procedural bar, there is no hearing on the constitutional challenge in *any* state or federal court.

Wainwright v. Sykes

433 U.S. 72 (1977).

MR. JUSTICE REHNQUIST delivered the opinion of the Court.

Respondent Sykes was convicted of third-degree murder after a jury trial in the Circuit Court of DeSoto County. He testified at trial that on the evening of January 8, 1972, he told his wife to summon the police because he had just shot Willie Gilbert. When the police arrived at respondent's trailer home, they found Gilbert dead of a shotgun wound, lying a few feet from the front porch. Shortly after their arrival, respondent came from across the road and volunteered that he had shot Gilbert, and a few minutes later respondent's wife approached the police and told them the same thing. Sykes was immediately arrested and taken to the police station.

Hear It

You can listen to the oral argument in *Sykes* at: http://www.oyez.org/cases/1970-1979/1976/1976_75_1578.

Once there, it is conceded that he was read his *Miranda* rights, and that he declined to seek the aid of counsel and indicated a desire to talk. He then made a statement, which was admitted into evidence at trial through the testimony of the two officers who heard it, to the effect that he had shot Gilbert from the front porch of his trailer home. There were several references during the trial to respondent's consumption of alcohol during the preceding day and to his apparent state of intoxication, facts which were acknowledged by the officers who arrived at the scene. At no time during the trial, however, was the admissibility of any of respondent's statements challenged by his counsel on the ground that respondent had not understood the *Miranda* warnings. Nor did the trial judge question their admissibility on his own motion or hold a fact-finding hearing bearing on that issue.

Respondent appealed his conviction, but apparently did not challenge the admissibility of the inculpatory statements. He later filed in the trial court a motion to vacate the conviction and, in the State District Court of Appeals and Supreme Court, petitions for habeas corpus. These filings, apparently for the first time, challenged the statements made to police on grounds of involuntariness. In all of these efforts respondent was unsuccessful. Having failed in the Florida courts, respondent initiated the present action under 28 U.S.C. § 2254, asserting the inadmissibility of his statements by reason of his lack of understanding of the *Miranda* warnings.

The simple legal question before the Court calls for a construction of the language of 28 U.S.C. § 2254(a), which provides that the federal courts shall entertain an application for a writ of habeas corpus "in behalf of a person in custody pursuant to the judgment of a state court only on the ground that he is in custody in violation of the Constitution or laws or treaties of the United States."

The area of controversy which has developed has concerned the reviewability of federal claims which the state court has declined to pass on because not presented in the manner prescribed by its procedural rules. The adequacy of such an independent state procedural ground to prevent federal habeas review of the underlying federal issue has been treated very differently than where the state-law ground is substantive. The pertinent decisions marking the Court's somewhat tortuous efforts to deal with this problem are: *Ex parte Spencer*, 228 U.S. 652 (1913); *Brown v. Allen*, 344 U.S. 443 (1953); *Fay v. Noia; Davis v. United States*, 411 U.S. 233 (1973); and *Francis v. Henderson*, 425 U.S. 536 (1976).

In *Fay v. Noia*, respondent Noia sought federal habeas to review a claim that his state-court conviction had resulted from the introduction of a coerced confession in violation of the Fifth Amendment to the United States Constitution. While the convictions of his two codefendants were reversed on that ground in collateral proceedings following their appeals, Noia did not appeal and the New York courts ruled that his subsequent *coram nobis* action was barred on account of that failure. This Court held that petitioner was nonetheless entitled to raise the claim in federal habeas, and thereby overruled its decision 10 years earlier in *Brown v. Allen*: "The doctrine under which state procedural defaults are held to constitute an adequate and independent state law ground barring direct Supreme Court review is not to be extended to omit the power granted the federal courts under the federal habeas statute."

As a matter of comity but not of federal power, the Court acknowledged "a limited discretion in the federal judge to deny relief to an applicant who had deliberately by-passed the orderly procedure of the state courts and in so doing has forfeited his state court remedies." In so stating, the Court made clear that the waiver must be knowing and "an intentional relinquishment or abandonment of a known right or privilege." Noting petitioner's "grisly choice" between acceptance of his life sentence and pursuit of an appeal which might culminate in a sentence of death, the Court concluded that there had been no deliberate bypass of the right to have the federal issues reviewed through a state appeal.

Florida procedure did, consistently with the United States Constitution, require that respondents' confession be challenged at trial or not at all, and thus his failure to timely object to its admission amounted to an independent and adequate state procedural ground which would have prevented direct review here. We thus come to the crux of this case. Shall the rule of *Francis v. Henderson*, barring federal habeas review absent a showing of "cause" and "prejudice" attendant to a state procedural waiver, be applied to a waived objection to the admission of a confession at trial? We answer that question in the affirmative.

Since *Brown v. Allen*, it has been the rule that the federal habeas petitioner who claims he is detained pursuant to a final judgment of a state court in violation of the United States Constitution is entitled to have the federal habeas court make its own independent determination of his federal claim, without being bound by the determination on the merits of that claim reached in the state proceedings. This rule of *Brown v. Allen* is in no way changed by our holding today. Rather, we deal only with contentions of federal law which were not resolved on the merits in the state proceeding due to respondent's failure to raise them there as required by state procedure. We leave open for resolution in future decisions the precise definition of the "cause" and "prejudice" standard, and note here only that it is narrower than the standard set forth in dicta in *Fay v. Noia*, which would make federal habeas review generally available to state convicts absent a knowing and deliberate waiver of the federal constitutional contention. It is the sweeping language of *Fay v. Noia*, going far beyond the facts of the case eliciting it, which we today reject.

The reasons for our rejection of it are several. The contemporaneous-objection rule itself is by no means peculiar to Florida, and deserves greater respect than *Fay* gives it, both for the fact that it is employed by a coordinate jurisdiction within the federal system and for the many interests which it serves in its own right. A contemporaneous objection enables the record to be made with respect to the constitutional claim when the recollections of witnesses are freshest, not years later in a federal habeas proceeding. It enables the judge who observed the demeanor of those witnesses to make the factual determinations necessary for properly deciding the federal constitutional question.

A contemporaneous-objection rule may lead to the exclusion of the evidence objected to, thereby making a major contribution to finality in criminal litigation. Without the evidence claimed to be vulnerable on federal constitutional grounds, the jury may acquit the defendant, and that will be the end of the case; or it may nonetheless convict the defendant, and he will have one less federal constitutional claim to assert in his federal habeas petition. If the state trial judge admits the evidence in question after a full hearing, the federal habeas court will gain significant guidance from the state ruling in this regard. Subtler considerations as well militate in favor of honoring a state contemporaneous-objection rule. An objection on the spot may force the prosecution to take a hard took at its whole card, and even if the prosecutor thinks that the state trial judge will admit the evidence he must contemplate the possibility of reversal by the state appellate courts or the ultimate issuance of a federal writ of habeas corpus based on the impropriety of the state court's rejection of the federal constitutional claim.

We think that the rule of *Fay v. Noia*, broadly stated, may encourage "sandbagging" on the part of defense lawyers, who may take their chances on a verdict of not guilty in a state trial court with the intent to raise their constitutional claims in a federal habeas court if their initial gamble does not pay off. The refusal of federal habeas courts to honor contemporaneous-objection rules may also make state courts themselves less stringent in their enforcement. Under the rule of *Fay v. Noia*, state appellate courts know that a federal constitutional issue raised for the first time in the proceeding before them may well be decided in any event by a federal habeas tribunal. Thus, their choice is between addressing the issue notwithstanding the petitioner's failure to timely object, or else face the prospect that the federal habeas court will decide the question without the benefit of their views. The failure of the federal habeas courts generally to require compliance with a contemporaneous-objection rule tends to detract from the perception of the trial of a criminal case in state court as a decisive and portentous event.

We believe the adoption of the *Francis* rule in this situation will have the salutary effect of making the state trial on the merits the "main event," so to speak, rather than a "tryout on the road" for what will later be the determinative federal habeas hearing. There is nothing in the Constitution or in the language of § 2254 which requires that the state trial on the issue of guilt or innocence be devoted largely to the testimony of fact witnesses directed to the elements of the state crime, while only later will there occur in a federal habeas hearing a full airing of the federal constitutional claims which were

Food for Thought

Are you persuaded? If Sykes' defaulted issue had been failure to object to a coerced confession, as in *Fay v. Noia*, with some strong evidence that the confession was involuntary, as opposed to a failure to understand *Miranda* warnings, do you think the Court would have reached out to change the rule? Is a state evidentiary rule like the "contemporaneous objection rule" sufficient to waive review of serious constitutional deficiencies? Is the failure to make a contemporaneous objection ineffective assistance of counsel?

not raised in the state proceedings. If a criminal defendant thinks that an action of the state trial court is about to deprive him of a federal constitutional right there is every reason for his following state procedure in making known his objection.

The "cause" and "prejudice" exception of the *Francis* rule will afford an adequate guarantee that the rule will not prevent a federal habeas court from adjudicating for the first time the federal constitutional claim of a defendant who in the absence of such an adjudication will be the victim of a miscarriage of justice. Whatever precise content may be given those terms by later cases, we feel confident in holding without further elaboration that they do not exist here. Respondent has advanced no explanation whatever for his failure to object at trial, and, as the proceeding unfolded, the trial judge is certainly not to be faulted for failing to question the admission of the confession himself. The other evidence of guilt presented at trial, moreover, was substantial to a degree that would negate any possibility of actual prejudice resulting to the respondent from the admission of his inculpatory statement.

Mr. Justice BRENNAN, with whom Mr. Justice MARSHALL joins, dissenting.

I believe that *Fay's* commitment to enforcing intentional but not inadvertent procedural defaults offers a realistic measure of protection for the habeas corpus petitioner seeking federal review of federal claims that were not litigated before the State. When one pierces the surface justifications for a harsher rule posited by the Court, no standard stricter than *Fay's* deliberate-bypass test is realistically defensible. Punishing a lawyer's unintentional errors by closing the federal court-house door to his client is both a senseless and misdirected method of deterring the slighting of state rules. It is senseless because unplanned and unintentional action of any kind generally is not subject to deterrence; and, to the extent that it is hoped that a threatened sanction addressed to the defense will induce greater care and caution on the part of trial lawyers, thereby forestalling negligent conduct or error, the potential loss of all valuable state remedies would be sufficient to this end. It is a misdirected sanction because even if the penalization of incompetence or carelessness will encourage more thorough legal training and trial preparation, the habeas applicant, as opposed to his lawyer, hardly is the proper recipient of such a penalty. Especially with fundamental constitutional rights at stake, no fictional relationship of principal-agent or the like can justify holding the criminal defendant accountable for the naked errors of his attorney. This is especially true, when so many indigent defendants are without any realistic choice in selecting who ultimately represents them at trial.

Points for Discussion

a. Procedural Default and Prejudice

In *Murray v. Carrier*, 477 U.S. 478 (1986), Justice O'Connor explained the cause and prejudice requirement:

> We think that the question of cause for a procedural default does not turn on whether counsel erred or on the kind of error counsel may have made. So long as a defendant is represented by counsel whose performance is not constitutionally ineffective under the standard established in *Strickland v. Washington*, we discern no inequity in requiring him to bear the risk of attorney error that results in a procedural default. Instead, we think that the existence of cause for a procedural default must ordinarily turn on whether the prisoner can show that some objective factor external to the defense impeded counsel's efforts to comply with the State's procedural rule. Without attempting an exhaustive catalog of such objective impediments to compliance with a procedural rule, we note that a showing that the factual or legal basis for a claim was not reasonably available to, counsel, or that "some interference by officials," made compliance impracticable, would constitute cause under this standard.

> Similarly, if the procedural default is the result of ineffective assistance of counsel, the Sixth Amendment itself requires that responsibility for the default be imputed to the State, which may not "conduct trials at which persons who face incarceration must defend themselves without adequate legal assistance." Ineffective assistance of counsel, then, is cause for a procedural default.

> Respondent does not dispute that the cause and prejudice test applies to procedural defaults on appeal, as we plainly indicated in *Reed v. Ross*. *Reed*, which involved a claim that was defaulted on appeal, held that a habeas petitioner could establish cause for a procedural default if his claim is "so novel that its legal basis is not reasonably available to counsel." That holding would have been entirely unnecessary to the disposition of the prisoner's claim if the cause and prejudice test were inapplicable to procedural defaults on appeal.

> We see little reason why counsel's failure to detect a colorable constitutional claim should be treated differently from a deliberate but equally prejudicial failure

Make the Connection

In Chapter 3, you learned that a successful ineffective assistance of counsel claim is difficult: it requires not only proof of deficient performance but also proof of a reasonable likelihood that the outcome of the trial would have been different. Failing to make a contemporaneous objection, while dooming a petitioner's ability to make the claim on habeas, will not necessarily be ineffective assistance of counsel.

by counsel to raise such a claim. The fact that the latter error can be characterized as a misjudgment, while the former is easily described as an oversight, is much too tenuous a distinction to justify a regime of evidentiary hearings into counsel's state of mind in failing to raise a claim on appeal.

The real thrust of respondent's arguments appears to be that on appeal it is inappropriate to hold defendants to the errors of their attorneys. Were we to accept that proposition, defaults on appeal would presumably be governed by a rule equivalent to *Fay v. Noia*'s "deliberate bypass" standard, under which only personal waiver by the defendant would require enforcement of a procedural default. We express no opinion as to whether counsel's decision not to take an appeal at all might require treatment under such a standard, but, for the reasons already given, we hold that counsel's failure to raise a particular claim on appeal is to be scrutinized under the cause and prejudice standard when that failure is treated as a procedural default by the state courts. Attorney error short of ineffective assistance of counsel does not constitute cause for a procedural default even when that default occurs on appeal rather than at trial. To the contrary, cause for a procedural default on appeal ordinarily requires a showing of some external impediment preventing counsel from constructing or raising the claim.

The habeas petitioner must show "not merely that the errors at trial created a possibility of prejudice, but that they worked to his actual and substantial disadvantage, infecting his entire trial with error of constitutional dimensions." Such a showing of pervasive actual prejudice can hardly be thought to constitute anything other than a showing that the prisoner was denied "fundamental fairness" at trial.

"In appropriate cases" the principles of comity and finality that inform the concepts of cause and prejudice "must yield to the imperative of correcting a fundamentally unjust incarceration." We remain confident that, for the most part, "victims of a fundamental miscarriage of justice will meet the cause-and-prejudice standard." But we do not pretend that this will always be true. In an extraordinary case, where a constitutional violation has probably resulted in the conviction of one who is actually innocent, a federal habeas court may grant the writ even in the absence of a showing of cause for the procedural default.

Make the Connection

Justice O'Connor leaves an opening for a miscarriage of justice if a claim is not allowed to proceed for a person who is probably actually innocent or a victim of "a fundamentally unjust conviction." As discussed in Part F below, while the Court pays lip service to the potential issue of executing or incarcerating the innocent, the standards for such a showing are insurmountably high and not well-defined.

b. State Court Review of Ineffective Assistance of Counsel Claims

In *Edwards v. Carpenter*, 529 U.S. 446 (2000), the Court held that a claim of ineffective assistance of counsel must be presented first to the State courts before the claim can serve as cause to excuse the procedural default of another habeas claim. In turn, a procedurally defaulted ineffective-assistance-of-counsel claim can be excused if the petitioner can satisfy the cause and prejudice standard with respect to the ineffective assistance claim itself.

While in *Coleman v. Thompson*, 501 U.S. 722 (1991), the Court held that counsel's failure to file timely notice of appeal in state court does not qualify as cause for procedural default on a claim, since the prisoner bears the risk of the negligence of his agent, the Court made an exception to that general rule in *Martinez v. Ryan*, 566 U.S. 1 (2012). In *Martinez*, the Court held that where, under state law, the initial-review collateral proceeding is the first proceeding when a prisoner may raise ineffective assistance claims, it is the equivalent of a direct appeal for those claims. Therefore, there is "cause" for a default on those claims if there is no counsel or deficient counsel at that initial-review collateral proceeding. As the dissent noted, this is the functional equivalent to requiring that the state provide counsel for collateral proceedings that provide the first occasion to raise a claim of ineffective assistance of counsel.

In *Trevino v. Thaler*, 133 S.Ct. 1911 (2013), the Court extended the *Martinez* exception regarding procedural default to a situation when a State's procedural framework, by reason of its design and operation, makes it highly unlikely that a defendant will have a meaningful opportunity to raise an ineffective-assistance-of-trial-counsel claim on direct appeal. In that event, the Court held the defendant may raise an ineffective assistance claim in a federal habeas court.

c. Cause and Prejudice

How does the "cause-and-prejudice" standard differ from the "fundamental miscarriage of justice" standard for excusing a procedural default?

"Prejudice" is a stricter standard than the "plain error" doctrine applicable to direct review because direct appeal is designed to afford a means for the *prompt* redress of miscarriages of justice. This standard "is out of place when a prisoner launches a collateral attack against a criminal conviction after society's legitimate interest in the finality of the judgment has been perfected by the expiration of the time allowed for direct review or by the affirmance of the conviction on appeal." Thus in *United States v. Frady*, 456 U.S. 152 (1982), prejudice did not follow simply from the fact that a jury instruction was erroneous (The instruction equated intent with malice and stated that the law presumes malice from the use of a weapon). The Court held that petitioner failed to show that the error "worked to his actual and substantial disadvantage, infecting his entire trial with error of constitutional dimensions," *i.e.,* prejudice must be evaluated by the effect of the error in the context of the whole trial, and the petitioner failed to contradict strong evidence that he had acted with malice.

Cause. In *Reed v. Ross,* 468 U.S. 1 (1984), the Court stated that cause existed for the defendant's failure to raise a due process challenge to shifting the burden of proof to the defendant on an issue of malice, because "burden shifting" was not held unconstitutional until several years after the procedural default. "Where a constitutional claim is so novel that its legal basis is not reasonably available to counsel, a defendant has cause for his failure to raise the claim in accordance with applicable state procedures." In contrast, in *Murray v. Carrier,* 477 U.S. 478 (1986), the Court found that the type of discovery claim in question "had been percolating in lower courts for years" at the time of the defendant's default. When the claim was actually raised in the defendant's case, it was not so novel as to excuse a procedural default.

Food for Thought

If petitioner can show "cause" under *Reed* because the "new rule" of law could not have been reasonably anticipated, does the petitioner then run afoul of *Teague v. Lane,* 489 U.S. 288 (1989), which held that "new rules of law" generally should not be applied retroactively to cases on "collateral review" such as habeas corpus? Professor Arkin characterized the interaction between *Reed* and *Teague* as "The Prisoner's Dilemma:"

> If a petitioner is able to show that his claim is based on a "new" rule of law, the habeas court will excuse his state procedural default, assuming petitioner can show actual prejudice. But, having shown that the rule under which he seeks relief was not available to him at the time he should have raised it in the state courts, the petitioner may well have won the battle under *Wainwright* only to lose the war to *Teague.* Under most circumstances, the petitioner will have just shown that the very rule under which he seeks relief is not retroactive unless he can fit it into one of the two [extremely limited] *Teague* exceptions.

Arkin, "The Prisoner's Dilemma: Life in the Lower Federal Courts After *Teague v. Lane,*" 69 N. Car. L. Rev. 371, 408 (1991). The two exceptions recognized in *Teague* are: (1) where the new rule places certain kinds of private conduct beyond the power of legislatures to proscribe, and (2) where the new rule requires procedures that are "implicit in the concept of ordered liberty" such as the right to counsel.

d. Apparent Futility

Suppose defense counsel says that she did not raise an issue in the state court proceedings because the state court would have been unsympathetic to the claim. Does the apparent futility of making an objection constitute cause? No, said the Court in *Engle v. Isaac,* 456 U.S. 107 (1982). The Court also rejected adoption of a rule requiring trial counsel to exercise "extraordinary vision" or to object to every aspect of the proceedings in the hope that some aspect might make a latent constitutional claim: "We have long recognized that the Constitution guarantees criminal defendants only a fair trial and a competent attorney. It does not insure that defense counsel will recognize and raise every conceivable constitutional claim. Where the basis of a constitutional claim is available, and other defense counsel have perceived and litigated that claim, the demands of comity and finality counsel against labeling alleged unawareness of the objection as a cause for a procedural default."

e. State Interference as Cause

In *Strickler v. Greene*, 527 U.S. 263 (1999), the Court explained the definition of "cause" when the failure to pursue a *Brady* claim will excuse the petitioner's default. A petitioner must prove that: 1) the prosecutor confirmed disclosure of all *Brady* material; 2) petitioner's reliance on the prosecutor's representations was reasonable; and 3) the prosecutor withheld evidence favorable to the defense. In *Amadeo v. Zant*, 486 U.S. 214 (1988), the Court held that governmental concealment of evidence that women and African-Americans were intentionally underrepresented on jury lists constituted cause for the defendant's failure to raise a timely challenge to the jury panel.

Hypo: *Lawyers Gone AWOL*

Cory Maples was found guilty of murder and sentenced to death. Maples sought post-conviction relief in Alabama state court alleging, among other things, ineffective assistance of counsel. His petition was written by two *pro bono* attorneys, both associated with the New York offices of the Sullivan & Cromwell law firm. As required by state law, the two attorneys engaged a lawyer in Alabama to move their admission *pro hac vice*. The Alabama lawyer made clear, however, that he would undertake no substantive involvement in the case. While Maples' state post-conviction petition was pending, his two lawyers left Sullivan & Cromwell. Their new employment disabled them from representing Maples. They did not inform Maples of their departure, and no other Sullivan & Cromwell attorney entered an appearance or otherwise notified the court. The trial court denied Maples' petition and notices of the order were posted to the two lawyers at Sullivan & Cromwell's address. When those postings were returned, unopened, the trial court clerk attempted no further mailing. The Alabama attorney also received a copy of the order, but did not act on it. With no attorney of record in fact acting on Maples' behalf, the 42-day period Maples had to file a notice of appeal expired. About a month later, an Alabama Assistant Attorney General sent a letter directly to Maples. The letter informed Maples of the missed deadline and notified him that he had four weeks remaining to file a federal habeas petition. Thereafter, Maples sought federal habeas relief. Does cause exist for Maples' procedural default? *Maples v. Thomas,*

565 U.S. 266 (2012); *see also Luna v. Kernan*, 784 F.3d 640 (9th Cir. 2015) (addressing similar issue of "egregious" attorney misconduct, but short of abandonment, leading to failure to meet one-year deadline).

F. Claims of Actual Innocence as "Gateways" to Federal Habeas Corpus Review

A common misperception, at least among the lay public, is that federal courts and ultimately the United States Supreme Court, sit as courts of last resort to correct any and all injustice done to American citizens. Justice Scalia, a frequent critic of expansive federal habeas review, recently explained in *Bousley v. United States*, 523 U.S. 614 (1998), it "would be marvelously inspiring to be able to boast that we have a criminal-justice system in which a claim of "actual innocence" will always be heard, no matter how late it is brought forward, and no matter how much the failure to bring it forward at the proper time is the defendant's own fault. But of course we do not have such a system, and no society unwilling to devote unlimited resources to repetitive criminal litigation ever could."

In *Herrera v. Collins*, 506 U.S. 390 (1993), the Court refused to recognize a claim of factual innocence as a free-standing constitutional claim subject to review on federal habeas corpus. Herrera was convicted of capital murder and sentenced to death. Ten years later, he filed a petition for federal habeas corpus relief, claiming that newly discovered evidence (that his dead brother had committed the murders) showed that he was actually innocent of the crimes. The Court stated that, after a final judgment, the presumption of innocence is no longer applicable. Moreover, a new claim of innocence is factually based, and habeas corpus relief is not a proper remedy for correcting factual errors. Instead a request for executive clemency is a proper remedy for innocence claims based upon new evidence that is discovered after the time for filing a new trial motion. The *Herrera* Court then assumed:

> for the sake of argument in deciding this case, that in a capital case a truly persuasive demonstration of 'actual innocence' made after trial would render the execution of a defendant unconstitutional, and justify federal habeas relief if there were no state avenues open to process such a claim. But because of the very disruptive effect that entertaining claims of actual innocence would have on the need for finality in capital cases, and the enormous burden that having to retry cases

based on often stale evidence would place on the States, the threshold showing for such an assumed right would necessarily be extraordinarily high.

The Court stated that Herrera failed to meet the Court's standard, because his affidavits were based mostly on hearsay, were obtained without the benefit of cross-examination, contained inconsistencies, and failed to overcome the strong trial proof of guilt.

> **Food for Thought**
>
> Why did the Court only assume "for the sake of argument" that it would be a violation of the Eighth Amendment's prohibition on "cruel and unusual punishment" to execute a person who is factually innocent? Would it be? Why the reticence?

Claims of innocence, however, are a vital component to petitioners' attempts to gain habeas review otherwise barred by the procedural default rule. In *Schlup v. Delo*, 513 U.S. 298 (1995), the Court described the nature of the role of innocence as a gateway requirement:

> As a preliminary matter, it is important to explain the difference between Schlup's claim of actual innocence and the claim of actual innocence asserted in *Herrera*. In *Herrera*, the petitioner advanced his claim of innocence to support a novel substantive constitutional claim, namely that the execution of an innocent person would violate the Eighth Amendment. Under petitioner's theory in *Herrera*, even if the proceedings that had resulted in his conviction and sentence were entirely fair and error-free, his innocence would render his execution a "constitutionally intolerable event." Schlup's claim of innocence, on the other hand, is procedural, rather than substantive. His constitutional claims are based not on his innocence, but rather on his contention that the ineffectiveness of his counsel and the withholding of evidence by the prosecution denied him the full panoply of protections afforded to criminal defendants by the Constitution. Schlup, however, faces procedural obstacles that he must overcome before a federal court may address the merits of those constitutional claims. Because Schlup has been unable to establish "cause and prejudice" sufficient to excuse his failure to present his evidence in support of his first federal petition, Schlup may obtain review of his constitutional claims only if he falls within the "narrow class of cases implicating a fundamental miscarriage of justice." Schlup's claim of innocence is offered only to bring him within this "narrow class of cases."

> Schlup's claim thus differs in at least two important ways from that presented in *Herrera*. First, Schlup's claim of innocence does not by itself provide a basis for relief. Instead, his claim for relief depends critically on the validity of his *Strickland* and *Brady* claims. Schlup's claim of innocence

is thus "not itself a constitutional claim, but instead a gateway through which a habeas petitioner must pass to have his otherwise barred constitutional claim considered on the merits." Schlup's conviction may not be entitled to the same degree of respect as one, such as Herrera's, that is the product of an error-free trial. Without any new evidence of innocence, even the existence of a concededly meritorious constitutional violation is not in itself sufficient to establish a miscarriage of justice that would allow a habeas court to reach the merits of a barred claim. However, if a petitioner such as Schlup presents evidence of innocence so strong that a court cannot have confidence in the outcome of the trial unless the court is also satisfied that the trial was free of nonharmless constitutional error, the petitioner should be allowed to pass through the gateway and argue the merits of his underlying claims.

Points for Discussion

a. Actual Innocence Showing

Food for Thought

What must be shown in support of an argument for actual innocence, thereby warranting relief from the procedural default rule? In *House v. Bell*, 547 U.S. 518 (2006), the Court held that petitioner had satisfied the difficult showing required by *Schlup*, and that his federal habeas proceeding therefore could go forward. DNA testing established that semen on the murder victim's clothing came from her husband rather than from House, the defendant; that evidence was the only forensic evidence linking House to the murder. In addition, House in his post-trial proceedings had presented evidence that the murder victim's husband had confessed to the murder. The Court found this to be the "rare" case when, if the jury had heard all the conflicting evidence, it likely would have viewed the record as a whole as creating reasonable doubt. Nonetheless, while House gained an opportunity for his petition to be heard, his strong showing was "not a case of conclusive exoneration" that *Herrera* contemplated would be necessary for relief as a free-standing claim. Do you agree?

In *Bousley v. United States*, 523 U.S. 614 (1998), Bousley pleaded guilty to drug and firearm charges, but reserved the right to challenge the quantity of drugs used in calculating his sentence. He unsuccessfully appealed his sentence, but did not challenge the plea's validity. He sought habeas relief, claiming that his guilty plea lacked a factual basis because the evidence did not show a connection between the firearms in the bedroom of the house and the garage where the drug trafficking occurred. The district court dismissed the petition. While Bousley's appeal was pending, the Supreme Court held that a conviction for using a firearm requires the prosecution to show "active employment of the firearm." In affirming dismissal of the habeas petition, the Eighth Circuit rejected Bousley's argument that the new Supreme Court case should be applied retroactively. Despite the fact that Bousley had procedurally defaulted on his claims, the Supreme Court held that Bousley should be permitted to make an actual innocence showing. The Court stated that actual innocence means factual innocence, not mere legal insufficiency. The prosecution is not limited to the existing record but may present any admissible evidence of petitioner's guilt. The actual innocence showing also must extend to charges that the prosecution had dropped or abandoned in the course of plea bargaining.

b. Innocence Overcomes AEDPA's Statute of Limitations.

In *McQuiggin v. Perkins,* 569 U.S. 383 (2013), the Court held that proof of actual innocence can overcome AEDPA's one-year statute of limitations for filing petitions, but the untimeliness will bear on the credibility of the evidence proffered to show actual innocence.

Executive Summary

AEDPA's Limitations on the Writ of Habeas Corpus. The Antiterrorism and Effective Death Penalty Act of 1996 (AEDPA) severely limited the availability of federal habeas corpus relief.

A Civil Action. A collateral attack on a criminal conviction requires filing of a separate lawsuit, which is civil in nature.

Time Limit on Filing. AEPDA has a one-year limitation for filing a petition for relief, and generally it prohibits the filing of successive petitions.

Exhaustion of State Remedies. Before filing a federal habeas petition, as a matter of comity a person must exhaust state remedies by presenting the claim to the state's highest court.

Requirement of Custody. A person may obtain federal habeas relief

Major Themes

a. Constitutional Errors—Habeas corpus is a collateral attack on a conviction that is a civil action brought by the convicted person against the party responsible for his or her custody, alleging federal constitutional errors in the trial or sentencing process.

b. Procedural Barriers—While known as "the Great Writ," beginning in the 1970s, the Court began to create more substantive and procedural barriers to federal habeas review of state convictions, and those barriers were enhanced by Congress in 1996 through passage of AEDPA.

c. Attorney Errors—Many prisoners never receive a federal habeas hearing on their federal constitutional claims, even if the errors may be serious and the prisoner may be innocent, due to their or their counsel's failure to meet all of the procedural requirements, whether through neglect or oversight.

only if he is in custody, which includes significant restraints on personal liberty as well as physical incarceration.

Claims on Habeas Must be "Federal." Federal habeas relief is available only for *federal* (not state) constitutional or statutory violations.

No Collateral Attack for Fourth Amendment Violations. If a person's Fourth Amendment claim was heard in state court, it cannot be considered by a federal court in a habeas proceeding.

Requirement to Preserve Issue or Show Cause and Prejudice. Failure to preserve an issue for appellate review precludes consideration in a habeas corpus proceeding unless there was cause for and actual prejudice from the failure to preserve the issue, or unless the petitioner can prove actual innocence.

Test Your Knowledge

To assess your understanding of the material in this chapter, click here to take a quiz.

For More Information

• RANDY HERTZ & JAMES S. LIEBMAN, FEDERAL HABEAS CORPUS PRACTICE & PROCEDURE (6th ed. 2011).

• WAYNE R. LAFAVE, JEROLD H. ISRAEL, NANCY J. KING & ORIN S. KERR, CRIMINAL PROCEDURE (5th ed. 2009).

• RUSSELL L. WEAVER, JOHN M. BURKOFF, CATHERINE HANCOCK, JANET HOEFFEL, STEVE FRIEDLAND & STEPHEN SINGER, PRINCIPLES OF CRIMINAL PROCEDURE Ch. 22 (6th ed. 2018).

Index

References are to page numbers.